D0004753

Hispanic Americans in Congress
1822–2012

PREPARED UNDER THE DIRECTION OF

THE COMMITTEE ON HOUSE ADMINISTRATION OF THE
U.S. HOUSE OF REPRESENTATIVES

DANIEL E. LUNGREN, CHAIRMAN

ROBERT A. BRADY, RANKING MINORITY MEMBER

BY THE

OFFICE OF THE HISTORIAN AND OFFICE OF THE CLERK
U.S. HOUSE OF REPRESENTATIVES

U.S. GOVERNMENT PRINTING OFFICE, WASHINGTON, DC, 2013

107th Congress
H. Con. Res. 90
House Document 108-225
U.S. Government Printing Office
Washington, DC: 2013

Library of Congress Cataloging-in-Publication Data

Hispanic Americans in Congress, 1822-2012 / prepared under the direction of the Committee on House Administration of the U.S. House of Representatives, Daniel E. Lungren, chairman, Robert A. Brady, ranking minority member, by the Office of the Historian and Office of the Clerk, U.S. House of Representatives.
pages cm
Editor, Matthew A. Wasniewski, Historian of the U.S. House of Representatives; co-editors, Albin Kowalewski, Laura Turner O'Hara, and Terrance Rucker, Office of the Historian, U.S. House of Representatives.
Summary: "A compilation of historical essays and short biographies about 91 Hispanic-Americans who served in Congress from 1822 to 2012"--Provided by publisher.
Includes bibliographical references and index.
1. Hispanic American legislators--Biography. 2. United States. Congress--Biography. I. Wasniewski, Matthew A. (Matthew Andrew), 1969- II. Kowalewski, Albin. III. O'Hara, Laura Turner. IV. Rucker, Terrance. V. United States. Congress. House. Office of the Historian. VI. United States. Congress. House. Office of the Clerk. VII. United States. Congress. House. Committee on House Administration.
E184.S75H5657 2012
920.009268'073--dc23
[B]

2012045668

For sale by the Superintendent of Documents, U.S. Government Printing Office
Internet: bookstore.gpo.gov Phone: toll free (866) 512-1800; DC area (202) 512-1800
Fax: (202) 512-2104 Mail: Stop IDCC, Washington, DC 20402-0001
ISBN 978-0-16-092028-8

ON THE COVER

Henry B. González of Texas is the longest-serving Hispanic American in congressional history. With years of experience as a civil rights proponent in San Antonio and Texas politics, González won a seat in the U.S. House in 1961 in a special election. He went on to serve more than 37 years, helped found the Congressional Hispanic Caucus, and became the chairman of the influential House Banking Committee.

Image courtesy of the U.S. House of Representatives Photography Office

House Concurrent Resolution No. 90

ONE HUNDRED SEVENTH CONGRESS, FIRST SESSION

SUBMITTED BY THE HONORABLE JOSÉ E. SERRANO

Resolved by the House of Representatives (the Senate concurring),

SECTION 1. PRINTING OF REVISED VERSION OF "HISPANIC AMERICANS IN CONGRESS". An updated version of House Document 103–299, entitled "Hispanic Americans in Congress" (as revised by the Library of Congress), shall be printed as a House document by the Public Printer, with illustrations and suitable binding, under the direction of the Committee on House Administration of the House of Representatives.

SEC. 2. NUMBER OF COPIES. (a) IN GENERAL.—Except as provided in subsection (b), in addition to the usual number, there shall be printed 30,700 copies of the document referred to in section 1, of which—(1) 25,000 shall be for the use of the Committee on House Administration of the House of Representatives; and (2) 5,700 shall be for the use of the Committee on Rules and Administration of the Senate. (b) ALTERNATIVE NUMBER.—If the total printing and production costs of the number of copies provided under subsection (a) exceed $220,000, there shall be printed the maximum number of copies of the document referred to in section 1 for which such total costs do not exceed $220,000, with distribution allocated in the same proportion as in subsection (a).

Agreed to December 7, 2001

COMPILED AND EDITED UNDER THE DIRECTION OF THE

COMMITTEE ON HOUSE ADMINISTRATION OF THE U.S. HOUSE OF REPRESENTATIVES

DANIEL E. LUNGREN, Chairman

ROBERT A. BRADY, Ranking Minority Member

DANIEL E. LUNGREN of California
GREGG HARPER of Mississippi
PHIL GINGREY of Georgia
AARON SCHOCK of Illinois
RICHARD NUGENT of Florida
TODD ROKITA of Indiana

ROBERT A. BRADY of Pennsylvania
ZOE LOFGREN of California
CHARLES GONZALEZ of Texas

KAREN L. HAAS, Clerk of the U.S. House of Representatives

MATTHEW A. WASNIEWSKI, Historian of the U.S. House of Representatives

OFFICE OF THE HISTORIAN, U.S. HOUSE OF REPRESENTATIVES

Co-editors: Albin J. Kowalewski, Laura Turner O'Hara, Terrance Rucker

Co-writers: Jacqueline Burns, Erin Hromada, Kathleen Johnson, Kenneth Kato, Joshua Litten, and Barry Pump

Contents

ALPHABETICAL LIST OF HISPANIC-AMERICAN MEMBERS OF CONGRESS VIII

INTRODUCTION 1

PART ONE: FORMER HISPANIC-AMERICAN MEMBERS OF CONGRESS

From Democracy's Borderlands: Hispanic Congressional Representation in the Era of U.S. Continental Expansion, 1822–1898 22

"Foreign in a Domestic Sense": Hispanic Americans in Congress During the Age of U.S. Colonialism and Global Expansion, 1898–1945 146

Separate Interests to National Agendas: Hispanic-American Members of Congress in the Civil Rights Era, 1945–1977 322

Strength in Numbers, Challenges in Diversity: Legislative Trends and Power Sharing Among Hispanic Americans in Congress, 1977–2012 472

PART TWO: CURRENT HISPANIC-AMERICAN MEMBERS OF CONGRESS 653

PART THREE: APPENDICES

Appendix A: Hispanic-American Representatives, Senators, Delegates, and Resident Commissioners by Congress, 1822–2012 710

Appendix B: Hispanic-American Representatives, Senators, Delegates, and Resident Commissioners by State and Territory, 1822–2012 724

Appendix C: Hispanic-American Members' Committee Assignments (Standing, Joint, Select) in the U.S. House and Senate, 1822–2012 727

Appendix D: Hispanic Americans Who Have Chaired Congressional Committees, 1881–2012 735

Appendix E: Hispanic-American Chairs of Subcommittees of Standing and Select Committees in the U.S. House and Senate, 1949–2012 737

Appendix F: Hispanic Americans in U.S. House Party Leadership Positions, 1987–2012 742

Appendix G: Hispanic-American Familial Connections in Congress 743

Appendix H: Congressional Hispanic Caucus and Congressional Hispanic Conference Chairmen and Chairwomen, 1976–2012 744

Appendix I: Constitutional Amendments, Treaties, and Major Acts of Congress Referenced in the Text 745

Appendix J: Original Text of Political Poems and Songs Referenced in Contextual Essays 749

Appendix K: Glossary 752

INDEX 755

Alphabetical List of Hispanic-American Members of Congress, 1822–2012*

Aníbal Acevedo-Vilá (2001–2005)

Joe Baca (1999–Present)

Herman Badillo (1971–1977)

Xavier Becerra (1993–Present)

Jaime Benítez (1973–1977)

Ben Garrido Blaz (1985–1993)

Henry Bonilla (1993–2007)

Albert G. Bustamante (1985–1993)

Francisco (Quico) Canseco (2011–Present)

Dennis A. Cardoza (2003–2012)

José Francisco Chaves (1865–1867; 1869–1871)

Dennis Chavez (1931–1935; 1935–1962)

Tony Coelho (1979–1989)

Antonio J. Colorado (1992–1993)

Félix Córdova Dávila (1917–1932)

Jorge Luis Córdova-Díaz (1969–1973)

Baltasar Corrada-del Río (1977–1985)

Jim Costa (2005–Present)

Henry Cuellar (2005–Present)

Eligio (Kika) de la Garza II (1965–1997)

Ron de Lugo (1973–1979; 1981–1995)

Federico Degetau (1901–1905)

Lincoln Diaz-Balart (1993–2011)

Mario Diaz-Balart (2003–Present)

Antonio M. Fernández (1943–1956)

Joachim Octave Fernández (1931–1941)

Antonio Fernós-Isern (1946–1965)

Bill Flores (2011–Present)

Luis G. Fortuño (2005–2009)

Jaime B. Fuster (1985–1992)

José Manuel Gallegos (1853–1856; 1871–1873)

Robert Garcia (1978–1990)

Charles A. Gonzalez (1999–Present)

Henry B. González (1961–1999)

Raúl M. Grijalva (2003–Present)

Luis V. Gutierrez (1993–Present)

Benigno Cárdenas Hernández (1915–1917; 1919–1921)

Joseph Marion Hernández (1822–1823)

Jaime Herrera Beutler (2011–Present)

Rubén Hinojosa (1997–Present)

Santiago Iglesias (1933–1939)

Raúl R. Labrador (2011–Present)

Octaviano A. Larrazolo (1928–1929)

Tulio Larrínaga (1905–1911)

Ladislas Lazaro (1913–1927)

Ben Ray Luján (2009–Present)

Manuel Luján, Jr. (1969–1989)

Tranquilino Luna (1881–1884)

Francisco Antonio Manzanares (1884–1885)

Matthew G. Martínez (1982–2001)

Mel Martinez (2005–2009)

Robert Menendez (1993–2006; 2006–Present)

Joseph M. Montoya (1957–1964; 1964–1977)

Néstor Montoya (1921–1923)

Luis Muñoz Rivera (1911–1916)

Grace Flores Napolitano (1999–Present)

Devin Nunes (2003–Present)

Solomon P. Ortiz (1983–2011)

Mariano Sabino Otero (1879–1881)

Miguel Antonio Otero (1856–1861)

Romualdo Pacheco (1877–1878; 1879–1883)

Bolívar Pagán (1939–1945)

Ed Pastor (1991–Present)

Francisco Perea (1863–1865)

Pedro Perea (1899–1901)

José Lorenzo Pesquera (1932–1933)

Pedro Pierluisi (2009–Present)

Jesús T. Piñero (1945–1946)

Santiago Polanco-Abreu (1965–1969)

Silvestre Reyes (1997–Present)

Bill Richardson (1983–1997)

David Rivera (2011–Present)

Ciro D. Rodriguez (1997–2005; 2007–2011)

Trinidad Romero (1877–1879)

Carlos A. Romero-Barceló (1993–2001)

Ileana Ros-Lehtinen (1989–Present)

Edward R. Roybal (1963–1993)

Lucille Roybal-Allard (1993–Present)

Marco Rubio (2011–Present)

Gregorio Kilili Camacho Sablan (2009–Present)

John Salazar (2005–2011)

Ken Salazar (2005–2009)

Linda T. Sánchez (2003–Present)

Loretta Sanchez (1997–Present)

José E. Serrano (1990–Present)

Albio Sires (2006–Present)

Hilda L. Solis (2001–2009)

Frank Tejeda (1993–1997)

Esteban Edward Torres (1983–1999)

Robert A. Underwood (1993–2003)

Nydia M. Velázquez (1993–Present)

* The closing date for this volume was September 1, 2012.

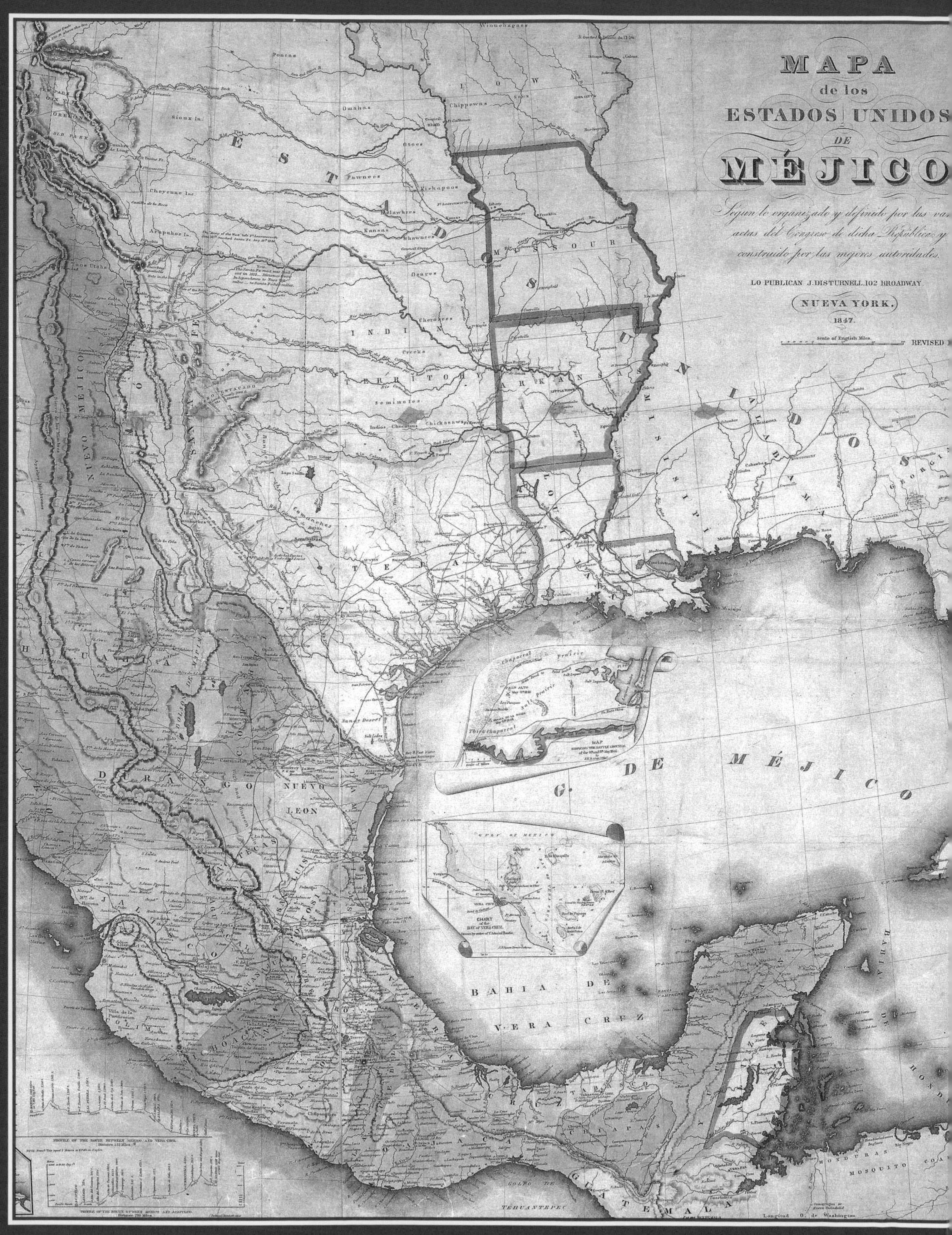

MAPA
de los
ESTADOS UNIDOS
DE
MÉJICO
Segun lo organizado y definido por las va
actas del Congreso de dicha República y
construido por las mejores autoridades.
LO PUBLICAN J. DISTURNELL, 102 BROADWAY
NUEVA YORK.
1847.
Scale of English Miles.
REVISED
IOWA
MISSOURI
ARKANSAS
LOUISIANA
INDIAN TERRITORY
TEJAS
NUEVO MÉJICO
CHIHUAHUA
DURANGO
NUEVO LEON
JALISCO
G. DE MÉJICO
BAHIA DE VERA CRUZ
CHIAPAS
OAXACA
GUATEMALA
HONDURAS
MOSQUITO
TEHUANTEPEC
CHART of the BAY of VERA CRUZ
Longitud 0. de Washington

Hispanic Americans in Congress
1822–2012

★ INTRODUCTION ★

On September 30, 1822, Joseph M. Hernández began his service in Congress as Florida's first Territorial Delegate, pioneering Hispanic-American representation in the American republic. Like other Hispanic Americans in the federal legislature during the 1800s, Hernández advanced from the periphery of the Union to hold a brief term in an office whose core duties were more diplomatic than legislative, working to turn the former Spanish colony where he was born into a state. *Hispanic Americans in Congress, 1822–2012*, chronicles the story of Hernández and the 90 Hispanics who followed him into Congress.[1] In helping to shape Congress, these *nuevomexicanos*, Puerto Ricans, Mexican Americans, Cuban Americans, and Guamanians, among others, enriched U.S. history.

The United States House, the Senate, and the career trajectories of their Hispanic Members have undergone extensive change during this span of nearly two centuries.[2] During our research for this book, several recurring themes raised the following questions: How did these individuals' experiences compare to those of other newly enfranchised Americans, particularly African Americans during Reconstruction and women in the early 20th century? To what degree did American expansion influence the story of Hispanic Americans in Congress? How did their decades-long status as statutory representatives with constituents at the fringes of the continental United States affect their legislative priorities and shape their legislative styles? What was their reaction to the political culture of Capitol Hill, and how did they overcome institutional barriers?

An 1847 map shows the states of Mexico and the southern United States at the time of the U.S.-Mexican War.

John Disturnell, *Mapa de los Estados Unidos de Méjico: Segun lo organizado y definido por las varias actas del Congreso de dicha república y construido por las mejores autoridades*, map (New York: J. Disturnell, 1847); from National Archives and Records Administration, Records of the U.S. Government, RG 11

Benigno Hernández of New Mexico, who served from 1915 to 1917 and 1919 to 1921 in the U.S. House, became the first *Hispano* to represent his state as a voting Representative.

Image courtesy of the Palace of the Governors Photo Archives (NMHM/DCA), 50403

EXPERIENCES OF HISPANIC AMERICANS AND OTHER MINORITIES IN CONGRESS

In some ways the history of Hispanic Members resembles that of other groups who had been newcomers to Congress. For example, by the 20th century, many Hispanic Members—like women and African Americans in Congress—had eventually come to view themselves as "surrogate" representatives for Hispanics nationwide, legislating for individuals far beyond the borders of their individual districts or states.[3] Additionally, like the stories of women and African-American Members of Congress, the story of Hispanic Americans in Congress occurred overwhelmingly in the U.S. House: Of the 91 Hispanic Americans who have served in Congress, only seven were Senators, and three of these served in the House first.[3]

Hispanic-American Members assimilating into the political culture of Capitol Hill participated in the same stages of development that women and African Americans did: pioneering, apprenticeship, and mature integration.[4] But although these stages were roughly proportional, they unfolded over a much longer time frame for Hispanic Members than for other groups because of reluctance against incorporating "foreign" peoples into the American body politic and because of the disadvantaged political status of the territories they represented. (Seventeen of the first 25 Hispanic Members of Congress—68 percent through the end of the Second World War—represented territorial possessions.)

Hispanic Members' story was unique in other aspects, too. After Reconstruction, black Americans experienced a prolonged period of contraction, decline, and exclusion that resulted from segregation and disfranchisement. From 1901 to 1929, there were no blacks in the federal legislature. Conversely, except for the period from the 49th through the 55th Congress (1885–1899)—due largely to political realignments in the New Mexico Territory rather than to direct disfranchisement—Hispanic Americans have consistently served in the federal legislature since the mid-1800s. From 1899 onward, at least one Hispanic American has served in each Congress. Unlike the pioneering women and African-American Members, who faced increased expectations and heightened scrutiny by the media, the earliest Hispanic Members elicited a muted reaction from the court of public opinion. In fact, the sparse coverage of New Mexican Territorial Delegates in Eastern newspapers and, particularly, the limited coverage of Puerto Rican Resident Commissioners by the mainland media, were considerable obstacles in researching this volume.

While seeking to advance within Congress and adapt to its culture, the early generations of Hispanic Members faced racial prejudices. Since there were relatively few of them, they also lacked the ability to organize legislative caucuses. More than one-third of them served as "statutory representatives," that is, as Delegates or Resident Commissioners who possessed circumscribed legislative powers.[5] For the most part, the Constitution did not contemplate such representation over the long term, leaving Congress to establish and manage these offices, whose powers were often strictly limited. Thus, their legislative strategies differed from those of most Representatives and Senators. Quite often, Hispanic-American statutory representatives functioned more like envoys or ministers without portfolio than lawmakers. Consequently, they often served as intercessors between the territorial governments and federal executive departments.

By the period after World War II, as Hispanic Representatives and Senators became more numerous, they cultivated legislative strategies that were common on Capitol Hill. Some pursued an institutionalist "work horse" strategy; adhering to the prevailing traditions and folkways of the House and Senate, they hoped to shape policies by attaining positions of influence on the inside.[6] Representative Henry B. González of Texas (1961–1999), who eventually chaired the powerful House Banking and Currency Committee, embodied such an approach. Though an advocate for civil rights since the early days of his political career, González eschewed identifying himself as a Member who supported Hispanic causes so as not to alienate others. In the 1960s, he repeatedly clashed with more-radical Hispanic activists in the Chicano movement, who embraced the name as a politicized term of self-identification. "Our task is to overcome political isolation, and it is a delicate path that makes the difference between attracting a friend and becoming isolated and alone," González once noted. "If we cry in an empty room, we may expect to hear only our own echoes."[7] Others, such as Ladislas Lazaro of Louisiana (1913–1927) and Edward Roybal of California (1963–1993), favored a methodical legislative style, diligently immersing themselves in committee work and policy matters.

Other individuals who embraced a "show horse" style were less common; circumventing prescribed congressional channels, they appealed directly to the public and media and became symbols for Hispanic civil rights. Many of the Puerto Rican Resident Commissioners—who were already relegated by their restricted role to the margins of institutional power—often bore the mantle of reform, claiming to speak on behalf of all Puerto Ricans. Among them were Luis Muñoz Rivera (1911–1916), Santiago Iglesias (1933–1939), and Antonio Fernós-Isern (1946–1965).

Ladislas Lazaro of Louisiana (right) was a country doctor whose civic service career began on the local school board. Lazaro eventually served in the Louisiana legislature before his 1912 election to the U.S. House. Here, he confers with Representative Joseph Walsh of Massachusetts (left) in 1921.

Image courtesy of the Library of Congress

FROM DEMOCRACY'S BORDERLANDS: HISPANIC-AMERICAN REPRESENTATION, 1822–1898

The congressional careers of the 10 Hispanic Americans who served during this era unfolded along with U.S. continental expansion. Each represented constituents whose native lands had been acquired by war or diplomacy from Spain or Mexico. For much of the 19th century, these lands lay at the far edges of the U.S. frontier. All but one of these Hispanic Americans—Representative Romualdo Pacheco of California—were Territorial Delegates, and the vast majority were from the New Mexico Territory, carved out of the lands ceded to the United States by Mexico in the wake of their conflict from 1846 to 1848.

The educational, professional, and social backgrounds of these Hispanic Members of Congress, particularly the eight Territorial Delegates from New Mexico, were strikingly similar. These Members were wealthy businessmen or landowners, well educated, and connected by fledgling political organizations and overlapping kinship networks. Their families had long played a governing role in the region in the era of Spanish rule predating Mexican independence. Several members of this cohort owned numerous Indian slaves; in Florida,

In the foreground, President William Howard Taft signs the New Mexico statehood bill. The United States, which acquired a vast swath of land in the Southwest ceded by Mexico after the U.S.-Mexican War, administered New Mexico as a territory for more than 60 years before admitting it to the Union in 1912. Most nineteenth-century Hispanic Americans in Congress were Delegates from New Mexico.

Image courtesy of the Library of Congress

Joseph Hernández operated massive plantations by using several hundred African-American slaves.

Their legislative strategies varied widely, though invariably they focused on basic infrastructure improvements, particularly roads and railways that would be important to any territory. None of these individuals were "surrogate representatives" in the sense that they represented Hispanic interests nationally, but several of them acted as ambassadors for their own Spanish-culture constituencies. José Manuel Gallegos, the first Hispanic Delegate from New Mexico, was a defrocked priest, a former Member of the Mexican legislative assembly, and an ardent Mexican nationalist. Gallegos understood implicitly that his overwhelmingly *nuevomexicano* constituency placed "peculiar demands" on Congress. "They are in their origins," he explained to the House, "alien to your institutions, your laws, your customs, your glorious history, and even strangers to your language.… I am, and have ever been, one of that very people."[8]

As Territorial Delegates, this generation of Hispanic Members of Congress had few substantive legislative accomplishments. The hurdles to effecting legislative change were numerous, although most were not as overt as the refusal by the House in 1854 to grant Delegate Gallegos an interpreter on the floor. (He spoke no English, and a clerk read his translated floor speeches throughout his House tenure). Far more subtle, but more profound, was the protean role of the Territorial Delegate in the 19th-century House. The institution, growing because of westward expansion, greeted the steady stream of territorial representatives in an improvisational fashion—putting in place an ad hoc system of representation whereby Congress crafted laws and set procedural rules that gave territories a limited voice in national affairs. Adding to the difficulty of addressing the interests of the large Hispanic population in the Southwest, too few Hispanic Members served at any one time to drive a legislative agenda. Except during three Congresses (the 45th through the 47th, 1877–1883), each with a pair of Hispanic Members who served simultaneously,

A *Puck* cartoon from 1902, *Waiting for Their Stars*, depicts three territories, New Mexico, Arizona, and Oklahoma, waiting to become states. Columbia promises, "Your stars shall be put on the flag just as soon as those politicians in Congress will let me." Oklahoma entered the Union in 1907; New Mexico and Arizona followed five years later.

Image courtesy of the Library of Congress

most of these individuals served their brief terms as the only Hispanic in the national legislature.

"FOREIGN IN A DOMESTIC SENSE," 1898–1945

The Spanish-American War of 1898 refashioned Hispanic representation in Congress. The short-lived war quickened America's rise as a world power and expanded its overseas empire to include the Philippines and Guam in the far Pacific and, closer to home, Puerto Rico in the Caribbean basin. Of the 15 Hispanic Americans who were elected or appointed to Congress in this era, eight were statutory representatives. (One was from the New Mexico Territory before its admission into the Union as a state in 1912, and seven were from Puerto Rico.)

For decades, territories on the North American continent had been organized with the understanding that they would eventually be incorporated as states. U.S. colonialism forced Congress to decide how overseas territories and peoples who were never expected to be admitted into the Union would be treated in the national legislature. Congress's solution to this problem was to create a piecemeal colonial administrative structure through a series of organic governing acts. Even the U.S. Supreme Court, in determining that such territories would remain unincorporated in a series of decisions known as the Insular Cases, was ambiguous about the status question: Puerto Ricans, the justices reasoned, were "foreign in a domestic sense."[9]

Congress set the administrative landscape for U.S. colonial rule in these far-flung locations—particularly in the case of Puerto Rico by the Foraker Act of 1900 and the Jones Act of 1917. Initially, the Foraker Act, which created the office of Resident Commissioner, greatly circumscribed Puerto Rico's representation in the U.S. federal government. Most officials, including the governor, and key administrators in the colonial government were presidential appointees, and Congress had authority to overrule any law passed by Puerto Rico's legislature. The Jones Act of 1917, while extending citizenship to Puerto Ricans, left the island's long-term status uncertain.

During this era, Resident Commissioners arguably had less power than Territorial Delegates. The first Resident Commissioner, Federico Degetau, could not even sit with other Members in the chamber. Eventually, Resident Commissioners were granted this privilege, along with a seat on the Insular Affairs Committee, which had jurisdiction over territories and overseas possessions. But the early Resident Commissioners were not permitted to join party caucuses, they could not vote in committee, and they had no vote on final legislation that reached the House Floor. Like earlier Territorial Delegates, they were not at their core legislators. Rather, they functioned like lobbyists or envoys, who could educate, debate, and testify on behalf of legislation, but were unable to vote their constituents' will.

Early Puerto Rican Resident Commissioners faced an uphill battle in making the case that territorial residents should participate in U.S. society and earn full citizenship rights. "A good deal has been said about the unpreparedness and the unfitness of our people for self-government," Tulio Larrínaga, the island's second Resident Commissioner, told congressional colleagues. "I wish every honest man …

Resident Commissioner Félix Córdova Dávila of Puerto Rico (far left) visits the White House in 1924 with other leaders from the island. The delegation pressed President Calvin Coolidge to grant Puerto Ricans the right to elect their own governor. Until the 1940s, Puerto Rican governors were appointed by U.S. Presidents.

Image courtesy of the Library of Congress

An image of the U.S. delegation to the Pan-American Conference in Rio de Janeiro in 1906. Puerto Rican Resident Commissioner Tulio Larrínaga is seated in the front row at the far left.

Image courtesy of the Library of Congress

Dennis Chavez of New Mexico was the first Hispanic American to serve in both the U.S. House (1931–1935) and Senate (1935–1962). Chavez was an early proponent of Hispanic civil rights nationally.

Image courtesy of the U.S. Senate Historical Office

President Harry S. Truman (left) rides in an open car in Puerto Rico in 1947 seated next to Governor Jesús Piñero. A year earlier, Truman had appointed Piñero as the first native Puerto Rican governor of the island. Piñero had previously served as Resident Commissioner in the U.S. House.

Image courtesy of the National Archives and Records Administration

to answer me this question: If every Territory and every State that has been admitted into this Union was better prepared than the island of Porto Rico is to-day? Look back to the different portions of this country which have been made States by acts of Congress. What was their population; what was their literacy; what was their wealth; what was their civilization as compared with the civilization of four hundred years of Porto Rico?"[10] Complicating matters was the fact that the Puerto Ricans themselves were divided nearly evenly into three factions regarding their future status: statehood, complete independence, or autonomy within a commonwealth structure.

Hispanic-American Members of Congress made notable gains in this era. Though he served only briefly and symbolically as the first Hispanic Senator, Octaviano Larrazolo of New Mexico (1928–1929) rose to prominence because of his long career as an advocate for *nuevomexicanos*, who he felt were marginalized and manipulated by the state's party structures. The next Hispanic to follow him—and the first to serve in both chambers—Dennis Chavez of New Mexico was arguably the first surrogate representative for Hispanics nationally; for instance, Chavez led a Senate panel that pushed for reforms in Puerto Rico during the early 1940s. As Hispanic Americans entered this apprenticeship phase on Capitol Hill, they gained more-prominent committee assignments. Joachim O. Fernández of Louisiana held powerful posts on the House Naval Affairs and Appropriations Committees in the 1930s, and during his brief stint in the U.S. House, Chavez chaired the Committee on Irrigation and Reclamation, which had a strong influence on policy in the Western states.

SEPARATE INTERESTS TO NATIONAL AGENDAS, 1945–1977

The Second World War marked another turning point for Hispanic representation in Congress. Of critical importance, it raised the expectations of returning Hispanic-American veterans, as it had for African-American servicemen; in fighting for democracy abroad, many believed that they had earned a greater measure of it, particularly in segregated locations, back home. An organized effort to attain broad civil rights ensued.

That movement followed two paths that converged by the end of the era. On the first path were individuals like Representatives González and Roybal; both were elected in the early 1960s but made their start in public service in the late 1940s, organizing local civil rights groups. Roybal founded the Community Service Organization (CSO) in southern California, and González created the Pan-American Progressive Association (PAPA) in San Antonio, Texas. CSO, PAPA, and similar groups that came into existence at that time advocated for education, housing, and employment issues important to their communities. By the 1960s, dissatisfaction with the pace of change led to the development of younger, more radical causes like the Chicano movement, which sought to spur local reforms and foster ethnic pride.

Meanwhile, Puerto Ricans experienced a different path to reform. In 1946, for the first time during U.S. colonial rule, a native Puerto Rican, former Resident Commissioner Jesús Piñero, was appointed to serve as governor. Then the Elective Governor Act of 1948 granted islanders the power to choose their governor at the polls instead of having one imposed on them by presidential fiat. Four years later, largely because of the work of Resident Commissioner Fernós-Isern and political titan Luis Muñoz Marín (the son of former Resident Commissioner Luis Muñoz Rivera), Congress granted Puerto Rico commonwealth status via Estado Libre Asociado (the Free Associated State)—a position that was short of statehood but one that extended federal programs and protections and fostered local autonomy. Resident Commissioners gained more privileges in the U.S. House during a series of institutional reforms in the 1970s, though they now competed with other voices representing insular interests in Washington, D.C.

The 12 Hispanic Americans elected to Congress in this era continued a period of institutional apprenticeship. This generation was the first in which the number of Hispanic voting Members of Congress (six) equaled the number of Hispanic nonvoting statutory representatives. Though statistically small, this trend portended greater possibilities for voting Members, who enjoyed privileges and powers statutory representatives did not, including the ability to accrue the requisite seniority for leadership positions. Hispanic Members continued to earn spots on key committees where none had served previously: In the 80th Congress (1947–1949) Antonio Fernós-Isern of Puerto Rico served on the House Armed Services Committee; in the 85th Congress (1957–1959) Joseph Montoya of New Mexico served on the House Judiciary Committee; in the 87th Congress (1961–1963) González served on the Banking and Currency Committee; and in the 89th Congress (1965–1967) Roybal served on the House Committee on Foreign Affairs. In the Senate, Dennis Chavez, who entered that chamber in 1935, rose to chair the Post Office and Post Roads Committee in the 79th Congress (1945–1947) and the powerful Public Works Committee in the 81st and 82nd Congresses (1949–1953) and again in the 84th Congress (1955–1957) until his death in 1962 during the 87th Congress (1961–1963).

Senator Joseph Montoya of New Mexico (right) speaks with President Lyndon Johnson (seated). At left is New Mexico's other Senator at the time, Clinton P. Anderson.

Image courtesy of the Lyndon B. Johnson Library/ National Archives and Records Administration

STRENGTH IN NUMBERS, CHALLENGES IN DIVERSITY, 1977–2012

Like their female and African-American colleagues, the post-civil rights era generation of Hispanic lawmakers created a legislative groundswell on Capitol Hill. The civil rights movement, the ensuing civil rights legislation of the 1960s, and court-ordered redistricting opened new avenues of political participation for many Hispanic Americans. Consequently, many more Hispanics were elected to political office at the state and national levels. Fifty-four of the 91 Hispanic Americans who served in Congress through 2012—nearly 60 percent—were seated after 1977. The overwhelming majority of these representatives (44 of 54) were elected as voting Members of Congress—a departure from the trend in the prior three generations of Hispanic Members. Moreover, in the 1970s, for the first time, Hispanic Members were elected from states outside the Southwest, including New York, New Jersey, and Illinois. With the election in 1989 of Ileana Ros-Lehtinen of Florida, who succeeded the late Claude Pepper, two more barriers were broken: Ros-Lehtinen became the first woman of Hispanic descent and the first person of Cuban descent to serve in Congress. These gains over several

Eligio (Kika) de la Garza of Texas chaired the House Agriculture Committee from 1981 to 1995, the second longest tenure of any chairman of that panel dating to its creation in 1820. Harold Cooley of North Carolina led the Agriculture Committee for 16 years in the 1940s and 1950s.

Collection of the U.S. House of Representatives, Photography Collection

A campaign button supports the election of Herman Badillo of New York to Congress. Badillo, who represented a district that encompassed parts of Queens, Manhattan, and the Bronx, was the first person of Puerto Rican descent to serve as a voting Representative in the U.S. Congress.

Collection of the U.S. House of Representatives

decades were punctuated by occasional surges, such as the one after the 1992 elections, when the number of Hispanics in Congress increased by one-third. Additionally, the elections of Mel Martinez of Florida and Ken Salazar of Colorado and the appointment and subsequent election of Robert Menendez of New Jersey meant there were more Latino Senators in the 109th Congress (2005–2007) than there had been in the entire history of Congress. No Hispanic Senators had served in the chamber since the departure of Joseph Montoya of New Mexico at the end of the 94th Congress (1975–1977).

The increase in Hispanic Americans from seven during the 95th Congress (1977–1979) to 31 in the 112th Congress (2011–2013) signaled that the time for formal organization and coordination had arrived. In December 1976, weeks before the opening of the 95th Congress (1977–1979), Representatives González of Texas, Roybal of California, Eligio (Kika) de la Garza of Texas, Herman Badillo of New York, and Puerto Rican Resident Commissioner Baltasar Corrada-del Río formally created the Congressional Hispanic Caucus (CHC). The group, though small, represented the amalgamation of various factions of the larger Hispanic civil rights movement, including activists, mainstream and middle-class reformers, and insular advocates. "The fact that we have joined together," the fledgling caucus declared, "is a sign of the growing power of our community, and we are looking forward to strengthening the Federal commitment to Hispanic citizens."[11] Indeed, in the following decades as its membership grew, the caucus pushed forward an ambitious legislative agenda. But policy perspectives within the caucus were far from monolithic. An eventual rift among Members over foreign policy toward communist Cuba led to the departure of Republican members of the CHC in 1997. And eventually, the objection by Hispanic Republicans to the CHC's treatment of an appeals court nominee in 2002 led to the creation of the Congressional Hispanic Conference in 2003.

During this era, Hispanic-American Members of Congress entered a mature phase of institutional development. As members of a cross-section of congressional committees, including the most coveted assignments, such as Appropriations, Ways and Means, and Rules, they were involved with legislation affecting every facet of American life. Representing districts that were electorally safe, many Hispanic Representatives enjoyed long careers that allowed them to accrue seniority and move into leadership positions. Since 1977, six Hispanic Members of Congress have chaired congressional committees—twice the number in the previous three eras combined. And for the first time, Hispanic Members have risen into the ranks of party leadership. The first, Representative Tony Coelho of California, chaired the Democratic Congressional Campaign Committee in the early 1980s and was elected Majority Whip in the 100th Congress (1987–1989) and again at the opening of the 101st Congress. (He served until he left the House in June 1989.) Robert Menendez chaired the House Democratic Caucus from 2002 until 2006, when he was appointed to the U.S. Senate. Previously, Menendez served as vice chairman of the caucus (1998–2002); Xavier Becerra of California filled that role from 2008 to 2012. Others on the leadership ladder have served as Chief Deputy Whips, including Bill

Tony Coelho of California helped the congressional Democrats establish a competitive campaign finance apparatus during the 1980s. Coelho became the Democratic Majority Whip, the highest elected House leadership position ever attained by a Hispanic American.

Collection of the U.S. House of Representatives, Photography Collection

Richardson of New Mexico (1993–1997), Menendez (1997–1999), and Ed Pastor of Arizona (1999–2013).

HISTORIOGRAPHY

The first edition of *Hispanic Americans in Congress* was published in 1995. Researched and written by the Library of Congress's Hispanic Division, it followed the same format that was used by the Office of the House Historian for the second editions of *Women in Congress* (1991) and *Black Americans in Congress* (1989). As with the third editions of the books on women and African Americans in Congress, this edition of *Hispanic Americans in Congress* features major changes, including expanded profiles of former Members, contextual essays that introduce the profiles chronologically and group them into generations, and appendices.

All the former Members who were included in the first edition of *Hispanic Americans in Congress, 1822–1995*, are also included in this publication. To compile the roster of Members elected after 1995, we used the official list of Hispanic Members of Congress of the Library of Congress's Hispanic Division. Another litmus test for self-identification was membership in the Congressional Hispanic Caucus or the Congressional Hispanic Conference.

Filipino Resident Commissioners, most of whom retained Spanish surnames, are not included in this publication because they identified themselves as Asian Pacific Islanders. Scholars in the Asian and Hispanic Divisions of the Library of Congress advised the Office of the Historian to include these Members in the forthcoming *Asian/Pacific Islander Americans* volume of the *Minorities in Congress* series.[12]

Members of the Congressional Hispanic Caucus pose on the East Front steps of the U.S. Capitol in 2004. The organization of the caucus in late 1976 marked the increasing power of Hispanics in electoral politics and their efforts to shape the legislative agenda in Congress.

Image courtesy of the U.S. House of Representatives Photography Office

TERMINOLOGY AND TRANSLATION

We use the term "Hispanic"—the U.S. government standard (and that of most state and local governments)—to identify persons who trace their origins to Spanish-speaking countries or regions, including Spain. During its 35-year history, the Congressional Hispanic Caucus, for instance, has included individuals with origins in Mexico, Cuba, Puerto Rico, and Portugal. In academic usage and even among some quarters in the general public, "Hispanic" can be a controversial label. Some prefer the term "Latino" to denote any individual, regardless of racial origin, who originates from a Spanish-speaking region in Latin America or the Caribbean. Others prefer to identify themselves as being from a particular country, using the terms "Mexican American" or "Chicano" to denote their roots in Mexico. However, even advocates for other more region- or country-specific terms acknowledge that, according to surveys of public opinion, most Americans prefer the designation "Hispanic."[13] Throughout this book, we strive to use terms that include a geographic area of origin. We also use the terms "Hispanic" and "Latino" interchangeably.

Many of the primary and secondary sources we consulted for this volume were written in Spanish. The Office of the Historian transcribed sections of original sources in Spanish for use in quotations in the biographical profiles and contextual essays; the original Spanish quotations appear in the endnotes. All paraphrased articles are cited, but not directly quoted, in the endnotes.

One example of Hispanic organization in the latter 20th century was the protest movement that united migrant farm workers who sought better pay and benefits.

Image courtesy of the Library of Congress

Manuel Luján, Jr., of New Mexico served in the U.S. House for nearly two decades and was a founding Member of the Congressional Hispanic Caucus in December 1976.

Collection of the U.S. House of Representatives

The Hispanic Division of the Library of Congress reviewed all quotations to ensure that the transcriptions and translations were grammatically correct. The Hispanic Division also added accents where applicable and modified the transcriptions to make them understandable to readers of modern Spanish. Original translations were prepared by Translations International, Inc.

METHODOLOGY AND USEFUL RESEARCH STRATEGIES

As with previous editions in the *Minorities in Congress* series, we consulted several standard sources that were indispensable during the compilation of this book. Inquiries into Members' congressional careers should begin with the *Biographical Directory of the United States Congress*. Maintained by the House Office of the Historian and the Senate Historical Office, this publication contains basic biographical information about Members, pertinent bibliographic references, and information about manuscript collections. Previous editions of the *Congressional Directory* also provided important biographical information, particularly for Puerto Rican Resident Commissioners. This Government Printing Office (GPO) publication, published once per Congress in recent Congresses but often once per session in earlier Congresses, dates to the early 19th century. From the 104th Congress (1995–1997) onward, the *Congressional Directory* is available at http://www.gpo.gov/fdsys/.

In the early phase of our research, we also consulted standard secondary references such as the *American National Biography*, the *Dictionary of American Biography*, and *Current Biography*. We used various editions of the *Almanac of American Politics* (Washington, D.C.: National Journal Inc.) and *Politics in America* (Washington, D.C.: CQ Press; Congressional Quarterly, Inc.; CQ-Roll Call, Inc.) as a starting point to research current Members and many former Members who served after 1971. We also consulted various editions of the United States Census for biographical information about Members by using ancestrylibrary.com at the Library of Congress, Washington, D.C. Many of these census citations appear in the notes.

Much of the information in this book was obtained from primary sources, particularly published official congressional records and scholarly compilations of congressional statistics. Following is a summary of the sources we consulted for information related to congressional elections, committee assignments, legislation, votes, floor debates, news accounts, and images.

- The election results for the biennial congressional elections from 1920 onward are available in the Clerk's "Election Statistics," published by GPO and available in PDF format at http://history.house.gov/institution/election-statistics/election-statistics. We used the names of current and former Members at the time of their election to Congress or their listing in congressional sources. Michael J. Dubin et al., *United States Congressional Elections, 1788–1997* (Jefferson, NC: McFarland and Company, Publishing, Inc., 1998) contains results for both general and special elections. For the results of elections for Territorial Delegates in New Mexico during the 19th century, we consulted W. G. Ritch, *The Legislative Blue Book of the Territory of New Mexico* (Albuquerque: University of New Mexico Press: 1968; reprint of 1882 edition);

the U.S. Department of State Territorial Papers, New Mexico, 1851–1872 (National Archives Microfilm Publication T17, Roll 2); General Records of the Department of State, Record Group 59, National Archives at College Park, College Park, MD (hereinafter referred to as NACP); and the U.S. Department of Interior Territorial Papers of New Mexico, 1851–1914 (National Archives Microfilm Publication M364, Roll 2); General Records of the Department of the Interior, Record Group 48, NACP. For results for elections for Puerto Rican Resident Commissioners that were held before 1940, our main source was Fernando Bayron Toro, *Elecciones y partidos políticos de Puerto Rico: 1809–2000* (Mayagüez, PR: Editorial Isla, 2003).

- For information on district boundaries and reapportionment, we relied on Kenneth C. Martis, *The Historical Atlas of Political Parties in the United States Congress, 1789–1989* (New York: Macmillan Publishing Company, 1989) and the three-volume work by Stanley B. Parsons et al., *United States Congressional Districts* (New York: Greenwood Press, 1986). Various editions of the *Congressional Directory* proved useful for consultation.
- Committee assignments and information about jurisdiction can be found in three indispensable scholarly compilations: David T. Canon, Garrison Nelson, and Charles Stewart III, *Committees in the U.S. Congress, 1789–1946*, four vols. (Washington, D.C.: CQ Press, 2002); Garrison Nelson, *Committees in the U.S. Congress, 1947–1992*, two vols. (Washington, D.C.: CQ Press, 1994); and Garrison Nelson and Charles Stewart III, *Committees in the U.S. Congress, 1993–2010* (Washington, D.C.: CQ Press, 2011). Committee rosters and information also are published in the *Congressional Directory*. However, this source does not indicate changes in committee composition that occur mid-Congress.
- Legislation, floor debates, roll call votes, bills, resolutions, and public laws dating back to the 1980s can be searched on the Library of Congress's THOMAS website at http://www.loc.gov. Two particularly useful print resources that discuss historical acts of Congress are Steven V. Stathis, *Landmark Legislation, 1774–2002: Major U.S. Acts and Treaties* (Washington, D.C.: CQ Press, 2002) and Brian K. Landsberg, ed., *Major Acts of Congress*, three vols. (New York: Macmillan Reference, Thompson-Gale, 2004). Floor debates about legislation can be found in the *Congressional Record* (1873 to the present), which is available from 1989 to present at the THOMAS website at http://www.loc.gov; an index of the *Record* from 1983 to the present is available at http://www.gpo.gov/fdsys/. Electronic copies of the *Annals of Congress* and the *Congressional Globe* (the predecessors of the *Congressional Record*) are available at http://www.loc.gov. We also consulted the official proceedings in the *House Journal* and the *Senate Journal*. For House roll call votes back to the second session of the 101st Congress, please visit http://history.house.gov. For Senate roll call votes back to the first session of the 101st Congress, check the U.S. Senate website at http://www.senate.gov/. For print copies of the *Congressional Directory*, the *Annals of Congress*, the *Congressional Globe*, the *Congressional Record*, the *House Journal*, or the *Senate Journal*, please consult a local federal depository

library. A GPO locator for federal depository libraries is accessible at http://catalog.gpo.gov/fdlpdir/FDLPdir.jsp. For presidential statements and addresses, we used John Woolley and Gerhard Peters, eds., *The American Presidency Project* at http://www.presidency.ucsb.edu.

Using an online database, we reviewed key newspapers for the historical periods included in this book, including the *Christian Science Monitor*, the *Los Angeles Times*, the *New York Times*, the *Wall Street Journal*, and the *Washington Post.* We also consulted microfilm editions of Spanish and Spanish-English newspapers, including the *Albuquerque* (NM) *Journal* (various editions); *El mundo* (San Juan, PR); *La correspondencia* (San Juan, PR); *La democracia* (San Juan, PR); the *San Juan Star* (San Juan, PR); the Santa Fe (NM) *Weekly Gazette* (various editions); and the Santa Fe *New Mexican* (various editions). News accounts and feature stories provided missing information, particularly for Members who served before 1945. All the newspaper articles are cited in the notes.

We consulted a number of primary source collections for biographical and legislative information. In addition to the U.S. Department of the Interior Territorial Papers (Record Group 48) and the U.S. Department of State General Records Files (Record Group 59), we consulted the Presidential State Files, Herbert Hoover Presidential Library, West Branch, IA; Records of the Office of Territories, Record Group 126; and the Records of the Bureau of Insular Affairs, Record Group 350, NACP; and the Records of the Congressional Hispanic Caucus, Record Group 233, National Archives, Washington, D.C. We also visited the Center for Southwest Research at the University of New Mexico (Albuquerque); the State Records Center and Archives and the Museum of New Mexico (Santa Fe) to review microfilm and photo collections of 19th- and early 20th-century New Mexico; and the Louisiana State University Libraries Special Collections (Baton Rouge).

BIBLIOGRAPHIC SOURCES

We hope this book will serve as a starting point for students and researchers. Accordingly, we have provided bibliographic information. When applicable, we have included information at the end of each profile about principal manuscript collections, other repositories with significant holdings, and oral histories. This information was drawn from the House and Senate records that were used to compile the *Biographical Directory of the United States Congress.*

The historical literature on Latino studies, which has become one of the most dynamic fields in the profession, has been created largely since the 1960s and is far too complex for a detailed discussion here. As often as possible, in the endnotes of the essays and profiles of this volume, we have pointed readers toward standard works on various aspects of Latino studies and congressional history. However, the following general studies of Hispanic-American politics and civil rights proved important. They include F. Chris Garcia and Gabriel R. Sanchez, *Hispanics and the U.S. Political System: Moving into the Mainstream* (Upper Saddle River, NJ: Pearson Prentice-Hall, 2008) and Maurilio E. Vigil, *Hispanics in Congress: A Historical and Political Survey* (Lanham, MD: University Press of America, 1996). For the rise of Chicano activism, two books by Juan Gómez-Quiñones are standard: *Chicano Politics: Reality & Promise,*

1940–1990 (Albuquerque: University of New Mexico Press, 1990) and *Roots of Chicano Politics, 1600–1940* (Albuquerque: University of New Mexico Press, 1994). Manuel G. Gonzales, *Mexicanos: A History of Mexicans in the United States*, second ed. (Bloomington: Indiana University Press, 2009), David Montejano, *Anglos and Mexicans in the Making of Texas, 1836–1986* (Austin: University of Texas Press, 1987), and John D. Skrentny, *The Minority Rights Revolution* (Cambridge: Belknap Press of Harvard University Press, 2002), are also useful histories. An important general reference work is Suzanne Oboler and Deena J. González, eds., *The Oxford Encyclopedia of Latinos & Latinas in the United States*, four vols. (New York: Oxford University Press, 2005).

For the history of America's relationship with Puerto Rico and overseas possessions with Hispanic populations, we found the following works to be useful. The standard overview of Puerto Rican-U.S. relations is César J. Ayala and Rafael Bernabe, *Puerto Rico in the American Century: A History since 1898* (Chapel Hill: University of North Carolina Press, 2007). Also helpful, though more focused on the U.S. perspective, are books by Surendra Bhana, *The United States and the Development of the Puerto Rican Status Question, 1936–1968* (Lawrence: The University Press of Kansas, 1975), Roland I. Perusse, *The United States and Puerto Rico: The Struggle for Equality* (Malabar, FL: Robert E. Krieger Publishing Company, 1990), and Truman R. Clark, *Puerto Rico and the United States, 1917–1933* (University of Pittsburgh Press, 1975). Other useful works that focus on specific aspects of Puerto Rican history during the era of American rule are Thomas G. Mathews, *Puerto Rican Politics and the New Deal* (Gainesville: University of Florida Press, 1960); Alfredo Montalvo-Barbot, *Political Conflict and Constitutional Change in Puerto Rico, 1898–1952* (Lanham, MD: University Press of America, 1997); and James L. Dietz, *Economic History of Puerto Rico: Institutional Change and Capitalist Development* (Princeton: Princeton University Press, 1986). To help us better understand the complicated Puerto Rican political landscape, we consulted Robert J. Alexander, ed., *Political Parties of the Americas* (Westport, CT: Greenwood Press, 1982) and Robert W. Anderson, *Party Politics in Puerto Rico* (Stanford, CA: Stanford University Press, 1965). Two political biographies also were important: A. W. Maldonado, *Luis Muñoz Marín: Puerto Rico's Democratic Revolution* (San Juan, PR: La Editorial Universidad de Puerto Rico, 2006) and Gonzalo F. Córdova, *Resident Commissioner Santiago Iglesias and His Times* (San Juan, PR: Editorial de la Universidad de Puerto Rico, 1993). For an introduction to the protean nature of Puerto Rico's status in the American empire, we consulted Christina Duffy Burnett and Burke Marshall, eds., *Foreign in a Domestic Sense: Puerto Rico, American Expansion, and the Constitution* (Durham, NC: Duke University Press, 2001) and Bartholomew H. Sparrow, *The Insular Cases and the Emergence of American Empire* (Lawrence: The University Press of Kansas, 2006).

A number of volumes helped us better understand the history of New Mexico, its status as a territory and push for statehood, and the U.S. Southwest generally. Useful general histories included Charles F. Coan, *A History of New Mexico*, three vols. (Chicago & New York: The American Historical Society, 1925); Jack E. Holmes, *Politics in New Mexico* (Albuquerque: University of

Admiral William Leahy (bottom right) speaks with Puerto Rican officials in 1939 about his new position as the island's governor. Among the officials are Resident Commissioner Santiago Iglesias (seated, center) and future Resident Commissioner Bolivar Pagán (standing second from right).

Image courtesy of the Library of Congress

New Mexico Press, 1967); Howard R. Lamar, *The Far Southwest, 1846–1912: A Territorial History*, rev. ed. (Albuquerque: University of New Mexico Press, 2000); and Robert W. Larson, *New Mexico's Quest for Statehood, 1846–1912* (Albuquerque: University of New Mexico Press, 1968). Laura E. Gómez, *Manifest Destinies: The Making of the Mexican American Race* (New York: New York University Press, 2007) and John M. Nieto-Phillips, *The Language of Blood: The Making of Spanish-American Identity in New Mexico, 1880s–1930s* (Albuquerque: University of New Mexico Press, 2004) offer compelling narratives about ethnic and racial identity in the territory in the decades after its control was transferred to the United States. For biographical information on early Territorial Delegates, the following were valuable guides: Carlos Brazil Ramirez, "The Hispanic Political Elite in Territorial New Mexico: A Study of Classical Colonialism" (Ph.D. diss., University of California–Santa Barbara, 1979); Gerald Arthur Theisen, "Jose Manuel Gallegos (1815–75): The First Mexican-American in the United States Congress" (Ph.D. diss., University of New Mexico, 1985); Ralph Emerson Twitchell, ed., *Leading Facts of New Mexican History*, vol. II (Cedar Rapids, IA: Torch Press, 1912); and Maurilio E. Vigil, *Los Patrones: Profiles of Hispanic Political Leaders in New Mexico History* (Washington, D.C.: University Press of America, 1980).

For a better understanding of the history of U.S. territorial acquisition and Manifest Destiny, we consulted George C. Herring, *From Colony to Superpower: U.S. Foreign Relations since 1776* (New York: Oxford University Press, 2008); Reginald Horsman, *Race and Manifest Destiny: The Origins of American Racial Anglo-Saxonism* (Cambridge: Harvard University Press, 1981); Thomas R. Hietala, *Manifest Design: American Exceptionalism & Empire* (Ithaca: Cornell University Press, 2003); Daniel Walker Howe, *What Hath God Wrought: The Transformation of America, 1815–1848* (New York: Oxford University Press, 2007); Walter LaFeber, *The American Age: U.S. Foreign Policy at Home and Abroad*, two vols. (New York: W. W. Norton, 1994); Eric T. L. Love, *Race over Empire: Racism & U.S. Imperialism, 1865–1900* (Chapel Hill: University of North Carolina Press, 2004); and Gordon S. Wood, *Empire of Liberty: A History of the Early Republic, 1789–1815* (New York: Oxford University Press, 2009).

The notion of representation on the periphery of a democracy, which is embodied by statutory representatives to Congress, is understudied and ripe for scholarly exploration. Nevertheless, the following works are helpful jumping-off points: Abraham Holtzman, "Empire and Representation: The U.S. Congress," *Legislative Studies Quarterly* 11, no. 2 (May 1986): 249–273; Arnold H. Leibowitz, *Defining Status: A Comprehensive Analysis of United States Territorial Relations* (Dordrecht, Netherlands: Martinus Nijhoff, 1989); Betsy Palmer, "Delegates to the U.S. Congress: History and Current Status," Congressional Research Service (CRS) Report for Congress (R40555), 6 January 2011, Library of Congress, Washington, D.C.; R. Eric Petersen, "Resident Commissioner from Puerto Rico," CRS Report for Congress (RL31856), 16 January 2009; Earl S. Pomeroy, *The Territories and the United States, 1861–1890: Studies in Colonial Administration* (Seattle: University of Washington Press, 1969; reprint of 1947 edition); José E. Rios, "The Office of the Resident

Commissioner of Puerto Rico" (M.A. thesis, Georgetown University, 1969); William R. Tansill, "The Resident Commissioner to the United States from Puerto Rico," *Revista juridica de la Universidad de Puerto Rico* 47, nos. 1–2, 1978: 68–106; and Nancy Jo Tice, "The Territorial Delegate, 1794–1820" (Ph.D. diss., University of Wisconsin, 1967).

For readers who are interested in acquiring reproductions of the photographs in this book, we have provided information for images from public, private, and commercial repositories. The photo collections we used are as follows: Prints and Photographs Division of the Library of Congress (Washington, D.C.); the Still Pictures Branch of the National Archives and Records Administration (College Park, MD); the Center for Southwest Research, University of New Mexico (Albuquerque); the Museum of New Mexico (Santa Fe); the Puerto Rican Cultural Institute (Chicago, IL); and the Las Vegas Citizens Committee for Historic Preservation (Las Vegas, NM). Others photographs were provided by the Collection of the U.S. House of Representatives; the Office of Photography, U.S. House of Representatives; the Collection of the U.S. Senate; and the U.S. Senate Historical Office. The images of current Members were provided by their offices, which are the point of contact for those seeking official images.

ACKNOWLEDGMENTS

The following individuals and institutions generously contributed their time and expertise in the textual and photographic research for this volume: Germain J. Bienvenu, Judy Bolton, and Barry Cowan of the Louisiana State University Libraries Special Collections in Baton Rouge, LA; Nancy Brown-Martinez and the staff of the Center for Southwest Research, University of New Mexico–Albuquerque; the staff of the Congressional Research Service, Library of Congress, Washington, D.C.; Jessie Kratz, Kris Wilhelm, and the staff of the Center for Legislative Archives, National Archives and Records Administration, Washington, D.C.; Nick Linville, Southeastern Archaeological Research, Jonesville, FL; Deborah Mekeel at The State Library of Florida, Tallahassee; Richard Peuser and the staffs at the branches for Textual Records, Microfilm, and Still Pictures Research, National Archives at College Park, MD; John Phelps, Curator of the Florida Historical Capitol, Tallahassee, FL; Melissa Salazar and staff, Archives and Historical Services, New Mexico State Records Center and Archives, Santa Fe; Howard Spencer at the Herbert Hoover Presidential Library, West Branch, IA; Faith Yoman and the staff at the New Mexico State Library, Santa Fe; and the staffs of the Fenwick Library at George Mason University, Fairfax, VA; the Franklin D. Roosevelt Presidential Library, Hyde Park, NY; the Harry S. Truman Presidential Library, Independence, MO; the Lauinger Library at Georgetown University, Washington, D.C.; the staff of the Newspaper and Current Periodical Reading Room of the Library of Congress, Washington, D.C.; and the staff of the Local History and Genealogy Reading Room at the Library of Congress.

A special thanks is in order for experts in Latino studies and Congress who graciously reviewed and commented on the manuscript: Georgette Dorn and Tracy North of the Hispanic Division, Library of Congress, and Historian Donald Ritchie, Associate Historian Betty Koed, and Assistant Historian Kate Scott of the

U.S. Senate Historical Office. We also thank Juan Manuel Pérez of the Hispanic Division, Library of Congress for reviewing and editing Spanish transcriptions.

We thank the supportive and collegial staff of the Office of the Clerk of the House of Representatives. Clerk of the House Karen L. Haas and Deputy Clerk Robert Reeves provided instrumental support. The Office of Communications in the Office of the Clerk designed the print and Web versions of this publication. For their collaboration and enthusiasm, we especially thank Phill McGowan, Communications Chief; Catherine Cooke, Manager of Integrated Communications; Mark Seavey, Senior Communications Designer; Chris Kelly, Senior Multimedia Developer; January Layman-Wood, Senior Content Developer; Kelsey Bensch, Content and Multimedia Producer; Malcolm Rouse-West, Design and Multimedia Producer; and Y. Michelle Haynes, Administrative Assistant. In addition, Government Printing Office designer Amy Ellis provided essential design support. We also thank Dale Thomas, Chief of the Legislative Resource Center, and copyeditor Marcie Kanakis for their help. The courteous and professional staff at the libraries of the U.S. House of Representatives and the U.S. Senate provided timely research assistance.

Lastly, we thank our colleagues in the Office of Art & Archives (OAA) in the Office of the Clerk for their help. OAA Chief and House Curator Farar Elliott and curatorial staff Karen McKinstry, Felicia Wivchar, and Britta Arendt vetted captions and credits related to artifacts from the House Collection. House Archivist Robin Reeder and archivists Heather Bourk and Alison Trulock provided information about manuscript collections, facilitated research visits to the National Archives, and acquired copies of rare images for this publication. Office Manager Selena Haskins and operations assistant Catherine Wallace performed the herculean task of handling project correspondence and keeping the writers on track while managing myriad other projects for the office.

Matthew A. Wasniewski, Historian

Co-editors: Albin J. Kowalewski, Laura Turner O'Hara, and Terrance Rucker

Co-writers: Jacqueline Burns, Erin Hromada, Kathleen Johnson, Kenneth Kato, Joshua Litten, and Barry Pump

NOTES

1 The closing date for the individuals included in this volume was September 1, 2012.

2 For a useful essay on surrogate representation within a larger discussion about "descriptive" versus "substantive" representation, see Michele L. Swers and Stella M. Rouse, "Descriptive Representation: Understanding the Impact of Identity on Substantive Representation of Group Interests," in *The Oxford Handbook of the American Congress*, Eric Schickler and Frances E. Lee, eds. (New York: Oxford University Press, 2011): 241–271.

3 The proportions (through June 2012) for African Americans are similar: a total of 132, 126 of whom have served in the House and six of whom have served in the U.S. Senate (4.5 percent of the total). A total of 277 women have served in Congress—238 in the House and 39 in the Senate (14 percent of the total); eight of the women with Senate service had served previously in the House.

4 See Office of History and Preservation, U.S. House of Representatives, *Women in Congress, 1917–2006* (Washington, D.C.: Government Printing Office, 2007): 1–5; *Black Americans in Congress, 1870–2007* (Washington, D.C.: Government Printing Office, 2008): 1–7.

5 See for example, Abraham Holtzman, "Empire and Representation: The U.S. Congress," *Legislative Studies Quarterly* 11, no. 2 (May 1986): 249–273.

6 For more on the "work horse" versus "show horse" styles, see James L. Payne, "Show Horses and Work Horses in the United States House of Representatives," *Polity* 12 (Spring 1980): 428–456.

7 For the quotation, see Thomas J. Foley, "'Brown Power' Parley Opens This Weekend,'" 22 October 1971, *Los Angeles Times*: A18. See also Jack Rosenthal, "U.S. Latins Vote Political Drive: Office in Capital Planned by Spanish-Speaking Unit," 25 October 1971, *New York Times*: 17.

8 *Congressional Globe*, House, 34th Cong., 1st sess. (23 July 1856): 1730.

9 For overviews of the Insular Cases, see James E. Kerr, *The Insular Cases: The Role of the Judiciary in American Expansionism* (Kennikat, NY: Kennikat Press, 1982): 3–13; Christina Duffy Burnett and Burke Marshall, "Between the Foreign and the Domestic: The Doctrine of Territorial Incorporation, Invented and Reinvented," in Christina Duffy Burnett and Burke Marshall, eds., *Foreign in a Domestic Sense: Puerto Rico, American Expansion, and the Constitution* (Durham, NC: Duke University Press, 2001): 1–36.

10 *Congressional Record*, House, 61st Cong., 2nd sess. (1 June 1910): 7241.

11 David Vidal, "Congressional Caucus Is Formed to Speak for Hispanic Population," 9 December 1976, *New York Times*: 32.

12 Memorandum, Georgette Dorn (chief, Hispanic Division, Library of Congress) to Matthew Wasniewski (deputy chief/historian, Office of History and Preservation, U.S. House of Representatives), 13 October 2010.

13 For general discussions of these various ethnic labels, see F. Chris Garcia and Gabriel R. Sanchez, *Hispanics and the U.S. Political System: Moving into the Mainstream* (Upper Saddle River, NJ: Pearson-Prentice Hall, 2007): 6–14; Kim Geron, *Latino Political Power* (Boulder, CO: Lynne Rienner Publishers, 2005): 3–4; and Suzanne Oboler, *Ethnic Labels, Latino Lives: Identity and the Politics of (Re)Presentation in the United States* (Minneapolis: University of Minnesota Press, 1995): i–xxi, 1–16.

Hispanic Americans in Congress

17th–112th Congresses (1821–2012)*

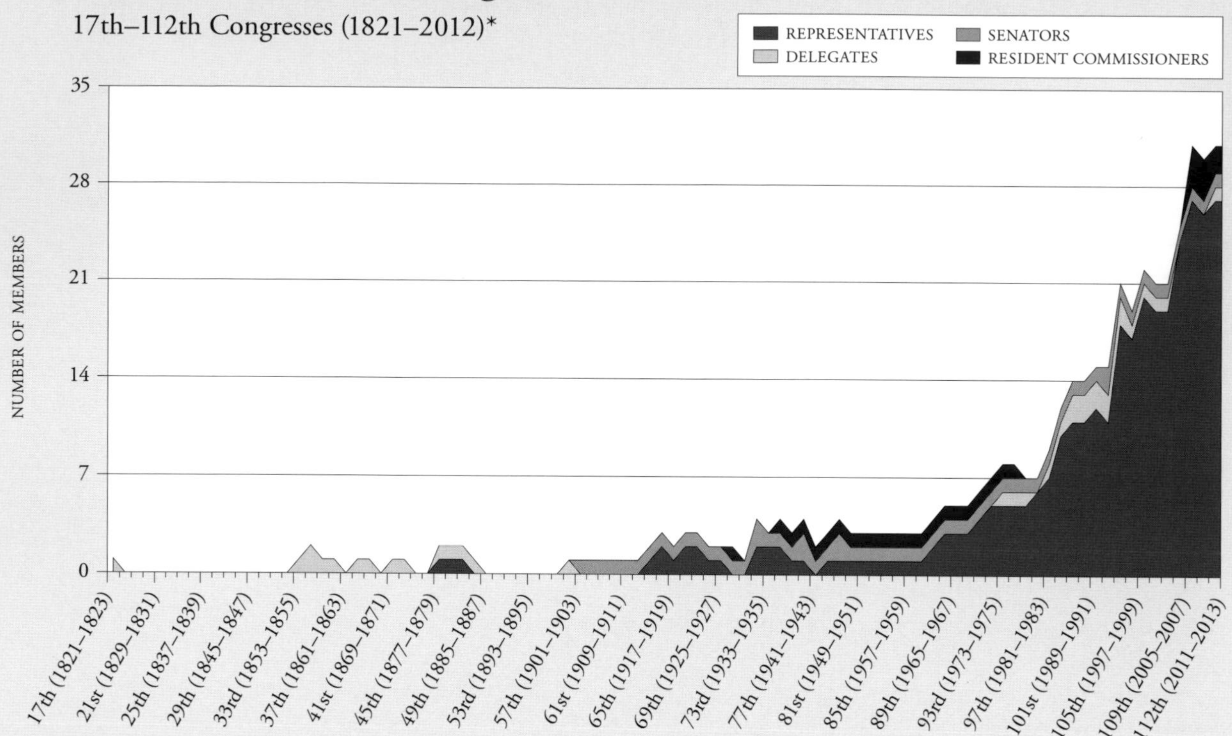

Hispanic Americans as a Percentage of Congress

17th–112th Congresses (1821–2012)*

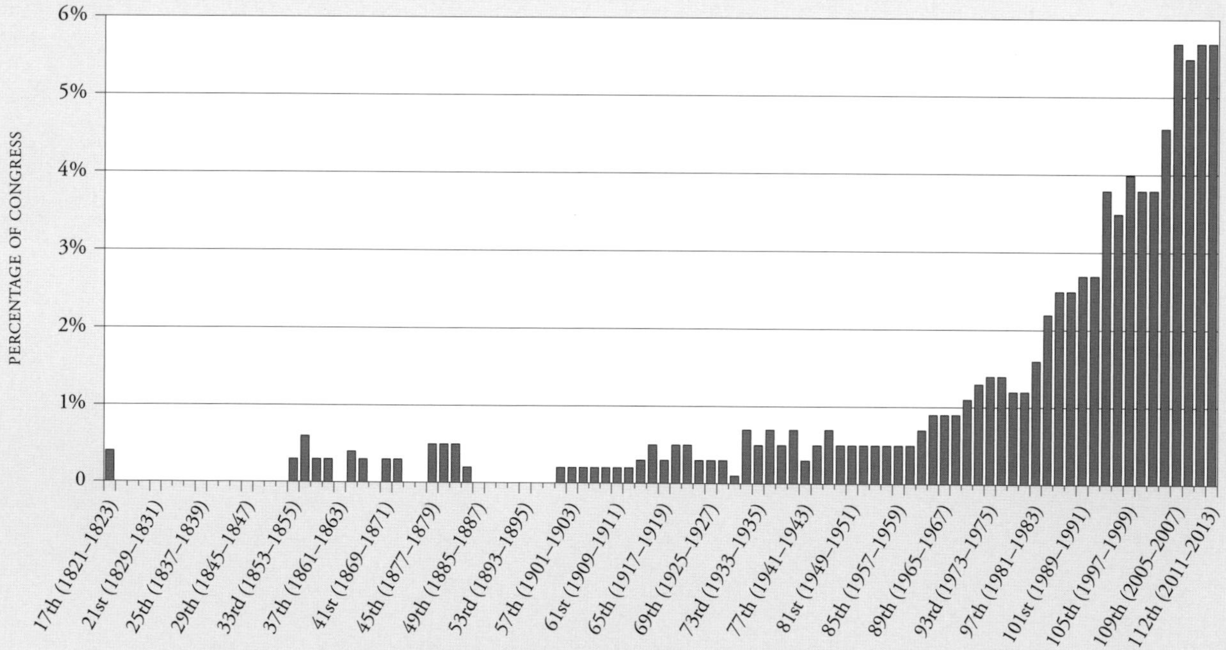

Source: Appendix A: Hispanic-American Representatives, Senators, Delegates, and Resident Commissioners by Congress, 1822–2012; Office of the Historian, U.S. House of Representatives; U.S. Senate Historical Office.

*112th Congress (2011–2013) as of September 1, 2012.

Hispanic-American Members by Office†
1821–2012*

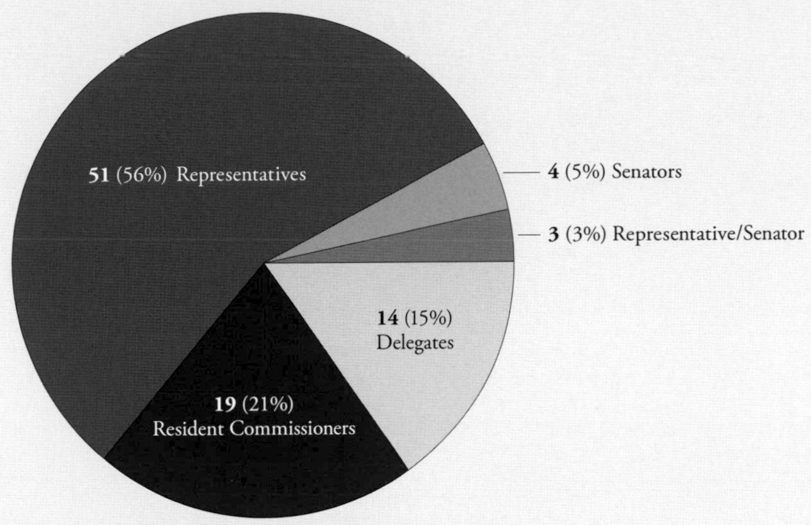

Length of Service of Hispanic-American Members of Congress‡
17th–112th Congresses (1821–2012)*

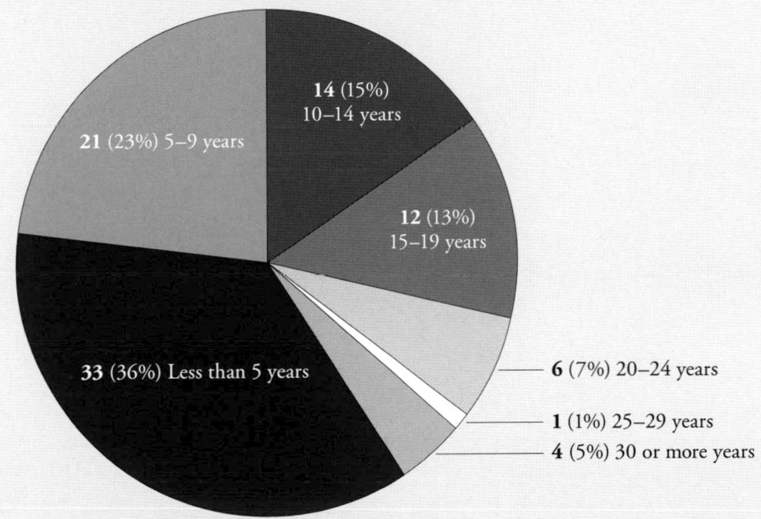

Sources: † Appendix A: Hispanic-American Representatives, Senators, Delegates, and Resident Commissioners by Congress, 1822–2012; ‡ *Biographical Directory of the United States Congress, 1774–2005* (Washington, D.C.: Government Printing Office, 2005); also available at http://bioguide.congress.gov.

*112th Congress (2011–2013) as of September 1, 2012.

★ PART ONE ★

Former Hispanic-American Members

From Democracy's Borderlands

HISPANIC CONGRESSIONAL REPRESENTATION IN THE ERA OF U.S. CONTINENTAL EXPANSION, 1822–1898

The story of Hispanic Americans' first century in Congress unfolded in conjunction with the drive for U.S. continental expansion. Through diplomacy or through war, the United States acquired territory once ruled by Spain (Florida and portions of Louisiana) and Mexico (Texas, New Mexico, Arizona, California, Nevada, Utah, and portions of present-day Colorado and Wyoming). Ten Hispanic Americans served in Congress before the Spanish-American War in 1898. With the exception of the first—Joseph Marion Hernández, a Territorial Delegate from Florida who served for a brief term during the 17th Congress (1821–1823)—and for Representative Romualdo Pacheco of California, all of them were Territorial Delegates from New Mexico. By incorporating these new possessions as territories, and eventually as states, Congress opened the door to Hispanic participation in the federal government. However, Hispanic representation in Congress consisted initially of a long line of Territorial Delegates with relatively brief tenures and limited powers who functioned more like lobbyists than traditional legislators.

Just weeks after José Manuel Gallegos triumphed in a contested election, becoming New Mexico's first Hispanic Territorial Delegate in the U.S. House, he faced the prospect of being a voiceless legislator, both literally and figuratively. A former priest from Mexico, Gallegos spoke no English, making him a bystander more than a participant on the House Floor. Unable to address the House or follow the debate, he relied on other Members to introduce resolutions for him, including Representative John Smith Phelps of Missouri, who at one point acted as Gallegos's interpreter.

Romualdo Pacheco was the first Hispanic American to serve as a voting Representative in the U.S. House. His California district extended from San Francisco Bay to the state's borders with Nevada and Mexico. Pacheco was also the first native Californian to serve as its governor.

Image courtesy of the Library of Congress

John Smith Phelps of Missouri served in Congress for nine terms (1845–1863). Phelps chaired the House Ways and Means Committee in the 35th Congress (1857–1859), but resigned his House seat to fight for the Union in the Civil War.

Image courtesy of the Library of Congress

Mexican-American War veteran William A. Richardson of Illinois succeeded Stephen A. Douglas in the House in 1847, serving for five terms. Upon Douglas' death in June 1861, Richardson was appointed to fill the unexpired term of the late Senator.

Image courtesy of the Library of Congress

Nevertheless, Gallegos was a savvy politician, having developed his skills on the "feudal frontier" of the legislature of Nuevo Mexico, which had been Mexico's most isolated province before its cession.[1] The American governor of the New Mexico Territory, David Meriwether, judged Gallegos to be "a shrewd, intelligent man" eager for knowledge about the operations of the Democratic Party, about which Gallegos admitted he knew very little.[2] Gallegos quickly enlisted key House allies to try to resolve his language problem, and on February 27, 1854, William A. Richardson of Illinois, chairman of the Committee on Territories, offered a resolution to allow Gallegos to bring an interpreter into the Hall of the House "in order that he may more effectually understand and participate in the proceedings of this body." However, Hendrick Wright of Pennsylvania immediately objected. Richardson responded, "Mr. Gallegos does not understand one word of the English language, which is the misfortune of his constituents; and this is not for his personal convenience, but for the convenience of the people that he represents."[3] Unmoved, Richardson's colleagues did not muster the two-thirds vote that was necessary to suspend the rules and have the resolution considered. This incident marked the second time in less than two months that a committee leader had failed Gallegos; earlier, Judiciary Committee chairman Frederick P. Stanton of Tennessee had tried unsuccessfully to secure an interpreter for Gallegos by introducing the matter as a privileged question.[4] The language barrier impeded Gallegos throughout his tumultuous term of service, which was cut short by another contested election. In a futile last-ditch attempt to save his seat in July 1856, Gallegos had a reading clerk present a translation of his appeal to the House.

The dismissal by the House of Gallegos's requests and of the interventions of two influential Members underscores the cultural divide between the people whose lands were acquired during the U.S.-Mexican War and the policymakers at the center of the U.S. government. The House's action also highlights the indifference many had to facilitating even the most basic level of political participation by territorial residents. Finally, the House's action illustrates the disadvantaged, even subservient, status of Territorial Delegates in the 19th-century Congress.

Although most of the *nuevomexicanos* who came to Congress had been influenced by American educational and cultural institutions, they, too, labored at a distinct institutional disadvantage.[5] Significantly, statutes and chamber rules denied them the most basic of all legislative privileges and duties: the right to vote on final legislation and the ability to serve on a committee. While their Hispanic heritage distinguished them from their congressional colleagues and made Anglo-Americans uneasy about their constituencies, it was their status as Territorial Delegates that precluded their becoming legislative actors. "Territories are really to be pitied; they are like children under a bad stepmother," commented a political observer from the New Mexico Territory in 1871. "There is no position so trying as that of the delegate in Congress from a territory. They have no vote—are the veriest beggars, relying entirely on the help of members, who have more than they can do in trying to help their own constituents."[6]

ERA OF U.S. CONTINENTAL EXPANSION

The history of Hispanic representation in Congress is entwined with that of U.S. continental expansion in the 19th century.[7] In the decades of rapid westward advance and settlement between the signing of the Adams-Onís Treaty of 1819 and the declaration of the Spanish-American War in 1898, the House nearly doubled in size.[8]

Thomas Jefferson, James Madison, and Westward Expansion

President Thomas Jefferson spearheaded westward expansion when the United States acquired the Louisiana territory from France in 1803 and sponsored Lewis and Clark's expedition (1805–1807). Jefferson's foreign policy goal to expand U.S. territory westward was intended to help the U.S. have greater freedom in dealing with foreign powers on the North American continent and to consolidate the power of the young republic. It required developing military strength and practicing shrewd diplomacy.[9] The policies Jefferson implemented, particularly regarding U.S. expansion in the modern Gulf Coast region, persisted through two more presidential administrations.

After securing the Louisiana territory, Jefferson and his successors focused on acquiring Spanish Florida—which encompassed all of modern-day Florida, as well as a strip running along the Gulf Coast to the Mississippi River. New possibilities for commerce and ports along the Gulf Coast were one rationale. National security was another: Florida offered strategic value in securing Louisiana, the Mississippi Territory, and Georgia. President James Madison employed his predecessor's tactics. In West Florida—which extended from Baton Rouge, on the east bank of the Mississippi River in modern-day Louisiana, to Pensacola, in the panhandle of modern-day Florida—U.S. settlers became the majority population from 1805 to 1810. The settlers resisted weakened Spanish rule and advocated for American sovereignty. In 1804 Congress passed the Mobile Act, which extended U.S. federal revenue laws to all territories ceded by France, including West Florida. The act also granted the President "discretionary authority" to take possession of the Mobile area.[10] In 1811 Madison asserted U.S. jurisdiction over the area and had incorporated West Florida into Louisiana. The United States annexed Mobile during the War of 1812.

Adams-Onís Treaty (Transcontinental Treaty)

Spain claimed the lands that constitute present-day Florida in addition to the land stretching from its panhandle westward, across the southern portions of modern-day Alabama and Mississippi to the eastern banks of the Mississippi River. General Andrew Jackson's invasion of Florida during the First Seminole War (1817–1818) spurred the Spanish government—fearing the loss of its claim to the territory—to the negotiating table. Benefiting from favorable geopolitical circumstances, Secretary of State John Quincy Adams entered into negotiations with Spanish diplomat Don Luis de Onís in 1819. In return for the United States' renouncing its tenuous claims to Texas and paying $5 million for U.S.

Considered the Father of the United States Constitution, James Madison of Virginia served four terms in the House (1789–1797). Like Thomas Jefferson, Madison saw the strategic value of securing the United States from foreign encroachment by acquiring East and West Florida.

James Madison (detail), Bradley Stevens (after Charles Willson Peale), 2002, Collection of the U.S. House of Representatives

Secretary of State John Quincy Adams of Massachusetts, the lead negotiator of the Adams-Onís Treaty, enjoyed a prominent political career as a foreign minister, U.S. Senator, and President before serving in the U.S. House of Representatives for nine terms (1831–1848).

John Quincy Adams, Ed Ahlstrom (after Jean-Baptiste-Adolphe Gibert), 2002, Collection of the U.S. House of Representatives

citizens' claims against Spain, Adams secured all of Spanish Florida, finalizing the Louisiana Purchase. The treaty also set a new boundary running from the mouth of the Sabine River on the Gulf Coast (on the eastern border of modern-day Texas) northwestward along portions of the Sabine, Red, and Arkansas Rivers, then westward on the 42nd parallel to the Oregon coast. It was the first boundary to traverse the U.S. continent.

The Adams-Onís Treaty also ushered in Congress's first Member of Hispanic descent; Joseph Marion Hernández served as Florida's first Territorial Delegate during the 17th Congress (1821–1823).[11] Pursuing an agenda that was typical for a Territorial Delegate, Hernández sought to secure infrastructure improvements that would benefit economic growth and bolster political arguments for Florida's admission into the Union as a state. A wealthy planter and military figure who had fought for Spanish interests in the Patriot War and the First Seminole War, Hernández helped bridge the transition from Spanish rule to American governance. It would be 30 years after Hernández's departure from the House in March 1823 until the next Hispanic Member arrived in Congress. Like many Territorial Delegates in the 19th century, Hernández returned home to a prominent career in local politics and business; he served in the legislature and led a militia in the Second Seminole War in the 1830s before making an unsuccessful bid for a U.S. Senate seat when Florida became a state in 1845.

Though the Adams-Onís agreement resolved one friction point, it created others. Critics charged that President James Monroe and Secretary of State Adams yielded legitimate claims to Texas, fueling later demands for Texas' "re-annexation," particularly by pro-slavery advocates in the 1830s. Moreover, the Adams-Onís Treaty validated Mexican ownership of lands that would become targets for U.S. expansion during the War with Mexico from 1846 to 1848.

Manifest Destiny

Powerfully articulated in the Monroe Doctrine of 1823, Adams's coolheaded geopolitical calculations provided later generations of U.S. officials with a road map for the advancement of American dominion in the Western Hemisphere. Meanwhile, Americans in the 1830s and 1840s justified their march across the continent under the rubric of "Manifest Destiny." Coined by a New York newspaper, the term described the popular desire for geographic expansion and, as such, was more a zeitgeist than an official foreign policy strategy in antebellum America.[12] Though derived from complex circumstances, Manifest Destiny was amenable to different political agendas and worldviews, and thus its appeal cut across regional, party, and class lines.[13] At the laying of the cornerstone of the Washington Monument on July 4, 1848, Speaker of the House Robert Winthrop captured the mood, employing a metaphor that evoked the era's ultimate symbol of progress: "The great American built locomotive 'Liberty' still holds it course, unimpeded and unimpaired; gathering strength as it goes," he said. "Nor can we fail to observe that men are everywhere beginning to examine the model of this mighty engine, and that not a few have already begun to copy its construction and to imitate its machinery.... The whole civilized world resounds with American opinions and American principles,"

Titled *American Progress. Westward the course of destiny. Westward ho!*, this print memorializes the movement of U.S. settlers across the continental United States during the 1840s and 1850s.

Image courtesy of the Library of Congress

he added. "Every vale is vocal with them. Every mountain has found a tongue for them."[14]

In the eyes of many observers there was little difference between federal policy and popular will. It was America's obligation, one pundit wrote in 1845, "to overspread and to possess the whole continent which providence has given us for the development of the great experiment of liberty and federated self government."[15] Such seemingly inevitable growth justified America's rapid acquisition of Western lands and amplified the nationalist sentiments of U.S. settlers in Texas and the Pacific Northwest in the 1840s.[16]

However, the concept of expansion veiled multiple motives and was advocated by Northerners and Southerners for different reasons. While many Americans supported it, such growth awakened sectional debates over slavery. The possibility of new Western lands forced the federal government to confront questions that had been somewhat mollified since the Missouri Compromise of 1820: Would new states allow slavery or oppose it? How would Congress maintain its balance of sectional interests? Expansionists, moreover, did not address the potential effects of rapid development on African Americans, American Indians, and Mexican citizens living in contested territories.[17]

Texas Revolution and Annexation

The boundaries that were ratified in the Adams-Onís Treaty, yielding Texas to New Spain, were swiftly altered in 1821 when Mexico replaced Spain as the sovereign, and U.S. settlers quickly began to cross into East Texas.[18] Throughout the 1820s, Anglos streamed into the Mexican province, outnumbering Hispanic Texans by two to one within a decade. The Mexican government sought to prohibit the slave trade, and in 1830 the Mexican Congress passed a law that suspended U.S. immigration into Texas.

In this political cartoon, Texas Army Commander-in-Chief Sam Houston (left) accepts the surrender of General Antonio López de Santa Anna. After achieving independence, Texas existed as an independent republic until its admission as a U.S. state in 1845.

Image courtesy of the Library of Congress

In 1834, the year after he assumed power, General Antonio López de Santa Anna dissolved the Mexican Congress and set up a dictatorship. Revolts erupted in several Mexican states. After the insurrection spread to Texas in June 1835 (largely because of issues related to the quartering of Mexican soldiers and because of the central government's collection of customs duties), a group of rebels in Anáhuac seized a Mexican garrison. Anglos Stephen Austin, William Travis, and Sam Houston became leading insurrectionaries. In March 1836, even as the Republic of Texas declared its independence, the Mexican Army under General Santa Anna massacred Texan forces at the Alamo in modern-day San Antonio and at Goliad, 100 miles to the southeast.[19] But under Sam Houston's command, the Army of Texas repelled Santa Anna's divided forces at the Battle of San Jacinto near modern-day Houston, killing roughly half of them and capturing nearly all the rest, including Santa Anna himself. Under the threat of death, Santa Anna ordered his forces to pull out of Texas and across the Rio Grande River, in effect recognizing Texan independence.[20]

During the next decade, the population in Texas increased from approximately 30,000 to 50,000 in 1835 to a total of approximately 125,000 to 140,000 in 1845. As members of a distinct minority who were suspected of disloyalty by Anglo settlers, Hispanic Texans were quickly excluded from the political process.[21]

With the population boom Texas' first president, Sam Houston, and subsequent leaders sought to join the United States. The Andrew Jackson administration (1829–1837) and the Martin Van Buren administration (1837–1841) demurred despite their unneutrality, fearing that annexation would provoke all-out war with Mexico—inviting a political backlash driven by critics who believed the push for Texas was linked to the extension of slavery in the Southwest.[22]

Sam Houston was a prominent war veteran and politician before moving to Texas in 1835. Houston served in the Texas congress and as its first president before his election to the U.S. Senate in 1846.

Image courtesy of the Library of Congress

But the John Tyler administration (1841–1845) was willing to proceed with annexation. Secretary of State Abel Upshur and his successor, John C. Calhoun, completed the negotiations, which were signed on April 12, 1844, and which made Texas eligible for admission as a U.S. territory, and perhaps later as one or more states. Additionally, the U.S. government assumed $10 million in Texan debt in exchange for public lands. The boundaries with Mexico were left unresolved.[23] On June 8, 1844, with public opinion stirred by antislavery activists after Senator Benjamin Tappan of Ohio leaked the provisions of the secret treaty to the press, the Senate rejected it with a vote of 35 to 16. But after the fall 1844 elections, in which James K. Polk triumphed, President Tyler pushed the treaty (H.J. Res. 46) through Congress. It passed the Democratic-controlled House 120 to 98 and the Senate 24 to 21. Tyler signed the treaty into law on March 1, 1845 (5 Stat. 797–798), three days before the end of his term. In the end, Texas was admitted as a state on December 29, 1845, with the proviso that it could be divided into as many as five states—a prospect that outraged and horrified abolitionist members of the Whig Party.[24]

War with Mexico and the Southwest

James K. Polk set an ambitious course when he assumed the presidency on March 4, 1845.[25] A strict Jacksonian, Polk accomplished what later historians have identified as three of four primary goals during the first session of the

29th Congress (1845–1847).[26] With the help of Democratic majorities in the House and the Senate, President Polk had lowered the tariff; he had created an independent treasury; and by diplomacy he had acquired the Oregon Territory from England. The acquisition of California from Mexico was all that remained of his original agenda. But unlike the acquisition of Oregon, taking possession of such coveted lands required an all-out war.[27]

Less than two years into Polk's presidency, many suspected but few knew about his grand designs for California. Revealing little, Polk sent diplomats to Mexico, pressuring the Mexican government not to interfere with the annexation of Texas. Moreover, Polk claimed that Mexico owed Americans living in Texas millions of dollars for seized and lost property. Mexican officials resisted, banishing Polk's diplomatic envoy. One historian notes, "Given the anti-American mood of their people, Mexican diplomats understood that any compromise with the United States at this time was tantamount to political suicide." An anxious Polk ordered U.S. troops to encamp just north of the Rio Grande River in an area that was claimed by both Mexico and the United States. After blockading the river and training its cannon on a nearby town, the U.S. military ignored Mexican requests to stand down. On April 25, 1846, a skirmish between Mexican and U.S. troops ignited hostilities. Mexican officials blamed the United States, while Polk blamed Mexico when he learned of the fighting two weeks later.[28]

Polk promptly appealed to Congress for "vigorous & prompt measure[s] to enable the Executive to prosecute the War."[29] Polk asked for 50,000 volunteers because "by the act of the Republic of Mexico, a state of war exists between that Government and the United States."[30] The bill (H.R. 145) met with little open resistance in the House and passed 174 to 14, with only Whigs opposed. Antislavery Whigs, like John Quincy Adams of Massachusetts and Joshua Giddings of Ohio, viewed the war with Mexico as proof that Southern interests intended to expand slavery westward.[31] Garrett Davis, a moderate Kentucky Whig, was the only one on the floor that day who voiced any opposition to the bill: "It is our own President who began this war," Davis declared. "He has been carrying it on for months in a series of acts. Congress, which is vested exclusively by the Constitution with war-making power, he has not designed to consult, much less to ask it for any authority."[32] Davis, despite his reservations, voted for the provision of troops and funding.

Horrified that the House had passed the bill in under two hours, Senator Thomas Hart Benton of Missouri told Polk that "19th Century war should not be declared without full discussion and much more consideration."[33] Others in the Senate bristled at Polk's demands. "War could not be made with Mexico," Senator John Crittenden reminded the body, "without touching the interests and exciting the jealousies of all nations trading with us." Like the House, the Senate eventually passed the bill with an overwhelming majority, 40 to 2.[34] Polk signed it into law (9 Stat. 9–10) the following day, May 13, 1846.

The war's nominal popularity in Congress disguised many people's reservations. Andrew Jackson Donelson, the former President's nephew, advised Polk to resolve the trouble quickly. "Nothing can be gained by a war with Mexico," he said. "We are not ready for another Annexation question, and

On Walker's reso: for ratification of Treaty of Annexation with Texas

8 June 1844.

YEAS.		NAYS.
	Allen	1
	Archer	2
1	Atchison	
	Atherton	3
2	Bagby	
	Barrow	4
	Bates	5
	Bayard	6
	Benton	7
	Berrien	8
3	Breese	

On June 8, 1844, the U.S. Senate refused to approve the ratification of a treaty annexing Texas to the United States. Shortly before he left office, President John Tyler, with the support of President-elect James K. Polk, maneuvered a joint resolution through both houses of Congress and signed the annexation treaty into law on March 1, 1845.

Original roll call vote on ratification of treaty to annex Texas; image courtesy of the National Archives and Records Administration

The first Speaker of the House to become President of the United States, James K. Polk was an Andrew Jackson protégé who quickly rose through the ranks of Tennessee politics. During Polk's term as President (1845–1849), the United States, through war and diplomacy, secured much of the American Southwest and long coveted Pacific Ocean ports along the West Coast.

Image courtesy of the Library of Congress

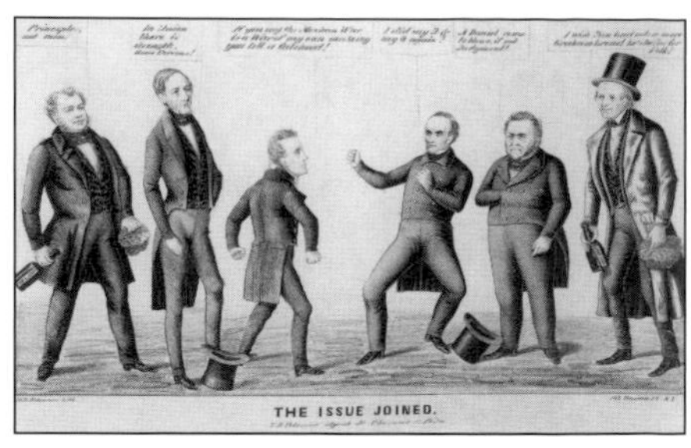

In this 1846 cartoon, President James K. Polk (center left) challenges Senator Daniel Webster of Massachusetts (center right) to a fight because of Webster's public criticisms of Polk's Texas policies. Supporters and critics of the war stand behind their respective advocates.

Image courtesy of the Library of Congress

the Mexicans are not fit for incorporation into our Union."[35] In the House, Giddings finally lambasted the war. It would, he noted, be long, expensive, and disgraceful, and given its "connection with slavery," he said, it threatened the "harmony and perpetuity of the Union."[36]

Treaty of Guadalupe Hidalgo

The Treaty of Guadalupe Hidalgo, signed by chief negotiator Nicholas P. Trist on February 2, 1848, and approved by the U.S. Senate on March 10, 1848, ended the war, opened a dramatically different chapter in U.S. relations with Mexico, and nearly completed America's continental empire.[37] The war, however, was not without cost; roughly 12,500 U.S. troops died (most from disease), and the federal government spent nearly $100 million.[38] Moreover, stiff Mexican resistance on the battlefield and at the negotiating table made the conflict last longer than the Polk administration anticipated. Popular support waned as the conflict continued, contributing to a change in control; the House flipped to a new Whig majority in the 1846 elections.[39] Moreover, "Mr. Polk's War" brought the country closer to fratricidal conflict: Would the new territories permit or outlaw slavery?

Even counting the human, financial, and political costs of the war, the Treaty of Guadalupe Hidalgo represented an American bonanza purchased at a discount. For the equivalent of nearly one-third of the landmass of the modern continental United States, American officials paid $15 million to Mexico and assumed $3.25 million in war claims by U.S. citizens.[40] In one fell swoop, America gained control of 530,000 square miles. From Mexico's vantage point, the United States gained over 900,000 square miles, including disputed Texas land claims Mexico had long considered illegitimate. The United States obtained nearly all of modern-day New Mexico and Arizona (whose southern portions were later acquired in the 1853 Gadsden Purchase); all of Nevada, Utah, and California, with its coveted deep water ports on the Pacific Ocean; and portions of present-day Colorado and Wyoming.[41] The war also engendered resentment among Mexicans and other Latin Americans, leaving many wary of U.S. motives.[42]

The Treaty of Guadalupe Hidalgo also began to address practical issues that arose from the fact that roughly 90,000 Mexican citizens, and substantially more American Indians of various tribes, were living in the newly acquired lands, most of them in what became modern-day New Mexico.[43] The treaty contained provisions pertaining to Mexican citizens—a group that included the nonitinerant Pueblo Indians—which guaranteed their U.S. citizenship and property rights, and permitted indigenous peoples to retain or renounce their Mexican citizenship in favor of U.S. citizenship. The treaty also extended blanket U.S. citizenship to any individual who had not made a declaration within one year of its ratification.

A Zia Pueblo family was photographed in the New Mexico Territory in 1885.

Image courtesy of the Library of Congress

But these guarantees were qualified. For instance, Pueblos, although they were Mexican citizens, were not accorded full civil and political rights. Instead, they were treated like the members of other Indian tribes in U.S. territory, who would eventually be moved to reservations and would not participate in territorial politics. For decades, congressional debates about New Mexican statehood were dominated by the question of whether *nuevomexicanos* were

This 1848 map outlines the territories acquired by the United States in the Treaty of Guadalupe Hidalgo. The borders of California, New Mexico, and Texas were later formalized as part of the Compromise of 1850.

E. Gilman, *Map of the United States Including Western Territories*, map (Philadelphia: P.S. Duval's Steam Lith. Press, 1848); from National Archives and Records Administration, Records of the U.S. House of Representatives, RG 233

white enough to achieve self-government, leading many *Hispano* politicians to accentuate their Spanish ancestry and to differentiate themselves from their Mexican and American Indian constituents.[44]

The Senate's consideration of the treaty amplified the calls of Manifest Destiny.[45] Thomas Ritchie, editor of the pro-Polk Washington *Daily Union*, wrote, "What we desire to obtain from Mexico is more of territory and less of population, but we have no objection to the acquisition of a few of her people along with the soil which we get." Senator Daniel S. Dickinson of New York explained that a "majority" of *nuevomexicanos* were members of "fated aboriginal races" who could "neither uphold government or be restrained by it" and therefore must "perish under, if they do not recede before, the influences of civilization."[46] Given prevailing racial prejudices and lingering concerns about the Catholicism of the Mexicans in the Southwest, the promises of citizenship as outlined by the treaty remained for decades largely unresolved, particularly in territories such as New Mexico and Arizona.

STATUTORY REPRESENTATION

Continental expansion forced Congress, particularly the House, to grapple with important representational questions. These issues were addressed in a patchwork manner. Like the territories they represented, which existed at the fringes of the United States' growing continental empire, 19th-century Delegates operated at the periphery of the House's power structure. Their influence, such as it was, depended upon statutes fixed by Congress and, just as significantly, on the sometimes-capricious nature of House Rules. This system had profound consequences for New Mexicans' representation in Congress.

From the very beginning, Congress has contended with the Constitution's silence on the issue of representation for U.S. territories. Over decades of improvisation, a system of "statutory representation" emerged that consists of laws crafted by Congress, complemented by evolving procedural rules in the House, giving territories a limited voice in the national legislature through the office of Territorial Delegate and, later, the Office of the Resident Commissioner.[47]

Territorial representation predated the First Federal Congress, which convened under the Constitution in 1789. Operating under the Articles of Confederation, the Continental Congress enacted the Northwest Ordinance of 1787 to create a government for the territory northwest of the Ohio River. That legislation provided for a Territorial Delegate, who was entitled to a seat in Congress but not to a vote on bills. From the outset, Delegates were seen as advocates who could foster awareness of and general discussion about territorial interests and perhaps even shape legislation during its formative stages, but also as individuals who were not fully empowered as legislators because they could not vote on final bills. After the Constitution was adopted, the First Federal Congress re-enacted the Northwest Ordinance in 1789, providing for a Delegate pending the establishment of a territorial legislature to elect the Delegate. A year later, Congress granted the Territory South of the River Ohio, which would become Tennessee, the privileges provided by the Northwest Ordinance. That territory sent the first Delegate, James White, to the federal capital in Philadelphia. White, who had represented North Carolina in the Continental Congress and who was the grandfather of future chief justice of the U.S. Supreme Court Edward Douglass White, presented his credentials to the House on November 11, 1794.

The concept envisioned by the unicameral Continental Congress now stood embodied in flesh and blood before a bicameral U.S. Congress. Representatives of the Third Congress (1793–1795) were understandably perplexed, and a vigorous discussion ensued on the House Floor. Was Delegate White a Member of the House? Or, did he belong in the Senate, since he—like every Senator—had been elected by the territorial/state legislature? Was he entitled to a seat in both chambers? If he was not fully a Member of the House, would he be given franking privileges? Could he be present when the House went into closed session? How would he be compensated, and should he be required to take the oath of office?[48]

Jonathan Dayton of New Jersey served in colonial and federal legislatures throughout his distinguished political career. A Revolutionary War veteran, Dayton also signed the U.S. Constitution in 1787 and served as Speaker of the House (1795–1799).

Jonathan Dayton (detail), Henry Harrison, 1911, Collection of the U.S. House of Representatives

Some, like Representative Zephaniah Swift of Connecticut, believed it was bad precedent to admit a person for whom "the Constitution has made no provision." Swift warned, "If we can admit a Delegate to Congress … we may with equal propriety admit a stranger from any quarter of the world."[49] William L. Smith of South Carolina believed that White was "no more than an Envoy to Congress … an Officer deputed by the people" of the territory. Jonathan Dayton of New Jersey, who chaired the Committee on Elections and would assume the Speakership in the following Congress, weighed in with a central conclusion: "Call him what you will, a member, a Delegate, or, if you please, a *nondescript*.... He is not a member. He cannot vote, which is the essential part." While conceding the right of debate to the Delegate, Dayton noted that the scope of the latter's power and participation was similar to that of "a printer [who] may be said to argue and influence, when he comes to this House, takes notes, and prints them in the newspapers."[50] The House seated White (he served for two years until Tennessee achieved statehood) and voted against requiring him to take the oath of office. Several months later, White was appointed to a select committee to study methods to promulgate U.S. laws more efficiently.[51]

Subsequent Delegates followed White's example, serving solely in the House, though more than two decades elapsed before the House established some clear definitions of Delegates' rights and responsibilities. Franking privileges were allowed, and eventually Delegates were required to take the oath of office. Starting with White, service on select committees became routine; occasionally Delegates chaired these select panels.[52] Moreover, at least one Delegate, William Henry Harrison of the Northwest Territory, served as a conferee to negotiate disputed legislation with the Senate.[53] Finally, in March 1817, the 14th Congress (1815–1817) passed a law stating that Delegates were to be seated exclusively in the House and elected to two-year terms to coincide with Representatives. Borrowing from the language of the Northwest Ordinance of 1787, the law also provided a fundamental guidepost that shaped the careers of Territorial Delegates for more than 150 years: "Each of the said delegates shall have a seat with a right of debating but not voting."[54] As will be discussed in the legislative interests section of this essay, the powers of a Delegate to serve on a committee also evolved slowly during the course of the 19th century and remained circumscribed, even after the rules were modified.

In the latter 19th century, because of their numbers (10 at their peak in the 42nd and 43rd Congress, 1871–1875), Delegates gained influence in Congress and in the city of Washington. Many of New Mexico's *Hispano* Delegates served during the high-water mark of territorial representation in the House in the 1870s and 1880s. "The territorial delegate increased in stature appreciably between 1861 and 1890," explains historian Earl Pomeroy. "Without the formal powers of a congressman, he acquired more of a congressman's influence and general functions. He was disseminator of information, lobbyist, agent of territorial officers, of the territorial legislature, and of his constituency, self-constituted dispenser of patronage. He interceded at times in almost every process of control over the territories, and generally no one challenged his right to intercede."[55]

In a system that contemplated Delegates as ministers without portfolio rather than traditional legislators, their power on Capitol Hill derived almost exclusively from their relationships and their access to leadership. Voting Members might exploit their seniority status, the collective power of their respective caucuses, or institutional rules to achieve their legislative goals. But for Delegates what mattered most was their position within the institution—their proximity to the Speaker, who held unfettered committee appointment powers in the late 19th century; to the chairmen of important committees; to a Representative, Senator, or even another Delegate who could represent specialized territorial interests before a standing committee—and their alignment with influential regional blocs.

In the process of representing constituencies who were culturally dissimilar from the majority-Anglo U.S. population, Hispanic-American Delegates amplified the diplomatist characteristics of their office. As the highest-ranking elected territorial officials, Delegates were intercessors between the frontier government and the federal legislature as well as between their constituencies and Cabinet-level officials. Joseph Hernández of Florida lobbied Secretary of State John Quincy Adams to help facilitate Spanish land grant verification; similarly, he sought to enlist the help of Secretary of War John C. Calhoun to support road construction. In borderland regions, where several distinct

An accomplished Civil War veteran, Delegate José Francisco Chaves of New Mexico served three terms in the U.S. House. After his congressional service, Chaves became an important political figure in the territory for the remainder of the nineteenth century.

Helen Haines, *History of New Mexico from the Spanish Conquest to the Present Time 1530–1890 with Portraits and Biographical Sketches of its Prominent People* (New York, NY: New Mexico Historical Publishing Company, 1891)

Delegate Francisco Perea used his position to influence the selection of federal appointees to the New Mexico Territory. Perea was an ardent supporter of the reservation system to maintain peace among Anglos, Hispanos, and American Indians in the territory.

Image courtesy of the Palace of the Governors Photo Archives (NMHM/DCA), 105371

cultural groups often competed for power, the Delegates served as facilitators. For instance, Hernández was instrumental in brokering the Treaty of Moultrie Creek between the James Monroe administration and the Seminole Indians. New Mexican Delegates Francisco Perea and José Francisco Chaves lobbied the Secretary of State and the President to appoint or remove territorial officials. Their motives frequently derived from competing impulses such as ensuring the efficiency of the territorial government or promoting their political allies—often by curtailing the careers of their political enemies.

In a less tangible sense, Hispanic-American Members of this era were cultural ambassadors. The office of Delegate provided a two-way circuit for cultural transmission that involved sending the territory federal policies and the appointees to implement them, and also receiving the representatives of a new, majority-Spanish heritage constituency. “Sir, I claim to be the representative of a people who have peculiar demands upon your justice and magnanimity,” said Delegate Gallegos, addressing the Speaker and the House by means of a translated speech. “They are in their origins, alien to your institutions, your laws, your customs, your glorious history, and even strangers to your language.... I am, and have ever been, one of that very people.”[56]

PRECONGRESSIONAL EXPERIENCE

Family Origins

Every Hispanic-American Member who served in the House during this era was born in a region of continental North America that had been under Spanish rule for centuries. Two were subjects of the Spanish crown: Joseph Marion Hernández, born in 18th-century Spanish Florida, and José Manuel Gallegos, born in present-day New Mexico during the Mexican Revolution, six years before Mexican independence. Romualdo Pacheco was born in Mexico’s Alta province in modern-day Santa Barbara, California. Of the remaining seven individuals, all but Tranquilino Luna were born in Nuevo Mexico, on the northern borderlands of the new nation of Mexico. Luna was born in New Mexico in 1849 before it became a territory, during the period of U.S. occupation after the war with Mexico.

All of the Hispanic-American Members came from upper-class backgrounds; some were landed gentry or even feudal barons, and others were from well-to-do merchant families. Hernández married into wealth and at one point owned more than 40,000 acres, three plantations, and dozens of slaves in Florida. Pacheco, whose father and namesake came from a leading Mexican family and died when he was an infant, benefited from his stepfather’s shipping fortune.

New Mexico provides the clearest example of the centralization of political power and economic privilege among the *nuevomexicano* elite. All of the 19th-century *Hispano* Delegates were members of the local ruling class. Most were the scions of prominent political dynasties or wealthy merchant families that had been in the region for two centuries. Many of these *Hispano* elites were further enmeshed by marriage or business ventures. Their power bases derived from their families’ control over massive Spanish land grants, county-level politics, or the emerging mercantile and industrial economies, and sometimes a combination of all three. Unlike the Anglo politicians, who tended to be lawyers, the *Hispano* elites were usually ranchers or merchants, or both. Compared to average Members of the U.S. Congress in this era, the members of this class had accumulated considerable wealth.[57] Collectively, 19th-century Hispanic Members had vast entrepreneurial experience, including commerce, plantation-scale agriculture, large-scale ranching operations, and mercantile pursuits. With respect to most other types of experience, such as military service or prior careers as legislators or practicing lawyers, these Members mirrored their House contemporaries.[58]

Most New Mexican *Hispano* Delegates were interrelated by blood or by marriage.[59] Particularly prominent were the Otero, Perea, and Chaves families. Francisco Perea, who represented the New Mexico Territory in the House during the Civil War, and his cousin José Francisco Chaves (Territorial Delegate from 1865 to 1871) were the grandsons of Francisco Xavier Chaves, governor of Nuevo Mexico in the 1820s. Their families dominated Bernalillo County, which encompassed Albuquerque. Mariano Otero (Delegate from 1879–1881), nephew of Miguel Otero, Sr. (Delegate from 1856–1861), married into the politically active Perea family; his brother-in-law, Pedro Perea, the cousin of Francisco Perea, served as Territorial Delegate from 1899 to 1901.

The fact that Members of Congress in this era tended to have privileged backgrounds was reflected in their access to higher education. From 1820 to 1900, the percentage of House Members who had graduated from or attended college rose from roughly 40 percent to better than 62 percent.[60] By that measure, the Hispanic Members of Congress during the 1800s were exceptionally well educated; eight of the 10 attended college, with two studying law and another, medicine. Gallegos, who attended seminary and was ordained in the Roman Catholic Church, became one of the few priests ever to serve in Congress. Like many of the New Mexican elite, half of this group attended colleges in Missouri at the northern terminus of the 800-mile-long Santa Fe Trail, attesting to the route's importance not only for trade but also for cultural exchange.[61]

Most of these Hispanic-American Members were born in the 1830s and 1840s and entered the House at a younger age than did the rest of the membership. The average age when they began serving in the House was 36.5 years. This figure was substantially lower than the average age (41.5 years) of the general population of House Members, which tended to be older each decade from the 1820s to the 1890s.[62] The youngest Hispanic-American Member elected during this era was New Mexico Territorial Delegate José Francisco Chaves, who entered the House at age 31; the oldest was Romualdo Pacheco of California, who had already enjoyed a long career in state politics when he came to the House at age 45.[63] One significant result of this trend, discussed later, was that these relatively youthful Members, particularly in the New Mexico Territory, engaged elder *nuevomexicanos* in political disputes with a decidedly generational edge.

The overwhelming majority (eight of 10) of the Hispanic Members in the 19th century had experience in elective political office; at least six served in the territorial legislature. In territorial New Mexico, the Anglos controlled many of the territorial appointments, such as governor, secretary, U.S. attorney,

A successful entrepreneur who served a term as New Mexico's Delegate to Congress (1879–1881), Mariano Otero aligned himself with the powerful Santa Fe Ring to expand his businesses and political influence. Otero lost both attempts to win re-election to the House in 1888 and 1890.

Image courtesy of the Miguel A. Otero Photograph Collection (PICT 000-021-0127), Center for Southwest Research, University Libraries, University of New Mexico

Delegate José Francisco Chaves of New Mexico served in the House during the late 1860s and early 1870s.

Image courtesy of the Library of Congress

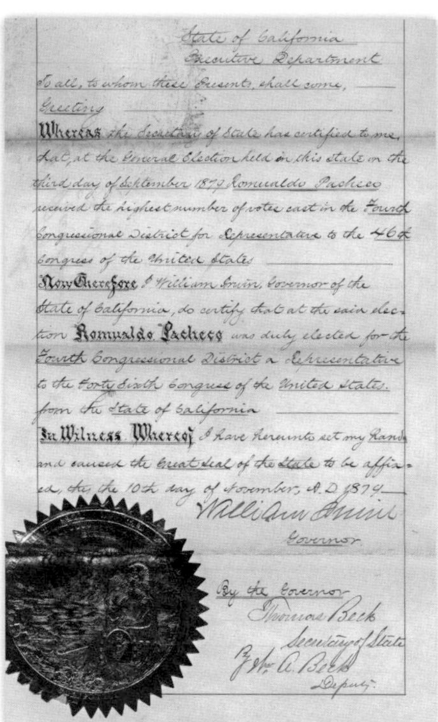

State of California
Executive Department
To all, to whom these Presents shall come,
Greeting
Whereas the Secretary of State has certified to me, that, at the General Election held in this State on the third day of September 1879 Romualdo Pacheco received the highest number of votes cast in the Fourth Congressional District for Representative to the 46th Congress of the United States
Now Therefore I William Irwin Governor of the State of California, do certify that at the said election Romualdo Pacheco was duly elected for the Fourth Congressional District a Representative to the Forty Sixth Congress of the United States from the State of California
In Witness Whereof I have hereunto set my hand and caused the Great Seal of the State to be affixed, this the 10th day of November, A.D 1879
William Irwin
Governor
By the Governor
Thomas Beck
Secretary of State
Deputy

On November 10, 1879, California Governor William Irwin certified Romualdo Pacheco's election as a U.S. Representative for California's Fourth District.

Romualdo Pacheco's original election certificate; image courtesy of the Center for Legislative Archives, National Archives and Records Administration

Dubbed the Great Compromiser, Henry Clay of Kentucky negotiated the Missouri Compromise of 1820 as Speaker of the House and helped devise the Compromise of 1850 as a U.S. Senator.

Henry Clay (detail), Guiseppe Fagnani, 1852, Collection of the U.S. House of Representatives

and district and supreme court justices, whereas the *Hispanos* controlled the territorial legislature since the overwhelmingly Hispanic population gave them a decided electoral advantage.[64] Gallegos served as a legislator in the Mexican government and as a delegate in the New Mexico Territory's legislative assembly in the early 1850s; between his terms as Delegate to Congress (1853–1856 and 1871–1873), he was the powerful and longtime speaker of the majority *Hispano* territorial legislature. Others had notable executive experience at the state and territorial level; Pacheco served as California's governor and treasurer, and Miguel Otero served briefly as the attorney general of the New Mexico Territory.

OVERVIEW OF NEW MEXICO POLITICS, 1848–1898

The story of the 19th-century Hispanic-American Members of Congress derives largely from the history of the *nuevomexicano* elites and their interactions with U.S. governing officials. Throughout this era, New Mexico's politics revolved around its territorial status and possible statehood, deferred initially because of the slavery issue and later because of longstanding prejudice against its Spanish-speaking, Roman Catholic inhabitants. New Mexico struggled for over 60 years—the longest of any contiguous state—to achieve statehood.

The U.S. military governed New Mexico until a civil territorial government was created under provisions of the Compromise of 1850. The provisions that Senator Henry Clay of Kentucky envisioned as passing in a single massive omnibus bill—the admission of California into the Union as a free state; the organization of New Mexico and Utah into territories, with no reference to their slavery status; and the resolution of the long-simmering Texas-New Mexico land disputes—passed both the Senate and the House as a series of separate measures. Part of a larger bill to settle the boundary with Texas, the New Mexico territorial measure carried the U.S. House by a tally of 108 to 97 on September 6, 1850, and was signed into law by President Millard Fillmore three days later.[65]

The politics of the New Mexico Territory, which developed over several decades, were driven more by local factionalism than by national issues; national political parties did not gain a toehold until after the Civil War. Historian Howard Lamar describes 1850s New Mexican politics as based on "cliques, usually led by one man and generally organized for the specific purpose of winning an election or controlling patronage." Neither Democrats nor Whigs existed in a national or regional sense out West in New Mexico, but local parties often defined themselves in relation to the party that was in power in Washington. For instance, many of the initial occupation politicians who were loyal Whigs while Millard Fillmore was President took to calling themselves "National Democrats" when Democrat Franklin Pierce became President in 1853. Their opponents went by several names, including "States Rights" Democrats and "Regular" Democrats.[66] Moreover, territorial politics were shaped by the comings and goings of federal administrators who owed their patronage positions to the majority national party in Washington, but in this fluid political environment, party affiliation was fleeting. Indeed, as Lamar observes, "Some thirty years after American conquest, New Mexican local politics were still based more on family alliance, cultural ties, anti-

Americanism, church faction, and crass economic interest than on any party principles.... The mere party labels Republican and Democrat became caricatures in this unique situation."[67]

While New Mexico politics were fractious to an extreme, Delegate elections—which occurred on the first Tuesday of September of odd years from 1853 until 1875—caused the territory's many political factions to unite around "two temporary parties" in what was then the only territory-wide election.[68] Usually, the defining issue in each of these contests was the division between the "native party" and a small but powerful pro-American faction. The former group, favoring home rule and the preservation of the social status quo, comprised some of the *nuevomexicano* elites. Their rivals were a group of wealthy *Hispanos* who aligned themselves with Anglo businessmen and military officials bent on facilitating the process of Americanization to modernize the territory and enrich themselves. The office of Delegate was an extremely important position from which both these groups sought to advance their agendas. Moreover, precisely because Delegates were the only federal officials elected popularly, they held tremendous sway and a legitimacy that was not often enjoyed by the appointed officials and administrators.[69]

During the Civil War, New Mexico was an important battleground in the far West.[70] Although allegiances were divided between the Confederacy and the Union, many *nuevomexicanos* remained loyal to the Union; Southern proponents suggested a pro-Confederate Arizona Territory be split from the original New Mexico Territory. Moving westward from Texas, the Confederate Army of the West occupied Santa Fe and Albuquerque in 1862, imprisoning the ardently pro-Union José Manuel Gallegos, who passed secrets to Union forces from his jail cell. Miguel Otero, though appointed secretary of the New Mexico Territory by President Abraham Lincoln, failed to receive Senate confirmation because of that chamber's long memories of his pro-Southern leanings. Inconclusive evidence suggests that despite his public displays of support for the Union, he supplied invading Confederate forces. Fearing violent reprisals by Unionists and pursuing entrepreneurial opportunities, Otero and his family left the territory and settled in Kansas for the remainder of the decade. José Francisco Chaves served as an officer in the First New Mexico Infantry Regiment, helping to repel the Confederate Army at the Battle of Valverde in 1863. With the Confederate campaign decisively checked at Valverde and Glorieta Pass, Chaves spent the final two years of the war as a lieutenant colonel, as the U.S. Army turned its attention to pacifying Navajo and Apache Indians.

Santa Fe Ring

The Civil War created new opportunities for Anglo lawyers and businessmen who had moved into the territory to seek their fortunes. A political scene with so much active ferment provided tantalizing opportunities for enterprising *Hispano*s who were willing to work with U.S. officials and Anglo outsiders to acquire greater political and economic dominance in the territory.

Built on a partnership between these two groups, the Santa Fe Ring was the first and perhaps the most notable political machine in New Mexico's history.[71] This Republican-oriented group dominated territorial politics in the

Homily in Verse

Translation of an excerpt from a campaign poem about Territorial Delegate Mariano S. Otero of New Mexico. From the Santa Fe Weekly New Mexican, *November 21, 1878.*

On July 30th
the convention met
to elect a delegate
to the Congress of the Union.

Republican Convention
You have come to good accord,
that Don Mariano S. Otero
be our delegate.

So then New Mexicans,
love your country,
vote for Mariano Otero,
drop Benito Baca.

Taking a closer look
and reflecting on the issue
New Mexico declares,
Elect our champion!

Republican Party,
you are assured
that all your friends
Work night and day.

Pay attention our friends,
be intelligent and valiant,
make sure the job goes
to our candidate.

This text is available in the original Spanish in Appendix J.

Delegate Francisco Manzanares of New Mexico served for a partial term during the 48th Congress (1883–1885). A successful entrepreneur, Manzanares owned a merchandising firm with offices in Colorado and the New Mexico Territory.

Helen Haines, *History of New Mexico from the Spanish Conquest to the Present Time 1530–1890 with Portraits and Biographical Sketches of its Prominent People* (New York, NY: New Mexico Historical Publishing Company, 1891)

A future Delegate and U.S. Senator, Thomas Catron of New Mexico managed the Santa Fe Ring, a confederation of Anglo and *Hispano* entrepreneurs who exerted political and economic dominance of the territory after the Civil War.

Image courtesy of the Library of Congress

latter 19th century, counting among its ranks nearly every governor of the territory and most federal officials from 1865 through the late 1880s. From the mid-1860s to the early 1880s, a string of *Hispanos* were elected Delegate on the Republican ticket. The Ring recruited lawyers, probate judges, land surveyors, doctors, and merchants, who combined forces for profit and political power. Through appointments to key territorial offices delivered by Republicans in Washington, D.C., and the support of the business class and a pliant press, they succeeded brilliantly. "Although located on the frontier," writes historian Howard Lamar, "the ring reflected the corporative, monopolistic, and multiple enterprise tendencies of all American business after the Civil War." Its chief means of influence was parlaying land into economic clout by purchasing, inflating, repackaging, and marketing a score of land grants doled out by Spanish rulers, and later by the U.S. government. The Santa Fe Ring's most grandiose venture involved its speculative promotion of the two-million-acre Maxwell Land Grant.[72]

Several *Hispano* Members of Congress were key Ring members or allies; Miguel Otero, Sr.; José Francisco Chaves; Mariano Otero; Francisco Manzanares; and the politically connected Perea family were all aligned with the Santa Fe Ring at some point in their careers. Miguel Otero, Sr., owned a piece of the sprawling Maxwell Land Grant. Chaves, despite some disagreements with the Santa Fe Ring, was particularly active as president of the territorial council after his tenure as Delegate. Mariano Otero proved useful as a longtime probate judge in Bernalillo County, and Manzanares was a partner with Stephen Elkins and Thomas Benton Catron in both the Maxwell Land Grant Company and the First National Bank of Santa Fe. Many of the *Hispano* Delegates who were not officially counted in its ranks sympathized with the Ring's larger desire to corporatize the territory. Only Gallegos, consistently portrayed by Ring candidates as a throwback to the corrupt, anti-modern rule of the Mexican regime, remained unaligned with the Ring. By the early 1890s, Elkins had gone back East, New Mexico's economy had diversified beyond the rampant land speculation of the early post-Civil War years, and the Santa Fe Ring faded in importance.

CRAFTING AN IDENTITY

Contested Elections

Article I, section 5 of the Constitution provides that "Each House shall be the Judge of the Elections, Returns, and Qualifications of its own Members." One of the earliest House committees was the Committee on Elections, created in 1789, with jurisdiction over election disputes and certification of House Members.[73]

While the House had always controlled the admission of its Members, the frequency of contested elections increased dramatically in the latter half of the 19th century because of Reconstruction—a majority of the disputed election results originated in the former Confederacy—and the admission of so many new territories to the Union. Several factors accounted for this exponential increase. The United States was almost evenly divided between the two traditional political parties; congressional majorities flip-flopped five times between 1870 and 1900. One scholar speculates that partisan competition and Southern disfranchisement directly influenced the incidence of contested elections, particularly during GOP-controlled Congresses. When a Republican majority in Congress could influence the outcome of a disputed election, the party encouraged its candidates to contest the results, viewing contested elections as an "institutional equalizer" for electing Southern GOP Representatives to the House and maintaining a majority, but both Democrat and Republican majorities abused the system.[74] "Great outrages have been committed by all parties which have controlled the House," noted Democratic Speaker Champ Clark of Missouri, whose House career began in 1893. Disputed elections in the 19th century "were so numerous as to become a burden," he added.[75]

The chaos, violence, and factionalism of the frontier's nascent political systems magnified the phenomenon, particularly in elections for Territorial Delegate, which involved many patchwork alliances to ensure a victorious majority. Seven of the 10 Hispanic-American Members in this era—José Manuel Gallegos, Miguel Antonio Otero, Francisco Perea, José Francisco Chaves, Romualdo Pacheco, Tranquilino Luna, and Francisco Manzanares—were involved in contested elections. Gallegos contended with three contested elections, the most of any Hispanic Member of the era.[76] "One unfortunate result of the complex struggle to win a delegate election was the resorting of each faction or party to fraud or intimidation to win," notes historian Howard Lamar. "The Americans, hampered by numerical inferiority, did not hesitate to use methods that would have ruined them politically in the states.… The New Mexicans, unused to the American concept of the franchise, were willing to sell this new thing—the vote—for some economic advantage."[77]

A variety of factors contributed to this phenomenon of contested territorial elections, including the absence of established parties; primitive electoral safeguards; and intense factionalism, which was manifested by a power struggle between older, Mexico-oriented *patrones* and younger, America-oriented *ricos*. As did congressional elections in the Reconstruction Era South, New Mexico's elections for Territorial Delegate routinely suffered from electoral abuses like stolen ballot boxes, voter fraud, intimidation, and violence. The frequency of these episodes paralleled that of the experiences of African-American politicians in the postwar South, but while black politicians often faced violent election contests that descended into overt racial hostility, contested elections during the early decades of the New Mexico Territory were more often manifestations of rivalry among local power elites and nascent parties in an ever-shifting political environment.[78] After Charles Clever's unsuccessful effort to contest José Francisco Chaves's election to the 40th Congress (1867–1869), Chaves wrote in an open letter to constituents: "I am aware that many of my friends of Mexican nativity entertained apprehensions that the fact of my being one of their race would be an obstacle in my way. But the sequel has happily dispelled that illusion, and will give to them a confident assurance that impartial justice will always await their demands in the House of Representatives and the government of the United States."[79] Of course, the fact that Radical Republicans retained a firm grip on the House and constituted a majority on the Elections Committee

They conclude the report as follows, (p. 15:)

"It appears that Gallegos's majority, upon which his certificate was awarded, was.............. .... 99 votes.
Your committee find, of Mexicans votes cast for Gallegos which they think ought to be rejected, 131 "

This gives Otero a majority of............ 32

Of the votes counted for Otero at the Mesilla precinct there were 72.
Of the votes counted for Gallegos at the Mesilla precinct there were.................................... 330
Deduct.................................... 72

Leaves.................................... 258
32

This vote being rejected, leaves Otero's majority.. 290

"Upon this state of facts your committee recommend the adoption of the following resolutions:
"*Resolved*, That José M. Gallegos is not entitled to a seat in this body as Delegate from the Territory of New Mexico.
"*Resolved*, That Miguel A. Otero is entitled to a seat in this body as such Delegate."

The privately published *Congressional Globe* detailed debates in the House and Senate. Pictured are the July 23, 1856, results of the contested election case between José Manuel Gallegos and Miguel Antonio Otero of the New Mexico Territory.

Congressional Globe, House, 34th Cong., 1st sess. (25 July 1856): 1730

Territorial Delegate José Francisco Chaves served in New Mexico's territorial legislature for almost three decades after his U.S. House career. During his service in Congress, Chaves tried on two occasions to expedite statehood for New Mexico.

Image courtesy of the Miguel A. Otero Photograph Collection (PICT 000-021-0056), Center for Southwest Research, University Libraries, University of New Mexico

Miguel Otero, Jr., who worked on his father's 1880 campaign for New Mexico Delegate against Tranquilino Luna, made history in 1897 when President William McKinley appointed him as the first (and only) *Hispano* governor of the New Mexico Territory.

Image courtesy of the Library of Congress

that decided in Chaves's favor worked to his advantage.

Clearly, election contests were contemplated in this era of shifting power in a closely divided House. In the wake of the 1880 election, Miguel Otero, Jr., who would serve as the first governor of Hispanic descent to be appointed in the New Mexico Territory, recalled, "What was done in Valencia County was but a sample of what was done by the Republican Party throughout the entire Territory." His father, the Democratic nominee who faced Republican Tranquilino Luna, "was urged by many of his friends to bring a contest.... But such a contest would have had to be fought out before Congress, and as the House of Representatives was then in the hands of the Republicans, my father thought it useless to go to the trouble and expense of the contest." Had his father "lived until the next election he would have been willing to enter the fray again and try conclusions" with Luna, Otero, Jr., wrote.[80]

Whether inspired by partisan gain or by racial discrimination, contested elections taxed Members' limited resources and sapped their ability to focus on constituents' needs. After a contested election fight with Gallegos that consumed three-quarters of the congressional term, Otero was awarded a House seat in July 1856. In a public letter to constituents, he explained that the harried transition had handicapped him further. Blaming Gallegos, Otero noted, "Although he promised me that he would transfer all the papers appertaining to the interests of New Mexico ... he nevertheless left the city without having complied with his promise, and in so doing he evinced a palpable and most reprehensible disregard for the welfare of the Territory." Otero complained of wasting precious time because he was obligated to check with every committee to find out whether any business initiated by Gallegos was still pending. Learning the legislative ropes would take time, he said, asking for his constituents' patience. "I am as yet, but young as the representative of my far-off people, and the fruits of my labors have not as yet been abundant," he wrote. "Give me time to plant, and I will endeavor to show that the laborer is worthy of his hire."[81]

Cultural Factionalism and *Nuevomexicano* Elites

In some cases disputes between candidates in New Mexico's elections for Delegate were unusually acrimonious because they were proxy contests for the territory's competing cultural regimes. The ferocity of the Gallegos-Otero contest in the mid-1850s reflected the gulf between New Mexico's two dominant *Hispano* factions: One favored the receding Spanish system, and the other adopted the insurgent Anglo-American model. Whereas Gallegos was "a pillar of the old native ruling class," oriented toward Mexican traditions and patterns of governance, Otero belonged to the *rico* class, which was openly aligned with the Americans.[82] Reared on revolutionary idealism, Gallegos's generation was imbued with an ardor to cultivate Mexican nationalism in the years after Mexico's independence from Spain. While such men bowed to the reality of American occupation and settlement, they favored the old culture and social mores, having spent their formative years in Mexican institutions. In their view, the territorial regime created by the Compromise of 1850 and the Treaty of Guadalupe Hidalgo was an instrument of American occupiers. *Hispanos* who conformed to the new political regime were mainly merchants, opportunistic individuals who did not get along with the pro-Mexican faction, and younger people like Otero who were educated in and familiar with U.S. institutions.[83]

When Gallegos won the 1855 election for Territorial Delegate by less than a 100-vote margin, Otero contested the result on multiple grounds, chief among them that ballots cast by Mexican citizens had inflated Gallegos's vote tally. Defending himself before the House through an interpreter, Gallegos stressed his personal ties, and those of most of his constituents, to Mexican culture, describing himself as "native to that very soil." Emphasizing the fact that Mexican-American constituents chose "me as their representative," he said, "I am not ashamed of whatsoever is common to them and to me." He judged the "sneers and jests" with which House Members had responded to his faltering English to be insults against all *nuevomexicanos*. "As I am their true representative under the laws, so I claim to be their true type in all that has been the subject of sarcasm and ridicule in the debates [about his contested election]," he said. "I receive it all as the representative of my people."[84]

In stark contrast, Otero, whose English had been refined in American colleges and who had spent considerable time in the Northeast and Midwest, claimed to defend "my people ... from the implied charge of having knowingly sent a representative who would boast of his incapacity, and claim his seat upon the very ground of being unable to fill it." He repeated salacious campaign allegations that Gallegos associated with corrupt clergymen who were "notoriously addicted to the grossest vices ... the disgrace of every gambling house and drinking saloon, and the open frequenters of brothels." Given the pervasive xenophobia of the 1850s, religion was a potent rhetorical device. The subtext was clear: A suspended Catholic priest, Gallegos was the creature of an alien political culture which Otero called the "Mexican party" faction and which he described as "indulging great hostility against the institutions of the United States."[85] This cultural clash resounded through the decades of New Mexico's territorial status. Years later when Gallegos challenged two-term incumbent Delegate José Francisco Chaves—another scion of a prominent family and an advocate of the territory's Americanization—many of the same patterns persisted. Gallegos's camp challenged Chaves's youth and chastised him for his facility with English: "He is much younger than Mr. Gallegos, superficial in appearance ... [and] attached to English to the point of hating his own language ... and, if you wish it, 'to the point of hating' his race." Chaves supporters painted Gallegos as "evidently inspired by hatred of Americans, their language and institutions, and directed to the Spanish speaking citizens, as he thinks they should entertain, and be swayed by ... the same sentiment."[86]

In the 1856 contested election, Otero played to more than religious bigotry against *nuevomexicanos* or generational friction among the *rico* elite; he drew a clear line between the elite he described as pure-blooded Spanish and the mixed-race Mexicans. In contrast to Gallegos, Otero claimed allegiance to the "American party"—by which he meant the pro-American faction of New Mexicans, not the national movement—but he described himself as being of "unmixed Spanish descent" and as part of the *nuevomexicano* elite who viewed U.S. annexation as salvation and "the only security from the perpetual discords and civil wars of Mexico."[87] "I confess I have always been attached

During his three terms in the House (1856–1861), Miguel Antonio Otero's pro-Southern sympathies and family connections drew him into an alliance with powerful southern Democrats. Otero lobbied for infrastructure appropriations—including a transcontinental railroad route through the South—to improve New Mexico's chances for statehood.

Image courtesy of the Library of Congress

Miguel Antonio Otero

Translation of an excerpt from a campaign poem about Delegate Miguel Antonio Otero of New Mexico. From the Santa Fe Weekly Gazette, *August 22, 1857.*

From high up in the empire,
the sun casts its rays
on our true democracy,
on our illustrious party,
on Miguel Antonio Otero;
on this beloved young man
showered with gifts
by the heavens;
we proclaim without apprehension
and, in my own judgment, without cowardice,
long live MIGUEL, long live ANTONIO
and long live OTERO as well.

This terrible administration
that governs this County
has subordinated
our liberty and action.
Now it is time and it is our chance
to be free from evil.
National Democracy
alert, alert we will be,
we nationals with greatest care,
will shed the blood
long live MIGUEL, long live ANTONIO
and long live OTERO as well.

Next September
we will have the elections
for our Delegate
to the Congress of the Union
and, also to remove
every corrupt official.
That all of our interests
be well represented
by our Delegate
a gift from the heavens,
long live MIGUEL, long live ANTONIO
and long live OTERO as well.

This text is available in the original Spanish in Appendix J.

to the institutions of this country, and to have been taught from childhood to look to this quarter for the political regeneration of my people," he added. However, Otero carefully avoided disassociating himself from the majority-*nuevomexicano* constituency, claiming he was a truer heir than Gallegos. "The sitting Delegate appeals to your *magnanimity* in favor of the people of New Mexico," Otero crowed. "When, sir, in the history of the race of which he claims to be a *type*, did Castilian blood ever congeal in the presence of power, and so far degrade itself as to seek to crawl into favor? I claim for New Mexico, not your magnanimity, but your fraternal justice."[88] By making this claim, Otero used a strategy that was common among the *rico* elite, who emphasized and even exaggerated their direct Spanish bloodlines and heritage. Questioning the "legitimacy" of this tactic, scholars like Laura Gómez and John M. Nieto-Phillips chronicle its repeated "articulation and its deployments in contexts of resistance and accommodation," but Otero and other like-minded *ricos* considered this strategy to be a crucial link in arguments for statehood, since they believed Congress needed to be convinced of *nuevomexicanos*' readiness for self-government based on their "whiteness." Scholars including Robert Larson, Gómez, and Nieto-Phillips maintain that racial fitness for self-government was a determinant in 19th-century debates about whether New Mexico should be admitted into the Union.[89]

Ironically, Miguel Otero would later be on the receiving end of the charge he leveled at Gallegos in the 1850s. In the intensely personal and bitter 1880 campaign for Territorial Delegate, Tranquilino Luna's supporters in the press depicted Otero as out of touch and a relic of the past. With Luna's victory, the editors of the *Daily New Mexican* called for an end to the politics of personality and for increasing engagement with national political issues. The editors predicted the "campaign of the future … will be one of argument and of discussion. The principles of the parties which the candidates who are running represent will be made the subject of criticism. Personalities will not figure to so great an extent. Politics will be lifted up to a higher plane and the whole method of conducting campaigns will be changed … the whole political atmosphere will be purer and cleaner."[90]

Social Experiences in Washington, D.C.

Groups that were newly admitted to the political process were often the subject of intense press coverage in Washington, D.C. Playing to public interest, the media customarily portrayed early African-American and women Members of Congress as spectacles and curiosities amid the capital's governing circles, which were overwhelmingly male, white, and Protestant.[91] But the Hispanic Members of the 19th century received little attention from contemporary political observers or Capitol Hill veterans. Though Benjamin Perley Poore, a D.C. journalist and editor of the early editions of the *Congressional Directory*, who recorded in his memoirs the Otero-Gallegos contested election, intimated that Gallegos's Catholicism made him the more conservative of the two, while the American-educated Otero possessed a "Democracy [that] was of the more liberal school," for the most part, the contemporaries of these Hispanic pioneers seemed largely oblivious to them.[92] There were too few to establish a distinctive presence, and their House careers, muted by their subordinate status as Delegates, usually lasted only one term. With the exception of Pacheco and Trinidad Romero (1877–1879) and Pacheco and Mariano Otero (1879–1881), no two Hispanics served in Congress simultaneously during this period.

Living arrangements were consequential for Members in Washington, D.C., which was rather provincial and sleepy throughout the 19th century. Scholars speculate that groups of Members living in boardinghouses and messes, particularly in the antebellum era, formed similar legislative agendas and voting blocs. While this theory has been disputed, clearly group living quarters often provided a sense of fraternity and company for individuals separated from family.[93] *Congressional Directory* listings suggest that only about a quarter of House Members brought their wives or families to Washington in the years before the Civil War. Primitive travel, shorter, more work-intensive sessions, and the relatively brief careers of most individuals serving in Congress accounted for this pattern. Even if they were married, the vast majority of Members lived as bachelors when Congress was in session. Most lived in boardinghouses run by women or roomed in hotels such as the National, Willard's, and Congressional. Not until after the Civil War did a greater proportion of Members—perhaps half—bring their families to Washington.

The *Congressional Directory* offers glimpses into the lives of Hispanic Delegates in the nation's capital. José M. Gallegos boarded at a residence several blocks from the Capitol during his service from 1853 to 1856, and at no point did he room with other Members of Congress. In contrast, Gallegos's political nemesis, Miguel Otero, Sr., had a connection to the region; his wife, the former Mary Josephine Blackwood, was a descendant of Maryland Senator Charles Carroll. Raised in Charleston, South Carolina, Mary Josephine belonged to the Southern aristocracy and seems to have contributed to her spouse's pro-Southern orientation in the 1850s. Otero roomed with two Maryland Representatives at a boardinghouse on Pennsylvania Avenue across the street from the National Hotel, which was popular among Southern Members in the antebellum years. Known for his assiduous courtship of key Southern leaders such as Jefferson Davis of Mississippi—who as Secretary of War (1853–1857) helped oversee surveys of a rail route to the Pacific—Otero eventually moved to the National and brought his wife to the capital for at least part of a term. One of the longest-serving Hispanics in the 19th century, Otero was one of only three Hispanic Members whose families accompanied them on the arduous journey to Washington. Another relatively long-serving Delegate, José Francisco Chaves, had his wife join him for one term in the late 1860s, and one-term Delegate Trinidad Romero roomed with his wife and daughter at the National Hotel for one session of the 45th Congress (1877–1879).

The *Congressional Directory* suggests that Romualdo Pacheco and Mariano Otero were the only Hispanic Members to live at the same location, renting rooms at the National Hotel during the 46th Congress (1879–1881). The two Republicans were known to work closely on legislation. Further, seating charts from various editions of the *Directory* for that Congress indicate that Pacheco and Otero occupied neighboring desks on their party's side of the chamber, along the south wall at the extreme left of the Speaker's rostrum.[94] The proximity

In 1885, Benjamin Perley Poore published a two-volume memoir, *Perley's Reminiscences of Sixty Years in the National Metropolis.* Students of Congress still use Perley's memoirs for insights on nineteenth-century life in Washington, D.C.

Image courtesy of the Library of Congress

Trinidad Romero, who served during the 45th Congress (1877–1879), served in New Mexico territorial politics before entering Congress. Romero also was one of a few *Hispanos* who served as a U.S. Marshal in the territory.

Image courtesy of the Citizens Committee for Historic Preservation, Las Vegas, New Mexico

Popular because of its proximity to the U.S. Capitol, the National Hotel was one of a number of establishments that Members of Congress used as their Washington residences during congressional sessions well into the 20th century.

Image courtesy of the Library of Congress

of their desks provides evidence of their working relationship since Members' desks functioned as their offices in the 19th century, before the construction of congressional office buildings.

The brevity of Hispanic-American Members' terms in the federal legislature suggests that they viewed their tenure in Washington as a means to advance their careers in territorial politics, particularly their business ventures. Miguel Otero, Sr., became a wealthy merchant as well as a partner and director of the Atchison, Topeka, and Santa Fe Railroad. In the 1890s his son, Miguel, Jr., became the only governor of Hispanic descent in the territory's history. After serving a single term in the U.S. House, Mariano Otero returned home to speculate in lucrative land grants through his ties to the Santa Fe Ring, making a fortune that rivaled his uncle's. Gallegos enlarged his fortune in farming and mercantile concerns and enjoyed a long tenure as speaker of the territorial house in the 1860s. José Francisco Chaves, who often aligned himself with the Santa Fe Ring, served eight terms as president of the powerful territorial council, effectively the New Mexico territorial senate. According to one scholar, he founded the New Mexican town of Torrance and dominated the politics of Valencia County as a result of his massive landholdings and his influence as a *patron*.[95]

LEGISLATIVE INTERESTS

Committee Assignments

Like their counterparts in other territories, the Hispanic-American Delegates lacked fundamental legislative tools. For much of the 19th century, Territorial Delegates were barred from serving on standing committees of the House. Particularly in the two decades before a standing committee system was formed in the 1810s, Delegates appointed by the Speaker might serve on select committees, and in rare instances, even chair those panels. Inconclusive evidence suggests that Delegates were seldom allowed to vote on committees, and the few occasions when they did were exceptions to the 1817 law that defined their power.[96]

The law that designated the District of Columbia a territory in 1871 entitled its Delegate in the House to sit on the Committee on the District of Columbia. Additionally, one of the 10 Delegates at the time was seated on the Committee on Territories, marking the first time Delegates were allowed to serve on standing House committees. When the House abolished the seat of the Delegate from the District of Columbia several years later, the remaining Delegates retained the right to serve on committees, but they still could not vote in committee.[97] Sparring over the 1871 resolution reserving two committee seats for Delegates, Representatives pointed out that Delegates would have the same status in committee as they did on the House Floor; one Representative said Territorial Delegates should act as "advisory members."[98] In 1876 the House approved with little debate a rule that expanded the scope of the standing committees on which Delegates could be seated to include Indian Affairs, Mines and Mining, and Public Lands but noted that "the said Delegates, in their respective committees, shall have the same privileges only as in the House," giving the Delegates the right to debate but not to vote.[99] Though there were challenges and possibly exceptions to that restriction, it remained intact until the 1970s.

Since all but one of the 10 Hispanic-American Members profiled during this era were Delegates, only four served on standing House committees. Representative Romualdo Pacheco of California was the first Hispanic Member to hold a standing committee assignment: a seat on the Public Lands Committee in the 45th Congress (1877–1879). He also served on the Private Land Claims and Public Expenditures Committees. Pacheco's committee assignments ranked roughly among the top third in terms of attractiveness to Members. He eventually chaired the Private Land Claims panel, making him the first Hispanic American to hold a leadership position in Congress. The committee, which existed for more than a century until its abolishment in 1911, reported general and special legislation to settle individual claims on public land. It was a significant panel for Members from Western states and territories, of which large swaths were owned by the federal government. Likewise, the Public Lands Committee, which managed all federal land, was a key assignment because it had jurisdiction over irrigation and reclamation, conservation, national parks, and mineral and water rights. After the Committee on Private Land Claims folded, its responsibilities were merged with those of the Public Lands Committee.[100]

A further expansion of the committees that were available to Delegates, due to a revision of House Rule XII in 1880, opened a seat on the House Coinage, Weights, and Measures Committee that appears to have been reserved by the Speaker for the New Mexican Delegate.[101] Mariano Otero, Tranquilino Luna, and Francisco Manzanares served on the Coinage, Weights, and Measures Committee, beginning with Otero during the 46th Congress (1879–1881). Created in 1864, Coinage, Weights and Measures was a decidedly middling assignment with little appeal for most Members. Its jurisdiction included standards of value for coinage (including gold and silver), legislation related to mints and assay offices, and national standards for weights and measurements.

In this circumscribed legislative landscape, Territorial Delegates often relied on other members of their cohort to advance their proposals. Future Speaker of the House Samuel Randall of Pennsylvania described the Delegates as "a quasi committee … they meet together both socially and in a legislative sense, and they will seek through one of their number to instruct and enlighten" pertinent committees on key territorial questions. The *New York Times* reported that once the House agreed to grant one Delegate a seat on the Territories Committee, the group organized "into a self-appointed committee," calling itself the "Territorial Syndicate," akin to a modern special-interest caucus. Its purpose was to arrange for individual Delegates serving on various committees to act as conduits for the other Delegates' legislative interests and concerns. "They will also consult with and aid each other in the preparation and passage of measures through both houses," the article said.[102] Clearly, this occurred in other cases, too, particularly when Delegates could ally themselves with Representatives from nearby states. For instance, Representative Pacheco worked closely with Delegate Mariano Otero of New Mexico, helping him look after territorial interests. In Otero's absence and at his request, Pacheco attempted to allocate more money to complete the construction of a jail and courthouse in Santa Fe.[103] He also presented a letter from territorial governor Lionel Sheldon, requesting that Congress approve the election of the New Mexico Legislative Assembly before the start of its next session.[104]

Infrastructure Improvements and Land Grants

Like many of their congressional colleagues, Hispanic Members in the latter 19th century were keenly interested in procuring federal dollars for infrastructure development and capital projects. This goal was particularly important for the Delegates, for whose territories basic public works improvements such as postal roads, railway lines, and federal buildings augured momentum toward statehood. However, disputed rights to land conferred previously by Spanish and Mexican authorities often complicated economic development, especially in the New Mexico Territory.[105]

Transportation projects were crucial to developing economies in the territories and far Western states, and from the 1850s through the 1880s, Congress actively promoted the growth of railroads in the United States.[106] Roadways and rails were ongoing concerns for Hispanic Members of Congress throughout this era. Delegate Joseph Hernández of Florida advocated for the construction of a 380-mile road along the Gulf of Mexico in the extreme western panhandle of the territory between Pensacola and St. Augustine, on the Atlantic coast. Hernández believed such an east–west route would boost economic development, facilitate the location and construction of a capital city, and make Florida an attractive candidate for statehood.[107] New Mexico Delegates followed the same pattern. Though hamstrung by the language barrier and all-consuming contested elections cases, Gallegos introduced a bill to construct a postal road between Albuquerque and California. His successor, Miguel Otero, Sr., courted powerful Southern Senators and Representatives in a bid to secure a major rail route through the New Mexico Territory. Romualdo Pacheco knew reliable transportation routes were crucial to the survival of the

This 1868 print, *Across the Continent: Westward the Course of Empire Takes Its Way*, shows the importance of railroads for U.S. settlement in the western territories.

Image courtesy of the Library of Congress

relatively remote economic outposts in the American Southwest and along the Pacific coast. Attuned to the needs of the shipping industry, he sought federal funds to dredge the harbor and improve the facilities in the Wilmington section of Los Angeles. He also sought congressional support to make the Los Angeles area the terminus for the Southern Pacific Railroad.

Congressional control over land grant issues was also an important aspect of territorial development, and Representative Pacheco had a prime perch from which to tend to the multitude of land claims and land grant issues that were central to politics in new territories and states. His assignments on the Public Lands Committee and his eventual chairmanship of the Private Land Claims Committee suited his interest in protecting the property rights of Western landowners. Several New Mexico Delegates who associated with the Santa Fe Ring, including Miguel Otero, Sr., and José Francisco Chaves, repeatedly brought before the House thorny land grant issues requiring the alteration or confirmation of long-standing Spanish or Mexican grants. Land grants formed one corner of a 19th-century golden triangle: By conferring rights to large tracts of land, Congress opened the way for territorial development by railroads and land speculators; territorial development, in turn, encouraged population growth and the possibility of statehood, and Santa Fe Ring members gambled on the prospect that statehood, once achieved, would boost property values.[108]

Indian Relations

One legacy of the United States' acquisition of lands ceded by Mexico was the inauguration of a new era in the federal government's policies toward American Indians. The Constitution prescribed powers to Congress (Article I, Section 8) "to regulate Commerce with foreign Nations, and among the several States, and with the Indian Tribes." From the beginning, Congress played a key role in negotiating treaties with various tribes. Reflecting their growing workload, the Senate and the House created standing committees on Indian affairs in 1820 and 1821, respectively. Congress approved the Indian Removal Act of 1830, initiated by the Andrew Jackson administration and premised on the idea that Eastern Indians could be relocated to the expanses of land west of the Mississippi River, freeing land for agriculture. It was during the implementation of Jackson's removal policies that Florida's Joseph Marion Hernández played a key role in the subjugation of the Seminoles during the 1830s. The mammoth land grabs of the 1840s, including the settlement of the Oregon Territory dispute and the acquisition of vast acreage with the Treaty of Guadalupe Hidalgo, brought more than a quarter-million people under U.S. control and into conflict with Anglo settlers heading west. In 1851 Congress created Indian superintendencies under the newly established Interior Department to manage tribal relations, and authorized Indian agents in New Mexico and Utah. At the request of many of these federal officials, the reservation system, whereby Indian tribes were relocated to lands under the stewardship of the U.S. government, emerged during the 1850s and accelerated during the Civil War.[109]

New Mexico's Bosque Redondo ("round grove of trees") was one such reservation that existed during the Civil War and its immediate aftermath. Sprawled across a million acres along the Pecos River in eastern New Mexico,

Before implementing Indian removal in the southeastern United States in the 1830s as President, Andrew Jackson of Tennessee garnered national attention for victories in Indian pacification campaigns after the War of 1812.

Image courtesy of the Library of Congress

Apache scouts were photographed at Apache Lake, Sierra Blanca range, Arizona Territory, in 1873.

Image courtesy of the Library of Congress

with Fort Sumner at its center, the Bosque Redondo was part of a two-pronged Indian pacification effort conceived by General James H. Carleton, the territory's military commander. Carleton aimed to subdue Apache and Navajo in the western reaches of the territory, who for centuries had fought against encroachment by Spanish and now Anglo settlers. "Carleton's Indian program was harsh and simple: to kill or capture the Indians until they agreed to surrender and live on a single reservation, where they could be taught Christianity and agriculture," notes historian Howard Lamar. At first the plan was ruthlessly efficient and widely praised by Anglo and *Hispano* New Mexicans. Forces initially mustered to turn back a Confederate advance rounded up thousands of Mescalero Apache and Navajos in 1863 and 1864, led by the First New Mexico Volunteer Cavalry under Colonel Kit Carson. By late 1864, more than 8,000 Indians (nearly three-quarters of the Navajo tribe) had been forced on a "Long Walk" eastward across barren stretches of the territory to the Bosque Redondo. Scores died on the journey. Moreover, their destination was ill-suited to hosting so large and diverse a group. Apache and Navajo were crowded together; longtime rivalries festered, and the prospect of violence grew. Despair set in when crops failed, federal supplies ran low, and many faced starvation. Once trumpeted as a winning strategy, the Bosque Redondo "now began to seem a fiasco," Lamar notes. In 1865 the Apaches left the reservation *en masse*; by 1868 the U.S. government had renegotiated a treaty with the Navajo, who were permitted to return to their native lands.[110]

The Bosque Redondo quickly became a political lightning rod. Pro- and anti-Carleton forces emerged, dominating the 1865 election for Territorial Delegate. The contest between nominal Republicans José Francisco Chaves and Francisco Perea focused largely on the controversy surrounding the reservation. Perea, the incumbent Delegate, supported Carleton's policy of using the military to round up Indians and relocate them to reservations. He considered his "imperative duty" the advocation of such a course of action and the procurement of the federal dollars necessary "to put these pests out of our way and reinstate our people in their rightful control" of "the destinies and prosperity of the beloved country for which our gallant forefathers endured and suffered so much in redeeming it from savage hands and reducing it to civilizing influences of our pure Christianity."[111] Chaves, an accomplished Indian fighter, criticized the resettlement because of his widely shared opposition to Carleton's authoritarian methods, as well as the economic ramifications, which involved the seizure of valuable grazing land along the Pecos River to host the tribes; the loss of a potential labor pool when captured Indians were "civilized" rather than pressed into servitude; and the federal government's repeated failures to supply the reservation with adequate supplies, leading to unrest.[112] On this last point, Delegate Chaves chastised the House during debate about a $50,000 appropriation to supply the Bosque Redondo. "I have noticed as a general thing members eulogize the enterprise, skill, and success of the Anglo-Saxon race," Chaves declared. "Although I am not of that race, still I can feel as proud as any of the glory of this great country. But I must be permitted also to say that great as we are, yet the United States has failed entirely and utterly in the attempt to solve the problem as to the best manner in which these Indians are to be treated so as to result in their civilization." Chaves pointed to Spanish and Mexican officials' relations with the Pueblo Indians as a model that was worthy of emulation.[113]

Slavery

The nature of New Mexico's forms of forced servitude—Indian slavery and peonage—did not fit neatly into the long and bitter debate about chattel slavery in the South, nor did it conform to prevailing conceptions of whiteness and blackness.[114] Territorial politics helped obfuscate Indian slavery since it was never legally sanctioned, and thus New Mexico's brands of servitude went largely unnoticed in the national debate during the antebellum era.

The practice of Indian slavery, which began in the 16th century, involved enslaving Indians captured during warfare, and their offspring, to work for planters and mine owners. Occasionally, Indian tribes captured and sold members of rival tribes to the Spaniards and later to the Mexicans; less frequently, Indians enslaved Spaniards and Mexicans. By one estimate, on the eve of the Civil War, as many as 3,000 American Indians were held as slaves in the New Mexico Territory.[115] In addition to Indian slavery, wealthy *Hispano* landowners practiced peonage using *nuevomexicano* laborers. Unlike chattel slavery, which was practiced primarily in the antebellum South, peonage was used mainly in territories that were formerly controlled by the Spanish.[116] Peons (derived from the Spanish *peón*, an unskilled laborer) became indebted to landowners for such things as rent, farming implements, and seeds and were paid a pittance to work off their debt. Most sank deeper into arrears, hence perpetuating their servitude. In some instances, a peon who had spent a lifetime in servitude would be "forced through continued and increased indebtedness to bind out his children."[117] In one such case the debt was reputed to be $5. Peonage was more visible than Indian slavery, both to conquering soldiers and to U.S. politicians. Northern abolitionists denounced it. In the wake of the war with Mexico, Representative George Perkins Marsh, a Vermont Whig, decried the practice as "that barbarous relic of ancient Roman law, *peonage*, of the servitude of an insolvent debtor to his creditor."[118]

Several Hispanic Delegates to Congress from this era drew on both the Spanish and Anglo-American models of slavery, and thus owed part of their higher economic status to their activities as slave masters and slave traders. By one estimate, Joseph Marion Hernández owned as many as 150 African-American slaves in a profitable but labor-intensive system of sugar and cotton production on his three Florida plantations. Among other tasks, Hernández's slaves performed the backbreaking work of draining and reclaiming swamplands for prime agricultural fields.[119]

Given the pervasiveness of Indian slavery and peonage among the *Hispano* elites in New Mexico, many of the New Mexican Delegates probably came from families that engaged in or profited directly from some form of forced servitude. However, since much of the practice was cultural and not codified in law, it is difficult to know which Delegates owned slaves or engaged in peonage. Based on census reports, court records, and newspaper accounts, Gallegos and several members of the extended Otero and Chaves families likely benefited directly from slavery.[120] Census records from 1860 indicate that Gallegos listed 21 servants in his household, including a Utah Indian named Josefa Gallegos; a seven-year-old Apache boy named Miguel Gallegos also is listed as a member of the household, although his status is ambiguous.[121] Tranquilino Luna, who was 11 years old at the time of the 1860 Census, lived in a home with 11 servants, one of whom was an Indian. Fifteen-year-old Mariano Otero lived in a household with two Indian servants, Dolores and Guadalupe. José Francisco Chaves and Francisco Perea, both independent adults in 1860, reported the presence of one and three female Indian servants, respectively, in their households.[122]

Controversy over territorial slavery stirred in Congress from the very beginning of U.S. involvement in New Mexico. In 1846, during the 29th Congress (1845–1847), as debate swirled about the potential westward expansion of slavery following the war with Mexico, Representative David Wilmot of Pennsylvania introduced an amendment to an appropriations request from the President. Later known as the Wilmot Proviso, the amendment echoed the language Thomas Jefferson first drafted to prohibit the expansion of slavery into the Northwest Territory in the 1780s. "That, as an express and fundamental condition to the acquisition of any territory from the Republic of Mexico ... neither slavery nor involuntary servitude shall ever exist in any part of said territory, except for crime, whereof the party shall first be duly convicted," Wilmot declared. The House adopted the proviso, but it never came to a vote in the Senate in the 29th Congress. Several versions of the proviso were passed by the House in the 30th Congress (1847–1849), but again it died in the Senate which was dominated by Southern Members.[123]

New Mexicans overwhelmingly approved the proposed constitution of 1850, which provided that New Mexico should enter the Union as a free state (prohibiting chattel slavery). But the Compromise of 1850, which conferred territorial status rather than statehood, was silent on the issue of slavery. In the 1850s, responding to both national impulses and local contingencies, New Mexicans shifted from an antislavery position to a pro-slavery position.[124] In 1857 the territorial legislature adopted a law that imposed severe restrictions on free blacks, mainly a 30-day moratorium on their presence in the territory; offenders could be fined, jailed, or sentenced to "hard labor."[125] The territory's slave code, engineered largely at Miguel Otero's insistence and passed in February 1859, established the federal Fugitive Slave Act in New Mexico, codified the sale of unclaimed slaves, dictated the relationship between masters and slaves, and limited the movements of slaves and free African Americans.[126]

These 1857 and 1859 laws were enacted as much for their message to key constituencies outside the territory as for the few who were directly affected by them. In practice, these codes applied only to a miniscule portion of New Mexico's population, probably the handful of slaves who had likely been brought into the territory as the personal servants of U.S. Army officers from the South. The 1850 Census, which listed nearly 58,000 non-Indians in the territory, recorded fewer than two dozen African Americans in all of New Mexico, which then spanned the bulk of present-day New Mexico and Arizona. By the next census, there were still only 64 blacks recorded in New Mexico.

Clearly, territorial disputes revolving "around slavery and the rights of free blacks were mostly about symbolic politics," in part because of "an understandable preoccupation with Euro-Americans as an audience," argues one historian.[127] This symbolism resonated with the key Southern Members of Congress, whose favor Otero curried to gain federal dollars for infrastructure improvements and a favorable ear for pro-statehood arguments. Throughout the 1850s, another study concludes, "national issues of free soil, slavery, and the tariff were discussed and debated by politicians and newspaper editors in New Mexico with great ferocity, but this was more for consumption in Missouri and Washington than it was for the local citizens."[128]

The slave code also revealed the powerful hand of *Hispano* elites, who were concerned with codifying and protecting the centuries-old practices of Indian slavery and peonage. Indeed, the Anglo officials who were drafting the bill seemed intent on appeasing affluent *Hispanos*, although references to peonage and Indian slavery were avoided.[129] Scholar Estévan Rael-Gálvez argues that Anglo-American officials through "lobbying efforts encouraged Mexicans to understand how regulating slavery and the protection of property in slaves, if not in name certainly in theory, [would] protect *their own system*, now being identified as peonage."[130]

The slave code's cruel and exacting provisions, including its prohibitions against interracial marriage and miscegenation, suggest that *Hispanos* sought to separate themselves from blacks. As Laura Gómez explains, the codes "reflected the preoccupation with pushing Mexican Americans up the racial hierarchy" while pushing blacks to the bottom.[131] Thus, the code balanced the concerns of several New Mexico factions by legalizing the territory's version of the "peculiar institution" of slavery by placing New Mexico in the pro-slavery column—an important step in Otero's mind toward statehood and toward receiving appropriations from powerful Southern politicians in a Democratic-led Congress—and by reaffirming the place of *Hispanos* relative to the place of blacks in the social order of the antebellum era.[132]

Weeks before Miguel Otero's tenure as Delegate expired at the end of the 36th Congress (1859–1861), Horace Greeley, the mercurial editor of the *New York Tribune* and a notorious Republican partisan, published a scathing editorial blasting New Mexico for the "signal atrocity and inhumanity" of its slave code and its long-standing peonage system. Greeley briefly criticized the Democratic administrations of Franklin Pierce and James Buchanan for what he described as their schemes to move New Mexico into the slave state column, but much of his bile was reserved for the mixed racial heritage of the territory. "The mass of the people are Mexicans—a hybrid of Spanish and Indian origin," he said. "They are ignorant and degraded, demoralized, and priest-ridden." The political system, he continued, was dominated by a handful of "able and unscrupulous men.... The masses are their blind, facile tools. There is no Press of any account; no Public Opinion; of course, no Republican party. Slavery rules all." Needless to say, Greeley flatly opposed the extension of statehood to the territory.[133]

Otero characterized Greeley's "unscrupulous exaggerations" as "utterly, maliciously, and basely false." But he did more than dutifully defend his constituents. Otero's lengthy refutation of racial mixing showed that his

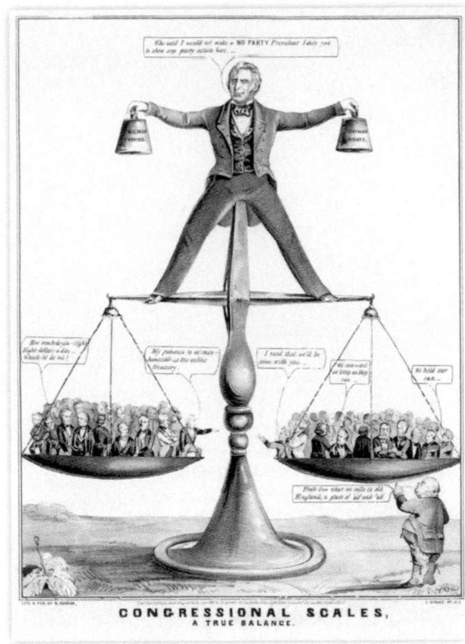

In this cartoon, President Zachary Taylor balances Northern and Southern interests by using the Wilmot Proviso and "Southern Rights." John Bull, an observer who symbolizes Great Britain, comments on the situation.

Image courtesy of the Library of Congress

The publisher of the *New York Tribune* and an intense partisan, Horace Greeley developed a national reputation as a provocateur. He served for one term as a Representative in the 30th Congress (1847–1849).

Image courtesy of the Library of Congress

Stephen Elkins served as a Union Army captain in the Civil War. A prominent politician in the New Mexico Territory, Elkins moved to West Virginia and served as a U.S. Senator from 1895 until his death in 1911.

Image courtesy of the Library of Congress

principal concern was drawing a distinct racial line. He emphasized the separateness of *Hispanos* like himself, who claimed descent from Spanish conquistadores, from those who were American Indians. "At the close of the seventeenth century … to the present day the Indians within the settlements have occupied pueblos or towns exclusively set apart for them, and they have scrupulously refrained from intercourse with the Spanish population excepting so far as became necessary for the ordinary transaction of business," Otero explained. Further, he noted the lack of intermarriage between the groups: The "two races have never amalgamated; and although the Spanish blood has sometimes manifested itself on the aboriginal race, and the Indian blood less frequently on the Spanish race, those instances are of rare occurrence—so rare as to render the sweeping allegation that the mass of the people of New Mexico are a hybrid race … grossly defamatory and shamefully mendacious."[134]

After the abolition of chattel slavery, federal officials viewed the practice of peonage in the New Mexico Territory more harshly. President Andrew Johnson issued a proclamation in June 1865 requiring all federal employees to discontinue peonage and to work to end the practice. Even after the ratification of the 13th Amendment in December 1865 and the Civil Rights Bill of 1866, Congress felt compelled to address directly New Mexico's forms of servitude. In the closing days of the 39th Congress (1865–1867), Massachusetts Senator Henry Wilson introduced S. 543, a bill "to abolish and forever prohibit the system of peonage in the Territory of New Mexico and other parts of the United States." Its three main provisions were to prohibit peonage and invalidate all supporting legislation; to impose penalties of up to $5,000 and five years in prison for all violations; and to obligate civil servants and soldiers to enforce the law. Radicals in both chambers backed the legislation—as did Santa Fe Ring leader Stephen Elkins, who was motivated as much by a desire to weaken *Hispano* elites as by altruism.[135] The bill passed the House with little debate on March 2, 1867, and was signed into law shortly thereafter.[136] Chaves, then a Territorial Delegate, did not address the House about the bill at any time during the 39th Congress.

Statehood

Perhaps the most complicated issue faced by the Territorial Delegates was statehood, both because of opposition in the national capital and because so many New Mexicans (both Anglos and *Hispanos*) were deeply ambivalent about it for so long.[137] From 1848 through 1898, the push for statehood grew in fits and starts. In the brief period leading up to the Compromise of 1850, statehood was promoted as a necessity to stave off Texan encroachment on the eastern section of the territory. In the 1870s, the ever-ambitious Santa Fe Ring championed statehood, in no small measure because many Ring members viewed themselves as natural administrators for a future state. And by the late 1880s, the movement gained renewed life as Anglos moved to the territory and became demographically equal to the *nuevomexicanos*.[138]

Among the Delegates of this era, Chaves was the most eloquent advocate for statehood, noting that until New Mexico was a full member of the Union, its laws and officials would be imposed by Congress and recalled at will. In an open letter to constituents, Chaves savaged the territorial appointment process: "Your governor ... and your judges ... are now elected by people who have never set foot on your soil, who are ignorant of the nature of your country and the needs of its people and who have no special interest in your well being." While "some of the servants sent from Washington ... have been capable, honorable, and trustworthy," Chaves acknowledged, "the preponderance have been the reverse." Chaves told his constituents they were "tormented by the insertion of politicians who ... finished their careers in the states and ... hope to find in your midst a new field for their political adventures." "Under a state government ... your laws would be your own laws, to be modified, amended, and repealed solely by your own will," he added.[139]

In this 1855 painting, Henry Clay of Kentucky speaks to Senate colleagues about the Compromise of 1850. The other members of the Great Triumvirate—Senators Daniel Webster of Massachusetts and John C. Calhoun of South Carolina—are seated nearby.

Image courtesy of the Library of Congress

Partisanship and prejudice created obstacles at the federal level. New Mexico's solid Republicanism in the latter 19th century worked to its detriment in Democratically controlled Congresses in the post-Reconstruction Era, particularly in those that were closely divided between the parties. But even more invidious was the portrayal—in the press and in speeches on the House and Senate Floors—of *nuevomexicanos* as indolent, ignorant, and irredeemably papist.[140] The pervasiveness of this sentiment during a debate on statehood at the end of the 50th Congress (1887–1889) caused Representative William McAdoo of New Jersey to complain that prejudice seemed to have trumped even political considerations. He described the Senate's stripping New Mexico from a House-passed omnibus statehood bill for the Dakotas, Montana, and Washington state as "a gross act of injustice to the people of New Mexico." The debate, he noted, had been colored by an "insidious calumniation and narrow-minded misrepresentation" of native New Mexicans. The territory's contributions to the

William McAdoo emigrated from Ireland to the United States in 1865. He served in the New Jersey state assembly before winning election to Congress for four terms. McAdoo chaired the House Committee on the Militia during the 50th Congress (1887–1889).

Image courtesy of the Library of Congress

One of the youngest Senators in congressional history, Albert Beveridge served for two terms (1899–1911). After losing re-election to the Senate in 1910, Beveridge ran unsuccessfully for governor of Indiana (1912) and two more times for the Senate (1914 and 1922).

Image courtesy of the Library of Congress

Union side in the Civil War were proof of the patriotism and loyalty of New Mexicans, McAdoo insisted. "These Spanish-Americans of New Mexico are Americans by birth, sympathy, and education, and have so testified on the field of battle."[141]

Although strong elements in the Eastern press and key politicians in Washington, D.C., were against New Mexican statehood, this opposition was not the main reason New Mexico remained a territory for more than 60 years. Indeed, many New Mexicans, if not most, seemed content to defer statehood. Of the *Hispano* Delegates from 19th-century New Mexico, only Miguel Otero, Francisco Perea, and Chaves ardently advocated statehood. Gallegos strenuously opposed it. Most Territorial Delegates were ambivalent or did not serve long enough in the national capital to record an opinion, reflecting most *nuevomexicanos'* perceptions of statehood as a threat to their economic and political status, and as the means by which their culture would be diluted. Anglo-Americans, particularly in the southern portions of the territory, thought statehood would only lead to tyranny imposed by a *nuevomexicano* majority until more Anglo settlers arrived. In fact, only small, vocal groups consistently championed the idea. Stephen Elkins, the Santa Fe Ring boss, saw statehood as a vehicle for the dominant Santa Fe class of politicians to cement their control of the state; a minority of *Hispano* elites considered statehood a means to achieve home rule and minimize Anglo usurpations.[142]

CONCLUSION

From 1885 to 1898, as the power of the New Mexico's *Hispano* elites began to wane during the final drive for statehood, there were no *Hispanos* serving in Congress.[143] The issue of race dominated debates and even internal territorial considerations about New Mexican statehood. Senator Albert Beveridge of Indiana, chairman of the Senate Committee on Territories from 1901 to 1911, who blocked the statehood initiative almost single-handedly, exemplified the predominant perspective. A 1902 committee report authored by Beveridge rejected statehood largely because of the territory's "Mexican element," a "mass of people, unlike us in race, language, and social customs" who had yet "to form a creditable portion of American citizenship."[144]

Notions of American exceptionalism and providential design that had impelled westward expansion had begun to clash with a resonant, underlying anxiety about incorporating culturally distinct peoples into the U.S. body politic. Gradually, Anglo politicians in the latter 19th century and the early 20th century became increasingly hesitant to invoke race as a rallying cry for U.S. territorial acquisition, particularly when encroachment on contiguous lands escalated to the seizure and administration of insular possessions.[145] Congress patched together a system of statutory representation for the territories in the 19th century, assuming that the territories would become states and that their second-class status in Congress would be temporary. The problem of statutory representation grew more complex as the United States acquired populated territories abroad, without immediate or long-term prospects for achieving statehood.

The 55th Congress (1897–1899), which declared war against Spain, was the last Congress to deliberate without a Member of Hispanic descent.

Though New Mexico continued to send *Hispanos* to Washington, the Spanish-American War of 1898 transformed Hispanic representation in Congress; in the aftermath of the war, Puerto Rico came under U.S. rule, and the office of Resident Commissioner was created to give Puerto Ricans a voice in the national legislature. The majority of the Hispanic Members of Congress who served between the conflict with Spain and World War II were Resident Commissioners. While the responsibilities of Territorial Delegates presaged those of Resident Commissioners in the U.S. House, the new office was in many ways distinct. Yet, like the New Mexico Delegates who preceded them, Puerto Rican Resident Commissioners sought to expand opportunities for their constituents, and in doing so, became ambassadors to the U.S. mainland for their island's culture and institutions.

NOTES

1 The quotation is from a chapter title in one of the standard works on the U.S. settlement of New Mexico: Howard R. Lamar, *The Far Southwest, 1846–1912: A Territorial History,* Rev. ed. (Albuquerque: University of New Mexico Press, 2000).

2 David Meriwether, *My Life in the Mountains and on the Plains*, edited by Robert A. Griffin (Norman: University of Oklahoma Press, 1966): 166–167.

3 *Congressional Globe*, House, 33rd Cong., 1st sess. (27 February 1854): 492.

4 The first attempt to secure Gallegos an interpreter was in early January; see *Congressional Globe*, House, 33rd Cong., 1st sess. (5 January 1854): 128.

5 Throughout this essay, the term *nuevomexicanos* will be used to describe New Mexicans of Hispanic and/or *mestizo* descent. The term *Hispano* will be used to differentiate New Mexicans of Hispanic and/or *mestizo* descent from New Mexican Caucasians, who will be referred to as "Anglos." For more on terminology, see Phillip B. Gonzales, "The Political Construction of Latino Nomenclatures in Twentieth Century New Mexico," *Journal of the Southwest* 35, no. 3 (Summer 1993): 158–172; John M. Nieto-Phillips, *The Language of Blood: The Making of Spanish-American Identity in New Mexico, 1880s–1930s* (Albuquerque: University of New Mexico Press, 2004): 2.

6 Letter to the Editor signed "Republican," 7 July 1871, (Santa Fe) *The Daily New Mexican*: 1.

7 For a brief summary of U. S. territorial expansion in the 19th century, see Bartholomew H. Sparrow, "Territorial Expansion," in Julian E. Zelizer, ed., *The American Congress: The Building of Democracy* (Boston & New York: Houghton Mifflin, 2004): 168–186. A more detailed treatment is Bradford Perkins, *The Cambridge History of American Foreign Relations, Vol. 1: The Creation of a Republican Empire, 1776–1865* (New York: Cambridge University Press, 1993).

8 See "Party Divisions of the House of Representatives, 1789 to Present" http://history.house.gov/Institution/Party-Divisions/Party-Divisions. In 1822, the year Hernández entered the House, there were 187 Representatives and four Delegates; on the eve of the Spanish-American War in 1898, the House had 357 Representatives and three Delegates.

9 Walter LaFeber, *The American Age: U.S. Foreign Policy at Home and Abroad.* Volume 1 to 1920 (New York: W. W. Norton, 1994; second ed.): 52–56; George C. Herring, *From Colony to Superpower: U.S. Foreign Relations since 1776* (New York: Oxford University Press, 2008): 109–112.

10 Herring, *From Colony to Superpower:* 109–112; Gordon S. Wood, *Empire of Liberty: A History of the Early Republic, 1789–1815* (New York: Oxford University Press, 2009): 374–376.

11 Although Hernández was elected at the end of September 1822, he did not arrive in Washington, D.C., until January, 1823; therefore, his six-month term was abbreviated to two months (January 8 to March 3, 1823).

12 The term "Manifest Destiny" was long assumed to be the work of New York news editor John O'Sullivan, but historians have recently questioned his authorship. New theories propose that well-known expansion proponent Jane Storm penned the phrase using the pseudonym "C. Montgomery." Daniel Walker Howe, *What Hath God Wrought*: *The Transformation of America, 1815–1848* (New York: Oxford University Press, 2007): 703.

13 For a concise overview, see Anders Stephanson, *Manifest Destiny: American Expansionism and the Empire of Right* (New York: Hill and Wang, 1995). See also Thomas R. Hietala, *Manifest Design: American Exceptionalism and Empire*, Rev. ed. (Ithaca, NY: Cornell University Press, 2003). For critical assessments, see Sam W. Haynes and Christopher Morris, eds., *Manifest Destiny and Empire: American Antebellum Expansionism* (College Station: Texas A&M University Press, 1997). For an illustration of expansionism's foothold in the Caribbean, see Tom Chaffin, *Fatal Glory: Narciso López and the First Clandestine U.S. War against Cuba* (Charlottesville: University of Virginia Press, 1996).

14 Robert C. Winthrop, "Oration Pronounced by the Honorable Robert C. Winthrop, Speaker of the House of Representatives of the United States, on the Fourth of July, 1848, on the Occasion of the Laying of the Corner-stone of the National Monument to the Memory of Washington" (Washington, D.C.: National Monument Society and J. & G. S. Gideon, Printers, 1848): 9–10.

15 As quoted in Stephanson, *Manifest Destiny*: 42.

16 Howe, *What Hath God Wrought*: 705; Reginald Horsman, *Race and Manifest Destiny: The Origins of American Racial Anglo-Saxonism* (Cambridge: Harvard University Press, 1981): 84–88, 92–94, 139–157.

17 See Horsman, *Race and Manifest Destiny*, pp. 208–228, for a discussion of where Mexicans fit in the worldview of white Americans in the 1840s.

18 Howe, *What Hath God Wrought*: 658–671; Matt S. Meier, *Mexican Americans, American Mexicans: From Conquistadors to Chicanos* (New York: Hill and Wang, 1993): 56–59.

19 David J. Weber, ed., *Foreigners in Their Native Land: Historical Roots of the Mexican Americans* (Albuquerque: University of New Mexico Press, 2003): 89–92.

20 Mexico's legislature subsequently refused to ratify the agreement, believing that Texan independence was the first step in U.S. expansion into the Southwest. See Weber, ed., *Foreigners in Their Native Land: Historical Roots of the Mexican Americans*: 114–115.

21 Bolstering the population growth were thousands of enslaved persons who were sold into the republic from the upper U.S. South, Cuba, and Africa. Weber, ed., *Foreigners in Their Native Land: Historical Roots of the Mexican Americans*: 145–147. By the 1890s and the early 20th century, "white primaries" and poll taxes intended to keep African Americans from voting largely kept Mexican Americans from voting as well.

22 See John M. Belohlavek, *'Let the Eagle Soar!': The Foreign Policy of Andrew Jackson* (Lincoln: University of Nebraska Press, 1985): 214–238.

23 Howe, *What Hath God Wrought*: 677–680.

24 *Senate Journal*, 28th Cong., 1st sess. (8 June 1844): 436–439; *Senate Journal*, 28th Cong., 2nd sess. (22 February 1845): 200; *House Journal*, 28th Cong., 2nd sess. (25 January 1845): 264, (1 March 1845): 541–542; Howe, *What Hath God Wrought*: 698–700; Stephen W. Stathis, *Landmark Legislation 1774–2002: Major U.S. Acts and Treaties* (Washington, D.C.: Congressional Quarterly Press, 2003): 68, 70.

25 For readable and concise biographies of Polk, see John Seigenthaler, *James K. Polk* (New York: Times Books, Henry Holt and Company, 2003); and Paul H. Bergeron, *The Presidency of James K. Polk* (Lawrence: University Press of Kansas, 1987).

26 During the 29th Congress there were 142 Democrats, 79 Whigs, and 6 Americans in the House of Representatives (with one vacancy). In the Senate, voters had elected 34 Democrats and 22 Whigs (there were two vacancies). See Kenneth C. Martis, ed., *The Historical Atlas of Political Parties in the United States Congress: 1789–1989* (New York: MacMillan, 1989): 98–99.

27 For a longer narrative of the events leading up to and after the U.S.-Mexican War, see Howe, *What Hath God Wrought*: 701–791; Sean Wilentz, *The Rise of American Democracy: Jefferson to Lincoln* (New York: W. W. Norton, 2005): 577–605; Herring, *From Colony to Superpower*: 194–207.

28 Manuel G. Gonzales, *Mexicanos: A History of Mexicans in the United States,* second ed. (Bloomington: Indiana University Press, 2009): 75–82, quotation on p. 76; see also, Herring, *From Colony to Superpower*: 197–200. For a summary of the public opinion of Mexicans during the war, see Jesús Velasco-Marquez, "Mexican Perceptions during the War," in Donald S. Frazier, ed., *The United States and Mexico at War: Nineteenth-Century Expansionism and Conflict* (New York: Macmillan, 1998): 338–339.

29 Milo Milton Quaife, ed., *The Diary of James K. Polk during his Presidency, 1845–1849*, vol. I (Chicago: A. C. McClurg & Company, 1910): 386.

30 *Congressional Globe*, House, 29th Cong., 1st sess. (11 May 1846): 795.

31 Wilentz, *The Rise of American Democracy*: 582–583; Leonard L. Richards, *The Life and Times of Congressman John Quincy Adams* (New York: Oxford University Press, 1986): 185–190.

32 *Congressional Globe*, House, 29th Cong., 1st sess. (11 May 1846): 794.

33 Quaife, ed., *Diary of James K. Polk*, vol. I: 392.

34 Like Garrett Davis, Crittenden and Senator William Upham opposed the language in the preamble condemning Mexico, but they eventually voted for the provisions. Other Senators did not attend the session and thus did not vote. *Congressional Globe*, Senate, 29th Congress, 1st sess. (12 May 1846): quotation on pp. 802, 804. For more information on public dissent and the war, see John H. Schroeder, *Mr. Polk's War: American Opposition and Dissent, 1846–1848* (Madison: University of Wisconsin Press, 1973).

35 Andrew J. Donelson to James K. Polk, 23 May 1846, in Wayne Cutler, ed., *Correspondence of James K. Polk*, vol. 11 (Knoxville: University of Tennessee Press, 2009): 172.

36 *Congressional Globe*, House, 29th Cong., 1st sess. (12 May 1846): 805.

37 The full text of the Treaty of Guadalupe Hidalgo of 2 February 1848 is available online at the Yale Law School's Avalon Project, http://avalon.law.yale.edu/19th_century/guadhida.asp (accessed 3 May 2010).

38 For casualty figures see, Howe, *What Hath God Wrought*: 752. Howe's discussion of the war is the most recent and balanced survey of the existing secondary literature on strategy, politics, and impact; see pp. 744–791.

39 Michael Holt, *The Rise and Fall of the American Whig Party: Jacksonian Politics and the Onset of the Civil War* (New York: Oxford University Press, 1999): 233–245.

40 For the most recent comprehensive treatment of the peace treaty, see Richard Griswold del Castillo, *The Treaty of Guadalupe Hidalgo* (Norman: University of Oklahoma Press, 1990). For a recent, balanced overview of the treaty process and its effects, see Howe, *What Hath God Wrought*: 800–811.

41 Herring, *From Colony to Superpower*: 205.

42 See Matt S. Meier and Feliciano Ribera, *Mexican Americans, American Mexicans: From Conquistadors to Chicanos* (New York: Hill and Wang, 1993; Rev. ed.): 6–68; quotation on p. 68. For a survey of Mexican historians' interpretations of the Treaty of Guadalupe Hidalgo—ranging from self-criticism to indictments of American aggrandizement—as well as an analysis of the treaty's legacy on the Chicano movement of the 20th century, see del Castillo, *The Treaty of Guadalupe Hidalgo*: 108–153.

43 The figure for the Hispanic population is from Howe, *What Hath God Wrought*: 809.

44 Gómez, *Manifest Destinies*: 81–115; John M. Nieto-Phillips, *The Language of Blood: The Making of Spanish-American Identity in New Mexico, 1880s–1930s* (Albuquerque: University of New Mexico Press, 2008): 47–48, 54.

45 For an insightful analysis of the potential for racial prejudice to act as a brake on expansion, see Horsman, *Race and Manifest Destiny*, 236–248; and Eric T. L. Love, *Race over Empire: Racism and U.S. Imperialism, 1865–1900* (Chapel Hill: University of North Carolina Press, 2004). See also Hietala, *Manifest Design*: 164.

46 Cited in Hietala, *Manifest Design*: 165–166. For the original speech, see *Congressional Globe*, Senate, 30th Cong., 1st sess. (12 January 1848): 157–160; quotation on p. 158.

47 Abraham Holtzman, "Empire and Representation: The U.S. Congress," *Legislative Studies*

Quarterly 11, no. 2 (May 1986): 249–273. A statistically small but numerically consequential group, statutory representatives have constituted over 1 percent of all House Members. Since 1789, 175 individuals have represented territories or insular possessions in the House (143 Delegates and 32 Resident Commissioners from Puerto Rico and the Philippines). This figure is based on data from the online *Biographical Directory of the United States Congress*, http://bioguide.congress.gov/ (accessed 3 February 2012). For the development of the office of Delegate from a procedural perspective, see Chapter 43 of *Hinds' Precedents of the House of Representatives*, vol. 2 (Washington, D.C.: Government Printing Office, 1907): 861–868.

48 *Annals of Congress*, 3rd Cong., 2nd sess. (17–18 November 1794): 884–891.

49 Ibid, 884.

50 Ibid., emphasis in original.

51 See Betsy Palmer, "Delegates to the U.S. Congress: History and Current Status," Report R40555, Congressional Research Service, Library of Congress, Washington, D.C.: 1–12; see especially, p. 7.

52 See, for example, *Hinds' Precedents*, for information on Delegate George Poindexter of the Mississippi Territory, who appears to have chaired at least two select committees: sections 1299 and 1303, pp. 865–866.

53 Palmer, "Delegates to the U.S. Congress: History and Current Status": 7.

54 *Statutes at Large*, Act of March 3, 1817, ch. 42, 3 Stat. 363. *Hinds' Precedents* notes that the language was replicated "verbatim" from the Northwest Ordinance Act of 1787. See section 1290, p. 861.

55 Earl S. Pomeroy, *The Territories and the United States* (Seattle: University of Washington Press, 1969; reprint of 1947 edition): 80.

56 *Congressional Globe*, House, 34th Cong., 1st sess. (23 July 1856): 1730.

57 For instance, in 2011 dollars, both Gallegos and Chaves were likely millionaires. Their known assets totaled in the high hundreds of thousands, roughly $725,000 and $950,000, respectively (using 1870 as the basis year). Mariano Otero also had accumulated more than $250,000 in 2011 dollars. Asset information for most other Hispanic Members of Congress from this era is incomplete. See the chart "Assets of Delegates Elected to the United States Congress," in Carlos Brazil Ramirez,"The Hispanic Political Elite in Territorial New Mexico: A Study of Classical Colonialism," Ph.D. diss., University of California–Santa Barbara (June 1979): 270. These figures were calculated using data from the historical Consumer Price Index. Other methods of calculation, including Gross Domestic Product, sometimes result in drastically different valuations. For a discussion of the difficulty involved in accounting for inflation conversion factors and determining the relative value of dollars over long periods, see Oregon State University's "Inflation Conversion Factors in final 2011 Dollars for 1774 to Estimated 2022" at http://oregonstate.edu/cla/polisci/individual-year-conversion-factor-tables (accessed 24 July 2012). For a detailed description of the involvement of the Otero, Perea, and Chaves clans in the lucrative trade along the Santa Fe Trail, see Susan C. Boyle, *Los Capitalistas: Hispano Merchants and the Santa Fe Trade* (Albuquerque: University of New Mexico Press, 1997). Ramirez provides a useful analysis of this cohort as well as comparisons with Anglo political elites on pp. 260–325.

58 See Allan G. Bogue, Jerome M. Clubb, Carroll R. McKibben, and Santa A. Traugott, "Members of the House of Representatives and the Process of Modernization, 1789–1960," *Journal of American History* 63 (September 1976): Tables 2 and 3, pp. 284, 286.

59 A number of Delegates from the New Mexico Territory were related by marriage. For detailed information, see Miguel Otero, Jr., to Ansel Wold, 9 November 1928, textual files of the *Biographical Directory of the United States Congress*, Office of the Historian, U.S. House of Representatives (hereinafter referred to as textual files of the *Biographical Directory of the United States Congress*). For background and detailed explanations of the familial relationships between the New Mexico Delegates, see Ramirez, "The Hispanic Political Elite in Territorial New Mexico: A Study of Classical Colonialism": 22–26, 284–288, 298, 300–301, 306–307, 312–313. Some of the bloodlines were quite complicated. Francisco Perea married Dolores Otero, a niece of Miguel Antonio Otero. Henry Connelly, who served as governor of the territory after the Civil War, married Dolores Perea,

the mother of José Francisco Chaves. When Chaves became a Delegate, his stepfather was governor of the territory.

60 Bogue et al., "Members of the House of Representatives and the Process of Modernization, 1789–1960": Table 1, p. 282.

61 Alvin R. Sunseri, *Seeds of Discord: New Mexico in the Aftermath of the American Conquest, 1846–1861* (Chicago, IL: Nelson-Hall, 1979): 68. "Some Mexican-Americans," notes Sunseri, "in a desperate effort to insure that their children would be prepared to deal with the Anglo-American invaders on more equal terms, sent them to school in Missouri."

62 Bogue et al., "Members of the House of Representatives and the Process of Modernization, 1789–1960": 275–302; see especially Table 6, p. 291. From 1820 to 1900, Members' median age at their entry into the House increased from 39 to 44 years.

63 The median age of the first generation of Hispanic-American Members of Congress elected to Congress (36.5 years) was far younger than that of the first generation of women elected to Congress (50 years), but just slightly younger than the average age of African-American Members during Reconstruction (41.5 years) and the early Jim Crow Era (36.95 years). In part, the median age for first-generation women in Congress (1917–1934) was higher because the professionalization of Congress (in which many politicians whose median terms of service rose significantly as they began to make a career of service in Washington) occurred over the course of several decades in the late 19th and early 20th centuries. For a comparative analysis of the background of pioneer cohorts of women and African Americans in Congress, see Office of History and Preservation, U.S. House of Representatives, *Women in Congress, 1917–2006* (Washington, D.C.: Government Printing Office, 2007): 24–26, and *Black Americans in Congress, 1870–2007* (Washington, D.C.: Government Printing Office, 2008): 22–25.

64 Ramirez, "The Hispanic Political Elite in Territorial New Mexico: A Study of Classical Colonialism": 557–558, 575. From the establishment of the territory in 1850 to 1880, *nuevomexicanos* dominated the territorial legislature. According to Ramirez, *nuevomexicanos* accounted for "more than sixty percent of men elected to the territorial council and over seventy percent of those elected to the House. They served over seventy percent of the terms in both houses and were reelected to office more often than Anglo-American legislators." See Ramirez, pp. 440–441 for specific figures.

65 *Congressional Globe*, House, 31st Cong., 1st. sess. (6 September 1850): 1762–1764.

66 Lamar, *The Far Southwest, 1846–1912: A Territorial History*: 88; see Horsman, *Race and Manifest Destiny*: 236–248, for Democrats' and Whigs' positions regarding New Mexico's admittance as a state.

67 Lamar, *The Far Southwest, 1846–1912: A Territorial History*: 114–117, quotation on p. 116. Lamar divides New Mexico's political evolution into three stages: 1) an unoccupied territory in which contending powers jockeyed for control during 1821 to 1846; 2) a frontier reliant upon the national government for defense and development from 1847 to 1864; 3) an assertion of local rights, the rise of a working political system, calculated use of outside aid for local benefit, and a growing sense of a distinct political identity from 1865 to 1912.

68 The election date was changed with the passage of a 1872 law that moved the election date of Delegates to the first Tuesday of November of the even-numbered year. See *Revised Statutes and Laws of the Territory of New Mexico in Force at the Close of the Session of the Legislative Assembly Ending February 2, 1865* (St. Louis: R. P. Studley & Co., 1865): 430; *Compiled Laws of New Mexico. In Accordance with an Act of the Legislature, approved April 3, 1884. Including the Constitution of the United States, the Treaty of Guadalupe Hidalgo, the Gadsden Treaty: The Original Act Organizing the Territory; The Organic Acts as now in force; The Original Kearny Code; and a List of Laws Enacted Since the Compilation of 1865.* (Topeka, KS: G. W. Crane & Co., 1885): 586.

69 Pomeroy, *The Territories and the United States, 1861–1890*: 80; Larson, *New Mexico's Quest for Statehood, 1846–1912*: 29–30, 36–40, 69–74; Lamar, *The Far Southwest, 1846–1912: A Territorial History*: 88–89. Lamar and Larson describe the political split between New Mexicans who wanted immediate statehood and those who preferred a territorial government. Pro-statehood advocates formed a faction under Richard Weightman, New Mexico's first Territorial Delegate, while pro-territory advocates united under Judge Joab Houghton. The

Weightman faction made an effort to promote *nuevomexicano* political candidates such as Gallegos, whereas the Houghton faction promoted primarily Anglo candidates. Larson writes that "the Spanish-speaking majority ... was hurt more than any other group by the political divisions and feuds" as one faction "scornfully exploited the Hispanos, and the other patronizingly sought their votes." The Weightman and Houghton factions fought for control of New Mexican politics through delegate elections and patronage appointments for the remainder of the 1850s. See also Ramirez, "The Hispanic Political Elite in Territorial New Mexico: A Study of Classical Colonialism": 261.

70 Larson, *New Mexico's Quest for Statehood*: 85–86. Larson lists two reasons for why *nuevomexicanos* remained loyal to the Union. First, Confederate rule meant Texan rule. For many New Mexicans, the Sibley invasion was another attempt by Texans who tried to take the Rio Grande Valley. Secondly, Confederate supporters' promotion of "the exclusive use of English in all legal proceedings by the Confederate Territory of Arizona ... made the territory's Spanish-speaking citizens more positive of the unsuitability of the Southern cause." For background on the Civil War in the American West and New Mexico, see Donald S. Frazier, *Blood and Treasure: Confederate Empire in the Southwest* (College Station: Texas A&M University Press, 1995); and Ray C. Colton, *Civil War in the Western Territories: Arizona, Colorado, New Mexico, and Utah* (Norman: University of Oklahoma Press, 1959). For more information about *nuevomexicano* experiences during the war, see Darlis A. Miller, "Hispanos and the Civil War in New Mexico: A Reconsideration," *New Mexico Historical Review* 54, no. 2 (April 1979): 105–123.

71 At the heart of the ring was the Santa Fe law partnership that included college friends and outsize personalities: Republicans Stephen Benton Elkins and Thomas Benton Catron. Before they joined forces, Elkins was U.S. District Attorney for New Mexico, and Catron was the territorial attorney general. Both men became successful politicians, advancing the Santa Fe Ring's interests along the way. For more information on both men, see "Thomas Benton Catron" and "Stephen Benton Elkins," *Biographical Directory of the United States Congress*, http://bioguide.congress.gov.

72 For an especially useful interpretation of the Santa Fe Ring's domination of territorial politics through land grant manipulations, see Lamar, *The Far Southwest, 1846–1912: A Territorial History*: 121–149. Lamar provides background on the Maxwell Land Grant (originally the Beaubien–Miranda claim), which dated to Spanish rule, on pp. 124–125. For the Santa Fe Ring's pro-statehood position, see Larson, *New Mexico's Quest for Statehood, 1846–1912*: 135–146.

73 For a summary of modern contested election practices, see Charles T. Howell "Contested Elections," in Donald Bacon et al., *Encyclopedia of the United States Congress*, vol. 2 (New York: Simon and Schuster, 1995): 568–570.

74 Jeffrey A. Jenkins, "Partisanship and Contested Election Cases in the House of Representatives, 1789–1902," *Studies in American Political Development* 18 (Fall 2004): 113.

75 Champ Clark, *My Quarter Century in Politics*, vol. 2 (New York: Harper & Brothers, 1920): 20.

76 In awarding Gallegos his seat against William Carr Lane in 1853, the Committee on Elections ruled that Pueblo Indians, who were considered citizens by the Mexican government, were not entitled to vote in territorial elections. In excluding the Pueblos from the political process, the House violated a key provision of the Treaty of Guadalupe Hidalgo that extended U.S. citizenship to those who renounced their Mexican citizenship as well as to those who had not elected Mexican citizenship one year after the treaty's ratification. See Ramirez, "The Hispanic Political Elite in Territorial New Mexico: A Study of Classical Colonialism": 267; and Mary Childers Mangusso, "A Study of the Citizenship Provisions of the Treaty of Guadalupe Hidalgo," M.A. thesis, University of New Mexico–Albuquerque, 1966: 78–88.

77 Lamar, *The Far Southwest, 1846–1912*: 91.

78 For the experience of early African-American Members, see Office of History and Preservation, *Black Americans in Congress, 1870–2007*: 25–30.

79 José Francisco Chaves, "Address," 9 March 1869, (Santa Fe) *The Daily New Mexican*: 1.

80 Miguel Otero, (Jr.), *My Life on the Frontier: 1864–1882* (Albuquerque: University of New Mexico Press, 1987; reprint of 1935 edition): 272–273.

81 Miguel Otero (Sr.), "Address of Hon. Miguel Otero to His Fellow Citizens of New Mexico," 6 March 1857, *Santa Fe Weekly Gazette*: 2.

82 Ramirez, "The Hispanic Political Elite in Territorial New Mexico: A Study of Classical Colonialism": 269, 271–273, 314.

83 For an analysis of factionalism in New Mexico politics, see Lamar, *The Far Southwest, 1846–1912: A Territorial History*: 51–117.

84 *Congressional Globe*, House, 34th Cong., 1st sess. (23 July 1856): 1730.

85 *Congressional Globe*, House, 34th Cong., 1st sess. (23 July 1856): 1733–1736. For more on the xenophobia of the 1850s, see Tyler Anbinder, *Nativism and Slavery: The Northern Know Nothings and the Politics of the 1850s* (New York: Oxford University Press, 1992): especially pp. xiii, 33–34, 43–50. The premier intellectual history of nativism remains John Higham, *Strangers in the Land: Patterns of American Nativism 1860–1925* (New York: Rutgers University Press, 1963; reprint Atheneum, 1973). For more information on how nativism influenced the primary political parties of the 1850s, see Eric Foner, *Free Labor, Free Soil, Free Men: The Ideology of the Republican Party before the Civil War* (New York: Oxford University Press, 1995; reprint of 1970 edition): 226–260.

86 "Democratic Proscription," 20 July 1871, (Santa Fe) *The Daily New Mexican*: 2; "Washington Correspondence," 24 July 1871, (Santa Fe) *The Daily New Mexican*: 1; "Gallegos' Cadet Appointment," 1 August 1871, (Santa Fe) *Daily New Mexican*: 1.

87 *Congressional Globe*, House, 34th Cong., 1st sess. (23 July 1856): 1733–1736.

88 Ibid., 1734.

89 Larson, *New Mexico's Quest for Statehood, 1846–1912*: 117–120, 123–125, 153–155, lists racialist and politically partisan motives for denying statehood to New Mexico in the 1870s; Laura E. Gómez, *Manifest Destinies: The Making of the Mexican American Race* (New York: New York University Press, 2007): 62–63, 71–78, 81–115; Nieto-Phillips, *The Language of Blood*: 8–11; 45–93; quotation on p. 9. However, some scholars disagree with Gómez's and Nieto-Phillips's approach. Charles Montgomery argues against analyzing New Mexican history from an "oppositional relationship, one marked by conflict, domination, resistance, and the virtually unbridgeable barrier of whiteness." Montgomery encourages scholars to study the "accommodative relationship" between elite *Hispanos* and Anglos in the early 20th century in "The Trap of Race and Memory: The Language of Spanish Civility on the Upper Rio Grande," *American Quarterly* 52, no. 3 (September 2000): 478–513. In the 1880 delegate election, Luna supporters accused Otero of pandering to *Hispano* constituents while making disparaging comments about them behind their backs.

90 "Our Victory," 6 November 1880, (Santa Fe) *The Daily New Mexican*: 2.

91 See, for example, Office of History and Preservation, *Women in Congress, 1917–2006*: 26–27, and *Black Americans in Congress, 1870–2007*: 30–32.

92 Benjamin Perley Poore, *Perley's Reminiscences of Sixty Years in the National Metropolis* (Philadelphia, PA: Hubbard Brothers, 1886): 456.

93 See, for example, James Sterling Young, *The Washington Community: 1800–1828* (New York: Columbia University Press, 1966), for an account that stresses the significant role of boardinghouses in organizing legislative behavior in the early 1800s. For a contrary view, see Allan G. Bogue and Mark P. Marlaire, "Of Mess and Men: The Boardinghouse and Congressional Voting, 1821–1842," *American Journal of Political Science* 19 (1975): 207–230. Bogue and Marlaire argue that influence of individual relationships within state delegations had a more determinative effect on voting patterns.

94 See for example, *Congressional Directory*, 46th Cong., 2nd sess. (Washington, D.C.: Government Printing Office, 1879).

95 Martha Durant Read, "Colonel Jose Francisco Chaves: A Short Biography of the Father of the New Mexico Statehood Movement," *Southwest Heritage* 8, no. 4 (Winter 1978–1979): 13–21, 30.

96 For more on this complex issue, see Palmer, "Delegates to the U.S. Congress: History and Current Status": 1–12; see especially pp. 7–10.

97 Certainly by 1884, when a proposal to grant Territorial Delegates the right to vote in

committee died in the Rules Committee, it is clear that Delegates were not empowered to act as full members of standing committees. See Palmer, "Delegates to the U.S. Congress: History and Current Status": 8.

98 See the floor debate in the *Congressional Globe*, House, 42nd Cong., 2nd sess. (13 December 1871): 117–118; for more on precedent, see *Hinds' Precedents of the House of Representatives*, vol. 2 (Washington, D.C.: Government Printing Office, 1907): 864–856.

99 *Congressional Record*, House, 44th Cong., 1st sess. (29 March 1876): 2035.

100 For a useful jurisdictional summary, see Charles E. Schamel, ed., et al., *Guide to the Records of the United States House of Representatives at the National Archives: 1789–1989 Bicentennial Edition* (Washington, D.C.: Government Printing Office, 1989): 89; 181–185; published as House Document no. 100–245, 100th Cong., 2nd sess. Eventually, the panel's responsibilities were transferred to the Banking and Currency Committee and the Interstate and Foreign Commerce Committee. For an analysis of committee attractiveness to Members, see Charles Stewart III, "Committee Hierarchies in the Modernizing House, 1875–1947," *American Journal of Political Science* 36, no. 4 (November 1992): 835–856; see especially Stewart's table on "Committee Attractiveness," pp. 845–846.

101 Schamel et al., *Guide to the Records of the United States House of Representatives at the National Archives*: 71–72.

102 *Congressional Globe*, House, 42nd Cong., 2nd sess. (13 December 1871): 118; "The National Capital: Territorial Syndicate," *New York Times* (14 December 1871): 1. Gallegos had been returned to the House for a single term and likely would have interacted with the syndicate, although there is no definitive evidence of his membership.

103 *Congressional Record*, House, 46th Cong., 3rd sess. (22 February 1881): 1955.

104 *Congressional Record*, House, 47th Cong., 1st sess. (21 December 1881): 241.

105 For more information about the competition for federal government resources between different sections of the United States in this era, see Richard F. Bensel, *Sectionalism and American Political Development: 1880–1980* (Madison: University of Wisconsin Press, 1984): 22–59, especially pp. 50–51. For a summary of a 19th-century Delegate's powers and privileges, see Pomeroy, *The Territories and the United States, 1861–1890*: 80–89. For a brief explanation of the complications of settling land grants in New Mexico, see Lamar, *The Far Southwest, 1846–1912*: 123–128.

106 For an overview of Congress and its efforts to promote railroad development and, later, regulation, see Wallace D. Farnham, "Railroads," in *The Encyclopedia of the U.S. Congress*, vol. 3 (New York: Simon and Schuster, 1995): 1660–1666. For a technical analysis of congressional land grant policy for railroads, see Lloyd J. Mercer, *Railroads and Land Grant Policy: A Study in Government Intervention* (New York: Academic Press, 1982).

107 Clarence Carter, ed., *The Territorial Papers of the United States, Vol. XXII: The Territory of Florida, 1821–1824* (New York: AMS Press, 1972; reprint of 1934 edition): 642–643.

108 See, for example, Larson, *New Mexico's Quest for Statehood*: 144–145. For a detailed overview of the New Mexico land grant issue, see Malcolm Ebright, *Land Grants and Lawsuits in Northern New Mexico* (Albuquerque: University of New Mexico Press, 1994).

109 For an overview of American Indians' experiences during three centuries of Spanish rule in the lands eventually acquired by the United States in the Mexican cession, see Albert H. Schroeder, "Shifting for Survival in the Spanish Southwest," in David J. Weber, *New Spain's Far Northern Frontier: Essays on Spain in the American West, 1540–1821* (Albuquerque: University of New Mexico Press, 1979): 237–255. For a survey of congressional Indian policy from 1789 forward, see Frederick E. Hoxie, "Indian Policy," in *The Encyclopedia of the U.S. Congress*, vol. 2 (New York: Simon and Schuster, 1995): 1112–1119; and Robert Bee, *The Politics of American Indian Policy* (Cambridge, MA: Scheckman, 1982).

110 See Lamar, *The Far Southwest, 1846–1912: A Territorial History*: 106–111. For a description of the Bosque Redondo Reservation experience from the Navajos' perspective, see Peter Iverson, *Diné: A History of the Navajos* (Albuquerque: University of New Mexico Press, 2002): 48–65. For more information on the Bosque Redondo, see "Bosque Redondo Memorial," New Mexico State Monuments Web Page, maintained by the New Mexico Department of Cultural Affairs, http://www.nmmonuments.org/inst.php?inst=8 (accessed 15 April 2010).

111 Francisco Perea, "To the People of New Mexico," 13 June 1863, *Santa Fe Weekly Gazette*: 2.

112 See Lamar, *The Far Southwest, 1846–1912: A Territorial History*: 106–111; and Robert M. Utley, *The Indian Frontier, 1846–1890*, rev. ed. (Albuquerque: University of New Mexico Press, 2003): 82–86.

113 *Congressional Globe*, House, 39th Cong., 2nd sess. (19 February 1867): 1344–1345.

114 Gómez, *Manifest Destinies: The Making of the Mexican American Race*: 81–115; Estévan Rael-Gálvez, "Identifying Captivity and Capturing Identity: Narratives of American Indian Slavery in Colorado and New Mexico, 1776–1934," Ph.D. diss., University of Michigan, 2002; and James F. Brooks, *Captives & Cousins: Slavery, Kinship, and Community on the Southwest Borderlands* (Chapel Hill: University of North Carolina Press/Omohundro Institute of Early American History and Culture, 2002). One classic study is L. R. Bailey's *Indian Slave Trade in the Southwest: A Study of Slave-Taking and the Traffic in Indian Captives* (Los Angeles: Westernlore Press, 1966).

115 Alvin R. Sunseri, *Seeds of Discord: New Mexico in the Aftermath of the American Conquest, 1846–1861* (Chicago, IL: Nelson-Hall, 1979): 59–64. For a more conservative estimate, of roughly 600 individuals, in 1860, see Lawrence Murphy, "Reconstruction in New Mexico," *New Mexico Historical Review* 43, no. 2 (April 1968): 100.

116 No single authoritative book exists on peonage in New Mexico in the latter half of the 19th century. A few works that address the practice are Sunseri, *Seeds of Discord*: 38–42; Clark S. Knowlton, "Patron-Peon Pattern among the Spanish Americans of New Mexico," *Social Forces* 41, no. 1 (October 1962): 12–17; and David J. Weber, *The Mexican Frontier, 1821–1846: The American Southwest under Mexico* (Albuquerque: University of New Mexico Press, 1982): 211–213. Pete Daniel, *The Shadow of Slavery: Peonage in the South, 1901–1969* (Urbana: University of Illinois Press, 1990), describes many of the aspects of peonage as it was practiced in the postbellum South before the civil rights movement.

117 Sunseri, *Seeds of Discord*: 40–41; Knowlton, "Patron-Peon Pattern among the Spanish Americans of New Mexico": 12–17; Weber, *The Mexican Frontier, 1821–1846*: 212. Knowlton identifies two predominant forms of the patron-peon relationship: large landowners and village patrons. In contrast to the perpetual condition of chattel slavery for African Americans in the U.S. South, Weber argues that a "peon was not legally a slave nor was peonage limited to one race. Peonage was viewed as a condition of class and bad fortune. A peon could … end his obligation by paying off his debt, and his condition was not hereditary."

118 "On Slavery in the Territories of Oregon, California, and New Mexico," *Congressional Globe*, Appendix, 30th Cong., 1st sess. (3 August 1848): 1072–1076; quotation on p. 1072. Derived from Spain, peonage foreshadowed some aspects of the share-cropping system that evolved in the postbellum South, but peonage commenced when a worker was forcibly restrained at a task (e.g., mining, herding, working as a domestic servant) because of indebtedness. For the Southern planter in 1900 and the New Mexican *rico* in 1850, peonage conferred many of the economic benefits and few of the disadvantages of chattel slavery. Overseers profited handsomely from the work of their laborers without expending a large outlay of capital to purchase them or providing for them in their old age. See Pete Daniel, *The Shadow of Slavery*: 16, 23–24. A synthetic treatment of peonage as it was practiced in the New Mexico Territory from the 1840s through the 1860s has not been published.

119 Linville, "Cultural Assimilation in Frontier Florida: The Life of Joseph M. Hernandez, 1788–1857": 17–19.

120 While some of the evidence is circumstantial, in its totality it is highly suggestive of complicity in slave-owning or trading. Unsurprisingly perhaps, it implicates the three Delegates who were the wealthiest *Hispanos* in Congress in that era. Miguel Otero's father, according to court records, was engaged in Indian slave trading in Taos; see Rael-Gálvez, "Identifying Captivity and Capturing Identity: Narratives of American Indian Slavery in Colorado and New Mexico, 1776–1934": 193, footnote 362. According to Lawrence Murphy, Chaves's family "owned more peons and Indian slaves than anyone in the Territory"; see Murphy, "Reconstruction in New Mexico": 101. Carlos Ramirez notes that Gallegos, according to 1860 Census records, listed 21 "servants" living in his household. See Ramirez, "The Hispanic Political Elite in Territorial New Mexico: A Study of Classical Colonialism": 269.

121 *Eighth Census of the United States, 1860: Population Schedule,* Santa Fe, Santa Fe, New Mexico Territory, microfilm, Roll M653_714, pages 491–92, http://search.ancestrylibrary.com (accessed 6 May 2010). Ten years later, after the Civil War, records indicate that Gallegos declared that three female Indian servants, all illiterate, lived in his household. See *Ninth Census of the United States, 1870: Population Schedule*, Santa Fe, Santa Fe, New Mexico Territory, microfilm, Roll M593_896, page 357A, http://search.ancestrylibrary.com (accessed 6 May 2010).

122 For Tranquilino Luna, see *Eighth Census of the United States, 1860: Population Schedule*, Los Lunas, Valencia, New Mexico Territory, microfilm, Roll M653_716, page 661. For Mariano Otero, see *Eighth Census of the United States, 1860: Population Schedule*, Valencia, Valencia, New Mexico Territory, microfilm, Roll M653_716, page 747. For José Francisco Chaves, see *Eighth Census of the United States, 1860: Population Schedule*, Los Pinos, Bernalillo, New Mexico Territory, microfilm, Roll M653_712, page 160. For Francisco Perea, see *Eighth Census of the United States, 1860: Population Schedule*, Alameda, Bernalillo, New Mexico Territory, microfilm, Roll M653_712, page 93. In 1870 Perea listed two of the same women as members of his household; one of them lived under his roof until she was in her 80s. See *Ninth Census of the United States, 1870: Population Schedule*, Bernalillo East, Bernalillo, New Mexico Territory, microfilm, Roll M593_893, page 40A, http://search.ancestrylibrary.com (accessed 6 May 2010).

123 For more on the Wilmot Proviso and the origins of the short-lived Free-Soil Party it spawned, see Eric Foner, "The Wilmot Proviso Revisited," *Journal of American History* 56 (1969): 262–279. For the original introduction of the bill, see *Congressional Globe*, House, 29th Cong., 1st sess. (8 August 1846): 1214–1217.

124 See Ganaway, *New Mexico and the Sectional Controversy*: 60–76, for a traditional interpretation that Anglo elites were responsible for the switch to a pro-slavery position. For an interpretation that places *Hispano* elites' need to preserve slavery at the center of the discussion, see Gómez, *Manifest Destinies*: 99–101.

125 Gómez, *Manifest Destinies*: 101–102.

126 For the full text of the 1859 New Mexico slave code as well as the text of a territorial law protecting peonage, see "Slavery in the Territory of New Mexico," House Rep. 508, 36th Cong., 1st sess. (10 May 1860): 1–8. This report from the House Judiciary Committee was to accompany H.R. 64, a bill "to disapprove and declare null and void all territorial acts and parts of acts heretofore passed by the Legislative Assembly of New Mexico which establish, protect, or legalize involuntary servitude or slavery." A lengthy minority dissent was appended to the report; see pp. 8–39. The House narrowly passed H.R. 64 on a 97 to 90 vote; see *Congressional Globe*, House, 36th Cong., 1st sess. (10 May 1860): 2045–2046. However, the bill died in the Senate Committee on Territories near the end of the session; see *Congressional Globe*, Senate, 36th Cong., 1st sess. (8 June 1860): 2743–2744.

127 Gómez, *Manifest Destinies*: 99; for a suggestion that these African-American slaves belonged to U.S. Army officers, see Brooks, *Captives & Cousins*: 309–310.

128 Lamar, *The Far Southwest, 1846–1912: A Territorial History*: 88.

129 Gómez, *Manifest Destinies*: 100. The territorial legislature subsequently passed bills protecting peonage slaves and Indian slaves as property. The territorial governor vetoed the latter measure.

130 See Rael-Gálvez, "Identifying Captivity and Capturing Identity: Narratives of American Indian Slavery in Colorado and New Mexico, 1776–1934": 197–198. Italics in original.

131 Gómez, *Manifest Destinies*: 103.

132 Ganaway, "Otero and the New Mexico Slave Code of 1859": 69–76; Sunseri, *Seeds of Discord*: 117–119. The code did not survive for long. An effort to repeal it was initiated during the same session in which it was enacted. With the start of the Civil War in 1861, the territorial assembly repealed the slave code. In Washington, John Bingham of Ohio introduced a bill on February 16, 1860, declaring the slave code null and void; a further provision of the bill sought to nullify the peonage law. It passed the House on a strict party-line vote but died in the Senate Committee on Territories. For a detailed discussion of *nuevomexicano* elites and American Indian slavery in New Mexico, see Gómez, *Manifest Destinies*: 105–112.

133 Horace Greeley, "New Mexico," 18 February 1861, *Santa Fe Weekly Gazette*: 2. The article was originally published December 3, 1860, in the *New York Tribune*.

134 Miguel Otero (Sr.), "To the Editor of the Constitution," 18 February 1861, *Santa Fe Weekly Gazette*: 2.

135 Gómez argues that Anglo advocacy against Indian slavery derived from just such an impetus: a political effort to undermine the hegemony of *nuevomexicano* elites in New Mexico. See Gómez, *Manifest Destinies*: 108–109.

136 *Congressional Globe*, House, 39th Cong., 2nd sess. (2 March 1867): 1/70; for a rudimentary overview of action by Radical Republicans in Congress, see Murphy, "Reconstruction in New Mexico": 99–115.

137 Two comprehensive sources on the statehood movement during the territorial decades are Larson, *New Mexico's Quest for Statehood, 1846–1912;* and Lamar, *The Far Southwest, 1846–1912: A Territorial History*.

138 Charles F. Coan, *A History of New Mexico*, vol. 1 (Chicago and New York: The American Historical Society, 1925): 387–388, 410–411; *Congressional Globe*, 41st Cong., 2nd sess. (24 January 1870): 709; *Congressional Globe*, Appendix, 41st Cong., 3rd sess. (3 March 1871): 244–247. Coan lists three attempts at achieving statehood in the 1860s and 1870s by the Legislative Assembly. As for efforts in Congress, José Francisco Chaves submitted a bill for statehood in 1870 (H.R. 954) and an enabling act for statehood in 1871, but neither one passed. Coan also notes that Delegate Stephen Elkins submitted bills in the 43rd and 44th Congresses (1873–1877) that failed to pass.

139 "Vuestro Gobernador … y vuestros jueces … son ahora elijidos por personas que jamas han pisado vuestro suelo, que ignoran el character de vuestro pais, las necesidades del pueblo, y que carecen de ningun interes especial en vuestro bien estar … no obstante que varios de los empleados que han sido mandados de Washington para que os sirvan, han sido cpaces, honrados y fieles, la preponderancia ha sido al contrario … Bajo un gobierno de Estado.… Vuestros leyes serian nuestras propias leyes, sujetas á ser modificadas, enmendadas y abrogadas unicamente por vuestra propia voluntad … atormentados por la introduccion de politicos, quienes tal vez ya habrian acabado su carrera en los estados y quienes esperan halla un campo Nuevo y propio en aventuras politicos." J. Francisco Chavez (Chaves), "A los ciudadanos de Nuevo Mejico," 4 May 1866, *Santa Fe New Mexican* (Santa Fe, NM): 4. Translated as "To the Citizens of New Mexico," by Translations International, Inc. (August 2010); Lamar, *The Far Southwest, 1846–1912*: 10–11. Lamar confirms Chaves's assertions, "More often than not, territorial appointees after 1865 were political hacks, defeated congressmen, or jobless relatives of congressmen and cabinet members. These appointees owed their loyalty neither to the territory nor to the branch of government they represented.…"

140 Larson, *New Mexico's Quest for Statehood, 1846–1912*: 123–125. For an example of such a portrayal, see Richard Melzer, "New Mexico in Caricature: Images of the Territory on the Eve of Statehood," *New Mexico Historical Review* 65 (October 1987): 335–360.

141 *Congressional Record*, House, 50th Cong., 2nd sess. (14 February 1889): 1910. Representative Francis Spinola of New York concurred: "I do not agree that it is good statesmanship to oppose the admission of New Mexico on account of the religious opinions of a large majority of its inhabitants." See p. 1906 of the same debate.

142 For discussions of distinct statehood impulses and public ambivalence, see Lamar, *The Far Southwest, 1846–1912: A Territorial History*: 64–70, 143–145, 161–169. Lamar notes that both "Spanish-Americans" and "Anglo-Americans" feared that statehood would entail the control of the government by the other group. See also Coan, *A History of New Mexico,* vol. 1: 410. Coan notes the even splits between the parties that sent New Mexican Delegates to Washington: "The democrats were successful in six out of nine elections between 1878 and 1892, while the republicans won in seven out of eight elections between 1894 and 1908."

143 Because of Republican squabbling and factionalism, Democrat Antonio Joseph won the Delegate's seat and held it for much of this period. See Larson, *The Far Southwest, 1846–1912: A Territorial History*: 169–170. Ramirez convincingly asserts that Joseph was not a *nuevomexicano*; see Ramirez, "The Hispanic Political Elite in Territorial New Mexico: A Study of Classical Colonialism": 304–305. For more information about Joseph, see *Biographical Directory of the United States Congress,* "Antonio Joseph," http://bioguide.congress.gov.

144 For an overview of Beveridge's opposition and congressional debate on statehood, see Larson, *New Mexico's Quest for Statehood, 1846–1912*: 214–225. See also "New Statehood Bill," Senate Rep. no. 2206, 57th Cong., 2nd sess. (10 December 1902): 1–31; quotation on p. 9.

145 Love, *Race over Empire: Racism and U.S. Imperialism, 1865–1900*: especially pp. 24–25, 196–200.

Hispanic-American Members by Office†

1822–1898

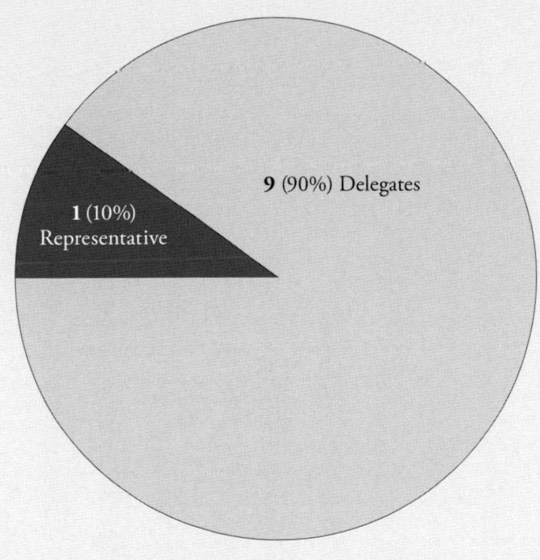

Hispanic-American Members by State and Territory†

First Elected 1822–1898

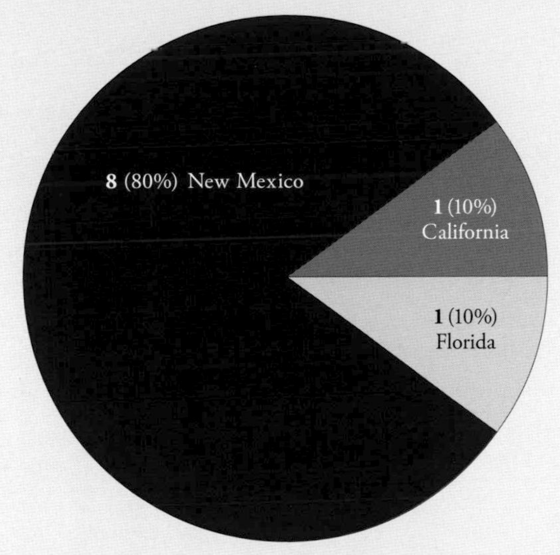

Party Divisions in the House of Representatives‡

17th Congress (1821–1823)*

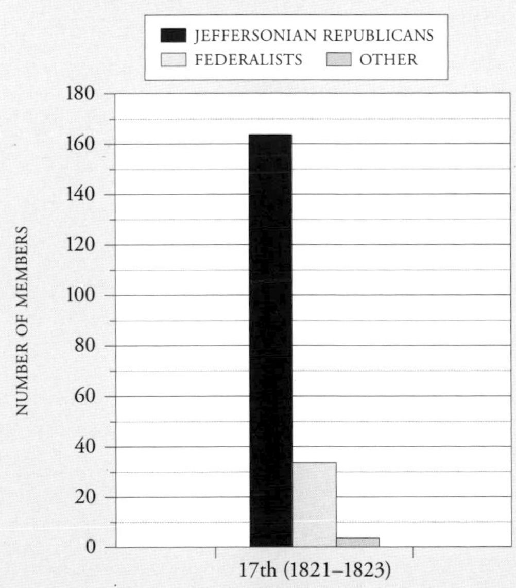

33rd–34th Congresses (1853–1857)*

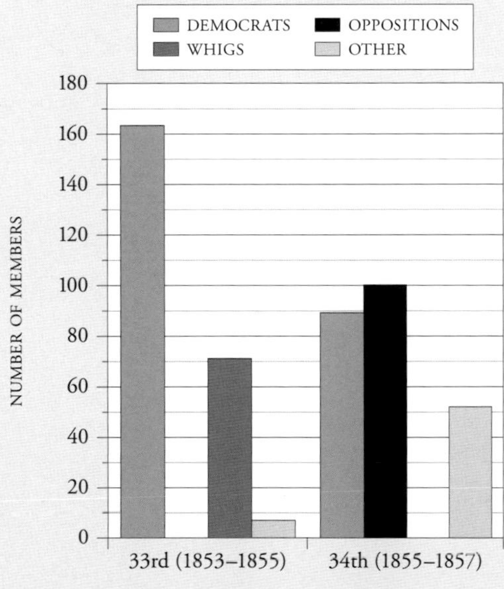

Sources: † Appendix A: Hispanic-American Representatives, Senators, Delegates, and Resident Commissioners by Congress, 1822–2012; Office of the Historian, U.S. House of Representatives; U.S. Senate Historical Office. ‡ *Biographical Directory of the United States Congress, 1774–2005* (Washington, D.C.: Government Printing Office, 2005); also available at http://bioguide.congress.gov.

*Party division totals are based on election day results.

Party Divisions in the House of Representatives

35th–55th Congresses (1857–1899)*

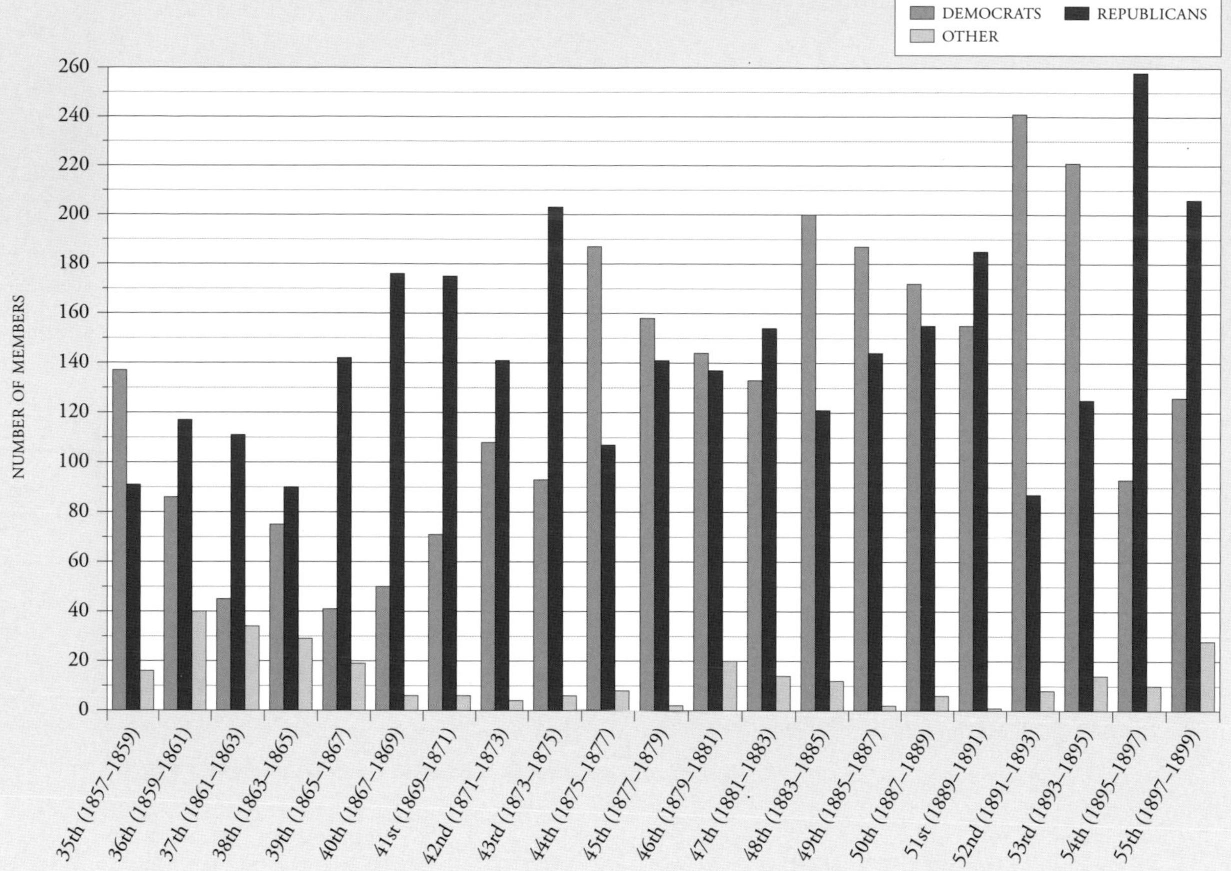

Source: Biographical Directory of the United States Congress, 1774–2005 (Washington, D.C.: Government Printing Office, 2005); also available at http://bioguide.congress.gov.

*Party division totals are based on election day results.

Congressional Service

For Hispanic Americans in Congress First Elected 1822–1884

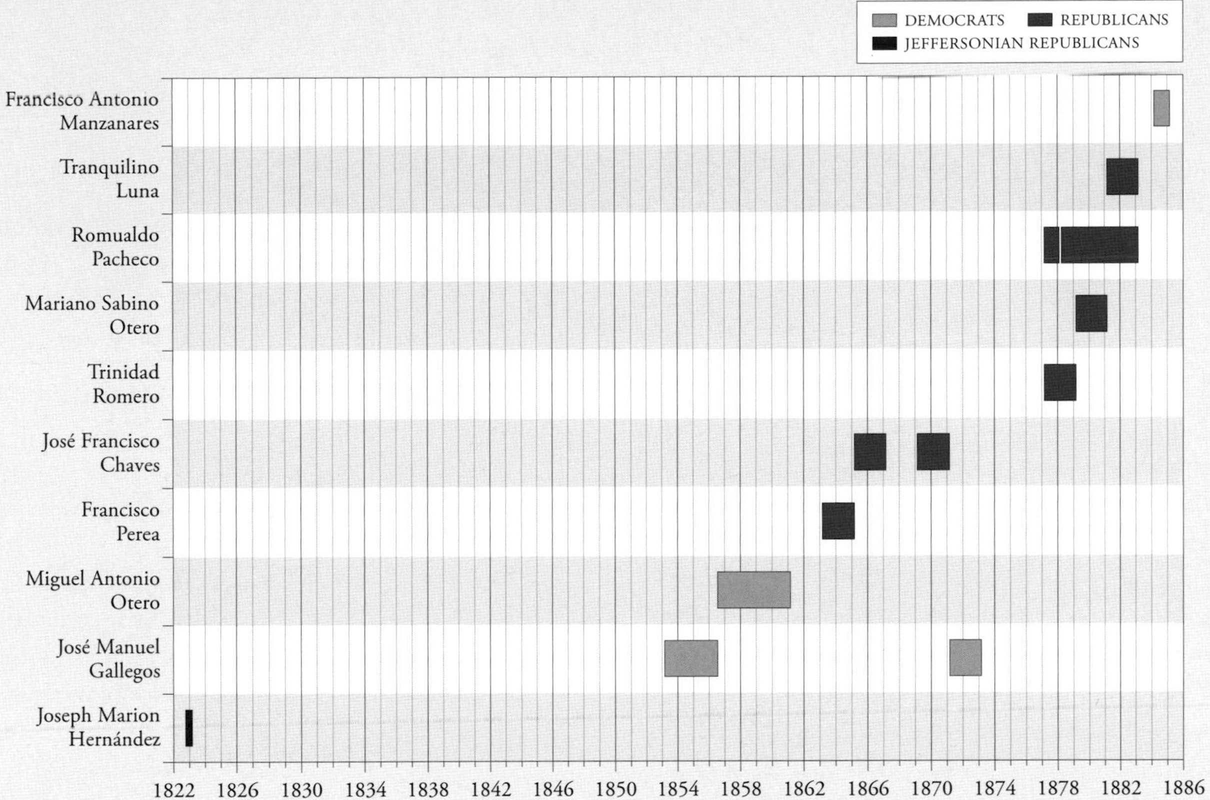

Joseph Marion Hernández
1788–1857

TERRITORIAL DELEGATE 1822–1823
JEFFERSONIAN REPUBLICAN FROM FLORIDA

Joseph Hernández, the first Hispanic Member of Congress and the first Territorial Delegate to represent Florida, bridged his state's cultural and governmental transition from Spanish colony to U.S. territory. Hernández fought first for Spain and later for the United States; he also earned—and lost—a fortune that included three plantations and numerous slaves. His complex life and career as a slave-owning, Indian-fighting politician cut from Jacksonian cloth embodied conflicting attitudes toward statehood, representation, and territorial conquest. Though brief, his service to the territory set an effective precedent, prompting the Washington *City Gazette* to declare, a "compliment is due to the zeal and industry of the honourable delegate from Florida, who during the session, appeared at all times attentive to the objects connected with the prosperity of his constituents and the interests of the Territory."[1]

José Mariano Hernández was born on May 26, 1788, in St. Augustine, Spanish Florida. He was the third of 10 children and the first son of Martín Hernández, Jr., and Dorotea Gomila, immigrants from the island of Minorca. The Hernándezes settled in St. Augustine in 1784, living in the northern section of the city, dubbed the Minorcan Quarter. Local residents earned their livelihoods by farming, fishing, and making handcrafts. Although the Hernándezes were not among St. Augustine's elite families, Martín Hernández was a skilled laborer and a slave owner, indicating that the family had some wealth. José Hernández attended local schools run by Catholic priests and worked with his father in carpentry. As an adolescent, he was educated in Savannah, Georgia, and Havana, Cuba. He returned to East Florida in 1811 after studying law, most likely in Cuba.[2]

During the Second Spanish Period (1783–1821), Spain regained territory lost to the British in the Seven Years' War (1756–1763). At that time, the Florida peninsula was divided between East and West Florida.[3] One historian describes Spanish East Florida as a "province virtually devoid of people, a place rich in land but poor in inhabitants." By 1811 the population numbered barely 4,000. St. Augustine and Fernandina, both coastal ports, were its only urban centers. The remainder of East Florida was "a scattering of forts, cotton and rice plantations, citrus groves, farms, cattle-ranching operations, sawmills, and lumber camps." Many of the colonial properties were nestled along the St. Marys, Nassau, and St. Johns Rivers. The area's major landmarks were military installations that guarded important routes on the rivers. East Florida society was a "small, somewhat self-contained world, one in which Spanish officials had to carefully balance Crown prerogatives against local needs and … defend Spanish interests with limited resources. Political life revolved entirely around the governor in his dealings with various factions of settlers." As a result of East Florida's physical isolation, small tax base, and limited funding from the Spanish government, local officials sought regional trade opportunities. In the 1790s, East Florida increased its trade with neighbors such as Mexico, Cuba, and the United States. However, territorial ambitions, economic competition, and distinct cultural differences between East Florida and its northern neighbors in Georgia and the Mississippi Territory poisoned their relations and plunged the region into armed conflict. In 1790 the king of Spain spurred increased settlement—and possible conflicts—by offering homestead grants to U.S. citizens.

A variety of factors stirred tensions between the settlers in Georgia and those in Florida. Economic competition played a major role. Both groups of settlers jockeyed for influence with the Florida Indians, who controlled lucrative trade markets and were potentially a significant

Image courtesy of the Library of Congress

force in an armed conflict. Also, much of the commerce in the Southern United States was based on access to rivers, many of which emptied into the Gulf of Mexico through the Floridas. Furthermore, control of the Floridas was a security issue because foreign powers could encroach into the Deep South by using the Florida route. Cultural conflicts deriving from differences in religious background (U.S. Protestants vs. Spanish Catholics) and great-power alliance (Spain was an ally of Great Britain, and memories of the American Revolution were still fresh) further divided the two groups. But their attitudes toward slavery drove the largest wedge between them. First, many of the conflicts regarding slavery developed from the differences between the black-white framework of Anglo-American jurisprudence and the more permeable three-race structure of Hispanic societies. Second, U.S. slaveholders were aware that Florida was a close haven for fugitive slaves, who could blend into Spanish or Seminole communities with relative ease. Third, the use of armed black soldiers in the Florida militia alarmed U.S. slaveholders, who feared possible slave revolts. Underlying all this was the lack of a clear governing authority, which encouraged violent acts of retribution. After 1790, neither the U.S. nor the Spanish authorities could effectively control border conflicts.[4]

For the next two decades, U.S. encroachment into East Florida, though sporadic, was sanctioned by two presidential administrations. President Thomas Jefferson and his Secretary of State, James Madison, sought to expand U.S. territory to the south and west of the original 13 colonies. Both men particularly coveted the Louisiana territory and the Floridas. After the Louisiana Purchase in 1803, Jefferson and Madison pressured Spain to cede the Floridas through a combination of economic inducement, military force, and slow advancement by U.S. settlers.[5]

The outbreak of what is known as the Patriot War developed out of U.S. settlers' resentment toward the Spanish government and their wanton desire to annex the territory for the United States. In March 1812, a group of self-proclaimed "Patriots" led by U.S. general George Mathews occupied the town of Fernandina and laid siege to St. Augustine. They declared victory in July 1812. The Madison administration supported the Patriots as a low-risk effort to foment instability in East Florida that could be used as a pretext for seizing new land and stopping British incursion into the region. However, when President Madison later withdrew his support, the initiative became a bloody, destructive war that lasted two more years. After returning to Florida, Hernández volunteered to join the Spanish military to defend the territory against U.S. expansionists.[6]

In February 1814, Hernández married Ana Hill Williams, a wealthy widow who lived in St. Augustine. Ana had at least nine children from her first marriage, including Guillermo, José Mariano Tomas, Eliza Ana, José Sam Gil, Juan Theofilio, Ana Teresa, Martín, Dorotea, and Louisa. Ana owned properties—among them, a 3,200-acre sugar cane plantation called Orange Grove—that allowed Hernández to become a prominent planter. Hernández also acquired a number of profitable land grants during the Patriot War.

In 1817 the First Seminole War erupted in the West Florida province. In January 1818 Andrew Jackson led a force of 4,800 men into the Spanish Floridas, seizing a fort and destroying Seminole settlements along the way. The campaign concluded in May 1818 with the formal cession of West Florida to the United States. Secretary of State John Quincy Adams and Spanish Ambassador Luis de Onís negotiated and signed a treaty of cession on February 22, 1819. After two years of diplomatic wrangling, the treaty was approved by the Senate on February 22, 1821. Although Hernández's role in the war remains ambiguous, it is clear that he benefited from the conflict by receiving more land grants from the Spanish government.[7] Ultimately, with the land that he purchased or inherited by marriage and the massive holdings he received as service grants from the Spanish crown, Hernández controlled 25,670 acres at the time of the U.S. annexation.[8]

Rather than fleeing with other Spanish settlers to Cuba, Mexico, or Texas, Hernández chose to stay and work with the new regime, changing his name from José Mariano to Joseph Marion. Hernández became friendly with the territory's first civil governor, William Pope DuVal, a

Jeffersonian Republican, a former Representative from Kentucky, and an ally of Andrew Jackson's. In April of 1822, DuVal submitted the names of Hernández and seven others as delegates to Florida's first legislative council. Hernández was also nominated to the brigadier generalship of the East Florida militia. The Florida legislative council selected Hernández to serve as Territorial Delegate, a decision that was confirmed by a three-day election (September 30 to October 2, 1822) in which Hernández faced no opposition.[9]

Hernández was sworn into the House on January 3, 1823.[10] As a Hispanic Catholic Representative in a Congress that was predominantly Anglo-American and Protestant, Hernández was entering uncharted territory. But Hernández was well qualified to usher in Florida's transition from Spanish to U.S. rule: He was bilingual, an established planter, and a well-known soldier who had fought in two major wars that determined Florida's territorial status. However, his legislative role was circumscribed, largely because of institutional restrictions on the powers of a Territorial Delegate. At the time, Territorial Delegates were prohibited from serving on standing House committees; thus, Hernández did not hold a committee assignment during his brief tenure.[11]

During Hernández's time in Congress, the finalization of Florida annexation by the United States involved two controversial issues, access to owning land or validating land deeds and the removal of Seminoles from the territory.[12] These overarching priorities shaped Hernández's four-pronged legislative agenda as Delegate: verifying the status of land grants as a result of their transition from Spanish to Anglo-American jurisprudence; advocating for infrastructural improvements; assisting Florida with its recovery from recent wars; and fostering relations among U.S. settlers and the remaining Spanish elites, Indians, and territorial authorities.

Hernández's first objective was to facilitate the verification of land claims from the Spanish government to the U.S. government. This was a personal issue as much as a diplomatic matter, given his extensive land holdings. On January 20, 1823, Hernández submitted a bill asking the House Committee on Public Lands to award "public lots and houses within the city of Pensacola" to the city instead of to the U.S. government. The next day, in a letter to Secretary of State John Quincy Adams, Hernández noted, "[It] is to be regreted Sir, that in a Territory so recently obtained from a forign Nation, whose Inhabitants are yet unacquainted with the System & Laws of Our Government, Should have had instances of … open Controvercy between its public functionaries" regarding these land claims. Hernández included a memorial from the St. Augustine city council and his own resolution. He asked Adams to "lay the enclosed papers before the President [Monroe], in order … to prevent … interference with the said property" until Congress rendered a decision.[13] On February 17, upon hearing that the Senate would reject the bill, Hernández appealed to Vice President Daniel D. Tompkins of New York to submit a bill creating an additional board of commissioners to settle the land claims.[14]

On behalf of the residents of St. Augustine, Hernández submitted a petition that lobbied for the separation of East and West Florida, outlining a plan for "a separate board of commissioners … to ascertain titles and claims to land" in East Florida and to permit settlement on public land.[15] The petition also requested that the "aid of Congress may be extended" toward building and maintaining transportation infrastructure and asked Congress to prohibit U.S. soldiers from voting for Territorial Delegates. The House sent the petition to five committees, each of which had jurisdiction over specific complaints.[16] Hernández also submitted a petition that called for a revision to the "assessment of taxes and the establishment of county courts."[17] In February 1823, Hernández objected to a bill that proposed forming a single board of commissioners; he argued that two boards were required because the dispensation of land grants in East Florida differed from that in West Florida. A new law (3 Stat. 754–756) resolved the issues regarding land claims and the formation of a board of commissioners described by Hernández in his legislation.[18]

Federal support for capital improvement projects such as roads, bridges, and canals was another priority. Hernández sought the construction of a 380-mile road

between St. Augustine and Pensacola, Florida's two largest settlements. A contemporary observed, "The best practicable track is about seven hundred miles, through an unsettled and savage wilderness, which is travelled with great hazard and difficulty."[19] Hernández also lobbied for new roads south of St. Augustine to facilitate the economic development of East Florida. In February 1823, Hernández submitted H.R. 275, which called for congressional funding for these routes, noting in a memorandum that a portion of the Pensacola–St. Augustine road "was originally opened by the British Government" during its occupation of the Floridas. After consideration by the Committee on Public Lands, a bill appropriating $15,000 for the project was passed by the House. On March 1, the bill was taken up by the Senate, where it was ordered to lie on the table but was not acted upon before the 17th Congress closed on March 3.[20] Hernández did not give up. In a March 11, 1823, letter to Secretary of War John C. Calhoun of South Carolina, Hernández insisted that a major roadway would benefit the military and the territorial government. He also believed it would facilitate the construction of a capital city and make Florida an attractive candidate for statehood.[21]

Hernández was a diplomatist as well as a legislator, promoting resolutions to conflicts with American Indians and seeking to smooth the transition from Spanish to U.S. rule. In the first decades of the 19th century, relations between Anglos and Indians often involved the imposition of racial separation. Although Hernández had interacted with Indians during his youth and adulthood, he conformed to the separatist practices of U.S. settlers. He encouraged the James Monroe administration to negotiate a treaty that would gather the Seminoles in one location and outline their relationship with the U.S. government. The resultant Treaty of Moultrie Creek, ratified in December 1823, compelled all Indians in Florida to move to a four-million-acre reservation with defined boundaries.[22]

When Hernández's term ended in March 1823, he prepared to run for a second term. A local newspaper endorsed his candidacy, stating, "In the faithful execution of the various and important trusts committed to him … his good sense and information on every subject connected with the interests and prosperity of this territory have inspired confidence and esteem in the Administration … and gained for Florida many warm and valuable friends on the floor of Congress."[23] Three opponents challenged the incumbent in the June 1823 election: Alexander Hamilton of St. Augustine and Farquar Bethune of Fernandina, both from East Florida; and Richard Keith Call, a Jackson acolyte who served on the territorial legislative council, from West Florida. According to one scholar, "Politics in Florida were largely of a personal nature as certain men of wealth and education became the natural leaders of political life on the frontier." In sum, voters were predisposed to support political candidates because of regional ties rather than party loyalties.[24] The candidates from East Florida split the vote three ways: Hernández garnered 252 votes to Hamilton's 249 and Bethune's 36. Call ran unopposed in West Florida, capitalizing on his service as the region's brigadier general of the militia, and with 496 votes he won a seat in the 18th Congress (1823–1825). Hernández's political career shifted to territorial politics with his appointment by President James Monroe to the territorial legislative council at the suggestion of Territorial Delegate Call. President John Quincy Adams renewed Hernández's appointment in 1825.[25]

Hernández ran for Delegate in 1825 against Joseph M. White, a Kentucky lawyer and politician who lived in Pensacola, and James Gadsden, a territorial council member who would eventually become known for negotiating the purchase of a portion of southern Arizona and New Mexico in 1853.[26] A laudatory editorial in the *East Florida Herald* reminded readers of Hernández's service in the House. Describing Hernández's efforts to secure passage of H.R. 275 and his facilitation of the Treaty of Moultrie Creek, the editor wrote, "We cannot but admit, that if talent or zeal deserve reward; if useful services call for some gratitude and acknowledgement … the claims of Gen. Hernández are paramount to those of every other candidate."[27] A rebuttal stressed White's superior qualifications and suggested that having a

Hispanic Delegate would be a liability for Florida. While no one would deny Hernández credit for his previous service, the writer argued, White was "better acquainted with our language, the organization of our political institutions, and the mode of transacting business in the councils of the nation." Hernández was almost left off the ballot. Announcing his candidacy in a public letter to local electors, he wrote that hearing rumors "I had withdrawn my name; I deem it a duty, that I owe to the public and my friends ... to put an end to any uncertainty, that may prevail on this subject."[28] In the general election, White prevailed with 742 votes, Gadsden placed second with 460 votes, and Hernández trailed with 362 votes.[29]

During the 1820s, Hernández established himself as a major territorial planter, producing some of Florida's biggest cash crops, including sugar cane and cotton. Contemporary publications noted the outstanding productivity of the Mala Compra and St. Joseph Plantations. However, Hernández's sugar cane and cotton crops required him to use between 60 and 150 slaves to run three massive plantations. Despite his agricultural success, Hernández was forced to sell large tracts of land during the mid-1820s to retire debts and make mortgage payments. In 1835 he borrowed money and used his estates as collateral to remain solvent.[30]

By this time, relations between white settlers and the Seminoles had deteriorated almost to the point of open conflict. Territorial authorities believed Indian removal policies that had been adopted in other parts of the Southeast would also work for Florida, and white settlers wanted to permanently eliminate Indian enclaves for fugitive slaves. Like other slave owners, Hernández was concerned about havens for fugitive slaves and about the possibility of armed rebellion by escaped slaves and the Seminoles. In response to the unrest, President Andrew Jackson sent a 700-man regular army force to coordinate the defense of East Florida. By late December 1835, black and Seminole insurgents had destroyed a half-dozen plantations in the St. Augustine area. A number of other devastating attacks in the region signaled the start of the Second Seminole War.[31]

Hernández returned to the battlefield in the Second Seminole War (1835–1842). According to his most recent biographer, he "was incredibly influential in shaping the course of ... the conflict" as the senior commander of the East Florida militia. He was responsible for ensuring the safety of civilians in East Florida and for protecting its complex of plantations, including his own. Hernández managed the defenses of the region with limited manpower in a territory that covered all of modern-day Florida except the Panhandle. Hernández contended with the militia, which was reluctant to fight away from home and with recalcitrant army regulars, who refused to follow his orders. After the arrival of reinforcements in March 1836 and a new field commander, Hernández played a significant role in the conflict, but was not the senior field commander. Throughout 1836, he helped recover slaves and prevented them from fleeing toward enemy lines.[32]

The war brought Hernández financial and political misfortune. In early 1836, the Seminoles attacked and destroyed 16 plantations in East Florida, among them Hernández's St. Joseph sugar cane operation. Compounding this loss, the U.S. Army requisitioned the Mala Compra Plantation. Mala Compra's use as a hospital, field headquarters, and supply depot, along with its abuse by soldiers, all but destroyed Hernández's home. Moreover, his workforce was greatly diminished. The war also brought Hernández unwanted national recognition. An informer led Hernández, two mounted companies of militia, and three companies of regular troops to a secluded camp of escaped slaves and Seminoles. Hernández's group captured dozens of enemy combatants, including a prominent leader who had organized the destruction of Hernández's St. Joseph plantation. In October 1837 he facilitated a meeting between U.S. forces and a group of prominent Seminole leaders that included Osceola.[33] Osceola's party arrived under a flag of truce but with no indication that they were willing to surrender. However, Hernández's commander, General Thomas Sidney Jesup, ordered Hernández to capture the men. Following orders, Hernández's 250-soldier contingent captured Osceola and 79 Seminoles. Within Florida, Hernández and Jesup were

hailed as heroes, but nationally, Jesup's decision to ignore the truce was criticized by the press. Although Hernández escaped censure, his association with the incident tarnished his political prospects. For the remainder of 1837, Hernández participated in expeditionary campaigns against Seminole insurgents in central and South Florida. In January 1838, he asked to be relieved from duty because of the war's toll on his personal fortunes. The Seminole War dragged on for four more years.[34]

Hernández attempted to revive his political career by running for the U.S. Senate. In the early 1840s, as Florida became more partisan with the Whig-Democrat divide, Hernández joined the Nucleus, a faction of conservative elites drawn from the ranks of planters, businessmen, and merchants. Like his counterparts, Hernández opposed single statehood for Florida; instead, he advocated for two states, East Florida and West Florida. His main competitor was David Levy, a Whig who tirelessly promoted the one-state concept. In July 1845, several months after Florida was admitted to the Union, Hernández, Levy, James D. Westcott, and Jackson Morton ran for Florida's two U.S. Senate seats. A majority of the Florida senate chose Levy and Westcott, who won handily with 41 votes each; Hernández and Morton received 16 votes each.[35]

Though his dreams of national office had ended, Hernández remained active in local politics, serving as mayor of St. Augustine in 1848. He eventually left Florida to reside in Matanzas, Cuba, in his later years and died on June 8, 1857.[36]

FOR FURTHER READING

Biographical Directory of the United States Congress, "Joseph Marion Hernández," http://bioguide.congress.gov.

Linville, Nick. "Cultural Assimilation in Frontier Florida: The Life of Joseph M. Hernandez, 1788–1857," (M.A. thesis, University of Florida, 2004).

MANUSCRIPT COLLECTIONS

Robert D. Farber University Archives and Special Collections Department, Brandeis University (Waltham, MA). *Papers*: Daniel Webster Collection, 1841–1843, five linear feet. The papers include a letter from Stephen White to Daniel Webster recommending Joseph Hernández as governor of Florida and an application from Hernández to Daniel Webster for the position. Both documents are dated July 13, 1841.

St. Augustine Historical Society Research Library (St. Augustine, FL). *Papers*: Hernández Family Biographical File, n.d., amount unknown. Persons represented include Joseph Hernández.

P. K. Yonge Library of Florida History, University of Florida (Gainesville). *Papers*: Miscellaneous Manuscripts Collection, c. 1822–1849, amount unknown. Correspondence by and relating to Joseph Hernández.

NOTES

1 "Mr. Hernandez," 12 April 1823, *East Florida Herald* (St. Augustine).

2 Nick Linville, "Cultural Assimilation in Frontier Florida: The Life of Joseph M. Hernandez, 1788–1857," (M.A. thesis, University of Florida, 2004): 3–6.

3 William S. Coker and Susan R. Parker, "The Second Spanish Period in the Two Floridas," in Michael Gannon, ed., *The New History of Florida* (Gainesville: University Press of Florida, 1996): 150. According to Coker and Parker, West Florida's borders "extended from the Chattahoochee and Apalachicola rivers on the east to the Mississippi River and the Isle of Orleans in the west. The Gulf of Mexico and the Louisiana lakes Borgne, Pontchartrain, and Maurepas formed its southern boundary." West Florida's urban populations were centered in Mobile, Baton Rouge, Natchez, and Pensacola, its capital.

4 James G. Cusick, *The Other War of 1812: The Patriot War and the American Invasion of Spanish East Florida* (Gainesville: University Press of Florida, 2003): 38–53; John Missall and Mary Lou Missall, *The Seminole Wars: America's Longest Indian Conflict* (Gainesville: University Press of Florida, 2004): 18. A small group of U.S. settlers organized a rebellion against the Spanish government from 1794 to 1795. In retribution, Spanish authorities arrested the conspirators and imprisoned them in Cuba, confiscated or destroyed private property, and used armed black soldiers to restore order. Embittered U.S. settlers, who owned property and slaves, fled across the border into Georgia and plotted to settle scores with the Spanish government. For a summary of the distinctions between U.S. and Spanish attitudes toward race, see Daniel L. Schafer, "'A Class of People Neither Freeman Nor Slaves': From Spanish to American Race Relations in Florida, 1821–1861," *Journal of Social History* 26, no. 3 (Spring 1993): 587–609, especially pp. 587–592.

5 George C. Herring, *From Colony to Superpower: U.S. Foreign Relations since 1776* (New York: Oxford University Press, 2008): 109–112; Gordon S. Wood, *Empire of Liberty: A History of the Early Republic, 1789–1815* (New York: Oxford University Press, 2009): 374–376. U.S. officials sought to exploit Spain's weakness

as a result of the Napoleonic wars by crafting the Mobile Act and fomenting a rebellion in Baton Rouge in 1810 that led to the annexation of West Florida, which bordered the Orleans Territory along modern-day Baton Rouge and extended eastward to Mobile.

6 Cusick, *The Other War of 1812: The Patriot War and the American Invasion of Spanish East Florida*: 293–299; Coker and Parker, "The Second Spanish Period in Two Floridas": 160–163; Linville, "Cultural Assimilation in Frontier Florida: The Life of Joseph M. Hernandez, 1788–1857": 7–8.

7 Linville, "Cultural Assimilation in Frontier Florida: The Life of Joseph M. Hernandez, 1788–1857": 10–11; Coker and Parker, "The Second Spanish Period in Two Floridas": 164; Daniel Walker Howe, *What Hath God Wrought: The Transformation of America, 1815–1848* (New York: Oxford University Press, 2008): 107–111; Missall and Missall, *The Seminole Wars:* 32–51.

8 Linville, "Cultural Assimilation in Frontier Florida: The Life of Joseph M. Hernandez, 1788–1857": 8–10, 35 (see footnote 17). In addition to Ana's Orange Grove Plantation, Hernández acquired an 800-acre sugar cane plantation, St. Joseph, in 1815. He acquired another 800-acre plantation called Mala Compra and a 375-acre extension called Bella Vista. Additionally, Hernández acquired two grants of 20,000 and 18,000 acres from the Spanish government for his services. To counter annexation by U.S. settlers and ensure that the best land would remain in the possession of Spanish settlers, Spanish governors in East Florida awarded land grants (called head-right or homestead grants) to Patriot War veterans like Hernández.

9 *Biographical Directory of the United States Congress*, "William Pope DuVal," http://bioguide.congress.gov; Linville,"Cultural Assimilation in Frontier Florida: The Life of Joseph M. Hernandez, 1788–1857": 12–13; Sidney Martin, *Florida during the Territorial Days* (Philadelphia, PA: Porcupine Press, 1974; reprint of 1944 edition): 47–48; Daniel L. Schafer, "U.S. Territory and State," in Michael Gannon, ed., *The New History of Florida*: 210–211; Joseph M. Hernández Certificate of Election (endorsed 20 November 1822), Committee on Elections (HR17A-H1), 17th Congress, Records of the U.S. House of Representatives, Record Group 233, National Archives, Washington, D.C. Two of the three sources provide conflicting versions of Hernández's election to Congress. Hernández's election certificate describes a three-day election that was won by Hernández. Sidney Martin, however, writes, "at the request of the Legislative Council, and after a make-shift election," Hernández was elected to Congress as a Territorial Delegate. Schafer echoes Martin's assertion that Hernández "was appointed by the legislative council in 1823" but lists the wrong date. Like Martin, Schafer writes, "All subsequent delegates were elected by the voters of the territory." The first popular election for a Territorial Delegate seat was in June 1823.

10 *Annals of Congress*, House, 17th Cong., 2nd sess. (3 January 1823): 482.

11 Linville, "Cultural Assimilation in Frontier Florida: The Life of Joseph M. Hernandez, 1788–1857": 13; no committee assignments for Hernández are listed in the *Annals of Congress*, the *House Journal*, or the *Congressional Directory* (17th Cong., 2nd sess.).

12 Schafer, "U.S. Territory and State": 215.

13 *House Journal*, 17th Cong., 2nd sess. (20 January 1823): 147; Clarence Carter, ed., *The Territorial Papers of the United States, Vol. XXII: The Territory of Florida, 1821–1824* (New York: AMS Press, 1972; reprint of 1934 edition): 604.

14 Carter, *Territorial Papers, Vol. XXII*: 619–622.

15 Herbert J. Doherty, Jr., "Political Factions in Territorial Florida," *Florida Historical Quarterly* 28, no. 2: 131–132. According to Doherty, "Floridians divided into factions favoring immediate statehood for the entire territory, favoring statehood separately for East and West Florida, or favoring no immediate steps toward that goal.... In East Florida as a whole the majority of the population favored division."

16 Martin, *Florida during Territorial Days*: 261–262; *House Journal*, 17th Cong., 2nd sess. (8 January 1823): 107–108.

17 "From Washington," *East Florida Herald* (St. Augustine), 8 February 1823; *House Journal*, 17th Cong., 2nd sess. (15 January 1823): 132. Although the article indicates that Hernández submitted a petition, the *House Journal* entry is not clear about such a submission. Hernández also worked behind the scenes for his constituents. In a February 18 letter to President James Monroe, Hernández endorsed two lawyers for Judge of the Inferior Court over Greenbury Geether, an incumbent who supported permitting U.S. Army soldiers who did not live in the Florida territory to vote for a Territorial Delegate. See Carter, *Territorial Papers, Vol. XXII:* 623–624.

18 Linville, "Cultural Assimilation in Frontier Florida: The Life of Joseph M. Hernandez, 1788–1857": 14. *Statutes at Large*, Act of March 3, 1823, Ch. 29, 3 Stat. 754–756. Sections 1 and 8 of the law pertained to Hernández's questions.

19 "Mr. Hernandez," *East Florida Herald* (St. Augustine), 12 April 1823: 3.

20 Carter, *Territorial Papers, Vol. XXII*: 633–635; *House Journal*, 17th Cong., 2nd sess. (5 February 1823) 197; (27 February 1823): 276. *Senate Journal*, 17th Cong., 2nd sess. (28 February 1823): 220; (1 March 1823): 242–243. "To the Electors of Florida," 1 February 1825, *East Florida Herald* (St. Augustine): 3.

21 Carter, *Territorial Papers, Vol. XXII*: 642–643.

22 Linville, "Cultural Assimilation in Frontier Florida: The Life of Joseph M. Hernandez, 1788–1857": 15–16; John K. Mahon, *History of the Second Seminole War, 1835–1842* (Gainesville: University Press of Florida, 1985; Rev. ed.): 39–46. For a historical overview of this period, see Michael D. Green, "The Expansion of

European Colonization to the Mississippi Valley, 1780–1880," in Bruce G. Trigger and Wilcomb E. Washburn, eds., *The Cambridge History of the Native Peoples of the Americas, Vol. 1: North America, Part 1*. (New York: Cambridge University Press, 1996): 461–538.

23 Letter to Editor by "A Floridian," 10 May 1823, *East Florida Herald* (St. Augustine).

24 Doherty, "Political Factions in Territorial Florida": 131.

25 Linville, "Cultural Assimilation in Frontier Florida: The Life of Joseph M. Hernandez, 1788–1857": 16–17; Herbert J. Doherty, Jr., *Richard Keith Call, Southern Unionist* (Gainesville: University Press of Florida, 1961): 27–28; Carter, *Territorial Papers, Vol. XXII*: 693.

26 John F. Stover, "Gadsden, James," *American National Biography* 8 (New York: Oxford University Press, 1999): 603–604. For more information about Joseph White, see Ernest F. Dibble, *Joseph Mills White: Anti-Jacksonian Floridian* (Cocoa: The Florida Historical Society Press, 2003).

27 *Pensacola Gazette and West Florida Advertiser* (Tallahassee), 16 April 1825: column C.

28 "To the Electors of Florida," 7 May 1825, *East Florida Herald* (St. Augustine): 1.

29 *Pensacola Gazette and West Florida Advertiser* (Tallahassee), 23 April 1825: column A; Dibble, *Joseph Mills White: Anti-Jacksonian Floridian*: 23–24.

30 Linville, "Cultural Assimilation in Frontier Florida: The Life of Joseph M. Hernandez, 1788–1857": 17–19. Linville cites comments from the *Farmer's Register*, a national newspaper: "General Hernandez … who has with great perseverance and success, overcome the laborious difficulties of clearing and draining new land; and has now under culture, upwards of 200 acres of these swamp lands, constituting by far the most valuable plantation, as respects soil, in Florida."

31 Linville, "Cultural Assimilation in Frontier Florida: The Life of Joseph M. Hernandez, 1788–1857": 19–20; Howe, *What Hath God Wrought: The Transformation of America, 1815–1848*: 98–107.

32 Linville, "Cultural Assimilation in Frontier Florida: The Life of Joseph M. Hernandez, 1788–1857": 20–25, 38 (footnote 51). According to Linville, "As the war progressed, Hernández collected written affidavits from officers who had taken supplies from his plantation. In June of 1836, his overseer made detailed notes of every item that was missing from his plantations."

33 For more information about Osceola, see Patricia R. Wickman, *Osceola's Legacy* (Tuscaloosa: University of Alabama Press, 2006; rev. ed.).

34 Linville, "Cultural Assimilation in Frontier Florida: The Life of Joseph M. Hernandez, 1788–1857": 25–29; Mahon, "History of the Second Seminole War," 241–218. The national reaction was so strong that Congress debated the "Osceola Incident" in the spring of 1838. For more information about Jesup, see Chester L. Kieffer, *The Maligned General: Thomas Sidney Jesup* (San Rafael, CA: Presidio Press, 1979).

35 George H. Haynes, *The Senate of the United States: Its History and Practice*, Vol. 1 (Boston: Houghton Mifflin, 1938): 81–85; Florida Senate, *A Journal of the Proceedings of the Senate of the First General Assembly of the State of Florida, at Its First Session* (Tallahassee, FL: Joseph Clisby, 1845): 27–28. Prior to the ratification of the 17th Amendment in 1913, U.S. Senators were elected by state legislatures. Article I, Section 4, of the U.S. Constitution gave states the authority to establish procedures for the election of Senators but reserved Congress's right to alter the election procedures as it saw fit. According to Haynes, "In the early years the choice was usually made by concurrent vote of the two [state] houses.… Later about half the states came to require that that election be made by a vote in joint convention." However, "insistence upon a majority vote for the same candidate in both branches of the legislature led not infrequently to deadlocks … it also presented a constant temptation to sharp practice for partisan advantage, and gave rise to election contests very embarrassing for the Senate to decide, since the point at issue was what constituted a legal 'house' or 'senate' in the state legislature." A series of embarrassing contested election cases in the mid-19th century compelled Congress to establish a set of uniform procedures for senatorial elections in 14 Stat. 243 (passed 25 July 1866). In the case of Florida in 1845, the Florida senate selected its U.S. Senators by a simple majority vote.

36 Linville, "Cultural Assimilation in Frontier Florida: The Life of Joseph M. Hernandez, 1788–1857": 29–32; *Biographical Directory of the United States Congress*, "Joseph Marion Hernández," http://bioguide.congress.gov.

"We think a passing compliment is due to the zeal and industry of the honourable delegate from Florida, who during the session ... [was] attentive ... [to] the prosperity of his constituents and the interests of the territory."

East Florida Herald, April 12, 1823

José Manuel Gallegos
1815–1875

TERRITORIAL DELEGATE 1853–1856; 1871–1873
DEMOCRAT FROM NEW MEXICO

José M. Gallegos, a prominent former priest and legislator, navigated the New Mexico Territory's chaotic political scene to become the first Hispanic of Mexican descent elected as a Territorial Delegate to Congress. The intense nationalism that accompanied his country's independence from Spain bound Gallegos and many of his constituents to the Mexican cultural and political institutions that the U.S. supplanted after the war with Mexico. Marred by multiple contested elections and complicated by his limited English, Gallegos's House service symbolized the challenges and contradictions inherent in the process of incorporating new lands and peoples into the growing nation.

José Manuel Gallegos was born in Abiquiú, New Mexico, on October 30, 1815, to Pedro Ignacio, the *alcalde* (mayor) and chief magistrate of the town, and Ana María Gavaldon. He attended a parochial school in Taos, New Mexico, where he became interested in theology, and may also have attended a private school in Abiquiú. From 1836 to 1839, he studied at the College of Durango, Mexico, to prepare for the Catholic priesthood.[1] Gallegos most likely graduated and was ordained by 1840. His mentors, including Padre Antonio José Martínez, studied in Durango during the Mexican Revolution, immersing themselves in secular politics as much as in sacred texts. Having committed to Mexican nationalism in their youth, they imparted that cultural identity to a young generation of seminarians like Gallegos, imbuing them with a deep sense of loyalty to the nascent Mexican state.[2]

Gallegos's independent nature made him a frequent source of concern for political and religious authorities. In 1840 he ran afoul of Governor Manuel Armijo, who accused Gallegos of having an affair with the wife of a corporal in the Mexican Army. Gallegos was sentenced to a three-year exile from Santa Fe, but his superior, a vicar, interceded and sent Gallegos to the parish of San Juan to avoid further controversy.[3] Gallegos served in San Juan from 1840 to 1845 and in the parish of Albuquerque from October 1845 to September 1852, becoming pastor of the latter parish in December 1847.

In July 1850, almost two years after the United States acquired New Mexico in the Treaty of Guadalupe Hidalgo, the Catholic Church placed the territory under the ecclesiastical control of the U.S. Catholic hierarchy. Pope Pius IX chose a young French missionary, John Baptiste Lamy, to manage the effort. Lamy was consecrated as a bishop in November 1850 and named J. Projectus Machebeuf as his deputy. Bishop Lamy and Machebeuf arrived in Santa Fe in August 1851, but the Vatican failed to inform the incumbent bishop, Antonio Zubiría y Escalante, about the administrative change. Local priests, including Gallegos, refused to recognize Lamy's authority until a formal transfer of power occurred. By January 1852, although Lamy had made the 1,500-mile trek to Durango to finalize the transfer of power, and had secured Zubiría's assent, many local priests still considered him illegitimate. Thus, Lamy began to replace the Mexican clergy with transplanted priests and nuns and to monitor recalcitrant priests like Gallegos.[4] For the remainder of the 1850s, these two factions of the Catholic Church fought for religious and political control of the territory. Lamy's faction grew as Anglo clergy came to New Mexico after the U.S. assumed control. Gallegos's faction consisted of priests of Mexican descent with a long history of service in the region.[5]

Because of his record, Gallegos proved an easy mark for Lamy, who questioned his competence, loyalty, and integrity and eventually suspended him from the priesthood in 1853.[6] Two reasons are cited for Gallegos's punishment. First, Gallegos left his parish to travel to Mexico without official permission and, upon his return,

Image courtesy of the Palace of the Governors Photo Archives (NMHM/DCA), 9882

tried to rally support among his parishioners against Machebeuf, whom Lamy had handpicked to succeed him.[7] Second, based principally on rumor and innuendo, Gallegos was charged with violating his vow of celibacy.[8]

Stinging from Lamy's suspension and "deprived of [his] living … by the new French bishop, to make way for the imported French priests of his own selection," Gallegos became a professional politician.[9] For much of the 1840s, Gallegos had been moonlighting as a legislator, and by the time of his dismissal as a priest, he had compiled a noteworthy political career. Although his run to serve as a deputy (a voting member) in the Mexican National Congress in 1843 was unsuccessful, he had gained valuable campaign experience. Before he turned 30, Gallegos had served as one of 19 electors who voted for a deputy and an alternate to the National Congress. The electors also chose seven *vocals* (representatives) to serve a four-year term in the Departmental Assembly. Among its duties, the assembly selected nominees for the office of governor by forwarding the list to the Mexican general government. It also responded to citizen protests about political affairs. Gallegos served in the First and Second Departmental Assemblies of New Mexico from 1843 to 1846, presiding for a single session of the First Assembly by filling in for a sick colleague.[10] In 1850, after the transfer of power to the United States, he campaigned for Democrat Richard H. Weightman, who won election as New Mexico's first Territorial Delegate to the U.S. Congress. In 1851 Gallegos was elected to the territorial council (upper house) of the First Legislative Assembly of the Territory of New Mexico as a representative of Bernalillo County.[11]

A year later, when Weightman declined to seek renomination as Delegate to the 33rd Congress (1853–1855), Gallegos ran for the vacant seat as a Democrat against William Carr Lane, New Mexico's territorial governor. While Gallegos won Weightman's endorsement and the support of the *nuevomexicano* clergy, Lane lined up the former priest's religious rivals, Lamy and Machebeuf, and his mentor, Antonio José Martínez. During the campaign, Gallegos's opponents worked hard to discredit him among his base of Hispanic Catholic voters by bringing up his alleged improprieties.[12] Political lines blurred in a campaign with such overt religious appeal. The *Santa Fe Weekly Gazette*, a Democratic organ, abandoned the party nominee and declared its support for Lane immediately after it printed the announcement of Gallegos's candidacy. The editors, who never challenged the propriety of a cleric's running for political office, wrote, "If they had selected a priest of good standing, the people would have no cause for complaint … but to select a priest, who is suspended for the grossness of his immorality, is to our conception, insulting to the voters of the Territory, as it is disrespectful to the Bishop and the Church." The editors also questioned Gallegos's citizenship and disparaged his English. "If he knew the English language he could give vent to such insignificant ideas as may be supposed to arise in heads as small as his," they wrote. "But as he does not know the language … he cannot have the poor privilege of [s]peaking nonsense."[13] Nevertheless, Gallegos prevailed in the September 1853 elections, defeating Lane by 445 votes.[14] The editors of the *Santa Fe Weekly Gazette* attributed the animus behind the race to cultural "strife" between Mexicans and Americans. "Padre Gallegos was supported by the Mexican population simply because he was a native Mexican," they proclaimed, "and the christening that he received by the [nominating] convention … was a mere cover and device to enable him and his friends to succeed more effectually in the contest they were about to wage against the Americans."[15]

Displeased with the outcome of the vote, Lane challenged the results before the largely unsympathetic House Committee on Elections, which was controlled by the Democratic majority. The committee threw out Lane's initial allegation that Gallegos did not meet citizenship requirements at the time of his election "for the reason that he had not been seven years a resident of the United States" because the Treaty of Guadalupe Hidalgo guaranteed U.S. citizenship to all who chose to remain in New Mexico after the transfer of control.[16] Lane then alleged voter fraud and ballot miscounts in certain counties. Many of Gallegos's votes, he claimed, were cast by "Mexican citizens" and should be disqualified. He also charged that votes cast by Pueblo Indians (not considered U.S. citizens at the time) inflated Gallegos's vote counts. Here Lane's appeals met with more success. The Elections Committee rejected ballots from a "precinct where all the votes were cast by Indians and the election was organized by the Indians and held by their chiefs without authority of law."[17] Territory-wide, the panel disqualified almost 4,000 votes—nearly half the total cast—reporting to the House that it discovered "many irregularities in the election and returns." Yet the House concluded that "these irregularities did not affect the substance of the election." Gallegos also had a powerful, if unlikely, ally in Thomas Hart Benton, the longtime Missouri Senator-turned-Representative. A political rival of Lane's, Benton apparently encouraged Missouri Democrats in New Mexico to oppose Lane and perhaps even worked in the capital city to help squelch Lane's election challenge.[18] In the final count, Gallegos prevailed, with 2,806 votes to Lane's 2,264.[19] Thus, Gallegos presented his credentials and was sworn in on December 19, 1853.[20]

Gallegos spent much of his first term familiarizing himself with an alien culture and legislative process. Unable to speak, read, or write English, he was reliant on bilingual New Mexican officials and Members of Congress to help him draft resolutions and legislative statements. Early in his first term, he sought to secure an interpreter by convincing key committee chairmen to make his case before the House. At first, he sought "per diem [money] out of the [House] contingent fund" to pay an interpreter. But the House refused even to debate that resolution.[21] Seven weeks later, based on the argument that Gallegos could not fully represent his constituents without using an interpreter, the chairman of the Committee on Territories, before which most of Gallegos's business pended, asked that the House permit a Spanish-speaking interpreter on the floor, implying that Gallegos would pay the costs. Two-thirds of the Members present voted against suspending the rules to consider the request, and it too died.[22] Despite this difficulty, Gallegos introduced three pieces of legislation: to pay for a wagon requisitioned by the U.S. Army in New Mexico; to request that the Committee on Military Affairs pay civilian officers in New Mexico Territory under military jurisdiction; and to establish a post road between Albuquerque, New Mexico, and California.[23]

Gallegos also sent home observations of Washington, D.C., and the Northern United States. He noted that Catholicism was openly practiced in several Northern states he had visited, though the congregations were comparatively small and located in poorer sections of cities. He wrote Governor David Meriwether that upon his arrival in December 1853, he had "visited the President and several Ministers of the Cabinet, [and] was received by all of them with deference and appreciation, as well as by many friends in the [House] Chamber." Gallegos also noted distinctions between the Anglo settlers eagerly streaming into the New Mexico Territory and the citizens in the nation's capital. "I have noticed the difference in the moral and political conduct displayed ... by our countrymen to the conduct that some Americans exhibit in our Territory," he wrote Lane, "and I am surprised to find an extraordinary difference.... hopefully in time we will enjoy the benefits that come with a peaceful and intelligent society."[24]

In 1855 Gallegos faced stiff opposition for re-election from an unabashedly pro-American faction within his own party.[25] His opponent was Miguel Otero, a prominent Democratic politician and a former personal secretary of Lane's. According to a biographer, Otero, who had attended St. Louis University and was bilingual, could "neutralize [Gallegos's] 'native son'" advantage as a viable alternative to *nuevomexicano* voters.[26] Otero allies rehashed the smear tactics of earlier campaigns, advertising Gallegos's dismissal from the Catholic Church. Bishop Lamy endorsed Otero and commanded clergy to support him. The initial count of the election results had Gallegos prevailing, with a razor-thin margin of 99 votes out of almost 14,000 cast.

Predictably, Otero contested Gallegos's election. Though he expanded on Lane's earlier challenge, lodging 11 individual complaints, he essentially repeated the core charge that Mexican citizens, who were not eligible to vote in the election, cast votes for the incumbent.[27] When Otero's side presented a list of names of disqualified voters, the House Committee on Elections accepted the testimony, and Gallegos complained that he had not been given sufficient notice or a list of disputed voters. The committee then made Gallegos responsible for ascertaining the citizenship of disputed voters. After reviewing the case for more than a year—more than half the congressional term—the committee reported to the full House that it had found Otero to be the victor.[28]

On July 23, 1856, when the House considered the contested election dispute, both men were permitted to make floor statements. A clerk read Gallegos's lengthy statement. Gallegos argued for his effectiveness as a "true" representative of New Mexico despite his inability to speak English. He noted, "The sneers and jests with which certain honorable members of this body have permitted themselves to treat the proposition that I should be heard by counsel … have produced no other effect upon me than that of painful disappointment at these exceptions to the generous spirit which I had been encouraged to expect from all the representatives of a free and magnanimous people." Gallegos then described the distinctive position that New Mexico and its people—like other territories acquired during the Mexican-American War—held in the newly expanded United States. His constituents were, he noted, "in their origin, alien to your institutions, your laws, your customs, your glorious history, and even strangers to your language." "I am not ashamed of whatsoever is common to them and to me," he added. He argued that as a Delegate, House Rules prohibited him from participating fully in floor debate and that what mattered more than giving speeches was "to be a true agent of his people, acquainted with their condition and their wants, and faithful and industrious in making them known." He dismissed Otero as one of those "inexperienced youths who have been educated out of their native Territory, so as to be more familiar with the language and condition and wants of others than those of whom they aspire to represent."[29]

Gallegos used the bulk of his speech to rebut Otero's case point by point. He denied allegations that the Roman Catholic Church helped secure his election. Just the opposite was true, he argued. "This foreign bishop [Lamy] did … intermeddle, by himself and his priests, not to support, but to crush me, and to secure the election of my opponent."[30] Gallegos also challenged the results of the election report that threw out more than 130 "Mexican votes" for him, dismissed testimony from key elected officials, and presented signed testimonies on his behalf from disputed polling places. He reiterated the provisions of the Treaty of Guadalupe Hidalgo, which extended citizenship to Mexicans after one year, and submitted additional testimony from the secretary of the territory that contradicted some of Otero's key claims. By his count, he had prevailed with close to 600 votes.[31]

Granted permission to speak on the floor, Otero rejected the argument that cultural familiarity with the populace trumped the English proficiency required to represent them on the floor of the House. "I protest against the assumption the personal deficiencies or errors of the gentleman are to be imputed by representation to the people of our territory," he said. Gallegos, he noted, broke his campaign promise that he would master English and would be "capable of representing the people here by his acquaintance with your language." Otero also defended Bishop Lamy, insisting that he was not "guilty of any interference whatever unless that could be called an interference which sought … to restrain the priesthood from the scandal of an active and zealous participation in the canvass" on Gallegos's behalf.[32] In the end, his forceful presentation, with carefully crafted allusions to his loyalty to the "American party" and Anglo political institutions, won the day. Even Pennsylvania's John Cadwalader, who studied the case and claimed to have "as strong an impression in favor of the sitting Delegate, as any member on this floor," was persuaded by Otero's case. The House overwhelmingly accepted the Election Committee's recommendation, granting Otero a seat by a 128 to 22 vote.[33]

Gallegos returned to New Mexico and eventually rebuilt a political career in the territory. In 1857 he was an unsuccessful candidate for the territorial assembly. Meanwhile, Otero's "American Party" aligned itself with Southern efforts to preserve and extend slavery into the territories. Dubbed the "National Democrats," the party swept its loyalists into power at the level of the territorial legislature, ensuring Otero a sympathetic base at home.[34] In 1859 Gallegos challenged Otero for the Delegate's seat to the 36th Congress (1859–1861). Having many of the same alliances still in place, Otero won. Again Gallegos turned his sights toward the territorial legislature, winning election handily in 1860. Re-elected three times, he served as speaker of the house for the Tenth, Eleventh, and Twelfth New Mexico Legislative Assemblies.[35]

During the Civil War, New Mexico became a pivotal battleground in the Western theater of operations. Many New Mexican U.S. military officers resigned their commissions to join the Confederate Army. Southern sympathizers lobbied for the separation of the New Mexico Territory into two territories, a pro-Confederate Arizona Territory and occupied New Mexico. In March 1862, the Confederate Army of the West, under the command of Henry L. Sibley, occupied Santa Fe and Albuquerque. The New Mexican government fled to Las Vegas, 50 miles east of Santa Fe. Gallegos, an ardent Union supporter, was imprisoned for his pro-Union sympathies and his position as speaker of the legislative assembly. During his incarceration, Gallegos met with a Union spy and supplied information to federal forces.[36] At the battles of Glorieta Pass and Valverde in 1863, the Union Army definitively repulsed the Confederate offensive and regained control of the territory.[37]

In 1863 Gallegos ran as a Democrat for the Delegate's seat against Francisco Perea, a well-regarded local politician and a Civil War veteran. Perea collected endorsements from a familiar ensemble of Gallegos's enemies: Bishop Lamy; James L. Collins, the editor of the *Santa Fe Weekly Gazette*; and Kirby Benedict, chief justice of the New Mexico supreme court. Benedict had considered running, but yielded when Gallegos won unanimous support at the nominating convention in June 1863. Perea, however, had the support of the *Gazette*; furthermore, his supporters neutralized the influence of the pro-Gallegos editor of the Santa Fe *New Mexican* by buying the paper. Perea's supporters employed tactics taken from the Lane and Otero campaigns, reminding voters of Gallegos's suspension from the priesthood. Gallegos's romantic relationship with a widow, Candelaria Montoya, begun after his suspension, was also the subject of salacious news reports.[38] More substantially, Gallegos was forced to jettison his longtime advocacy of gradual statehood for New Mexico and embrace immediate statehood to co-opt the position from Perea.[39] The initial results showed that Perea won the election. However, because of a variety of irregularities in various counties, the governor "had the vote reconstructed from the tallies kept by election officials in the precincts, and these were tabulated in place of the actual ballots." According to the recount, Perea had won the majority of the votes.[40] Gallegos and his supporters contested the results, arguing that the governor had exceeded his authority. The case came before the House Committee on Elections and seemed to hinge on the inability of the Gallegos camp to take testimony from witnesses, as it had been instructed to, "either before the chief justice of the Territory or a probate judge." Gallegos complained that he needed more time to assemble a case and that his options were limited given that one of the two available judges "resided in an inaccessible part of the Territory" and the other, Benedict, "was a violent political opponent." One of Gallegos's supporters, Secretary of the Territory William F. M. Arny, traveled to Washington to advocate for Gallegos; the contestant himself did not undertake the journey. Unconvinced, the Committee on Elections did not grant Gallegos an extension and awarded the seat to Perea.[41]

After the election, Gallegos participated in a number of business dealings and repositioned himself as a Constitutional Union loyalist.[42] He served as the territorial treasurer (1865–1866) and as quartermaster general of New Mexico (1868). In between, he served another term as speaker of the territorial house. Then, based on a recommendation from Delegate Charles Clever, whom he had campaigned for the previous year, Gallegos was appointed Superintendent of Indian Affairs by President Andrew Johnson until a suitable military replacement was found in November 1868. In this position, Gallegos managed the transfer of American Indians to reservations and oversaw affairs among Indians, Anglos, and *nuevomexicano* settlers.[43]

After serving briefly as Santa Fe County treasurer, Gallegos ran for the Delegate's seat in the summer of 1871. His opponent was Republican nominee José Francisco Chaves, the three-term incumbent and a cousin of Gallegos's 1863 rival, Francisco Perea. Gallegos believed Chaves had played an instrumental role in foiling his 1863 campaign. José D. Sena, another Republican, split from the party and ran for the seat as an Independent. The election was accompanied by violence. On August 27, 1871, Gallegos was scheduled to speak at a rally in Mesilla, New Mexico, but the Republicans staged a counter-rally. Whether Gallegos was present after the speeches is unclear, but the two groups met in the town plaza. Tensions flared, a shot was fired, and a riot commenced, leaving nine dead and 40 wounded. The Republican split virtually guaranteed Gallegos's victory; he prevailed with 50 percent of the vote versus 34 percent and 16 percent for Chaves and Sena, respectively. Unlike the results of Gallegos's previous elections, this win was so convincing, it was not contested.[44]

Gallegos claimed his seat at the opening of the 42nd Congress (1871–1873) as a more savvy and seasoned national legislator. One scholar notes that Gallegos was "a much more effective politician … in 1871 than he had been in 1853" because of his "effective functioning in the bicultural political reality of New Mexico." Gallegos's two decades as a territorial legislator and federal appointee provided a wealth of experience. He also understood a Territorial Delegate's power to pressure federal appointees in Santa Fe because of his access to and influence on their bosses in Washington.[45] During his term, Gallegos submitted petitions for constituents as well as bills to build military roads throughout the New Mexico Territory and organize a public school system. He took a special interest in supporting Pueblo Indians because of his experience as Superintendent of Indian Affairs. According to one scholar, Gallegos advocated a conciliatory approach toward American Indians, especially the Pueblos, because he had been the pastor of a number of Pueblo villages throughout New Mexico. Although Gallegos was a Democrat, he supported his Republican colleagues by advocating for Republican territorial appointees to the Ulysses S. Grant administration.[46]

Gallegos ran for re-election in 1873. Unlike in the 1871 race, in which the Republican vote was split between Chaves and Sena, in 1873 the Republicans fielded one candidate, Stephen B. Elkins. A Missouri native who came to New Mexico during the war, he eventually led the Santa Fe Ring, a notorious political machine that dominated New Mexico politics in the last decades of the 19th century. Elkins unseated the incumbent by a comfortable margin, 62 to 38 percent. After the 1873 race, Gallegos retired from politics and returned to the territory. He died of a stroke on April 21, 1875, in Santa Fe, New Mexico.[47]

FOR FURTHER READING

Biographical Directory of the United States Congress, "José Manuel Gallegos," http://bioguide.congress.gov.

Chavez, Fray Angelico. *Très Macho—He Said; Padre Gallegos of Albuquerque, New Mexico's First Congressman* (Santa Fe, NM: William Gannon, 1985).

Theisen, Gerald Arthur. "Jose Manuel Gallegos (1815–1875): The First Mexican American in the United States Congress," (Ph.D. diss., University of New Mexico, 1985).

MANUSCRIPT COLLECTIONS

Archives of Archdiocese of Durango (Durango, Mexico). *Papers*: 1836–1839, one file consisting of Gallegos's seminary records.

Huntington Library (San Marino, CA). *Papers*: Ritch Collection, 1862. Consists of one broadside, an address signed by Gallegos and others, urging resistance by the people of the New Mexico Territory to the Confederate force advancing from Texas.

New Mexico State Records Center and Archives (Santa Fe). *Papers*: Manuel Alvarez Papers, 1825–1856, two linear feet. Gallegos is included among the correspondents. *Papers*: Benjamin M. Read Collection, 1704–1926, seven linear feet. Subjects include Gallegos. Material related to Gallegos exists in several additional collections.

NOTES

1 Gerald Arthur Theisen, "Jose Manuel Gallegos (1815–1875): The First Mexican American in the United States Congress," (Ph.D. diss., University of New Mexico, 1985): 6–7, 12; Fray Angelico

Chavez, *Très Macho–He Said: Padre Gallegos of Albuquerque, New Mexico's First Congressman* (Santa Fe, NM: William Gannon, 1985): 3–4, 12.

2 Chavez, *Très Macho–He Said*: 9; Theisen, "Jose Manuel Gallegos (1815–1875)": 12. Chavez notes that although Gallegos's 1875 obituary lists his graduation date as 1835, "this is clearly a mistake, since at age twenty he was much too young to be ordained. The year 1840 ... appears to be the correct date, since at age twenty-five he was of the right canonical age for ordination. It is also in this same year that he first appears as an ordained priest in the local church records." Theisen asserts that Gallegos graduated in November 1839.

3 Chavez, *Très Macho–He Said*: 10–11.

4 Theisen, "Jose Manuel Gallegos (1815–1875)": 74–81. For biographical information about Lamy, see Elizabeth Zoe Vicary, "Lamy, John Baptiste," *American National Biography*, 13 (New York: Oxford University Press, 1999): 96–97; Paul Horgan, *Lamy of Santa Fe* (Middletown, CT: Wesleyan University Press, 2003; reprint of 1975 edition). The most recent biography about Machebeuf is Lynn Bridgers, *Death's Deceiver: The Life of Joseph P. Machebeuf* (Albuquerque: University of New Mexico Press, 2007).

5 "Jose Manuel Gallegos" in Maurilio Vigil, *Los Patrones: Profiles of Hispanic Political Leaders in New Mexico History* (Washington, D.C.: University Press of America, 1980): 40; Ralph Emerson Twitchell, *The Leading Facts of New Mexican History*, Vol. 2 (Cedar Rapids, IA: Torch Press, 1912): 309.

6 Biographers conclude that Gallegos was suspended rather than excommunicated. See, for example, the treatment of Gallegos's status in *The American Catholic Historical Researches*, 21 (Philadelphia, PA: Martin I. J. Griffin, 1904): 110–113.

7 Chavez, *Très Macho–He Said*: 16, Theisen, "Jose Manuel Gallegos (1815–1875)": 85–88. According to Theisen, Gallegos rallied parishioners to his defense multiple times. In one attempt, "950 citizens of Albuquerque petitioned the bishop" on Gallegos's behalf. Gallegos also "moved into the rectory and tried to preach." Gallegos tried again courting a couple dozen of the most powerful people in the city. After Machebeuf stood his ground, "850 parishioners brought signed formal complaints against the management of the parish by the French vicar." Gallegos received support from other *nuevomexicano* priests such as Antonio José Martínez, who appealed to Rome to criticize Bishop Lamy's actions. Gallegos himself sent a letter to Pope Pius IX that criticized Lamy's and Machebeuf's efforts to assert control and remove *nuevomexicano* priests. The actions of Gallegos and his allies sound similar to "la junta de ignación" (a mass meeting of indignation). According to Phillip B. Gonzales, *nuevomexicanos* used these forms of protest "to publicly voice their objection to Anglo prejudice and provided key forums for developing a protest-oriented 'Hispano' identity." See Phillip B. Gonzales, "La Junta de Ignación: Hispanic Repertoire of Collective Protest in New Mexico, 1884–1933," *Western Historical Quarterly* 31, no. 2 (Summer 2000): 161–86, especially pp. 161–167.

8 "Jose Manuel Gallegos," in Vigil, *Los Patrones*: 40–44; Chavez, *Très Macho–He Said*: 45–47. Although Vigil blames Bishop Lamy for Gallegos's demotion, Chavez blames Machebeuf. One scholar alleges that Lamy punished Gallegos "as part of a campaign to replace Mexican clerics with outside priests." See, for example, Alvin R. Sunseri, *Seeds of Discord: New Mexico in the Aftermath of the American Conquest, 1846–1861* (Chicago, IL: Nelson-Hall, 1979): 133. According to Marc Simmons, various sources allege that Gallegos's "personal conduct ... was licentious in the extreme. Among his closest cronies were ... rich stockmen ... at whose ebullient house parties he danced, drank, and gambled. He knew all the politicians and leading merchants and had business dealings with many of them. On the side, he ran a string of freight wagons ... and operated a general store in Albuquerque.... A store owned by a man of the cloth was bad enough, but Gallegos added insult to injury by keeping it open on Sundays and by having his mistress help out at the counter." Marc Simmons, *Albuquerque, a Narrative History* (Albuquerque: University of New Mexico Press, 1982): 146–149. This version of events is corroborated by Samuel Ellison, a New Mexican transplant who arrived with Kearny's army in 1846. Ellison noted that Gallegos was "suspended by Archbishop Lamy for concubinage." See J. Manuel Espinosa, ed., "Memoir of a Kentuckian in New Mexico, 1848–1884," in *New Mexico Historical Review* 8, no. 1 (January 1938): 8. Gerald Theisen cites an 1840 case investigated by the U.S. Consul in Santa Fe in which 25-year-old Gallegos was caught having an affair with a woman. Theisen notes that "granting [that] this 'great scandal' did indeed happen, perhaps such behavior among the New Mexican clergy was not so commonplace, or it would not have been so described." See Theisen, "Jose Manuel Gallegos (1815–1875)": 23.

9 Theisen, "Jose Manuel Gallegos (1815–1875)": 88–89. The quotation comes from *Congressional Globe*, House, 34th Cong., 1st sess. (23 July 1856): 1730.

10 Theisen, "Jose Manuel Gallegos (1815–1875)": 28–29; Lansing B. Bloom, "New Mexico under Mexican Administration-VI; Part III-New Mexico as a Department, 1837–1846," *Old Santa Fe* Vol. 2, no. 2 (October 1914): 158–159, 164–165.

11 W. G. Ritch, *The Legislative Blue-Book of the Territory of New Mexico* (Albuquerque: University of New Mexico Press, 1968; reprint of 1882 edition): 101; Robert W. Larson, *New Mexico's Quest for Statehood, 1846–1912* (Albuquerque: University of New Mexico Press, 1968): 29–30, 36–40, 69–74; Howard R. Lamar, *The Far Southwest, 1846–1912: A Territorial History*, rev. ed. (Albuquerque: University of New Mexico Press, 2000): 88–89. Lamar and Larson describe the political split between the New Mexicans who wanted immediate statehood and those who preferred a territorial government. Pro-statehood advocates formed a faction under Richard Weightman, New Mexico's first Territorial Delegate, and pro-territory advocates united under Judge Joab

Houghton. The Weightman faction made an effort to promote *nuevomexicanos* like Gallegos for political office. The Houghton faction promoted primarily Anglo candidates. Larson writes that "the Spanish-speaking majority … was hurt more than any other group by the political divisions and feuds" as one faction "scornfully exploited the Hispanos, and the other patronizingly sought their votes." The Weightman and Houghton factions fought for control of New Mexican politics through elections for Territorial Delegates and patronage appointments for the remainder of the 1850s. For more information about Weightman, see *Biographical Directory of the United States Congress,* "Richard Hanson Weightman," http://bioguide.congress.gov.

12 Opponents tried to tie Gallegos to another suspended priest, Benigno Cárdenas, as a sign of his moral corruption. See "The Letter of Cardenas to Gallegos," 3 September 1853, *Santa Fe Weekly Gazette*: 2.

13 "Padre Gallegos nominated for Congress," 13 August 1853, *Santa Fe Weekly Gazette*: 2. For another editorial critical of Gallegos, see "Defense of Padre Gallegos," 27 August 1853, *Santa Fe Weekly Gazette*: 2. For concerns about Gallegos's serving as a Delegate and issues of the separation of church and state, see "The True State of the Case," 27 August 1853, *Santa Fe Weekly Gazette*: 2–3.

14 Twitchell, *The Leading Facts of New Mexican History*: 309; Theisen, "Jose Manuel Gallegos (1815–1875)": 88–93; José Manuel Gallegos certificate of election (endorsed 1 October 1853), Committee on Elections (HR33A-J1), 33rd Congress, Records of the U.S House of Representatives, Record Group 233, National Archives, Washington, D.C. (NA). Gallegos won with 4,971 votes; Lane earned 4,526 votes.

15 "Padre Gallegos' Democracy and Our Position," 10 September 1853, *Santa Fe Weekly Gazette*: 2.

16 Theisen, "Jose Manuel Gallegos (1815–1875)": 100.

17 Chester H. Rowell, *A Historical and Legal Digest of All the Election Cases in the House of Representatives of the United States from the First to the Fifty-Sixth Congress, 1789–1901* (Westport, CT: Greenwood Press, 1976; reprint of 1901 edition): 140.

18 Sunseri, *Seeds of Discord*: 133; Lamar, *The Far Southwest, 1846–1912*: 90. For more information about Benton, see *Biographical Directory of the United States Congress*, "Thomas Hart Benton," http://bioguide.congress.gov.

19 Twitchell, *The Leading Facts of New Mexican History*: 309; Theisen, "Jose Manuel Gallegos (1815–1875)": 101–104; Rowell, *A Historical and Legal Digest of All the Election Cases in the House of Representatives of the United States from the First to the Fifty-Sixth Congress, 1789–1901*: 140; José Manuel Gallegos certificate of election; 33rd Congress; RG 233, NA.

20 *Congressional Globe*, House, 33rd Cong., 1st sess. (19 December 1853): 62–63. Gallegos was sworn in on December 19, 1853, and the House formalized the decision on February 24, 1854. See *Congressional Globe*, House, 33rd Cong., 1st sess. (24 February 1854): 475.

21 *Congressional Globe*, House, 33rd Cong., 1st sess. (5 January 1854): 128.

22 *Congressional Globe*, House, 33rd Cong., 1st sess. (28 February 1854): 492.

23 *Congressional Globe*, House, 33rd Cong., 1st sess. (27 February 1854): 490; F. G. Franklin, "Foreigner Held Seat," *Washington Post* (6 January 1902): 4. Theisen asserts, "Throughout his first term of office, Gallegos was able to introduce pre-translated statements, but his constituents literally were denied his voice in the House of Representatives." See Theisen, "Jose Manuel Gallegos (1815–1875)": 106–107, 114–116; "A Survey of Public Lands in New Mexico–a Bill before Congress for That Purpose," 3 June 1854, *Santa Fe Weekly Gazette*: 2 records that Senator James Shields of Illinois submitted S. 220 on Gallegos's behalf. The bill passed the Senate but did not come to a final vote in the House. See *House Journal*, 33rd Cong., 1st sess.: 1426, and *Senate Journal*, 33rd Cong., 1st sess.: 734; J. Manuel Espinosa, ed., "Memoir of a Kentuckian in New Mexico, 1848–1884," in *New Mexico Historical Review*, 13, no. 1 (January 1938): 8. Samuel Ellison, a New Mexican transplant who arrived with Kearny's army in 1846, notes that Gallegos "procured the first appropriation of $20,000 & $50,000 for a capital [*sic*] & penitentiary."

24 Theisen, "Jose Manuel Gallegos (1815–1875)": 114–116; "He visitado al señor Presidente y a los varios Ministros del Gabinete, todos ellos me recivieron [*sic*] con concideracion [*sic*] y apracio [*sic*], así mismo me reconocen muchos amigos de la cámara a que correspondo.… He observado el contraste de la conducta moral y política que guardan nuestros compatriotas en estos mundos respecto a la que observan algunos americanos en nuestro Territorio, y con sorpresa distingo … ojalá que con el tiempo [illegible] los goces que brinda una sociedad pacífica é inteligente." José Manuel Gallegos, "Carta Interesante del Sr. Gallegos," *Santa Fe Weekly Gazette*, 11 March 1854: 3. Translated as "An Interesting Letter from Mr. Gallegos" by Translations International, Inc. (December 2009)

25 Lamar, *The Far Southwest, 1846–1912*: 90.

26 Theisen, "Jose Manuel Gallegos (1815–1875)": 107, 151 (footnote 10). Theisen explains, "It was not inconsistent to be a National Democrat within the territory and a Democrat nationally.… In 1853, Gallegos was not nationally affiliated with a party. Even though he was nominated by a convention … which said it was that of the Democratic party.… However, the editor of the *Santa Fe Weekly Gazette* … went to great lengths to explain how [Gallegos] had not 'endorsed the democratic platform laid down by the Baltimore convention.'"

27 Ibid., 107–110.

28 Ibid., 107–114; Rowell, *A Historical and Legal Digest of All the*

Contested Election Cases in the House of Representatives of the United States from the First to the Fifty-Sixth Congress, 1789–1901: 144–145.

29 *Congressional Globe*, House, 34th Cong., 1st sess. (23 July 1856): 1730.

30 Ibid.

31 Ibid., 1730–1732.

32 Ibid., 1733–1736.

33 Ibid., 1736; Vigil, *Los Patrones*: 40–41; for an alternative account of the Gallegos-Otero contest, see Horgan, *Lamy of Santa Fe*: 230–236.

34 Theisen, "Jose Manuel Gallegos (1815–1875)": 120–124.

35 Ibid., 125–127; "The Result," 24 September 1859, *Santa Fe Weekly Gazette*: 2–3. Although the results of the election are illegible in the English section of the newspaper, the Spanish section states that Otero won by a 1,169-vote margin ("Cuando nuestros lectores sepan que el Hon. M. A. Otero ha sido re-electo por la mayoría larga de 1169 votos."). The National Archives' Center for Legislative Archives was unable to locate Otero's 1859 election certificate, nor were the certified election results preserved in the Department of State Territorial Papers, New Mexico, 1851–1872 (National Archives Microfilm Publication T17, Roll 2); General Records of the Department of State, Record Group 59; National Archives at College Park, College Park, MD (NACP). Therefore, the *Santa Fe Weekly Gazette* articles may be the only existing primary source for the results of the 1859 elections for Territorial Delegate for New Mexico.

36 Theisen, "Jose Manuel Gallegos (1815–1875)": 130–132. After the occupation, Gallegos served as foreman for a grand jury in a U.S. District Court that indicted two dozen New Mexicans for collaborating with the Confederacy. Although Gallegos's former opponent Miguel Otero was suspected of collaboration, he was not indicted. Otero and his family moved to Missouri in 1862 in anticipation of a possible indictment. After the Civil War ended, all the cases were dismissed.

37 Ibid., 130. For more information about New Mexico during the Civil War, see Lamar, *The Far Southwest, 1846–1912*: 97–121; Ray C. Colton, *Civil War in the Western Territories: Arizona, Colorado, New Mexico, and Utah* (Norman: University of Oklahoma Press, 1959); Donald S. Frazier, *Blood and Treasure: Confederate Empire in the Southwest* (College Station: Texas A&M University Press, 1995).

38 During the campaign, an infamous poem titled, "El Padrecillo" (The Father), was published in the *Santa Fe Weekly Gazette*. The poem reiterated many of the charges of corruption and salaciousness that dogged Gallegos for much of his political career. The poem describes examples of Gallegos partisans that fleeced the voters while Gallegos remained conspicuously oblivious to their crimes. See "El Padrecillo," 11 July 1863, *Santa Fe Weekly Gazette*: 4. In December 1868, Gallegos married Candelaria Montoya in an Episcopal ceremony. He was 51 and she was in her mid-30s. Candelaria had two daughters, Josefa and Felipita, and a son, Pantaleon, from a previous marriage. Gallegos adopted them all. Theisen, "Jose Manuel Gallegos (1815–1875)": 166, 170; Chavez, *Très Macho–He Said*: 99–102.

39 Theisen, "Jose Manuel Gallegos (1815–1875)": 137.

40 Ibid., 132–143. Theisen notes an example in which the votes for one county were not counted because the poll books were burned.

41 Rowell, *A Historical and Legal Digest of All the Contested Election Cases in the House of Representatives of the United States from the First to the Fifty-Sixth Congress, 1789*–1901: 188; Theisen, "Jose Manuel Gallegos (1815–1875)": 143–146.

42 Theisen, "Jose Manuel Gallegos (1815–1875)": 146–149.

43 See Theisen, "Jose Manuel Gallegos (1815–1875)": 171–177; U.S. Office of Indian Affairs, *Office Copy of the Laws, Regulations, etc., of the Indian Bureau, 1850* (Washington, D.C.; Government Printing Office, 1874): 49–50. For a detailed study of the Office of Indian Affairs, see Laurence F. Schmeckebier, *The Office of Indian Affairs: Its History, Activities, and Organization* (New York: AMS Press, 1972; reprint of 1927 edition).

44 Theisen, "Jose Manuel Gallegos (1815–1875)": 177–179.

45 Ibid., 178–179.

46 *Congressional Globe*, Index, 42nd Cong., 2nd sess.: 201; *Congressional Globe*, Index, 42nd Cong., 3rd sess.: 227; Theisen, "Jose Manuel Gallegos (1815–1875)": 172–174, 179–182. According to Theisen, Gallegos "introduced a total of nine bills and one joint resolution" during his term.

47 Theisen, "Jose Manuel Gallegos (1815–1875)": 182–184; "José Manuel Gallegos" in Vigil, *Los Patrones*: 42–43; "The Death of Gallegos," 23 April 1875, *Daily New Mexican* (Santa Fe): 1; Ritch, *The Legislative Blue-Book of the Territory of New Mexico*: 93. Elkins earned 10,643 votes to Gallegos's 6,582. For an alternative account of the 1871 election for Delegate, see Oscar Lambert, *Stephen Benton Elkins* (Pittsburgh, PA: University of Pittsburgh Press, 1955): 39–40.

Miguel Antonio Otero
1829–1882

TERRITORIAL DELEGATE 1856–1861
DEMOCRAT FROM NEW MEXICO

The second Hispanic Delegate to serve the New Mexico Territory, and the longest-serving Hispanic Member in the 19th century, Miguel Otero belonged to a powerful business family.[1] A successful entrepreneur, Otero engaged in politics as a full-contact sport and was, in the words of one scholar of New Mexico territorial affairs, "dynamic, intelligent, and very much on the political make."[2] His rise to public office symbolized the emergence of a new generation of New Mexican politicians: a bilingual social elite that bridged the territory's Hispanic and Anglo worlds. In a bid to advance the cause of New Mexican statehood, Otero aligned himself with Southern Democrats, who supported the expansion of slavery into the territories.

Born in Valencia, New Mexico, on June 21, 1829, Miguel Antonio Otero was the youngest son of Vicente and Doris Gertrudis Chaves y Aragon Otero.[3] Vicente Otero was a farmer, a merchant, and occasionally a judge under the Mexican government. He also served as an *alcalde* (mayor) and in the New Mexican government. The family lived comfortably, if not lavishly. Even before the outbreak of the Mexican-American War, the Oteros displayed an attraction for American culture. At least one biographer claimed Otero "was one of the first New Mexicans to travel east to the United States for an education." Moreover, the Otero clan developed an "aristocratic flair that would distinguish them from other Hispanics in New Mexico. They were well-received and regarded by the Anglo-American community in or outside New Mexico. They would be decidedly pro-American rather than pro-Mexican in nationalistic sympathies and would … be more identified with Anglo-American culture and values than most Hispanics." Otero was educated in private and parochial schools and attended St. Louis University from 1841 until the outbreak of the Mexican-American War in 1846, when he returned to New Mexico at his family's request. The following year he enrolled at Pingree College, a small school in Fishkill, New York, where he served as a teacher and as an assistant to the principal. He began studying law with a local attorney and continued under the tutelage of senior attorneys in New York City and St. Louis from 1849 to 1852, when he passed the Missouri bar exam.[4]

While studying in St. Louis, Otero befriended fellow law student William G. Blackwood, who introduced the New Mexican to his visiting sister, Mary Josephine Blackwood. Otero married her in 1857. Raised by a maternal aunt in Charleston, South Carolina, Mary Josephine was a descendant of the family of Senator Charles Carroll of Maryland and, as her son recalled many years later, "quite a society woman and popular, well known and admired" by her peers wherever the Oteros resided.[5] The marriage connection contributed to Otero's Southern sympathies during the secession crisis and the Civil War. A year after his marriage, Otero arranged to have his new brother-in-law, William, appointed as a New Mexico supreme court judge. Miguel and Mary Josephine had four children: Page Blackwood; Miguel, Jr.; Gertrude Vincentia; and Mamie Josephine. Gertrude died as a child.[6] Many years later, under the William McKinley administration, Miguel, Jr., became the only Mexican American appointed to serve as governor of the New Mexico Territory.

Otero, who set up a private law practice, immediately immersed himself in territorial politics. In 1852 he became the private secretary to territorial governor William Carr Lane, the former mayor of St. Louis, serving until Lane's term expired in 1853. While Lane ran unsuccessfully against José Manuel Gallegos for the Territorial Delegate's seat in Congress, the 23-year-old Otero won election in

Image courtesy of the Palace of the Governors Photo Archives (NMHM/DCA), 152218

September 1852 to represent his home county, Valencia, in New Mexico's Second Legislative Assembly. In 1854 Otero was appointed attorney general for the territory; he served in that position until his election to Congress.[7]

In 1855 Otero opposed Gallegos, the incumbent Democratic Delegate, for a seat in the 34th Congress (1855–1857). Otero's faction in the nascent territorial political scene was drawn from Democrats and former Whigs who supported the policies of the Millard Fillmore administration. Over time, they came to be identified as "National Democrats" because they supported the national administration's policies. Another local faction of Democrats disagreed with many of the positions of the emerging national party. Otero's candidacy was calculated to defuse Gallegos's appeal to *nuevomexicano* constituents and signaled the ascendancy of a younger generation of public servants whose sympathies were more American than Mexican.[8] Political opponents filled the newspapers with salacious innuendos meant to discredit Gallegos, a defrocked Catholic priest, and to question his ability to serve honorably. Bishop John Baptiste Lamy, Gallegos's rival, endorsed Otero and encouraged the clergy to support him. Charges of voting impropriety flew throughout the election. Critics questioned whether a Delegate like Gallegos, who spoke no English, could adequately represent the territory's interests in Congress. According to contemporary sources, Otero "employed every means at his disposal to achieve victory, and was ably assisted by his Anglo friends." In one instance, four Otero supporters "accosted" a courier conveying poll books from Rio Arriba County, a Gallegos stronghold, to Santa Fe. The Otero camp insisted that the books were stolen to retaliate for Gallegos supporters' sacking the returns from polling places in Valencia County that favored Otero.[9] Initially the returns showed that Gallegos won with a razor-thin plurality: 99 votes out of nearly 14,000 cast (6,914 for Gallegos versus 6,815 for Otero).

Otero contested Gallegos's election on 11 grounds, chief among them the charge that votes cast by Mexican citizens had inflated Gallegos's totals.[10] Otero claimed that nearly 2,000 votes cast in Santa Fe and Rio Arriba Counties belonged to inhabitants who had chosen to remain Mexican citizens under the eighth article of the Treaty of Guadalupe Hidalgo and who were thus ineligible to vote for U.S. Territorial Delegates.[11] Through his lawyer, Gallegos questioned the validity of the article in the treaty and countered that an act of Congress was required for the establishment of a tribunal to determine citizenship requests. In effect, he argued that the provision was null because it had never been properly administered. However, as the House Committee on Elections pointed out in its report on the case, the territorial governor had in 1849 established "registers of enrolment … [for inhabitants who wished] to elect to retain the character of Mexican citizens." Gallegos also challenged the validity of the occupation government, countering that the declarations it collected were suspect. The Committee on Elections rejected that argument, noting that any act of Congress would have abrogated that portion of the treaty and, moreover, that the military government's efforts sufficed. "It would be a mere mockery to say that they had the right to retain the character of Mexican citizens, and yet could not do so, because no mode of doing it had been prescribed by law," the report concluded. Further, in examining evidence at the precinct level, the committee determined that Otero had actually prevailed by 290 votes.[12]

The full House received the committee report on May 10, 1856, and shortly before the end of its session, on July 23, 1856, consented to hear both the incumbent and the challenger make their arguments on the floor. In a statement read by a clerk, Gallegos stressed his social and cultural ties to New Mexicans as their "true" representative. He also rejected the perception that "the influence of the Roman Catholic church was brought into the contest at the polls." While he did not directly address the more scurrilous personal charges leveled against him in the campaign, he defended his record and noted that by denigrating his inability to address the House in English, his colleagues had insulted his constituents. He also introduced evidence from the secretary of the territory that contradicted some of Otero's claims.[13]

Otero's lengthy and powerful rebuttal—strengthened in great measure by his fluent and humorous delivery—

questioned Gallegos's ability to represent New Mexicans without knowing English. He defended church officials Gallegos had attacked for conspiring against him, and he spent much of the speech detailing his claims that disqualified voters had tipped the vote in Gallegos's favor. Finally, he stressed his own deep ties to the territory, noting, "I am happy to entertain the thought that I am the first native citizen of that acquired Territory who has come to the Congress of our adopted fatherland, and address it in the language of its laws and its Constitution."[14] In a stirring coda, Otero added a line that was meant to distinguish him from the Anglo politicians moving into the territory: "I come here, not as a successful adventurer from the restless waters of political speculation; I come here because my people sent me." By a margin of 128 to 22, the House approved the committee report and awarded the seat to Otero.[15]

By law and tradition, the House refused to assign Delegates a seat on standing committees, so Otero never held a committee post during his House career. During the remainder of his first term (August 1856 to March 1857) Otero "won renown by opposing army operations in New Mexico and advocating a more vigorous policy against the Indians."[16] He petitioned for the territory to receive two Indian Agents, representatives of the U.S. government who worked with American Indian tribes. Otero proposed a number of bills, among them a measure to secure appropriations for the completion of government buildings. He also wanted to improve New Mexico's transportation infrastructure, in part by pushing for the transcontinental railroad to pass through New Mexico. He sought to stimulate more mail service between Independence, Missouri, and Santa Fe, and late in the session he submitted a resolution seeking land grants to build a road from Springfield, Missouri, to the Pacific coast via Albuquerque. These bills were referred to committee but did not receive consideration in the waning months of the 34th Congress. In all, Otero claimed to have acquired $116,000 in appropriations for the territory.[17]

In March 1857 Otero received the Democratic nomination for Delegate to the 35th Congress (1857–1859). His main opponent was Republican Spruce M. Baird, a local judge and a powerful territorial politician.[18] Otero ran on his record of securing essential resources for the territory, promising constituents that if they returned him to office greater rewards would follow. During the campaign, the *Santa Fe Weekly Gazette*, an organ of the Democratic Party, declared, "If the present delegate has done his duty in Congress toward his constituents let his services be rewarded."[19] During the campaign, an opposition newspaper leveled the potent charge that Otero and the Democratic Party were agitating for immediate statehood. Otero deflected the charge, asserting that while the ultimate goal ought to be the "eventual erection of New Mexico into a State Government," it should first achieve a measure of economic self-sufficiency and a larger population to provide stability. In his words, the territory should wait until its "great dormant resources [were] developed and made a means of revenue to her treasury." Otero added that "an influx of immigration" would result in "our savage Indian neighbors quieted and ourselves and property protected."[20] Otero won with a large majority: 59 to 41 percent of the vote.[21] During the 1859 election for Territorial Delegate for the 36th Congress (1859–1861), Otero won by a margin of 1,169 votes.[22]

During his second term, Otero sought additional internal improvements for New Mexico. He obtained a $600,000 annual grant for the Butterfield Overland Mail and acquired construction funds for a road from Fort Smith, Arkansas, to the Colorado River via New Mexico. He also ensured that the territory became a land district, enabling constituents to register for land grants and temporarily preventing settlers in the western portions of the territory (modern-day Arizona) from forming a separate territory. Otero acquired funds to support a geological survey for New Mexico, complete work on the territorial capitol building, and secure $75,000 in appropriations for the Superintendent of Indian Affairs.[23] In a public letter, Otero notified his constituents that he had acquired more than $700,000 in appropriations for road construction in the territory. He also sought to "obtain a twice monthly mail service from Santa Fe to

Independence (Missouri) … [and] a weekly mail service from Santa Fe to Las Cruces."[24]

During the late 1850s, Otero's territorial political faction evolved into a party with Southern sympathies, particularly regarding the preservation and expansion of slavery into the territories. Dubbed "National Democrats," the party swept into power at the level of the territorial legislature, ensuring that Otero had a sympathetic home audience for his legislative agenda in Washington.[25] Indeed, although his role shaping national politics was circumscribed, Otero exerted an extraordinary amount of influence on politics in the New Mexico Territory.

Increasingly, Otero's actions were driven by his central desire to court Southern congressional leaders to promote his vision for the territory's development.[26] During his final term in the 36th Congress (1859–1861), he sought with renewed vigor to direct the transcontinental railroad through New Mexico as a means to spur internal improvements, commerce, and business investments. The effort merged Otero's interest in developing the territory's infrastructure with his desire to put the territory on the path to statehood.

To convince congressional Democrats of the viability of a Southern route, Otero pressured the New Mexico legislature to charter the Southern Pacific Railroad. As an additional incentive, he encouraged the New Mexico legislature to pass a code protecting the right of masters to capture slaves in the territory. By taking this action, he hoped to solicit the support of Jefferson Davis of Mississippi, who was known to have desired a similar railway route.[27] In a letter to Alexander Jackson, secretary of the territory and an advocate for slavery, Otero argued that "the laws of the United States, the Constitution, and the decisions of the Supreme Court on the Dred Scott case, established property in slaves in the Territories." He wrote that he hoped Jackson would "perceive at once the advantage of such a law for our territory" and that he expected Jackson to "take good care to procure its passage." Jackson did.[28] Otero lobbied other state officials, suggesting that failure to approve a slave code would curtail his influence with key Southern politicians. On February 3, 1859, after the overwhelmingly majority-*nuevomexicano* Eighth Legislative Assembly voted for its passage, the territorial governor signed "An Act for the Protection of Slave Property in this Territory," into law. Though the code was repealed in 1861, it contained many significant provisions. Among them was that stealing or abetting in the escape of slaves, including any action taken to induce them to abandon their owners, was punishable by fines or imprisonment.[29]

By the late 1850s, Otero had assembled the beginnings of a territory-wide machine in New Mexico. He was well connected with the Southern governor and secretary; he had managed to place his brother-in-law on the territorial supreme court; he had influence with the territory's major newspaper, the *Santa Fe Weekly Gazette*; and he also counted James L. Collins, the newspaper's editor, and the federally appointed Superintendent of Indian Affairs as an ally.[30] Nevertheless, Otero, who served as a delegate to the Democratic National Convention in Charleston, South Carolina, in 1860, chose not to run for a fourth term in the U.S. House.[31] His decision was forced in part by the emergence of the Republican Party and by the waning power of pro-Southern sympathizers in New Mexico after the divisive 1860 presidential election. In a public letter that was remarkable for its ambivalence about the cause for secession given his earlier flirtations with Southern Members of Congress, Otero wrote that he awaited "with almost breathless suspense … the consequences that must result from this awful manifestation, on the part of the Northern people … to disregard the equal rights which Southern people claim in the common territory belonging to the United States." He bemoaned the fact that "this glorious Union is to be dissolved and broken up before the great and noble mission for which it was formed and intended by its founders, is consummated. And for what? For the accursed negro." Otero advocated that, if the Union dissolved, New Mexico should enter a "Union with the Pacific free States, west of the great prairies. If California and Oregon declare their independence of this Government, I am for joining them. Our resources are similar to theirs, our interest therefore [is] the same." Still, he believed secession to be unnecessary and, while

emphasizing his fealty to the Democratic Party, he confirmed his commitment to the Union: "I think it would be, to say the least, imprudent to secede.... You may rest assured that as long as there is no direct violation, or an overt act committed by the administration of Mr. Lincoln, against the institutions of the South and its constitutional rights I can be nothing else than a Union man."[32]

Such a position made Otero a palatable political appointee for the newly installed Abraham Lincoln administration, which was eager to keep New Mexico in the Northern fold. On the eve of the outbreak of the Civil War, Otero accepted President Lincoln's appointment as secretary of the territory, but he served in that position for less than a year because the Senate withheld its final confirmation in light of Otero's publicly declared sympathy with the South.[33] In a letter to Secretary of State William H. Seward, Otero attributed his "rejection" to "malicious and false representations made against me by unprincipled, personal, and political enemies in the States and in the Territory," but he assured Seward that despite this outcome he would not "be the less loyal ... nor become less zealous in contributing my feeble efforts ... in behalf of the preservation of the Union, the constitution and the laws of the United States."[34]

Otero exploited his congressional connections and government experience in the private sector. His first venture was a Kansas City, Missouri-based firm that he formed with a partner, David Whiting. Hinting at its future success, Whiting & Otero also maintained a New York City office. During the Civil War, Otero's firm played a controversial role during the Confederate invasion of New Mexico. The inventory from Otero's stores (reported to contain $200,000 in merchandise) helped sustain the Confederate Army of the West, which sacked Albuquerque in March 1862 under General Henry Sibley. Whether Otero volunteered the supplies or was forced to comply is unclear.[35] A Chicago newspaper alleged that Otero was "very bitter against the government and intended to arouse these simple people to rebellion."[36] Charges of Otero's disloyalty to the Union dogged him throughout the Civil War and afterward. Once, Union soldiers arrested Otero because, according to his son, "Some of my father's political enemies in New Mexico had proffered certain charges against him to the military authorities at Leavenworth [Kansas]." However, Otero was released based on "the findings of the Santa Fe Military Court, as well as a personal letter from General [Edwin S.] Canby, which completely exonerated him."[37]

In 1864 Otero left New Mexico to pursue business interests in Kansas City and in Leavenworth, where he worked as a silent partner in a forwarding and commission firm. In 1867 Otero, with his brother Manuel, and Scottish immigrant John Perry Sellar formed one of the largest merchandising firms in the Southwest: Otero, Sellar, and Company. Otero retired from the business in 1871 but remained active in the company up to 1881.[38] In the 1870s, Otero served as an agent for the Atchison, Topeka, and Santa Fe Railroad, lobbying on its behalf before the New Mexico territorial government. In this position, he continued to pursue one of his goals in Congress: bringing major railroads through New Mexico to spur economic development. He also served on the board of directors of the New Mexico and Southern Pacific Railroad Company and arranged for its passage through the territory. Eventually, Otero and Sellar, among others, incorporated the San Miguel National Bank in Las Vegas, New Mexico, in 1879.[39] Returning to New Mexico in the 1870s, Otero was a stakeholder in the Maxwell Land Grant, one of the largest land grants in New Mexico.[40] According to his son, Otero, Sr., continued to dabble in politics when he lived briefly in Colorado. He was elected county treasurer of Las Animas County, Colorado, although a deputy served in his place. Otero was nominated for lieutenant governor.[41]

In the summer of 1880, the Democratic Party prevailed upon Otero to run for the Delegate's seat in the 47th Congress (1881–1883), but he lost to Tranquilino Luna, a successful entrepreneur. Much of the campaign took on a generational bent as Otero, a first-generation assimilationist, faced a younger competitor who was comfortable in the *Hispano* and the Anglo communities of the territory. Luna's supporters criticized Otero's 1850s career, particularly his Southern sympathies, as well as his

departure from New Mexico in the 1860s to pursue his business interests, and Luna highlighted Otero's failure to protect land grants that *Hispano* landowners lost under U.S. rule. Also, Otero's age was considered a strike against him. In a close election, Luna won 52 to 48 percent.[42] Less than two years later, on May 30, 1882, Otero died in Las Vegas, New Mexico, from complications of pneumonia.[43]

FOR FURTHER READING

Biographical Directory of the United States Congress, "Miguel Antonio Otero (Sr.)," http://bioguide.congress.gov.

Ganaway, Loomis Morton. "Otero and the New Mexico Slave Code of 1859," in *New Mexico and the Sectional Crisis, 1846–1861* (Philadelphia, PA: Porcupine Press, 1976; reprint of 1944 edition): 60–76.

Otero, Miguel Antonio, Jr., *My Life on the Frontier, 1864–1882* (Albuquerque: University of New Mexico Press, 1987; reprint of 1935 edition).

Otero, Miguel Antonio, Sr., *The Indian Depredations in the Territory of New Mexico* (Washington, D.C.: n.p., 1859).

_____. *Address to the People of New Mexico* (Santa Fe, NM: n.p., 1860).

_____. *An Abolition Attack upon New Mexico, and a Reply by the Hon. M. A. Otero* (Santa Fe, NM: n.p., 1861).

Speer, William S. and John Henry Brown, eds., *The Encyclopedia of the American West* (Easley, SC: Southern Historical Press, 1978; reprint of 1881 edition): 30–32.

MANUSCRIPT COLLECTIONS

Harvard University, Graduate School of Business Administration (Cambridge, MA). Has credit reports on Miguel Otero and Otero, Sellar, & Co.

New Mexico State Library (Santa Fe). *Papers*: Felipe Chavez Papers, 1810–1913, 2.5 linear feet. Subjects include Miguel Otero.

University of New Mexico Library, Special Collections (Albuquerque), Gross, Kelly, & Company Collection. Contains business records of Otero, Sellar & Co.

NOTES

1 Otero was the longest-serving Hispanic-American Member in the 19th century based on the length of his service from the time of his swearing-in (4 years, 8 months, and 13 days). By the same method of calculation, Gallegos (who was not seated as a new Member until December 19, 1853, because of an election challenge) is by a narrow margin the second-longest-serving Hispanic-American Member in the 19th century (4 years, 7 months, and 4 days).

2 Alvin R. Sunseri, *Seeds of Discord: New Mexico in the Aftermath of the American Conquest, 1846–1861* (Chicago, IL: Nelson-Hall, 1979): 133.

3 Some biographers suggest that Otero's parents were born in Spain, but this seems unlikely since a study examining records of Catholic marriages that took place in New Mexico between 1693 and 1846 found that just 10 persons out of more than 13,000 listed Spain as their parents' birthplace. See Laura E. Gómez, *Manifest Destinies: The Making of the Mexican American Race* (New York: New York University Press, 2007): 98.

4 Mark L. Gardner, "Otero, Miguel Antonio," *American National Biography* 16 (New York: Oxford University Press, 1999): 822–823 (hereinafter referred to as *ANB*); "Miguel A. Otero" in Maurilio E. Vigil, *Los Patrones: Profiles of Hispanic Political Leaders in New Mexico History* (Washington, D.C.: University Press of America, 1980): 45–48; Miguel Otero, Jr., to Ansel Wold, 26 May 1927, textual files of the *Biographical Directory of the United States Congress*, Office of the Historian, U.S. House of Representatives (hereinafter referred to as textual files of the *Biographical Directory of the United States Congress*); Carlos Brazil Ramirez, "The Hispanic Political Elite in Territorial New Mexico: A Study of Classical Colonialism," (Ph.D. diss., University of California–Santa Barbara, 1979): 274. Otero had two brothers, Antonio José and Manuel Antonio. In his memoir, Otero, Jr., asserts that his father graduated from St. Louis University in 1849, although this is not confirmed by other sources. However, in a 5 April 1926 letter in the *Biographical Directory* files, Otero, Jr., states that his father graduated from Fishkill in 1852.

5 Miguel Antonio Otero, Jr., *My Life on the Frontier, 1864–1882* (Albuquerque: University of New Mexico Press, 1987; reprint of 1935 edition): 284–285.

6 Gardner, "Otero, Miguel Antonio," *ANB*; "Miguel A. Otero," in Vigil, *Los Patrones*: 46; Otero, *My Life on the Frontier, 1864–1882*: 285.

7 Gardner, "Otero, Miguel Antonio," *ANB*; Gómez, *Manifest Destinies: The Making of the Mexican American Race*: 98; "Hon. Miguel A. Otero," in William S. Speer and John Henry Brown, eds., *The Encyclopedia of the New West* (Easley, SC: Southern Historical Press, 1978; reprint of 1881 edition): 30–32; Otero, Jr., to Wold, textual files of the *Biographical Directory of the United States Congress*. Gardner questions whether Otero served as attorney general under Governor David Meriwether's administration, noting that while his son Miguel, Jr., claims he did, Gardner's sources did not confirm this. An 1881 biography states that President Franklin Pierce offered Otero the position of U.S. Attorney in 1851 but that Otero declined. Gardner also differs from the 1881 biography

on the location of Otero's first law practice; whereas Gardner and Otero, Jr., report the location as Albuquerque, Otero's 1881 biographer reports that the office was in Valencia County.

8 Howard R. Lamar, *The Far Southwest, 1846–1912: A Territorial History*, rev. ed. (Albuquerque: University of New Mexico Press, 2000): 88–89; Robert W. Larson, *New Mexico's Quest for Statehood, 1846–1912* (Albuquerque: University of New Mexico Press, 1968): 29–30, 69–74. Lamar and Larson describe the political split between the New Mexicans who wanted immediate statehood and those who preferred a territorial government. Pro-statehood advocates formed a faction under Richard Weightman, New Mexico's first Territorial Delegate, and pro-territory advocates united under Judge Joab Houghton. The Weightman faction tried to promote *nuevomexicano* politicians for political office, but the Houghton faction promoted primarily Anglo candidates. Larson writes that "the Spanish-speaking majority … was hurt more than any other group by the political divisions and feuds" as one faction "scornfully exploited the Hispanos, and the other patronizingly sought their votes." The Weightman and Houghton factions fought for control of New Mexican politics through elections for Territorial Delegate and patronage appointments for the remainder of the 1850s.

9 Sunseri, *Seeds of Discord*: 133.

10 "Results of the Election for Delegate," 22 September 1855, *Santa Fe Weekly Gazette*: 2; Gerlald A. Theisen, "José Manuel Gallegos (1815–1875): The First Mexican-American in the United States Congress," (Ph.D. diss., University of New Mexico, 1985): 107–110.

11 For the House Election Committee's report on the Otero-Gallegos case, see House Miscellaneous Document no. 57, *Cases of Contested Elections in Congress, from 1834 to 1865, Inclusive*, 38th Cong., 2nd sess. (1865): 177–185. Otero's principal complaint about Mexican citizens voting for Gallegos is on pp. 178–179. For more information on the case, see Theisen, "José Manuel Gallegos (1815–1875)": 107–114; Chester H. Rowell, *A Historical and Legal Digest of All the Contested Election Cases in the House of Representatives of the United States from the First to the Fifty-Sixth Congress, 1789–1901* (Westport, CT: Greenwood Press, 1976; reprint of 1901 edition): 144–145.

12 *Cases of Contested Elections in Congress, from 1834 to 1865, Inclusive*: 179.

13 *Congressional Globe*, House, 34th Cong., 1st sess. (23 July 1856): 1730–1732.

14 Ibid., 1734.

15 Ibid., 1736.

16 Gardner, "Otero, Miguel Antonio," *ANB*; Sunseri, *Seeds of Discord*: 133.

17 "Bills and Propositions for New Mexico," 28 February 1857, *Santa Fe Weekly Gazette*: 2; Otero, "Address of Hon. Miguel Antonio Otero to His Fellow Citizens of New Mexico." For a detailed argument for building an intercontinental railroad through New Mexico, see Miguel Otero, "Pacific Railroad," in *Congressional Globe*, Appendix, 35th Cong., 1st sess. (25 May 1858): 415–418.

18 For more information about Baird, see Clarence Wharton, "Spruce McCoy Baird," *New Mexico Historical Review* 27, no. 4 (October 1952): 300–314.

19 "Baird and Otero," 11 July 1857, *Santa Fe Weekly Gazette*: 2.

20 "Mr. Otero and a State Government," 29 August 1857, *Santa Fe Weekly Gazette*: 2.

21 Sunseri, *Seeds of Discord*: 134. The official results were 8,498 votes for Otero and 5,986 for Baird. See Certified Election Results of 1857 Territorial Delegate Race in "Copy of Executive Journal of the Territory of New Mexico from the 1st Day of December 1856, to the 30th Day of November 1857, Inclusive," in Department of State Territorial Papers, New Mexico, 1851–1872 (National Archives Microfilm Publication T17, Roll 1), General Records of the Department of State, Record Group 59, National Archives at College Park, College Park, MD (NACP). One scholar attributes Baird's defeat to "his former relations with Texas and … having held a territorial appointment under the whig administration" of President Millard Fillmore. See also Loomis Morton Ganaway, "Otero and the New Mexico Slave Code of 1859," in *New Mexico and the Sectional Controversy, 1846–1861* (Philadelphia, PA: Porcupine Press, 1976; reprint edition): 62.

22 "The Result," 24 September 1859, *Santa Fe Weekly Gazette*: 2–3. The results of the vote are illegible in the English section of the newspaper, but the Spanish section states that Otero won by 1,169 votes. ("Cuando nuestros lectores sepan que el Hon. M. A. Otero ha sido re-electo por la mayoria larga de 1169 votos.") The National Archives' Center for Legislative Archives could not locate Otero's 1859 election certificate, nor were the certified election results preserved in the Department of State Territorial Papers, New Mexico, 1851–1872 (T17, Roll 2), RG 59, NACP. Therefore, the *Santa Fe Weekly Gazette* articles may be the only existing primary source for the results of the 1859 elections for Territorial Delegate in New Mexico.

23 Sunseri, *Seeds of Discord*: 134.

24 "Conseguir un correo semi-mensual de Santa Fé a Independencia … Además un correo seminario [*sic*] de Santa Fé a los [*sic*] Cruces." "Miguel Otero, Sr., Cámara de Representantes," 28 March 1857, *Weekly Gazette* (Santa Fe, NM): 2. Translated as "House of Representatives" by Translations International, Inc. (December 2009). Although Otero describes his success in this letter, there is no indication that his proposed bills passed. Throughout the 35th Congress, Otero submitted a number of bills that were referred to committees and quietly shelved. For examples, see *Congressional Globe*, House, 35th Cong., 1st sess. (20 January 1858): 346; and *Congressional Globe*, House, 35th Cong., 2nd sess. (23 December 1859): 200. However, New Mexico received a number

of appropriations for the construction of roads between major settlements, smaller towns, and military forts. See *Congressional Globe*, Appendix, 35th Cong., 1st sess.: 579.

25 Theisen, "José Manuel Gallegos (1815–1875)": 120–124; Lamar, *The Far Southwest, 1846–1912*: 90–91. Lamar notes that "Otero's election symbolized the ever-shifting center of power in New Mexico. Where Delegates [Richard] Weightman and Gallegos played second fiddle to the governor or depended upon others to help them, Otero was a man of ability and many projects. As a Democrat with Southern connections, he stood ready to forward the course of the South."

26 Historians disagree about the motivation for New Mexico's adoption of a slave code in 1859. Traditionally, scholars have viewed the territory's position on slavery as a calculated decision made to promote its chances for statehood. Initially inclined toward an antislavery position, territorial leadership assumed a pro-slavery tilt during the 1850s, largely to cultivate powerful Southern leaders in Congress. More recently, scholars have argued that the slave codes legalizing black chattel slavery were adopted principally because of *nuevomexicano* elites' interest in protecting the long-standing and far more extensive practices of Indian slavery and peonage. But while making this argument, Laura Gómez concedes that Otero's position on slavery also was likely influenced by larger, national interests. See Gómez, *Manifest Destinies*: 100, 104; Larson, *New Mexico's Quest for Statehood, 1846–1912*: 64–65.

27 Theisen, "José Manuel Gallegos (1815–1875)": 124–127; Sunseri, *Seeds of Discord*: 134–135; Gómez, *Manifest Destinies*: 100–101. Gómez cites an alternative explanation from Estévan Rael-Gálvez, who argues that New Mexico legislators "enacted a slave code that legalized black chattel slavery in order to better protect their real interest in slavery—the enslavement of Indians taken captive from nomadic tribes and sold into Mexican households." See Estévan Rael-Gálvez, "Identifying and Capturing Identity: Narratives of American Indian Slavery, Colorado, and New Mexico, 1776–1934," (Ph.D. diss., University of Michigan, 2003). But Gómez cites an even more basic impulse, self-protection, behind the legislation: "Given the fragility to Mexican Americans' claims to whiteness, Mexican elites' actions regarding African Americans can credibly be seen as a means of distancing themselves from the group undeniably at the bottom of the American racial order."

28 Ganaway, "Otero and the New Mexico Slave Code of 1859": 67–68; Gómez, *Manifest Destinies*: 100, writes that Jackson was the "likely author" of the code.

29 Ganaway, "Otero and the New Mexico Slave Code of 1859": 69–76; Sunseri, *Seeds of Discord*: 117–119. The code did not survive very long. A repeal measure was submitted during the 1859–1860 session of the territorial assembly. With the start of the Civil War in 1861, the slave code was repealed by the assembly. In Washington, Representative John Bingham of Ohio introduced a bill on February 16, 1860, to declare it null and void. A further provision of the bill would have nullified the peonage law. Although the bill passed the House based on strict party lines, it died in the Senate Committee on Territories. For a detailed discussion about *nuevomexicano* elites and American Indian slavery in New Mexico, see Gómez, *Manifest Destinies*: 105–112. Gómez notes that when the territorial slave code passed, 34 of the 37 New Mexico territorial legislators were *nuevomexicanos* (p. 102). See also "The New Mexico Territorial Assembly, 1858–1859," *New Mexico Historical Review*, 37, no. 1 (January 1962): 77–80.

30 Lamar, *The Far Southwest: 1846–1912: A Territorial History*: 91.

31 Gardner, "Otero, Miguel Antonio," *ANB*.

32 "From Washington City," 8 December 1860, *Santa Fe Weekly Gazette*: 2.

33 Gardner, "Otero, Miguel Antonio," *ANB*; "Miguel A. Otero," in Vigil, *Los Patrones*: 46; Otero, *My Life on the Frontier*: 1–2; Otero, Jr., to Wold, textual files of the *Biographical Directory of the United States Congress*. Although the Lincoln administration sought to retain Otero's allegiance to the Union, there is conflicting information about the positions he was offered. According to Vigil, President Lincoln offered Otero an appointment as minister to Spain, but Otero declined, preferring to serve as secretary of the territory. According to information supplied by Miguel Otero, Jr., the *Biographical Directory of the United States Congress* notes that Otero served as territorial secretary and acting governor for one year; there are no primary sources to corroborate this claim. In fact, according to Otero, Jr.'s memoirs, his father refused the appointment to concentrate on his firm, which included banking, wholesale, and retailing.

34 Miguel A. Otero to Henry H. Seward, 1 September 1861, Department of State Territorial Papers, New Mexico, 1851–1872 (T17, Roll 2), RG 59, NACP.

35 Gardner, "Otero, Miguel Antonio," *ANB*; Jerry D. Thompson, *Henry Hopkins Sibley: Confederate General of the West* (College Station: Texas A&M Press, 1996): 275.

36 "Our New Mexico Letter," 13 January 1862, *Chicago Tribune*: 2. The article alleges that Otero sent this letter while he was under consideration for secretary of New Mexico Territory in early 1861. The writer further alleges that the article was "distributed in pamphlet form in the Spanish language and distributed by Otero all over the Territory.... For obvious reasons these were never printed in English."

37 Otero, Jr., *My Life on the Frontier, 1864–1882*: 4–5.

38 Gardner, "Otero, Miguel Antonio," *ANB*; Lamar, *The Far Southwest: 1846–1912*: 125–126; Otero, Jr., to Wold, textual files of the *Biographical Directory of the United States Congress*. For more information about the Otero, Sellar Company, see Daniel T. Kelly, *The Buffalo Head: A Century of Mercantile Pioneering in the Southwest* (Santa Fe, NM: Vergara Publishing Company, 1972): especially pp. 3–34.

39 Ramirez, "The Hispanic Political Elite in Territorial New Mexico: A Study of Classical Colonialism," 280–282; Otero, Jr., *My Life on the Frontier, 1864–1882*: 268–269. For more on Otero's numerous business dealings, see Gardner, "Otero, Miguel Antonio," *ANB*; Lamar, *The Far Southwest, 1846–1912*: 125–126, 153. Lamar credits Otero with helping to establish and charter the New Mexico and Southern Pacific Railroad. As for his own firm, Lamar writes, "The Atchison, Topeka, and Santa Fe celebrated its entrance into New Mexico on January 1, 1879, at which time Vice-President Otero drove a golden spike into a tie that lay on the Colorado-New Mexico line." (Gardner writes that Otero drove in the golden spike in December 1878.) Otero, Jr., claims that his father refused money for his hard work and that when urged to submit a bill for his services, Otero, Sr., declined, saying, "I was working for New Mexico, and I am satisfied if my Territory gets the benefit of my labors."

40 Lamar, *The Far Southwest, 1846–1912: A Territorial History*: 125–126.

41 Otero, Jr., to Wold, textual files of the *Biographical Directory of the United States Congress*.

42 Otero, Jr., *My Life on the Frontier*: 270–273; W. G. Ritch, *The Legislative Blue-Book of the Territory of New Mexico* (Albuquerque: University of New Mexico Press, 1968; reprint of 1882 edition): 93. The official vote count was 10,385 for Luna to Otero's 9,562.

43 "The Distinguished Dead," 2 June 1882, *Rocky Mountain News*: 4.

Francisco Perea
1830–1913

TERRITORIAL DELEGATE 1863–1865
REPUBLICAN FROM NEW MEXICO

Francisco Perea capitalized on his family's prominence and his military service to propel his career in territorial and national politics. The first Republican Hispanic-American Member of Congress, he dedicated his single term as Territorial Delegate to serving his constituents and containing the Indian threat to settlers by championing a controversial reservation system.

Perea was born in Las Padillas, New Mexico, on January 9, 1830, to Juan Perea and Josefa Chaves de Perea. Perea's maternal grandfather, Francisco Xavier Chaves, was Mexico's governor of the New Mexico province in the 1820s, and two of Perea's maternal uncles eventually succeeded his grandfather. Perea's father served in the Fourth Departmental Congress in 1846 and in the New Mexico Legislative Assembly in 1852 and 1857. After the U.S. war with Mexico, José Leandro, Perea's paternal uncle, represented Bernalillo County in the First Legislative Assembly. Years later, his cousins Pedro Perea and José Francisco Chaves would serve as New Mexico's Legislative Delegates to the U.S. Congress. Francisco studied at a local Bernalillo school in 1836 and 1837. He and his cousin José Chaves attended a Santa Fe school in 1837 and 1838, and Francisco transferred to a school in Albuquerque the following academic year. From 1839 to 1843, Perea tutored his younger siblings. Like many elite New Mexicans, he received a college education in Missouri, mastering English (again, with his cousin José F. Chaves) at Jesuit College in St. Louis from 1843 to 1845. While the Mexican-American War raged on, Perea traveled to New York City's Bank Street Academy in 1847, completing his studies in 1849. During this sojourn, Perea and a colleague visited East Coast cities including Philadelphia, Baltimore, and Washington, D.C.; they also traveled to northern New York and Chicago.

Perea returned to New Mexico in 1850 to pursue a career in business that included ranching, trade, and commerce. He served as a distributor of manufactured goods to New Mexicans by importing products from cities such as St. Louis, and Independence, Missouri, at the head of the Santa Fe Trail. He also herded sheep to California for sale in the markets. After making a fortune selling sheep, Perea invested in the Atlantic and Pacific Railroad. Perea married twice. He had 18 children with his first wife, Dolores Otero (a niece of Territorial Delegate Miguel Antonio Otero's), whom he wed in 1851, but many of them died in infancy. Dolores died in 1866. In 1875 Perea married Gabriela Montoya, with whom he had 18 more children, but only 10 were living at the time of his death.[1]

Perea entered politics when he was elected to New Mexico's Eighth Legislative Assembly in 1858 for a two-year term representing Bernalillo County.[2] Aside from his pedigree, his motivation to run for political office is unclear. A staunch Republican, Perea considered Abraham Lincoln's election to the presidency in 1860 to be fortuitous for the Union. The news of Lincoln's election, Perea recalled, "was celebrated by immense processions of men and boys marching through the principal streets to the music of many brass bands, the firing of cannon, and the discharging of anvils."[3] Nevertheless, New Mexican loyalties were split between pro-Confederate Democrats and pro-Union Republicans; the territory became a flashpoint for conflict during 1861 and 1862.

In the summer and fall of 1861, Perea advocated for New Mexico to remain in the Union by appealing to "every prominent man in the … territory." In light of New Mexico's precarious condition, Lincoln authorized Governor Henry Connelly to raise two full regiments and four battalions of four companies each. Perea organized a volunteer battalion at his own expense and was commissioned as a regimental lieutenant colonel.[4]

Image courtesy of the National Archives and Records Administration

Dubbed "Perea's Battalion," the unit was stationed near Albuquerque, where its namesake commander led various campaigns against Apaches and Navajos in 1861 and 1862. The battalion also saw action in the Apache Canyon at the Battle of Glorieta Pass, a pivotal engagement that forced the Confederates out of New Mexico in March 1862. Shortly thereafter, Perea resigned his commission and returned to civilian life.[5]

In January 1863, Perea ran for the position of Territorial Delegate to the U.S. House in the 38th Congress (1863–1865), winning the Republican nomination that June. He outlined his proposed legislative priorities in a public letter that was printed in New Mexico newspapers. Perea's experience fighting Indians convinced him that the two cultures could not coexist. He condemned past treaties as "worse than useless," suggesting that American Indians were liable "to do wrong in accordance with the instincts of the savage nature." Justifying his solution—to remove Indians to reservations—he argued, "It will be acting the part of wisdom in our own behalf and the part of philanthropy on behalf of the savages … [there] they may be compelled to earn their subsistence by the labor of their own hands, and have the opportunity given them to cultivate the habits and enjoy the blessings of civilization and Christianity."[6]

The economic leg of his platform was closely associated with suppressing American Indians, particularly the Apaches, because their removal would open more land to settlers and allow the exploitation of New Mexico's mineral resources. Perea believed mining would determine the territory's financial fortunes. "Nothing can give our Territory as much prominence in the eyes of the people throughout the United States as the fact of the existence of rich gold producing mines in our midst," he wrote. To remove the Indians, Perea promised that as Delegate, he would make "every exertion I can put forth … to strengthen the hands of our [military] Department commander and give him sufficient force to expel the savages from the bounteous fields which should now be furnishing profitable employment to thousands of our people."[7]

Perea advised against implementing statehood in the midst of war, noting that the issue might be exploited by "men ambitious of place and power" and arguing that public sentiment did not support it.[8] Nevertheless, he urged continued support for the Lincoln administration, asserting, "It is the duty of all citizens to occupy themselves with the stern realities with which we are confronted and do all in their power to maintain the integrity of the government." He left no doubt that as Delegate, he would exert "the whole of my influence … in favor of the reestablishment of the Union as it was and the enforcement of the constitution as it is."[9]

Perea's opponents were José Manuel Gallegos and Judge Joab Houghton, a former chief justice of the superior court under New Mexico's military government and an associate of Miguel Otero's brother Antonio José.[10] Houghton dropped out of the race in July 1863 and threw his support to Perea.[11] Gallegos, a prominent but controversial priest-turned-politician, served as a Territorial Delegate in the 33rd and 34th Congresses (1853–1857), but was unseated in his second term after Miguel Otero contested his election. However, Gallegos remained a power in territorial politics, serving as speaker in the Tenth, Eleventh, and Twelfth Legislative Assemblies (1860–1862).[12] Although Gallegos ran as a Democrat, he was pro-Union and was imprisoned during the Confederate occupation of Santa Fe, but his party designation left him open to charges of collaborating with secessionists.

Perea's supporters resurrected tactics other territorial politicians had used against Gallegos, advertising his suspension from the Catholic priesthood and his affiliation with a cadre of activist priests before the American occupation. A seamy campaign poem entitled *El Padrecillo* ("The Father"), circulated by Perea's backers, mocked Gallegos's connections to administrative corruption and his obliviousness to such ethical lapses. The poem also publicized Gallegos's controversial relationship with Candelaria Montoya, a widow.[13] According to one account, Perea visited nearly every part of the territory and frequently spoke to crowds.[14] The initial results showed that Perea won the election, with 7,231 votes to Gallegos's 6,425.[15] However, a variety of seeming irregularities in various

counties persuaded Republican governor Henry Connelly to have "the vote reconstructed from the tallies kept by election officials in the precincts, and these were tabulated in place of the actual ballots." The recount confirmed Perea's majority.[16] Gallegos and his supporters contested the results, arguing that Connelly had exceeded his authority, but when Gallegos was denied an extension to obtain more testimony from voters, his case fell apart, and the House Committee on Elections awarded the seat to Perea.[17]

Like the other Delegates of the era, Perea was not permitted to sit on a standing committee when he was sworn in to the 38th Congress (1863–1865). Nevertheless, he submitted bills regarding a range of constituent services and personal legislative interests; but because Republicans controlled the chamber and tended to support the development of national infrastructure, Perea's initiatives enjoyed only modest success.[18] In early 1864, Perea requested funds to construct a military road between Taos, New Mexico, and the territorial capital of Santa Fe. Another measure requested financial aid for communities in the New Mexico Territory and the newly created Arizona Territory, and a third measure asked for the implementation of boundaries between the New Mexico, Colorado, and Arizona Territories. Perea responded to the needs of military veterans by submitting private relief bills and requesting payments for volunteer companies that served against hostile Indian tribes and in the Mexican-American War. All the bills were read and submitted to the appropriate committees, but no action was taken.[19] Perea tried to secure money for surveying land in New Mexico in H.R. 786, a miscellaneous appropriations bill, but he was unsuccessful.[20] True to his campaign promise, he took particular interest in a Senate bill that requested "aid in the settlement, subsistence, and support of the Navajo Indian captives upon a reservation in the Territory of New Mexico." The bill mustered enough votes to pass, but Senator William Windom of Minnesota killed it using a parliamentary tactic.[21]

During his tenure, Perea became close friends with President Lincoln, to whom he was introduced by former New Mexico Territorial Delegate John S. Watts in 1864. "I met the President in the White House, in company with a number of senators, representatives, and others," Perea recalled. Perea went to see Lincoln "time after time on business connected with complaints against [territorial] officials and other difficulties." Perea reported that he "occupied the seat in the pit of the theater directly under the Lincoln box" on the evening of April 14, 1865. "I heard the shot fired by [John Wilkes] Booth," he said.[22] Also, Perea served as one of three delegates to the Republican National Convention in Baltimore, Maryland, in 1864.[23] According to a contemporary account, Perea "bore aloft the Star Spangled banner, over which streamed a pure white penant bearing … the motto: 'New Mexico–the Union and the Monroe Doctrine forever.' The flag and its motto attracted great attention and elicited loud applause."[24]

Perea used his influence as a Territorial Delegate to persuade federal officials in Washington, D.C., to attack political opponents and promote the careers of his allies back home. During the contested election case, Perea wrote a number of letters to Secretary of State William H. Seward about the professional conduct of William F. M. Arny, the territorial secretary and a committed ally of José Manuel Gallegos. In one letter, Perea enclosed documents alleging that Arny's performance had alienated constituents. Perea also noted that Arny had "undertaken to come to Washington with(out) leave" from territorial superiors to hire lawyers to represent Gallegos in February 1864.[25] A month later, Perea informed Seward about Arny's support of Gallegos, neglecting to tell him about Governor Connelly's relationship with the Perea family. Perea wrote, "It becomes obvious beyond question, that he has been not only instrumental in exciting a contest for my seat in Congrefs, but that the principal object … is to act as an agent in behalf of the contestant." Perea considered Arny's conduct "reprehensible, in disturbing the political quietude of the Territory by agitating this contest, after the voice of the people had spoken and their decision had been announced in the form of law" and asked that he be removed.[26]

Early in 1865, Perea became involved in a dispute between the New Mexico and Colorado Territories concerning The Conejos, a large tract of land on New Mexico's northern border that was ceded to Colorado upon its incorporation in 1861. In a published letter to James Ashley of Ohio, Chairman of the House Committee on Territories, Perea alleged that "the sole purpose of such a severance was to give evenness and symmetry to the southern boundary of Colorado … at the serious expense of New Mexico." Perea noted that the "population of Los Conejos … are almost entirely Mexicans. They are foreign in language … from the great body of the people of Colorado. The laws of that Territory are enacted and published only in the English language, which they do not understand and the legislative discussions and deliberations are conducted in the same language." Perea emphasized the Conejans' foreignness, their affinity for Spanish institutions, and their incompatibility with Colorado Anglos and American jurisprudence. He deemed the situation "utterly repugnant to the true principles of liberty" and requested its immediate amelioration.[27]

Perea insisted that New Mexican citizenship would satisfy the cultural aspirations of the Conejans. He noted that one of the earliest acts of the New Mexico territorial government was to declare "that the principles of the civil law should prevail in all civil causes that might arise before their courts; and the Congress of the United States, in approving that legislation … manifested its appreciation of their desire to preserve and perpetuate their ancient and venerated system of jurisprudence."[28] New Mexicans, Perea maintained, were uniquely suited to managing this still-foreign people. Although "they have formed a patriotic fondness for this government, and are now earned and true in their allegiance to their new sovereign, the change was not a matter of their own choice. The acquisition of their country was the fruit of war waged by the United States against their native land, and by every consideration of justice and humanity they are entitled to the enjoyment of their native language, and their system of law and domestic usages, so long … as they do not conflict with the principles of the general government." Perea submitted the bill in the waning weeks of the session, and the Committee on Territories did not act on it. After acquiring the region, Colorado retained it through its territorial period (1861–1876); today Los Conejos remains part of that state.[29]

Perea began running for re-election in January 1865. In a glowing editorial, the *Santa Fe Weekly Gazette* noted that he had been a highly effective legislator and had stood firm in his support of the Lincoln administration. While admitting Perea's "efforts have secured but very meager appropriations—sums far below the amounts obtained by his predecessors," the editors blamed the war for siphoning off federal funds. Alluding to the tempestuous tenures of earlier Territorial Delegates, they appealed to constituents to keep Perea in office because he was experienced. In an effort to defuse potential contenders' use of a native-son platform, the editors suggested that replacing Perea would be "unfair to the Mexican people as a race" because it would deprive New Mexicans of an incumbent with seniority. Other Members of Congress "are possessed of advantages which the New Mexican people are unwilling to give to their own sons," they wrote. If Perea "is successfully opposed by a native, that native will be no further advanced than his predecessor.… Thus always we shall have inexperienced Representatives, and so always be subjected to the same imputation and disadvantages."[30] To Perea, the editors wrote, "[You are] worthy of our confidence; you have done your work well and are entitled to the reward of re-election to the place which for two years you have so worthily filled."[31] Perea responded that he was "grateful to the public for past favors" [and] would "endeavor to continue to merit their approbation" upon being re-elected.[32]

Perea's acceptance letter for the Republican nomination in July 1865 outlined his successes and his plans for another term. Adopting the party platform, he acknowledged that much of his energy was focused on containing "our deadly enemies" the Navajo Indians. As part of that platform, he embraced a developing military-led effort to forcibly remove Navajos to a reservation known as the Bosque Redondo in eastern New Mexico. Perea noted, "I have steadfastly, in Congress, before the Committees on Indian Affairs in both Houses and before the Interior and War Departments of the Government, advocated the policy which is now observed of keeping that tribe on the Reservation at the Bosque Redondo." After vigorously defending the policy, he added, "Those who oppose the Government in its efforts to thus relieve us of our despoilers are the worst enemies the Territory can have." If he was re-elected for another term, Perea promised, "I shall continue to use all the influence I possess to have the reservation system made permanent and in this way, secure lasting peace with the Indians."[33]

Perea's principal election opponent was his cousin, José Francisco Chaves. Although both men were Republicans, they represented distinct territorial factions. Perea was nominated to lead the Union Party ticket. Unionists, explains historian Howard Lamar, "supported the Indian reservation policy ... praised General [James H.] Carleton and the troops participating in the Indian campaigns, recognized the supremacy of the United States Government, and condemned Abraham Lincoln's assassination." Chaves was an Administration Party candidate. The Administration faction's loyalties were identical to those of Unionists, but they opposed Carleton's policy of forcing the Navajos onto the Bosque Redondo Reservation.[34]

Perea noted that although he and Chaves were "connected by the most endearing ties of consanguinity," his cousin had "allowed himself to pass into the hands of my enemies, the enemies of my political friends and, as I hold, the enemies of the Territory."[35] The campaign hinged on the Bosque Redondo Reservation experiment. Perea fully supported its expansion, whereas Chaves opposed it. Chaves also criticized Perea's efforts to regain Los Conejos. Throughout the summer of 1865, Perea's political standing suffered from his association with the controversial General Carleton, who was eventually removed from his post.[36] Chaves prevailed, with a 58 to 42 percent victory.[37]

Afterward, Perea returned to his business activities in New Mexico and, according to his eulogist W. H. H. Allison, retained a large amount of political influence by controlling federal appointments to the territory under President Andrew Johnson's administration. Later, Perea was elected to the territory's Sixteenth and Twenty-Sixth Legislative Assemblies (1866–1867 and 1886–1887, respectively) as a representative of Bernalillo County. In 1881 Perea owned and operated a resort hotel in Jemez Springs, New Mexico, where he also served as postmaster from 1894 to 1905. Perea died in Albuquerque at age 83 on May 31, 1913.[38]

FOR FURTHER READING

Allison, W. H. H. "Colonel Francisco Perea," in Ralph Emerson Twitchell, ed., *Old Santa Fe: A Magazine of History, Archaeology, Genealogy, and Biography* 1, no. 2 (October 1913): 210–222.

Biographical Directory of the United States Congress, "Francisco Perea," http://bioguide.congress.gov.

NOTES

1 "Francisco Perea," in Maurilio E. Vigil, *Los Patrones: Profiles of Hispanic Political Leaders in New Mexico History* (Washington, D.C.: University Press of America, 1980): 53–55; "Francisco Perea," in Matt S. Meier, *Mexican American Biographies: A Historical Dictionary, 1836–1987* (Westport, CT: Greenwood Press, 1988): 175; W. H. H. Allison, "Francisco Perea, Delegate to 38th Congress, Dies at Home Here," 22 May 1913, *Albuquerque Morning Journal*: 1. This obituary was reprinted verbatim in W. H. H. Allison, "Colonel Francisco Perea," in Ralph Emerson Twitchell, ed., *Old Santa Fe: A Magazine of History, Archaeology, Genealogy, and Biography*, vol. 1, no. 2 (October 1913): 210–222. See also Carlos Brazil Ramirez, "The Hispanic Political Elite in Territorial New Mexico: A Study of Classical Colonialism," (Ph.D. diss., University of California–Santa Barbara, 1979): 274, 285.

2 W. G. Ritch, *The Legislative Blue Book of the Territory of New Mexico* (Albuquerque: University of New Mexico Press, 1968; reprint of 1882 edition): 105–106.

3 Allison, "Francisco Perea, Delegate to 38th Congress."

4 Ibid.

5 "Francisco Perea," in Vigil, *Los Patrones*: 53–55; Ralph Emerson Twitchell, ed., *Leading Facts of New Mexican History*, vol. 2 (Cedar Rapids, IA: Torch Press, 1912): 399–400; Allison, "Francisco Perea, Delegate to 38th Congress." According to Twitchell, Perea "engaged in repairing his houses and fortune, both of which had been severely wrecked by the invading Texans" during 1863.

6 Francisco Perea, "To the People of New Mexico," 13 June 1863, *Santa Fe Weekly Gazette*: 2.

7 Perea, "To the People of New Mexico."

8 Ibid.

9 Ibid.

10 For a brief biography of Houghton, see Twitchell, *Leading Facts of New Mexico History*, vol. 2: 272–273, 398–399.

11 "The Canvass for Delegate," 4 July 1863, *Santa Fe Weekly Gazette*: 2.

12 Ritch, *The Legislative Blue Book of New Mexico*: 107–109; *Biographical Directory of the United States Congress*, "José Manuel Gallegos," http://bioguide.congress.gov.

13 "The Canvass for Delegate." The *Santa Fe Weekly Gazette* described Gallegos as a "disgraced priest, adulterer, sacreligist, [and] trickster."

14 Allison, "Francisco Perea, Delegate to 38th Congress." Some of Gallegos's supporters "had favored the dissolution of the union of the state, and later had welcomed the advent into the territory of the Texas Rangers."

15 Certified Election Results of New Mexico Delegate's Race, Copy of Record of Executive Proceedings of the Territory of New Mexico from the 10th Day of November 1862 to the 28th Day of October 1863, Department of State Territorial Papers, New Mexico, 1851–1872 (National Archives Microfilm Publication T17, Roll 2), General Records of the Department of State, Record Group 59, National Archives at College Park, College Park, MD (NACP).

16 Gerald Arthur Theisen, "Jose Manuel Gallegos (1815–75): The First Mexican-American in the United States Congress," (Ph.D. diss., University of New Mexico, 1985): 132–143. Theisen writes that votes for one county could not be counted because the poll books were burned.

17 Chester H. Rowell, *A Historical and Legal Digest of All the Contested Election Cases in the House of Representatives of the United States from the First to the Fifty-Sixth Congress, 1789–1901* (Westport, CT: Greenwood Press, 1976; reprint of 1901 edition): 188; Theisen, "Jose Manuel Gallegos (1815–75)": 144–145.

18 For an overview of Congress's activities during the Civil War, see Mark Neely, "The Civil War," in Julian Zelizer, ed., *The American Congress: The Building of Democracy* (New York: Houghton Mifflin, 2004): 207–223.

19 *Congressional Globe*, House, 38th Cong., 1st sess. (11 January 1864): 149–150; *Congressional Globe*, House, 38th Cong., 1st sess. (5 April 1864): 1425; *Congressional Globe*, House, 38th Cong., 1st sess. (11 April 1864): 1532; *Congressional Globe*, House, 38th Cong., 1st sess. (10 May 1864): 2207. For a summary of Perea's legislative activities, see "Col. Perea," 30 January 1864, *Santa Fe Weekly Gazette*: 2.

20 *Congressional Globe*, House, 38th Cong., 2nd sess. (1 March 1865): 1260. Perea objected to New Mexico's allocation of $5,000 because the Colorado Territory (part of which belonged to New Mexico prior to its creation in 1861) was receiving $15,000 for its surveys. Perea pointed out, "New Mexico is paying $150,000 a year in the United States Treasury, while in Colorado … there is not even a collector of revenue yet." However, Delegate Hiram Bennet of Colorado argued, "Surveys have not been ordered in Colorado … for two years previous to this appropriation." He also noted, "New Mexico has a large amount of private lands, and consequently there is less of the public domain [there] than in Colorado." Perea withdrew his amendment after Bennet's explanation.

21 *Congressional Globe*, House, 38th Cong., 1st sess. (29 June 1864): 3389. Perea supported and tried to acquire appropriations for the Bosque Redondo Reservation experiment and took credit for his efforts in "Col. Perea's Acceptance," 8 July 1865, *Santa Fe Weekly Gazette*: 2. For background, see Peter Iverson, *Diné: A History of the Navajos* (Albuquerque: University of New Mexico Press, 2002).

22 "Mr. Lincoln Was Always Intensely Interested in Affairs of New Mexico," 12 February 1909, *Albuquerque Morning Journal*: 1, 2.

23 Allison, "Francisco Perea, Delegate to 38th Congress": 1. Allison claims that in 1864 New Mexico "was for the first time represented in a national convention." However, Miguel Otero had attended the Democratic National Convention in Charleston, South Carolina, in 1860.

24 "From Washington City," 23 July 1864, *Santa Fe Weekly Gazette*: 2; Allison, "Francisco Perea, Delegate to 38th Congress." Perea's obituary states that he attended the Republican National Convention with two other delegates from New Mexico, "which was for the first time represented in a national convention."

25 Francisco Perea to William H. Seward, 20 February 1864, Department of State Territorial Papers, New Mexico, 1851–1872, RG 59, NACP. Gallegos authorized Arny to represent him and to hire legal representation when necessary. See José Manuel Gallegos to William F. M. Arny, 6 February 1864, Department of State Territorial Papers, New Mexico, 1851–1872, RG 59, NACP. Perea took particular issue with Arny's "abandonment of his post of duty without lawful permission to come here for the purpose of prosecuting that contest." Perea continued, "And it is still more worthy of condemnation in the assault he has insidiously made … on the rectitude of his co-officials of the Territory, for the purpose of gaining a personal or political end."

26 The spelling "Congrefs" is from Perea's original. Francisco Perea to William H. Seward, 21 March 1864, Department of State Territorial Papers, New Mexico, 1851–1872, RG 59, NACP. Although Perea claimed Arny did not get permission from the governor to visit Washington, José Gallegos wrote that the New Mexico legislative assembly, where Gallegos had a great deal of support, authorized Arny's trip to Washington. See José Manuel Gallegos to William F. M. Arny, 5 February 1864, Department of State Territorial Papers, New Mexico 1851–1872, RG 59, NACP. Perea suggested that the documents he had sent Seward (a memorial from Gallegos and affidavits by Arny confirming Gallegos's election complaints) indicated that Arny had lied to officials in Washington about political developments in the territory. Perea penned additional letters calling for Arny's ouster, but the State Department did not act on his requests. See Francisco Perea to William H. Seward, 26 June 1864, and Francisco Perea to William H. Seward, 6 March 1865, Department of State Territorial Papers,

1851 1872, RG 59, NACP. Arny continued to serve as secretary and also spearheaded the effort to outlaw slavery in the territory. For biographical information about Arny, see Lawrence R. Murphy, *Frontier Crusader: William F. M. Arny* (Tucson: University of Arizona Press, 1972), especially pp. 124–132, for the 1863 contested election case and Perea's complaints to Secretary of State Seward. For information about Arny and slavery in New Mexico, see Alvin R. Sunseri, *Seeds of Discord: New Mexico in the Aftermath of the American Conquest, 1846–1861* (Chicago: Nelson-Hall, 1979): 41–42. For an overview of the period, see Lawrence R. Murphy, "Reconstruction in New Mexico," *New Mexico Historical Review* 43 (April 1968): 99–115.

27 Perea further asserted that the Conejans "can neither take an intelligent part in legislation, nor understand from their laws … either the rights they confer or the obligations they impose; and they must remain in darkness as to the character of the laws under which they live, until the government of the United States shall, at its own great expense, have those laws translated into their native tongue." This lack of understanding "is tantamount to their exclusion from every share in the legislation of the country." See Francisco Perea, "Letter of Hon. Francisco Perea to Hon. Jas M. Ashley, Chairman of the Committee on Territories, of the House of Representatives, Reclaiming a Certain Portion of the Territory of New Mexico, Which Has Been Included in the Boundaries of Colorado," 18 February 1865, *Santa Fe Weekly Gazette*: 1. See also "Shame, Where Is Thy Blush?" 11 March 1865, *Santa Fe Weekly Gazette*: 2.

28 Perea, "Letter of Hon. Francisco Perea to Hon. Jas M. Ashley, Chairman of the Committee on Territories."

29 Ibid. See "The Conejos," 1 July 1865, *Santa Fe Weekly Gazette*: 2; for E. C. Ingersoll's letter to Perea explaining why the bill did not progress. The committee endorsed Perea for re-election to Congress by sending the *Santa Fe Weekly Gazette* a letter attesting to Perea's professionalism and effectiveness as an advocate for New Mexico. For background information about Los Conejos, see Ray C. Colton, *The Civil War in the Western Territories: Arizona, Colorado, New Mexico, and Utah* (Norman: University of Oklahoma Press, 1959): 197–198; William A. Keleher, *Turmoil in New Mexico, 1846–1868* (Santa Fe: Sunstone Press, 2008; reprint of 1952 edition): 126–127. Los Conejos, "being the extreme northern portion of New Mexico, was severed from New Mexico and annexed to the territory of Colorado by act of congress approved February 28, 1861. The sole purpose of the severance, affecting 3,000 native born New Mexicans, was to give evenness and symmetry to the southern boundary of Colorado. Hon. Francisco Perea … belatedly protested against the severance, in a letter written to James M. Ashley, chairman of the Committee on Territories in the House … and attempted to reclaim the lost territory for New Mexico, contending the act of severance had passed without consultation or warning."

30 "Congressional Election," 25 February 1865, *Santa Fe Weekly Gazette*: 2.

31 "Hon. Francisco Perea," 14 January 1865, *Santa Fe Weekly Gazette*: 2. According to the article, Perea secured "$100,000 for the Navajos, nearly $23,000 for the legislative fund, $50,000 for the general and incidental expenses of the Indian Superintendency in the Territory, $25,000 for deficiencies, and other amounts sufficient to keep in operation the various civil offices of the Territory."

32 Francisco Perea, "A Card," 14 January 1865, *Santa Fe Weekly Gazette*: 2. Perea wrote this opinion piece on 6 December 1864.

33 "Col. Perea's Acceptance," 8 July 1865, *Santa Fe Weekly Gazette*: 2.

34 Colton, *The Civil War in the Western Territories*: 197–198; Howard R. Lamar, *The Far Southwest, 1846–1912: A Territorial History*, rev. ed. (Albuquerque: University of New Mexico Press, 2000): 109–112. By the 1864 presidential election, New Mexico Republicans had split into three groups, as Lamar explains, "the regulars, consisting of Governor [Henry] Connelly, Delegate Perea, and Judge John S. Watts, who openly declared for Lincoln; another faction, led by Connelly's own secretary [of the territory], W. F. M. Arny, who supported [Salmon] Chase and the Radicals [Republicans]; and still a third group, who were actually old-time Democrats and wanted [George B.] McClellan for President." By the 1865 Delegate election, Chaves "ran on a pro-Arny and anti-Bosque ticket, while his cousin Francisco Perea … defended the General."

35 Colton, *The Civil War in the Western Territories*: 197–198; Lamar, *The Far Southwest, 1846–1912: A Territorial History*: 109–112; "Col. Perea's Acceptance."

36 Allison, "Francisco Perea, Delegate to 38th Congress"; Martha Durant Read, "Colonel Jose Francisco Chaves: A Short Biography of the Father of the New Mexico Statehood Movement," *Southwest Heritage* 8, no. 4 (Winter 1978–1979): 13–21, 30; for more information about Carleton, see Aurora Hunt, *Maj. Gen. James H. Carleton (1814–73), Western Frontier Dragoon* (Glendale, CA: Arthur H. Clark Company, 1958). The *Santa Fe Weekly Gazette* published a September 1864 letter from Chaves to Perea describing Chaves's opposition to the reservation in "Chavez and the Reservation Question," 5 August 1865, *Santa Fe Weekly Gazette*: 2.

37 Certified Election Results of 1865 Delegate Election, 21 September 1865 entry of Governor's Journal, Copy of the Executive Records of the Territory of New Mexico, Department of State Territorial Papers, New Mexico, 1851–1872, RG 59, NACP. The official totals were 8,571 votes for Chaves and 6,180 votes for Perea.

38 Allison, "Francisco Perea, Delegate to 38th Congress"; Ritch, *New Mexico Blue Book*, 111; Territory of New Mexico, *Report of the Secretary of the Territory, 1905–1906 and Legislative Manual 1907* (Albuquerque, NM: Morning Journal, 1907): 169.

José Francisco Chaves
1833–1904

TERRITORIAL DELEGATE 1865–1867; 1869–1871
REPUBLICAN FROM NEW MEXICO

Like many of his 19th-century contemporaries, three-term Territorial Delegate José Francisco Chaves, used his distinguished military service as a route to political office. A prominent militia commander and a Union officer during the Civil War, Chaves began as a local power broker working with key politicians in Santa Fe. Elected to Congress at the end of the Civil War, Chaves emerged as a strong supporter of New Mexican statehood when he made a memorable speech on the House Floor. In an open letter to constituents, Chaves pointed out the disadvantages of New Mexico's remaining a territorial possession. "You are not the owners of your own laws or of your own servants [political representatives]," Chaves declared. "Therefore, you are not essentially a free people, but rather a subordinate, dependent community, governed … by the pleasure or whim of men who live far from your borders, who in their public actions towards you are sometimes governed by individual influences and rarely act with due concern for your true condition and your needs."[1]

José Francisco Chaves was born on June 27, 1833, in Los Padillas, Bernalillo County, New Mexico, to Mariano Chaves and Dolores Perea. Like their cousins Francisco and Pedro Perea, the Chaves family played a prominent role in New Mexico's military and political affairs. Chaves's paternal grandfather, Francisco Xavier Chaves, was governor of New Mexico after Mexico won its independence from Spain in 1821. Chaves's father was a prominent military officer and an aide to Mexican general Manuel Armijo, who suppressed the Pueblo Revolt of 1837. José Chaves was educated in Chihuahua, Santa Fe, and St. Louis. Like the sons of many elites in New Mexico, Chaves attended college in Missouri, studying at St. Louis University from 1841 to 1846.[2] "The heretics are going to over-run all this country," Mariano Chaves told his son before sending him to St. Louis. "Go and learn their language and come back prepared to defend your people."[3] Chaves returned to New Mexico and may have fought in the Mexican-American War. Afterward, he completed his education in New York, attending private academies in New York City and in Fishkill. He also studied medicine for one year at the College of Physicians and Surgeons in New York City before returning to New Mexico in 1852. From 1853 to 1857, he managed the family ranch. Chaves married Mary Bowie of California in 1857, and they raised a daughter, Lola, and a son, Francisco. After Mary died in 1874, Chaves married Mariana Armijo and adopted her son, James. Mariana passed away in 1895.[4]

Chaves's career in local politics began at the same time he became active in territorial military affairs. In 1859 and 1860, he took part in military expeditions against hostile Navajos, whose attacks on U.S. settlements resulted in approximately 300 deaths and $1.5 million in stolen property. Chaves had been elected to the Ninth Legislative Assembly (1859–1860) as a representative of Valencia County, but because of his military commitment, he served just one term. At the outbreak of the Civil War in 1861, Chaves served as a major in a volunteer regiment of the First New Mexico Infantry to defend the territory against a Confederate army led by General Henry Sibley. During the war, Chaves served at Fort Union, near Santa Fe, and at Fort Craig. He also fought in the Battle of Valverde and in skirmishes near Albuquerque.[5] Chaves was promoted to a lieutenant colonel for his service.

After the Confederates were definitively repulsed in late 1862, the Union Army in the Southwest targeted the Apaches and the Navajos. Chaves led four companies of infantry into lands west of Santa Fe to harass the Navajos and protect U.S. settlers.[6] The goal was to compel their surrender and move them to the newly formed Bosque

Image courtesy of the Miguel A. Otero Photograph Collection (PICT 000-021-0057), Center for Southwest Research, University Libraries, University of New Mexico

Redondo Reservation in eastern New Mexico, an area that was hundreds of miles from Navajo territory. Failure to comply, the army warned, would mean annihilation.[7] Chaves helped establish Fort Wingate, where he assumed command and assisted Colonel Kit Carson to harass and attack the Navajos in the summer of 1863. Years later Chaves recalled, "The instructions which I received from General [James H.] Carleton … were to call in some of their principal [Navajo] men and notify them that a vigorous war would be waged against them for their many depredations against the citizens, and that all those who claimed to be good Indians and who wished to save themselves, their families, and their property, must come … into Fort Wingate, and that they would be transported to the Bosque Redondo … they would be taught to live like the whites … and that they would be fed, cared for, and protected by the Government until they should be capable of doing so themselves."[8] Honorably discharged from the army in 1865 after six years of pacifying the Apaches and Navajos, Chaves publicly criticized the territory's "subjection or destruction" policies, particularly the Bosque Redondo Reservation experiment.[9]

After his discharge, Chaves entered the legal profession and became involved in territorial politics full-time.[10] His first campaign for elective office suggested considerable personal ambition and a commitment to undercut the Bosque Redondo program. When Chaves declared his intention to seek the Republican nomination for Delegate—one of the territory's most coveted offices—in the 39th Congress (1865–1867), he directly challenged the one-term incumbent, his first cousin Francisco Perea. Although both men were Republicans, they represented different territorial factions of the party; Perea, the Union Party and Chaves, the Administration Party. In most respects, there was little daylight between these two groups that supported the U.S. federal government, but the Unionists supported General Carleton's controversial Indian reservation policy, which the Administrationists denounced.[11]

Chaves campaigned on two central issues: renewed efforts to recover the Los Conejos region, along the New Mexico-Colorado border, and opposition to the Navajo resettlement policy. As Delegate, Perea had submitted a bill for the return of the Los Conejos region to New Mexico and had written about it extensively. But Chaves supporters hinted that Perea's inability to get the bill passed was due either to apathy or weakness.[12] The removal of Indians also proved to be a complex issue, and the realities of the campaign trail compelled Chaves to temper some of his opposition to the Navajo resettlement policy.[13] In some places, noted an observer, Chaves "is opposed to the Bosque Reservation; and in [another area] he is in favor of it. In San Miguel he is in favor of the Reservation but opposed to its management." At other times, Chaves "dislikes [saying] anything on the subject but is rather inclined to favor it."[14] Eventually Chaves's opponents construed his resistance to the reservation as a repudiation of the territorial and federal government policies he had defended as a military officer—a stance that was incompatible with the role of a Territorial Delegate. Critics warned voters that Chaves was "a man who is unalterably opposed to the welfare of the country." The territorial government "has expended much money in [the Bosque Redondo's] establishment and is willing to spend more for its maintenance," they said. If voters "are contented with what it has done and is doing for us in this behalf, there will be no difficulty" in choosing the right candidate for the job.[15]

A bitter feud among establishment *Hispanos*, animated by overt appeals to the Anglo minority, was on full display. During the campaign, Chaves's opponents criticized his speaking style and his attacks on members of the elite. One critic wrote Chaves's "stock in trade … is abuse of prominent gentlemen in the Territory. If free use of abuse towards other people be an evidence of his fitness for Congressional honors he certainly would be the man for the place." The writer also judged Chaves's "ambition far overvaults his capacity."[16] Perea downplayed his cousin's challenge, intimating that Chaves was being manipulated by political enemies. Meanwhile, Chaves's camp claimed that the military was actively suppressing supporters and that Chaves's opponents were fostering racial tensions to promote an anti-Chaves voting bloc.

"The American inhabitants, including Germans, Irishmen, and all others born beyond New Mexico … are openly appealed to by his enemies to combine as a race against him." Chaves's supporters cited a speech in which he advocated that *Hispano* troops should be led by *Hispano* officers. Describing Chaves as "just towards all classes of citizens," the writer observed, "Some Americans, if they have a difficulty with a Mexican citizen, do not hesitate in trying to arouse the feeling of race among his countrymen, against the Mexican. These practices are not fair nor right, and if persisted in must lead to bad consequences."[17]

Ultimately, Perea's political standing suffered from his association with General Carleton, who had conceived and executed the plan for the Bosque Redondo. When Carleton was dismissed as commander of the Military Department of New Mexico, Chaves supporters used the incident to question Perea's political integrity, noting that Chaves "in his speeches and conversation wherever he went through the Territory took decided ground against the official acts of the 'Military Autocrat' of New Mexico, and boldly denounced the policy … in overriding the just claims of the citizens of the Territory."[18] Perea's political camp used time-honored methods to undercut the challenger: "Greenbacks and whisky flowed freely, and all sorts of tricks were resorted to in order that he might be politically prostrated."[19] But the Bosque Redondo issue proved potent, and Chaves won, garnering 58 percent of the vote to Perea's 42 percent.[20]

During Chaves's first term he lobbied for statehood and for the acquisition of the Los Conejos section for New Mexico.[21] As was generally the case for Territorial Delegates of this era, Chaves was not permitted to serve on a standing House committee. A bill he submitted to restore the Los Conejos region to New Mexico was referred to the House Committee on Territories, where it died.[22] Although Chaves disagreed with Carleton's "subjection or destruction" policy, he believed American Indians should be moved to facilitate Anglo and *Hispano* settlement, and submitted a bill that would place Utes, Apaches, Comanches, and Kiowas on reservations.[23] The Confederate occupation of the territory prevented the completion of construction projects that had been authorized in previous appropriations legislation, and in making his case to renew these projects, Chaves spoke of New Mexicans' loyalty even in the face of hardship. "I appeal to the generosity and liberality of this House to allow sufficient money to build up these buildings for my people, who, though they came into this Union not willingly, but by the fortunes of war, and who are a people of foreign extraction, are and have been as loyal as any people in the world," Chaves said. Though the underlying bill passed, Chaves's amendment was not adopted.[24] Chaves also submitted resolutions from the Legislative Assembly of New Mexico calling for relief from the damage caused by the 1861–1862 Confederate occupation and for appropriations for the completion of the territorial capitol and a penitentiary.[25]

Additionally, Chaves sought to persuade constituents to support statehood for New Mexico. Anticipating dissent, he argued that paying higher taxes for the ability to shape New Mexico's political future was worth the cost. "In exchange for the taxation entailed by the increase in expenses, you will have your laws entirely under your own control and the acts of your legislature will not be subject to rescission or abrogation by a higher authority, as they are now and will continue to be if you remain in your present politically dependent condition." Chaves also told constituents, with statehood, "you will have the high privilege of electing your own officials, who will be answerable to you for their conduct [and] … to remove them from their jobs … at your pleasure when they are unfaithful, instead of being obliged to send your complaints to this city [Washington, D.C.], [where] … they are received with negligence and indifference, and frequently scorned."[26]

During his re-election bid for the 40th Congress (1867–1869), Chaves ran against Democrat Charles P. Clever, a successful lawyer, a Civil War veteran, and the publisher of the *Santa Fe Weekly Gazette*. In his acceptance letter, Chaves thanked the delegates to the Republican convention. "I know and feel that there are among the members … gentlemen who from their talents, experience, and large interests in the Territory are better fitted to fill the important position [of Delegate] ... the results of the last convention are more gratifying to me; for it shows that what little I may have done in my official capacity has received the commendation of a majority of my constituents, and they are willing for a second time to entrust their interests in my hands."[27] Chaves had to contend with perceptions that he had compiled a paltry legislative record. Supporters argued that his inability to win substantial legislative victories reflected Congress's preoccupation with Reconstruction. One editorialist wrote, "The time of Congress was fully occupied with its consideration, leaving but little opportunity to consider the affairs and interests of the territories, which being without votes in Congress, without political power, could take no part and have no voice" in the deliberations. Moreover, supporters argued, opponents "with a zeal ... and a mendacity perfectly astonishing" undermined him by "creating a prejudice against him to impair his influence, by misrepresenting him, slandering him, villifying him ... in all places where the venom of their poisoned tongues could."[28]

The election was one of the most protracted and contentious in New Mexican history, leaving the territory without representation in Congress for nearly two years. According to initial tallies, Chaves won with 1,123 votes versus Clever's 577, though numerous discrepancies—seemingly attributable to chicanery by Clever's supporters—marred the results.[29] In Rio Arriba County, where the majority voted for Chaves, Clever supporters stole the ballot box. In a precinct of Tierra Amarilla County that had never before polled 100 votes, 464 were cast, all but 12 for Clever. "Protect us from the shameful, the abominable results of the guilty works of the men who ... in the late canvass [have] shown conclusively that they have neither regard for the interests of the people of New Mexico, nor respect for their rights," the editors of the *New Mexican* entreated the Republican-dominated Congress.[30] Chaves contested the results, alleging that alterations made in poll books after the election cost him several hundred votes. The committee also investigated charges of voter intimidation in Rio Arriba County. The case consumed nearly all of the 40th Congress.[31] At its conclusion, the House Committee on Elections voted unanimously for Chaves. In his summation on the House Floor, Solomon N. Pettis of Pennsylvania said the committee's decision hinged on the poll books. The facts of the case, Pettis noted, "disclosed a state of fraud and piracy upon the ballot-box, and a disregard of the laws not equaled by anything that ever before [came] under my observation in regard to any election." The committee stated, "It was upon these frauds ... which were proved by witnesses before the committee, that we came to our conclusion."[32] Chaves retained a 389-vote majority and was thus awarded the seat, but his victory was pyrrhic, since there were less than two weeks left in the 40th Congress.[33]

Chaves's re-election to the House in 1869 for a seat in the 41st Congress (1869–1871) was comparatively trouble-free. His challenger was Vicente Romero, a successful entrepreneur described by the *Santa Fe New Mexican* as politically weak and lacking in organization.[34] Chaves defeated Romero, with 57 to 43 percent of the vote. One observer suggested that Chaves's re-election was due to lingering public resentment about "the frauds of 1867, by which he was kept out of his seat ... for near two years."[35]

During Chaves's term in the 41st Congress, he submitted eight petitions, 26 bills, and one joint resolution.[36] Many of his legislative initiatives involved infrastructure improvements such as the construction of wagon roads and post roads, as well as the construction of a capitol building in Santa Fe.[37] Chaves submitted a bill requesting a land grant for the Atchison, Topeka, and Santa Fe Railroad, a bill seeking funding in the 1870 Indian Appropriations Bill (H.R. 1169), and a bill defining New Mexico's northern boundaries using land surveys in the territory.[38]

Chaves spent much of his time initiating the statehood process, with little success. He submitted H.R. 954, a bill to authorize New Mexicans to "form a constitution and State government preparatory to their admission into the Union on an equal footing with the original States"; the bill was not considered and died at the end of the Congress. The issue of statehood was a sore subject for some New Mexicans. Twenty-five years after New Mexico was annexed by the United States, it remained a territory, although many New Mexicans who had known nothing but territorial government were opposed to changing the status quo. In an eloquent floor speech, Chaves told colleagues New Mexicans felt that without statehood they had "no part in the general legislation of this country, and only a limited and subordinate part … which directly relates to their own local interests." New Mexicans, according to Chaves, were "anxious to assume that relation to the Government of the United States which will … advance their local interests, and will enable them, through their Senators and Representatives in Congress, to demand … protection and consideration from the Government which they now have to solicit as a matter of grace."[39] The act that would enable New Mexico's statehood failed to pass because of political gridlock.[40]

Chaves faced other obstacles, including New Mexico's lackluster reputation among territorial military appointees, who often expressed "deep regret that the Territory was ever acquired from Mexico." Other critics charged, "The people of New Mexico … are not republican in spirit," a dig at their patriotism as well as an expression of doubt about their fitness for self-rule.[41] According to one scholar, racial and religious prejudices toward *nuevomexicanos* made statehood a difficult cause.[42] Another scholar notes that New Mexicans' own ambivalence, reflected in the divided support for statehood between Anglos and *Hispanos*, further doomed Chaves's efforts.[43]

Chaves ran for a fourth term in 1871 against a formidable opponent, veteran Democrat and speaker of the territorial assembly José Manuel Gallegos. Gallegos had served as Territorial Delegate in the 33rd and 34th Congresses (1853–1857) and had run for the seat unsuccessfully in 1859 and 1863, blaming Chaves for his 1863 loss. Chaves's path to re-election was further complicated when Republican José D. Sena split from the party to run as an Independent, taking votes away from Chaves.[44] The *Daily New Mexican*, which backed Chaves in the 1865, 1867, and 1869 races, supported Sena's nomination in 1871. Even after Chaves secured the support of the nominating convention, the editors promised only "to abide by the action of the Santa Fe Convention," saying, "We will do all we can … to secure his election to Congress."[45] Chaves's campaign stressed that a three-term Republican Delegate could do better for New Mexico than a freshman Democrat in a Republican-majority Congress. "Chaves, by his long service … has fully established his republicanism, he has the entire political and personal confidence of the administration and of the Congress," wrote "A Republican," a frequent newspaper correspondent, "and I venture that there is not a single one of them who would not serve him personally." Again, Chaves's opponents charged that he had failed to bring home federal dollars. But "A Republican" warned, Gallegos's election dooms "the fate of appropriations for public improvements of any kind of character; it defeats any enabling act [for statehood]," and any other beneficial legislation for the territory.[46] The election was marred by violence. On August 27, 1871, in the town of Mesilla, Republicans and Democrats formed two processions. The groups provoked each other, causing a riot; nine men were killed, and approximately 50 were injured.[47] In the end, Chaves could not overcome the Republican split, and Gallegos won, capturing 50 percent of the vote compared to 34 percent for Chaves and 16 percent for Sena.[48]

Like many of his predecessors, Chaves re-immersed himself in New Mexico politics after leaving Washington. He became a powerful political player through his interaction with the Santa Fe Ring, a group composed mainly of Republican lawyers and business professionals who dominated New Mexican politics. A number of sources alleged that Chaves controlled a political machine out of Valencia County.[49] He served as attorney for the Second Judicial District from 1875 until 1877. He also represented Valencia County as a member of the territorial council in New Mexico's Legislative Assembly for 12 terms (1875–1904), presiding over the council for seven terms. Chaves was renowned for his skill as a parliamentarian in the assembly. A colleague noted that Chaves's success "was due not only to his familiarity with the rules of procedure, but to his wonderful memory which enabled him to keep in mind … the most tangled jumbles of resolutions offered, motions to amend, of the acceptance or rejection of amendments, offers of substitutes, motions to lay on the table, and all such matters … which would have driven a less capable man to the confines of distraction."[50] He also presided over the 1889 state constitutional convention. Finally, Chaves served as New Mexico's superintendent of public instruction from 1901 to 1903 and was appointed historian of New Mexico, although he died before filling the appointment.[51]

On November 26, 1904, Chaves was killed by a rifle shot in Pinos Wells, New Mexico, while dining with friends.[52] Immediately, three posses fanned out to search for the assassin. Three days later, Domingo Valles, who had an arrest record for stealing livestock, was captured. According to Chaves's friend and eulogist, Frank W. Clancy, "There had been a series of grievous offenses in Torrance county, such as stealing of stock, destruction of property, burning of houses and fences, and other like things, and … [Chaves] was active in seeking evidence to punish the malefactors, and there is no doubt that this activity on his part brought about the murder." Clancy prosecuted the case against Valles, who was defended by future governor and U.S. Senator Octaviano Larrazolo. Clancy believed Valles was "the scoundrel who fired the fatal shot which killed Colonel Chaves," but Larrazolo's defense was so convincing that Valles was acquitted. No one else was ever charged with the crime.[53]

Chaves's funeral was one of the largest ever held in Santa Fe. His body lay in state at the capitol with an honor guard. Several hundred people paid their respects before the funeral, at which former Territorial Delegate Pedro Perea was a pallbearer.[54] Chaves was interred at the U.S. National Cemetery in Santa Fe.

FOR FURTHER READING

Biographical Directory of the United States Congress, "José Francisco Chaves," http://bioguide.congress.gov.

Read, Martha Durant. "Colonel José Francisco Chaves: A Short Biography of the Father of the New Mexico Statehood Movement." *Southwest Heritage* 8, no. 4 (Winter 1978–1979): 13–21, 30.

Walter, Paul A. F., ed. *Colonel José Francisco Chaves, 1833–1924* (Santa Fe: Historical Society of New Mexico, 1926).

MANUSCRIPT COLLECTION

Arizona Historical Society (Tucson). *Papers:* Herman H. Heath Papers, 1867–1869, one folder. Contains correspondence from Chaves discussing New Mexico politics. There is also a miscellaneous biographical file for Chaves in the historical society's general collection.

NOTES

1 "No sois dueños de vuestras propias leyes ni de vuestros propios empleados. Por lo tanto, no sois esencialmente un pueblo libre, sino una comunidad subordinada y dependiente, gobernada … sino por el placer o capricho de hombres que residen distante de vuestros, límites, quienes, en sus actos públicos hacia vosotros, son algunas veces gobernados por influjos individos [*sic*] y raras veces obran con debido concimiento de vuestra verdadera condición y de vuestras necesidades." J. Francisco Chavez (Chaves), "A los ciudadanos de Nuevo Mejico," 4 May 1866, *The New Mexican* (Santa Fe, NM): 4. Translated as "To the Citizens of New Mexico," by Translations International, Inc. (August 2010).

2 "J. Francisco Chavez," in Maurilio E. Vigil, *Los Patrones: Profiles of Hispanic Political Leaders in New Mexico History* (Washington, D.C.: University Press of America, 1980): 56–62; Carlos Brazil Ramirez, "The Hispanic Political Elite in Territorial New Mexico: A Study of Classical Colonialism," (Ph.D. diss., University of California–Santa Barbara, 1979): 285. According to an obituary for Chaves's cousin Francisco Perea ("Francisco Perea, Delegate to 38th Congress, Dies at Home Here," 22 May 1913, *Albuquerque Morning Journal*: 2), "early in the spring of 1843" a number of boys including Perea, Chaves, and future Delegate Miguel Otero attended school in St. Louis. Vigil states that Chaves attended school from 1841 to 1846.

3 Ralph Twitchell, *The Leading Facts of New Mexican History*, vol. 2 (Cedar Rapids, IA: Torch Press, 1912): 400–401. This quotation also appears in a few other biographies about Chaves.

4 Ramirez, "The Hispanic Political Elite in Territorial New Mexico": 287; Twitchell, *The Leading Facts of New Mexican History*: 400–401; "By the Bullet of a Dastardly Assassin," 27 November 1904, *Santa Fe New Mexican*: 1; "Suspected Assassin of Colonel J. Franco Chaves Captured by Game Warden P. B. Otero," 28 November 1904, *Santa Fe New Mexican*: 1.

5 "J. Francisco Chavez," in Vigil, *Los Patrones*: 57; Frank McNitt, *Navajo Wars: Military Campaigns, Slave Raids, and Reprisals* (Albuquerque: University of New Mexico Press, 1972): 385–392, 398–399. McNitt states that Chaves participated in the 1859–1860 campaigns because of settlers' anxiety about Navajo incursions that resulted in 300 deaths and $1.5 million in stolen property.

Governor Abraham Rencher and Colonel Thomas T. Fauntleroy agreed to form a battalion of five citizen companies. The governor reported to Secretary of State Lewis Cass that Chaves's group "had cut swathes through Navajo cornfields, captured thousands of their livestock, and returned with about one hundred Navajo women and children … as captives." For a different perspective, see Peter Iverson, *Diné: A History of the Navajos* (Albuquerque: University of New Mexico Press, 2002): 41–48.

6 Ray C. Colton, *The Civil War in the Western Territories: Arizona, Colorado, New Mexico, and Utah* (Norman: University of Oklahoma Press, 1959): 125. Brigadier General James H. Carleton, commander of the Department of New Mexico, wrote on September 22, 1862, that he ordered Chaves and his four companies "to move into Navaho country … to punish them for stealing livestock and killing a large number of white people."

7 Colton, *The Civil War in the Western Territories*: 136–138. Carleton told Navajo leaders they had until July 1863 to move to the Bosque Redondo Reservation, after which "any Navaho seen by the soldiers … was to be treated as hostile. Orders were given to kill every male Navaho Indian who could be found who was capable of bearing arms and to take women and children as prisoners." For a detailed study, see Gerald Thompson, *The Army and the Navajo: The Bosque Redondo Experiment, 1863–1868* (Tucson: University of Arizona Press, 1976).

8 *Congressional Globe*, Appendix, 39th Cong., 2nd sess. (2 March 1867): 150. Chaves knew this "not only because I commanded at Fort Wingate, but also for the reason that I interpreted from Spanish to English to General Carleton himself what Indians said to the Navajo interpreter."

9 For Chaves's army service generally, see "J. Francisco Chavez," in Vigil, *Los Patrones*: 57–58; W. G. Ritch, *The Legislative Blue-Book of the Territory of New Mexico* (Albuquerque: University of New Mexico Press, 1968; reprint of 1882 edition): 107; "The Cruel Assassin's Bullet," 28 November 1904, *Daily Citizen* (Albuquerque): 1; "Escorted to His Final Resting Place," 30 November 1904, *Santa Fe New Mexican*: 1. For Chaves's position on the Indian removal policy, see Martha Durant Read, "Colonel Jose Francisco Chaves: A Short Biography of the Father of the New Mexico Statehood Movement," *Southwest Heritage* 8, no. 4 (Winter 1978–1979): 16. For more information about Chaves's commanding role at Fort Wingate, see Robert Utley, *Frontiersmen in Blue: The United States Army and the Indian, 1848–1865* (Lincoln: University of Nebraska Press, 1981; reprint of 1967 edition): 238–241.

10 Ramirez, "The Hispanic Political Elite in Territorial New Mexico": 287; Read, "Colonel Jose Francisco Chaves": 16. Ramirez states that Chaves studied law and passed the bar in the 1840s, whereas Read states that Chaves studied law and passed the bar after he retired from the military in 1863.

11 Colton, *The Civil War in the Western Territories*: 197–198; Howard R. Lamar, *The Far Southwest, 1846–1912: A Territorial History*, rev. ed. (Albuquerque: University of New Mexico Press, 2000): 109–112. By the 1864 presidential election, New Mexico Republicans had split into three groups: "the regulars, consisting of Governor [Henry] Connelly, Delegate Perea, and Judge John S. Watts, who openly declared for Lincoln; another faction, led by Connelly's own secretary [of the territory], W. F. M. Arny, who supported [Salmon] Chase and the Radicals [Republicans]; and still a third group, who were actually old-time Democrats and wanted [George B.] McClellan for President." By the 1865 election for Territorial Delegate, Chaves "ran on a pro-Arny and anti-Bosque ticket, while his cousin Francisco Perea … defended the General."

12 Colton, *The Civil War in the Western Territories*: 197–198; William A. Keleher, *Turmoil in New Mexico, 1846–1868* (Santa Fe: Sunstone Press, 2008; reprint of 1952 edition): 126–127. The area of Los Conejos, "being the extreme northern portion of New Mexico, was severed from New Mexico and annexed to the territory of Colorado by act of Congress approved February 28, 1861. The sole purpose of the severance, affecting 3,000 native born New Mexicans, was to give evenness and symmetry to the southern boundary of Colorado. Hon. Francisco Perea … belatedly protested against the severance, in a letter written to James M. Ashley, chairman of the Committee on Territories in the House … and attempted to reclaim the lost territory for New Mexico, contending the act of severance had passed without consultation or warning."

13 Read, "Colonel Jose Francisco Chaves": 16.

14 The *Santa Fe Weekly Gazette* published an 1864 letter in which Chaves advised Perea not to support the reservation system because of political opposition in San Miguel County. Also published were some articles Chaves wrote for the *Santa Fe New Mexican,* as well as formal petitions he wrote in 1864 and 1865 prior to his candidacy that were critical of the reservation system. See "Chavez and the Reservation Question," 5 August 1865, *Santa Fe Weekly Gazette*: 2. The article lists Chaves's 1864 letter to Perea, three articles from the *Santa Fe New Mexican* objecting to the reservation, a formal petition protesting the reservation that was signed by 1,974 residents of San Miguel County, and statements from Chaves's April 1865 nominating convention rejecting the addition to the platform of a statement supporting the reservation.

15 "The Issue to Be Decided," 26 August 1865, *Santa Fe Weekly Gazette*: 2.

16 "Chavez on the Stump," 22 July 1865, *Santa Fe Weekly Gazette*: 2.

17 "Desperation," 4 August 1865, (Santa Fe) *The New Mexican*: 2. The writer notes, "None of [Chaves's] friends are surprised at this—they have seen that every dollar of patronage, and every means of influence in the hands of the commander of this Department were to be exerted to the fullest extent to defeat Colonel Chavez."

18 "Francisco Perea, Delegate to 38th Congress, Dies at His Home Here."

19 "The Election—the Result," 6 October 1865, (Santa Fe) *The New Mexican*: 2.

20 September 21, 1865, entry of Governor's Journal Certifying Delegate Election Results, Copy of the Executive Records of the Territory of New Mexico, Department of State Territorial Papers, New Mexico, 1851–1872 (National Archives Microfilm T17, Roll 2), General Records of the Department of State, Record Group 59, National Archives at College Park, College Park, MD (NACP). The official results—8,571 votes for Chaves and 6,180 votes for Perea—were printed in "Territorial Election," 30 September 1865, *Santa Fe Weekly Gazette*: 2.

21 Read "Colonel Jose Francisco Chaves": 16; Robert W. Larson, *New Mexico's Quest for Statehood, 1846–1912* (Albuquerque: University of New Mexico Press, 1968): 86–88.

22 *Congressional Globe*, House, 39th Cong., 1st sess. (22 January 1866): 350.

23 *Congressional Globe*, House, 39th Cong., 1st sess. (13 February 1866): 811–812. Chaves also lobbied for appropriations for relief (although it is not clear why) for towns and villages in New Mexico and Arizona. See *Congressional Globe*, House, 39th Cong., 1st sess. (19 February 1866): 919.

24 *Congressional Globe*, House, 39th Cong., 1st sess. (28 July 1866): 4307. Chaves proposed an amendment to H.R. 715, a bill to fund the construction of penitentiaries in the territories and to secure $40,000 to build other public buildings, but the bill was not adopted.

25 *Congressional Globe*, House, 39th Cong., 2nd sess. (7 February 1867): 1073; *Congressional Globe*, House, 39th Cong., 2nd sess. (14 February 1867): 1246–1247. Chaves also submitted private relief bills and proposals for increases in territorial judges' salaries.

26 "Como equivalente para la tazacion [*sic*] incidente al aumento de los gastos, tendreis vuestras leyes enteramente bajo vuestro propio dominio, y los actos de vuestra Legislatura no seran sujetos, á revisión y abrogación de una autoridad más alta, como lo son ahora, y como continuaran, mientras permanesereis [*sic*] en vuestra presente, dependiente condición política … tendreis el alto privilegio de elijir [*sic*] vuestros propios oficiales, quienes os seran responsables por su conducta … remover de su empleo, á vuestro placer cuando fueran infieles, en lugar de estar obligados de mandar vuestras quejas á esta ciudad, en donde se atienden con negligencia é indiferencia, y frecuentemente menopreciadas." Chavez (Chaves), "A los ciudadanos de Nuevo Méjico." Translated as "To the Citizens of New Mexico," by Translations International, Inc. (August 2010).

27 "Col. Chaves' Letter of Acceptance," 27 April 1867, (Santa Fe) *The New Mexican*: 2.

28 "Review," 18 May 1867, (Santa Fe) *The New Mexican*: 2.

29 "The Result," 21 September 1867, (Santa Fe) *The New Mexican*: 2.

30 According to the Santa Fe *New Mexican*, the probate judge in Dona Ana County unilaterally "went over the … poll books of his county, and wrote the word 'rejected' across the names of *two hundred and thirty-one Chaves voters*." Votes from entire precincts in Mora and Socorro Counties were summarily disqualified by the Secretary of the Territory, W. F. M. Arny. See "The Result." [Italics in the original.] Usually, territorial officials produced two copies of the voting tallies, one for the secretary of the territory and the other for the probate judge. Historian Howard Lamar writes, "Probate judges also controlled the election machinery, which meant that they had a major voice in determining who should be elected to the Assembly, who would become delegate, and who would succeed to local office." See Lamar, *The Far Southwest, 1846–1912: A Territorial History*: 76.

31 "The Copperheads Running off the Witnesses of Col. Chaves," 4 February 1868, (Santa Fe) *The New Mexican*: 2.

32 *Congressional Globe*, House, 40th Cong., 3rd sess. (20 February 1869): 1423–1424. For an example of witness intimidation during the investigation of the contested election case, see "The Copperheads Running Off the Witnesses of Col. Chaves."

33 Chester H. Rowell, *A Historical and Legal Digest of All the Election Cases in the House of Representatives of the United States from the First to the Fifty-Sixth Congress, 1789–1901* (Westport, CT: Greenwood Press, 1976; reprint of 1901 edition): 225. For a detailed summary about the contested election case, see the explanation of S. N. Pettis of Pennsylvania in *Congressional Globe*, Appendix, 40th Cong., 3rd sess. (18, 20 February 1869): 203–205. For Charles Clever's rebuttal, see *Congressional Globe*, Appendix, 40th Cong., 3rd sess. (20 February 1869): 248–258. For Chaves's public letter thanking his constituents for their support, see "Address," 9 March 1869, (Santa Fe) *The Daily New Mexican*: 1. Interestingly, Stephen B. Elkins, a future Territorial Delegate and U.S. Senator, represented Chaves during the contested election case.

34 "The Canvass," 31 August 1869, (Santa Fe) *The Daily New Mexican*: 1; "The Gazette Mourneth," 17 September 1869, (Santa Fe) *The Daily New Mexican*: 1. For more information about Romero, see Ramirez, "The Hispanic Political Elite in Territorial New Mexico": 288.

35 "The Finality of Our Delegate Election," 24 September 1869, (Santa Fe) *The Daily New Mexican*: 1. Chaves earned 8,194 votes; and Romero earned 6,273.

36 *Congressional Globe*, Index, 41st Cong., 2nd sess.: CCXLVI.

37 *Congressional Globe*, House, 41st Cong., 2nd sess. (20 December 1869): 240; *Congressional Globe*, House, 41st Cong., 2nd sess. (7 February 1870): 1088; *Congressional Globe*, House, 41st Cong., 2nd sess. (19 March 1870): 2095.

38 *Congressional Globe*, House, 41st Cong., 2nd sess. (24 January 1870): 709; *Congressional Globe*, House, 41st Cong., 2nd sess. (19 March 1870): 2095; *Congressional Globe*, House, 41st Cong.,

2nd sess. (28 April 1870): 3074; *Congressional Globe*, House, 41st Cong., 2nd sess. (2 June 1870): 4018.

39 *Congressional Globe*, House, 41st Cong., 3rd sess. (3 March 1871): 245.

40 "Washington Correspondence," 10 July 1871, (Santa Fe) *The Daily New Mexican*: 1. The correspondent blamed the failure of the enabling act on presidential politics: "But for the pending presidential election of 1872, the enabling act would have passed Congress; but the democrats determined the vote of New Mexico should not be given to Grant in 1872 ... as they also did the enabling act for Colorado."

41 "Washington Correspondence."

42 Larson, *New Mexico's Quest for Statehood, 1846–1912*: 93, 125–126.

43 Read, "Colonel José Francisco Chaves": 16–17.

44 Gerald Arthur Theisen, "Jose Manuel Gallegos (1815–1875): The First Mexican American in the United States Congress," (Ph.D. diss., University of New Mexico, 1985: 177–179).

45 No title, 13 May 1871, (Santa Fe) *The Daily New Mexican*: 1. Chaves may have lost support because of the publication of a critical letter by New Mexico chief justice Kirby Benedict, who accused Chaves of slander in 1870. For more information, see 4 May 1871, (Santa Fe) *The Daily New Mexican*: 1. For a copy of the letter in question, see Aurora Hunt, *Kirby Benedict, Frontier Federal Judge* (Glendale, CA: Arthur H. Clark Company, 1961): 196.

46 "Washington Correspondence," 14 July 1871, (Santa Fe) *The Daily New Mexican*: 1. One writer charged Chaves "has proved himself an utter failure because of his failing to get these [securing land for public works] and other appropriation for the benefit of the Territory." Chaves supporters blamed congressional Democrats' intransigence: "The [Democratic] leaders that passed these resolutions know ... that the defeat of all New Mexican measures ... was the work of the democratic members in the House." See A Republican, "Washington Correspondence," 20 July 1871, (Santa Fe) *The Daily New Mexican*: 1. For a similar charge, see "Political Misrepresentations," 2 September 1871, (Santa Fe) *The Daily New Mexican*: 1.

47 Twitchell, *Leading Facts of New Mexican History*, vol. 2: 400–401; Theisen, "Jose Manuel Gallegos (1815–75)": 177–179. According to Twitchell, no one was indicted or punished for the riot. For a contemporary report, see "The Mesilla Riot" and "Great Riot in Mesilla," 1 September 1871, (Santa Fe) *The Daily New Mexican*: 1.

48 Theisen, "Jose Manuel Gallegos (1815–75)": 177–179; "Official Vote for Delegate," 19 September 1871, (Santa Fe) *The Daily New Mexican*: 1. The official tally was 7,670 votes for Gallegos, 5,285 for Chaves, and 2,534 for Sena. Interestingly, in late July 1871, a writer who alleged that Democrats encouraged Sena to run claimed, "There is no more chance of the election of Gallegos now that Sena is running than there was before, because ... Sena will take few or no votes from the republican party but probably will take from the democratic party many votes which they would have retained if only two candidates were in the field." See A Republican, "Washington Correspondence," 26 July 1871, (Santa Fe) *The Daily New Mexican*: 1.

49 Read, "Colonel Jose Francisco Chaves": 18; Lamar, *The Far Southwest, 1846–1912: A Territorial History:* 142–143; Territory of New Mexico, *Report of the Secretary of the Territory, 1903–1904, and Legislative Manual, 1905* (Santa Fe: The New Mexican Printing Company, 1905): 48 opposite. According to Lamar, Chaves's split with the Ring came after the contested election case of Tranquilino Luna and Francisco Manzanares. In the 1884 election for Delegate, Chaves supported Independent candidate William L. Rynerson until the end, when he threw his support to Democratic candidate Antonio Joseph over Republican candidate L. Bradford Prince and Independent candidate E. L. Brown. Chaves also advocated moving the state capital from Santa Fe to Albuquerque to dilute the Ring's influence. During the debate, as "rival contestants showed up to claim Council seats from [nearby counties], the Santa Feans, fearful of losing the capital, hastily seated the antiremoval delegates. This was the breaking point. [Chaves] ... already itching for a fight and always a brilliant organizer, set up his own council of insurgent members. Thomas Catron, leading the antiremoval forces, pushed through an act that permanently located the capital in Santa Fe. But the price paid was open rupture within the Republican Party" [in New Mexico].

50 *Report of the Secretary of the Territory, 1905–1906 and Legislative Manual, 1907* (Albuquerque: Morning Journal, 1907): 168–178; Paul A. F. Walter, ed., *Colonel Jose Francisco Chaves, 1833–1924* (Santa Fe: Historical Society of New Mexico, 1926): 5–6. This English translation of the title contains an error: "1924" should be "1904," the year Chaves died. The original, Spanish title contains the correct year.

51 Read, "Colonel Jose Francisco Chaves": 18–19. For more about the constitutional convention and Chaves's role, see Larson, *New Mexico's Quest for Statehood, 1846–1912*: 147–168.

52 "By the Bullet of a Dastardly Assassin"; "The Cruel Assassin's Bullet." Accounts of Chaves's assassination differ. According to the Santa Fe newspaper, Chaves "fell dead with a bullet piercing his lungs just over the heart and passing out of the body and imbedding itself several inches in the wall." The Albuquerque newspaper reported that "the bullet struck the head, and penetrated the brain."

53 "Suspect Valles at Santa Fe," 30 November 1904, *The Daily Citizen* (Albuquerque): 1; "Suspected Assassin of Colonel J. Franco Chaves Captured by Game Warden P. B. Otero"; Walter, ed., *Colonel Jose Francisco Chaves, 1833–1924*: 9–10; Read, "Colonel Jose Francisco Chaves": 20.

54 "Escorted to His Final Resting Place."

Romualdo Pacheco
1831–1899

UNITED STATES REPRESENTATIVE 1877–1878; 1879–1883
REPUBLICAN FROM CALIFORNIA

Born in California while it was still Mexican territory, Romualdo Pacheco was the privileged stepson of a prominent merchant and landowner on the Pacific frontier. An avid outdoorsman who won fame for his prowess as a hunter, and a member of elite society in San Francisco and Santa Barbara, Pacheco defended the rights of landowners and promoted industry in his growing state. "Romualdo Pacheco … was indisputably the most illustrious Californio of his time," noted a contemporary. "[He was] a magnificent physical specimen whose brain matched his brawn."[1]

José Antonio Romualdo Pacheco, Jr., was born October 31, 1831, in Santa Barbara, California. His mother, Ramona Carillo, belonged to a prominent Mexican family.[2] Pacheco's father, a native of Guanajuato, Mexico, and a captain in the Mexican army, had arrived in California in 1825. He was killed outside Los Angeles five weeks after his namesake's birth, while protecting Mexican governor Manuel Victoria in the waning days of Mexico's war for independence from Spain. Pacheco's mother subsequently married John Wilson, a Scottish sea captain. The couple's wealth afforded Romualdo and his older brother, Mariano, a comfortable childhood. In 1838 the two boys sailed to Hawaii on their stepfather's ship, the *Don Quixote*, to attend Oahu Charity School in Honolulu, an English-language institution run by missionaries and family friends. Pacheco became fluent in English and French and, after returning to California in 1843, he had to re-learn Spanish.[3] Pacheco went to work on his stepfather's shipping fleet, learning navigation skills and studying with a private tutor. In 1846, during the Mexican-American War, while Pacheco was transporting cargo up the California coast on a vessel flying the Mexican flag, the U.S.S. *Cyane* stopped and searched his ship near Monterey. Permitted to continue his journey, Pacheco was stopped again near the coast of San Francisco, where he was allegedly imprisoned briefly by the U.S. military.[4] Pacheco was a wealthy businessman and rancher by 1848 when he accepted U.S. citizenship, which he was granted by the Treaty of Guadalupe Hidalgo.[5] He subsequently worked on his parents' estates north of Los Angeles, in San Luis Obispo County, becoming an expert horseman, and dabbled a year later in the mining business during the California Gold Rush.

Pacheco eventually answered the familial call to political service when California became a state in 1850. Profoundly interested in protecting the rights of Southern California landowners, his stepfather, John Wilson, was San Luis Obispo County's first treasurer and served on the county's first board of supervisors in 1852. After California joined the Union in 1850, Pacheco's brother, Mariano, was elected to the state legislature and served a single term before poor health forced him to retire in 1853.[6] Carrying on the family tradition, Pacheco entered the political arena, serving as a superior court judge for San Luis Obispo County from 1853 to 1857 and then as a state senator until 1862. Initially a Democrat, Pacheco ran for re-election as a Union Party candidate in 1861 because of his deep disdain for slavery and his disapproval of the secession crisis; Pacheco was one of the first prominent Hispanic Americans to speak out against African-American slavery.[7] In 1863 Pacheco joined the Republican Party, and California Governor Leland Stanford appointed him to fill a vacancy for state treasurer; he won election for a full term later that year. Also in 1863, Governor Stanford commissioned Pacheco as a brigadier general in the California state militia to command Hispanic troops in the First Brigade of California's "Native Cavalry."[8] Maintaining ties to his father's birthplace, Pacheco became a key contact for Mexican President Benito Juárez, connecting his

Romualdo Pacheco, Daniel Greene, 2005,
Collection of the U.S. House of Representatives

UNION
RAILROAD MAP

emissaries with prominent Californians who supported his war against France in 1864.[9] In 1863 Pacheco married Mary Catherine McIntire, a Kentucky playwright who became one of California's first published female authors.[10] The couple had a daughter, Maybella Ramona, and a son, Romualdo, who died at age seven.

In 1867 Pacheco lost a re-election bid for state treasurer; however, he returned to the state senate in 1869. At the Republican state convention in 1871, Pacheco was nominated for lieutenant governor under the winning ticket headed by Newton Booth. When Booth accepted an appointment to the U.S. Senate, Pacheco became governor of California in 1875, serving from February to December. The first Hispanic American and the first native Californian to serve as governor, Pacheco focused on building new government facilities and services and on mediating between Spanish-speaking Californians of Mexican descent and settlers from the Eastern United States and elsewhere.[11] His experience as a rancher made him an expert with a lasso, and he was acclaimed as the only California governor known to have lassoed a grizzly bear.[12] Pacheco withdrew his name from nomination for a full term as governor in 1875 when he realized he had little chance of winning in the fractious GOP state convention. He ran unsuccessfully as an Independent candidate for lieutenant governor.

In 1876 Pacheco entered a race for a U.S. House seat representing a large southern portion of the state that was mostly on the frontier, stretching from the peninsula just south of San Francisco to Mono County and the Nevada border in the east, and nearly 500 miles south to the Mexican border.[13] He received the Republican nomination at the district convention on August 10, 1876. Facing Democratic incumbent Peter D. Wigginton, Pacheco campaigned on the development of California ports, emphasizing his maritime experience. The San Luis Obispo *Tribune* reported that in a meeting in that city on Christmas Day 1875, Pacheco was "greeted with loud applause [as] he proceeded to give some of his experiences as a sailor on the Pacific Coast.... From experience he knew that the matter of protecting our harbor was perfectly feasible."[14] Wigginton enjoyed more support from the newspapers in the district, including the endorsement of the *Tribune*, but Pacheco's heritage appealed to the district's majority-Hispanic, or "native-Californian," population.[15] Pacheco initially won the election by a single ballot—19,104 votes to Wigginton's 19,103—but the incumbent contested Pacheco's narrow victory.[16] Upon investigation, the California secretary of state observed that two votes for Wigginton that were cast in Monterey County were missing from the total certified by the county's board of elections; he accused the tally clerk of changing the final count after the board adjourned and refused to certify Pacheco's election. Pacheco petitioned his case all the way to the California supreme court after the clerk testified that he had altered the vote count to correct a clerical error, based on evidence found in board members' notes.[17] The court upheld Pacheco's election, ordering the secretary of state to issue the certificate of election. Carrying this document and the endorsement of the state's Democratic governor, Pacheco traveled to Washington.

Convening on October 15, 1877, the Democratic-controlled 45th Congress (1877–1879) attempted to block Pacheco's swearing-in based on Wigginton's contest, then pending before the Committee on Elections. With the support of a resolution adopted by voice vote and sponsored by House Republican Floor Leader James Garfield of Ohio, Pacheco took the oath of office on October 17, 1877.[18] The first Hispanic Member with full voting rights, Pacheco was unable to pursue many of his legislative initiatives in his first term. The Committee on Elections—made up of a majority of Democrats—upheld Wigginton's contest on January 31, 1878.[19] Though the committee's majority agreed with the California supreme court's decision regarding the votes cast in Monterey County, ballot irregularities elsewhere in the district reversed Pacheco's razor-thin victory. State law permitted precinct judges to challenge ballots having any extraneous "impression, device, color, or thing."[20] Judges rejected several ballots for both Pacheco and Wigginton because of this law, and because several voters were not residents of the state or district. After examining more than two dozen individual ballots, the committee ruled that Wigginton had prevailed by four votes. The full House concurred on February 7, 1878, by a party-line vote of 136 to 125, unseating Pacheco.[21]

After Wigginton returned to his San Francisco law practice at the end of the 45th Congress, Pacheco again ran for a House seat in 1878. In his next two elections, Pacheco faced accusations from popular Democratic newspapers in the district that he was too attached to the national Republican Party and distanced from his constituents by his wealth.[22] The editors denounced Pacheco for ignoring his constituents and failing to grant them plum federal patronage jobs. "He has always received their passionate aid and has enjoyed the dignity and emoluments of public office through their votes," charged Santa Barbara's Spanish-language Democratic newspaper *La gaceta*, "but none of their class has ever been appointed to any position or favored for their influence!"[23] Yet his electoral victories were often determined by "the Spanish vote," and he successfully campaigned in both English and Spanish. In September 1879 he defeated Democrat Wallace Leach and James Ayers, a third-party Workingmen's candidate, taking 40 percent, with 15,391 votes. In 1880 he won re-election, defeating Leach by only 191 votes and winning with 46 percent and 17,768 votes. Workingmen's candidate J. F. Godfrey siphoned off 9 percent, with a little more than 3,000 votes.

Republicans assigned Pacheco to three standing committees over the course of his career: Public Lands, Private Land Claims, and Public Expenditures.[24] Though they were not considered particularly desirable, these assignments reflected Pacheco's preference for working within an intimate committee setting rather than making lengthy floor speeches.[25] He focused his legislative efforts, balancing the rights of landowners in California with a venture to protect and expand the harbors and railroads that were the economic lifelines for his remote Western district. Pacheco attempted to improve the harbor in the Wilmington section of Los Angeles by requesting an amendment allocating money in a rivers and harbors appropriation bill. Citing the lack of safe ports for riding out storms along more than 500 miles of California coast, Pacheco also stressed the region's importance as the endpoint for the Southern Pacific Railroad. "I would state from my own personal knowledge of the great wealth and importance of Southern California, its rapidly increasing commerce, and the importance of having that point a secure harbor for shipping," Pacheco argued. The House rejected the amendment by a narrow 78 to 74 vote.[26] The Democratic majority in the 45th and 46th Congresses (1877–1881) meant that Pacheco was typically defeated; of the 50 bills he introduced, only two—both private bills introduced on behalf of individuals—became law. Yet, noting his interest in protecting Western landowners, the GOP leadership made him chairman of the Committee on Private Land Claims in the 47th Congress (1881–1883) when the Republicans regained a majority. Pacheco was the first Hispanic Member to chair a full committee.

Pacheco broke his silence on national issues in a debate on the House Floor over a bill restricting Chinese immigration, on February 23, 1882. Addressing the nearly 50 percent increase in Asian residents in California from 1870 to 1880, Pacheco threw his support behind stemming the flow of Asian immigration.[27] "The subject [of Asian immigration] is of such vital importance to this country, and especially to the Pacific coast," Pacheco declared, "that I should fail [in] my duty did I not earnestly advocate its passage and state my reasons for doing so."[28] Espousing the anti-Chinese rhetoric that had been popular among wealthy Californians for decades—which was taking hold nationally in an era of increasing tensions among working-class laborers—Pacheco argued that Chinese immigrants in California, primarily single men brought to work railroad and mining operations, were taking white laborers' jobs and degrading the moral character of California's cities.[29] "It is necessary to see with our own eyes the insidious encroachments of the Mongolian upon every branch of labor, every avenue of industry," Pacheco noted. "They are taking in our factories and workshops, at the plow, beside the loom, yea in our very kitchens and laundries, the place of the white laborer."[30] Pacheco described Chinese culture as "unchanged, unchangeable, fixed, as immovable as the

decrees of fate." "His ancestors have also bequeathed him the most hideous immoralities," he said. "The imagination shrinks back appalled at the thought of the morals of a hundred thousand men without families," Pacheco added, appealing to 19th-century attitudes toward large populations of single men.[31] Drawing a parallel between Chinese immigration in California and the African slave trade earlier in the century, Pacheco appealed for Eastern support by invoking California's sacrifices during the Civil War: "When our great civil war broke out and ravaged and desolated the land, though the Pacific States were far removed from the scene of strife, were they slow to offer their aid?… [Californians] ask merely that the evil already done to them shall be restricted to its present proportions."[32] The Chinese Exclusion Act, which suspended the immigration of all Chinese laborers and denied citizenship to Asian immigrants, passed the House on March 23 by a vote of 167 to 66 (with 59 Members not voting).[33] Pacheco joined half the GOP Members (60 of the affirmative votes) and all seven Representatives from Western states in approving the measure.[34]

Pacheco did not run for re-election in 1882, but returned to California as one of its most prominent residents. After working as a partner in a San Francisco stock brokerage, he was appointed as an envoy to the Central American republics by President Benjamin Harrison in 1890. In July 1891 Harrison named him minister plenipotentiary to Honduras and Guatemala; however, he lost the patronage post upon the election of Democratic President Grover Cleveland in 1893. Pacheco retired to the home of his brother-in-law, Henry R. Miller, in Oakland, California, where he died of Bright's disease on January 23, 1899. His obituary in the *Los Angeles Times* said, "We have public men who might well copy in some measure the pose of mind, the calm dignity, the graceful honesty and gentle manliness of Romualdo Pacheco."[35]

FOR FURTHER READING

Biographical Directory of the United States Congress, "Romualdo Pacheco," http://bioguide.congress.gov.

Conmy, Peter Thomas. *Romualdo Pacheco: Distinguished Californian of the Mexican and American Periods* (San Francisco: Grand Parlor, Native Sons of the Golden West, 1957).

Genini, Ronald, and Richard Hitchman. *Romualdo Pacheco: A Californio in Two Eras* (San Francisco: Book Club of California, 1985).

MANUSCRIPT COLLECTION

Only a few scattered letters relating to Pacheco exist. See Pacheco's entry in the *Biographical Directory of the United States Congress* for more details, http://bioguide.congress.gov.

NOTES

1 Quoted in Ronald Genini and Richard Hitchman, *Romualdo Pacheco: A Californio in Two Eras* (San Francisco: The Book Club of California, 1985): vii. The authors do not provide the source of the quotation.

2 Most scholars agree on this date, but Peter Conmy notes that Pacheco's baptismal record lists his birthday as September 20, 1831. Peter Thomas Comny, *Romualdo Pacheco: Distinguished Californian of the Mexican and American Periods* (San Francisco: Grand Parlor, Native Sons of the Golden West, 1957): 4–5. A romanticized account of Pacheco's parents' courtship can be found in Winifred Davidson, "Romualdo's Ramona," 21 June 1931, *Los Angeles Times*: K11.

3 Conmy, *Romualdo Pacheco*: 5.

4 All Pacheco's major biographers note that the U.S. Navy stopped Pacheco's ship, but only Carmen E. Enciso and Tracy North mention his brief imprisonment. Enciso and North, *Hispanic Americans in Congress, 1822–1995* (Washington, D.C.: Government Printing Office, 1995): 94.

5 Leonard Schlup, "Pacheco, Romualdo" *American National Biography* 16 (New York: Oxford University Press, 1999): 882–883 (hereinafter referred to as *ANB*).

6 Genini and Hitchman, *Romualdo Pacheco*: 48–49.

7 Enciso and North, *Hispanic Americans in Congress*: 94.

8 Ibid.

9 Ibid.

10 Schlup, "Pacheco, Romualdo," *ANB*; Conmy, *Romualdo Pacheco*: 11–12.

11 Schlup, "Pacheco, Romualdo," *ANB*.

12 For accounts of Pacheco's exploits as an outdoorsman, see, for example, "Gleanings from the Mails," 15 March 1875, *New York Times*: 2; "Pacheco's Prowess," 13 April 1878, *San Francisco Chronicle*: 1; T. C. Crawford, "Pacheco as a Hunter," 8 December 1890, *Chicago Daily Tribune*: 6.

13 Stanley B. Parsons et al., *United States Congressional Districts, 1843–1883* (New York: Greenwood Press, 1986): 151–152.

14 Quoted in Genini and Hitchman, *Romualdo Pacheco*: 148.

15 "The Pacific States," 9 September 1876, *New York Times*: 2; Genini and Hitchman, *Romualdo Pacheco*: 148–149.

16 Michael J. Dubin et al., *U.S. Congressional Elections, 1788–1997* (Jefferson, NC: McFarland & Company, Inc., 1998): 236.

17 Chester H. Rowell, *A Historical and Legal Digest of All the Contested Election Cases* (Washington, D.C.: Government Printing Office, 1901): 322–323.

18 *Congressional Record*, House, 45th Cong., 1st sess. (17 October 1877): 91–93.

19 See House Committee on Elections, *Case of Wigginton vs. Pacheco*, 45th Cong., 1st sess., 31 January 1878, H. Rep. 118.

20 Rowell, *A Historical and Legal Digest of All the Contested Election Cases*: 323.

21 Ibid., 323–324. One Democrat, Clarkson Potter of New York, voted in Pacheco's favor *Congressional Record*, House, 45th Cong., 2nd sess. (7 February 1878): 836–837. See also "Democratic Unscrupulousness," 8 February 1878, *New York Times*: 1.

22 Dubin et al., *U.S. Congressional Elections, 1788–1997*: 248, 250; See, for example, "Notas Politicas," *La gaceta* (Santa Barbara, CA), 9 October 1880: 2; "Notas Politicas," *La gaceta* (Santa Barbara, CA), 23 October 1880: 2; [Untitled article], *La gaceta* (Santa Barbara, CA), 23 October 1880: 2. Translated by Translations International, Inc. (February 2010).

23 "Él siempre ha recibido la ardiente ayuda de éstos, y ha gozado la dignidad y emolumentos de posición oficial por sus sufragios, pero ninguno de su clase jamás ha sido nombrado á alguna posición ó favorecido por su influencia!" "Opiniones de la prensa," *La gaceta* (Santa Barbara, CA), 16 October 1880: 2. Translated as "Opinion of the Editors," by Translations International, Inc. (February 2010).

24 David T. Canon et al., *Committees in the U.S. Congress, 1789 to 1946*, vol. 3 (Washington, D.C.: Congressional Quarterly Press, 2002): 796. Pacheco also served on the Select Committee on the Death of President Garfield; see *Congressional Record*, House, 47th Cong., 1st sess. (9 December 1877): 64. Canon does not list Pacheco as a member of the select committee; see David T. Canon et al., *Committees in the U.S. Congress, 1789 to 1946*, vol. 4 (Washington, D.C.: Congressional Quarterly Press, 2002): 301.

25 From the 45th to the 53rd Congresses (1877–1895), all three committees were of middling desirability; see Charles Stewart III, "Committee Hierarchies in the Modernizing House, 1875–1947," *American Journal of Political Science* 36 (1992): 845–846.

26 *Congressional Record*, House, 46th Cong., 3rd sess. (15 February 1881): 1642.

27 The Asian population in California was 49,310 in the 1870 Census and 75,218 in the 1880 Census. However, the influx in immigration generally in California increased by a similar percentage in this decade. The Asian population was 8.5 percent of the total population in 1870, but it increased only slightly, to 8.7 percent of the total population, in 1880. See Appendix A-1 "Race and Hispanic Origin for the United States: 1790 to 1990," in Campbell Gibson and Kay Jung, "Historical Census Statistics on Population Totals by Race, 1790 to 1990, and by Hispanic Origin, 1970 to 1990, for Large Cities and Other Urban Places in the United States," U.S. Census Bureau, http://www.census.gov/population/www/documentation/twps0076/twps0076.html (accessed 3 February 2010).

28 *Congressional Record*, House, 47th Cong., 1st sess. (23 February 1882): 2210.

29 For more information on the national politics of Asian immigration, specifically in the debate and passage of the Chinese Exclusion Act of 1882, see Andrew Gyory, *Closing the Gate: Race, Politics, and the Chinese Exclusion Act* (Chapel Hill: University of North Carolina Press, 1998).

30 *Congressional Record*, House, 47th Cong., 1st sess. (23 February 1882): 2210.

31 Ibid., 2211.

32 Ibid.

33 Ibid., 2227–2228.

34 Gyory, *Closing the Gate:* 238. President Chester A. Arthur vetoed the original bill. The House and Senate re-adopted a similar bill that temporarily excluded Chinese immigration. Arthur signed the bill into law on May 6, 1882. Pacheco supported the new measure; see *Congressional Record*, House, 47th Cong., 1st sess. (17 April 1882): 2973–2974.

35 "Romualdo Pacheco," 26 January 1899, *Los Angeles Times*: 8.

Trinidad Romero
1835–1918

TERRITORIAL DELEGATE 1877–1879
REPUBLICAN FROM NEW MEXICO

Considered one of the "most widely known and influential politicians of New Mexico in the territorial days," Trinidad Romero, a successful merchant and entrepreneur, served a single term as a Territorial Delegate to Congress. His short time in the House, like that of many other New Mexican Delegates of the era, marked but a brief moment in a long career in various territorial offices.[1]

Trinidad Romero was born June 15, 1835, in Santa Fe, New Mexico, to Miguel Romero and Josefa Delgado. Miguel had extensive experience in the American occupation government. He was appointed *alcalde* (mayor) of Santa Fe by General Stephen Kearny during the military occupation period and was a founder of the Republican Party in New Mexico. The second of 10 children, Romero was educated by private tutors and also received some formal schooling.[2] He left Santa Fe at age 15 and moved 50 miles east to Las Vegas, New Mexico, where he "engaged extensively in sheep and cattle raising … also in the general merchandising business, which through careful management, yielded him a large profit."[3] Romero assisted his father with freighting goods via ox teams between St. Louis, Missouri, and Las Vegas, New Mexico, in 1851. The business prospered since Las Vegas lay astride the Santa Fe Trail, which connected Santa Fe with Independence, Missouri. The family also took advantage of the burgeoning railroad industry to form a merchandise conglomerate. The senior Romero and three of his sons, including Trinidad, founded the Romero Mercantile Company in 1878, with Miguel serving as the company's first president. Trinidad succeeded his father and later yielded the post to one of his brothers. The business prospered, enabling the family to build branch stores in other New Mexican towns. Romero married Valeria Lopez, the daughter of a Las Vegas, New Mexico, sheriff. The couple had eight children: Serapio; Bernardo; Roman; Miguel; Epimenia; Trinidad, Jr.; Valeria; and Margarita. The family's wealth was considerable; Romero was a prominent landowner in San Miguel County, and his holdings included a 3,000-acre ranch and the sprawling El Puertocito Grant, which he owned with his brother, Eugenio, a prominent politician.[4]

Romero became politically active in the 1860s as a result of his business activities. Elected to the territorial house of representatives in 1863, he served for one term.[5] He also served as probate judge of San Miguel County in 1869 and 1870. During the 1860s, Romero emerged as one of the leaders of the Republican Party in San Miguel County, which encompassed his political base in Las Vegas, and which had experienced considerable growth. At the time, San Miguel County was in the north-central portion of the territory; later, portions of it were carved out to form Guadalupe County in the south. Canyons and highlands shaped the northwestern landscape of San Miguel, which stretched from the Sangre de Cristo Mountains and was drained by the Pecos River. The 655,000-acre Pablo Montoya Grant yawned across the western part of the county, sustaining some of the largest cattle-ranching operations in the territory. By 1880 the Santa Fe Railroad had been built across the northwestern section of San Miguel.[6]

In 1876 Romero ran for the Delegate's seat in the U.S. House for the 45th Congress (1877–1879) when Stephen B. Elkins, a powerful attorney and the incumbent Delegate, chose not to run for re-election.[7] Elkins controlled New Mexico's most potent political machine, the Santa Fe Ring, a network of business, legal, and political elites who dominated territorial affairs. Romero received not only Elkins's endorsement, but also the unanimous nomination of the Republican territorial

Helen Haines, *History of New Mexico from the Spanish Conquest to the Present Time 1530–1890 with Portraits and Biographical Sketches of its Prominent People* (New York, NY: New Mexico Historical Publishing Company, 1891)

convention.[8] In a glowing editorial highlighting Romero's business acumen, a partisan supporter asked, "If you had to choose one of these candidates with whom to entrust your private business … would you not rather trust the man who has guided his own business affairs with the most discretion[?] Every voter would do so in his own business; then why will you not act as wisely when you entrust a man with your public business[?]"[9] Romero defeated Democrat Pedro Valdez, a two-term member of the territorial assembly (and former speaker) with 56 percent of the vote in a relatively clean election.[10]

When Romero claimed his seat in the U.S. House in October 1877 at the opening of the 45th Congress, he was given no committee assignments. (Territorial Delegates had only recently been granted the privilege of serving on standing committees, and no New Mexico Delegate would serve on a committee until 1880.) Nevertheless, Romero exercised his right to submit legislation, introducing eight bills that reflected his preoccupation with constituent services. The purposes of the bills ranged from seeking pension relief for individuals to confirming land claims in New Mexico. Romero also sought compensation for former Delegate Francisco Perea's battalion of militia that fought against the Confederate Army from November 1861 to January 1862.[11]

Much of his legislative work was frustrated because his party did not control the House. Romero's rights and privileges were curtailed by House Rules that favored the Democratic majority, and his weakness was compounded by the fact that he was a freshman. Moreover, his legislative priorities ranked low because of his status as a nonvoting Delegate. Frustrated at his inability to obtain financial relief for farmers whose crops were damaged by a grasshopper infestation in Rio Arriba and Taos Counties, Romero apologized to a local judge in a public letter. "Thrice have I attempted by introducing a resolution for the purpose, but thrice my resolution has been defeated," he wrote. Since the House calendar, which prioritizes the legislation the chamber will debate and vote upon, was determined by the majority party, Romero's bills were listed at the bottom of the agenda or ignored altogether.[12] "If the House would have acted on the private calendar at its due time, the bill … would have passed a long time since," Romero explained. "But unfortunately it was not done, not on account of time, but on account of politics and demagogueism which predominate in the present Congress and seems to absorb the whole attention of its members." After promising to continue fighting for federal relief money, Romero closed his public letter by offering "one hundred head of sheep, as my private contribution for the relief of those that are in most need."[13]

Like many of his contemporaries who served as Territorial Delegates—party placeholders who treated their positions as stepping stones to new political or business ventures in the territory—Romero declined to seek re-election in the 46th Congress (1879–1881). He returned to his business activities in the territory and remained active in local politics, serving as a U.S. Marshal from 1889 to 1893. Romero was one of only a handful of *nuevomexicanos* to hold this position in the 19th century. He also edited the *Campaign Bulletin*, a short-lived newspaper that covered aspiring New Mexican Republican politicians.[14] By 1891, a historical survey of the territory noted that although Romero had "lost two fortunes … through his indomitable will and ambitious and energetic spirit he … is to-day reputed to be one of the [most] successful men of New Mexico."[15] On August 28, 1918, Romero died in Las Vegas, New Mexico.[16]

FOR FURTHER READING

Biographical Directory of the United States Congress, "Trinidad Romero" http://bioguide.congress.gov.

NOTES

1 "Trinidad Romero Dies at Las Vegas at Age of 83 Years," 29 August 1918, *Santa Fe New Mexican*: 5. For a brief description of the evolution of congressional careers in the 19th century, see Linda L. Fowler, "Congressional Careers," in Donald C. Bacon, Roger H. Davidson, and Morton Keller, eds., *The Encyclopedia of the United States Congress*, vol. 3 (New York: Simon & Schuster, 1995): 1379–1383.

2 "Trinidad Romero," in Maurilio E. Vigil, *Los Patrones: Profiles of Hispanic Political Leaders in New Mexico History* (Washington, D.C.: University Press of America, 1980): 63–69; Helen Haines, *History of New Mexico from the Spanish Conquest to the Present Time, 1530–1890* (New York: New Mexico Historical Publishing Co., 1890): 360–363. According to Vigil, Romero did not receive any formal schooling, but according to Haines, Romero "received the benefits of a common school education in Santa Fe." See also Carlos Brazil Ramirez, "The Hispanic Political Elite in Territorial New Mexico: A Study of Classical Colonialism," (Ph.D. diss., University of California–Santa Barbara, 1979): 297.

3 Haines, *History of New Mexico from the Spanish Conquest to the Present Time, 1530–1890*: 360.

4 Ibid., 363; Ramirez, "The Hispanic Political Elite in Territorial New Mexico": 297.

5 W. G. Ritch, *The Legislative Blue Book of New Mexico* (Albuquerque: University of New Mexico Press, 1968; reprint of 1882 edition): 110.

6 For a description of San Miguel County, see Charles F. Coan, *A History of New Mexico,* vol. 1 (Chicago: The American Historical Society, Inc., 1925): 545–548.

7 "The Republican Candidate," 15 September 1876, (Santa Fe) *Daily New Mexican*: 1.

8 "The Convention Thursday," 16 September 1876, (Santa Fe) *Daily New Mexican*: 1.

9 "For Delegate," 24 October 1876, (Santa Fe) *Daily New Mexican*: 3.

10 "Trinidad Romero," in Vigil, *Los Patrones: Profiles of Hispanic Political Leaders in New Mexico History*: 63–69; Ralph E. Twitchell, *Leading Facts of New Mexico History*, vol. 2 (Cedar Rapids, IA: Torch Press, 1912): 406–407; "The Official Vote of New Mexico," 12 December 1876, (Santa Fe) *Daily New Mexican*: 1. The final tally had Romero with 9,591 votes against Valdez's 7,418. These election results are confirmed in the *Congressional Directory*, 45th Cong., 2nd sess. (Washington, D.C.: Government Printing Office, 1878): 76. For biographical and career information about Valdez, see Ritch, *The Legislative Blue Book of New Mexico,* 106, 110; and Ramirez, "The Hispanic Political Elite in Territorial New Mexico": 296–297. Valdez served in the Eighth Legislative Assembly (1858–1859) and Fourteenth Legislative Assembly (1863–1865). According to Ramirez, Valdez submitted the 1859 slave code bill on behalf of Territorial Delegate Miguel Antonio Otero and territorial secretary Alexander Jackson.

11 *Congressional Record*, Index, 45th Cong., 2nd sess.: 479; *Congressional Record*, Index, 45th Cong., 3rd sess.: 269; *Congressional Record*, House, 45th Cong., 2nd sess. (10 April 1878): 2422.

12 Roger H. Davidson and Walter Olezsek, *Congress and Its Members*, 10th ed. (Washington, D.C.: CQ Press, 2008): 246.

13 "The Appropriation for the Taos Sufferers," 15 June 1878, (Santa Fe) *Weekly New Mexican*: 2.

14 Ramirez, "The Hispanic Political Elite in Territorial New Mexico": 297.

15 Haines, *History of New Mexico from the Spanish Conquest to the Present Time, 1530–1890*: 360.

16 "Trinidad Romero," in Vigil, *Los Patrones: Profiles of Hispanic Political Leaders in New Mexico History*: 67; "White House Callers," 8 November 1889, *Los Angeles Times*: 5; "Trinidad Romero Dies at Las Vegas at Age of 83 Years."

Mariano Sabino Otero
1844–1904

TERRITORIAL DELEGATE 1879–1881
REPUBLICAN FROM NEW MEXICO

A successful rancher and banker, Mariano Otero enjoyed a short-lived career in elective office that was emblematic of the web of business and familial connections among the territorial political elite. His uncle, Miguel Antonio Otero, Sr., served as New Mexico's Delegate to the U.S. House from 1856 to 1861. His cousin, Miguel Antonio Otero, Jr., built a career as a powerful state politician, eventually becoming the only Hispanic-American governor of the New Mexico Territory. In accepting the nomination in 1878 to run as the Republican nominee for Territorial Delegate, Otero wrote, "The confidence manifested by the unanimity of my nomination arouses in me the most profound emotions of gratitude and an earnest determination to spare no effort and hesitate at no sacrifice of my personal convenience to discharge worthily the duties of the position."[1] His fleeting career at the federal level coincided with the declining influence of the Republican Party in late 19th-century New Mexico.

Mariano Sabino Otero was born in Peralta, Valencia County, New Mexico, on August 28, 1844, to Juan Otero and his wife, whose name is not known. He was educated in private and parochial schools in New Mexico and then studied at St. Louis University. Upon returning to New Mexico, Otero became a sheep and cattle rancher and later moved into banking. The Otero family dominated Valencia County, which at one time stretched from Texas to California. The eastern part of the county was bordered by the San José, Rio Puerco, and Rio Grande Rivers; the west was bordered by streams that flowed into the Zuñi River. The sprawling county was separated by the Continental Divide, with the Zuñi Mountains in its northwest quadrant.[2] Mariano Otero relocated to Albuquerque and married Filomena Perea, the sister of Pedro Perea, a rising politico who eventually served as a Delegate in Congress. The couple had five children: Margarita; Frederick; Alfredo; Mariano, Jr.; and Dolores.[3]

Otero became active in politics when he served as probate judge in Bernalillo County from 1871 to 1879. In 1874 state Democrats nominated him for congressional Delegate, but he declined their offer, perhaps because of the responsibilities of managing his business empire; he not only achieved great success in ranching, marketing, and commerce, but he also owned the Nuestra Señora de la Luz de los Lagunitas Land Grant, which comprised more than 39,000 acres.[4]

In 1878 the state Republican Party nominated Otero to run for the Delegate's seat. This time Otero reluctantly accepted the nomination. Santa Fe's *New Mexican*, a mouthpiece for the GOP, noted Otero's "superior qualifications for the position are well known to the entire community and … [he] is universally recognized and respected as a gentleman of fine ability." The newspaper noted that Otero "did not seek the nomination; in fact [he] earnestly entreated the delegates to nominate another man; but so strong was the feeling in his favor that no heed was given to his declination … and [he] was nominated by acclamation."[5] In his acceptance letter, Otero thanked the committee. As "the candidate of the Republican party," he expressed pride in "its record and achievements and loyal[ty] to its principles." If elected, Otero promised to "earnestly endeavor to fairly represent all the people and the interests of every section of the Territory, faithfully, honestly, and to the very best of my ability." Otero also indicated his desire and expectation that his political opponents would place the welfare of the territory above expedient political maneuvering, and asked for "the sympathy and assistance not only of my political friends and supporters but of all my fellow citizens whose intelligence and patriotism impels them to regard as

Image courtesy of the Palace of the Governors Photo Archives (NMHM/DCA), 10327

paramount to all other considerations the welfare and the prosperity and happiness of [the New Mexican] people."[6] As was often the case in New Mexican politics of this era, the opposing political candidate was a relative. Democrat Benito Baca was a successful entrepreneur who came from a prominent political family in San Miguel County, in the north-central portion of the territory, and was married to a niece of Otero's uncle, Miguel Antonio Otero, Sr. Baca's campaign was hamstrung by health issues. Suffering from carbuncle, a bacterial skin infection that causes large boils, Baca underwent a painful surgery but recovered to run in the election.[7]

Otero traversed the territory, visiting Valencia, Socorro, and San Miguel Counties, some of the most populated portions of New Mexico. The editors of the Santa Fe *New Mexican* predicted, "Old reliable Republican counties will give larger republican majorities than ever before." They also reported dissatisfaction within Democratic sectors: "Not only are republicans aroused by the disreputable course of the democrats … but many respectable democrats [who] are disgusted with the course of that party, and not willing to bear any share in the responsibilities for the vile slanders … have repudiated the party and its candidate, and are working for Otero."[8] Otero was so popular that one political observer wrote a "Homily in Verse" lauding his nomination and urging readers to vote for him: "So then New Mexicans, love your country, vote for Mariano Otero, drop Benito Baca; taking a closer look and reflecting on the issue New Mexico declares, Elect our champion!"[9] Esteem for the two candidates energized the bases of their parties, resulting in a large turnout. The popular vote was split nearly down the middle. Otero prevailed on Election Day with 9,739 votes to Benito Baca's 9,067, translating into a narrow 52 to 48 percent margin of victory. The editors of the *New Mexican* considered the 1878 election "among the most fairly and most closely contested elections that have transpired since the organization of the territory" and attributed the closeness of the election to the Republicans' disorganization early in the race and the Democrats' efficiency rallying supporters.[10]

Elected to the 46th Congress (1879–1881), Otero was sworn in on March 19, 1879.[11] Under new House Rules enacted during his tenure, he became the first New Mexican Territorial Delegate—and only the second Hispanic-American Member of Congress—to earn a committee assignment, on the Committee on Coinage, Weights, and Measures. Otero tended primarily to constituent services by submitting pension and relief requests for individuals in the territory as well as bills supporting the education of Pueblo Indian children. Also, like many of his predecessors, he sought to secure federal appropriations for local projects.[12]

When it came time for the 1880 elections, Otero declined to seek renomination after serving a single term. He returned to New Mexico, where he pursued his business interests and a career in state politics. By 1884 Otero had affiliated himself with powerful Republican oligarchs like Stephen Elkins and Thomas Catron, along with his relatives José Francisco Chaves and Miguel Otero in the Santa Fe Ring.[13] From 1884 to 1886, he served as commissioner of Bernalillo County. He also served as a delegate to the 1889 territorial constitutional convention.[14]

By the late 1880s, Otero's connections to the Santa Fe Ring had renewed his interest in the coveted Delegate post. In 1888 and 1890 he ran as a Republican, but he lost both times by narrow margins to Antonio Joseph because of the GOP's factionalism and Joseph's wide popularity.[15] During the 1888 campaign, Otero was well received throughout the territory. A newspaper account reported, "Expressions of gratitude are being received from all over the county [Dona Ana] about the nomination of Mariano S. Otero … [who] is so well known in this county that there is no need to praise him in our area."[16] A man who identified himself as "a Mexican" appealed to *Hispano* constituents in a campaign poem: "O valiant Mexican!/If you want to be protected…./Cast your vote and your support/For Otero, our champion." The poem then exhorted voters, "Be free! Be proud!/Noble blood runs in your veins/Have Courage! The world is yours!/Take the chains off your neck."[17] But Joseph prevailed, with 53.5 percent of the vote to Otero's 46.5 percent.

In the 1890 race, Joseph suffered the political fallout from his failure the previous year to support the proposed draft of the New Mexico state constitution. The Republican organ, the Santa Fe *Daily New Mexican,* portrayed Otero as a progressive, business-oriented candidate who would resolve land grant issues and move New Mexico forward.[18] In fact, a major plank of Otero's platform was to resolve some of the outstanding land titles that plagued New Mexico.[19] In other sections of the territory, Otero was "pushing the battle to the wall, and … being ably seconded by local leaders and county committees."[20] One editor wrote, Otero "represents the party which has declared itself in favor of those measures of public policy which are best calculated to promote the material interests of New Mexico, and … puts those principles into practice."[21] Nevertheless, the Democratic incumbent won by a 53 to 47 percent margin that was nearly identical to the one he had polled two years earlier.[22]

Otero's second unsuccessful campaign effectively ended his quest to rejuvenate his career in elective politics. During the 1890s, he served as president of the Albuquerque Bank of Commerce. On February 1, 1904, Otero died of a stroke at age 59.[23]

FOR FURTHER READING

Biographical Directory of the United States Congress, "Mariano Sabino Otero," http://bioguide.congress.gov.

RESEARCH COLLECTIONS

New Mexico State Records Center and Archives (Santa Fe). Otero is included among the correspondents in the Governor L. Bradford Prince papers, 1889–1893.

University of New Mexico, Center for Southwest Research (Albuquerque). Otero is included among the correspondents in the Charles Lanman correspondence, 1860–1868.

NOTES

1 "Mr. Otero's Letter of Acceptance," 17 August 1878, (Santa Fe) *The New Mexican*: 2.

2 Charles Coan, *A History of New Mexico*, vol. 1 (Chicago and New York: The American Historical Society, 1925): 551–552.

3 "Mariano Otero," in Maurilio E. Vigil, *Los Patrones: Profiles of Hispanic Political Leaders in New Mexico History* (Washington, D.C.: University Press of America, 1980): 74–76; "Hon. M. S. Otero: His Sudden Death from Apoplexy Early This Morning at His Residence," 1 February 1904, *Albuquerque Daily Citizen*: 1; "Warring Republican Factions," 10 October 1890, *New York Times*: 2; *Tenth Census of the United States, 1880: Population Schedule, Bernalillo, Bernalillo, New Mexico Territory*, Roll T9_802, page 29.3000, http://search.ancestrylibrary.com (accessed 5 June 2010).

4 Carlos Brazil Ramirez, "The Hispanic Political Elite in Territorial New Mexico: A Study of Classical Colonialism," (Ph.D. diss., University of California–Santa Barbara, 1979): 298–299.

5 "Our Candidate," 3 August 1878, (Santa Fe) *The New Mexican*: 2.

6 "Mr. Otero's Letter of Acceptance."

7 "Death of Don Benito Baca," 25 June 1879, (Las Cruces, NM) *Thirty-Four*: 1; "Honor to the Dead: The Territorial Press on the Death of Don Benito Baca," 2 July 1879, (Las Cruces, NM) *Thirty-Four*. Baca was born on March 10, 1849, to Juan Maria Baca and Dolores Sandoval de Baca. Juan Maria Baca was a prominent political leader and probate judge in San Miguel County and one of the founders of its county seat, Las Vegas. Benito studied at a private school in Santa Fe and graduated from St. Louis University. He worked for Otero, Sellar, and Company for three years and managed a large family estate in Las Vegas. Baca married Emilia Otero, a niece of former Territorial Delegate Miguel Antonio Otero, Sr., in 1873. After the election, Baca underwent a second surgical procedure but died on June 21, 1879. For more information about Baca, see Benjamin M. Read, *Illustrated History of New Mexico* (New York: Arno Press, 1976; reprint of 1912 edition): 732–733; and Ramirez, "The Hispanic Political Elite in Territorial New Mexico: A Study of Classical Colonialism": 298–299.

8 "The Campaign," 21 September 1878, (Santa Fe) *The New Mexican*: 2.

9 "Pues bien, Nuevo Mejicanos/Teneis amor por la Patria/Votad por Mariano Otero/Dejad á Benito Baca/Dando una mirada electa/ Reflejando la cuestion/El Nuevo Méjico grita/Electo nuestro campeón," Un Viajero (A Traveler), "Homilía en Verso," 2 November 1878, *The New Mexican* (Santa Fe, NM): 2. Translated as "Homily in Verse," by Translations International, Inc. (December 2009).

10 "The Official Count on Delegate," 7 December 1878, (Santa Fe) *The New Mexican*: 2; "Lessons of the Campaign," 16 November 1878, (Santa Fe) *The New Mexican*: 2.

11 *Congressional Record*, House, 46th Cong., 1st sess. (19 March 1879): 19.

12 See listings in the *Congressional Record* Index, 46th Cong., 2nd sess.: 644.

13 Robert W. Larson, *New Mexico's Quest for Statehood, 1846–1912* (Albuquerque: University of New Mexico Press, 1968): 144.

14 For more information about the 1889 territorial constitutional convention, see Larson, *New Mexico's Quest for Statehood, 1846–1912*: 147–168.

15 "Overtaken by the Pale Rider," 1 February 1904, *Santa Fe New Mexican*: 1; Ramirez, "The Hispanic Political Elite in Territorial New Mexico: A Study of Classical Colonialism": 299; Coan, *A History of New Mexico*, vol. 1: 409.

16 "De todos [*sic*] partes de el [*sic*] condado vienen espreciones [*sic*] de gratificación sobre la nominación de Don Mariano S. Otero … es tan bien conocido en este condado que no hay necesidad de elogiarlo en nuestra parte," "Egos Políticos," 11 September 1888, *El observador fronterizo* (Las Cruces, NM): 1. Translated as "Political Egos" by Translations International, Inc. (December 2009).

17 Coan, *A History of New Mexico*, vol. 1: 490; "Mejicano valiente!/Si deseas protección … Da tu voto y soporte/A Otero nuestro campeón … Sois libre! Tienes orgullo!/Sangre noble corre en tus venas/Ten valor! El Mundo es tuyo!!/Quitate del pezcueso [sic] las cadenas," "Viva Otero," 30 October 1888, *El observador fronterizo* (Las Cruces, NM): 1. Translated as "Long Live Otero" by Translations International, Inc. (December 2009).

18 "Another Lie Exploded," 23 October 1890, (Santa Fe) *Daily New Mexican*: 2; "Warring Republican Factions," 10 October 1890, *New York Times*: 2. According to this article in the *New York Times*, Otero's support splintered when he became involved in a feud with his Perea relatives over the choice of Bernalillo County sheriff. Otero voted for Perfecto Armijo, while the Perea clan supported a relative, José L. Perea, for the position. By mid-October, wrote the *New York Times*, Otero "dropped his Territorial canvass against Anthony Joseph … and says he will devote his time here to defeating the Pereas." While the *New Mexican* alleged that the *New York Times* story was a lie, this incident, whether or not it actually occurred, illustrates the intense political competition between the Oteros and the Pereas.

19 "Mr. Joseph's Course on the Land Court Bill," 15 October 1890, (Santa Fe) *Daily New Mexican*: 2.

20 "Cheering News for M. S. Otero," 23 October 1890, (Santa Fe) *Daily New Mexican*: 2.

21 "The Only Question," 1 November 1890, (Santa Fe) *Daily New Mexican*: 2. See also "A Business Reason Why M. S. Otero Should Be Elected," 30 October 1890, (Santa Fe) *Daily New Mexican*: 2.

22 "Statement of the Vote of the Territory of New Mexico for Delegate to the Fifty-Second Congress, Cast at the November Election 1890, as Declared by the Secretary of the Territory, December 6, 1890," Copy of the Executive Proceedings of the Territory of New Mexico, July 1, 1889–December 31, 1899, National Archives Microfilm Publication M364, Roll 2, Interior Department Territorial Papers, New Mexico, 1851–1914, Records of the Department of the Interior, Record Group 48; National Archives at College Park, College Park, MD. The election results are also listed in Coan, *A History of New Mexico,* vol. 1: 409.

23 "Mariano Otero," in Vigil, *Los Patrones*: 74; "Hon. M. S. Otero: His Sudden Death from Apoplexy Early This Morning at His Residence."

"I HOLD THAT NO CITIZEN HAS THE RIGHT TO REFUSE TO SERVE HIS COUNTRY IN ANY PUBLIC POSITION TO WHICH HIS FELLOW CITIZENS MAY CALL HIM."

Mariano Otero
(Santa Fe) *The New Mexican*, August 17, 1878

Tranquilino Luna
1849–1892

TERRITORIAL DELEGATE 1881–1884
REPUBLICAN FROM NEW MEXICO

Tranquilino Luna was a transitional figure in New Mexico politics. A successful rancher and entrepreneur, Luna ran for the Territorial Delegate's seat in the U.S. House against Miguel A. Otero, a seasoned political veteran and a patron of early territorial politics. Their 1880 election campaign displayed the stark divide between the older, founding generation of territorial politicos and a successor generation bent on dictating the terms of New Mexico's political future. Once in Congress, Luna introduced a bill to create a state government and bring New Mexico into the Union. However, his controversial 1882 election sparked a conflict between warring political factions throughout the territory and prematurely ended his House career.

Tranquilino Luna was born on June 29, 1847, in Los Lunas, Valencia County, Mexico, to Antonio Jose Luna and Isabella Baca. According to one scholar, Antonio was quite wealthy. A merchant-farmer, Luna "grazed 45,000 sheep and had an annual income of $25,000 at the height of his career."[1] Tranquilino Luna's family was active in politics; his grandfather, Juan Baca, had served three terms in the territorial assembly as a representative of Valencia County.[2] One of nine children, Luna was educated in local public schools. Like the other offspring of affluent *nuevomexicanos* in the territory, Luna was sent to college in the United States. After graduating from the University of Missouri at Columbia, Luna returned to New Mexico to work in the livestock industry. In the late 1860s he married Amalia Jaramillo. The couple had one son, Maximiliano, who later became one of Theodore (Teddy) Roosevelt's Rough Riders in the Spanish-American War.[3]

In 1878 Republicans nominated Luna for Delegate at their convention, but "for the sake of harmony" he declined the offer to make way for Mariano S. Otero, whom he "promised to support … heartily." Two years later, when Otero declined nomination for a second term, Luna sought to run for Delegate in the 47th Congress (1881–1883). In August 1880, the Republican Party unanimously nominated him as its candidate. The *Daily New Mexican* described the new nominee as a "man of kindly, energetic, and enterprising disposition and exceedingly popular among all classes, both of Americans and Mexicans wherever known."[4] In his acceptance speech at the nominating convention, Luna assured supporters, "I pledge most solemnly if elected to do all that lays in my power for the development and prosperity for the people, and … the many and varied interests of our beloved Territory." He vowed to address infrastructure improvements, including the expansion of the railroads. His campaign received a boost from the support of former Delegate José Francisco Chaves, a major political patron who campaigned for Luna in the northern counties of the territory.[5] Luna's Democratic opponent was another towering figure in territorial politics, Mariano Otero's uncle, Miguel Otero, Sr., who had served as Territorial Delegate during the 34th through the 36th Congresses (1855–1861). At the time of Otero's tenure, the New Mexico territorial government was controlled by "National Democrats," who aligned themselves with the Democratic presidential administrations in Washington and supported preserving slavery and secession.[6] A Southern sympathizer, Otero tried to move New Mexico toward statehood and economic development by allying himself with powerful Southern Members of Congress. Although publicly Otero took a middle course on secession, questions about his loyalty forced him in 1860 to relocate with his family to Missouri, where they remained for the better part of a decade. This left him open to accusations in 1880 that he was little more than a carpetbagger, "a gentleman who was born in New Mexico but has lived for a great portion of his life in Colorado and Kansas."[7]

Image courtesy of the Palace of the Governors Photo Archives (NMHM/DCA), 9978

A major campaign issue was the impact on territorial development of old land grants approved by the Spanish, Mexican, and New Mexican governments for prominent families. The question of whether the United States would honor individual claims to these large swaths of land when it acquired New Mexico had been resolved by the Treaty of Guadalupe Hidalgo, but their private ownership hindered settlement and curtailed business opportunities created by the rise of the transcontinental railroad.[8] Otero campaigned on the promise to resolve the impasse, though critics noted that he had been responsible—or at least had raised no objections—to efforts to secure patents for some of the largest grants in the 1850s.[9]

Memories of Otero's pro-Southern inclinations lingered in 1880, and his political opponents attacked this facet of his congressional service. Otero tried to turn his prior service to his advantage, arguing that experience trumped old political arguments. "I am acquainted with members of Congress; am conversant with the rules and methods by which business is done in the house ... and could go at once to work for the Territory without losing time in becoming acquainted with the details of parliamentary rules," Otero asserted. "Luna knows nothing of these things, and the five or six months which he would lose in learning them, would be employed by me profitably." Opponents countered that Congress had changed in Otero's two-decade absence. "Congressmen have died and disappeared and there remain few of Otero's colleagues, even those having long since forgotten him," wrote the *Daily New Mexican.* The newspaper's editors also insinuated that Otero was too old, that he possessed "no longer the manhood and ambition which might have urged him to prominence in past years and ... has not now the energy which should have produced work from him."[10]

Critics also charged Otero with pandering to *Hispano* constituents, whom they said he had denigrated as a Delegate in the 1850s. "In addressing himself to our Mexican residents he adroitly identifies with them and their interests and is full of ... sympathy and affection for his own race," wrote the editors of the *Daily New Mexican.* "No one would think from the cunning addresses that Otero is ashamed that he was born a Mexican, but it is so."[11] Otero's camp countered by accusing "Luna of being implicated in land-grant feuds" and of "being an enemy of the Mexican."[12] Another Otero supporter, exemplifying the highly personalized politics of Territorial Delegate elections, warned Luna about the futility of campaigning in Las Vegas, New Mexico, an Otero stronghold. "Tranquilino, stay at home, and forever give up the mistaken idea that you were cut out for a Congressman. It takes brains to be a member of Congress as well as a thorough familiarity with parliamentary usages and a keen insight into the needs of a rapidly-growing Territory. You certainly have common sense enough to know that you lack these requirements."[13]

Although Luna's supporters attacked Otero, Luna stated he did "not believe in the policy or decency of personal abuse or mud throwing. Of the Democratic nominee," he continued, "personally I have none but kind words to speak. Of his and his newspapers' policy of personality and no argument, I confidently leave the voters to judge." Luna's pledge not to turn the campaign into a personal popularity contest suggested a shift in the territorial elections in the 1880s in which national issues took precedence over the cult of personality.[14] Luna focused on issues such as settling land grants and instituting a comprehensive public education system in the territory. "I believe in full and free education by compulsion if necessary," he said. "The school house speaks volumes, and wherever you find it you find a progressive, useful, and worthy people."[15] In the end, Luna defeated Otero, with 53 to 47 percent of the vote.[16] Although the newspapers reported no widespread voter abuse or fraud, Miguel Otero, Jr., recalled, "Rumors of great frauds ... were rife on the streets of every town in the Territory, and the Democrats made preparations to do what they could to check such tactics. But their results were unavailing." Otero, Jr., was dispatched to Socorro County "to watch for evidence of fraudulent practices" and to Valencia County, "where it was said they voted the sheep." In Valencia County, he claimed a precinct cast nearly 1,000 votes for Luna but not one for his father. The precinct "turned out … to be merely a sheep camp belonging to the Luna family," but given the Republican control of the House, Miguel Otero, Sr., did not contest the election.[17]

When Luna claimed his seat at the opening of the 47th Congress (1881–1883), he received the committee assignment Mariano Otero had held in the previous Congress. The Committee on Coinage, Weights, and Measures had jurisdiction over the standardization of weights and measurements and over any legislation affecting currency. Though not eagerly sought after by most House Members, the assignment was useful to Delegates from states with large mining interests, such as New Mexico. Like many other Territorial Delegates, Luna worked largely behind the scenes, not in the public eye making floor speeches. Typical of new Members, he focused on constituent services, submitting bills for pension relief and resolving land claims.[18] Luna submitted two bills to clarify land grant rights; one of the bills, H.R. 1923, was submitted as a substitute on Luna's behalf by Representative Romualdo Pacheco of California, chairman of the Committee on Private Land Claims.[19] Luna also submitted H.R. 1922 to provide for the formation of a state government in the territory. The bill was referred to the Judiciary Committee, where it eventually died at the end of the congressional term. Luna submitted H.R. 7443 to amend the Organic Act of New Mexico by modifying Texas' northern and western boundaries to settle border disputes that had festered since the Compromise of 1850.[20]

Luna sought a second term in the 48th Congress (1883–1885), telling a reporter he had "been importuned by a number of friends to consent to run, and after repeated importunities had finally given his consent." Bucking the unspoken expectation that Territorial Delegates serve only one term, Luna acknowledged that while he had not voiced his disagreement with the custom to "rapidly rotate the incumbent out of office … he had always thought it a bad practice, [because] a delegate could hardly get to work effectively in a single term of congress."[21] Luna's opponent was Democrat Francisco Manzanares, a successful entrepreneur-turned-politician. The press portrayed Manzanares as the unknown candidate, echoing Luna that he was better qualified because of his familiarity with Washington, D.C. Although many Territorial Delegates of the era had been successful businessmen, one observer wrote of Manzanares, "A man who has devoted the better … part of his life to his own private affairs cannot be expected to take up and successfully fill a new and uncongenial position." Moreover, this critic believed that Manzanares lacked "opinions on grave public questions."[22] Although Luna's campaign activity was hamstrung by his convalescence from a debilitating illness, he was described by an observer as "so well known throughout the territory that he needs no introduction … [being] personally acquainted with almost everyone of weight."[23]

Luna prevailed over Manzanares, with 53 to 47 percent of the vote, and served for the first year of the 48th Congress (1883–1885).[24] But while the territory certified the election, Manzanares disputed the results, charging that there had been voting irregularities in several counties, most notably in Luna's political base of Valencia County. One political observer, while absolving Luna of direct involvement, suggested that his political patron José Francisco Chaves was responsible for instigating "frauds committed by irresponsible parties … in Bernalillo and Valencia counties."[25] Manzanares appealed to the House Committee on Elections, which was controlled by the new Democratic majority and favorably disposed toward his complaint. The committee reviewed evidence from different precincts, closely examining inconsistencies in poll books that suggested partial or complete forgeries of voting returns.

Meanwhile, Luna's term of service was consumed by the contested election, though he continued to serve on the Committee on Coinage, Weights, and Measures and submitted relief bills for constituents.[26] In its final report, the House Committee on Elections disqualified 2,357 votes it deemed fraudulent, swinging the election to Manzanares by a margin of more than 900 votes.[27] Luna's congressional service ended when the House concurred with the committee's findings and seated Manzanares on March 5, 1884. Miguel Otero, Jr., whose father had

considered appealing the 1880 election against Luna on similar grounds, noted approvingly, "When the frauds and stealing were shown, Francisco A. Manzanares secured his seat, to the entire satisfaction of the people of New Mexico."[28] The episode ended tragically when Melchior Luna, one of Luna's relatives, fatally wounded Manuel Sanchez, a Manzanares supporter, following an argument. According to a witness, "Harsh words followed between the men, whereupon Luna drew his Colt's forty-five caliber revolver and sent a bullet through Sanchez's body, entering in the breast and coming out the back." Sanchez died the following morning.[29]

After his departure from the House, Luna returned to New Mexico to focus on his business activities. In 1892 he served as a delegate to the Republican National Convention in Minneapolis, Minnesota. He also succeeded his late brother as sheriff of Valencia County, serving until his death in Peralta, New Mexico, on November 20, 1892, of complications from what was likely dysentery.[30]

FOR FURTHER READING

Biographical Directory of the United States Congress, "Tranquilino Luna," http://bioguide.congress.gov.

NOTES

1 Carlos Brazil Ramirez, "The Hispanic Political Elite in Territorial New Mexico: A Study of Classical Colonialism," (Ph.D. diss., University of California–Santa Barbara, 1979): 300. The 1860 Census notes that Antonio Luna's personal estate was valued at $63,500. See *Eighth Census of the United States, 1860: Population Schedule,* Los Lunas, Valencia, New Mexico Territory, Roll M653_716, page 661, http://search.ancestrylibrary.com (accessed 6 May 2010).

2 W. G. Ritch, *Legislative Blue Book of New Mexico* (Albuquerque: University of New Mexico Press, 1968; reprint of 1882 edition): 100–103. Baca served in the First Legislative Assembly (1851–1852) and in the territorial council of the Third and Fourth Legislative Assemblies (1853–1855).

3 "Tranquilino Luna," in Maurilio E. Vigil, *Los Patrones: Profiles of Hispanic Political Leaders in New Mexico History* (Washington, D.C.: University Press of America, 1980): 77–79.

4 "Our Next Delegate," 5 August 1880, (Santa Fe) *Daily New Mexican*: 4.

5 "Tranquilino Luna," 5 August 1880, (Santa Fe) *Daily New Mexican*: 1; "Our Next Delegate"; Tranquilino Luna, "Luna's Acceptance," 25 August 1880 *Campaign Bulletin*: 1. One article notes that some of the Valencia County Democrats attempted to sabotage the deal but that Luna's intervention preserved the agreement that Otero would be the nominee.

6 Howard R. Lamar, *The Far Southwest, 1846–1912: A Territorial History*, rev. ed. (Albuquerque: University of New Mexico Press, 2000): 88. According to Lamar, Territorial Delegate elections revealed "the multitudinous factions that split [local politicians] into two temporary parties." Because "Whigs were in national office when New Mexico became a territory, a large number of the first American politicians … declared loyalty to that party. When the [Franklin M.] Pierce administration assumed office in 1853, however, many local Whigs conveniently took refuge under the rubric 'National Democrat.' Those in opposition … were called … regular Democrats. Rather than parties, New Mexico had cliques, usually led by one man and generally organized for the specific purpose of winning an election or controlling patronage."

7 "Apart from Politics," 6 October 1880, (Santa Fe) *The Daily New Mexican*: 2. Some sources say the Otero family left New Mexico in 1862, whereas others give a date as late as 1864. In light of the Unionist reprisals that occurred after the Confederate occupation of the territory, 1862 or 1863 seems to be the most plausible date.

8 See Lamar, *The Far Southwest, 1846–1912: A Territorial History*: 123–133. The land grant issue involved two vexing questions: How could numerous grants from three distinct governments (Spain, Mexico, and New Mexico) be recognized, and under which legal tradition, Anglo-American or Spanish, would they be recognized? According to Lamar, there were three kinds of grants, "one to a community, usually for grazing purposes, a second to an individual for some outstanding service … and a third to the various Indian pueblos." When the first U.S. Surveyor General came to New Mexico in 1854, he faced a challenge of settling "over one thousand claims … of which 197 involved large private grants," with contradictory instructions from Congress. The net result was the lack of "a public domain in New Mexico, while … it guaranteed that long legal battles climaxed by acts of Congress would characterize the history of the New Mexican land system." Until the establishment of a Court of Private Land Claims in 1891, pitched legal battles between different groups were the norm for settling land grants. For a detailed history of the land grant issue, see Malcolm Ebright, *Land Grants and Lawsuits in Northern New Mexico* (Albuquerque: University of New Mexico Press, 1994).

9 "Otero's Pretensions," 1 October 1880, (Santa Fe) *The Daily New Mexican*: 2. Critics charged that "nineteen grants in New Mexico were confirmed by one act of Congress while Otero sat in his Delegate's seat and listened without objection or protest." The *Daily New Mexican* estimated that during Otero's tenure, "no less than two thirds of all land grants ever confirmed in New Mexico were patented … [which] included by far the largest land grants,

the Maxwell, Mora, Beck, and Ortiz among them." One article (18 October 1880, (Santa Fe) *The Daily New Mexican*: 1) asserts that not only was the "Mora grant … confirmed while Otero represented New Mexico in Congress … he owns a part of it. Will his friends say that he did not exert himself to have this grant confirmed?" For a detailed description of the land grants that were confirmed during Otero's terms as Delegate, see "Facts for the Miners," 29 October 1880, (Santa Fe) *The Daily New Mexican*: 2.

10 "Otero's Pretensions."

11 No title, 3 October 1880, (Santa Fe) *The Daily New Mexican*: 2. The article quotes Otero as saying to the House, "Gentlemen, do not judge me by the rest of my race. I am not utterly ignorant nor have I been reared in degradation and immorality; though I am a native of New Mexico." See also "Friend or Foe," 21 October 1880, (Santa Fe) *The Daily New Mexican*: 2. The themes of Otero's ignoring the needs of New Mexicans during his tenure by casting a blind eye toward revising the land grant system and his setting himself apart from his *Hispano* constituents dogged him throughout the campaign.

12 "Put Up or Shut Up," 18 October 1880, (Santa Fe) *The Daily New Mexican*: 2.

13 No title, 23 October 1880, *Las Vegas Weekly Optic*: 2.

14 See, for example, Lamar, *The Far Southwest, 1846–1912: A Territorial History*: 174–177.

15 "Luna at Home," 26 October 1880, (Santa Fe) *The Daily New Mexican*: 2.

16 "Votes cast for delegate to 47th Congress. Statement as canvassed by the Secretary of the Territory," (National Archives Microfilm Publication M364, Roll 1) Interior Department Territorial Papers, New Mexico, 1851–1914, Records of the Department of the Interior, Record Group 48, National Archives at College Park, College Park, MD (NACP). Official election statistics also were published in "The Official Count," 22 November 1880, *Santa Fe Weekly New Mexican*: 3. Vote totals were 10,835 for Luna and 9,562 for Otero.

17 Miguel Otero, Jr., *My Life on the Frontier: 1864–1882* (Albuquerque: University of New Mexico Press, 1987; reprint of 1935 edition): 270–271. Almost 50 years after the 1880 election, Otero, Jr., remained bitter about his father's defeat, as evidenced in Otero, Jr.'s autobiography: "The result showed that under any fair and honest count my father would have been declared elected by a handsome majority, but through the basest and most barefaced frauds ever practiced in any country, he was robbed of his victory, and Tranquilino Luna declared elected."

18 David T. Canon et al., *Committees in the U.S. Congress, 1789 to 1946: Member Assignments*, vol. 3 (Washington, D.C.: CQ Press, 2002): 653; *Congressional Record*, Index, 47th Cong., 1st sess.: 256; *Congressional Record*, Index, 47th Cong., 2nd sess.: 96–97.

19 *Congressional Record*, House, 47th Cong., 1st sess. (19 December 1881): 207; *Congressional Record*, House, 47th Cong., 1st sess. (6 June 1882): 4581; *Congressional Record*, Index, 47th Cong., 1st sess.: 589, 711. Luna submitted H.R. 1923 on December 19, 1881; Pacheco resubmitted the bill as a substitute amendment (H.R. 6404) on June 19, 1882, to the Committee on Private Land Claims, where it died.

20 *Congressional Record*, House, 47th Cong. 2nd sess. (29 January 1883): 1735.

21 "Hon. Tranquilino Luna," 4 August 1882, *Las Vegas Daily Gazette*: 4.

22 "Manzanares and Luna," 18 October 1882, (Santa Fe) *Daily New Mexican*: 2.

23 "Hon. Tranquilino Luna," 3 November 1882, (Santa Fe) *Daily New Mexican*: 2.

24 "General Election 1882—Votes as returned, counted, and declared for Delegate to 48th Congress," (M364, Roll 1) Territorial Papers of the United States, New Mexico, 1851–1914, RG 48, NACP. The results, 15,062 votes for Luna and 13,378 votes for Manzanares, were certified 29 November 1882.

25 "Manzanares vs. Luna," 6 March 1884, (Santa Fe) *Daily New Mexican*: 2; Martha Durant Read "Colonel José Francisco Chaves: A Short Biography of the Father of the New Mexico Statehood Movement," *Southwest Heritage* 8, no. 5 (Winter 1978–1979): 18; Lamar, *The Far Southwest, 1846–1912: A Territorial History*: 142–143. Chaves was dogged by charges that he ran a political machine out of Valencia County throughout his career. He was also charged with colluding with the Santa Fe Ring, although he actively worked against the Ring on a number of occasions.

26 *Congressional Record* Index, 48th Cong., 1st sess.: 268. For more details about the 1884 contested election case, see Lamar, *The Far Southwest, 1846–1912: A Territorial History*: 142–143.

27 Chester Rowell, *A Historical and Legal Digest of All the Contested Election Cases in the House of Representatives of the United States from the First to the Fifty-Sixth Congress, 1789–1901* (Westport, CT: Greenwood Press, 1976; reprint of 1901 edition): 399–400.

28 Otero, Jr., *My Life on the Frontier: 1864–1882*: 272–273.

29 "Fatal Tragedy Growing out of Election Contest," 24 February 1883, *Las Vegas Daily Gazette*: 2. It is unclear what charges, if any, were brought against Melchior Luna.

30 "Tranquilino Luna," in Vigil, *Los Patrones*: 77–78; "At the Capital: Blaine's Resignation and the Sensation and Comment It Caused," 5 June 1892, *St. Louis Post-Dispatch*: 2; "New Mexico's Loss," 22 November 1892, *Los Angeles Times*: 2. Luna died "after an illness of one month with inflammation of the bowels, brought on from flux."

Francisco Antonio Manzanares
1843–1904

TERRITORIAL DELEGATE 1884–1885
DEMOCRAT FROM NEW MEXICO

An accomplished entrepreneur, Francisco Manzanares was a reluctant candidate for New Mexico Territorial Delegate in the U.S. House. Urged on by friends and political supporters, Manzanares—who had never clearly allied himself with either major political party—accepted the Democratic nomination, noting that his preference was to remain immersed in the booming business opportunities in the district and admitting he was a political neophyte. "My life has been spent in active business pursuits and I do not pretend to be versed in the methods of distinctions of the politician," he said.[1] As it turned out, Manzanares endured not only the rigors of the territorial campaign, but also a contested election that consumed half a congressional term. Serving just a year, Manzanares returned contentedly to his business interests at the close of the 48th Congress (1883–1885).

Francisco Antonio Manzanares was born in Abiquiú, New Mexico, on January 25, 1843, to José Antonio Manzanares and Maria Manuela Valdez. José Manzanares represented his family's home county, Rio Arriba, in the New Mexico Territory's First Legislative Assembly (1851–1852) and in the territorial council of the Third, Fourth, and Sixth Legislative Assemblies (1853–1855; 1856–1857).[2] Manzanares attended the Taos school of Padre Antonio José Martínez, a prominent local priest who had mentored José Manuel Gallegos, New Mexico's first *nuevomexicano* Delegate to the U.S. House. Manzanares attended St. Louis University from 1863 to 1864. After leaving the university, Manzanares worked one year at Chick, Browne, and Company, a merchandising firm in Kansas City, Missouri. He then moved to New York City to study in a commercial college and worked in a bank. When he returned to Chick, Browne, and Company, Manzanares took advantage of the burgeoning railroad industry by expanding the firm's business to cities that served the Kansas Pacific and the Atchison, Topeka, and Santa Fe Railroads. Propelled by his ambition and work ethic, he rose from company clerk to partner in four years by buying interest from a senior partner. Renamed Browne & Manzanares, the firm moved to Las Vegas, New Mexico, and competed with commissioning firms such as Otero, Sellar, and Co. and the Romero firm. Eventually, Browne & Manzanares established branches in five cities in New Mexico and Colorado.[3] In 1871 Manzanares married Ofelia Baca, the daughter of Benito Baca, a cousin and Democratic opponent of Mariano S. Otero's in the 1878 race for Delegate. The couple had two children, Antonio, Jr., and Manuel.[4]

Manzanares's fortunes increased as the scope of his business activities widened. The newly renamed Browne & Manzanares Company became so successful that it opened a wholesaling firm in Las Vegas, New Mexico, where Manzanares lived. By 1885 the firm had become a stock company, with branches in three locations in New Mexico and Colorado. Manzanares contributed to the territory's economic development through his involvement in forming the First National Bank of Las Vegas, the First National Bank of Santa Fe, and the First National Bank of Raton. Manzanares also formed a wholesale grocery business with branches throughout the territory. He enjoyed close ties with the Republican-dominated Santa Fe Ring, serving as a trustee of the Maxwell Land Grant Company and, with other Ring members, as a co-director of the First National Bank of Santa Fe.[5]

In 1882 Manzanares received the Democratic nomination to challenge the incumbent Territorial Delegate, Tranquilino Luna, for a seat in the 48th Congress. One observer noted, "Nobody was more surprised to know the action of the Democratic convention than Manzanares

Image courtesy of the Palace of the Governors Photo Archives (NMHM/DCA), 48967

himself." The same observer noted that when Manzanares received word of his nomination, he hesitated and at "first wanted to know all the circumstances that led up to this ... and wondered whether he may refuse to be a candidate before leaving the city on much more important business than politics."[6] From the outset, Manzanares was uncertain about leaving behind his growing business empire for the rigors of campaigning. In his acceptance letter, Manzanares frankly acknowledged his lack of political experience, writing that although he appreciated "the high honor conferred upon me by selecting me from the masses of many fellow citizens as one fitted to represent the interests of our territory ... I have been reluctant to accept the nomination, but the urgent solicitation of many of my fellow citizens and personal friends of every shade of political opinion and from every portion of the Territory ... constrains me to forgo my personal preferences."[7]

Assessing the Luna-Manzanares contest, Republican political operative William A. Breeden suggested that part of Manzanares's reluctance to accept the Democratic nomination may have been his conflicting political loyalties. "It is a known fact that Sr. Manzanares stated ... that he did not know whether he was a Republican or a Democrat and that he would have to investigate and examine the records and the principles of the two parties before being [able] to determine to which party he belonged," Breeden said. He described Manzanares as "a man who flirts with both political parties, who seeks and asks for the smiles and favors of each party and refuses to declare his allegiance to either." While urging Republicans to rally behind Luna, he warned Democrats that "with all of [Manzanares's] changing around and his avoidances and his attempts to avoid the question, although he tried to be a candidate through the Democratic Party, [Manzanares] also wants to avoid being the candidate of the party."[8]

Press coverage of the race juxtaposed Manzanares's lack of political experience with his effort to win one of the most coveted seats in territorial politics. Predictably, Luna's supporters emphasized his experience navigating Washington's political scene, portraying Manzanares as an inexperienced businessman who would be beyond his capabilities representing territorial interests in the national capital.[9] Luna, who had tried to push New Mexico toward statehood and to settle some of the territory's outstanding land claims, was himself breaking with convention by running for a second term, because a string of previous Delegates had served one term.[10] Luna won the election, with 53 percent to Manzanares's 47 percent.[11]

Although Luna was declared the winner, and the territory certified the results, Manzanares contested the election because of alleged voting irregularities in a number of precincts, particularly in Luna's political base of Valencia County.[12] One Republican-leaning newspaper stated, "We believe that Mr. Manzanares was fairly elected by the voters of New Mexico, and we have never hesitated to say that we believed he was entitled to his seat, and there is not an honest man in the Territory or either political party who will deny the justice or fairness of this action by the House."[13] The House Committee on Elections, controlled by the newly installed Democratic majority, reviewed the evidence and disqualified nearly 2,400 votes that were determined to be fraudulent. Inconsistencies in the poll books suggested that at least portions of these votes had been forged. After deducting these votes, the committee determined that Manzanares had prevailed by nearly 940 votes.[14] Midway through the congressional term, the House Committee on Elections overturned the election results and awarded Manzanares the seat.[15]

Sworn into the House on March 5, 1884, Manzanares served on the Committee on Coinage, Weights, and Measures (the only committee New Mexico Territorial Delegates had served on until that point).[16] He submitted bills for pension relief for individual constituents and bills for infrastructure improvements, to provide funds for a hospital, to construct a school for American Indians, and to reserve land for a university.[17] He added an amendment to the 1886 Indian Appropriations Bill (H.R. 7970) that secured $25,000 to establish an industrial school for Indian students in Santa Fe.[18] At the end of his term, a newspaper called Manzanares "the best delegate in Congress ever sent by Democratic votes in this Territory." The editors of the newspaper continued,

"The people, irrespective of party, acknowledge the fact that he has faithfully discharged the duties of a delegate and has fully lived up to the trust reposed in him. Mr. Manzanares retires to private life with the esteem and confidence of the people of New Mexico, and may count on many a Republican vote should he ever again desire official honors."[19]

Manzanares declined to serve for a second term and returned to managing his business empire in New Mexico and Colorado. One newspaper noted that Manzanares "accomplished what he desired in the passage of various important bills which he had prepared for the aid of the Territory, and in demolishing the political ring in the Territory"—the latter part of the statement referring to his success as a candidate who was not endorsed by the Santa Fe Ring. He remained active in New Mexico politics and continued to be an important figure in Democratic Party circles.[20] In 1886 and 1897, Manzanares served as a county commissioner. He also participated in the 1889 New Mexico constitutional convention.[21]

In 1902 Manzanares sold his interest in Browne & Manzanares for a 5,000- to 6,000-acre plot of land in San Miguel County and a cash settlement.[22] After a long bout with a stomach disease, he died in Las Vegas, New Mexico, on September 17, 1904, "surrounded by the clamor and tears of … dear children and beloved sisters, who had been called ahead of time to his death bed."[23] Manzanares was interred in Mount Calvary Cemetery in Las Vegas.

FOR FURTHER READING

Biographical Directory of the United States Congress, "Francisco Antonio Manzanares," http://bioguide.congress.gov.

Haines, Helen. *History of New Mexico from the Spanish Conquest to the Present Time, 1530–1890: With Portraits and Biographical Sketches of Its Prominent People* (New York: New Mexico Historical Publishing Co., 1891): 515–519.

Meier, Matt S. *Mexican American Biographies: A Historical Dictionary, 1836–1987* (Westport, CT: Greenwood Press, 1988): 130.

MANUSCRIPT COLLECTION

Library of Congress (Washington, D.C.). *Papers*: Benjamin Harrison Papers, 1787–1940. Contains two letters sent by Manzanares to the Benjamin Harrison administration.

NOTES

1 "At Last," 11 October 1882 (Santa Fe) *Daily New Mexican*: 1.

2 W. G. Ritch, *The Legislative Blue Book of the Territory of New Mexico* (Albuquerque: University of New Mexico Press, 1968; reprint of 1882 edition): 101–104; Carlos Brazil Ramirez, "The Hispanic Political Elite in Territorial New Mexico: A Study of Classical Colonialism," (Ph.D. diss., University of California–Santa Barbara, 1979): 302. Manzanares's father also served as prefect of Rio Arriba County under the military administration of the United States in 1849. José Manzanares later fought for the Union in the Civil War and served as a United States Indian Agent.

3 Helen Haines, *History of New Mexico from the Spanish Conquest to the Present Time, 1530–1890* (New York: New Mexico Historical Publishing, Co., 1891): 51; "Francisco A. Manzanares," in Maurilio E. Vigil, *Los Patrones: Profiles of Hispanic Political Leaders in New Mexico* (Washington, D.C.: University Press of America, 1980): 80; Ramirez, "The Hispanic Political Elite in Territorial New Mexico": 302. The branches were in El Moro, Carson City, Granada, and La Junta, Colorado; and Socorro, New Mexico.

4 Ramirez, "The Hispanic Political Elite in Territorial New Mexico: A Study of Classical Colonialism": 298. For biographical information about Benito Baca, see Benjamin M. Read, *Illustrated History of New Mexico* (New York: Arno Press, 1976; reprint of 1912 edition): 732.

5 Ramirez, "The Hispanic Political Elite in Territorial New Mexico: A Study of Classical Colonialism": 303; Haines, *History of New Mexico from the Spanish Conquest to the Present Time, 1530–1890*: 519; "Francisco A. Manzanares" in Vigil, *Los Patrones*: 81. According to Haines, Browne & Manzanares Company became "one of the largest houses in the Southwest, having branches in Las Vegas, Socorro, and Trinidad, Col." According to Vigil, Manzanares's grocery stores were located in "Granada, La Junta, and Trinidad in Colorado, and Otero and Springer in New Mexico."

6 "Cuando se hace la pregunta directa sobre si aceptaría la nominación [*sic*] de la democracia. El señor Manzanares titubio [*sic*] un momento y dijo que no sabía todavía. Quería primero ponerse al tanto de todas las circumstancias que la trajeron a cabo-y a ver que había negado a ser un candidato antes de salir de la ciudad, con un negocio de mucha mayor importancia para el que la política, y ninguno estaba más sorprendido de saber el proceder de la convención democrática que el mismo Manzanares. La decisión se ha hecho," 12 October 1882, (Santa Fe) *Daily New Mexican*: 3. Translated as "The Decision Has Been Made," by Translations International, Inc. (January 2010).

7 "At Last," 11 October 1882, (Santa Fe) *Daily New Mexican*: 2.

8 "Ciertamente no debían ni pueden afectar la situación, ni cambiar la mayoría republicana del territorio … Manzanares ha declarado muy recientemente que no sabía si era republicano o demócrata y que tendria que investigar y examinar los registros y principios de los dos partidos antes que pudiese determinar a cual pertenecía." William A. Breeden, "La aceptación analizada," 19 October 1882, (Santa Fe) *Daily New Mexican*, 3. Translated as "Acceptance Analyzed," by Translations International, Inc. (January 2010).

9 "Manzanares and Luna," 18 October 1882, (Santa Fe) *Daily New Mexican*: 2.

10 "Hon. Tranquilino Luna," 4 August 1882, *Las Vegas Daily Gazette*: 4.

11 "General Election 1882—Votes as returned, counted, and declared for Delegate to 48th Congress," National Archives Microfilm Publication M364, Roll 1, Interior Department Territorial Papers of the United States, New Mexico, 1851–1914, RG 48, National Archives at College Park, College Park, MD (NACP). The results (15,062 votes for Luna and 13,378 for Manzanares) were certified on 29 November 1882.

12 For newspaper coverage of the contested election, see "Manzanares vs. Luna," 6 March 1884, (Santa Fe) *Daily New Mexican*: 2; Martha Durant Read "Colonel José Francisco Chaves: A Short Biography of the Father of the New Mexico Statehood Movement," *Southwest Heritage* 8, no. 4 (Winter 1978–1979):18. José Francisco Chaves, a former Delegate and Luna's political ally, was dogged throughout his career by charges that he ran a political machine out of Valencia County. He was also charged with colluding with the Santa Fe Ring, although he actively worked against it on a number of occasions.

13 Haines, *History of New Mexico from the Spanish Conquest to the Present Time, 1530–1890*: 516.

14 Chester Rowell, *A Historical and Legal Digest of All the Contested Election Cases in the House of Representatives of the United States from the First to the Fifty-Sixth Congress, 1789–1901* (Westport, CT: Greenwood Press, 1976; reprint of 1901 edition): 399–400.

15 Rowell, *A Historical and Legal Digest of Contested Election Cases*: 399–400; "New Mexico's Loss," 22 November 1892, *New York Times*: 2. According to this obituary, "the Democratic House of Representatives gave the seat to Manzanares."

16 *Congressional Record*, Index, 48th Cong., 1st sess.: 282; *Congressional Record*, Index, 48th Cong., 2nd sess.: 110.

17 *Congressional Record*, House, 48th Cong., 1st sess. (5–6 March 1884): 1621, 1655; *Congressional Record*, Index, 48th Cong., 1st sess.: 282.

18 *Congressional Record*, House, 48th Cong., 2nd sess. (22 January 1885): 922, 930; *Congressional Record*, House, 48th Cong., 2nd sess. (3 March 1885): 2533, 2544; Senate Committee on Appropriations, 48th Cong., 2nd sess., 1885, S. Rep. 1283: 1, 4.

19 Haines, *History of New Mexico from the Spanish Conquest to the Present Time, 1530–1890*: 516.

20 Ramirez, "The Hispanic Political Elite in Territorial New Mexico: A Study of Classical Colonialism": 302–304; Howard R. Lamar, *The Far Southwest: A Territorial History, 1846–1912,* rev. ed. (Albuquerque: University of New Mexico Press, 2000): 142–143; Territory of New Mexico, *Report of the Secretary of the Territory, 1903–1904, and Legislative Manual, 1905* (Santa Fe: The New Mexican Printing Company, 1905): 48–opposite; "Francisco A. Manzanares," in Vigil, *Los Patrones:* 82. Lamar argues that one long-term effect of the factional squabbling among Republicans was the loss of the Delegate's seat for more than 10 years. By the summer of 1884, the Republicans had divided into two main factions, the Santa Fe Ring and a group of Valencia County Republicans led by José Francisco Chaves who "jointly denounced Secretary Ritch, Governor Sheldon, and the whole Santa Fe Ring" at their county convention. At the Republican territorial convention, Chave[s] and delegates from the southern and western counties left the convention in protest." In the wake of the standoff, "new faces and new forces … persuaded the Democrats to pass over the conservative Manzanares to choose Antonio Joseph" as their candidate. As the nation tended to vote Democratic in the 1884 elections, so did New Mexico, and Joseph defeated Republicans L. Bradford Prince and William Rynerson, the latter a member of the territorial council. Joseph won 45 percent of the vote; Prince, 36 percent; and Rynerson, 19 percent. Vigil does not state which county Manzanares served as commissioner, but most likely it was San Miguel or Valencia.

21 Robert W. Larson, *New Mexico's Quest for Statehood, 1846–1912* (Albuquerque: University of New Mexico Press, 1968): 156.

22 Ramirez, "The Hispanic Political Elite in Territorial New Mexico": 303.

23 "En medio de los clamores y lágrimas de sus queridos hijos y amadas hermanas, quien [*sic*] habían sido llamadas con anticipación á su lecho de muerte … sufría, hacía ya algunos años, de complicaciones en su organism interno … una inflamacion de los intestinos y estómago que al fin paralizó la acción de estos órganos importantes." "Don Francisco A. Manzanares," 17 September 1904, *La voz del pueblo* (Las Vegas, NM): 4. Translated as "Francisco A. Manzanares" by Translations International, Inc. (January 2010).

"IF MY FELLOW CITIZENS SEE FIT TO ELECT ME AS THEIR DELEGATE IT WILL BE MY ENDEAVOR TO . . . SERVE THE TERRITORY TO THE BEST OF MY ABILITY AND WITH WHATEVER KNOWLEDGE OF ITS WANTS AND INTERESTS I MAY POSSESS."

Francisco Antonio Manzanares
(Santa Fe) *Daily New Mexican*,
October 11, 1882

"Foreign in a Domestic Sense"

HISPANIC AMERICANS IN CONGRESS DURING THE AGE OF U.S. COLONIALISM AND GLOBAL EXPANSION, 1898–1945

On October 15, 1900, *La correspondencia*, a San Juan daily newspaper, described the qualities of a Resident Commissioner, a position recently created by the Foraker Act (31 Stat. 77–86) to provide Puerto Rico with representation in the U.S. House. The writer stated that such a "representative must be worthy of the trust of those he represents. He must earn that trust through his history, which is a record of the things he has accomplished for the good of the homeland, a justification of his intellectual qualities, a demonstration of his character, and evidence of his love of freedom."[1] Yet, the first Resident Commissioner, Federico Degetau, was not even allowed to set foot on the House Floor when the 57th Congress (1901–1903) assembled in December 1901. Many in Congress questioned the very existence of the position of Resident Commissioner and the ability of Puerto Ricans to participate in a democratic society. Many Members of Congress were confused by the island's ambiguous position within the United States, classified as neither a state nor a territory. "Now, Mr. Chairman, Puerto Rico is either in the United States or out of it," Representative Amos Cummings of New York declared during debate on the Foraker Act. "If the island is out of the United States, we have no business legislating for her here in any way whatever, and if she is in the United States, she is in the same condition as Arizona, New Mexico, Oklahoma, and the other Territories." He concluded by suggesting facetiously that the Foraker Act "ought to be amended so as to be entitled, 'An act to make a temporary purgatory for the island of Puerto Rico.'"[2]

The colonial conquests of the late 19th century, particularly in Puerto Rico and the Philippines, marked the first time the U.S. took control over large indigenous

---

An 1898 map depicts the Caribbean basin and prominent battles of the Spanish-American War, along with inserts of Havana and Santiago, Cuba, and San Juan, Puerto Rico. The war spanned from the Caribbean to the Pacific islands of Guam and the Philippines.

Eugenia A. Wheeler Goff, *Goff's Historical Map of the Spanish-American War in the West Indies*, map (Chicago: Fort Dearborn Publishing Company, 1899); from Library of Congress, Geography and Map Division, http://www.loc.gov/item/98687149

GOFF'S HISTORICAL MAP OF THE
SPANISH-AMERICAN WAR
IN THE
WEST INDIES, 1898
Copyrighted, 1899, by EUGENIA WHEELER GOFF, and HENRY SLADE GOFF, authors of Goff's Historical Maps for Schools and Families.
FORT DEARBORN PUB. CO.
MAP ENGRAVERS AND PUBLISHERS
CHICAGO, ILL.
SAN JUAN
ISLAND OF PUERTO RICO
ATLANTIC OCEAN
HAVANA
CITY AND HARBOR.
GULF OF MEXICO
GENERAL STAFF MAP COLLECTION
FILE COPY
Do not mark or mutilate. Return to Map Room as soon as possible. Get your receipt.
SAN SALVADOR OR CAT ISLAND
ELEUTHERA
GT. BAHAMA
New Providence I.
Ft. Nassau
GT. BAHAMA CHANNEL
GT. INAGUA
HAITI OR ST. DOMINGO I.
WINDWARD PASSAGE
MONA PASSAGE
SANTO DOMINGO
PUERTO RICO
JAMAICA
KINGSTON
PUERTO PRINCIPE
SANTIAGO DE CUBA
MANZANILLO
PTO. CUANTANAMO
Bombarded, Aug. 12.
Vessels under Merry repulsed, Ensign Bagley killed, May 11.
Occupied by Americans, Aug. 11.
First permanent landing of American troops (600 marines under Col. Huntington) U. S. flag first raised in Cuba, June 10. Marines attacked, June 11, 12, 13, aided by Cubans under Laborda routed Spanish camp, June 14. batteries bombarded June 15, 17. Miles sailed for Puerto Rico, July 21.
PEDRO BANK
Portland Rock
Morant Keys
CANEY-Battle, July 1-2
LA QUASINA
SHAFTER'S ROUTE
Battle of Siboney or La Quasina, June 24.
Landing place of Siboney
Landing place of Baiquiri
Shafter landed, June 21-23.
Baiquiri
Siboney
Campo Rico
Santa Barbara
Firmeza
Quentuqui
La Moco
Magote
Prudencia
Altares
Demajayabo
SEA

This image of Ladislas Lazaro of Louisiana was taken during his first term of congressional service. Elected on the strength of Woodrow Wilson's 1912 progressive platform, Lazaro served for eight terms (1913–1927) until his death in March 1927.

Image courtesy of the Library of Congress

populations outside the continental United States. The newly acquired territories had little or nothing in common with Anglo-American culture and political traditions, and the United States sought to manage them on a long-term basis, with the expectation that they would remain territories rather than incorporated states. Their assimilation was particularly difficult given the prevailing race relations in the United States, which led to the systematic disfranchisement and segregation of African-American citizens. An influx of immigration from Southern and Eastern Europe, as well as Asia, changed the racial and ethnic composition of many U.S. regions and heightened nativist fears about increasing urban poverty and labor tension.[3]

Of all the Hispanic Americans elected to Congress before the end of the Second World War, the overwhelming majority (17 of 25, or 68 percent) were statutory representatives, Delegates or Resident Commissioners with circumscribed legislative powers that were defined by Congress rather than the Constitution. A century of American hemispheric expansion and colonial acquisition shaped these positions. Not until 1913, when Ladislas Lazaro of Louisiana entered the House, did a Hispanic American represent in Congress a state or territory that had not been ceded by the Spanish empire or the Mexican government.

More than half the Hispanic Members of Congress who were first elected between 1898 and 1945 were Puerto Rican Resident Commissioners, a new class of statutory representative. Their story dominates that of the Hispanic Members during this era, and their careers were characterized by their attempts to balance the island's local needs with its economic, political, and cultural interests, which were all increasingly intertwined with the United States. The story of New Mexican Members is separate but parallel to that of the Puerto Ricans in the early 20th century. Only Senator Dennis Chavez of New Mexico bridged the gap in the 1940s. In the first clear example of surrogate representation among Latino Members, Chavez addressed issues that were significant to Hispanics beyond his prescribed state boundary when he focused on the economic needs of Puerto Ricans following World War II.[4]

But with no more than three Hispanic individuals serving simultaneously throughout this era—an insufficient number to create a voting bloc or an issues caucus—legislating was often lonely and isolating. Luis Muñoz Rivera, the poet-turned-politician, clearly understood this reality. Like the New Mexico Delegates before him and the Resident Commissioners who would follow him, he labored under the constraints of House Rules that limited his ability to represent and legislate. His awareness of being relegated to the margins of institutional power magnified Muñoz Rivera's sense that he was engaged in a solitary undertaking. Serving as Resident Commissioner in the 1910s, he wrote a friend in Puerto Rico, "I am here alone, in tomb-like isolation, mixing with people who speak a different tongue, who have no affinity with my way of life, who are not even hostile ... but indifferent, cold, and rough as the granite stones which support their big Capitol."[5]

PRECONGRESSIONAL AND WASHINGTON EXPERIENCES

Family/Ethnic Roots

The Hispanic Members of Congress of this era were products of an increasingly interconnected geopolitical landscape. Nearly half (seven of 15) were born outside the United States. Five were born in Puerto Rico under Spanish rule; one was born in Mexico (Larrazolo), one was born in Spain (Iglesias), and another spent much of his youth in Spain (Degetau). Those who were American citizens from birth lived in Louisiana or the New Mexico Territory nearly their entire lives. Like 19th-century *nuevomexicano* politicians, who hailed from politically connected families, Delegate Pedro Perea followed his cousin Francisco Perea and brother-in-law Mariano Otero into politics. Puerto Rican politicians, too, had familial connections. Resident Commissioner Luis Muñoz Rivera's son, Luis Muñoz Marín, was a major figure in Puerto Rican politics throughout the middle of the 20th century, serving as Puerto Rico's first elected governor from 1948 to 1964. Félix Córdova Dávila's son, Jorge Luis Córdova-Diaz, served as Resident Commissioner from 1969 to 1973. Santiago Iglesias took on Bolívar Pagán as his protégé, and according to one account raised him after his parents died.[6] Pagán eventually married Iglesias's daughter and served out his late father-in-law's term.

The son of Resident Commissioner Luis Muñoz Rivera, Luis Muñoz Marín (right) dominated Puerto Rican politics as a party leader, president of the Puerto Rican senate, and governor of the Puerto Rican commonwealth for more than two decades.

Image courtesy of the Library of Congress

Age Relative to the Rest of the Congressional Population

The cohort of Hispanic Americans who entered Congress between 1898 and 1945 was slightly older (47 years old) than the average group of Members when they were first elected (45 years old) and far older than the first generation of Hispanic Americans in Congress, who were on average a decade younger (36.5 years). While this difference in age can be explained by the trend toward older Members entering Congress, it is also attributable to the fact that these Hispanic lawmakers spent the first part of their careers deeply involved in state or territorial politics. Because of their advanced age, six of the 15 died in office.

During this era, the oldest Hispanic Member in Congress at the time of his first election was Octaviano Larrazolo of New Mexico, who was elected at age 69 to a brief and symbolic term as the first Hispanic Senator. The youngest Hispanic Member during this era was 34-year-old Representative Joachim O. Fernández of Louisiana, a former state legislator who hitched his political wagon to Huey P. Long's insurgent political machine in the late 1920s and early 1930s.

Education, Professions, and Prior Political Experience

In most other respects, the members of this group mirrored their contemporary House colleagues. Eighty percent had some college education, with roughly half studying law.[7] Five (Degetau, Larrazolo, Pagán, Félix Córdova Dávila, and José Pesquera) were practicing lawyers. Five (Degetau, Muñoz Rivera, Iglesias, Pagán, and Néstor Montoya) were journalists or writers, which was a direct route to political office for many Puerto Ricans in this era.

With regard to political experience, the members of this group stood out from their House contemporaries. All but two of the 15 Hispanic Members of Congress in this era (87 percent) served in statewide or territory-wide office; 12 of them served in their state legislatures before their election to Congress.[8] By comparison, less than half the House membership had experience in statewide office during this same period. Some of the Hispanic Members also had held key leadership posts at the state or territorial level. In 1903 Néstor Montoya was the speaker of the New Mexico territorial assembly; Pagán was both president *pro tempore* and majority floor leader in the Puerto Rican senate in the 1930s. In 1932, longtime judge Félix Córdova Dávila resigned his post as Puerto Rican Resident Commissioner to serve on the insular supreme court.

In this 1928 photo, newly elected New Mexican Senator Octaviano Larrazolo and his daughter Marie pose on the steps of the U.S. Capitol. Larrazolo's election as the first *Hispano* governor of New Mexico inspired other *Hispano* candidates to run for elected office.

Image courtesy of the Library of Congress

D.C. Residences and Careerism in Congress

During this era, as more politicians began to view Congress as a career rather than as a stepping stone to another position, Members began relocating their families to Washington, D.C. From their arrival, Representative Ladislas Lazaro of Louisiana and his family were fixtures of Washington society. When Lazaro's daughter Eloise debuted in 1913, the *Washington Post* ran a large photograph of her, pronouncing her "one of the most beautiful of the younger members of the congressional set."[9] Another Lazaro daughter, Elaine, married South Trimble, Jr., son of the longtime and popular Clerk of the House.

Like most Resident Commissioners, Luis Muñoz Rivera spent much of his time in the capital as a bachelor. He resided in the upscale neighborhoods of northwest Washington, D.C., along with many other Members of Congress. For a time he rented an apartment in The Highlands, just off Connecticut Avenue near the Kalorama neighborhood; he later moved to The Benedick, a bachelor apartment just west of the White House on I Street. His teenage son, Luis, lived with him while attending Georgetown Preparatory High School and Georgetown Law School. Like many congressional family members of the time, Luis took a position as his father's personal secretary, working in his office on the second floor of the House Office Building (now the Cannon House Office Building).[10]

Santiago Iglesias employed members of his large family in his congressional office. He brought several of his daughters to the city after his election, taking up residence in an apartment in the Wisteria Mansions on Massachusetts Avenue near the American Federation of Labor (AFL) building, where he had spent time in labor organization efforts. He later purchased a four-bedroom duplex on Porter Street in northwest Washington, into which he moved his family, after renting out his home in San Juan. Iglesias's daughters, Libertad and Igualdad, were two of the three staff members in his congressional office. His daughter Laura took over Igualdad's position when she married Resident Commissioner Bolívar Pagán in 1933.[11]

Unlike Representatives, who moved into the House Office Building right away, Resident Commissioners received their office assignments in 1910, two years after the building opened.[12] New Mexico Representative Néstor Montoya described the building's amenities: "This building, which is located two blocks from the capitol, has couriers for the members, telephone and telegraph offices, special restaurants and everything needed for comfort."[13] At the time, most Members kept only a skeleton staff in Washington and maintained no official district staff or offices. Ladislas Lazaro, for instance, had one full-time staffer: a personal secretary, Isom Guillory, from his home town of Ville Platte. His closest political confidant was J. P. Trosclair, the postmaster in Opelousas, one of the largest towns in his sprawling southwestern Louisiana district. Because Lazaro often spent long stretches of time in Washington with his family, he did not have the benefit of a politically astute wife or child in the district. During Lazaro's first several terms, Trosclair was his eyes and ears in his home district, and he became adept at sniffing out Lazaro's potential primary challengers. Lazaro relied on Trosclair to analyze local politics, to pass messages to political allies, and to promote stories about his legislative successes.

Opened in 1908, the House Office Building (now named for Speaker Joe Cannon of Illinois), pictured above, enabled Members to conduct business in comfortable offices and convene hearings in larger committee rooms.

Image courtesy of the Library of Congress

PUERTO RICO

The predominant development in the story of Hispanic-American Members of Congress during this era was the ambiguous absorption of Puerto Rico into the national fold. The island territory was neither fully part of the United States nor an independent country. "Since [Puerto Rico] was subject to the sovereignty of and was owned by the United States, *it was foreign to the United States in a domestic sense*," pronounced Justice Henry Brown in the Supreme Court's landmark *Downes v. Bidwell* (182 U.S. 244) decision in 1901—which was intended to clarify the island's position, but ended up only adding a new layer of uncertainty instead.[14] Primarily as a result of this contradic decision, Congress governed Puerto Rico through a series of statutes that enabled the United States to extract island resources and exploit its strategic location at the center of the Caribbean while paying little attention to the economic, cultural, and political realities on the island. Lawmakers found themselves in the position of "fabricat[ing] the jurisdictional fiction of an unincorporated territory," notes a scholar, effectively "relegating the island to the perpetual status of a ward who will never become part of his patron's family."[15]

U.S. Expansionism and the Caribbean

Although the United States began acquiring Caribbean territories in the late 1800s, the impetus for such acquisitions was based on Manifest Destiny—the concept that the United States had a moral claim on territory stretching to the Pacific Ocean and beyond—and on the 1823 Monroe Doctrine, which asserted that European nations should not meddle in the Western Hemisphere. The desire for security and control of economic resources such as sugar and tobacco also fueled some U.S. policymakers' ambitions for Caribbean territory during the antebellum era.[16]

Though the Civil War temporarily halted America's focus on the Caribbean, by the 1880s, large American businesses sought new markets, and the U.S. government desired influence beyond the North American continent. Within U.S. society, the emergence of a social elite and the travels of entrepreneurs, tourists, missionaries, and settlers also encouraged the public to look at expanding the United States' role in world affairs. Even anti-expansionists such as President Grover Cleveland had a mixed record as far as pursuing an aggressive foreign

A prominent Civil War veteran, William McKinley of Ohio served for seven terms in the House before being elected governor of Ohio. Elected President in 1896, McKinley was felled by an assassin in Buffalo, New York, in September 1901, six months into his second term.

Image courtesy of the Library of Congress

The accidental sinking of the U.S.S. *Maine* in Havana's harbor killed 266 U.S. sailors. With a rallying cry, "Remember the Maine, to hell with Spain," many newspapers blamed Spain for the incident. Popular sentiment compelled Congress to declare war in April 1898.

Image courtesy of the Library of Congress

policy and checking U.S. expansionist initiatives in the early 1890s.[17] Territorial expansion was a key platform for President William McKinley during the 1896 and 1900 elections, especially the expansion southward into the Caribbean where an American-owned isthmian canal was being built to connect the Atlantic and Pacific oceans.[18]

Spanish-American War

When Cuban revolutionaries began calling for independence from Spain in 1895, the United States found itself in an awkward situation given Cuba's proximity and its strategic Caribbean location. The American press began sensationalizing the events in Cuba, and popular opinion rallied behind the revolutionaries. McKinley and his deputies pressured Spanish officials to stop the uprising before it became uncontrollable, warning that failure to comply might precipitate American intervention.[19]

By February 1898 the diplomatic situation had deteriorated and the relationship between the U.S. and Spain was tottering. The explosion on February 15 of the U.S.S. *Maine*, an American battleship newly arrived in Havana Harbor, killed 266 sailors and became the tipping point for American intervention. Though the circumstances of the explosion were unclear, many, including some in Congress, blamed Spain.[20] President McKinley resisted the immediate calls for war, but with conditions in Cuba expected to worsen, he acknowledged the conflict in a message to Congress on April 11.[21] He blamed Spain and demanded an end to the war to protect U.S. interests and promote peace in the Caribbean. The House voted 325 to 19 in favor of war, passing a joint resolution that stopped short of recognizing an independent Cuban government. But the Senate added language to the House measure recognizing the Cuban Republic three days later on April 16, by a 67 to 21 vote.[22] When the conference committee convened, negotiations lasted until after one o'clock in the morning. The final resolution acknowledged Cuban freedom but did not acknowledge Cuba as a republic. Congress formally declared war on April 25.[23]

On July 25, 1898, the United States invaded Puerto Rico as part of an American strategy to capture Spanish holdings in the Caribbean. The Spanish Army put up little resistance to the invasion, and some rural peasants even formed mobile bands to resist their former colonizers.[24] Two future Resident Commissioners watched the assault from different perspectives. As a leader in the Autonomist Party and having recently won home rule for Puerto Rico from the Spanish government, Luis Muñoz Rivera watched the invasion with dismay. His political rival, Santiago Iglesias, whom Muñoz Rivera had imprisoned for his labor agitation at the outbreak of the war, nearly died when an American shell struck the prison. Upon his release, he aided the American invaders by serving as an interpreter. Hostilities ended August 12, 1898, and the United States installed a military government in Puerto Rico on October 18. The Treaty of Paris, which was signed December 10, 1898, ended the war, with Spain ceding Puerto Rico, Guam, and the Philippines to the United States. Among those present at the treaty's signing in France was future Resident Commissioner Federico Degetau.

Overview of Puerto Rican Politics, 1898–1900

Puerto Rican politics differed from those of the other islands in the Spanish Caribbean and from those of other U.S. territories. Unlike Cuba and the Dominican Republic—which were characterized by revolutionary militarism and authoritarianism, respectively—Puerto Rico followed a tradition of working within the existing colonial system to liberalize civil government on the island.[25] By the time the United States acquired Puerto Rico at the end of the Spanish-American War the island's political elite, who would shape the first generation of relations with the United States, already had a long history of working within a colonial framework. By 1869 the Spanish Cortes in Madrid had seated the first Puerto Rican delegates. Over time Puerto Rican businessmen and politicians became inclined to favor "electoral and parliamentary solutions to its colonial dilemma," thus reinforcing "a defining characteristic of the island's political culture," relative economic stability with rigid class lines.[26]

Autonomists, who sought self-rule within the Spanish imperial orbit, dominated island politics by the 1880s. They formed Liberal and Conservative factions that often reflected the platforms of major parties in Madrid. Moreover, they constantly advanced their case for ever-greater measures of home rule by contrasting the island's record as a faithful outpost of the empire with Cuba's insurrectionist movement. For instance, the Autonomist faction, led by Luis Muñoz Rivera, contributed "loyalty and support for the Liberal Party in the Spanish Cortes in exchange for concessions of enhanced self-rule." Muñoz Rivera declared to Spanish officials, "We are Spaniards and wrapped in the Spanish flag we shall die."[27] He and future Resident Commissioner Federico Degetau were among those who traveled to Madrid in 1895 to secure home rule for Puerto Rico from the Spanish government.

The United States' victory in the Spanish-American War moved Puerto Rico's trajectory away from self-rule, frustrating and traumatizing Puerto Rico's political elites "to the extent that more than a century later, those wounds continued to ooze with no end in sight."[28] Instead of political autonomy, which Spain had promised, the United States implemented two years of military rule under three different governors: Major John Brooke, General Guy Henry, and General George W. Davis—all of whom had backgrounds as Indian fighters, leaving Puerto Ricans dismayed at the unlikelihood of their political recognition.[29] After the United States occupied the island in 1898, Muñoz Rivera wrote a poem likening his efforts to achieve political autonomy for Puerto Rico to Sisyphus's eternal task of pushing a huge rock up a hill, only to have it roll back down.[30]

The Foraker Act and Its Discontents

In 1900 the U.S. ended its military occupation of Puerto Rico and attempted to define the island's position within the federal orbit. Beginning as H.R. 6883, a bill to apply U.S. customs and internal revenue laws in Puerto Rico, the Foraker Act was the first law to define Puerto Rico's territorial status in the early 20th century. The bill was introduced by its chief sponsor, House Ways and Means Chairman Sereno Payne of New York, in January 1900.[31] Senate

Joseph Foraker of Ohio, chairman of the Senate Committee on Pacific Islands and Puerto Rico, was a Civil War veteran. Foraker also served as governor of Ohio for two terms before his election to the U.S. Senate.

Image courtesy of the Library of Congress

John C. Spooner of Wisconsin supported the acquisition of the Philippines, Puerto Rico, and Guam as U.S. territories, but opposed their permanent annexation.

Image courtesy of the Library of Congress

bill S. 2264, introduced by Joseph Foraker of Ohio, simultaneously provided a "temporary civil government for Porto Rico." A report that accompanied the bill recommended "the election of a Delegate to the U.S. House of Representatives, who shall be allowed a seat but not vote in that body."

Two types of opposition emerged. Some Members argued that the legislation did not go far enough, challenging the notion that a single individual could represent more than one million, a constituency significantly larger than any House Member's. Also, the provision fell significantly short of Puerto Rico's representation in the Spanish Cortes, which included four senators and 12 deputies.[32] Other Members, such as Senator John C. Spooner of Wisconsin, believed the legislation went too far. Spooner felt territories such as Puerto Rico and Hawaii would never become states and that the election of a Delegate held out a false promise of eventual statehood. "There is no difference between a Delegate in Congress and a member except in the matter of a vote. It has always been considered a pledge of statehood," Spooner argued. "I am not yet ready, nor are we called upon now, to give that *quasi* pledge of statehood, or to imply that they will ever reach a condition where it shall be either for their interests, or certainly for ours, to let them be one of the members of this Union."[33]

A small Puerto Rican delegation representing a diverse range of political interests appealed for a civil government during debate on the Foraker Act. Among the members of the delegation was future Resident Commissioner Tulio Larrínaga, who was then a municipal engineer of San Juan and a member of the Puerto Rican Federal Party. Testifying before several House and Senate committees about conditions on the island, he called for free trade with the United States, advocated territorial status for Puerto Rico, and discussed universal male suffrage.[34] "Puerto Rico needs a civil government even more than free trade," he told the House Committee on Ways and Means. "The people want to feel that they have become in a tangible manner attached to the United States and [that Puerto Rico is] not a mere dependency."[35]

The House passed Payne's bill by a vote of 172 to 160. The Senate replaced the language in the House bill with its own, adding such extensive amendments that the bill was eventually named for its Senate sponsor. President McKinley signed the Foraker Act (31 Stat. 77–86) on April 12, 1900. The law established a colonial regime, administered by the U.S. President and the Congress, and designated the island an "unorganized territory"; thus, while Puerto Ricans were not granted U.S. citizenship, those who swore loyalty to the United States would receive its protection. The act placed absolute power in the hands of a governor appointed by the President and an 11-member executive council that comprised a majority of U.S. appointees who directed the island's six principal administrative bureaus. The law also created a 35-member house of delegates that would be popularly elected every two years, but undermined its authority by vesting the executive council with unchecked veto power. Additionally, it provided that "qualified voters" would elect biennially a Resident Commissioner who would be "entitled to official recognition as such by all Departments" and given a seat in the U.S. House. Finally, the law anticipated, but stopped short of, instituting a system of free trade. Instead it established a reduced ad valorem tariff of 15 percent for all Puerto Rican merchandise entering the United States and all U.S. goods entering Puerto Rico.[36] Although the Foraker Act was economically generous in some respects—it exempted the island from U.S. taxes, for example—many Puerto Ricans were bitterly disappointed because it left the island's political status unresolved and created an undemocratic administrative structure.[37]

Future Resident Commissioner Luis Muñoz Rivera emerged as the voice of mainstream discontent with the Foraker Act. Addressing the Puerto Rican house of delegates in 1908, he characterized American political leaders as "petty kings" and the house of delegates as an institution serving little purpose because its laws were "wrecked on that perpetual reef" of the U.S.-appointed governor's council. Even in oppressed countries like Ireland and Hungary, the lawmakers were natives, Muñoz Rivera noted, but "the members of the Porto Rican senate are Americans, and we are given the laws of Montana, of California.... The inventors of this labyrinth find pleasure in repeating that we are not prepared [for self-government]," he said. "I wish to return the charge word for word ... that American statesmen are not prepared to govern foreign colonies so different in character and of such peculiar civilization."[38]

This 1899 image of La Fortaleza emphasizes its defensive capabilities. Built in the 16th century to guard San Juan Bay from naval attacks, it has served as the Puerto Rican governor's residence for more than 400 years.

Image courtesy of the Library of Congress

Insular Cases

The Foraker Act also raised questions about American citizenship for Puerto Ricans. Since the passage of the Northwest Ordinance in 1787, most territories within the continental United States achieved statehood by following well-established guidelines.[39] The Insular Cases, which were eventually heard by the U.S. Supreme Court, stemmed from debate about whether overseas territories such as Puerto Rico should be considered foreign or domestic for tax purposes, but the question on most Americans' minds, was whether Puerto Ricans would be entitled to full citizenship under the new civil government.[40] Of the Insular Cases heard before the Supreme Court, scholars consider *Downes v. Bidwell* (182 U.S. 244, 1901), *Dorr v. United States* (195 U.S. 138, 1904), *Balzac v. Porto Rico* (258 U.S. 298, 1922), and *Rasmussen v. United States* (197 U.S. 516, 1925) to be the most important because they delineated the entitlements of incorporated versus nonincorporated territories. The Supreme Court ruled that nonincorporated territories would receive "fundamental" constitutional protections including "freedom of expression, due process of law, equal protection under the law ... [and] protection against illegal searches," but not the full range of constitutional protections enjoyed by U.S. citizens.[41] The Supreme Court classified Puerto Rico, the Philippines, and Pacific territories acquired after 1898 as nonincorporated territories. Incorporated territories received full constitutional protections because they were considered part of the United States.[42] Puerto Ricans were considered "citizens of Porto Rico," a designation that gave rise to the term "U.S. national," a person who receives fundamental constitutional protections but is not entitled to full civil or constitutional rights.

The court was deeply divided over the groundbreaking decision in *Downes v. Bidwell*. In a 5 to 4 decision, the Justices wrote five different opinions (one majority, with two separate concurrences, and two dissenting), reflecting an array of views.[43] In effect, the ambiguous ruling reinforced the Supreme Court's marginal role in territorial jurisdiction, thus preserving—and arguably strengthening—Congress's absolute authority over Puerto Rico's status.

William A. Jones sponsored an act that outlined independence for the Philippine Islands. A 14-term U.S. Representative, Jones attended the Virginia Military Institute as an adolescent and helped to defend Richmond, Virginia, from the Union Army during the Civil War.

Collection of the U.S. House of Representatives

The Jones Act of 1917: Origins and Discontents

Frustrated with the Foraker Act, the Puerto Rican Union Party led a revolt against then-governor Regis Post and the executive council in 1909, accusing them of deliberately resisting calls for political reform on the island. After a large portion of its legislative agenda was rejected, the Puerto Rican house of delegates submitted petitions protesting the Foraker Act to the U.S. Congress and to President William Howard Taft, and threatened to adjourn without passing vital budget and appropriations bills. Congress amended the Foraker Act to enable it to pass Puerto Rico's budget bills if the house of delegates failed to act, and American officials became newly aware of Puerto Rico's grievances with its governing legislation.[44]

Woodrow Wilson's ascent to the presidency increased the likelihood that the Foraker Act would be amended. In 1912 Wilson campaigned on a promise to ensure U.S. citizenship and home rule for Puerto Ricans.[45] From 1912 to 1914, Insular Affairs Committee chairman William A. Jones of Virginia, who had previously opposed the Foraker Act, introduced bills on six occasions calling for a new constitutional government for Puerto Rico and U.S. citizenship for its residents. None of them gained any traction, but two events in 1914 added to the island's importance in the eyes of U.S. officials: the completion of the Panama Canal and the start of the First World War. The canal's role as a vital connection between the Atlantic and Pacific Oceans highlighted Puerto Rico's strategic value as a stopover for maritime commercial traffic. This was especially the case for ships coming from Europe, but the start of World War I strengthened fears that the Caribbean would be dragged into the conflict. Puerto Rico had served for centuries as a Spanish outpost, and in the early 20th century it was crucial to U.S. plans to protect the Panama Canal from German U-boats patrolling Caribbean shipping lanes.[46]

Though the Wilson administration was preoccupied with events in Europe, the Bureau of Insular Affairs (BIA) argued that cementing the political bonds between Puerto Rico and the mainland would pay significant dividends. "The word loyalty will have a greater meaning [for Puerto Ricans] if we admit them to the conglomerate of our citizenship," read a 1912 internal BIA memo. "Otherwise, there will always be discontent[ed] elements that will agitate for breaking the bond."[47] Also, U.S. military planners were eager to assemble a volunteer Puerto Rican home guard and a Puerto Rican regiment to protect the island and defend the Canal Zone, respectively. Puerto Ricans' newly acquired U.S. citizenship made recruitment easier. On an island with roughly one million inhabitants, hundreds of thousands of men registered for the draft; more than 17,000 were selected.[48] The island also exceeded its fundraising quota for Liberty Loan bond drives. "We have been at your side in the hour of crisis and the people who are good to share the responsibilities, hardships, and sacrifices at any great emergency and who are quick to respond to the call of public duty, should also be good to share the prerogatives and advantages of your institutions and of American citizenship in normal times," said Resident Commissioner Félix Córdova Dávila.[49]

This 1912 photo shows the construction of the Panama Canal. The locks are visible but the gates have not yet been built. World War I made the U.S. government aware of Puerto Rico's importance in relation to the canal.

Image courtesy of the Library of Congress

Introduced by House Insular Affairs Chairman Jones—and following on the heels of the First Jones Act (39 Stat. 545-556), which in August 1916 had increased Filipino autonomy and pledged independence as soon as practicable—the Second Jones Act (39 Stat. 951-968), which pertained to Puerto Rico, was less sweeping than the Foraker Act and retained much of the colonial structure. While the new legislation increased membership in the territorial house from 35 representatives to 39 and created for the first time a popularly elected senate with 19 members, it reserved Congress's right to annul or amend bills passed by the insular legislature and it required that directors of four of the six major government departments—agriculture and labor, health, interior, and treasury—be appointed by the U.S. President with the advice and consent of the territorial senate. The two remaining department heads, the attorney general and the commissioner of education, would be named solely by the President.[50] As a scholar of Puerto Rican politics notes, the Jones Act "barely nodded in the direction of [the] American principle of government by consent of the governed," and though it provided some "coveted gains," it hardly fulfilled most Puerto Ricans' aspirations.[51] Most significant, rather than deferring to Puerto Ricans on the issue of citizenship, the final version of the Jones Act conveyed new constitutional obligations.

Citizenship was a controversial subject on an island whose political leaders struggled to define its relationship with the United States. For example, Luis Muñoz Rivera initially argued against granting Puerto Ricans U.S. citizenship in the debate over the Jones Act, following the lead of his Union Party, which eliminated statehood from its platform in 1912. However, he personally

Sixty-fourth Congress of the United States of America;

At the Second Session,

Begun and held at the City of Washington on Monday, the fourth day of December, one thousand nine hundred and sixteen.

AN ACT

To provide a civil government for Porto Rico, and for other purposes.

Be it enacted by the Senate and House of Representatives of the United States of America in Congress assembled, That the provisions of this Act shall apply to the island of Porto Rico and to the adjacent islands belonging to the United States, and waters of those islands; and the name Porto Rico as used in this Act shall be held to include not only the island of that name but all the adjacent islands as aforesaid.

BILL OF RIGHTS.

SEC. 2. That no law shall be enacted in Porto Rico which shall deprive any person of life, liberty, or property without due process of law, or deny to any person therein the equal protection of the laws.

That in all criminal prosecutions the accused shall enjoy the right to have the assistance of counsel for his defense, to be informed of the nature and cause of the accusation, to have a copy thereof, to have a speedy and public trial, to be confronted with the witnesses against him, and to have compulsory process for obtaining witnesses in his favor.

That no person shall be held to answer for a criminal offense without due process of law; and no person for the same offense shall be twice put in jeopardy of punishment, nor shall be compelled in any criminal case to be a witness against himself.

That all persons shall before conviction be bailable by sufficient sureties, except for capital offenses when the proof is evident or the presumption great.

The Jones–Shafroth Act (39 Stat. 951-968) guaranteed full citizenship rights to Puerto Ricans. The act also extended the term of Resident Commissioners from two to four years. This law was superseded by the Commonwealth Act of 1952.

Original Jones–Shafroth Act; image courtesy of the National Archives and Records Administration

embraced the prospect of U.S. citizenship for Puerto Ricans. After eventually endorsing the Jones Act on the House Floor, Muñoz Rivera proceeded to explain why many Puerto Ricans rejected it. "My countrymen, who, precisely the same as yours, have their dignity and self respect to maintain, refuse to accept a citizenship of an inferior order, a citizenship of the second class, which does not permit them to dispose of their own resources nor to live their own lives nor to send to this Capitol their proportional representation," he said.[52] Muñoz Rivera never saw the Jones Act implemented; he died before President Wilson signed it into law on March 2, 1917.

Intended to pacify Puerto Rico's concerns and strengthen America's grip on the Caribbean Basin during wartime, the Jones Act only made Puerto Rico's political situation more complex. "Rather than solving the status question, the Jones Act intensified the status struggle," placing Resident Commissioners at the center of the debate observes historian Luis Martínez-Fernández."[53]

The Ongoing Question of Puerto Rican Status

What the Foraker Act, the Insular Cases, and the Jones Act failed to finally determine was Puerto Rico's political status as a nonincorporated American territory. According to Martínez-Fernández, the early decades of U.S. rule in Puerto Rico were driven by a policy of "bifurcation and fragmentation" as U.S. authorities played favorites with factions of the island's political elite in an attempt "to retain the island as a territorial conquest of ambiguous political status."[54] Puerto Rican politicians were also split on the question of status. The popularity of three broad options—statehood, complete independence, and some measure of autonomy within the colonial structure—waxed and waned among Puerto Rico's political elites.

By virtue of their participation in the American federal government most Resident Commissioners either advocated a form of colonial autonomy or pursued statehood. At the heart of the matter was the constant struggle to achieve a balance between federal and local control of Puerto Rico's internal affairs. One scholar describes Luis Muñoz Rivera as a "master trapeze artist in Puerto Rico's ideological wars" because at one point in his career he embraced all three status options.[55] But this balancing act was difficult for Muñoz Rivera, who was caught between his deep emotional and cultural attachment to his Hispanic heritage and Puerto Rican independence and his pragmatic impulse to accept U.S. citizenship. Here was the essential autonomist dilemma: Whereas statehood threatened to subsume local Puerto Rican issues, complete independence might limit the island's economic opportunities.[56] The divisiveness of this issue both on and off the island led a *Washington Post* reporter to observe in 1924, "What the ultimate status of Porto Rico will be is a matter still lying in the capacious lap of the gods."[57]

Pivoting on the issues of autonomy, statehood, and independence, Puerto Rican political parties underwent a number of transformations in the early 20th century (see table on page 160). One scholar describes the insular political scene of the 1920s as a "kaleidoscope" with the "disappearance of some parties, the birth of new ones, and the merger of others" and as a jumble of "personality clashes, factions within parties, and changing political credos." Adding another layer of complexity, these developments always "operated within the framework of United States control."[58] Félix Córdova Dávila discussed Puerto Ricans' quandary: testifying before the House Committee on Insular Affairs during the 70th Congress (1927–1929), "This uncertainty [in status] brings as a result a divided public opinion; some of the people advocating independence, others statehood, and others full self-government," he told his colleagues."We are not to be blamed for the different views that are striking our minds. It is not our fault. If there is any fault at all, it belongs exclusively to the doubtful position we are left in through the failure of the American Congress to define our status." Continuing, Córdova Dávila delineated Puerto Rico's identity crisis:

> Are we foreigners? No; because we are American citizens, and no citizen of the United States can be a foreigner within the boundaries of the Nation. Are we a part of the Union? No; because we are an unincorporated Territory under the rulings of the Supreme Court. Can you find a proper definition for this organized and yet unincorporated Territory, for this piece of ground belonging to but not forming part of the United States? Under the rulings of the courts of justice we are neither flesh, fish, nor fowl. We are neither a part nor a whole. We are nothing; and it seems to me if we are not allowed to be part of the Union we should be allowed to be a whole entity with full and complete control of our internal affairs.[59]

Shifting American policy had a direct influence on the confusing political alliances in Puerto Rico. "The political situation here is more complex and scrambled than it has been for many years," wrote Harwood Hull in the *New York Times* in 1932, a year that saw at least three party transitions. "Party lines have been broken and re-formed in recent months."[60]

CRAFTING AN IDENTITY
The Office of Resident Commissioner

The position of Resident Commissioner, which Congress created for Puerto Rico, echoed the island's ambiguous status.[61] Like Territorial Delegates, the Resident Commissioner had legislative responsibilities, but unlike Territorial Delegates, the Resident Commissioner was "entitled to official recognition as such by all [executive] Departments." Also, although the Resident Commissioner was a Member of Congress, he was obligated to present his certificate of election to the State Department as if he were a foreign diplomat.[62] The first Resident Commissioner, Federico Degetau, said it was "difficult, from a reading of the law, for many people to determine whether the commissioner was elected by the people to represent them or to represent the government of the island … in other words, whether he is an official of the local or of the Federal Government."[63]

The creation of the office of Resident Commissioner was a compromise: While recognizing that the residents of Puerto Rico, and later those of the Philippines, deserved some federal representation, Members of Congress were tacitly precluding the possibility that these overseas territories would

Table—Political Parties of Puerto Rico, Founded 1898 through 1945[a]

POLITICAL PARTY	PERIOD	DESCRIPTION	RESIDENT COMMISSIONER(S)
Partido Federalista (Federal Party)	1898–1904	Supported internal autonomy and eventual independence. Backed primarily by coffee growers who were critical of U.S. trade policy that negatively affected their crop.[b]	Luis Muñoz Rivera
Partido Republicano (Republican Party)	1898–1932	Supported eventual statehood. Backed by commercial powers with economic ties to the United States, including sugar producers. Continued as the Pure Republicans after 1924.[c]	Federico Degetau José Lorenzo Pesquera (unofficially)
Partido de Unión (Union Party)	1904–1932	Born of an alliance between dissident members of Partido Republicano and Partido Federalista. Initially supported a "catch-all" program of independence, statehood, and autonomy and stood firmly in favor of amending the Foraker Act of 1900 to include a greater degree of self-government. Eventually embraced autonomy after eliminating statehood from the platform in 1912 and independence in 1922.[d]	Luis Muñoz Rivera Tulio Larrínaga Félix Córdova Dávila
Alianza (Alliance)	1924–1932	Derived from factions in both the Partido de Unión and Partido Republicano. Took a pragmatic approach, supporting autonomy and believing statehood and independence were politically unfeasible in Washington.[e]	Félix Córdova Dávila
Partido Socialista (Socialist Party)	1915–1948[f]	Born of the political wing of the Federación Libre de Trabajadores (Free Federation of Labor), a labor union with ties to the American Federation of Labor. Informed by the global political movement, the Party initially considered itself an extension of the American Socialist Party; formal ties between the two parties ceased in 1924. Supported statehood but focused primarily on social justice and aiding impoverished Puerto Ricans.[g]	Santiago Iglesias Bolívar Pagán
Partido Nacionalista (Nationalist Party)	1922–1960s	Split from the Partido de Unión, advocating complete cultural and political independence from the United States. Never carried a significant electoral base, peaking with an unsuccessful electoral alliance with the Liberal Party in 1932. Turned toward violence following the 1932 electoral loss amid crippling economic depression. Followers carried out a number of attempted assassinations, several successfully.[h]	N/A
Coalición (Coalition)	1924	An electoral agreement between a wing of the Partido Republicano and the Partido Socialista for the 1924 election cycle. Both parties campaigned on the issue of statehood but maintained separate platforms.[i]	Santiago Iglesias
Partido Unión Republicana (Union Republican Party)	1932	Derived from portions of the Alianza and the Partido Republicano. Sought statehood but favored independence over contemporary colonial arrangement. Organized in January 1932 and absorbed into the Coalición in October 1932.[j]	José Lorenzo Pesquera (unofficially)
Coalición (Coalition)	1932–1940	An electoral fusion agreement between the Partido Unión Republicana and Partido Socialista. Supported statehood and the social justice platforms advocated by the Socialistas. Opposed local New Deal interventions.	Santiago Iglesias Bolívar Pagán
Partido Liberal (Liberal Party)	1932–1940	Organized from factions of the Partido de Unión and Partido Republicano. Criticized the U.S. government for its perceived neglect of Puerto Rico's political and economic needs, and supported independence. Provided local support for New Deal programs specific to Puerto Rico. Factions split over support for Tydings legislation in 1936, calling for immediate and complete political and economic independence.[k]	N/A
Partido Popular Democrático (PPD or Popular Democratic Party)	1938–present	Organized by Luis Muñoz Marín shortly after he left the Partido Liberal. The PPD was a key supporter of a series of social and economic reforms in the 1930s and 1940s. Supported the formation of the Estado Libre Asociado (Free Associated State) in 1952 and thereafter supported autonomy within the commonwealth status. Dominant on the island from the 1940s to the late 1960s.[l]	Jesús T. Piñero[m]

ever become states.[64] An early Senate Report on the Foraker Act mentioned "the election of a Delegate to the House of Representatives," and although the suggestion "met with some objection," a Senate committee concluded, "It is certainly a modest representation for 1,000,000 people."[65] Senator John C. Spooner of Wisconsin reasoned, "No Congress gives a Delegate to a people except upon the theory that the time is come when they shall be admitted to statehood." He opposed Puerto Rican statehood, saying the island's residents "know nothing of us, nothing of our ways ... nothing of our system, nothing of our institutions." He later vowed to support the Foraker Act only if Congress granted Puerto Rico "a commissioner, whose status shall enable him to represent their necessities and wants to the Congress."[66]

The final version of the Foraker Act provided for the election of a Resident Commissioner, whose position was defined in two sentences.[67] The Resident Commissioner served a two-year term and would earn the same salary as any other Member of Congress. Candidates had to be citizens of Puerto Rico and at least 30 years old—which was five years older than the constitutional requirement for Representatives—and literate in English.[68] After presenting his credentials to the State Department, the Resident Commissioner was recognized by Congress as the representative for Puerto Rico, who could lobby Members and government officials on the island's behalf. However, the act's

---

a General sources defining Puerto Rico's political parties, including visual interpretations, are available in Richard E. Sharpless, "Puerto Rico," in Robert J. Alexander, ed., *Political Parties of the Americas* (Westport, CT: Greenwood Press, 1982): 611–623; César Ayala and Rafael Bernabe, *Puerto Rico in the American Century: A History since 1898* (Chapel Hill: University of North Carolina Press, 2007): 143 (see especially Figure 7.1); Truman R. Clark, *Puerto Rico and the United States, 1917–1933* (Pittsburgh, PA: University of Pittsburgh Press, 1975): 77.

b Sharpless, "Puerto Rico": 617; Ayala and Bernabe, *Puerto Rico in the American Century*: 52–55.

c Sharpless, "Puerto Rico": 621–622; Ayala and Bernabe, *Puerto Rico in the American Century*: 52–55.

d Sharpless, "Puerto Rico": 623; Ayala and Bernabe, *Puerto Rico in the American Century*: 55.

e Ayala and Bernabe, *Puerto Rico in the American Century*: 59; Clark, *Puerto Rico and the United States, 1917–1933*: 80–82.

f The last Socialist territorial senator, Bolívar Pagán, won his final term as a Socialist in 1948. See Fernando Bayron Toro, *Elecciones y partidos políticos de Puerto Rico, 1809–2000* (Mayagüez, PR: Editorial Isla, 2003): 212.

g Gonzalo F. Córdova, *Resident Commissioner Santiago Iglesias and His Times*: 134; Ayala and Bernabe, *Puerto Rico in the American Century*: 61–68.

h Sharpless, "Puerto Rico": 617–618; Ayala and Bernabe, *Puerto Rico in the American Century*: 105–107.

i Bayron Toro, *Elecciones y partidos políticos de Puerto Rico*: 161.

j Córdova, *Resident Commissioner Santiago Iglesias and His Times*: 231–232; Clark, *Puerto Rico and the United States, 1917–1933*: 144–145.

k Sharpless, "Puerto Rico": 617; Ayala and Bernabe, *Puerto Rico in the American Century*: 100, 115–116; Córdova, *Resident Commissioner Santiago Iglesias and His Times*: 158.

l Sharpless, "Puerto Rico": 620–621.

m Other individuals who served as Resident Commissioner from the PPD served after 1945.

Sisifo (Sisyphus) excerpt

By Luis Muñoz Rivera (1902), *referencing Greek mythology in speaking of Puerto Rico's political position after the United States won control of the island from Spain.*

V.

Resigned
but indomitable, with the proud and rough
dignity of someone who is fulfilling his destiny
and that relies on his valor, little by little
the titan arrives at the plain and looks
for the crag that defies his strength.
He stares at it, walks around it,
studies its centuries-old caves
and puts his shoulder to the giant mass.
It's all useless. He is attacked by monsters
with infernal thunder and stung by reptiles
with their venomous tongues.
The crowd, doubtful of success,
applauds the whole time but from a distance
as if they were fearful of a fast collapse.
The block resists the bold push,
the beasts that hide in its cavities
redouble their enormous joy
and Sisyphus, breathless, stops,
reflects, and starts all over again.

The original Spanish is in Appendix J.

ambiguity, coupled with Congress' uncertainty about Puerto Rico's readiness for democratic government, led it to deny the Resident Commissioner speaking privileges and even access to the House Chamber.

The limits of Degetau's power were immediately apparent, but Degetau used committee testimony and the aid of sympathetic Members to push legislation beneficial to Puerto Rico. He also employed press interviews and lobbied executive branch officials. Members of Congress and the media realized the frustration Degetau experienced and, in May 1902, a *Baltimore Sun* editorial noted that John Lacey of Iowa had submitted a resolution to extend floor privileges to Degetau. "Mr. Degetau's official functions have begun and ended with this designation, and if he succeeds in getting even so far as across the threshold of one of the lobbies at the Capitol, where he may inspire but not exhale the legislative atmosphere, he is doing about all he can reasonably expect to do," it said. Degetau is "driven to the second-hand method of buttonholing members, just [as] any untitled lobbyist is privileged to do." Also noted by the *Sun* was the inconsistency in Degetau's position relative to that of the Delegate from Hawaii, Robert Wilcox, who could take a seat on the House Floor, make motions, and serve on committees.[69] "Both, according to the Supreme Court construction, are United States Territories," the editorial observed. "So that under this broad yet somewhat flexible ruling Porto Rico ought to have the same rights of representation as are accorded to Hawaii, which does not seem to bear to this country the same commercialist importance as does the island only a few hundred miles off the coast of the United States."[70]

On March 18, 1902, Henry Cooper of Wisconsin, chairman of the House Committee on Insular Affairs, inserted the "Resident Commissioner" position into an amendment to the House Rules that would allow various people—from "private secretaries" to "judges of the Supreme Court"—access to the House Floor.[71] The House spent little time debating the resolution before adopting the final version on June 28; however, the victory was incomplete. Just before the bill passed, John Dalzell of Pennsylvania, who brought it to the floor, assured his colleagues that the amendments would not give the Resident Commissioner privileges that were equal to those of the Territorial Delegates; although the bill would allow the Resident Commissioner to be present on the House Floor, it would not allow him to speak on record or vote.[72] The Resident Commissioner "was put on a par with the clerks of House committees, heads of executive departments, foreign ministers, and the Librarian of Congress in having access to the House Chamber," notes a scholar.[73] Though several measures sought to enhance the privileges of the Puerto Rican Member, they remained unchanged until the passage of the Jones Act, which gave the Resident Commissioner the same rights as the other Members of the House, lengthening his term from two to four years; reducing the minimum age qualification to 25 years; and providing him franking privileges, stationery, and money to hire a clerk.[74]

The status of Resident Commissioners and Territorial Delegates was decidedly secondary compared with that of their voting colleagues. While Resident Commissioners and Territorial Delegates were eventually allowed to hold committee assignments and introduce legislation as third-party candidates, they did not receive support from the Democratic Caucus or the Republican

Conference. However, because statutory representatives lacked official ties to a major party, they could seek the support of both Democrats and Republicans. Many Resident Commissioners used their circumscribed office to the fullest extent possible by participating in committee debate, introducing amendments, testifying before House and Senate panels, and cajoling and lobbying Members from both chambers in private conversations and at social gatherings. Clarence Miller of Minnesota, a high-ranking Republican on the Insular Affairs Committee, recalled that Resident Commissioner Luis Muñoz Rivera was "persistent and solicitous" regarding the creation of a more democratic government in Puerto Rico. "I do not know of anyone who could have been more insistent than he has been during all these years," he said.[75]

Puerto Ricans in Washington

Hispanic Americans in Congress regularly experienced racial prejudice. Many white Members subscribed to decades-old beliefs that stereotyped Hispanics, especially Puerto Ricans, as "dark-skinned, childlike, poor, and primitive" and unfit to govern themselves.[76] When the United States acquired Puerto Rico in 1899, Secretary of War Elihu Root said, "Before the people of Porto Rico can be fully entrusted with self-government, they must first learn the lesson of self-control and respect for the principles of the constitutional government."[77]

Puerto Rico's first Resident Commissioner, Federico Degetau, challenged these assumptions by engaging those who held them, and he questioned their capacity for citizenship. Degetau discussed Puerto Ricans' "fitness" and "ability" to embrace a republican form of government in numerous interviews. He also responded to charges from "white supremacist" officeholders, including former Secretary of the Navy Hilary Herbert, who in 1901 classified Puerto Ricans as an "inferior race." As "a member of an 'inferior' race," Degetau wrote Herbert, "I suppose that your theory is the result of a careful study of the people of Puerto Rico."[78] "Americans think we have savages and Indians in Porto Rico," Degetau observed. "Why, we have no more Indians than you have in Chicago. People ask me where the natives in the party are. I tell them that I am a typical native."[79] Later Degetau defended an appropriation to maintain a "Porto Rican regiment" in the U.S. Army. When future Speaker James Beauchamp (Champ) Clark of Missouri cited racial stereotypes as a reason for nixing the funding, Degetau noted that after the regiment visited Washington, "the public in the capital expected to see men of an inferior race, of small stature and sallow complexion, and they found that by their physical appearance the Porto Ricans did not differ from the other soldiers.... On account of their military bearing and dexterity, they obtained continuous applause; their moral conduct won them unanimous praise." Supporting Degetau, Representative Frank Mondell of Wyoming asserted that Puerto Rico should have a regiment for its protection, and the House defeated Clark's amendment, 89 to 47.[80]

Luis Muñoz Rivera challenged the assumptions of cantankerous Speaker Joseph Cannon of Illinois. During debate over the Jones Act, Cannon objected to extending Puerto Ricans citizenship because he believed they were unfit for self-rule.[81] The cigar-chomping Illinoisan, who noted that Puerto Rico has "great tobacco and makes pretty good cigars," believed the "racial question"

This 1905 image shows the "Porto Rican Battalion" marching in a procession along Pennsylvania Avenue in Washington, D.C. Resident Commissioners Federico Degetau and Tulio Larrínaga prevented the dissolution of the regiment by preserving its funding in House appropriations bills.

Image courtesy of the Library of Congress

As Speaker and chairman of the House Rules Committee, Joe Cannon of Illinois held an extraordinary amount of power until insurgent Republicans allied with Democrats to challenge his iron-fisted control of the House in 1910. Thereafter, Speakers were barred from holding committee chairmanships.

Collection of the U.S. House of Representatives, Photography Collection

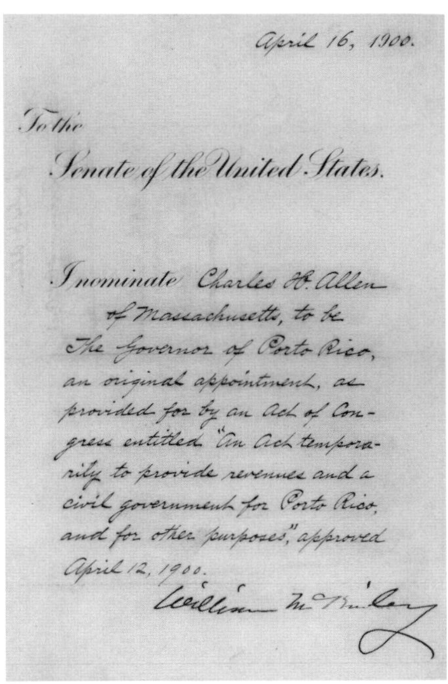
April 16, 1900.

To the

Senate of the United States.

I nominate Charles H. Allen of Massachusetts, to be The Governor of Porto Rico, an original appointment, as provided for by an Act of Congress entitled "An Act temporarily to provide revenues and a civil government for Porto Rico, and for other purposes," approved April 12, 1900.

William McKinley

In this April 1900 letter to the U.S. Senate, President William McKinley nominates Charles H. Allen to serve as the first civilian governor of Puerto Rico in accordance with the Foraker Act of 1900.

Image courtesy of the National Archives and Records Administration

and "climatic conditions" disqualified most of the islanders from governing themselves. Cannon further suggested that the infrastructure improvements and reforms to education and business that had been enacted on the island since the Spanish-American War resulted largely from American "enterprise and capital" and vehemently opposed statehood. "God forbid that in [Muñoz Rivera's] time or my time, there should be statehood for Puerto Rico as one of the United States," he said.[82]

Muñoz Rivera rejected Cannon's belief that Puerto Ricans should be denied U.S. citizenship. "Mr. Chairman, Porto Rico, deprived of its natural sovereignty, depends upon the generosity and chivalry of American lawmakers," he said from the well of the House shortly after Cannon's speech. "I consider it very unfortunate that a Porto Rican is obliged to hear on this floor remarks offensive to the dignity of his native land … it is not our fault that we are compelled to come here and ask for the enactment of legislation, of a constitution, which should be our undeniable right to make, according to American principles, ourselves. I must conclude, declaring emphatically that I am as proud to be a Porto Rican as the gentleman from Illinois is proud of being an Illinoisan, and as every gentleman on this floor is proud of being an American."[83] The House Floor and galleries erupted in applause when Muñoz Rivera finished speaking.

The Language Barrier

Many Hispanic Members of this era were bilingual or learned English so they could work with U.S. government officials. Santiago Iglesias was a translator for American forces during the Spanish-American War, and improved his English while working and attending school in New York. He spoke prolifically on the House Floor.[84] Octaviano Larrazolo, like many New Mexican politicians, and Tulio Larrínaga of Puerto Rico were fluent in both English and Spanish. Larrínaga headed the English department in the cultural center of the Puerto Rican Arts and Sciences Association starting in 1876, and Ladislas Lazaro often used both French and English while campaigning in Louisiana.

Resident Commissioners continued to study English after they assumed office. A brilliant orator in Spanish and a longtime resident of New York City, Muñoz Rivera began to study English at age 50 in preparation for his service in Washington, D.C. "I will go to a mountain or a beach, with my books, practice English without speaking another language," he confided to a friend in 1911. "When I master it, I will feel better prepared…. I have progressed a lot. I need much more," he said.[85] José Pesquera studied English in Pennsylvania from 1901 to 1902, but still had difficulty communicating with President Herbert Hoover's administration in 1932. In an effort to defend himself against Pesquera's charge that the War Department neglected Puerto Rico after the 1932 San Cipriano hurricane, Deputy Chief of Staff George Van Horn Moseley said he preferred to communicate with an administration official who often accompanied the Resident Commissioner, since Pesquera "sometimes has a little difficulty communicating in English over the phone."[86]

Córdova Dávila spoke for many in Puerto Rico when he noted, "Language is a factor of unquestioned importance. English has not yet reached the heart of the [Puerto Rican] people, nor is it reasonable to expect this ever to come about." "The language of a people constitutes the voice of its soul, the means of expressing its feelings, and its personality. Love for the vernacular is ingrained in the individual. To deprive him of his native tongue would be heartless and cruel."[87] Nearly two decades later, Bolívar Pagán promoted increased English language instruction in Puerto Rico by supporting a $300 million proposal to rehabilitate the Puerto Rican school system. Pagán, assuaging fears that Puerto Rican children were not learning enough English, testified that English was taught as a separate subject in the early years of primary school but thereafter became the main language of instruction.[88]

"Porto Rico" to "Puerto Rico"

Maintaining Puerto Rico's Spanish heritage included changing its official name from "Porto Rico" back to the original Spanish, "Puerto Rico." The United States used "Puerto Rico" in diplomatic correspondence before the Spanish-American War but used the anglicized spelling "Porto Rico" in the Treaty of Paris, which ended the conflict. Gervasio Luis Garcia traces the origin of the phonetic English spelling to a *National Geographic* article, published in 1899 by journalist Robert T. Hill. His use of "Porto Rico" went against the wishes of the *Geographic*'s editors, who printed the following disclaimer: "The form 'Puerto Rico' is that commonly used by the people of the island itself and by those of other Spanish-speaking countries, and is good Spanish.… The Editors wish it to be understood that in this trifling matter they are not establishing a precedent."[89] Hill's decision to use the anglicized name was based on arguments that were entrenched at the turn of the century: that "Porto Rico" had been used internationally for more than 300 years and provided English speakers a way to pronounce the island's Spanish name and that "Puerto Rico" was "un-American." Concluding that the change in Puerto Rico's name was an extension of the United States' geographical conquest, Gervasio Garcia noted in 2000 that, "Naming was a form of domination; the imperial appetite was not sated until it appropriated every bit of the island, even its name."[90]

Puerto Ricans did not consider the name change "trifling." On December 18, 1931, Félix Córdova Dávila introduced a joint resolution (H.J. Res. 149) that would change "Porto Rico" back to "Puerto Rico," and submitted a petition from the Puerto Rican senate to the House Committee on Insular Affairs deeming "Porto Rico" an "impure idiomatic compound" and requesting reversion of the territory's official name so "full justice will thus be done to our history, our language, and our traditions."[91] Resident Commissioner José Pesquera steered the bill after succeeding Córdova Dávila in April 1932, but the seemingly innocuous legislation met with sturdy resistance. On May 11, in a debate that was riddled with interruptions regarding unrelated issues, opponents of the bill maintained that "Porto" was the standard English spelling. Changing the name would create unnecessary "expense of changing dies for postage stamps, for [Puerto Ricans'] currency, for their bonds, and many other things merely to gratify the sentimental whim of the local inhabitants."[92] But most Members defended the change. Ralph Lozier of Missouri noted Puerto Ricans "are now loyal American citizens," arguing, "There is no reason, either in the history, language or traditions of these Spanish-speaking people to support

Seventy-second Congress of the United States of America;
At the First Session,

Begun and held at the City of Washington on Monday, the seventh day of December, one thousand nine hundred and thirty-one.

JOINT RESOLUTION

To change the name of the island of "Porto Rico" to "Puerto Rico."

Resolved by the Senate and House of Representatives of the United States of America in Congress assembled, That from and after the passage of this resolution the island designated "Porto Rico" in the Act entitled "An Act to provide a civil government for Porto Rico, and for other purposes," approved March 2, 1917, as amended, shall be known and designated as "Puerto Rico." All laws, regulations, and public documents and records of the United States in which such island is designated or referred to under the name of "Porto Rico" shall be held to refer to such island under and by the name of "Puerto Rico."

Speaker of the House of Representatives.

~~Vice President of the United States and~~ President of the Senate. pro t

On December 7, 1931, Congress passed S.J. Res. 36, which changed the spelling of "Porto Rico" to "Puerto Rico" in official U.S. records, documents, and communications.

Original joint resolution to change the name of the island of "Porto Rico" to "Puerto Rico"; image courtesy of the National Archives and Records Administration the legitimacy of the foreign term 'Porto,' used in connection with their island habitation."[93] The House eventually passed S.J. Res. 36 (in lieu of H.J. Res. 149) 88 to 31; without debate, the Senate concurred, changing the name in May 1932.[94]

The passage of the resolution was a symbolic victory in the battle to maintain Puerto Rico's cultural heritage. Speaking for Córdova Dávila after his departure from the House, Resident Commissioner of the Philippines Camilo Osias said to his colleagues, "Never underrate the importance of individual and national sentiment in human affairs.... The change of the spelling of the name of Porto Rico may seem trivial to some, but to the inhabitants of that island it is fundamental, priceless, all important." By voting for the measure, "you are investing in friendship" and working to "evoke the eternal gratitude" of the Puerto Rican people," he said.[95]

Political and Ethnic Shifts in New Mexico

The issue of cultural heritage was also important for New Mexican Hispanics during this era as changing racial demographics shifted New Mexican politics, upsetting traditional political alliances between Anglos and *nuevomexicanos*.

Since the mid-19th century, three groups of settlers with divergent interests had had an understanding that characterized the territory's politics. According to a historian of turn-of-the-century New Mexico, "a Spanish-speaking elite, backed by New Mexico's majority population of [poor Hispanic] voters, shared power with an outnumbered but well-organized and growing Anglo minority."[96] At the root of this arrangement were the state's demographics. Hispanics, with their shrinking but still large majority, dominated elections at the town and county level, giving them influence over many of the state's everyday affairs in the territorial legislature. Meanwhile, given their disproportionate wealth

THE CANVASSING BOARD OF THE

STATE OF NEW MEXICO

To All to Whom These Presents Shall Come, Greeting:

This is to Certify, that OCTAVIANO A. LARRAZOLO

was duly and regularly elected in accordance with law to the office of UNITED STATES SENATOR(SHORT TERM ENDING MARCH 4, 1929) *at the General Election held in the said State of New Mexico on the* Sixth *day of November, in the year One Thousand Nine Hundred and* Twenty-eight, *as shown by the returns of said election on file in the office of the Secretary of State, and as declared and determined by the State Canvassing Board, consisting of the Governor, the Secretary of State, and the Chief Justice of the State of New Mexico.*

IN TESTIMONY WHEREOF, We have hereunto set our hands and caused to be affixed the Great Seal of the State of New Mexico, this Third *day of* December, *A. D.* 1928 *and of the Independence of the United States the One Hundred and* Fifty-Second.

GOVERNOR OF NEW MEXICO.

CHIEF JUSTICE OF NEW MEXICO.

SECRETARY OF STATE OF NEW MEXICO.

Octaviano Larrazolo's three-decade political career in New Mexico culminated with his election to the U.S. Senate in November 1928.

Octaviano Larrazolo's original election certificate; image courtesy of the National Archives and Records Administration and federal connections, Anglos controlled many of New Mexico's appointed positions, including the office of territorial governor.[97] As a result of this arrangement, neither group of New Mexicans sustained influence over the other throughout the 19th century.[98] But with the majority of Anglo and Hispanic voters registered as Republicans, this resulted in an era of "Republican domination."[99] Pedro Perea benefited from this agreement; bolstered by the territory's Republican machine in his 1898 election campaign, he ousted an Anglo incumbent in an election that mirrored the parties' national platforms but reflected racial stereotypes of the time.

The long-standing political dynamic that dominated New Mexico's territorial period began to dissolve as Anglo migrants from Texas and Oklahoma flocked to the cheap, oil-rich land in eastern New Mexico. Their arrival upset the demographic structure that had sustained the territory's balance of power; from 1900 to 1910, New Mexico's population grew from 195,310 to 327,301.[100] Many of the Anglo newcomers were middle-aged, financially secure Democrats who brought their racial and ethnic prejudices to New Mexico. Ignoring the genealogical, class, and regional distinctions among their *nuevomexicano* neighbors, they labeled many as "Mexican," a derogatory term. These settlers resuscitated the Democratic Party and subverted the political arrangement between Anglos and Hispanics that had defined the territory for six decades.[101] Their predominance in territorial politics led Octaviano Larrazolo in 1911 to leave the Democratic Party, to which he had been loyal since first entering politics in 1885. In a public letter of resignation, he noted this treatment "forced me to the humiliating conviction that in the Democratic party of New Mexico there exists an element of intolerance that should not be countenanced or encouraged." Moreover, he wrote, that element "is strong enough … to make me apprehensive of the future welfare of a very large number of people in New Mexico."[102]

In addition to reinvigorating the Hispanic electorate, scholars generally credit Larrazolo with helping to develop a political arrangement between Anglo and *nuevomexicano* leaders from both parties.[103] A "gentlemen's agreement" had segregated political contests so that Anglos ran only against Anglos and Hispanic candidates faced only Hispanics at the nominating conventions. As a result, more *nuevomexicano* politicians ran for local offices in the 1910s and 1920s. Regarding congressional elections, the record is mixed. Benigno Cárdenas Hernández, who belonged to the Republican Old Guard of Rio Arriba County, benefited both from the "native son movement," which encouraged *nuevomexicanos* to run for local political office, and from his party connections. He defeated a three-term Anglo incumbent in 1914, lost to an Anglo opponent in 1916, and was re-elected against an Anglo opponent in 1918. Hernández's successor, Néstor Montoya, ran against a prominent local politician, Antonio Lucero, in 1920, but lost the nomination to *nuevomexicana* Adelina Otero-Warren in 1922. Larrazolo was elected governor in 1918.[104]

Dennis Chavez's political career coincided with a shift in New Mexico's ethnopolitical culture, following the national trend favoring the Democratic Party and resulting in more-competitive elections; although his father was a Republican, Chavez joined the Democratic Party because of the GOP's perceived abuse of patronage. After serving one term in the New Mexico state house and working as a loyal party operative, Chavez won a House seat in 1930 and served for two terms. In 1934 Chavez took on progressive Republican Bronson Cutting for a U.S. Senate seat.[105]

In this undated photograph, Senator Dennis Chavez (left) and a constituent from New Mexico (right) participate in a Senate committee hearing.

Image courtesy of the Dennis Chavez Pictorial Collections (PICT 000-394-0433), Center for Southwest Research, University Libraries, University of New Mexico

LEGISLATIVE INTERESTS

Committee Assignments

Hispanic Members held far more committee assignments in this era than they did during the 19th century. Seven sat on Insular Affairs, four on Public Lands, four on Indian Affairs, and three on Territories. In part this trend reflected more-liberal House Rules concerning standing committees. Pedro Perea of New Mexico, who served a single term in the 56th Congress (1899–1901), became the first Hispanic Delegate from that territory to hold an assignment on a committee other than the obscure Coinage, Weights, and Measures panel. Perea held four committee assignments, including seats on the important Post Office and Post Roads Committee and the Territories Committee.

Resident Commissioners experienced a trajectory in their committee assignments that was similar to that of New Mexico's Delegates. From 1900 to 1904, the Resident Commissioner received no committee assignments. After 1904 Federico Degetau received a seat on one panel on the Insular Affairs Committee, which had legislative jurisdiction over Puerto Rico's administration. In 1933 Santiago Iglesias became the first Resident Commissioner to sit on additional committees. He and Bolívar Pagán both served on four panels: Agriculture, Insular Affairs, Territories, and Labor. Pagán, who represented Puerto Rico during World War II when the United States constructed a major naval facility on the island, added two more prominent committee assignments—Naval Affairs and Military Affairs—to his considerable workload.[106]

These more numerous assignments reflected the broad legislative agendas of their constituencies, and meant they held more desirable and more powerful committee positions than their predecessors. In the aggregate, Pedro Perea's assignments were impressive; Post Office and Post Roads was a top-tier committee assignment in the 56th Congress, and his assignment on Military Affairs was a good one. Also, in the decade after the Spanish-American War, the Insular Affairs Committee ranked among the top third in terms of desirability among House Members. When Iglesias served on the Agriculture Committee in the 1930s, amid the Great Depression, the Dust Bowl, and the flood of New Deal legislation, that panel was the third most desirable in the House.[107] Without a doubt, the Hispanic Member who secured the most plum assignments was Representative Joachim Fernández, Huey Long's New Orleans-based lieutenant. As a freshman, Fernández received a top-tier assignment, the Naval Affairs Committee. After serving three terms on Naval Affairs, he left for the exclusive Appropriations Committee, which was the second-most-powerful committee in the House and the panel charged with allocating federal money.[108]

However, the ascendancy of Hispanic Members to committee leadership positions remained slow. Before 1970, Resident Commissioners, like Delegates, could not attain seniority on committees; as a result, no matter how many years they served on a committee, they were still outranked by voting Members.

Although House Rules stipulated that the Delegates and the Resident Commissioner would receive the same powers and privileges as other Members, the tradition of seniority applied only when the Delegates and the Resident Commissioner determined rank among themselves.[109] In this era, only two Hispanic Members, Dennis Chavez of New Mexico and Ladislas Lazaro of Louisiana, chaired House committees. During the 73rd Congress (1933–1935), his second and final term in the House, Chavez led the Irrigation and Reclamation Committee, a panel of immense importance to Western Members whose states depended on their ability to access water. Lazaro held the gavel on the minor Enrolled Bills Committee, which standardized the legislative language of approved bills and prepared them for the President's signature, and became the Ranking Member on the influential Merchant Marine and Fisheries Committee before his untimely death in 1927. Chavez eventually chaired two Senate panels, including the influential Public Works Committee. Antonio M. Fernández of New Mexico, elected to the House late in this era, chaired the Memorials Committee for a single term before it was disbanded in 1947.

The Great Depression and the New Deal

The economic collapse marking the beginning of the Great Depression in 1929 hit Puerto Rico especially hard because it highlighted the island's dependence on U.S. economic policy and on a single cash crop: sugar. "The coming of the Great Depression simply made manifest the severity of conditions that debilitated the island economy," writes economic historian James Dietz. "It did not create or invent them."[110] Declines in manufacturing and agricultural output were not as severe as those on the mainland because production had faltered throughout the 1920s.[111] Two hurricanes in 1928 and 1932 had decimated entire economic sectors. The tobacco industry, which was the second-largest industry on the island, had grown steadily through the early part of the century under American trade barriers; however, the 1928 San Felipe hurricane nearly leveled production.[112] The 1932 San Cipriano hurricane also caused upwards of $30 million in damage, some of which Resident Commissioner José Pesquera sought to repair with federal aid. Dietz likens the storms' effect to those of the Dust Bowl drought that devastated the Midwestern United States in the early 1930s.[113]

Moreover, purchasing power on the island declined severely during the 1930s. In the 1920s, Puerto Rico received as much as 94.1 percent of its goods from the United States, more than 39.5 percent of which was food.[114] Dependent on imports from the mainland for basic necessities, including rice, beans, lard, and milk, the average Puerto Rican spent 94 percent of his or her income on food in 1930.[115] The situation worsened between 1930 and 1933; with wages already at their lowest level since the United States occupied the island in 1898, Puerto Ricans saw a 30 percent decline in per capita income. A similar, if not more severe, rise in the cost of living mirrored this drop; prices for necessities rose by a third from 1932 to 1933.[116]

Extending New Deal benefits to Puerto Rico tested the Resident Commissioners' ability to balance desires for local control with the distribution of federal aid on the island. Early in the economic crisis, Félix Córdova Dávila and José Pesquera attempted to stem losses by appealing to President Herbert Hoover

Rexford Guy Tugwell (left) was one of the principal architects of the New Deal. Here he is seen riding with FDR in a car through Greenbelt, Maryland, a federally built planned community that Tugwell conceived. He would serve as governor of Puerto Rico from 1941 to 1945.

Image courtesy of the Library of Congress

to extend to Puerto Rico the Reconstruction Finance Corporation, a program that funneled federal tax revenue to local banks.[117] When Franklin D. Roosevelt ascended to the presidency in 1933, he urged a series of emergency economic policies and social welfare programs known collectively as the New Deal, and sought to include Puerto Rico in much of this legislation."One thing that seemed to be very clear was that your problems here on the island are very much the same kind of problems that we have in many other parts of the United States," Roosevelt noted on a 1934 visit to San Juan. "They are social problems and economic problems, and the same methods that we use to solve them in other parts of the country will be applied here in Puerto Rico."[118] In the early 1930s, Santiago Iglesias spent nearly his entire congressional career balancing the needs of Puerto Ricans vis-à-vis New Deal legislation. Iglesias successfully sought Puerto Rico's inclusion in the Federal Deposit Insurance Corporation (FDIC), a program to regulate banking. Though unsuccessful at including Puerto Rico in the initial Social Security Act of 1935, Iglesias managed to extend some of the legislation's benefits to children and rural communities in a 1937 amendment.[119]

Not all New Deal programs aided displaced Puerto Ricans. The Agricultural Adjustment Act (AAA), passed in May 1933, inflated the cost of living as federal policy subsidized mainland farmers, who then produced less, driving up the costs of goods and services for Puerto Rican consumers. Additionally, under the AAA, the island's farmers were exempt from the provisions of the law and the insular government lost its right to save a percentage of the tax revenue con exports.[120] Iglesias attempted to remedy the legislation's damaging effects byretaining the taxes on agricultural products as originally set forth in the Jones Act.[121]

Most notably, the economic collapse highlighted the island's dependence on the cultivation of sugarcane and the production of its only export crop: sugar. Nearly 95 percent of all Puerto Rican exports went to the continental United States. Accounting for nearly 15 percent of the entire U.S. market, Puerto Rican sugar was hugely profitable during World War I with little competition from warring European nations, but the industry collapsed after Europe returned to its pre-war production in the 1920s.[122] The economic pressures accompanying the onset of the Depression, combined with the decline of the sugarcane industry, were felt island-wide. Already hovering at 36 percent in December 1929, unemployment rates soared to 65 percent by 1933.[123] As a result, the years 1933 and 1934 saw widespread labor unrest, and thousands of workers from every economic sector went on strike.[124]

The Sugar Act, or Jones–Costigan Act, of 1934 (48 Stat. 670–679) proved to be particularly damaging, and amending it became a focus for Resident Commissioners Santiago Iglesias and Bolívar Pagán. As part of the Department of Agriculture's efforts to further regulate American sugar in light of plummeting prices, the legislation established quotas for each sugar-producing region based on output from 1925 to 1933. As demanded by the State Department, Cuba, which had been subjct to American trade barriers, received the largest quota for sugar cane after the market declined. Beet producers in the mainland

United States lobbied Congress to gain a significant share of the quota. As an incorporated territory, Hawaii also received a substantial quota, leaving Puerto Rico and the soon-to-be-independent Philippines with the greatest reductions in production allotments.[125] The legislation passed after Puerto Rico was assigned an insufficient 800,000-ton quota, with expected production exceeding more than a million tons.[126]

A year after the Sugar Act's passage, Iglesias submitted a resolution from the insular legislature attesting to the act's devastating effect on the island's sugar industry. "The Puerto Rican sugar industry is not only suffering from an abnormal situation but also is being punished by not as yet having received a satisfactory agreement whereby the sugar employers and the workers in general are compensated by the terrible cuts in production in the island," read the resolution.[127] In 1937, when the Sugar Act was up for reauthorization, Iglesias pleaded, "It seems to me this great Nation should not consider treating citizens of one part of the United States differently from citizens of other parts of the United States."[128] But instead of providing Puerto Rico with a sugar quota for export to the continental United States, the law limited the island to providing only for its own consumption.[129]

"The Great Social Laboratory"

Roosevelt and his academic advisors, known as the Brains Trust, also orchestrated a series of micromanaged relief projects on the island, which proved to be a turning point in Puerto Rico's colonial relationship with the United States. The island's dire economic situation demonstrated severe weaknesses in the colonial system. Members of the Roosevelt administration, notably Ernest Gruening and Rexford Guy Tugwell, determined that historically there had not been enough federal intervention in Puerto Rico. Referred to as "the great social laboratory," the island became an experiment in localized government reform as well as a jumping-off point for American diplomacy in Latin America.[130] While this policy fostered a previously absent professional class, it also had the unintended effect of radicalizing the Nationalist movement.

From left, Puerto Rican Governor Rexford Guy Tugwell chats with Elmer Ellsworth, a PPD official, and naval officer Vernon de Mars at La Fortaleza, the governor's residence in San Juan. Tugwell's successor, Resident Commissioner Jesús T. Piñero, became the first native-born Puerto Rican to serve as governor of the island.

Image courtesy of the Library of Congress

Luis Muñoz Marín was elected as the first governor of the Commonwealth of Puerto Rico in 1948. His party colleague (and appointed gubernatorial predecessor) Jesús Piñero helped to push the Elective Governor Act of 1948 through Congress.

Image courtesy of the Library of Congress

A major change in the U.S. government's oversight over Puerto Rico involved transferring the island's jurisdiction from the War Department to the Interior Department, establishing the Division of Territories and Island Possessions (DTIP) on May 29, 1934. The move placed the management of all U.S. territories in a single office and, more significant, moved Puerto Rico out of the military's jurisdiction.[131] Embracing the change, two local leaders, Puerto Rican agronomist Carlos Chardón and Liberal Party leader Luis Muñoz Marín—the son of former Resident Commissioner Luis Muñoz Rivera—proposed an economic aid plan that focused on breaking up the sugar conglomerates. Published as the *Report of the Puerto Rico Policy Commission*, the provision was popularly known as Plan Chardón.[132] The Roosevelt administration initially embraced the plan and, in an effort to implement it, Roosevelt also created the Puerto Rican Reconstruction Administration (PRRA) in 1936.[133] Gruening was named the agency's administrator, and led a bureaucracy of 53,000 employees at its peak, making him "the political and economic czar over Puerto Rican affairs," in the words of one historian.[134] The PRRA eventually "grew into a vast apparatus, staffed by a new generation of reform-minded professionals," according to other historians.[135]

Resident Commissioner Santiago Iglesias offered qualified opposition to the creation of the PRRA and the implementation of Plan Chardón. While noting that the plan was "expected to inaugurate a new era of social justice," he disapproved of its failure to address the needs of the cane workers. "A large percentage of our population is composed of peasants whose only source of livelihood is derived from their work in the cane fields," he observed. "The standard of living and education among the poorer classes, although constantly improving, is not as high as we should like to see it, and there is a dire need for improvement."[136] Additionally, as a Coalitionist, he rejected the PRRA's tendency to favor the Liberal Party in filling its patronage positions, accusing Muñoz Marín and Chardón of creating a "supergovernment" beyond the scope of the local legislature.[137] Indeed, led by Coalitionists in the insular legislature, the PRRA soon succumbed to the battle for local control. Puerto Rican administrators, including Chardón, resigned following administrative differences with Gruening, depriving the agency of a local face. Gruening resigned from the PRRA under a cloud in 1939.[138]

Gruening's oversight over the PRRA, described by one observer as "one of the most repressive periods in U.S. rule," centered on larger foreign political implications rather than on altruistic concerns to alleviate Puerto Rican suffering.[139] Economic intervention on the island was linked to Latin America generally and served as a way to test the "Good Neighbor" Policy. In his first inaugural address, President Roosevelt promised to intervene to help alleviate the effects of economic depression on the United States' Latin American neighbors. Interpreted as an "early version of foreign aid," U.S. policy in Puerto Rico was a means to establish a better relationship with Latin America.[140]

Government intervention in the form of the PRRA also drastically shifted the makeup of the Puerto Rican economy. Agriculture's share of the island's economy dropped from nearly 50 percent in 1929 to 30 percent a decade later. However, an increase in the number of government workers mirrored this decline. The number employed by the federal or insular government in 1939 was more than double the number in 1929 (making up 32 percent versus 14 percent of the national income).[141] The result was a new, politically minded, white-collar class of Puerto Rican men and women who helped transform the island's politics later in the 20th century.[142]

Puerto Rican Independence

The economic upheaval of the Great Depression initiated a wave of anti-Americanism in Puerto Rico that crested in the mid-1930s. Formed in 1922 when the dominant Partido de Unión (Union Party) dropped independence from its platform, the Partido Nacionalista (Nationalist Party), who called for complete Puerto Rican independence, were never a significant force in their own right, but an electoral alliance with the Partido Liberal (Liberal Party) in the 1932 election as well as an increase in deadly protests catapulted them into the public eye. On February 23, 1936, members of the Nationalist Youth Movement, Hiram Rosado and Elías Beauchamp, assassinated insular police commissioner Francis Riggs. The two young men were arrested at the scene and taken to a police station. Claiming the youths had attempted to steal their weapons, the arresting officers shot both assassins dead while they were in custody. Puerto Ricans of all political stripes condemned the outburst of violence and agreed with Resident Commissioner Santiago Iglesias, who on the House Floor called the act a "tragic and brutal assassination" and a "dastardly crime" and demanded an independent investigation.[143] Among others, Nationalist leader Albizu Campos was indicted for murder. After the initial trial ended in a hung jury, a new panel found all the defendants guilty. Campos received a sentence of 10 years but was paroled after six.

The increase in violence attracted attention in the U.S. Congress, but congressional reaction reflected a callousness toward issues regarding Puerto Rican status. On April 23, 1936, Senator Millard Tydings of Maryland, chairman of the Committee on Territories and Insular Affairs and a personal friend of the deceased Riggs, introduced S. 4529. The bill granted Puerto Rico independence if the island's voters approved it in a plebiscite but provided little political or financial aid for such a transition. Moreover, the bill levied a draconian 25 percent tariff on goods exported from Puerto Rico to the United States, a move that would choke an already ailing economy. "Senator Tydings' presentation of the bill was the act of an angry man," notes a scholar. "There was no statesmanship about it."[144] Puerto Ricans denounced the bill as an attempt to discredit independence and some city halls, plazas, and schools lowered the American flag at the news of its introduction.[145] Resident Commissioner Santiago Iglesias swiftly condemned the Tydings Bill. "I certainly am sorry that I have lived to see the day the great American Government would ask our people to commit suicide," he chided. "That is what independence, as it has been offered, means."[146]

The bill did not gain much traction and eventually died; however, it generated much congressional ire. Tydings introduced a version of his bill five times over the next decade.[147] The legislation also incited Nationalist violence. While campaigning in October 1936, Santiago Iglesias suffered a gunshot

Senator Millard Tydings of Maryland, a World War I veteran elected to the Maryland house of delegates, later served in the U.S. House for two terms and in the Senate for four terms.

Image courtesy of the Library of Congress

In this 1898 cartoon, Uncle Sam offers a suit of "stars and stripes" to a young Puerto Rican. The question of Puerto Rico's assimilation and status remained a constant source of political disagreement on the island and in Congress.

Image courtesy of the Library of Congress

This 1899 image, "Uncle Sam's Burden," shows a U.S. soldier carrying three dark-skinned children (representing the Philippines, Puerto Rico, and Cuba) in a backpack made out of the U.S. flag.

Image courtesy of the Library of Congress

The Puerto Rico Governor's office was used as a reward for political supporters, as was the case when President Warren G. Harding appointed Emmet Montgomery Reily, of Kansas City, to the post in 1921. Reily's tumultuous tenure as governor lasted for less than two years.

Image courtesy of the Library of Congress

wound during an assassination attempt. Five suspects were apprehended, and Iglesias continued his campaign event with a bandaged arm. On March 21, 1937, Nationalists planning to demonstrate in Ponce as part of Palm Sunday festivities had their parade license revoked. After they demonstrated anyway, armed police officers fired into the crowd, killing 21 people and wounding more than 100. Two police officers were among the dead.[148] The violence, which peaked with the disaster in Ponce, and Senator Tydings's extreme reaction to it were symptomatic of Puerto Rico's nebulous relationship with the United States. It was Tydings's attempt to address the island's legal status directly on the Senate Floor that transformed a local matter to an issue of national prominence.

Puerto Rico's Continental Governors

The attempts by Resident Commissioners to balance home rule with federal intervention created numerous political battles with Puerto Rico's continental governors. The Foraker and Jones Acts empowered the U.S. President to appoint a territorial governor for Puerto Rico, with the advice and consent of the U.S. Senate.[149] There were 19 appointees from 1900 to 1946, with mixed results.[150] Many Puerto Ricans considered continental governors illegitimate and treated them accordingly. Appointees were beholden only to their presidential patrons and therefore were not directly accountable to those they governed. "As long as the governor kept in the good graces of a president, there was little likelihood that even the opposition of some members of Congress would put his job in jeopardy," observes a scholar.[151] Most had little familiarity with the island before they were appointed. Puerto Ricans often reflexively dismissed the governor's authority. Governor Theodore Roosevelt, Jr. (1929–1932) quipped that unless an appointee had been born in Puerto Rico, he could be the "Archangel Gabriel" and still fail to win the "backing of the community."[152] The son of the "Rough Rider" and the U.S. President was one of the more popular appointees. Upon accepting his post, he read as much as he could about Puerto Rico and attempted to learn Spanish; throughout his tenure, he earned Puerto Ricans' respect by speaking, however brokenly, in their native tongue.[153] However, most governors were frequently at odds with the local political elites. Two in particular clashed with Resident Commissioners, who called for their removal, revealing another fault line between local and federal forces.

E. Mont Reily

Emmet Montgomery Reily, or E. Mont Reily, as he preferred to be called, was a Kansas City newspaper editor and a Republican political operative who was appointed territorial governor of Puerto Rico by President Warren G. Harding in May 1921. While Harding sought to reward Reily for supporting him early in his campaign, he wanted to keep the abrasive Missourian far from Washington, D.C. Even before Reily arrived on the island in midsummer of 1921, his "tactlessness and ineptitude" had alienated many Puerto Ricans.[154] The governor's post required the deft hand and managerial agility of a seasoned statesman, but Reily behaved as though he was a city ward boss, inserting into prominent civil offices Kansas City cronies who had no knowledge of Spanish or basic administrative experience. Most vexing to Puerto Ricans, Reily advocated

"100% Americanism," meaning he expected island residents to speak English, salute only the U.S. flag, and adopt the mainland's culture, excluding their Spanish heritage.

Resident Commissioner Félix Córdova Dávila led the campaign to oust Reily from office, appealing to Congress to investigate the governor for malfeasance and gross incompetence. On March 2, 1922, Córdova Dávila delivered a lengthy speech asking colleagues "to protest against and ask relief from the acts of an unprincipled, un-American, and altogether unfitted administrator."[155] He listed Reily's numerous violations of the letter and the spirit of the Jones Act, chief among them disregarding the legislative powers of the insular senate and removing judiciary and executive officials arbitrarily and without cause. To underscore the power and importance of regional perceptions of U.S. rule in Puerto Rico, Córdova Dávila reminded Members that Puerto Rican relations with "the Latin-American people are very close, and the success of the United States in the policy of friendship and brotherhood with our neighbors of the Latin race will depend to a great extent on the success in Porto Rico." In this respect the Resident Commissioner deemed Reily "more an enemy of the people of the United States than of the island."[156] Less than a week later, Córdova Dávila presented to the House a resolution adopted by the Puerto Rican senate by a 15 to 3 majority, declaring Reily to be "a vulgar agitator and an irresponsible despot." The resolution requested that Congress formally investigate the governor and asked President Harding to remove him from office.[154]

Benjamin G. Humphreys of Mississippi, a Democrat and a former chairman of the Committee on Territories, took to the House Floor in April 1922 to argue for a House investigation into Reily's tenure as governor. The chairman of the

An eight-term House incumbent, Horace M. Towner of Iowa had a cordial relationship with Resident Commissioner Félix Córdova Dávila. Governor Towner supported two bills that Córdova Dávila submitted in 1924 and 1928 to enable the island to select its own governor.

Image courtesy of the Library of Congress

Horace M. Towner of Iowa was inaugurated as governor of Puerto Rico after he resigned from the House in April 1923.

Image courtesy of the National Archives and Records Administration

Appointed by Governor William B. Leahy to serve the remainder of Santiago Iglesias's term as Resident Commissioner, Bolivar Pagán, Iglesias's son-in-law, sought New Deal programs for Puerto Rico. Pagán also had a contentious relationship with appointed Governor Rexford Guy Tugwell for the remainder of his congressional career.

Image courtesy of the Library of Congress

Rules Committee, Philip Campbell of Kansas, interjected that the President should decide the matter or that Reily should request an inquiry to clear his name; while the House had the power to impeach Reily, Campbell noted that doing so would be "wholly impracticable" because it would take too long.[158]

The House never launched an inquiry, but Reily resigned in February 1923, citing health issues. Evidence suggests that President Harding's patience had been exhausted and that Reily was prodded to leave. The President named Reily's successor in short order, tapping House Insular Affairs Committee chairman Horace Towner of Iowa in early March. Towner immediately set about conciliating the dominant Union Party. During a brief tribute to Towner on the House Floor, Córdova Dávila read a cable from the president of the Puerto Rican senate expressing the island's "great enthusiasm" for Towner's appointment.[159]

World War II and Rexford Tugwell

For the United States, World War II reinforced the importance of Puerto Rico's location. "Puerto Rico is in a strategic position from the defense standpoint of the Nation and will play an important role in America's defense program," Secretary of the Interior Harold Ickes informed speaker of the Puerto Rican house Miguel Angel García Méndez in June 1940. "A high degree of loyalty and willingness to make great personal sacrifices are demanded of each of us.... It seems to me incumbent upon every Puerto Rican, as it is upon every citizen of the United States, to set aside prejudices and selfish interests in order to meet the challenge that confronts us as a result of the European situation."[160] The construction of the Roosevelt Roads military base on the eastern tip of Puerto Rico in 1943 not only highlighted federal interest in the island's strategic importance, but also led to an improved infrastructure such as new facilities including airports, harbors, docks, highways, and housing developments. Resident Commissioner Bolívar Pagán noted Puerto Rico's role as the "Gibraltar of the Caribbean ... the American watchdog at the entrance of the Panama Canal."[161] Pagán addressed Puerto Rico's combat role in a speech just before the vote declaring war on Japan on December 8, 1941: "On behalf of these 2,000,000 American citizens of Puerto Rico I can pledge the fortunes, the lives, and the honor of my people to fight and die for this great country," he intoned.[162]

Puerto Rico's economic recovery was short-lived due to German U-boat activity during the war which limited shipping traffic in the Caribbean.[163] By 1942 Puerto Rico was virtually without basic goods, including beans, milk, eggs, meat, and cattle feed.[164] The inability to export local products compounded food shortages. A record low of 7,263 tons of cargo reached the island in September 1942—representing 7 percent of the monthly average for 1940.[165] Throughout the war, prices for imported food rose by more than 90 percent.[166] The only meat for sale in Puerto Rican markets was pigs' ears and tails and soaring prices on these products forced the Office of Price Administration, the agency charged with organizing wartime rationing, to intervene and fix prices.[167] Though few people died of starvation, malnourishment, particularly among the poor, proved to be a lasting problem.[168]

Puerto Rican Governor Rexford Guy Tugwell soon came under attack for Puerto Rico's wartime distress. Described as "too handsome to get any sympathy," Tugwell was a "brainstruster" hired from Columbia University in 1932 by the newly elected President Roosevelt, and served in the Department of Agriculture for most of his federal career. Tugwell's outspoken defense of the New Deal often made him the "whipping boy" for Roosevelt's detractors and a lightning rod for the media. Tugwell's advocacy of government land use planning eventually earned him the moniker "Rex the Red" from critics who equated his approach with that of Communist bureaucrats in the Soviet Union.[169] Known for his lofty vocabulary, soft-spokenness, and direct action, Tugwell was eventually forced to leave the Roosevelt administration in 1936 because of his controversial reputation. In July 1941, Roosevelt named Tugwell chancellor of the Universidad de Puerto Rico (University of Puerto Rico). After Governor Guy Swope resigned the following August, the President tapped him to fill the vacancy.

Tugwell's appointment drew howls of protest, especially from Resident Commissioner Bolívar Pagán, whose opposition stemmed primarily from local political rivalries. Tugwell favored Pagán's political rival, Luis Muñoz Marín, and the Partido Popular Democrático (Popular Democratic Party). Yet the Resident Commissioner also had allies in Congress, who disapproved of the governor's work during the New Deal, including the powerful House Rules Committee, whose members accused Tugwell of engaging in communist activities while administering the Farm Subsidy Administration (FSA).[170] Detractors also noted that congressional committees led by Democrats and tasked with overseeing the governor's performance, were generally ignorant of the island's current events.[171] Senator Arthur Vandenberg, a Michigan Republican, submitted a bill in January 1943 to remove Tugwell as part of a larger investigation of Roosevelt's New Deal initiatives.[172] Vandenberg described him "as a starry eyed crystal gazer whose reddish dreams have already cost us hundreds of millions of dollars," adding that Puerto Rico had a "Tugwell crisis" as well as a food crisis.[173] The Senate Committee on Territories approved the legislation on January 18, 1943.[174] Representative Fred Crawford of Michigan introduced a House resolution threatening to annul seven laws passed under Tugwell's administration, calling the governor "a dictator over the agriculture and the sugar industry."[175]

Bolstered by congressional support, Pagán and his attacks on the governor soon made headlines during Puerto Rico's food crisis. A proposed and desperately needed $15 million emergency food program, which Pagán supported with the stipulation that Tugwell resign, brought the situation to a head. Primarily out of disdain for Tugwell, conservative elements in Congress allied with Pagán. In a House Agriculture Committee hearing on the food aid bill, Representative Harry Coffee of Nebraska accused Tugwell of conducting "experiments in national socialism," and the hearing soon dissolved into a forum to critique Tugwell's leadership. The ongoing battle over food aid inspired two congressional committees, one of them headed by New Mexico Senator Dennis Chavez, to investigate the situation in Puerto Rico.[176]

The Chavez and Bell Committees

The desperate situation in Puerto Rico, allusions to communism, and the underlying partisanship exacerbated the problems in America's colonial relationship with Puerto Rico, and on January 28, 1943, the Senate passed a resolution authorizing the Committee on Territories and Insular Affairs to create an investigatory subcommittee to explore the situation on the island. The vote limited the study to Puerto Rico's economic and social considerations rather than a full investigation into its political machinations, and Senator Chavez was selected to chair the committee. Using a political strategy that political scientists later dubbed "surrogate representation," the New Mexican Senator took responsibility for the welfare of Hispanic Americans beyond his state's borders.[177] "Suppose we do let them starve," Chavez said to the Senate. "Congress is responsible for those people," he noted. "I want to feed those people … and that's all."[178]

The Subcommittee on Senate Resolution 26, as it was formally known, flew to Puerto Rico in early February 1943. "We have no preconceived ideas nor bring any conclusions on the subject matter of our study, and only want to visit the Island with the idea of helping Puerto Rico," Chavez said after landing.[179] The Chavez committee toured Puerto Rico, concluding that the island had an "almost unsolvable" crisis wherein population growth outstripped its capacity for food production.[180] The subcommittee recommended that the United States begin transporting the unemployed to the mainland to alleviate work shortages and bolster the wartime labor force throughout the country.[181] More to the point, the Chavez committee, and eventually the Senate, supported $50 million in funding over two years for public works programs on the island.[182]

Five months later, the House of Representatives sent an equivalent subcommittee to Puerto Rico to conduct its own investigation. Led by Democrat Representative C. Jasper Bell of Missouri, the panel dissected the island's political culture, especially Governor Tugwell's leadership, often excluding from its consideration the wartime food shortage. According

Senator Dennis Chavez of New Mexico (right) discusses the installation of government radio stations with law professor Herbert Wright of The Catholic University of America during a Senate Interstate Commerce Committee hearing in May 1938.

Image courtesy of the Library of Congress

to Tugwell, the House subcommittee had "prejudged the entire situation" and was conducting hearings to expose graft and corruption rather than exploring the underlying economic problems. Moreover, Tugwell said, "the majority of the Committee was obviously interested in discrediting the Chavez Committee's work."[183] The House investigation, with its broader jurisdiction, was indeed more critical than Chavez's hearings, which early on placed responsibility with the War Shipping Administration, but eventually refused to directly assign blame.[184] Ultimately, the subcommittee report concluded, "Political leaders in Puerto Rico have chartered a course which will eventually destroy individual liberties of the people and enslave them eventually by setting up a form of government wholly alien to our own."[185] Though the subcommittee recommended more study, its members clearly wanted Tugwell dismissed. "We have no experiences from circumstances and conditions on the mainland which can be used as the basis for solving Puerto Rico's problems," the committee report said.[186] The subcommittee's wish had nearly come true in early 1943, when the Senate's Territories Committee voted 9 to 3 in favor of terminating Tugwell's tenure.[187]

CONCLUSION

The investigations by the Chavez and Bell committees were a prelude to a new era in which Puerto Ricans took greater control over their local affairs. While the committees' recommendations provided the framework for a modified set of insular guidelines, Puerto Rico retained its uncertain status in the annals of American policy. It remained stuck between annexation and independence, and much of the confusion stemmed from diplomatic and cultural misunderstandings between lawmakers and the island's inhabitants.[188] "Puerto Rico is a Protean affair," said Senator Homer Bone of Washington, who sat on the Chavez committee. "Just as you think you have sized it up, it turns into something else." He spoke for many in Congress when he concluded, "I am slightly confused." [189] Even Senator Chavez had once called Puerto Rico's situation "baffling."[190]

Congressional action regarding Puerto Rico for the first half of the 19th century proved to be a series of experiments in colonial policy. Puerto Rican Resident Commissioners navigated these waters from a position of relative isolation and little power, in an attempt to protect the needs and the heritage of their constituents while appealing to American markets and protection. Like other statutory representatives, Resident Commissioners were limited; their ability to legislate was in the hands of their colleagues. One such colleague, Senator Chavez, sought to aid and clarify the mainland's relationship with Puerto Rico. Chavez promoted increased autonomy for the island, and surprised many Puerto Ricans when he advocated incorporating the territory into the national narrative. "I want Puerto Rico to take a place in the American scheme of things as Americans," he told the press. "On independence, as far as I'm concerned, you can forget about it." Puerto Rico's economy, he believed, would be better served if Puerto Rico remained a U.S. affiliate rather than an independent country.[191] "I would like to see Puerto Rico run her own affairs—as Americans," Chavez said.[192]

"A place in the American scheme of things as Americans" was the impulse behind the post–World War II Hispanic civil rights movement, as returning veterans sought to advance Hispanic political participation to promote a more egalitarian society. Dennis Chavez himself would turn away from Puerto Rican issues to focus on national concerns and the needs of his New Mexican constituents. The island would undergo a significant political transformation under the dominant Popular Democratic Party. Advancing in the ever-present struggle between local and federal control, Puerto Ricans would win by 1950 the right to elect their own governor and write their own constitution. Though the establishment of the Puerto Rican commonwealth in 1952 would provide Puerto Ricans a measure of autonomy, many of the difficulties that arose from the island's arbitrary relationship with the United States in the first half of the century would persist. And though Resident Commissioners would experience only incremental changes in their ability to participate in Congress, an increasing overall number of Hispanic Members would result in better organization. The creation of the Congressional Hispanic Caucus in 1976 would partially alleviate the "tomb-like isolation" lamented by Luis Muñoz Rivera more than a half-century before.[193]

NOTES

1 "El representante debe merecer la confianza del representado: esa confianza ha debido obteneria con su historia, en la cual estén consignados los hechos que ha realizado en la lucha por el bien de la patria, justificadas sus condiciones intelectuales, demostrado su carácter, y evidenciado su amor a la libertad." Un Imparcial, "Gatell y Degetau: A elegir." *La correspondencia* (San Juan, PR), 15 October 1900: 2. Translated as "Gatell and Degetau: To the Polls," by Translations International, Inc. (May 2009).

2 *Congressional Record*, House, 56th Cong., 1st sess. (28 February 1900): 2420.

3 Many historians consider this era the age of "scientific racism," that is, the systematic exclusion of nonwhites due to white supremacism, from participation in America's politics, economy, and society. For an overview, see Devon G. Peña, "Scientific Racism," in Suzanne Oboler and Deena J. González, eds., *The Oxford Encyclopedia of Latinos and Latinas in the United States*, vol. 4 (New York: Oxford University Press, 2005): 87–93. Eric T. L. Love thoroughly examines the historiography of race and empire in *Race over Empire: Racism & U.S. Imperialism, 1865–1900* (Chapel Hill: University of North Carolina Press, 2004): 1–26.

4 For a discussion of surrogate representation using modern examples, see Jane Mansbridge, "Should Blacks Represent Blacks and Women Represent Women? A Contingent 'Yes,'" *Journal of Politics* 61 (1999): 628–657.

5 Quoted in Mack Reynolds, *Puerto Rican Patriot: The Life of Luis Muñoz Rivera* (New York: Crowell-Collier Press, 1969): 87.

6 "Appoints Bolivar Pagan," 27 December 1939, *New York Times*: 9; "Memorial Services Held in the House of Representatives of the United States, Together with Remarks Presented in Eulogy of Santiago Iglesias, Late a Resident Commissioner from Puerto Rico," (Washington, D.C.: Government Printing Office, 1941): 33.

7 On average, 78 percent of House Members from 1900 to 1950 had some postsecondary education. Roughly half (56 percent) practiced law. See Allan G. Bogue et al., "Members of the House of Representatives and the Processes of Modernization, 1789–1960," *Journal of American History* 63, no. 2 (September 1976): 275–302.

8 Senator Octaviano Larrazolo was one of these individuals, having served as a state representative and as governor of New Mexico before his Senate service.

9 "Louisiana Beauty Who Is to Enter Washington Society This Winter," 19 November 1913, *Washington Post*: 4.

10 For information on living arrangements and on Muñoz Rivera's son's office position, see A. W. Maldonado, *Luis Muñoz Marín: Puerto Rico's Democratic Revolution* (San Juan, PR: La Editorial Universidad de Puerto Rico, 2006): 31–33.

11 Gonzalo F. Córdova, *Resident Commissioner Santiago Iglesias and His Times* (Editorial de la Universidad de Puerto Rico, 1993): 271.

12 CLXXVI Cannon's Precedents § 245 (p. 417); *Congressional Record*, House, 61st Cong., 2nd sess. (7 January 1910): 406; *House Journal*, 61st Cong., 2nd sess. (7 January 1910): 131.

13 "Yo fuí asignado las oficinas No. 145, en el edificio de Miembros de la Cámara … Este edificio que esta dos cuadras del capitolio, contiene oficina del teléfono y telégrafo, restaurantes especiales y todo lo necesario para la comodidad." Néstor Montoya, "Notas de Washington," *La bandera americana* (Albuquerque, NM), 18 March 1921: 2. Translated as "Notes from Washington" by Translations International, Inc. (July 2009).

14 *Downes v. Bidwell*, 182 US 244 (27 May 1901).

15 Gervasio Luis Garcia, "I Am The Other: Puerto Rico in the Eyes of North Americans, 1898," *Journal of American History* 87, no. 1 (June 2000): 44.

16 See Robert E. May, *The Southern Dream of a Caribbean Empire*, rev. ed. (Athens: University of Georgia Press, 1991). For a comprehensive account of 19th-century territorial expansion, see George C. Herring, *From Colony to Superpower: U.S. Foreign Relations since 1776* (New York: Oxford University Press, 2008).

17 The classic work on American imperialism at the turn of the 20th century remains Walter LaFeber, *New Empire: An Interpretation of American Expansion, 1860–1898,* 35th Anniversary ed. (Ithaca: Cornell University Press, 1998). See also Jeannette P. Nichols, "The United States Congress and Imperialism, 1861–1897," *Journal of Economic History* 21, no. 4 (December 1961).

18 Herring, *From Colony to Superpower*, 304–309; George Thomas Kurian, ed., *The Encyclopedia of the Republican Party*, vol. 2 (Armonk, NY: M. E. Sharpe, 1997): 457–462.

19 For more information on the buildup to the war and its effects on America's political culture, see Herring, *From Colony to Superpower*; LaFeber, *New Empire*; Robert L. Beisner, *From the Old Diplomacy to the New, 1965–1900* (Wheeling, IL: Harlan Davidson, 1986); and Charles S. Campbell, *Transformation of American Foreign Relations, 1865–1900* (New York: HarperCollins, 1976).

20 John L. Offner, *An Unwanted War: The Diplomacy of the United States and Spain over Cuba, 1895–1898* (Chapel Hill: University of North Carolina Press, 1992): 122–123. For example, the *New York Times* reported that "the Maine's 250 perished through the treachery and murderous ingenuity of the Spanish." See "National Capital Topics," 6 March 1898, *New York Times*: 13.

21 Historians debate the role of the *Maine* incident in provoking the war. See Louis A. Perez, Jr., "The Meaning of the Maine: Causation and the Historiography of the Spanish-American War," *Pacific Historical Review* 58 (Aug. 1998): 293–322.

22 *Congressional Record*, House, 55th Cong., 2nd sess. (13 April 1898): 3820 3821; "Congress Tells Spain to Go," 14 April 1898, *Chicago Daily Tribune*: 1. The Senate had concurred with the House in a 51 to 37 vote earlier in the evening of April 16. *Congressional Record*, Senate, 55th Cong., 2nd sess. (16 April 1898): 3993; "The Senate for Free Cuba," 17 April 1898, *New York Times*: 1.

23 "Cuba Free," 19 April 1898, *Boston Globe*: 1; "An Act Declaring that War Exists Between the United States of American and the Kingdom of Spain," 30 Stat. 364. See also Lewis L. Gould, *The Presidency of William McKinley* (Lawrence: University Press of Kansas, 1980): 84–88.

24 Luis Martínez-Fernández, "Puerto Rico in the Whirlwind of 1898: Conflict, Continuity, and Change," *OAH Magazine of History* 12, no. 3 (Spring 1998): 26.

25 Luis Martínez-Fernández, "Political Culture in the Hispanic Caribbean and the Building of U.S. Hegemony, 1868–1945," *Revista Mexicana del Caribe* 6, no. 11 (2001): 14.

26 Martínez-Fernández, "Political Culture in the Hispanic Caribbean and the Building of U.S. Hegemony, 1868–1945": 14–15.

27 Ibid., 19.

28 Ibid., 17.

29 Tomás Sarramía Roncero, *Los gobernadores de Puerto Rico* (San Juan, PR: Publicaciones Puertoriqueñas, Inc., 1993); Roberto H. Todd, *Desfile de gobernadores de Puerto Rico* (San Juan, PR: Imprenta Baldrich, 1943).

30 Luis Muñoz Rivera, *Tropicales* (New York: H. M. Call Printing Company, 1902): 147–152.

31 Jose A. Cabranes, *Citizenship and the American Empire* (New Haven: Yale University Press, 1979): 26–35.

32 Senate Committee on Pacific Islands and Porto Rico, *Temporary Civil Government for Porto Rico*, 56th Cong., 1st sess., 1900, S. Rep. 249, 14–15.

33 *Congressional Record*, House, 56th Cong., 1st sess. (28 February 1900): 2429–2430. See debate on the bill on pp. 2401–2430, especially the quotations on pp. 2402–2407, 2410–2412, 2414, 2424, and 2426; William R. Tansill, "The Resident Commissioner to the United States from Puerto Rico," *Revista Juridica de la Universidad de Puerto Rico* 47, nos. 1–2 (1978): 69–72.

34 See, for example, Hearing before the Senate Committee on Pacific Islands and Porto Rico, *Industrial and Other Conditions of the Island of Puerto Rico, and the Form of Government Which Should be Adopted for It*, 56th Cong., 1st sess. (5 February 1900): 176–182. R. B. Horton, ed., House Committee on Insular Affairs, *Committee Reports, Hearings, and Acts of Congress Corresponding Thereto*, 56th Cong., 1st and 2nd sess. (Washington, D.C.: Government Printing Office, 1904): 337.

35 "Puerto Rico Is Able to Support Itself," 22 March 1900, *New York Times*: 5.

36 "An Act Temporarily to Provide Revenues and Civil Government for Porto Rico, and other Purposes" (Foraker Act), 31 Stat. 77–86, 1896–1901; Stephen W. Stathis, *Landmark Legislation 1774–2002: Major Acts and Treaties* (Washington, D.C.: CQ Press, 2003): 148–149.

37 For an account of Muñoz Rivera's reaction to the Foraker Act in the context of his son's coming of age in a political family, see Maldonado, *Luis Muñoz Marín*: 27–28.

38 Hon. Luis Muñoz Rivera, "Are the Porto Rican People Prepared for Self-Government," extract from remarks of Hon. Tulio Larrínaga in the House of Representatives, 8 May 1908 (Washington, D.C.: Government Printing Office, 1908): 7.

39 Northwest Ordinance, Section 12, Article 5. For a description of the evolution of territorial incorporation, the classic study is Max Farrand, *Legislation of Congress for the Government of the Organized Territories of the United States, 1789–1895* (Buffalo, NY: William S. Hein, 2000; reprint of 1896 edition). A more recent study is James E. Kerr, *The Insular Cases: The Role of the Judiciary in American Expansionism* (Kennikat, NY: Kennikat Press, 1982): 3–13. For a succinct overview, see Christina Duffy Burnett and Burke Marshall, "Between the Foreign and the Domestic: The Doctrine of Territorial Incorporation, Invented and Reinvented," in Christina Duffy Burnett and Burke Marshall, eds., *Foreign in a Domestic Sense: Puerto Rico, American Expansion, and the Constitution* (Durham, NC: Duke University Press, 2001): 1–36. For a recent interpretation, see Burnett, "Untied States: American Expansion and Territorial Deannexation," *University of Chicago Law Review* 72, no. 3 (Summer 2005): 797–879.

40 Bartholomew Sparrow, *The Insular Cases and the Emergence of American Empire* (Lawrence: University Press of Kansas, 2006): 10, 40–55.

41 Efrén Rivera Ramos, "Insular Cases," in Oboler and González eds., *The Oxford Encyclopedia of Latinos and Latinas in the United States*, vol. 2: 386–387.

42 Sparrow, *The Insular Cases and the Emergence of American Empire*: 5, 257. Sparrow cites the number of cases as 35, whereas Pratt cites it as 14. Another study cites the number of cases as 22. Regardless of the number, the three studies agree on the important cases that defined the concepts of "incorporation" and "nonincorporation" of territories; Walter F. Pratt, Jr.,"Insular

Cases," in Kermit L. Hall, ed. *The Oxford Companion to the Supreme Court of the United States*, 2nd ed. (New York: Oxford University Press, 2005): 500–501.

43 Sparrow, *The Insular Cases and the Emergence of American Empire*: 86.

44 Roland I. Perusse, *The United States and Puerto Rico: The Struggle for Equality* (Malabar, FL: Robert E. Krieger Publishing Company, 1990): 19–20; Alfredo Montalvo-Barbot, *Political Conflict and Constitutional Change in Puerto Rico, 1898–1952* (Lanham, MD: University Press of America, 1997): 63–64.

45 Perusse, *The United States and Puerto Rico*: 20.

46 Donald A. Yerxa, "The United States Navy in Caribbean Waters during World War I," *Military Affairs* 51, no. 4 (October 1987): 182, 185; Burnett, "Untied States: American Expansion and Territorial Deannexation": 797–879; César J. Ayala and José L. Bolívar, *Battleship Vieques: Puerto Rico from World War II to the Korean War* (Princeton: Markus Wiener, 2011).

47 "La palabra lealtad tendrá mayor significado si lo admitimos al conglomerado de nuestra ciudadanía. De lo contrario, siempre habrá elementos descontentos que agitarán a favor de la cuptura del lazo." Quoted in María Eugenia Estades Font, *La presencia militar de Estados Unidos en Puerto Rico, 1898–1918: Intereses estratégico y dominación colonial* (Río Piedras, PR: Ediciones Huracán, 1988): 209. Translated as *The Military Presence of the United States in Puerto Rico 1898–1918: Strategic Interests and Colonial Domination* by Translations International, Inc. (May 2010).

48 For Córdova Dávila's complete committee testimony regarding the bill, see Hearings before the Committee on Territories and Insular Possessions, *The Civil Government of Porto Rico, Part 2*, 68th Cong., 1st sess. (9 March 1924): 87–92.

49 Ibid.

50 The governor and the President also retained veto power over legislation. Stathis, *Landmark Legislation*: 174.

51 José E. Rios, "The Office of Resident Commissioner of Puerto Rico," unpublished M.A. thesis, Georgetown University (9 May 1969): 11–12.

52 *Congressional Record*, House, 64th Cong., 1st sess. (5 May 1916): 7471, 7473.

53 Martínez-Fernández, "Political Culture in the Hispanic Caribbean and the Building of U.S. Hegemony, 1868–1945": 33.

54 Ibid., 29.

55 Maldonado, *Luis Muñoz Marín*: 35.

56 Héctor Luis Acevedo, "Luis Muñoz Rivera and the Foundations of Contemporary Autonomism," in *Perspectivas sobre Puerto Rico en homenaje a Muñoz Rivera y Muñoz Marín* (San Juan, PR: Fundación Luis Muñoz Marín, 1997): 36.

57 "Territories and Statehood," 23 June 1924, *Washington Post*: 6.

58 Truman R. Clark, *Puerto Rico and the United States, 1917–1933* (University of Pittsburgh Press, 1975): 76; see especially chapter 4.

59 Hearings before the House Committee on Insular Affairs, *Popular Election of the Governor of Porto Rico*, 70th Cong., 1st sess. (16 May 1928): 22.

60 Harwood Hull, "Puerto Rico Facing Doubtful Election," 18 September 1932, *New York Times*: E8.

61 Though the position of Resident Commissioner was initially created for Puerto Rico, the Philippines also sent Resident Commissioners to Congress from 1902 until it achieved independence in 1946.

62 Foraker Act, 31 Stat. 77, 86.

63 R. B. Horton, ed., Committee on Insular Affairs, House of Representatives, *Committee Reports, Hearings, and Acts of Congress Corresponding Thereto* (Washington, D.C.: Government Printing Office, 1903): 34.

64 Tansill, "The Resident Commissioner to the United States from Puerto Rico": 69.

65 Senate Committee on Pacific Islands and Porto Rico, *Temporary Civil Government for Porto Rico*, 56th Cong., 1st sess. (5 February 1900), S. Rep, 249: 14–15.

66 *Congressional Record*, House, 56th Cong., 1st sess. (2 April 1900): 3632.

67 According to the Foraker Act, "qualified voters" in Puerto Rico were those "who have been bona fide residents for one year and who possess the other qualifications of voters under the laws and military orders in force on the first day of March, nineteen hundred." Such qualifications were subject to change per executive council restrictions. (31 Stat. 77, 83).

68 Foraker Act, 31 Stat. 77–86.

69 Starting in 1850, Territorial Delegates were first allowed to make motions, except for the motion to reconsider, which is dependent on the right to vote on the House Floor. See XLIII *Hinds' Precedents* § 1292 (pp. 862–863); *Congressional Globe*, House, 31st Cong., 1st sess. (20 August 1850): 1607.

70 "Commissioner in Name Only," 17 May 1902, *Baltimore Sun*: 4.

71 H. Res. 169, amending House Rule XXIV, 57th Cong., 1st sess.; Tansill, "The Resident Commissioner to the United States from Puerto Rico": 72.

72 *Congressional Record*, House, 57th Cong., 1st sess. (28 June 1902): 7608.

73 Tansill, "The Resident Commissioner to the United States from Puerto Rico": 72–73.

74 Ibid., 79–82.

75 *Congressional Record*, House, 64th Cong., 2nd sess. (5 May 1916): 7473.

76 Jorge Duany, "Race and Racialization," in Oboler and González, *The Oxford Encyclopedia of Latinos and Latinas in the United States*, vol. 3: 535. See pp. 537–538 for a detailed discussion of racial stereotypes about Puerto Ricans.

77 Elihu Root, *The Military and Colonial Policy of the United States: Addresses and Reports* (Cambridge, MA, 1916). Quoted in Gervasio Luis Garcia, "I Am The Other: Puerto Rico in the Eyes of North Americans, 1898," *Journal of American History* 87, no. 1 (June 2000): 39–40.

78 "Not an Inferior People," 30 June 1901, *Washington Post*: 5.

79 "Seek Statehood for Porto Rico," 31 October 1901, *Chicago Daily Tribune*: 2.

80 *Congressional Record*, 58th Cong., 3rd sess. (19 January 1905): 1088–1090; "Porto Rican Heard in House," 20 January 1905, *San Francisco Chronicle*: 13.

81 For more on the relationship between Cannon and Muñoz Rivera, see Hon. Luis Muñoz Rivera, "Are the Porto Rican People Prepared for Self-Government," extract from remarks of Hon. Tulio Larrínaga in the House of Representatives, 8 May 1908 (Washington, D.C.: Government Printing Office, 1908): 7.

82 *Congressional Record*, Appendix, 64th Cong., 1st sess. (5 May 1916): 1036–1037.

83 *Congressional Record*, House, 64th Cong., 1st sess. (5 May 1916): 7484.

84 "Memorial Services Held in the House of Representatives of the United States, Together with Remarks Presented in Eulogy of Santiago Iglesias, Late a Resident Commissioner from Puerto Rico," (Government Printing Office, 1941): 32.

85 Maldonado, *Luis Muñoz Marín*: 32.

86 George Van Horn Moseley to Walter H. Newton, 19 October 1932; Presidential States File; Puerto Rico, General Correspondence; Herbert Hoover Papers; Herbert Hoover Presidential Library, West Branch, IA.

87 Hearings before the House Committee on Insular Affairs, *Popular Election of the Governor of Porto Rico*, 70th Cong., 1st sess. (16 May 1928): 23.

88 "Ickes Assails School Policy in Puerto Rico," 8 April 1943, *Christian Science Monitor*: 13.

89 Robert T. Hill, "Porto Rico," *National Geographic* 10, no. 3 (March 1899): 112n.

90 Garcia, "I Am the Other:" 49–51.

91 House Committee on Insular Affairs, *Correct the Spelling of the Name of the Island of Porto Rico,* 72nd Cong., 1st sess., 1932, H. Rep. 585, 2.

92 *Congressional Record*, House, 72nd Cong., 1st sess. (11 May 1932): 10031.

93 Ibid., 10028.

94 *Congressional Record*, House, 72nd Cong., 1st sess. (13 May 1932): 10074.

95 *Congressional Record*, House, 72nd Cong., 1st sess. (11 May 1932): 10030.

96 As quoted in Charles Montgomery, "Becoming 'Spanish-American': Race and Rhetoric in New Mexico Politics, 1880–1928," *Journal of American Ethnic History* 20, no. 4 (Summer 2001): 60.

97 Carolyn Zeleny, *Relations between Spanish-Americans and Anglo-Americans in New Mexico* (New York: Arno Press, 1974; reprint of 1966 edition): 203–207; Ernest B. Fincher, *Spanish Americans as a Political Factor in New Mexico, 1912–1950* (New York: Arno Press, 1974): 101–109.

98 Charles Montgomery, "The Trap of Race and Memory: The Language of Spanish Civility on the Upper Rio Grande," *American Quarterly* 52, no. 3 (September 2000): 490.

99 Regarding the Republican voting base, see Jack E. Holmes, *Politics in New Mexico* (Albuquerque: University of New Mexico Press, 1967): 148–153; Fincher, *Spanish-Americans as a Political Factor in New Mexico*: 101, 103.

100 Holmes, *Politics in New Mexico*: 9; Montgomery, "The Trap of Race and Memory: The Language of Spanish Civility on the Upper Rio Grande": 480–481.

101 Phillip B. Gonzales, "The Political Construction of Latino Nomenclatures," *Journal of the Southwest* 35, no. 2 (Summer 1993): 161. Regarding the new settlers, see Gerald D. Nash, "New Mexico in the Otero Era: Some Historical Perspectives," *New Mexico Historical Review* 67, no. 1 (January 1992): 4. Regarding the changing definition of "Mexican," see Montgomery, "The Trap of Race and Memory": 491–493. See especially, Montgomery, "Becoming 'Spanish-American'": 59–84. Fincher describes the period from 1911 to 1930 as a "Republican-Democrat balance of power." See Fincher, *Spanish-Americans as a Political Factor in New Mexico*: 101.

102 As quoted in Paul F. Larrazolo, *Octaviano A. Larrazolo* (New York: Carlton Press, Inc., 1986): 76–77.

103 Montgomery, "The Trap of Race and Memory": 481, 488.

104 Holmes, *Politics in New Mexico:* 227–231. There is still debate as to whether a "gentlemen's agreement" existed from 1911 to the end of New Mexico's nominating convention system in 1938. Political scientist Jack Holmes attempts to quantify convention nominations issued to *nuevomexicano* candidates for both the Democratic and Republican parties. More important, he has estimated the number of interparty matches that resulted in these nominations. Holmes surmises that out of the "thirteen state conventions of each party from 1911 through 1938, the Democrats allotted fifty-one nominations to candidates of Hispanic surname, and the Republicans, fifty-nine.... Just short of 63 percent of the fifty-nine Republican Hispanic nominations went to candidates for congress, secretary of state, auditor, and corporation commissioner; 75 percent of the fifty-one Democratic Hispanic nominations were for the same offices; and most of the occurrences of matching in the convention era are found in those nominations." He also estimates that out of a possible "fifty-one matched or Hispanic versus Hispanic candidacies ... a total of thirty-five matches did occur."

105 Juan Gómez-Quiñones, *Roots of Chicano Politics, 1600–1940* (Albuquerque: University of New Mexico Press, 1994): 331–333; For a detailed discussion of the effects of the Democratic-Republican realignment on the 1934 U.S. Senate race, see Holmes, *Politics in New Mexico*: 170–174.

106 It is unclear why Resident Commissioners received the additional assignments. See R. Eric Peterson, "Resident Commissioner from Puerto Rico," 16 January 2009, Report RL31856, Congressional Research Service, Library of Congress, Washington, D.C.: 3; Tansill, "The Resident Commissioner to the United States from Puerto Rico": 83; Rios, "The Office of Resident Commissioner of Puerto Rico": 44–45.

107 Charles Stewart III, "Committee Hierarchies in the Modernizing House, 1875–1947," *American Journal of Political Science* 36 (1992): 845–846.

108 Stewart, "Committee Hierarchies in the Modernizing House, 1875–1947."

109 Tansill, "The Resident Commissioner to the United States from Puerto Rico": 86–87.

110 James L. Dietz, *Economic History of Puerto Rico: Institutional Change and Capitalist Development* (Princeton: Princeton University Press, 1986): 136.

111 Dietz, *Economic History of Puerto Rico*: 137.

112 Thomas G. Mathews, *Puerto Rican Politics and the New Deal* (Gainesville: University of Florida Press, 1960): 6–7; see also Teresita A. Levy, "The History of Tobacco Cultivation in Puerto Rico, 1899–1940," PhD diss., The City University of New York, 2007.

113 Dietz, *Economic History of Puerto Rico*: 137.

114 Córdova, *Resident Commissioner Santiago Iglesias and His Times*: 285; Clark, *Puerto Rico and the United States, 1917–1933*: 109–110.

115 Manuel R. Rodríguez, *A New Deal for the Tropics: Puerto Rico during the Depression Era, 1932–1935* (Princeton: Markus Wiener Publishers, 2010): 23.

116 Statisics on the Puerto Rican economy following the stock market crash in 1929 can be found in Rodríguez, *A New Deal for the Tropics*: 1–2; Dietz, *Economic History of Puerto Rico*: 136–143; and Ayala and Bernabe, *Puerto Rico in the American Century*: 96.

117 *Congressional Record*, House, 72nd Cong., 1st sess. (10 May 1932): 9966–9967.

118 "Remarks in San Juan, Puerto Rico," 7 July 1934, in John T. Woolley and Gerhard Peters, *The American Presidency Project* (Santa Barbara, CA), http://www.presidency.ucsb.edu/ws/?pid=14722 (accessed 15 February 2011).

119 See Marietta Morrissey, "The Making of a Colonial Welfare State: U.S. Social Insurance and Public Assistance in Puerto Rico," *Latin American Perspectives* 33, no. 1 (January 2006): 23–41.

120 The only commodity protected under the AAA and produced in Puerto Rico was tobacco, a shrinking industry. See Dietz, *Economic History of Puerto Rico*: 147; Rodríguez, *A New Deal for the Tropics*: 32–33.

121 *Congressional Record*, House, 74th Cong., 1st sess. (28 February 1935): 2748.

122 For more information on the sugar industry under the Foraker Act, see Ayala and Bernabe, *Puerto Rico in the American Century:* 33, 35, 38; Dietz, *Economic History of Puerto Rico*: 108–109; Mathews, *Puerto Rican Politics and the New Deal*: 4–5.

123 Rodríguez, *A New Deal for the Tropics*: 23; Henry Wells, *The Modernization of Puerto Rico: A Political Study of Changing Values and Institutions* (Harvard University Press, 1969): 114.

124 Ayala and Bernabe, *Puerto Rico in the American Century*: 96.

125 Ibid., 100–101; Córdova, *Resident Commissioner Santiago Iglesias and His Times*: 305; "The Sugar Act of 1937," Yale *Law Journal* 47, no. 6 (April 1938): 984–985.

126 Dietz, *Economic History of Puerto Rico*: 171; see especially Table 3.8. Despite receiving a larger quota, Cuban sugar producers were hindered by continued trade barriers in the Jones–Costigan Act that affected Cuban sugar but not domestic sugar. See Ayala, *American Sugar Kingdom: The Plantation Economy of the Spanish Caribbean, 1898–1934* (University of North Carolina Press, 1999): especially chapters 3 and 8.

127 *Congressional Record*, House, 74th Cong., 1st sess. (21 February 1935): 2430.

128 *Congressional Record*, House, 75th Cong., 1st sess. (5 August 1937): 8317; see also Santiago Iglesias "Puerto Rico Talks Back," *Congressional Record*, Appendix, 75th Cong., 1st sess. (8 July 1937): A1708–1710.

129 Sugar Act of 1937, P.L. 75-414, 50 Stat. 905. Pagán took up Iglesias's mantle on sugar quotas after the former's death. Yet his request went unheeded. See "Increase Sought in Sugar Quota for Puerto Rico," 6 January 1940, *Wall Street Journal*: 9; Dietz, *Economic History of Puerto Rico:* 171–172; see especially Table 3.8.

130 Pedro Cabán, "Puerto Rico, Colonialism In," in Oboler and González, eds., *The Oxford Encyclopedia of Latinos and Latinas in the United States*, vol. 3: 518.

131 For more on Gruening, see Robert David Johnson, "Anti-Imperialism and the Good Neighbour Policy: Ernest Gruening and Puerto Rico Affairs, 1934–1939," *Journal of Latin American Studies* 29, no. 1 (February 1997): 89–110. See also Robert David Johnson, *Ernest*

Gruening and the American Dissenting Tradition (Cambridge: Harvard University Press, 1998), especially chapter 4.

132 Several sources provide detailed outlines of the Chardón Plan. See, for example, Ayala and Bernabe, *Puerto Rico in the American Century*: 101–103; Dietz, *Economic History of Puerto Rico:* 149–150; Mathews, *Puerto Rican Politics and the New Deal*: 157–158; Rodríguez, *A New Deal for the Tropics*: 128–135; and Johnson, "Anti-Imperialism and the Good Neighbour Policy": 98–99.

133 Dietz, *Economic History of Puerto Rico*: 147; Mathews, *Puerto Rican Politics and the New Deal*: 130; Ayala and Bernabe, *Puerto Rico in the American Century*: 97.

134 Johnson, "Anti-Imperialism and the Good Neighbour Policy": 96.

135 Ayala and Bernabe, *Puerto Rico in the American Century*: 102.

136 *Congressional Record*, House, 74th Cong., 1st sess. (7 February 1935): 1676.

137 Mathews, *Puerto Rican Politics and the New Deal*: 169; Ayala and Bernabe, *Puerto Rico in the American Century*: 104; Rodríguez, *A New Deal for the Tropics*: 136.

138 The Chardón Plan collapsed due to lack of funding by 1941, and the agency limped along until its liquidation in 1955. Rodríguez, *A New Deal for the Tropics*: 136–137; Johnson, "Anti-Imperialism and the Good Neighbour Policy": 99, 109–110.

139 Dietz, *Economic History of Puerto Rico*: 148.

140 Johnson, "Anti-Imperialism and the Good Neighbour Policy": 98.

141 Dietz, *Economic History of Puerto Rico*: 138; see especially Table 3.1.

142 "Justo Pastor Rivera explica los planes de la PRERA," 6 January 1935, *El mundo*: 89. The article is quoted in Rodríguez, *A New Deal for the Tropics*: 71.

143 *Congressional Record*, House, 74th Cong., 2nd sess. (24 February 1936): 2716; "Puerto Rico Probe of Killings Begun," 25 February 1936, *Baltimore Sun*: 2.

144 Frank Otto Gatell, "Independence Rejected: Puerto Rico and the Tydings Bill of 1936," *The Hispanic American Historical Review* 38, no. 1 (February 1958): 36, 44. Representative Marion Zioncheck of Washington claimed that with U.S. Marine protection, he could clean up the "Puerto Rican mess" in a week. See Gatell, "Independence Rejected: Puerto Rico and the Tydings Bill of 1936:" 36.

145 Ayala and Bernabe, *Puerto Rico in the American Century*: 112.

146 *Congressional Record*, House, 74th Cong., 2nd sess. (19 May 1936): 7522.

147 Perusse, *The United States and Puerto Rico*: 29. See Gatell, "Independence Rejected: Puerto Rico and the Tydings Bill of 1936": 36.

148 Ayala and Bernabe, *Puerto Rico in the American Century*: 116. According to Ronald I. Perusse, 19 people were killed. See Perusse, *The United States and Puerto Rico*: 24–25.

149 Foraker Act, 31 Stat. 81.

150 Sarramía Roncero, *Los gobernadores de Puerto Rico*. This figure includes Jesus Piñero, who was appointed by President Harry S. Truman and served from 1946 to 1949 as the first native governor. See also Todd, *Desfile de gobernadores de Puerto Rico*.

151 Clark, *Puerto Rico and the United States, 1917–1933*: 163.

152 Ibid., 164.

153 Ibid., 135, 140–141.

154 Ibid., 48–75; quotation on p. 74.

155 *Congressional Record*, House, 67th Cong., 2nd sess. (2 March 1922): 3301–3310; quotation on p. 3301.

156 Ibid., 3301, 3306.

157 *Congressional Record*, House, 67th Cong., 2nd sess. (8 March 1922): 3583–3584.

158 *Congressional Record*, House, 67th Cong., 2nd sess. (12 April 1922): 5406–5410.

159 *Congressional Record*, House, 67th Cong., 4th sess. (1 March 1923): 5037–5038.

160 Harold Ickes to Garcia Mendez, 4 June 1940, Doc 9-9-82- Politics-Elections-1940; Classified

Files, 1907–1951; Office of Territories, Record Group 126; National Archives at College Park, College Park, MD (hereinafter referred to as RG 126; NACP).

161 *Congressional Record*, House, 77th Cong., 1st sess. (8 December 1941): 9528.

162 Ibid.

163 "Sugar Storage Space in Cuba, Puerto Rico Adequate for Present," 13 April 1942, *Wall Street Journal*: 10.

164 "Moves in Congress to Oust Tugwell," 18 November 1942, *New York Times*: 16.

165 Office of Statistics, Office of the Governor and Division of Territories and Island Possessions, Department of the Interior, *The Puerto Rican Economy during the War Year of 1942*, June 1943: 2, Notes and Publications File, Box 19, William A. Brophy and Sophie Aberle Brophy Papers, Harry S. Truman Library, Independence, MO.

166 Dietz, *Economic History of Puerto Rico*: 203.

167 Howard M. Norton, "Pig Tails, Ears, Only Meats in Puerto Rico Last Month," 18 December 1942, *Baltimore Sun*: 3.

168 Dietz, *Economic History of Puerto Rico*: 204.

169 Michael V. Namorato, "Tugwell, Rexford Guy," *American National Biography*, 21 (New York: Oxford University Press, 1999): 923–925 (hereinafter referred to as *ANB*).

170 "'Red Activities' of FSA Assailed by House Group," 11 March 1942, *Chicago Daily Tribune*: 5.

171 "Dr. Tugwell in Puerto Rico," 20 November 1942, *Chicago Daily Tribune*: 14.

172 John Fisher, "Vandenberg Bill Urges Ending of Tugwell Regime," 8 January 1943, *Chicago Daily Tribune*: 9.

173 Chesly Manly, "Senate Blocks Quiz of Tugwell Rule on Island," 28 November 1942, *Chicago Daily Tribune*: 9.

174 "Senate Group Votes Bill to Oust Tugwell," 19 January 1943, *Chicago Daily Tribune*: 1; "Senators Back Bill to Remove Tugwell," 19 January 1943, *New York Times*: 17; "Senate Committee Favors Ousting of Tugwell," 19 January 1943, *Washington Post*: 5.

175 "Tugwell: Give Puerto Rico More Self-Rule," 12 February 1943, *Christian Science Monitor*: 3.

176 Robert F. Whitney, "Puerto Rico Asks for Food," 13 December 1942, *New York Times*: E10.

177 Mansbridge, "Should Blacks Represent Blacks and Women Represent Women? A Contingent 'Yes.'" See also Representative Edward Roybal of California's eulogy of Chavez: *Congressional Record*, House, 88th Cong., 1st sess. (31 January 1963): 1536.

178 "Puerto Rican Aid Sought," 30 October 1942, *Baltimore Sun*: 9; Paul W. Ward, "Ickes Opposes Plan to Probe Puerto Rico," 19 November 1942, *Baltimore Sun*: 1.

179 As quoted in Enrique Lugo-Silva, *The Tugwell Administration in Puerto Rico, 1941–1946* (Rios Piedras, PR: self-published): 96. The subcommittee never seems to have adopted an official name. The name "Subcommittee on Senate Resolution 26" comes from Senate Committee on Territories and Insular Affairs, *Economic and Social Conditions in Puerto Rico*, 78th Cong., 1st sess. (15 December 1943) S. Rep. 628.

180 As quoted in "Senators Question Tugwell in San Juan," 14 February 1943, *New York Times*: 28.

181 Senate Committee on Territories and Insular Affairs, *Economic and Social Conditions in Puerto Rico*, 78th Cong., 1st sess., 1943, S. Rep. 628, 35.

182 "Puerto Rican Aid Backed in Senate," 3 April 1943, *Christian Science Monitor*: 3; "Passes Puerto Rico Bill," 13 May 1943, *New York Times*: 4.

183 Tugwell to Ickes, 18 June 1943, San Juan, PR, 9-8-59- Social & Economic Conditions-Investigations-Bell Committee General; RG 126; NACP.

184 The subcommittee report did, however, express frustration with federal officials' inability to coordinate their efforts or work together. "Chavez Report Thus Far Gives OK to Tugwell," 8 January 1943, *Christian Science Monitor*: 9; "Chavez Group Decries Rifts on Puerto Rico," 17 July 1943, *Christian Science Monitor*: 7.

185 House Committee on Insular Affairs, *Investigation of Political, Economic, and Social Conditions in Puerto Rico*, 79th Cong., 1st sess., 1945, H. Rep. 497: 36.

186 House Committee on Insular Affairs, *Investigation of Political, Economic, and Social Conditions in Puerto Rico*: 42. See also Pete McKnight, "Puerto Rico Split in Bell Hearing," 21 June 1943, *Baltimore Sun*: 1.

187 "Senate Committee Favors Ousting of Tugwell," 19 January 1943, *Washington Post*: 5.

188 Ayala and Bernabe, *Puerto Rico in the American Century*: 208.

189 Homer T. Bone to B. W. Thoron, 17 May 1944, Bethesda, MD., 9-8-59- Social & Economic Conditions- Investigations- Bell Committee (Part No. 1); RG 126; NACP.

190 Chavez Subcommittee to William A. Brophy, unknown date, 9-8-68 (Part No. 4)- Government- Organic Act- Amendments- Advisory Committee to the President- General; RG 126; NACP.

191 "Puerto Ricans Hail Prospect of Self Rule," 10 March 1943, *Christian Science Monitor*: 3; Ayala and Bernabe, *Puerto Rico in the American Century*: 150.

192 "U.S. Senate Investigators in Puerto Rico," 10 February 1943, *Christian Science Monitor*: 3.

193 Quoted in Reynolds, *Puerto Rican Patriot*: 87.

Party Divisions in the House of Representatives

56th–78th Congresses (1899–1945)*

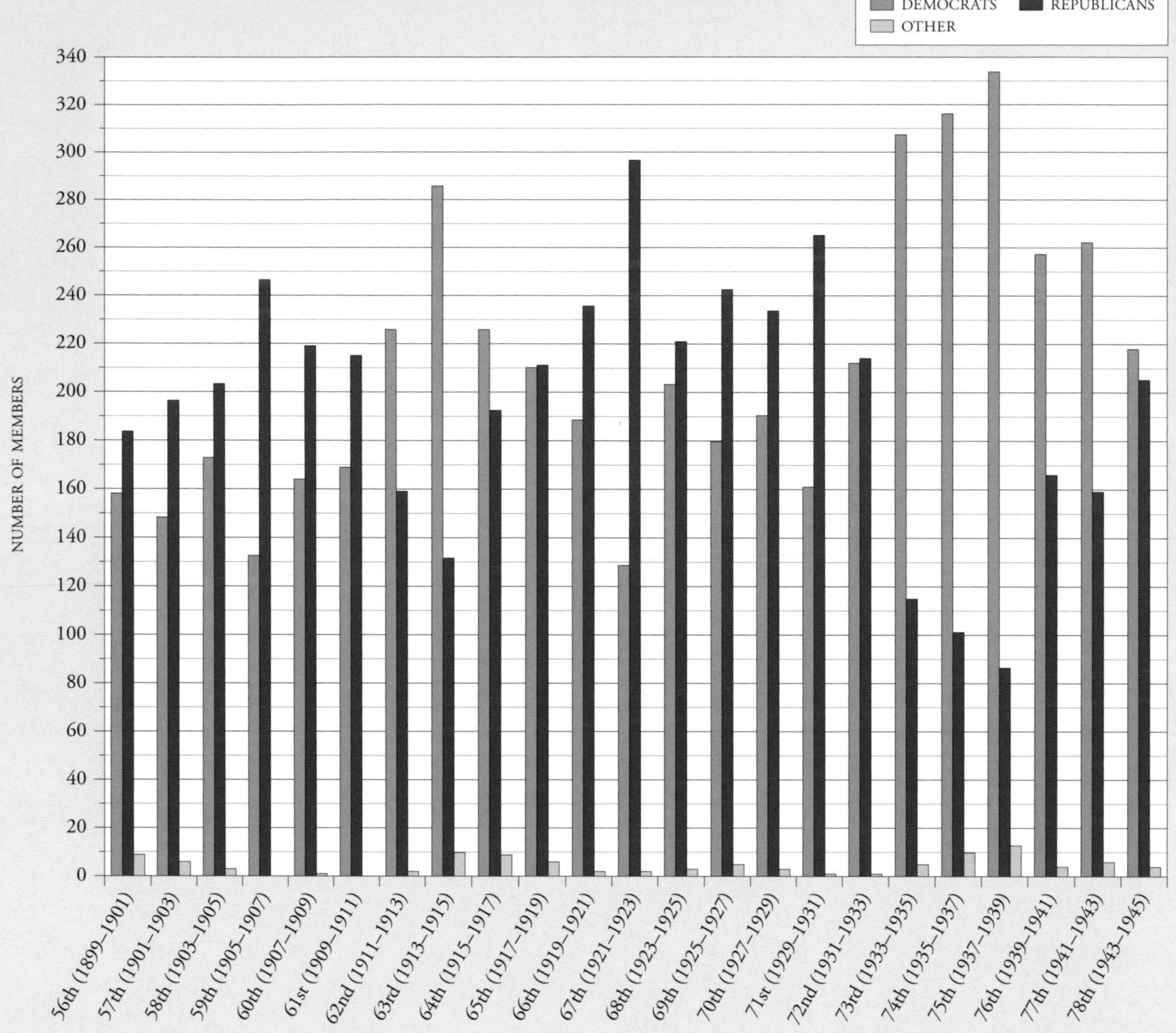

Source: Biographical Directory of the United States Congress, 1774–2005 (Washington, D.C.: Government Printing Office, 2005); also available at http://bioguide.congress.gov.; Office of the Historian, U.S. House of Representatives.

*Party division totals are based on election day results.

Party Divisions in the Senate

56th–78th Congresses (1899–1945)*

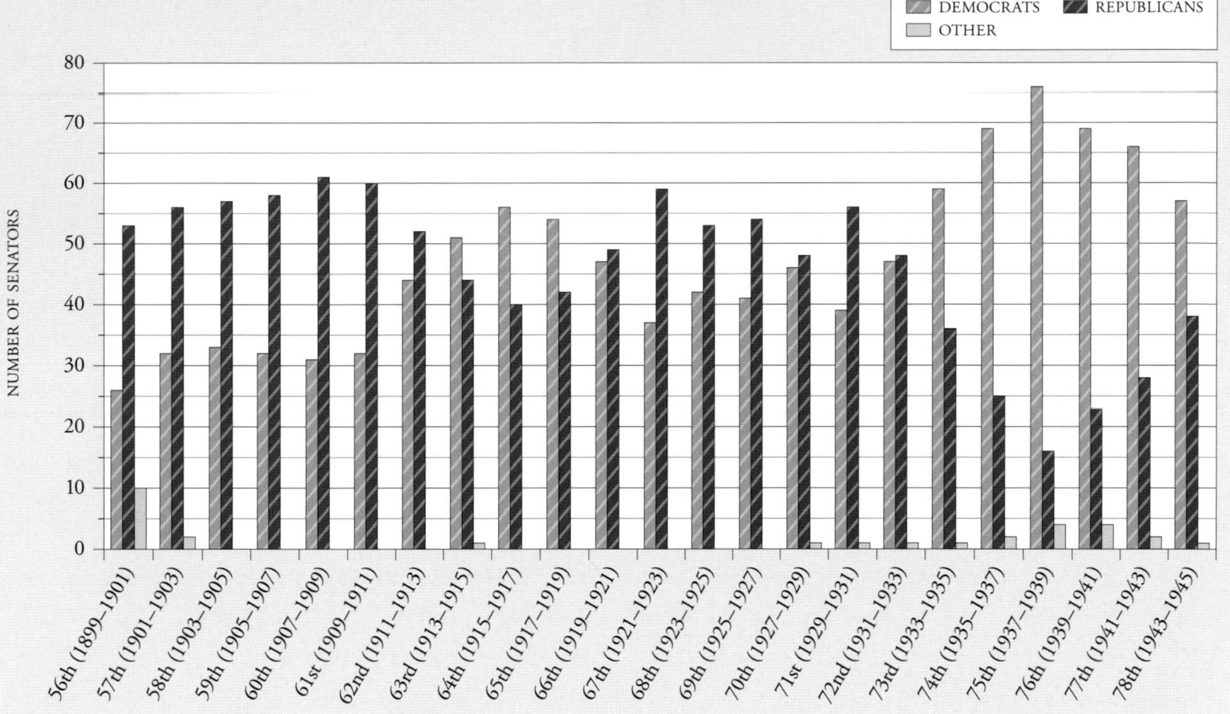

Source: Biographical Directory of the United States Congress, 1774–2005 (Washington, D.C.: Government Printing Office, 2005); also available at http://bioguide.congress.gov.

*Party division totals are based on election day results.

Hispanic-American Members by Office
1898–1945

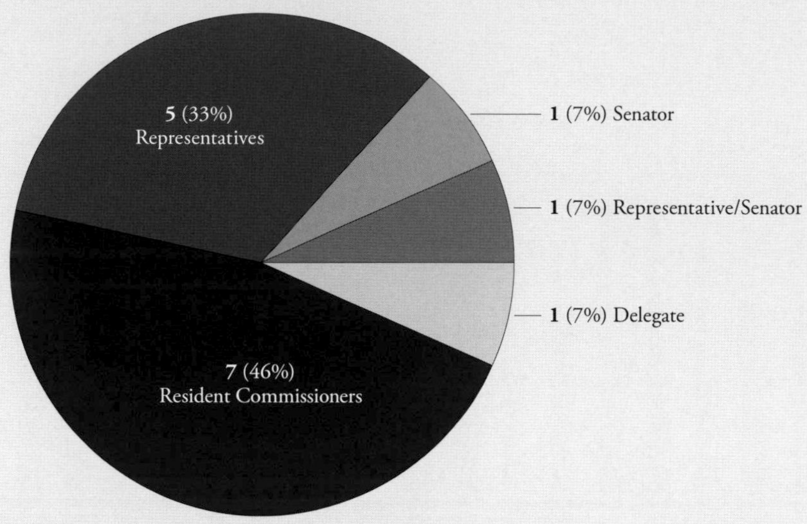

Hispanic-American Members by State and Territory
First Elected 1898–1943

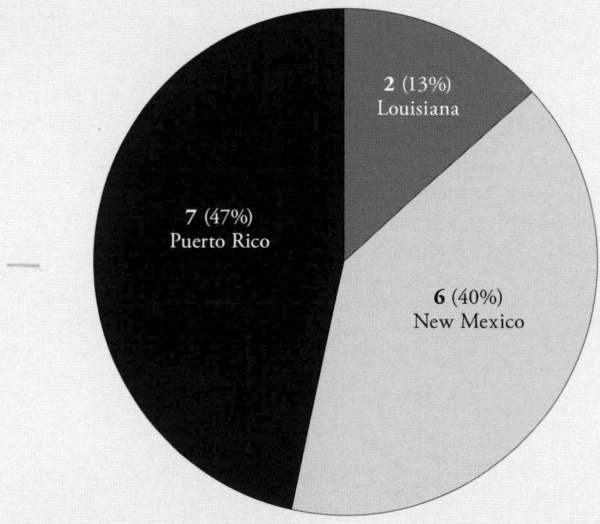

Source: Appendix A: Hispanic-American Representatives, Senators, Delegates, and Resident Commissioners by Congress, 1822–2012; Office of the Historian, U.S. House of Representatives; U.S. Senate Historical Office.

Congressional Service

For Hispanic Americans in Congress First Elected 1898–1942

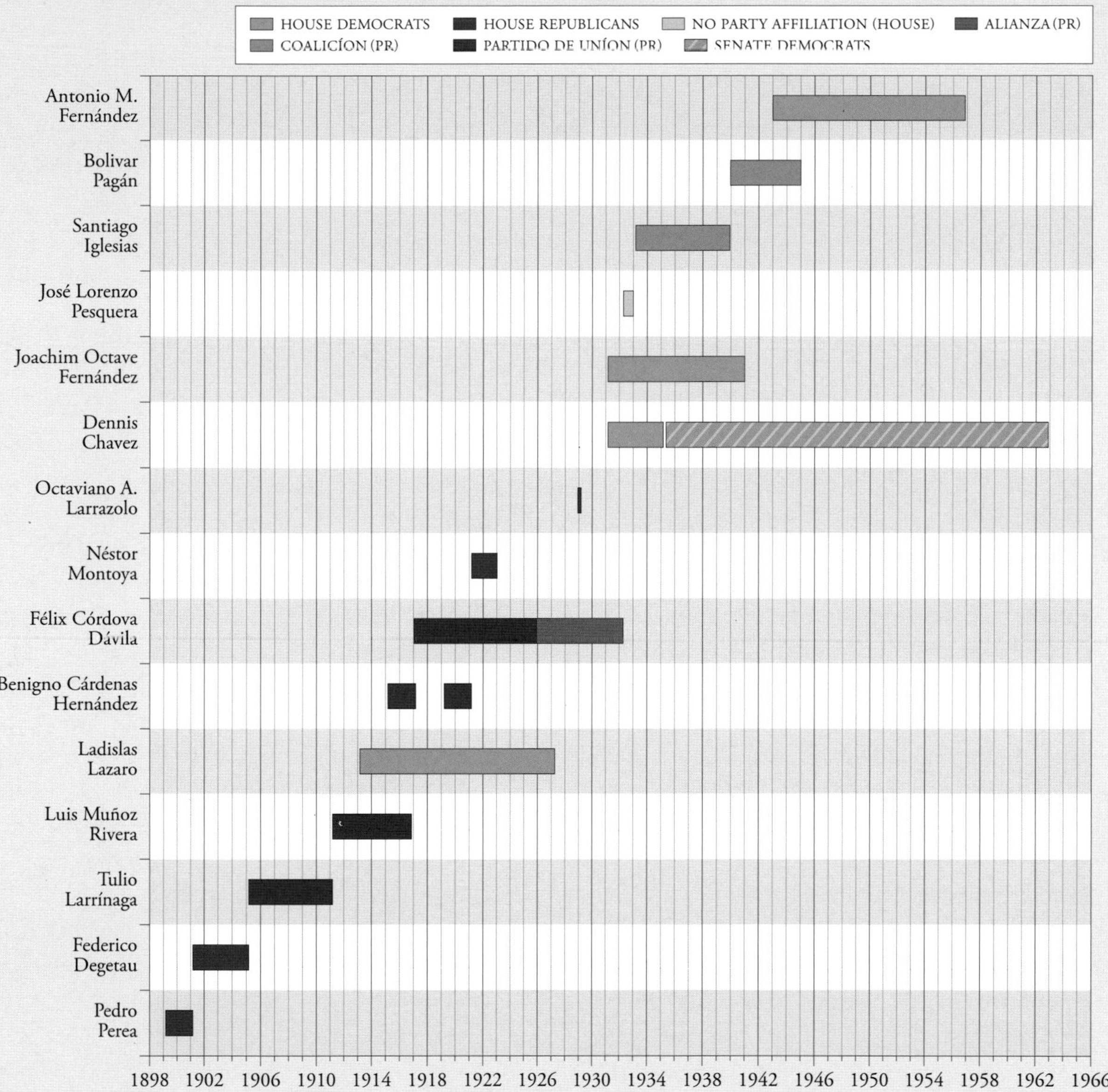

Pedro Perea
1852–1906

TERRITORIAL DELEGATE 1899–1901
REPUBLICAN FROM NEW MEXICO

Pedro Perea, a member of a prestigious New Mexican political family, followed in the footsteps of his cousin Francisco, who served as a Territorial Delegate in the 38th Congress (1863–1865), and in those of his brother-in-law, Mariano Otero, who served in the 46th Congress (1879–1881). Like many other 19th-century Delegates from New Mexico, Pedro Perea served a single term in Congress before returning to a prosperous business career in the territory. An obituary characterized him as "an uncompromising Republican, broad minded, careful and earnest in his desire to see New Mexico take her place in the front ranks of the sisterhood of States."[1]

Perea was born in Bernalillo, Sandoval County, New Mexico—just north of Albuquerque—on April 22, 1852, to José Leandro and Dolores Chavis Perea. Perea's father was a prominent merchant and a local politician; his mother managed the family home. Perea grew up in a wealthy household with eight siblings and three servants.[2] He attended St. Michael's College in Santa Fe; Georgetown College in Washington, D.C.; and St. Louis University, where he earned a degree in 1871. Perea returned to New Mexico and he formed a merchandising business with his brother that specialized in farming and ranching.[3] Before formally entering politics, Perea used his status and influence to secure funding to expand the Santa Fe road.[4] Perea married Emelia Montoya, and the couple had one son, Abel.[5]

Perea's formal political experience began when he was elected to New Mexico's 27th Legislative Assembly (1886–1888) to represent Bernalillo County as a member of the territorial council. He served four two-year terms, three of them consecutive (1886–1892, 1894–1896), and focused on the territory's financial and appropriations issues.[6] In 1890 Perea continued to pursue business opportunities while serving as a territorial councilman, eventually becoming president of the Bank of Santa Fe from 1890 to 1894.[7] Perea's political career was closely aligned with the Santa Fe Ring, a Republican faction that dominated politics in New Mexico for much of the post–Civil War era. Perea's political patron was Thomas B. Catron, a powerful lawyer and landowner who had been an associate of Perea's father's in the 1870s and served as a Territorial Delegate in the 54th Congress (1895–1897). In 1896 Perea served as a delegate to the Republican National Convention in St. Louis, where William McKinley was nominated as the party's presidential candidate. One year later, Perea, with Catron's support, was considered for a federal appointment as New Mexico's governor along with 20 other candidates. The administration passed over Perea for Miguel Otero, Jr., the son of Territorial Delegate Miguel Otero, Sr., and a prominent party operative in his own right.[8] Members of the Ring objected not only to the administration's choice of Miguel Otero for governor, but also to the actions of the sitting Delegate, Harvey Fergusson, who proposed statehood for New Mexico in the 55th Congress (1897–1899). Consequently the Ring rallied behind Perea's bid for Delegate to oust Fergusson, which served as a check on Otero's position, and helped maintain the Ring's political influence in Washington and throughout the territory.[9] Perea, enthusiastically nominated by local Republicans, was endorsed as a "hard working, efficient … and influential delegate, who will deserve and enjoy the good will and favorable opinion of his fellow members and the people of New Mexico." Another endorsement said the "interests of New Mexico require that a protectionist be at the national capital to look after the … territory, and Mr. Perea is that man."[10] Perea ran on his business acumen and legislative experience, and as an advocate for New Mexico's farmers, miners, and ranchers.[11]

During the election campaign, Perea's ethnicity became

Image courtesy of the Palace of the Governors Photo Archives (NMHM/DCA), 50570

a dominant issue. According to pro-Perea sources, the Fergusson campaign would "attempt to raise the race question during the campaign and will endeavor to incite race passions and bitterness." The goal was "to divide what is called the Mexican vote … and then advise and induce the so-called American voters to cast their ballots for the Democratic candidate." Pro-Republican newspapers responded by vigorously defending Perea's reputation.[12] The topic of race was particularly divisive in the southeastern section of the territory known as Little Texas. A local Eddy County newspaper presented voters with a choice between "Pedro Perea, a full-blooded Mexican, and Hon. Harvey B. Fergusson, the best delegate New Mexico ever had in Congress."[13] Perea's supporters responded in an editorial that Perea was "a native of this territory, born in 1852, and his ancestors came to this country over 200 years ago and have been residents and leading citizens … ever since." Citing his education in U.S. schools in St. Louis, Washington, D.C., and Santa Fe, supporters stressed that Perea's "father became an American citizen by absolute choice, in 1848."[14]

The race-baiting tactic failed, and Perea beat Fergusson with a decisive 52 to 47 percent of the vote.[15] In an editorial postmortem, the *Santa Fe New Mexican* noted that Perea had accomplished the impossible and that his victory was "only the second time the Republicans have carried the territory since 1880." The editorial also noted that Perea overcame a "popular Democratic candidate and a Democratic majority of 2,000 … in a four weeks' campaign." One scholar concluded that Perea's victory "reestablished the unquestioned political dominance of New Mexico's Old Guard Republicans" over Fergusson and his Democratic supporters.[16]

Elected to the 56th Congress (1899–1901), Perea served on four committees: Post Office and Post Roads, Military Affairs, Private Land Claims, and Territories.[17] This assignment contrasted sharply with those of his predecessors; each had held a single seat that was preordained for New Mexico Delegates since the 46th Congress (1879–1881): Coinage, Weights, and Measures.[18]

When Perea entered the House, New Mexico's territorial apprenticeship had been in existence for 54 years. Like his predecessor, Harvey Fergusson, Perea took an aggressive stand for New Mexican statehood. On the day he was sworn into the House, Perea submitted H.R. 57, a bill "to enable the people of New Mexico to form a constitution and state government." Referred to the Committee on Territories, it languished and eventually died.[19] Perea also submitted bills for the establishment of roads and for agricultural interests and private bills for constituent needs. He convinced the federal government to restore Santa Fe's border to its area prior to the U.S. occupation of New Mexico in 1846.[20] Unfortunately, Perea's initiatives were crippled as a result of political infighting between Catron and Governor Otero; they broke down completely when Otero dismissed Perea's term as useless and Perea accused Otero of actively working against him.[21] Perea did not run for re-election to the 57th Congress (1901–1903).[22]

When Perea returned to New Mexico, Governor Otero appointed him territorial insurance commissioner, a position he held until his death. Perea died of acute gastritis on January 11, 1906, in Bernalillo, New Mexico. He was 54.[23]

FOR FURTHER READING

Biographical Directory of the United States Congress, "Pedro Perea," http://bioguide.congress.gov.

MANUSCRIPT COLLECTIONS

University of New Mexico, Center for Southwest Research (Albuquerque). *Papers*: Thomas B. Catron Papers, 1692–1934, approximately 259 boxes. Perea is included among the correspondents.

Papers: Marion Dargan Papers, 1890–1943, 4.2 cubic feet. Subjects covered include Perea.

NOTES

1 "Death Overtakes Peoples' Leader," 11 January 1906, *Santa Fe New Mexican*: 1.

2 *Eighth Census of the United States, 1860: Population Schedule,* Alameda, Bernalillo, New Mexico Territory, Roll M653_712, page 93, http://search.ancestrylibrary.com (accessed 6 January 2011). According to the census, José Leandro Perea owned real estate worth $25,000 and personal property worth $200,000.

3 "Pedro Perea," in Maurilio E. Vigil, ed., *Los Patrones: Profiles of Hispanic Political Leaders in New Mexico History* (Washington, D.C.: University Press of America, 1980): 84–86; Carlos Brazil Ramirez, "The Hispanic Political Elite in Territorial New Mexico: A Study of Classical Colonialism," Ph.D. diss., University of California–Santa Barbara, 1979: 306.

4 "Death Overtakes Peoples' Leader"; "Distinguished New Mexican Closes Career," 11 January 1906, *Santa Fe New Mexican*: 1.

5 *Tenth Census of the United States, 1880: Population Schedule,* Bernalillo, Bernalillo, New Mexico, Roll 802, page 7A, Library of Congress, Washington, D.C., http://search.ancestrylibrary.com (accessed 6 January 2011).

6 Territory of New Mexico, *Report of the Secretary of the Territory, 1905–1906 and Legislative Manual 1907* (Albuquerque: Morning Journal, 1907): 170–173. For accounts of Perea's work on the territorial council, see, for example, "Pedro Perea," 20 October 1890, *The Daily New Mexican* (Santa Fe): 2; Mr. Perea's Record as a Legislator," 13 October 1898, *Santa Fe New Mexican*: 2; "Friend of Albuquerque," 18 October 1898, *Albuquerque Daily Citizen*: 2; "Our Next Delegate," 19 October 1898, *Albuquerque Daily Citizen*: 2; "Hon. Pedro Perea, Republican Candidate for … ," 22 October 1898, *Santa Fe New Mexican*: 2; "Mr. Perea's Legislative Record," 24 October 1898, *Santa Fe New Mexican*: 2; "Perea and the Miners," 2 November 1898, *Santa Fe New Mexican*: 2.

7 "Pedro Perea," *Los Patrones*: 84; Ramirez, "The Hispanic Political Elite in Territorial New Mexico": 306–307.

8 Ramirez, "The Hispanic Political Elite in Territorial New Mexico": 306–307; Ralph Twitchell, *Leading Facts of New Mexican History*, vol. II (Cedar Rapids, IA: Torch Press, 1912): 523. According to Twitchell, the fact that Senator Stephen B. Elkins of West Virginia—a former New Mexico Delegate who favored Perea—failed to keep an appointment with McKinley and Secretary of the Interior Cornelius Newton Bliss helped Otero win the seat. In his memoirs, Miguel Otero, Jr., cites his longtime friendship with William McKinley as the primary reason for his appointment. See Miguel Otero, *My Nine Years as Governor of the Territory of New Mexico, 1897–1906* (Albuquerque: University of New Mexico Press, 1940): 1–28.

9 Robert W. Larson, *New Mexico's Quest for Statehood: 1846–1912* (Albuquerque: University of New Mexico Press, 1968): 194–196.

10 For information about Perea's nomination, see "Pedro Perea Nominated," 1 October 1898, *Santa Fe New Mexican*: 4; and "County Republicans," 30 September 1898, *Albuquerque Daily Citizen*: 1. For Perea's endorsements, see "The Republican Nominee for Delegate," 3 October 1898, *Santa Fe New Mexican*: 2; and "A Practical Man Needed," 8 October 1898, *Santa Fe New Mexican*: 2.

11 "Hon. Pedro Perea, Republican Candidate for … "

12 "A Dangerous Game to Play," 11 October 1898, *Santa Fe New Mexican*: 2; for an example, see "An American Citizen," 22 October 1898, *Albuquerque Daily Citizen*: 2. In "Campaign of Abuse," 13 October 1898, *Santa Fe New Mexican*: 2. An editor for the *New Mexican* wrote: Democrats "admit his ability, concede his honesty and that his public and private life is beyond criticism, but close each paragraph with sneers at his candidacy. They do not have the manhood to come out and give their real reason, which is racial prejudice.… They will not vote for any one unless he speaks the dialect of West Virginia with a limpid drawl." For a colleague's defense of Perea, see José D. Sena, "Hon. Pedro Perea's Campaign," 4 November 1898, *Santa Fe New Mexican*: 2.

13 "Race Issue Talk," 21 October 1898, *Albuquerque Daily Citizen*: 2. The article reports, "All over this territory the democrats are working the race prejudice racket for all it is worth." See also "They Will Not Succeed," 20 October 1898, *Santa Fe New Mexican*: 2.

14 "An American Citizen," 22 October 1898, *Albuquerque Daily Citizen*: 2.

15 Twitchell, *Leading Facts of New Mexican History*: 543; Territory of New Mexico, *Report of the Secretary of the Territory, 1903–1904, and Legislative Manual, 1905* (Santa Fe: The New Mexican Printing Company, 1905): 48. Perea received 18,722 votes, and Fergusson received 16,659.

16 Calvin A. Roberts, "H. B. Fergusson, 1848–1915: New Mexico Spokesman for Political Reform," *New Mexico Historical Review* 57, no. 3 (July 1982): 246–247; "Perea's Election," 11 November 1898, *Santa Fe New Mexican*: 2. Roberts writes that the 1898 campaign was difficult for Fergusson: "Silver disappeared as a dominant issue, replaced by popular enthusiasm for the war with Spain, which benefited Republicans." Also, Fergusson was blamed for his supporters' race-baiting tactics.

17 Garrison Nelson et al., eds., *Committees in the U.S. Congress, 1789–1946*, vol. 3 (Washington, D.C.: CQ Press, 1994): 817.

18 Of Perea's nine Hispanic predecessors in Congress in the 19th century, only three New Mexican Delegates (Mariano Otero, Tranquilino Luna, and Francisco Manzanares) served on committees, as a result of changes to the House Rules in 1871 and 1880. They served on the Committee on Coins, Weights, and Measures, whose jurisdiction included the standardization of coin values, legislation related to mints and assay offices, and the creation of national standards for weights and measures. Manzanares also served on the House Select Committee on the New Orleans Exposition. According to political scientist Charles Stewart III, the Committee on Coins, Weights, and Measures was ranked 53rd out of 69 committees in terms of its attractiveness to Members. Conversely, Perea's committee assignments were very desirable (Military Affairs ranked 13th, Post Office and Post Roads ranked 14th, Private Land Claims ranked 25th, and Territories ranked 29th). For an analysis of committees' attractiveness to Members during this period, see Charles Stewart III, "Committee Hierarchies in the Modernizing House, 1875–1947," *American Journal of Political Science* 36, no. 4 (November 1992): 835–856; see especially Stewart's table on "Committee Attractiveness," pp. 845–846.

19 *Congressional Record*, House, 56th Cong., 1st sess. (4 December 1899): 10. Perea submitted this bill the day he was sworn into office. The bill was printed in "The New Mexico Statehood Bill," 11 December 1899, *Santa Fe New Mexican*: 1.

20 *Congressional Record*, House, 56th Cong., 1st sess. (14 March 1900): 2884–2886. Perea provided legal documentation about the city's original area to support his claims.

21 Larson, *New Mexico's Quest for Statehood*: 196–197. Interestingly, Larson dismisses Perea's tenure because he "was not a dynamic, forceful personality." In making this assessment, Larson compares Perea's efforts to those of his peers: Delegate John F. Wilson of Arizona, who submitted two statehood bills and was assisted by a companion bill sponsored by Senator Clarence Clark of Wisconsin; and Delegate Dennis Flynn of Oklahoma, who submitted three statehood bills. None of these bills became law.

22 *Congressional Record*, Index, 56th Cong., 1st sess.: 545; "Pedro Perea," in *Los Patrones*: 85.

23 "Death Overtakes Peoples' Leader."

"Pedro Perea will be the next delegate to congress. He is the man needed at Washington … and he can then secure some good legislation for New Mexico."

Santa Fe New Mexican, October 11, 1898

Federico Degetau
1862–1914

RESIDENT COMMISSIONER 1901–1905
REPUBLICAN FROM PUERTO RICO

The first Puerto Rican Resident Commissioner in the United States Congress, Federico Degetau had a distinguished résumé as a celebrated legal scholar, novelist, and politician in Puerto Rico and Spain. He was thoroughly grounded in legal theory and political action, and as a student of American jurisprudence, Degetau welcomed the prospect of U.S. rule. But his reaction soured when the new administrators curbed Puerto Rican civil rights and denied them full American citizenship. When House Rules prohibited Degetau from speaking—or even sitting—in the chamber, he lobbied for greater parliamentary privileges and served Puerto Ricans by extralegislative means: speaking to the media, communicating with the executive branch, and representing constituents before the U.S. Supreme Court.

Federico Degetau y González was born in Ponce, Puerto Rico, on December 5, 1862. He had no siblings. His mother, María Consolación González y Sánchez Páez, came from a prominent political family in San Juan. His father, Mathías Degetau, was a lawyer from a large German family. When the elder Degetau died in 1863, the family moved from San Juan to Ponce. Degetau's mother relied on relatives to provide for the family, particularly for her son's primary and secondary education. Six years later, the Degetaus returned to San Juan. In 1874 the family moved to Spain and lived in Cádiz and Barcelona. After studying at universities in Granada, Salamanca, and Valladolid, Degetau received a bachelor's degree in philosophy from the Universidad de Madrid in 1879. He later studied civil engineering but after a year switched to medicine, and by 1883 had decided to study law. In 1888, Degetau graduated with a doctor of laws degree from the Universidad de Madrid and began publishing articles in a variety of newspapers and journals.

For a brief period, he pursued a career in literature and journalism, writing short novels and articles. His first novel, *¡Qué Quijote!* (1883), was published in an anthology distributed in Puerto Rico and Spain. By 1895, Degetau had published five books ranging from short stories to an autobiography and a study of the pedagogical system of Froebel, a German educator who promoted kindergarten study.[1]

Degetau's dual-career track informed his political views. In May 1882 he published his first essay in a Madrid newspaper, *La correspondencia*. In November 1887 Degetau founded the periodical *Isla de Puerto Rico*. Published for only three months, it was dedicated to the overthrow of the Spanish governor, General Romualdo Palacios. Degetau's articles appeared in numerous Puerto Rican publications, enhancing his reputation as a political activist. He returned to Spain in 1896 with a commission of like-minded liberals to negotiate greater autonomy for the island. Degetau remained in Spain to represent Ponce in the Cortes, Spain's parliamentary body. During the Spanish-American War, he traveled to France to celebrate the signing of the Treaty of Paris, and eventually returned to Puerto Rico in November 1898. He married Ana Moreno Elorza y Valeriano, on March 1, 1902, in Council Bluffs, Iowa. The couple adopted Fernando Bonifacio Sánchez and his sister, Plácida.[2]

With the cession of Puerto Rico to the United States via the Treaty of Paris, Degetau, along with many others, welcomed the new regime. After Degetau returned to the island, U.S. military governor Guy Henry dissolved the cabinet and, on December 6, 1898, established four posts: secretary of state, secretary of justice, secretary of the provincial government, and secretary of the treasury. Degetau was secretary of the provincial government until

Image courtesy of the National Archives and Records Administration

his resignation on March 23, 1899. He also served as minister of development, first deputy mayor of San Juan, and director of public instruction.[3]

In April 1899, Degetau initiated a campaign to organize new political parties on the island, based on his personal conviction that Puerto Ricans deserved U.S. citizenship and autonomy, which were not conferred by the Foraker Act, which had been approved the following year.[4] Degetau and the Republicans had as a primary goal the "definitive… annexation of Puerto Rico to the United States," through the "Declaration of Puerto Rico as a territory, as a means of later becoming a state of the Federal Union."[5] Degetau extolled the U.S. system of government, based on the Declaration of Independence and the Constitution, as a "new political society … in which individual freedom was safeguarded against all possible aggression of tyranny, in which the old, ruinous theory of 'paternal governments'… was disappearing with the new affirmation of government of the people by the people themselves."[6] For Degetau, "these principles, by which order and social wellbeing are founded on the conscience of every people and not on soldiers' bayonets in the service of a governor, are what we claim for our country," he said in 1900.[7]

That year, as his party's nominee for the newly created post of Resident Commissioner to the U.S. Congress, Degetau asked for support "not because of personal merit, but rather because [of] your approval of the principles that I have just described."[8] Degetau's opponent was Federal Party nominee Manuel Gatell, a former postal employee and pharmacist.[9] Some critics painted Gatell as a puppet of Luis Muñoz Rivera, the Federalist leader. "What responsibility is Mr. Gatell assuming towards the country if he is elected? None," rejoined a critic. "All his responsibilities would be towards Muñoz Rivera who chose him, and *he* will say what will be required of Gatell as Commissioner."[10]

Degetau criss-crossed the island on a two-week campaign tour, speaking to crowds in both Republican and Federalist strongholds in major cities such as Arecibo, Aguadilla, Mayagüez, and Ponce.[11] At the end of the trip, Degetau responded to a series of attacks by Luis Muñoz Rivera's island-wide newspaper, *La democracia*, that claimed his stump speeches had been inflammatory: "The people of Puerto Rico are tired of the politics of insults and indecencies that can only establish hatreds and disorder within the country … upon announcing my modest name, the vast majority of the country has responded, because Federalists and Republicans throughout the Island can attest that in none, in not one, of my speeches or my articles have I offended or insulted Mr. Muñoz or anyone, as *La democracia* claims."[12] Indeed, Degetau's popularity as a political dissident in Spain and his activities during the period of military rule in Puerto Rico conferred a large advantage.

Federalists eventually called for an election boycott to protest U.S. officials' perceived bias toward Republicans, who had not been prosecuted for political violence. As a result, the Republicans swept the elections and gained majority control of the inaugural session of the island's newly created house of delegates.[13] Degetau defeated Gatell on November 6, 1900, with an overwhelming majority of the vote (98 percent). Renominated in September 1902, Degetau ran in the general election on November 4 against Federalist Felipe Cuebas Arredondo, earning 46 percent of the vote to his opponent's 22 percent.[14]

When Degetau arrived on the mainland, he participated in a small media tour of New York and Washington, D.C. The press posed many familiar questions: Was Puerto Rico fit to be a territory? Did a majority of islanders prefer statehood or independence? Wasn't benevolent U.S. rule preferable to the supposed cruelties of life under Spanish governance? Degetau expressed his admiration for the U.S. form of government and responded that most Puerto Ricans wanted a territorial government. "That is, they want t/he same privileges that you accord to the people of Arizona, Indian Territory, Oklahoma, and other Territories," he noted, characterizing Puerto Ricans dissenting from this viewpoint as lower-class and ignorant of the U.S. system of government.[15] Degetau suggested that by developing its natural resources to improve its infrastructure, educational system, and economy, Puerto Rico could achieve statehood. Describing the Republican approach as gradualist, he distanced himself from the Federalists, whom he portrayed as impatient and overly zealous in their pursuit of statehood. "My people want to become root and branch Americans [but] we cannot do it too quickly. We recognize that we are naturally Americans, and that our future is part of the future of this country," he said.[16]

With the start of the 57th Congress (1901–1903), Degetau's status as a Member of Congress became a matter of public speculation. Degetau had no floor privileges, nor was he permitted to hold committee assignments; yet his salary was commensurate with that of other House Members. Indeed, his role in the House resembled that of lobbyists, who sought to persuade Members to vote in a manner they deemed beneficial. One observer noted that Degetau's primary function seemed to be to "advise and assist committees concerning Porto Rican legislation." Nevertheless, the media treated Degetau like a celebrity, and Senators and Representatives "cordially welcomed" him. The House Post Office received a "considerable [amount] of mail" before his arrival, and Representative Henry Allen Cooper of Wisconsin, Chairman of the Committee on Insular Affairs, welcomed Degetau and strove to "make him at home in the quarters of that committee." The Resident Commissioner told his colleagues, "The Porto Rican people … want to become Americans in the full sense as fast as possible, and they also hope their representative will be accorded the rank of delegate, for as commissioner the island has less representation than it had under Spain."[17]

One of Degetau's major goals was to put Puerto Rico on the path to statehood. Using a media-savvy strategy to circumvent his inability to speak on the House Floor, he announced his plans to propose a bill to provide Puerto Rico territorial status in preparation for statehood. "All that is required to make Porto Rico one of the most productive countries in the world is the introduction of American capital," Degetau noted. "Millions of dollars are awaiting investment, but not a cent will be put into the island until the country is provided with suitable and stable laws for its government," he said.[18] In his second term he also pushed for H.R. 11592, a bill conferring U.S. citizenship on Puerto Ricans, but the bill was referred to the Committee on Insular Affairs and died there.[19] During debate on an army appropriations bill (H.R. 17473), Degetau noted that colleagues referred to him as the "delegate from Porto Rico." Gently correcting them, he explained, a "bill giving legal expression to that sentiment—providing for a delegate from Porto Rico—was unanimously recommended by the Committee on Insular Affairs and unanimously approved by the House during the last days of Congress. A similar bill … is at present on the Calendar, but until now I am, in the language of the law, only a 'Resident Commissioner.'"[20]

Though barred by House Rules from serving on committees, Degetau participated in hearings before Chairman Cooper's Committee on Insular Affairs—a recently formed panel with oversight of civil government and infrastructure in U.S. possessions overseas, including the Philippines, Guam, and Puerto Rico—testifying on H.R. 14083, a bill to grant Puerto Rico a Delegate in place of a Resident Commissioner.[21] Degetau argued that the Resident Commissioner's status was muddled. While the Foraker Act provided for the election of an official to represent Puerto Rico, Degetau acknowledged, it was "difficult … for many people to determine whether the commissioner was elected by the people to represent them or to represent the government of the island, and also whether he represents the island as a part of the American Union or as a distinct political body; in other words, whether he is an official of the local or of the Federal Government."[22]

In June 1902, 18 months after Degetau entered Congress, he finally received floor privileges when Representative Cooper submitted H. Res. 169, amending House Rule 34 to provide Degetau a seat on the House Floor.[23] After a sustained campaign in which numerous Members submitted bills on Degetau's behalf, he received floor privileges and membership on the Committee on Insular Affairs (without seniority) in February 1904 as a result of H. Res. 158, sponsored by John Dalzell of Pennsylvania.[24]

Congress lifted the moratorium on Degetau's participation in floor debate so late in his career that he participated in debate in relatively few instances, although he eloquently defended his countrymen against racial stereotypes late in his final term in the House. During the debate of an annual army appropriation bill in the Committee of the Whole, James Beauchamp (Champ) Clark of Missouri, a future Speaker of the House, moved an amendment to strike out the appropriation for a provisional army regiment in Puerto Rico.[25] In opposing that amendment, Degetau reminded his colleagues that Puerto Rico had avoided a bloody revolution because of its reasoned appeals to the Spanish government. "Without recourse to violence, [Puerto Ricans] accomplished as great reforms as any other people ever accomplished, [and] do not need military force to coerce them into the performance of their present duty," he noted. Degetau also challenged racist arguments that Puerto Ricans were temperamentally unfit to serve as soldiers. "No, we are not 'hot-blooded Spaniards,'" he declared. "It is true that the immense majority of us Porto Ricans are of Spanish ancestry.... It is true also that we have long loved American institutions, and through this love we are loyally Americans, who have won our American citizenship."[26] Degetau highlighted the distinguished record of the Puerto Rican regiment's commanding officers and concluded his speech by emphasizing Puerto Rico's sense of duty and patriotism. "Every Porto Rican who is aware of the sacredness of this civic duty feels proud of every opportunity that may be offered to him in the military as well as in the civic avenues of life," Degetau said to prolonged applause, "of maintaining and defending, with the other American citizens, for the welfare and progress of mankind, the same ideal of justice articulated in the Constitution and symbolized in the flag." Supporting Degetau's position, Frank Mondell of Wyoming asserted that Puerto Rico should have a regiment for its protection, and Clark's amendment was defeated, 89 to 47.[27]

Degetau maintained his status as a practicing attorney and was admitted to the bar of the U.S. Supreme Court in April 1901. His admission to the bar was controversial because of his uncertain status as a U.S. citizen, but when Solicitor General John K. Richards introduced him as a member of the Puerto Rican supreme court bar, "there was no objection to his admission and Mr. Degetau walked to the clerk's office and took the oath of office."[28] Degetau sought to clarify the ambiguity surrounding Puerto Rican citizenship by participating in legal disputes that would force U.S. officials to specify the status of Puerto Ricans' citizenship. He interacted with Members of Congress and corresponded with executive branch officials such as the Secretary of State and the President of the United States about matters affecting Puerto Rico, especially the inconsistent policies followed by the Department of the Treasury with regard to Puerto Ricans' immigration status.[29] Degetau also represented Puerto Ricans whose citizenship was in question. He successfully represented Juan Rodríguez, who challenged the Navy Department's refusal to register him for employment at the Washington Navy Yard because his citizenship was in doubt. The District of Columbia Court of Appeals ruled that Rodríguez was eligible for civil service employment and ordered the navy to reverse its decision.[30]

Degetau participated in one U.S. Supreme Court case, *Gonzalez v. Williams*, by filing an amicus curiae brief. The case involved Isabel González, an unmarried pregnant woman who emigrated from Puerto Rico to New York City in 1902. Based on her ethnicity, gender, and pregnancy, immigration authorities at Ellis Island deemed her an alien and refused her entry. González challenged the ruling in court, arguing that she was a U.S. citizen. Degetau illustrated the inconsistencies between the Treasury Department's enforcement of immigration restrictions toward González and its printed regulations. He challenged a circuit court's decision against González, describing the implied legal assumptions of the transfer of sovereignty (and citizenship) from Spain to the United States resulting from the imposition of military government in 1898, the provisions of the Treaty of Paris, and *Hawaii v. Mankichi*.[31] Asserting that the "accepted principle in international law [is] that the nationality of a person follows the nationality of the territory in which such person is born," Degetau argued that the Puerto Rican case was "a clear case of collective naturalization as distinguished from individual naturalization, that happens when a country or province becomes incorporated in another country ... the citizens of Porto Rico forming the same body politic with the other citizens of the United States and obeying and supporting the same Constitution and … the same statutory laws that all the other citizens of the United States obey and support."[32] Degetau's view was that since the cession of Puerto Rico and its people by Spain to the United States released islanders from their political obligations to Spain, and since the islanders took an oath to support the Constitution of the United States, it followed that Puerto Ricans acquired de facto (or territorial) citizenship under Section 7 of the Foraker Act. The court narrowly ruled in González's favor by declaring that Puerto Ricans were not aliens; however, the Justices did not rule that Puerto Ricans were U.S. citizens.[33]

By August 1903, Degetau had split from the Republican Party, an action that contributed to his decision not to run for a third term.[34] After his congressional term expired in 1905, Degetau served as chancellor at the Universidad de Puerto Rico and continued his career as a lecturer. He was also an accomplished painter. Degetau died in Santurce, Puerto Rico, on January 20, 1914, and was interred at Cementerio de San Juan (San Juan Cemetery).[35]

FOR FURTHER READING

Biographical Directory of the United States Congress, "Federico Degetau," http://bioguide.congress.gov.

Degetau y González, Federico. *Juventud* (Madrid: A. Avrial, 1894).

______. *Cuentos* (Madrid: A. Avrial, 1894).

______. *El ABC del sistema Froebel* (Madrid: J. Perales y Martinez, 1896).

______. *The Political Status of Porto Rico* (Washington, D.C.: Globe Printing Company, 1902).

Erman, Sam. "Meanings of Citizenship in the U.S. Empire: Puerto Rico, Isabel Gonzalez, and the Supreme Court, 1898 to 1905," *Journal of American Ethnic History* 27, no. 4 (Summer 2002): 5–33.

Mergal Llera, Angel M. *Federico Degetau: Un orientador de su pueblo* (New York: Hispanic Institute, 1944).

MANUSCRIPT COLLECTION

Universidad de Puerto Rico, Centro de Investigaciones Históricas (Rio Piedras, PR). *Papers*: Angel M. Mergal Papers, 1887–1917, approximately 2,300 items. Correspondence, speeches, newspaper clippings, press releases, testimonials, and other papers relating to the career of Federico Degetau.

NOTES

1 "Federico Degetau," in Federico Rives Tobar, *100 biografías de puertorriqueños ilustres* (New York: Plus Ultra Educational Publishers, Inc., 1973): 213–215; "Nace don Federico Degetau y González en Ponce, Puerto Rico, el 5 de diciembre de 1862. Fueron sus padres doña María Consolación González y Sánchez Páez y don Mathías Degetau. Doña Consuelo pertenecía a una prestigiosa familia de la capital … Don Matías Degetau perteneció a una numerosa familia hamburguesa … Por carta que escribió Flavius Dede al Licenciado Federico Martín, el 28 de septiembre de 1863, nos enteramos de la muerte del Sr. Degetau, ocurrida a principios del mes … La familia González y Sánchez Páez habíase trasladado de la Capital a Ponce … La inteligente señora mantuvo a través de toda su vida relaciones con los parientes y amigos de su esposo, consagrándose a la educación de su hijo … Poco más de seis años tenía el niño cuando llegó a San Juan … Con este acendrado amor por todo lo puertorriqueño, y este profundo respeto por todo lo español, salían doña Consuelo, su hijo … en las postrimerías del 1874 … El Havre, luego Burdeos, Lisboa, y finalmente Cadíz, donde Federico se aclimataría a la Península … La esperanza de hallar en la selecta colonia puertorriqueña de Barcelona ambiente más propicio para la educación de su hijo, le deciden por la Capital de Cataluña … En 1879 terminaba su bachillerato en Filosofía … En junio de 1879 … comienza sus studios en Ingeniería Civil … El próximo años le tenemos estudiando medicina … En enero de 1883 publica en la colección La Biblioteca Pequeñita, su novela *¡Qué Quijote!*, que fué reproducida en periódicos de provincias, incluso Puerto Rico … En 1887 toma los exámina en Salamanca, en mayo de 1888 vuelve a Granada, donde se exámenes en Derecho Procesal y Mercantil, finalmente el 30 de junio de 1888 toma sus exámenes en Madrid, y le es extendido el correspondiente Título, por el Ministerio de Fomento, el 29 de octubre de 1888." Angel M. Mergal, *Federico Degetau: Un orientador de su pueblo* (New York: Hispanic Institute in the United States, 1944): 30–31, 34–36, 39–41, 44–50. Translated as "Mergal Biography Degetau-part 1-ENG," by Translations International, Inc. (June 2010).

2 "El primer artículo de Madrid, que haya llegado a nuestra noticia, se publicó en *La Correspondencia* … En 1887 edita, redacta y distribuye el periodico Isla de Puerto Rico, fundado y mantenido exclusivamente para derrocar el gobierno del General Romualdo Palacios, de infeliz memoria en aquella provincia española … En 1896 vuelve a Puerto Rico. Se le designa para formar parte de una comisión, enviada a Madrid por los partidos liberales de la Isla … Degetau permanence en España y representa luego a la Isla como Diputado a Cortes por el distrito de Ponce … en su carácter personal, a las reuniones que en París celebran los plenipotenciarios de España y Estados Unidos para poner fin a la Guerra hispano-

americana. Regresó a Puerto Rico el 22 de noviembre de 1898 … El 1 de marzo de 1902 don Federico Degetau y González … y doña Ana Moreno Elorza y Valarino contraían matrimonio en Council Bluffs, Iowa … No hubo hijos de este matrimonio. Bonifacio Sánchez y su hermana Plácida, los chicos avileses, fueron adoptados también por doña Ana … El 22 de noviembre regresa a su isla." Mergal, *Federico Degetau: Un orientador de su pueblo*: 43–46, 50–51. Translated as "Mergal Biography-Degetau-part 1-ENG," by Translations International, Inc. (June 2010).

3 Degetau's major biographer notes that the structure of the government was intended to ensure the participation of the major political parties but dismissed this as "a useless attempt." "Bajo la nueva bandera, aún sin ciudadanía determinanda, Degetau desempeña el Ministerio de Fomento en el gobierno temporero del general Henry. Acepta la designación para primer Teniente Alcalde de San Juan … Asume la Dirección de la Instrucción pública en la ciudad Capital … El 22 de noviembre regresa a su isla. El 6 de diciembre el gobernador militar Henry disuelve el Gabinete autonómico y establece en su lugar cuatro departamentos: Secretario de Estado … Secretario de Justicia … Secretario de Gobernación, don Federico Degetau, Secretario de Hacienda … A juzgar por la composición de este gobierno, se pensó en satisfacer ambos bandos políticos. Intento inútil. Don Federico renunció el 23 de marzo de 1899." Mergal, *Federico Degetau: Un orientador de su pueblo*: 50, 165. Translated by Translations International, Inc. (June 2010).

4 César J. Ayala and Rafael Bernabe, *Puerto Rico in the American Century: A History since 1898* (Chapel Hill: University of North Carolina Press, 2007): 52–53. During this period, Puerto Rican social elites divided into two main parties. Both were committed to the concept of *autonomía*, which stood for individual rights for citizens and a capacity for self-government. The two parties, Partido Federal (Federal Party) and Partido Republicano (Republican Party) advocated different methods to achieve similar goals. The Republican Party used a gradualist approach, refusing to openly condemn U.S. rule, seeking instead to adapt to the system while displaying unconditional loyalty in order to acquire statehood. The Federal Party, on the other hand, offered a vigorous critique of American colonial policies while holding out for statehood. Although the Federalists eventually abandoned the statehood concept, they promoted a policy of gradual reforms, called autonomism, within the existing colonial structure.

5 "Primera. Anexión definitiva y sincera de Puerto Rico a los Estados Unidos. Segunda. Declaración Territorio para Puerto Rico, como medio de ser luego un Estado de la Unión Federal." Federico Degetau y González. "Al País." 8 October 1900, *La correspondencia* (San Juan, PR): 2. Translated as: "To Our Country," by Translations International, Inc. (May 2009). This article may have been the first of four manifestos that Degetau published in Puerto Rican newspapers. According to Angel Mergal, Degetau's major biographer, the other manifestos were published on May 31, 1901, September 12, 1902, and August 31, 1904. See Mergal, *Federico Degetau: Un orientador de su pueblo*: 178–179.

6 "Una nueva sociedad política en que la libertad del individuo estaba garantizada contra toda agresión posible de la tiranía: en que la vieja funesta teoría de los 'gobiernos paternales' … se desvanecía ante la nueva afirmación del gobierno del pueblo por el pueblo mismo." Federico Degetau y González. "Al País," 8 October 1900, *La correspondencia* (San Juan, PR): 2. Translated as "To Our Country," by Translations International, Inc. (May 2009).

7 "Esos principios que hacen radicar el orden y bienestar social en la conciencia del pueblo y no en las bayonetas de soldados que sirvan a un gobernante, es lo que revindicamos para nuestro país." Federico Degetau y González. "Al País," 8 October 1900, *La correspondencia* (San Juan, PR): 2. Translated as "To Our Country," by Translations International, Inc. (May 2009).

8 "A reclamar en Washington para nuestro pueblo el derecho a la plenitud de la ciudadanía americana, me ha sido conferido por mi Partido … Y no por merecimientos personales, sino porque vuestra aprobación a los principios que acabo de exponer, es lo que significa ese voto vuestro dado a mi nombre." Federico Degetau y González. "Al País," 8 October 1900, *La correspondencia* (San Juan, PR): 2. Translated as "To Our Country," by Translations International, Inc. (May 2009).

9 "Manuel Gatell: Ex-dependiente de farmacia, ex-empleado subalterno de correos." Un Imparcial. "Gatell y Degetau: A elegir," 15 October 1900, *La correspondencia* (San Juan, PR): 2. Translated as "Gatell y Degetau: To The Polls," by Translations International, Inc. (May 2009). For more information about Gatell, see the following anonymous article that lists "XXX" as the author: XXX, "Remitido: Gatell y Degetau," 16 October 1900, *La correspondencia*: 2.

10 "Qué responsibilidad contrae Gatell ante si el país sale electo? Ninguna. Todas sus responsibilidades serán ante Muñoz que lo elige, y éste dirá cuando a él se las exijan, que Gatell fué el Comisionado." Un Imparcial, "Remitido": A XXX y á "El País," 17 October 1900, *La correspondencia* (San Juan, PR): 2. Translated as "Notice: To XXX and to El País," by Translations International, Inc. (May 2009). For XXX's response defending Gatell's qualifications, see XXX, "Remitido: Cuatro palabras, Gatell y Degetau," 18 October 1900, *La correspondencia*: 2.

11 "Los pueblos de Arecibo, Aguadilla, Mayagüez, Ponce, Juana Daz, y Humacao, serán visitados por este ciudadano dignísimo, de palabra fácil y de una ilustración vasta en todos los problemas que afectan a la futura vida política del país." "Degetau González," 11 October 1900, *La correspondencia*: 2. Translated as "Degetau González," by Translations International, Inc. (May 2009); "Regreso de Degetau," 30 October 1900, *La correspondencia*: 2. Degetau navigated the island for two weeks, leaving San Juan and visiting cities such as Arecibo in the central-western section, Aguadilla and Mayagüez on Puerto Rico's west coast, Ponce and Juana Díaz on the southern coast, and Humacao in the southeast corner of the island. Degetau

visited Gurabo and Caguas, which he describes in Federico Degetau, "Sección neutral," 1 November 1900, *La correspondencia*: 2.

12 "Por lo demas mi viaje de propaganda ha dado ocasión al país para demostrar: 1o Que el pueblo puertorriqueño está cansado de una política de insultos y de procacidades que sólo puede determinar odios y desórdenes en lo interior … y al aclamar mi modesto nombre, la inmensa mayoría del país lo ha hecho porque a federales y republicanos de toda la isla les consta que en ninguno, absolutamente en ninguno de mis discursos, ni de mis artículos, he ofendido, ni insultado al Sr. Muñoz ni a nadíe, como afirma 'La Democracia'." Federico Degetau, "Sección neutral," 1 November 1900, *La correspondencia* (San Juan, PR): 2.

13 Sam Erman, "Meanings of Citizenship in the U.S. Empire: Puerto Rico, Isabel González, and the Supreme Court, 1898 to 1905," *Journal of American Ethnic History* 27 (Summer 2008): 10. See also Julian Go, *American Empire and the Politics of Meaning: Elite Political Cultures in the Philippines and Puerto Rico during U.S. Colonialism* (Durham, NC: Duke University Press, 2008): 25–55 for cultural precepts used by Federal Party predecessors in 1898 and 1899, especially *retraimiento*.

14 *First Annual Report of Charles H. Allen, Governor of Porto Rico, Covering the Period from May 1, 1900, to May 1, 1901*, Senate Document 79, 57th Cong., 1st sess. (1901): 123. Degetau won with 58,937 votes, and Gatell earned only 148 votes; Fernando Bayron Toro, *Elecciones y partidos políticos de Puerto Rico: 1809–2000*. (Mayagüez, PR: Editorial Isla, 2003): 120. Out of a total of 158,924 votes, Degetau's party earned 73,823, while the Federal Party earned 34,605. A third party earned 2,788. For information about Arredondo and Degetau's renomination in the 1902 election, see "Federal Candidates Nominated," 14 September 1902, *San Juan News*: 1; and "Degetau to Run Again for Commissioner," 16 September 1902, *San Juan News*: 1.

15 "Porto Ricans Improving," 3 December 1900, *New York Times*: 7.

16 "Views of Porto Rico's Delegate," 3 December 1900, *Washington Post*: 1.

17 "Porto Rican Commissioner," 15 December 1900, *Washington Post*: 4; "Right to Floor Questioned," 8 December 1900, *Washington Post*: 4. See also William R. Tansill, "The Resident Commissioner to the United States from Puerto Rico: An Historical Perspective," *Revista jurídica de la Universidad de Puerto Rico* 47, nos. 1–2 (1978): 68–106. For biographical information about Cooper, see "Henry Allen Cooper," *Biographical Directory of the United States Congress*, http://bioguide.congress.gov.

18 "Statehood Their Aim," 25 December 1900, *New York Times*: 11. No bills proposing that Puerto Rico be made a territory were submitted during the 2nd session of the 56th Congress. See *Congressional Record*, Index, House, 56th Cong., 2nd sess.: 222.

19 *Congressional Record*, Index, 58th Cong., 2nd sess.: 149–150, 307.

20 *Congressional Record*, House, 58th Cong., 3rd sess. (19 January 1905): 1086.

21 David T. Canon, Garrison Nelson, and Charles Stewart III, eds., *Committees in the U.S. Congress, 1789–1946*, vol. 3 (Washington, D.C.: CQ Press, 2002): 617; National Archives and Records Administration, *Guide to the Records of the United States House of Representatives at the National Archives: 1789–1989, Bicentennial ed.*, 100th Cong., 2nd sess., H. Doc. 100–245. (Washington, D.C.: Government Printing Office: 1989): 195–196.

22 R. B. Horton, ed., House Committee on Insular Affairs, *Committee Reports, Hearings, and Acts of Congress Corresponding thereto, Committee on Insular Affairs, House of Representatives*, 57th Cong., 1st and 2nd sess. (Washington, D.C.: Government Printing Office, 1903): 34–37. For Degetau's testimony about granting supervisory authority over Puerto Rico's public lands to the Secretary of the Interior, see pp. 426–430.

23 Tansill, "The Resident Commissioner to the United States from Puerto Rico": 72–73.

24 Ibid., 79–82. See pp. 74–79 for two other unsuccessful attempts to obtain speaking privileges and to change Degetau's status from Resident Commissioner to Delegate, See also "Voice for Porto Rico," 3 February 1904, *Washington Post*: 4; "Delegate from Porto Rico," 3 February 1904, *New York Times*: 6. For floor debate on the approval of speaking privileges for Degetau. See *Congressional Record*, House, 58th Cong., 2nd sess. (2 February 1904): 1523–1529

25 Gilberto N. Villahermosa, *Honor and Fidelity: The 65th Infantry in Korea, 1950–1953* (Washington, D.C.: Center of Military History, U.S. Army, 2009): 1–4. The regiment was a unit of two battalions of volunteer infantry authorized by Congress in 1899 and 1900.

26 *Congressional Record*, House, 58th Cong., 3rd sess. (19 January 1905): 1088. See pp. 1083–1084 for Clark's statements. The full debate is on pp. 1082–1090.

27 Ibid., 1088–1090; "Porto Rican Heard in House," 20 January 1905, *San Francisco Chronicle*: 13.

28 "Admission of Mr. Degetau," 1 May 1901, *Washington Post*: 3; United States Department of Justice, Office of the Solicitor General, "John K. Richards," http://www.justice.gov/osg/aboutosg/osghistpage.php?id=9 (accessed 28 February 2011).

29 Erman, "Meaning of Citizenship in the U.S. Empire": 10–11. Erman states that Degetau consistently "lobbied the chairman of the House Committee on Insular Affairs, Henry Allen Cooper, and sent letters to the secretary of state concerning inconsistent treatment of Puerto Rican migrants." Erman describes two instances in which Degetau "intervened in a Puerto Rican man's appeal of a U.S. military commission sentence. And he applied, personally, for a U.S. passport identifying him as a U.S. citizen and for admission to the bar of the U.S. Supreme Court. While these efforts did not produce immediate results, Degetau was personally well received when he made them."

30 "Status of a Porto Rican," 20 May 1904, *Washington Post*, 12; "Porto Rican Eligible," 8 March 1905, *Washington Post*: 6; WestlawNext, *U.S. Ex Rel. Rodriguez v. Bowyer* 1905 WL 17637 (App. D.C.), https://a.next.westlaw.com/ (accessed 24 May 2010).

31 Erman, "Meaning of Citizenship in the U.S. Empire": 5; *U.S. Supreme Court Records & Briefs*: 53-I: Part VII; 192 U.S. 1-149 (Reel 633): 21–31 (hereinafter referred to as *U.S. Supreme Court Records & Briefs*).

32 *U.S. Supreme Court Records & Briefs*: 35.

33 Ibid., 5, 42–43; Erman, "Meaning of Citizenship in the U.S. Empire": 20–23. Erman analyzes Degetau's brief as a statement from "an official, male, and Puerto Rican perspective." According to Erman, Degetau reinterpreted U.S. colonialist precedents with "the contention that Puerto Ricans were not 'natives' in a colonial sense." Erman points out that Puerto Ricans differed from Native Americans and Filipinos in that under Spanish sovereignty, "Puerto Ricans enjoyed such rights as representation in the national legislature, national citizenship accompanied by constitutional protections … and broad autonomy, continuing that even after U.S. annexation of Puerto Rico, Spain let Puerto Ricans be military officers, embassy officials, and senators." In essence, according to Erman, Degetau argued that Puerto Ricans were "fit" to acquire U.S. citizenship. Erman states that Degetau "portrayed a population actively and naturally blending into the United States against which barriers to citizenship seemed out of place … Puerto Rican citizenship was territorial citizenship, coexisting with the U.S. citizenship that the Fourteenth Amendment guaranteed to all those born within the U.S. nation."

34 "En agosto de 1903 vuelve a Puerto Rico. Sus actividades en la política republicana a empezaban a estar en desacuerdo con el partido, y decide no presentar su candidatura para las próximas elecciones." Mergal, *Federico Degetau, Un orientador de pueblo*: 52. Translated as "Mergal Biography Degetau-part 1-ENG," by Translations International, Inc. (June 2010).

35 "Federico Degetau Died This Morning," 20 January 1914, *The Times* (San Juan): 1. For obituaries and reminiscences in Spanish, see "Federico Degetau," 20 January 1914, *El tiempo*: 1; "El entierro de Degetau," 21 January 1914, *La correspondencia*: 1; "El entierro de Degetau Gonzalez: Sentida manifestacion," 21 January 1914, *La democracia*: 1; "El entierro de Federico Degetau," 21 January 1914, *El tiempo*: 1; "Federico Degetau: Notas intimas," 22 January 1914, *La democracia*: 1.

"Thus far Mr. Degetau's official functions have begun and ended with this designation [of Resident Commissioner], and if he succeeds in getting even so far as across tiie threshold of one of the lobbies of the Capitol ... he is doing about all he can reasonably expect to do."

Baltimore Sun, May 17, 1902

Tulio Larrínaga
1847–1917

RESIDENT COMMISSIONER 1905–1911
UNIONIST FROM PUERTO RICO

An engineer by training, Tulio Larrínaga, Puerto Rico's second Resident Commissioner in Congress moved into politics when Puerto Rico became a U.S. territory. Like his predecessor, Federico Degetau, Larrínaga used the Resident Commissioner's ministerial powers and his own political savvy to encourage and cajole U.S. politicians to reform the island's civil government. In particular, Larrínaga sought to modify or eliminate aspects of the Foraker Act that infringed on Puerto Ricans' popular sovereignty and limited the Resident Commissioner's ability to represent constituents. "Everybody on the floor of this House knows that it is only due to the courtesy of the Committee on Rules … not by any law of Congress, that the Commissioner from Porto Rico is allowed the privilege of the floor," Larrínaga declared.[1]

Tulio Larrínaga y Torres Vallejo was born in Trujillo Alto, Puerto Rico, on January 15, 1847. He attended the Seminario Conciliar de San Ildefonso in San Juan. Larrínaga studied civil engineering at Rensselaer Polytechnic Institute in Troy, New York, from 1865 to 1868 and graduated from the University of Pennsylvania in Philadelphia in 1871. Among Larrínaga's projects were the preparation of a topographical map of Kings County, New York, and his work for an engineering firm involved in the construction of Grand Central Station in New York City. Returning to Puerto Rico in 1872, Larrínaga served as a municipal architect of San Juan. He also helped found Ateneo Puertorriqueño (the Puerto Rican Arts and Sciences Association) in 1876 and served as the head of the English department in the cultural center. He was a member of the Royal Economic Society of Friends of the Nation and the insular library commission. In 1879 Larrínaga married Berthy Goyro Saint Victor. The couple raised Tulio, Jr.; Berta; Concepción; and two other children.[2]

Larrínaga is credited with building the first railroad in Puerto Rico—a short line that ran from San Juan several miles south to Rio Piedras—and with introducing American rolling stock to the island. He served for 10 years as an engineer of the Provincial Deputation, working extensively on the construction of San Juan Harbor and on roads elsewhere on the island. He also directed the works of the 1893 Puerto Rico exposition as a member of its jury. Cayetano Coll y Toste, a prominent historian and writer, observes that Larrínaga's engineering successes benefited from his ability to maneuver in political circles, reminiscing that he was "able to gain the good will of Unconditional Party leader Pablo Ubarri, who exercised great influence over the island administration." "One can go far with friends in high places," he added. Larrínaga first became involved in politics when Puerto Rico achieved autonomy from Spain in 1897, joining the Partido Liberal de Puerto Rico (Liberal Reform Party of Puerto Rico). When Puerto Rico came under American governance in 1898, Larrínaga served as the subsecretary of public works and as assistant secretary of the interior under the autonomous government.[3]

In 1900, along with Luis Muñoz Rivera and others, Larrínaga founded the Partido Federalista de Puerto Rico (Federal Party of Puerto Rico), which advocated Puerto Rico's joining the United States as a territory but retaining control of local institutions. (In 1904 Larrínaga would join the Partido de Unión (Union Party), the successor to the Partido Federalista, which promoted local autonomy while reforming political ties between the United States and Puerto Rico.) During the initial debates over the structure of a civil government for Puerto Rico in early 1900, Larrínaga came to Washington with a political delegation advocating for home rule. He testified before

Image courtesy of the Puerto Rican Cultural Institute

the Senate Committee on Pacific Islands and Porto Rico regarding S. 2264, a precursor bill to the Foraker Act. Larrínaga called for free trade between the United States and Puerto Rico, advocated for territorial status, and discussed universal male suffrage.[4] When he testified before the House Committee on Insular Affairs, Larrínaga argued that Puerto Ricans "expect the American Government will give them a Territorial form of government; that they will have some Congressional representation of one or two members," citing Puerto Rico's voting experience with Spain as a precedent.[5] During the deliberations on the Foraker Act, Larrínaga told the Ways and Means Committee, "Puerto Rico needs a civil government even more than free trade. The people want to feel that they have become in a tangible manner attached to the United States and not a mere dependency."[6]

Larrínaga began his elective career as a member of the insular house of delegates for the district of Arecibo in 1902.[7] In 1904 he won election as Resident Commissioner to the 59th Congress (1905–1907); he served a total of three terms, winning by a comfortable margin each time. His opponent in 1904 was Republican Mateo Fajardo Cardona. Larrínaga's Union Party polled 62 percent against the Republicans' 38 percent. Larrínaga was re-elected to the 60th Congress (1907–1909), again by 62 percent, against Republican candidate Ledo Francisco Paria Capo. Two years later, he polled 64 percent of the vote against Republican Roberto Todd and Socialist Santiago Iglesias, a future Resident Commissioner.[8] Larrínaga interpreted his party's electoral domination as proof of Puerto Ricans' displeasure with the provisions of the Foraker Act, particularly the appointed executive council, which often undermined acts of the popularly elected insular house of delegates—which Unionists had consistently pressured Congress to revise or repeal. Such electoral results, he noted, show "very clearly that our people are more determined … to stop the encroaching tendency of that upper house or executive council."[9]

During his tenure in the House, Larrínaga served on the Committee on Insular Affairs, created to oversee civil government and infrastructure issues pertaining to the United States' territories overseas, including the Philippines, Guam, and Puerto Rico.[10] Unlike his predecessor, Federico Degetau, who was hamstrung by his lack of floor and speaking privileges, Larrínaga enjoyed these privileges from the outset of his congressional career and was well versed in advocating for Puerto Rican interests in Washington. During his first term, in the 59th Congress, Larrínaga submitted six bills and two petitions. Three of the bills dealt with reforming the structure of the civil government as defined by the Foraker Act. He also submitted a bill to amend the law limiting the number of Puerto Ricans who were admitted to the U.S. Military Academy at West Point and a bill to expand improvements to San Juan Harbor.[11] Additionally, Larrínaga appealed to President Theodore Roosevelt "for a greater measure of self-government" for Puerto Rico. "The people of Porto Rico were being treated as if they were not capable of self-government," Larrínaga told Roosevelt, and the acts of the house of delegates "were practically annulled by the executive council."[12]

In an editorial about self-rule in Puerto Rico, Larrínaga criticized the *Washington Post* for describing council members of San Juan municipalities as "self-styled" politicians. "Those representatives have been selected by the most genuine representation of the people of Porto Rico, for the members of the municipal council … are elected directly by the vote of the people, as well as the house of delegates," Larrínaga countered. He described his election as a mandate to liberalize American rule on the island by reforming the Foraker Act. "The people of Porto Rico sent me here to Washington by the largest vote ever cast in the country to tell Congress and the American people that we wished to elect our senate as we elect the members of the house of delegates, so that we could make our own laws and manage our own local affairs," Larrínaga wrote.[13] In the press and on the House Floor, Larrínaga took exceptional offense to the executive council, first, because he objected to the council's selection by the President of the United States instead of by popular vote; and second, because he objected to the council's extraordinary power to alter measures approved by the popularly elected house of delegates. In a floor speech, Larrínaga stressed that for "many years we have been putting up with all the encroachment of our masters in that executive council ... we have cooperated with our local government to the verge of humiliation; but the time has come ... when we are no longer disposed to allow them to go beyond the limits fixed by the organic act ... for the genuine representation of the people in the lower house."[14] During the second session of the 61st Congress (1909–1911), chairman of the House Committee on Insular Affairs Marlin Olmsted of Pennsylvania submitted H.R. 23000 on Larrínaga's behalf, a bill designed to replace the Foraker Act with a more generous system of Puerto Rican self-government. Whereas the Foraker Act was a "temporary act" that became permanent, the new bill would provide a permanent government for the island. House debates on the bill demonstrated Larrínaga's more forceful tack, emphasizing the shortcomings and anti-democratic tendencies of the Foraker Act while appealing for greater self-sovereignty on the island. Larrínaga compared his bill to the Constitution of the United States. When asked "whether I preferred the present organic act of Porto Rico to this bill now before the House ... with the provision [in this bill] giving us collective citizenship ... my answer ... is I do," he said. Larrínaga noted that Chairman Olmsted believed "that the upper house under the present Foraker Act hindered the lower house from enacting any legislation whatsoever." Larrinaga continued, "He had the honesty to say ... what the Porto Ricans have been saying and protesting against every day for the last ten years; that you have not given to the people of Porto Rico any power whatsoever to enact their own laws."[15] After extensive debate, the bill passed the House on June 15, 1910, and was referred to the Senate Committee on Pacific Islands and Porto Rico, where it died.[16]

In January 1906, Larrínaga submitted to the House a memorial petition from the municipal councils of 52 towns in Puerto Rico. The petition requested that voters continue to be permitted to elect the members of the house of delegates by popular vote and that the presidentially appointed executive council be replaced with an insular senate of 14 members also elected by popular vote. As for the directors of the island's six principal administrative departments, who were selected by the President, the petition asked that they "be appointed by the governor of Porto Rico with the advice and consent of the insular senate." The petition was submitted to the Committee on Insular Affairs, and no further action was taken.[17] In 1907 Larrínaga and the house of delegates lobbied President Theodore Roosevelt, unsuccessfully, to select a native Puerto Rican to serve as secretary of Puerto Rico to administer the insular government's executive-branch duties.[18]

On November 21, 1906, President Roosevelt visited Puerto Rico en route from a visit to the Panama Canal. He was greeted by a number of political dignitaries, including Larrínaga. During his visit, Roosevelt promised to "continue to use every effort to secure citizenship for Porto Ricans. I am confident that this will come in the end," he continued. "My efforts will be unceasing to help you along the path of true self-government, which must have for its basis union, order, liberty, justice, and honor." When Roosevelt returned to the United States, he vigorously lobbied Congress to grant full citizenship to Puerto Ricans, including an appeal in his sixth Annual Message to Congress.[19] Five days after submitting the Annual Message, Roosevelt delivered a special message to Congress praising the natural beauty of the island and the effectiveness of its government and reiterating his belief in the "desirability of conferring full American citizenship upon the people of Porto Rico." "I cannot see how any harm can possibly result from it, and it seems to me a matter of right and justice to the people of Porto Rico," Roosevelt insisted. "They are loyal, they are glad to be under our flag, they are making rapid progress along the path of orderly liberty." In the *New York Times*, Larrínaga noted, "Mr. Roosevelt's visit had a healthful influence on the political feeling of the country. There was a sentiment of discouragement prevailing on the island. The people thought they were forgotten, but this feeling has now dissipated."[20]

To supplement such public statements, Larrínaga quietly pressured Roosevelt and Insular Affairs Committee chairman Henry Cooper of Wisconsin to move legislation. Seizing the momentum generated by Roosevelt's visit to the island, Cooper introduced H.R. 17661, a bill to grant full citizenship to Puerto Ricans. As Larrínaga rounded up the support from other Members, he commented, "The present relation we bear to the United States is ridiculous.... When I went to Europe recently I could say I was a member of the House, yet had to admit I was not an American citizen." Larrínaga noted that "Spaniards and other foreigners may come to the island, and after a short time become naturalized as American citizens, but the people of Porto Rico, who have lived all their lives there, must remain without citizenship." When Cooper brought the bill to the House Floor, James Beauchamp (Champ) Clark of Missouri, a future Speaker of the House, objected to debating the bill on the grounds that it "ought to be considered in a full House." Cooper attempted to schedule a debate for unanimous consent in the next week, but Clark objected again. This resistance effectively killed the bill.[21]

During his second term in the 60th Congress (1907–1909), Larrínaga honed his forceful criticisms of the Foraker Act, tying Puerto Rican dissatisfaction to anti-American sentiment. During a debate about the disapproval of certain laws of the Territory of New Mexico, Larrínaga criticized the Foraker Act as a "leaden block that closed the sepulcher where the liberties and rights of a million freemen are buried.... Instead of ... self-government ... you will find ... the executive is mixed with the legislative, and officers that are appointed by the Executive go down there to make the laws for a people whose customs they do not know; for a people whose faces they have never seen before ... and for a people whose laws and language they do not know." Larrínaga also discussed the economic policies in the act that crippled Puerto Rico's economy and "ruined the country, because no provision was made to protect our main industry, the industry of the poor man, the coffee industry." Larrínaga dismissed U.S. statesmen, including House Speaker Joe Cannon, who claimed credit for enhancing Puerto Rico's economy and political standing. "I hear every day in the political campaign here, 'We have made Porto Rico prosperous.' I wish you had," he declared. "Then no discontent would exist, and perhaps I could be looked upon by my countrymen with more kind regard. I wish you had made Porto Rico happy, but you have not, Mr. Speaker."[22]

Like his predecessor Degetau, Larrínaga counted among his major legislative interests the retention of the Puerto Rico regiment of the U.S. volunteer infantry from the U.S. Army. The regiment comprised two battalions of volunteer infantry that were authorized by Congress in 1899 and 1900. Introduced on Larrínaga's behalf by Chairman of the Committee on Military Affairs John Hull of Iowa, H.R. 18618 provided for the establishment of the Puerto Rico Provisional Regiment as a full infantry regiment in the U.S. Army. The House passed the bill with a small majority, but three times Larrínaga then attempted to persuade his colleagues to concur with the Senate's amendments; eventually the House passed the revised bill and President Roosevelt signed it into law on May 27, 1908.[23]

To promote his constituents' livelihoods, Larrínaga tried to shield Puerto Rican export markets from exorbitant tariffs.[24] In 1907 he corresponded with President Roosevelt, Secretary of State Elihu Root, and various subordinates about the negotiations for French tariffs that would adversely affect Puerto Rico's ailing coffee industry. The French, in a commercial agreement with the United States, proposed a "maximum tariff of 300 francs per 100 kilograms of coffee imported into the French markets," Larrínaga wrote. "This [tariff rate] would mean the closing of those markets to our main staple. We depend wholly today on France and Cuba for the disposal of four-fifths of our coffee crop, and you can well imagine, Mr. President, what a terrible blow the closing of those markets would be to the island," he continued.[25] Larrínaga also appealed to Root, writing the tariff issue is "a question of life and death to our coffee-planters. As long as our coffees do not receive protection at our home markets, we shall have to depend upon foreign markets for their sale ... to preserve the existence of our plantations."[26] Root informed Larrínaga that the 1908 Commercial Agreement between the United States and France "provided for the application of the minimum rate ... in return for certain specified concessions in favor of products of the United States,

including Porto Rico" and would take effect in February 1908. In the final agreement, products such as coffee were imported "at the rates of the minimum tariff or at the lowest rates" applicable, though such concessions could be revoked by the French president if additional tariffs were added.[27] Larrínaga's lobbying efforts probably saved the Puerto Rican coffee industry. His interest in foreign affairs received a boost when President Roosevelt selected him as a U.S. delegate to the Pan-American Conference in Rio de Janeiro. He also represented the United States at interparliamentary conferences, in Berlin in 1908 and in Brussels in 1910.[28]

Larrínaga secured appropriations and used his experience as an engineer to promote infrastructure projects in Puerto Rico. He had extensive experience with the construction of San Juan Harbor during his tenure as chief engineer for the project, and later, in 1908, he corresponded with Secretary of the Interior James R. Garfield about improvements. After securing a $657,000 appropriation for the dredging of San Juan Harbor, Larrínaga stressed to Garfield that the project should begin immediately, despite the protests of Governor Regis H. Post. Congress's approval to fund the project was "in accordance with specific plans prepared by the War Department, and we cannot expend a single dollar out of that appropriation for any other part of the work than that fixed in those plans," Larrínaga reminded Secretary Garfield.[29]

Larrínaga retired at the end of the 61st Congress and returned to his engineering career. He remained politically active by serving on the territorial executive council. On April 28, 1917, he died of heart trouble in Santurce, a suburb of San Juan.[30]

FOR FURTHER READING

Biographical Directory of the United States Congress, "Tulio Larrínaga," http://bioguide.congress.gov.

Larrínaga, Tulio. *Brief of Honorable Tulio Larrinaga* (Washington, D.C.: n.p., 1908).

_____. *Civil Government for Puerto Rico* (Washington, D.C.: n.p., 1910).

NOTES

1 *Congressional Record*, House, 61st Cong., 1st sess. (31 March 1909): 672.

2 "Tulio Larrínaga," in Federico Ribes Tovar, ed., *100 Biografías de puertorriqueños ilustres* (New York: Plus Ultra Educational Publishers, Inc., 1973): 195–197; Clarence Russell Williams, "Larrínaga, Tulio," *Dictionary of American Biography*, 6 (New York: American Council of Learned Societies, 1933): 8–9 (hereinafter referred to as *DAB*); *Thirteenth Census of the United States, 1910: Population Schedule*, Santurce, Puerto Rico, Roll T624_1778, page 32B, Library of Congress, Washington, D.C., http://search.ancestrylibrary.com (accessed 11 January 2012); National Archives and Records Administration; *U.S. Passport Applications, Hawaii, Puerto Rico, and Philippines, 1907–1925*; ARC Identifier 1244181/MLR Number A1_542; Box 4340; vol. 29, Library of Congress, Washington, D.C., http://search.ancestrylibrary.com (accessed 11 January 2012). Two of the Larrínaga children are neither listed in the Thirteenth Census nor in U.S. passport records.

3 Ronald I. Perusse, *The United States and Puerto Rico: The Struggle for Equality* (Malabar, FL: Robert E. Krieger, 1990): 5–6; Williams, "Larrínaga, Tulio," *DAB;* "Supo captarse la buena voluntad del cacique máximo incondicional, don Pablo Ubarri, que ejercía gran influencia en la adminstración insular.… Y el que a buen árbol se arrima, buena sombra le cae encima." Cayetano Coll y Toste, "Tulio Larrinaga," in *Puertorriqueños ilustres.* (Barcelona: Ediciones Rumbos, 1963): 300. Translated as "Tulio Larrinaga," by Translations International, Inc. (September 2010).

4 "Tulio Larrínaga," in Federico Ribes Tovar, ed., *100 Biografías de puertorriqueños ilustres*: 197; Hearing before the Senate Committee on Pacific Islands and Porto Rico, *Industrial and Other Conditions of the Island of Puerto Rico, and the Form of Government Which Should Be Adopted for It*, 56th Cong., 1st sess. (5 February 1900): 176–182.

5 R. B. Horton, ed., House Committee on Insular Affairs, *Committee Reports, Hearings, and Acts of Congress Corresponding Thereto*, 56th Cong., 1st and 2nd sess. (Washington, D.C.: Government Printing Office, 1904): 337. Larrínaga, who testified on March 12, 1900, also discussed the condition of the railroads, literacy and education of Puerto Ricans with regard to suffrage and the coffee and sugar markets.

6 "Puerto Rico Is Able to Support Itself," 22 March 1900, *New York Times*: 5.

7 Fernando Bayron Toro, *Elecciones y partidos políticos de Puerto Rico, 1809–2000* (Mayagüez, PR: Editorial Isla, 2003): 121.

8 Toro, *Elecciones y partidos políticos de Puerto Rico, 1809–2000*: 125–132; Larrínaga's opponents are listed in "Candidatos Republicanos en Ponce," 20 Septiembre 1904, *La correspondencia*: 4; "Ellos y nosotros," 29 Septiembre 1906, *El aguila*: 1;

"Candidaturas: Relación de los candidates presentados al gobierno," 19 Octubre 1908, *La democracia*: 1.

9 *Congressional Record*, House, 60th Cong., 2nd sess., (26 January 1909): 1451. Larrínaga noted, "In 1904, the Union party, the one more strenuously opposed to the Foraker Act, carried the elections by an overwhelming majority; in 1906 we carried the whole island, electing every member to the lower house; in 1908 we swept the island from one end to the other."

10 David T. Canon, Garrison Nelson, and Charles Stewart III, eds., *Committees in the U.S. Congress, 1789 to 1946*, vol. 3 (Washington, D.C.: CQ Press, 2002): 617; National Archives and Records Administration, *Guide to the Records of the United States House of Representatives at the National Archives: 1789–1989, Bicentennial ed.*, 100th Cong., 2nd sess., H. Doc. 100-245. (Washington, D.C.: Government Printing Office, 1989): 195–196.

11 *Congressional Record*, Index, 59th Cong., 1st sess., 534.

12 "Complaint from Porto Rico," 30 May 1905, *Washington Post*: 6. For a similar proposal, see "Porto Ricans Dissatisfied," 19 January 1906, *Washington Post*: A1.

13 Tulio Larrínaga, "Appeal for Porto Rico," 7 August 1905, *Washington Post*: 5; the editorial that Larrínaga responded to is "Home Rule in Porto Rico," 1 August 1905, *Washington Post*: 6. For another rebuttal of a *Washington Post* editorial that casts Puerto Rico in a negative light, see Tulio Larrínaga, "The Porto Rican Election," 13 March 1906, *Washington Post*: A1.

14 *Congressional Record*, House, 60th Cong., 2nd sess. (26 January 1909): 1451. For a detailed critique of an appropriations amendment to the Foraker Act by Larrínaga, see *Congressional Record*, House, 61st Cong., 1st sess. (24 May 1909): 2340–2346.

15 *Congressional Record*, House, 61st Cong., 2nd sess. (1 June 1910): 7240.

16 *Congressional Record*, Index, 61st Cong., 2nd sess.: 298.

17 *Congressional Record*, House, 59th Cong., 1st sess. (16 January 1906): 1168; "Porto Rico Wants Change," 16 January 1906, *Washington Post*: 5; "Porto Rico's Governor Tells Island's Needs," 5 December 1906, *New York Times*: 7; *Congressional Record*, Index, 59th Cong., 1st sess.: 530.

18 "Want Native as Secretary," 9 March 1907, *The Sun* (Baltimore, MD): 11; Senate Committee on Pacific Islands and Porto Rico, *Annual Report of the Governor of Porto Rico for the Fiscal Year Ending June 30, 1907*, 60th Cong., 1st sess., 1907, S. Doc. 92: 7. Incoming governor Regis H. Post discussed the appointment of a Puerto Rican secretary with Roosevelt. Post opposed the appointment because of his perception that Puerto Rico could not govern itself, so Roosevelt appointed William F. Willoughby to the position on April 18, 1907. See also "Gov. Post Sees President," 31 March 1907, *New York Times*: 5.

19 "President's Pledge to Porto Ricans," 22 November 1906, *New York Times*, 2; "Presidente en Ponce," 21 November 1906, *La correspondencia*: 1; Theodore Roosevelt, "Sixth Annual Message," 3 December 1906, in John T. Woolley and Gerhard Peters, *The American Presidency Project*, http://www.presidency.ucsb.edu/ws?pid=29547 (accessed 22 February 2011).

20 "Porto Rico's Governor Tells Island's Needs," 5 December 1906, *New York Times*: 7; Theodore Roosevelt, "Special Message," 11 December 1906, in Woolley and Peters, *The American Presidency Project* http://www.presidency.ucsb.edu/ws?pid=69671 (accessed 22 February 2011).

21 *Congressional Record*, House, 59th Cong., 2nd sess. (7 December 1906): 172–173; "Citizenship for Porto Rico," 7 December 1906, *Washington Post*: 4.

22 *Congressional Record*, House, 60th Cong., 1st sess. (9 May 1908): 6027–6028.

23 Gilberto N. Villahermosa, *Honor and Fidelity: The 65th Infantry in Korea, 1950–1953* (Washington, D.C.: Center of Military History, U.S. Army, 2009): 1–4; *Congressional Record*, House, 60th Cong., 1st sess. (8 May 1908): 5955–5962; *Congressional Record*, House, 60th Cong., 1st sess. (23 May 1908): 6841, 6868; *Congressional Record*, House, 60th Cong., 1st sess. (25 May 1908): 6905; *Congressional Record*, Index, 60th Cong., 1st sess.: 701; An Act Fixing the Status of the Porto Rico Provisional Regiment of Infantry, P.L. 60-142, 35 Stat. 392.

24 César J. Ayala and Rafael Bernabe, *Puerto Rico in the American Century* (Chapel Hill: University of North Carolina Press, 2007): 33–38, 45–47.

25 Letter from Tulio Larrínaga to Theodore Roosevelt, 7 May 1907, Numerical and Minor Files of the Department of State, 1906–1910 (National Archives Microfilm Publication M862, Roll 478), National Archives at College Park, MD (NACP).

26 Letter from Tulio Larrínaga to Elihu Root, 7 June 1907, Numerical and Minor Files of the Department of State, 1906–1910, NACP.

27 Letter from Elihu Root to Tulio Larrínaga, 28 January 1908, Numerical and Minor Files of the Department of State, 1906–1910, NACP; "Additional Commercial Agreement, Signed at Washington, January 28, 1908," in U.S. Department of State, *Papers Relating to the Foreign Relations of the United States with the Annual Message of the President Transmitted to Congress December 8, 1908* (Buffalo, NY: William S. Hein & Co., Inc., 2008; reprint of 1912 edition): 329.

28 "Tulio Larrinaga," in Tovar, ed., *100 Biografías de puertorriqueños ilustres*: 195–197; Williams, "Larrinaga, Tulio," *DAB*. For an overview of the conference, see A. Curtis Wilgus, "The Third International American Conference at Rio de Janeiro, 1906," *Hispanic American Historical Review* 12, no. 4 (November 1932): 420–456.

29 Letter from Tulio Larrínaga to James R. Garfield, 8 March 1908, Territories: Porto Rico: Improvement of San Juan Harbor, File 9-8-31, Classified Files, 1907–1951, Office of Territories, Record Group

126, NACP. Larrínaga also dissuaded the Secretary from seeking to change the work plans because "obtaining authorization for change in the program already laid out … would, therefore, imply new legislation by Congress; and even admitting that the Administration would favor such legislation … such a course of procedure would probably take more time than is necessary for the completion of the first part of the work."

30 "Tulio Larrinaga Dead," 30 April 1917, *The Times* (San Juan): 1; For Spanish-language obituaries, see "Tulio Larrinaga," 30 April 1917, *El tiempo*: 1; "Entierro de Sr. Larrínaga," 30 April 1917, *La correspondencia*: 1; "Don Tulio Larrínaga," 30 April 1917, *La correspondencia*: 1. There is some disagreement about when Larrínaga served on the executive council and for how long, but all these articles indicate that he served on the executive council at some point after his congressional service. Larrínaga's *Biographical Directory* entry indicates that he served only in 1911; the *DAB* says, "President Wilson appointed him a member of the Executive Council," but does not mention the year. The first edition of *Hispanic Americans in Congress* indicates that Larrínaga served from 1913 to 1917. See Williams, "Larrínaga, Tulio" *DAB*; "Tulio Larrinaga" in Carmen E. Enciso and Tracy North, eds., *Hispanic Americans in Congress, 1822–1995* (Washington, D.C.: Government Printing Office, 1995): 67–68; *Biographical Directory of the United States Congress,* "Tulio Larrínaga," http://bioguide.congress.gov.

Luis Muñoz Rivera
1859–1916

RESIDENT COMMISSIONER 1911–1916
UNIONIST FROM PUERTO RICO

The leading voice for Puerto Rican autonomy in the late 19th century and the early 20th century, Luis Muñoz Rivera struggled against the waning Spanish empire and incipient U.S. colonialism to carve out a measure of autonomy for his island nation. Though a devoted and eloquent nationalist, Muñoz Rivera had acquired a sense of political pragmatism, and his realistic appraisal of Puerto Rico's slim chances for complete sovereignty in his lifetime led him to focus on securing a system of home rule within the framework of the American empire. To that end, he sought as the island's Resident Commissioner to shape the provisions of the Second Jones Act, which established a system of territorial rule in Puerto Rico for much of the first half of the 20th century. Though displeased with its obvious deficiencies, he ultimately supported the act as a stepping stone to autonomy. "Give us now the field of experiment which we ask of you," he told the House during floor debate on the Jones Act, "that we may show that it is easy for us to constitute a stable republican government with all possible guarantees for all possible interests."[1]

Luis Muñoz Rivera was born on July 17, 1859, in Barranquitas, a rural town in central Puerto Rico, roughly halfway between San Juan and Ponce. He was the eldest son of Luis Ramón Muñoz Barrios and Monserrate Rivera Vásquez. His mother died when he was 12, and he was responsible for helping to raise and tutor his nine brothers.[2] His father was a landowner and merchant and eventually became mayor of Barranquitas. Muñoz Rivera's family was politically active during the 1860s and 1870s as the debate over Spanish colonial rule intensified and two primary political factions emerged in Puerto Rico. His father was a leading member of the Conservative Party, which supported rule by governors appointed by Spain, while an uncle was a Liberal Party loyalist and a proponent of home rule. Muñoz Rivera attended the local common (public) school between ages 6 and 10, and then his parents hired a private tutor to instruct him. According to several accounts, Muñoz Rivera was largely self-taught and read the classics in Spanish and French. As a young man, he wrote poetry about his nationalist ideals, eventually becoming a leading literary figure on the island and publishing two collections of verse: *Retamas* (1891) and *Tropicales* (1902). To make a living, Muñoz Rivera initially turned to cigar manufacturing and opened a general mercantile store with a boyhood friend. His father had taught him accounting, and he became, according to one biographer, a "moderately successful businessman."[3]

Muñoz Rivera married Amalia Marín Castillo in 1893.[4] A stage actress, Amalia was the daughter of Ramón Marín y Solá, a playwright and journalist, and an oft-persecuted advocate for Puerto Rican autonomy. She was "tough-minded, opinionated, demanding" and devoted to their child, Luis Muñoz Marín. With Muñoz Rivera immersed in island politics, the marriage was not a happy one, and the couple eventually separated.[5] Muñoz Marín became a transitional political figure in his own right, serving as the island's first popularly elected governor and helping to found the Commonwealth of Puerto Rico.

Muñoz Rivera's long career in public service began in the 1880s, merging familial political instinct with his penchant for writing and speaking. In 1883 he joined the Liberal Party in Barranquitas, and by at least one account he won his first political office, a seat on the town council, as a Liberal candidate.[6] In 1885, again running as a Liberal, he lost a bid for a seat in the provincial assembly. He attracted the attention of Román Baldorioty de Castro, the "elder statesman" of the Liberal Party, who embraced him as a protégé.[7] In March 1887, Muñoz Rivera cofounded the Partido Autonomista (Autonomist Party), which

Image courtesy of the Puerto Rican Cultural Institute

sought to create an autonomist Puerto Rican government under the Spanish colonial system. In 1887 the Spanish governor of Puerto Rico, Romualdo Palacio y González, instituted a political crackdown against Autonomists, called *los compontes*. Many, including Muñoz Rivera's future father-in-law, were jailed before Palacio was replaced by a more moderate governor. Several years later, Muñoz Rivera himself was jailed briefly.[8] It was the first of many occasions on which he was harassed, formally charged, or detained for agitating against the government. After Baldorioty de Castro died in 1889, Muñoz Rivera assumed leadership of the Autonomist Party. He won a seat in the provincial assembly representing a district that encompassed Caguas, but his election was challenged, and his term expired before he could claim the seat.[9]

Throughout his career, Muñoz Rivera used his writing skills to advance his political agenda. In July 1890, he founded the daily newspaper *La democracia* in Ponce, using his father-in-law's printing press.[10] The newspaper pointed out the injustices of the colonial regime overseen by the governor while lobbying major political factions in Madrid to support Autonomist policy goals. *La democracia* was the first of several newspapers founded by Muñoz Rivera as political mouthpieces.

As the leader of the Autonomist Party, Muñoz Rivera steered a middle course. He spurned the entreaties of pro-Spanish factions and also rejected efforts by the *separatista* movement, which sought a complete break with Spanish and, later, American imperial rule. He believed that the best option for Puerto Rico was to ally itself with metropolitan political parties; without financial resources or activism among youth and the peasantry, the possibility of a revolution for complete independence appeared remote. This middle-of-the-road position permitted Muñoz Rivera a moderate stance for dealing with Spanish officials: He could criticize the violence of the Cuban insurrectionists while rejecting the Spanish misrule that incited it.[11] Throughout his decades of advocating for Puerto Rican autonomy, Muñoz Rivera continued to reject armed revolt, revealing his pragmatic way of thinking. Mob violence would provide ready ammunition for critics who argued that Puerto Ricans were "unprepared" for self-rule. Moreover, such resistance had no prospect of success. "A revolution in an island 100 miles long by 30 miles wide, crossed everywhere by roads and dominated by forces immensely superior would be nonsensical and useless," Muñoz Rivera explained in a letter to the *Washington Post*.[12] His middle-of-the-road stance also derived from countervailing cultural currents, for while he championed Puerto Rican autonomy, he displayed a lifelong affinity for Spain, which he regarded as the Mother country. Late in his career, Muñoz Rivera said Puerto Ricans "had a hundred causes of affection toward Spain. She gave us her blood, her laws, her language, and the pride of her legendary traditions and of her remarkable progress."[13]

In 1895, Muñoz Rivera and other Autonomist commissioners traveled to Madrid and persuaded Spanish Liberal Party leader Praxedes M. Sagasta to sign a pact promising that Puerto Rico would be granted home rule if he came to power. In return, the Autonomist Party was eventually dissolved, and the new Puerto Rican Liberal Party, which Muñoz Rivera helped found in 1897—and for which he established the newspaper *El liberal* in San Juan—endorsed that agreement. In November 1897, after coming to power, Sagasta hurriedly granted the Autonomist Charter, without approval by the Spanish parliament (the Cortes), to quell revolutionary ardor in the islands and to forestall U.S. intervention.

As the island's foremost diplomat, Muñoz Rivera was appointed secretary of grace, justice and government when the home-rule cabinet was formed in February 1898.[14] Later that spring he was elected head of a new executive council formed in July 1898. But Puerto Rico's hard-won political status was short-lived. Days after the new government was formed, the USS *Maine* exploded at anchor and sank in Havana Harbor. By late April, Spain and the United States were at war. On July 25, just a week after Muñoz Rivera's newly elected government had convened for business, U.S. Army troops landed at Guánica, on the southwestern side of the island. By mid-August, the island was under U.S. military rule. Muñoz Rivera's governing cabinet sought to resign en masse, but the initial military governor refused to accept the resignation when the formal transfer of sovereignty was concluded in October 1898. When a new commanding general, Guy V. Henry, assumed command and tried to curtail the cabinet's powers, Muñoz Rivera abruptly resigned.

For a long period Muñoz Rivera was engaged as a diplomat for Puerto Rican autonomy, playing much the same role he had under imperial Spain. In 1899 at the behest of sugar cane plantation owners, he lobbied officials in Washington to reduce trade barriers between the island and the mainland United States, particularly for agricultural products. He founded the newspaper *El territorio*, which voiced the concerns of Puerto Rican landowners. A year later, he organized the Federal Party, establishing the newspaper *El diario de Puerto Rico* as its voice. Muñoz Rivera and his followers, known as Muñocistas, were labeled anti-American, and Partido Republicano mobs, supporting statehood under the United States, ransacked his print shop and attacked his home. To protect his family, Muñoz Rivera moved to the town of Caguas, 15 miles south of San Juan.

Rebuffed by political opponents and colonial administrators, Muñoz Rivera relocated to New York City to assess America's political attitudes toward its new colonial venture in the Caribbean. In April 1901, the family took up residence in an apartment along Fifth Avenue, blocks from the modern-day Flatiron District. There Muñoz Rivera founded the bilingual *Puerto Rican Herald* newspaper to initiate a dialogue on Puerto Rican autonomy and to launch a public relations effort to topple the Foraker Act (31 Stat. 77–86), which had imposed American rule in Puerto Rico. In the *Herald's* first issue was an open letter to President William McKinley in which Muñoz Rivera lambasted the Foraker Act as a disgrace to the United States and Puerto Rico, writing that it possessed "not the slightest shade of democratic thinking."[15]

In 1904 Muñoz Rivera returned from New York City to reconstitute a political movement after the dissolution of the Federal Party. With José de Diego, he cofounded the Unionist Party which, as he wrote in the *Puerto Rican Herald*, sought to secure "the right of Puerto Rico to assert its own personality, either through statehood or independence. If the United States continues to humiliate and shame us," wrote Muñoz Rivera, "we can forget about statehood and support independence, with or without U.S. protection."[16] The Unionist platform was more elastic than that of the Republican Party, which sought statehood. Muñoz Rivera won a seat with the Partido de Unión in the Puerto Rican house of delegates in 1906 and was re-elected twice, serving until 1910. He chaired the ways and means committee and advocated tirelessly for self-rule.

In 1910 the Puerto Rican voters elected Muñoz Rivera to serve a two-year term as Resident Commissioner in the U.S. House of Representatives. On the strength of a Unionist surge (carrying 51 of 66 municipalities), he defeated his Partido Republicano opponent with 55 percent of the popular vote in the November 6, 1910, general election.[17] Muñoz Rivera was re-elected in 1912 and 1914 by comfortable margins as the Partido de Unión ticket prevailed, with 61 percent and 53 percent of the vote, respectively.[18]

In the era when Muñoz Rivera served in the House, Resident Commissioners and Territorial Delegates could hold committee assignments and introduce legislation, but they could not vote on final measures on the House Floor. Furthermore, as a third-party candidate, Muñoz Rivera had neither the support that was conferred by a membership in the Democratic Caucus nor the Republican Conference. Like his predecessors Tulio Larrínaga and Federico Degetau, Muñoz Rivera received a seat on the Insular Affairs Committee. Since that committee had jurisdiction over laws affecting the United States' overseas possessions and territories, it was a natural fit for the Resident Commissioner. This panel drafted the penultimate piece of legislation establishing Puerto Rico's political status. It was Muñoz Rivera's only committee assignment during his three terms in the House, and because he did not caucus with the Republicans or the Democrats, he never advanced in seniority.[19]

World War I spurred fears of German naval incursions into the Caribbean Basin. Anticipating such concerns, Resident Commissioner Muñoz Rivera supported a bill to strengthen a U.S. Army regiment on the island by increasing it from approximately 560 to 1,900 men, many of them native Puerto Ricans. It was, he argued, sounding like naval strategist Alfred Mahan, necessary for the protection of such a "strategic … advanced base." Muñoz Rivera sought to allay fears that such a force might serve as a training ground for revolutionaries. He noted, "These Latin soldiers … will emulate the tranquil valor, the bold intrepidity of the Anglo-Saxon soldiers of this hemisphere. Rest assured that they will defend, with no care for the sacrifice of their own lives, the rights and the flag of this Nation, for they well know your splendid history, for they realize in maintaining the supremacy of your national character and influence they maintain the principles of modern freedom and civilization." The Resident Commissioner believed such service was an opportunity to demonstrate Puerto Ricans' character and their worthiness for self-rule. It would prove, Muñoz Rivera waxed, "that there is in the forests of Porto Rico good timber out of which to make heroes … they will be heroes following and defending the Star-Spangled Banner."[20] Though the Caribbean did not play host to any significant naval battles during the First World War, the region "stood quietly as the keystone of American national security," foreshadowing its strategic commercial importance in World War II.[21] Puerto Rico's readiness also demonstrated its loyalty to the United States, drawing the attention of President Woodrow Wilson's administration and serving as an impetus for the passage of the Jones Act in 1917.[22]

Geostrategic concerns created a window of opportunity for serious discussion of autonomy for Puerto Rico. Capitalizing on this opening, Muñoz Rivera introduced a bill in early 1914 to establish a civil government in Puerto Rico that increased the prospect for home rule and circumscribed the power of the presidentially appointed governor. It differed markedly from legislation authored by Insular Affairs Committee Chairman William A. Jones of Virginia. In February 1914 Muñoz Rivera testified about the Jones Bill before the Senate committee with jurisdiction over the United States' insular possessions. The bill in its present form, Muñoz Rivera noted, "cannot fill the necessities of the Porto Rican people, nor represent what my country expects from a Democratic Congress" which "in its national platforms of 1900, 1904, and 1908, declared that no nation has the right to govern a people against its will. But with my country, a greater injustice is being perpetrated by denying its right to home rule, which, from the very first day of American sovereignty, it insistently claimed."[23]

In light of the dissension in Puerto Rico regarding the issue of home rule versus statehood or complete independence, Muñoz Rivera asked his congressional colleagues to strip from the legislation provisions that would extend American citizenship to Puerto Ricans. Testifying before Chairman Jones and the House Insular Affairs Committee in March 1914, Muñoz Rivera explained that the purpose of his bill was not to protest perceived deficiencies in the chairman's bill, but to express Puerto Ricans' desire for independence. He intimated that while the Unionist Party had stripped Puerto Rican statehood from its platform in November 1913, he still believed that outcome was desirable. However, he emphasized that the Puerto Rican people would overwhelmingly reject any bill that would "make us citizens of an inferior class," adding, "If we can not be one of your States; if we can not constitute a country of our own, then we will have to be perpetually a colony, a dependency of the United States. Is that the kind of citizenship you offer us? Then that is the citizenship we refuse."[24] Among other amendments Muñoz Rivera requested were the qualification of the presidentially appointed governor's veto power (allowing the legislature to override a veto by a two-thirds majority). He also proposed that the territory be divided into political units by a board composed of the chief justice of the Puerto Rican supreme court and two additional members appointed by the island's political parties instead of by the territorial cabinet. He insisted that public funds be deposited in Puerto Rican banks rather than in financial institutions in New York and other U.S. cities. He also proposed the creation of a public service commission composed of cabinet members, an auditor, the president of the territorial senate, and the speaker of the territorial house.[25] Some of his suggestions—such as a proposal to extend the Resident Commissioner's term of service from two to four years—were incorporated into the act, but others were watered down as they moved through both chambers, and still others were simply ignored.[26] Perhaps most significantly, Chairman Jones, expressing the committee's widely shared concerns about Puerto Rico's political stability, opposed any bill that did not extend U.S. citizenship. "To postpone the settlement of this question means, in my judgment, that it will become a very live and most disturbing political issue in Porto Rico," Jones remarked during the hearing.[27]

Muñoz Rivera believed the Second Jones Act to be little more than a half measure, though he accepted it as a step toward eventual autonomy. On May 5, 1916, Chairman Jones yielded the floor to Muñoz Rivera during debate on the bill, marking the legislative and oratorical pinnacle of the Resident Commissioner's congressional career. In the longest and most passionate speech he made in the House, Muñoz Rivera declared that while Puerto Ricans would have welcomed U.S. citizenship in 1898 had statehood then been offered, they no longer hoped for or desired such an outcome. He thanked Chairman Jones and the Ranking Republican, Representative Towner, for having "endeavored to make this bill … a democratic measure, acceptable to all of my countrymen." Describing the creation of a full elective legislature as "a splendid concession" to American principles and Puerto Rican rights, he attacked the abeyance of local powers imposed by an appointed council. But in the end, he supported the Jones Act despite its imperfections: "This bill can not meet the earnest aspirations of my country. It is not a measure of self-government ample enough to solve definitely our political problem.… But, meager and conservative as the bill appears … we sincerely recognize its noble purposes and willingly accept it as a step in the right direction and as a reform paving the way for other more acceptable and satisfactory which shall come a little later, provided that my countrymen will be able to demonstrate their capacity, the capacity they possess, to govern themselves."[28] The Jones Act passed the House several weeks later on a voice vote.[29]

Afterward, Muñoz Rivera returned to Puerto Rico, his health weakened by the burden of his political responsibilities. With the extension of the Resident Commissioner's term of service from two to four years, pending ultimate passage of the legislation, there were no elections in Puerto Rico in the fall of 1916. But even without the difficulties of campaigning, Muñoz Rivera declined rapidly. He died of an infection from a ruptured gall bladder on November 15, 1916, in Santurce, a suburb of San Juan. Puerto Ricans were plunged into mourning. The revered political leader's body lay in state in San Juan. His funeral procession weaved 150 miles across the island from the capital to Ponce and then back to Barranquitas for burial. More than 1,000 automobiles followed the hearse bearing Muñoz Rivera's body. "Never before has Porto Rico paid a like tribute to any man," reported the Associated Press. "As the funeral procession passed through various cities and towns thousands of people bared their heads and placed wreaths and flowers either on the hearse or in the road over which it passed.… Everywhere the demonstrations of grief and affection were such that the burial was delayed for more than a day."[30] Girls in white dresses with black sashes threw flowers at the head of the casket, while musicians followed playing the national anthem, "La Borinqueña," as the casket was carried into the local church.[31] Muñoz Rivera was interred in Barranquitas in a mausoleum in San Antonio de Padua Cemetery, appropriately named for a Catholic saint who was revered for his inspiring, eloquent oratory.

FOR FURTHER READING

Biographical Directory of the United States Congress, "Luis Muñoz Rivera," http://bioguide.congress.gov.

Monclava, Lidio Cruz. *Luis Muñoz Rivera: Los primeros 10 años de su vida politica* (San Juan, PR: Instituto de Cultura Puertorriqueña, 1959).

Reynolds, Mack. *Puerto Rican Patriot: The Life of Luis Muñoz Rivera* (New York: Crowell-Collier Press, 1969).

Rivera, Jose A. *The Political Thought of Luis Muñoz Marin* (Princeton, NJ: Xlibris Corporation, 2002).

Sterling, Philip, and Maria Brau. *The Quiet Rebels; Four Puerto Rican Leaders: José Celso Barbosa, Luis Muñoz Rivera, José de Diego, Luis Muñoz Marín* (Garden City, NY: Doubleday, 1968).

NOTES

1 *Congressional Record*, House, 64th Cong., 1st sess. (5 May 1916): 7473.

2 This is according to a juvenile biography by Mack Reynolds, *Puerto Rican Patriot: The Life of Luis Muñoz Rivera* (London: Crowell-Collier Press, 1969): 45–46.

3 See *Congressional Directory*, 62nd Cong., 1st sess. (1911): 119; Errol D. Jones, "Muñoz Rivera, Luis," *American National Biography* 16 (New York: Oxford University Press, 1999): 101 (hereinafter referred to as *ANB*).

4 Jones, "Muñoz Rivera, Luis," *ANB*: 101.

5 A. W. Maldonado, *Luis Muñoz Marín: Puerto Rico's Democratic Revolution* (San Juan, PR: La Editorial Universidad de Puerto Rico, 2006): 27–28.

6 Jones, "Muñoz Rivera, Luis," *ANB*: 101. Other biographies note that this was the year he joined the town's Partido Liberal branch, but do not mention his election.

7 Philip Sterling and Maria Brau, *The Quiet Rebels: Four Puerto Rican Leaders: José Celso Barbosa, Luis Muñoz Rivera, José de Diego, Luis Muñoz Marín* (Garden City, NY: Zenith Books/Doubleday, 1968): 40–41. The "elder statesman" quotation is in Sterling and Brau, *The Quiet Rebels*: 41.

8 Maldonado, *Luis Muñoz Marín*: 18.

9 Following some of the few sources in English that provide summaries of Muñoz Rivera's early career: Sterling and Brau, *The Quiet Rebels*: 35–61; Mack Reynolds, *Puerto Rican Patriot: The Life of Luis Muñoz Rivera* (London: Collier-Macmillan Limited, 1969). A recapitulation of Muñoz Rivera's 1889 run for the provincial assembly is on p. 42.

10 Maldonado, *Luis Muñoz Marín*: 17–18.

11 César J. Ayala and Rafael Bernabe, *Puerto Rico in the American Century: A History since 1898* (Chapel Hill: University of North Carolina Press, 2007): 23–24.

12 "Defends Porto Rico," 25 July 1911, *Washington Post*: 3.

13 Hon. Luis Muñoz Rivera, "Are the Porto Rican People Prepared for Self-Government," extract from remarks of Hon. Tulio Larrínaga in the House of Representatives, 8 May 1908 (Washington, D.C.: Government Printing Office, 1908): 6. For an appreciation of Muñoz Rivera as a pragmatist who sought to reconcile sometimes-contradictory beliefs, see Maldonado, *Luis Muñoz Marín*: 19.

14 This position is described as being the most important one in that first cabinet. One source notes that the word "grace" was used to denote that mercy and justice were applied equally. One of Muñoz Rivera's roles as secretary was to issue pardons and paroles. See Sterling and Brau, *The Quiet Rebels*: 47–48.

15 Maldonado, *Luis Muñoz Marín*: 28.

16 Jones, "Muñoz Rivera, Luis," *ANB*: 101.

17 *Congressional Directory*, 63rd Congress (Washington, D.C.: Government Printing Office, 1914): 128. Figures are approximate. Election results in other published sources vary. For instance, Fernando Bayron Toro suggests that the Union Party captured 63 percent of the vote. See *Elecciones y partidos políticos de Puerto Rico, 1809–2000* (Mayagüez, PR: Editorial Isla, 2003): 136.

18 Bayron Toro, *Elecciones y partidos políticos de Puerto Rico, 1809–2000*: 140, 144.

19 Standard sources, such as the *Congressional Directory*, do not list any committee assignments for Muñoz Rivera in the 63rd Congress (1913–1915), though this omission may be an error.

20 *Congressional Record*, Extension of Remarks, Appendix, House, 54th Cong., 2nd sess. (21 March 1916): 600.

21 Donald Yerxa, "The United States Navy in Caribbean Waters during World War I," *Military Affairs* 51 (October 1987): 186. See also Donald Yerxa, *Admirals and Empire: The United States Navy and the Caribbean, 1898–1945* (Columbia: University of South Carolina Press, 1991): 35–76.

22 Luis Martínez Fernández, "Political Culture in the Hispanic Caribbean and the Building of US Hegemony, 1868–1945," *Revista Mexicana del Caribe* 11 (2002): 7–55.

23 Hearings before the Senate Committee on Pacific Islands and Porto Rico, United States, *A Civil Government for Porto Rico*, 63rd Cong., 2nd sess. (25 February 1914): 6–9.

24 Hearings before the Senate Committee on Pacific Islands and Porto Rico, *A Civil Government for Porto Rico*, 63rd Cong., 2nd sess. (2 March 1914): 54; quotation from p. 57. Muñoz Rivera represented this position faithfully, though he seemed not to share the concern of many in his party that conferring citizenship on Puerto Ricans would undercut the island's eventual autonomy. "It seems to me that by granting to the Porto Ricans American citizenship the Congress of the United States will not deprive itself of the right to later grant to Porto Rico full independence," Muñoz Rivera responded to Horace Mann Towner of Iowa. "It seems to me that [the] Congress of the United States is supreme under all circumstances." "A great number of my constituents do not coincide with my own opinions," he added. "I am here to represent the Porto Rican people; I am not here to represent my own personal ideas."

25 Ibid., 54–56.

26 For instance, the final bill vested the insular legislature with the power to override the governor's veto, but it made potential overrides subject to review and ultimately to a possible veto by the U.S. President.

27 Ibid., 58. In 1916 committee hearings, Muñoz Rivera continued to press for the postponement of Puerto Rican citizenship. At a critical juncture in U.S. wartime relations with other Latin American and Caribbean nations, he noted, "From the standpoint of American national interest, this question of citizenship should be left undecided for the present, in order to prevent a possible embarrassment." See Hearings before the House Committee on Insular Affairs, *A Civil Government for Porto Rico*, 63rd Cong., 2nd sess. (13, 15 January 1916): 10–11.

28 *Congressional Record*, House, 64th Cong., 1st sess. (5 May 1916): 7471.

29 Ibid., 7471–7473; *Congressional Record*, House, 64th Cong., 1st sess. (23 May 1916): 8510–8511.

30 "His Corpse Was Borne 150 Miles over Roads Strewn with Flowers," 28 November 1916, *Atlanta Constitution*: 1.

31 Maldonado, *Luis Muñoz Marín*: 38.

Ladislas Lazaro
1872–1927

UNITED STATES REPRESENTATIVE 1913–1927
DEMOCRAT FROM LOUISIANA

Representative Ladislas Lazaro, a country doctor from southwest Louisiana, was the second Hispanic American to serve in Congress with full voting rights. Propelled into national office in 1912 as a supporter of Democrat Woodrow Wilson's Progressive platform, Lazaro tended to the agricultural interests of his Louisiana district in the bayou country dotted with rice, cotton, and sugar cane plantations. He focused largely on protective tariffs and on improving farmers' access to markets through waterway and railway projects—an issue of primary importance to planters and businessmen who sought to deliver commodities to ports like New Orleans and Lake Charles. Addressed affectionately by colleagues and constituents alike as "Doctor" or "Doc," Lazaro was esteemed for his patient, dispassionate counsel. He was the second Hispanic American ever to chair a standing committee and, by the early 1920s, the longest-serving Hispanic Member to that point.[1]

Ladislas Lazaro was born on June 5, 1872, on the Lazaro plantation near Ville Platte, Louisiana, in St. Landry Parish, part of which is now Evangeline Parish.[2] Lazaro was the child of Marie Denise Ortego, a daughter of one of Ville Platte's founding Hispanic families, and Alexandre Lazaro, an émigré from the town of Risan, in what is now Montenegro in the Balkans.[3] The family lived on a plantation, which Lazaro's father farmed. When Ladislas was 12 years old, his father died; his mother then moved the family into Ville Platte. Ladislas Lazaro's lifelong friend René Louis De Rouen observed that Lazaro had a middle-class upbringing and was surrounded by local boys from similar stations in life, "neither very rich nor poor," knowing of "no hunger that he was not sure of satisfying and of no luxury which enervates the mind or body."[4] Lazaro attended local public and private schools in St. Landry Parish. He attended St. Isadore's College (a preparatory school now named Holy Cross High School) in New Orleans. In 1894 Lazaro graduated from the Louisville Medical College in Kentucky and began practicing as a family physician in Washington, Louisiana, a hamlet 15 miles southeast of Ville Platte. Lazaro married the former Mary (Mamie) Curley of Lake Charles, Louisiana, on December 21, 1895.[5] They raised three daughters—Elaine, Mary, and Eloise—and a son, Ladislas, Jr. Lazaro's medical practice thrived at the turn of the century, and he eventually was chosen by his colleagues to serve as first vice president of the state medical society in 1907.

Education issues in St. Landry Parish kindled Lazaro's interest in politics when his children became old enough to attend the local schools. In 1904 he was appointed to the parish school board; two years later he became board president. He pushed for agricultural high schools, establishing the first in St. Landry Parish. In July 1907 he declared his candidacy for a state senate seat that encompassed his home parish, along with neighboring Evangeline and Acadia Parishes. His platform centered largely on cleaning up the state government's employment and spending practices, although it also focused on improving funding for health and education. In addition, Lazaro advocated for agricultural interests, calling particularly for the increased study of scientific farming practices. "The future of this country is largely agricultural, and no effort should be spared to place it in position to compete successfully with scientifically trained rivals," he said. Lazaro's politics derived from a common Progressive impulse, a faith that rationality and scientific methodology would improve society by fostering a better-educated citizenry and a renewed commitment to public service.[6] Lazaro ran unopposed and won re-election, again without opposition, in 1912. In Baton Rouge, he

Image courtesy of the Library of Congress

served as chairman of the committee on charitable and public institutions and also as a member of the education committee. His principal legislative accomplishments were securing more funds for charity hospitals and helping to pass the first state appropriation for agricultural high schools.[7]

In 1912 Representative Arsène Pujo, a Lake Charles lawyer who served five terms in the House and rose to chair the Banking and Currency Committee when Democrats gained control of the chamber in 1911, abruptly announced that he would not seek re-election to a sixth term.[8] The district he represented, then Louisiana's 7th Congressional District, encompassed eight parishes in southwestern Louisiana, stretching eastward from the Texas border to the southern center of the state—including Opelousas and Lake Charles (the latter had roughly 11,500 inhabitants according to the 1920 Census)—and terminating 50 miles west of the state capital of Baton Rouge. It was the least-populated congressional district in the state, with just over 165,000 inhabitants, and it overlapped the parishes that composed Lazaro's state senate district. Primarily rural, the district had an economy that was mainly agricultural; its chief crops were rice and cotton.

In July 1912 Lazaro declared his candidacy in an address in Ville Platte. His opposition in the primary included Phillip J. Chappius, a lawyer from Acadia Parish and a former mayor of Crowley, Louisiana; and John W. Lewis of Opelousas, a longtime political opponent who attacked Lazaro's state senate record as failing his rural constituency. Lazaro attached himself to the Democratic platform adopted at the national convention in Baltimore, Maryland, where Woodrow Wilson was nominated as the party's presidential candidate. His campaign was a Progressive laundry list borrowed largely from the national party's planks.[9]

But as often occurred in Louisiana's factionalized politics in the early 20th century, the campaign revolved largely around the personalities of the candidates and the byzantine network of political loyalties that undergirded them.[10] In the one-party South, Democratic primaries often placed this personality-cult spectacle on full display. During the campaign, an anonymous circular purported by the press (but denied by Lewis's campaign) to have been distributed by Lewis's supporters, intimated that Lazaro's Catholicism disqualified him from holding office.[11] More substantively, Lewis attacked Lazaro's fidelity to the legislative program of then-Louisiana Governor Luther Hall. Lazaro refuted Lewis's attacks across the district, addressing gatherings in English and French. Chappius, whose campaign seemed to focus more on Lewis than on Lazaro, ran well ahead in his home parish of Acadia, while Lazaro carried Evangeline and Calcasieu Parishes, the latter encompassing Lake Charles. Lewis defeated Lazaro in Cameron and St. Landry Parishes, but by relatively narrow margins. Lazaro won in the three-way contest with 3,422 votes, or roughly 38 percent of the vote; Lewis trailed with 32 percent; and Chappius finished third with 30 percent.[12] In the general election, Lazaro easily beat Socialist candidate Otis Putnam, winning 87 percent of the vote. With this victory, Lazaro became the first Hispanic American to represent Louisiana in Congress and, eventually, the longest-serving Hispanic Representative until the generation of Members elected during the 1960s.[13]

When he took his seat in the 63rd Congress (1913–1915), Lazaro was assigned to three committees: Merchant Marine and Fisheries; Enrolled Bills; and Coinage, Weights, and Measures, assignments he would keep for the rest of his career. In 1915 he assumed the chairmanship of the Enrolled Bills Committee, a lower-tier panel whose handful of members oversaw the preparation of the bills awaiting the President's signature.[14] By his final term in the House, after Republicans had gained control of the chamber, Lazaro was the Ranking Minority Member on the Merchant Marine and Fisheries Committee. The assignment to the Merchant Marine and Fisheries Committee, an upper-tier panel in terms of its attractiveness to Members during the bulk of Lazaro's service, proved an important one for the Louisianan.[15] It provided him a prime platform for tending to the transportation issues that were central to the agricultural business in his district and for promoting federal funding for Louisiana's myriad waterways projects.[16]

The district remained unchanged during Lazaro's tenure, partly because Congress failed to reapportion House seats after the 1920 Census.[17] Lazaro faced opposition in the general election only twice in his subsequent seven re-election campaigns: In 1914 and 1916 he defeated a Republican candidate and a Socialist candidate with 86 percent and 95 percent of the vote, respectively.[18] His only significant electoral challenge occurred in the 1916 primary, when many in his district were infuriated by his support of Democratic gubernatorial candidate Rufus Pleasant over Progressive John Parker. Lazaro had tried to avoid publicly endorsing either camp and had even cut short a campaign trip for Pleasant that he had been urged to take by the state Democratic committee. Pleasant won, but Progressives in the district ran two candidates from Lake Charles against Lazaro in the Democratic primary on September 2: T. Arthur Edwards, a lawyer and district attorney, and Judge Alfred Barbee.[19] Edwards campaigned vigorously. Pointedly attacking Lazaro's record, he told a crowd, "It would be a pity to spoil a good fisherman and hunter [Barbee] by making a congressman of him. You voters made a poor congressman out of Lazaro, who was a good physician."[20] But such rhetorical flourishes could not diminish Lazaro's record of constituent service. He ultimately prevailed with 55 percent of the vote, carrying seven of the eight parishes in the district. Edwards finished second, with 25 percent of the vote.[21] Firmly established after the primary, Lazaro was promoted by friends and supporters for Louisiana's 1920 gubernatorial race, but he declined to enter the contest, and there is no evidence that he ever seriously considered running for any public office besides a House seat.[22] By 1923 he was the dean of the Louisiana delegation and so well placed that his biennial campaign rationale was simple: Constituents would be unwise to turn him out for a less-experienced candidate. "No one," he wrote a local newspaper editor, "whether he is running a farm, store, bank or any other business will discharge a faithful and efficient employee merely to take on a new one, and the business of Government is the same as any other business."[23]

Above all else, Lazaro was keenly sensitive to the interests of the large portion of his constituents who were farmers, partly because of a personal connection. He managed his family plantation, even while in Congress, and sought annually to bring crops to market. As he explained to Harry Kapp of the Louisiana Farm Bureau Federation, "Everything I have is invested in the farm I live on, and my only money crop is cotton. Therefore I am vitally interested in doing all I can to help the farmer."[24]

Just weeks after the opening of the 63rd Congress, freshman Lazaro boldly proclaimed his opposition to a tariff bill authored by fellow Democrat Oscar Underwood of Alabama, chairman of the House Ways and Means Committee. The Underwood–Simmons Tariff, as it became known, put sugar on the free list and slashed rates on other imported agricultural products, such as cotton, by 50 percent. The bill particularly threatened Louisiana's numerous small-scale rice growers by opening American markets to less-expensive Asian rice. In a speech inserted into the appendix of the *Congressional Record*, Lazaro based his opposition on personal beliefs and on the overwhelming wishes of his constituents—and availed himself of a rule that allowed members of the Democratic Caucus to vote independently of the party on issues where their campaign pledges diverged from the party's position. Halving the rice tariff, Lazaro warned, "would prove the ruin and disaster of this growing industry, which is the mainstay and the foundation upon which rests the business interest of my section and upon which it depends." Such a calamity, he added, would eventually affect the consumer. For when Asian rice would be "dumped upon our shores in sufficient quantities to drive out and ruin the domestic industry … the imported rice of the Orient will be controlled by trusts and combinations, and the poor American consumer will pay a higher price for this staple food."[25] When the Underwood Tariff came to the House Floor for a vote later that fall—passing by a vote of 255 to 104—Lazaro was one of only four Democrats to oppose it (two of the other dissenters were also Louisianans).[26]

When the opportunity came in 1922 to boost tariff rates to protect the rice and sugar industries, Lazaro firmly supported the Fordney–McCumber Tariff, which reset rates to levels that had been established in 1897 by the Dingley Tariff. On this matter, Lazaro and much of the Louisiana delegation were in opposition to the deeply ingrained 19th-century anti-tariff bias of most other Southern Members of Congress and were in line with "the modern agricultural and manufacturing interests of the New South," wrote one historian.[27]

Lazaro consistently monitored big farm bills that affected his agricultural constituency. In 1926 two leading members of the congressional farm bloc, House Agriculture Committee Chairman Gilbert N. Haugen of Iowa and Senate Agriculture and Forestry Committee Chairman Charles McNary of Oregon, introduced legislation to provide the first government support for the distressed farming industry by subsidizing the sale of surplus U.S. crops overseas. But the McNary–Haugen Bill presented Lazaro with a dilemma: Whereas Louisiana rice growers initially opposed the legislation, cotton growers supported an amended version. Lazaro opposed the initial McNary–Haugen measure, arguing that it favored Midwestern and Western farmers, particularly wheat producers, and put Southerners at a disadvantage. "To be frank with you," he wrote to a friend, "I cannot think of any legislation that could be more harmful to agriculture than this measure.... This whole propaganda back of the McNary–Haugen Bill comes from a radical element in the West, and they are trying to brow-beat the Administration into giving them a subsidy out of the Treasury at the expense of the taxpayers, including our Southern farmers."[28] But in 1927 Lazaro dropped his opposition to the bill when an amended version that rice growers felt would promote better price structures emerged from committee. When the House passed the measure on February 17, 1927, Lazaro was in a minority of three members from the Louisiana delegation to support it. Congress passed the McNary–Haugen Farm Relief Bill twice, in 1927 and in 1928, only to have President Calvin Coolidge veto both versions. Though McNary–Haugen failed to become law, it set the parameters about the debate over farm subsidies and supports that prevailed in the coming decades.[29]

Lazaro focused not just on trade policy and farm support, but also on transportation issues that affected farmers. Here his Merchant Marine assignment proved invaluable. The shipping shortage during the First World War that nearly devastated the Southern cotton industry convinced Lazaro of the need to augment the American Merchant Marine and national shipping infrastructure. "Transportation, like taxes, mingles with the cost of goods in every step of their making," he explained in 1917 on the eve of U.S. intervention. "For this reason conveyance from one community to another and from one country to another helps to make a people great, efficient, progressive, prosperous and powerful. This is why the broad-minded, farseeing, unselfish American citizen now begins to pause, think, and ask for legislation more and more with regard to transportation."[30] World War I proved that America must boost its shipping capacity far beyond its ability to haul only a tenth of its total commerce. Speaking on behalf of a 1919 bill to greatly expand funding for the merchant marine, Lazaro told colleagues, "It is just as foolish for a nation to depend on foreign ships to carry on its foreign business as it would be for a department store to depend on its competitors to deliver its goods to its customers."[31] With the input and approval of Lazaro's panel, and broad bipartisan backing, the Jones Merchant Marine Act passed both chambers and was signed into law in 1920. The act committed the United States "to do whatever was necessary to develop and encourage the maintenance" of a merchant marine sufficient to handle the majority of American commerce "and serve as a naval or military auxiliary in time of war or national emergency, ultimately to be owned and operated privately by the citizens of the United States." The bill repealed wartime emergency shipping legislation, restructured the U.S. Shipping Board, and directed that entity to promote more shipping routes and facilitate the expansion of the merchant marine fleet.[32]

Like many Members of the Louisiana and Texas delegations, Lazaro advocated allocating federal funds to complete the Intracoastal Waterway canal project from New Orleans to Corpus Christi. A longtime advocate for reining in railroad rates that cut into farmers' profit margins, he believed the waterway was vital to agricultural development in the region. "I represent a district that is altogether agricultural," he testified before the House Committee on Rivers and Harbors in 1926, "and one of our biggest problems today is the question of freight rates, and I do not think that we can have any relief in this country in that line until we develop and use our waterways."[33] Lazaro's seat on the Merchant Marine Committee provided him a prime perch from which to make that argument, and he was instrumental in securing a $16 million appropriation for the section of the canal linking the Mississippi River with Galveston, Texas.[34] The modern Gulf Intracoastal Waterway stretches from Brownsville, Texas, to Fort Myers, Florida, and by the end of the 20th century it was used to transport commodities worth tens of billions of dollars.[35]

Lazaro's positions on national issues were often those held by many Southern Members of Congress. His stand on two major constitutional amendments in the 65th Congress—the 18th Amendment, establishing the prohibition of alcohol, and the 19th Amendment, granting women the right to vote—was anchored in the widely shared Southern sensitivity concerning federal interference in states' rights. Both issues, he insisted, should be decided by direct ballot in individual states, not by federal statute. Believing alcohol was medicinal, Lazaro, along with two of his seven Louisiana colleagues, voted against the Prohibition Amendment that passed the House in December 1917 and became law in January 1919 after its ratification by the states.[36] He also opposed a string of proposed measures granting women the right to vote—including two votes by the House that passed the 19th Amendment by wide margins in January 1918 and May 1919—on the grounds that the states would be yielding too much power to the federal government.[37] "We have had our experience with the Federal Government interfering with suffrage once before," during Reconstruction, Lazaro explained in 1916 campaign literature, "and I do not think our people are willing to take any chances with a measure of this kind, which would reopen old sores and compel us to assume the burden of eliminating the negro woman's vote."[38]

As the Ranking Member of the Merchant Marine and Fisheries Committee, Lazaro was one of four House managers appointed to the conference committee that hammered out an important measure. Passing the House and Senate as the Radio Act of 1927, the measure represented Congress's first comprehensive attempt to regulate broadcasting. It created the Federal Radio Commission to oversee licensing and to regulate the nascent broadcasting industry "as public convenience, interest, or necessity requires." But it split the ultimate authority for controlling radio broadcasts among disparate entities: the three branches of the military, the Secretary of Commerce, and the Interstate Commerce Commission. Arguing for the measure on the House Floor, Lazaro admitted on behalf of the conferees: "While we do not claim this bill to be perfect, we feel it is the very best that could be agreed upon at this time. With the absolute chaos in the air and the demand of the public for relief, I think it is our duty to pass this measure at this time."[39] Lazaro's speech won applause, and shortly thereafter the House agreed to the conference report by voice vote. Within less than a decade, the growth of the broadcasting industry demonstrated the necessity for centralized control over the administration of the airwaves, leading to the passage of the landmark Communications Act of 1934.[40]

The 1927 Radio Bill marked Lazaro's legislative swan song. Late in the 69th Congress (1925–1927), Lazaro's health deteriorated, eventually necessitating abdominal surgery. Following an operation on March 9, 1927, Lazaro seemed to make a strong recovery, but then his condition worsened, and he died on March 30 at Garfield Hospital in Washington, D.C., of complications from an abscess. Word of his death shocked political observers and friends alike, most of whom were unaware of the severity of his illness. The *Clarion-Progress* of Opelousas mourned, "A pall of gloom overhangs St. Landry parish at the loss of its beloved statesman, citizen, and friend."[41] Condolence letters and telegrams flooded the Lazaro home in Washington, D.C. "Death intervened to end untimely a public career of genuine usefulness," observed the New Orleans *Times-Picayune*, adding, "Louisiana has no representative at the national capital more loyal than he, and both the state and his district were given many proofs of his devotion to their interests. His passing is therefore accounted a serious loss to the commonwealth and will be widely and sincerely mourned."[42] Befitting Lazaro's position as dean of the Louisiana delegation, a large congressional party escorted his body by train to Opelousas, where thousands of mourners waited. Lazaro's passing was a personal loss to many in his home parish, distinct from the political void left by his absence. On the 20-mile ride north to Ville Platte, those in the funeral entourage were awestruck by the outpouring of "grief ... unmistakably manifested everywhere." The district's numerous farmers and their families, many of them Lazaro's former patients, lined the route, and students and faculty stood outside each schoolhouse to pay their respects as a funeral procession of more than 300 vehicles wound along the highway. "Never have I seen anything like it—mile after mile on public roads, vehicles of all kinds carrying people bowed down with grief, not one of them in the spirit of curiosity, but genuine sorrow and regret," recalled Representative James Z. Spearing of Louisiana.[43] Lazaro was interred in the Old City Cemetery in Ville Platte.

FOR FURTHER READING

Biographical Directory of the United States Congress, "Ladislas Lazaro," http://bioguide.congress.gov.

MANUSCRIPT COLLECTION

Louisiana and Lower Mississippi Valley Collections, Louisiana State University (Baton Rouge). *Papers*: 1894–1928, seven feet. Personal, medical practice, and congressional papers and correspondence, several photographs, and memorabilia. Includes copies of political speeches, House bills, government reports, political broadsides, and correspondence pertaining to state and local political campaigns. Lazaro's interests in agriculture and the tariff questions related to the rice industry also are reflected. Finding aid in repository.

NOTES

1 As only the second Hispanic Representative in Congress—after Romualdo Pacheco of California, who served from 1879 to 1883—Lazaro was also only the second Hispanic Member who was eligible to chair a committee.

2 The area had been settled by persons of French and Spanish origin in the late 1700s and lay on the edge of the Mamou Prairie, from which the town took its name. Ville Platte, derived from the French for "flat town," was incorporated shortly before the Civil War and eventually lay along the Texas and Pacific Railway. Clare D'Artois Leeper, *Louisiana Places* (Baton Rouge: Legacy Publishing Company, 1976): 246.

3 Sources are inconclusive about whether Lazaro had any siblings. At least one internal memo in Lazaro's files, discussing the disposition of his House salary upon his death, referenced a sister named Belle. See the untitled memorandum of 22 December 1922, C-38, Congressional File, Box 3, Folder 27, October–December 1922 Papers of Ladislas Lazaro, Louisiana and Lower Mississippi Valley Collections, Louisiana State University, Baton Rouge (hereinafter referred to as Papers of Ladislas Lazaro). No other biographical sources, including Lazaro's obituaries, list siblings. Information on Lazaro's paternal relatives is included in a long letter from his cousin Lazar Popovich. See Papers of Ladislas Lazaro, Popovich to Lazaro, 10 April 1922.

4 De Rouen was born in Ville Platte and was two years Lazaro's junior. He succeeded Lazaro in a special election on August 23, 1927. His reminiscences are included in a set of memorial addresses for Lazaro delivered on the House Floor in May 1928. See *Congressional Record*, House, 70th Cong., 1st sess. (13 May 1928): 8589.

5 Glenn R. Conrad, ed., *A Dictionary of Louisiana Biography: Vol. I, A to M* (New Orleans: Louisiana Historical Association, 1988): 493.

6 Speeches from Lazaro's first Louisiana senate campaign can be found in the Papers of Ladislas Lazaro, C-37, Congressional File, Box 1b, Folder 1: 1907–1913.

7 Papers of Ladislas Lazaro, C-39, Typewritten Speeches and Speech Notes, n.d., Box 6, Folder 52, undated biographical profile of Lazaro.

8 Pujo, who was also in charge at the time of an influential special committee looking into the trusts and financial combinations—which received much press attention in an election year—told the press he was retiring because he was "sick" of the election cycle and the pace of Members' lives. See, for example, "43 in House to Retire," 2 September 1912, *Baltimore Sun*: 9; and William L. Altdorfer, "A Startling Exodus of Statesmen from Public Office," 5 May 1912, *Washington Post*: SM4.

9 As Lazaro told constituents, he unreservedly endorsed "Federal control and support of levees; tariff for revenue, limited to the necessity of government conducted honestly and economically and with efficiency; a revision of the tariff in the people's interest

without injuring any legitimate industry; a tariff on rice, sugar and lumber; the full exercise of the state of their reserved power; the income tax; publicity and curtailment of campaign expenses; primaries in selecting residential candidates; the election of the United States Senators by the people; vocational and agricultural education; good roads and drainage; a department of labor represented in the President's Cabinet." Papers of Ladislas Lazaro, C-37, Congressional File, Box 1b, Folder 1: 1907–1913.

10 V. O. Key, Jr., *Southern Politics in State and Nation*, 2nd ed. (Knoxville: University of Tennessee Press, 1977): 156–182.

11 "Circular Sent Causes Anger—Brings in Religion," 2 September 1912, *The Daily-Picayune* (New Orleans): 3.

12 "Lewis and Lazaro," 6 September 1912, *The Daily-Picayune* (New Orleans): 1, 10. Local newspapers speculated that the race might be close enough to force a runoff primary on September 24, 1912, but there is no evidence that a runoff was ever held.

13 Of the Hispanic representatives whose careers ended before World War II, only Félix Córdova Dávila, a Puerto Rican Resident Commissioner, served longer in Congress. Dávila was in office roughly eight months longer than Lazaro. Dennis Chavez of New Mexico served two terms in the House (1931–1935) before being appointed to a vacancy in the U.S. Senate in May 1935, winning election to the remainder of the term, and being re-elected four times. He served until his death in 1962.

14 Enrolled Bills Committee chairmanship and composition information in *Congressional Directory*, 64th Congress (Washington, D.C.: Government Printing Office, 1916): 185; *Congressional Directory*, 65th Congress (Washington, D.C.: Government Printing Office, 1917): 187. Lazaro was just the second Hispanic American to chair a standing congressional committee; Romualdo Pacheco was the first.

15 Charles Stewart III, "Committee Hierarchies in the Modernizing House, 1875–1947," *American Journal of Political Science* 36, no. 4 (November 1992): 835–856; see especially Stewart's table on "Committee Attractiveness," p. 845. Created in 1887, the Merchant Marine and Fisheries Committee had gradually acquired jurisdiction over a wide range of maritime matters, including all policy affecting water transportation, shipping and shipbuilding, registering and licensing vessels, navigation, the Coast Guard, lighthouses, the Panama Canal, and, eventually, regulations governing radio communications. See, for example, Kathleen A. Dolan, "Merchant Marine and Fisheries Committee, House," in the *Encyclopedia of the U.S. Congress*, vol. 3 (New York: Simon and Schuster, 1995): 1391–1392.

16 The Agriculture Committee was a prominent assignment at this point and seemingly an attractive panel for a Member from a rural district. There is no mention in any of Lazaro's existing papers or in press accounts that he sought a seat on the Agriculture Committee, which typically was dominated by Southerners. Only a handful of Louisianans served on the panel in the first half of the 20th century, and only one (James Aswell) served during Lazaro's tenure.

17 For more information on the reapportionment battle during the 1920s, see Charles Eagles, *Democracy Delayed: Congressional Reapportionment and the Urban-Rural Conflict in the 1920s* (Athens: University of Georgia Press, 1990).

18 "Election Statistics, 1920 to Present," http://history.house.gov/institution/election-statistics/election-statistics. For results prior to 1920, see Michael J. Dubin et al., *U.S. Congressional Elections, 1788–1997* (Jefferson, NC: McFarland & Company, Inc., 1998).

19 References to the campaign can be found in the 20 August 1916, New Orleans *Times-Picayune*: C4.

20 "Edwards Attacks Lazaro's Record," 24 August 1916, New Orleans *Times-Picayune*: 5.

21 For results, see the 15 September 1916, New Orleans *Times-Picayune*: 3.

22 Lazaro's correspondence does not indicate that he ever seriously considered a run for statewide office.

23 Ladislas Lazaro to Albert Tate, 14 June 1924, Papers of Ladislas Lazaro, Box 4.

24 Letter of 4 May 1926, Lazaro to Harry F. Knapp, Papers of Ladislas Lazaro, C-40, Congressional File, Box 8, Folder 81, MS 1113.

25 *Congressional Record*, Appendix, 63rd Cong., 1st sess. (28 April 1913): 16–18. For more on Congress and tariff policy throughout U.S. history, see Robert W. Barrie, *Congress and the Executive: The Making of U.S. Foreign Trade Policy, 1789–1986* (New York: Taylor & Francis, 1987); Robert W. Barrie, "Tariffs and Trade," in *The Encyclopedia of the U.S. Congress*, vol. 4, Donald Bacon et al., ed., (New York: Simon and Schuster, 1995): 1909–1923.

26 *Congressional Record*, House, 63rd Cong., 1st sess. (30 September 1913): 5274; "Tariff Bill Passes House, 254 to 103," 1 October 1913, *New York Times*: 1.

27 Christopher M. Lee, "Organization for Survival: The Rice Industry and Protective Tariffs, 1921–1929," *Louisiana History* 35, no. 4 (Fall 1994): 454.

28 Lazaro to L. N. McCollister, 2 June 1924, Papers of Ladislas Lazaro, Box 4; Unaddressed Letter from Lazaro to "Dear Friend," 24 June 1926, Papers of Ladislas Lazaro, Box 5.

29 For more on the McNary–Haugen legislation, see Darwin N. Kelly, "The McNary–Haugen Bills, 1924–1928," *Agricultural History* 14 (1940): 170–180; Steve Neal, *McNary of Oregon: A Political Biography* (Portland: Oregon Historical Society, 1985).

30 Ladislas Lazaro, "The High Cost of Living," *Congressional Record*, Extension of Remarks, Appendix, 64th Cong., 2nd sess. (27 February 1917): 553.

31 *Congressional Record*, House, 66th Cong., 1st sess. (8 November 1919): 8152.

32 See Stathis, *Landmark Legislation*: 181. The act was named for Senator Wesley Livsey Jones of Washington state, chairman of the Senate Commerce Committee, http://bioguide.congress.gov. For more on the act, see Michael McClintock, "Merchant Marine Act of 1920," in Brian K. Landsberg, ed., *Major Acts of Congress*, vol. 2 (New York: Thompson-Gale, 2004): 267–270; Clinton H. Whitehurst, Jr., *The U.S. Merchant Marine: In Search of an Enduring Maritime Policy* (Annapolis, MD: Naval Institute Press, 1983); and Clinton H. Whitehurst, Jr., *The U.S. Shipbuilding Industry: Past, Present, and Future* (Annapolis, MD: Naval Institute Press, 1986).

33 Hearings on the Subject of the Improvement of the Louisiana and Texas Intracoastal Waterway from the Mississippi River, at or Near New Orleans, LA., to Corpus Christi, Tex., held before the Committee on Rivers and Harbors, House of Representatives, 69th Congress, 1st sess. (19 and 23 March 1926): 52.

34 In fact, Lazaro's obituaries list his work on the canal as one of his prime legislative accomplishments. For example, see "Dr. Lazaro, Dean of Congressmen, Dead at Capital," 31 March 1927, New Orleans *Times-Picayune*: 1.

35 See a history of the Gulf Intracoastal Waterway in *The Handbook of Texas Online*, http://www.tshaonline.org/handbook/online/articles/GG/rrg4_print.html (accessed 7 October 2009).

36 *Congressional Record*, House, 65th Cong., 2nd sess. (17 December 1917): 469–470. Louisiana eventually became the 14th state to ratify the amendment, on 3 August 1918.

37 See the roll call tallies for both dates: *Congressional Record*, House, 65th Cong., 2nd sess. (10 January 1918): 810; and *Congressional Record*, House, 66th Cong., 1st sess. (21 May 1919): 93–94.

38 Lazaro campaign pamphlet 1916, page 8; Papers of Ladislas Lazaro. His opposition to women's suffrage had been long-standing; in the state senate he asked in a 1910 floor speech, "Why should [a] woman long for some other sphere in which to serve when she can exhibit all that is grand and beautiful and glorious and christianlike [*sic*] in the domestic circle?... To the woman who wants to vote to better our government I would say in the language of Roosevelt, stay at home and 'raise good citizens and you need not worry about our government.'"

39 *Congressional Record*, House, 69th Cong., 2nd sess. (29 January 1927): 2578.

40 See House Rpt. no. 1886, "Conference Report on Regulation of Radio Communication," 69th Congress, 2nd sess. (27 January 1927): 1–19. For a history of broadcast regulator acts, see Robert W. Van Sickel, "Communications Act of 1934," in Brian K. Landsberg, ed., *Major Acts of Congress*, vol. 1 (New York: MacMillan/Thompson-Gale, 2004): 142–146.

41 "Dr. L. Lazaro Dies in Washington," 1 April 1927, *Clarion-Progress* (Opelousas, LA): 1.

42 "Representative Lazaro," 31 March 1927, New Orleans *Times-Picayune*: 8.

43 *Congressional Record*, House, 70th Cong., 1st sess. (13 May 1928): 8592.

"THE DUTY OF ONE ASPIRING TO POLITICAL LEADERSHIP IS TO THINK WITH HIS PEOPLE AND WITH COURAGE ENDEAVOR TO POINT OUT THE PATH OF HONOR AND PROSPERITY. HIS AIM SHOULD BE, NOT TO ACT THE PART OF THE DEMAGOGUE AND CUNNINGLY WATCH FOR THE FAVORING BREEZES OF POPULAR PASSION BUT TO ACT THE PART OF THE CONSTRUCTIVE STATESMAN AND TO HEROICALLY AND SINCERELY GIVE DIRECTION TO PUBLIC OPINION."

Ladislas Lazaro
From a state senate speech c. 1907

Benigno Cárdenas Hernández
1862–1954

UNITED STATES REPRESENTATIVE 1915–1917; 1919–1921
REPUBLICAN FROM NEW MEXICO

Benigno Hernández was the first Hispanic American from New Mexico elected to the U.S. House of Representatives. He rose through the ranks of local politics in an era of Republican dominance. Elected two years after New Mexico was admitted to the Union in 1912, Hernández benefited from a rich tradition of Territorial Delegates who had tended to their constituents' needs. Hernández's loss of his congressional seat during the Democratic resurgence in the 1916 elections and return to the House after Republican gains in the 1918 midterms reflected national trends.

Benigno Cárdenas (B. C.) Hernández was born in Taos, New Mexico, to Juan J. and Maria M. Hernández, on February 13, 1862. Juan was an adobe mason, and Maria maintained the household. Benigno was the third of 15 children. He attended local schools but had little formal education. Instead, Hernández learned the sheep-ranching and mercantile trades while living in Ojo Caliente, Lumberton, and Tierra Amarilla in Rio Arriba County. He returned to Taos in 1882, working as a clerk until 1888. Hernández lived in a number of communities while building a merchandising business. In 1904 he joined Amador & Company, a firm specializing in sheep, cattle, and merchandising. In 1898 Hernández married Frances Whitlock; the couple had three children: B. C., Jr.; John W.; and Isabel.[1]

Hernández served as probate clerk and recorder in Tierra Amarilla from 1900 to 1904 and was then elected to a two-year term as county sheriff. Hernández served as Rio Arriba's treasurer and collector from 1908 to 1912 and as receiver in the state land office from 1912 to 1914 before returning to his business activities. He also served as a delegate to the Republican National Convention in 1912 and in 1916.[2] One scholar counted Hernández as a member of the "Old Guard," a Republican contingent that used a "political establishment of considerable skill and permanence ... [in] ... dominant counties of the Rio Grande and Upper Pecos valleys." Many of the Old Guard Republicans were successful entrepreneurs who not only "achieved a measure of independence from politics" but also spoke for "a union of business and similar groups with government." Because they wielded significant influence over political and business affairs at the county level, the Old Guard Republicans had an extraordinary amount of political leverage at the state and national levels.[3]

Although Hernández's rationale for seeking a seat in the U.S. House in 1914 remains unclear, most likely he hoped to capitalize on the political winds of fortune, which were shifting at the state and national levels.[4] However, some considered Hernández's nomination to be part and parcel of the New Mexican Republican Party's machine politics.[5] At least one contemporary observer believed Hernández's run was a party decision based on the strategic placement of New Mexico Republicans in the 1916 elections.[6]

Hernández ran against an incumbent who was a three-term House veteran and the favorite of the New Mexican political establishment. Democrat Harvey Butler Fergusson had served as New Mexico's Territorial Delegate in the 55th Congress (1897–1899) and had then run two unsuccessful campaigns before winning election in 1912 as one of the new state's two U.S. Representatives. During the nomination process, both New Mexico's major newspapers, the Republican *Albuquerque Morning Journal* and the Democratic *Santa Fe New Mexican*, endorsed Fergusson over Hernández. The *New Mexican* commented, "Mr. Hernandez has about as much [chance] of being elected as the proverbial snowball." The Republican nominee "is not widely known throughout the state; his achievements for the state have been nil; he has no special strength with the native people and none with the English-speaking

Collection of the U.S. House of Representatives, Photography Collection

population," the editors wrote.[7] However, a Republican political operative noted that Hernández was a favorite in three counties with large numbers of Hispanic voters; one of these was Santa Fe County, a populous area encompassing the state capital.[8] Acknowledging the need to increase his profile with voters, Hernández welcomed the statewide campaign. "I do not deny that there are plenty of places in New Mexico where I am not well known," he told supporters. "I believe that the people of the northern counties know me better than those of the southern counties but I shall visit every county. I think the voters are desirous of seeing the men they are to consider as nominees and for this reason I shall speak all over the state."[9]

The Republican-leaning editors of the *Albuquerque Morning Journal* insinuated that Hernández's run was racially motivated. When a reader asked if the paper would "support B. C. Hernandez if he were an Anglo instead of a Spanish-American," the editors claimed they objected to Hernández because he could not adequately represent New Mexico in Washington, D.C. The newspaper "would welcome the election of a native citizen to either house of congress or to the governorship … provided his ability was such as to reflect credit on the citizenship of New Mexico," the editors wrote, but instead "it is understood that he was nominated … solely because he was a Spanish-American."[10]

The *Albuquerque Morning Journal*'s allegations of Hernández's financial mismanagement during his term as county treasurer became increasingly rampant as Election Day approached.[11] Hernández vigorously defended his reputation and considered suing the paper for libel. "When my term of office ended I turned over to my successor … the books and records pertaining to the office," read Hernández's published rebuttal of the charges. "I stated … that there might be some errors … and suggested that a final settlement be deferred until the books could be investigated by the traveling auditor of the state and I could be checked out." Republican Committee Chairman Charles Ely submitted affidavits from one of the county commissioners to verify Hernández's rebuttal.[12] By mid-October 1914, the paper had charged that Hernández "failed utterly to discharge his responsibility and properly bear his trust as treasurer of the county of Rio Arriba," making his quest for national office "utterly inconceivable."[13] Despite the controversy, Hernández continued campaigning across the state against Fergusson and third-party candidates alongside prominent Republicans such as Senator Thomas Catron, who had dominated New Mexico politics since the 1870s as an architect of the Santa Fe Ring.[14] Progressive Party candidate Francis C. Wilson warned voters, "You will give one man a double vote. Senator Catron will vote in the senate and over in the house of representatives" if Hernández is elected. Wilson believed Hernández's only platform was race. "I have heard Hernandez … in Taos," he said, "and in that talk he never showed for the fraction of a second that he knew there is a congress … or that there are national issues. But from fifteen points of his circle he comes back to: 'Vote for me; I am Spanish-American.'"[15]

Hernández accumulated a majority of the vote (51.3 percent), prevailing against Fergusson, Wilson, and another opponent.[16] Much of his support came from northern counties.[17] "I should not be human if I did not feel elated over my election," Hernández said. "It was one of the peculiar features of this campaign that I myself did not have a chance to vote for I was campaigning … and did not get back to Tierra Amarilla to cast my ballot." Hernández credited his victory to third-party voters and dissatisfied Fergusson supporters who either stayed home or voted for other candidates. He minimized the importance of using race as a campaign issue, saying the tactic "may have worked to a certain extent, but I do not believe that it cut such a big figure as compared with the other causes."[18]

Hernández's legislative interests included pension relief for his constituents and the resolution of their land claims, natural resource development, and national defense. After taking his seat in the 64th Congress (1915–1917), Hernández served on the Indian Affairs and the Irrigation of Arid Lands Committees. He submitted bills that reflected his constituents' needs, such as financial relief for individuals, as well as bills for public works projects. Expanding New Mexico's infrastructure was a special

interest of his. Speaking in support of a bill that would provide federal money for the construction of roads on National Forest lands, Hernández argued, "New Mexico and other western states can not afford ... to survey, construct, and maintain all the roads ... but these communities are perfectly willing to meet the Federal Government half way and do their share of road building aided by the Federal Government, as proposed by this bill."[19] Hernández also dealt with social issues such as women's suffrage. Suffragists in New Mexico challenged Senator Catron and Hernández to support the cause, but Catron resolutely opposed it, while Hernández remained noncommittal.[20]

Much of Hernández's legislative agenda focused on security and national defense. The ongoing civil wars in Mexico due to the political upheaval from the 1910 revolution were an immediate security concern in New Mexico. By 1915 the Woodrow Wilson administration, in concert with other nations, recognized the regime of Venustiano Carranza, a regional governor who became president and pledged to uphold constitutionalism, liberal capitalism, and international law.[21] One of Carranza's regional rivals was Francisco (Pancho) Villa, a bandit-turned-charismatic revolutionary who led the Division del Norte, a force that possessed artillery, troop trains, and limited air support. On March 9, 1916, Villa led 1,500 men from Mexico into Columbus, New Mexico; killed at least 17 U.S. citizens; and destroyed property before retreating. Villa's forces also killed 18 U.S. engineers in Mexico.[22] The American public demanded a quick, decisive reprisal. Representative Frank Mondell of Wyoming criticized the Wilson administration, charging that it "first interfered with the domestic affairs of the Republic south of us, and then continued its meddlesome interference until there was not a faction ... that did not hate the American name." [23] The day after the attack, Hernández condemned the escalating violence on the Mexico-New Mexico border. He said, "The people of New Mexico on the border have been suffering like the people of Texas, like the people of Arizona, and if the [Venustiano] Carranza regime to-day is unable to take care of conditions down there.... The people of New Mexico have a militia now, and undoubtedly will assist the national authorities in controlling and trying to apprehend the assassins who have committed these latest outrages." Hernández's colleagues applauded his speech.[24]

One of the Wilson administration's greatest concerns was tempering the U.S. response to Villa's raid. Faced with mounting public pressure and a restless Congress that could push him into a full-scale invasion in an election year, President Wilson decided on a limited engagement; he ordered 12,000 troops, led by General John J. Pershing, to enter Mexico to arrest Villa. Carranza, who sent his own force into northern Mexico to arrest Villa, warned Wilson that such an invasion could lead to full-scale war. Pershing's forces, dubbed the "Punitive Expedition," pushed 350 miles into Mexico but did not find Villa because of the hostile terrain, the lack of cooperation from local citizens, and Villa's skill in evasion. U.S. forces fought with some of Carranza's men on June 21; nine U.S. soldiers and 30 Mexican soldiers were killed, and a larger number were wounded. To resolve the crisis, Wilson and Carranza formed a joint commission to resolve the incident and drafted agreements about border procedures. Villa did not invade the United States again, and the two nations avoided a full-scale conflict.[25]

Hernández advocated limited support for U.S. involvement in World War I during his first term. In 1915 he supported a resolution sponsored by Jeff McLemore of Texas warning Americans not to sail on vessels of belligerent nations such as Great Britain, France, or Germany so as to avoid capture or death. In 1916 Hernández supported diplomatic engagement with Germany, stating, "We should first exhaust our diplomacy and warn our people to avoid danger, and when we have done all in our power toward preventing war ... and our diplomacies are exhausted, we will then be unflinching in our solemn duty."[26] Along with diplomacy, he supported the National Defense Act of 1916 (H.R. 12766), which reorganized the U.S. Army into an active duty force, a reserve, and the National Guard. The act also increased the size of the U.S. Army and spurred the creation of a modern munitions-production infrastructure.[27]

At the start of his 1916 re-election campaign, Hernández announced his intention to win a second term, declaring, "I have served to the best of my ability as a representative in congress, and I would like to go back for another term." Citing his experience as an incumbent, he said, "I think I could render better service [to the state in] another term, because I have learned how the work is done." Throughout the campaign, he promoted the Republican Party platform, which consisted of strict neutrality regarding the conflict in Europe along with a simultaneous increase in the nation's defense. Hernández also campaigned against the Wilson administration's policies of dialogue and limited engagement with Mexico, which he called "a long series of blunders." "I believe that Mexico policies will do more than any other one thing to bring about the defeat of Mr. Wilson," Hernández said.[28] His opponent was William Walton, a prominent lawyer who was serving in the state senate and had also represented Grant County in the 34th Legislative Assembly (1901–1902).[29] The *Albuquerque Morning Journal* again refused to endorse Hernández. The editors resurrected the unsubstantiated charges of Hernández's negligence as treasurer of Rio Arriba County, concluding, "Mr. Hernandez should not have been elected [in 1914] ... [and] should not be re-elected this year" because of his lackluster record in Congress.[30]

At the national level, the Republican Party's presidential nominee, Supreme Court Justice Charles Evans Hughes, could not unify Republican progressives and Old Guard conservatives. Hughes's platform was difficult to distinguish from Wilson's neutrality policies, partially because he could not afford to alienate isolationist Midwesterners, many of whom were of German descent, with pro-war rhetoric.[31] Hughes's ambiguous national platform, which lacked a compelling counter-argument to neutrality, complicated the efforts of many national Republican candidates to distinguish themselves from Democratic opponents. Along with fellow Republicans Frank A. Hubbell, a candidate for the U.S. Senate, and future U.S. Senator Holm O. Bursum, then seeking the governorship, Hernández campaigned around the state.[32]

Hernández lost re-election to Walton in a close race (49 to 48 percent), partly because of the success of President Wilson's "peace" campaign message and legislative successes supported by both Republicans and progressives.[33] Wilson not only won re-election, but he also brought a number of Democrats into Congress on his coattails. Republicans suffered because of voters' tepid enthusiasm for Hughes and the split between progressives and conservatives within the party.[34] Within New Mexico, the press suggested that Hernández's inattentiveness to constituent needs and his focus on national issues cost him at the polls. In an election postmortem, the *Albuquerque Morning Journal* acknowledged, "Few people in the state ... believed that B. C. Hernandez would be beaten for Congress," but the newspaper reported that in his home county of Rio Arriba, Hernández "failed to receive more than about one-half the plurality" he had won in 1914. "Hernandez paid little attention to anything except national politics," observed the editor, noting that the state's representatives in Washington should have been focused on key issues such as securing federal lands. "He made a few speeches on matters pertaining to his state, but they were merely perfunctory ... and got him nowhere."[35]

After his electoral loss, Hernández threw himself into supporting New Mexico's mobilization efforts for World War I. He served on the executive committee of the New Mexico council of defense. As one of the most prominent *nuevomexicano* council members, Hernández wrote dispatches about the draft, the war, and New Mexican participation in the war in Spanish. He also opposed the Industrial Workers of the World and supported the Wilson administration's repression of labor during the war.[36]

In 1918 Hernández's electoral hopes were revived when Walton left the House to pursue a Senate run against Albert Fall in 1918. Hernández announced his candidacy and ran on a platform that stressed his experience and success in Washington. He highlighted his ability to secure more than $1 million in federal money for New Mexican roads and reminded critics who accused him of pacifism that his "only boy ... voluntarily enlisted and [had] gone to the front." Hernández "pledged that he

would vote for all measures necessary to win the war."[37] The once-hostile *Santa Fe New Mexican* now endorsed Hernández, noting that he would do what was necessary to help prosecute the war.[38] To underscore Hernández's fitness on military matters, Julius Kahn of California, the well-respected chairman of the House Military Affairs Committee, gave him a ringing endorsement. Kahn burnished Hernández's credentials in military preparedness by recalling his support for various bills: "While a member of the house … he was independent and fearless in his votes. I know [that] especially with reference to the legislation of the … national defense act." Kahn recalled, "Hernández repeatedly voted while the house was in a committee of the whole, considering the measure for an expansion of our military establishment, and when you consider that that law was passed only seven months before Germany served her notice upon us that she would destroy our ships … it shows that Mr. Hernández had vision and was looking into the future when he cast those votes."[39] Hernández's principal challenger was Democrat G. A. Richardson, a judge from the Pecos Valley. In the general election, Hernández prevailed with 51 percent of the vote to Richardson's 48 percent; a third-party candidate, W. B. Dillon, won the small remainder of the votes.[40]

When he claimed his seat in the 66th Congress (1919–1921), Hernández served on the Indian Affairs, Irrigation of Arid Lands, and Public Lands Committees.[41] Hernández submitted bills for pension and estate relief, public works projects, and legislation for veterans.[42] In a floor speech on Memorial Day 1919, Hernández paid tribute to New Mexico's veterans of the Civil War, the Spanish-American War, and the First World War. Hernández noted that during World War I, about "5,000 men … voluntarily enlisted in all branches of the Army and Navy," with "15,000 or more … drafted under the provisions of the selective service law." Unfortunately, "eleven hundred casualties marked the price paid by sons of our State in the World War." He paid special notice to the families of fallen servicemen, noting, "When we are paying tribute to our heroes, let us not forget the mothers, the widows, and their orphans" in the aftermath of the conflict.[43] Hernández also supported H.R. 487, a bill to provide employment and homes for military and naval veterans by developing state or federally owned land. Touting the support of the American Legion of New Mexico, which comprised 3,000 veterans, Hernández told the House such an endorsement "indicates that the people of New Mexico are intensely interested in this legislation, and they are willing to lend their aid by giving up part of the lands that were ceded to that State by the Federal Government, and … the funds derived by the sale and rentals of other lands ceded by the Federal Government" prior to New Mexico's statehood. Introduced by House Majority Leader Frank Mondell of Wyoming, the bill was submitted to the Committee on Public Lands, where it eventually died.[44]

One of Hernández's lasting legislative successes was the passage of H.R. 14669, a bill to consolidate forest lands in the Carson National Forest, near Taos, New Mexico, whose enactment (P.L. 66-382) authorized the Secretary of the Interior to exchange land with private landowners for the benefit of the national park. Hernández submitted the bill at the end of the congressional session. After a small debate about the equity of value between private and federal land, the bill passed the House and the Senate and was signed by the President during the waning hours of the 66th Congress.[45]

Hernández declined to serve in Congress for a third term and returned to New Mexico. President Warren Harding appointed him collector of internal revenue and he remained in that office through the 1920s, eventually serving as director of internal revenue. Hernández resigned in 1933 as Democrats regained power in New Mexico. He remained active in New Mexican politics until he moved to California in 1946. He died in Los Angeles on October 18, 1954.[46]

FOR FURTHER READING

Biographical Directory of the United States Congress, "Benigno Cárdenas Hernández," http://bioguide.congress.gov.

NOTES

1 *Ninth Census of the United States, 1870: Population Schedule*, Red Willow Indian Reservation of Taos Juan Santisteben, Taos, New Mexico Territory, Roll M593_896, page 684B, Library of Congress, Washington, D.C., http://search.ancestrylibrary.com (accessed 13 January 2011). Charles F. Coan, "Benigno Cardenas Hernandez" in *A History of New Mexico*, vol. 2 (Chicago and New York: The American Historical Society, 1925): 120–121; "Benigno 'B. C.' Hernandez" in Maurilio Vigil, *Los Patrones: Profiles of Hispanic Political Leaders in New Mexico History* (Washington, D.C.: University Press of America, 1980): 143–145; "Former State Congressman Dies at 92," 19 October 1954, (Santa Fe) *The New Mexican*: 1. According to this obituary, Hernández's "only formal schooling consisted of three months of class work one winter under a traveling school teacher." Although the census form notes that Juan Hernández worked as an adobe mason in 1870, Coan states that he "spent his life as a rancher and stock raiser" and died with the title "don." Coan also states that Benigno "acquired his early education in private and public schools in Taos."

2 Coan, "Benigno Cárdenas Hernández"; *Biographical Directory of the United States Congress*, "Benigno Cárdenas Hernández," http://bioguide.congress.gov.

3 Jack Holmes, *Politics in New Mexico* (Albuquerque: University of New Mexico Press, 1967): 148, 176–177. Holmes notes that within 11 counties, the Old Guard members were "one or more individuals of political energy and acumen who could direct the local work necessary to win elections, act in concert with other politicians, and work successfully at the higher level of strategy and abstraction required by state and national politics."

4 Calvin A. Roberts, "H. B. Fergusson, 1818–1915: New Mexico Spokesman for Political Reform," *New Mexico Historical Review* 57 (July 1982): 251–252. Roberts argues that "partisan politics … helped oust Fergusson in favor of Republican Ben C. Hernandez. Despite an appeal by [President Woodrow] Wilson to the voters of New Mexico that Fergusson be returned to his seat, age and ill health robbed [Fergusson] of his zest and vigor of campaigning." Hernández's run could also be seen as part of the "native-son" movement fostered by Octaviano A. Larrazolo in 1911 to encourage Hispanic politicians to seek public office in New Mexico. See Carolyn Zeleny, *Relations between the Spanish-Americans and Anglo-Americans in New Mexico* (New York: Arno Press, 1974; reprint of 1966 edition): 220–225.

5 "As to B. C. Hernandez," 31 August 1914, *Albuquerque Morning Journal*: 4. For Hernández's nomination as the political machine's cynical choice, see "A Moral Issue," 15 October 1914, *Albuquerque Morning Journal*: 6.

6 "The Optics Explanation," 16 September 1914, *Albuquerque Morning Journal*: 6. The editors insisted that "wound up with the candidacy of Mr. Hernandez is the candidacy of Senator [Thomas B.] Catron to succeed himself two years from now. He [Catron] forced the nomination of Hernandez because he did not want a native [that is, Hispanic] candidate in the field for the senatorship in 1916." For more information about the "gentlemen's agreement" to wage only Anglo versus Anglo and Hispanic versus Hispanic political campaigns, see Zeleny, *Relations between the Spanish-Americans and Anglo-Americans in New Mexico*: 229–230.

7 "Our Best Wishes," 25 August 1914, *Santa Fe New Mexican*: 2.

8 "Santa Fe County for Hernandez for Congress," 13 August 1914, *Santa Fe New Mexican*: 6. The operative stated, "With Hernandez we could beat Fergusson."

9 "Candidates Are Preparing for a Whirlwind Tour of 26 Counties," 29 August 1914, *Santa Fe New Mexican*: 4.

10 "As to B. C. Hernandez."

11 In one article, the editors charged that Hernández had "marked as paid over $800 in taxes when they were not paid … also that he marked as paid some $360 in merchandise licenses alleged not to have been paid." However, the newspaper also alleged "that Hernández made good the amounts when demand was made by the traveling auditor." See "Owing to Scandal Made Public in Connection with Official Acts Hernandez May Resign from Ticket," 13 September 1914, *Albuquerque Morning Journal*; "Hernandez Will Take Steps to Protect Himself in Court's Intimation of Chairman Ely," 14 September 1914, *Santa Fe New Mexican*: 1.

12 "Chairman Ralph C. Ely's Comprehensive Statement in Vindication of Personal Honesty of Hernandez," 24 September 1914, *Albuquerque Morning Journal*: 1, 6.

13 "More Evidence of Carelessness by Hernandez," 14 October 1914, *Albuquerque Morning Journal*: 3; "Mr. Hernandez Was Also Very Careless in the Year A.D. 1909," 13 October 1914, *Santa Fe New Mexican*: 1; "Impossible," 14 October 1914, *Santa Fe New Mexican*: 4. Governor William McDonald gave the press a report alleging that in 1909, Hernández fell $2,447 short in his accounts and did not realize his mistake until an auditor pointed it out to him.

14 "Catron Stumping New Mexico with B. C. Hernandez," 21 September 1914, *Albuquerque Morning Journal*: 3. For biographical information about Catron, see the *Biographical Directory of the United States Congress*, "Thomas Benton Catron," http://bioguide.congress.gov/.

15 "Speaker Rips Mask Off G.O.P. Rascals and Incompetents," 2 November 1914, *Santa Fe New Mexican:* 5.

16 Michael J. Dubin et al., *United States Congressional Elections, 1788–1997: The Official Results of the Elections of the 1st through 105th Congresses* (Jefferson, NC: McFarland & Company, Inc., 1998): 401.

17 "Hernandez Will Go to Congress as Successor to H. B. Fergusson," 4 November 1914, *Albuquerque Morning Journal*: 1; "Majority for

Hernandez in State Grows as Returns Come In," 5 November 1914, *Albuquerque Morning Journal*: 1.

18 "Hernandez Admits Race Issue Was Used in Election; Says Wilson Helps," 5 November 1914, *Santa Fe New Mexican*: 3.

19 *Congressional Record*, Appendix, 64th Cong., 1st sess.: 1340–1341.

20 Joan M. Jensen, "'Disfranchisement Is a Disgrace': Women and Politics in New Mexico, 1900–1940," *New Mexico Historical Review* 56, no. 1 (January 1981): 18. Jensen quotes an activist who dismissed Hernández as Catron's puppet as saying, Catron "simply put Hernandez in Congress before our citizens know what was being done." Jensen argues that Catron's position on women's suffrage made him a political liability to Republicans in the 1916 elections, but is unclear whether this contributed to his re-election defeat.

21 Kendrick A. Clements, *The Presidency of Woodrow Wilson* (Lawrence: University Press of Kansas, 1992): 96–100. For a brief summary of the rise of Carranza during the Mexican Revolution, see John Mason Hart, "The Mexican Revolution, 1910–1920," in Michael C. Meyer and William H. Beezley, eds., *The Oxford History of Mexico* (New York: Oxford University Press, 2000): 435–466.

22 Jim Tuck, "Villa, Pancho," *American National Biography* 22 (New York: Oxford University Press, 1999: 358–359; Walter LaFeber, *The American Age: U.S. Foreign Policy at Home and Abroad, Volume 1–To 1920,* 2nd ed. (New York: W. W. Norton, 1994): 280–281; "Punishment, Not Intervention, Wilson Plan," 10 March 1916, *Los Angeles Times*: 11. For a detailed description of the raid and the subsequent U.S. response, see Friedrich Katz, *The Life and Times of Pancho Villa* (Stanford, CA: Stanford University Press, 1998): 560–582.

23 For a summary of Mondell's criticisms, see "House Debates Villa Raid," 10 March 1916, *New York Times*: 3; *Congressional Record*, House, 64th Cong., 1st sess. (9 March 1916): 3874–3875.

24 *Congressional Record*, House, 64th Cong., 1st sess. (10 March 1916): 3907.

25 Clements, *The Presidency of Woodrow Wilson*, 100–101; Katz, *The Life and Times of Pancho Villa,* 566–570.

26 *Congressional Record*, Appendix, 64th Cong., 1st sess.: 514. For the text of the resolution, see *Congressional Record*, Appendix, 64th Cong., 1st sess. (18 February and 8 March 1916): 361–365, 453–454.

27 Steven V. Stathis, *Landmark Legislation, 1774–2002* (Washington, D.C.: Congressional Quarterly Press, 2003): 172–173; *Congressional Record*, House, 64th Cong., 1st sess. (23 March 1916): 4731. During his first term, Hernández submitted H.R. 5755, which would have paid $2,000 in contested-election expenses to the widow of Tranquilino Luna, a Territorial Delegate from New Mexico in the 47th and 48th Congresses (1881–1885). The House did not reimburse the Luna family. For more information, see *Congressional Record*, House, 64th Cong., 1st sess. (15 December 1915): 294.

28 "Not Dickering, Says Hernandez, and Candidate Only for Congressman; First Statement by Returning Official," 7 August 1916, *Santa Fe New Mexican*: 3. Hernández emphasized that his candidacy was limited to Congress because a small number of *nuevomexicano* caucus delegates asked him to run for governor to maintain a balance of Anglo and *Hispano* officeholders. See "Native Editor Says G.O.P. Must Divide the Ticket Along Racial Lines," 19 August 1916, *Santa Fe New Mexican*: 2.

29 "William B. Walton," in Coan, *A History of New Mexico,* vol. 2: 38–39; Territory of New Mexico, *Report of the Secretary of the Territory, 1905–1906, and Legislative Manual 1907* (Albuquerque, NM: Morning Journal, 1907): 176. Like Hernández, Walton dealt with caucus delegates who sought a balance between Anglo and *Hispano* officeholders by nominating him to the governor's race. See "Grant County Here To See That Billy Walton Secures Nomination," 29 August 1916, *Santa Fe New Mexican*: 3; "De Baca Boom for Governorship Rapidly Getting Out of Control among Delegates," 30 August 1916, *Santa Fe New Mexican*: 3.

30 "The Real Issue in New Mexico," 20 October 1916, *Albuquerque Morning Journal*: 6.

31 Clements, *The Presidency of Woodrow Wilson*: 133–134; George Thomas Kurian, ed., *The Encyclopedia of the Republican Party,* vol. 2 (Armonk, NY: M. E. Sharpe, 1997): 475–479; Patricia A. Behlar, "Charles Evans Hughes," in Kurian, ed., *The Encyclopedia of the Republican Party,* vol. 1 (Armonk, NY: M. E. Sharpe, 1997): 271–272.

32 "Bergere Opening Hernandez Campaign," 1 September 1916, *Santa Fe New Mexican*: 5; "G.O.P. Candidates Leave Tonight for Campaign Tour of Mora and San Miguel," 11 September 1916, *Santa Fe New Mexican*: 5; "Hernandez and Hubbell Speak in Mora County," 14 September 1916, *Albuquerque Morning Journal*: 3; "Republican Candidates Pleased With Trip," 20 September 1916, *Albuquerque Morning Journal*: 5; "Long Distance Talking Record Is Won by G.O.P.," 21 September 1916, *Albuquerque Morning Journal*: 5; "Hernandez Gets Warm Reception from Taos Crowd," 3 October 1916, *Albuquerque Morning Journal*: 5; "Mexican Policy of Wilson Big Factor in Race for The House," 21 October 1916, *Albuquerque Morning Journal*: 1.

33 Manuel Martinez, *The New Mexico Blue Book or State Official Register, Nineteen Hundred and Nineteen* (Santa Fe: New Mexico Secretary of State, 1919): 274.

34 Clements, *The Presidency of Woodrow Wilson*: 133–134; Betty Glad, "Hughes, Charles Evans," *American National Biography* 11 (New York: Oxford University Press, 1999): 416–421.

35 "The Defeat of Hernandez," 13 November 1916, *Albuquerque Morning Journal*: 6.

36 Phillip Gonzales and Ann Massman, "Loyalty Questioned: Nuevomexicanos in the Great War," *Pacific Historical Review* 75, no. 4 (November 2006): 647–648. For more information about the New Mexico Council of Defense, see Walter M. Danburg, "The State Council of Defense," in Lansing B. Bloom, ed., *New Mexico in the Great War.* (Santa Fe: El Palacio Press, 1927): 22–39. For a scholarly overview of the National Council of Defense and its state equivalents, see William J. Breen, *Uncle Sam at Home: Civilian Mobilization, Wartime Federalism, and the Council of National Defense, 1917–1919* (Westport, CT: Greenwood Press, 1984). For an overview of the effects of questions of loyalty and patriotism on labor repression during this period, see David M. Kennedy, *Over Here: The First World War and American Society,* Twenty-Fifth Anniversary ed. (New York: Oxford University Press, 2004): 66–75.

37 "Hernandez 100 Percent Yank, Is Catron Tribute," 3 October 1918, *Santa Fe New Mexican*: 5.

38 "Tested and Found Right," 19 October 1918, *Santa Fe New Mexican*: 4.

39 "Fall and Hernandez Are Endorsed by Kahn of California on Records," 24 October 1918, *Santa Fe New Mexican*: 3.

40 Martinez, *The New Mexico Blue Book or State Official Register: Nineteen Hundred and Nineteen*: 237.

41 David T. Canon, Garrison Nelson, and Charles Stewart III, eds., *Committees of the U.S. Congress, 1789–1946,* vol. 3 (Washington, D.C.: Congressional Quarterly Press, 2002): 492.

42 *Congressional Record*, Index, 66th Cong., 1st sess.: 9393–9394; *Congressional Record*, Index, 66th Cong., 2nd sess.: 9519; *Congressional Record*, Index, 66th Cong., 3rd sess.: 4823. Hernández again submitted an unsucessful bill (H.R. 7373) to provide relief ($2,000) for the estate of Tranquilino Luna. See *Congressional Record*, House, 66th Cong., 1st sess. (15 July 1919): 2666.

43 *Congressional Record*, Appendix, 66th Cong., 1st sess.: 8843–8844.

44 *Congressional Record*, Appendix and Index, 66th Cong., 1st sess. (11 November 1919): 9138–9139, 9700.

45 *Congressional Record*, Index, 66th Cong., 3rd sess.: 4944; *Congressional Record*, House, 66th Cong., 3rd sess. (1 March 1921): 4211–4212; Carson National Forest Act, P.L. 66-382, *Statutes at Large*, 41 Stat. 1364, 1914–1921.

46 The reason Hernández decided to retire remains unclear. For more on his postcongressional career, see Vigil, *Los Patrones: Profiles of Hispanic Political Leaders in New Mexico History*: 144; "Former State Congressman Dies at 92," 19 October 1954, *The New Mexican*: 1; "B. C. Hernandez, Former N.M. Representative, Dies," 20 October 1954, *Albuquerque Journal*: 14.

"I represent a State whose citizens are most patriotic. Long before we came into the sisterhood of States they had shown ... to the world their patriotism by offering their services and enlisting with the men from the North, from the South, and from the East in the defense of their flag and their country."

Benigno Cárdenas Hernández
Congressional Record Appendix, March 8, 1916

Félix Córdova Dávila
1878–1938

RESIDENT COMMISSIONER
UNIONIST FROM PUERTO RICO 1917–1924
ALLIANCE FROM PUERTO RICO 1924–1932

With lawyerly precision, Félix Córdova Dávila persisted in his demands that U.S. authorities resolve Puerto Rico's status, challenging them to live up to their own democratic rhetoric. As a member of the Partido de Unión (Union Party), which controlled the island's politics in the early 20th century, Córdova Dávila continued the campaign of his predecessor, Luis Muñoz Rivera, to secure greater political freedom for Puerto Ricans. Córdova Dávila believed that the island ought to be given complete independence if the United States failed to grant it statehood in a timely fashion. His proposals were seriously considered by Congress but were ultimately turned aside. By the time he retired, Córdova Dávila had served nearly 15 years in the House—longer than any other Hispanic Member of Congress until that point. "Under the rulings of the courts of justice we are neither flesh, fish, nor fowl," he testified at a committee hearing late in his career. "We are neither a part nor a whole. We are nothing; and it seems to me if we are not allowed to be part of the Union we should be allowed to be a whole entity with full and complete control of our internal affairs."[1]

Félix Córdova Dávila was born to Lope Córdova and Concepción Dávila on November 20, 1878, in Vega Baja, on the north coast of Puerto Rico, about 30 miles west of San Juan.[2] He attended the local public schools in Manati, a few miles west of his birthplace. At age 20, Córdova Dávila enrolled at the National University School of Law, now The George Washington University Law School, in Washington, D.C. He graduated with bachelor's and master's degrees in law and returned to Puerto Rico, where he passed the bar in 1903 and established his own practice in San Juan. In 1904 Córdova Dávila was appointed judge of the court in Caguas, about 20 miles south of San Juan, in the island's interior. That same year he was appointed judge of the municipal court and was transferred to Manati, where he served until 1908, when he received the Unionist nomination for a seat in the Puerto Rican house of delegates and was reappointed judge in Manati. He refused both offers, taking a temporary position as district attorney for the Aguadilla district, near the island's northwest tip. Shortly thereafter he was appointed district court judge in Guayama, in the south (1908–1910); in Arecibo, in the north (1910–1911); and in San Juan (1911–1917). In 1906 Córdova Dávila married Mercedes Diaz. The couple raised three boys: Jorge Luis, Félix, and Enrique. Jorge Luis Córdova-Díaz eventually followed his father's career trajectory, serving briefly on the supreme court of Puerto Rico and then as Resident Commissioner from 1969 to 1973. Mercedes died in early October of 1918, in Washington, D.C., during the influenza pandemic that swept America and the world; she was 33 years old.[3] On July 9, 1919, Córdova Dávila married Patria Martinez of Mayaguez. Their daughter, Aida, died as a teenager.[4]

Córdova Dávila first sought elective office in 1917, when he received the Partido de Unión's nomination to run for the vacancy created by the sudden death of Luis Muñoz Rivera in November 1916. Córdova Dávila was elected to the House in a scheduled general election on July 16, 1917; Partido de Unión captured 52 percent of the vote, outpolling Republicans and Socialists, who captured 34 and 14 percent of the vote, respectively.[5] Under the provisions of the Second Jones Act, also known as the Organic Act of Puerto Rico—which was signed into law by President Woodrow Wilson in March 1917 and which Muñoz Rivera had backed as a first step to rectifying the Foraker Act—elections for Puerto Rican Resident Commissioners would occur every four years, beginning in the 1920 election. Córdova Dávila was re-elected to three subsequent terms. In 1920 he won 51 percent of the vote,

Image courtesy of the Library of Congress

with Republican and Socialist candidates receiving roughly 26 and 24 percent of the vote, respectively. In 1924 the Republican Party split; one faction joined the Unionists to form the Alianza (Alliance), while the faction known as the Constitutional Historical Party joined the Socialists to form the Coalición (Coalition). Córdova Dávila was re-elected on the Alliance ticket with 64 percent of the vote.[6] Four years later, with the same party configuration, in an election described as "the most hotly contested and closest … held in the history of the island," Córdova Dávila secured a third term, but with just 52 percent of the vote compared with his opponent's 48 percent.[7]

Córdova Dávila took his seat in the House on August 7, 1917, in the middle of the first session of the 65th Congress (1917–1919).[8] On July 9, 1918, he received his first committee assignment, Insular Affairs, the panel Resident Commissioners were typically assigned to since it had jurisdiction over all legislation affecting America's overseas possessions, including Puerto Rico. From this panel Córdova Dávila's predecessor, Luis Muñoz Rivera, sought to shape the 1917 Organic Act, known as the Jones Act. During Córdova Dávila's tenure on the Insular Affairs Committee, where he served for the rest of his House career, the panel was headed by Representative Horace Mann Towner of Iowa, who became chair when the Republicans took control of the House in 1919. Towner wielded the gavel until 1923, when President Warren G. Harding appointed him Governor of Puerto Rico, an office he held until 1929. Córdova Dávila's connection to Towner proved beneficial.

One of Córdova Dávila's major tasks was to extend to Puerto Rico certain laws and federal programs that were already in place in the mainland United States, such as vocational education, construction of rural post roads, and programs to improve health care for mothers and infants, which Towner had championed in the House through the Sheppard–Towner Act. But Córdova Dávila did not want to extend all American laws to Puerto Rico. When the island's suffragists, inspired by the ratification in 1920 of the 19th Amendment, granting U.S. women the right to vote, sought to extend the franchise to Puerto Rican women, Córdova Dávila's support was tepid. Testifying before the Senate Committee on Territories and Insular Affairs and the House Committee on Insular Affairs, he expressed support for women's right to vote and his "honest and sincere conviction" that women's influence would benefit electoral politics in Puerto Rico. However, he favored the institution of a Spanish-literacy qualification without regard to the sex of the voter, partially because the Partido de Unión feared that the Partido Socialista (Socialist Party) would benefit from universal suffrage. Believing Puerto Rico had the right to legislate its own affairs, he refused to acquiesce to the demands of the Puerto Rican Women's Suffrage Association that he bring the issue before the U.S. Congress.[9] As a committee witness, he told Senator Millard Tydings of Maryland that the Puerto Rican legislature should be allowed to determine voting qualifications without interference from the U.S. Congress. "To be frank," he said, "I do not believe you are qualified to legislate in local matters in Porto Rico. You do not know Porto Rico. We are better qualified than you are. So you should let Porto Ricans handle their own local affairs."[10] In 1928 Puerto Rican voters approved an amendment that extended the vote to women, along with an amendment that required all new voters to take a literacy test. In April 1929 the insular legislature passed a law granting suffrage to women.[11]

Like Muñoz Rivera, Córdova Dávila spent the bulk of his time pursuing the Partido de Unión's primary goal of liberalizing Puerto Rico's system of self-government. Each Congress he introduced bills to amend the Organic Act of 1917. These bills sought a greater measure of home rule, including a civil government with a governor elected by the people instead of one who was appointed by the U.S. President, and authority for Puerto Ricans to draft their own constitution. These bills were usually referred to committees, where they died. Nevertheless, Córdova Dávila's efforts gave voice to Puerto Rican frustrations with the Jones Act. In February 1919 on the House Floor, he demanded that the United States clarify whether the island would ultimately be granted statehood or complete autonomy. "If you think … we are an insular piece of ground, with a considerable population, far removed from any physical relation with the States and Territories; if you think that on account of our differences in language, ethnology, and habits we can never form a part of the American federation; if we can not be a star in that glorious heaven of blue with its stripes of red and white … then we must demand that the American people give us the freedom that is our God-given right," he told the House. Following Córdova Dávila's speech, the Unionist and Republican Parties in the insular legislature agreed to press jointly for either statehood or independence and sent Córdova Dávila a congratulatory message thanking him "for the splendid and just exposition of our political situation before the American people."[12]

Córdova Dávila's efforts in the 1920s were hampered by the Republican administrations' general disinterest and by a coincident period of gubernatorial instability in Puerto Rico. In fact, Córdova Dávila led the effort to recall the widely unpopular Governor Emmett Montgomery Reily. The relationship between the governor and the Resident Commissioner started badly when Reily commanded Córdova Dávila to ask the Puerto Rican assembly to raise the salaries of some friends he had inserted into public office. "Increase the salaries of these offices, do not cut the appropriations of the governor, and we will get along all right," Reily said. When the two men clashed later over Reily's removal of the Puerto Rican attorney general who had been appointed by the previous governor, Córdova Dávila warned Reily, "You are going to fail. Porto Rico will welcome an executive, but not a boss." Reily eventually denounced Córdova Dávila as a "professional double-crosser" and warned President Warren Harding against meeting personally with him, saying, "*Every* Puerto Rican professional politician carries a pistol, and I do not think you should ever see Córdova unless your Secretary or someone else is present."[13]

On the House Floor, Córdova Dávila repeatedly voiced Puerto Ricans' discontent with Reily. When he asked the House to consider impeaching and recalling Reily, the governor's defenders and senior Members demurred, citing the President's jurisdiction.[14] The House never launched an inquiry, but Reily's inartful politics soon proved to be his undoing, and Washington officials recalled him in early 1923. Horace Towner, the former chairman of the House Insular Affairs Committee, was named Reily's successor. In a brief tribute to Towner on the House Floor, Córdova Dávila read a cable from the president of the Puerto Rican senate expressing the islanders' "great enthusiasm" for his appointment.[15] Towner continued to have a working relationship with Córdova Dávila, and he appointed many members of the Partido de Unión to advisory positions and other prominent posts.[16]

In late 1923, with Towner ensconced as governor, Córdova Dávila mounted a campaign for an even more ambitious overhaul of the Jones Act. Among the chief reforms he sought were the popular election of a Puerto Rican governor empowered to appoint a cabinet and directors for the island's departments; legislative powers for local issues vested solely in the Puerto Rican legislature, that is, without being subject to veto by the U.S. President or to revision by the U.S. Congress; and the extension to Puerto Rico of "measures of a national character that tend to promote education, agriculture, and other sources of knowledge or wealth" in the same proportion they were provided to American states. Overarching all these proposals was the request that "Congress, as well as the President of the United States, declare their intentions as regards the final status of the island of Puerto Rico." On January 11, 1924, Córdova Dávila assured his colleagues that he spoke not of a "complaint," but of the islanders' "cherished dream." "We have no grievances, but we have aspirations—the fond hope of all people to control their own affairs," he said on the House Floor. "Experience has taught us that unnecessary delay in the recognition of the rights of any people has always been a cause of unrest and dissatisfaction. On the other hand, the granting of more liberal laws and the establishment of justice by the great powers in their overseas territories has always removed misgivings and prejudices and created a spirit of everlasting gratitude in the bosoms of the people favored by such concessions."[17]

Horace Mann Towner traveled with the delegation to support the reform in meetings with the President and before congressional panels. On January 24, 1924, the delegation—Towner, Puerto Rican senate president Antonio R. Barceló, speaker of the house Miguel Guerra, and insular senators and representatives from the Unionist, Republican, and Socialist Parties—met with President Calvin Coolidge at the White House to press for the popular election of the Puerto Rican governor. On January 26, 1924, with the delegation watching from the House Gallery, Córdova Dávila spoke about the memorial passed by the Puerto Rican legislature that had been presented to President Coolidge. The President's response was noncommittal and patronizing: "My suggestion is that you cooperate, one with the other, and attempt to harmonize your difficulties, if any arise, and all work together for the common welfare.... The only way to prepare for something better to-morrow is to do well the duties that come to us to-day."[18]

Several days later, on February 2, Córdova Dávila introduced H.R. 6583, a measure that proposed self-government and an elective governor. As a member of the delegation, Towner testified on behalf of the bill. All the insular politicians considered the fact that Puerto Ricans were by law American citizens and that many had served the Allied cause in the First World War as evidence of their readiness for greater autonomy.[19] Appearing before the Senate Committee on Territories and Insular Possessions in early March, Córdova Dávila argued that Puerto Ricans' patriotism and loyalty proved their fitness for greater self-rule.[20] He closed by invoking the benefits of a more liberal approach to Puerto Rico, particularly since West Indian, Latin American, and South American nations monitored U.S. policy. "Even the whole world is watching the policy of the United States in connection with Porto Rico and the Latin American countries to determine how the experiment will succeed of establishing a perfect understanding between the two great families inhabiting the Western Hemisphere, the Anglo-Saxon and the Latin," Córdova Dávila noted. "If you are to succeed in destroying the misgivings and the prejudices that have so long existed against you and in their stead developing a sincere, permanent, and fraternal union, which the geographical position of your republican neighbors in Central and South America renders so desirable, then the foundations for the success of such a policy must be laid in Porto Rico."[21] Within six weeks, the House Committee on Insular Affairs reported the bill favorably for the consideration of the whole House, but for reasons that remain unclear the bill never came up for consideration.[22] Meanwhile, a similar bill backed by Senator William King of Utah worked its way to approval in the Senate. S. 2448 was similar to the Córdova Dávila measure, although the first gubernatorial election would be pushed back to 1932. After the Coolidge administration signaled its support for the bill's passage, proponents grew hopeful when the Senate version was to be taken up in the House on the unanimous-consent calendar. But when the bill was called up in early June 1924, Representative Guinn Williams of Texas, an influential Democrat on the Insular Affairs Committee, objected, and it was referred back to the committee, from which it failed to emerge before the congressional term ended several days later.[23]

In 1928 Córdova Dávila pushed once again for a bill to allow the popular election of a governor. Momentum for the effort built because Governor Towner again endorsed the reform. Moreover, Representative Fiorello LaGuardia introduced his own bill to provide for the direct election of the governor, differing from Córdova Dávila's bill in that it granted universal suffrage to Puerto Ricans. LaGuardia testified before the House Insular Affairs Committee. "I do not know of an instance in the history of human liberty where we have the happy coincidence that the appointed governor sent to an island possession is inclined to agree not only with the right but the desirability of an elective governor for the island," he said.[24] Córdova Dávila, arguing on that same day before the committee for his own version of the bill, noted the "unrest and dissatisfaction" and the "constant agitation" about the question of the governor's direct election as well as the status issue. Statehood, he said, would be "acceptable," but only "with our customs, with our traditions, with our language, and with everything, that is part of our existence."[25] In a familiar refrain, he attacked the Supreme Court's Insular Cases, which he said had placed the status of Puerto Rico in a "very peculiar" light. "It is hard for me to understand how Porto Rico can be foreign to the United States in a domestic sense and not foreign in an international sense," Córdova Dávila told the committee. While Puerto Rican courts had ruled that in conferring citizenship, the Jones Act had indeed incorporated the island into the United States, the U.S. Supreme Court had reversed these judgments in cases such as *Balzac v. Porto Rico*. "The fathers of this country never dreamed of an empire with possessions foreign to the United States in a domestic sense, belonging to but not forming part of the Union," Córdova Dávila lectured the committee members. "You have to face this problem with courage, intelligence, and statesmanship. You cannot escape the responsibilities assumed by this country when the American flag was raised in Porto Rico. You can not be democratic at home and autocratic abroad. You can not have democracy within the continental limits of the United States and an empire in the so-called insular possessions. You have to be consistent with your principles. If not, you should discontinue the teachings of American ideals in Porto Rico, as it is unfair and cruel to instill in the minds of the Porto Ricans the principles of democracy and the liberal institutions of this country and deny them at the same time a decent status in the establishment of a government based upon these principles."[26]

Córdova Dávila had been saying these things for a decade, and his frustration was palpable. His attempts at political reform faltered largely because of systemic impediments. He faced a largely indifferent, Republican-controlled House and a string of GOP executives who had no particular interest in liberalizing Puerto Rican politics, either because they were averse to further embroiling the United States in overseas affairs or because they feared that destabilizing the status quo would undermine business and strategic interests.[27] Moreover, without a vote to trade on the House Floor, he had little leverage with voting Representatives, who had their own legislative agendas and constituencies to tend to. During a 1928 committee hearing on suffrage, Córdova Dávila told the chairman of the Insular Affairs Committee that while a handful of Members, including Representatives Charles Underhill of Massachusetts, Ralph Gilbert of Kentucky, and Frederick Dallinger of Massachusetts, took an interest in the problems of Puerto Rico, most Members did not. "I do not mean to seriously reflect on you gentlemen, and I am not blaming you for that," Córdova Dávila told Chairman Edgar Kiess of Pennsylvania. "You have big problems, national and international, and you have to pay attention to your other duties. You have a congressional district to serve and you have no time to spare for consideration of the important and intricate problems of Porto Rico. It is unquestionable that we are more qualified than you to handle our own affairs. At all events, the right to the control of our affairs is inherently and necessarily ours."[28]

On April 4, 1932, Córdova Dávila submitted a letter of resignation to the Speaker to accept an appointment as associate justice of the supreme court of Puerto Rico.[29] He formally resigned his seat on April 11 and departed for Puerto Rico. One of his colleagues, Resident Commissioner Camilo Osias of the Philippines, said the Puerto Rican judge "endeared himself by his genial nature and gentlemanly qualities. He served his people efficiently and faithfully."[30] Republican Joseph Hooper of Michigan described Córdova Dávila as "a distinguished man, distinguished in his profession as a lawyer, in his love of service to literature, and in the arduous work which he performed here on behalf of his beloved island."[31] A month after Córdova Dávila left office, the House approved the Senate version of a measure he had authored, changing the island's official name from "Porto Rico" to "Puerto Rico" to do "justice to the history, language, and traditions of the island."[32] He served on the court for about five years and was the voice of caution and compromise in May 1936 when the island was rattled by a wave of school strikes and shutdowns. "Anarchy and demagogy never provided a foundation for a happy and prosperous people," he noted.[33] Poor health forced Córdova Dávila to resign his post.[34] He died December 3, 1938, in Condado, Puerto Rico, and was interred in Fournier Cemetery in San Juan.

FOR FURTHER READING

Biographical Directory of the United States Congress, "Félix Córdova Dávila," http://bioguide.congress.gov.

MANUSCRIPT COLLECTION

Filson Historical Society (Louisville, KY). *Papers*: Arthur Yager Papers, 1913–1921, 1.75 cubic feet. Correspondents include Félix Córdova Dávila.

NOTES

1 Hearings before the House Committee on Insular Affairs, *Popular Election of the Governor of Porto Rico*, 70th Cong., 1st sess. (16 May 1928): 22.

2 Córdova Dávila's parents' names are listed in Conrado Asenjo, ed., *Quien es quien en Puerto Rico: Diccionario biografico de record personal* (San Juan, PR: Real Hermanos, Inc., 1936): 52.

3 "Deaths Reported," 9 October 1918, *Washington Post*: 14.

4 See Córdova Dávila's biographical entries in the *Congressional Directory*, 65th Congress (Washington, D.C.: Government Printing Office, 1919): 126; *Congressional Directory*, 68th Congress (Washington, D.C.: Government Printing Office, 1924): 127. Family names were provided by a great-grandson of Córdova Dávila's through César J. Ayala, a scholar of Puerto Rican-U.S. relations.

5 Fernando Bayron Toro, *Elecciones y partidos políticos de Puerto Rico, 1809–2000* (Mayagüez, PR: Editorial Isla, 2003): 149.

6 For more on the formation of these coalitions, see Truman R. Clark, *Puerto Rico and the United States, 1917–1933* (Pittsburgh, PA: University of Pittsburgh Press, 1975): 80–82.

7 For election results listing official returns for the parties, but not for individual candidates, see "Twenty-Fifth Annual Report of the Governor of Puerto Rico," House Document no. 220, 69th Cong., 1st sess. (22 January 1926): 67–68; "Twenty-Ninth Annual Report of the Governor of Puerto Rico," House Document no. 202, 71st Cong., 2nd sess. (5 December 1929): 83.

8 The Resident Commissioner seemed to be an afterthought. The *Record* for that day, which contained the first speech by the first woman in Congress (Jeannette Rankin of Montana) does not mention the Resident Commissioner's seating or his taking the oath of office, which for many years was optional for Delegates.

9 Córdova Dávila's views were aligned with those of the majority in the insular legislature, who believed the issue fell under its jurisdiction and was a means to "reaffirm and exercise its power," as provided under the Jones (Organic) Act of 1917.

10 Hearing before the Senate Committee on Territories and Insular Possessions, *Woman Suffrage in Porto Rico,* 70th Cong., 1st sess. (25 April 1928): 20–25; quotation on p. 21. This decision appears to have been as much a matter of principle for Córdova Dávila as it was motivated by concerns over the potential electoral gains by the Partido Socialista. As he told the House Insular Affairs Committee, which was considering an amendment to the Organic Act of 1917, "It seems to me, there is nothing more local to the people of Puerto Rico than this very question." However, he conceded, "If there ever should be an exception to that principle, this proposition comes nearer to justifying an exception to that policy than anything I know of." See Hearings before the Committee on Insular Affairs, U.S. House of Representatives, *Suffrage for Porto Rico*, 70th Cong., 1st sess. (30 April 1928): 10–11.

11 Alfredo Montalvo-Barbot, *Political Conflict and Constitutional Change in Puerto Rico, 1898–1952* (Lanham, MD: University Press of America, 1997): 92–93. See also "Twenty-Ninth Annual Report of the Governor of Puerto Rico," House Document no. 202, 71st Cong., 2nd sess. (5 December 1929).

12 *Congressional Record*, House, 65th Cong., 3rd sess. (12 February 1919): 3209–3212, quotation on p. 3212; "Puerto Rican Parties Demand Statehood," 2 March 1919, *New York Times*: 10.

13 *Congressional Record,* House, 67th Cong., 2nd sess. (2 March 1922): 3302; Clark, *Puerto Rico and the United States, 1917–1933*: 56, 62.

14 *Congressional Record*, House, 67th Cong., 2nd sess. (17 March 1922): 4040–4044; *Congressional Record*, House, 67th Cong., 2nd sess. (12 April 1922): 5406–5410.

15 *Congressional Record*, House, 67th Cong., 4th sess. (1 March 1923): 5037–5038.

16 Clark, *Puerto Rico and the United States, 1917–1933*: 78; Hearings before the Senate Committee on Territories and Insular Possessions (Part 2), *The Civil Government of Porto Rico*, 68th Cong., 1st sess. (9 March 1924): 90.

17 *Congressional Record*, House, 68th Cong., 1st sess. (11 January 1924): 861–862.

18 *Congressional Record*, House, 68th Cong., 1st sess. (26 January 1924): 1470.

19 Montalvo-Barbot, *Political Conflict and Constitutional Change in Puerto Rico, 1898–1952*: 89.

20 See Córdova Dávila's complete committee testimony regarding the bill in Hearings before the Senate Committee on Territories and Insular Possessions, *The Civil Government of Porto Rico* (Part 2), 68th Cong., 1st sess. (9 March 1924): 87–92. The island also exceeded its quota for money raised by Liberty Loan bond drives. "We have been at your side in the hour of crisis and the people who are good to share the responsibilities, hardships, and sacrifices at any great emergency and who are quick to respond to the call of public duty should also be good to share the prerogatives and advantages of your institutions and of American citizenship in normal times,"

Córdova Dávila said. The Resident Commissioner believed that a Puerto Rican native would be more attuned to the "people," the "customs," and the "psychology" of the islanders. Moreover, Córdova Dávila noted that Governor Towner had exceptional leadership qualities and was willing to forgo office in the mainland United States to serve in Puerto Rico. Córdova Dávila's belief that those who possessed Towner's administrative qualities were more likely to pursue political careers in the mainland United States implies that the pool of potential governors was shallow.

21 Hearings before the Senate Committee on Territories and Insular Possessions, *The Civil Government of Porto Rico* (Part 2): 90–92.

22 H. Rep. 291, "Amend the Organic Act of Porto Rico," 68th Cong., 2nd sess. (13 March 1924): 1–6.

23 Clark, *Puerto Rico and the United States, 1917–1933*: 89–90.

24 Hearings before the House Committee on Insular Affairs, *Popular Election of the Governor of Porto Rico*, 70th Cong, 1st sess. (16 May 1928): 4.

25 *Popular Election of the Governor of Porto Rico*: 17, 18–19.

26 Ibid., 22–23.

27 Montalvo-Barbot, *Political Conflict and Constitutional Change in Puerto Rico, 1898–1952*: 92.

28 Hearings before the House Committee on Insular Affairs, *Suffrage for Porto Rico*, 70th Cong., 1st sess. (30 April 1928): 12.

29 *Congressional Record*, House, 72nd Cong., 1st sess. (4 April 1932): 7419.

30 *Congressional Record*, 72nd Cong., 1st sess. (11 April 1932): 8240.

31 *Congressional Record*, House, 72nd Cong., 1st sess. (31 May 1932): 11938.

32 See H. Rep. 585, "Correct the Spelling of the Name of the Island of Porto Rico," 72nd Cong., 1st sess. (20 February 1932): 1–2; Córdova Dávila introduced the resolution as H.J. Res. 149. It cleared the Committee on Insular Affairs, and a Senate measure, S.J. Res. 36, was adopted by unanimous consent in lieu of the House bill. See also *Congressional Record*, 72nd Cong., 1st sess. (11 May 1932): 10030–10033.

33 "Moderation Urged on Puerto Ricans," 15 May 1936, *New York Times*: 11.

34 "Felix Cordova Dead; Puerto Rican Jurist," 4 December 1938, *New York Times*: 60.

Néstor Montoya
1862–1923

UNITED STATES REPRESENTATIVE 1921–1923
REPUBLICAN FROM NEW MEXICO

The second Hispanic from New Mexico to serve as a voting representative in the U.S. House, Néstor Montoya entered politics with a different perspective from that of his nonvoting predecessors. The editor of a prominent newspaper for over 20 years, Montoya used his role as a journalist to advocate fair treatment of his fellow *nuevomexicanos*, in print, on the street, and in politics. Although Montoya served only one term in Congress, his public life spanned almost 40 years. Like his contemporary Octaviano Larrazolo, Montoya had a political career that differed from those of his predecessors because he was an early surrogate representative for *nuevomexicano* interests. Reflecting on his career in public service, Montoya noted, "Activity, constancy, tact, and insistency are necessary qualifications to make your contributions and obtain results. Many times you have to wait for the … moment and not miss it … among so many that are doing the same thing."[1]

Néstor Montoya was born in Albuquerque, New Mexico, to Teodosio and Encarnación (Cervantes) Montoya, on April 14, 1862. He attended public schools in Albuquerque and graduated in 1881 from St. Michael's, a college preparatory academy in Santa Fe, after which he worked in a merchandising business for an uncle. Beginning in 1884, Montoya's bilingualism enabled him to find a variety of federal positions. He worked as a clerk for the U.S. Postal Service for four years and for the U.S. Treasury in Santa Fe. He also worked as an interpreter for the First, Second, and Fourth Judicial Districts. In 1886 Montoya, then a loyal Democrat, traveled to New Mexico with Territorial Delegate Antonio Joseph, speaking in support of Joseph's re-election to the House. Montoya and his wife, Florence, had six children: Néstor, Jr.; Paul; Theodore; Frances; Aurelia; and Estefanita.[2]

Montoya's dual career in journalism and politics began in Las Vegas, which served as the county seat for San Miguel County. Located at the end of the Santa Fe Trail in the northeast section of the territory, Las Vegas was the first New Mexican city many Easterners encountered. Founded in 1835, it grew rapidly during the next 40 years. The expansion of the Atchison, Topeka, and Santa Fe Railroad, with Las Vegas as its hub, brought large numbers of Anglo-Americans to the county, drastically altering the city's cultural and economic composition. Moreover, the explosive growth in farming and ranching that resulted from Anglo settlement led to large land purchases, severely disrupting the lifestyles of local *nuevomexicano* farmers. Many rural families had lived and worked on communal plots for years, and sometimes for generations. By 1889 active *nuevomexicano* resistance emerged when a group of vigilante farmers called Las Gorras Blancas (the White Caps) took arms, rode through the county, and "cut fences, burned crops and buildings, tore up railroad tracks … and terrorized unsympathetic landowners."[3] At the same time Las Gorras Blancas emerged, Montoya and E. H. Salazar founded *La voz del pueblo*, a Spanish-language newspaper that voiced the grievances of displaced farmers and other *nuevomexicanos* whose livelihoods had been destroyed by these socioeconomic changes. The newspaper, a four-page weekly that Montoya owned and edited for a year before selling it to a colleague, served as an outlet for the venting of local unrest while providing news of interest to *nuevomexicanos*.[4] Montoya's journalistic ventures supplemented his political activism, thus giving him an influential voice in New Mexican politics for his entire career in public service.

As a result of the civil unrest, some of San Miguel County's disaffected citizens formed El Partido Popular

Image courtesy of the Library of Congress

(the Popular Party) in 1890 to protest the rampant takeover of land and the displacement of *nuevomexicano* farmers. The party, which Montoya joined, was a combination of Anglo and *Hispano* elites who were dissatisfied with Republican rule, along with working-class and Socialist dissidents who sympathized with the political insurgents. The party's effectiveness at the polls boosted third-party candidates to major victories in the 1890 and 1892 territorial elections. Although he was a Democrat, Montoya also was one of the movement's beneficiaries. In 1889 Montoya was elected to the 29th Legislative Assembly (1890–1892), representing San Miguel County in the territorial house of representatives. After his first term in the legislature, Montoya moved to Albuquerque in 1895. In 1900 he founded another newspaper, *La bandera americana*, which he edited and managed for the rest of his life.[5] Montoya also started a Spanish-language press association and served as its president. This association merged with newspaper editors in eastern New Mexico to form a state press association in 1912. Montoya served as its president until his death.[6]

Montoya's political career progressed steadily in the 1900s. In 1902 he was elected to the 35th Legislative Assembly, (1903–1905) representing Bernalillo County, and served as speaker of the territorial house. Montoya was re-elected to serve as a member of the territorial council during the 36th Legislative Assembly (1905–1907).[7]

In 1910 he was a delegate to the New Mexico state constitutional convention and chaired its elective franchise committee.[8] He was part of an *Hispano* Republican coalition that secured constitutional provisions for protecting civil rights such as voting and education. During the 1910s, Montoya served on a number of boards, including the University of New Mexico's Board of Regents and, during World War I, on the Bernalillo County draft board. He also served as secretary of the Republican central committee of Bernalillo County for eight years.[9]

In 1920 Montoya was nominated by the Republican Party to run for New Mexico's At-Large seat in the U.S. House. His opponent was Antonio J. Lucero, a prominent Democrat. Lucero was a journalist and assistant editor of the *La voz del pueblo*, the newspaper which Montoya had founded decades earlier in Las Vegas. He also served as chief clerk of the territorial council in the 31st Legislative Assembly (1894–1896) and as New Mexico's first secretary of state for two terms (1912–1917).[10]

Montoya's campaign reflected the Republicans' 1920 platform, which called for women's suffrage, infrastructure improvements, tax reform, and fair wages. He crisscrossed the state discussing a variety of local and national issues while promoting Republican candidates at the state level.[11] Lucero, on the other hand, was an aggressive campaigner who affiliated himself with Richard Hanna, the Democratic nominee for governor. Lucero ran on a platform that advocated U.S. entry into the League of Nations and supported the Volstead Act, which provided the statutory framework for the newly adopted 18th Amendment (Prohibition) to the U.S. Constitution. He also pledged to support legislation for World War I veterans.[12]

During the election, Montoya fought for control of his newspaper against Frank Hubbell, a prominent entrepreneur who served in the territorial legislature and had run against Thomas Catron for U.S. Senator in 1916.[13] Hubbell was president of the newspaper's publishing company, while Montoya and his 21-year-old daughter, Frances, who served as treasurer, managed its day-to-day affairs. In September 1920, Hubbell, acting as majority shareholder, convinced the board of directors to remove Montoya as editor. The next month Hubbell forcibly evicted Frances and two other staffers from the newspaper's offices. When Frances resisted, Hubbell called the sheriff to escort her off the premises. The sheriff arrived to find that the "girl was struggling with him" and arrested Hubbell for assault. Frances "fell in a faint" and "was delirious when [bystanders] put her in a taxicab." Upon hearing the news, Montoya stopped campaigning and rushed back to Albuquerque.[14] *La bandera americana* lambasted Hubbell and, regarding Montoya, noted "The machines, paper or press would not matter at all to him personally if they had been taken by force, but it is an indignity and humiliation that this assault was committed … against an innocent girl, the sight of which terrorized the entire community."[15]

The conflict between Montoya and Hubbell also involved a political dimension; Montoya, who ran as a Republican, treated the newspaper as a Republican organ, but Hubbell supported the Democratic ticket. Montoya secured an injunction to destroy issues that had been published under Hubbell's watch, noting they "did not conform to my political policy." Also, Montoya argued that he had been ousted without due authority and requested an injunction for the maintenance of the status quo until a final decision was rendered.[16] According to media coverage, the court awarded Montoya a permanent injunction, enabling him to remain editor of *La bandera americana*, agreeing that Hubbell and his son had conspired to wrest the newspaper from Montoya "for the purpose of influencing voters not to support Montoya … [but instead] to support his opponent, A. Lucero."[17] Despite the controversy, Montoya beat Lucero with 52 to 47 percent of the vote; A. J. McDonald, a third-party candidate, received the remainder of the vote.[18]

Elected to the 67th Congress (1921–1923), Montoya won spots on the House Committees on Indian Affairs and the Public Lands. Such assignments were important to representatives from Western states with sprawling tracts of federal land and numerous American Indian reservations.[19] During his term, Montoya submitted petitions for constituents' pensions and petitions for public works projects in New Mexico.[20] One of the bills Montoya supported, H.R. 10874, was designed to increase compensation for World War I veterans. A father whose three sons served in the war, Montoya told his colleagues, "It is our duty … to recognize, approve, and exalt said qualities by national recognition and pride.… In casting my vote for the bill I do so not as a partisan or in a partisan spirit, but as an American, as Representative of my state, New Mexico, performing a duty to the best part of our citizenship—the American soldier."[21] Although the bill passed the House and the Senate, it was vetoed by President Warren Harding. The House then overrode the President's veto, but the Senate did not.[22]

At the end of the first session, Montoya wrote a public letter to his constituents about his activities as their Representative. Montoya listed his efforts to secure numerous public works appropriations for the state, including an "allocation of $150,000 for a site and new federal building in Silver City" and an "allocation of $18,000 to pave the streets around the federal building in Santa Fe." Both measures (H.R. 2900 and H.R. 2901) were submitted for consideration to the appropriate committees, where they died. Montoya also sought protections and exemptions for Indian reservations; H.R. 2904 requested a commission to "ascertain and determine the rights of persons occupying Pueblo Indian lands in the State of New Mexico," but this proposal also died in committee.[23] During the 1921 summer recess, Montoya campaigned throughout New Mexico for Holm Bursum, a prominent Republican who was appointed to the Senate in March 1921 and elected to a full term that September.[24]

Montoya announced his renomination bid in July 1922. His platform consisted not only of promoting national legislation, but also of "actively helping in the passage of the Smith–McNary reclamation bill," which allowed states to provide land and employment to military and naval veterans. Montoya also reminded voters of his service: "In the year and a half that I have served constantly as your member of congress I have attended to hundreds of matters confided to me by my constituents … I have attended to many land matters before the interior department, general land office … Indian matters, immigration matters, claims, pensions, post office matters, mail routes and rural carriers, by the hundreds."[25] One local newspaper endorsed Montoya because of his ability to acquire "things of great benefit for the working people of this state, in addition to always keeping an eye on the appointments that have to be made to fill federal offices in this state, which are by his recommendations."[26] However, Montoya entered the race with a divided political base. He acknowledged that Independents could vote against the Republican ticket throughout the state and within his home county of Bernalillo. He also cited the 1920 Hubbell controversy, noting that Hubbell "was one of the most active workers … and fought the whole republican ticket." One weapon Montoya wielded was control over the selection of the state's postmasters. In the words of an observer, "Representatives control the appointment of all postmasters ... a prerogative in which the senators do not interfere ... New Mexico has a great many postmasters, and Montoya has recommended the appointment of all of them."[27]

However, larger changes caused problems for Montoya. After the 19th Amendment, guaranteeing women's suffrage, passed in 1919, New Mexico ratified it in February 1920. In 1921 the state amended its constitution to permit women to hold public office, despite opposition from many *Hispano* men. Many Republican women threw their support for the At-Large Representative seat to Adelina "Nina" Otero-Warren, a suffrage advocate from Santa Fe who served in a number of public appointed positions. Many Santa Feans rallied to support Otero-Warren's candidacy, and as a result, Montoya received only marginal support in the state capital, even though he actively supported women's suffrage. Montoya's supporters began a disinformation campaign questioning whether Otero-Warren's campaign should be taken seriously. At the nominating convention, delegates elected Otero-Warren with 446½ to Montoya's 99½ votes.[28] Despite his crushing loss, Montoya stumped for Otero-Warren, calling her "my successor in the Congress of the United States." "It is going to be my mission ... to inform the people of this state what a woman can do in Congress," he told an audience. However, Otero-Warren lost to John Morrow, a prominent Democratic politician.[29] Alice Robertson, the first woman from Oklahoma elected to Congress, said when Montoya "came back and told me about [his nomination defeat], he did so in the most beautiful, most chivalrous, and most courteous way, speaking in highest terms of the lady and his hopes for her election."[30]

Montoya returned to the House for the two remaining sessions. Two months before the end of his term, Montoya died in his Washington home, on January 13, 1923. As was customary, the House adjourned for one day and reserved another to honor Montoya's memory. An escort of five Representatives and one Senator traveled to New Mexico to attend his funeral.[31] Ten Members submitted memorial addresses to honor Montoya.

Montoya's predecessor and friend, Benigno Cárdenas Hernández, wrote two obituaries, one for the *Congressional Record* and the other appeared for *La bandera americana*. In the latter, Hernández said Montoya was "one of the favorite sons of this state, and [an] exemplary citizen ... who reflected the honor and credit to our Spanish-speaking people. He was always a faithful defender of the Hispanic-American people, which today sheds its tears of true sorrow as a tribute to his remembrance."[32] The House also agreed to H. Res. 494, which authorized the payment of one month's salary to Frances and Néstor Montoya, Jr., who had served as their late father's congressional aides.[33]

FOR FURTHER READING

Biographical Directory of the United States Congress, "Néstor Montoya," http://bioguide.congress.gov.

Gutiérrez, Ezekiel. "Néstor Montoya: Un hombre derecho." *La Herencia del norte* 23 (Fall 1999): 20.

United States House of Representatives, 67th Cong., 4th sess., 1923. *Néstor Montoya: Memorial Addresses Delivered in the House of Representatives of the United States in Memory of Néstor Montoya, Late a Representative from New Mexico* (Washington, D.C.: Government Printing Office, 1924).

NOTES

1 Néstor Montoya, "Nestor Montoya Is a Candidate for House Seat," 5 July 1922, *Albuquerque Morning Journal:* 7.

2 *Fourteenth Census of the United States, 1920*: Old Albuquerque, Bernalillo, New Mexico, Roll T625_1074, page 14B, Library of Congress, Washington, D.C., http://search.ancestrylibrary.com (accessed 18 January 2012); *Thirteenth Census of the United States, 1910*: Old Albuquerque, Bernalillo, New Mexico, Roll T624_913, page 18A, http://search.ancestrylibrary.com (accessed 18 January 2012); Helen Haines, *History of New Mexico from the Spanish Conquest to the Present Time, 1530–1890* (New York: New Mexico Historical Publishing Co., 1891): 424–427; "Nestor Montoya," in Maurilio E. Vigil, *Los Patrones: Profiles of Hispanic Political Leaders in New Mexico History* (Washington, D.C.: University Press of America, 1980): 146–148; "Montoya Suddenly Dies in Washington," 13 January 1923, *Santa Fe New Mexican*: 1; "Nestor Montoya, State's Representative in House, Dies at Washington

Home," 14 January 1923, *Albuquerque Morning Journal*: 1; B.C. Hernández, "Obito por el Hon. B. C. Hernández," 19 January 1923, *La bandera americana*: 1. Translated as "Obituary by the Hon B.C. Hernández" by Translations International, Inc. (July 2009). One obituary notes that Montoya's mother was "a direct descendant of the famous Spanish author Cervantes."

3 Doris L. Meyer, *Speaking for Themselves: Neomexicano Cultural Identity and the Spanish-Language Press, 1880–1920* (Albuquerque: University of New Mexico Press, 1996): 46–50; Robert J. Rosenbaum, *Mexicano Resistance in the Southwest* (Dallas, TX: Southern Methodist University Press, 1998; reprint of 1981 edition): 99–101, 168. For a summary of the actions of Las Gorras Blancas and reactions from law enforcement, see especially pp. 103–110. One of the group's targets was former Territorial Delegate Francisco Manzanares, who owned land in San Miguel County.

4 Rosenbaum, *Mexicano Resistance in the Southwest*: 118–119; for a detailed explanation of the role of Spanish-language newspapers in territorial New Mexico, see Meyer, *Speaking for Themselves*: 3–17. For an overview of the territorial press in New Mexico, see Porter Stratton, *The Territorial Press of New Mexico, 1834–1912* (Albuquerque: University of New Mexico Press, 1968).

5 Rosenbaum, *Mexicano Resistance in the Southwest*: 123–134, 137–139; see also pp. 169 and 178 for charts that detail the results for San Miguel County's elections in 1890 and 1892; "Nestor Montoya, State's Representative in House, Dies at Washington Home"; Territory of New Mexico, *Report of the Secretary of the Territory, 1905–1906, and Legislative Manual 1907* (Albuquerque, NM: Morning Journal, 1907): 172, 177–178. Montoya served as editor and manager of *La bandera americana* until the publication of the issue dated 10 November 1922.

6 "Nestor Montoya, State's Representative in House, Dies at Washington Home"; Stratton, *The Territorial Press of New Mexico, 1834–1912*: 66.

7 Territory of New Mexico, *Report of the Secretary of the Territory, 1905–1906, and Legislative Manual 1907*: 172, 177–178; "Nestor Montoya," in Vigil, *Los Patrones: Profiles of Hispanic Political Leaders in New Mexico History*: 147. Vigil writes, "In 1892 Montoya was elected to the territorial House of Representatives from Santa Fe County and continues in the body through 1903, when he served as Speaker of the House of Representatives." The Territorial Blue Books list Montoya's service years as 1889 and 1903–1907, with no service in between.

8 Dorothy I. Cline, *New Mexico's Constitution: A 19th Century Product* (Santa Fe, NM: The Lightning Tree, 1985): 63; Territory of New Mexico, *Report of the Secretary of the Territory, 1909–1910, and Legislative Manual, 1911* (Santa Fe: New Mexican Printing Company, 1911): 126; "Nestor Montoya," in Vigil, *Los Patrones: Profiles of Hispanic Political Leaders in New Mexico History*: 147.

9 Helen Haines, *History of New Mexico from the Spanish Conquest to the Present Time, 1530–1890* (New York: New Mexico Historical Publishing Co., 1891): 424–427; "Nestor Montoya," in Vigil, *Los Patrones: Profiles of Hispanic Political Leaders in New Mexico History*: 147; "Nestor Montoya, State's Representative in House, Dies at Washington Home": 1. Haines notes that Montoya was a "Democrat in politics" in 1891; by 1910 Montoya had switched to the Republican Party.

10 Territory of New Mexico, *Report of the Secretary of the Territory, 1905–1906, and Legislative Manual 1907*: 173; Benjamin M. Read, *Illustrated History of New Mexico* (New York: Arno Press, 1976; reprint of 1912 edition): 753; "Office of the Secretary, New Mexico's First Secretary of State," http://www.sos.state.nm.us/History/PastSOS.html (accessed 21 September 2010).

11 "Republican Platform in Brief," 9 September 1920, *Albuquerque Morning Journal*: 4; "Mechem Rally at Belen Not Up to Hanna's," 7 October 1920, *Albuquerque Morning Journal*: 1; "Republican Speakers Address 100 Voters at Los Griegos Rally," 12 October 1920, *Albuquerque Morning Journal*: 1; "Montoya Smashes Speed Records in Disposing Instantly of Principal Issues," 30 October 1920, *Santa Fe New Mexican*: 1.

12 "Hanna Tour Presages Smashup for Bosses," 20 September 1920, *Santa Fe New Mexican*: 1; "Wants Law to Hit The Vote-Buyers," 1 October 1920, *Santa Fe New Mexican*: 1; "Antonio Lucero," 2 October 1920, *Santa Fe New Mexican*: 4; "Lucero States His Stand for Welfare of Ex-Service Men," 30 October 1920, *Santa Fe New Mexican*: 8. The *Santa Fe New Mexican* endorsed Lucero for the House seat in "Antonio Lucero," 2 October 1920, *Santa Fe New Mexican*: 4.

13 Frank Hubbell was a powerful rancher who operated a large business empire in New Mexico. He owned a merchandising company and a public works company, which he sold to the city of Albuquerque, and served as director of a life insurance company. Hubbell also had an extensive political résumé, having served as chairman of the Republican County Central Committee of Bernalillo County and as chairman of the state Republican committee. For a brief biography, see Charles F. Coan, *A History of New Mexico*. vol. 2 (Chicago and New York: American Historical Society, Inc., 1925): 44–46.

14 "Montoya's Daughter Is Ejected by Hubbell, Girl Delirious as a Result, Family Reports Father Ends Speaking Tour; Hurries Home," 7 October 1920, *Albuquerque Morning Journal*: 3. Montoya eventually sued Hubbell for $30,000 for alleged injuries to his daughter. "To Ask $30,000 of F. A. Hubbell, Montoya States," 8 October 1920, *Albuquerque Morning Journal*: 2.

15 "El Sr. Montoya ha estado ocupado en la campaña del estado … sin pensar por un momento que el Sr. Hubbell buscará ventaja y en su ausencia y de una manera violentá, por la fuerza, tomará posecion [*sic*] de la oficina, y para hacerlo cobardemente cometió un ultraje encontra de la Señorita Frances Montoya … por cuya violencia, lastimaduras en los jalones, moretones en los brazos … nada le hubiera importado de máquinas, papeles o que a él personalmente lo hubieran tirado por la fuerza, si hubieran podido

pero es una indignidad y humillación que tal ultraje se cometiera ... encontra de una niña inocente cuyo espectáculo terrorizó a toda a la comunidad." "Debido a la accion de Frank A. Hubbell de haberse apoderado de la imprenta por la fuerza y violencia," *La bandera americana*: (Albuquerque, NM): 9 October 1920: 1. Translated as "Due to Frank A. Hubbell's Taking Control of the Printery by Force and Violence" by Translations International, Inc. (January 2011); *Fourteenth Census of the United States, 1920:* Old Albuquerque, Bernalillo, New Mexico, Roll T625_1074, page 14B, lists Frances's age.

16 "Burns Issue of Paper Opposing His Candidacy," 10 October 1920, *Albuquerque Morning Journal*: 4. According to this article, during the trial, Montoya was "confronted every few minutes with the difficulty of explaining checks signed, rent paid and tax returns made by himself in the name of the company and under his signature as an official of that company." Montoya acknowledged that "in 1907 La Bandera has been incorporated and later that, $2100 in stock had been issued to him and $5100 to Frank Hubbell, although neither paid for this stock in cash at the time." The article also states that Montoya admitted "he and Hubbell were among a number of men who contributed to the organization of La Bandera in 1901 and that they had run it on a 50-50 basis ... before its incorporation." While the signed checks indicate that Hubbell was an official and Montoya a secretary, Montoya said he and Hubbell each played a role "as it existed" at that time. See "Montoya Fight for Newspaper Given Hearing," 14 October 1920, *Albuquerque Morning Journal*: 4.

17 "Hubbell and Son Conspired to Secure La Bandera, Is Held by the District Court," 20 October 1920, *Santa Fe New Mexican*: 2; "Hubbell Will Take Case to Supreme Court," 16 October 1920, *Albuquerque Morning Journal*: 4. After the verdict was rendered, Hubbell announced that he would appeal to the state supreme court and would publish another Spanish-language newspaper that would promote Democratic policies. For an alternative version of the court decision, see "Frank A. Hubbell: Prohibido permanente de interfirir con 'La bandera americana,'" 15 October 1920, *La bandera americana*: 1.

18 "Election Statistics, 1920 to Present," http://history.house.gov/institution/election-statistics/election-statistics. Lucero wrote Montoya a congratulatory letter. A copy of the letter, along with Montoya's response is included in "El hon. Antonio Lucero congratula a don Nestor Montoya," 19 October 1920, *La bandera americana*: 2.

19 David T. Canon, Garrison Nelson, and Charles Stewart III, eds., *Committees in the U.S. Congress, 1789–1946: Member Assignments*, vol. 3 (Washington, D.C.: CQ Press): 736. These committees, which were important for Montoya's constituents and for Members from Western states, ranked near the middle or the bottom in terms of attractiveness to Members. According to Charles Stewart, the House Committees on Indian Affairs and Public Lands ranked 37.5 and 49.5, respectively, out of a total of 69 committees, from 1875 to 1947. However, among committees continually in existence, both committees ranked somewhat higher in terms of attractiveness to Members: Indian Affairs ranked 17th, and Public Lands 23rd out of a total of 29 committees. For more information about committee attractiveness in this period, see Charles Stewart III, "Committee Hierarchies in the Modernizing House, 1875–1947," *American Journal of Political Science* 36, no. 4 (November 1992): 835–856. The charts chronicling committee attractiveness are on pp. 845–846 and p. 848.

20 *Congressional Record*, Index, 67th Cong., 1st sess.: 215; *Congressional Record*, Index, 67th Cong., 2nd sess.: 198.

21 *Congressional Record*, House, 67th Cong., 2nd sess. (24 March 1922): 4453.

22 *Congressional Record*, Appendix and Index, 67th Cong.: 399.

23 "Un proyecto pide de que el gobierno apropie $150,000 para un sitio y un nuevo edificio federal en Silver City ... apropriación por $18,000 para pavimentar las calles al derredor del edificio federal en Santa Fé." "Montoya en el congreso," *La bandera americana* (Albuquerque, NM), 22 April 1921: 1. Translated as "Montoya in Congress," by Translations International, Inc. (January 2011); *Congressional Record*, Appendix and Index, 67th Cong., 1st sess.: 452; *Congressional Record*, House, 67th Cong., 1st sess. (13 April 1921): 218. Montoya submitted eight bills for consideration, all of which died in committee.

24 For more information about Bursum, see *Biographical Directory of the United States Congress*, "Holm Olaf Bursum," http://bioguide.congress.gov. For a description of Montoya's campaign activities on Bursum's behalf, see "El representante," 19 August 1921, *La bandera americana*: 2; "Para Washington," 7 October 1921, *La bandera americana*: 1; "Montoya espera el desarrollo de reclamacion," 14 October 1921, *La bandera americana*: 1.

25 "Nestor Montoya Is a Candidate for House Seat," 5 July 1922, *Albuquerque Morning Journal*: 7. Montoya also promoted the Smith–McNary bill to his *Hispano* constituents. For example, see "Montoya: Haciendo buen trabajo para el desarrollo de terreno," 17 January 1922, *La bandera americana*: 1.

26 "Cosas de grande beneficio para el pueblo trabajador de éste estado, además de estar siempre vigilando también que los nombramientos que se tienen que hacer para llenar oficinas federales en este estado los cuales están bajo sus recomendaciones." "El primer: Canonazo de la ampaña congresional," *La bandera americana* (Albuquerque, NM), 30 June 1922: 2. Translated as "The First Cannon Shot of the Congressional Campaign" by Translations International, Inc. (January 2011).

27 "Party Unity Is Necessary, Says Nestor Montoya," 10 July 1922, *Albuquerque Morning Journal*: 3.

28 Charlotte Whaley, *Nina Otero-Warren of Santa Fe* (Albuquerque: University of New Mexico Press, 1994): 94–97; "Republicans Nominate Dr. C. L. Hill, Dona Ana County, for Governor,"

9 September 1922, *Albuquerque Morning Journal*: 1, 2. The amendment passed because of Anglo support in the counties of "Little Texas" in southeastern New Mexico. For a detailed description of the women's suffrage movement in New Mexico, see Joan M. Jensen, "'Disfranchisement Is a Disgrace': Women and Politics in New Mexico, 1900–1940," *New Mexico Historical Review* 56, no. 1 (January 1981): 6–35.

29 "Republicans on Campaign Tour Well Received," 23 September 1922, *Albuquerque Morning Journal*: 3; "Election Statistics, 1920 to Present," http://history.house.gov/institution/election-statistics/election-statistics. For a detailed account of this race, see Elizabeth Salas, "Ethnicity, Gender, and Divorce: Issues in the 1922 Campaign by Adelina Otero-Warren for the U.S. House of Representatives," *New Mexico Historical Review* 70, no. 4 (October 1995): 367–382.

30 United States, House, 67th Cong., 4th sess., 1923. *Néstor Montoya. Memorial Addresses Delivered in the House of Representatives of the United States in Memory of Néstor Montoya, late a Representative from New Mexico* (Washington, D.C.: Government Printing Office, 1924): 32. For more information about Alice Robertson, see *Biographical Directory of the United States Congress,* "Alice Mary Robertson," http://bioguide.congress.gov/.

31 "Montoya Dies Suddenly in Washington," 13 January 1923, *Santa Fe New Mexican*: 1; "Nestor Montoya, State's Representative in House, Dies at Washington Home."

32 "Uno de los hijos predilectos de este estado, un excelente ciudadano … que reflejaba honor y crédito a nuestra gente de habla española. Siempre fue fiel defensor del pueblo hispanoamericano, que hoy derrama lágrimas de sincero pesar como un tributo a su memoria." Hernández, "Obito por el Hon. B. C. Hernández." Translated as "Obituary by the Hon. B. C. Hernández" by Translations International, Inc. (July 2009).

33 *Congressional Record*, House, 67th Cong., 4th sess. (26 January 1923): 2527–2528.

Octaviano A. Larrazolo
1859–1930

UNITED STATES SENATOR 1928–1929
REPUBLICAN FROM NEW MEXICO

In 1928 Octaviano A. Larrazolo, a free-thinking Republican lawyer from New Mexico who immigrated to the United States as a boy, was elected the first Hispanic Senator in U.S. history. A champion of equal opportunity who was known throughout the state as the "silver-tongued orator"—a reference to his eloquent rhetoric in Spanish and English—Larrazolo built a political career around his persistent defense of Hispanic civil rights. He managed to transcend New Mexico's machine politics, and though he made enemies in both parties, he was "the great champion of the Spanish-American people, always uncompromising in his concern for their welfare.... He was their acknowledged spokesman," said his fellow New Mexican Senator Sam Bratton.[1]

Octaviano Ambrosio Larrazolo was born on December 7, 1859, to Octaviano Larrazolo, an affluent landowner, and Donaciana Larrazolo in El Valle de Allende, Chihuahua, Mexico.[2] Larrazolo grew up in relative comfort and was taught to read and write while he was young. He later attended school in town but withdrew after being beaten by his teacher.[3] His situation changed rapidly during the mid-1860s when the Larrazolo family was left destitute after supporting Benito Juárez's revolt against the French occupation of Mexico. In 1863 French troops ransacked the Larrazolos' home after forcing the family to give them quarter.[4]

In late November 1870, as his family struggled with insolvency, Larrazolo left home to attend school in the United States under the care of John B. Salpointe, a Catholic bishop.[5] For the next five years, Larrazolo attended private schools in Tucson, Arizona, and Las Cruces, New Mexico. After completing his primary studies in 1875, Larrazolo enrolled at St. Michael's College in Santa Fe, New Mexico.[6] A year later, he left St. Michael's and returned to Tucson, where he worked odd jobs, selling shoes and teaching classes.[7] Unsure about his future, he briefly considered joining the priesthood before he accepted a teaching position in San Elizario, Texas.[8] Fluent in English and Spanish, Larrazolo taught during the day and studied law at night. In preparation for a legal career, Larrazolo became a U.S. citizen on December 11, 1884, and registered with Texas' Democratic Party. In 1885 he was appointed clerk of the U.S. District and Circuit Courts for the Western District of Texas.[9] He married Rosalia Cobos in 1881, and they had two sons, Juan Bautista and José Maria, and a daughter, Rosalia. His wife died in 1891, the day after their daughter was born, and the following year Larrazolo married María Garcia, with whom he had nine children: Octaviano Ambrosio, Josefina, Carlos G., Luis Fernando, Heliodoro A., Maria, Justiniano Santiago, Pablo Frederico, and Rafael E.[10]

Larrazolo began his political career in the winter of 1886, winning the clerkship of El Paso's district court. He was re-elected in 1888 and admitted to the Texas bar the same year. Larrazolo was elected district attorney for Texas' 34th Judicial District in El Paso in 1890 and again in 1892.[11] After his second term, Larrazolo moved to New Mexico and opened a law office in Las Vegas, where he quickly became enmeshed in Democratic politics and earned a reputation as a captivating speaker.

In 1900, 1906, and 1908, Larrazolo ran unsuccessfully for the office of Territorial Delegate to the U.S. Congress. As a Democrat, Larrazolo faced an uphill struggle from the start because New Mexico's majority-Hispanic population leaned Republican. Moreover, he ran for office as New Mexico's political structure underwent a fundamental change.

As a Hispanic Democrat, Larrazolo was a minority member of the state's minority party, and as the new, predominantly Anglo-Democratic population grew, it became more resistant to the ambitions of Hispanic

Image courtesy of the Library of Congress

politicians. Despite receiving little support from his own party's base in east New Mexico, Larrazolo nearly won the elections of 1906 and 1908 because he managed to court Hispanic Republicans in the central and western parts of the state.[12] "The election would have been won if the eastern Democratic counties had but given the head of the ticket the same support they gave the balance of the ticket," a frustrated Larrazolo told the Democratic Territorial Central Committee.[13] Tensions peaked in 1910 when Democrats refused to send Hispanic delegates to New Mexico's constitutional convention and ultimately opposed provisions that guaranteed Spanish speakers their civil rights.[14]

Chastened by his experiences, and unwilling to associate with "a party whose principle of 'equal rights to all'" was "but a shining platitude," Larrazolo broke with New Mexico's Democrats in 1911.[15] In many respects it was a difficult decision, since the Republicans offered few alternatives. Throughout the 1900s, Larrazolo's relationship with the Republican Party had been notably confrontational, and while Anglo-Democrats shunned him, the GOP repeatedly mocked him and accused him of race-baiting.[16] Republican newspapers criticized Larrazolo and his supporters for "working the race prejudice racket for all they are worth," and claimed that Larrazolo had "appealed to race hatred in the Spanish-speaking sections of the Territory."[17] As late as 1908, the *Santa Fe New Mexican* accused Larrazolo of "posing as a high-toned decendant [*sic*] of the kings of Spain and as a noble Spaniard of the bluest blood, although he was born in Chihuahua, Mexico in what the New Mexican is informed, is an Indian settlement."[18]

Abandoned by Democrats and a perennial target for Republicans, Larrazolo began to set his own course. In 1910, as he stumped in favor of New Mexico's constitution, Larrazolo attacked the machine politics that he felt were exploiting Hispanic voters across the state. "I do not believe that it is the duty of a citizen to surrender his conscience to any man or any set of men, or to any party of any name," he said.[19] "If it is true that there are bosses over you and you are not free," he told his listeners, "you … have allowed yourselves to be controlled by other men but you will be controlled by bosses only as long as you permit the yoke to rest on you." Larrazolo asked if New Mexico would approve a constitution guaranteeing civil protections, or whether Hispanic New Mexicans would essentially "remain in slavery." Larrazolo seemed to sense that New Mexico was dangerously close to following the lead of the American South, where Jim Crow laws had systematically stripped African Americans of their rights in the half-century since congressional Reconstruction. "Every native citizen must unite in supporting this constitution because it secures to you people of New Mexico your rights—every one of them; the rights also of your children and in such a manner that they can never be taken away," he continued. It was imperative that Hispanics support the constitution, he told them, "if you want to acquire your freedom and transmit this sacred heritage in the land hallowed by the blood of your forefathers who fought to protect it." "Do not wait until you are put in the position of Arizona which in two years will be able to disfranchise every Spanish speaking citizen."[20] Larrazolo feared that without voting rights, Hispanic landowners would be forced to sell out to the railroad.[21]

His speech in 1910 was a milestone. Larrazolo had forced both parties to acknowledge the concerns of Hispanic New Mexicans, and in doing so he became the most vocal leader of his generation. A year later, still attacking New Mexico's political system, Larrazolo said he had registered as a Republican so that he could "administer equal rights to all." Addressing a group of Hispanic Republicans, Larrazolo said, "I have not come to you to ask you to wage war, my friends who are descendants of the noble conquistadores, with the Anglo-Saxon race," because whether they liked it or not New Mexico needed the Anglos' capital investments.[22]

Having been cast by both parties as a race agitator, Larrazolo remained nonetheless a powerful influence in state politics. Many Republicans blamed him for the numerous Democratic victories in the first election after New Mexico attained statehood. Though neither Anglo-Democrats nor Anglo-Republicans, nor even moderate

Hispanics, liked what he said about "slavery," "bosses," "freedom," "war," and their "sacred heritage," they could not ignore him. Larrazolo had wide name recognition, spoke eloquently, and was not afraid to break with his party to protect Hispanic civil rights.[23] Though a registered Republican, he campaigned for Hispanic candidates of both parties, among them his close friend Democrat Ezequiel C. de Baca, who became governor in 1916.[24]

Two years later, in 1918, New Mexican Republicans nominated Larrazolo for governor. Democrats had already selected their own Hispanic candidate, Felix García. Despite Larrazolo's reputation as a political liability, Republican leaders hoped he would draw votes both from older Anglo conservatives and Hispanic voters. Accepting his party's nod during World War I, Larrazolo challenged the GOP to exert the strong leadership it had shown during the Civil War. "The Republican party is the only one which knows the science of making men free," he said. "It made this union free. Why is it not the party in conjunction with the allies in these later days to be entrusted with the task of making the whole world free?"[25]

Though Larrazolo touted the Republican Party's "noble heritage," he struggled to clarify his own past, and his reputation for generating controversy gave many voters pause.[26] Factionalism and personal rivalries continued to divide Hispanic voters, and some worried that Larrazolo's bold approach would undermine his earlier accomplishments. Anglos, too, were skeptical, and to allay fears that he would favor Hispanic interests over New Mexican interests, Larrazolo declared, "I shall put into practice the principles that I have defended and on account of which undoubtedly I have made many enemies. Those principles are: 'Equal rights and privileges for all citizens of New Mexico without regard to ancestry.'"[27] Amid a crippling drought and a statewide outbreak of the flu, Larrazolo won by a scant 1,319 votes.[28]

Larrazolo's ambitious agenda as governor (1919 to 1921) was alternately supported and attacked by Republicans. Larrazolo appealed to the federal government for drought relief, created a department of public health, and as a pioneer in the idea of public domain, urged the national administration to cede unused federal lands to the states. For his efforts he was named president of the League of Public Lands.[29] In 1919 Larrazolo declared martial law to quell a strike by coal miners in McKinley and Colfax Counties, and with a majority-Republican legislature, passed measures that restricted child labor, mandated regular school attendance, raised schoolteachers' salaries, and ensured that bilingual instruction was available in New Mexico's schools. But Larrazolo had an independent streak during a period in New Mexican politics when independent minds were scorned, and he had spent his formative years as a Democrat. He backed the passage of the 19th Amendment, and unlike the state and national legislatures, supported President Woodrow Wilson's call for a League of Nations. He was derided nationally after he pardoned Mexican troops accused of killing American citizens during Pancho Villa's raid, prompting the *Chicago Daily Tribune* to observe, "New Mexico seems to have been reclaimed by Mexico … without even taking the trouble to secede."[30] But it was his decision to pass income tax legislation that finally alienated his party at home. Business owners and miners threatened lawsuits, and the Republican legislature, led by old guard conservatives, repealed the measure. But Larrazolo vetoed the repeal, at great political cost, and the income tax remained.[31] As his term ended, Republican dissenters vowed, "No more Old Mexico in New Mexico."[32]

Though Larrazolo was not renominated for governor, he was not away from politics for long.[33] He moved back to El Paso and opened a law office, but returned to New Mexico two years later. Despite his chronic asthma, Larrazolo spoke throughout the state, and in 1923 he was nominated by the state legislature for the governorship of Puerto Rico. Although President Harding appointed another candidate, Larrazolo used his renewed popularity as a springboard back into public service. He lost election to a seat on the state supreme court in 1924, but was elected to the state house of representatives from Bernalillo County in 1927.[34] As a state legislator, Larrazolo addressed some of the same concerns he did as governor, chief among them state land ownership and land reclamation.[35]

Shortly after Larrazolo won re-election to New Mexico's house of representatives in 1928, Democratic U.S. Senator Andrieus A. Jones died. Republican Bronson M. Cutting, who had been appointed to Jones's seat, asked Larrazolo to run for the unexpired term set to end six months later on March 4, 1929. The Republican Party ran Larrazolo for the unexpired term and Cutting for the full term. By the time Larrazolo reluctantly accepted his party's nomination in September 1928, the unexpired term was nearly complete. In a final, lasting attack on New Mexico's political arrangement, he demanded at the nominating convention that the 1928 Republican ticket be split evenly between Anglo and Hispanic candidates.[36] Larrazolo's stance troubled some Pecos Valley Republicans, but older party stalwarts noted that he had advocated for split tickets as early as 1911, and that his nomination passed because he had long been "an outstanding champion of the native people."[37] Larrazolo promised he would work in Washington "to keep respected the name and reputation of the Spanish-American people," and New Mexico's Republican press rallied behind him.[38] Larrazolo won the Senate race that year with nearly 56 percent of the vote, becoming the first Hispanic Senator. The *Los Angeles Times*, which had once charged Larrazolo with race-baiting, believed he would make a fitting ambassador to Mexico once his term ended.[39] But Larrazolo's doctors cautioned him against moving to Washington since he was 69 and in poor health.

Larrazolo presented his credentials and was sworn into office on December 7, 1928, but his arrival in Washington garnered little national attention. The *Washington Post* commented only that his election was "a striking illustration of the melting pot" before noting that Larrazolo had violated the rules of decorum and shocked fellow Senators by lighting a cigarette on the chamber floor.[40] The Mexican Senate, on the other hand, proud that a native son had climbed to the heights of American politics, wired Larrazolo a message with its "greetings and best wishes," which a Senate clerk read on the floor.[41]

In keeping with his legislative interests, Larrazolo was appointed to the Agriculture and Forestry, Public Lands and Surveys, and Territories and Insular Possessions Committees, but shortly into his tenure he came down with the flu.[42] Having missed votes because of his illness, he went home over the winter recess. Returning to Washington shortly after the beginning of the new year, Larrazolo introduced S. 5374 "to provide for a military and industrial school for boys and girls in the State of New Mexico."[43] It would be his only legislative action. Ten days later, on January 25, a gravely ill Larrazolo returned to New Mexico for good. On his behalf in early February, Senator Otis F. Glenn of Illinois introduced S. 5682, to settle outstanding claims with Mexico. While at home, Larrazolo suffered a stroke, and his formal term in the Senate ended in March as he recuperated with his family.[44] Larrazolo's health continued to deteriorate over the next year. He died on April 7, 1930.[45]

FOR FURTHER READING

Biographical Directory of the United States Congress, "Octaviano Ambrosio Larrazolo," http://bioguide.congress.gov.

Córdova, Alfred C. and Charles B. Judah. "Octaviano Larrazolo: A Political Portrait," Division of Research, Department of Government (Albuquerque: University of New Mexico, 1952).

Gonzalez, Phillip B. "Race, Party, Class: The Contradictions of Octaviano Larrazolo," in Norman Gross, ed., *Noble Purposes: Nine Champions of the Rule of Law* (Athens: Ohio University Press, 2007).

Larrazolo, Paul F. *Octaviano A. Larrazolo* (New York: Carlton Press, Inc., 1986).

Vigil, Maurilio E. *Los Patrones: Profiles of Hispanic Leaders in New Mexico History* (Washington, D.C.: University Press of America, 1980).

Walter, Paul A. F. "Octaviano Ambrosio Larrazolo." *New Mexico Historical Review* 7 (April 1932): 97–104.

MANUSCRIPT COLLECTIONS

New Mexico State Records Center (Santa Fe) *Papers*: Governor Octaviano A. Larrazolo Papers, 1918–1920, 12 linear feet. The collection contains the official papers of Octaviano A. Larrazolo during his time as governor. *Papers*: Luis E. Armijo Papers, c. 1911, 1916, one linear foot. Collection includes letters written and received by Octaviano A. Larrazolo.

University of New Mexico, Center for Southwest Research (Albuquerque). *Papers*: 1841–1981, 1.25 linear feet and one oversized folder. The Octaviano A. Larrazolo Papers consist of material relevant to his political career and family, primarily between 1885 and 1930. Also included are a handful of photographs. A finding aid is available in the repository.

NOTES

1 *Congressional Record*, Senate, Appendix, 71st Cong., 2nd sess. (12 May 1930): 9140. The most recent treatment of Larrazolo's life is Phillip B. Gonzalez, "Race, Party, Class: The Contradictions of Octaviano Larrazolo," in Norman Gross, ed., *Noble Purposes: Nine Champions of the Rule of Law* (Athens: Ohio University Press, 2007): 95–109.

2 Alfred C. Córdova and Charles B. Judah, "Octaviano Larrazolo: A Political Portrait," Division of Research, Department of Government (Albuquerque: University of New Mexico, 1952): 1.

3 Octaviano A. Larrazolo, Unpublished memoir: 12 (MSS 614 BC, Octaviano A. Larrazolo Papers, Center for Southwest Research, General Library, University of New Mexico).

4 Larrazolo, Unpublished memoir: 5–6, 15.

5 Ibid., 16–29.

6 Ibid., 25–26; Paul F. Larrazolo, *Octaviano A. Larrazolo* (New York: Carlton Press, Inc., 1986): 28, 30–31.

7 Larrazolo, *Octaviano A. Larrazolo*: 34.

8 Ibid., 33–34, 37; Maurilio E. Vigil, *Los Patrones: Profiles of Hispanic Leaders in New Mexico History* (Washington, D.C.: University Press of America, 1980): 122.

9 Larrazolo, *Octaviano A. Larrazolo*: 43, 45–46; Córdova and Judah, "Octaviano Larrazolo": 2.

10 Vigil, *Los Patrones*: 122; Larrazolo, *Octaviano A. Larrazolo*: 42, 46–47, 49, 85–87.

11 Vigil, *Los Patrones*: 122; Córdova and Judah, "Octaviano Larrazolo": 2.

12 Larrazolo lost all three races by close margins. In 1900 Larrazolo lost to Republican Bernard S. Rodey by 3,700 votes out of 39,414 total cast, or about 9 percent. In 1906 Larrazolo lost to Republican William H. Andrews, Jr., by .58% (266 votes out of a total 45,775). He lost to Andrews again in 1908 by .69% (388 votes out of a total 55,580). See *Report of the Secretary of the Territory, 1909–1910 and Legislative Manual, 1911* (Santa Fe: New Mexican Printing Company, 1911): 138–140. See also Charles Montgomery, "Becoming 'Spanish-American,'" *Journal of American Ethnic History* 20 (Summer 2001): 71; Phillip B. Gonzales, "The Political Construction of Latino Nomenclatures in Twentieth-Century New Mexico," *Journal of the Southwest* 35 (Summer 1993): 161. Though Larrazolo was a Hispanic Democrat in the predominantly Hispanic Republican section of north-central New Mexico, he benefited from what one political scientist calls "organized groups of dissidents from the majority [Republican] party." See Jack E. Holmes, *Politics in New Mexico* (Albuquerque: University of New Mexico Press, 1967): 154. See also "Republicans Put Strong Ticket in Field at Capital," 4 October 1918, *Santa Fe New Mexican*: 1.

13 As quoted in Larrazolo, *Octaviano A. Larrazolo*: 75.

14 Charles Montgomery, *The Spanish Redemption: Heritage, Power, and Loss on New Mexico's Upper Rio Grande* (Berkeley: University of California Press, 2002): 81."Impending statehood portended the rapid expansion of Anglo American control in New Mexico at the same time that the importation of racial prejudice was palpably evident in the region," writes Phillip B. Gonzales. See Gonzales "The Political Construction of Latino Nomenclatures in Twentieth-Century New Mexico," *Journal of the Southwest*: 158–167, as quoted on p. 166.

15 "Gov. Mills and O. A. Larrazolo Fires [*sic*] Volleys at Democratic Party," 26 September 1911, *Santa Fe New Mexican*: 3.

16 Republicans, too, incited racial strife, but given their dependence on Hispanic voters, they were quick to divert attention from such political maneuvering. Montgomery, *The Spanish Redemption*: 79.

17 "Showing Larrazolo's Duplicity," 8 October 1908, *Santa Fe New Mexican*: 4; "Larrazolo's Dirty and Cowardly Campaign Should Lose," 17 October 1908, *Santa Fe New Mexican*: 4; "Campaign in Territory Is Bitter One," 18 October 1908, *Los Angeles Times*: I4.

18 "Should Be Defeated," 27 October 1908, *Santa Fe New Mexican:* 4. For more information on race, ethnicity, and politics in New Mexico at the turn of the 20th century see Montgomery, "Becoming 'Spanish-American,'" *Journal of American Ethnic History*: 59–84; Montgomery, *The Spanish Redemption*: 73–75.

19 "Vote for the Constitution Declares O. A. Larrazolo," 21 December 1910, *Santa Fe New Mexican*: 3; Carolyn Zeleny, *Relations between the Spanish-Americans and the Anglo-Americans in New Mexico* (New York: Arno Press, 1974): 200.

20 "Vote for the Constitution Declares O. A. Larrazolo."

21 "Republicans Put Strong Ticket in Field at Capital," 4 October 1918, *Albuquerque Morning Journal*: 1.

22 "Gov. Mills and O. A. Larrazolo Fires [*sic*] Volleys at Democratic Party"; see also Gonzales, "The Political Construction of Latino Nomenclatures": 166.

23 Republicans branded such words as treason. Montgomery, *The Spanish Redemption*: 82.

24 Montgomery, "Becoming 'Spanish-American,'" *Journal of American Ethnic History*: 72; Larrazolo, *Octaviano A. Larrazolo*: 90–91.

25 "Fall and Larrazolo Last Night's Results; Fall States Case," 3 October 1918, *Santa Fe New Mexican*: 1, 3.

26 "O. A. Larrazolo, Republican Candidate for Governor, Issues Statement of Position to Voters," 30 October 1918, *Santa Fe New Mexican*: 3.

27 Montgomery, *The Spanish Redemption*: 84–85. An earlier political scientist noted that "the shift of population [ran] strongly against areas at the base of Republican strength in the period 1900–1920." See Holmes, *Politics in New Mexico*: 148; Córdova and Judah, "Octaviano Larrazolo": 20. As quoted in Larrazolo, *Octaviano A. Larrazolo*: 102.

28 Paul A. F. Walter, "Octaviano Ambrosio Larrazolo," *New Mexico Historical Review* 7 (April 1932): 102.

29 Córdova and Judah, "Octaviano Larrazolo": 22–24; Larrazolo, *Octaviano A. Larrazolo*: 107–108.

30 "Is New Mexico Quitting Us Cold?," 30 November 1920, *Chicago Daily Tribune*: 8.

31 For an overview of his time as governor, see Vigil, *Los Patrones*: 124–126; Walter, "Octaviano Ambrosio Larrazolo": 102–103; Larrazolo, *Octaviano A. Larrazolo*: 103–159.

32 As quoted in Montgomery, *The Spanish Redemption*: 84.

33 In fact, Larrazolo was the last Hispanic governor of New Mexico until 1974. See Montgomery, *The Spanish Redemption*: 88.

34 Larrazolo, *Octaviano A. Larrazolo*: 169, 174.

35 Ibid., 177–178.

36 Ibid., 179. Larrazolo's insistence on equal opportunity for Hispanic candidates sparked lasting change, but Anglos continued to control many offices, and the state in general remained relatively poor. Montgomery, *Spanish Redemption*: 88.

37 "Republicans to Put up Ticket Today," 12 September 1928, *Santa Fe New Mexican*: 2; "The G.O.P. Ticket," 17 September 1928, *Santa Fe New Mexican*: 4.

38 "Larrazolo Makes Eloquent Plea for Justice for Spanish Race," 12 September 1928, *Santa Fe New Mexican*: 4; "O. A. Larrazolo," 17 September 1928, *Santa Fe New Mexican*: 4.

39 "Election Statistics, 1920 to Present," http://history.house.gov/institution/election-statistics/election-statistics; "From Adobe Hut to Senate," 11 November 1928, *Los Angeles Times*: 10.

40 "From a Senator's Diary," 13 January 1929, *Washington Post*: M15.

41 *Congressional Record*, Senate, 70th Cong., 2nd sess. (17 December 1928): 733. The message was wired to Larrazolo by Bronson Cutting.

42 "Senate Hard Hit by 'Flu' Wave," 13 January 1929, *Los Angeles Times*: 7.

43 *Congressional Record*, Senate, 70th Cong., 2nd sess. (15 January 1929): 1712.

44 "Republican Lead Rises in Senate," 8 November 1928, *New York Times*: 4.

45 *Congressional Record*, Senate, 70th Cong., 2nd sess. (4 February 1929): 2738; Larrazolo, *Octaviano A. Larrazolo*: 188.

"EVERY NATIVE CITIZEN MUST UNITE IN SUPPORTING THIS CONSTITUTION BECAUSE IT SECURES TO YOU PEOPLE OF NEW MEXICO YOUR RIGHTS — EVERY ONE OF THEM; THE RIGHTS ALSO OF YOUR CHILDREN AND IN SUCH A MANNER THAT THEY CAN NEVER BE TAKEN AWAY."

Octaviano A. Larrazolo
Santa Fe New Mexican, December 21, 1910

Dennis Chavez
1888–1962

UNITED STATES REPRESENTATIVE 1931–1935
UNITED STATES SENATOR 1935–1962
DEMOCRAT FROM NEW MEXICO

The first Hispanic Democrat elected to the U.S. Senate, Dennis Chavez changed the face of New Mexican and national politics. Over his 31-year career, Chavez never strayed far from the New Deal liberalism that first won him election to national office. Through ambitious public works legislation, Chavez modernized the country's infrastructure and national defense systems. But it is perhaps his civil rights agenda, which broadened the idea of American citizenship, that Chavez is best remembered for. As Representative Henry B. González of Texas said, "the fact that a man with a surname such as Chavez was able to contribute as magnificently as the Senator did will forever be an inspiration to those of us who cannot escape our names."[1]

The third of eight children, Dionisio (Dennis) Chavez was born in early April of 1887 or 1888 to David Chavez and Paz Sanchez Chavez in Los Chavez, Valencia County, New Mexico.[2] Chavez's father maintained a small farm in the Rio Grande Valley and worked for neighboring ranches when the need arose. As there was no school in town, the younger Chavez tended the family's sheep and cattle with his father. David Chavez had been appointed the Republican Party's precinct chairman and was also a justice of the peace.[3]

During Chavez's childhood the railroad came to central New Mexico, forever transforming the territory by bringing new people, ideas, and jobs to the region. In 1895, seeking new opportunities and an education for their children, Chavez's parents moved the family to a section of south Albuquerque known as Barelas. Chavez's father took a job with the railroad and enrolled Dennis in the nearby Presbyterian Mission School, where he learned English. Dennis later transferred to St. Mary's Elementary School and then attended Albuquerque's public schools.[4]

In the seventh grade Chavez withdrew from school to help support his family. He worked as a delivery boy for Highland Grocery, creating a minor scandal in 1903 when he refused to serve a group of railroad workers who had been hired to break a labor strike. Three years later, Chavez began working as an engineer for the city of Albuquerque, eventually rising to assistant city engineer.[5] In 1911 Chavez married Imelda Espinosa. The couple had three children: Dennis, Jr., and daughters, Gloria and Ymelda.

As a youngster, Chavez became a Democrat because he blamed Republicans for the low standard of living in the American Southwest. "Republicans were in control of everything," he later remembered, "and under them, English-speaking communities had schools, Spanish-speaking communities had none."[6] "My relatives and everyone I knew were Republicans," he said in 1948, "but I became a Democrat before I could vote because I disapproved of the inequalities condoned by the Republican Party."[7] At the time, Chavez's political leanings tended to cut against the grain, as many *Hispanos*—including Octaviano Larrazolo, who became the first Hispanic U.S. Senator—were leaving the Democratic Party. Although Anglo Democrats had begun taking steps to limit *Hispano* political involvement, Chavez, as his campaign literature later said, "saw in the Democratic party a political philosophy that placed human rights above property rights."[8]

Shortly into his tenure with the city of Albuquerque, Chavez became active in state politics. In 1908 he spoke in support of then-Democrat Octaviano Larrazolo, an unsuccessful candidate for Territorial Delegate, and two years later he worked as a translator for Democrat William McDonald, a successful gubernatorial candidate.[9] In 1916 Chavez ran for the clerkship of Bernalillo County while he rallied support for other Democratic nominees across the state. Though Chavez lost, Democrat Ezequiel C. de Baca won the governorship, and Democrat Andreius A. Jones was elected to the U.S. Senate. In appreciation, de Baca

Image courtesy of the Library of Congress

appointed Chavez state game warden, but Chavez lost the patronage job when the governor died a few months later. For the next year, Chavez worked as an editor, a court interpreter, and a partner in an engineering firm until he was offered a legislative clerkship in Senator Jones's Washington office. In 1917 Chavez moved his young family to Washington, D.C., and enrolled in night classes at Georgetown University Law School. After graduating in 1920, he returned home to Albuquerque, where he began practicing law.[10]

Chavez was successful in defending organized labor and as a defense counsel in high-profile murder cases, and he used his popularity as a springboard into elected office. Two years out of law school, Chavez won a seat in the state house of representatives in 1922. Though Chavez served only one term, his progressive agenda made him a rising star in the Democratic Party.[11] Frequent speaking engagements kept his name in the public arena, and in 1930 Chavez formally filed as a candidate for the U.S. House of Representatives. During the campaign, Chavez kept his platforms simple and in line with the Democratic agenda: He supported a higher tariff, advocated more-aggressive veterans' legislation, called for federal aid for transportation, and sought state ownership of public lands.[12] In a crowded Democratic field at the nominating convention (New Mexico had no direct primary at the time), Chavez won his party's nod on the second ballot.[13]

His candidacy was well-timed. State Republicans were reeling from internal divisions, and the onset of the Great Depression had undercut the GOP's national agenda.[14] New Mexico's At-Large seat in the U.S. House of Representatives required a statewide campaign, and Chavez stumped in both English and Spanish from the traditionally Democratic, heavily Anglo counties of eastern New Mexico to the predominantly *Hispano* and Republican jurisdictions of north and central New Mexico. He spoke about water and labor rights and chastised Republicans for their inability to raise wages, lower unemployment, and direct relief to the state. Chavez garnered crucial endorsements from pro-labor groups and major newspapers and from the influential Club politico independiente de Nuevo Mexico.[15] His Republican opponent, incumbent Representative Albert G. Simms, spoke widely on the tariff and Prohibition, but failed to court the numerous swing votes of the state's Independent-leaning Republicans.[16] On Election Day, Chavez won, with nearly 56 percent of the vote; nationally, Democrats won control of the House of Representatives by a narrow margin.[17]

In the 72nd Congress (1931–1933), Chavez had a heavy workload for a first-term Member, serving on committees that fit with his interests: Public Lands, Irrigation and Reclamation; World War Veterans' Legislation; Public Buildings and Grounds; Indian Affairs; and War Claims.[18] Exhausted, Chavez wrote to a friend, "If you think that being a Congressman is a sinch [*sic*], please get over it.... I have to work long hours everyday; sometimes at night and even on Sundays."[19] During his first term Chavez allocated much of his time to constituent services, filing for pensions and introducing private relief bills. Although Chavez was instrumental in acquiring property for schools in the state, his biographers consider his most ambitious achievement to be the modification of the Reconstruction Finance Corporation (RFC), a federal program that made loans to banks to bolster failing businesses and municipal treasuries.[20] Under Chavez's direction, the RFC refinanced its loans to a number of Southwestern irrigation projects. Chavez later augmented his agenda for agricultural relief by sponsoring a freeze on payments for government loans to fund irrigation projects.[21]

Chavez's legislative interests complemented the increasingly popular notion that the federal government was responsible for the country's financial health and its general quality of life. Federal initiatives had begun to strengthen New Mexico's economy, and as Chavez prepared for his re-election campaign, he linked his fortunes with those of presidential candidate Franklin D. Roosevelt and his running mate, Speaker of the House John Nance Garner of Texas, one of Chavez's allies.[22] Still widely popular, Chavez received an additional boost in the 1932 campaign when New Mexico's Progressive Party fused with the statewide Democratic ticket.[23] With nominal opposition, Chavez captured 29 of New Mexico's 31 counties, winning by nearly 42,000 votes.[24]

The national Democratic tide that swept the 1932 election made Chavez an influential Member of a large House majority. With his new seniority, Chavez assumed greater responsibility in his preferred policy areas. During the 73rd Congress (1933–1935), Chavez sat on the Public Lands Committee and the Indian Affairs Committee and chaired the Committee on Irrigation and Reclamation.[25] As the son of a rancher, Chavez knew firsthand the difficulties of farming the arid Southwest, and he used his chairmanship to address water-use legislation, refusing to tackle new bills until the committee finished existing projects.[26] One of his biggest legislative efforts culminated in the passage of the Pueblo Lands Bill, which compensated Pueblos and Anglos for the land and the access to water they had lost because of confusing or undocumented property titles.[27]

Chavez became increasingly popular in his district as his support for President Roosevelt's series of economic programs, called the New Deal, brought jobs to the Southwest; by the mid-1930s, the Civilian Conservation Corps (CCC) had employed nearly 34,000 New Mexicans. Chavez's popularity almost catapulted him to the U.S. Senate after New Mexico's senior Democratic Senator, Sam Bratton, resigned in 1933.[28] Ultimately Chavez was not appointed to the Senate, but New Mexico's governor agreed to back him for a seat on the state's Democratic National Committee and in his anticipated challenge to New Mexico's Republican Senator, Bronson Cutting, in the 1934 election.[29]

In the House, Chavez strengthened New Mexico's ties to the national administration, supporting projects for new roads and federal subsidies for bean growers. In September 1934 he was chosen as the Democratic candidate to challenge the incumbent Senator Cutting.[30] The owner of the *Santa Fe New Mexican* and the state's leading Progressive, Cutting had seen his power wane in recent months. His support for the New Deal had angered Republicans, and a recent quarrel with President Roosevelt had soured his relationship with Democrats. But both Chavez and Cutting were popular among Hispanic voters, and the two ran on similar platforms, touting their New Deal successes and the federal money directed to the state.[31] Observers called the race "topsy-turvy" because Cutting, a Republican, often seemed more liberal than Chavez, who was a Democrat.[32] Chavez lost "the most sharply contested election in New Mexico's history," as it was later characterized, by only 1,284 votes.[33] Chavez challenged the election results, citing widespread voter fraud, and petitioned the Senate for a recount.[34] Cutting returned to New Mexico to prepare his defense, but on his way back to Washington, he was killed in a plane crash over Missouri. Five days later, New Mexico governor Clyde Tingley appointed Chavez to fill Cutting's vacant seat.[35] As the new Senator took the oath of office on May 20, 1935, five of Cutting's Progressive colleagues walked out: Hiram Johnson of California, George Norris of Nebraska, Gerald P. Nye of North Dakota, Robert La Follette of Wisconsin, and Henrik Shipstead of Minnesota.[36]

In one biographer's opinion, Chavez used his first year in the Senate to lay the groundwork for a successful campaign in 1936. His work ethic, combined with his calculated use of state and federal patronage, helped Chavez create "an airtight political machine" back home.[37] In Washington, his record proved to be exceedingly liberal: He supported strengthening the Agricultural Adjustment Act and the Social Security Act, backed numerous pro-labor bills, and spoke out on behalf of women's rights. His ability to win appropriations for building projects made him hugely popular; Chavez, along with the rest of the New Mexico delegation, had secured nearly five million dollars in federal funds by the end of 1936.[38] The country's economic woes dominated the 1936 election, and Chavez defeated his Republican challenger, Miguel A. Otero, Jr., with nearly 56 percent of the vote.[39]

Chavez's early Senate career was not without controversy. In 1938 a federal grand jury indicted 73 people in New Mexico for "graft and corruption" in the management of New Mexico's Works Progress Administration (WPA).[40] Among the accused were Chavez's sister, son-in-law, nephew, secretary, and close Democratic operatives.

Additional reports regarding "the greatest scandal ever uncovered in the State," revealed that 17 of Chavez's relatives worked for the WPA, which one Republican-leaning newspaper called "the Chavez family relief association."[41] Though juries found all Chavez's relatives to be innocent, the episode haunted him during later elections.[42] In 1940, while the WPA issue was still fresh, Chavez survived a close Democratic primary (the first direct primary in New Mexico's history) against three-term Democratic Representative John J. Dempsey but then crushed his Republican challenger in the general election.[43] The issue resurfaced in 1946 when Republican Patrick J. Hurley, who had been Secretary of War under President Herbert Hoover, courted the military vote, characterizing the election as "War Veterans vs. Payroll Veterans." But despite attacks on Chavez's long association with the New Deal, and the WPA scandal, Chavez won the race by about 3 percent.[44]

Though Chavez lost the veteran vote in 1946, World War II had been a transformative period for him. From the outset, he supported the Neutrality Acts of 1935, 1936, and 1937. The war movements in Europe, Chavez told the Senate in 1937, were "but heralds of a New World catastrophe.... Our role in the event of such a disaster should be well defined. Such a war will not be our war; we must not be dragged into it."[45] As the country mobilized, Chavez straddled a fine line: Although he backed measures to ensure domestic security, including Roosevelt's call for a larger navy and air force, and supported the Selective Service and Training Act, he opposed the adoption of lend-lease legislation.[46] After the bombing of Pearl Harbor, Chavez supported U.S. involvement in World War II and began working for veterans' benefits, especially for the many New Mexican prisoners of war in the Pacific Theater. For two years Chavez directed communication between his constituents who had relatives in the South Pacific and the Navy and War Departments, and although Chavez failed to pass a bill promoting low-ranking officers and enlisted men by one grade for every year of their captivity, he was praised across New Mexico for his efforts.[47]

Early in the war, Chavez, then a junior member of the Committee on Territories and Insular Affairs, pushed to strengthen the country's ties with Latin America.[48] In 1943 he was appointed chairman of the Subcommittee on Senate Resolution 26, an ad hoc five-member group investigating the federal government's relationship with Puerto Rico. After hearings that winter, the subcommittee concluded that Puerto Rico's population had outpaced its ability to provide for its residents.[49] Many critics, on and beyond Puerto Rico, faulted America's nebulous colonial policy, but few observers could point to a single solution. Chavez called the situation "baffling."[50] The island's long-term and temporary problems could "only be met in one way," Chavez said, "with a full knowledge that the people are American citizens and not foreigners."[51] Chavez, like many in Puerto Rico, sought to update the country's insular policy and supported phasing out presidential appointments and implementing measures for the direct election of Puerto Rican governors.[52]

Building on the momentum from his investigation of Puerto Rico, Chavez moved to codify recent executive orders ensuring the right to work and sought to create a Fair Employment Practices Commission (FEPC) to monitor the public and the private sectors for discriminatory hiring practices. This issue was of particular concern to Chavez's *Hispano* constituents, since, as he said in 1944, "Many of our people in the Southwest have been discriminated against economically."[53] On June 23, 1944, Chavez introduced legislation to establish the FEPC (S. 2048), and was appointed chairman of an Education and Labor subcommittee to oversee the bill's consideration. Though the 78th Congress (1943–1945) adjourned before voting on the bill, Chavez re-introduced it (S. 101) shortly into the 79th Congress (1945–1947) and immediately ran into stiff opposition.[54] Numerous states, including Chavez's, had already rejected fair-employment bills, and Chavez received no support from New Mexico's senior Senator, Carl Hatch, when Southern Senators blocked the legislation.[55] Chavez's final plea to "divest our way of every element of bigotry and hypocrisy" made little difference; his bill died in the Senate on February 9, 1946.[56] "This is only the beginning," Chavez said disappointedly on the floor. "We cannot have [the country] divided. We cannot have one country for the South and another country for the other States of the United States."[57]

Despite his frustration, Chavez continued to believe that direct federal action could improve the country's living conditions, especially in his native Southwest. In 1949 he became chairman of the Committee on Public Works, assuming partial control over the nation's infrastructure. Created by the Legislative Reorganization Act of 1946, the Public Works Committee oversaw flood control and river improvement; water power and pollution; buildings and grounds owned by the federal government; and the upkeep of federal highways and post roads.[58] A decade of war mobilization had put many building projects on hold, and when Chavez assumed the chairmanship, government surveys estimated that upwards of $100 billion would be needed to improve schools, roads, sewers, hospitals, airports, and parks.[59] Chavez's chairmanship of Public Works and his high rank on Appropriations helped him to authorize and fund such projects.[60]

As chairman, Chavez outlined a series of long-term committee goals. He looked favorably on bills that incorporated multiple concerns, and sought matching appropriations schedules. Chavez learned early on that the key to a successful bill was "merely a tightening up for economy purposes without policy change."[61] With his increasing influence, Chavez set about solving the Southwest's water problem. Under his leadership, the committee investigated land reclamation along the Rio Grande, water access in central Arizona, flood control in Idaho and Nevada, and completed hydroelectric projects in Washington. The construction of the Jémez Dam, just north of Albuquerque, in 1950 was a signal accomplishment for Chavez, now New Mexico's senior Senator. "For years I have envisioned the time when the Rio Grande would be harnessed for its entire path through New Mexico," he said during a visit to the project. "I wish to say that I am proud of having fathered the Middle Rio Grande project as you see it today."[62]

As the national budget adjusted after World War II, Chavez's faith in New Deal federalism suddenly seemed outdated. Coupled with Republican Dwight Eisenhower's victory in the presidential election, all signs pointed to a resurgent nationwide conservatism. In 1952 Chavez survived another close re-election campaign against his old foe Republican Patrick J. Hurley, winning by roughly 2 percent.[63] Hurley challenged the election results, and though the Senate's Rules and Administration's Subcommittee on Privileges and Elections recommended that Chavez be unseated, the full Senate voted in March 1954 to allow Chavez to retain his Senate membership.[64]

After Chavez survived the contested election, his dual appointments on the Appropriations and Public Works Committees solidified his legacy as one of the Senate's leading liberals. Early in his career, Chavez, like most junior Senators, had had a large committee load. Before the Legislative Reorganization Act of 1946, he sat on Foreign Relations (74th and 75th Congresses); Indian Affairs (74th–79th Congresses); Irrigation and Reclamation (74th–79th Congresses); Post Office and Post Roads (74th–79th Congresses); Public Buildings and Grounds (74th–76th Congresses); Appropriations (76th–79th Congresses); Education and Labor (77th–79th Congresses); and Territories and Insular Affairs (77th–79th Congresses).[65] But as he gained seniority, Chavez was assigned to fewer and more-powerful committees.

Early in the Cold War, Chavez moved to protect America's international military supremacy. As chairman of the Appropriations Subcommittee on Defense Spending in the late 1950s, Chavez fought against attempts to cut funding for national security. "The Russians are bending every effort to catch up and, if possible, over take us in the development of modern military forces," he noted.[66] The political instability in East Asia reaffirmed Chavez's commitment to creating modern defense systems, and he directed many of the jobs that resulted to the Southwest.[67] Research on missile defense and nuclear energy drove new employment at Holloman Air Force Base, Kirtland Air Force Base, White Sands Proving Grounds, and the areas surrounding Albuquerque.[68]

But for Chavez, foreign threats mattered less than America's civil liberties. Chavez was one of the first Senators to question the political expediency of claims that

the U.S. State Department had fallen under communist influence. Referring to accusations leveled by Senator Joseph McCarthy of Wisconsin, Chavez warned that fear mongering threatened America's intellectual freedom. "I contend that once men are tried for the heresy of thinking a democracy is robbed of its intellectual yeast," he said in May 1950.[69] "It matters little if the Congress appropriates hundreds of millions of dollars to check the erosion of the soil if we permit the erosion of our civil liberties, free institutions, and the untrammeled pursuit of truth." In the end, Chavez told his Senate colleagues, "A man is ... measured by what he does in relation to his times, and the fact that we do our assigned duty adequately may not be enough; sometimes we must step out and sound the alarm." Four years later Chavez, along with 66 other Senators, voted to censure McCarthy for having impeded "the constitutional processes of the Senate."[70]

Chavez suffered from declining health in the late 1950s. After surviving stomach cancer and then throat cancer, he died of a heart attack on November 18, 1962. President John F. Kennedy remembered Chavez as "a leading advocate of human rights," and Lyndon Johnson, a close Senate colleague, said, "His heart was always with the lowly and those who needed help."[71] Throughout his career, Chavez was "a good public servant and that's about the highest thing you can say about a man," said former President Harry Truman, also a close friend of Chavez's.[72] Four years later, the state of New Mexico donated a bronze sculpture of Chavez to the National Statuary Hall Collection in the U.S. Capitol.

FOR FURTHER READING

Biographical Directory of the United States Congress, "Dennis Chavez," http://bioguide.congress.gov.

Diaz, Rosemary T. "*El Senador*, Dennis Chavez: New Mexico Native Son, American Senior Statesman, 1888–1962," (Ph.D. diss., Arizona State University, 2006).

Lujan, Joe Roy. "Dennis Chavez and the Roosevelt Era, 1933–1945," (Ph.D. diss., University of New Mexico, 1987).

_____. "Dennis Chavez and the National Agenda: 1933–1946." *New Mexico Historical Review* 74 (January 1999): 55–74.

Vigil, Maurilio and Roy Lujan. "Parallels in the Career of Two Hispanic U.S. Senators." *Journal of Ethnic Studies* 13 (Winter 1986): 1–20.

MANUSCRIPT COLLECTIONS

Library of Congress, Manuscript Division (Washington, D.C.). *Papers*: In the Clinton Presba Anderson Papers, c. 1938–1972. Persons represented include Dennis Chavez.

University of New Mexico, Center for Southwest Research (Albuquerque). *Papers*: c. 1921–1963, 383 linear feet. The Dennis Chavez Papers cover many aspects of his political career. The collection includes Chavez's personal and congressional correspondence, records pertaining to legislation and committee activity, maps, photographs, and memorabilia. Topics include New Mexico and national politics, natural resources, American Indian affairs, national defense, Latin America, and labor.

Yale University (New Haven, CT). *Papers*: John Collier Papers, c. 1922–1968, 52.25 linear feet. Persons represented include Dennis Chavez.

NOTES

1 *Congressional Record*, House, 88th Cong., 1st sess. (31 January 1963): 1536.

2 There is some confusion about Dennis Chavez's birthdate. The *Biographical Directory of the United States Congress* lists Chavez's birthdate as April 8, 1888, but Rosemary T. Diaz's study states that Chavez was born April 7, 1887. According to the same study, Chavez himself claimed he was born April 4, 1888, and stood by that date throughout his life. See Edward Lahart, "The Career of Dennis Chavez as a Member of Congress, 1930–1934" (M.A. thesis, University of New Mexico, 1958): 2; Roy Lujan, "Dennis Chavez and the Roosevelt Era, 1933–1945," (Ph.D. diss., University of New Mexico, 1987): 5; *Biographical Directory of the United States Congress, 1774–2005* (Washington, D.C.: Government Printing Office, 2005): 812; Rosemary T. Diaz, "*El Senador*, Dennis Chavez: New Mexico Native Son, American Senior Statesman, 1888–1962," (Ph.D. diss., Arizona State University, 2006): 40–46.

3 Diaz, "*El Senador*": 42–43.

4 Lujan, "Dennis Chavez and the Roosevelt Era": 6–7.

5 Ibid., 9–10.

6 As quoted in Diaz, "*El Senador*": 95. Chavez once said of a local Republican operative and friend of his father's: "I saw him abuse citizens in a way that would have meant a fist fight if nothing else if he had treated me in the same way." Quoted in Lujan, "Dennis Chavez and the Roosevelt Era": 13, see also pp. 8–9; Rosemary T. Diaz, "*El Senador*": 43.

7 *Congressional Record*, Senate, Appendix, 80th Cong., 2nd sess. (2 February 1948): A1007.

8 As quoted in Lahart, "The Career of Dennis Chavez as a Member of Congress, 1930–1934": 11.

9 Lujan, "Dennis Chavez and the Roosevelt Era": 11.

10 Ibid., 13–15.

11 Lahart, "The Career of Dennis Chavez as a Member of Congress, 1930–1934": 21–22.

12 As quoted in Lahart, "The Career of Dennis Chavez as a Member of Congress, 1930–1934": 31–32.

13 Ibid., 36–37; Lujan, "Dennis Chavez and the Roosevelt Era, 1933–1945": 41.

14 Lujan, "Dennis Chavez and the Roosevelt Era": 35. A political scientist argues that the liberalism of the 1930s arrived later in New Mexico than it did elsewhere in the country. See Jack E. Holmes, *Politics in New Mexico* (Albuquerque: University of New Mexico Press, 1967): 198–213.

15 Lahart, "The Career of Dennis Chavez as a Member of Congress, 1930–1934": 40–43; Lujan, "Dennis Chavez and the Roosevelt Era": 43, 45.

16 Lahart, "The Career of Dennis Chavez as a Member of Congress, 1930–1934": 43–44; Diaz, "*El Senador*": 173–174.

17 There is some discrepancy regarding the number of votes Chavez received. State election results show Chavez winning by little more than 17,000 votes. The number used here is the official figure recorded by the Clerk of the U.S. House of Representatives. See "Election Statistics, 1920 to Present," http://history.house.gov/institution/election-statistics/election-statistics. For state results, see Diaz, "*El Senador*": 177.

18 *Congressional Directory*, 72nd Cong., (December 1932): 205; Diaz, "*El Senador*":180.

19 As quoted in Diaz, "*El Senador*": 184.

20 Diaz, "*El Senador*": 181–184; Lujan, "Dennis Chavez and the Roosevelt Era": 63–65.

21 Lujan, "Dennis Chavez and the Roosevelt Era": 66–68; Diaz, "*El Senador*": 183–184.

22 Diaz, "*El Senador*": 189.

23 Lahart, "The Career of Dennis Chavez as a Member of Congress": 75–76.

24 "Election Statistics, 1920 to Present," http://history.house.gov/institution/election-statistics/election-statistics.

25 Garrison Nelson et al., *Committees in the U.S. Congress, 1789–1946: Member Assignments,* vol. 3 (Washington, D.C.: CQ Press, 2002): 190.

26 Diaz, "*El Senador*": 192.

27 House Committee on Indian Affairs, *Payment of Claims to Indian Pueblos*, 73rd Cong., 1st sess., 1933, H. Rep. 123, 3; *Congressional Record*, House, 73rd Cong., 1st sess. (15 May 1933): 3434–3439.

28 Diaz, "*El Senador*": 198; Lujan, "Dennis Chavez and the Roosevelt Era": 85–87.

29 Lujan, "Dennis Chavez and the Roosevelt Era," 100–103. See also Lahart, "The Career of Dennis Chavez as a Member of Congress, 1930–1934": 90–94.

30 Democrat Carl Hatch, who had been appointed to Bratton's seat, was quite popular, leaving Chavez to challenge Cutting, the only non-Democrat in the Senate from New Mexico. Lahart, "The Career of Dennis Chavez as a Member of Congress, 1930–1934": 96–99, 106–107.

31 Cutting wrote the Republican platform, which included particulars not seen in the Democratic agenda, namely a government takeover of Federal Reserve banks, Social Security, and wartime arms production. See Arthur Sears Henning, "Cutting Fights Hard to Retain Seat in Senate," 21 October 1934, *Chicago Daily Tribune*: 9. For more on the 1934 election, see Richard Lowitt, *Bronson M. Cutting: Progressive Politician* (Albuquerque: University of New Mexico Press, 1992): 274–285.

32 Arthur Sears Henning, "Cutting Fights Hard to Retain Seat in Senate," 21 October 1934, *Chicago Daily Tribune*: 9.

33 "New Deal Battles Cutting, Early Ally," 5 November 1934, *Washington Post*: 2; "Election Statistics, 1920 to Present," http://history.house.gov/institution/election-statistics/election-statistics. There is some discrepancy in the historical record concerning the number of votes. The U.S. Senate Historical Office claims that Cutting won by 1,261 votes. See Anne M. Butler and Wendy Wolff, *United States Senate: Election, Expulsion and Censure Cases, 1793–1990* (Washington, D.C.: Government Printing Office, 1995): 356. For more information on the 1934 contest in the Senate, see Lowitt, *Bronson M. Cutting*: 285–310.

34 "Chavez Declares He Is U.S. Senator," 16 November 1934, *Washington Post*: 2; "Chavez Files Cutting Election Contest; Fraud, Unlawful Use of Money Charged," 26 February 1935, *New York Times*: 1.

35 Butler and Wolff, *United States Senate*: 356–357. "Chavez Named for Cutting's Seat in Senate," 12 May 1935, *Chicago Tribune*: 5; "Chavez Is Named to Cutting's Seat," 12 May 1935, *New York Times*: 2; Bliss Isely, "Senator Chavez, Cutting's Successor, Scion of Pioneers," 19 May 1935, *Washington Post*: B4.

36 Having gone to the Supreme Court, progressive William Borah of Idaho, too, missed Chavez's swearing-in. Though he did not walk out with the others, Borah told the press he was there "in spirit." "Progressives 'Cut' Chavez in Senate," 21 May 1935, *New York Times*: 13; "6 Walk Out As Chavez Takes Cutting's Seat," 21 May 1935, *Chicago Daily Tribune*: 2. As quoted in Lowitt, *Bronson M. Cutting*: 310.

37 Lujan, "Dennis Chavez and the Roosevelt Era": 136, 140, 146.

38 Roy Lujan, "Dennis Chavez and the National Agenda, 1933–1946," *New Mexico Historical Review* 74 (January 1999): 60.

39 "Election Statistics, 1920 to Present," http://history.house.gov/institution/election-statistics/election-statistics; "Chavez Wins by 20,000," 6 November 1936, *New York Times*: 2; Diaz, "*El Senador*": 232–235.

40 See Lujan, "Dennis Chavez and the Roosevelt Era": 248.

41 "73 Leaders in New Mexico Politics Are Indicted for WPA Violations," 21 October 1938, *New York Times*: 1; Lujan, "Dennis Chavez and the Roosevelt Era": 252–253. During the 1930s, the *Chicago Tribune* took a hard line against Roosevelt and the New Deal. See Donald A. Ritchie, *Reporting from Washington: The History of the Washington Press Corps* (New York: Oxford University Press, 2005): 7–10; Joseph Ator, "Senator Chavez Gets 17 Kin on Public Pay Roll," 29 October 1938, *Chicago Daily Tribune*: 4.

42 "Sets WPA 'Fraud' Trial," 24 November 1938, *New York Times*: 32. The *Chicago Daily Tribune* reported that 45 of the 73 would stand trial. See "U.S. Puts 45 on Trial Tomorrow in Relief Scandal in N. Mexico," 29 January 1939, *Chicago Daily Tribune*: 21; "Link 2 Relatives of U.S. Senator to WPA Scandal," 2 February 1939, *Chicago Daily Tribune*: 8; "Six More Convicted of W.P.A. Corruption," 30 March 1930, *Los Angeles Times*: 5; "Jury Acquits Nine in W.P.A. Politics Case," 15 April 1939, *Los Angeles Times*: 2. Many people, including the defense attorney, believed the trials were a smear campaign against Chavez that was orchestrated by his former ally, Governor Tingley. See Lujan, "Dennis Chavez and the Roosevelt Era": 275.

43 The Associated Press called the primary "one of the most hotly contested battles of State political annals." "Chavez and Dempsey Close in Senate Race," 16 September 1940, *New York Times*: 9. Dempsey returned to the House of Representatives in the 82nd Congress (1951–1953) and served four consecutive terms until he died in office in 1958. For more on the direct primary, see Lujan, "Dennis Chavez and the Roosevelt Era": 219–220; and Holmes, *Politics in New Mexico*: 198–218. "Election Statistics, 1920 to Present," http://history.house.gov/institution/election-statistics/election-statistics.

44 Walter M. Harrison, "Arthritic St. George Has Chavez on Skewer," 27 October 1946, *Washington Post*: B1. Hurley petitioned the Senate Campaign Investigations Committee to look into Chavez's victory, but to no avail. See "Hurley Asks Investigating Chavez Vote," 14 November 1946, *Washington Post*: 2; "Chavez Retains New Mexico Seat," 8 November 1946, *New York Times*: 17; "Election Statistics, 1920 to Present," http://history.house.gov/institution/election-statistics/election-statistics.

45 Lujan, "Dennis Chavez and the Roosevelt Era": 404; *Congressional Record*, Senate, 75th Cong., 1st sess. (10 August 1937): 8602; "Chavez Scores Nazis Before Senate Group," 13 May 1938, *New York Times*: 14.

46 Lujan, "Dennis Chavez and the National Agenda": 61–62.

47 Ibid., 63–65; *Congressional Record,* Senate, 78th Cong., 1st sess. (2 December 1943): 10207–10213.

48 In 1938 he authored a bill permitting the United States to erect radio towers in Southern California to broadcast anti-fascist messages to Latin America. Despite a hearing before the Interstate Commerce Committee, Chavez's measure failed to pass during the 75th or the 76th Congress (1937–1941). See Lujan, "Dennis Chavez and the Roosevelt Era": 404–412, 415. On the Chavez–McAdoo bill, see "U.S. Radio Station Asked to Further Pan-Americanism," 4 March 1938, *Washington Post*: X5; "To Act on Federal Radio Station," 10 May 1938, *New York Times*: 6; "U.W. Radio and 3,000 Students Urged to Link South America," 12 May 1938, *Christian Science Monitor*: 5; "On Capitol Hill," 19 May 1938, *Washington Post*: X2; "Bill Asks Pan-American Radio," 28 April 1939, *New York Times*: 38.

49 "Puerto Rican Aid Sought," 30 October 1942, *The Sun*: 9; Paul W. Ward, "Ickes Opposes Plan to Probe Puerto Rico," 19 November 1942, *The Sun*: 1; "Senators Question Tugwell in San Juan," 14 February 1943, *New York Times*: 28; Senate Committee on Territories and Insular Affairs, *Economic and Social Conditions in Puerto Rico*, 78th Cong., 1st sess., 1943, S. Rep. 628.

50 Chavez Subcommittee to William A. Brophy, unknown date, 9-8-68 (Part No. 4)-Government-Organic Act-Amendments-Advisory Committee to the President-General, Box No. 861, RG 126, National Archives, College Park. The island's appointed governor was critical of U.S. colonial policy and faulted preceding national administrations for not clarifying the country's constitutional obligations toward Puerto Rico. See "Tugwell Hints Puerto Ricans Nearing Revolt," 27 September 1943, *Atlanta Journal Constitution*: 8; William D. Carter, "Tugwell Blames Lack of Policy for Troubles of Puerto Rico," 27 September 1943, *Washington Post*: 15. For the New Deal and anti-imperialism, see Robert David Johnson, *Ernest Gruening and the American Dissenting Tradition* (Cambridge: Harvard University Press, 1998): 113–152.

51 "Chavez Demands End of Tugwell 'Guinea Pig' Rule," 23 February 1943, *Chicago Daily Tribune*: 9.

52 "Puerto Ricans Hail Prospect of Self Rule," 10 March 1943, *Christian Science Monitor*: 3.

53 "Spanish-Americans Ask Fair Play, Says Chavez," 19 October 1944, *Los Angeles Times*: 12.

54 Hearings before a Senate Subcommittee of the Committee on Education and Labor, *Fair Employment Practices Act*, 78th Cong., 2nd sess. (30, 31 August and 6, 7, 8 September 1944). See also Lujan, "Dennis Chavez and the Roosevelt Era": 515; "Negro Group Prays before Senators," 1 September 1944, *New York Times*: 15. For the committee report, see Senate Committee on Education and

Labor, *Prohibiting Discrimination in Employment Because of Race, Creed, Color, National Origin, or Ancestry*, 79th Cong., 1st sess., 1945, S. Rep. 290.

55 *Congressional Record*, Senate, 79th Cong., 2nd sess. (8 February 1946): 1154–1155; *Congressional Record*, Senate, 79th Cong., 1st sess. (6 January 1945): 80; Lujan, "Dennis Chavez and the Roosevelt Era": 522–524; "Senators Approve Extension of FEPC," 24 May 1945, *New York Times*: 14.

56 "Anti-Bias Measure Backed by Chavez," 20 March 1945, *New York Times*: 12.

57 *Congressional Record*, Senate, 80th Cong., 2nd sess. (9 February 1946): 1219.

58 Garrison Nelson, ed., *Committees in the U.S. Congress, 1947–1992,* vol. 1, (Washington, D.C.: CQ Press, 1993): 117.

59 Jay Walz, "Public Works Backlog Is Put at $100 Billion," 17 July 1949, *New York Times*: E7; Garrison Nelson, ed., *Committees in the U.S. Congress, 1947–1992,* vol. 2: (Washington, D.C.: Congressional Quarterly Press, 1993): 117.

60 In 1950, Chavez was chairman of the Appropriations subcommittee on Labor-Federal Security. See Jerry Kluttz, "The Federal Diary," 2 June 1950, *Washington Post*: M19.

61 "Senate Group Cuts Road Aid $120 Million," 25 February 1950, *Washington Post*: B5. As Diaz writes, Chavez "turned the focus toward the completion of major projects, project operation and maintenance, and potential expansion needs for existing projects." For a full summary of Chavez's committee overhaul, see Diaz, "*El Senador*": 307–309.

62 For a summary of Chavez's water-use legislation and congressional activity, see Diaz, "*El Senador*": 264–268; *Congressional Record*, Senate, Appendix, 81st Cong., 2nd sess. (10 May 1950): A3489. For more on Congress's role in water policy, see Paul Charles Milazzo, *Unlikely Environmentalists: Congress and Clean Water, 1945–1972* (Lawrence: University Press of Kansas, 2006.)

63 "Election Statistics, 1920 to Present," http://history.house.gov/institution/election-statistics/election-statistics; Jeffery A. Jenkins, "Partisanship and Contested Elections in the Senate, 1789–2002," *Studies in American Political Development* 19 (Spring, 2005): 72; Butler and Wolff, *United States Senate: Election, Expulsion and Censure Cases*: 399–400.

64 Butler and Wolff, *United States Senate: Election, Expulsion and Censure Cases*: 401–402; William S. White, "Senate Unit Votes to Unseat Chavez," 17 March 1954, *New York Times*: 1; "New Mexico's Senator," 23 March 1954, *Washington Post*: 10; William S. White, "Chavez Sustained in Senate as All Democrats Back Him," 24 March 1954, *New York Times*: 1; "Chavez Election Is Upheld; Grand Jury Scores Hurley," 26 September 1954, *New York Times*: 1.

65 For a list of committees, see Nelson et al., *Committees in the U.S. Congress, 1789–1946,* vol. 3: 190.

66 As quoted in Philip Potter, "Defense," 22 June 1956, *Baltimore Sun*: 1.

67 Allen Drury, "Senators Weigh Cut in Military," 4 April 1955, *New York Times*: 17; "Battle Opens over Boost in Defense Fund," 22 June 1956, *Chicago Daily Tribune*: 2.

68 Diaz, "*El Senador*": 285–287.

69 *Congressional Record*, Senate, 81st Cong., 2nd sess. (12 May 1950): 6974.

70 Ibid., 6969. See also "New Senate Drive to Fight M'Carthy," 15 May 1950, *New York Times*: 51; William S. White, "Budenz Uses Catholic Church as a 'Shield,' Chavez Says," 13 May 1950, *New York Times*: 1; "Ten Senators Urge Repeal of Red Law," 2 October 1950, *New York Times*: 7. For the censure vote, see *Congressional Record*, Senate, 83rd Cong., 2nd sess. (2 December 1954): 16392.

71 "JFK Calls Chavez Death 'Great Loss,'" 20 November 1962, *Washington Post*: B5; "Shock and Sorrow Expressed at Death," 19 November 1962, *Santa Fe New Mexican*: 1.

72 "Truman Calls Sen. Chavez 'Great Man,'" 19 November 1962, *Los Angeles Times*: 19.

Joachim Octave Fernández
1896–1978

UNITED STATES REPRESENTATIVE 1931–1941
DEMOCRAT FROM LOUISIANA

Joachim O. Fernández, a native New Orleanian and a veteran of the city's tangled political scene, served as a U.S. Representative during the tumultuous 1930s. Attentive to his east New Orleans constituency, he sought federal dollars for major infrastructure improvements to revive employment during the Great Depression and supported the expansion and modernization of the U.S. Navy. With a seat on the Naval Affairs Committee and later on, the Appropriations Committee, he was well situated to achieve these goals. But Fernández's political fortunes were entwined with those of the statehouse political machine ruled by Huey P. Long, the flamboyant and ruthless boss of Louisiana politics. Fernández jettisoned the city Democrats who helped launch his political career and migrated his allegiance to Long's organization, embarking on a decade-long House career that benefited from Long's largesse. "I fought the city machine, and by the grace of God and the help of Senator Long I was elected to Congress," said Fernández on the House Floor.[1]

Joachim Octave (Joe) Fernández was born in New Orleans, Louisiana, on August 14, 1896, to Octave Gonzales Fernández and Mary (Benson) Fernández. According to census records, Octave's father, V. G. Fernández, was born in Spain and emigrated to the United States, where he worked as a merchant. Octave Fernández, a native New Orleanian, served in the Louisiana state house of representatives and died in office in 1921. Joachim was the second of six children who were raised in the family home on Dauphine Street in eastern New Orleans, several blocks north of the Mississippi River.[2] He completed the elementary grades at public school and a local private school, Cecil Barrois, but did not attend high school or college. He worked as an expert on shipping fees and storage tariffs. On June 3, 1920, Fernández married the former Viola Murray, a native of Covington, Louisiana, who had lived in New Orleans for nearly two decades. They raised four children: Florau, Mercedes, June Rose, and Joachim, Jr. Viola died on May 7, 1947, and Fernández subsequently married Jessie Nosacka.[3]

Fernández's political career began in 1921, the same year his father died, when he was elected as a delegate to the Louisiana state constitutional convention. He then won election to the Louisiana legislature and served for much of the 1920s. From 1924 to 1928, he represented New Orleans' Ninth Ward in the eastern portion of the city, where his family resided, in the state house of representatives. From 1928 through 1930, Fernández held a seat in the state senate encompassing the Eighth and Ninth Wards. Initially he was a party regular and was endorsed by the New Orleans Democratic machine.

Fernández's political star in Louisiana followed the arc of Huey Pierce Long's ascendancy. Long built his power base as a member of the state railroad commission from 1918 to 1928. Elected governor of Louisiana in 1928, "the Kingfish" won election as a U.S. Senator in November 1930, although he delayed taking his seat until January 1932. Long portrayed himself as a champion of the people and demonstrated a keen ability to develop a formidable, intensely loyal political organization. He controlled the state legislature, a massive patronage apparatus, and a portion of the congressional delegation. Long thrived on the one-party Southern Democratic system, where policy issues tended to be de-emphasized and politics were driven by intense factionalism and intense personalities. In the words of an eminent scholar of Southern politics, "Huey P. Long's control of Louisiana more nearly matched the power of a South American dictator than that of any other American state boss … [even the strongest of whom] were weaklings alongside the Kingfish."[4]

Image courtesy of the Library of Congress

A product of New Orleans' hardscrabble electoral scene, Fernández was "marvelously adept at sniffing the political winds" and plotting his course accordingly.[5] During his successful bid for the state senate in 1928, Fernández ran as an anti-Long candidate, but after taking office, he switched his allegiance to the Kingfish and introduced Long's initiatives, including utility bills to bring natural gas into New Orleans. Over time, Fernández became known locally as "Bathtub Joe" because when unwanted callers, particularly New Orleans newspaper reporters, phoned him at home, he instructed his wife to tell them he was taking a bath.[6]

In 1930 the Louisiana 1st District encompassed much of New Orleans, including the Third through the Ninth Wards—sweeping from the modern-day Central Business District eastward through the French Quarter and ending at the Industrial Canal—and the Fifteenth Ward, which included Algiers, on the south bank of the Mississippi River. From the eastern portions of the city, the district swung south into the bayous, taking in Plaquemines and St. Bernard Parishes, which were Long's strongholds. Long, who was running for his Senate seat simultaneously, recruited Fernández to run in the district and lent him his formidable support against the six-term incumbent, Democrat James O'Connor. In throwing his allegiance behind Long, Fernández irrevocably severed his ties to City Hall and the Old Regulars Democratic machine. Founded shortly after the Civil War, the Old Regulars were "the only genuine big-city machine in the South" and were ruled by fewer than two dozen ward leaders, who controlled an army of 2,000 volunteers. For years they enjoyed disproportionate power because they controlled the state's largest city and thus had a large hand in electing the governor.[7] By defecting to the Long faction in 1930, and taking over as the group's leader in New Orleans' Ninth Ward, Fernández pitted himself against his old allies and their impressive political apparatus. As Paul Maloney, Long's handpicked candidate in the 1930 election for the neighboring 2nd District, recalled, Long was assembling his own pliant component of the congressional delegation: "Jimmie O'Connor was the Congressman in the first district. Jack String was the Congressman in the second district, both had been in Congress for a good many years and both able men. When Huey Long then decided to run for the Senate and he wanted me, and when he got me, he thought he might just as well put somebody else up there [than] Jimmie O'Connor, and he got J. O. Fernández."[8]

In the September 10 primary, Fernández prevailed over O'Connor by a slender margin, 24,937 to 23,425 votes. O'Connor carried the city wards by several thousand votes, but Fernández ran his strongest in St. Bernard Parish, a largely rural swath of bayous that stretched south and east from Orleans Parish, and in neighboring Plaquemines Parish where he benefited from Long's accord with a local sheriff who led the principal political faction. The challenger received 5,061 votes in the two parishes compared with the incumbent's 322 votes.[9] In the 1930 general election, Fernández faced the only opposition he would ever encounter in November of an election year, the hapless Republican nominee John B. Murphy, whom he trounced by a margin of 30,629 to 1,335. Again the country parishes broke overwhelmingly in favor of Fernández and other Long-ites. As longtime New Orleans political reporter Hermann B. Deutsch noted, "The astonishing figures added the words 'a St. Bernard count' to Louisiana's political colloquial speech."[10] In his subsequent four general elections, Fernández ran unopposed, and the district boundaries were not altered.[11]

As a freshman, Fernández received an unusually favorable assignment on the Naval Affairs Committee, the forerunner to the modern Armed Services Committee.[12] It was a natural fit for a Member who hailed from a strategic maritime district that was home to the once-thriving Algiers Naval Station, a nearly one-square-mile repair and maintenance facility directly across the Mississippi River from New Orleans. With as many as 1,600 civilian workers during World War I, Algiers had fallen into disuse by the time Fernández entered Congress. By 1933 the navy had decommissioned the Algiers dry dock, and its civilian employees numbered barely one dozen.[13] Fernández served on the Naval Affairs Committee from the 72nd through the 74th Congresses (1931–1937) before winning a seat on the influential Appropriations Committee in the

75th Congress (1937–1939), where he remained until leaving the House. On Appropriations he served on the subcommittee with oversight of naval expenditures.[14] Both the Naval Affairs and the Appropriations assignments ranked extremely high in terms of their attractiveness to Members of the House.[15]

Fernández's legislative workload primarily involved bills to assist individuals with issues such as pension adjustments, benefits, or discharge from military service.[16] Like many of his colleagues, he also sought federal dollars to advance local projects that involved acquiring land for the construction of levees, bridges, and streets; erecting public buildings such as post offices and a Veterans Administration hospital in Orleans Parish; surveying several bayous; establishing a Coast Guard station on Lake Pontchartrain, astride the northern part of the city; and securing mail contracts for local shipping companies. Throughout the 1930s, he also introduced a series of bills to establish Chalmette National Historical Park—now Chalmette Battlefield and National Cemetery, which is part of Jean Lafitte National Historical Park and Preserve, seven miles southeast of the city—to commemorate the Battle of New Orleans during the War of 1812.

When Fernández claimed his seat on the Naval Affairs Committee in 1931, the newly installed chairman was Carl Vinson, who would chair the panel for three decades, pumping vast resources to military planners who created the most powerful navy in the world by the end of the Second World War.[17] From bill proposals to reports, Fernández's work on the committee supported that expansion effort, particularly when it benefited the maritime facilities and interests of the port of New Orleans. In 1935, he supported an effort to permanently assign naval officers to the navy's burgeoning aeronautical engineering branch. Previous officers had rotated out, creating continuity problems.[18] Another measure doubled the amount of money the navy could spend, to $600,000 every two years, to repair damage or upgrade equipment on existing ships. In the early 20th century, Fernández wrote in a committee report that the old cap was "quite sufficient." But, he explained, possibly with an eye toward boosting traffic at the Algiers facility, "In these later years, the situation has become increasingly onerous, due to the increasing age of the ships and the improvements in the art of naval warfare, notably, the introduction of airplanes, improvements in torpedoes, and gunnery devices."[19] He supported a bill providing that military law would be applied to all individuals held in military prisons, regardless of their enlistment status. It would, Fernández explained, "eliminate the cumbersome, expensive, and unsatisfactory system of prosecuting in the Federal courts men whose enlistments have expired."[20] Finally, he authored a measure to provide $25,000 per year in federal money, matching a state appropriation, to establish a nautical school in New Orleans "for the instruction of young men in navigation, marine engineering, and other nautical subjects," similar to schools in other major U.S. ports, such as New York and San Francisco.[21]

Fernández's House career was often entwined with Long's bid to cement his statewide power by wresting control of New Orleans' politics from the Old Regulars. By the fall of 1934, Long ran a slate of victorious candidates in the city, but his tactics—including instructing the subservient governor to call out the National Guard in New Orleans during the elections to intimidate the machine, which controlled the police force—raised criticisms.[22] Louisiana Representative Jared Y. Sanders, Jr., of Baton Rouge, the son of a former Congressman and Louisiana governor and a member of the anti-Long faction, compared Long's rule with that of Adolph Hitler and Joseph Stalin, calling him "the dictator" and a "ruthless, vicious, and corrupt" foe of democracy.[23] Fernández blunted Sanders's attack in a House Floor speech that received national press coverage.[24] Intimating that Sanders's father had employed his own heavy-handed tactics as governor, Fernández insisted that the 1934 Louisiana elections were by comparison "fair and square" and that Sanders was "unduly alarmed." He did admit, however, that his electoral success was due to his ties with Long's faction "because the people are with Senator Long."[25] Also, he inserted into the *Record* a number of news articles, including some by anti-Long outlets, attesting to the fairness of the elections.

Long's assassination in September 1935 at the state capitol building in Baton Rouge dealt a blow to Fernández's electoral fortunes. Eulogizing the Kingfish, Fernández noted, "This man who dared champion the cause of the masses went before the people of his beloved State, and he triumphed each successive time with greater majorities."[26] When Sam H. Jones, whom Fernández opposed, was elected governor in early 1940, carrying the First District by 17,000 votes, the warning signs were clear. Realizing his vulnerability, Fernández tried to head off primary opposition by advertising the accomplishments of his decade-long career. He inserted a speech into the *Congressional Record* stressing his attention to constituent services and his support for appropriations for the New Deal's Works Progress Administration (later the Works Projects Administration) to augment the city's infrastructure.[27]

F. Edward Hébert, a political columnist and city editor for the New Orleans *States* newspaper, had covered and helped publicize a series of revelations later dubbed the Louisiana Scandals about graft, corruption, and tax evasion by Long-ites.[28] In 1940 Hébert challenged Fernández in the Democratic primary, having garnered the support of the Old Regulars including New Orleans mayor Robert Maestri, former governor and disgruntled Long acolyte, James Noe, and Governor Jones. As an incumbent, Fernández enjoyed the support of local labor unions, with whom Hébert had always had a rocky relationship because he opposed the formation of a guild at the *States*. Fernández also received letters of support from Speaker of the House William B. Bankhead of Alabama and Majority Leader Sam Rayburn of Texas. Hébert assailed Fernández's inability to bring home enough federal money for the state despite his prime committee assignments. Hébert labeled the incumbent "Joe-Joe Zero," explaining years later that the epithet summarized "what my opponent had accomplished during ten years in Congress." Hébert dismissed the support of Bankhead and Rayburn as an acknowledgment of Fernández's party fealty, which he claimed trumped loyalty to his Louisiana constituency. "I can well believe that [Rayburn] heartily approved Mr. Fernandez because while the congressman from Louisiana saw to it that Mr. Rayburn was getting fifty to sixty millions of dollars for Corpus Christi, Louisiana was getting not one red dime."[29]

That charge was exacerbated when the retired Algiers Naval Station dry dock was relocated to Pearl Harbor in the spring of 1940. "The Algiers yard goes on rusting" under Fernández's watch, complained the editors of the New Orleans *Item* newspaper. To bolster the facility, constituents needed a Representative with "strong character, exceptional address, and dogged persistence." "It long ago became apparent that Mr. Fernandez by no means fills the bill," the editors continued. "Even if he and his colleagues had not been ward-heeling down here for the corrupt statehouse machine … it would have made no difference. For Mr. Fernandez simply lacks the qualifications required of a man who handles assignments of that sort." But the criticisms were not entirely accurate. After the navy mothballed Algiers, Fernández sought a use for the facility and arranged for the navy to allow the National Youth Administration to move in. The New Orleans Congressman also inserted a proviso into the Naval Supply Act of 1938, which President Franklin D. Roosevelt signed into law, calling for money to be expended "as may be necessary incident to the utilization of the Naval Station, New Orleans, LA., for vessels to be placed and maintained in a decommissioned status." As war loomed in Europe and Asia, Fernández lobbied Roosevelt to recommission Algiers by reinvesting in a facility that could refurbish up to 20 older destroyers and build light cruisers. He reminded the President that an enhanced naval presence in the Gulf of Mexico might deter interference in the region.[30]

Fernández responded to his Algiers critics by publishing his efforts in the *Congressional Record* Appendix and taking a thinly veiled swipe at Hébert by dismissing the "so-called learned college and university graduates, who get paid to push a pen behind an editor's desk and try to mold public opinion."[31] Soon afterward he directly attacked Hébert's credibility and work as a reporter.

Hébert countered by stressing Fernández's ties to the Long faction and urged New Orleanians to purge the last vestiges of the regime and vote for the candidate

approved by Governor Jones. Fernández, he concluded, was one of "this mob of diehards who can't understand the writing on the wall. They can't believe that after twelve years of ruthless plunderbund they have been counted out by the free and independent people of the state."[32] On primary day, Hébert, joined by Hale Boggs, who ousted Representative Maloney in the adjoining district, prevailed over Fernández by a two to one margin. The election brought four pro-Jones candidates into the House, making five of the eight Louisiana delegation members allies of the reform movement spurred by the Louisiana Scandals. Fernández briefly entered the 1942 primary against Hébert, but dropped out early. Hébert cruised to re-election that year.[33]

Days after leaving the House in January 1941, Fernández was called to active duty as a lieutenant commander in the U.S. Naval Reserve. He served in that capacity until late September 1943, when he was appointed collector of internal revenue for the district of Louisiana. He served in that post for three years. In the fall of 1945, Fernández unexpectedly entered the mayoral race, adopting a 16-point reform package and promising civic improvement. Within months, he again surprised political observers by bowing out of the race and endorsing longtime incumbent Robert Maestri, who was unseated by reformer DeLesseps (Chep) Morrison.[34]

After retiring from politics, Fernández worked as a tax consultant. In 1951 he was hired by the state of Louisiana as a revenue examiner and as head of the income tax department. Fernández retired in New Orleans, where he passed away shortly before his 82nd birthday on August 8, 1978, after an extended illness. He was interred in Metairie Cemetery.[35]

FOR FURTHER READING

Biographical Directory of the United States Congress, "Joachim Octave Fernández," http://bioguide.congress.gov.

NOTES

1 *Congressional Record*, House, 74th Cong., 1st sess. (1 February 1935): 1372, 1374.

2 Information on Octave Fernandez was extracted from the 1880 and 1910 Federal Censuses and from a brief obituary in the New Orleans *Times-Picayune* (28 November 1920): 4. The 1910 census records list four additional siblings: Adele (15 years), Mary (11 years), John (8 years), and Elarita (5 years). According to the obituary, Mary's name was actually Marie. See "Fernandez Rites Friday," 10 August 1978, New Orleans *Times-Picayune*: 12. A death notice for Fernández lists another sibling, Louis, who was deceased. See "Death Notices," 11 August 1978, New Orleans *Times-Picayune*: 14. For census information, see *Tenth Census of the United States, 1880: Population Schedule*, New Orleans, Orleans, Louisiana, Roll 462_1254462, page 598B; and *Thirteenth Census of the United States, 1910: Population Schedule*, New Orleans, Orleans, Louisiana, Roll T624_522, page 4A, Library of Congress, Washington, D.C. http://search.ancestrylibrary.com (accessed 23 October 2012).

3 Glenn R. Conrad, ed., *A Dictionary of Louisiana Biography: Volume I, A to M* (New Orleans: The Louisiana Historical Association, 1988): 299; see also Viola Fernández's death notice in the New Orleans *Times-Picayune* (8 May 1947): 2.

4 For an overview of Louisiana politics of the era, see V. O. Key, Jr., *Southern Politics in State and Nation* (Knoxville: University of Tennessee Press; reprint 2006): 156–182, quotation on p. 156. For an important account about Long and his popular appeal, see Alan Brinkley, *Voices of Protest: Huey Long, Father Coughlin, & the Great Depression* (New York: Vintage, 1983).

5 T. Harry Williams, *Huey Long* (New York: Vintage Books, 1981): 300.

6 Williams, *Huey Long*: 300.

7 For more on the Old Regulars, sometimes referred to as the Choctaws in relation to a club associated with the machine, see Williams, *Huey Long*: 188–190; see also Allan P. Sindler, *Huey Long's Louisiana: State Politics, 1920–1952* (Baltimore, MD: Johns Hopkins Press, 1956), especially pp. 22–26 and 98–116.

8 T. Harry Williams Papers, Ms. 2489, Series IV. Oral History Interviews, Box 19, folder 109, interview with Paul Maloney on June 26, 1957: 14.

9 See "Tuesday's Primary Results," 11 September 1930, *New Orleans Times-Picayune.* Incredibly, Long outpolled his opponents by 3,979 to 9 votes. Moreover, the vote tally exceeded the eligible voting population by at least 1,500 votes. Cited in an Associated Press wire story published as "Harris's Lead Grows," 11 September 1930, *Washington Post*: 2.

10 Hermann B. Deutsch, "New Orleans Politics—The Greatest Free Show on Earth," in Hodding Carter, ed., et al., *The Past as Prelude:*

New Orleans, 1718–1968 (New Orleans: Tulane University Press, 1968): 331–332; Williams, *Huey Long*: 539–540. This figure is from Williams; Deutsch tallies the vote at 2,700 to 7.

11 "Election Statistics, 1920 to Present," http://history.house.gov/institution/election-statistics/election-statistics.

12 Fernández's predecessor, James O'Connor, held the Naval Affairs assignment for two terms in the 1920s, and from the 1890s onward, a Member of the Louisiana delegation usually served on the panel.

13 Joachim O. Fernández, "My Answer to the Unfair and Uncalled for Newspaper Attacks–Sufferers of Atavism," *Congressional Record*, House, Extension of Remarks, 76th Cong., 3rd sess. (18 June 1940): 3981–3985. Statistics in the appendix about the number of ships and the number of personnel at the Algiers Naval Station were reprinted by Fernández.

14 Fernández referenced this assignment on the House Floor: See *Congressional Record*, 76th Cong., 1st sess. (4 May 1939): 5125.

15 Charles Stewart III, "Committee Hierarchies in the Modernizing House, 1875–1947," *American Journal of Political Science* 36, no. 4 (November 1992): 835–856; see especially Stewart's table "Committee Attractiveness," p. 845. Appropriations ranked second throughout the 1930s; Naval Affairs ranked eighth.

16 House Committee on Naval Affairs, *George Dewey Hilding*, 73rd Cong., 1st sess., 1933, H. Rep. 93: 1–11.

17 Eventually dubbed "the Admiral," Vinson was also known as "the Father of the Two-Ocean Navy." For more on Vinson, see James F. Cook, *Carl Vinson: Patriarch of the Armed Forces* (Macon, GA: Mercer University Press, 2004).

18 House Committee on Naval Affairs, *Authorize the Assignment of Officers of the Line of the Navy for Aeronautical Engineering Duty Only, and for Other Purposes*, 74th Cong., 1st sess., 1935, H. Rep. 541:1–3.

19 House Committee on Naval Affairs, *Increasing the Statutory Limit of Expenditure for Repairs or Damages to Naval Vessels*, 74th Cong., 1st sess., 1935, H. Rep. 241: 1–4.

20 House Committee on Naval Affairs, *Provide for Better Administration of Justice in the Navy*, 72nd Cong., 1st sess., 1932, H. Rep. 577: 1–3.

21 House Committee on Naval Affairs, *Providing a Nautical School at the Port of New Orleans, La.*, 72nd Cong., 1st sess., 1932, H. Rep. 838: 1–3.

22 For more on this period of Long's reign of power in Louisiana politics, particularly as it relates to his efforts to make inroads in New Orleans, see Garry Boulard, *Huey Long Invades New Orleans: The Siege of a City, 1934–36* (Gretna, LA: Pelican, 1998). For an overview of the Long era in Louisiana politics, including the anti-Longs and the formation of the reform effort in state politics, see the edited compendium of previously published essays in Edward F. Haas, ed., *The Louisiana Purchase Bicentennial Series in Louisiana History, Volume VIII: The Age of the Longs: Louisiana 1928–1960* (Lafayette: Center for Louisiana Studies, 2001).

23 *Congressional Record*, House, 74th Cong., 1st sess. (1 February 1935): 1368–1369.

24 In a House Floor speech, Fernández had enthusiastically endorsed an unsuccessful effort to deny Sanders his House seat after his victory in the spring 1934 special election was contested. In retaliation, weeks before the Louisiana congressional primaries, Sanders publicly beseeched then-Majority Leader Joseph W. Byrns of Tennessee to dispatch a House committee to monitor the Louisiana elections because of the "inconceivable" conditions created by the Long machine and alluded to Fernandez's primary as an example. In early September, Sanders sent a telegram asking President Franklin D. Roosevelt to block Governor O. K. Allen's mobilization of the Louisiana National Guard, which he interpreted as an attempt by the Long faction to intimidate voters. See *Congressional Record*, House, 73rd Cong., 2nd sess. (16 April 1934): 1519; "Long Issue Debated in the House," 2 February 1935 *New York Times*: 5; *Congressional Record*, House, 74th Cong., 1st sess. (1 February 1935): 1372–1375.

25 *Congressional Record*, House, 74th Cong., 1st sess. (1 February 1935): 1372, 1374.

26 *Congressional Record*, House 74th Cong., 2nd sess. (21 April 1936): 5808.

27 See Joachim O. Fernández, "I Am a Candidate for Re-election," *Congressional Record*, House, Extension of Remarks, 76th Cong., 3rd sess. (11 March 1940): 1331–1333.

28 For Hébert's account of the campaign, see F. Edward Hébert with John McMillan, *Last of the Titans: The Life and Times of Congressman F. Edward Hébert of Louisiana* (Lafayette: Center for Louisiana Studies, The University of Southwestern Louisiana, 1976): 154–160. For more on the downfall of the Long regime, see Betty M. Field, "The Louisiana Scandals," in *The Louisiana Purchase Bicentennial Series in Louisiana History, Volume VIII: The Age of the Longs*: 271–284.

29 Hébert, *Last of the Titans*: 157–158.

30 *Congressional Record*, House, Extension of Remarks, 76th Cong., 3rd sess. (18 June 1940): 3982–3983.

31 Ibid., 3981.

32 Hébert, *Last of the Titans*: 159.

33 Ibid., 168. Hébert went on to an epic career as an old-line Dixiecrat—serving 18 consecutive terms in the House and eventually chairing the Armed Services Committee.

34 See Edward F. Haas, *DeLesseps S. Morrison and the Image of Reform: New Orleans Politics, 1946–1961* (Baton Rouge: Louisiana State University Press, 1974): 28–33. Fernández claimed he left the race because he did not have the backing of prominent politicians, including the governor. Some speculated that the mayor had planted Fernández as a stalking horse or that Fernández had profited by backing out. In actuality, Fernández agreed to withdraw if Maestri would pay his campaign expenses (roughly $35,000), though he refused to accede to the mayor's wish that he wait to withdraw from

the race until the filing deadline had passed. Hébert, who subscribed to the theory that the Old Regulars had planted Fernández in the race, observed, "Fernández being put forward as a reformist candidate almost defies imagination, but clearly demonstrates how silly politics was in New Orleans." Hébert, *Last of the Titans*: 229–230.

35 "Fernandez Rites Friday."

José Lorenzo Pesquera
1882–1950

RESIDENT COMMISSIONER 1932–1933
NONPARTISAN FROM PUERTO RICO

One of the few Members to be appointed to the U.S. House of Representatives, rather than elected, José Pesquera served nearly a year as a nominally nonpartisan Resident Commissioner during a period of political and economic upheaval in Puerto Rico and the United States.[1] Trained as a lawyer, Pesquera was passionate about farming, and he spent his short congressional career attempting to bolster Puerto Rican agricultural and economic interests in the midst of the Great Depression. "I must give special recognition to the good farmers … who, regardless of their political affiliations were the driving force behind the idea of my candidacy," Pesquera declared upon his nomination. "I will make every effort to be capable of being worthy of the honor conferred on me and of the trust that everyone has placed in me."[2]

José Lorenzo Pesquera was born in Bayamón, Puerto Rico, just southwest of San Juan, on August 10, 1882, to José J. Pesquera and Inés Dávila.[3] He attended a primary and secondary school run by his maternal uncle and graduated from the Provincial Institute of Puerto Rico with a degree in secondary education in 1897. He subsequently studied English at Keystone State Normal School, in Kutztown, Pennsylvania, from 1901 to 1902. In 1904 he earned his law degree from West Virginia University in Morgantown and was admitted to the state's bar. Shortly afterward, Pesquera returned to Puerto Rico, where he was admitted to the territory's bar and opened a law practice. He also engaged in dairy farming. On December 25, 1908, he married Encarnación López del Valle from Toa Alta.[4] In 1917 Pesquera won election as a Partido Republicano (Puerto Rican Republican) to the territorial house of representatives, where he served until 1920. The Partido Republicano was generally aligned with small-business interests on the island and sympathized with, but had no official ties to, the mainland GOP.[5] In 1927 Pesquera was appointed director of the Agricultural Association of Puerto Rico, a powerful advocacy group for the territory's land-owning farmers. Throughout his tenure, he served on several economic commissions to the United States, and he was frequently in contact with Members of the U.S. Congress.[6]

On April 11, 1932, Puerto Rican Resident Commissioner Félix Córdova Dávila resigned to become an associate justice on the territory's supreme court. His departure came amid a series of political realignments—primarily related to Puerto Rico's relationship with the United States—leading into the November 1932 elections.[7] Tasked with appointing Dávila's replacement, Puerto Rican governor James R. Beverley, a recent Hoover administration appointee and a former U.S. Attorney General, navigated the volatile political landscape by soliciting suggestions for nominees from the island's political parties.[8] The ensuing political scramble sparked protests against the partisan nature of the nomination process. Editorials in major newspapers confirmed the widespread belief that, because Resident Commissioners were elected every four years as part of a party slate, the governor should appoint a representative of the former Alianza (Alliance), which had been absorbed by the Partido Unión Republicano (Union Republican Party), out of respect for Dávila's former affiliation. "In my opinion," Rafael Cuevas Zequeira wrote Governor Beverley, removing his name from the list of nominees, "the function of the Governor of Puerto Rico, in good government ethics and considering the political nature of the position of resident commissioner, consists of filling the ministerial duty to fill the vacancy created through the resignation of the office that the people elected and appointing the candidate chosen by the majority party."[9]

As the Unión Republicano loyalist considered the "least political" among the front-runners, Pesquera soon

Image courtesy of the Puerto Rican Cultural Institute

emerged as the leading candidate and received support from influential business groups on the island. Telegrams supporting him began trickling into Governor Beverley's office.[10] On the afternoon of April 15, just before the Puerto Rican senate prepared to adjourn indefinitely, the governor submitted Pesquera's name for consideration.[11] Early in the evening, the senate appointments committee ruled in Pesquera's favor. When the full senate took up the appointment in the early-morning hours of April 16, Santiago Iglesias and the Partido Socialista (Socialist Party) launched the strongest opposition to Pesquera's nomination. At a quarter past two in the morning, a packed gallery listened to Iglesias's lengthy speech opposing the nominee.[12] He rejected the appointment based on political attacks Pesquera had made as president of the Alianza Agricultural (Agricultural Alliance) against the territory's house and senate leaders. Pesquera's supporters included Unión Republicano president Rafael Martínez Nadal, who defended him against charges that he represented only large international conglomerations on the island, noting that his organization also defended small farmers. "As of this time he will no longer be president of the Farmers Association and will become the defender of all the country's interests in the U.S. Congress," *La correspondencia* wrote, paraphrasing Martínez Nadal: "There he will defend farmers' interests with the same energy as he will defend the interest of laborers and all other interests of Puerto Rico."[13] The senate overwhelmingly approved Pesquera's nomination at three o'clock in the morning by a vote of 11 to 3; all the Socialista senators opposed it, and the Partido Liberal (Liberal Party) members abstained from voting.[14] Pesquera left for Washington a day later, telling *La correspondencia,* "My dearest wish is to negotiate the legislation most advantageous to the country and I will direct all my activities in the north to achieving that goal."[15] He was sworn in on April 28, 1932.[16] Though Pesquera claimed no party affiliation, the *New York Times* described him as "nominally a Republican."[17] Pesquera took a seat on the Insular Affairs Committee.[18]

Pesquera arrived in Washington during one of the most tumultuous periods in Puerto Rican history under U.S. rule.[19] Interconnected factors created political instability. Absentee agricultural corporations monopolized an industry that was overly dependent on exports of cash crops, including sugar, tobacco, and coffee. Low agricultural wages and poor living standards, along with a booming population, magnified the effects of the worldwide depression in Puerto Rico; by 1933 the island's unemployment rate stood at 65 percent.[20] Pesquera promised to address national issues that were pertinent to economic recovery, including control over Puerto Rico's alcohol sales. An amendment to the Jones Act of 1917, which granted Puerto Ricans U.S. citizenship, allowed them to hold a referendum to extend Prohibition to the island. In July 1917, they voted nearly two to one to ban the sale and consumption of alcohol, primarily out of loyalty to the U.S. The law frequently went unenforced, however, and by the early 1930s, selling alcohol was suggested as a method for raising revenue for the cash-strapped insular government.[21] "Prohibition … is a problem with deep economic and moral implications for our people," Pesquera observed. "As to what Prohibition represents to the island's public finances, it suffices to say that with the revenue we used to take in from income tax and other taxes on imports and the sale of liquors, we would have enough to balance our budget completely, to free some of the country's farmers and merchants from their burdens and to continue building public works to attest to our desire for progress and comfort." He vowed to request the "right to write our internal regulations in matters of Prohibition," noting that "[t]his would be perfectly legal if we bear in mind that it is the Volstead Act that governs our island, not the Eighteenth Amendment to the Constitution."[22] With 15 percent of Puerto Rico's foreign trade costs going to freight alone, Pesquera also promised to amend shipping laws to prohibit all but U.S. flag ships from transporting goods between the mainland and Puerto Rico so as to end competition between international freighter services. He also believed that reducing tariffs and taxes to create "free zones" of trade in Puerto Rico "would give an extraordinary impulse to our economic life."[23]

However, Pesquera's first action in Congress concerned a different goal. His first and longest speech on the House Floor advocated a bill introduced by his predecessor, Córdova Dávila, to change the territory's name from "Porto Rico," the official U.S. government spelling since the Foraker Act passed in 1900, back to the original "Puerto Rico." Pesquera was one of the final Members to speak about the issue. "Puerto Rico is the name we have given to our fair land. Puerto Rico is the word associated with the tombs of our parents and the cradles of our sons. Puerto Rico is the word we have consecrated as representative of our patriotic sentiments," he declared. Further, Pesquera compared the islanders' attachment to the traditional spelling with a mother's sentimental attachment to a ribbon in her daughter's hair. "We know that this Congress of the United States is not willing to impose itself upon the patriotic feelings of the people of Puerto Rico, and we know that we are going to have the restitution that we are asking for in this bill which is of no significance whatever to the United States from an economic standpoint," he said. "But which is of immense significance to the high feelings and patriotic sentiment of one and a half millions of American citizens in the island of Puerto Rico."[24] The arguments in favor of the legislation did not fall on deaf ears, and in May 1932 the House concurred in a voice vote with a Senate Joint Resolution that changed the territory's name back to "Puerto Rico."[25]

Having scored a cultural victory, Pesquera spent the majority of his truncated term seeking immediate relief for his constituents from economic depression. He requested an extension of the Reconstruction Finance Corporation (RFC) benefits and loans to Puerto Rico.[26] Initiated at the request of President Herbert Hoover in January 1932, and dubbed "a millionaire's dole" by New York Representative Fiorello La Guardia, the RFC funneled federal tax revenue directly to failing banks.[27] On May 10, Pesquera introduced a bill extending the RFC's benefits to Puerto Rico, but the bill died in the Committee on Banking and Currency.[28]

On June 10, during a debate on another bill establishing a system of federal home-loan banks to forestall a run of foreclosures linked to the Great Depression, Republican Representative Louis McFadden of Pennsylvania offered an amendment extending the bill's benefits to Puerto Rico. Proponents accused McFadden, a former banker, of burdening the bill with amendments to prevent its final passage, but McFadden argued that the bill was unfair to the island territory. "Puerto Rico is one of the best sources of trade with the United States that there is in the Atlantic," he explained. "I think it would be a particular hardship on Puerto Rico, and would be a discrimination against it, to keep it from receiving the benefits of this particular legislation." Pesquera entered the debate, noting that the 1917 Jones Act dictated the "intention of this Congress to make Puerto Rico participate, as a community of American citizens, in all legislation that is contemplated to be of benefit to the rest of the American citizens." Fielding questions on the soundness of Puerto Rican banks—and reassuring incredulous Members that Puerto Ricans held home loans—Pesquera described the island's bleak financial situation. "We are not asking alms," he declared. Conceding that Puerto Ricans did not pay federal taxes, Pesquera emphasized the territory's role as a trading partner with the mainland. "We are your sixth best customer in the whole world," he observed. "If it is true that the taxpayers of this country may have to make a little sacrifice in order to give us the benefits of this law, it is also true that they, being the business men of this country, are going to continue to get a benefit in their business with the island of Puerto Rico."[29] The amendment passed moments later, 55 to 26.[30] President Hoover signed the Federal Home Loan Bank Act into law on July 22, 1932.[31]

Pesquera had been in office less than six months when the island's ever-shifting political parties chose their candidates for the upcoming election. With the Partido Unión Republicano and the Partido Socialista merging into the Coalición in response to the newly organized Partido Liberal, the nomination of candidates for Resident Commissioner for the 1932 election was bitter and chaotic. A colorful editorial appeared in early September in *El mundo*, a newspaper that generally supported the Partido Unión Republicano, promoting Pesquera as the candidate most likely to represent "the anonymous legion

of informed citizens whose political leanings do not tend toward blind fanaticisms … whose sincere love for their native soil does not brood in brains disturbed by hunger or by fear and whose daily bread does not depend on election results." The author described him "as the logical, unquestionable representative to Washington for the next term, and as a person who should be sent there, not only by one party alone, but by the entire people of Puerto Rico united."[32] However, Pesquera did not approve of his party's political merger. In a dramatic move at the Agricultural Association Convention on September 11, Pesquera officially left the Partido Unión Republicano and threatened to form a new, agrarian-backed party.[33] Enemies and allies alike called for his resignation.[34] "Pesquera has hoped to sacrifice the farmers cause to his foolhardy, feverish ambition to hold on to the office of Resident Commissioner," spat Socialista vice president Bolívar Pagán.[35] Pesquera's old ally, Rafael Martínez Nadal, dismissed Pesquera as an unskillful representative in Washington. If not for his aides and other Puerto Ricans lobbying Congress, including Santiago Iglesias, Martínez Nadal claimed, "Pesquera would probably have lost a month in wandering the streets of Washington, looking for the government offices."[36] Partido Liberal leaders considered nominating Pesquera at their convention later in September, primarily in an attempt to court the members of the powerful Agricultural Association. However, Pesquera declined the nomination, throwing his support behind the eventual nominee, Fernández García.[37]

Pesquera's defection allowed him to act independently in Washington, a freedom he embraced after Puerto Rico was devastated by the San Cipriano Hurricane, whose eye passed over the territory on the night of September 26 and 27, 1932. Estimating winds of more than 120 miles per hour, the local National Weather Bureau office noted that "only the heaviest construction of masonry and concrete, with cemented tile roofs, came out of the zone of heavy damage unscathed." The death toll reached 225, with 3,000 more reported injured.[38] Pesquera sent President Hoover a memorandum seeking immediate relief for the thousands of homeless residents, requesting U.S. Army supplies including "tents, cots and blankets" and immediate government loans to three local banks to restore public confidence.[39] Receiving a response he characterized as "disheartening," he visited the President on October 1.[40]

Failing to capture aid or attention from the Hoover administration, Pesquera publicized the administration's equivocal response in a politically calculated move. Submitting a letter he sent to Senator Robert Wagner of New York, a frequent advocate of Puerto Rican issues, to several Spanish-language newspapers, Pesquera outlined his correspondence with the Hoover White House as well as with the War Department, which was assigned to the relief efforts. He blasted the administration's refusal to provide 5,000 tents and 30,000 cots and blankets, despite their "admitting they have these supplies and transport facilities for immediate shipment." Pesquera's insinuation that the U.S. government purposely neglected Puerto Rico after the destructive storm landed on the front page of English- and Spanish-language newspapers in New York and Puerto Rico.[41] "The Administration's attitude is as amazing as it is heartless," he seethed. "[T]he War Department has always furnished these supplies to victims of similar disasters not only in the United States but throughout the world." Alluding to the upcoming 1932 election, Pesquera said, "It seems to me that Puerto Rico is doubly unfortunate in that the calamity has come when [the] continental United States is engaged in a political campaign and politically minded officials seem to think that distressed communities on the mainland will complain if succor is afforded Puerto Rico while denied to other American communities. Isn't this 'playing politics with human misery?'" he asked.[42]

Pesquera's publicity captured the attention of Hoover officials, who were engaged in a close and highly charged campaign against Democratic candidate Franklin Delano Roosevelt centering on a referendum in Hoover's approach to economic relief in the Great Depression. Puerto Ricans were generally unhappy with Hoover's relief efforts, and their sentiments were shared by the Puerto Rican diaspora living in New York City, who increasingly were agitating for aid.[43] "The Porto Ricans are complaining," New York state Republican committee chairman J. W. Krueger wrote

the White House. "[A]nd this is valuable ammunition to the Democratic candidates and orators at this time."[44] Krueger added that Pesquera had become "one of the leading speakers and an important figure at practically all the Democratic meetings among Puerto Ricans" in New York City.[45] Another New York City GOP observer implored the administration, "As you probably know, thousands of Porto Ricans have settled in this City. They are, of course, citizens, and after being here one year, have the right to vote. For some reason, which many of us have been unable to fathom, an impression has gone forth amongst them that nothing has been done to alleviate the conditions in Porto Rico caused by the recent tornado."[46]

Given the administration's belief that the Resident Commissioner represented Hoover as a Beverley appointee, and thus as a Republican, talk of political retribution abounded. Krueger noted, "Something ought to be done with Pesquera … who should be severely called to account for his activities here in the Democratic campaign."[47]

The White House made good on the threat, authorizing Krueger to "make a suggestion to this Commissioner as to whether he had considered that his appointment came from Governor Beverley and that his misrepresentations of the President's action and position might be very embarrassing to the Governor."[48] Krueger allegedly confronted Pesquera, pressuring him to desist and asserting that his criticism "was an untruth and a serious reflection on the President, who, he knows, has done a lot for the Puerto Ricans in the past two years."[49]

Working with Governor Beverley, Pesquera continued to pressure the Hoover administration, primarily because both politicians faced enormous pressure from Puerto Ricans to act. George Van Horn Moseley, a War Department official, met with Pesquera to discuss the issue and later paraphrased the Resident Commissioner's response as, "You must realize that I am the Resident Commissioner and this request has been made on me, and it is up to me to produce."[50] On October 3, Pesquera met with officials from the Emergency Relief Division of the RFC to follow up on a request made by Governor Beverley for a $5 million loan toward immediate relief under Title I of the federal organization's founding legislation.[51] The meeting ended poorly for Pesquera. Though he requested funds through various provisions of the act, RFC officials claimed the organization was not designed to provide relief from natural disasters and demanded to know precisely how many people had been affected and how much money was needed before drawing any permanent conclusions; they estimated that $1 million would suffice for the remainder of 1932.[52] The Puerto Ricans did not receive the supplies they requested, and on October 12, the RFC approved a meager $750,000 relief loan.[53]

Pesquera's anger with the Hoover administration resulted in his official endorsement of Roosevelt in the presidential election on November 3, and he encouraged Puerto Ricans living in New York to vote accordingly. "I believe we need a Democratic victory to ensure full recognition of the rights we Puerto Ricans have as American citizens," he told *El mundo.* "We have not received the recognition from the Republican administration and the stance of the War Department as regards sending materials to aid the victims of the last storm shows we cannot hold out hope that the Republican administration will cooperate with us, not even for humanitarian reasons."[54] He also spoke freely about local politics. When Santiago Iglesias secured the Coalición's nomination for Resident Commissioner, Pesquera published a statement attacking this decision, arguing that Iglesias's nominally "red" ties would be harmful to the island's cause in Washington.[55] "If the Republican Union Party has decided not to choose a man from within its own ranks but rather one from within the Socialist Party to hold Puerto Rico's only representative office in the U.S. Congress," Pesquera said, "it is obvious that the Republican Union [Party] will not have a chance to maintain its principles in Washington, because it has surrendered that privilege to the Socialist Party." He concluded, "And if this is not surrender, let God be the judge."[56]

After the Coalición handily won a majority in the election, elevating Iglesias to Resident Commissioner, Pesquera returned to his law practice and agricultural pursuits in Bayamón, where he died on July 25, 1950.

FOR FURTHER READING

Biographical Directory of the United States Congress, "José Lorenzo Pesquera," http://bioguide.congress.gov.

NOTES

1 Several other Resident Commissioners were appointed to the U.S. House. Appointments from Puerto Rico to fill vacancies are permitted under the Jones Act of 1917 (39 Stat. 964). The following Resident Commissioners were also appointed to their first term: Quintin Paredes of the Philippines (1935), Joaquin Elizalde of the Philippines (1938), Bolívar Pagán of Puerto Rico (1939), Carlos Romulo of the Philippines (1944), Antonio Fernós-Isern of Puerto Rico (1946), and Antonio Colorado of Puerto Rico (1992).

2 "Pero debo consignar mi especial reconocimiento a los buenos agricultores… quienes, sin distinción de matices políticos fueron los iniciadores del movimiento de opinión que se verficó en mi favor … Si … realizaré todos aquellos esfuerzos de que sea capaz para hacerme digno del honor que se me ha confiado y de la confianza que en mi se ha depositado por todos." "'Si el senado aprueba mi nombramiento realizaré todos aquellos esfuerzos'," 15 April 1932, *El mundo* (San Juan, PR): 1. Translated as "'If the Senate Approves My Appointment I Will Make Every Effort'" by Translations International, Inc. (June 2010).

3 Pesquera had at least one brother, Mariano R. Pesquera. See Ansel Wold to Marino [*sic*] R. Pesquera, 12 September 1947, textual files of the *Biographical Directory of the United States Congress*, Office of the Historian, U.S. House of Representatives (hereinafter referred to as textual files of the *Biographical Directory of the United States Congress*); Mariano R. Pesquera to Ansel Wold, 2 October 1947, textual files of the *Biographical Directory of the United States Congress*.

4 "Don José L. Pesquera falleció el martes en ciudad Bayamón," 27 July 1950, *El mundo* (San Juan, PR): 12. Pesquera's obituary does not mention any children.

5 For more information on the Puerto Rican Republican Party, see Robert J. Alexander, ed., *Political Parties of the Americas: Canada, Latin America, and the West Indies*, The Greenwood Historical Encyclopedia of the World's Political Parties (Westport, CT: Greenwood Press, 1982): 621–622. Discussion on the Puerto Rican political party's ties with mainland Republicans and Democrats can be found in Gonzalo F. Córdova, *Resident Commissioner Santiago Iglesias and His Times* (Editorial de la Universidad de Puerto Rico, 1993): 239–240.

6 "'Si el senado aprueba mi nombramiento realizaré todos aquellos esfuerzos'"; Jose E. Rios, "The Office of Resident Commissioner of Puerto Rico," (M.A. thesis, Georgetown University, 9 May 1969): 83. For the Agricultural Association's activities, see, for example, "Porto Rican's Dispute with Land Bank Ends," 5 September 1931, *Baltimore Sun*: 2; "Mexico May Join the League of Nations," 5 September 1931, *Washington Post*: 2; "El senado considerará esta tarde la designacíon del lcdo. José L. Pesquera para comisionado residente," 15 April 1932, *La correspondencia* (San Juan, PR): 1.

7 Truman R. Clark, *Puerto Rico and the United States: 1917–1933* (University of Pittsburgh Press, 1975): 158; César J. Ayala and Rafael Bernabe, *Puerto Rico in the American Century: A History since 1898* (Chapel Hill: University of North Carolina Press, 2007): 59, see also the chart on p. 143; Córdova, *Resident Commissioner Santiago Iglesias and His Times*: 235, 242–246.

8 The Jones Act permits the governor to appoint the Resident Commissioner to fill a vacancy with the advice and consent of the Puerto Rican senate. See Act of March 2, 1917, 39 Stat. 964.

9 "La función del Gobernador de Puerto Rico, en buena ética de gobierno, considerada la naturaleza politica del cargo de Comisionado Residente, se reduce a mi modo de ver, a cumplir el deber ministerial de cubrir la vacante ocasionada por la renuncia del funcionario que el pueblo eligiera designado al candidato merecedor de la confianza del partido de la mayoría" ["Cuevas Zequeira retira su nombre de la terna," 14 April 1932, *El mundo* (San Juan, PR): 1. Translated as "Cuevas Zequeira Withdraws His Name from the Slate" by Translations International, Inc. (June 2010)]; Rafael Rivera Santiago, "El lcdo. José L. Pesquera debe renunciar," 13 September 1932, *El mundo* (San Juan, PR); Cordova, *Resident Commissioner Santiago Iglesias and His Times*, 234–235.

10 Córdova, *Resident Commissioner Santiago Iglesias and His Times*, 234; "Y de la terna que se le envió, seleccionó al menos, políticos de los candidatos políticos que le fueron sometidos: Al Lede, Pesquera." Rafael Rivera Santiago, "El lcdo. José L. Pesquera debe renunciar." Translated as "José L. Pesquera Should Resign" by Translations International, Inc. (June 2010).

11 "Pesquera fue confirmado esta madrugada por el senado ," 16 April 1932, *La correspondencia* (San Juan, PR): 1.

12 "El senado confirm ayer el nombramiento de Pesquera," 17 April 1932, *El mundo* (San Juan, PR): 1.

13 "[D]esde este momento [Pesquera] dejará de ser el Presidente de la Asociación de Agricultores para convertirse en el defensor de todos los intereses del país en el Congreso Americano. Allí defenderá los intereses Agrícolas con el mismo calor que defenderá los intereses obreros y todos los demás intereses de Puerto Rico." "Pesquera fue confirmado esta madrugada por el senado." Translated as "The Senate Confirmed Pesquera This Morning" by Translations International, Inc. (June 2010).

14 "Gets Washington Post," 17 April 1932, *New York Times*: 6; "Pesquera fue confirmado esta madrugada por el senado;" Santiago, "El lcdo. José L. Pesquera debe renunciar." For evidence of Pesquera's broad support throughout the island, especially from the Puerto Rican Republicans, see, for example, Luis Herrera, "La liga de asociaciones de dirige al Partido Union Republicana," 25 April 1932, *La correspondencia* (San Juan, PR): 1; P. H. Behr, "El Coronel

Behr le dirige una expresiva carta," 26 April 1932, *El mundo* (San Juan, PR): 1.

15 "Mi más caro anhelo [illegible] gestionar la legislación más provechosa para el país y a conseguir ese fin consagraré en el Norte todas mis actividades." "Dice el Comisionado Residente," 21 April 1932, *La correspondencia* (San Juan, PR): 1. Translated as "Resident Commissioner Says" by Translations International, Inc. (June 2010).

16 *Congressional Record*, House, 72nd Cong., 1st sess. (28 April 1932): 9142.

17 "Gets Washington Post," 17 April 1932, *New York Times*: 6. It is unclear why Pesquera did not claim Union Republican affiliation while serving in Congress. The fluctuating party divisions in Puerto Rico at the time may have precluded his claiming an official affiliation.

18 There is no documentation that Pesquera was assigned committees. However, he appears in the roster for the Insular Affairs Committee as an Independent Member in 1932 and as a Republican Member in 1933. See, for example, Hearing before the House Insular Affairs Committee, *Provide a Government for American Samoa*, 72nd Cong., 1st sess. (20 and 22 May 1932): II; Hearing before the House Insular Affairs Committee, *Provide a Civil Government for the Virgin Islands of the United States*, 72nd Cong., 2nd sess. (19, 20, 21 January 1933): II.

19 Ayala and Bernabe, *Puerto Rico in the American Century*: 95.

20 Robert David Johnson, "Anti-Imperialism and the Good Neighbour Policy: Ernest Gruening and Puerto Rican Affairs, 1934–1939," *Journal of Latin American Studies* 29, no. 1 (February 1997): 95; Clark, *Puerto Rico and the United States, 1917–1933*: 106.

21 Truman R. Clark, "Prohibition in Puerto Rico, 1917–1933," *Journal of Latin American Studies* 27, no. 1 (February 1995): 81, 85–86, 95.

22 "La Prohibición ... es un problema de hondas implicaciones económicas y morales para nuestro pueblo.... En cuanto a lo que representa la Prohibición en las finanzas públicas insulares, baste decir que con los ingresos que antes percibíamos por concepto de rentas internas y otros tributos sobre la importación y venta de licores, tendríamos bastante para equilibrar perfectamente nuestro presupuesto, para libertar de algunas de sus cargas a los agricultores y comerciantes del país y para perseverar en la construcción de obras públicas que diesen fe de nuestro afán de progreso y de confort.... [N]uestro derecho a redactar nuestros reglamentos internos en materia de Prohibición. Esto sería perfectamente legal si tenemos en cuenta que es la Ley Volstead la que rige en nuestra isla y no la enmienda dieciocho de la Constitución nacional." "Los planes que se propone desarrollar Pesquera," 22 April 1932, *El mundo* (San Juan, PR): 1. Translated as "Plans That Pesquera Proposes to Undertake" by Translations International, Inc. (June 2010).

23 "Creo que el establecimiento de una zona franca en Puerto Rico daría un impulso extraordinario a nuestra vida económica; no solamente por la vida financiera que ello traería a nuestra isla, ... sino también porque nos daría las ventajas extraordinarias de adquirir... nuestras necesidades en numerosos productos a precios de la extrema competencia entre las industrias mundiales." ("Los planes que se propone desarrollar Pesquera.")

24 *Congressional Record*, House, 72nd Cong., 1st sess. (11 May 1932): 10030.

25 To change the name of the island of "Porto Rico" to "Puerto Rico," Public Law 72-20.

26 "Los planes que se propone desarrollar Pesquera."

27 David M. Kennedy, *Freedom from Fear: The American People in Depression and War, 1929–1945* (New York: Oxford University Press, 1999): 84–85.

28 H.R. 11988, *Congressional Record*, House, 72nd Cong., 1st sess. (10 May 1932): 9966–9967.

29 *Congressional Record*, House, 72nd Cong., 1st sess. (10 June 1932): 12624.

30 Ibid., 12625.

31 Kennedy, *Freedom from Fear*, 82–83; 47 Stat. 725.

32 "Ellos forman la legión anónima de ciudadanos conscientes cuyo partidismo político no está tenido de fanatismos elegos ni de apasionamientos ridículos ... y cuyo sincero amor al suelo patrio no se empolla en cerebros turbados por el hambre o por el miedo y cuyo pan nuestro de cada día no depende del resultado de las elecciones.... [José L. Pesquera, siendo] el lógico e indiscutible representante a Washington por el próximo término y debiendo ser enviado allí no por un partido solo, sino por el pueblo entero de Puerto Rico en unión." Rafael Arroyo Zeppenfeldt, "José L. Pesquera: El hombre del destino," 9 September 1932, *El mundo* (San Juan, PR): 5. Translated as "José L. Pesquera: The Man of the Hour" by Translations International, Inc. (June 2010).

33 Córdova, *Resident Commissioner Santiago Iglesias and His Times*, 247; "La asamblea de la Asociación de Agricultores acordó gestionar 'Cómo un acto reinvidicador que el nombre del Sr. José L. Pesquera sea en cualquier forma postulado para el cardo de Comisionado Residente en Washington,'" 12 September 1932, *El mundo* (San Juan, PR): 6. "El Comisionado Residente don José L. Pesquera se retira del Partido Republicano," 12 September 1932, *La democracia* (San Juan, PR): 1.

34 J. Córdova Chirino, "La vanidad del Sr. Pesquera," 13 September 1932, *La correspondencia* (San Juan, PR): 4; Santiago, "El lcdo. José L. Pesquera debe renunciar."

35 "Pesquera ha pretendido sacrificar la causa de los agricultores a su ambición descabellada y delirante de continuar en la silla de Comisionado Residente." "Pesquera y Landron le han dado un cuartelazo," 13 September 1932, *El Mundo* (San Juan, PR):

1. Translated as "Pesquera and Landron Have Risen Up" by Translations International, Inc. (June 2010).

36 "Pesquera hubiera perdido probablemente un mes en andar por las calles de Washington buscando las oficinas del gobierno." Rafael Martínez Nadal, "El Sr. Pesquera es el que menor participación tiene," 17 September 1932, *El Mundo* (San Juan, PR): 1. Translated as "Mr. Pesquera Has Had the Least Involvement" by Translations International, Inc. (June 2010).

37 Harwood Hull, "Puerto Rico Facing Doubtful Election," 18 September 1932, *New York Times*: E8; "La asamblea de la asociación de agricultores acordó gestionar 'cómo un acto reinvidicador que el nombre del Sr. José L. Pesquera sea en cualquier forma postulado para el cardo de Comisionado Residente en Washington,'" 12 September 1932, *El mundo*: 6.

38 W. J. Humphreys, "West Indian Hurricanes of August and September, 1932," Volume 60 (9), *Monthly Weather Review* (1932): 178, http://ams.allenpress.com/perlserv/?request=get-toc&issn=1520-0493&volume=60&issue=9 (accessed 24 March 2010).

39 "Ask Relief at Once for Puerto Ricans," 2 October 1932, *New York Times*: 27; "Estoy preparando y a el terreno todos tienen los mejores deseos," 3 October 1932, *El mundo* (San Juan, PR): 3.

40 "Desalentadora" ["Las gestiones que hicieron Beverley y Pesquera"], 13 October 1932, *El mundo* (San Juan, PR): 1; Appendix E - The President's Calendar, 1 October 1932, *Public Papers of the Presidents of the United States: Herbert Hoover* (Washington, D.C.: Government Printing Office, 1977): 1235. Though references to and summaries of the memorandum exist, the document itself was not archived. See, for example, Lawrence Richey to Hon. Patrick H. Hurley, 1 October 1932; Presidential States File; Puerto Rico, General Correspondence; Herbert Hoover Papers; Herbert Hoover Presidential Library, West Branch, IA (hereinafter referred to as Presidential States File, Hoover Library). Other correspondence between Pesquera and President Hoover and Pesquera and Secretary of War Patrick L. Hurley was reprinted in *El mundo*. See, for example, "Pesquera se dirige nuevenmente al Presidente y al Secretario de la Guerra," 4 October 1932, *El mundo* (San Juan, PR): 2.

41 "Sharp Criticism to Government's Indifference to Pto. Rico's Distress," 8 October 1932, *El universal* (English section): 1; "La actitud de la administración estan desconcertante como despiadada," 12 October 1932, *El mundo* (San Juan, PR): 2.

42 "Sharp Criticism to Government's Indifference to Pto. Rico's Distress."

43 See, for example, James J. Lanzetta to Herbert Hoover, telegram, 28 September 1932, Presidential States File, Hoover Library; United Puerto Rico Republican Club (New York, NY) to Hoover, telegram, 7 October 1932, Presidential States File, Hoover Library.

44 Clark, *Puerto Rico and the United States: 1917–1933*: 156–157; J. W. Krueger to Lawrence Richey, 11 October 1932; Presidential States File, Hoover Library.

45 J. W. Krueger to Walter H. Newton, 31 October 1932; Presidential States File, Hoover Library; Krueger to Newton, 20 October 1932; Presidential States File, Hoover Library. Krueger appends a newspaper article confirming Pesquera's presence at a New York meeting of the Spanish American Citizens Democratic Club. See, Nickols, "Political Briefs," 29 October 1932, *El universal* (English section): 1.

46 Isaac Seigel to Walter H. Newton, 20 October 1932; Presidential States File, Hoover Library.

47 J. W. Krueger to Lawrence Richey, 20 October 1932; Presidential States File, Hoover Library.

48 Walter H. Newton to J. W. Krueger, 2 November 1932; Presidential States File, Hoover Library.

49 Krueger to Newton, 31 October 1932; Presidential States File, Hoover Library.

50 George Van Horn Moseley to Walter H. Newton, 19 October 1932; Presidential States File, Hoover Library.

51 Beverley's request is recorded in "Chronological Record of Action Taken by the Bureau of Insular Affairs and Puerto Rican Authorities Re Hurricane of September 27, 1932," File 856-121, General Classified Files, 1898–1945, General Records Relating to More Than One Island Possession, Records of the Bureau of Insular Affairs, Record Group 350, National Archives at College Park, College Park, MD (hereinafter referred to as RG 350, NACP): 7.

52 Edward A. Stockton, Jr., "Memorandum for Records," 3 October 1932, File 856-121, RG 350, NACP; Stockton, "Memorandum for Records," 4 October 1932, File 856-121, RG 350, NACP.

53 Short to Beverley, telegram, 1 October 1932, File 856-121, RG 350, NACP; "El gobernador no solo ha estado ocupandose de nuestra suerte," 17 October 1932, *El mundo* (San Juan, PR): 1. The Puerto Rican senate eventually rejected some of the Reconstruction Finance money because the Liberal Party did not support the payment structure. See "Cablegrams que se cruzaron el viernes ultimo," 24 October 1932, *El mundo* (San Juan, PR): 2; "Considero cruel la actitud de la minoria Liberal," 26 October 1932, *El mundo* (San Juan, PR): 1; "Pesquera formó un juicio sin datos sobre la situación," 27 October 1932, *La democracia* (San Juan, PR): 1; "La mayoria demusetra haber puesto el interes pardista," 3 November 1932, *El mundo* (San Juan, PR): 1.

54 "No hemos tenido ese reconocimiento de parte de la administración republicana y la actitud del Departamento de la Guerra en lo que respecta al envío de materiales para ayudar a las víctimas del último temporal demuestra que no podemos abrigar esperanzas de que

la administración republicana coopere con nosotros, ni aún por humanidad." "'Se necesita un triunfo Demócrata para asegurar el pleno reconocimiento,'" 3 November 1932, *El mundo* (San Juan, PR): 3. Translated as "Democrat Victory Needed to Ensure Full Recognition" by Translations International, Inc. (June 2010).

55 Harwood Hull, "Puerto Rico Facing Doubtful Election," 18 September 1932, *New York Times*: E8; "El mantenimiento de los principios de la Unión Republicana esta vinculado," 10 September 1932, *El mundo* (San Juan, PR): 1.

56 "Si la Unión Republicana no ha querido escoger de su seno un hombre, sino que lo ha escogido del seno del Partido Socialista, para que ostente la única representación de Puerto Rico en el Congreso de los Estados Unidos, es obvio que la Unión Republicana no tendrá oportunidad de mantener sus principios en Washington, puesto que le ha cedido al Partido Socialista el privilegio de mantener los suyos. Y si esto no es rendición que venga Dios y lo vea." "El mantenimiento de los principios de la Unión Republicana está vinculado," 10 September 1932, *El mundo* (San Juan, PR): 1. Translated as "Maintaining the Principles of the Republican Union Is Linked" by Translations International, Inc. (June 2010).

Santiago Iglesias
1872–1939

RESIDENT COMMISSIONER 1933–1939
COALITIONIST FROM PUERTO RICO

Imprisoned in San Juan when the Americans invaded Puerto Rico in 1898, Santiago Iglesias was a fiery labor organizer who frequently ran afoul of Spanish authorities. Eventually embracing American democratic principles, Iglesias became known as "Mr. Liberty" and the "He-Cinderella of Porto Rico."[1] Born in poverty in Spain, Iglesias, the former radical who was eventually considered the "dean of the Puerto Rican politicians" and a "staid and dependable" public servant, was elected Resident Commissioner during a period of political upheaval.[2] A tireless legislator, Iglesias espoused Puerto Rican statehood along with greater local control, increased federal financial assistance, and close political ties to the mainland United States. "Puerto Rico is American socially, politically," he concluded in his maiden speech on the House Floor. "And its trade, its practices, and its industry pile and flourish under the American flag.... Since 1917 all Puerto Ricans have been American citizens, and this citizenship is the same brand as that of New Yorkers, or Californians, or Minnesotans, or Down-in-Mainers."[3]

Santiago Iglesias was born on February 22, 1872, in La Coruña, Spain. His father, Manuel Iglesias, was a carpenter.[4] Iglesias's mother, Josefa Pantín, worked in a cigar factory to support her family, and Santiago Iglesias left school at age 12 to become a carpenter's apprentice. Early in his training, he took part in a violent strike, his first act in a lifelong struggle to reform labor rights.[5]

In 1887 Iglesias joined the Spanish Socialist Party and moved to Cuba, where he took a job in a furniture factory. His work with organized labor, including rallying laborers to lobby for a 12-hour workday, led to his frequent dismissal from and constant movement between jobs. Iglesias's involvement with the Cuban War for Independence in 1895 drew the ire of Spanish authorities. He attempted to escape to England in 1896; however, after arousing the suspicions of his fellow passengers aboard the ship, which was to route through Spain on its way to Great Britain, he disembarked in San Juan, Puerto Rico, on December 26.[6]

Iglesias's arrival marked the beginning of a labor movement in Puerto Rico that was previously nonexistent because of oppressive Spanish labor laws.[7] As a carpenter helping to reinforce San Juan's military fortifications, Iglesias began organizing his fellow laborers. Two days after he arrived, Iglesias met with local labor leaders to discuss starting a newspaper to promote their causes.[8] Iglesias's impassioned speech in that initial meeting, advocating participation in the international labor movement and decrying colonialism, vaulted him to the unofficial position of the island's labor leader. Taking advantage of the eroding Spanish colonial infrastructure in Puerto Rico, Iglesias quickly organized meetings, educational programs, and literature designed to unite laborers. He refrained from publicly supporting the political factions that were emerging in the late 1890s as Spain promised autonomy to Puerto Rico, believing that the local political elite cared little about the working people. After Iglesias organized his first mass meeting of workers on March 27, 1898, Luis Muñoz Rivera, then a member of the Spanish Autonomist Cabinet, ordered his arrest, but Iglesias fled to the other side of San Juan Harbor. Two weeks later, amid the confusion caused by the outbreak of the Spanish-American War, Iglesias attempted to escape to New York, but Spanish authorities captured and incarcerated him in San Juan. Iglesias spent the rest of the war in prison. He was nearly killed when an American bomb hit his jail cell on May 12.[9]

The Spanish government attempted to deport Iglesias, but before that occurred, Washington asked Madrid to release all political prisoners in October 1898. Iglesias

Image courtesy of the National Archives and Records Administration

immediately returned to his labor-organizing activities, receiving protection from the island's U.S. military commander, General John R. Brooke, for whom Iglesias was an interpreter. Soon afterward Iglesias founded the first official organized labor group on the island, the Federación Regional de los Trabajadores (Puerto Rican Federation of Laborers), and presided over the group's initial meeting on October 20, 1898.[10]

Iglesias's labor activities redoubled after the United States acquired Puerto Rico as a territory in February 1899. He pitted himself against his longtime political enemy Muñoz Rivera, the founder of the Partido Federalista (Federal Party), by allying occasionally with José Celso Barbosa, the founder of the Partido Republicano (Puerto Rican Republican Party), Muñoz Rivera's rival and a sometime friend to Iglesias.[11] Ultimately, his refusal to take clear sides resulted in a split in the Puerto Rico Federation of Laborers.[12] Iglesias headed up the Federación Libre de Trabajadores (Free Federation of Laborers), a faction insisting on labor's independence from the political wrangling.[13] Frequently imprisoned, and ill as a result of his activism, Iglesias managed to organize a large general strike starting August 1, 1900, to protest the severe devaluation of the Spanish *peso* after the Foraker Act demanded its exchange for American dollars. Though the strikers were unsuccessful, the month of violence that followed the strike solidified the power of the Federación Libre de Trabajadores.

Realizing he needed to link with U.S. trade unions, Iglesias moved to New York to seek out sympathetic labor leaders. He worked as a carpenter in Brooklyn while learning English and taking night classes at Cooper Union College.[14] He also became an American citizen.[15] Iglesias convinced the American Federation of Labor (AFL) to organize in Puerto Rico, and with the blessing of AFL president Samuel Gompers, met with Presidents William McKinley and Theodore Roosevelt.[16] With Gompers's and Roosevelt's support, Iglesias returned to Puerto Rico as the island's AFL organizer, but upon his arrival in 1901, Iglesias was arrested for failing to appear for a court date for charges that he broke a Spanish law prohibiting conspiracy to raise wage labor.[17] Gompers paid Iglesias's bail, but in December, Iglesias was sentenced to slightly more than three years in prison. Supporters appealed his case to the Puerto Rican supreme court, and after Iglesias served seven months, the court overturned his sentence. Bolstered by Gompers's advocacy, and garnering headlines about his legal battles in major mainland newspapers, Iglesias rose to national prominence. A year later, he married Justa Bocanegra of Aguadilla, Puerto Rico. The couple raised 11 children: Santiago Angel, Josefina, Libertad, Fraternidad, América, Igualdad, Justicia, Laura, Luz, Manuel, and Eduardo. Many of their names reflected their father's political beliefs.[18]

For the next three decades, Iglesias merged politics with labor activism as the Federación Libre (Free Federation) became more powerful. He edited a series of Spanish-language newspapers promoting labor causes; in addition to the *Ensayo oberero* (1897–1899), Iglesias helped publish the *Porvenir social* (1899–1900), the *Unión oberera* (1903–1906), and the *Justicia* (1914–1925).[19] In 1906 and 1908, he ran for Resident Commissioner on the Federación Libre ticket, but his party lost handily to the Partido de Unión (Unionist Party) and its candidate, Tulio Larrínaga.[20] In 1915 Federación Libre workers met in Cayey, Puerto Rico, and formed their own political arm, which they designated the Partido Socialista (Puerto Rican Socialist Party). Though he did not officially lead the party until 1920, Iglesias was one of its founders and remained the party's spokesperson for the rest of his life.[21] Representing his new party, Iglesias was elected to the Puerto Rican territorial senate, where he served from 1917 to 1933. With Gompers, Iglesias founded the Pan American Federation of Labor (PAFL).[22]

Iglesias won election as Resident Commissioner to Congress primarily because of a coalition between his Partido Socialista and the Partido Unión Republicana (Union Republican Party). Although Socialistas had traditionally focused more on economic reform than on Puerto Rico's status and because Iglesias believed stronger ties to the American mainland would benefit poorer Puerto Ricans, the two parties were linked by the issue of status.[23]

The Coalición (Coalition), which favored statehood, faced off with the newly formed Partido Liberal (Liberal Party), which was led by territorial senator Luis Muñoz Marín, and espoused independence.[24] The Coalición leadership agreed in June 1932 to back a candidate from the Partido Socialista for Resident Commissioner, a candidate from the Partido Unión Republicana as president of the territorial senate, and a candidate from the party that received the most votes for speaker of the territorial house.[25] Amid thunderous applause, the Socialist convention unanimously nominated Iglesias for Resident Commissioner.[26] The Partido Unión Republicana signaled its solidarity by nominating Iglesias in September. When the pact was formalized in October, he was officially the Coalición candidate.[27]

The 1932 election was unique in that Puerto Rican women were permitted to vote providing they (like men) passed a literacy test. In addition, the scramble to overturn new, local election law that purposely favored large, established political parties left little time for campaigning.[28] With three parties on the ballot—the Coalición, the Partido Liberal, and the Partido Nacionalista (Nationalist Party)—the question of Puerto Rico's status became a primary issue during the campaign, along with the economic problems resulting from the Great Depression, which were manifested by a decrease in Puerto Rico's per capita income of approximately 30 percent between 1931 and 1933.[29] Iglesias campaigned on a familiar platform, emphasizing social justice, economic aid, and reform. "I am accused of being a radical, a Socialist who would as resident commissioner be concerned with the working classes only," he said. Indeed, Iglesias's opponents highlighted his many jail sentences, including his imprisonment during the U.S. invasion.[30] Iglesias brushed off these attacks, likening himself to the Democratic presidential candidate, New York Governor Franklin D. Roosevelt, and his supporters. "They stand for social justice, democratic institutions and humanity—for individual freedom and private rights," he noted. Iglesias also asserted that he planned to be a dedicated representative of Puerto Rico in Congress. "In speaking of Congress," he noted, "I do not have charity in mind. It is cooperation."[31] In line with the Coalición, Iglesias did not support independence, believing that Puerto Rico's becoming a U.S. territory was the best option for the working classes. Iglesias faced Partido Liberal candidate Benigno Fernández García, formerly a Partido Unión candidate for the territorial house of representatives and a floor leader for the Alianza (Alliance). Nacionalista candidate Julio Medina González, who favored independence, also entered the race.[32]

Despite interruptions by the powerful September San Cipriano hurricane—whose devastation forced a special legislative session—and political wrangling that lasted through the summer, the fall campaign went relatively smoothly. Election Day, November 8, 1932, was "as colorful as a carnival," with supporters flying their parties' flags. Despite the political shifts and economic difficulties surrounding the contest, the election was one of the quietest since 1900.[33] Eighty-five percent of registered voters turned out to elect officials by party slates. The Coalición won with 35 percent of the vote, elevating Iglesias to the Resident Commissioner. The Partido Liberal trailed with 29 percent of the vote, and the Nacionalistas garnered less than 1 percent.[34]

Iglesias arrived in Washington after attending an AFL convention in Cincinnati, eventually settling his large family in a duplex in northwest Washington. Sworn in on the Opening Day of the 73rd Congress (1933–1935), he became the first Resident Commissioner to receive committee assignments in addition to a seat on the Insular Affairs Committee, traditionally reserved for the representative from Puerto Rico. Iglesias was also named to the Agriculture, Labor, and Territories Committees. He still lacked the right to vote and the ability to accrue seniority on committees, but at that time lawmakers considered the Agriculture Committee to be one of the most attractive committee assignments in the House.[35]

The new Resident Commissioner educated his colleagues about Puerto Rican history, government, and economic issues, speaking frequently and protractedly on the House Floor about matters that affected his home island. His first speech on March 29, 1933, introduced his colleagues to his two greatest concerns during his service on Capitol Hill: Puerto Rico's economic rehabilitation and the clarification of the territory's political and cultural connection with the mainland United States. Furthermore, he emphasized the economic problem Puerto Rico faced as a result of the Depression and asked that the territory be included in economic rehabilitation plans proposed by newly elected President Roosevelt. "As you all know," he said, using a sentence he would invoke frequently, "Puerto Rico stands literally at the crossroads of the world, at the entrance to the Caribbean region and on a direct line between east and west, north and south."[36]

During his two terms in office, Iglesias doggedly pursued Puerto Rico's inclusion in New Deal legislation for the financial relief of banks and individuals. On March 12, 1935, he argued in favor of incorporating Puerto Rican banks under the Federal Deposit Insurance Corporation (FDIC), a program to guarantee bank deposits that was created as part of the Glass–Steagall Banking Act of 1933.[37] Iglesias eventually succeeded in having Puerto Rican banks included among those of other territories under the legislation's protection.[38] He also fought for the inclusion of Puerto Rico under the umbrella of Social Security, yet succeeded only late in his career in securing coverage for Puerto Ricans under two sections of the legislation: Section 5 funneled aid through the Children's Bureau in the Department of Labor, and section 6 provided money aimed primarily at rural communities via the U.S. Public Health Service.[39]

At other times Iglesias had to shift tactics to block the effects of New Deal legislation. He unsuccessfully attempted to combat the negative effect of the Agricultural Adjustment Act (AAA), passed in May 1933, on the prices of food imports in Puerto Rico. A later amendment to the AAA, the Sugar Act of 1934 (also known as the Jones–Costigan Act) proved particularly damaging to Puerto Rico's depressed sugar industry.[40] The bill attempted to regulate sugar production by assigning quotas to American sugar producers in various regions. Puerto Rico's allotment—nearly 40 percent lower than the expected output in the following year—proved severely inadequate. Moreover, quotas assigned to Cuba, the Philippines, Hawaii, and mainland producers were much higher.[41] "Puerto Rico feels it is entitled to be treated with the same consideration that has been accorded to the domestic producers of sugar," Iglesias railed. "Puerto Rico wants to be recognized as an integral part of the United States and be recognized in the same way as any other domestic community of the mainland or any other part or territory of the United States."[42]

But it was Iglesias's response to the debate over Puerto Rico's status that drew the most attention during his career on Capitol Hill. On January 3, 1935, on the Opening Day of the 74th Congress (1935–1937), Iglesias introduced a bill granting Puerto Rico statehood.[43] Outlining the history of the island's acquisition by the United States from the invasion of the island in 1898 through the passage of the Jones Act in 1917, he explained his reasoning. "The loyalty and sincerity of purpose of the people of Puerto Rico are far above any possible question," he declared. "We have done our duty and played our part in the sorrows and happiness of the Nation." He further noted, as he would frequently, that Puerto Rico's population, according to the 1930 Census, exceeded the combined populations of Nevada, Wyoming, New Mexico, Arizona, and Vermont, which were established states. He also cited his limited rights as Resident Commissioner. "I desire that you bear in mind that Puerto Rico, not having a vote in Congress, cannot exercise the great influence which may be exercised by the representatives of the several States of the Union," he said.[44] Iglesias's initial bill languished in the Committee on Territories, but after a year, almost to the day, Iglesias made a similar appeal.[45]

Iglesias's statehood bill was soon overshadowed by the introduction of a vindictive piece of legislation calling for Puerto Rico's independence from the United States—contingent on complete economic severance during the severe financial crisis—from Senator Millard Tydings of Maryland, a close friend of the late Puerto Rican police chief E. Francis Riggs, who had been assassinated by Nacionalista extremists in February 1936. In a rare moment of unanimity with the island's Partido Liberal spokesman Luis Muñoz Marín, Iglesias deemed the Tydings legislation "unjust, arbitrary, and devastating for Puerto Rico … a destructive measure and [one that] certainly will bring nothing but despair among the people who love American democracy."[46]

In the thick of the debate over the Tydings legislation, Iglesias faced his first re-election campaign. As in past elections, the primary issue was Puerto Rico's status, but in 1936 the issue took on national importance. "For the first time the offensive has been taken by those opposed to independence," observed the *New York Times*. "They say the outcome of the election will make it unnecessary for Congress to order an independence plebiscite."[47] Also, the election was the first conducted under universal suffrage laws; men and women, voters—both literate and illiterate—were now eligible to vote, and a record number registered.[48] Despite fears dating back to Spanish rule about unescorted women entering polling places, one observer noted, "Women voters came to the voting places and departed, with or without escorts, with seemingly no more concern than when they go shopping."[49] To facilitate voter turnout, the island government shut down universities for Election Day.[50] Since Partido Liberal leader Muñoz Marín called for a boycott of the election because of his disdain for the Tydings legislation, Iglesias faced a weakened candidate, Dr. J. A. López Antongiorgi, a surgeon who had long been based in New York.[51]

Iglesias campaigned vigorously for his statehood bill, denouncing the Tydings legislation and the independence movement generally. On October 27, 1936, in Mayagüez, Puerto Rico, Iglesias received a flesh wound to his right arm when Nacionalista Domingo S. Crespo fired off five rounds from the 1,000-person crowd that had gathered to hear Iglesias speak.[52] The police quickly apprehended the shooter, and four other suspects were arrested later. An investigation revealed that the would-be assassin had also taken aim at two other people on the podium: Maria Luisa Arcelay, the island's only female legislator, and speaker of the territorial house M. A. García Méndez.[53] One week later, Iglesias returned to the podium in the Plaza Principal with a bandage on his arm. Again, he spoke in favor of Puerto Rican statehood, noting "The welfare of the island people is obtainable only within the liberality of American institutions."[54] He later denounced Nacionalista violence in a letter to the *Washington Post*, writing, "There is no necessity or excuse for violence where freedom exists as it does in Puerto Rico. It is a very small minority, without any important standing among the masses of the people."[55] Aided by the boycott by the Partido Liberal, the Coalición won handily, extending Iglesias's term in Washington and winning three-quarters of the territorial senate and house.[56] Iglesias's return to Washington was a blow to the independence movement. "Puerto Rico prefers to go along with Uncle Sam rather than set up shop for herself as an independent republic," declared the *New York Times*.[57]

After the 1936 election, Iglesias became the face of the anti-independence movement in Puerto Rico. To combat the publicity received by the Tydings legislation, he wrote a long editorial in the *Christian Science Monitor*: "In answer to the frequent questions which are put to me, as to whether the people of Puerto Rico want to become independent," he wrote, "my reply is a forceful, emphatic, unqualified … 'No! How could they, in view of what the United States has meant to them!' … They know there is no other explanation for the fact that they have more to eat than before; that they have a better balanced diet, better clothing, a higher percentage of people in school and a higher rate of literacy and knowledge of the English language than any of the comparable Caribbean and other countries; that they have more miles of railroads and more miles of highways per hundred square miles than any of those countries."[58] The Tydings legislation languished in the Senate Committee on Territories and Insular Affairs.

Iglesias's second term was quieter than his first; he was less active on the House Floor but provided lengthy treatises in the *Congressional Record* Appendix. In 1939 the AFL sent Iglesias back to Mexico and Cuba to revive the PAFL. Having contracted malaria, he was weakened by a fever and died a week after returning from his trip, on December 5, 1939, in Washington's Garfield Hospital. Speaker William Bankhead of Alabama appointed a committee to attend funeral services in Puerto Rico, where Iglesias lay in state in San Juan, while flags on the island flew at half-staff.[59] More than 200,000 people attended his funeral, where House Labor Committee chair Representative Mary Norton of New Jersey spoke on behalf of the Members of Congress.[60] Bolívar Pagán, elected to succeed his father-in-law, memorialized Iglesias on the House Floor. "A hard worker, a bold fighter, and beloved leader for my land on the seas," Pagán noted. "[Iglesias] had devoted more than 40 years to the awakening to the betterment, to the welfare, and to the social and economic freedom of our common people."[61] He later described his father-in-law as "a live wire, a human dynamo, an energetic, honest, and far-sighted statesman at the service of the people."[62] Iglesias was buried in San Juan Cemetery.

FOR FURTHER READING

Biographical Directory of the United States Congress, "Santiago Iglesias," http://bioguide.congress.gov.

Gonzalo F. Córdova, *Resident Commissioner Santiago Iglesias and His Times* (Editorial de la Universidad de Puerto Rico, 1993).

MANUSCRIPT COLLECTION

University of Virginia, Alderman Library (Charlottesville). *Papers*: Santiago Iglesias Pantin Papers, 1915–1937, one reel microfilm. Papers are mostly in Spanish.

NOTES

1 "Memorial Services Held in the House of Representatives of the United States, Together with Remarks Presented in Eulogy of Santiago Iglesias, Late a Resident Commissioner from Puerto Rico" (Government Printing Office, 1941): 31 (hereinafter referred to as "Memorial Services"); Harwood Hull, "A He-Cinderella of Puerto Rico," 6 October 1929, *Baltimore Sun*: MP11.

2 Thomas Mathews, *Puerto Rico and the New Deal* (Gainesville: University of Florida Press, 1960): 16.

3 *Congressional Record*, House, 73rd Cong., 1st sess. (29 March 1933): 1003.

4 Iglesias' primary biographer, Gonzalo F. Córdova, states that Iglesias's father died before he was born, but Gregg Andrews writes in *American National Biography* that Iglesias was 12 when his father died. At least one older brother, Eduardo, immigrated to Argentina and was never heard from again. See Gonzalo F. Córdova, *Resident Commissioner Santiago Iglesias and His Times* (Editorial de la Universidad de Puerto Rico, 1993): 45; Gregg Andrews, "Iglesias, Santiago," *American National Biography*, 11 (New York: Oxford University Press, 1999): 631 (hereinafter referred to as *ANB*).

5 Historians disagree about the first time Iglesias participated in the labor movement. Córdova notes that this occurred in 1882, although Iglesias would have been 12 years old, and reports that the master carpenter in Iglesias's shop influenced him by imbuing him with Socialist and Marxist ideology. See Córdova, *Resident Commissioner Santiago Iglesias and His Times*: 45–46. Andrews notes that Iglesias masterminded the 1884 walkout as a protest against his employer. See Andrews, "Iglesias, Santiago," *ANB*.

6 Carmen E. Enciso and Tracy North, *Hispanic Americans in Congress, 1822–1995* (Washington, D.C.: Government Printing Office, 1995), 64; Córdova, *Resident Commissioner Santiago Iglesias and His Times*: 47.

7 César J. Ayala and Rafael Bernabe, *Puerto Rico in the American Century: A History since 1898* (Chapel Hill: University of North Carolina Press, 2007): 17; Córdova, *Resident Commissioner Santiago Iglesias and His Times*: 50–51.

8 Córdova, *Resident Commissioner Santiago Iglesias and His Times*: 51.

9 Ibid., 53–62.

10 Ibid., 65; Ayala and Bernabe, *Puerto Rico in the American Century:* 17.

11 For an explanation of Puerto Rican political parties, see Figure 1 in the contextual essay for this section.

12 The interactions among the three men are documented in detail in Córdova, *Resident Commissioner Santiago Iglesias and His Times*, chapter 2.

13 Ayala and Bernabe, *Puerto Rico in the American Century:* 17; Córdova, *Resident Commissioner Santiago Iglesias and His Times*: 71.

14 "Memorial Services": 32.

15 Córdova, *Resident Commissioner Santiago Iglesias and His Times*: 101.

16 Ibid., 96.

17 William George Whittaker, "The Santiago Iglesias Case, 1901–1902," *The Americas* 24, no. 4 (April 1968): 381.

18 "Santiago Iglesias," *Dictionary of American Biography, Supplements 1–2: To 1940* (American Council of Learned Societies, 1944–1958). Reproduced in Biography Resource Center. Farmington Hills, MI: The Gale Group, 2003, http://galenet.galegroup.com/servlet/BioRC (accessed 20 November 2003) (hereinafter referred to as *DAB*); "Porto Rican Gives His Daughters Unusual Names," 17 September 1939, *Chicago Tribune*: G7.

19 *DAB.*

20 Ibid. See also Enciso and North, *Hispanic Americans in Congress, 1822–1995*: 64. Under the provisions of the Foraker Act, Resident Commissioners faced re-election every two years, until 1917. See Abraham Holtzman, "Empire and Representation: The U.S. Congress," *Legislative Studies Quarterly* 11, no. 2 (May 1986): 254.

21 Córdova, *Resident Commissioner Santiago Iglesias and His Times*: 134.

22 Ibid.

23 Ayala and Bernabe, *Puerto Rico in the American Century*: 65; "Political Parties in Puerto Rico," File 719-82, Entry 5; General Classified Files, 1898–1945; General Records Relating to More Than One Island Possession; Records of the Bureau of Insular Affairs, Record Group 350; National Archives at College Park, College Park, MD (hereinafter referred to as RG 350; NACP); Iglesias to George H. Dern, Secretary of War, 14 March 1933, File 719-82, RG 350, NACP.

24 Ayala and Bernabe, *Puerto Rico in the American Century*: 100; Harwood Hull, "Puerto Rico Facing Doubtful Election," 18 September 1932, *New York Times*: E8.

25 Córdova, *Resident Commissioner Santiago Iglesias and His Times*: 242.

26 "Name Iglesias for Post," 5 August 1932, *New York Times*: 7.

27 Córdova, *Resident Commissioner Santiago Iglesias and His Times*: 244–246.

28 Electoral law dictated that, to receive space on the ballot, new or poorly polling parties were required to present petitions with the signatures of at least 10 percent of the total number of voters in the previous election. Thus, the Liberal Party, a new political entity, and the Nationalists, who had polled a meager 329 votes in the previous election, were forced to circulate these documents to gain a place on the ballot. Urged by then-Resident Commissioner José Pesquera, the insular legislature pushed through the compromise brokered among Pesquera, Iglesias, and Governor James Beverley, allowing all three parties on the ballot. Liberal leader Antonio Barceló had championed the law as president of the insular senate and leader of the large and powerful Alliance Party in 1928. Ironically, the breakup in the Alianza put him in the position of opposing his own law. See Mathews, *Puerto Rican Politics and the New Deal*: 35–38.

29 Mathews, *Puerto Rico and the New Deal*: 40; Ayala and Bernabe, *Puerto Rico in the American Century*: 96.

30 Truman R. Clark, *Puerto Rico and the United States, 1917–1938* (University of Pittsburgh Press, 1975): 123.

31 "Iglesias Restates His Stand," 27 October 1932, *Porto Rico Progress*: 10; available in File 719-49, RG 350, NACP.

32 If he won, Medina González planned to go to Washington as a plenipotentiary minister instead of as Resident Commissioner, demanding Puerto Rico's separation from the United States (Córdova, *Resident Commissioner Santiago Iglesias and His Times*: 252–254).

33 Harwood Hull, "Puerto Rico Poll Calmest in Years," 27 November 1932, *New York Times*: E7.

34 Votes for Partido Unión Republicana and votes for the Partido Socialista were counted separately in the balloting but were combined in the final result. The Partido Unión Republicana polled 19 percent, and the Socialistas polled 17 percent [Córdova, 256; "Puerto Rico Elections: General Election of 1932, 3 May 1934, File 9 8 82-Politics-Elections-1932; Classified Files, 1907–1951; Office of Territories, Record Group 126; National Archives at College Park, College Park, MD (hereinafter referred to as RG 126; NACP)].

35 R. Eric Peterson, "Resident Commissioner from Puerto Rico," 16 January 2009, Report RL 31856, Congressional Research Service, Library of Congress, Washington, D.C.: 3; Charles Stewart III, "Committee Hierarchies in the Modernizing House, 1875–1947," *American Journal of Political Science 36* (November 1992): 845.

36 *Congressional Record*, House, 73rd Cong., 1st sess. (29 March 1933): 1003.

37 *Congressional Record*, House, 74th Cong., 1st sess. (12 March 1935): 3490.

38 Federal Deposit Insurance Corporation, *A History of the FDIC 1933–1983*, http://www.fdic.gov/bank/analytical/firstfifty/chapter3.html (accessed 17 September 2010).

39 "Hopes for Security Law," 15 August 1937, *New York Times*: 22; *Congressional Record*, Appendix, 76th Cong., 1st sess. (16 March 1939): 1026–1028.

40 Sugar Act of 1934, P.L. 73-213, 48 Stat 670.

41 Ayala and Bernabe, *Puerto Rico in the American Century*: 100–101; Córdova, *Resident Commissioner Santiago Iglesias and His Times*: 305; "The Sugar Act of 1937," *Yale Law Journal* 47, no. 3 (April 1938) 984–985; James L. Dietz, *Economic History of Puerto Rico: Institutional Change and Capitalist Development* (Princeton University Press, 1986): 171 (see especially Table 3.8).

42 *Congressional Record*, House, 73rd Cong., 2nd sess. (15 February 1934): 2621–2623.

43 Córdova, *Resident Commissioner Santiago Iglesias and His Times*: 312; H.R. 1394.

44 *Congressional Record*, House, 74th Cong., 1st sess. (3 January 1935): 35.

45 *Congressional Record*, House, 74th Cong., 1st sess. (5 June 1935): 8715.

46 "Puerto Rican Bill Draws More Fire," 28 April 1936, *New York Times*: 8.

47 "Iglesias Campaigns Again in Puerto Rico," 2 November 1936, *New York Times*: 12.

48 "Iglesias Elected by Puerto Ricans," 5 November 1936, *New York Times*: 20; "Iglesias Campaigns Again in Puerto Rico."

49 "Puerto Rico Vote Favors U.S. Ties," 15 November 1936, *New York Times*: E10.

50 Ibid.

51 Ibid.; Frank Otto Gatell, "Independence Rejected: Puerto Rico and the Tydings Bill of 1936," *The Hispanic American Historical Review* 38, no. 1 (February 1958): 40.

52 "Iglesias Is Wounded in Puerto Rican Talk," 27 October 1936, *New York Times*: 4.

53 "Push Puerto Rico Inquiry," 17 November 1936, *New York Times*: 17.

54 "Iglesias Campaigns Again in Puerto Rico."

55 Santiago Iglesias, "Puerto Rico Affairs," 26 March 1937, *Washington Post*: 8.

56 Gatell, "Independence Rejected: Puerto Rico and the Tydings Bill of 1936": 42; "Puerto Rico Vote Favors U.S. Ties," 15 November 1936, *New York Times*: E10. When examined separately, Liberals were still the single largest polling party (over Socialists and Republicans). See "Estadisticas de las elecciones celebradas en Puerto Rico el 3 de Noviembre de 1936," File 9-8-82-Politics-Elections-1936, RG 126, NACP.

57 "Iglesias Elected by Puerto Ricans." "An independence plebiscite would only favor the opponents of island Americanism," Iglesias told reporters. "For many years I have insisted at Washington that the vast majority of the island people want only union with the people of the United States. Yesterday's election again proves this."

58 Santiago Iglesias, "Puerto Rico and Independence," 12 April 1937, *Christian Science Monitor*: 1.

59 "Santiago Iglesias, Labor Leader, Dies," 6 December 1939, *New York Times*: 32; "Iglesias Lies in State," 12 December 1939, *New York Times*: 16; "Crowd Carries Body of Iglesias to Grave," 13 December 1939, *New York Times*: 27.

60 "Memorial Services": 33.

61 Pagán married Iglesias's daughter Igualdad in 1933. See "Daughter of Island Envoy Wed Here," 28 September 1933, *Washington Post*: 8; "Memorial Services": 29.

62 "Memorial Services": 32.

"We have rejected all formulas of a colonial government. We consider this formula disgraceful and not compatible with the civil dignity of our Nation.... We want and are anxious to be recognized as an integral part of the States of the Union, [and] to lead our future along that line."

Santiago Iglesias
House Floor Speech, June 5, 1935

Bolívar Pagán
1897–1961

RESIDENT COMMISSIONER 1939–1945
COALITIONIST FROM PUERTO RICO

Dubbed "Puerto Rico's best-read man" by the *New York Times*, Bolívar Pagán was highly educated and a prolific writer.[1] Pagán married a daughter of his mentor, labor leader and political giant Santiago Iglesias, and upon the older man's sudden death, filled his seat as Puerto Rico's Resident Commissioner in the U.S. House of Representatives. Pagán pursued his father-in-law's economic initiatives in Congress, particularly the defense of the island's sugar industry against strict quotas. However, Puerto Rico's strategic location during the Second World War and the appointment of a controversial governor eventually consumed Pagán's congressional career.

Bolívar Pagán was born in Guayanilla, a suburb of Ponce in southwestern Puerto Rico, on May 16, 1897, to Emilio Pagán and Elisa Lucca.[2] Pagán received his early education in Adjuntas, before moving to Ponce for secondary school, where he excelled at writing, winning the Insular School literary prize in 1915. After graduating from Ponce High School in 1916, he worked as a journalist for several local newspapers: *El día de Ponce*, *Nosotros*, *Renacimiento*, and *Puerto Rico ilustrado*. He eventually edited *La idea* and *La aurora*. In 1919, under the tutelage of Puerto Rican Partido Socialista (Socialist Party) founder Santiago Iglesias, he became vice president of the party. Pagán received his law degree at the University of Puerto Rico at Rio Piedras in 1921, was accepted to the bar, and set up practice in San Juan. In 1922 he served as a judge in Fajardo, Puerto Rico, on the island's eastern coast. Frequently part of a team of politicians lobbying Washington, Pagán was particularly active in efforts to obtain statehood for the island.[3]

Pagán made two unsuccessful bids as a Partido Socialista candidate, for the Puerto Rican house of representatives in 1924, and for the Puerto Rican senate in 1928; however, in 1925 he began a four-year term as the San Juan city treasurer.[4] Pagán finally attained a seat in the insular senate as a Coalición (Coalition) candidate in 1932 and served from 1933 to 1939, rising to president *pro tempore* and majority floor leader. In 1936 and 1937, he was also the city manager for San Juan. Personally and politically allied to Iglesias, then the island's Resident Commissioner in the U.S. Congress, Pagán married Iglesias's daughter Igualdad in 1933.[5]

After Iglesias's unexpected death on December 5, 1939, the Jones Act permitted Governor William B. Leahy to appoint a successor to serve out Iglesias's elected term, which ended in January 1941.[6] Since Iglesias belonged to the Coalición, Leahy asked each of the two parties that formed the pact—the Socialistas, led by Pagán, and the Partido Unión Republicana (Republican Union Party)—to submit the name of a candidate. However, the Unión Republicana leaders honored the terms of the Coalición, which called for a Socialista member to fill the Resident Commissioner post. On December 26, Leahy officially named Pagán to the post.[7] He was sworn in on January 3, 1940, and inherited his late father-in-law's assignments on the Agriculture, Insular Affairs, and Territories Committees.[8]

Much of Pagán's work continued his father-in-law's legacy, including the advocacy of Puerto Rico's economic and political interests in various New Deal relief and employment programs. Pagán fought to increase Puerto Rican quotas for sugar exports to the continental United States, an issue Iglesias pursued when Congress passed emergency regulations on domestic production in 1934 and 1937. Pagán's request to increase Puerto Rico's sugar quota by nearly two-thirds went unheeded, despite restrictions on the industry, whose production exceeded its 1938 quota by nearly one-third.[9]

Pagán also continued Iglesias's quest for Puerto Rican statehood and greater local control over the government,

Image courtesy of the Library of Congress

but he considered calls for the island's independence tantamount to "economic suicide."[10] On April 12, 1940, Pagán submitted two bills. The first called for the local election of the island's governor starting the following November; the governor would appoint his own cabinet, the island's auditor, and seven of the island's positions on the supreme court (an increase from five). Pagán also called for the popular election of a vice president, who would serve as the island's president of the senate. The second bill called for a constitutional convention to consider the island's statehood. Both bills, however, died in committee.[11] The following month, Pagán was a signatory to a letter to President Franklin D. Roosevelt claiming that Governor Leahy had assumed extraconstitutional powers by appointing two cabinet ministers without the advice or consent of the insular senate. Deeming the move an "embarrassing situation," the letter stated that the governor's arbitrary exercise of power gave "no credit to the United States as a champion and safeguard of democracy," at a time when "absolute dictatorship in Europe had put democracy and modern civilization in actual jeopardy."[12]

Pagán faced a changed political landscape in his first election as the incumbent. Two new political entities, the Partido Popular Democrático (Popular Democratic Party, or PPD) and the Partido Unificación Tripartita (Tripartite Unification Party)—dissident factions of the former Coalición and Partido Liberal—petitioned to be on the ballot. The PPD, led by Luis Muñoz Marín, had broken with Partido Liberal allies in 1937 over the issue of immediate independence. As a result, Muñoz Marín tabled the independence issue to focus on social reform and began campaigning in force for the 1940 election. The PPD nominated Dr. Antonio Fernós-Isern, a local physician. The Unificación Tripartita, backed by laborers, chose Puerto Rican speaker Miguel Angel García Méndez as its candidate.[13] Pagán's Coalición stood by its desire for statehood; the incumbent "expresses himself as vigorously pro American," noted Governor Leahy.[14]

The political upheaval and continued economic depression translated into a violent campaign. In a July 31 telegram to Interior Secretary Harold Ickes, Governor Leahy noted, "The political controversy here is getting hotter from day to day. We hope it will not explode into violence although there has already been reported some scattered bombing without any casualties more serious than shaken nerves."[15] Although three people were killed and 15 were injured during the polling, federal observers considered the violence an improvement over the status quo.[16] "Our local election here is reported as the most peaceful election of recent years," Governor Leahy told Secretary Ickes. "Only two persons were assassinated," he reported erroneously, "and only three ballot boxes were burned."[17] The PPD was confident of victory leading up to Election Day. However, surprisingly, the Coalición held together. As a result of the continued and largely pragmatic alliance of the Unión Republicanas and the Socialistas under the Coalición banner, Pagán prevailed; official returns put the Coalición on top with 222,423 votes (39 percent), barely edging out the PPD's 214,857 votes (38 percent). Unificación Tripartita and a minor political entity—the Partido Agrícola Pura (Pure Agriculture Party), which polled just over 1,000 votes—garnered a combined total of 131,571 votes (23 percent).[18]

From his perch on the House Committee on Labor in the 77th Congress (1941–1943), Pagán addressed the issue of sugar quotas.[19] He rallied against a lopsided vote to raise quotas for mainland producers and refiners of beet and cane sugar that would further restrict quotas for the territories and other producers of cane sugar.[20] The vote took place after only 40 minutes of debate, without committee hearings, and despite the warnings of President Roosevelt, Secretary of State Cordell Hull, and Secretary of Agriculture Claude Wickard. Though Agriculture Committee chairman Hampton Fulmer of South Carolina assured his colleagues the new quotas would not raise sugar prices, opponents of the proposal disagreed. The Florida delegation was among the groups that lobbied the hardest against the proposal, to protect its burgeoning production of cane sugar. Texas and Louisiana beet producers opposed Florida and the sugarcane-producing territories.[21] Pagán read a letter from the President into the *Congressional Record*: "The Administration has not recommended sugar legislation," the letter said. "It must also be recognized that a quota and allotment structure may, under conditions now current, conflict with national and defense requirements," continued the letter, alluding to the growing threat to the United States from the Second World War and to its interest in protecting U.S. territories. Moreover, unstable foreign areas in Cuba and the British West Indies would be under a "virtual embargo," Secretary Hull had noted. Recognizing the need for stability in sugar-producing regions after the United States entered World War II on December 8, 1941, the Senate amended the legislation on December 15, striking the quota reductions but lowering the price for raw sugar for three years.[22]

Pagán initially approved of Roosevelt's foreign policy toward Latin America, praising the President's "iron pact" speech, in which FDR proclaimed his intention to defend South America against Nazi incursion and pledged "whole hearted and faithful support of your leadership of this nation and the whole democratic world."[23] In the 78th Congress (1943–1945), Pagán gained additional assignments on the Military Affairs and Naval Affairs Committees, reflecting Puerto Rico's selection before the war as the site for a $30 million army and naval base.[24] The committee assignments recognized Puerto Rico's strategic importance to the U.S. war effort. Dubbed the "Pearl Harbor of the Caribbean," Puerto Rico became a key location for combating Nazi submarines believed to be roaming the sea.[25]

A food shortage caused by German U-boat attacks on Caribbean shipping drew national attention to the antipathy between Pagán and Puerto Rico's appointed governor, Rexford Tugwell. Pagán first aired local dissatisfaction with Tugwell, a former member of Roosevelt's "Brains Trust," when Tugwell was appointed chancellor of the University of Puerto Rico in July 1941. Pagán called the move "the most anti-Puerto Rican manoeuvre ever attempted," noting that no small state university—let alone "the little university of the small and hungry Puerto Rico"—paid its chancellor the exorbitant annual salary of $15,000 that was offered to Tugwell. The selection of a "continental American" as chancellor was also insulting, Pagán said, because it implied that the island could not oversee its own institutions. Pagán's political opponent Luis Muñoz Marín supported Tugwell's appointment, partly because of a campaign promise to isolate the university from politics.[26] Pagán claimed their alliance benefitted the PPD and Tugwell at Puerto Ricans' expense. In return, Pagán was frequently accused of attacking Tugwell strictly for political purposes.[27]

Shortly after Tugwell accepted his appointment as university chancellor in August 1941, Puerto Rican governor Guy Swope resigned, and President Roosevelt quickly tapped Tugwell for the vacancy. Muñoz Marín spoke at Tugwell's nomination hearing, and Pagán vocally opposed the appointment.[28] As early as January 1942, he called for Tugwell's removal from the post, writing that the governor was "disregarding in Puerto Rico all the principles that the United States forces and democratic peoples are fighting for thruout the world." He accused Tugwell of aligning with the minority PPD to create despotic political rule and of collecting two federal salaries because he received $10,000 annually as governor while retaining his pay as university chancellor.[29] Pagán requested Tugwell's recall several times throughout the next year, but the Roosevelt administration, advertising itself as sympathetic to the plight of Latin American governments, ignored him.[30] Noting that Tugwell threatened to impose martial law to squelch protest against him, Pagán again described his rule as anti-American: "In this way Tugwell is an American Quisling, [he] is doing a good job for the axis powers."[31]

Pagán's battle against the Tugwell administration eventually led to a showdown over a proposed $15 million emergency food program for Puerto Rico. The package stipulated a reduction in sugar production, long anathema to Puerto Rican politicians, along with seeds for food crops to displace cane fields. Pagán was incensed that local politicians were never consulted about the program, a course he claimed was typical of Tugwell. Pagán supported the food aid legislation, observing that the submarine attacks had decimated ships carrying more than two-thirds of the island's food supplies from the mainland.[32] However, he opposed the initial proposal, promising to introduce another $15 million food program, without stipulations, that would include "safeguards for its administration so that the economic structure of Puerto Rico will not be unnecessarily affected."[33]

The committee eventually approved an aid bill introduced by Pagán as promised, but in a blow to Tugwell added an amendment offered by Representative William Poage of Texas stipulating that the money would not be appropriated while the governor was in office.[34] Despite his opposition to Tugwell's regime, Pagán expressed doubt about the amendment, fearing it would delay the approval of the desperately needed food aid. Yet, following the committee's nearly unanimous vote, Pagán expressed satisfaction with the outcome.[35] "The members of the agriculture committee do not have confidence in Tugwell and the proviso approved with the bill is merely a declaration against Tugwell," he noted. "I hope that Tugwell will interpret the proviso as a request of the committee on agriculture that he be withdrawn from the governorship of Puerto Rico."[36] Angered by the amendment, Interior Secretary Ickes accused Pagán of seeking publicity instead of the relief of his constituents, beginning several rounds of public hostility between the two. "The Resident Commissioner of Puerto Rico has again demonstrated that he is more concerned with politics than with the feeding of the people of Puerto Rico," Ickes told reporters. Pagán responded by saying, Ickes "demonstrat[ed] that he doesn't know what he is talking about."[37] When Ickes was called before the House Insular Affairs Committee to testify on Tugwell's rule, committee members ended up serving as "volunteer referees." Pagán's questioning of the Interior Secretary degraded into a shouting match as Ickes, professing to misunderstand Pagán's accent and accusing him of "playing politics," frequently asked Pagán to repeat himself. Representative Ed Gossett of Texas eventually moved to close the hearing, noting, "I don't want to sit here and listen to the secretary and Mr. Pagan argue."[38]

Part of Pagán's fight to dismiss Tugwell included the submission of several bills for the direct election of the Puerto Rican governor, requiring an amendment to the Jones Act, which established the island's local government. Ironically, Tugwell was the first to suggest the idea to Roosevelt, who approved of his plan on July 4, 1942. However, in an effort to maintain some control over the strategically located island, the Tugwell plan kept the appointed governor in place until the 1944 election cycle. Secretary Ickes supported the plan, but two days later Pagán introduced a bill that allowed the direct election of the governor in the upcoming 1942 election, calling for Tugwell's immediate resignation and for election plans to move forward.[39] New York Representative Vito Marcantonio, a radical member of Congress whose East Harlem district included a large Puerto Rican population, opposed both plans, arguing that neither went far enough and he called for the "immediate, unconditional freedom" of Puerto Rico. Citing the large number of absentee corporate landowners on the island, Marcantonio claimed that only Puerto Rico's independence would satisfy the requirements of the Atlantic Charter and secure the full cooperation of Latin American nations.[40] Ignoring both Pagán and Marcantonio, Roosevelt officially endorsed the Tugwell plan in a message to Congress on March 9, 1943, in which he appointed to a committee headed by Ickes an equal number of Puerto Rican and "continental" residents to recommend the changes in the Jones Act to require the direct election of the island's governor.[41] Pagán was not selected to serve on the committee, but supported its final plan to allow Puerto Rico to elect its own governor.[42]

Pagán called one last time for Tugwell's resignation. On May 1, 1944, he declared that Puerto Ricans were on the brink of revolution. "If the American flag had not been waving over Puerto Rico, the people would have already gone into open revolt by arms," he told reporters. He also charged the governor with living in a plush mansion despite the island's poverty. "Tugwell's dictatorial attitude can be matched only by Hitler's and Mussolini's," he said.[43] Pagán was more diplomatic in a letter to Roosevelt, writing, "Many Congressmen, who are acquainted with the Puerto Rican situation, argue that the reform measure [proposed by Tugwell] would be fake if Puerto Ricans do not have since now a new governor, respected and trusted by all."[44] Tugwell called Pagán's assertions "irresponsible," declaring, "We in Puerto Rico are as peaceful as other Americans who happen to live in Wichita or Seattle."[45] "Mr. Pagán has perhaps lost touch with the real Puerto Rico," Tugwell spat. "His return from Washington [last year], triumphant over thousands of hungry fellow-citizens, evidently went to his head a little. That's the only way I can account for his delusions of revolution."[46] In September, Pagán threatened in a letter to the President to boycott the election if he did not remove Tugwell, a move the White House strongly denounced.[47]

Pagán decided not to run for re-election in 1944 because of another political realignment. A new coalition of the Partidos Unión Republicana and Socialista, and dissident factions of the former Partido Liberal allied to combat the growing strength of the PPD. The agreement included putting forward a former Liberal for Resident Commissioner, and Colonel Manuel Font topped the new Coalición ticket.[48] Early predictions boasted a PPD victory in the fall of 1944, partly as a vindication of the policies of Tugwell, who according to the minority party, was maligned strictly for political purposes.[49] In an election watched closely by mainland observers, including New Mexico Senator Dennis Chavez, the PPD, which was headlined by the candidate for Resident Commissioner, Jesus T. Piñero, won 65 percent of the votes, handily defeating the Coalición's 35 percent.[50] The issue of Puerto Rico's status crept back into the campaign. Leading the victorious party, Luis Muñoz Marín declared he would call for a plebiscite to vote on independence.[51]

Pagán served in the island senate until the PPD absorbed his Partido Socialista in the late 1940s, after which he resumed his law practice on the island.[52] He also wrote a two-volume political history of Puerto Rico, from the U.S. invasion in 1898 through 1953. After completing a draft of his manuscript in 1960, he was diagnosed with cancer. He underwent an operation but died 17 months later in San Juan on February 9, 1961.[53]

FOR FURTHER READING

Biographical Directory of the United States Congress, "Bolívar Pagán," http://bioguide.congress.gov.

Pagán, Bolívar. *Crónicas de Wáshington* (San Juan, PR: Biblioteca de Autores Puertorriqueños, 1949).

_____. *Historia de los partidos políticos Puertorriqueños, 1898–1956* (San Juan, PR: Librería Campos, 1959).

_____. *Proccerato Puertorriqueño del siglo XIX: Historia de los partidos políticos Puertorriqueños, desde sus orígines hasta 1898* (San Juan de Puerto Rico: Editorial Campos, 1961).

NOTES

1 "Appoints Bolivar Pagan," 27 December 1939, *New York Times*: 9.

2 Libertad I. Moore to Ansel Wold, 16 January 1940, textual files of the *Biographical Directory of the United States Congress*, Office of the Historian, U.S. House of Representatives (hereinafter referred to as textual files of the *Biographical Directory of the United States Congress*). A newspaper article indicates that Santiago Iglesias raised Pagán alongside his 11 children after Pagán was orphaned at a young age, but even in his eulogy of Iglesias on the House Floor, Pagán never confirmed this. "Appoints Bolivar Pagan," 27 December 1939, *New York Times*: 9; "Memorial Services Held in the House of Representatives of the United States, Together with Remarks Presented in Eulogy of Santiago Iglesias, Late a Resident Commissioner from Puerto Rico," (Washington, D.C.: Government Printing Office, 1941): 33.

3 See, for example, "Offers Puerto Rico Plan," 6 June 1939, *New York Times*: 5; "Resident Commissioner of Puerto Rico Named," 27 December 1939, *Baltimore Sun*: 9.

4 Moore to Wold, textual files of the *Biographical Directory of the United States Congress*.

5 "Daughter of Island Envoy Wed Here," 28 September 1933, *Washington Post*: 8. It is not known whether the couple had any children.

6 Second Jones Act of 1917, PL 64-368, 39 Stat. 964.

7 "May Succeed Iglesias," 21 December 1939, *New York Times*: 16; "Report Post for Pagan," 24 December 1939, *New York Times*: 9; "Appoints Bolivar Pagan."

8 *Congressional Record*, House, 76th Cong., 3rd sess. (3 January 1940): 6. In what appears to be a formality under the provisions of the Jones Act (39 Stat. 964), the Puerto Rican senate confirmed Pagán's appointment on February 17. See "Pagan Confirmed by Puerto Ricans," 18 February 1940, *Washington Post*: 15. Several other Resident Commissioners were appointed to the House. Appointments from Puerto Rico to fill vacancies are permitted under the Jones Act of 1917 (39 Stat. 964). Other Resident Commissioners who were appointed are José Pesquera of Puerto

Rico (1932), Quintin Paredes of the Philippines (1935), Joaquin Elizalde of the Philippines (1938), Carlos Romulo of the Philippines (1944), Antonio Fernós-Isern of Puerto Rico (1946), and Antonio Colorado of Puerto Rico (1992). See *Biographical Directory of the U.S. Congress*, http://bioguide.congress.gov.

9 James L. Dietz, *Economic History of Puerto Rico: Institutional Change and Capitalist Development* (Princeton: Princeton University Press, 1986): 171–172, see especially Table 3.8.

10 "Pagan, 61, Is Dead of Cancer," *San Juan Star*, 10 February 1961, available in the textual files of the *Biographical Directory of the United States Congress.*

11 H.R. 9360 and H.R. 9361; "Pleads for Puerto Rico," 13 April 1940, *New York Times*: 6; *Congressional Record*, House, 76th Cong., 3rd sess. (12 April 1940): 4464.

12 "Puerto Ricans Protest Leahy Rule, Is Report," 22 May 1940, *Baltimore Sun*: 4.

13 César J. Ayala and Rafael Bernabe, *Puerto Rico in the American Century: A History since 1898* (Chapel Hill: University of North Carolina Press, 2007): 136–137, 142; "New Party Is Strong in Puerto Rico Vote," 7 November 1940, *New York Times*: 6; "Results in Closely Contested Races for Seats in the House," 7 November 1940, *Washington Post*: 6.

14 William D. Leahy to Harold Ickes, 16 November 1940, Doc. 9-9-82-Politics-Elections-1940; Classified Files, 1907–1951; Office of Territories, Record Group 126; National Archives at College Park, College Park, MD (hereinafter referred to as RG 126; NACP).

15 William D. Leahy to Harold Ickes, 31 July 1940, Doc. 9-8-82-Politics-Elections-1940, RG 126, NACP.

16 "Puerto Rico Vote Split," 9 November 1940, *New York Times*: 8.

17 "Puerto Rico Vote Split"; William D. Leahy to Harold Ickes, 6 November 1940, Doc. 9-9-82-Politics-Elections-1940; RG 126; NACP.

18 Fernando Bayron Toro, *Elecciones y partidos políticos de Puerto Rico, 1809–2000* (Mayagüez: Editorial Isla, 2003): 191–194; "Puerto Rico Vote Split"; "Total Number of Votes Cast in the Last Election by Each Political Party for Commissioner to Washington," Doc. 9-8-82-Politics-Elections-1940; RG 126; NACP.

19 David T. Canon et al., *Committees in the U.S. Congress, 1789 to 1946*, vol. 3 (Washington, D.C.: CQ Press, 2002): 797.

20 *Congressional Record*, House, 77th Cong., 1st sess. (1 December 1941): 9297.

21 "Mainland Sugar Wins House Help," 2 December 1941, *New York Times*: 19.

22 Senate Committee on Finance, *Extension of Sugar Act of 1937*, 77th Cong., 1st sess., S. Rep. 907; P.L. 77-386, 55 Stat. 872–873.

23 Associated Press, "Controlled Nazi Press Blames 'Jewish Suggesters' to F.D.R.," 29 May 1941, *Atlanta Constitution*: 6.

24 Canon et al., *Committees in the U.S. Congress, 1789 to 1946*, vol. 3: 797; "Puerto Rico Base Work Progressing, Leahy Reports," 2 January 1940, *Washington Post*: 4.

25 John Lear, "Rexford Tugwell under Fire as Governor of Puerto Rico," 1 March 1942, *Washington Post*: B3; Lear, "Tugwell Stirs Up a Tropical Storm," 8 March 1942, *Baltimore Sun*: SC10.

26 "Assails Naming Tugwell," 30 July 1941, *New York Times*: 5.

27 Surendra Bhana, *The United States and the Development of the Puerto Rican Status Question, 1936–1968* (Lawrence: The University Press of Kansas, 1975): 41, 46–47.

28 Hearing before the Senate Committee on Territories and Insular Affairs, *Nomination of Rexford G. Tugwell*, U.S. Senate, 77th Cong., 1st sess. (6, 12, 13, and 18 August 1941).

29 "Brand Tugwell a Quisling; Call for His Ouster," 22 January 1942, *Chicago Daily Tribune*: 7; "Tugwell Called American Quisling," 22 January 1942, *Baltimore Sun*: 13; "Tugwell Removal Asked by Puerto Rico Official," 3 February 1942, *Atlanta Constitution*: 12.

30 "Tugwell Worse Governor, Says Plea for Recall," 29 October 1942, *Chicago Daily Tribune*: 9; "Tugwell's Recall Urged," 29 October 1942, *New York Times*: 25; "Tugwell under New Attack on Ouster of Aid," 12 November 1942, *Chicago Daily Tribune*: 13; John Lear, "Rexford Tugwell under Fire as Governor of Puerto Rico," 1 March 1942, *Washington Post*: B3; Lear, "Tugwell Stirs Up a Tropical Storm," 8 March 1942, *Baltimore Sun*: SC10.

31 "Brand Tugwell a Quisling; Call for His Ouster"; "Tugwell Called American Quisling."

32 "Claims Tugwell Tries Nazi Ideas in Puerto Rico." 17 October 1942, *Chicago Tribune*: 14.

33 Eugene Rachlis, "Puerto Rican Opposes Plan for Food Fund," 21 June 1942, *Washington Post*: 9.

34 John Fisher, "Millions Voted Puerto Rico if Tugwell Quits," 18 November 1942, *Chicago Daily Tribune*: 1; "Moves in Congress to Oust Tugwell," 18 November 1942, *New York Times*: 16. The latter claims "Representative Page" introduced the amendment, but there was no one named "Page" on the House Agriculture Committee in the 77th Congress. However, Representative William Poage of Texas served on the committee. See *Congressional Directory*, 77th Cong., 2nd sess. (Washington, D.C.: Government Printing Office, 1941): 197.

35 Accounts of the committee vote differ. Chairman Fulmer claimed the vote was unanimous, but reporters noted two dissenters. See Paul Ward, "House Group Adopts Device to Oust Tugwell from Office," 18 November 1942, *Baltimore Sun*: 1.

36 "Moves in Congress to Oust Tugwell," 18 November 1942, *New York Times*: 16; John Fisher, "Millions Voted Puerto Rico If Tugwell Quits," 18 November 1942, *Chicago Daily Tribune*: 1.

37 "Pagan Disputes Ickes," 20 November 1942, *New York Times*: 11.

38 William Moore, "Tugwell Debate with Ickes Fags a Puerto Rican," 25 February 1943, *Chicago Daily Tribune*: 11.

39 James B. Reston, "Right of Electing Governor Planned for Puerto Ricans," 4 July 1942, *New York Times*: 1; "Election of Governor Planned for Puerto Rico," 5 February 1943, *Atlanta Constitution*: 3; "Plans Being Made to Let Puerto Rico Elect Its Governor," 5 February 1943, *Baltimore Sun*: 11.

40 "Offers Bill to Aid Puerto Rico in '42," 7 July 1942, *New York Times*: 10. Pagán frequently found himself trading barbs with Marcantonio. See, for example, *Congressional Record*, House, 76th Cong., 3rd sess. (26 April 1940): 5148–5155.

41 Franklin D. Roosevelt, "Message to Congress on Local Election of a Governor of Puerto Rico," in John T. Woolley and Gerhard Peters, *The American Presidency Project*, http://www.presidency.ucsb.edu/ws/?pid=16371 (accessed 28 September 2010); "Home Rule Asked for Puerto Rico," 10 March 1943, *New York Times*: 3.

42 "Puerto Rican Rule to Come Up Tomorrow," 18 July 1943, *Chicago Daily Tribune*: 16; "Ickes, Seven Others Seek Workable Formula for Puerto Rican Home Rule," 18 July 1943, *Washington Post*: M8; "Back Puerto Rico Bill," 6 August 1944, *New York Times*: 16.

43 "Puerto Ricans Held on Verge of Revolt," 1 May 1944, *Christian Science Monitor*: 11; "Tugwell Rule Brews Revolt, Asserts Critic," 2 May 1944, *Chicago Daily Tribune*: 8; "Puerto Rico Revolt Hinted; Tugwell Ouster Demanded," 2 May 1944, *Los Angeles Times*: 2; "Assails Tugwell as 'Like Hitler'," 2 May 1944, *New York Times*: 9; "Puerto Rico Revolt Said Seething," 2 May 1944, *Atlanta Constitution*: 3.

44 Bolivar Pagán to Franklin D. Roosevelt, 6 June 1944, Doc. 9-8-82-Politics-General, RG 126, NACP.

45 "Tugwell Denies His Regime Is Dictatorship," 4 May 1944, *Chicago Daily Tribune*: 5.

46 "Puerto Rico Safe, Tugwell Declares," 4 May 1944, *New York Times*: 5.

47 Franklin D. Roosevelt to Bolivar Pagán, 9 October 1944, Doc. 9-8-82-Politics-Elections-General, RG 126, NACP.

48 Bayron Toro, *Elecciones y partidos políticos de Puerto Rico*: 202.

49 "Tugwell in Puerto Rico," 19 March 1944, *Washington Post*: B5.

50 Elmer Ellsworth and J. T. Piñero to Bolivar Pagán, 4 May 1944, Doc. 9-8-82 – Politics-Elections-Legislation, U.S., RG 126, NACP. Some results separate the remaining Partido Liberal votes from the Coalición votes. Taken separately, the Partido Liberal won 38,630 votes, the Socialistas won 68,107, and the Unión Republicanas won 101,779 votes. "Total Number of Votes Cast in Last Election by Each Political Party for Commissioner in Washington," Doc. 9-8-82-Politics-Elections-1944, RG 126; *Congressional Record*, Extension of Remarks, 79th Cong., 1st sess. 22 January 1945; 9-8-82-Politics-Elections-1940; RG 126; NACP.

51 Paul W. Ward, "New Measure on Puerto Rico," 21 December 1944, *Baltimore Sun*: 7.

52 Pagán won his final senate term as a Socialista in 1948. See Bayron Toro, *Elecciones y partidos políticos de Puerto Rico, 1809–2000*: 212.

53 "Puerto Rican Ex-Official," 10 February 1961, *Washington Post*: B4; "Bolivar Pagan, 61, Puerto Rican Aide," 10 February 1961, *New York Times*: 24. According to Social Security records, Pagán was born in 1897, which would have made him 64 when he died. However, his obituaries state that he died at age 61.

Antonio M. Fernández
1902–1956

UNITED STATES REPRESENTATIVE 1943–1956
DEMOCRAT FROM NEW MEXICO

Antonio M. Fernández rose from a modest background to become an influential and noteworthy politician. As New Mexico's longest-serving Representative in the mid-20th century, he tirelessly defended his constituents. While concentrating on issues affecting the military and American Indians—two core groups in his At-Large district—he preferred to stay out of the limelight, focusing on compromise and diligent research. "Political leaders are necessary in our party system of Government," Fernández once remarked, "but the men chosen by the people to serve in Congress can best do so if when elected they devote their time at their posts without too much regard for their own political fortunes, and certainly without attempting to direct and control the political fortunes of others."[1]

Antonio M. Fernández was born in Springer, in northwestern New Mexico, on January 17, 1902, to José Estevan and Maria Anita Fernández. Educated as a child in a one-room country schoolhouse, Fernández went on to attend New Mexico Normal University (now Highlands) in Las Vegas, New Mexico. After college, he married Cleofas Chavez on June 9, 1924. The couple had five children: Anita; Dolores; Antonio, Jr.; Orlando; and Manuel. Fernández worked in the office of a local judge and served as a court reporter in the Eighth Judicial District of New Mexico from 1925 to 1930. After earning a law degree at Cumberland University Law School in Lebanon, Tennessee, in 1931, Fernández was admitted to the bar in New Mexico and began practicing in Raton, New Mexico. He worked as an assistant district attorney of the Eighth Judicial District of New Mexico in 1933, and a year later he opened a law practice in Santa Fe. Before serving in the U.S. House, Fernández held a series of elected and appointed positions. In 1935 he represented Colfax County in the New Mexico house of representatives. As a state legislator, he introduced and shepherded the first Rural Electrification Authority Act to passage.[2] After leaving office, Fernández was chief tax attorney for the New Mexico state tax commission before serving as assistant attorney general from 1937 to 1941. He then worked for the New Mexico public service commission in 1941 and 1942.

Reapportionment after the 1940 Census altered New Mexico's political landscape when the state gained a second seat in the U.S. House of Representatives. Fernández's legal background, political experience, and extensive public service attracted him to federal office, and in the 1943 Democratic primary, he joined four other contenders for the two At-Large seats. Incumbent Representative Clinton Anderson easily topped the field to secure the first House seat, while Fernández and New Mexico state corporation commissioner Robert Valdez battled for the second spot. Amid allegations of voter fraud and irregularities by both Fernández and Valdez, the New Mexico state canvassing board led an investigation that included several recounts in the disputed precincts. On October 7, 1942, nearly one month after the primary, the board ruled that Fernández had won the nomination by a slim 45-vote margin.[3]

In the general election, Fernández again placed second behind Representative Anderson, but he defeated his nearest Republican opponent, William A. Sutherland, by nearly 14,000 votes to earn a seat in the 78th Congress (1943–1945).[4] Fernández was usually the second highest vote getter, but in New Mexico's At-Large campaigns that was enough to win re-election. In 1950, however, he placed ahead of former Democratic New Mexico governor John Dempsey by 504 votes. During his tenure in the House, Fernández served alongside Democrat Georgia Lee Lusk, the first woman to represent New Mexico, and Democrat John E. Miles, New Mexico's governor from 1939 to 1942.[5]

Image courtesy of the Library of Congress

Fernandez's committee assignments reflected the interests and priorities of his southwestern state. In his first term, Fernández served on a host of committees: Claims; Indian Affairs; Insular Affairs; Irrigation and Reclamation; Mines and Mining; Public Lands; and Elections No. 1. During the 79th Congress (1945–1947), he retained his assignments, with the exception of Mines and Mining; in its place he chaired the Committee on Memorials. After the Legislative Reorganization Act of 1946 merged disparate committees with overlapping jurisdictions, Fernández served on the modified Public Lands Committee, a combination of four of his previous committee assignments (Indian Affairs, Irrigation and Reclamation, Insular Affairs, and Mining) during the 80th Congress (1947–1949).

Elected in the midst of World War II, Fernández ardently represented his military constituents when he arrived at the Capitol. He drew attention to the issue of absentee voting for servicemen and consistently supported increased federal funding for New Mexico military personnel. During debates on amendments to the Vocational Rehabilitation Act of 1943—legislation aimed at assisting disabled individuals, including war veterans—Fernández reminded his colleagues of the sacrifices New Mexico servicemen had made for the war effort, including a large number of troops who had suffered through the Bataan Death March in the Japanese-occupied Philippines. "New Mexico has more of her men in the armed forces injured and prisoners today than any other State except possibly Texas," he remarked. Fernández proposed that his state should receive additional compensation from the government since the "wounded in battle are not distributed on an equal basis between the states" and since New Mexico relied disproportionately on federal aid.[6]

During his first term in office, Fernández supported the Servicemen's Readjustment Act, better known as the GI Bill of Rights, which passed the House on May 18, 1944. Among its chief provisions were tuition benefits for college-bound veterans and low-interest home mortgage loans. During the floor debate, Fernández took exception to a provision in the bill that would require returning soldiers to prove that the war had interrupted their educational pursuits, saying, "the people of New Mexico would resent discrimination against a large proportion of their boys serving in the war, who because of lack of facilities, lack of opportunity, and lack of more encouragement, went to work at an early age instead of to school."[7] The House eventually adopted a compromise measure that required servicemen older than 24 to verify an interruption in schooling.[8] The landmark legislation sailed through the House and Senate, with no dissenting votes.

After the war, Fernández continued to work on behalf of military personnel in New Mexico by assisting veterans and their families to process compensation claims. On October 18, 1951, he testified before the House Interstate and Foreign Commerce Committee to recommend the swift passage of legislation ensuring financial compensation for American prisoners of war. "I appear only because I feel we owe it to the people of my State, who in proportion to their numbers furnished the largest contingent of any State to the heroic defense of Bataan."[9] Throughout his House service, Fernández publicized the bravery of New Mexican POWs stationed in the Philippines during World War II. To honor their service and sacrifice, including the infamous Bataan Death March, in which American and Filipino soldiers who had surrendered were brutalized by the Japanese, Fernández lobbied for the rank promotion of prisoners of war in the Pacific Theater. Many of them were New Mexico Guardsmen. "Promotion," Fernández maintained, "is only a token of the Nation's gratitude for the valor of all those men who held the Japanese at bay for many months without hope of rescue." Their families, he added, looked "to Congress for some recognition of the aggravated circumstances under which they fell."[10]

In the 78th and 79th Congresses, Fernández introduced legislation to establish a military aviation academy. One of the earliest Members of Congress to vocalize the need for a separate air force training facility, Fernández sought to make New Mexico a leading contender in a competitive process that involved several states vying to host the new military academy. Emphasizing his state's vast space and temperate climate—both favorable for flying—Fernández added, "New Mexico has shown a spirit which should be recognized by the Nation and rewarded with something more tangible than praise."[11] In keeping with his determination to recognize the sacrifices made by the military, Fernández observed that an aviation academy located in New Mexico would be a fitting tribute and a "perpetual memorial" to the many soldiers of his state who had been involved in the Bataan Death March. But despite the support of Senator Dennis Chavez of New Mexico, who also introduced similar legislation, the Air Force ultimately built its facilities in Colorado Springs, Colorado.[12]

In the 81st Congress (1949–1951), Fernández relinquished his seat on Public Lands for a spot on the influential Appropriations Committee. A member of the Military Appropriations Subcommittee because of his knowledge of and experience with military affairs, Fernández also served on the Appropriations subcommittee responsible for the District of Columbia. Fernández quickly earned a reputation as an advocate for the District who lobbied for increased federal aid for the nation's capital. The New Mexico Representative reminded his colleagues of the unique and complex situation posed by the District. "We must operate within a balanced budget for the District, against the background of needs for operation, maintenance, and particularly capital outlay, far above the money available," he observed.[13] According to Fernández, Congress had the responsibility to promote the public welfare of D.C. residents by providing adequate funding for their schools, police, and hospitals without placing an onerous tax burden on the District.[14]

Fernández sought to acquire federal aid for his Native-American constituents, especially the Navajo and Hopi tribes, two of the most destitute groups in the nation.[15] In 1949 Fernández took center stage in a heated debate with John Collier, the former head of the Bureau of Indian Affairs. A major proponent of a 10-year, $88 million appropriation that authorized new schools, roads, hospitals, and resource development on reservation lands, Fernández introduced an amendment that would place the Navajos and Hopis under state jurisdiction. The New Mexico Representative contended that American Indians should be afforded the same rights as other state residents, including access to state courts.[16] Although Collier supported the underlying impetus of the Navajo-Hopi rehabilitation bill, which first passed the House on July 14, 1949, he criticized Fernández's rider and launched a public battle for its removal from the legislation.[17] Collier used his position as a nationally recognized advocate for Native Americans to voice concern that states could manipulate their new jurisdictional power to seize control of Navajo and Hopi rights to water—an essential resource in the arid Southwest. He also speculated that shifting jurisdiction from the federal government to states could undermine Native-American independence by hindering tribal organization.[18] Fernández took to the House Floor to defend his amendment, which he maintained would lead to a better quality of life and increased rights for the Navajos and Hopis. "It is time that we took some positive steps toward the final assimilation, education, and rehabilitation of the Indians as real citizens rather than perpetuate their segregation to the point of absurdity," he asserted.[19] Fernández adamantly denied that his amendment would provide states the authority to undermine any federal treaties with American Indian tribes and claimed that Collier "deliberately attempted to mislead the public."[20] Amid the growing controversy and concern about the potential flaws and ambiguity of the measure, President Harry S. Truman vetoed the Navajo-Hopi Bill on October 17, 1949.[21] More than five months later, on April 6, 1950, the House passed a revised economic aid bill for the Navajos and Hopis—a compromise measure with the Senate that eliminated Fernández's amendment. The President signed the bill into law on April 19, 1950.[22]

Throughout his House tenure, Fernández called for government intervention to assist the many impoverished people in New Mexico. An unswerving advocate of increased educational opportunities for the children of his state, he proposed Congress allocate federal funds to build new schools and improve existing facilities, particularly those for Hispanic Americans and American Indians. However, he balked at the notion of increased financial responsibility at the state level for American-Indian

education. "My State is desperately trying to educate the native children, the Spanish-speaking children of that State," Fernández observed.[23] He explained that although he thought the education was essential for Native Americans' increased independence and improved welfare, the state was not in a position to take on this responsibility.

Fernández also sought to help his constituents by using land grants. During the 78th Congress, he introduced legislation on behalf of Hispanic Americans living in northern New Mexico. Lamenting their challenging circumstances, Fernández asked for a federal land grant to accommodate a series of trade schools in the impoverished region: "Those good people, hedged in on very small holdings, starting life under a handicap by reason of inadequate familiarity with the language of the country and unable to compete with the industrial life of those who have followed from other States, come before you asking only that some of the land which once surrounded them and which would have provided for their increase, be set aside to their State in trust and on condition that the proceeds thereof be used for trade schools."[24]

On October 25, 1956, Fernández collapsed while campaigning for an eighth consecutive term in Congress. He suffered a stroke and was hospitalized for the remainder of the campaign. Despite well-publicized reports of his poor health, voters re-elected Fernández to demonstrate their loyalty; he finished behind fellow Democrat John Dempsey but defeated his closest Republican opponent, Dudley Cornell, by more than 13,000 votes.[25] After suffering a second stroke and lapsing into a coma, Fernández died on November 7, 1956, the day after his election to the 85th Congress (1957–1959). "I know of no member of Congress who was more able, upright and devoted to the service of the people he represented," Representative Dempsey said. "He made understanding and brilliant contributions to his state and country which will stand as a monument to his sterling character."[26] Majority Leader and future Speaker of the House John McCormack of Massachusetts remembered Fernández as "a great man in this body; not great so much as any speeches are concerned but great in the real sense of greatness, in the contributions he made in committee to the production of legislation."[27] Shortly after Fernández's death, New Mexico state party leaders considered his widow as a possible candidate for the vacant House seat.[28] Ultimately, however, Democratic Lieutenant Governor Joseph Montoya received the party's nomination and won the April 9, 1957, special election for the state's second At-Large House seat.[29]

FOR FURTHER READING

Biographical Directory of the United States Congress, "Antonio M. Fernández," http://bioguide.congress.gov.

MANUSCRIPT COLLECTION

Yale University Library, Manuscripts and Archives (New Haven, CT). *Papers*: John Collier Papers, 1910–1987, 52.25 linear feet. Subjects include Antonio Manuel Fernández.

NOTES

1 "Fernandez Speaks at Farmington Rally," 10 September 1942, *Albuquerque Journal*: 9.

2 Maurilio E. Vigil, "Antonio M. "Tony" Fernandez," in *Los Patrones: Profiles of Hispanic Political Leaders in New Mexico History* (Washington, D.C.: University Press of America, 1980): 154–156; "Death Takes Tony Fernandez, Winner in Congressional Race," 7 November 1956, (Santa Fe) *New Mexican*: 1.

3 "Fernandez Appears Victor in New Mexico," 7 October 1942, *Christian Science Monitor*: 8; "Valdez Demands Recounts of Vote in 7 Precincts," 23 September 1942, *Albuquerque Journal*: 1; "45 Vote Divisions Still Disputed," 30 September 1942, *Albuquerque Journal*: 2; "Fernandez Wins Congress Nomination by 45 Votes," 8 October 1942, *Albuquerque Journal*: 2.

4 "Election Statistics, 1920 to Present," http://history.house.gov/institution/election-statistics/election-statistics.

5 For information on Congresswoman Lusk, see Office of History and Preservation, Office of the Clerk, *Women in Congress, 1917–2006* (Washington, D.C.: U.S. Government Printing Office, 2006): 254–257.

6 *Congressional Record*, House 78th Cong., 1st sess. (10 June 1943): 5665.

7 *Congressional Record*, House, 78th Cong., 2nd sess. (17 May 1944): 4608.

8 "Withdraws Rival to GI Bill of Rights," 18 May 1944, *New York Times*: 20; "Veteran Bill Unanimously Approved by Both Houses," 14 June 1944, *Washington Post*: 1.

9 *Congressional Record*, House, 82nd Cong., 2nd sess. (3 June 1952): A3403.

10 *Congressional Record*, House, 78th Cong., 2nd sess. (19 September 1944): 7952.

11 *Congressional Record*, House, 78th Cong., 2nd sess. (26 April 1944): 3715.

12 "Colorado Site Picked for New Air Academy," 25 June 1954, *Los Angeles Times*: 4; *Congressional Record*, House, 78th Cong., 2nd sess. (2 May 1944): A2091; "Johnson Asks 'West Point of Air'; Bill for Academy Plan Due Today," 1 August 1949, *New York Times*: 1.

13 *Congressional Record*, House, 83rd Cong., 1st sess. (2 June 1953): 5918.

14 *Congressional Record*, House, 83rd Cong., 1st sess. (14 June 1954): 8182–8183.

15 For historical information on American Indians, see H. B. Shaffer, "Changing Status of American Indians," in *Editorial Research Reports*, 1954, Volume 1 (Washington, D.C.: CQ Press. Retrieved Feb. 23, 2009, from CQ Press Electronic Library, CQ Researcher Online, http://library.cqpress.com/cqresearcher/cqresrre1954052600; and pp. 10–13 of P. Katel, "American Indians," *CQ Researcher* 16: 361–384. Retrieved Feb. 23, 2009, from CQ Researcher Online, http://library.cqpress.com/cqresearcher/cqresrre2006042800.

16 Mary Spargo, "Fernandez Scores Collier on Indian Bill," 11 October 1949, *Washington Post*: 2.

17 *Congressional Record*, House, 81st Cong., 1st sess. (14 July 1949): 9506.

18 "Ex-Commissioner Scores Indian Bill," 26 September 1949, *New York Times*: 28.

19 *Congressional Record*, House, 81st Cong., 1st sess. (2 August 1949): 10646.

20 *Congressional Record*, House, 81st Cong., 1st sess. (10 October 1949): 14167–14168.

21 "President Vetoes Navajo-Hopi Bill," 18 October 1949, *New York Times*: 29; Jack Goodman, "Indians Turn Thumbs Down on Big Gift with Strings," 23 October 1949, *New York Times*: E10.

22 *Congressional Record*, House, 81st Congress, 2nd sess. (6 April 1950): 4901–4902; "House Passes Indian Aid Bill," 7 April 1950, *New York Times*: 2; "President Signs Bill to Aid Indians; Hails 10-Year Rehabilitation," 20 April 1950, *New York Times*: 1.

23 *Congressional Record*, House, 80th Cong., 1st sess. (25 April 1947): 4070.

24 *Congressional Record*, House, 78th Cong., 2nd sess. (13 January 1944): A154.

25 "Election Statistics, 1920 to Present," http://history.house.gov/institution/election-statistics/election-statistics.

26 "Top State Leaders Express Sorrow at Death of Rep. A. M. Fernandez," 8 November 1956, *Albuquerque Journal*: 2.

27 *Congressional Record*, House, 85th Cong., 1st sess. (22 January 1957): 853–854.

28 "Mrs. Fernandez Being Proposed for Congress," 9 November 1956, *Albuquerque Journal*: 1.

29 "Democrat's Success in New Mexico Hailed," 11 April 1957, *New York Times*: 6.

Separate Interests to National Agendas

HISPANIC-AMERICAN MEMBERS OF CONGRESS IN THE CIVIL RIGHTS ERA, 1945–1977

In June 1952 two long-running but often dissimilar paths of Hispanic-American congressional history converged, if only for a moment. At issue was the transformation of Puerto Rico from a colonial territory to a U.S. commonwealth. Under Puerto Rico's proposed constitution, the island's new government, the Estado Libre Asociado (Free Associated State or ELA), would be linked to the U.S. mainland by matters involving foreign affairs, but its authority to govern locally would be enhanced. Congress initially approved the concept, but quickly split over a constitutional human rights provision that had wide support among the Puerto Rican people.

In the U.S. Senate, one faction sought to establish Congress's ability to approve or reject amendments to the island's constitution, essentially stripping Puerto Ricans of sovereignty.[1] One such advocate bluntly argued that Congress essentially had the option to "give them a constitution or not give it to them." Dennis Chavez of New Mexico, on the other hand—often that chamber's lone proponent for boosting Hispanic civil rights—pushed back: "The Puerto Ricans did not ask us to take [their political rights]; we took them," he said. In areas of the world where the U.S. was then working to contain the spread of communism, including in the Caribbean Basin, Chavez noted that America's efforts would be aided by treating Puerto Ricans with more equanimity.[2] Chavez's intervention in the debate foreshadowed an important trend in this era—the increasing cooperation among advocates for Hispanic issues on a national scale. In this instance, the amendment giving Congress the right to void amendments to the island's constitution was stripped from the final legislation; likewise the language regarding human rights was removed from the constitution.[3]

Henry B. González of Texas is the longest-serving Hispanic American in congressional history. With years of experience as a civil rights proponent in San Antonio and Texas politics, González won a seat in the U.S. House in 1961 in a special election. He went on to serve more than 37 years, helped found the Congressional Hispanic Caucus, and became the chairman of the influential House Banking Committee.

Henry B. González, Jesse Trevino, 1997, Collection of the U.S. House of Representatives

This union poster urges consumers to boycott buying lettuce and grapes to support efforts to improve working conditions for migrant farmworkers.

Image courtesy of the Library of Congress

This era in the history of Hispanic Americans in Congress is best narrated from two perspectives. The first involves Mexican-American strides toward civil rights reforms in the mainland United States, which were enabled by Chavez and other Hispanic Congressmen; the second, Puerto Rico's evolution from territory to commonwealth, made possible by a long line of reform-minded Resident Commissioners like Fernós-Isern. Widely divergent at the beginning of this period, these perspectives became inextricably intertwined by its end: Local agendas became state agendas, state policy interests became regional agendas, and regional agendas became national agendas. The policy interests of Hispanic Americans from diverse cultural and geographical backgrounds became increasingly similar, as well. The creation of the Congressional Hispanic Caucus at the close of this era consolidated these agendas, lending them additional strength.

In the 30 years after World War II, Hispanic Americans living in the Southwest and Puerto Rico experienced remarkable changes that redefined their elected representatives' legislative careers. Prior to the global conflict, Mexican Americans in the Southwest lived in segregated communities with limited opportunities for social or political advancement. As occurred during the disfranchisement of African Americans in the South, local and state governments erected roadblocks such as poll taxes and English literacy tests to restrict Hispanics' electoral participation and moved polling places beyond the reach of their segregated communities.[4] During the 1930s and 1940s, a small number of politically active middle-class Hispanics formed local organizations that challenged segregation in the courts and in their communities. During World War II, the industrial mobilization of the United States increased employment opportunities and enabled more Hispanic Americans to enlist in the military. The war also led Hispanic-American activists and Members of Congress to press for civil rights.

Rapid grass-roots organizing, often occurring simultaneously throughout the country, nationalized Mexican-American political issues during the 1940s and 1950s as civil rights organizations fought segregation, enabling future Members of Congress to parlay local activism into statewide and nationwide careers. By the early 1960s, some prominent Hispanic civil rights organizations had begun mobilizing into regional and national associations, not only to promote their social agendas but also to register new voters and propel Mexican-American politicians into local, state, and federal offices. At the same time, working-class activists formed grass-roots organizations that promoted Hispanic-American issues and inspired the Chicano movement, which emphasized a positive self-image for Hispanics in the face of discrimination. By the late 1960s, dissatisfaction with the Democratic Party and uneven progress toward achieving social and political equality had emboldened college-bound and working-class Hispanics to embrace more-activist tactics, to hold their elected representatives accountable through protests, and to form third parties such as La Raza Unida, a movement that conveyed ethnic pride while enabling local activists to initiate social and political change.[5]

Puerto Ricans had a different experience. Before World War II, islanders elected their representatives in the insular house and senate, but they could not elect their own governor. Moreover, any decisions made by Puerto Rico's legislature could be nullified or modified by the executive council, a board of non-Puerto Ricans selected by the U.S. President. From its inception in 1917, Puerto Rican Resident Commissioners had worked to mitigate the effects of the Jones Act and gain more autonomy (and federal resources) for the island. However, after the creation of the Estado Libre Asociado (ELA) in 1952, the role of Resident Commissioners had changed from advocating for greater autonomy to that of a "cost-plus lobbyist" who appealed to Democrats and Republicans for resources in a nonconfrontational manner, according to a political observer.[6] For much of this period, Resident Commissioners debated the role and function of the office. Even as Puerto Rican Resident Commissioners acquired more institutional privileges after the passage of the Legislative Reorganization Act of 1970, their overall power and influence in Washington and Puerto Rico decreased because of the passage of the Elective Governor Act of 1948 and the institution of commonwealth status in 1952. Eventually, Mexican-American activists in the Southwest and Puerto Rican activists in the Caribbean and the Northeast, increasingly unified by the civil rights movement and the Chicano movement, began to combine their resources. By the early 1970s, as Resident Commissioners gained influence in the House, the Hispanic-American Members of Congress, who once worked separately, began working together to improve the welfare of Hispanic Americans across the United States, and in 1976 they formed the Congressional Hispanic Caucus.

A political cartoon from the early twentieth century depicts Puerto Rico in shackles, an allusion to U.S. tariff rates that hurt sugar and tobacco producers on the island. The issue of more equitable agricultural tariff rates was a consistent one.

Image courtesy of the Library of Congress

PRECONGRESSIONAL EXPERIENCE

Family/Ethnic Roots

Like their predecessors, the Hispanic Members of this era frequently hailed from politically connected families. Puerto Rican Resident Commissioner Jaime Benítez was born into a literary family; his ancestors included several famous 19th-century poets. Texas Representative Eligio (Kika) de la Garza II, descended from a Spanish land grant family, traced his roots to Southern Texas as far back as the 18th century. Ron de Lugo, the Virgin Islands' first Delegate to Congress, was descended from the original Spanish settlers in the Caribbean; his grandfather emigrated from Puerto Rico to the Virgin Islands in 1879. New York's Herman Badillo became the first Puerto Rican-born U.S. Representative, having migrated to New York City with his guardian in 1941, like thousands of others who left the island to seek economic opportunities on the mainland. Four other Hispanic Members also followed their parents into political service. Jorge Luis Córdova-Díaz spent his youth learning English and observing the congressional tenure of his father, Resident Commissioner Félix Córdova Dávila, in the 1920s. New Mexican Senator Joseph Montoya's father was sheriff of Sandoval County in the late 1920s; Texas Representative Henry González's father served as mayor of Mapimi, Mexico; and New Mexico Representative Manuel Luján, Jr.'s father served six years as mayor of Santa Fe, New Mexico, before running for a seat in the U.S. House and the governorship of New Mexico in the 1940s.

Eligio (Kika) de la Garza of Texas, first elected to the House in 1964, served 32 years and was the longtime chairman of the Agriculture Committee.

Image courtesy of the Library of Congress

Edward Roybal of California was elected in 1949 to the Los Angeles City Council—the first Hispanic American to serve in that post in the twentieth century. Elected to the U.S. House in 1962, Roybal served 30 years, chaired an Appropriations subcommittee, and cofounded the Hispanic Caucus.

Collection of the U.S. House of Representatives, Photography Collection

Age Relative to the Rest of the Congressional Population

Whereas Members of Congress were typically younger in this era, Hispanic-American Representatives, Senators, and Resident Commissioners as a whole were older than their congressional contemporaries and, on average, older when they were first elected (about 47.4 years old) than were past generations of Hispanic-American Members.[7] The youngest Member during this era was Kika de la Garza, who was sworn in at age 37 on January 4, 1965. The oldest was Resident Commissioner Jaime Benítez, who was 64 on his first day in office, January 3, 1973.

The advanced median age of the Hispanic-American Members of this generation was a byproduct of their long political service before their election to Congress. Puerto Rican Resident Commissioners, especially, rose to prominence with their contemporary Luis Muñoz Marín, who was also born in the late 19th century, and with his dominant Partido Popular Democrático (Popular Democratic Party, or PPD), which was formed in 1938. All the Resident Commissioners from this period except Jorge Luis Córdova-Díaz were allied initially with the powerful Muñoz Marín, whose political career started in the 1920s and spanned more than 40 years. The youngest Resident Commissioner, Santiago Polanco-Abreu, who was 44 when he took office in 1965, represented the next generation of PPD politicians who were groomed under Muñoz Marín.[8]

Education, Professions, and Prior Political Experience

All but one Hispanic-American Member in this era had held a political office at the local or state level, and some attained powerful positions in their municipalities.[9] Joseph Montoya was one of the youngest members of the New Mexico state house of representatives in 1936 (at age 21). He eventually served as majority leader before serving a single term in the state senate and then three years as lieutenant governor. Resident Commissioner Santiago Polanco-Abreu entered the insular house of representatives almost immediately after college in 1947 and eventually served as speaker in 1963. Henry González served in the San Antonio city council and the Texas state senate before making a long-shot bid for Texas governor in 1958. California Representative Edward Roybal was the first Hispanic to be elected to the Los Angeles city council since the early 1880s and served in that body from 1949 to 1963. Herman Badillo worked his way up through the Democratic Party in local clubs and campaigns in East Harlem, becoming Bronx borough president in 1965 and running unsuccessfully for New York City mayor in 1973 and 1977.

Another commonality among postwar Hispanic Members was higher education; with the exception of Ron de Lugo, who served in the U.S. Army, all these Members pursued some form of higher education. Eight of the 12 pursued graduate degrees, and consistent with the general congressional trend, all but two were lawyers.[10]

CRAFTING AN IDENTITY

Committee Assignments and Leadership

Several members of this generation of Hispanic Americans in Congress held prominent committee assignments. Like their House colleagues, many sat on committees that reflected their legislative interests.[11] Four individuals served as committee chairs. Henry González and Kika de la Garza led standing committees (the Banking, Finance and Urban Affairs Committee and the Agriculture Committee, respectively) after serving long apprenticeships. Republican Manuel Luján was the Ranking Member on two committees.[12] Although he did not chair a standing committee, Joseph Montoya held prominent committee posts early in his congressional career, serving on the Judiciary Committee as a freshman and on the House Appropriations Committee in his second term. Montoya later served on the Senate Appropriations Committee after he was elected to that chamber in 1964.

Initially, Resident Commissioners operated under the Legislative Reorganization Act of 1946, which limited their participation to the House Committees on Agriculture, Armed Services, Insular Affairs, and Interior and Insular Affairs (formerly called Public Lands) and prevented them from voting in committees, gaining seniority, or wielding the chairman's gavel. That changed after the Córdova Amendment was adopted as part of the Legislative Reorganization Act of 1970, making Resident Commissioners more like full Members.[13] Had he been permitted as Resident Commissioner to accrue seniority, Antonio Fernós-Isern would have been the senior member of the Committee on Insular Affairs. "He [has] been a most able member of [the] Committee on Interior and Insular Affairs and is the most senior member in point of longevity," Chairman Wayne Aspinall of Colorado said of Fernós-Isern.[14]

Although this generation of Hispanic-American Members made significant strides—serving for multiple terms of service, acquiring attractive committee assignments, and gaining seniority so as to become chairman or Ranking Members—none served in a party leadership position.

Numbers of Hispanic Americans in Congress

The cohort of Hispanic Americans in Congress grew during this era, despite the fact that for more than a decade—from the 79th to the 86th Congresses (1945–1961)—there were just three Hispanic-American Members serving simultaneously. Senator Dennis Chavez of New Mexico, At-Large Representative Antonio Fernández of New Mexico, and Resident Commissioner Antonio Fernós-Isern served for much of this period. New Mexico and Puerto Rico continued to send the most Hispanic Americans to Congress and to re-elect the most Hispanic-American Members to consecutive terms. Fernós-Isern served for a total of 18 years (1946–1965). Fernández served in the House for 13 years until his untimely death in 1956. There were still three Hispanic-American Members after Fernández's successor, Joseph Montoya, was elected in 1957. However, the number of Hispanic-American Members began to increase with the election of Henry González in 1961. At the start of the 88th Congress (1963–1965), there were four Hispanic-American Members in the House with the election of Edward Roybal of California. After Dennis Chavez died

New Mexico's Dennis Chavez was the first Hispanic Member to serve in both houses of Congress. Elected to office during the New Deal, he served in the House for two terms before winning election to the Senate. Throughout his career, Chavez supported public works projects, national defense, and civil rights issues.

Image courtesy of the U.S. Senate Historical Office

in 1962, it was another two years until Hispanic-American Joseph Montoya was elected to the Senate. By the start of the 92nd Congress (1971–1973), the number of Hispanic-American Members had increased with the election of Ron de Lugo of the Virgin Islands. However, Hispanic Americans were still grossly underrepresented relative to their percentage of the general population, which was concentrated in the Southwest. "Seven million voters have but six elected officials, one Senator and five Members of Congress," Montoya noted on the Senate Floor in 1972. "Three million Chicanos in California have but one congressman, Edward R. Roybal … [in] New York City … one and a half million Puerto Ricans have but one representative … in the person of Herman Badillo."[15]

In this undated photograph, Herman Badillo of New York (right) talks with Ronald Dellums of California (left) on the steps of the U.S. Capitol.

Image courtesy of the Moorland-Spingarn Research Center, Howard University

Legislative Interests

Their small numbers meant that the Hispanic Members of Congress lacked influence to push a legislative agenda for much of this period. Often, even while major civil rights bills worked their way through Congress, these Members remained on the legislative sidelines. Historian Juan Gómez-Quiñones notes that although these Members "did not have a major impact on legislation … [they] contributed to the informational and coordinative resources available to Mexican American organizations" and secured employment for Hispanic Americans in other areas of the federal government.[16] Many Hispanic legislators worked behind the scenes to lay the groundwork for the passage of significant bills. Representative Antonio Fernández helped Fernós-Isern shepherd legislation that enabled Puerto Rico to elect its own governor and establish the island as a commonwealth. Fernández guided the Elective Governor Act of 1948 (P.L. 80-362) to passage by blocking an amendment that would have altered the measure; he also authorized legislation for the ELA, despite charges by more-conservative Members that he was promoting socialism.[17] Within the New Mexico delegation, Senator Chavez worked with Fernández and Joseph Montoya to promote legislation that helped the state. In one case, the delegation secured passage of S. 107 (P.L. 87-483), a bill that authorized the Department of the Interior to build an irrigation project for Navajo Indians along the Colorado River for $221 million in 1962.[18]

Throughout this period, Hispanic Americans in Congress broadly supported the emerging civil rights agenda, including the Civil Rights Act of 1964, the Voting Rights Act of 1965, and its extensions in 1970 and 1975, but by the late 1960s, there were divisive opinions on certain pieces of legislation. In 1968 Joseph Montoya introduced S. 740, a bill to establish a presidential Cabinet committee to develop recommendations for jobs for Hispanic Americans. According to Montoya, passage of the bill would "assure that Federal programs are reaching all Spanish Americans, Mexican Americans, Puerto Rican Americans, Cuban Americans, and all other Spanish-speaking and Spanish-surnamed Americans, to provide the assistance they need, and to seek out new programs that might be necessary to handle programs that are unique to such persons."[19] Although Representatives Luján, Roybal, and de la Garza voted to pass the bill, Henry González voted against it because it lacked "powers to act, and none to compel action. Nor have we given any mandate to the Executive to Act," he said. "What we have done … is to create an illusion and we are calling that help."[20] The bill passed the Senate with minor amendments and then passed the House with a few amendments, becoming law (83 Stat. 838, 1969–1970) on December 30, 1969.[21]

Although they worked hard within the institution and helped improve the experience of Hispanic Americans nationwide, Hispanic-American Members also spent considerable time on their districts. As the Representative of a district with high levels of unemployment, Luján supported legislation to extend tax credits to businesses in economically deprived states like New Mexico. Luján's district included several American Indian reservations, and throughout his tenure he supported tribal sovereignty, including the return of land titles to Taos Pueblos and financial assistance for tribal economic development.[22] Like most Western Congressmen (of both parties), Luján sought to protect local water rights and opposed what he saw as excessive federal control over New Mexico's water resources. Luján's regional focus and attention to his district easily won him re-election for most of his congressional career.[23] Herman Badillo also adopted a district-centered approach. With his many disadvantaged constituents in mind, Badillo consistently supported legislation to help the poor, including initiatives to increase employment, provide comprehensive child care, and start community development programs.[24]

Unidos Meeting of 1971

In June 1971, Representative Badillo announced that a number of Puerto Rican and Mexican-American activists met to discuss "the formation of a Chicano-Boricua coalition or alliance … to demand specific legislation and programs aimed at meeting the needs of the Spanish-speaking community."[25] In September 1971, four Hispanic Members of the 92nd Congress—Representatives Badillo, Roybal, and Luján and Senator Montoya—agreed to sponsor a national conference to bring together Southwestern Mexican-American and Northeastern Puerto Rican civil rights groups and to reach out

From left to right: Senator Joseph Montoya of New Mexico and Representatives Edward Roybal of California and Herman Badillo of New York attend the Unity Conference in October 1971.

Image courtesy of the National Archives and Records Administration

Hispanic activists pushed mainstream civil rights groups and elected officials to pursue economic and social reforms with greater vigor. Here, young Chicano movement members display protest signs in 1970.

Image courtesy of the Library of Congress

to the growing Cuban-American community in South Florida.[26] Badillo and Roybal served as co-chairmen, and Montoya was the keynote speaker. The National Spanish-Speaking Coalition Conference, under the banner Unidos (Unity), took place in Arlington, Virginia, on October 23 and 24, 1971.[27] Roybal described one of his primary goals, "We want to set up an organization with political muscle … [because] Spanish-speaking people have been short-changed by the federal government for too long." Both chairs "hoped the conference would develop solutions to problems … such as job discrimination in both public and private employment, bilingual education, economic development, housing and community action programs." Not all Hispanic Americans in Congress agreed that working together to further Hispanic-American political concerns was the best course, however. Representatives González and de la Garza disassociated themselves from the conference, attracting widespread media attention. González was concerned that the conference might lead to the "creation of an isolated position.… Our task is to overcome political isolation, and it is a delicate path that makes the difference between attracting a friend and becoming isolated and alone," he said.[28] In the end, the coalition erected political platforms and legal strategies to combat discrimination by filing a lawsuit against four federal agencies and calling for an investigation by the Justice Department of police brutality against Hispanic Americans.[29] The conferees also agreed to create a national political action campaign to promote legislation and monitor law enforcement.[30]

DEPRESSION, WAR, AND CIVIL RIGHTS
Hispanics in the Southwest

Before 1910, Mexican immigrants traveled frequently between the United States and Mexico because of the light enforcement of the borders. Many came to the United States temporarily to look for work or visit family or friends. Despite stronger laws restricting European and Asian immigrants from the 1900s to the 1920s, "transnational movement back and forth between the United States and Mexico remained largely unhindered, and the border between the two countries went virtually unregulated."[31] In part, this reflected the needs of U.S. farmers, particularly in the West and the Southwest, for Mexican field workers. By 1929 the Southwest was responsible for 40 percent of the United States' total fruit and vegetable output.[32] To support this level of production and the region's economic status, growers relied heavily on the inexpensive labor of Mexican workers.[33]

Mexican immigrants also played a prominent role in the rail and mining industries. For example, Mexicans made up 43 percent of Arizona's copper-mining workforce, and by 1922 they constituted 85 percent of the railroad workforce in the Southwest.[34] Various groups began to protest as their presence expanded. Small farmers objected because they were forced to compete with larger farms that employed cheaper Mexican labor. Organized labor also objected, fearing that the overuse of immigrant labor would depress wages.[35] Thus, in the 1920s, many unions operated under an informal agreement to exclude Mexicans and lobbied the federal government to regulate Mexican immigration. The American Federation of Labor (AFL) was particularly active, attempting to promote emigration restrictions in Mexico through its relationship with that country's major labor organization.[36] However, both proponents and opponents of Mexican immigration agreed that it was undesirable for Mexicans to become permanent members of U.S. society, and supporters of Mexican labor sought to assuage concerns that Mexicans were seeking integration.[37]

An image of the Santa Rita pit copper mine in southwestern New Mexico in 1940—at the time the largest such mine in the world. In the early 20th century, Mexican workers accounted for nearly half the copper-mining workforce in the U.S. Southwest.

Image courtesy of the Library of Congress

Immigration restriction gained momentum during the 1920s. With the creation of the Border Patrol in 1925, the federal government began trying to curb illegal immigration.[38] Tipping the fragile balance in favor of those opposing Mexican labor was the realization that, contrary to the assurances of Mexican labor supporters, Mexicans became permanent members of U.S. society. From 1910 to 1920, for example, Mexican immigrants were the leading foreign-born group in California, and by 1930 they constituted 19 percent of its immigrant population.[39] At the same time, California's naturalization rate for Mexicans was declining. In light of these facts, reform groups that had previously supported integration began advocating increased limitations on Mexican immigration.[40]

In the face of such restrictions, younger generations of immigrants had begun building communities and a common cultural identity in the United States, nurtured by emerging Spanish-language media in urban areas like Los Angeles, California, and San Antonio, Texas.[41] In Southwestern states, Mexican Americans lived under a modified Jim Crow system that limited their movement and hampered their opportunities for social and economic advancement. Across the Sunbelt, the enforcement of legal segregation in workplaces, housing, and schools was common. Texas instituted rigid segregation, whereas New Mexico protected *nuevomexicanos'* civil rights under its constitution but tended to separate the races in social settings. California used what one scholar calls "race-based legal distinctions and selective law enforcement" to enforce segregation. By the 1930s, a small but politically active middle class emerged and challenged these barriers of "political disparateness, ideological ambiguousness, economic exploitation, social fragmentation, and educational discrimination," according to one historian.[42] These activists began to fight the Anglo-dominated political

A Mexican onion picker pauses in a field near Tracy, California, in 1935. During the Great Depression, various U.S. groups sought to prevent the employment of migrant workers who were seen as competition for scarce jobs.

Image courtesy of the Library of Congress

establishment by forming *mutualistas* (mutual aid societies) and social clubs to improve living conditions, publicize civil rights issues, and confront segregation practices directly.[43]

Repatriation During the Great Depression

While Mexican Americans experienced racial discrimination during the early 20th century, the degree of prejudice varied according to regional economic conditions. Predictably, the Great Depression marked a period of extreme hardship for Mexican immigrants and Mexican Americans. After the stock market crashed on Thursday, October 24, 1929, industrial production fell by 50 percent, and investment dwindled to a trickle. Job losses increased sharply, and by 1932 the U.S. unemployment rate was 25 percent. Neither the agricultural market nor its increasingly mechanized means of production was immune to these hardships. The Depression forced many rural Southwestern residents into the cities in search of work and support. Los Angeles, in particular, was attractive to Mexicans because of the *barrios* (neighborhoods), which had been established by earlier generations of immigrants. By 1930 Los Angeles' Mexican population was second only to Mexico City's.[44]

As the Depression wore on and job opportunities shrank, workers became more desperate, and animosity toward Mexican immigrants and Mexican Americans intensified. The devastating Dust Bowl in the Midwest and the South aggravated the situation, forcing farmers westward in droves in search of employment. In response, white Americans pressured employers to exclude noncitizens, sometimes resulting in the exclusion of non-whites, even if they were citizens. For example, California's legislature adopted a law in 1931 prohibiting companies that conducted business with the government from employing noncitizens in public jobs.[45] Similar discrimination pervaded the welfare system, as people of Mexican descent consumed a decreasing share of public benefits. This trend developed as the Mexican population grew, constituting a steady proportion of those who were eligible for benefits, especially in urban areas, where unemployment skyrocketed.[46]

The Vigues, an immigrant family from Mexico, stand outside their dilapidated shack in Austin, Texas, in the early 1940s. The U.S. Housing Authority, created during the New Deal, began to address the needs of impoverished Southwestern residents by developing public housing projects.

Image courtesy of the Library of Congress

Soon after the stock market crash, federal and local governments began formulating plans to repatriate Mexican workers in the United States. In 1930, echoing sentiments throughout the Southwest, President Herbert Hoover denounced Mexicans as a factor contributing to the Depression and ordered the Labor Department to develop a deportation program.[47] Eager to recover skilled workers for its economy, the Mexican government obligingly identified them and paid for their transportation to Mexico.[48] The program was initiated in Southern California under the direction of the federal government, with state and local government support, and expanded throughout the Southwest. In 1931 alone, anywhere from 50,000 to 75,000 individuals returned to Mexico. Los Angeles lost approximately one-third of its Mexican population during this period.[49] Between 1929 and 1935, more than 400,000 people were repatriated to Mexico, including U.S. citizens of Mexican descent. Approximately 85,000 more Mexicans returned to Mexico voluntarily. Most repatriates continued to live in poverty.[50] Some attempted to return to the United States, but they were denied entry by federal border authorities.[51]

In 1929 Mexican Americans in San Antonio, Texas, founded the League of United Latin American Citizens (LULAC), which sought to challenge and eliminate segregation and to protect these citizens' constitutional rights. The group was formed at a crucial time, when anti-Mexican sentiment threatened to erupt. With the establishment of the draft and a high enlistment rate for Hispanic Americans during World War II, some of LULAC's advisors were employed by the U.S. government as liaisons to the Hispanic-American community.[52]

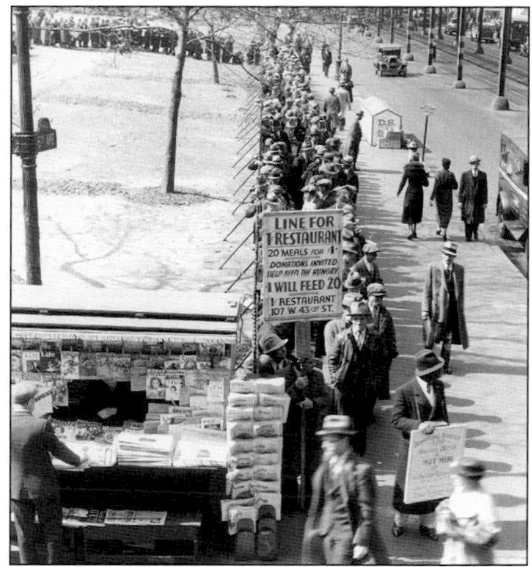

Hundreds stand in a line wrapping around a New York City block, waiting for bread handouts in 1932. The Great Depression plunged the nation into a prolonged, severe economic crisis. The U.S. unemployment rate reached nearly 25 percent; for minority groups it was much higher.

Image courtesy of the Franklin D. Roosevelt Library/ National Archives and Records Administration

Hispanic Americans During World War II

As the United States moved closer to war with the Axis powers, Hispanic Americans, like many other Americans, experienced a rapid change in their social status. Historian Manuel Gonzales estimates that as many as 750,000 Hispanic-American men and women saw active service in the war. Along with the option to participate in the military, an expansion in wartime manufacturing enabled thousands of Mexican Americans to enter the workforce.[53]

U.S. government officials realized that incorporating racial minorities into the war effort was pivotal to achieving victory, and to promoting free-market capitalism abroad after the war.[54] Mitigating domestic and racial discrimination benefited emerging political constituencies at home, and policymakers also viewed the issue as a matter of national security: In highlighting human rights abuses and racial discrimination perpetrated by Nazi Germany and Imperial Japan, the United States invited criticism from its enemies, who pointed to legal segregation in the South and the marginalization of ethnic minorities elsewhere.[55] American officials wanted to maintain positive relations with allies such as Mexico, whose diplomats received numerous complaints about racial discrimination from Mexican immigrants in the United States. Mexican officials sought to protect Mexican immigrants and Mexican Americans by complaining to the U.S. State Department about their treatment. The Franklin D. Roosevelt administration responded by monitoring discriminatory practices in the Southwest and promoting work exchanges between the two countries.[56]

Senator Dennis Chavez of New Mexico introduced legislation during World War II to create a permanent Fair Employment Practices Commission. Chavez believed such a step would advance the rights of Hispanic Americans nationwide.

Image courtesy of the Library of Congress

Dennis Chavez and the Creation of the Fair Employment Practices Committee

On June 25, 1941, President Roosevelt issued Executive Order 8802, which declared "full participation in the national defense program by all citizens of the United States, regardless of race, creed, color, or national origin" based on "the firm belief that the democratic way of life within the Nation can be defended successfully only with the help and support of all groups within its borders." The order required that the federal government, unions, and defense industries "provide for the full and equitable participation of all workers."[57] Roosevelt's mandate also created the Fair Employment Practices Committee (FEPC) in the federal Office of Personnel Management to investigate complaints about unjust hiring practices. Thousands availed themselves of the FEPC mechanism. From July 1, 1943, to June 30, 1944, the committee logged more than 4,000 complaints, nearly 80 percent of which involved discrimination based solely on race.[58] Much of the remaining 20 percent involved ethnic and religious intolerance, which Senator Dennis Chavez of New Mexico found particularly troubling given its effect on his constituents.[59]

The FEPC's work underscored Chavez's efforts on behalf of the nation's veterans, particularly those in his Southwestern constituency. "If they go to war, they are called Americans—if they run for office, they are Spanish-Americans, but if they are looking for jobs, they are referred to as damn Mexicans," Chavez noted.[60] In its report to the President, the employment committee concurred with Chavez and urged the establishment of policies to protect labor rights. "Wartime gains of Negro, Mexican-American and Jewish workers are being lost through an 'unchecked revival' of discriminatory practices," the committee concluded. Moreover, minorities who served in the war had more difficulty finding work than did their white contemporaries. Without direct action, civil unrest would undoubtedly follow and "be a cause of embarrassment to the United States in its international relations," reported the *New York Times*.[61]

On June 23, 1944, Chavez introduced a bill to establish a permanent Fair Employment Practices Commission. Appointed chairman of an Education and Labor subcommittee that oversaw issues related to fair employment, Chavez used the subcommittee hearings to demonstrate the extent of discrimination in the United States, whose effects made the creation of an employment commission a national concern.[62] Though the 78th Congress (1943–1945) adjourned before the Senate considered his bill, Chavez reintroduced it during the 79th Congress (1945–1947). Days later, Southern Senators filibustered it.[63] The bill's opponents framed employment discrimination as a local issue that was outside Congress's purview; numerous state governments, including Chavez's own, had already rejected fair employment bills. Democrat Carl Hatch, New Mexico's senior Senator, called the bill unconstitutional, arguing, "When we attempt to force by law tolerance, respect, mutual good will, and such things, we are only aggravating the conditions which we seek to improve."[64] Republican Robert Taft of Ohio had similar concerns and expressed reservations that overregulation would hamper free trade.[65] Supporters pointed out that the legislation encompassed transportation and communication issues and affected interstate commerce.[66] As Senate Majority Leader Alben Barkley of

Kentucky considered possible areas for compromise, the bipartisan opposition dug in its heels, and the Senate voted against cloture. "It took the crucifixion of Christ to redeem the world," Chavez remarked, disheartened but not surprised. "It took intestinal fortitude to bring about the Declaration of Independence. It took ordinary American decency to bring about the Constitution to the United States. It took the death of Americans during the Civil War to find out that this was one country. It took this vote today to find out that a majority cannot have its will."[67] Undeterred, Chavez fought to protect the civil rights of all citizens until his death in 1962.

The Bracero Program

After the United States entered World War II, the need for agricultural production and labor increased dramatically. The cessation of trade with Europe eliminated a major supplier of agriculture products, and large numbers of domestic workers left the agricultural workforce for the military or higher-paying defense work.[68] While there were roughly one million domestic migrant workers in 1940, that number decreased to approximately 60,000 by 1942.[69] Foreseeing such shortages, cotton and vegetable growers in the Southwest petitioned Congress to permit the hiring of temporary laborers.[70] Analyzing the labor needs of the agricultural sector in the late 1940s, President Harry S. Truman's Commission on Migratory Labor stated, "The demand for migratory labor is thus essentially twofold: To be ready to go to work when needed, to be gone when not needed."[71]

While the United States was eager to recruit Mexican workers who had been displaced during the previous decade, the Mexican government based its cooperation on the establishment of standards for workers' wages, housing, and food as well as worker protections if demand for farm labor declined. Moreover, the Mexican government required contracts in Spanish and insisted that the United States pay workers' transportation across the border.[72] In 1943 Congress

A family of Mexican laborers travel north of the U.S. border in 1944 to participate in the Bracero Program, which brought temporary workers to the United States. During World War II, such laborers filled positions in the agriculture and railroad industries vacated by U.S. men who joined the military.

Image courtesy of the National Archives and Records Administration

authorized the Bracero Program with large majorities in both chambers. President Roosevelt signed the bill into law (P.L. 78-45) on April 23, 1943.[73]

Initially the Bracero Program proved popular; immigrant workers earned a living while the Mexican economy benefited from worker remittances.[74] However, many employers ignored the protections in the 1943 agreement, subjecting *braceros* (seasonal farm workers) to excessive costs, poor food and housing, exposure to harmful substances, and discrimination.[75] Eventually an agreement between the worker and the grower replaced the contract between the U.S. government and the *bracero*, effectively undermining the federal government's oversight role. To limit transportation costs, farmers insisted that recruitment centers be located close to the U.S.-Mexico border, but this promoted illegal immigration, as workers who were ineligible for the Bracero Program were also a short distance from the border.[76]

In this undated photograph, children work as farm laborers beside their adult counterparts.

Photograph by Paul Fusco, Magnum Photos; image courtesy of the Library of Congress

Judiciary Committee Chairman Emanuel Celler of New York attempted to include employee sanctions by submitting amendments to the Agricultural Act of 1949. "Without the sanctions," Celler said, "you have here an engraved invitation for the predatory interests along the border … to go into Mexico and induce people, smugglers, and procurers" to illegally transport laborers to the U.S. to work on "the plantations and on the ranches, and on the huge farms."[77] Democratic Representative Antonio Fernández of New Mexico vehemently disagreed, asserting, "If what you want is to starve every illegal Mexican alien out of this country; it is most effective." Fernández criticized the amendment, saying it "affects and punishes a lot of other laborers who are not Mexican aliens, but Americans.… A man of my nationality, American, but of Mexican and Spanish descent, would be very adversely affected in his efforts to obtain employment." He predicted the amendment would require "the farmer to become [a] policeman, an investigator, an informer, or run the risk of being a criminal.… He will employ only the Mexican with an immigration card and the Negro to the exclusion of Americans who look, speak, and have names like the Mexican nationals," Fernández said.[78] After spirited debate, an overwhelming majority rejected Celler's amendment.

Congressional opponents of the Bracero Program focused on its negative effect on domestic employment. Senator Chavez, speaking in 1943 on the initial authorization of the Bracero Program, stated, "[In] justice to ourselves and in justice to the boys who are doing the fighting, our own citizens should have the opportunity of working on our farms. They should be given the opportunity to pick citrus fruits and vegetables in Florida, and cotton in the Southwest."[79] Later, Representatives George McGovern of South Dakota and Eugene McCarthy of Minnesota insisted the agreement disadvantaged small family farmers competing with large farms with the ability to hire *braceros*.[80] While the agreement restricted the *braceros* to agricultural or railroad work, there was concern that *braceros* remaining in the United States after their contract had expired could easily move into the industrial sector.[81]

Support for the program eroded as opposition grew louder by the 1960s. Stricter regulations by the Department of Labor greatly reduced the number of *braceros* who were admitted, as labor organizations such as the AFL-CIO gained more influence. In addition, the mechanization of agriculture lessened the need for Mexican labor. While the reauthorization of the measure in 1951 had passed with strong support, the 1961 and 1963 reauthorizations were far more contentious.[82] The program eventually expired in 1964.[83]

Cars cross the international border between Juarez, Mexico, and El Paso, Texas, in the late 1930s. U.S. shoppers during the Great Depression took advantage of a favorable exchange rate by traveling into Mexico to buy goods.

Image courtesy of the Library of Congress

Illegal Immigration and the End of the Bracero Program

While the Bracero Program lacked provisions to discourage illegal immigration, it was generally believed that the availability of a legal route to the American labor market would reduce illegal entry. However, illegal immigration increased during the operation of the Bracero Program. Many Mexicans who were not qualified to participate in the program crossed the border illegally and found work with growers who wanted to keep operating costs low. Texas, particularly, relied on undocumented labor to augment its workforce after being expelled from the Bracero Program for noncompliance.[84]

Under pressure from the Mexican government to increase the regulation of illegal immigration, the U.S. Border Patrol initially redirected its scarce resources to the U.S.-Mexico border, doubling the number of officers on patrol.[85] Immigration and Naturalization Service (INS) apprehension rates skyrocketed during the next decade, rising from 11,715 in 1943 to 885,587 in 1953, with Mexicans constituting a growing proportion of that number.[86] Growers in the Southwest and their Members in Congress routinely pressed the INS to relax its enforcement of immigration law, especially when labor was in high demand. Also, as a study pointed out, Congress consistently failed to fund the INS at levels commensurate with its task. Thus, while the INS assigned more agents to work along the border, its total force was cut by a third from 1942 to 1951.[87]

In 1951 President Truman's Commission on Migratory Labor released a report blaming low wages in the Southwest and social ills on illegal immigration: "The magnitude … has reached entirely new levels in the past 7 years.… In its newly achieved proportions, it is virtually an invasion," the report said.[88] After touring Southern California in August 1953 to assess the impact of illegal immigration, President Dwight D. Eisenhower's Attorney General, Herbert Brownell, Jr., pushed Congress to enact sanctions against employers

A rocket-shaped campaign button touted Edward Roybal of California in the 1960s. Roybal, like other Hispanic politicians of the era, got his start in local politics after World War II and emerged on the national scene in the 1960s.

Collection of the U.S. House of Representatives

of undocumented workers and to confiscate the vehicles that were used to bring them to the United States.[89] While neither proposal became law, the administration moved forward on plans for a deportation operation.[90] On June 9, 1954, INS Commissioner General Joseph Swing announced the commencement of "Operation Wetback."[91] The first phase of the operation began in California and Arizona.[92] Its effectiveness depended on publicity as well as manpower. Extensive media coverage that often exaggerated the strength of the Border Patrol, as well as targeted displays of strength, gave the impression of a greater force. In many regions, this strategy convinced thousands who had entered the U.S. illegally to repatriate voluntarily. In Texas, for example, more than 63,000 individuals returned to Mexico of their own volition; U.S. officials detained an additional 42,000 persons in July 1954. An INS report later indicated that the agency apprehended nearly 1.1 million individuals.[93] The INS operation won at least tacit support from several key groups; the Mexican government, labor groups, and even Mexican-American civil rights groups acknowledged the labor problem, but they withheld extensive criticism.[94] While the raids disrupted the growing seasons in California and Arizona, the government pacified farm owners with promises of additional *bracero* labor.[95] Though the program was touted as a success, its effects were short-lived; illegal entry exploded again after the United States terminated the Bracero Program in 1964.[96]

Hispanic Interests and Political Representation After World War II (1945–1970)

The end of the war was a watershed moment in the development of Hispanic-American political activism. Hispanic troops had fought in theaters across the globe, and returning veterans began taking advantage of education and job training programs. Better credentials led to better jobs, "with more workers than ever before entering skilled and semiskilled positions," writes historian Juan Gómez-Quiñones. As a direct offshoot of this development, veterans flooded civic groups like LULAC, Texas' GI Forum (created in 1948), and Los Angeles' Community Service Organization (CSO; cofounded by veteran and future Representative Edward Roybal in 1947), whose cumulative effect was to galvanize political awareness, register voters, and generate leadership throughout the Southwest. Conditions varied, however, and Hispanic-American politicians had different experiences in each state. In New Mexico, numerous Hispanic Americans served in positions at the state and local level, where well-organized networks of Hispanic voters could swing results in close elections. During this period, New Mexico sent three Representatives to Congress who served multiple terms (Fernández, 13 years; Montoya, 19 years, including a dozen years in the Senate; and Luján, 20 years) and attained prominent positions.[97] California and Texas had stricter segregation practices, whose effects on Hispanic Americans varied greatly. The number of Hispanic Americans in Texas who were actively involved in politics was second only to the number in New Mexico. Despite Jim Crow segregation, Hispanics actively participated in counties and municipal wards throughout Texas.[98]

The Civil Rights Movement and Its Influence on Mexican Americans

By 1960, grass-roots organizations like LULAC, the GI Forum in Texas, and the CSO in Los Angeles had successfully challenged legal segregation in the courts.[99] As historian Gómez-Quiñones states, years of organized protest by African Americans in the South provided Hispanic Americans west of the Mississippi with a model for their civil rights campaigns. Before long, a national movement emerged. Since the country's major political parties seemed unwilling to adopt the concerns of their Hispanic constituencies, community leaders began organizing groups with broad agendas. The Mexican American Political Association (MAPA) was formed in 1959 out of frustration with the Democratic Party's general indifference to Hispanic-American concerns. The Political Association of Spanish-Speaking Organizations (PASSO) was founded in 1960 to nurture political talent and encourage Hispanic candidates to run for office. Though electoral results were mixed, such efforts provided valuable political experience for future candidates.[100]

Edward Roybal of California and Henry González of Texas organized "Viva Kennedy" clubs in their states in support of John Kennedy's 1960 presidential campaign. Within two years, both men would win election to the U.S. House.

Private Collection

1960 Presidential Election and Mexican-American Politics

Despite Hispanic Americans' political successes at the local, state, and regional levels, victories at the national level were fewer and farther between in the first half of the 20th century. Mexican Americans had participated in Democratic National Co;entions since the 1940s, but according to Gómez-Quiñones they "were not widely recognized electorally as a significant factor in the national presidential elections."[101] However, in 1959, the John F. Kennedy campaign encouraged the formation of "Viva Kennedy" clubs to mobilize Hispanic-American voters for the 1960 presidential election. Mexican-American politicos such as future Congressman Henry González organized club activities in Texas (and served as state co-chair), and Edward Roybal, as MAPA's chair, used political networks to rally Hispanic-American voters around the Kennedy

Puerto Rican Governor Luis Muñoz Marín and his wife, Inés, host President John Kennedy and First Lady Jacqueline Kennedy during the president's tour of Latin American nations in 1962.

Image courtesy of the National Archives and Records Administration

César Chávez, a farm worker, civil rights advocate, and labor leader, cofounded the National Farm Workers Association (later the United Farm Workers).

Image courtesy of the Library of Congress

Senator Joseph Montoya of New Mexico was a leading supporter of the Bilingual Education Act.

Image courtesy of the U.S. Senate Historical Office

candidacy. Kennedy himself devoted considerable resources toward addressing the concerns of Hispanic voters, visiting and campaigning in areas with large concentrations of Mexican Americans. He "shared with most of them a Roman Catholic religious heritage, and had a wife who spoke to them in Spanish," Gómez-Quiñones observes. That year 85 percent of Mexican Americans nationally voted for Kennedy.[102]

The political mobilization of Mexican-American voters during the election had far-reaching consequences. The "Viva Kennedy" clubs enabled activists to muster large numbers of potential voters through registration drives and grass-roots initiatives. Both González (in 1961) and Roybal (in 1962) used this energized political base to win election to the U.S. House of Representatives after Kennedy's victory.

Rise of the Chicano Movement

Lingering dissatisfaction with Democratic inattention to Mexican-American concerns fueled another challenge to the status quo.[103] Many civil rights organizations had developed from a small but politically active middle class in urban areas, and many Mexican-American activists "faced … a juncture between integration and self-determination" that emerged from the inconsistent results of lobbying for civil rights since the late 1940s. By the early 1960s, a number of grass-roots movements that consisted mainly of urban working-class and agricultural workers in the Southwest used more confrontational tactics to protest segregationist practices. Although established civil rights organizations refused to support these groups, college students provided a receptive audience. Calling themselves Chicanos, these activists demanded immediate social reforms through the acquisition of political power. According to Gómez-Quiñones, instead of working within a system that benefited Hispanic Americans only marginally, Chicanos augmented conventional civil rights protest strategies by aggressively promoting radical social change for working-class groups in Mexico and the United States.[104]

The Chicano movement challenged "the assumptions, politics, and principles of the established political leaders, organizations, and activity within and outside the [Mexican-American] community." Newer organizations like the United Farm Workers (led by César Chávez) and the Crusade for Justice worked alongside established organizations like LULAC and MAPA to represent the interests of middle- and working-class Mexican Americans in the 1960s.[105]

For much of the decade, the Kennedy and Johnson administrations had maintained working relationships with the country's Hispanic population, but by 1966 these partnerships had begun to fray. During an EEOC meeting in March 1966, representatives from LULAC and the GI Forum criticized the commission for its inattention to Hispanic concerns and its lack of a Hispanic representative or staff member. Fifty representatives walked out in protest. In response, the administration added a Hispanic member and sponsored the creation of the Inter-Agency Cabinet Committee on Mexican-American Affairs, an initiative Senator Montoya endorsed wholeheartedly.[106] Montoya, who also guided the Bilingual Education Act toward final passage in 1968, often used his influence to support the Chicano movement while shepherding legislation that benefited Hispanic Americans nationwide.

Hispanic-American Members of Congress reacted to social movements outside the institution in various ways. In a 1967 Senate Floor speech, Montoya spoke about Hispanic Americans' living conditions and about their desire to attain equality without sacrificing their ethnic identity. "Most Spanish-Americans are near or at the bottom of the economic heap ... [and] usually lag even behind Negroes in years of schooling attained, with some 30 percent of the Spanish-surnamed male adults being categorized as functional illiterates," he said. Citing contributing factors such as a "lack of job skills, inadequate schooling, and language problems," Montoya described the effects of social discrimination on Mexican Americans in the Southwest and cited their attempts to bridge the cultural gap by learning English and following some Anglo-American customs. Hispanic Americans "clearly want equal opportunity and full acceptance now, not in the distant and hypothetical future, and they do not believe that their difference—either presumed or real—from Anglo-Americans offers any justification for denial of opportunity and acceptance" within U.S. society.[107]

Henry González, on the other hand, showed little patience for the efforts of separatists and radicals in the Chicano movement. "No matter how worthy their ideals may be, [they] have fallen into the spell and trap of reverse racism," he declared.[108] In April 1969, González denounced several key leaders of the Mexican American Youth Organization (MAYO)—which used inflammatory rhetoric to mobilize young political activists in the Southwest and was key to the establishment of the party La Raza Unida—as "purveyors of hate."[109] He also attacked quasi-government entities such as the Ford Foundation, which provided grants to promote Hispanic engagement in politics but which, González insisted, did little to monitor the funding or prevent its distribution to radical groups.[110] González distinguished efforts to develop pride in one's ethnicity and organize communities from cultural chauvinism, racial hatred, and self-aggrandizement. "The tragic thing is that in situations where people have honest grievances, dishonest tactics can prevent their obtaining redress," González noted, "and where genuine problems exist, careless or unthinking or consciously mean behavior can unloose new forces that will create new problems that might require generations to solve. I want to go forward, not backward; I want the creation of trust, not fear; and I want to see Americans together, not apart," he said.[111]

Much of the problem was generational.[112] In the same way González recoiled at La Raza Unida's youthful idealism, Chicano activists scorned him as a *patron* from an earlier era who was more concerned with his status in the Mexican-American community than with advancing Chicano issues. Harsher critics believed he cared more about Anglo interests than about those of his Latino constituency. "Gonzalez is criticized by many Mexican-American militants for being a *Tío Thomas*, or Uncle Tom," noted the *Dallas Morning News* in 1969.[113]

Henry González of Texas was an early proponent of Hispanic civil rights in the years after World War II. González, however, became concerned that tactics adopted by activists in the 1960s and 1970s threatened to marginalize Hispanic Americans.

Image courtesy of the U.S. House of Representatives Photography Office

Hilda Hernandez of New York City (left), who emigrated from Puerto Rico, registers to vote in 1960. An unidentified man reviews registration materials.

Image courtesy of the Library of Congress

PUERTO RICO

Puerto Rican Migration and Political Participation

Since the late 19th century, Puerto Rico's relationship with the United States has been characterized by the continual migration of people from the island to the mainland. Some scholars have characterized this as "one of Puerto Rico's most constant historical realities."[114] Driven largely by economic and political conditions, the earliest migrants tended to be educated elites and artisans who had fled the island to escape Spanish tyranny. But after the United States took control of Puerto Rico in 1898, bringing with it a modicum of political stability, large-scale agribusinesses took root, transforming the island's traditional domestic economy. U.S. capital flowed south as mainland-controlled sugar, coffee, and needlework sectors reshaped Puerto Rico's means of production. The change to a consumer-driven economy created a new working class, and close relations between labor organizations in Puerto Rico—particularly Santiago Iglesias's Federación Libre de los Trabajadores (Free Federation of Laborers, or FLT)—and the American Federation of Laborers (AFL) created a direct connection between mainland industry and Puerto Rican laborers. The FLT actively encouraged Puerto Ricans to work in mainland factories, and after the Jones Act of 1917 granted Puerto Ricans U.S. citizenship, Puerto Rican migration increased even more. The number of Puerto Ricans in the mainland United States—numbered at 1,513 in 1910—swelled tenfold by 1920 and grew another 500 percent in the following decade. The Great Depression and World War II slowed the rate of increase, but the number of Puerto Ricans arriving on the mainland continued to climb.[115]

By the 1950s, the flow of Puerto Ricans to the mainland United States had increased so drastically that historians dubbed the phenomenon the "Great Migration." An estimated 470,000 people—or 21 percent of the island's total population—left Puerto Rico for the United States between 1950 and 1960.[116] By the end of the decade, 30 percent of all native-born Puerto Ricans were living on the mainland, primarily in *colonias*, dense, centralized neighborhoods inhabited predominantly by Puerto Ricans and other Hispanic Americans.[117] The earliest Puerto Rican migrants settled in New York City; before 1920 they clustered in East Harlem on the Upper East Side, an area that came to be known as Spanish Harlem or El Barrio.[118] In 1950, 80 percent of mainland Puerto Ricans lived in New York City.[119] By the mid-1970s, 12 percent of New York City's inhabitants claimed Puerto Rican roots.[120]

Puerto Rican migrants in the mid-20th century occupied the lower rungs of the U.S. labor market, taking jobs as domestic workers, in manufacturing, and in the service and maintenance industries.[121] Generally, Puerto Ricans did not fare as well as other migrant groups. A 1976 report from the U.S. Commission on Civil Rights stated that within the Puerto Rican community on the mainland, the "incidence of poverty and unemployment ... is more severe than that of virtually any ethnic group in the United States."[122] By the late 1960s and early 1970s, both New York-based Puerto Ricans and new migrants began moving out of New York City, which was hit hard by the recession. Large migrant populations settled in industrial Northeastern and Midwestern cities, including Philadelphia, Chicago, Gary (Indiana), Lorain (Ohio), Paterson

(New Jersey), and Hartford and Bridgeport (Connecticut). By the early 1970s, more than 30 U.S. cities had populations of more than 10,000 Puerto Ricans.[123]

Puerto Rico's insular government contributed to this exchange of people and goods. Machines replaced men as the preferred form of labor on the island's sugar plantations, and Puerto Rico began hemorrhaging agricultural jobs. Its manufacturing industry struggled to compensate, and the island was left with catastrophic unemployment rates. With more workers than available work, island officials sought ways to alleviate the pressure on the island's economy. Invoking his medical training, Resident Commissioner Antonio Fernós-Isern sought policies for "a good emergency 'bloodletting,' scientifically carried out" to spark the economy. He hoped encouraging islanders to move to the mainland would help reduce what he called Puerto Rico's "hypertension."[124] Officials in New York noted that the new migrants were unprepared for life on the mainland; they spoke very little English and arrived with few job prospects.

In 1947 Puerto Rican officials opened the Migration Office in response to these problems. (In 1951 the office became the Migration Division of the Puerto Rico department of labor.) The office served to recruit Puerto Rican labor for growing industries in the mainland United States, to regulate the flow of new migrants and help them find jobs, and to defend laborers from abuse.[125] One Puerto Rican cabinet official observed, "You cannot stop Puerto Rican people from coming to the United States, for they are citizens. They have been coming to New York City by themselves without Government aid in the past. We want to step in to give them some guidance about the housing, the weather and where they can find a job."[126]

PPD officials lobbied for easy transportation between the island and the mainland, particularly on routes between New York and San Juan. Until the 1940s, steamships were the primary mode of transportation, but in the 1960s, jet-powered aircraft made the journey significantly easier. One San Juan-based commercial airline adopted the slogan, "Board Flight 55 and take a leap to New York," referencing both the flight number and the $55 cost.[127] Through the efforts of Puerto Rican politicians, one-way air travel between the two cities dropped as low as $35.[128] The effect of the migration and the rate of Puerto Rican political participation, especially in New York City, is the subject of some debate. Compared to African Americans—who also migrated in large numbers from the South to the industrial Northeast—and to other ethnic immigrant urban communities, Puerto Ricans lacked strong political motivations to leave Puerto Rico; their reasons for leaving were almost strictly economic. "European immigrants came to New York City hoping to become citizens, while Puerto Ricans came as migrant workers," writes historian James Jennings. Their sense of being temporary residents meant that they generally avoided politics. "Puerto Rican migrants did not perceive themselves as American citizens who could demand equal treatment before the law. These migrants saw themselves more as mere workers in someone else's country," Jennings states.[129] Indeed, cheap transportation enabled many Puerto Ricans to travel back and forth to the island, lessening the migrants' typical tendency to assimilate into their new neighborhoods. While several historians point to robust pre–World War II organizations that addressed broad community issues, other scholars are

Antonio Fernós-Isern, Puerto Rico's Resident Commissioner to the U.S. Congress from 1946 to 1965, played a key role in winning commonwealth status for the island in the early 1950s. Fernós-Isern also advocated the movement of Puerto Ricans to the mainland United States.

Image courtesy of the National Archives and Records Administration

This poster from the late 1930s promoted Puerto Rico as a tourist destination for mainland U.S. citizens. In the decades after World War II, air travel made the island even more accessible, and opened up new possibilities for Puerto Ricans seeking to relocate in mainland cities such as New York.

Image courtesy of the Library of Congress

Elected to the U.S. House in 1970, Herman Badillo of New York was the first person of Puerto Rican descent to serve as a full-fledged voting Representative.

Collection of the U.S. House of Representatives, Photography Collection

not convinced Puerto Rican migrants actively sought such political agency.[130] "Puerto Ricans generally thought they had little to gain in American politics," said Bernardo Vega, a Puerto Rican critic who was based in New York during the early 20th century.[131]

Most historians agree that the major American political parties were slow to embrace Puerto Ricans as a constituency. "Neither of the two parties, not the Democratic nor the Republican, was seriously interested in the support of the Puerto Ricans," Vega observed.[132] Puerto Ricans' earliest link to American politics was between its extreme Nationalist wing and the leftist American Labor Party. Represented most vocally by U.S. Congressman Vito Marcantonio—an American Labor Party member who represented East Harlem in the late 1930s and 1940s—New York-based Puerto Ricans developed a "troublesome" reputation that was unwelcome in the post–World War II, anti-communist, Cold War atmosphere.[133]

The first generation of Puerto Rican politicians within the U.S. party system gained influence by using a measured approach, rising through the ranks and avoiding issues that were strictly Puerto Rican. Representative Badillo, for example, entered New York City politics through the reform wing of the Democratic Party, focusing on stemming corruption and promoting government efficiency. "Badillo's political entree with this group therefore reflected a moderate orientation toward working in a middle-class, relatively mainstream context rather than a political identity limited to a Latino constituency," writes historian Sherrie Baver.[134] Though he addressed issues affecting Puerto Ricans in his district, Badillo distanced himself from El Barrio's radical heritage. For example, he vocally opposed naming a Harlem public school after Pedro Albizu Campos, an activist for Puerto Rican independence who had endorsed terrorist activities in the 1930s.[135] Badillo also worried that federally funded antipoverty programs in New York City encouraged ethnic isolation rather than cooperation.[136]

Before long, the civil rights movement revived a more radical Puerto Rican political community, especially in New York. The adoption of the Estado Libre Asociado (Free Associated State) in Puerto Rico in the early 1950s not only undercut the independence movement, but it also sparked renewed migration to the mainland, where urban industrialization had flourished after the war. Consequently, many leaders in and around Manhattan began addressing the economic needs of El Barrio and other popular Puerto Rican enclaves.[137] On the national level, the political mobilization of African Americans made the Democratic Party more amenable to minority interests, and by the 1960s Puerto Ricans, as people of color, confronted the notion of social justice.[138]

Antecedents of the Estado Libre Asociado (ELA)

Throughout the early 1940s, congressional conservatism generally blocked any progress toward greater Puerto Rican autonomy.[139] During the Second World War, because of Puerto Rico's strategic location at the entrance to the Caribbean Sea, Congress chose not to address the issue of the island's relationship to the United States, whether as a territory, a state, or an independent country.[140] But after 1945, several developments encouraged officials to reconsider Puerto Rico's status. The first, and perhaps the most influential, was a response to the political and symbolic leadership of future governor Luis Muñoz Marín and his powerful political party, the PPD, which was formed in 1938. Muñoz Marín and the PPD promoted a moderate position of supporting an autonomous relationship with the United States instead of immediate independence.[141] The economic success of Muñoz Marín's mid-1940s industrialization plan, dubbed "Operation Bootstrap," also fostered a growing belief on the mainland that Puerto Rico had reached a critical level of economic and political maturity.[142] A second, equally powerful justification for revisiting the federal-insular relationship was the "international atmosphere of decolonization" that emerged after World War II.[143] Under pressure from the newly created United Nations, President Truman advocated self-determination and self-government for colonies, including Puerto Rico, as part of the "Four Points" in his 1949 inaugural address.[144]

As early as 1943, the Puerto Rican legislature requested that islanders be permitted to elect their governor as the next step toward self-government. Muñoz Marín and his PPD ally Antonio Fernós-Isern sought this right as a step toward greater autonomy, and the move seemed appropriate after President Truman's appointment of the first native-born governor, Jesús Piñero, in 1946. The men's congressional allies—Chairman of the House Insular Affairs Subcommittee on Territories and Insular Possessions Fred Crawford of Michigan and Senator Hugh Butler of Nebraska—introduced a bill permitting the island's voters to elect their own governor in 1947. Reported favorably by committees in both houses, the Crawford–Butler Elected Governor Act (P.L. 80-362) passed with widespread bipartisan support in the final minutes of the first session of the 80th Congress (1947–1949).[145] The measure was the first major change to Puerto Rican governance since the Jones Act in 1917.[146] "Indeed," wrote a historian, "the climate in Congress for insular autonomy was remarkably favorable."[147]

President Harry Truman is greeted upon his arrival in San Juan, Puerto Rico, in 1948. Shaking Truman's hand is Jesús Piñero, governor of Puerto Rico; to Truman's immediate right is president of the insular senate and future governor Luis Muñoz Marín.

Image courtesy of the National Archives and Records Administration

"In the Nature of a Compact": The Development of ELA

Despite the new legislation, the federal-insular relationship remained confusing and outdated. Attempts to tack a status referendum onto the Crawford–Butler Act failed before the bill came to the floor, but supporters used debate over the legislation to promote the idea of a "compact" between the United States and Puerto Rico.[148] Fernós-Isern outlined his views on this political relationship in an address at Princeton University on May 5, 1948, redefining Puerto Rico not as a state of the union or as an independent republic, but as an intermediate "Autonomous State" or a "Federated Republic."[149] A fixation on independence or statehood had created "worshippers of different sects," Fernós-Isern said the following October. He called on Puerto Ricans to unite, not as a colony but as a dominion of the United States, aligned with the mainland with regard to international matters but governed locally under its own constitution.[150]

Historians credit Muñoz Marín and Fernós-Isern with navigating the autonomous option, which became the ELA, through treacherous political waters in Congress and Puerto Rico.[151] Fernós-Isern, a physician, and Muñoz Marín, a writer, bonded over a "non-legalistic, non-doctrinaire approach" to Puerto Rico's status issues. In the Resident Commissioner's estimation, the key to shepherding a status change through Congress was to simplify the legislation.[152]

Resident Commissioner Antonio Fernós-Isern, left, and Governor Luis Muñoz Marín, right, were key allies in the fight to achieve the Estado Libre Asociado (ELA). Puerto Rico's attorney general, Victor Gutierrez Franqui, is between the men.

Image courtesy of the National Archives and Records Administration

The two PPD leaders abandoned the aggressive tactics that were pursued in previous status fights; instead of attacking past U.S. policy toward its "shameful colony," the two argued that Puerto Rico had earned the right to escape "centuries of poverty and injustice."[153]

Introduced on March 13, 1950, Fernós-Isern's 59-line bill (H.R. 7674) followed his simple, straightforward strategy.[154] "In the nature of a compact" between the United States and Puerto Rico, the bill authorized Puerto Ricans to conduct a plebiscite on the bill's basic provisions. If voters approved, the Puerto Rican legislature would call a constitutional convention to draft a document that would require popular consent before its submission to the U.S. Congress for final approval.[155] "This is not statehood," Fernós-Isern explained to his colleagues. "Puerto Rico will continue to be represented in Congress by its Resident Commissioner. This is not independence. Puerto Ricans will continue proudly to be American citizens, in a common loyalty to our common institutions.... Mr. Chairman, I confidently say that the present political aspirations of the people of Puerto Rico are embodied in this bill."[156]

After sailing through committees in both chambers, the bill encountered minimal but vocal opposition on the House Floor. Representative Marcantonio of New York—a frequent advocate for independence who represented a large number of Harlem-based Puerto Ricans—argued vehemently against it, as did Jacob Javits, also of New York.[157] Marcantonio characterized the bill as "merely a snare and a delusion and a fraud perpetuated" on Puerto Ricans. "We are giving them nothing," he declared. "This bill is a scheme to deprive the people of Puerto Rico to pass on their own future status."[158] His parliamentary tactic—to remove the enacting clause and recommit the bill to the House Committee on Public Lands—failed spectacularly by vote of 260 to 1; Marcantonio's was the lone vote in its favor.[159] Indeed, most Members saw the PPD's overwhelming victory in the 1948 elections as a mandate for the bill and believed it recognized Puerto Rico's political maturity. House Public Lands Committee Ranking Member Fred Crawford described the bill as "a decided step forward toward human liberty and the right of a people to develop within themselves that responsibility which means freedom under the law."[160] The final bill passed on a voice vote in both chambers, becoming Public Law 600 after President Truman signed it on July 3, 1950.[161] Fernós-Isern called on Puerto Ricans to unite with mainland Americans in observing "independence day" on the 4th of July.[162] "The great victory in all this is not for any party," he noted, "but for the entire people of Puerto Rico who after a whole generation have overcome their blindness."[163] More than three-quarters (76.5 percent) of Puerto Ricans approved Public Law 600 in a plebiscite vote on June 4, 1951.[164]

Fernós-Isern presided over the subsequent constitutional convention, but Muñoz Marín himself drafted the document's preamble, which along with the first and second articles, was deemed a "value-oriented" provision, defining the island's ideals and political culture.[165] The third, fourth, and fifth articles of the bill distributed power among the legislature, executive branch, and judicial system.[166] The convention overwhelmingly approved a final draft, 88 to 3, on February 5, 1952.[167]

Section 20 of the constitution contained a bill of rights that extended beyond the U.S. Constitution's. Borrowed from the United Nations' Universal Declaration of Human Rights, it protected the right to work, a standard of living "adequate for health and well-being," social services, and special care for women and children.[168] "The Constitution contains a comprehensive Bill of Rights which not only incorporates the traditional American guarantees to the individual, but also reflects recent advances in respect to social and economic matters," Fernós-Isern explained. "With respect to the latter, however, it is worth noting that the Constitution carefully adapts its statement of social and economic rights to the realities of the Puerto Rican situation," he said.[169] Fernós-Isern counted on the Puerto Rican electorate's ability to create and amend its own constitution to justify the island's new status with no interference from Congress beyond its assurance that the document was within the parameters of U.S. law.[170] Puerto Rican voters approved the constitution by a margin of more than 4 to 1 in a plebiscite on March 3, 1952.[171]

The meaning of Puerto Rican sovereignty and Congress's future role on the island became the focus of debate in the U.S. House during the 82nd Congress (1951–1953). Given that congressional oversight was limited to ensuring that the Puerto Rican constitution fit the parameters of Public Law 600, the objectives were to create a republican government, include a bill of rights, and attain majority approval by the Puerto Rican people before submitting the document to Congress and the President for final approval.[172] It was unclear whether Congress could amend articles it deemed unacceptable, but both houses soon took this approach over Fernós-Isern's objections.[173]

The House Interior and Insular Affairs Committee unanimously supported the constitution, reporting H.J. Res. 430 without amendment on April 30, 1952, but Chairman John Murdock of Arizona noted "a good deal of opposition" to Section 20 because the committee believed it was too socialistic, and he encouraged its removal.[174] The debate centered on the ideological intention behind, the legality of, and the acceptance of the extensive bill of rights. Support was not split along partisan lines.[175] Members against amending argued that Congress could only ensure the constitution met the requirements of Public Law 600 and that amending it or weighing in on policy would renege on the

Vito Marcantonio of New York, whose district included Puerto Rican neighborhoods in Harlem, favored complete independence for the island rather than commonwealth status.

Image courtesy of the Library of Congress

Fred L. Crawford, Ranking Member of the House Public Lands Committee, described the bill permitting Puerto Ricans the right to draft a constitution under commonwealth status as "a decided step forward toward human liberty."

Image courtesy of the Library of Congress

President-elect John Kennedy and Puerto Rican Governor Luis Muñoz Marín met in Washington, D.C., in January 1961.

Image courtesy of the Library of Congress

agreement established by the law.[176] "Our enactment of Public Law 600 has no meaning unless it means that we entrusted the people of Puerto Rico the responsibility of writing law on which their government is to [be] based," noted Lloyd Bentsen of Texas. Bentsen recognized that the statement in Section 20 represented the "goals toward which Puerto Rico intends to work."[177] One of the bill's most vocal allies, Representative Reva Bosone of Utah, was the first to note that passage would profoundly shape future U.S. relations with Latin America. "I have always thought that probably our best friends were and would be the South American countries," Bosone said. "I am convinced … that our tie, our link with South America is Puerto Rico.… In my opinion it would be wrong not to pass this constitution, and the effect of it would be tremendous on our good will and saving face in the confidence of the Puerto Rican people. All of this will in turn be reflected in our relationship with South America."[178]

Though Cold War rhetoric provided a strong rationale to pass the constitution, it also drove the desire to strike Section 20. Insular Affairs Committee Chairman Murdock eventually submitted an amendment to delete this portion of the bill of rights.[179] Supporters included Republican Representative John Wood of Idaho, who called "this strange bill of rights" an "entirely unworkable thing in our form of society."[180] Most Members who spoke favored Murdock's amendment, which passed on voice vote, and argued that Congress's right to reject the constitution extended to rejecting portions of it.[181]

Representative Reva Bosone of Utah favored granting Puerto Rico greater autonomy in crafting its constitution in the early 1950s. Bosone reasoned that such a policy would promote stronger ties between the United States and the island and, by extension, South American nations.

Collection of the U.S. House of Representatives, Photography Collection

The Senate Committee on Interior and Insular Affairs upheld the House amendment in its report on S.J. Res. 151. South Carolina Senator Olin Johnston's attempt to assert absolute congressional authority to approve or reject the Puerto Rican constitutional amendment under the ELA provoked a sharp exchange with Dennis Chavez of New Mexico.[182] But the amendment, which some observers described as a "poison pill," passed by voice vote.[183] The House-Senate conference committee deleted the Johnston amendment, but in doing so also struck Section 20. Furthermore, any additional amendments could not alter the arrangements made under Public Law 600 and the remainder of the Jones Act.[184]

To Fernós-Isern, the final measure represented a significant victory and proved that the relationship between Puerto Rico and the United States was a balanced "compact." Congress still maintained ultimate oversight over Puerto Rico's internal affairs, and with the Jones Act in place, the final law created a "moral" compact between Puerto Rico and the United States rather than fundamentally altering their legal relationship.[185] Moreover, Fernós-Isern's strategy had achieved a resolution to the status issue, which many Puerto Ricans had sought for half a century.[186] With President Truman's signature, the ELA took effect July 25, 1952, the anniversary of the American invasion of Puerto Rico in the Spanish-American War.[187] Fernós-Isern and Muñoz Marín joined 35,000 people in front of the capitol in San Juan to raise the new flag, which boasted five red and white vertical stripes with a single white star in a blue triangle, a design that Puerto Rican revolutionaries had hoisted against Spain in 1895.[188]

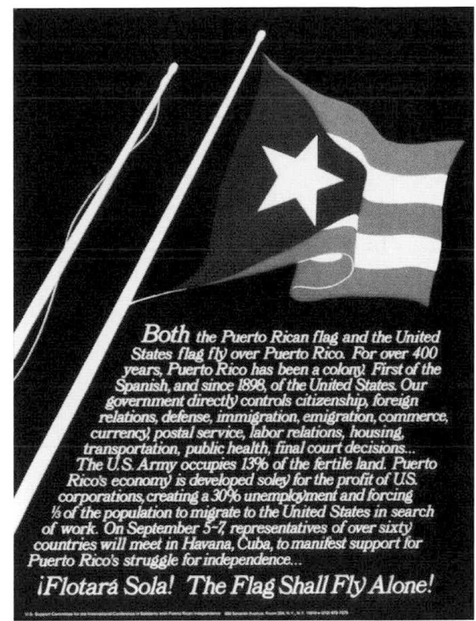

A poster, depicting the Puerto Rican flag in the decades after commonwealth status was granted, supports complete Puerto Rican independence. Alluding to a century of U.S. rule in Puerto Rico, it also declares that one day the Puerto Rican flag shall fly alone.

Image courtesy of the Library of Congress

Reactions to the ELA

International reaction to the ELA's passage did not disappoint its supporters. In May 1952, the Organization of American States' publication arm, *Americas*, observed that the new Puerto Rican constitution "enhance[d] the international prestige of the United States as the defender of democracy, for under the island's new status even an opportunistic political or a local poet could hardly call Puerto Ricans 'colonials.'"[189] The U.S. delegation to the United Nations, which included Fernós-Isern, reported in 1953 that Puerto Rico was now a self-governing territory. Fernós-Isern convinced the UN General Assembly to pass Resolution 748, relieving the United States from reporting on Puerto Rico's decolonization efforts.[190] While serving in Congress, Fernós-Isern also celebrated subsequent ELA anniversaries, praising Puerto Rican progress under the new political structure. "The people of Puerto Rico have proved they are politically mature," he reported in 1954. "They are not going to be stampeded into suicide and jump through the separatist window into the turmoil of today's international struggle, nor will they break their backs trying to carry burdens and assume financial responsibilities for which they lack the necessary strength."[191]

Yet support for the ELA was far from universal. Detractors noted that the underlying status structure remained unchanged; Puerto Rico was still a U.S. territory. "The Congress of the United States … agreed to accept the Commonwealth status on the understanding that the phrase 'in the nature of a compact' did not mean that Congress was irrevocably giving up its jurisdiction over Puerto Rican matters, internal and external," historian Surendra Bhana concludes.[192] The ELA faced several court challenges in the late 20th century.[193]

The honeymoon period that followed the adoption of the ELA barely lasted into the next decade. As early as 1959, Fernós-Isern, under pressure from statehood advocates in Puerto Rico, introduced H.R. 9234, popularly known as the Fernós–Murray Bill, to clarify the intent of Public Law 600. The measure died in committee, but within the next five years Fernós-Isern served on a congressionally established commission to study the future relationship between the United States and Puerto Rico.[194] The commission's findings concluded

Jaime Benítez, who served as Resident Commissioner from 1973 to 1977, remained a steadfast supporter of commonwealth status despite continued widespread disagreement among the Puerto Rican populace.

Image courtesy of the Library of Congress

that three alternatives—statehood, commonwealth, and independence—were viable. The results, announced in 1966, sparked a plebiscite on July 23, 1967, wherein a relatively low turnout of voters chose to continue under the auspices of the ELA.[195] Given the pro-commonwealth results, pro-statehood Resident Commissioner Jorge Luis Córdova-Díaz, who won office in 1968, estimated that building enough support for statehood to convince Congress to act would take 25 more years. "The time is not yet ripe [for statehood]," he said in 1970, "but surely it is coming when the great preponderance of our people will clearly express its will in this sense."[196] Future Resident Commissioner Jaime Benítez continued to support commonwealth status. "I believe that the immense majority of my fellow Puerto Ricans are now and will continue to be as far as one may foresee into the future spiritually committed, soberly and progressively so, in spite of intervening confusions, exasperations, difficulties, and misunderstandings, to permanent association and union with the U.S," he said in 1968. The key feature of the island's status, he reiterated, was its flexibility as a "middle of the road approach."[197] The idea of statehood, he said later, was "unmitigated nonsense."[198] Benítez defeated the incumbent, Córdova-Díaz, as the PPD's candidate for Resident Commissioner in 1972, indicating that after 20 years, status remained one of the most contentious issues on the island.

The Nationalists and the ELA

The most vocal and violent detractors of Public Law 600 and the ELA was the Partido Nacionalista (Nationalist Party). As early as the fall of 1950, radical Nacionalistas launched two attacks in Puerto Rico: On October 27, they led an armed uprising in at least seven Puerto Rican towns; three days later, they attempted to assassinate Muñoz Marín at the governor's mansion in San Juan. A total of 33 Nacionalistas died.[199]

Nacionalistas also struck in Washington during the debate on Public Law 600. On November 1, 1950, New York-based Puerto Rican Nacionalistas attacked Blair House, President Truman's temporary home on Lafayette Square, across from the White House. Though the President was unharmed, one of the two assassins and a White House police officer were killed. Resident Commissioner Fernós-Isern condemned the attack as the work of a small, extremist minority and was quick to distance Puerto Rico from the violence. "I am a physician. Perhaps I might find in the intricacies of psychiatry an explanation for this type of behavior and for the reasoning or lack of reasoning behind it," he told his colleagues on the House Floor. "But outside of that, I can say this: Thank God this type of behavior and reasoning is not typical of the people of Puerto Rico."[200] He linked the violent wing of the Partido Nacionalista with "traitorous" United States communists in an "unholy marriage."[201] In a visit to the White House on November 17, Fernós-Isern delivered a letter to President Truman expressing the regrets of the Puerto Rican people.[202] After the remaining assassin was sentenced to execution, Fernós-Isern delivered a letter that was signed by 119,000 Puerto Ricans who were thankful the President had been spared. Weighing 57 pounds, the letter denounced the "arbitrary act of violence ... by a small group of fanatic Nationalists."[203]

On March 1, 1954, Nacionalista extremists struck the U.S. Congress. Three armed men and one woman posing as journalists sprayed the House Chamber with gunfire from the southwest corner of the public galleries. At least 243 Members of Congress and many staff members, in the middle of a vote on Mexican farm labor legislation, dove for cover under chairs or tables and behind the rostrum. Five Members were wounded, two seriously. Fernós-Isern, who was a trained doctor and was in his office during the shooting because he couldn't vote, ran toward the Capitol after hearing about the attack to see if he could help the medical personnel. Capitol Police stopped him for security reasons, confining him to his office on the seventh floor of the New (Longworth) House Office Building.[204] Fernós-Isern denounced the shooters the same way he had denounced Truman's would-be assassins and accused Puerto Ricans in New York of being "communist dupes." The shooters "are certainly out of touch with the political situation in Puerto Rico," he said.[205] "Can it be the doing just of Puerto Rican Nationalists?" he asked a *Baltimore Sun* journalist rhetorically. "Who benefits? Certainly not Puerto Rico."[206]

On March 1, 1954, Puerto Rican nationalists attacked the U.S. Capitol, raining gunfire onto the House Floor from the public galleries. Five Representatives were injured in the fusillade. Suspects Lolita Lebrón, Rafael Cancel Miranda, and Andrés Figueroa Cordero are led away shortly after being detained by Capitol Police and bystanders.

Image courtesy of the Library of Congress

Governor Muñoz Marín also flew to Washington on March 2 to express his condolences. The governor visited all the wounded Congressmen, except Michigan Representative Alvin Bentley, who was unable to receive visitors, and called on President Eisenhower at the White House.[207] Later Muñoz Marín stood in the well of the House, shook hands with Members, and received a standing ovation. Speaker Joe Martin of Massachusetts, who had ducked behind the rostrum to avoid the rampage, voiced his support for the Puerto Rican government. "A few gangsters can't break up the friendship of great nations," he said.[208]

Changes in the Role of the Resident Commissioner

Puerto Rico's evolution from territory to commonwealth resulted in some changes to the role of the Resident Commissioner. Prior to World War II, the Resident Commissioner's role consisted largely of securing funding and resources while working to acquire greater autonomy under the Jones

Resident Commissioner Antonio Fernós-Isern (center) and Governor Luis Muñoz Marín (left) extend their sympathy to House Speaker Joseph Martin of Massachusetts (right) after radical Puerto Rican nationalists attacked Members in the House Chamber in 1954.

Image courtesy of the National Archives and Records Administration

Act of 1917. Resident Commissioners functioned as foreign ambassadors, congressional legislators, lobbyists, and publicity agents for Puerto Rican tourism and industry.[209] Jesús Piñero's brief tenure as Resident Commissioner during the 79th Congress (1945–1947) exemplifies the multiple roles of the office. Both Piñero and his successor, Antonio Fernós-Isern, worked closely with PPD leader Luis Muñoz Marín to improve Puerto Rico's economic situation by acquiring federal aid and attracting investment capital to the island. The two also worked to obtain airline routes between Puerto Rico and the mainland United States and spoke for and represented Puerto Rico on the mainland.

While the passage of Public Law 600 did not legally change the duties or privileges of the Resident Commissioner, scholar José Rios notes that the Resident Commissioner assumed two additional obligations under the new Puerto Rican constitution: the "legal obligation to insure that Congress did not approve legislation that could be in conflict with the status of the Commonwealth" and "the obligation to support those changes in the association with the United States that the people of Puerto Rico should propose."[210] Fernós-Isern, with the support of Senator James Murray of Montana, tried to enhance the Resident Commissioner's role as an ambassador to the executive branch, among other things, by sponsoring H.R. 9234 during the 86th Congress (1959–1961), but the bill never passed.[211] Greater autonomy for Puerto Rico also meant that the other elective offices, including those of the governor and the insular legislature, took on increased stature in Puerto Rico. For example, when the speaker of the insular house, Santiago Polanco-Abreu, was handpicked by Muñoz Marín as the PPD candidate for Resident Commissioner, many of his supporters viewed his selection as a career step backward and akin to "political exile" because it isolated him from the party during a crucial transition period.[212] But with the U.S. Congress expected to tackle the question of Puerto Rico's status, others believed the Resident Commissioner's job was more important than ever.[213]

Expanding the Rights of Territorial Delegates and the Resident Commissioner

During this period, Territorial Delegates often joined the Resident Commissioner to address issues common to their constituents. In the 1950s, Delegates Joseph Farrington of Hawaii and Bob Bartlett of Alaska, along with Resident Commissioner Fernós-Isern, formed an informal caucus they jokingly called the "three cadets." "We compared notes and exchanged ideas. We understood each other, and I think we understood each other's problems," Fernós-Isern noted.[214] On April 10, 1972, Congress passed H.R. 8787 (P.L. 92-271), creating positions for Delegates to represent Guam and the U.S. Virgin Islands in the House starting in the 93rd Congress (1973–1975).[215] While lobbying for the position he eventually won, Ron de Lugo mirrored the argument put forth by Fernós-Isern with the passage of the ELA. "Let me make it perfectly clear that we in the Virgin Islands do not seek independence, nor do we by urging passage of H.R. 8787 seek statehood," de Lugo told the Senate Subcommittee on Territories and Insular Affairs. "We seek only, in a limited way, a voice to articulate the needs of the people of the Virgin Islands within the framework of the national legislature."[216] De Lugo's strategy of testifying before House and Senate subcommittees and committees was one that was often used by Resident Commissioners to discuss economic and political needs, and to attempt to eliminate some of the bureaucracy from Congress's territorial governance.

The growing number of statutory representatives made great strides in obtaining more rights within the legislative process. Political tremors in Puerto Rico during the late 1960s sent shock waves from San Juan to Washington. For nearly 20 years, the PPD, which was responsible for creating and nurturing the island's commonwealth status, remained virtually unchallenged. The pro-commonwealth plebiscite in 1967 seemed to reaffirm the island's confidence in the Popular Democrats and to solidify Puerto Rico's unique relationship with the federal government. But less than a year later, the PPD lost elections islandwide to the upstart, pro-statehood Partido Nuevo Progresista (New Progressive Party, or PNP). Social ills like poverty, crime, and corruption hurt the PPD's popularity, and the new PNP administration provided an ambitious, new agenda that included statehood. "The depth and desire for change in the Puerto Rican electorate was underestimated by all the politicians," said an editorial in San Juan's leading English-language newspaper shortly after the election.[217]

Delegate Ron de Lugo of the Virgin Islands, in pressing for greater representation for his territory in Congress, employed many of the same arguments as Resident Commissioners had for Puerto Rico.

Image courtesy of the Library of Congress

The Puerto Rican electorate's "desire for change" extended the duties and responsibilities of the Resident Commissioner, which had been a talking point during the 1968 campaign for the office. Until that point, the Resident Commissioner's role in the House had been unique. The Resident Commissioner sat on committees whose jurisdictions affected Puerto Rico, but could not gain seniority or vote during markup. He could introduce legislation on the House Floor but was unable to vote on its final passage. Thus, the office of the Resident Commissioner often functioned more like a lobbying operation than a seat in the national legislature.[218] For nearly a generation, this arrangement satisfied the PPD's commonwealth program; Puerto Ricans maintained U.S. citizenship, their cultural identity, and a degree of independence in exchange for a muted role in federal politics.

But such thinking began to change with the retirement of the initial group of PPD leaders. Amid the rise of the pro-statehood PNP in the late 1960s, many voters reassessed their expectations for the office of Resident Commissioner. Whereas the PPD tended to concern itself only with legislation that might influence Puerto Rico's commonwealth status, the PNP promised to refashion the Resident Commissioner's seat.[219] When Jorge Luis Córdova-Díaz won election in 1968, he set in motion a series of events that made the office of Resident Commissioner significantly more influential.

Like earlier Resident Commissioners, Córdova-Díaz lamented his nonvoting status. "I can sit in the chamber and have my colleagues tell me how lucky I am not to have to vote on a controversial issue," he said in 1970. "But I itch to vote. I don't have any political muscle." It all made "getting even the smallest of things" for Puerto Rico difficult, not to mention larger items, such as food stamps, which he struggled to procure.[220] Córdova-Díaz considered the office

Carl Albert of Oklahoma was Speaker of the House when the chamber adopted new rules that expanded the powers of Delegates and Resident Commissioners.

Carl Albert, Charles B. Wilson, 1973, Collection of the U.S. House of Representatives

of Resident Commissioner to be unequal to representing nearly three million people.[221] Even future Speaker Carl Albert of Oklahoma conceded, "I think it is important to note that the role of Resident Commissioner is unique in the Congress. The man who serves in this capacity must find his own way among men and women whose status is rather different and in many ways easier."[222]

Córdova-Díaz offered an amendment as part of the Legislative Reorganization Act of 1970 (P.L. 91-510) that permitted the Resident Commissioner to vote in committee. Córdova-Díaz was certain the amendment would fail in the Senate. "I can't complain that I've been ignored," he said after the bill passed the House, "but I feel if the bill is passed [by the Senate] the chances are better that I'll be listened to. These department heads are well aware that I haven't had the vote and now they'll realize that someday they might need me. So I feel they'll be more responsive when I ask them for something."[223] When the amendment unexpectedly cleared the Senate, the office of Resident Commissioner assumed more direct power than ever before.[224] On the Opening Day of the 92nd Congress (1971–1973), the House implemented the rights that were won by Córdova-Díaz, declaring that statutory Members would "serve on standing committees in the same manner as Members of the House" and would have the right to accrue seniority.[225] Statutory representatives intended to continue to try to obtain more rights in Congress, especially the right to vote on the House Floor. Asked about full voting rights for Delegates on the House Floor, de Lugo responded, "The fact that I'm here shows you how far we've come."[226]

HISPANIC AMERICANS IN CONGRESS AND THE COLD WAR

The pressure to live up to the rhetoric about spreading democratic principles abroad increased during the Cold War, and the defense of human rights was an even larger concern for the Harry S. Truman administration. According to one scholar, President Truman shared three goals with later Cold War Presidents: countering Soviet propaganda about U.S. hypocrisy regarding racial equality; convincing nonaligned nations in Africa, Latin America, and Asia of the United States' belief in racial egalitarianism; and leveraging the civil rights movement to enact domestic reforms.[227]

With the escalation of the Cold War between the United States and the Soviet Union in the 1950s, Hispanic-American Members of Congress pursued their legislative interests in an era of decolonization abroad, anti-communist sentiment at home, and conflicts designed to contain communist expansion in Europe, Asia, and Latin America. Senator Dennis Chavez held a particularly powerful position early in the Cold War era; as chairman of the Senate Appropriations Subcommittee on Defense in the late 1950s, Chavez wielded great influence over the Eisenhower administration's defense spending. He opposed the President's attempt to cut national security outlays with the New Look program and viewed any reduction in the country's military preparedness as unwise in the wake of the inconclusive resolution of the Korean War in 1953.[228] Military buildups were the foundation for Chavez's domestic Cold War agenda, and he believed no amount of money was too great for national security. His New Mexico constituency benefited greatly from the arms race.

The country's sophisticated military infrastructure created new jobs, which Chavez directed to the Southwest.[229]

Chavez's anti-communism had its limits, however, and he resented the state of public discourse in the early 1950s. As the Senate investigated accusations by Senator Joseph McCarthy of Wisconsin that communists had infiltrated the State Department, Chavez tried to reorient the chamber's moral—and constitutional—compass. He was one of McCarthy's earliest critics. At great personal risk, Chavez spoke out against McCarthy's accusations, telling the Senate he felt obligated to "step out and sound the alarm."[230] The rampant claims of treason, most without substantive evidence, noted New Mexico's Senator, "[bred] hysteria and confusion—a course so dangerous that few dare to oppose the drift lest they be the next marked for destruction."[231]

But anti-communist rhetoric cut both ways. During his 1962 House campaign, Joseph Montoya outlined his hard-line bona fides and the value of his seat on the House Appropriations Committee. In a speech to constituents, he reminded voters that he "consistently voted against seating Communist China in the United Nations" and "supported the authorization of funds to carry on the work of the House Un-American Activities Committee." He adamantly opposed aid to countries like India, which remained neutral in the struggle between the superpowers; supported anti-communist authoritarian regimes abroad; and sought to strengthen U.S. ties with Latin America. When reactionaries at home accused Montoya of harboring communist sympathies, he pointed to his foreign policy commitments abroad as evidence to the contrary.[232]

Hispanic politicians had varied responses to the Vietnam War. Those who were initially patient became vehemently critical by the time President Richard Nixon assumed control. In 1971 Montoya submitted an amendment seeking the immediate withdrawal of the United States from Vietnam. In May of the same year, Edward Roybal joined a lawsuit with 27 other Democratic lawmakers demanding an immediate end to the war. According to the *Los Angeles Times*, Roybal's affidavit was one of 15 filed in U.S. district court proclaiming "that military appropriations and authorization bills should not be taken as a form of war declaration."[233] Herman Badillo, who also entered Congress in 1971,

Dennis Chavez of New Mexico was one of a handful of U.S. Senators who denounced the tactics of their red-baiting, anticommunist colleague Joseph McCarthy of Wisconsin—pictured at the right of the photo. The full Senate eventually censured McCarthy for abusing his powers and bringing the Senate into "dishonor and disrepute."

Image courtesy of the Library of Congress

made no secret of his opposition to the Vietnam War, publicly criticizing the Nixon administration's approach to ending the conflict and supporting many of the antiwar amendments and bills considered by the House. "We … should be reasserting the responsibility of Congress to shape our foreign and military policy by bringing the war to an end—now," he said.[234] Kika de la Garza had a different opinion. He described public antiwar demonstrations as an "insult to our servicemen and their families" and "a continuing attempt to wreck the American Government and to bring anarchy to our country."[235] As the representative of a district that sent a significant number of constituents

Cuban refugees in New York City watch President John Kennedy's televised October 1962 speech in which he announces a naval "quarantine" of the island during the Cuban Missile Crisis. Cold War conflicts in Latin America created new waves of immigrants to the U.S. and increasingly diverse Latino communities.

Image courtesy of the Library of Congress

to fight in the war, de la Garza supported the Nixon administration's strategy for a gradual withdrawal from Vietnam. "If you become involved in a military conflict you go out and win, using all the resources at your command," he said, describing his support for the President as a patriotic duty.[236]

The Puerto Rican Resident Commissioners had a range of opinions concerning the struggle against communism. While rector of the Universidad de Puerto Rico from 1941 to 1966, future Resident Commissioner Jaime Benítez omitted political affiliation from the hiring process to ensure academic freedom.[237] As a result, he frequently risked his own reputation to protect professors from charges of communism by insular and federal authorities.[238] In March 1966, Resident Commissioner Santiago Polanco-Abreu submitted a concurrent resolution expressing the Puerto Rican legislature's support for the Vietnam War. Polanco-Abreu said the resolution "condemns all actions tending to weaken the efforts of the United States in its struggle to preserve peace and democratic justice in the world, as now in Vietnam, and to check Communist aggression."[239] His successor, Jorge Luis Córdova-Díaz, made no remarks about the Vietnam War on the House Floor, but he publicly disputed Herman Badillo's contention that a disproportionate number of Puerto Ricans had served in Vietnam.[240]

THE FOUNDING OF THE CONGRESSIONAL HISPANIC CAUCUS

On December 8, 1976, Representatives Badillo, González, de la Garza, and Roybal and Puerto Rican Resident Commissioner-elect Baltasar Corrada-del Río announced the formation of the Congressional Hispanic Caucus (CHC).[241] While several of the founding Members had served in Congress since the 1960s, they had not formed a group to focus on issues that were important to Hispanic Americans. Since 1971, Badillo had urged the creation of a Hispanic Caucus to foster greater unity among the Hispanic Members.[242] The founders of the CHC stated that their mission was "to develop programs … to increase opportunities for Hispanics to participate in and contribute to the American political system" and to "reverse the national pattern of neglect, exclusion and indifference suffered for decades by Spanish-speaking citizens of the U.S."[243] "The fact that we have joined together is a sign of the growing power of our community, and we are looking forward to strengthening the Federal commitment to Hispanic citizens," the caucus declared.[244] Roybal was the CHC's first chairman. For reasons that were not specified, Representative Luján and outgoing Resident Commissioner Benítez, as well as Delegate de Lugo, did not join the caucus.

CONCLUSION

From the end of World War II to the mid-1970s, Hispanic-American Members of Congress faced momentous changes outside the institution. They responded by emphasizing the improvement of national conditions over local and regional interests. As local civil rights organizations in the Southwest and the Northeast organized, gaining influence and challenging discriminatory practices, Hispanic-American Members continued to serve their constituents by acquiring resources, promoting legislation, and learning institutional mores so as to become more powerful and effective legislators. As middle- and working-class Mexican Americans mobilized to challenge discrimination during the civil rights era, some Mexican-American Members of Congress used their influence to push through civil rights legislation and lobbied the Kennedy and Johnson administrations on behalf of their constituents. By the late 1960s, dissatisfaction with the uneven progress of the civil rights movement prompted a more confrontational stance that demanded immediate social benefits in exchange for political support.

Despite divisions regarding tactics, Hispanic-American Members began to promote the legislative interests that were common to Mexican-American and Puerto Rican civil rights activists. The elimination by the Civil Rights Act of 1964 and the Voting Rights Act of 1965 (and its various extensions) of many legalistic barriers to voting and political participation set the stage for an increase in the number of Hispanic-American Members, with an enhanced ability to gain access to important committees, acquire seniority, and serve as chairmen or Ranking Members or within party leadership. Ideological differences and disagreements over policy sometimes proved divisive, but as Hispanic-American Members acquired more institutional power, their often similar legislative interests enabled them to work toward common goals as members of the Congressional Hispanic Caucus.

NOTES

1 *Congressional Record*, Senate, 82nd Cong., 2nd sess. (23 June 1952): 7842, 7846; A. W. Maldonado, *Luis Muñoz Marín: Puerto Rico's Democratic Revolution* (San Juan: La Editorial Universidad de Puerto Rico, 2006): 318–319, 322.

2 *Congressional Record*, Senate, 82nd Cong., 2nd sess. (23 June 1952): 7846.

3 Quoted in Maldonado, *Luis Muñoz Marín: Puerto Rico's Democratic Revolution*: 321–322; David M. Helfeld, "Congressional Intent and Attitude toward Public Law 600 and the Constitution of the Commonwealth of Puerto Rico," *Revista juridicia de la Universidad de Puerto Rico* 21, no. 4 (May–June 1952): 299, 302; *Congressional Record*, Senate, 82nd Cong., 2nd sess. (23 June 1952): 7841, 7846. Chavez was reacting to remarks by Senator Olin Johnston of South Carolina who said, "We have received nothing from Puerto Rico in return for all we have given them, all the millions of dollars that we have spent in Puerto Rico. We have asked for nothing in return in the form of taxes or anything else.... In relation to the Constitution of Puerto Rico I can say that we can give them a constitution or not give it to them: I want the Puerto Ricans to know this."

4 Rodolfo Espino III, "Political Representation," in Suzanne Oboler and Deena J. González, eds., *The Oxford History of Latinos and Latinas in the United States,* vol. 3 (New York: Oxford University Press, 2005): 424–431.

5 Ignacio García, "La Raza Unida Party," in Oboler and González, eds., *The Oxford History of Latinos and Latinas in the United States,* vol. 2: 473–475.

6 Walter S. Priest, "What Lies Ahead for Polanco?" 15 November 1964, *San Juan Star*: 3.

7 Overall, Hispanic-American Representatives were about the same age as their congressional counterparts (43.4 years), but the average age of the Puerto Rican Resident Commissioners when they were first elected was considerably older (55.8 years). See Allan G. Bogue et al., "Members of the House of Representatives and the Processes of Modernization, 1789–1960," *Journal of American History* 63, no. 2 (September 1976): 291 (see especially Table 6). This figure includes Joseph Montoya of New Mexico, who served in the House from 1957 to 1964 and in the Senate from 1964 to 1976.

8 Córdova-Díaz was not a member of the PPD; he was a member of the Partido Acción Cristiana (Christian Action Party) and the Partido Nuevo Progresista (New Progressive Party).

9 Jorge Luis Córdova-Díaz was appointed to serve on the bench of the supreme court of Puerto Rico. He did not serve as a legislator until he was elected Resident Commissioner in 1968.

10 From 1940 to 1950, 50.7 percent of House Members were lawyers; from 1950 to 1960, 52 percent practiced law. See Bogue et al., "Members of the House of Representatives and the Processes of Modernization, 1789–1960": 284 (especially Table 2). It is unclear whether Ron de Lugo attended college.

11 Herman Badillo was initially assigned to the Committee on Agriculture, but lobbied for, and got a spot on the Education and Labor Committee with the support of the Democratic Study Group and Speaker Carl Albert of Oklahoma.

12 Ralph Nader Congress Project, *Citizens Look at Congress: Jorge L. Córdova, Resident Commissioner from Puerto Rico* (Washington, D.C.: Grossman Publishers, 1972). Jorge Luis Córdova-Díaz caucused with the Republican Party during the second half of his term of service in the House.

13 William R. Tansill, "The Resident Commissioner to the United States from Puerto Rico: An Historical Perspective," *Revista juridica de la Universidad de Puerto Rico*, 47, nos. 1–2 (1978): 83.

14 *Congressional Record*, House, 88th Cong., 2nd sess. (1 October 1964): 23426.

15 *Congressional Record*, Senate, 92nd Cong., 2nd sess. (7 August 1972): 27010. Interestingly, Montoya does not list Jorge Luis Córdova-Díaz, the Puerto Rican Resident Commissioner, or Ron de Lugo, the Delegate for the Virgin Islands, who were nonvoting Members of the House.

16 Juan Gómez-Quiñones, *Chicano Politics, Reality and Promise, 1940–1990* (Albuquerque: University of New Mexico Press, 1990): 94–95.

17 Maldonado, *Luis Muñoz Marín: Puerto Rico's Democratic Revolution*: 259–260; Surendra Bhana, *The United States and the Development of the Puerto Rican Status Question, 1936–1968* (Lawrence: The University Press of Kansas, 1975): 103–104; *Congressional Record*, House, 82nd Cong., 2nd sess. (28 May 1952): 6169.

18 "Candidate's Stand on Issues," n.d., 1962 file," Box 64, Folder 1 (MSS 386 BC), Joseph M. Montoya Papers, University of New Mexico Center for Southwest Research, Albuquerque (hereinafter referred to as Montoya Papers, CSWR).

19 *Congressional Record*, Senate, 91st Cong., 1st sess. (18 December 1969): 39945.

20 *Congressional Record*, House, 91st Cong., 1st sess. (16 December 1969): 39400–39401.

21 *Congressional Record*, Index, 91st Cong.: 1579; "An Act to Establish the Cabinet Committee on Opportunities for Spanish-Speaking People, and for Other Purposes," P.L. 91-181, 83 Stat. 838, 1969–1970.

22 Ralph Nader Congress Project, *Citizens Look at Congress: Manuel Luján, Jr.* (Washington, D.C.: Grossman Publishers, 1972): 8.

23 *Politics in America, 1982* (Washington, D.C.: Congressional Quarterly Inc., 1981): 791; "Election Statistics, 1920 to Present" http://history.house.gov/Institution/Election-Statistics/Election-Statistics/.

24 See, for example, Badillo's stance on unemployment, *Congressional Record*, House, 92nd Cong., 2nd sess. (2 March 1972): 6689–6690.

25 *Congressional Record*, House, Extension of Remarks, 92nd Cong, 1st sess. (4 June 1971): 18267.

26 "Latin Parley Is Called by Four from Congress," 26 September 1971, *New York Times*: 77.

27 Will Lissner, "Coalition Sought by Puerto Ricans," 30 September 1971, *New York Times*: 43; Jack Rosenthal, "U.S. Latins Vote Political Drive," 25 October 1971, *New York Times*: 17.

28 Thomas J. Foley, "'Brown Power' Parley Opens This Weekend," 22 October 1971, *Los Angeles Times*: A18.

29 Jack Rosenthal, "Latin Americans Sue U.S. on Rights," 23 October 1971, *New York Times:* 31; "Hispanic-Americans Complain about Frequent Police Abuses," 24 October 1971, *Chicago Tribune*: A22.

30 Rosenthal, "U.S. Latins Vote Political Drive."

31 Nicholas De Genova, "Immigration Policy, Twentieth Century," in Oboler and González, eds., *The Oxford History of Latinos and Latinas in the United States*, vol. 2: 353.

32 Manuel Gonzales, *Mexicanos: A History of Mexicans in the United States*, 2nd ed. (Bloomington: Indiana University Press, 2009): 123.

33 Kunal M. Parker, "Citizenship and Immigration Law, 1800–1824: Resolution of Membership and Territory," in Michael Grossberg and Christopher Tomlins, eds., *The Cambridge History of Law in America: The Long Nineteenth Century (1789–1920)*, vol. 2 (New York: Cambridge University Press, 2008): 197–199.

34 Gonzales, *Mexicanos: A History of Mexicans in the United States*: 122–123.

35 David Montejano, *Anglos and Mexicans in the Making of Texas, 1836–1986* (Austin: University of Texas Press, 1987): 182.

36 Montejano, *Anglos and Mexicans*: 190; Harvey A. Levenstein, "The AFL and Mexican Immigration in the 1920s: An Experiment in Labor Diplomacy," *The Hispanic American Historical Review* 48, no. 2 (May 1968): 206–219.

37 Parker, "Citizenship and Immigration Law, 1800–1924," in Grossberg and Tomlins, *The Cambridge History of Law in America,* vol. 2: 200; Montejano, *Anglos and Mexicans*: 187–188.

38 Parker, "Citizenship and Immigration Law, 1800–1924," in Grossberg and Tomlins, *The Cambridge History of Law in America,* vol. 2: 200.

39 George J. Sánchez, *Becoming Mexican American: Ethnicity, Culture, and Identity in Chicano Los Angeles* (New York: Oxford University Press, 1993): 96.

40 Sánchez, *Becoming Mexican American*: 105.

41 Gonzales, *Mexicanos: A History of Mexicans in the United States*: 121–122; Juan Gómez-Quiñones, *Roots of Chicano Politics, 1600–1940* (Albuquerque: University of New Mexico Press, 1994): 297–301; Mae M. Ngai, *Impossible Subjects: Illegal Aliens and the Making of Modern America* (Princeton, NJ: Princeton University Press, 2004): 129–130.

42 Richard Steele, "Mexican Americans in the 1940s: Perceptions and Conditions," in Richard Griswold del Castillo, ed., *World War II and Mexican American Civil Rights* (Austin: University of Texas Press, 2008): 9–17; Gonzales, *Mexicanos: A History of Mexicans in the United States*: 113–125, 163–168. Like New Mexico, California sought to guarantee Hispanics' civil rights in the 19th century through the 1879 state constitution, but Hispanics' political power declined throughout the 1870s. The quotation is from Gómez-Quiñones, *Roots of Chicano Politics, 1600–1940*: 295–296.

43 For a detailed description of the formation of these groups, see Gómez-Quiñones, *Roots of Chicano Politics, 1600–1940*: 311–318.

44 Gonzales, *Mexicanos: A History of Mexicans in the United States*: 140–142. Gonzales notes that Los Angeles had "97,116 Mexicanos living within its city limits."

45 Sánchez, *Becoming Mexican American*: 211.

46 Ibid., 212–213.

47 Ibid., 213–214.

48 Victor C. Romero, "Deportation Cases and Legislation," in Oboler and González, eds., *The Oxford Encyclopedia of Latinos and Latinas in the United States,* vol. 1: 496.

49 Gonzales, *Mexicanos: A History of Mexicans in the United States*: 148.

50 Sánchez, *Becoming Mexican American*: 217.

51 Ibid., 220.

52 Benjamin Marquez, *LULAC: The Evolution of a Mexican American Political Organization* (Austin: University of Texas Press, 1993): 17–34; Richard Steele, "The Federal Government Discovers Mexican Americans," in Griswold del Castillo, ed., *World War II and Mexican American Civil Rights*: 23–31; Gómez-Quiñones, *Chicano Politics: Reality and Promise, 1940–1990*: 40–41.

53 Gonzales, *Mexicanos: A History of Mexicans in the United States:* 163–164; Steele, "The Federal Government Discovers Mexican Americans," in Griswold del Castillo, ed., *World War II and Mexican American Civil Rights*: 20–21; Gonzales, *Mexicanos: A History of Mexicans in the United States*: 168–169.

54 For an overview of efforts to promote democracy abroad in the 20th century, see Tony Smith, *America's Mission: The United States and the Worldwide Struggle for Democracy in the Twentieth Century* (Princeton, NJ: Princeton University Press, 1995).

55 John D. Skrentny, *The Minority Rights Revolution* (Cambridge, MA: Belknap Press of Harvard University Press, 2002): 21–25.

56 Steele, "The Federal Government Discovers Mexican Americans," in Griswold del Castillo, ed., *World War II and Mexican American Civil Rights:* 23–24; Gómez-Quiñones, *Chicano Politics; Reality and Promise, 1940–1990*: 36–37.

57 "Executive Order 8802: Establishing the Committee on Fair Employment Practices," 25 June 1941, published as part of the American Presidency Project, University of California, Santa Barbara, http://www.presidency.ucsb.edu (accessed 1 February 2008). For a discussion of FDR's political position, see Harvard Sitkoff, *A New Deal for Blacks: The Emergence of Civil Rights as a National Issue* (New York: Oxford University Press, 1978): 320–323. See also David M. Kennedy, *Freedom from Fear: The American People in Depression and War, 1929–1945* (New York: Oxford University Press, 1999): 768.

58 Joe Roy Lujan, "Dennis Chavez and the Roosevelt Era, 1933–1945," (Ph.D. diss., The University of New Mexico, 1987): 476.

59 "Spanish-Americans Ask Fair Play, Says Chavez," 19 October 1944, *Los Angeles Times*: 12.

60 As quoted in Rosemary T. Diaz, "*El Senador*, Dennis Chavez: New Mexico Native Son, American Senior Statesman, 1888–1962," (Ph.D. diss., Arizona State University, 2006): 331,

see also 330–338.

61 Jay Walz, "FEPC's Life Ends with No Hope Held for Early Revival," 1 July 1946, *New York Times*: 1.

62 Lujan, "Dennis Chavez and the Roosevelt Era": 515 and all of Chapter 11; "Negro Group Prays before Senators," 1 September 1944, *New York Times*: 15. For the committee report, see Senate Committee on Education and Labor, *Prohibiting Discrimination in Employment Because of Race, Creed, Color, National Origin, or Ancestry*, 79th Cong., 1st sess. (24 May 1945), S. Rep. 290.

63 *Congressional Record*, Senate, 79th Cong., 1st sess. (6 January 1945): 80; Lujan, "Dennis Chavez and the Roosevelt Era": 522–524; "Senators Approve Extension of FEPC," 24 May 1945, *New York Times*: 14.

64 *Congressional Record*, Senate, 79th Cong., 2nd sess. (8 February 1946): 1154–1155.

65 *Congressional Record*, Senate, 79th Cong., 2nd sess. (9 February 1946): 1194, 1196.

66 Lujan, "Dennis Chavez and the Roosevelt Era": 539.

67 *Congressional Record*, Senate, 80th Cong., 2nd sess. (9 Feb. 1946): 1219.

68 Gonzales, *Mexicanos: A History of Mexicans in the United States*: 170.

69 Juan Roman García, *Operation Wetback: The Mass Deportation of Mexican Undocumented Workers in 1954* (Westport: Greenwood Press, 1980): 3; Sánchez, *Becoming Mexican American:* 220.

70 García, *Operation Wetback: The Mass Deportation of Mexican Undocumented Workers in 1954*: 3; Sánchez, *Becoming Mexican American:* 220; Kitty Calavita, *Inside the State: The Bracero Program, Immigration, and the I.N.S.* (New York: Routledge, 1992): 19. According to Sánchez, the internment of Japanese Americans in 1942 aggravated the labor shortage.

71 As quoted in Calavita, *Inside the State*: 21.

72 Gilbert Paul Carrasco, "Bracero Program," in Oboler and González, eds., *The Oxford Encyclopedia of Latinos and Latinas in the United States*, vol. 1: 220.

73 *Statutes at Large*, 57 Stat. 70, 1940–1943. For a detailed description of the Bracero Program in the 1950s and 1960s, see Ngai, *Impossible Subjects: Illegal Aliens and the Making of Modern America*: 138–147.

74 Gonzales, *Mexicanos: A History of Mexicans in the United States*: 173–174.

75 Carrasco, "Bracero Program," in Oboler and González, eds., *Oxford Encyclopedia of Latinos and Latina,* vol. 1*:* 221.

76 Calavita, *Inside the State*: 27–28; Carrasco, "Bracero Program," in Oboler and González, eds., *Oxford Encyclopedia of Latinos and Latinas,* vol. 1: 221.

77 *Congressional Record,* House, 82nd Cong., 1st sess. (27 June 1951): 7254.

78 Ibid., 7260, 7261, 7264. The amendment was rejected 125 to 55.

79 *Congressional Record,* House, 78th Congress, 1st sess. (8 April 1943): 3104.

80 Gonzales, *Mexicanos: A History of Mexicans in the United States*: 173–174. For McCarthy's views, see *Congressional Record*, House, 87th Cong., 1st sess. (23 May 1961): 8596.

81 Carrasco, "Bracero Program," in Oboler and González, eds., *Oxford Encyclopedia of Latinos and Latinas,* vol. 1: 223; Gonzales, *Mexicanos: A History of Mexicans in the United States*: 174.

82 García, *Operation Wetback*: 142.

83 Gonzales, *Mexicanos: A History of Mexicans in the United States*: 173.

84 Joseph Nevins, "Deportations of Mexican-Origin People in the United States," in Oboler and González, eds., *Oxford Encyclopedia of Latinos and Latinas,* vol. 1: 496.

85 Kelly Lytle Hernández, "The Crimes and Consequences of Illegal Immigration: A Cross-Border Examination of Operation Wetback, 1943 to 1954," *Western Historical Quarterly* 37, no. 4 (Winter 2006): 427.

86 Hernández, "The Crimes and Consequences": 429; Calavita, *Inside the State*: 217.

87 Calavita, *Inside the State*: 32–36.

88 Nevins, "Deportations of Mexican-Origin People in the United States," in Oboler and González, eds., *Oxford Encyclopedia*, vol. 1: 497; Calavita, *Inside the State*: 47.

89 García, *Operation Wetback*: 159–160.

90 Ibid., 175.

91 Undocumented workers were often called *mojados* or "wetbacks." The term "wetback" first came into use around 1929 to define a person who illegally immigrated across the Rio Grande from Mexico to the United States. Although "wetback" is not classified by the *Oxford English Dictionary* or by most major U.S. dictionaries as offensive, its origins are controversial. See *The Oxford English Dictionary*, 2nd ed., Vol. XX, comp. J. A. Simpson and E. S. C. Weiner (Oxford: Clarendon Press, 1989), s.v. "wet." For one scholar's perspective about the term's offensiveness, see García, *Operation Wetback*: xvi.

92 Garcia, *Operation Wetback*: 183.

93 Ibid., 217.

94 Nevins, "Deportations of Mexican-Origin People in the United States," in Oboler and González, eds., *Oxford Encyclopedia*, vol. 1: 497.

95 García, *Operation Wetback*: 192–193, 207.

96 Gonzales, *Mexicanos: A History of Mexicans in the United States*: 177.

97 Gómez-Quiñones, *Chicano Politics: Reality and Promise, 1940–1990*: 45–48.

98 Ibid., 75–77. Hispanic Texans' participation varied according to the election procedures in their locality.

99 Gonzales, *Mexicanos: A History of Mexicans in the United States:* 181–190; Marquez, *LULAC: The Evolution of a Mexican American Political Organization:* 53–55. Gonzales identifies two cases: *Mendez et al. v. Westminster School District of Orange County* (1947) and *Delgado v. Bastrop Independent School District* (1948), which dismantled de jure school segregation in California and Texas, respectively. LULAC was involved in both class action lawsuits.

100 Gómez-Quiñones, *Chicano Politics: Reality and Promise, 1940–1990*: 66–67; Gonzales, *Mexicanos: A History of Mexicans in the United States*: 189–190.

101 Gómez-Quiñones, *Chicano Politics: Reality and Promise, 1940–1990*: 88–89.

102 Ibid., 88–92; Louis F. Weschler and John F. Gallagher, "Viva Kennedy," in Rocco J. Tresolini and Richard T. Frost, eds., *Cases in American National Government and Politics* (Englewood Cliffs, NJ: Prentice-Hall, Inc., 1966): 53–59; Eugene C. Lee and William Buchanan, "The 1960 Election in California," *Western Political Quarterly* 14, no. 1, part 2 (March 1961): 309–326.

103 Gómez-Quiñones, *Chicano Politics: Reality and Promise, 1940–1990*: 92.

104 Gonzales, *Mexicanos: A History of Mexicans in the United States*, 194–195; Gomez-Quinones, *Chicano Politics, Reality and Promise, 1940–1990*: 104–105. For a summary of the Chicano movement, see Jorge Mariscal, "Chicano/a Movement," in Oboler and González, eds., *Oxford Encyclopedia of Latinos and Latinas in the United States*, vol. 1: 320–321.

105 Gómez-Quiñones, *Chicano Politics, Reality and Promise, 1940–1990*: 101–105. See also pp. 92–97.

106 Ibid., 93–96, 108.

107 *Congressional Record*, Senate, 90th Cong., 1st sess. (18 May 1967): 13242–13243.

108 *Congressional Record*, House, 91st Cong., 1st sess. (3 April 1969): 8590–8591.

109 For more on MAYO, see Gómez-Quiñones, *Chicano Politics: Reality and Promise, 1940–1990*: 110–112, 128–131; Armando Navarro, "Mexican American Youth Organization," in Oboler and González, eds., *Oxford Encyclopedia*, vol. 3: 122–123; *Congressional Record*, House, 91st Cong., 1st sess. (29 April 1969): 10779. For a longer discussion, see *Congressional Record*, House, 91st Cong., 1st sess. (28 April 1969): 10522–10527.

110 See, for example, *Congressional Record*, House, 91st Cong., 1st sess. (16 April 1969): 9308–9309.

111 *Congressional Record*, House, 91st Cong., 1st sess. (22 April 1969): 9952.

112 Ralph Nader Congress Project, *Citizens Look at Congress: Henry B. Gonzalez: Democratic Representative from Texas* (Washington, D.C.: Grossman Publishers, 1972): 17.

113 "Rep. Gonzalez Strikes Back at 'Uncle Tom' Criticism," 29 May 1969, *Dallas Morning News*.

114 Edna Acosta-Belén and Carlos E. Santiago, *Puerto Ricans in the United States: A Contemporary Portrait* (Boulder, CO: Lynne Rienner Publishers, 2006): 28.

115 Acosta-Belén and Santiago, *Puerto Ricans in the United States*: 28–29, 46–47.

116 Ibid., 81.

117 J. Hernández-Alvarez, "The Movement and Settlement of Puerto Rican Migrants within the United States, 1950–1960," *International Migration Review* 2, no. 2 (Spring 1968): 40–41. In 1960, 85 to 90 percent of Puerto Ricans lived in *colonias*. Ibid., 51.

118 Acosta-Belén and Santiago, *Puerto Ricans in the United States*: 54–57; Angelo Falcon, "A History of Puerto Rican Politics in New York City: 1860s to 1945," in James Jennings and Monte Rivera, eds., *Puerto Rican Politics in Urban America* (Westport, CT: Greenwood Press, 1984): 21, 35; Hernández-Alvarez, "The Movement and Settlement of Puerto Rican Migrants within the United States": 47–50.

119 Acosta-Belén and Santiago, *Puerto Ricans in the United States*: 85.

120 César J. Ayala and Rafael Bernabe, *Puerto Rico in the American Century: A History since 1898* (Chapel Hill: University of North Carolina Press, 2007): 180–181.

121 Ayala and Bernabe, *Puerto Rico in the American Century*: 197.

122 "The Migrants," *The Wilson Quarterly* 4, no. 2 (Spring 1980): 141.

123 Ayala and Bernabe, *Puerto Rico in the American Century*: 180–181; Hernández-Alvarez, "The Movement and Settlement of Puerto Rican Migrants within the United States, 1950–1960": 41, 43.

124 "Letter to the Times: Economy of Puerto Rico," 7 August 1947, *New York Times*. 20.

125 Ayala and Bernabe, *Puerto Rico in the American Century*: 195; Acosta-Belén and Santiago, *Puerto Ricans in the United States*: 78.

126 "Guidance Is Asked for Puerto Ricans," 28 October 1947, *New York Times*: 17.

127 Translated by the authors from "En el Jet 55, a Nueva New York en un brinco." See Acosta-Belén and Santiago, *Puerto Ricans in the United States*: 70.

128 Ayala and Bernabe, *Puerto Rico in the American Century*: 194; "The Migrants": 144–145.

129 Jennings, "Introduction: The Emergence of Puerto Rican Electoral Activism in Urban America": 5, 6.

130 Falcon, "A History of Puerto Rican Politics in New York City: 1860s to 1945": 15, 18. The earliest of these organizations, including the Hermandad Puertorriqueña en América (Porto Rican Brotherhood of America), were formed in 1923 to help migrants adjust to life on the mainland and to offer protection from civil rights abuses. It also inspired the Liga Puertorriqueña e Hispana (Puerto Rican and Hispanic League) in 1927 as well as a variety labor and civic clubs. See Acosta-Belén and Santiago, *Puerto Ricans in the United States*: 56.

131 Quoted in Falcon, "A History of Puerto Rican Politics in New York City: 1860s to 1945": 22; Acosta-Belén and Santiago, *Puerto Ricans in the United States*: 70.

132 Quoted in Falcon, "A History of Puerto Rican Politics in New York City: 1860s to 1945": 22.

133 Jennings, "Introduction: The Emergence of Puerto Rican Electoral Activism in Urban America," in Jennings and Rivera, eds., *Puerto Rican Politics in Urban America*: 7; Sherrie Baver, "Puerto Rican Politics in New York City: The Post-World War II Period," in Jennings and Rivera, eds., *Puerto Rican Politics in Urban America*: 44–45. The first Puerto Rican elected to state office, Oscar Garcia Rivera, who won a state assembly seat representing East Harlem in 1937, ran on a Republican-American Labor fusion platform. See Falcon, "A History of Puerto Rican Politics in New York City: 1860s to 1945": 32.

134 Baver, "Puerto Rican Politics in New York City: The Post-World War II Period": 43, 46.

135 Peter Kihss, "Badillo Decries Name for School," 20 April 1976, *New York Times*: 9.

136 Murray Schumach, "New Congressional Panel Will Investigate City's Antipoverty Agencies," 4 April 1971, *New York Times*: 38.

137 Baver, "Puerto Rican Politics in New York City: The Post-World War II Period": 49, 53; Jennings, "Introduction: The Emergence of Puerto Rican Electoral Activism in Urban America": 8.

138 Jennings, "Introduction: The Emergence of Puerto Rican Electoral Activism in Urban America": 10–11.

139 Surendra Bhana, *The United States and the Development of the Puerto Rican Status Question, 1936–1968* (Lawrence: The University Press of Kansas, 1975): 93.

140 Bhana, *The United States and the Development of the Puerto Rican Status Question, 1936–1968*: 110.

141 For a more detailed analysis of the PPD's shift on status, see Robert W. Anderson, *Party Politics in Puerto Rico* (Stanford, CA: Stanford University Press, 1965): 55–57; Bhana, *The United States and the Development of the Puerto Rican Status Question, 1936–1968*: 73–92; Richard E. Sharpless, "Puerto Rico," in Robert J. Alexander, ed., *Political Parties of the Americas* (Westport, CT: Greenwood Press, 1982): 620–621.

142 Helfeld, "Congressional Intent and Attitude toward Public Law 600 and the Constitution of the Commonwealth of Puerto Rico": 309–310.

143 Alfredo Montalvo-Barbot, *Political Conflict and Constitutional Change in Puerto Rico, 1898–1952* (Lanham, MD: University Press of America, 1997): 118–120.

144 The push for greater Puerto Rican autonomy had bipartisan backing in Congress. See Bhana, *The United States and the Development of the Puerto Rican Status Question, 1936–1968*: 101–102, 116; A. W. Maldonado, *Luis Muñoz Marín: Puerto Rico's Democratic Revolution* (San Juan: La Editorial Universidad de Puerto Rico, 2006): 285–286; Helfeld, "Congressional Intent and Attitude toward Public Law 600": 260.

145 A. W. Maldonado, who later served as the *San Juan Star*'s chief Washington correspondent, recalls the last-minute passage in detail in his biography of Luis Muñoz Marín. See Maldonado, *Luis Muñoz Marín: Puerto Rico's Democratic Revolution*: 260–261.

146 The Senate stripped the final legislation of the additional powers permitted the governor by the House proposal, including the ability to appoint members of the Puerto Rican supreme court. Under the final provision, Congress also retained the right to annul Puerto Rican laws. See Joseph Hearst, "New Puerto Rico Law Held Step for Autonomy," 10 August 1947, *Chicago Daily Tribune*: 4.

147 Bhana, *The United States and the Development of the Puerto Rican Status Question, 1936–1968*: 99.

148 Ibid., 100.

149 Antonio Fernós-Isern, "The Significance of the Reform," (lecture, Woodrow Wilson School of Public and Foreign Affairs, Princeton University, Princeton, NJ, May 5, 1948), published by the Office of Puerto Rico, Washington, D.C.; Helfeld, "Congressional Intent and Attitude toward Public Law 600": 259. The concept of an autonomous relationship with the United States had antecedents as far back as the 1920s. See Bhana, *The United States and the Development of the Puerto Rican Status Question, 1936–1968*: 109.

150 Bhana, *The United States and the Development of the Puerto Rican Status Question, 1936–1968*: 114–115, 140.

151 Ayala and Bernabe, *Puerto Rico in the American Century*: 163; Maldonado, *Luis Muñoz Marín: Puerto Rico's Democratic Revolution*: 316; Bhana, *The United States and the Development of the Puerto Rican Status Question, 1936–1968*: 134.

152 Maldonado, *Luis Muñoz Marín: Puerto Rico's Democratic Revolution*: 286.

153 Ibid., 287, 292. Muñoz Marín and Fernós-Isern did not want to upset Puerto Rico's favorable economic relationship with the United States, which specified that federal taxes collected on the island were diverted to Puerto Rican coffers. Seeking a voting representative in Congress was also unacceptable, as that would entail the assumption of a federal tax burden.

154 Ibid., 291.

155 Helfeld, "Congressional Intent and Attitude toward Public Law 600": 258; "Puerto Rico Constitution," *CQ Almanac 1950*, 6th ed. (Washington, D.C.: Congressional Quarterly, 1951): 409.

156 *Congressional Record*, House, 81st Cong., 2nd sess. (30 June 1950): 9585. Senator Joseph O'Mahoney of Wyoming and Senator Butler introduced a similar measure in the Senate, S. 3336, on March 31. The Senate and House versions were nearly identical, but the Senate version contained two more clauses highlighting Puerto Rico's right to self-government. See also Bhana, *The United States and the Development of the Puerto Rican Status Question, 1936–1968*: 126.

157 Representative Jacob Javits of New York also criticized the measure because it limited Puerto Ricans' status options, though Javits ultimately supported the bill. See "Puerto Rico Constitution": 409; http://library.cqpress.com/cqalmanac/cqal50-1378197; Helfeld, "Congressional Intent and Attitude toward Public Law 600": 269.

158 *Congressional Record*, House, 81st Cong., 2nd sess. (30 June 1950): 9586.

159 "Puerto Rico Constitution": 409; http://library.cqpress.com/cqalmanac/cqal50-1378197. Marcantonio's amendment was the only one that stood for a roll call vote. The final measure passed by voice vote. See Montalvo-Barbot, *Political Conflict and Constitutional Change in Puerto Rico:* 132; *Congressional Record*, House, 81st Cong., 2nd sess. (30 June 1950): 9601–9602.

160 Quoted in Helfeld, "Congressional Intent and Attitude toward Public Law 600," 269; *Congressional Record*, House, 81st Cong., 2nd sess. (30 June 1950): 9601. The Legislative Reorganization Act of 1946 had placed the jurisdiction of the Insular Affairs Committee (which the act also abolished) under the Public Lands Committee.

161 *Congressional Record*, House, 81st Cong., 2nd sess. (30 June 1950): 9602.

162 "Puerto Rico Hails Its 'Independence,'" 5 July 1950, *New York Times*: 24.

163 "Puerto Rico Hails Its 'Independence.'"

164 Ayala and Bernabe, *Puerto Rico in the American Century*: 168.

165 Maldonado, *Luis Muñoz Marín: Puerto Rico's Democratic Revolution*: 312–313; Helfeld, "Congressional Intent and Attitude toward Public Law 600": 272–273. See also Montalvo-Barbot, *Political Conflict and Constitutional Change in Puerto Rico*: 135; Bhana, *The United States and the Development of the Puerto Rican Status Question, 1936–1968*: 145.

166 The remaining four articles covered municipal organization, taxes, government salaries, and other administrative tasks. See Montalvo-Barbot, *Political Conflict and Constitutional Change in Puerto Rico*: 135–136.

167 S. Gálvez Maturana, "Constituyente aprueba proyecto de constitución con votación de 88 a 3," 5 February 1952, *El mundo* (San Juan, PR): 1.

168 Antonio Fernós-Isern, *Original Intent in the Constitution of Puerto Rico*, 2nd ed. (Hato Rey, PR: Lexis-Nexis of Puerto Rico, Inc., 2002): 48. The bill of rights was authored by a committee chaired by future Resident Commissioner Jaime Benítez.

169 Fernós-Isern, *Original Intent in the Constitution of Puerto Rico*: xii.

170 Maldonado, *Luis Muñoz Marín: Puerto Rico's Democratic Revolution*: 315.

171 Bayron Toro, *Elecciones y partidos políticos de Puerto Rico, 1809–2000*: 215; "Caribbean Charter," 9 March 1952, *Washington Post*: B4; "Letters to the Times," 17 March 1952, *New York Times*: 20; Montalvo-Barbot, *Political Conflict and Constitutional Change in Puerto Rico*: 135–136; Anthony Leviero, "Truman Endorses Puerto Rican Code," 23 April 1952, *New York Times*: 10.

172 Helfeld, "Congressional Intent and Attitude toward Public Law 600": 263; "Puerto Rico Constitution": 409; http://library.cqpress.com/cqalmanac/cqal50-1378197; Bhana, *The United States and the Development of the Puerto Rican Status Question, 1936–1968*: 151.

173 Helfeld, "Congressional Intent and Attitude toward Public Law 600": 277; Bhana, *The United States and the Development of the Puerto Rican Status Question, 1936–1968*: 123.

174 "Puerto Rico Constitution," in *CQ Almanac 1952*, 8th ed. (Washington, D.C.: Congressional Quarterly, 1953): 231–232, http://library.cqpress.com/cqalmanac/cqal52-1381241; Helfeld, "Congressional Intent and Attitude toward Public Law 600": 275; Montalvo-Barbot, *Political Conflict and Constitutional Change in Puerto Rico*: 136–137; House Committee on Insular Affairs, *Approving the Constitution of the Commonwealth of Puerto Rico Which Was Adopted by the People of Puerto Rico on March 3, 1952*, 82nd Cong., 2nd sess., 1952, H. Rep. 1832; *Congressional Record*, House, 82nd Cong., 2nd sess. (28 May 1952): 6167–6168.

175 Helfeld, "Congressional Intent and Attitude toward Public Law 600": 293–295.

176 Ibid., 289.

177 *Congressional Record*, House, 82nd Cong., 2nd sess. (28 May 1952): 6169.

178 Ibid., 6172.

179 The amendment also altered Section 5, which mentioned compulsory education, to permit Puerto Ricans to use private schools. See *Congressional Record*, House, 82nd Cong., 2nd sess. (28 May 1952): 6181.

180 *Congressional Record*, House, 82nd Cong., 2nd sess. (28 May 1952): 6175.

181 See, for example, the remarks of Noah Mason of Illinois; *Congressional* Record, House, 82nd Cong., 2nd sess. (28 May 1952): 6172–6173.

182 Maldonado, *Luis Muñoz Marín: Puerto Rico's Democratic Revolution*: 318–319; quoted on 321–322; Helfeld, "Congressional Intent and Attitude toward Public Law 600": 302; *Congressional Record*, Senate, 82nd Cong., 2nd sess. (23 June 1952): 7841. Critics on the Senate Floor and in Puerto Rico accused Senator Johnston of taking vengeance on the Muñoz Marín administration. (Muñoz Marín had earlier rejected a request from Leonard Long, a contractor and a friend of Senator Johnston's, for a special tax exemption in Puerto Rico.) The *Washington Post*, the *New York Times*, and *El mundo* ran editorials against Johnston. See, for example "Human Rights in Puerto Rico," 27 May 1952, *New York Times*: 26; "Nullification," 25 June 1952, *Washington Post*: 14. Columnist Drew Pearson lobbied on behalf of Muñoz Marín. See Maldonado, *Luis Muñoz Marín: Puerto Rico's Democratic Revolution*: 319.

183 *Congressional Record*, Senate, 82nd Cong., 2nd sess. (23 June 1952): 7848, 7851; Maldonado, *Luis Muñoz Marín: Puerto Rico's Democratic Revolution*: 322; Helfeld, "Congressional Intent and Attitude toward Public Law 600": 299; *Congressional Record*, Senate, 82nd Cong., 2nd sess. (23 June 1952): 7846.

184 "Puerto Rico Constitution": 231–232; http://library.cqpress.com/cqalmanac/cqal52-1381241; Helfeld, "Congressional Intent and Attitude toward Public Law 600": 304.

185 Ayala and Bernabe, *Puerto Rico in the American Century*: 164, 169; Bhana, *The United States and the Development of the Puerto Rican Status Question, 1936–1968*: 165. Muñoz Marín concluded, "The bill's importance is moral rather than practical." Quoted in Ayala and Bernabe, *Puerto Rico in the American Century*: 169; from Zapata Oliveras (Spanish source).

186 Maldonado, *Luis Muñoz Marín: Puerto Rico's Democratic Revolution*: 298.

187 Ibid., 321.

188 Ibid., 327; "Puerto Rico Hoists Flag of Autonomy," 26 July 1952, *New York Times*: 11.

189 Quoted in *Political Conflict and Constitutional Change in Puerto Rico, 1898–1952*: 141. Other news magazines proclaimed a similar end of colonialism on the island; see, for example, "Retreat from Power," *New Republic* 126, no. 22 (2 June 1952): 8.

190 Ayala and Bernabe, *Puerto Rico in the American Century*: 172–173.

191 *Congressional Record*, House, 83rd Cong., 2nd sess. (26 July 1954): 12088.

192 Bhana, *The United States and the Development of the Puerto Rican Status Question, 1936–1968*: 165.

193 See Ayala and Bernabe, *Puerto Rico in the American Century*: 173–174 for an overview of the court challenges.

194 "Puerto Rico Commission," in *CQ Almanac 1964*, 20th ed. (Washington, D.C.: Congressional Quarterly, 1965): 434–435; see http://library.cqpress.com/cqalmanac/cqal64-1304813/ (accessed 8 May 2012).

195 Roland I. Perusse, *The United States and Puerto Rico: The Struggle for Equality* (Malabar, FL: Robert E. Krieger, 1990): 43.

196 *Congressional Record*, House, 91st Cong., 2nd sess. (23 April 1970): 12996.

197 Pedro Roman, "Benitez Says Island's Future Depends on Bonds with U.S.," 10 August 1968, *San Juan Star*: 3.

198 Interview with Jaime Benítez, Former Resident Commissioner of Puerto Rico, "Should Puerto Rico Be a State?: No," 11 April 1977, *U.S. News & World Report*: 47.

199 Montalvo-Barbot, *Conflict and Constitutional Change in Puerto Rico*: 134.

200 *Congressional Record*, House, 81st Cong., 2nd sess. (30 November 1950): 16004.

201 "400 in Puerto Rico Lay Down All Arms," 3 November 1950, *New York Times*: 1.

202 "Assassin Enters Plea of Not Guilty; Judge Delays Setting Date For Trial," 18 November 1950, *New York Times*: 8; "Rulers of the World Felicitate Truman," 3 November 1950, *New York Times*: 20.

203 Paul P. Kennedy, "Truman Assassin Sentenced to Die," 7 April 1951, *New York Times*: 1.

204 John Fisher, "5 Congressmen Shot Down," 2 March 1954, *Chicago Daily Tribune*: 1; "Communist Plot Charged," 2 March 1954, *New York Times*: 19.

205 Fisher, "5 Congressmen Shot Down"; "Communist Plot Charged."

206 "Attack Seen Red Inspired," 2 March 1954, *Baltimore Sun*: 7. Fernós-Isern also revealed that New York police had informed him the previous month that communists "mingled" with members of the Independence Party of Puerto Rico in the city and that he was "not ready to absolve" communist complicity.

207 John Fisher, "Congressmen Gun Victims All May Live," 3 March 1954, *Chicago Daily Tribune*: 1.

208 William M. Blair, "Regrets Voiced by Muñoz Marín," 3 March 1954, *New York Times*: 14. Speaker Martin relates a vivid account of the March 1 shooting in Joe Martin, *My First Fifty Years in Politics, as told to Robert J. Donovan* (New York: McGraw-Hill, 1960): 216–220.

209 José E. Rios, "The Office of Resident Commissioner of Puerto Rico," M.A. thesis, Georgetown University, 1969: 54. Rios worked in the office of Resident Commissioner Santiago Polanco-Abreu from 1964 to 1968.

210 Rios, "The Office of Resident Commissioner of Puerto Rico": 50.

211 Ibid., 51–52, 55.

212 "The Editor's Sunday Memo," 23 August 1964, *San Juan Star*: 19; "The Editor's Sunday Memo," 30 August 1964, *San Juan Star*: 19.

213 "Polanco Abreu: A Will With an IBM's Grasp," 17 August 1964, *San Juan Star*: 15; Margot Preece, "Resident Commissioner or House Member—Problem for Polanco," 21 August 1964, *San Juan Star*: 3.

214 *Congressional Record*, House, 83rd Cong., 2nd sess. (21 June 1954): 8548.

215 The House had already authorized a Delegate for the District of Columbia on September 22, 1970. See P.L. 91-405, 84 Stat. 852.

216 Hearing before the Senate Subcommittee on Territories and Insular Affairs, Committee on Interior and Insular Affairs, *Guam and the Virgin Islands Delegate to the House of Representatives*, 92nd Cong., 2nd sess. (16 March 1972).

217 "Depth of Change," 7 November 1968, *San Juan Star*: 29.

218 "I'm a lobbyist on the inside, and the inside part of that is important," Resident Commissioner Córdova-Díaz once said. See Robert L. Asher, "'Congressman' without a Vote," 26 July 1970, *Washington Post*: B6.

219 Harry Turner, "Polanco in Congress," 23 October 1968, *San Juan Star*: 25; Eddie Lopez, "Why the Populars Lost," 8 November 1968, *San Juan Star*: 30; Harry Turner, "Cordova Diaz Talks of 'New Approach,'" 5 December 1968, *San Juan Star*: 1.

220 Robert F. Levey, "A Nonvoting Delegate Tells of His Frustrations on Hill," 5 April 1970, *Washington Post*: 53; Ralph Nader Congress Project, *Citizens Look at Congress: Jorge L. Córdova, Resident Commissioner from Puerto Rico* (Washington, D.C.: Grossman Publishers, 1972): 1; Richard L. Madden, "Badillo Says U.S. Programs Are Excluding Puerto Ricans," 5 May 1971, *New York Times*: 16; "51% in Puerto Rico Get Food Stamps," 8 October 1975, *Los Angeles Times*: 12.

221 Levey, "A Nonvoting Delegate Tells of His Frustrations on Hill." As quoted in Asher, "'Congressman' without a Vote." See also "Around Town," 21 September 1970, *Washington Post*: A22.

222 *Congressional Record*, House, 88th Cong., 2nd sess. (1 October 1964): 23425.

223 George Gedda, "House Gives P.R. Commissioner Vote," 16 September 1970, *San Juan Star*: 1.

224 For a cursory treatment of what one historian calls the "Córdova Amendment," see Tansill, "The Resident Commissioner to the United States from Puerto Rico: An Historical Perspective": 83, 98–100.

225 *Congressional Record*, House, 92nd Cong., 1st sess. (21 January 1971): 14. The House later extended these rights to the new Delegates from Guam and the U.S. Virgin Islands.

226 Philip Shenon, "In the House, But without Votes," 12 April 1985, *New York Times*: A14.

227 Skrentny, *Minority Rights Revolution*: 28–33.

228 Philip Potter, "Defense," 22 June 1956, *Baltimore Sun*: 1; Allen Drury, "Senators Weigh Cut in Military," 4 April 1955, *New York Times*: 17; George C. Herring, *From Colony to Superpower: U.S. Foreign Relations since 1776* (New York: Oxford University Press, 2008): 659. The "New Look" program was the Dwight D. Eisenhower administration's strategy to contain communist expansion while controlling the U.S. defense budget.

229 Diaz, "*El Senador*": 285–287.

230 *Congressional Record*, Senate, 81st Cong., 2nd sess. (12 May 1950): 6969. See also "New Senate Drive to Fight M'Carthy," 15 May 1950, *New York Times*: 51; William S. White, "Budenz Uses Catholic Church as a 'Shield,' Chavez Says," 13 May 1950, *New York Times*: 1; "Ten Senators Urge Repeal of Red Law," 2 October 1950, *New York Times*: 7; Diaz, "*El Senador*": 242–303.

231 *Congressional Record*, Senate, 81st Cong., 2nd sess. (12 May 1950): 6969.

232 *Congressional Record*, House, 86th Cong., 1st sess., (16 July 1959): 13925–13926. See also Untitled campaign speech, "1962 file?-5 min. TV," Box 64, Folder 1, Montoya Papers-CSWR; Gómez-Quiñones, *Chicano Politics: Reality and Promise, 1940–1990*: 44–45.

233 "Roybal Again Facing Cavnar in 30th District," 26 October 1970, *Los Angeles Times*: C2; "13 Congressmen Seek Injunction to Halt War," 26 May 1971, *Los Angeles Times*: A4.

234 *Congressional Record*, House, 92nd Cong., 1st sess. (24 March 1971): 7912.

235 *Congressional Record*, House, 91st Cong., 1st sess. (6 November 1969): 33259.

236 *Congressional Record*, House, 91st Cong., 1st sess. (10 February 1970): 3195–3196.

237 Carmen Hilda Sanjurjo, "The Educational Thought of Jaime Benítez, Chancellor of the University of Puerto Rico from 1942 to 1966," (Ph.D. diss., Columbia Teachers College, 1986): 80.

238 The U.S. House of Representatives' Special Committee to Investigate Un-American Activities, chaired by Martin Dies, Jr., of Texas, was among the groups looking into the political sympathies of university faculty. "Benítez Opposed in Puerto Rico," 1 November 1942, *New York Times*: 34; "Lovett Appointment Defended by Puerto Rico University Head," 4 April 1944, *Chicago Daily Tribune*: 11; "Defends Naming Lovett," 4 April 1944, *New York Times*: 10.

239 *Congressional Record*, House, 89th Cong., 2nd sess. (3 March 1966): 4814–4815.

240 For Badillo's and Córdova-Díaz's statements, see *Congressional Record*, House, 92nd Cong., 1st sess. (4 May 1971): 13343–13349. For Córdova-Díaz's rebuttal of Badillo's statements about Puerto Rican participation in the Vietnam War, see *Congressional Record*, House, 92nd Cong., 1st sess. (5 May 1971): 13580.

241 John A. Garcia, "Congressional Hispanic Caucus," in Oboler and González, eds., *The Oxford Encyclopedia of Latinos and Latinas in the United States,* vol. 1: 396.

242 Maurilio E. Vigil, "The Congressional Hispanic Caucus: Illusions and Realities of Power," *Journal of Hispanic Policy* 4 (1989–1990): 19.

243 Vigil, "The Congressional Hispanic Caucus": 23.

244 David Vidal, "Congressional Caucus Is Formed to Speak for Hispanic Population," 9 December 1976, *New York Times*: 32.

Party Divisions in the House of Representatives

79th–94th Congresses (1945–1977)*

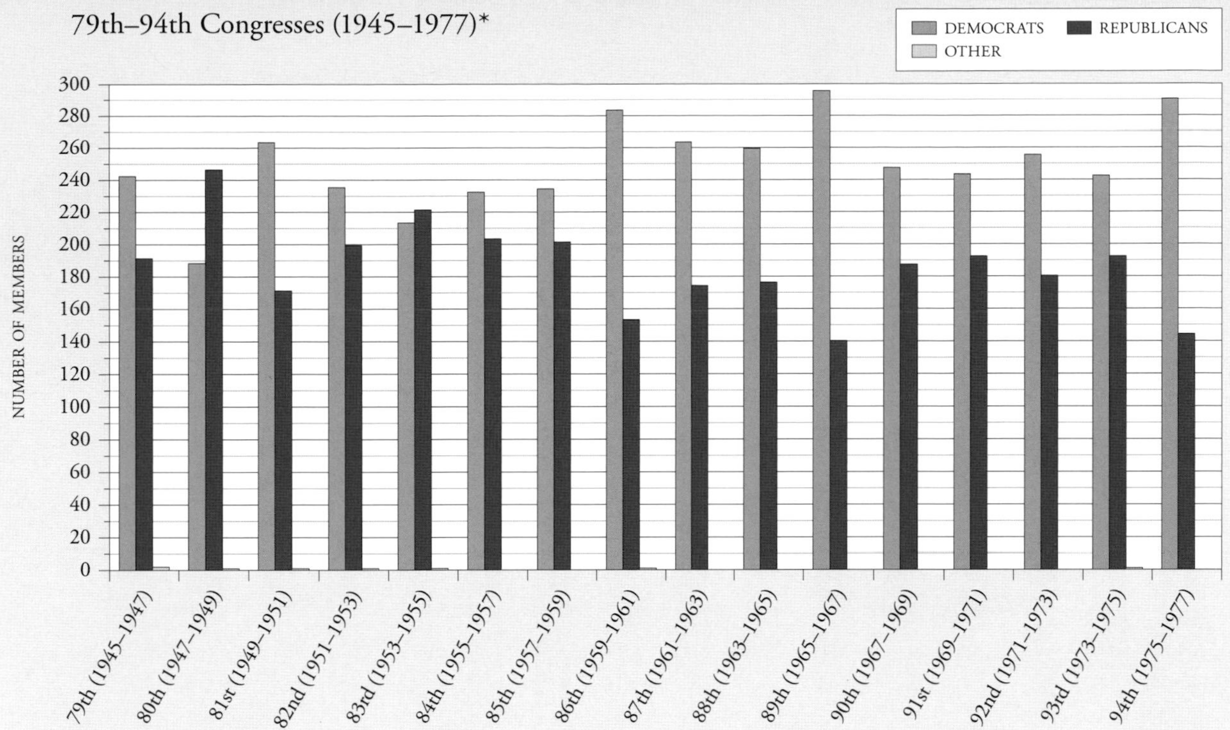

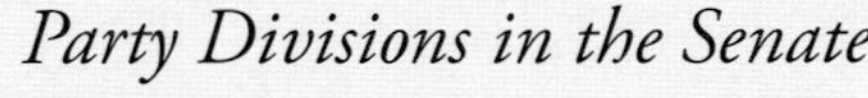

Party Divisions in the Senate

79th–94th Congresses (1945–1977)*

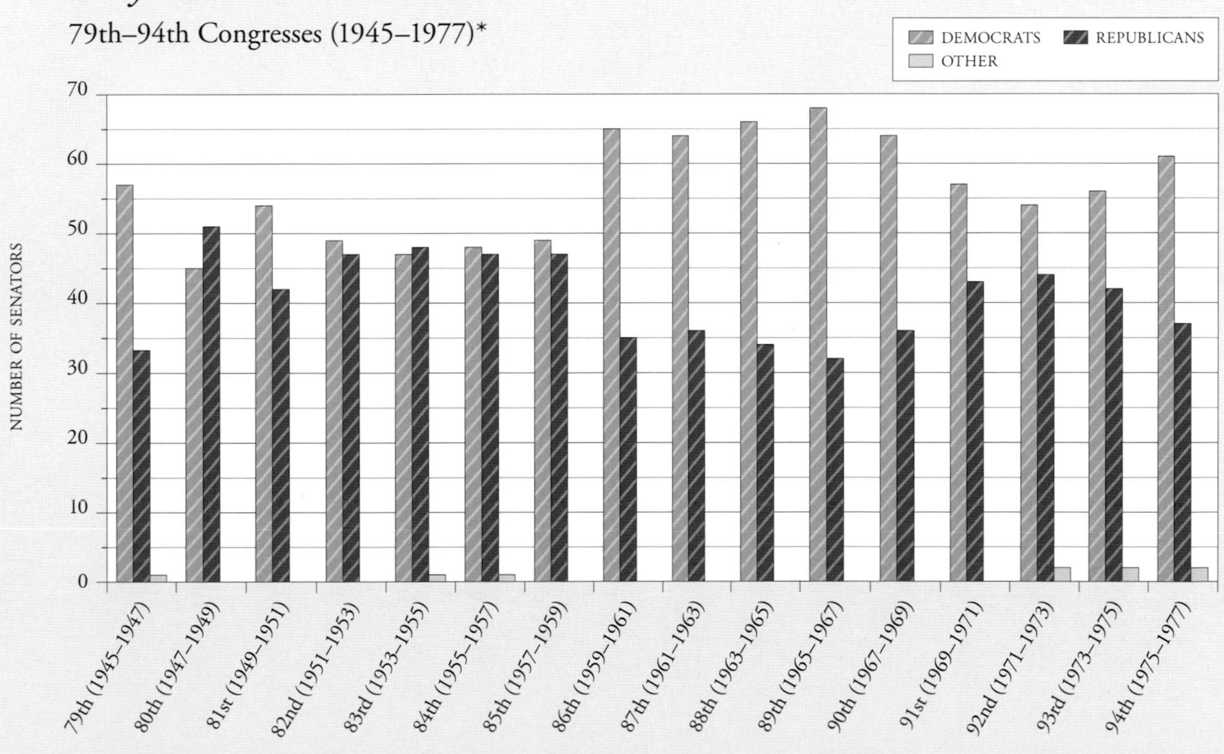

Source: Biographical Directory of the United States Congress, 1774–2005 (Washington, D.C.: Government Printing Office, 2005); also available at http://bioguide.congress.gov.; Office of the Historian, U.S. House of Representatives; U.S. Senate Historical Office.

*Party division totals are based on election day results.

Hispanic-American Members by Office†

1945–1977

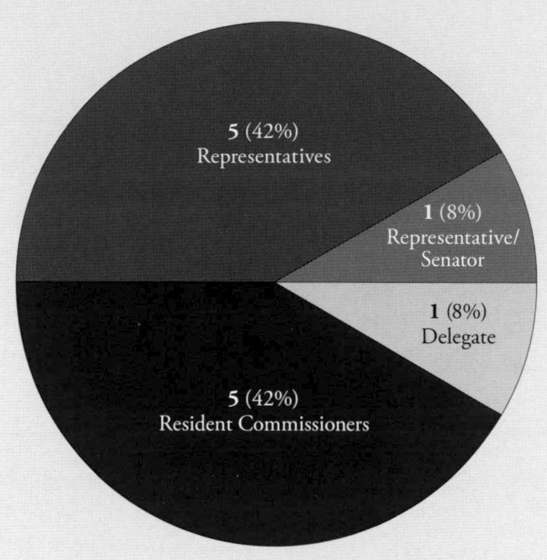

Hispanic-American Members by State and Territory†

First Elected 1945–1977

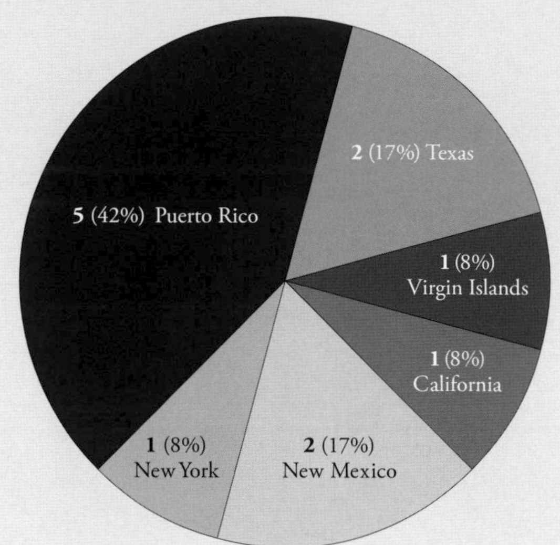

Puerto Rican Population Growth in the United States‡

1900–2010*

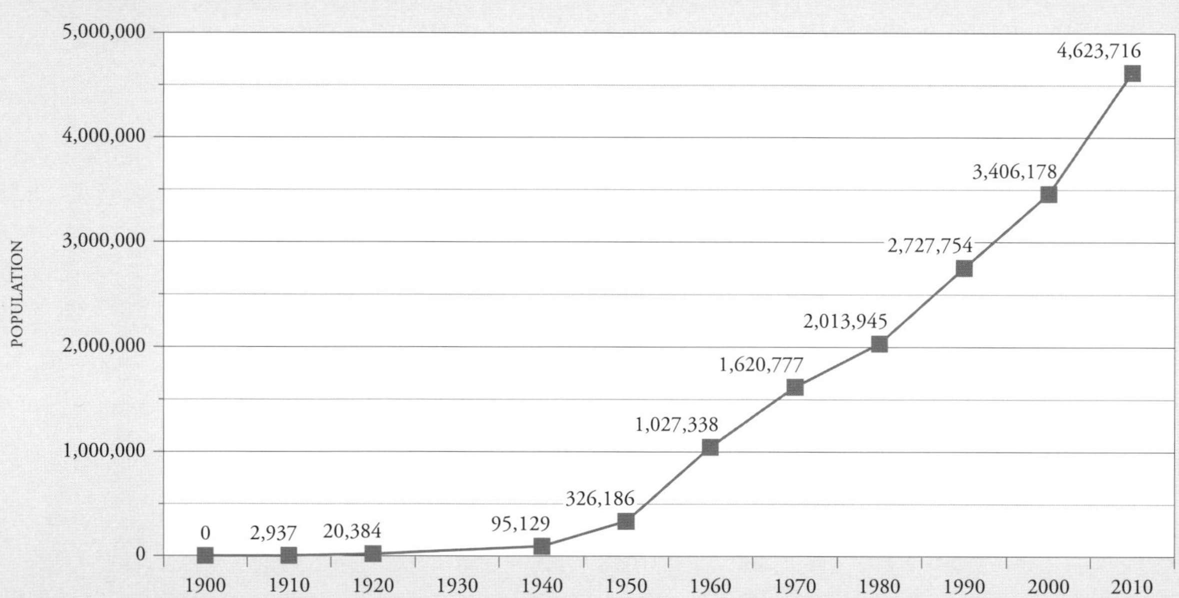

Sources: † Appendix A: Hispanic-American Representatives, Senators, Delegates, and Resident Commissioners by Congress, 1822–2012; Office of the Historian, U.S. House of Representatives; U.S. Senate Historical Office. ‡ U.S. Census Bureau; *Historical Statistics of the United States: Earliest Times to the Present, Millenial Edition*, eds. Richard Sutch and Susan B. Carter. Vol. 1. Cambridge: Cambridge University Press, 2006.

*See the U.S. Census's footnotes on their methodology over time for determining the question of "Spanish Origin." No data was taken for the year 1930. Data includes all Puerto Ricans both in Puerto Rico and on the mainland United States.

Congressional Service

For Hispanic Americans in Congress First Elected 1944–1976

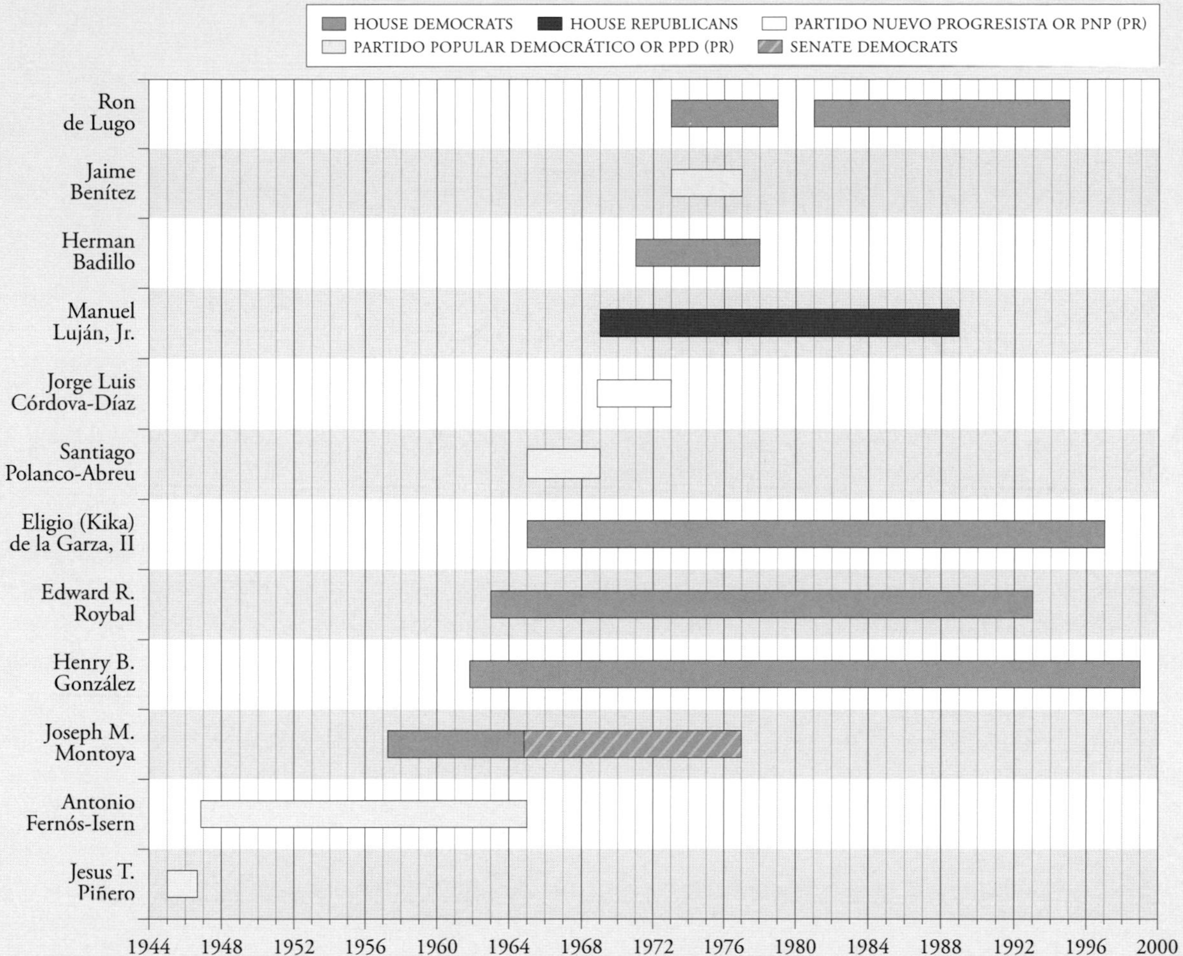

Jesús T. Piñero
1897–1952

RESIDENT COMMISSIONER 1945–1946
POPULAR DEMOCRAT FROM PUERTO RICO

A prominent landowner-turned-politician, Jesús Piñero parlayed his concern for the poor and his desire to perpetuate his family vocation into a political career. After an apprenticeship in local politics, Piñero allied himself with Luis Muñoz Marín at a pivotal time in Puerto Rican politics. Piñero's fortuitous associations and hard work enabled him to serve in Puerto Rico's senate and ultimately in the U.S. Congress. During his short tenure as Resident Commissioner, Piñero sought economic aid for Puerto Rico. His congressional career ended when President Harry S. Truman tapped him to serve as the first native-born governor of Puerto Rico in the island's 500-year history. On the eve of his winning the Resident Commissioner's seat, Piñero said, "By representing you in Washington, I will fulfill the mission that the people assigned me.... I did not ask for the assignment ... but I accept it because it is my duty ... and because I love the opportunity to serve the people."[1]

One of six siblings, Jesús Toribio Piñero was born in Carolina, Puerto Rico, on April 16, 1897, to Emilio and Josefa Jiménez Sicardo Piñero. The Piñeros were wealthy and owned a sugar plantation. After Piñero's mother died in 1905, the family moved to Rio Piedras, a suburb of San Juan, Puerto Rico's capital. Piñero studied at Xavier Preparatory School in Baltimore, Maryland, and graduated from Central High School in San Juan in 1914. He attended the University of Puerto Rico for two years and the University of Pennsylvania's School of Engineering until 1918. After returning to Puerto Rico, Piñero prepared to serve in the U.S. Army, but World War I ended before he arrived at the front. From 1918 to 1926, Piñero devoted himself to the family business, sugar cultivation. In 1931 Piñero married Aurelia Bou Ledesma. The couple raised two children, Haydee, and José Emilio. [2]

In 1926 Piñero began participating in various political groups. He was elected chair of Carolina's municipal assembly in 1928, where he served until 1933. While serving as chair, Piñero took a particular interest in improving educational opportunities for the poor and for peasant laborers. Piñero's accomplishments included opening a vocational school and teaching the poor about improving their lives, using motion picture technology.[3] Piñero's political activities took a significant turn when he became president of the Puerto Rico Sugar Cane Farmers Association. It was in this capacity that he traveled to Washington, D.C., to contest the Jones–Costigan Act (48 Stat. 670; 1928–1934), which established limits on the amount of sugar the United States could import from its territories. During this trip, Piñero worked with Luis Muñoz Marín, a member of the Puerto Rican senate and the son of former Resident Commissioner Luis Muñoz Rivera. The two men participated in a mission to obtain financial aid for Puerto Rico from the U.S. government to mitigate the destruction inflicted by a pair of hurricanes in 1928 and 1932 and the economic crisis resulting from the Great Depression. Their efforts helped obtain for the island a relief package worth more than $70 million and led to the eventual creation of the Puerto Rico Reconstruction Administration. Piñero became a member of its board in 1935. In 1936 he ran, unsuccessfully, for a Puerto Rican senate seat from the district of Humacao on the Partido Liberal (Liberal Party) ticket. After his defeat, Piñero joined Muñoz Marín's newly formed Partido Popular Democrático (Popular Democratic Party, or PPD) in 1938.[4]

The emergence of the PPD changed Puerto Rico's electoral landscape and signaled a significant change in thinking about the island's relationship with the United States. Formed out of the remains of the Partido Liberal in

Image courtesy of the Library of Congress

1938, the PPD promoted gradual political autonomy for Puerto Rico during the 1940 elections. Appealing to an emerging middle class and rural constituents, the PPD promised land and labor reforms that would benefit both. Muñoz Marín asserted that support for the PPD would be a vote for immediate social reforms instead of a vote to resolve Puerto Rico's political status. The PPD also sought support from the labor movement. One of the main differences between the Partido Liberal and the PPD concerned the issue of Puerto Rico's status. Whereas the Partido Liberal focused on Puerto Rico's eventual status as a state or an independent nation, the PPD focused on industrializing the island to improve its social and economic welfare. With the rise of the PPD, Piñero's association with the party, and his close ties to Muñoz Marín, contributed to his rapid political ascent. The PPD eventually gained power in the 1940 elections and remained as the island's dominant political party until 1968.[5]

The 1940 elections became a three-way race between the PPD and two other parties: the Coalición (the Coalition), a merger of the Republicans and Socialists; and La Unificación Puertorriqueña Tripartita (the Tripartite Puerto Rican Unification), which consisted of the remnants of Republican, Socialist, and Liberal Party insurgents. The results of the election split political power between the Coalición, which selected the Resident Commissioner, and the PPD, which controlled the Puerto Rican senate. Both groups shared power in the Puerto Rican house of representatives.[6] Piñero was elected to the Puerto Rican house of representatives by promoting the PPD platform in 1940.[7] During his tenure, Piñero served on four committees: treasury; agriculture; police, civil service and elections; and industry and commerce, which he chaired. He submitted bills for public works projects such as roads and buildings as well as bills for other public resources. He also submitted plans for special funds to combat diseases, such as malaria, and to provide aid for insolvent mothers.[8]

Piñero was one of a number of candidates for Resident Commissioner in the summer of 1944. Although Piñero received mixed reviews, he was fully endorsed by PPD leader Muñoz Marín.[9] After Piñero won the nomination, he faced three challengers. His main opponent was Manuel Font, a U.S. Army officer and a nominee of El Partido Union (the Union Party). During the campaign, *La democracia*, a party newspaper founded by Muñoz Marín's father, Luis Muñoz Rivera, described Piñero's political background and his relationship with Muñoz Marín. The newspaper commended Piñero's nomination, touting his "intimate knowledge of the procedures, manners, and methods that could be employed with the greatest success in Washington in benefit of the people of Puerto Rico" and dismissed Font as a "man of frankly conservative tendencies."[10] Piñero, the editors continued, "is not a flashy figure … he does his work quietly, with plausible honor, natural in a man that feels a duty [to] his party and his people and serves with marked devotion."[11] In a radio interview during the campaign, Piñero said the "federal government supplies certain economic and financial aid to the people of Puerto Rico … [as] a principle of responsibility and of justice, instead of mere charity or of a simple gift or of favors that you want to do what you can." Piñero observed that many in Congress did not feel an obligation to assist Puerto Ricans and said that the Resident Commissioner's task was to educate policymakers "that, while the people of Puerto Rico need help for things beyond their control … that help must be considered as a right, not as a right that is strictly demanded with the risk of creating prejudice against it, but as [a] right which is achieved by agreements within a friendly process of … understanding and mutual good faith."[12] Piñero garnered a comfortable 65 percent majority on Election Day.[13]

As the incoming Resident Commissioner, Piñero faced an immediate public relations challenge. His predecessor, Bolívar Pagán, a Socialist who had opposed the PPD, attacked the policies of controversial governor Rexford Guy Tugwell, Muñoz Marín, and the actions of the PPD. Piñero sought to dispel the negative perceptions of the Puerto Rican government that had been cultivated by Pagán and to regain the trust of alienated Members of Congress. Muñoz Marín sent Piñero a 10-page memorandum regarding his goals and the assignments he was expected to complete. Piñero was to "be Muñoz's presence in Washington; create a positive image of the Popular Party and its work on the island; and avoid at all cost ... any controversy regarding the topic of the political situation in Puerto Rico."[14] Piñero served on the following House committees: Agriculture, Insular Affairs, Labor, Military Affairs, Mines and Mining, Naval Affairs, and Territories. Some of the committees were highly desirable assignments for shaping broad policy (e.g., Naval Affairs and Agriculture), whereas others were valuable assignments for addressing local needs (e.g., Territories and Labor).[15]

When Piñero arrived in Washington in late December 1945, he met with a number of his political counterparts in executive branch agencies like the Department of the Interior, along with Senator Dennis Chavez and Representative Antonio Fernández of New Mexico, the other Hispanic-Americans Members of the 79th Congress (1945–1947).[16] One of Piñero's early initiatives was to procure aid for Puerto Rican veterans of World War II, with the help of the Puerto Rico Department of the American Legion in Washington.[17]

Piñero pursued a variety of legislative interests. His main goals were to secure economic aid for the island and to pursue Muñoz Marín's initiative of gaining greater autonomy by advocating for a plebiscite that would determine whether Puerto Rico would become an independent country or part of the United States. Like his political patron, Piñero tried to enact immediate reforms that would aid the Puerto Rican people.[18] Most of Piñero's legislation consisted of private relief bills submitted on behalf of his constituents. Among his other duties, Piñero served as an economic advocate for Puerto Rico, meeting with officials about agricultural matters, securing airline routes between the continental United States and Puerto Rico, and protecting Puerto Ricans' citizenship rights.[19] He was particularly interested in defending agricultural interests and in ensuring that Puerto Ricans were treated as U.S. citizens instead of U.S. nationals.[20] Piñero was also interested in making sure the territories received some kind of representation. He submitted H.R. 7172, a bill to amend the Organic Act of the Virgin Islands, to provide the Virgin Islands with a Resident Commissioner, and lobbied for representation in Congress.[21]

The question of Puerto Rico's political status in relation to the United States came to a head when Senator Millard Tydings of Maryland, who chaired the Senate Committee on Territories and Insular Possessions, began to push new legislation in 1945. Tydings's bill, which called for Puerto Rico's immediate independence and for a plebiscite to convene a constitutional convention, illustrated the split between Muñoz Marín, who promoted Puerto Rico's gradual movement away from its current government structure, and opposition figures within the PPD, who favored Puerto Rico's immediate independence. Muñoz Marín and Piñero wanted Puerto Ricans to choose between independence, statehood, and a form of government called "dominion status." After receiving the approval from the Puerto Rican legislature, Piñero submitted a House version of his bill (H.R. 3237), and Tydings submitted a companion bill in the Senate (S. 1002) in May 1945.[22] During a speech on the House Floor, Piñero said the "people in Puerto Rico [should] decide democratically what they want and what course they wish to take."[23] However, C. Jasper Bell of Missouri, the chair of the House Committee on Insular Affairs, said his committee would not act on the bill unless the Senate disposed of the Tydings Bill in July 1945.[24] In an op-ed to the *Washington Post*, Piñero described the bills as "a reminder to Congress as well as to the people of the United States that two million Puerto Ricans ... ardently desire something better than the status of a subject, colonial people." He also reiterated Muñoz Marín's desire that "no particular form of political status should be forced upon Puerto Rico, that Congress should define the possibilities and permit the people to choose" their desired form of government.[25]

On behalf of the Puerto Rican legislature, Piñero met with President Truman on August 21, 1945, to ask for support for the Tydings–Piñero bill.[26] Truman took a middle course, encouraging Congress to reach a solution that would be acceptable to the majority of Puerto Ricans while taking care not to yield its constitutional authority over unincorporated territories. To the three types of government outlined in the Tydings–Piñero bill Truman added a fourth option that enabled the people to elect their own governor. "It is now time … to ascertain from the people of Puerto Rico their wishes as to the ultimate status which they prefer, and, within such limits as may be determined by the Congress, to grant them the kind of government which they desire," Truman declared in October.[27]

Piñero contrasted the wave of postwar immigration with Puerto Rico's dependent status. After observing, "One half of the world's population is made up of dependent peoples under some form of colonial rule," Piñero noted that colonial powers such as France and Great Britain had relinquished some control to their colonies. Piñero judged the United States' relationship with Puerto Rico to be ironic. "In view of our own origin as a free nation, we today hold sovereignty over dependent peoples, all of them American citizens, but denied the rights that American citizenship symbolizes to the rest of the world," he said. Piñero characterized U.S. sovereignty over the territories as benevolent, but noted, "Benign rule does not excuse our failure to live up to our American principles of granting the fullest enjoyment of … democracy to all citizens under the Stars and Stripes."[28] Although the Tydings–Piñero bill died in committee, the idea of a plebiscite to determine the structure of Puerto Rico's government persisted, culminating in the passage of the Elective Governor Act in 1947.

During the second session of the 79th Congress, Piñero continued to perform his duties as Resident Commissioner, and he also became involved in the selection of a new governor for Puerto Rico. Governor Tugwell's tenure was scheduled to end in June 1946, and Secretary of the Interior Julius Krug suggested Piñero as his successor. Krug's recommendation was seconded by the Puerto Rican legislature in July 1946.[29] Upon receiving the news of his appointment by President Truman, Piñero responded, "I feel deeply honored.… If this appointment is confirmed by the United States Senate, I will recommend myself to Divine Providence to guide me and I will ask for the cooperation of all of the people of Puerto Rico so that I may serve better both the interest of the federal government as well as the people of my island."[30] An editorial in *El mundo*, Puerto Rico's largest daily newspaper, advised readers to "interpret the appointment of Mr. Jesús T. Piñero … as a demonstration of faith in our ability to govern our own affairs. In that sense, the event merits the distinction of figuring among the most important milestones in our history and … [is a possible] precursor of other definitive measures in relation to the political status of Puerto Rico," the editorial continued.[31] The Senate confirmed Piñero's nomination on July 27, 1946. From his confirmation until his swearing-in as governor, Piñero was both Resident Commissioner and governor-elect. During that time, Piñero visited New York City, where he was greeted by the Mayor William O'Dwyer and the New York city council. He was honored with a reception after he visited Spanish Harlem.[32]

Piñero was sworn in as governor on September 3, 1946. A contemporary observer noted that Piñero was "considered by most Puerto Ricans as an interim governor, holding office only until the people achieve their long-cherished ambition to determine their permanent political status by … plebiscite."[33] One of Piñero's major legislative achievements was the passage of the Elective Governor Act (61 Stat. 770) in August 1947. The statute enabled Puerto Ricans to elect a governor by popular vote in the 1948 election cycle. Submitted by Fred Crawford of Michigan, H.R. 3309 met with little opposition in Congress. President Truman called the bill "a great step toward complete self-government," saying, "I sincerely hope that the action of the Congress will meet with the approval of the people of Puerto Rico."[34] Piñero and his successor, Antonio Fernós-Isern, attended the signing ceremony along with Crawford and a number of other government officials.[35] The act enabled Luis Muñoz Marín to run successfully for a four-year term as Puerto Rico's first elected governor.

Piñero also pursued legislative interests such as social services for the poor, land reform, and infrastructure improvements, including the purchase of a public utilities company and its oversight by a public service commission.[36]

He continued to serve as the island's ambassador by praising the island's successes in the media and advocating more opportunities for business and travel between Puerto Rico and the mainland.[37] After Muñoz Marín's election, Piñero retired from politics and returned to his business interests. At age 55, he died of a heart attack in his sleep in Canovanas, Puerto Rico, on November 19, 1952. Piñero was buried in Carolina Cemetery in Carolina, Puerto Rico.[38]

FOR FURTHER READING

Biographical Directory of the United States Congress, "Jesús T. Piñero," http://bioguide.congress.gov.

Partsch, Jaime. *Jesús T. Piñero: El exiliado en su patria* (Rio Piedras, PR: Ediciones Huracán, 2006).

MANUSCRIPT COLLECTION

Universidad del Este (Carolina, PR). *Papers*: 1897–1952, Collection includes audio and video of oral histories, photographs, films, and documents.

NOTES

1 "Yo quiero hacer claro ante ustedes ... que al representarlos a ustedes en Washington cumpliré la misión que el pueblo me encomienda.... Yo no he solicitado la encomienda ... La acepto porque es deber mío ... y porque amo la oportunidad de servir al pueblo." "Jesús T. Piñero, candidato Popular para Comisionado Residente," 5 November 1944, *El mundo* (San Juan, PR): 7. Translated as "Jesús T. Piñero, Popular Candidate for Resident Commissioner" by Translations International, Inc. (July 2011).

2 Olga Jiménez Wagenheim, "Piñero, Jesús Toribio," *American National Biography* 17 (New York: Oxford University Press, 1999): 542–543 (hereinafter referred to as *ANB*); Teofilo Maldonado, "Piñero dice su labor primordial sera hacer que el pueblo Americano comprenda bien al nuestro," 3 December 1944, *El mundo*: 7. For an extensive history of the Piñero family, see Jaime Partsch, *Jesús T. Piñero: El exiliado en su patria* (Rio Piedras, PR: Ediciones Huracán, 2006): 14–18.

3 Wagenheim, "Piñero, Jesús Toribio," *ANB.*

4 Wagenheim, "Piñero, Jesús Toribio," *ANB*; César J. Ayala and Rafael Bernabe, *Puerto Rico in the American Century: A History since 1898* (Chapel Hill: University of North Carolina Press, 2010): 100–101. For more information about Munoz Marín, see Olga Jiménez Wagenheim, "Muñoz Marín, Luis," *ANB* 16 (New York: Oxford University Press, 1999): 99–100. For a more extensive biography, see A. W. Maldonado, *Luis Muñoz Marín: Puerto Rico's Democratic Revolution* (San Juan: Editorial Universidad de Puerto Rico, 2006).

5 Wagenheim, "Piñero, Jesús Toribio," *ANB.*

6 Ayala and Bernabe, *Puerto Rico in the American Century*: 136–138, 142–144. For a detailed explanation of the 1940 election, see Fernando Bayron Toro, *Elecciones y partidos políticos de Puerto Rico, 1809–2000* (Mayagüez, PR: Editorial Isla, 2003): 191–197.

7 Wagenheim, "Piñero, Jesús Toribio," *ANB;* Partsch, *Jesús T. Piñero: El exiliado en su patria*: 66.

8 Partsch, *Jesús T. Piñero: El exiliado en su patria,* 66–70.

9 For a description of Piñero's nomination in English, see Ayala and Bernabe, *Puerto Rico in the American Century*: 153–154; and Rexford G. Tugwell, *The Stricken Land: The Story of Puerto Rico* (New York: Greenwood Press, 1968): 664. For detailed descriptions of Piñero's nomination in Spanish, see Partsch, *Jesús T. Piñero: El exiliado en su patria,* 70–75; and "Populares postulan a Piñero para comisaria," 21 August 1944, *El mundo*: 1, 4, 21.

10 "Tiene un conocimiento íntimo de los procedimientos, las maneras, los metodos que con mayor exito pueden emplearse en Washington en beneficio del pueblo de Puerto Rico ... merece la entera confianza del pueblo de Puerto Rico; saben que no violará ningún compromiso contraído por su partido con el pueblo de Puerto Rico, tanto el mandato económico que ha de dar." "El candidato a Washington, Jesús T. Piñero," 2 September 1944, *El mundo*: 1. Translated as "The Candidate to Washington, Jesús T. Piñero," by Translations International, Inc. (July 2011).

11 "Es hombre de tendencias francamente conservadoras. Unionista y luego liberal, su actitud corresponde en términos generales a la de un conservador del republicanismo a ultranza.... No es Piñero figura de relumbrón. Modesto y desinteresado, su obra la hace en silencio, con probidad plausible, propia de un hombre que se debe a su partido y a su pueblo y le sirve con marcada devoción." Wilfredo Braschi, "Dos candidatos," 13 September 1944, *El mundo*: 2. Translated as "Two Candidates," by Translations International, Inc. (July 2011).

12 "El principio de que el Gobierno Federal suministre cierta ayuda económica y financiera al pueblo de Puerto Rico es un principio de responsibilidad y de justicia, en vez de ser un principio de mera caridad o sencilla dádiva o de favores que se quiere buenamente hacer.... Muchos de nuestros amigos en Washington ... no comparten este criterio ... su actitud, con toda sinceridad y con toda buena fe. Pero hay que irles demostrando que, mientras el pueblo de Puerto Rico necesite ayuda, por ... esa ayuda se debe considerar como un derecho; no como un derecho que se reclama a rajatabla con riesgo de crear prejuicio contra él, sino como un derecho sobre el cual se llega a acuerdos dentro de un procedimento de amistad, de convencimiento, de comprensión y de mútua buena

fe." "Piñero expone la labor hará en Washington," 31 October 1944, *La democracia* (San Juan, PR): 1, 5. Translated as "Piñero Explains What Work Will Do in Washington," by Translations International, Inc. (July 2011).

13 "Election Statistics, 1920 to Present," http://history.house.gov/institution/election-statistics/election-statistics.

14 "Ser la presencia de Muñoz en Washington; crear una imagen positiva del Partido Popular y su labor en la isla; y evitar a toda costa que se desarrolle ninguna polémica sobre el tema de la situación política de Puerto Rico." Partsch, *Jesús T. Piñero: El exiliado en su patria*: 78. Translated as "The Commissioner's Agenda," by Translations International, Inc. (July 2011).

15 David T. Canon et al., eds., *Committees in the U.S. Congress, 1789–1946*, vol. 3 (Washington, D.C.: CQ Press, 2002): 830; Charles Stewart III, "Committee Hierarchies in the Modernizing House, 1875–1947," *American Journal of Political Science* 36 (1992): 845–846. Piñero's committee assignments varied widely in terms of their attractiveness to Members. According to Stewart's ranking of the desirability of 69 committees from this time period, Piñero's assignments to the House Committees on Naval Affairs and Agriculture ranked highest (7th and 8th, respectively). Military Affairs ranked 13th, Labor ranked 19th, Insular Affairs ranked 23rd, Mines and Mining ranked 25th, and Territories ranked 29th.

16 "Piñero prestara hoy juramento come comisionado en Washington," 3 January 1945, *El mundo*: 6.

17 "La cooperacion de Piñero para los veteranos," 2 January 1945, *El mundo*: 1, 16.

18 One of Piñero's early initiatives was the creation of an insular office that would plead Puerto Rico's case beyond the halls of Congress. For more information about this, see "Piñero hacia Washington en mes diciembre," 14 November 1944, *El mundo*; Charles McCabe,"Emilio Colon designado para la oficina insular en Washington," 17 September 1945, *El mundo*; "Oficina en Wáshington estará establecida en mes diciembre," 16 November 1945, *El mundo*.

19 For an example of Piñero's interest in protecting the Puerto Rican sugar market, see "Piñero escribe a la OAP y CCA sobre el azucar," 31 January 1945, *El mundo*: 14. For examples of Piñero's securing airline routes between Puerto Rico and the United States, see "Lanzaran un ataque contra las tarifas de la Pan American," 2 April 1945, *El mundo*: 1, 15; Ruth Broom, "Piñero procura contactos con la Cia. Grace," 4 November 1945, *El mundo*: 1, 3. Piñero also sought money for Puerto Rican farmers. For example, see Jean Van Vraken, "Piñero urge aprobacion de los fondos para extension agricola," 16 February 1946, *El mundo*: 1, 24. For information about Piñero's investigation of Puerto Rican soldiers' forced labor alongside Japanese prisoners of war in Hawaii, see Charles McCabe, "Piñero urge se investigue el caso de puertorriqueños en el Hawaii," 11 December 1945, *El mundo*: 1, 14.

20 *Congressional Record*, Index, 79th Cong., 2nd sess.: 640, 657. Piñero submitted H.R. 5975, a bill to amend the Nationality Act of 1940 to preserve the citizenship of a Puerto Rican born outside of the United States, and H.R. 6701, a bill to preserve the nationality of citizens residing abroad. Both bills died in committee.

21 Ibid., 668. Piñero also advocated for voting representation for the Virgin Islands. See J. T. Piñero, "Virgin Islands," 27 March 1946, *Washington Post*: 8.

22 Ayala and Bernabe, *Puerto Rico in the American Century*: 156; *Congressional Record* Index, 79th Congress, 1st sess: 757, 777, 886. For information about the deliberation and submission of H.R. 3237, see "Pedira el plebiscite la Comision Legislativa," 5 May 1945, *El mundo*: 1, 16. For a contemporary analysis of the bill, see Luis Muñoz Morales, "El Bill Tydings–Piñero; Alternativas-Plebiscito," 3 June 1945, *El mundo*: 9. The bill was popularly known as the Tydings–Piñero Bill.

23 *Congressional Record*, House, 79th Cong., 1st sess. (16 May 1945): 4660.

24 Charles McCabe,"No habra audiencias por ahora sobre el Bill Tydings–Piñero," 6 June 1945, *El mundo*: 1, 18. Congress considered three bills that called for greater political autonomy for Puerto Ricans: the Tydings plebiscite bill; the Tydings–Piñero Bill, advocating three solutions (H.R. 3237); and a bill authored by Vito Marcantonio of New York (H.R. 2781), advocating full independence. Marcantonio's bill died in committee. For a description of the bill, see *Congressional Record*, Index, 79th Cong., 1st sess.: 875; Ruth Broom, "Bill de Piñero detenido en el Comite Camara," 18 July 1945, *El mundo*: 2, 3.

25 J. T. Piñero, "Puerto Rico to Test U.S. Policy," 20 May 1945, *Washington Post*: B3.

26 "Piñero visito ayer al Pres. Truman," 22 August 1945, *El mundo*: 1, 6. During a 15-minute meeting, Piñero told Truman that the Puerto Rican legislature had voted on two occasions to dissolve the current form of government and that its intention was to decide how the government would be run in the future. Piñero said Truman was sympathetic to Puerto Ricans' point of view.

27 Harry S. Truman, "Special Message to the Congress on Puerto Rico," October 16, 1945, in John T. Woolley and Gerhard Peters, The American Presidency Project [online]. Santa Barbara, CA, http://www.presidency.ucsb.edu/ws/?pid=12314 (accessed 19 July 2012).

28 *Congressional Record*, House, 79th Cong., 2nd sess. (19 March 1946): 2424. Piñero submitted an editorial about Puerto Rico's status and, one week earlier, a critique of U.S. rule as an editorial in the *New York Times*. See *Congressional Record*, Appendix, 79th Cong., 2nd sess.: A1490–A1491.

29 For more information about Krug, see "Ex-Interior Secretary Dies," 28 March 1970, *Washington Post*: B6; and "J. A. Krug, 62, Dies; Was Truman Aide," 28 March 1970, *New York Times*: B6; "For Piñero as Governor," 10 July 1946, *New York Times*: 44.

30 "Me siento profundamente honrado, y acepto con la mayor humildad la designación que me han otorgado hoy el Presidente de los Estados Unidos.... Si el nombramiento es confirmado por el Senado de Estados Unidos, me encomendaré a la Divina providencia pare que me guíe y pediré la cooperación de todo el pueblo de Puerto Rico para asi servir mejor tanto los intereses del Gobierno Federal como los del pueblo de mi Isla." Jean Van Vraken, "Piñero recibió el nombramiento con su característica modestia," 27 July 1946, *El mundo*: 1. Translated as "Piñero Received the Appointment with His Characteristic Modesty," by Translations International, Inc. (August 2011). For a positive contemporary reaction to Piñero's nomination, see E. L. Bartlett, "Piñero 'Appointment,'" 1 August 1946, *Washington Post*: 6. Bartlett, a House colleague of Piñero's, served as Territorial Delegate to Alaska.

31 The editors also hoped Piñero's "public management can result in a new era of civil achievements for the community" while eschewing political partisanship from the PPD. The editors warned, "It is necessary to think not only of the great responsibility that the party that is in power will assume.... By claiming partisan loyalties, the Popular Democratic Party will push Mr. Pinero toward partiality, privilege and favoritism ... then its failure of the recognition that has been given to Puerto Rico would not come as a surprise." However, if the PPD "is willing to provide facilities for a better government ... and positions itself in a generous and honest position of Puerto Ricanism, then it must contribute powerfully to the triumph of Mr. Piñero in this difficult mission." "Debemos interpretarlo como un inicio del reconocimento de nuestro derecho al gobierno propio y una demostración de fe en nuestra habilidad para regir nuestros propios asuntos. En tal sentido, el acontecimiento merece la distinción de figurar entre los principales jalones de nuestra historia ... ser precursor de otras medidas definitivas en relación con el status político de Puerto Rico ... a la esperanza de que su gestión pública pueda resultar en una nueva era de realizaciones cívicas para la comunidad ... hay que pensar no solo en la gran responsibilidad que en ello tendrá el gobernador Piñero, sino también en la gran responsabilidad que asumirá el partido que está en el poder.... Si reclamando lealtades partidaristas, el Partido Popular Democrático empujara al señor Piñero a la parcialidad, al privilegio y al favoritism ... entonces no habrían de extrañar su fracaso y el fracaso del reconocimento que se le ha hecho a Puerto Rico ... el partido en el poder se dispone a brindar facilidades para una mejor obra de gobierno, y condena y destruye las malas prácticias y se sitúa en generosa e íntegra posición de portorriqueñismo, entonces habrá de contribuir poderosamente al triunfo del señor Piñero en su difícil encomienda." "El nombramiento de Piñero," 26 July 1946, *El mundo*: 6. Translated as "Piñero's appointment" by Translations International, Inc. (August 2011).

32 "Mayor to Greet Piñero," 26 July 1946, *New York Times*: 47; "Piñero Is Honored at City Ceremony," 26 August 1946, *New York Times*: 23.

33 "Puerto Rico Hails Governor Piñero," 4 September 1946, *New York Times*: 35; Paul Blanshard, "Puerto Rico Moves a Step Ahead," 4 August 1946, *New York Times*: 92.

34 Harry S. Truman, "Letter to Governor Piñero of Puerto Rico upon the Signing Bill Providing for an Elected Governor," in John T. Woolley and Gerhard Peters, The American Presidency Project [online]. Santa Barbara, CA, http://www.presidency.ucsb.edu/ws/?pid=12725 (accessed 18 April 2011).

35 C. P. Trussell, "President Enacts Puerto Rico Poll," 6 August 1947, *New York Times*: 20.

36 Wagenheim, "Piñero, Jesús Toribio," *ANB*.

37 For examples, see "Piñero Cites Gains by Puerto Ricans," 23 July 1948, *New York Times*: 7; "Puerto Rico 'Letter' Seeks New Industry," 3 August 1948, *New York Times*.

38 Wagenheim, "Piñero, Jesús Toribio," *ANB;* "Jesús T. Piñero falleció a los 55 mientras dormía," 20 November 1952, *El mundo*: 1, 12; *Biographical Directory of the United States Congress*, "Jesús T. Piñero," http://bioguide.congress.gov.

Antonio Fernós-Isern
1895–1974

RESIDENT COMMISSIONER 1946–1965
POPULAR DEMOCRAT FROM PUERTO RICO

An "unpretentious and likable physician," Antonio Fernós-Isern served in the public health sector for several decades, but the high point of his career in public service was his tenure as Puerto Rico's longest-serving Resident Commissioner in the U.S. House of Representatives.[1] "Resembling an Old World diplomat" in his pince-nez, "Tony," as he was known to his colleagues, saw Puerto Rico through some of the most transformative decades of its relationship with the United States.[2] A principal architect of the Estado Libre Asociado (Free Associated State, or ELA)—a relationship between the United States and Puerto Rico—Fernós-Isern, along with his close friend and political ally Luis Muñoz Marín, shaped Puerto Rico's autonomous status for the second half of the 20th century. Regularly defending his American connections and those of his homeland against public and sometimes violent calls for the island's independence, Fernós-Isern told his colleagues, "Our life, my life, and those of [the people] who now struggle in Puerto Rico, is the American life."[3]

Antonio Fernós-Isern was born in San Lorenzo, Puerto Rico, located in the eastern-central mountains, on May 10, 1895.[4] When he was three years old, U.S. troops invaded Puerto Rico in the Spanish-American War. "I watched American soldiers come into my little town of San Lorenzo and raise the American Flag," Fernós-Isern recalled. "I now know there were only five soldiers. At the time, I thought it was a whole battalion. I made friends with the soldiers. In fact, the first English words I learned, I learned from them."[5] Fernós-Isern attended elementary school and high school in Puerto Rico before enrolling in a medical preparatory program at the Pennsylvania Normal School in Bloomsburg. He earned his M.D. from the University of Maryland College of Physicians and Surgeons and School of Medicine in College Park in 1915.[6] Fernós-Isern completed his residency in cardiology in 1933 at Columbia University.

Fernós-Isern worked as a physician in Caguas, Puerto Rico, northwest of his hometown, before taking on a series of positions in public health. He served as the health officer for San Juan in 1919 and as Puerto Rico's assistant commissioner of health from 1920 to 1921 and from 1923 to 1931. He became commissioner of health in 1931 but resigned in 1933 when the Coalición (the Coalition) took power, working on the faculty of the School of Public Health School of Tropical Medicine until 1935. As a member of the new Partido Popular Democrático (Popular Democratic Party, or PPD), Fernós-Isern returned to his position as commissioner of health in 1942, serving during a U-boat blockade in World War II that left Puerto Ricans without food imports and close to starvation.

Representing the PPD and seeking agrarian and industrial reform for the island, Fernós-Isern ran for Resident Commissioner in 1940, but lost to Coalitionist Bolívar Pagán.[7] However, when Resident Commissioner Jesús Piñero was appointed governor of Puerto Rico in 1946, he announced his support for the PPD and tapped Fernós-Isern as his replacement.[8] Fernós-Isern's appointment surprised some Puerto Rican observers because it had been rumored that PPD leader Luis Muñoz Marín planned to select a younger man for the post. Fernós-Isern's political ideas were not well known, but his alleged advocacy of the island's independence was not considered particularly desirable in a representative to Congress.[9] One observer noted that Fernós-Isern had earned the post because of his narrow loss to Bolívar Pagán in 1940. Also, his stately demeanor was deemed beneficial for the post. "Fernós is generally praised for his personality and his broad knowledge of English," noted a reporter for *El mundo*. "In manners and appearance Fernós has the personal air of distinction of many members of the Latin

Image courtesy of the Library of Congress

American diplomatic corps, and some circles that know Fernós express the opinion that he will be an 'ambassador at the same time he is a congressman.'"[10] Though he traveled to Washington in August to meet with Piñero and familiarize himself with his duties, Fernós-Isern did not take office until September 11, 1946. The PPD's hegemony over Puerto Rico's politics throughout the 1950s and early 1960s ensured his re-election. Winning on a party slate by margins as high as 68 percent—often in four-way races between various political parties—during some of the most peaceful elections in the island's electoral history, with some of the largest voter turnouts, Fernós-Isern served 18 years, the longest tenure of any Resident Commissioner.[11] With his wife, Gertrudis (Tula) Delgado—an active member and an officer of the Puerto Rican Women's Club in Washington—he moved to 1513 Woodley Place in Northwest Washington.[12] From his sixth-floor suite in the Longworth House Office Building, Fernós-Isern accepted assignments on the Committees on Agriculture, Armed Services, and Public Lands beginning in the 80th Congress (1947–1949); he remained on these committees for the rest of his career.[13] Despite his inability as Resident Commissioner to accrue seniority on committees, Fernós-Isern increased his influence on the Agriculture Committee, which was then among the top ten House committees in terms of desirability to Members.[14]

Like his predecessors, Fernós-Isern focused first on the ailing Puerto Rican economy. Despite efforts at land reform and industrialization, Puerto Rico's per capita income was one-fourth of the U.S. average. By 1950 a drop in federal expenditures and depressed rum sales in the United States caused the island's normally "boom and bust" economy to flounder.[15] "Present conditions in Puerto Rico are simply unbelievable," Fernós-Isern observed. "Eighty percent of the population are the underprivileged classes with an income not beyond $500 a year. There is terrific economic pressure on the people."[16] Fernós-Isern pushed for and finally achieved full old-age and survivor benefits for Puerto Ricans under the Social Security Act in 1951; disability benefits were extended in 1955.[17] He also fought discrimination against native Puerto Ricans in federal jobs. A 1952 agriculture appropriation bill stipulated that the salaries for federal employees from the mainland who were based in Puerto Rico would be 25 percent higher—because of a cost of living adjustment—than those of native Puerto Ricans with similar federal jobs. "The reason for the extra pay, as I understand it, is that the cost of living, at comparable standards, has been found to be higher in the offshore areas than in the mainland," Fernós-Isern observed. "I maintain that if this is true it holds equally if your name is Smith or Martinez."[18]

U.S. import regulations on Puerto Rican sugar were a particular focus for Fernós-Isern, as they had been for the island's Resident Commissioners since the Jones–Costigan Act of 1934. In 1947 the House and Senate predicted a surplus after sugar had remained scarce during World War II. Both houses considered legislation restricting imports of Puerto Rican sugar, and a *Washington Post* reporter predicted a "hot floor fight" over the quotas assigned to various sugar-producing regions. Cuba's quota, in particular, was slated to increase, as that nation increased its wartime production at the behest of the United States.[19] Puerto Rico's quota of 910,000 tons was well below the island's capacity for production. Fernós-Isern and longtime island advocate Representative Fred L. Crawford of Michigan, who chaired the Insular Affairs Subcommittee on Territories and Insular Possessions, led the opposition to the bill, noting the restrictions on Puerto Rico's ability to refine its own product, which Fernós-Isern estimated would bring in $20 million a year, adding to an unfair balance of trade between Puerto Rico and the mainland.[20] "It is only fair that the rules of trade be applied to the island without discrimination," Fernós-Isern observed. "We have no other market than the mainland market."[21] But neither Crawford nor Fernós-Isern offered any amendments to the final bill because Fernós-Isern claimed it was too late. "Conversations went on," he noted. "Most of the sectors engaged in sugar production are agreed, and we do not want, even if we could, and we cannot, to upset the apple cart."[22] When the Sugar Act was slated for renewal in 1951, Fernós-Isern and Crawford lobbied for a higher quota. "Sugar is the backbone of the Puerto

Rican economy," Fernós-Isern stated. After the 1948 act, he noted, "Puerto Rico was not given a marketing quota sufficient to take care of its production. This hit us in the Achilles heel of our economy: 1948, 1949, 1950, and 1951 have been years of anguish for Puerto Rico."[23] Fernós-Isern's and Crawford's efforts increased Puerto Rico's quota to a more reasonable 1,080,000 tons.[24]

Puerto Rico's weak economy drove its residents' migration to the United States, particularly to the El Barrio neighborhood in New York's Upper East Side. In 1947 the Welfare Council of New York estimated that the city's population added between 1,500 and 3,000 Puerto Ricans each week.[25] Fernós-Isern attributed this wave of migration to the island's sugar dependence and its "half-way" industrialization—conditions he sought to ameliorate—coupled with its 110 percent increase in population between 1900 and 1940.[26] He promoted migration along with relief for overburdened New York City social programs, suggesting the Puerto Rican legislature establish an agency to advise migrants to the city.[27] Fernós-Isern also compared the state of the island's public health with that of postwar Europe.[28]

Fernós-Isern's focus on migration to the mainland carried over to demands for more transportation options. He proposed a measure to increase the number of steamboats for passengers between the island and the mainland, authorizing the Maritime Commission to cover half the cost of new vessels for Puerto Rican trade. (Under the current law, construction subsidies were available only for ships used for foreign trade along essential routes.) Fernós-Isern insisted the bill to increase the number of lines above prewar levels would help promote tourism on the island and boost the local economy.[29] In a rare move, the U.S. Chamber of Commerce supported the subsidy, citing the need to construct more vessels and increase foreign trade.[30]

Fernós-Isern's legacy in the House was the transformation of the relationship between the U.S. government and Puerto Rico. Assisted by political maneuvering on the part of Muñoz Marín, Fernós-Isern changed Puerto Rico from a territory that was governed by the relatively restrictive provisions of the 1917 Jones Act to a free associated state—an autonomous position unique to Puerto Rico. Fernós-Isern capitalized on the international attention on the island's status that resulted from Governor Rexford Tugwell's controversial leadership throughout the 1940s as well as on the drive toward decolonization after the Second World War.[31]

On August 4, 1947, President Harry S. Truman signed the Crawford–Butler Act, marking the first time an unincorporated U.S. territory was permitted to elect its own governor, and fulfilling a request made by the Puerto Rican legislature as early as 1943.[32] Chairman Crawford sponsored the bill in the House, and a similar piece of legislation was introduced in the Senate by Hugh Butler of Nebraska. Fernós-Isern remained quiet during House debate on the bill but spoke extensively in its favor during committee hearings. "What are the political aspirations of the people of Puerto Rico?" he asked the Senate Subcommittee on Territories and Insular Affairs. "The political aspirations of the people of Puerto Rico may be summed up by stating that we consider ourselves as belonging in the world of democracy.... Our maturity within a democratic republican system of government should indeed be recognized" after a half century.[33] In 1948, Muñoz Marín and his PPD Party won handily, making Muñoz Marín the first elected governor of Puerto Rico and returning Fernós-Isern to office.

Considering his party's windfall victory in the 1948 election as a mandate, Fernós-Isern sought the autonomy denied to Puerto Ricans by the Crawford–Butler legislation. During Governor Muñoz Marín's visit to Washington, Fernós-Isern introduced H.R. 7674 on March 13, 1950, calling for a constitutional government in Puerto Rico.[34] The bill called for a plebiscite to determine the island's status, a move that was supported by both houses of the territorial legislature. The legislature would then call a constitutional convention to act on the voters' decision, and the resultant document would be subject to a popular vote in Puerto Rico, with final approval coming from the U.S. President and Congress. The final bill would supersede related portions of the Jones Act of 1917.[35]

When the bill was introduced, Fernós-Isern said to his colleagues, "The charter upon which this local government is based has never been adopted by the people of Puerto Rico. That such a charter be substituted by a constitution of the people's adoption is now a fitting and necessary step in order to perfect the democratic nature of our system of government."[36] The legislation slid easily through Congress, based largely on testimony from Puerto Rican and American officials declaring its advantages for Puerto Ricans and its importance for international relations.[37] Fernós-Isern's bill passed both houses on voice votes, with very little opposition.[38] President Truman signed Public Law 600 on July 3, 1950.

Fernós-Isern chaired the constitutional convention, which began September 17, 1951. The final document contained a preamble and nine articles declaring Puerto Rico's loyalty to the United States and its Constitution and a bill of rights as well as a passage from the United Nations' Declaration of Human Rights that conferred the right to work and the right to basic health care. A final draft was submitted to Governor Muñoz Marín on February 21, 1952, and Puerto Rican voters agreed to the constitution by plebiscite with a margin of more than 4 to 1 on March 3, 1952.[39]

But in Congress, Members debated the constitution's specifications for providing services to poor Puerto Ricans. Both houses amended the bill before passing it, most significantly striking rights from the borrowed United Nations document. House amendments also clarified that nonsectarian schools would receive the same funding as parochial schools. Some Members argued that the protections were so broad, they had a socialistic or communistic tinge.[40] Fernós-Isern, who had submitted his own annotated version of the document to Members of Congress before the debates, was quick to point out that the constitution abided by the criteria set forth in Public Law 600 and also addressed the specific needs of Puerto Ricans.[41] "Puerto Rico is a poor country. The people have a low level of existence," he noted. "They expect more of the Government than they would, if they had at least the income or the average income of the poorest State of the Union."[42] He defended the clauses in question, noting that the document granted Puerto Rico a certain level of autonomy. Fernós-Isern felt Congress's role stopped at making sure the document complied with Public Law 600 and the U.S. Constitution. "This is a Constitution for Puerto Rico and for Puerto Rican conditions.... We do not understand that if Congress approves our constitution, Congress will subscribe to the provisions of our constitution, section by section as if it were adopted by the Congress itself," he argued. "If such were the case, if the constitution were adopted by Congress as a law of Congress, it would be no constitution at all. It would be an organic act. We have understood that the constitution was to be submitted to Congress so that Congress would make sure that we complied with the requirements Congress laid down for us."[43] Fernós-Isern reluctantly endorsed the House amendments, primarily in an attempt to see the bill through to final passage.[44]

Fernós-Isern praised and defended the ELA throughout the 1950s. In 1953 he was appointed an alternate delegate representing Puerto Rico and the United States at the United Nations, where he helped the U.S. government make the case that Puerto Rico was fully self-governing and no longer a colonial possession.[45] The Resident Commissioner gave annual addresses on the House Floor commemorating the July 25 anniversary of the ELA, updating Members on Puerto Rico's progress, and praising the commonwealth compact. "Its march of progress is steady. Under it, freedom is assured to all in Puerto Rico.... Peace and law and order prevail. Prosperity is vigorously manifested. Unemployment is down. Living standards are elevated," he noted in 1953. "The people of Puerto Rico are happy, and they thank God they can be happy in freedom, in peace, and in prosperity."[46]

Fernós-Isern's assessments drew increased opposition from the Nacionalistas (Nationalists), who plotted in the year following the creation of the commonwealth compact to assassinate him and Muñoz Marín.[47] On the afternoon of March 1, 1954, Nacionalistas attacked the House Chamber, shooting into the crowded well and wounding five Members. When the House reconvened the next afternoon, Fernós-Isern, who had been in his office during the shooting, was the first Member recognized to speak, and he walked to the well while his colleagues applauded.[48] "Mr. Speaker, on no occasion could I address this House with deeper sorrow," he intoned. "To add to my consternation, the name of the dear island of my birth was invoked by the reckless vandals who staged this terrible deed yesterday.... The bullets that were shot did not only sorely hurt five of our colleagues; they all hit the heart of Puerto Rico." Fernós-Isern also submitted resolutions of condemnation from Governor Muñoz Marín and from the Puerto Rican legislature.[49] Security increased significantly around the Capitol complex after the shooting, and Fernós-Isern and his wife received 24-hour police bodyguards.[50] The shooting was Fernós-Isern's most vivid memory of his House service.[51]

Reacting toward the end of his House career to violence by the Nacionalistas and increasing demands for Puerto Rican statehood, Fernós-Isern sought various amendments to Public Law 600 to give Puerto Rico even more autonomy. On March 23, 1959, he submitted H.R. 5926, the Puerto Rico Federal Relations Act (or the Fernós–Murray bill), to replace Public Law 600 with "Articles of Permanent Association" between the people of Puerto Rico and the United States. The bill sought no immediate changes to Puerto Rico's status but attempted to clarify language left over from the Jones Act and unaddressed by Public Law 600; as Muñoz Marín said, H.R. 5926 was a "cosmetic job" to do away with "warts and other blemishes" of previous legislation.[52] But Fernós-Isern withdrew the bill on the advice of Muñoz Marín in the face of sturdy resistance from bureaucracies in the territory and within the federal government. Congressional views toward the territories had also changed; Hawaii and Alaska were close to achieving statehood, lending more support to this movement. Fernós-Isern submitted a second bill addressing some of the most vehement protests, but that measure did not make it out of committee. Moreover, the failure of both bills was a significant blow to the PPD's power, but Muñoz Marín and Fernós-Isern were undeterred.[53] The former wrote President John F. Kennedy on June 10, 1962, near the 10th anniversary of the commonwealth, stating his intention to ask the insular legislature to seek a plebiscite revisiting Puerto Rico's status with the United States. Kennedy agreed, and the two also sought to secure Puerto Ricans the right to vote in U.S. presidential elections. Protesters who opposed the upcoming plebiscite broke into Fernós-Isern's office and destroyed papers, furniture, and photographs of President Kennedy and Governor Muñoz Marín.[54]

In March 1963 Representative Wayne Aspinall of Colorado submitted H.R. 5945, a bill to create a commission to study Puerto Rican status. Fernós-Isern spoke of his support for the measure, outlining the political history of Puerto Rico and the United States beginning with the Foraker Act. Of the ELA, he observed, "It was not possible at that time this pioneering effort in self-government within the framework of an association were [*sic*] created to [attain] a point of perfection. Experience and realities would assert themselves and determine the necessary adjustments."[55] In 1964 following the bill's passage, Fernós-Isern served as a representative of the PPD on the United States-Puerto Rico Commission on the Status of Puerto Rico.

Fernós-Isern did not run for re-election as Resident Commissioner in 1964; instead, he ran for and won a seat in the insular senate.[56] "I decided that a new generation, coming behind us, should take over," he told his House colleagues. "I thought it was time that I go back to Puerto Rico and enjoy what years of life I may still be granted by the Lord; to enjoy the breezes and the sunshine and the beautiful views of Puerto Rico."[57] Members filled nearly a dozen pages of the *Congressional Record* with tributes to their longtime colleague, noting his role in creating the commonwealth. "Dr. Fernós established in the House a reputation for effective, dedicated work," observed future Speaker Carl Albert of Oklahoma. "He also established his place among the greatest of our political geniuses because of his role in the creation of the Commonwealth relationship between Puerto Rico and the United States. Puerto Rico's broadened political ties and major economic and social reforms might not have been realized had Dr. Fernós failed to supply the skill and persistence to

accomplish the required legislation."[58] The *Washington Post* noted Fernós-Isern "has earned not gaudy celebrity.... His methods have been those of quiet persuasion, and he has eschewed hucksterism and humbug."[59] Fernós-Isern served four years in the Puerto Rican senate before retiring in 1969. He remained in Puerto Rico until his death from a heart attack in San Juan on January 19, 1974. "A force on the move has been halted, and the lights of Puerto Rico have been dimmed," said president of the Puerto Rican senate Cancel Rios as Fernós-Isern lay in state in the capitol in San Juan.[60] The former Resident Commissioner was laid to rest in the National Cemetery in Old San Juan.

FOR FURTHER READING

Biographical Directory of the United States Congress, "Antonio Fernós-Isern," http://bioguide.congress.gov.

Fernós-Isern, Antonio. *Estado libre asociado de Puerto Rico: Antecedentes, creación y desarrollo hasta la época presente* (Rio Piedras, PR: Editorial de la Universidad de Puerto Rico, 1988).

_____. *Original Intent in the Constitution of Puerto Rico: Notes and Comments Submitted to the Congress of the United States* (Hato Rey, PR: Lexis-Nexis Puerto Rico, 2002).

NOTES

1 "Envoy to Congress," 25 September 1964, *Washington Post*: A24.

2 A. W. Maldonado, *Luis Muñoz Marín: Puerto Rico's Democratic Revolution* (San Juan: La Editorial Universidad de Puerto Rico, 2006): 258; Members used Fernós-Isern's nickname in their tributes to him upon his retirement from Congress. See, for example, *Congressional Record*, House, 88th Cong., 2nd sess. (10 September 1964): 21944; *Congressional Record*, House, 88th Cong., 2nd sess. (1 October 1964): 23426, 23429; and *Congressional Record*, House, 88th Cong., 2nd sess. (4 October 1964): 24018.

3 *Congressional Record*, House, 82nd Cong., 2nd sess. (28 May 1952): 6180.

4 There is no information on Fernós-Isern's parents or siblings.

5 *Congressional Record*, House, 83rd Cong., 1st sess. (16 February 1953): 1121.

6 Fernós-Isern later received an honorary law degree from this institution. See "Degree to Be Given," 19 March 1961, *Washington Post*: B6; "Seven to Be Awarded GW Honorary Degrees," 31 May 1961, *Washington Post*: A4.

7 Richard E. Sharpless, "Puerto Rico," in Robert J. Alexander ed., *Political Parties of the Americas* (Westport, CT: Greenwood Press, 1982): 620; Fernando Bayron Toro, *Elecciones y partidos políticos de Puerto Rico, 1809–2000* (Mayagüez, PR: Editorial Isla, 2003): 191–194.

8 Appointments to fill vacancies for Puerto Rican Resident Commissioners are permitted under the Jones Act of 1917 (39 Stat. 964). The following Resident Commissioners were appointed to their first terms: José Pesquera of Puerto Rico (1932), Quintin Paredes of the Philippines (1935), Joaquin Elizalde of the Philippines (1938), Bolívar Pagán of Puerto Rico (1939), Carlos Romulo of the Philippines (1944), and Antonio Colorado of Puerto Rico (1992). See *Biographical Directory of the United States Congress*, http://bioguide.congress.gov/.

9 Charles McCabe, "Aluden a su actitud pro independencia," 14 August 1946, *El mundo*: 1; Representative Vito Marcantonio of New York also refers to Fernós-Isern's support for independence in debate on Public Law 600. *Congressional Record*, House, 81st Cong., 2nd sess. (30 June 1950): 9587. There are no sources in English regarding Fernós-Isern's political views on the status issue before his work on Public Law 600, but Luis Muñoz Marín's transition on this issue is well documented. See, for example, Surendra Bhana, *The United States and the Development of the Puerto Rican Status Question, 1936–1968* (Lawrence: University Press of Kansas, 1975): 73–92.

10 "En modales y apariencia, Fernós tiene el aire personal de distinction de muchos miembres del cuerpo diplomatic latinoamericano y algunos circulos que conocen a Fernós opinan que éste sera un 'embajador a la vez que congresista.'" Charles McCabe, "Aluden a su actitud pro independencia," 14 August 1946, *El mundo*: 1. Translated as "They Refer to His Pro Independence Activity" by Translations International, Inc. (August 2011).

11 Bayron Toro, *Elecciones y partidos políticos de Puerto Rico, 1809–2000*: 210, 216–217, 223–224, 229–231, 239.

12 "Puerto Rican League Plans Party Sunday," 19 December 1947, *Washington Post*: C7; *Congressional Record*, House, 88th Cong., 2nd sess. (1 October 1964): 23429; "Spring Is Time for a Change, Organizations Elect New Heads," 29 May 1953, *Washington Post*: 26; "Puerto Rican-American Group to Honor Officers," 22 June 1951, *Washington Post*: C4. According to the *Congressional Directory*, Fernós-Isern and his wife had no children, but obituaries mention three children: Manuel; Antonio, Jr.; and Maria Delores. *Congressional Directory*, 86th Congress (Washington, D.C.: Government Printing Office, 1960): 181; Connie Arena, "Island Mourns Passing of Fernos Isern," 21 January 1974, *San Juan Star*: 1.

13 Fernós-Isern's offices were located in the Longworth House Office Building throughout his career. From 1947 to 1950 he occupied suite 1632, and from 1951 to 1964 he occupied suite 1710. *Congressional Directory*, various editions.

14 Garrison Nelson, *Committees in the U.S. Congress, 1947 to 1992*, vol. 2 (Washington, D.C.: Congressional Quarterly, Inc., 1994):

293. The Legislative Reorganization Act of 1946 also stipulated which committees Resident Commissioners could serve on (Act of August 2, 1946, ch. 753, 60 Stat. 830 § 122); Charles Stewart III, "Committee Hierarchies in the Modernizing House, 1875–1947," *American Journal of Political Science* 36 (1992): 848.

15 James L. Dietz, *Economic History of Puerto Rico: Institutional Change and Capitalist Development* (Princeton University Press, 1986): 204–205.

16 "Aid Planned Here for Puerto Ricans," 12 January 1947, *New York Times*: 25.

17 Marietta Morrisey, "The Making of a Colonial Welfare State: U.S. Social Insurance and Public Assistance in Puerto Rico," *Latin American Perspectives* 33, no. 1 (January 2006): 32.

18 *Congressional Record*, House, 82nd Cong., 1st sess. (9 May 1951): 5131.

19 "Sugar Act of 1948." In *CQ Almanac 1947*, 3rd ed., 02-388-02-393. Washington, D.C.: Congressional Quarterly, Inc. 1948. http://library.cqpress.com/cqalmanac/cqal47-1398114 (accessed 19 July 2012).

20 John W. Ball, "Congress Sees Sugar Surplus for Five Years," 10 July 1947, *Washington Post*: 7.

21 *Congressional Record*, House, 80th Cong., 2nd sess. (20 April 1948): 4655.

22 *Congressional Record*, House, 80th Cong., 1st sess. (9 July 1947): 8560.

23 *Congressional Record*, House, 82nd Cong., 1st sess. (13 August 1951): 9893–9894.

24 "Sugar Act Extended." In *CQ Almanac 1951*, 7th ed., 02-92-02-95. Washington, D.C.: Congressional Quarterly, Inc. 1952. http://library.cqpress.com/cqalmanac/cqal51-1405903 (accessed 19 July 2012).

25 "Aid Planned Here for Puerto Ricans," 12 January 1947, *New York Times*: 25; "Puerto Rican Drift to Mainland Gains," 31 July 1947, *New York Times*: 25.

26 "Aid Planned Here for Puerto Ricans."

27 "Immigrant Aid Urged for Puerto Ricans," 30 October 1947, *New York Times*: 51.

28 "Health Funds Asked to Aid Puerto Ricans," 18 May 1949, *New York Times*: 29.

29 "Puerto Rico Seeks More Ship Service," 6 June 1949, *New York Times*: 37.

30 Helen Delich, "Merchant Ship Aid Advocated," 28 April 1950, *Baltimore Sun*: 7.

31 Alfredo Montalvo-Barbot, *Political Conflict and Constitutional Change in Puerto Rico, 1898–1952* (Lanham, NY: University Press of America, Inc., 1997): 117–118.

32 C. P. Trussell, "Present Enacts Puerto Rico Poll," 6 August 1947, *New York Times*: 20.

33 Hearing before the Senate Subcommittee on Territories and Insular Affairs, Committee on Public Lands, *To Amend the Organic Act of Puerto Rico*, 80th Cong., 1st sess. (21 June 1947): 5–6, 9–10.

34 "Puerto Rico Backs New Charter," 31 March 1950, *New York Times*: 11.

35 "Puerto Rico Constitution." In *CQ Almanac 1950*, 6th ed., 409. Washington, D.C.: Congressional Quarterly, Inc. 1951. http://library.cqpress.com/cqalmanac/cqal50-1378197 (accessed 19 July 2012).

36 *Congressional Record*, Extension of Remarks, 81st Cong., 2nd sess. (14 June 1950): A1898–A1899.

37 Montalvo-Barbot, *Political Conflict and Constitutional Change*: 127–131.

38 "Puerto Rico Gets Chance to Write Constitution as Truman Signs Bill," 4 July 1950, *New York Times*: 30.

39 Bayron Toro, *Elecciones y partidos políticos de Puerto Rico, 1809–2000*: 215; "Caribbean Charter," 9 March 1952, *Washington Post*: B4; "Letters to the Times," 17 March 1952, *New York Times*: 20; Montalvo-Barbot, *Political Conflict and Constitutional Change*: 135–136; Anthony Leviero, "Truman Endorses Puerto Rican Code," 23 April 1952, *New York Times*: 10.

40 "Puerto Rican Code Approved by House," 29 May 1952, *New York Times*: 28.

41 Fernós-Isern's document submitted to Members of Congress was republished as *Original Intent in the Constitution of Puerto Rico*, 2nd ed. (Hato Rey, PR: Lexis-Nexis of Puerto Rico, Inc., 2002).

42 *Congressional Record*, House, 82nd Cong., 2nd sess. (13 May 1952): 5124.

43 Ibid., 5124–5125.

44 Maldonado, *Luis Muñoz Marín*: 318–320; "Puerto Rican Code Approved by House," 29 May 1952, *New York Times*: 28.

45 *Congressional Record*, House, 88th Cong., 2nd sess. (10 September 1964): 21945.

46 *Congressional Record*, Extension of Remarks, 83rd Cong., 1st sess. (23 July 1953): A4604.

47 "Attack Seen Red Inspired," 2 March 1954, *Baltimore Sun*: 7; "Puerto Rican Bares Plot against Ike," 14 September 1954, *Baltimore Sun*: 1; Robert M. Hallett, "Slaying Plot Cites Puerto Rico Group," 14 September 1954, *Christian Science Monitor*: 1.

48 C. P. Trussell, "Shooting in House Causes Increase in Capitol Guards," 3 March 1954, *New York Times*: 1.

49 *Congressional Record*, House, 83rd Cong., 2nd sess. (2 March 1954): 2484.

50 "Puerto Rican Official Guarded," 2 March 1954, *New York Times*: 17.

51 *Congressional Record*, House, 88th Cong., 2nd sess. (1 October 1964): 23424.

52 Price Day, "Run and Freedom," 18 May 1959, *Baltimore Sun*: 14.

53 Roland I. Perusse, *The United States and Puerto Rico: The Struggle for Equality* (Malabar, FL: Robert E. Krieger Publishing Company, 1990): 38–39.

54 "Vandals Raid Office of Puerto Rico Aide," 7 August 1962, *New York Times*: 8.

55 *Congressional Record*, House, 88th Cong., 1st sess. (23 October 1963): 20126.

56 Fernós-Isern announced his intention to retire when Muñoz Marín decided not to run for re-election for governor, in order to revitalize the PPD. See Bayron Toro, *Elecciones y partidos políticos de Puerto Rico, 1809–2000*: 239.

57 *Congressional Record*, House, 88th Cong., 2nd sess. (1 October 1964): 23431.

58 Ibid., 23424.

59 "Envoy to Congress."

60 Arena, "Island Mourns Passing of Fernos Isern."

"We know that we are members of this great community of the United States, in our own way, in that little island in the Caribbean. But we should not exist as a possession. How can 2,200,000 American citizens be only a possession? We must be a free people in a free American commonwealth."

Antonio Fernós-Isern
House Floor Speech, May 28, 1952

Joseph M. Montoya
1915–1978

UNITED STATES REPRESENTATIVE 1957–1964
UNITED STATES SENATOR 1964–1977
DEMOCRAT FROM NEW MEXICO

A liberal Democrat who spent almost 40 years in public service, Joseph M. Montoya was a 20-year veteran of New Mexico state politics before he came to Congress, and a Cold Warrior who supported U.S. global efforts to contain communism. Within that context, Montoya served his constituency by soliciting federal funds for defense and social programs in New Mexico. His longtime colleague Manuel Luján, Jr., said, "Senator Montoya was exactly what every public servant should be—a true servant of the people who elected him. No person was too insignificant … and no problem brought to him by a constituent was ever too small for him to try to solve."[1]

Joseph Manuel Montoya was born on September 24, 1915, to Tomás and Frances de La Montoya, in Peña Blanca, Sandoval County, New Mexico. Tomás was a county sheriff, and Frances taught elementary school. Montoya attended parochial elementary schools. When Tomás became sheriff of Sandoval County around 1929 or 1930, the Montoya family moved to Bernalillo. Montoya graduated from Our Lady of Sorrows High School in Bernalillo, New Mexico, and from Regis College in Denver, Colorado, in 1934. Then he moved to Washington, D.C., where he worked for the U.S. Department of Labor and attended Georgetown University Law School, earning an LL.B. in 1938. In 1940 Montoya married Della Romero, a nurse. The couple had three children: Joseph II, Patrick, and Linda.

In 1939 Montoya returned to New Mexico full time and gained admission to the bar. His public service had been underway since 1936, when he became one of the youngest members to serve in New Mexico's house of representatives (he was elected at age 21). After his re-election in 1938, he served as majority leader from 1939 to 1940.[2] In 1940 Montoya won a state senate seat, which he held for five years (1941–1946). He also served as majority whip and chairman of the judiciary committee.[3] He was elected lieutenant governor in 1946 and served from 1947 to 1951.[4] In 1950 Montoya ran against Antonio Fernández in the Democratic primary for an At-Large U.S. House seat. After failing to topple the incumbent, Montoya spent a year away from politics, but in 1952 he was re-elected to the state senate. After one term (1953–1954) he was re-elected lieutenant governor in 1954; he served two terms (1954–1957) before running for the U.S. House.[5]

With the blessing of Democratic Party leaders, Montoya ran for a vacant seat in the 85th Congress (1957–1959) after the sudden death of Fernández, the eight-term incumbent who died the day after he was re-elected in November 1956.[6] Montoya sought to hold the Dwight D. Eisenhower administration accountable for its government spending. "I think it is up to the Democrats in Congress to point out to the administration just how reckless and irresponsible its fiscal policies have been," Montoya noted during the campaign. Montoya told constituents he would secure federal resources for New Mexico. "It is more important than ever that our state have representatives who can work with the majority in Congress to protect such federal projects as our atomic energy installations and our missile test and experimental bases which are not only essential to the state's economy but are vital to national security as well," he said.[7] Montoya pledged to develop closer ties between the United States and Latin America, saying, "It is just as important to us to strengthen democratic forms of government in the countries to the South as it is to Europe and Asia."[8]

Montoya's opponent was Thomas Bolack, a state legislator from Farmington, New Mexico, who later became governor. Montoya's party affiliation was advantageous since registered Democrats outnumbered Republicans five to two. Also, he was "a long-experienced politician with contacts all over the state" and had "a following that will go to the trouble of

Image courtesy of the Library of Congress

voting without a lot of spending and effort." The observer noted, "Bolack's gamble is on winning the admiration of the huge independent vote; he's on the side of the popular president ... and he's not a piker in the pocketbook."[9]

By late March, Montoya's campaign was in trouble. His poll numbers began to slip because of tepid support from organized labor and the party's inability to mobilize Hispano voters. Some of Montoya's organized-labor advocates were tainted by scandals, and the Republican distribution of state house patronage jobs to Latino voters in the community fragmented Montoya's once-monolithic support. "Democrats of influence have not stepped forward to help him ... [and] some local Demo leaders are secretly supporting the Republican," noted an editorial. Bolack "had the benefit of heavy spending in the newspapers, television, radio, and roadside advertising in the early part of his campaign."[10] Eight days before the election, Senators Clinton Anderson and Dennis Chavez, along with Representative John J. Dempsey, endorsed Montoya.[11] He prevailed in the special election on April 9, 1957, with 53 percent of the vote to Bolack's 47 percent.[12] Montoya was re-elected to his At-Large seat (New Mexico had two at the time) for three more terms, with pluralities in the four-way 1958 race (32 percent) and in the six-way 1962 general election (29 percent). In 1962 he won with a 53 percent majority.[13]

Montoya first served on the House Judiciary Committee during the 85th Congress; the assignment was a prestigious one for a freshman member. In Montoya's second term, he earned a seat on the influential Appropriations Committee, where he remained until he moved to the Senate.[14] Montoya delineated the advantage of his position during his re-election campaign in 1962. "It means that there is a New Mexican among the most influential men in the House," he said. "It means this New Mexican's opinions count heavily in the decisions which insure that your tax money is spent only where necessary for our Nation's strength and well-being. It means that through one man, New Mexico speaks with double strength: once in the Appropriations Committee and again in the full House."[15]

Montoya aggressively advocated for federal aid for state education programs and public works projects. Although all of the bills he proposed died in committee, Montoya established a reputation as an ambitious legislator.[16] Montoya tried to secure financial and material aid for veterans and lobbied for federal workers.[17] He advocated government support, particularly farm subsidies and funding to train seasonal workers for other occupations, as well as federal aid for depressed rural and industrial areas and public infrastructure projects.[18] He also tried to expand educational opportunities for students because he believed providing for education was a "national responsibility as well as a local one."[19] During his House tenure, Montoya supported the Vocational Education Act of 1963 (H.R. 4955), which he noted would provide New Mexico an allotment—"almost double what my State is receiving under present programs. These funds are sorely needed to construct area vocational schools, improve vocational education facilities and train additional young people ... to successfully enter the labor market," Montoya said.[20] The House passed the bill on August 6, and President John F. Kennedy signed it into law (P.L. 88-210) on December 18.[21]

In these and other undertakings, Montoya emphasized constituent service. Like many Members from Western states, he pursued federal subsidies to develop New Mexico's natural resources. In 1962 Montoya secured an early victory when the New Mexico delegation won passage of S. 107 (P.L. 87-483), a bill authorizing the Department of the Interior to build an irrigation project for Navajo Indians along the Colorado River for $221 million. Montoya described the project as a major contribution to the "future development of Northern New Mexico, Albuquerque, and the Middle Rio Grande Valley."[22] He also routinely submitted legislation to extend Social Security benefits to his constituents and to other U.S. citizens.

Montoya also honed his anti-communist bona fides. Running for re-election in 1962, he reminded voters that he disapproved of efforts to seat Communist China in the United Nations, voted to fund the continued work of the controversial communist-hunting House Un-American Activities Committee, and sponsored legislation to block U.S. aid to communist regimes. He also invited "voters to look at copies of the hearings on Appropriations where I have stated in no uncertain terms that I oppose aid to foreign countries dominated by the Communist philosophy [and] … countries which are neutralist in thinking, such as India, Ghana, Brazil, Mali, and others." These overt expressions of devotion to U.S. society neutralized charges of communist sympathy leveled against Montoya and other politicians of his generation, especially those who challenged racial discrimination.[23]

The death of New Mexico's Senator Dennis Chavez on November 8, 1962, set off a scramble for a successor, which Montoya soon joined.[24] In 1963 the state legislature replaced direct primaries with pre-primary nominating conventions, centralizing party control over nominations for office. This development allowed Montoya to preempt any primary opponents by conserving his resources for the general election against Republican Edwin L. Mechem, who had resigned as governor to fill the Chavez vacancy.[25] Montoya's nomination in 1964 was endorsed by New Mexico's senior Senator, Clinton Anderson, and by President Lyndon B. Johnson. One newspaper noted that Montoya had the advantage of "the growing support in New Mexico for President Johnson, which is expected to aid the entire ticket, and the loyalty of Spanish-American voters to candidates with Spanish names," especially in the northern portion of the state. Mechem, meanwhile, was widely criticized as a "self-appointed senator."[26] A major state newspaper, Santa Fe's *New Mexican*, endorsed Montoya based on his experience of working with New Mexico's congressional delegation and his ability to steer federal dollars to the state.[27] Montoya also benefited from national Democrats' strategy to attack the "extreme" positions of Republican presidential nominee Senator Barry Goldwater of Arizona. Montoya used the same strategy to criticize Mechem's political record.[28] President Johnson visited New Mexico to campaign for the challenger. "I think this state needs Joe Montoya; I think this nation needs Joe Montoya; I think I need Joe Montoya," he said.[29] In the 1964 election, Montoya beat Mechem with 55 percent of the vote, winning both the unexpired term and the full term beginning January 3, 1965. Since his term as Senator began November 4, 1964, he had seniority over the other Senators elected to the 89th Congress (1965–1967). Montoya earned 53 percent of the vote in his 1970 Senate re-election campaign.[30]

Long considered the consummate institutional insider, Montoya eagerly began learning Senate procedure by "taking his turn presiding over the Senate during slow periods" and embracing his committee assignments. His "network of committee and subcommittee memberships … enabled him to wield influence on a specific program or proposal from different positions of authority."[31]

Montoya began his Senate service on three committees: Public Works, Agriculture, and Government Operations. Four years later, in 1969, he moved to the Senate Appropriations Committee. He also served on the Select Committee on Small Business and the Select Committee on Presidential Campaign Activities, and on the Joint Committees on Atomic Energy and Bicentennial Arrangements. Montoya chaired a number of subcommittees during his Senate tenure.[32]

Montoya's bilingual education initiatives merged his interest in supporting education with broader civil rights issues. He supported the Bilingual Education Act of 1968, a bill sponsored by Senator Ralph Yarborough of Texas. An amendment to the National Defense Education Act of 1958 (NDEA) and the Elementary and Secondary Education Act of 1965 (ESEA), it provided financial assistance for bilingual programs in Spanish and English. Sponsors emphasized that the bill could help the United States in its fight against communism. Opposition was minimal, and the bill was approved as a package of amendments added to the ESEA.[33] But the Johnson administration was ambivalent about implementing the bill's bilingual education components, which were seriously underfunded the first year. Montoya advocated proper funding since bilingual education was "heralded as the first real sign of national concern for the plight of the Spanish and Mexican Americans, the Indians, and the Puerto Ricans who are trapped by linguistic circumstance in the cycle of poverty," noting that the administration's request to provide only one-third of the authorized funding "was met with astonishment and great disappointment" by the program's supporters. Congress eventually appropriated $7.5 million, a fraction of the $30 million that was authorized by the original legislation.[34]

Montoya sought to link Hispanic-American issues with the broader civil rights movement in the 1960s and 1970s. In January 1968, Montoya introduced S. 740, a bill that established a Presidential Cabinet Committee on Opportunities for Spanish-Speaking People. In a Senate Floor speech, Montoya said the bill's enactment would "mark the turning point for all Spanish-speaking people of this Nation as they continue their quest for full equality of opportunity." He staked his personal and professional prestige on the measure's passage. As "the only U.S. Senator of Spanish heritage, I pledge to my people that I shall keep careful watch, that I shall keep careful surveillance over the activities of this new Cabinet-level committee to insure that it carries out its work in the dedicated spirit I know it is capable of."[35] Montoya said the measure was necessary to "assure that Federal programs are reaching all Spanish Americans, Mexican Americans, Puerto Rican Americans, Cuban Americans, and all other Spanish-speaking and Spanish-surnamed Americans, to provide the assistance they need, and to seek out new programs that might be necessary to handle programs that are unique to such persons."[36] Although the bill had prominent supporters, such as Senator Yarborough and Edward Roybal of California in the House, other members, such as Representative Henry González of Texas, objected to its lack of specifics and questioned its effectiveness.[37] After several amendments, the bill cleared both chambers and became law (83 Stat. 838; 1969) on December 30, 1969.[38]

Like many Members of Congress who had emphasized their credentials as Cold Warriors, Montoya supported President Johnson's Vietnam policies, voting in his waning months in the House, for example, for the Gulf of Tonkin Resolution (H.J. Res. 1145), which authorized the use of military force in Vietnam in August 1964.[39] Montoya supported the Vietnam War as fulfilling U.S. obligations to maintain regional security and preserve access to strategic natural resources. In 1967, even as support for the war soured, Montoya reminded his colleagues, "Members of this body debated and discussed the implication of our involvement in Southeast Asia. In the end, we determined overwhelmingly that our national interest was involved in that part of the world."[40] Like many of his congressional colleagues, Montoya gradually became more critical, first calling for reforms within South Vietnam in 1968 and a year later suggesting gradual disengagement. "After a decade of steadily increasing U.S. military and economic support," he said, "Saigon [must] begin justifying the faith the American people have been asked to place in its sincerity in developing a government responsible to the people."[41] Montoya later objected to the Richard M. Nixon administration's expansion of the war into Cambodia in 1970 because such an invasion would result neither in victory nor in a quick withdrawal from Vietnam.[42] By 1971, Montoya had submitted an amendment to provide for the immediate withdrawal of the United States from Vietnam "within 4 months after the date of the presidential election" and to "allow the President of the United States to make a finding … which would assure the Congress that the Republic of Vietnam has followed democratic processes in selection of its President."[43] Although the amendment was not adopted, calls for more immediate withdrawal increased inside and outside Congress until the final pullout of U.S. combat troops in 1973.

By the early 1970s, Montoya faced questions regarding his personal, political, and financial matters. Despite Montoya's history of late tax filings, the Internal Revenue Service (IRS) had not audited him since he chaired the Senate Appropriations Subcommittee on Treasury, Postal Service, and General Government, which controlled the IRS budget allocation. The IRS did, however, investigate charges that Montoya had created seven dummy committees to launder $100,000 in campaign contributions. In 1975 critics pounced on revelations that Montoya's extensive real estate investments throughout New Mexico had made him a millionaire. Montoya denied using his political position for personal financial gain. "If I owned all of the property or had an interest in every business my enemies say I have, I'd be the richest man in New Mexico," he countered.[44] But these revelations damaged Montoya's political reputation

beyond repair. His opponent in the 1976 general election, Republican Harrison "Jack" Schmitt, a former astronaut, campaigned on honesty and transparency.[45] According to a leading newspaper, perceptions of Montoya's corruption, along with shrinking support from his base, enabled Schmitt's decisive win, with 57 percent of the vote. After the election, Montoya was implicated in the "Koreagate" scandal, in which a number of Members of Congress allegedly accepted illegal campaign contributions from foreign agents who sought to influence U.S. policy toward South Korea.[46]

Montoya suffered from failing health throughout 1977. After traveling to Washington, D.C., in the spring of 1978 to seek medical care, Montoya died of liver and kidney failure on June 5. He was interred at Rosario Cemetery in Peña Blanca, New Mexico.[47]

FOR FURTHER READING

Biographical Directory of the United States Congress, "Joseph Manuel Montoya," http://bioguide.congress.gov.

Vigil, Maurilio and Roy Lujan. "Parallels in the Career of Two Hispanic U.S. Senators," *Journal of Ethnic Studies* 13 (Winter 1986): 1–20.

MANUSCRIPT COLLECTIONS

Gerald R. Ford Library (Ann Arbor, MI). *Papers*: 1974–1977. Correspondence and briefing papers. Finding aid.

Library of Congress Manuscript Division (Washington, D.C.). *Papers*: Correspondence in Clinton Presba Anderson papers, 1938–1972. A finding aid is available to researchers.

National Archives and Records Administration Center for Legislative Archives (Washington, D.C.). *Papers*: 1961. In Richard Fenno Research Interview Notes collection.

University of New Mexico, Center for Southwest Research (Albuquerque). *Papers*: 1938–1978, 523 feet. Primarily reflects Montoya's career in the U.S. Senate and includes personal and congressional papers and correspondence, photographs, and memorabilia. A finding aid is available but access to some records is restricted to researchers.

NOTES

1 *Congressional Record*, House, 95th Cong., 2nd sess. (5 June 1978): 16252.

2 "James I. Matray, "Montoya, Joseph Manuel," *American National Biography*, 15 (New York: Oxford University Press, 1999): 713–714 (hereinafter referred to as *ANB*); "Joseph Montoya," in Maurilio E. Vigil, ed., *Los Patrones: Profiles of Hispanic Political Leaders in New Mexico History* (Washington, D.C.: University Press of America, 1980): 157–163; *Congressional Record*, Senate, 95th Cong., 2nd sess. (22 June 1978): 18507; Elizabeth F. Gonzales, *The New Mexico Blue Book: State Official Register, 1937–1938* (Santa Fe: Secretary of State, 1938): 12; Jessie M. Gonzales, *The New Mexico Blue Book: State Official Register, 1939–1940* (Santa Fe: Secretary of State, 1940): 22, 24; "Peña Blanca Residents Ignore Montoya Funeral," 9 June 1978, (Santa Fe) *The New Mexican*: A1, A2.

3 "Joseph Montoya," in Vigil, ed., *Los Patrones:* 157–158; Jessie M. Gonzales, *The New Mexico Blue Book: State Official Register, 1941–1942* (Santa Fe: Secretary of State, 1942): 19; Cecilia Cleveland, *New Mexico Blue Book, 1943–1944* (Santa Fe: Santa Fe Press, 1944): 37; Cecilia Cleveland, *New Mexico Blue Book, 1945–46* (Santa Fe: Quality Press, 1946): 84.

4 Matray, "Montoya, Joseph Manuel," *ANB*; Vigil, 158; Alicia Romero, *New Mexico Blue Book, 1947–1948* (Santa Fe, Southwestern Publishing, Co., 1948): 38; Alicia Romero, *New Mexico Blue Book*, 1949–1950 (Santa Fe, n.p., 1950): 66.

5 "Joseph Montoya," in Vigil, ed., *Los Patrones*: 158; Campbell, "Sen. Montoya Rites to Be in Santa Fe," 6 June 1978, *Albuquerque Journal*: A3.

6 Will Harrison, "Joe Montoya Presses Hard for Blitz in House Race," 18 December 1956, (Santa Fe) *The New Mexican*: 11. Because Montoya was outside the Dennis Chavez faction of New Mexico politics, he sought support from New Mexico's other senator, Clinton Anderson, who was also an ally of Fernández's.

7 "Joe Stresses Need of Dem in Congress," 20 March 1957, (Santa Fe) *The New Mexican:* 12.

8 "20 Years of Service Cited by Little Joe," 1 April 1957, (Santa Fe) *The New Mexican:* 1; see also "Joe Stresses Use of Atom in Hill Talk," 2 April 1957, (Santa Fe) *The New Mexican* for details about a speech in which he "favored broadening the already important role being played by the scientific laboratories in the state."

9 Will Harrison, "Congressional Race Pits Two Successful Businessmen," 3 March 1957, (Santa Fe) *The New Mexican*: 7B. Harrison caustically notes that the outcome of the election "seems to hinge on the size of the vote attracted to the polls. A little vote is good for Montoya, his racial friends and party regulars are sure to show up. A big vote would favor Bolack."

10 Will Harrison, "Joe Needs Big Push to Keep Race Edge," 27 March

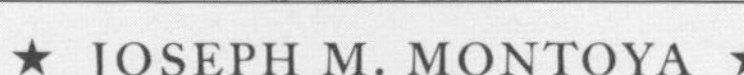

1957, (Santa Fe) *New Mexican*: 7. Harrison predicts a Bolack victory "unless Montoya finds new support and a remedy for his weakening position. Organized labor at this date isn't much of a recommendation and Montoya's anticipated 65 per cent of the Spanish-American vote is becoming doubtful."

11 "20 Years of Service Cited by Little Joe."

12 Ernestine D. Evans, *New Mexico Election Returns, 1911–1969* (Santa Fe: Secretary of State, 1970); "Montoya's Edge over 8,000: Voting Heavy with 130,000 Ballots Cast," 10 April 1957, (Santa Fe) *New Mexican*: 1.

13 "Election Statistics, 1920 to Present," http://history.house.gov/institution/election-statistics/election-statistics.

14 Garrison Nelson et al., eds., *Committees in the U.S. Congress, 1947–1992: Volume 2: Member Assignments* (Washington, D.C.: CQ Press, 1993): 631–632.

15 "Experience and Seniority," 9-62, Box 64, Folder 1 (MSS 386 BC), Joseph M. Montoya Papers, University of New Mexico Center for Southwest Research, Albuquerque, New Mexico (hereinafter referred to as Montoya Papers, CSWR); Untitled campaign speech, "1962 file?-5 min. TV," Box 64, Folder 1, Montoya Papers, CSWR.

16 *Congressional Record*, Index, 85th Congress, 1st sess., 533; *Congressional Record*, Index, 85th Congress, 2nd sess., 469; "Campaign, 1959 File," Box 64, Folder 1, Montoya Papers, CSWR. Among the bills Montoya submitted were requests for federal aid for the construction of schools (H.R. 13009 and H.R. 10697) and an irrigation project for Navajo Indians (H.R. 12170). None of these bills became law.

17 *Congressional Record*, Index, 86th Cong., 2nd sess.: 457.

18 Matray, "Montoya, Joseph Manuel," *ANB*.

19 "Candidate's Stand on Issues, n.d., 1962 file," Montoya Papers, CSWR.

20 "Joseph Montoya," in Vigil, ed., *Los Patrones:* 158–159; *Congressional Record*, Index, 88th Cong., 2nd sess.: 476–477, 765; *Congressional Record*, House, 88th Cong., 1st sess. (6 August 1963): 14278. Vigil is incorrect about Montoya's sponsoring the Wilderness Act of 1964, a Senate bill (S. 4). Montoya did not speak about the bill on the House Floor.

21 For a brief description of the passage of the Vocational Education Act of 1963, see "Vocational Schools, NDEA." CQ Press Electronic Library, CQ Almanac Online ed., http://library.cqpress.com/cqalmanac/cqal63-1316888 (accessed 21 August 2009). Originally published in *CQ Almanac 1963* (Washington: Congressional Quarterly, Inc., 1964).

22 "Candidate's Stand on Issues," n.d., 1962 file," Montoya Papers, CSWR.

23 Untitled campaign speech, "1962 file?-5 min. TV," Box 64, Folder 1, Montoya Papers, CSWR; Juan Gómez-Quiñones, *Chicano Politics: Reality and Promise, 1940–1990* (Albuquerque: University of New Mexico Press, 1990): 44–45. According to Gómez-Quiñones, as Mexican-American politicians challenged discrimination in the 1950s, "they demonstrated a defensive commitment to expressing loyalty and patriotism; a fear of addressing any problem that might cast doubt on the community's or individual's patriotism; and zealous devotion to staying within the conventions and accepted norms of behavior of the society and its institutions."

24 "Senate Seat Goal Is Set by Montoya," 20 August 1963, *Washington Post*: A6. According to one political scientist, New Mexico Democrats were unable to challenge Mechem because of intraparty disorganization. See Frederick C. Irion, "The 1962 Election in New Mexico," *The Western Political Quarterly* 16, no. 2 (June 1963): 448–452.

25 "Pre-Primary Repeal Asked," 24 February 1964, (Santa Fe) *The New Mexican*: 1, 2; "Joseph Montoya," in Vigil, ed., *Los Patrones*: 158–160; Maurilio Vigil and Roy Lujan, "Parallels in the Career of Two Hispanic U.S. Senators," *The Journal of Ethnic Studies* 13, no. 4 (Winter 1986): 11; "Election Statistics, 1920 to Present," http://history.house.gov/institution/election-statistics/election-statistics. Vigil and Lujan charge that Mechem's appointment "had broken the unwritten agreement which reserved one of two New Mexico Senate seats for an Hispanic." They also describe Montoya's successful effort to convince the state legislature "to pass legislation adopting the pre-primary convention which ensured that the party organization would certify candidates for the primary election." The legislation in question is "Laws of 1963, Chapter 317," in *New Mexico State Session Laws*, 26th Legislature, Regular Session, Ch. 311–325: 1048–1143.

26 Ted Hulbert, "New Mexico: A Clear Choice," 13 October 1964, *Christian Science Monitor*: B8; Bill Feather, "Johnson 'Needs' Joe Montoya," 28 October 1964, (Santa Fe) *The New Mexican*: 1; Will Harrison, "Montoya Holds Hard Core Vote," 25 October 1964, (Santa Fe) *The New Mexican*: A3. Harrison identifies these counties as "Guadalupe, Mora, Rio Arriba, Taos, Santa Fe, San Miguel, Sandoval, Valencia, and Socorro."

27 "The Race for U.S. Senate: We Endorse Montoya," 18 October 1964, (Santa Fe) *The New Mexican*: 4.

28 A. Spencer Hill, "The 1964 Election in New Mexico, " *The Western Political Quarterly* 18, no. 2 (June 1965): 499–501; "Montoya Pulls Bandwagon into Sierra County Today," 15 October 1964, (Santa Fe) *The New Mexican*: A6; "Joe Montoya Hurls Blast at Mechem," 21 October 1964, (Santa Fe) *The New Mexican*: A1, A2; Mike Browne and Bill Feather, "Council for Livable World Becomes Senatorial Campaign Issue in State," 21 October 1964, (Santa Fe) *The New Mexican*: 5; Bill Feather, "Dems Campaign in South Sector," 22 October 1964, (Santa Fe) *The New Mexican*: A2; Mike Browne, "Mechem Runs Down List in Attack on Demo Administration Policies," 22 October 1964, (Santa Fe) *The New*

Mexican: B5; Bill Feather, "Montoya Flays His Opponent," 23 October 1964, (Santa Fe) *The New Mexican*: 7; Bill Feather, "Montoya Says Mechem Gets Contributions from Birch Society," 29 October 1964, (Santa Fe) *The New Mexican*: A3; "Montoya-Mechem Race Gets Major Share of Attention," 1 November 1964, (Santa Fe) *The New Mexican*: B1. For a synopsis of Montoya and Mechem's voting records, see Helene C. Monberg, "NM Senate Race Offers Choice of Conservative, Liberal," 30 October 1964, (Santa Fe) *The New Mexican*: 13.

29 Feather, "Johnson 'Needs' Joe Montoya: President Makes Personal Appeal for Congressman." The issue of civil rights also emerged during Montoya's 1964 Senate campaign. Although he voted for the Civil Rights Act of 1964 (H.R. 7152) as a Representative in February 1964, Montoya responded as follows to a public question on the need for further congressional action on civil rights: "I do not feel that further congressional action is necessary on civil rights" because "present … legislation encourages community action in furtherance of the extension of civil rights to people who might feel aggrieved." However, in a prepared speech to the National Association for the Advancement of Colored People (NAACP), Montoya said, "A quiet revolution is taking place in the field of race relations in the United States." He praised the passage of the law as "the most important [act] enacted by the Congress on the subject of civil rights in this century and possibly the most positive stroke in behalf of liberty since the enactment and ratification of the Fourteenth Amendment." See "Draft Statement of Remarks on Civil Rights," Box 64, Folder 19, Montoya Papers, CSWR.

30 "Election Statistics, 1920 to Present," http://history.house.gov/institution/election-statistics/election-statistics.

31 Vigil and Lujan, "Parallels in the Career of Two Hispanic U.S. Senators": 11, 13.

32 Nelson, *Committees in the U.S. Congress*, 1947–1992, vol. 2: 631–632. Charles B. Brownson, ed., *Congressional Staff Directories*, various ed. (Washington, D.C.: 1969–1971); *Congressional Staff Directory*, 92nd–94th Congresses (Washington, D.C.: Government Printing Office, 1972–1976). Montoya chaired the Senate Appropriations Committee's Subcommittees on the Legislative Branch and Treasury, Post Office, and General Government; and the Senate Committee on Public Works' Subcommittee on Economic Development (as special and standing subcommittees) throughout his Senate career. He also chaired the Senate Select Committee on Small Business' Subcommittee on Government Procurement and the Joint Atomic Energy Committee's Subcommittee on Energy Agreements for Cooperation.

33 John D. Skrentny, *The Minority Rights Revolution* (Cambridge: Belknap Press of Harvard University Press, 2002): 192–195, 203–204. For a detailed study of the Bilingual Education Act, see Gilbert Sanchez, "An Analysis of the Bilingual Education Act, 1967–1968," (Ed.D. diss., University of Massachusetts–Amherst, 1973).

34 Skrentny, *Minority Rights Revolution*: 204–207; *Congressional Record*, Senate, 90th Cong., 2nd sess. (6 September 1968): 26010–26011. Montoya also supported the reauthorization of the Bilingual Education Act of 1974. For details, see Skrentny, *Minority Rights Revolution*: 225–228. See *Congressional Record*, Senate, 90th Cong., 1st sess. (11 October 1967): 28550–28551, and *Congressional Record*, Senate, 91st Cong., 1st sess. (20 March 1969): 7034–7035, for two examples of Montoya's supporting bilingual education programs in the Southwest United States.

35 *Congressional Record*, Senate, 91st Cong., 1st sess. (25 September 1969): 27119. For an extensive description of the Cabinet Committee and its activities, see Montoya's testimony before the Senate Committee on Government Operations, "Establish an InterAgency Committee on Mexican-American Affairs," 91st Cong., 1st sess., 1969: 1–29.

36 *Congressional Record*, Senate, 91st Cong., 1st sess. (18 December 1969): 39945.

37 See *Congressional Record*, House, 91st Cong., 1st sess. (16 December 1969): 39391–39401 for Roybal's statement (p. 39395) and González's statement (p. 39401). According to Gilbert Sanchez, one reason González did not support the bill was the political feud between President Johnson and the bill's sponsor, Senator Ralph Yarborough of Texas. See Sanchez, "An Analysis of the Bilingual Education Act, 1967–68": 68–69.

38 *Congressional Record*, Index, 91st Cong.: 1579; *Statutes at Large*, 83 Stat. 838, 1969.

39 *Congressional Record*, House, 88th Cong., 1st sess. (7 August 1964): 18555.

40 *Congressional Record*, Senate, 90th Cong., 1st sess. (5 October 1967): 27992–27993. These pages contain a forceful defense of the war effort by Montoya.

41 Matray, "Montoya, Joseph Manuel," *ANB*; *Congressional Record*, Senate, 90th Cong., 2nd sess. (25 January 1968): 1002–1004; *Congressional Record*, Senate, 91st Cong., 1st sess. (4 February 1969): 2669–2770. Although the *ANB* entry asserts that Montoya began opposing the war in 1967, Montoya's Senate Floor speeches demonstrate that he consistently supported the war effort throughout 1967 and 1968.

42 See *Congressional Record*, Senate, 91st Cong., 2nd sess. (18 March 1970): 7873. For another of Montoya's critiques of the expansion of the Vietnam War to Cambodia, see *Congressional Record*, Senate, 91st Cong., 2nd sess. (30 April 1970): 13560–13561.

43 *Congressional Record*, Senate, 92nd Cong., 1st sess. (13 September 1971): 31431.

44 Matray, "Montoya, Joseph Manuel," *ANB*; "Montoya Says He Assumed '70 Fund Drive Was Legal," 29 June 1973, *Wall Street Journal*: 5; George Lardner, Jr., "Montoya Confirms Campaign Forgery," 29 June 1973, *Washington Post*: A1.

45 Matray, "Montoya, Joseph Manuel," *ANB*; Jack Anderson and Les Whitten, "IRS Quietly Auditing Montoya Taxes," 24 March 1976, *Washington Post*: B6. An internal IRS investigation in 1975 revealed that auditors had halted an examination of Montoya's returns after misinterpreting a directive at a time when the agency was criticized for alleged harassment of Nixon's political enemies. Although Montoya's failure in 1970 to report out-of-state campaign contributions violated a 1972 state law, no hard evidence was uncovered confirming that Montoya actively circumvented the law. For more information about Schmitt, see *Biographical Directory of the United States Congress,* "Harrison Hagan Schmitt," http://bioguide.congress.gov.

46 Matray, "Montoya, Joseph Manuel," *ANB*; Montoya submitted a financial disclosure statement in the *Congressional Record*. See *Congressional Record*, Senate, 94th Cong., 1st sess. (18 December 1975): 41550; "Joseph M. Montoya," 6 June 1978, (Santa Fe) *New Mexican*: A4. According to the *New Mexican*, Montoya "became one of Watergate's victims because of the public's new demands for integrity and openness from public officials." The newspaper also noted that "the state's voter make-up changed.... The large solid block of Spanish voters which had helped in so many campaigns had dissipated." The voters that took their place were "newcomers who did not understand ... [Montoya's] ... old-school personal brand of politics and were turned off instead of aroused by his fiery, but often stilted speeches." For more information about the "Koreagate" scandal, see "Koreagate," in Mark Grossman, ed., *Political Corruption in America: An Encyclopedia of Scandals, Power, and Greed*, vol. 1. 2nd ed. (Millerton, NY: Grey House Publishing, 2008): 276.

47 Matray, "Montoya, Joseph Manuel," *ANB*; Bruce Campbell, "Sen. Montoya Rites to Be in Santa Fe," 6 June 1978, *Albuquerque Journal*: A1.

"I shall go to Washington as a Democrat, and I shall remain a Democrat. However, in matters vital to the welfare of our state and our nation, I shall cast my votes according to . . . the best interests of the public I represent — and that public includes all the people of our state."

Joseph M. Montoya
(Santa Fe) *The New Mexican*, April 10, 1957

Henry B. González
1916–2000

UNITED STATES REPRESENTATIVE 1961–1999
DEMOCRAT FROM TEXAS

Henry González served 37 years in the House, making him the longest-serving Hispanic Member in Congress. A pioneering, populist figure in Texas state politics, he was revered by his hometown constituents, who knew him as "Henry B." González rejected radical reformers, pursuing a strategy of effecting change from within the system. His pugnacious style and undeterred commitment to causes and programs he held dear often left him marginalized by those in power at the national level. "Given that the power to influence decisions that affect our lives is concentrated in the established systems of our government, I felt that I could contribute by participating in that process," González wrote. "There is a place for those who remain outside these processes, but I felt that I could contribute by influencing policy from the inside. Yet even on the inside I have largely remained an outsider because of my refusal to surrender my independence."[1]

Enrique (Henry) Barbosa González was born on May 3, 1916, in San Antonio, Texas, to Leonides González Cigarroa and Genevieve Barbosa Prince de González. His father's ancestors immigrated to Mexico from the Basque region of Spain and settled in the state of Durango, in northern Mexico, where many of them worked as silver miners; his mother was of mixed Scottish and Hispanic ancestry.[2] In 1911 Gonzaléz's parents fled Durango during the Mexican revolution, leaving behind their upper-middle-class life in Mapimi, where Leonides was mayor. Establishing a secure economic footing in the United States was difficult for the González family, which grew to include Henry and his five siblings. Leonides served as editor of San Antonio's *La prensa* newspaper, and the family home became a salon for expatriate Mexican intellectuals and politicians. Encouraged by his parents, Henry immersed himself in literary classics and in key Western political tracts. Henry attended the local public schools, learning English and working part-time during elementary school to help support his family. He graduated from Jefferson High School in 1935 and attended San Antonio College, where he earned an associate's degree in 1937. For two years he attended the University of Texas in Austin, studying engineering and law, but he put his educational plans on hold during the Great Depression because he could not find enough work to pay his tuition.[3] In 1943 González graduated with a bachelor of laws degree (LL.B.) from the St. Mary's University School of Law in San Antonio, which granted him an honorary J.D. degree in 1965.[4] During World War II, he served as a navy and an army intelligence censor for radio broadcasts and cable traffic. From 1943 to 1946, González was assistant chief probation officer for Bexar County's juvenile court. He resigned from his post as chief probation officer when a local judge forbade him to hire an African American for his staff. Later Gonzaléz worked for the San Antonio Housing Authority, eventually managing a housing project on the western edge of the city.[5] He married the former Bertha Cuellar in 1940 and they raised eight children: Henry B., Jr.; Rose Mary; Charles; Bertha; Stephen; Genevieve; Francis; and Anna Marie.

González's work in probation and public housing gave him entrée to thousands of homes in the city and hence wide name recognition, which helped him to found the Pan American Progressive Association (PAPA) in 1947. Organizing businessmen to contribute to the larger community "responded to my belief that we in the Hispanic community needed to quit complaining about how bad things were and instead do something to help ourselves," he recalled years later.[6]

González later resigned from PAPA, but fighting segregation remained a major component of his early

Image courtesy of the U.S. House of Representatives Photography Office

activism in local and state politics. Running on a platform to better serve the "neglected people" around San Antonio, González lost election to the Texas state house in 1950, but gained a reputation as a grass-roots organizer and a solid populist whose platform emphasized "manpower versus money power."[7] Three years later he secured a seat on the San Antonio city council as a member of an anti-administration group dubbed the San Antonians that swept to victory largely because of González's campaigning; one newspaper described González as "a young man with a razor-sharp wit and a wide smile." He was a driving force steering legislation that ended segregation in the city's parks and recreation facilities, a victory he called "particularly sweet" since, as a child, he was once forced to leave a city swimming pool because he was Hispanic.[8]

In 1956 González shocked the Lone Star State by winning election to the Texas senate. The *San Antonio News* called González's win a "staggering upset against long odds" considering President Dwight Eisenhower's comfortable victory in González's district. González ran an energetic campaign as "a man—not a name" and avoided ethnic appeals, helping him to win the confidence of his overwhelmingly Anglo constituency. González became the first Mexican American elected to the Texas senate and the first Mexican-American senator in more than a century.[9] His victory was a potent symbol of the opportunities in state and national politics that would become available to Hispanic Americans over the next decade.

Nevertheless, González's time in Austin was often combative and frustratingly hostile. Colleagues referred to him as "that Mexican," and he found himself fighting regular attempts by the legislature to circumvent national civil rights legislation. Twice González filibustered measures that would have resegregated Texas' public schools. He spoke roughly 40 hours in all against bills he called hateful, intending, he said, "to fight every one of them to the last ditch."[10] "It may be some can chloroform their conscience," González said. "But if we fear long enough, we hate, and if we hate long enough, we fight."[11]

Seeking to effect lasting change, González set his sights on higher office. He waged an unsuccessful gubernatorial campaign in 1958, driving across the state in the family station wagon before being outspent five to one by the incumbent. Three years later, he lost the special election for the U.S. Senate seat vacated by Lyndon B. Johnson when he became Vice President.[12]

González polled well in urban areas and across South Texas in both his losses, and when Paul Kilday, a 12-term Democratic incumbent who represented the greater San Antonio area, resigned to accept a nomination to the Court of Military Appeals, González entered the special election primed to fill the vacancy. "Barefooted. I ran what I call 'barefooted,'" he said years later. "I didn't have any financial backing. I even had to borrow the money to pay the filing fee in my first race."[13] His principal opponent was John Goode, Jr., a former GOP chairman for Bexar County and a self-described "militant conservative" who frequently railed against the John F. Kennedy administration's New Frontier programs. González, who had taken to calling himself a "consiberal" (liberal on human rights, conservative on property rights and taxes), attacked Goode as an isolationist who "exudes the attitude of defeatism and cynicism."[14] Former President Dwight D. Eisenhower campaigned on Goode's behalf. Kennedy endorsed González, and Vice President Johnson, along with Mexican film star and comedian Cantinflas, came to San Antonio to stump on González's behalf in a campaign that became a referendum on Kennedy's first year in office and a GOP attempt to crack Texas' solidly Democratic House delegation. Days before the election, Johnson said to a crowd, "The eyes of the whole world are on us. They want to see whether we're bigots, whether we're going to be prejudiced or whether we'll all go out and vote for a good American."[15] In an extremely heavy special election turnout, González defeated Goode by a 55 to 44 percent margin on November 4, 1961, becoming the first Hispanic American to represent Texas in the U.S. Congress.[16] In a state where segregation laws undermined the voting rights of thousands of black, Hispanic, and poor voters, this was a remarkable feat. González called the results "a reaffirmation of faith in the Democratic leadership of President Kennedy and Vice President Johnson."[17]

When González entered the House in 1961, his district, the Texas 20th, encompassed Bexar County and the city of San Antonio. Over time, redistricting transferred portions of the county to adjacent districts including the majority-Anglo residential neighborhoods to the north and the poor Mexican-American communities to the south, but the 20th District retained its San Antonio core over the decades. In the 1960s Hispanic Americans constituted a narrow majority of the district, but by the 1990s they made up nearly 70 percent of its population.[18] In his 18 re-election efforts, González often ran unopposed in the primary and was never seriously challenged in the general election.[19]

When he arrived in the House, González sought his predecessor's seat on the influential Armed Services Committee to allow him to meet the needs of the numerous military installations and military personnel in his district. González asked Vice President Johnson to help him attain the seat on Armed Services, but Speaker John McCormack of Massachusetts withheld it to avoid provoking more-senior Members seeking the assignment. González was appointed to the Committee on Banking and Currency, which remained his principal committee assignment although its name changed several times during his long career.

Longtime Banking Committee Chairman Wright Patman of Texas took González under his wing and mentored him. González benefited from the connection to the state delegation since Texans controlled key leadership and committee posts at the time, and Patman was someone González could identify with; he was "commonly labeled a populist, and he was very much a representative of the people," González recalled.[20] Patman counseled González: "Henry, you just stay on this committee and quit making a wave about Armed Services, and you'll end up as chairman."[21] As a junior member, González actively supported key New Frontier and Great Society legislation including the Housing Act of 1964, the Equal Opportunities Act of 1964, the Civil Rights Act of 1964, and the Library Service Act of 1964. Chairman Patman appointed González to be a special liaison for Latin American affairs, and González waged a public campaign against the Bracero Program. Instituted during the Second World War to offset workers lost to military duty, the program permitted U.S. farmers and agricultural businesses to use Mexican laborers to harvest crops, but González denounced its employers because the *braceros* received low wages, poor health care benefits, and substandard housing.[22]

Like many of his generation who fought against segregation, González believed the best way to effect change was to work within the system: to achieve positions of power so that he could advance the civil liberties of all his constituents. "I have never palmed myself off as some sort of ethnic leader," he said, and while other Hispanic Members of Congress supported efforts to organize "Brown Power" movements and believed they spoke on behalf of Hispanics nationwide, González did not.[23] "What I fear is creation of an isolated position, for a minority must develop a means to enlist majority support," he said at the height of the Chicano movement. "Our task is to overcome political isolation, and it is a delicate path that makes the difference between attracting a friend and becoming isolated and alone. If we cry in an empty room, we may expect to hear only our own echoes."[24] González's approach informed his position on representation in the House. He helped found the Congressional Hispanic Caucus in 1976 but eventually became disenchanted with it, ostensibly because he disapproved of its fundraising with lobbyists and its dues structure, though he also believed the group's focus had become too narrow. "Isolating oneself in the tribe means strangulation," he told a reporter.[25] González never served as the group's chairman, and eventually he quit the caucus.[26]

González left his legislative mark as a member of the Banking and Currency Committee, where he rose steadily through the ranks. During the 92nd Congress (1971–1973) he was elevated to the chairmanship of the Subcommittee on International Finance (later the Subcommittee on International Development, Institutions, and Finance), where he remained through the 96th Congress (1979–1981).[27] In the 97th Congress (1981–1983), González took over the gavel of the Subcommittee on Housing and Community Development; he relinquished that post when the Republicans took control of the House after the 1994 elections. During his tenure as chairman of the International

Finance panel, González routinely attached a rider known as the "González Amendment" to international banking bills. The purpose of the amendment was to protect U.S. citizens from expropriation by countries that received loans from international development institutions to which the United States contributed. González's successful amendment to a foreign aid bill in 1972 required U.S. representatives to international financial institutions, such as the World Bank, to vote against loans for countries that seized property without compensating the U.S. citizens and businesses that were affected.[28]

González became chairman of the Banking and Currency Committee in 1989 at the start of the 101st Congress. His gruff style sometimes rankled Democrats as well as Republicans.[29] However, as one political almanac wrote, the "open and gentlemanly way" González led the panel contrasted with the turbulent tenure of the previous chairman, Fernand J. St. Germain, endearing the Texas Representative to many committee members.[30] Under González's leadership, the Banking Committee handled a raft of legislative initiatives, including flood insurance reform, affordable-housing initiatives, credit for small businesses, and stronger laws to prevent financial crimes like money laundering and bank fraud.

The largest issue to come before the panel was the Savings and Loan Crisis of the late 1980s—the United States' most grievous economic crisis since the Great Depression and its costliest financial scandal to that point in U.S. history. Intended to promote homeownership after World War II, years of deregulation had left the savings and loan industry with little oversight. Banks invested in junk bonds and took risks in the real estate market, plunging many financial institutions and their depositors into insolvency. González had warned about the collapse of the banking industry since the early 1980s, and he faulted Congress for having "all but completely abdicated" its responsibility to oversee domestic and foreign investments.[31] After the crash, González helped direct the massive savings and loan bailout in the spring of 1989, keeping committee hearings open to the public for nearly two years. The *Almanac of American Politics* called González's work on the bill a "first-class job," in no small part because González was "utterly independent" of banking lobbyists.[32]

Sponsored by González, the Financial Institutions Reform, Recovery, and Enforcement Act (H.R. 1278, P.L. 101-73) provided a $50 billion federal outlay to close or sell off hundreds of the failed savings and loan associations. It also created the Resolution Trust Corporation (RTC)—a budgetary agency with a five-year lifespan—to replace the Federal Savings and Loan Insurance Corporation and hiked thrifts' capital requirements, forcing investors to contribute more of their own money and discouraging the risky speculation that caused the crisis. In addition to his general leadership on the bill, González authored two amendments; the first gave state and local public housing agencies a three-month right of first refusal to acquire residences being held by the Resolution Funding Corporation (RFC), and the second expanded the RTC's oversight to include public officials and private real estate brokers. The full House Banking and Currency Committee approved the amended bill by a vote of 49 to 2 on May 2. The bill then passed the House 320 to 97 on June 15. González assigned all 51 members of his committee to conference with the Senate to negotiate a final version of the legislation. While many House Democrats found the solution to fund the bailout unpalatable, the conference report passed the House on August 5 by a vote of 201 to 175 and was signed by President George H. W. Bush.[33]

Another centerpiece of González's tenure as chairman was the push to overhaul the public housing system for the first time since the mid-1970s. The Cranston–González National Affordable Housing Act of 1990 (S. 566, P.L. 101-625) started as a González-sponsored measure in the House (H.R. 1180) after the Ronald Reagan administration cut funding to popular housing programs, but was modified substantially as the House and Senate reconciled their differences. Chaired by González, the Subcommittee on Housing and Community Development considered 147 amendments during the markup, eventually approving the bill by voice vote before sending it to the full committee and then to the House Floor. The full House approved the bill in a 378 to 43 vote on August 1, 1991.[34]

Later that fall, Chairman González successfully shepherded through Congress a provision that created the National Housing Trust, lowering mortgage rates for first-time homebuyers and providing funding for down payments. As signed into law, the measure authorized nearly $57 billion in federal spending for a variety of programs, including rent subsidies, public housing, and financial aid for the elderly and disabled, with the aim of increasing the housing stock by more than 350,000 units. For the first time, the federal government issued block grants to meet the housing needs of state and local agencies; this provision was backed by Republicans who were hoping to limit direct spending on housing projects. Again, the committee consideration process was open and often chaotic, and when House and Senate conferees met to reconcile their versions of the measures, González resisted efforts to end public housing construction, eventually getting Home Ownership Made Easy (HOME) grants, portions of which had to be spent directly on the construction of affordable housing. "I have seen what public housing can do," González said, recalling his years in San Antonio. "I would hope we'd not [kill] this—not just out of respect for me—but out of responsiveness to the poor."[35] The conference report passed the House on October 25 by voice vote, and the measure was signed into law by President Bush on November 28, 1991.

González capped off the hectic 1991 session by fighting the Bush administration and most of the House Banking Committee over the best way to overhaul the federal deposit insurance system. The general fund that underwrote the investments of millions of Americans in member banks was "broke," González pointed out, and needed to be replenished if the New Deal era system was to survive. While others advocated a takeover by private industry, González called on Congress to front the capital required by the general fund. On November 21 the House passed an omnibus bill that ultimately cleared the Federal Deposit Insurance Corporation (FDIC), which governs America's banking industry, with a $30 billion line of credit at the U.S. Treasury. The bill also strengthened regulations controlling the nation's insurance system and gave federal regulators more tools. Finally, the bill contained a provision backed by González that created an FDIC program giving low-income persons and state and local agencies the ability to acquire single- and multifamily housing units being disposed of by banks.[36]

González also used his chairmanship to make the Federal Reserve System (the Fed) more accountable. Time and again, González reminded his colleagues that the Fed "was not struck from the brow of Jove, the Greek God. It is an institution that is the creature of Congress."[37] As such, González argued, the Fed could and should be called to account by Congress, though historically Congress had been reluctant to do so. The Fed constituted the primary "example of the abuse of openness in the federal government," González once wrote.[38] Largely through dint of congressional hearings, González revealed that the Fed had kept minutes of its meetings for years while denying the existence of official transcripts, destroyed many of its unedited meeting records, falsified records regarding a fleet of more than 50 expensive airplanes it maintained, and authorized billions of dollars in loans to foreign countries without congressional approval. González also condemned the system as elitist because its senior staff included few minorities. In the early 1980s, González tried without success to initiate impeachment proceedings against Fed chairman Paul Volcker. González's accomplishments included the requirement that the Federal Open Market Committee (FOMC) make the minutes of its meetings public in a timely fashion.[39]

González's insistence on greater transparency in executive branch agencies was rooted in his belief that by gradually relinquishing its coequal constitutional powers over fundamental issues like war powers and the budget, Congress had created a permissive environment in which a long line of Presidents had chosen "to usurp leadership, authority, and power." In 1992, González wrote of a "tremendous disequilibrium" between the executive and legislative branches of government. "Congress today has been relegated to a position of nay-saying, that is, of trying to restrict an agenda set by the President, rather than to

set an agenda of its own," he wrote. "This role of objector rather than initiator is a weak one."[40]

González's efforts to demystify the Federal Reserve System followed a pattern of legislative initiatives on which his position isolated him from most of his colleagues. The creation of a special committee to investigate the assassination of President John F. Kennedy in Dallas in 1963 highlighted González's tenacity on a controversial issue. González had been seated in the fifth car in Kennedy's motorcade.[41] Like many Americans, he came to doubt the conclusions of the Warren Commission, created to investigate the circumstances around Kennedy's death. "I suppose I really had questions from the start as to why he died, who killed him, and what direction had the bullets come from," González wrote years later in a book that alleged the assassination was a conspiracy to overthrow the U.S government. After testimony at the Watergate hearings indicating that Kennedy may have been killed in retaliation for the botched Bay of Pigs incident early in his presidency, González introduced a resolution to create a special House committee to investigate Kennedy's assassination and the 1968 assassination of civil rights leader Reverend Martin Luther King, Jr. "We need to know why [the assassinations] happened, what the net effect of these events have had on us, and how to prevent their happening again," he noted.[42]

González became chairman of the House Select Assassinations Committee on February 2, 1977, but while the committee was still organizing, he ran into perhaps the most damaging experience of his House career. González became involved in an acrimonious public dispute with the committee's chief counsel, Richard A. Sprague, and after his efforts to remove Sprague from the committee met with tepid backing from House leadership and the unanimous disapproval of his fellow committee members, González resigned less than a month after becoming chairman, on March 2, 1977.[43]

In the decades that followed, González was often the lone voice for a long list of causes. He repeatedly urged a full investigation into the murder of Judge John W. Wood in San Antonio, arguing that the killing had been a conspiracy by organized crime. In 1982 when indictments were handed down against five individuals, FBI director William Webster thanked González for providing the impetus for the investigation.[44] Twice González recommended the impeachment of President Ronald Reagan: for his initiation of the U.S. invasion of Grenada in 1983 and for his alleged role in the Iran-Contra affair. González's committee also uncovered $3 billion in U.S. loans that were made to Iraq through an Italian bank based in Atlanta, Georgia. The loans were ostensibly intended as agricultural credits, but it was later revealed that they were converted for Saddam Hussein's military purposes. This episode and President George H. W. Bush's failure to obtain a formal declaration of war from Congress before the first Gulf War early in 1991 prompted a later effort by González to impeach President Bush.[45]

"It was fitting that González represented the area of arid Texas scrubland where the legendary Alamo stands," writes Robert Cwiklik, who authored a book about the powerful bank lobby in Congress. "Over the years, he'd often been the last man at the fort, fighting the hopeless battles.... But populists like González didn't find Washington, land of the done deal, a very welcoming place. He'd long been dismissed by insiders, who no more liked his polyester suits of yellow and green than his principled, sourly uncompromising stands."[46] González cared little what people said about him, and he relished his reputation as "the Don Quixote of the House," once proudly telling a reporter about his "great big satchel at home just crammed full of lost causes."[47] At the conclusion of legislative business on many days, González frequently delivered lengthy special orders speeches which he titled, "my advice to the privileged orders." Shunning D.C. society, González rented a small apartment and refused to move his family to the capital; thus, most weekends he returned to San Antonio. González's lifestyle was largely due to his intent to remain independent from special-interest groups and others seeking to curry his favor. "I still haven't gotten the tips of my shoes dirty," González noted, long after he became a force in the House.[48] "The people elected me with no conditions attached," he remarked late in his career. "No debt to pay to anybody. Not beholden to a particular group. I was free to be guided by my own conscience."[49]

In September 1997 Representative González, who was 81 and in failing health, announced his retirement from the House. "I am proud of a long list of achievements and hard-won battles for a better community and a better country," he said. "Now, with a full and grateful heart, I must declare that it is time for me to come home."[50] At the start of the 106th Congress (1999–2001), González's son Charles succeeded him; they were the first Hispanic father-son pair of Representatives.[51] Jim Leach of Iowa, who succeeded González as chairman of the Banking and Currency Committee when the Republicans gained control of the chamber in 1995, memorialized González's service in a tribute on the House Floor: "An old-fashioned liberal, Henry never had a conflict of interest. He did not simply advocate, he lived campaign reform. His only special interest was his constituents. He never let them down, nor did they ever countenance an alternative."[52] González died in San Antonio on November 28, 2000, and was interred there at San Fernando Cemetery II.[53]

FOR FURTHER READING

Auerbach, Robert D. *Deception and Abuse at the Fed: Henry B. Gonzalez Battles Alan Greenspan's Bank* (Austin: University of Texas Press, 2008).

Biographical Directory of the United States Congress, "Henry B. González," http://bioguide.congress.gov.

González, Henry B. "The Relinquishment of Co-Equality by Congress," *Harvard Journal on Legislation* 29 (Summer 1992): 331–356.

Pycior, Julie Leininger. "Henry B. Gonzalez," in Kenneth E. Hendrickson, Michael L. Collins, and Patrick Cox, eds., *Profiles in Power: Twentieth-Century Texans in Washington* (Austin: University of Texas Press, 1993).

Rodriguez, Eugene. *Henry B. Gonzalez: A Political Profile* (New York: Arno Press, 1976).

MANUSCRIPT COLLECTION

University of Texas, The Center for American History (Austin). *Papers*: 1946–1998, approximately 500 cubic feet. The Henry B. González Papers comprise correspondence, committee records, campaign files, schedules, personal schedules, appointments, legislative files, photographs, video and audiotapes, memorabilia, and artifacts. Included are records documenting González's service as an elected member of the San Antonio city council, the Texas state senate, and the U.S. Congress. The bulk of the records document González's tenure as a U.S. Representative from Texas (1961–1998). A finding aid is available in the repository and online.

NOTES

1 Henry González, "From Participation to Equality," in Philip L. Fetzer, ed., *The Ethnic Moment: The Search for Equality in the American Experience* (Armonk, NY: M. E. Sharpe, 1996): 172.

2 Gonzalez, Henry B.," *Current Biography Year Book, 1993* (New York: H. W. Wilson and Company, 1993): 214.

3 "González, Henry B.," *American National Biography Online.*

4 "Henry Barbosa González," in *Notable Latino Americans: A Biographical Dictionary*, Matt S. Meier, ed. (Westport, CT: Greenwood Press, 1997): 183–184.

5 Eugene Rodriguez, Jr., *Henry B. Gonzalez: A Political Profile* (New York: Arno Press, 1976): 57–58.

6 González, "From Participation to Equality": 156, 158.

7 Rodriguez, *Henry B. Gonzalez*: 50–57; quotation on p. 55.

8 González, "From Participation to Equality": 162; see also Juan Gómez-Quiñones, *Chicano Politics: Reality and Promise, 1940–1990* (Albuquerque: University of New Mexico Press, 1990): 58; Rodriguez, *Henry B. Gonzalez*: 60–72.

9 Antonio Navvaro, a native Texan of Spanish descent, was appointed a state senator in 1846. See Rodriguez, *Henry B. Gonzalez*: 77.

10 "Integrationists in Texas Lose Fight; to Try Again," 4 May 1957, *Washington Post*: A10; "Bias Delays Pledged: Two Texas Senators Plan New Segregation Filibusters," 4 May 1957, *New York Times*: 43.

11 "Texas: For Whom the Bells Toll," 13 May 1957, *Time*: 27.

12 "Texas Race Poses Integration Test," 11 May 1958, *New York Times*: 52; Rodriguez, *Henry B. Gonzalez*: 86–87.

13 Michelle Garcia, "Henry B. Gonzalez's Last Stand," 8 November 1998, *Fort Worth Star-Telegram*: E1.

14 Dave Harmon, "His Crusades Over, Henry B. Returns Home; San Antonio Democrat Leaves," 3 January 1999, *Austin American-Statesman*: A1.

15 "Texas G.O.P. Predicts Victory in Special Race for House Seat," 3 June 1961, *New York Times*: 8; "All-Out House Race Nearing Close in Texas," 29 October 1961, *Chicago Tribune*: 9; "The Ex-President," 4 November 1961, *Christian Science Monitor*: 9; "A Bias-Free Vote Asked by Johnson," 4 November 1961, *New York Times*: 10; "Gonzalez, Democrat, Is Winner in Texas Race for House Seat," 5 November 1961, *New York Times*: 1; "Victory Conceded by Goode: 'New Frontiersman' Gonzalez Wins Congress Seat in Texas Election," 5 November 1961, *Washington Post*: A1.

16 For election results, see Michael J. Dubin et al., *United States Congressional Elections, 1788–1997* (Jefferson, NC: McFarland & Company, Inc., 1998): 629. The *New York Times* claimed that the turnout set a record for Texas special elections; see "Democrats Cheer Victory in Texas," 6 November 1961, *New York Times*: 42.

17 "Texas Winner Claims an O.K. for Kennedy," 6 November 1961, *Chicago Tribune*: 3.

18 "Election Statistics, 1920 to Present," http://history.house.gov/institution/election-statistics/election-statistics; and various editions of the *Congressional Directory* and the *Almanac of American Politics* (1972 to present).

19 "Election Statistics, 1920 to Present," http://history.house.gov/Institution/Election-Statistics/Election-Statistics/.

20 González, "From Participation to Equality": 165.

21 Julie Leininger Pycior, "Henry B. Gonzalez," in *Profiles in Power: Twentieth-Century Texans in Washington* (Austin: University of Texas Press, 2004, Rev. ed.): 302.

22 For a useful overview of the Bracero Program, see Gilbert Paul Carrasco, "Bracero Program," in *The Oxford Encyclopedia of Latinos and Latinas in the United States*, Suzanne Oboler and Deena J. González, eds., vol. 1 (New York: Oxford: 2005): 220–224. The following regional studies of the Bracero Program are also useful: Erasmo Gamboa, *Mexican Labor and World War II: Braceros in the Pacific Northwest, 1942–1947* (Austin: University of Texas Press, 1990); Ernesto Galarza, *Farm Workers and Agri-Business in California, 1947–1960* (Notre Dame, IN: University of Notre Dame Press, 1977).

23 *Politics in America, 1990* (Washington, D.C.: Congressional Quarterly, Inc., 1989): 1488.

24 For the quotation, see Thomas J. Foley, "'Brown Power' Parley Opens This Weekend,'" 22 October 1971, *Los Angeles Times*: A18. See also Jack Rosenthal, "U.S. Latins Vote Political Drive: Office in Capital Planned by Spanish-Speaking Unit," 25 October 1971, *New York Times*: 17.

25 Paul Houston, "Rep. Gonzalez: He Packs a Punch When It Gets Tense," 15 July 1990, *Los Angeles Times*: A1.

26 The date of González's departure from the Congressional Hispanic Caucus is unclear, though it was likely between 1986 and 1987.

27 The name of the Banking and Currency Committee eventually was changed to Banking, Finance, and Urban Affairs; the name of González's subcommittee was changed to International Development, Institutions, and Finance in the 94th Congress.

28 See, for instance, David R. Francis, "Nixon Acts to Stifle Congress: Tough Stand on Expropriation," 22 January 1972, *Christian Science Monitor*: 8.

29 Robert M. Garsson, "Will Gonzalez Punish His Challengers, or Cultivate Them?" 10 December 1990, *The American Banker*. González had a frosty relationship with House leaders, including Speaker Thomas Foley of Washington. Some complained privately that González ignored subcommittee chairmen and operated "in a vacuum." Just before the start of the 102nd Congress, González's opponents sought to remove him from the chairmanship of the Banking and Currency Committee, but González survived a vote in the Democratic Caucus, 163 to 89.

30 *Politics in America, 1990* (Washington, D.C.: Congressional Quarterly, Inc., 1989): 1485.

31 *Congressional Record*, House, 98th Cong., 1st sess. (25 April 1983): 9610.

32 *Almanac of American Politics, 1992* (Washington, D.C.: National Journal Inc., 1991): 1225. For González's independence on the bill to bail out savings and loan associations, see Paul Duke, Jr., "House Banking Panel Chief Gonzalez, Despite Doubts of Critics, Helps Keep Thrift Bill Tough," 19 July 1989, *Wall Street Journal*: A16. This was a point of pride for González who, as early as 1954, was known to have rejected a gift of $14,000 in bank stock from a San Antonio lobbyist. See Vincent J. Burke, "Offered $14,000 Bank Stock, Lawmaker Says," 4 August 1964, *Los Angeles Times*: 4; *Congressional Record*, House, 101st Cong., 1st sess. (4 April 1989): 5365.

33 "Sweeping Thrift Bailout Bill Cleared," *Congressional Quarterly Almanac*, 101st Cong., 1st sess., 1989, vol. XLV (Washington, D.C.: Congressional Quarterly, Inc., 1989): 117–133.

34 For a comprehensive summary of the measure and House action on the measure, see "U.S. Housing Programs Overhauled: Bill Aimed to Increase Stock of Affordable Homes," *Congressional Quarterly Almanac, 1990* (Washington, D.C.: Congressional Quarterly, Inc., 1990): 631–647.

35 "U.S. Housing Programs Overhauled": 643.

36 *Congressional Quarterly Almanac, 1991* (Washington, D.C.: Congressional Quarterly, Inc., 1991): 76–78.

37 *Congressional Record*, House 98th Cong., 2nd sess. (4 June 1984): 14821.

38 González, "From Participation to Equality": 168.

39 For more on González's efforts to introduce transparency at the Federal Reserve Bank, which routinely led to conflict with powerful Fed Chairman Alan Greenspan, see Robert D. Auerbach, *Deception and Abuse at the Fed: Henry B. Gonzalez Battles Alan Greenspan's Bank* (Austin: University of Texas Press, 2008).

40 Henry B. Gonzalez, "The Relinquishment of Co-Equality by Congress," *Harvard Journal on Legislation* 29 (Summer 1992): 331–356; quotations on pp. 331, 355–356.

41 Arthur Schlesinger, Jr., *A Thousand Days: John F. Kennedy in the White House* (New York: Fawcett Premier, 1965): 932–935, quotation on p. 935. González had been Kennedy's ally from the

early days of his presidential campaign and had known Kennedy as a young U.S. Representative. Along with Senator Dennis Chavez of New Mexico, González was a national co-chairman of the "Viva Kennedy" Clubs, aimed at bringing out the Mexican-American vote for the Democratic presidential nominee. On November 21, 1963, González hosted Kennedy in San Antonio, whose residents welcomed the President warmly. González accompanied Kennedy on the rest of the trip, through Houston and on to Dallas, joking as they disembarked from Air Force One, "Well, I'm taking my risks. I haven't got my steel vest yet."

42 Michael Canfield and Alan J. Weberman, *Coup d'Etat in America: The CIA and the Assassination of John F. Kennedy* (New York: The Third Press/Joseph Okpaku Publishing Company, Inc., 1975): xvii–xviii.

43 Among his complaints, González cited the committee and staff as "an administrative nightmare" and characterized Sprague, a former Philadelphia prosecutor, as "insubordinate, and insulting, not to mention disloyal." David Burnham, "Gonzalez, Assailing His Committee, Quits as Assassination Inquiry Head," 3 March 1977, *New York Times*: 1; George Lardner, Jr., "Gonzalez Submits Resignation from JFK-King Panel," 3 March 1977, *Washington Post*: A1; T. R. Reid, "Rep. Gonzalez, Sprague Told to Work Together," 26 February 1977, *Washington Post*: A2; George Lardner, Jr., "Rep. Gonzalez Trying to Fire Sprague," 11 February 1977, *Washington Post*: A1; David Burnham, "Sprague Ouster Is Upset by Panel on Assassination," 11 February 1977, *Washington Post*: A1. González also claimed that interference by organized crime had undermined the investigation. Some speculated that the House would dissolve the panel with González's departure, but its leadership was transferred to Representative Louis Stokes of Ohio. Eventually, the panel, whose activities were covered widely in the media, filed a report that Kennedy was likely killed as part of a conspiracy. For more on the committee and its work, see Sylvia Meagher, *Master Index to the JFK Assassination Investigations: The Reports and Supporting Volumes of the House Select Committee on Assassinations and the Warren Commission* (Metuchen, NJ: Scarecrow Press, 1980). González's dispute with Sprague damaged his reputation among his House colleagues. For an analysis of González's ostracism by the establishment, see Christopher Hitchens, "No Fool on the Hill," *Harper's Magazine* 285 (October 1992): 84–96.

44 *Current Biography, 1993*: 216.

45 Some of González's actions did not endear him to his colleagues. After steering the savings and loan bailout to a successful conclusion in the summer of 1989, González pursued an investigation of Charles Keating and the Keating Five, a group of Senators (four of them Democrats) who came under intense scrutiny for their connections to the head of the failed Lincoln Savings and Loan Bank, which cost U.S. taxpayers roughly $3 billion.

46 Robert Cwiklik, *House Rules: A Freshman Congressman's Initiation to the Backslapping, Backpedaling, and Backstabbing Ways of Washington* (New York: Villiard Books, 1991): 121–122.

47 Harmon, "His Crusades Over, Henry B. Returns Home; San Antonio Democrat Leaves." Some of González's critics were far less charitable. Late in González's career, *Politics in America* observed that he was "all but dismissed in the House as a flake"; see *Politics in America, 1990*: 1485. "His dedication to principle has sometimes reduced his effectiveness," observed a biographer; see Meier, "Henry Barbosa González," 183; Bicknell Eubanks, "Gonzalez: A Sturdy Liberal," 10 November 1961, *Christian Science Monitor*: 16.

48 Christopher Marquis, "Henry Gonzalez, 84; Served 37 Years in House," 20 November 2000, *New York Times*: A33. González also had a reputation for being gruff and pugnacious. In October 1963, González was one of fewer than two dozen House lawmakers who voted to abolish the House Un-American Activities Committee. Republican Representative Ed Foreman of Texas was quoted in several papers as having called the San Antonio Congressman a communist in response to González's vote. González confronted Foreman on the House Floor, and a physical altercation ensued. See "Capitol Hill Rematch Is Off," 30 October 1963, *Washington Evening Star*; and Jerry Doolittle, "'One-Punch' Gonzalez Doesn't Faze Foreman," 30 October 1963, *Washington Post*: A1. In 1986, González allegedly assaulted a constituent at a San Antonio diner after he overheard the man call him a communist. The district attorney, whom González later called a coward, charged González with misdemeanor assault, but the charges were eventually dropped. Pycior, "Henry B. Gonzalez": 303; Rodriguez, *Henry B. Gonzalez*: 125–127; Renee Haines, "Congressman Charged with Assaulting Constituent," 5 May 1987, United Press International.

49 Garcia, "Henry B. Gonzalez's Last Stand."

50 "Longtime Rep. Henry B. Gonzalez Plans Retirement," 4 September 1997, Associated Press; Catalina Camia, "Gonzalez Departure Will Be End of Era; Texas Iconoclast Championed Host of Causes for Democrats," 5 September 1997, *Dallas Morning News*: 1A.

51 Edward Roybal and Lucille Roybal-Allard became the first father-daughter pair of U.S. Representatives when Roybal-Allard succeeded her father in his Los Angeles-area district at the start of the 103rd Congress (1993–1995). Félix Córdova Dávila (1917–1932) and Jorge Luis Córdova-Díaz (1968–1973), a father-son team of Puerto Rican Resident Commissioners, were the first Hispanic parent-child combination in Congress.

52 *Congressional Record*, House, 105th Cong., 1st sess. (7 October 1997): 21519. For the rest of the tributes, see pp. 21517–21525.

53 For an obituary, see Christopher Marquis, "Henry Gonzalez, 84; Served 37 Years in House," 29 November 2000, *New York Times*: A33.

Edward R. Roybal
1916–2005

UNITED STATES REPRESENTATIVE 1963–1993
DEMOCRAT FROM CALIFORNIA

In his 30 industrious years on Capitol Hill, Edward R. Roybal rose to power by shaping legislation on behalf of the underprivileged. Serving the sick and the elderly, nonprofits, and non-native English speakers, Roybal never seemed to waver from the progressive course he first set as a member of the Los Angeles city council. A cofounder of the Congressional Hispanic Caucus (CHC) and its first chairman, Roybal was among the country's most influential Hispanic politicians. Later, as chairman of a House Appropriations subcommittee, he underwrote many of the most important federal programs, making him one of the most influential Members of the House. "If we don't invest in the Hispanic population today," he cautioned in 1987, "we will pay the consequences tomorrow."[1]

Edward Ross Roybal was one of 10 children born to Baudilio Roybal, a carpenter, and Eloisa (Tafoya) Roybal on February 10, 1916, in Albuquerque, New Mexico.[2] Like many families in the Southwest, Roybal's family had lived in the region for eight generations, since it was controlled by the Spanish. When he was six, Edward and his family moved to Los Angeles, California, settling on the east side in the barrios near Boyle Heights. He attended the local public schools and graduated from Roosevelt High School in 1934. For much of the next year, he worked for the Civilian Conservation Corps before studying accounting and business administration at the University of California, Los Angeles, and Southwestern University, also in the city. From 1942 until 1944 he worked as a public-health educator with the California Tuberculosis Association, and he later served four years as director of health education for the Los Angeles County Tuberculosis and Health Association.[3] Late in the Second World War, Roybal served as an accountant for an infantry unit in the U.S. Army. He married the former Lucille Beserra on September 27, 1940, and the couple raised three children: Lucille; Lillian; and Edward, Jr.

Like many veterans, particularly Latino veterans, Roybal was motivated by his wartime experience to challenge discrimination in Southern California, especially its effects on economic, education, and housing conditions around Los Angeles.[4] After an unsuccessful bid in 1947 for a seat on the Los Angeles city council, Roybal helped start the Community Service Organization (CSO), which sought to ally the city's diverse neighborhoods, using strategies outlined by noted reformer Saul Alinsky. Roybal was the group's first president and its primary spokesman, and in addition to pushing an array of progressive issues, the CSO quickly became the core of Roybal's political base.[5] Two years later, at Alinsky's urging, and with the support of local labor unions and, eventually, several newspapers, Roybal mounted a second attempt for a city council seat.

In 1949, backed by this broad coalition, Roybal won the election, becoming the first Hispanic to serve on the Los Angeles city council since 1881 and one of the highest-ranking Latinos in California municipal government.[6] Roybal's sweeping civil rights agenda, along with his diverse campaign staff and his drive to register voters, contributed to his decisive victory against incumbent Parley P. Christensen. Roybal won the general election with 63 percent of the vote, and despite redistricting and shifts in population over the next decade, he went on to win re-election by huge margins in 1951, 1953, 1957, and 1961.[7]

Neither Roybal's widespread support in his district nor his position on the city council inoculated him against the prevalent discrimination in the rest of Los Angeles. At his initial council meeting, Roybal was introduced as "our new Mexican councilman who also speaks Mexican." Years later, Roybal alluded to that incident as a defining moment

Collection of the U.S. House of Representatives, Photography Collection

in his political career. "I'm not Mexican," he said. "I am a Mexican American. And I don't speak a word of Mexican. I speak Spanish."[8]

Roybal was in the minority on the city council, and the dominant conservative members were indifferent to much of his agenda. "They thought I would fall flat on my face," he said later. "They felt right along that I was not their equal."[9] Nevertheless, he chaired the public health and welfare committee and developed a reputation as a stalwart liberal who took stands on matters of principle despite the potential for criticism from voters and the outright derision of his colleagues. During the Cold War, for instance, Roybal was the only person who voted against the Subversive Registration Bill and its mandatory oaths of loyalty to the U.S. government.[10] This independence persisted throughout Roybal's career on Capitol Hill; Roybal "voted his conscience, even when people made fun of him," recalled a principal aide.[11]

Roybal's strength was constituent service; he attended district functions, served as a general ombudsman for everyday issues, and worked with the city to defuse tensions between the Mexican-American community and the Los Angeles police.[12] Moreover, as the most visible Hispanic officeholder in Los Angeles, he was the primary "spokesman for communities of color," according to one historian. In a highly publicized episode, Roybal fought the city after it ceded a huge swath of residential land to its professional baseball team, displacing many Mexican-American families—even though the location was outside his council district.[13] In 1954 he launched an unsuccessful campaign for lieutenant governor of California, and in 1958, he narrowly lost a bid to become the first Latino member of the Los Angeles County board of supervisors.[14]

In 1962, after California gained eight additional seats in the U.S. House because of a population increase, Roybal entered the race for the newly created 30th District seat spanning his Eastside council district, downtown Los Angeles, and portions of Hollywood to the west. His platform reflected many of the community issues he had pursued during his 13 years on the council, including job creation, education, housing, and urban renewal. The CSO and the labor unions backed Roybal, but the state's Democratic Party remained uncommitted since it had drawn the district with another candidate in mind. Chief among Roybal's opponents in the primary was William F. Fitzgerald, a professor at Loyola University. Three other minor candidates filled out the field. The Los Angeles County Democratic central committee did not endorse either of the two leading candidates in the run-up to the June 1962 primary, but Roybal secured the support of state controller and future U.S. Senator Alan Cranston shortly before the election. With strong grass-roots backing and wide name recognition, Roybal easily captured the Democratic nomination by a three to one margin.[15]

Flush with a public endorsement from President John F. Kennedy, Roybal faced nine-term incumbent and Republican torchbearer Gordon L. McDonough in the 1962 general election. McDonough had lost much of his political base when the state legislature redrew California's congressional map, giving Democrats a significant registration advantage in the new district.[16] In a midterm election during which Democrats comfortably retained control of the House, Roybal won with nearly 57 percent of the vote.[17] In his subsequent 14 bids for re-election, he was never seriously challenged in the Democratic primary, and he never received less than two-thirds of the vote in the general election.[18] Early on, Roybal said, "Since I want to make my own decisions I shouldn't accept any contributions which I couldn't easily repay."[19] By 1980 his re-election bid was known as "one of the least expensive campaigns in the House of Representatives."[20]

In the House, Roybal developed a low-key, behind-the-scenes approach that some described as elegant. He had what the *Los Angeles Times* called a "quiet energy," and a major political study in the 1990s dubbed Roybal "durable." "Despite a style few would call dynamic, he has become a part of the political landscape in the Hispanic neighborhoods of East Los Angeles," the study said. "He was a quiet ground-breaker," recalled a senior aide. "Many of his accomplishments go unrecognized because he did things in a quiet way."[21]

As a freshman at the start the 88th Congress (1963–1965), Roybal hoped to serve on the Foreign Affairs Committee because of his interest in U.S.-Latin American policy, but instead he was assigned to the Interior and Insular Affairs Committee and later to the Post Office and Civil Service Committee.[22] In two years he won a seat on Foreign Affairs and left his previous assignments. After serving on the Veterans' Affairs Committee in the 91st Congress (1969–1971), Roybal relinquished the Foreign Affairs and the Veterans' Affairs assignments in 1971 for a seat on the exclusive Appropriations Committee. By the time he retired two decades later, Roybal had become chairman of the Appropriations Committee's Subcommittee on Treasury, Postal Service, and General Government. He was also a longtime member of the House Select Committee on Aging, which he chaired from 1983 to 1993 (98th–102nd Congresses).

Roybal tended to think locally and legislate nationally, balancing the needs of his Los Angeles constituency with those of America's growing Hispanic population. His pleas to strengthen the country's public services, especially those benefitting large minority populations, were passionate and effective. He supported the progressive agendas of the Kennedy and Lyndon B. Johnson administrations but opposed the continuation of the government's Bracero Program, which exploited immigrant farm workers.[23]

Education reform represented an early but short-lived victory for Roybal, who had grown frustrated with the inability of the public school system to meet the needs of an increasingly diverse society. Though Roybal's education bill did not make it out of committee in 1967, he provided crucial testimony in a Senate hearing in Los Angeles. "Up to now in our schools, millions of young people who speak a language other than English have been cheated or damaged or both by ill-informed educational policies which have made of their bilingualism an ugly disadvantage in their lives."[24] After bilingualism was cast as both a civil right and a matter of national defense, education reform progressed in a relatively straightforward manner during in the late 1960s. A provision of the Elementary and Secondary Education Amendments of 1967, the Bilingual Education Act outlined a three-year appropriations schedule to fund bilingual programs, including increases in the amount of money awarded each year.[25] Fourteen years later, Roybal found himself in another fight for access to bilingual instruction. "The children of our community continue to be shortchanged by this nation's educational system—a system, that Hispanics, like all Americans, help support through the billions of tax dollars they pay," he lamented in a letter to the editor in the *Washington Post*.[26]

Early during his tenure on the Foreign Affairs Committee, Roybal emerged as an outspoken critic of the Vietnam War, citing the high casualty rate among Hispanic-American troops and its devastating effect at home.[27] Joining other lawmakers, Roybal filed an injunction to end the conflict, arguing later that more-progressive domestic policies could help stop the destruction. Many Hispanic soldiers enlisted "to obtain some form of specialized training" because they could not afford to pay for college, he noted. But, he asked, "Is not the loss of one's life perhaps too high tuition to pay for education?"[28]

Roybal's tendency to speak out against such inequities, which began during his days on the Los Angeles city council, set the course for the rest of his congressional career. "Yes, there was discrimination when I first came here.... There were instances in which invitations were extended but not to the congressman from California," he told a reporter in 1987.[29] But as in the past, Roybal's perseverance forced others to take notice, and by the early 1970s he spoke of his valuable relationships with other Members.[30] Roybal's understated political style masked an ambitious legislative energy; in the 93rd Congress alone (1973–1975) he introduced 242 bills.[31] Roybal's drive extended well beyond the House Chamber, and in 1976 he helped found the Congressional Hispanic Caucus (CHC), a legislative service organization that monitored policy directly affecting the nation's Hispanic communities.[32] Like the CSO, the CHC, despite its small size, had a national presence, encouraging Jimmy Carter just days into his presidency to hire more Hispanic Americans in his administration.[33] Sensitive to the needs of the nation's growing immigrant population, the

CHC also pushed the Census Bureau to more accurately identify changes in the country's shifting demographics. "We cannot expect federal programs to serve Hispanics equitably unless they have adequate information on this population," Roybal said.[34]

Roybal's agenda was progressive but moderate during his career, irking his more radical constituency, and in 1970 the Congress of Mexican-American Unity refused to support his re-election bid. "The move was sparked by young, militant Chicano delegates who said Roybal was not responsive enough to political currents in the Mexican-American community," observed the *Los Angeles Times*; a law student went so far as to call him "a dormant congressman."[35] But Roybal consistently managed to influence the political system from within, and he spoke out against injustices that were usually ignored in national debates. The *Los Angeles Times* threw its support behind Roybal, describing him as "an eloquent, effective spokesman for minorities, since he went to Congress."[36]

With his growing reputation, Roybal undertook efforts to marshal Hispanic politicians across the country. During his chairmanship of the CHC, he also directed the National Association of Latino Democratic Officials (NALADO), a party organization, and the National Association of Latino Elected and Appointed Officials (NALEO), a nonpartisan catchall league offering guidance to the country's varied Hispanic interest groups.[37] Unsurprisingly, the activities of the CHC, NALADO, and NALEO often mutually reinforced each other, with NALEO organizing voter registration drives in the late 1970s and early 1980s as part of a push to make U.S. citizenship more accessible.[38] When Roybal died two decades later, NALEO reported a roster of more than 6,000 members.[39]

Roybal's career was not without controversy. In 1978 he became ensnared in a widely reported ethics investigation that involved a number of sitting and former Members and a lobbyist, Tongsun Park. That year the House Ethics Committee charged Roybal with four counts of failing to disclose campaign donations, accepting campaign funds for personal use, and giving false and misleading testimony.[40] Roybal acknowledged a "mistake in judgment" but said he had "too much respect to willfully or intentionally lie" about what had happened.[41] The committee found Roybal guilty on three of four counts and unanimously recommended a formal censure—the second-most-severe punishment under House Rules—which would strip him of his seniority and his standing in committee.[42]

Many viewed this punishment as being overly harsh, and Roybal's constituents as well as House Democrats in Washington were outraged. Censure was far more serious than the reprimand that was suggested for two white Members from California, Charles H. Wilson and John McFall, who were also found guilty of taking money and misleading the investigation. In Los Angeles, Hispanic interest groups protested the verdict. The president of the influential National Council of La Raza called the proceedings an attempt "to render ineffective the leading Hispanic voice in the House," and in Washington the CHC and the Congressional Black Caucus (CBC) questioned whether Roybal had received a fair trial.[43] When the full House voted on Roybal's punishment, the California delegation managed to reduce it to a reprimand. "This is certainly a victory for me, for the civil rights of all congressmen, and for all Americans who believe in the constitutional rights to equal justice," Roybal said. It also demonstrated "the potential strength of the Hispanic community when it unifies behind a cause," he noted.[44]

The ethics case had little effect on Roybal's career. His constituents in Los Angeles remained loyal, and in the next decade he became chairman of the Appropriations Subcommittee on Treasury, Postal Service, and General Government and chairman of the Select Committee on Aging.[45] During the 1980s, Roybal became "the conscience of the House" on immigration policy, as Representative Barbara Boxer of California dubbed him. Another Democrat said that he had assumed "national leadership of the Hispanic community" at a time when Hispanic-American voters had more influence than ever before.[46]

Roybal knew the country needed to update its immigration policy, but he disagreed with the series of bills in the early 1980s that would have made naturalization possible for millions of immigrants living in the United

States while imposing heavy fines on businesses with undocumented employees. Afraid that the bill would cause widespread discrimination, Roybal and his colleagues pressured House leadership in the fall of 1983, and the measure never went to the floor for votes.[47] Encouraged, a year later they submitted a separate immigration measure that would better enforce existing labor laws, but the bill never made it out of committee.[48] When the much-debated Immigration Reform and Control Act—complete with the economic sanctions Roybal had opposed—became law in 1986, he railed against it but agreed to work with officials to address his constituents' concerns. "If it fails in Los Angeles it will fail everywhere," he said.[49] Still fighting a year later, Roybal introduced an amendment offering amnesty to families that qualified for residency.[50]

Roybal broadened his legislative agenda in the latter half of his career, largely after he became chairman of the Select Committee on Aging. As he had fought ethnic and racial discrimination, Roybal worked in the 1980s to combat age discrimination. He had become alarmed at how little people knew about the care that was provided to elderly and dependent persons.[51] Roybal's generation had lived through the Depression and fought in World War II, and as chairman he focused on hospice care and protection for America's seniors. He also sought to protect housing programs and seniors' Social Security benefits. Roybal believed proper medical and health care was as much a consumer issue as a matter of human dignity, and in 1986 and in 1987, he introduced the "Homecare Quality Assurance Act," which included "a federal bill of rights for home care consumers." Senior abuse and neglect were among the concerns Roybal brought to the nation's attention in late July 1986 in a hearing before the Select Committee on Aging titled the "Black Box of Home Care Quality."[52]

Under Roybal's leadership, the Treasury, Postal Service, and General Government Subcommittee took a measured approach to federal spending. With jurisdiction over agencies ranging from the General Services Administration (GSA) to the U.S. Postal Service, Roybal's subcommittee was responsible for much of the basic administration of the U.S. government.[53] Foremost among the subcommittee's embattled policy issues were postal subsidies and federal funding for the IRS and the U.S. Customs Service. Faced with a deepening recession, Roybal and fellow Democrats advocated bolstering each program. "If you want to do something about the deficit, you can't continue to reduce money for agencies that produce revenues for the Treasury of the United States," he said in 1985.[54] Roybal was a pragmatic chairman, and six years later when the subcommittee had a tight spending limit, he omitted all pork barrel expenditures (special projects requested by individual Members) from the House legislation. "The rest of the committee felt that the chairman's idea made sense," a House Democrat confided.[55] In Roybal's 10 years at the helm of the Treasury, Postal Service, and General Government Subcommittee, its annual spending grew from $10 billion to nearly $23 billion, reflecting the gradual growth in federal obligations.[56]

Despite his position as chairman, Roybal made few headlines—a testament to his quiet and efficient style. He had a good relationship with his staff; for example, of the 1989 Treasury bill, Roybal said, "The language is not acceptable to the staff, and I can't work with a staff that's not happy."[57] With House colleagues, Roybal was firm, but evenhanded. Asked by a reporter if he would pressure the committee's Ranking Minority Member about a spending measure, Roybal smiled and said, "I'm not going to put any pressure on him.... I'm going to ask him for help."[58]

Called "a model of dignity" by the *Los Angeles Times*, Roybal announced his retirement in 1992.[59] Redistricting that resulted from the 1990 Census had severed his traditional power base in East Los Angeles. That fall, his daughter Lucille Roybal-Allard won election to the House as a Democrat from a new district that included constituents who had once been her father's.

After leaving the House, Roybal retired and moved back to Los Angeles, where he lived for 12 more years, deeply involved in the community he had long served. On October 24, 2005, Roybal died of respiratory failure at a Pasadena hospital.[60] In Washington, Senator Ken Salazar of Colorado noted that Roybal had inspired him to go into public service. "He fought social injustice on the streets, in our classrooms, and in the halls of Congress," Salazar said.

"Throughout his life, he gave voice to the disenfranchised and offered hope to the sick."[61]

FOR FURTHER READING

Biographical Directory of the United States Congress, "Edward Ross Roybal," http://bioguide.congress.gov.

Ralph Nader Congress Project. *Citizens Look at Congress: Edward R. Roybal, Democratic Representative from California* (Washington, D.C.: Grossman Publishers, 1972).

Underwood, Katherine. "Process and Politics: Multiracial Electoral Coalition Building and Representation in Los Angeles' Ninth District, 1949–1962," (Ph.D. diss., University of California–San Diego, 1992).

MANUSCRIPT COLLECTION

Special Collections, Chicano Studies Research Center, University of California, Los Angeles (Los Angeles). *Papers*: 1919–2003, 732 linear feet. The collection spans Roybal's tenure on the Los Angeles city council and in the U.S. House of Representatives as well as his personal and family history. It contains images, personal correspondence, and correspondence relating to his official duties. A finding aid is available online.

NOTES

1 George Ramos, "Edward R. Roybal, 1916–2005: Pioneer in Latino Politics in Los Angeles," 26 October 2005, *Los Angeles Times*: A1.

2 Names and occupations from Ramos, "Edward R. Roybal, 1916–2005: Pioneer in Latino Politics in Los Angeles"; and *The Dictionary of Hispanic Biography* (Gale, 1998). See also Katherine Underwood, "Pioneering Minority Representation: Edward Roybal and the Los Angeles City Council, 1949–1962," *Pacific Historical Review* 66 (August 1997): 404.

3 Matt S. Meier, *Mexican American Biographies: A Historical Dictionary, 1836–1987* (Westport, CT: Greenwood Press, 1988): 199–200; *Biographical Directory of the United States Congress*, "Edward Ross Roybal," http://bioguide.congress.gov. See also Sanford D. Horwitt, *Let Them Call Me Rebel: Saul Alinsky—His Life and Legacy* (New York: Alfred A. Knopf, 1989): 227.

4 Ricardo Romo, *East Los Angeles: History of a Barrio* (Austin: University of Texas Press, 1983): 167–168; Edward J. Escobar, "Bloody Christmas and the Irony of Police Professionalism: The Los Angeles Police Department, Mexican Americans, and Police Reform in the 1950s," *Pacific Historical Review* 72 (May 2003): 181.

5 For more on this partnership, the CSO, and the 1949 city council election, see George J. Sánchez, "'What's Good for Boyle Heights Is Good for the Jews': Creating Multiracialism on the East Side during the 1950s," *American Quarterly* 56 (September 2004): 633–661; Horwitt, *Let Them Call Me Rebel*: 227–235; Kenneth C. Burt, "The Power of a Mobilized Citizenry and Coalition Politics: The 1949 Election of Edward R. Roybal to the Los Angeles City Council," *Southern California Quarterly* 85 (Winter, 2003): 413–438; and especially Katherine Underwood, "Process and Politics: Multiracial Electoral Coalition Building and Representation in Los Angeles' Ninth District, 1949–1962," (Ph.D. diss., University of California–San Diego, 1992): 96–114.

6 Ramos, "Edward R. Roybal, 1916–2005: Pioneer in Latino Politics in Los Angeles"; Matt S. Meier et al., *Notable Latino Americans: A Biographical Dictionary* (Westport, CT: Greenwood Press, 1997): 343; Romo, *East Los Angeles: History of a Barrio*: 169.

7 Terms on the city council were lengthened to four years in 1953. See Underwood, "Pioneering Minority Representation": 410–412.

8 Quoted in Ramos, "Edward Roybal, 1916–2005: Pioneer in Latino Politics in Los Angeles." A similar version of this incident is included in "Roybal Recalls Prejudice inside Council, Congress," 27 July 1987, *Los Angeles Times*: 8.

9 "Roybal Recalls Prejudice inside Council, Congress."

10 For an in-depth examination of the city council's makeup and Roybal's initiatives, see Underwood, "Process and Politics: Multiracial Electoral Coalition Building and Representation in Los Angeles' Ninth District, 1949–1962": 154–248. See also Irasema Coronado, "Roybal, Edward," in the *Oxford Encyclopedia of Latinos and Latinas in the United States* Vol. 4 (New York: Oxford University Press, 2005): 40; Ralph Nader Congress Project, *Citizens Look at Congress: Edward R. Roybal, Democratic Representative from California* (Washington, D.C.: Grossman Publishers, 1972): 12; "Chairmen of 15 Council Committees Announced," 7 July 1949, *Los Angeles Times*: A1.

11 Ramos, "Edward R. Roybal, 1916–2005: Pioneer in Latino Politics in Los Angeles."

12 See, for example, Underwood, "Process and Politics: Multiracial Electoral Coalition Building and Representation in Los Angeles' Ninth District, 1949–1962": 165–167, 209–215. For a shorter treatment, see Underwood, "Pioneering Minority Representation: Edward Roybal and the Los Angeles City Council, 1949–1962": 399–425. For the relationship between Roybal and the city police

during Roybal's tenure on the city council see Escobar, "Bloody Christmas and the Irony of Police Professionalism": 181–183.

13 Underwood, "Process and Politics": 167–170, 201, 215–221.

14 The latter election, which was subjected to several recounts, and which Roybal eventually lost to Ernest Debs, left lingering resentment in the Latino community, which suspected that Roybal had been denied the seat because of his ethnicity. Ramos, "Edward R. Roybal, 1916–2005: Pioneer in Latino Politics in Los Angeles."

15 See Underwood, "Process and Politics": 254–258.

16 "McDonough Will Run in New District," 11 August 1961, *Los Angeles Times*: B1; "Know Your Candidates: McDonough, Roybal Tangle in 30th Dist.," 19 October 1962, *Los Angeles Times*: A1.

17 "Roybal Says Victory Backs Up Kennedy," 8 November 1962, *Los Angeles Times*: 14.

18 Meier, *Mexican American Biographies*: 199. After Roybal left, it was 23 years before another Hispanic legislator won election to Los Angeles' city council. See Underwood, "Pioneering Minority Representation: Edward Roybal and the Los Angeles City Council, 1949–1962": 424.

19 Ralph Nader Congress Project, *Citizens Look at Congress: Edward R. Roybal:* 7.

20 Quoted in Roger Smith, "25th Congressional District: Roybal Apparently Coasting in—Again," 29 October 1980, *Los Angeles Times*: C9. See also Ralph Nader Congress Project, *Citizens Look at Congress: Edward R. Roybal*: 4, 7.

21 "Roybal Recalls Prejudice inside Council, Congress"; *Politics in America, 1990* (Washington, D.C.: Congressional Quarterly Inc., 1989): 170; Ramos, "Edward R. Roybal, 1916–2005: Pioneer in Latino Politics in Los Angeles." See also Ralph Nader Congress Project, *Citizens Look at Congress: Edward R. Roybal:* 1.

22 For more background, see "Roybal May Get Post He Seeks," 13 January 1963, *Los Angeles Times*: 16.

23 "Bracero Plan to Be Opposed by Rep. Roybal," 10 January 1963, *Los Angeles Times*: 10.

24 Hearing before the Senate Special Subcommittee on Bilingual Education of the Committee on Labor and Public Welfare, *Bilingual Education*, 90th Cong., 1st sess. (24 June 1967): 415. A record of the remainder of Roybal's statement and the rest of the questioning that took place that day is on pp. 411–420.

25 Elementary and Secondary Education Amendments of 1967, P.L. 90-247, 81 Stat. 783–820. For more on the bilingual education reform of the 1960s, see John D. Skrentny, *The Minority Rights Revolution* (Cambridge, MA: Harvard University Press, 2002): 179–229; and Ralph Nader Congress Project, *Citizens Look at Congress: Edward R. Roybal*: 16.

26 Edward Roybal, "Bilingual? Si!," 12 February 1981, *Washington Post*: A18.

27 "Roybal Again Facing Cavnar in 30th District," 26 October 1970, *Los Angeles Times*: C2; "13 Congressmen Seek Injunction to Halt War," 26 May 1971, *Los Angeles Times*: A4; "Roybal Backs Chicano Viet Moratorium," 25 August 1970, *Los Angeles Times*: A4. See also Ralph Nader Congress Project, *Citizens Look at Congress: Edward R. Roybal*: 5, 8–9.

28 "Roybal Backs Chicano Viet Moratorium."

29 "Roybal Recalls Prejudice inside Council, Congress."

30 Ralph Nader Congress Project, *Citizens Look at Congress: Edward R. Roybal*: 1.

31 The only one of the 242 bills that became law was H.R. 1367, a private relief measure, enacted on December 5, 1973.

32 David Rodriguez, *Latino National Political Coalitions: Struggles and Challenges* (New York: Routledge, 2002): 65.

33 "Carter Pledges More Jobs for Hispanics, Roybal Says," 11 May 1978, *Los Angeles Times*: A2.

34 Ellen Hume, "Progress Cited in Data on Hispanics," 13 December 1978, *Los Angeles Times*: B12.

35 Bill Boyarsky, "Latino Political Group Refuses to Endorse Roybal Reelection," 16 February 1970, *Los Angeles Times*: 3. See also Ralph Nader Congress Project, *Citizens Look at Congress: Edward R. Roybal*: 1, 16.

36 "Congressional Endorsements," 27 October 1970, *Los Angeles Times*: B6.

37 Rodriguez, *Latino National Political Coalitions*: 70; William Gildea, "An Evening for Hispanic Unity," 18 October 1977, *Washington Post*: B4; "Roybal Heads New Latin Group," 14 December 1975, *Los Angeles Times*: A35.

38 Kenneth Reich, "Hispanics Plan Voter Registration Drive," 5 August 1979, *Los Angeles Times*: A24; Lee May, "Citing Black Gains, Latino Group Sets Sights on Resources in Private Sector," 21 September 1983, *Los Angeles Times*: B14; Jay Matthews, "Latino Politicians Urge Citizenship for Constituents," 22 November 1986, *Washington Post*: A8.

39 Ramos, "Edward R. Roybal, 1916–2005: Pioneer in Latino Politics in Los Angeles."

40 Ellen Hume, "Accused of Lying in Korean Probe," 14 September 1978, *Los Angeles Times*: B1.

41 Ellen Hume, "May Have Pocketed Cash, Roybal Says," 14 September 1978, *Los Angeles Times*: 1.

42 "Rare Full-House Censure of Roybal Recommended," 27 September 1978, *Los Angeles Times*: A2.

43 Charles R. Babcock, "Hispanics Assail Roybal Penalty," 7 October 1978, *Washington Post*: A5; "Efforts Pressed to Ease Penalty on Rep.

Roybal," 12 October 1978, *Washington Post*: A3; Robert L. Jackson, "Groups Try to Soften Roybal Censure," 13 October 1978, *Los Angeles Times*: B20.

44 Some Members criticized the whole review process. Ronald V. Dellums of California, a member of the CBC, questioned the legitimacy of the Ethics Committee, pointing out that none of its Members were African American or Hispanic. Others in the Democratic Caucus believed Roybal's lighter punishment indicated a retreat from Congress's efforts to reform after the Watergate Scandal, just four years earlier. See Charles R. Babcock, "House Votes Reprimands for Roybal, McFall and Wilson," 14 October 1978, *Washington Post*: A7; Thomas B. Edsall, "Democrats Back away on Penalties," 7 December 1978, *The Sun*: A1.

45 Roybal won more than 67 percent of the vote in the 1978 general election and nearly 70 percent of the vote in the 1980 general election. See "Election Statistics, 1920 to Present," http://history.house.gov/institution/election-statistics/election-statistics.

46 Steven V. Roberts, "Roybal Digs in His Heels on Immigration," 10 June 1984, *New York Times*: E3.

47 For more on the early immigration debate, see *CQ Almanac*, 97th Congress, 1st Session, 1981 (Washington, D.C.: Congressional Quarterly, Inc., 1982): 422–424; *CQ Almanac*, 97th Congress, 2nd Session, 1982 (Washington, D.C.: Congressional Quarterly, Inc., 1983): 409; *CQ Almanac*, 98th Congress, 2nd Session, 1984 (Washington, D.C.: Congressional Quarterly, Inc., 1985): 229–238; Robert Pear, "Immigration and Politics," 6 October 1983, *New York Times*: A1; James Fallows, "Immigration Bill Stirs up Melting Pot of Controversy," 5 February 1984, *Los Angeles Times*: D1; "Immigration Compromise?" 15 February 1984, *Los Angeles Times*: C4.

48 For the period between Roybal's bill and the eventual passage of the Immigration Reform and Control Act of 1986, see Margaret Shapiro, "Hispanic Caucus Counters Bill on Aliens," 2 February 1984, *Washington Post*: A4; Fallows, "Immigration Bill Stirs up Melting Pot of Controversy"; Margaret Shapiro, "Immigration Measure Produces Sharp Divisions in House Hispanic Caucus," 18 March 1984, *Washington Post*: A2; Robert Pear, "Immigration Bill Is Hardly Home Free," 8 April 1984, *New York Times*: E2; Roberts, "Roybal Digs in His Heels on Immigration"; Robert Pear, "The Hesitant House," 8 May 1984, *New York Times*: A14; Spencer Rich, "House Chooses 29 Conferees on Immigration Legislation," 7 September 1984, *Washington Post*: A9; Frank del Olmo, "Immigration Reform Claws at Fence," 31 May 1985, *Los Angeles Times*: B5. See also *Congressional Record*, House, 99th Cong., 2nd sess. (3 October 1986): 28320–28324.

49 The first quotation is from Mary McGrory, "Still Gripped by Fear," 26 November 1987, *Washington Post*: 2; the second quotation is from Marcia Chambers, "Many Questions Aimed at New Alien Law," 5 December 1986, *New York Times*: A21. For more on the law, see *CQ Almanac*, 99th Congress, 2nd Session, 1986 (Washington, D.C.: Congressional Quarterly, Inc., 1987): 61–67.

50 "Keep Immigrants' Families Together," 4 April 1987, *Chicago Tribune*: 10.

51 Ellen Hume, "2 Californians Will Chair House Panels on Children, the Elderly," 24 November 1982, *Los Angeles Times*: B3.

52 Hearing before the House Select Committee on Aging, *Black Box of Home Care Quality*, 99th Cong., 2nd sess. (29 July 1986). See also Victor Cohn, "Waiting for the Nurse to Show," 14 October 1986, *Washington Post*: H8.

53 *CQ Almanac*, 99th Congress, 1st Session, 1985 (Washington, D.C.: Congressional Quarterly, Inc., 1986): 330.

54 The mail subsidies supported nonprofit organizations operating on limited budgets. Quoted in *CQ Almanac*, 99th Congress, 1st Session, 1985 (Washington, D.C.: Congressional Quarterly, Inc., 1986): 331.

55 Quoted in *CQ Almanac*, 102nd Congress, 1st Session, 1991 (Washington, D.C.: Congressional Quarterly, Inc., 1992): 593.

56 See *CQ Almanac*, 1982–1992.

57 Dan Morgan, "Pride, Projects Drive Deal-Making on U.S. Spending," 3 October 1989, *Washington Post*: A6.

58 David Rogers, "Senate Approval of Last Spending Bills Clears Way for Budget Talks with House," 2 October 1989, *Wall Street Journal*: A16.

59 "Roybal Recalls Prejudice inside Council, Congress."

60 Ramos, "Edward R. Roybal, 1916–2005: Pioneer in Latino Politics in Los Angeles."

61 *Congressional Record*, Senate, 109th Cong., 1st sess. (27 October 2005): 24136.

"If we don't invest in the Hispanic population today, we will pay the consequences tomorrow."

Edward R. Roybal

Eligio (Kika) de la Garza II

1927–

UNITED STATES REPRESENTATIVE 1965–1997
DEMOCRAT FROM TEXAS

With his election to the U.S. House in 1964, Kika de la Garza broke through the barrier of Anglo-American political dominance in his South Texas district. The first Hispanic to chair a standing committee in the House since 1945, he steadfastly promoted programs to strengthen and support the country's agricultural sector throughout his 32-year tenure in Congress.[1] "There is a tremendous gap between the consumer and the fellow who rides on the tractor or who is picking the fruit," de la Garza said. "I would like to be remembered as the chairman ... [who was] a factor in legislative programs in bringing together groups that represent agriculture, the farmers and ranchers and consumers—that somehow each one would admit that he couldn't exist without the other."[2]

Eligio (Kika) de la Garza II was born September 22, 1927, in Mercedes, Hidalgo County, Texas, to Darío de la Garza and Elisa Villarreal. Descended from Spanish land grantees, his family had lived in South Texas since the first part of the 18th century. Kika was educated at Our Lady of Guadalupe Catholic School and Mission High School and served in the U.S. Navy from 1945 to 1946. He continued his education at Edinburg Junior College and the U.S. Army Field Artillery School in Fort Sill, Oklahoma. From 1950 to 1952 he served in the U.S. Army, fighting in the Korean War as a second lieutenant with the 37th Division Artillery. De la Garza earned a law degree from St. Mary's University in San Antonio after he was discharged from the army and later received an honorary Doctor of Law degree from the same institution.[3] He married Lucille Alamia, and the couple raised three children, Jorge, Michael, and Angela.[4]

De la Garza began his political career after he returned from his army service in Korea, winning election to the Texas house of representatives in 1951.[5] He served in that body from 1952 to 1964.[6] During his tenure in the Texas house, he was involved in the absorption of Pan American University into the University of Texas system and in the creation of the Texas Water Commission and a coastal wetlands preserve. He was also influential in establishing the nation's first state-run system of English instruction for preschool children.[7] Additionally, de la Garza was employed during this time by a law firm, as the Texas legislature met only for a total of four months every two years.[8]

In 1964 five-term Democratic Representative Joe Kilgore of Texas announced his intent to retire from the U.S. House of Representatives. His district encompassed the southernmost portion of Texas, bordering Mexico, and most of the population was concentrated along the Rio Grande. The majority of his constituents were Hispanics who were predominantly employed in irrigation or in farming cotton and produce. In many instances, large numbers of poor Mexican-American farmhands were financially dependent on a single landowner. This large Hispanic population ensured that the district would consistently vote Democratic in national elections, but the region's political structure was dominated by the powerful, more conservative Anglo ranchers, bankers, and lawyers in Brownsville, Harlingen, McAllen, Edinburg, and Mission.[9]

As Kilgore prepared to step down, de la Garza and fellow state representative Lindsey Rodriguez prepared to secure the Democratic nomination for the open seat. An ardent supporter of President Lyndon B. Johnson, Rodriguez was significantly more liberal than de la Garza. With the backing of the Political Association of Spanish-Speaking Organizations (PASSO), Rodriguez characterized de la Garza as disconnected from the needs of poor Hispanics in the district and as a puppet for Anglo business interests. Despite Rodriguez's attacks, de la Garza won Kilgore's endorsement and significantly outraised his opponent, cruising to a primary victory by a margin of nearly two to one. With a

Eligio (Kika) de la Garza II, Jena Rawley-Whitaker, 1996, Collection of the U.S. House of Representatives

solidly Democratic constituency behind him, he easily defeated his Republican opponent, veterinarian Joe Coulter from Brownsville, with 69 percent of the vote.[10] De la Garza became the first Mexican American to represent the region and the second Mexican American from Texas to be elected to Congress, after Representative Henry B. González from San Antonio. De la Garza was re-elected by considerable margins throughout his tenure in the House, securing at least 70 percent of the vote in the 1966 to 1990 elections. In 1992 he received 60 percent of the vote, and in the Republican wave of 1994, he won with 59 percent.[11]

On January 4, 1965, Eligio de la Garza became a Member of the 89th Congress (1965–1967). He was given a seat on the Agriculture Committee, where he served for the rest of his congressional career. He sat on the Merchant, Marine and Fisheries Committee during the 92nd to the 96th Congresses (1971–1981) and on the International Relations Committee during the 95th Congress (1977–1979).[12]

De la Garza's primary focus was agriculture, and he used his seat on the Agriculture Committee to further the interests of his rural constituency. In the 1960s the salinity of the Rio Grande was a matter of great importance to his district, as crops were being destroyed as a result of irrigation drainage in Mexico that increased the level of salt in the lower portion of the river. De la Garza introduced H.R. 11880, which divided the responsibility for maintaining the river between the two countries. "This is the type of legislation, Mr. Speaker, that I favor," he said on the House Floor shortly before its passage. "Where two nations share jointly the costs of a project, and where the local people also share. This is truly democracy at work; this is truly the good neighbor policy at work."[13] In the 90th Congress (1967–1969), de la Garza was named chairman of the Agriculture Committee's Departmental Operations Subcommittee, which he led through the 96th Congress (1979–1981).[14] De la Garza worked throughout his career to pass legislation that would benefit sugar and cotton farmers, such as the Sugar Act Amendments of 1971 and the Emergency Agricultural Act of 1978, which included an amendment authored by de la Garza to raise rates for cotton loans from 44 to 48 cents.[15] He successfully amended the Food and Agricultural Act of 1977 to establish a support program for sugar prices that was similar to the government's support program for the prices of commodities such as milk and honey.[16] Speaking in support of the amendment on the House Floor, he said, "[The] situation is this: The sugar industry in the United States is in very serious, drastic circumstances because of the chaotic situation that the sugar industry finds itself in throughout the world … this is a small attempt to assist the American producer to just hold his head above water."[17]

De la Garza also worked to further the influence and visibility of Hispanic Americans in Congress. In 1976 he joined with Herman Badillo of New York, Henry B. González of Texas, Edward R. Roybal of California, and Puerto Rican Resident Commissioner Baltasar Corrada-del Río to form the Congressional Hispanic Caucus (CHC). De la Garza served as chairman of the caucus from 1989 to 1991, when the Hispanic community was becoming more politically diverse. While Hispanics had traditionally been affiliated with the Democratic Party in the 20th century, Representative Ileana Ros-Lehtinen of Florida and Delegate Ben Blaz of Guam were elected as Republicans in the 1980s. "The fact is the Hispanic community politically is a spectrum from right to left, like any other community," de la Garza said. He suggested that the Hispanic community could operate like a European parliamentary system, with distinct divergent blocs forming coalitions on core issues. In the end, "jobs are jobs, and homes are homes, and schools are schools," he said.[18] However, like fellow Texan Henry B. González, de la Garza did not seek membership in the CHC to legislate solely for the Hispanic community. "There are people here in Washington, for example, who make a living of ethnic legislation," de la Garza said. "But [if] a fellow doesn't have a job, I try to get him a job whether his name is González or Smith."[19] De la Garza and González had also declined to attend the 1971 Brown Power Meeting that predated the CHC because they believed isolating "Hispanic" issues was an ineffective way to secure Latino rights and equality.[20] De la Garza's votes for key civil rights legislation evidenced

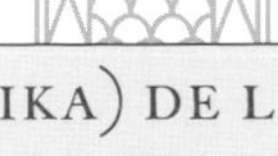

his egalitarianism; he voted in favor of the Voting Rights Act of 1965 (and its extensions in 1970 and 1975), the Elementary and Secondary Education Amendments of 1967, and the Civil Rights Restoration Act of 1987.[21]

At the opening of the 97th Congress (1981–1983), Agriculture Chairman Thomas Foley of Washington stepped down to serve as Democratic Whip, and de la Garza was the expected successor. Many younger Democrats on the committee, including subcommittee chairmen, supported Ed Jones of Tennessee, viewing de la Garza as an "autocratic hatchetman for Foley" who would not defer to the subcommittees. But the Democratic Caucus rejected the effort to scuttle de la Garza in a vote of 110 to 92.[22] "Be calm. Be courteous," Foley counseled de la Garza as the Texan prepared to accept the Agriculture Committee gavel.[23] Throughout his tenure as chairman, de la Garza sought to foster a conciliatory and collaborative environment among the committee members. He allowed subcommittees considerable latitude to craft legislation within their specialties, often sitting in on hearings to educate himself on the issues. "[H]e has been completely fair and balanced in handling the committee," commented Representative Jim Weaver of Oregon, who chaired the Forests, Family Farms, and Energy Subcommittee.[24]

Chairman de la Garza was tested early on when the Agriculture Committee crafted the 1981 farm legislation. Constrained by budgetary caps, and by a presidential veto if Congress exceeded the caps, de la Garza was at the center of intense negotiations, particularly regarding price support.[25] After the House passed a $16.2 billion measure by a 192 to 160 vote, the House and Senate struggled to close the $6 billion divide between their proposals.[26] "This is perhaps one of the most difficult moments I have had in my legislative career, which is some 28 years," de la Garza lamented as he introduced the final $11 billion omnibus bill that had been crafted through conference committee.[27] The legislation passed the House 205 to 203.[28] De la Garza also effectively used his chairmanship to form coalitions opposing cuts in agricultural spending proposed by the Ronald Reagan and George H. W. Bush administrations. De la Garza defeated two such measures that were being considered as part of the 1990 Food and Agricultural Resources Act; one barred subsidies to farmers earning more than $100,000 annually, and the other reduced the price support per pound of sugar by 2 cents. Likening such measures to "sending a mechanic who works on diesels to do brain surgery," he proclaimed that supporting agriculture was necessary for American prosperity.[29] On the House Floor, de la Garza declared, "So the bottom line is, it is jobs in the United States of America, farmers in the United States of America.… You cannot cut it anymore. You cannot hide it anymore. It is jobs, jobs, jobs in the USA."[30]

De la Garza was also on the front lines crafting multibillion-dollar disaster relief legislation. By July 1988, 43 percent of the country was suffering from one of the worst droughts in the nation's history. As co-chairman of the Congressional Drought Relief Task Force, de la Garza urged Congress to provide relief. "We want to give these farmers hope," he said.[31] He then guided through the chamber a $3.9 billion relief bill, stressing the positive effects of the legislation. "We provide help for the farmer now, because by helping him, we help all of our rural citizens. There is an interdependence between the farmer, the agri-businessman and all others who go to make up the fabric of rural America," he said.[32]

De la Garza's efforts to protect the agriculture industry extended to the debates on immigration reform that took place in the 1980s. An initial immigration reform package faltered in 1983, largely because of the Hispanic Caucus's influence. When the Immigration Control and Legalization Amendments Act of 1986 (H.R. 3810) was brought to the House Floor, de la Garza sponsored an amendment to prohibit immigration officials from entering agricultural operations without a search warrant or the owner's consent.[33] "[Fourth Amendment] constitutional protections are applicable to persons conducting businesses in office buildings and it is not apparent why persons conducting businesses in fields are less deserving of this basic constitutional benefit," de la Garza said when he introduced his amendment. "This amendment is particularly important … because it will ensure that farming operations will not be disrupted by broad scale, random raids. Work stoppages are very costly to the farmer, especially when the crops need harvesting in a timely manner."[34] The amendment was adopted by a 221 to 170 vote.[35] De la Garza voted against the final bill, however.

In the 103rd Congress (1993–1995), de la Garza was at the center of efforts by the William J. (Bill) Clinton administration to reorganize the federal government, including the U.S. Department of Agriculture (USDA) and the Federal Crop Insurance Group. While he supported the administration's objectives, de la Garza opposed efforts to reduce the federal deficit solely by cutting agriculture. Yet he acknowledged that the complexity of the department and its agencies were leading to severe inefficiencies. "People have to wait for months to get the department to say yea or nay. Somehow there appears to be a breakdown in communications," he said. De la Garza backed the administration's proposals to reduce employment, close or consolidate field offices, and merge department agencies, believing it was vital "to consolidate, to streamline, and to make, in 1994, the Department of Agriculture [that] President Lincoln wanted it to be in 1862."[36]

In 1993 de la Garza lobbied forcefully for passage of the North American Free Trade Agreement (NAFTA), arguing that the trade deal would increase the nation's agricultural trade surplus. "Open access to the Mexican market will lock in the export gains we have won and allow trade growth to continue," he argued. "NAFTA is in the best economic interests of most family farmers here in the United States and for the vast majority of our agriculture-related businesses."[37] While the majority of Hispanics from the Southwest supported the trade agreement, Members of Congress representing Puerto Rico, Cuban-American constituencies, and some Mexican-American constituencies opposed the agreement for economic and foreign policy reasons. Florida Representatives Lincoln Diaz-Balart and Ros-Lehtinen, for example, who were of Cuban descent, opposed the agreement because they objected to Mexico's cordial relationship with the Fidel Castro regime in Cuba. Representative Robert Menendez of New Jersey, who was also of Cuban descent, opposed the agreement because he believed it did nothing to protect American jobs and would encourage companies to invest outside the United States.[38]

The 1995 shift in the House majority ended de la Garza's 14-year chairmanship of the Agriculture Committee—the second longest in that panel's history.[39] In the 104th Congress (1995–1997) he served as the ranking Democrat on the committee. While in the minority, de la Garza opposed Republican efforts to transition the nation's agricultural business to a market-driven industry by ending the federal government's 60-year-old subsidy program. The proposal sought to cut $13.4 billion in farm subsidies and to free producers to choose their own crops. However, de la Garza and many of his fellow Democrats, as well as farm-state Republicans, were apprehensive about how the plan would affect farmers.[40] "Farmers in every region of this country have very grave concerns" about this "sudden and dramatic abandonment by the government of its role in sharing the farmers' risk," de la Garza cautioned.[41] Although he opposed the portion of the Republican welfare reform plan that would cut billions from the food stamp program, he was not wholly opposed to Republican initiatives. Viewed in the House as a conservative lawmaker, de la Garza frequently aligned himself with conservative Democrats and Republicans. He introduced a constitutional amendment for a balanced budget in every Congress since his election, except for the 98th (1983–1985), and he introduced a constitutional amendment to allow prayer in schools in every Congress since the 90th (1967–1969).[42] While no Democratic Congress was willing to pursue these amendments, Republicans made the balanced budget amendment a pillar of their agenda. "I've always been one to say that sometimes the impossible just takes a little longer," de la Garza remarked.[43]

On December 18, 1995, de la Garza announced his intent to retire from the House at the close of the 104th Congress in January 1997, expressing his desire to continue performing public service in the private sector. "I feel I can continue outside of elective office to make a contribution," he said. "There are many more things I would like to do and I want to do them while I am in good health and young enough."[44] Referred to as "a Secretary of State of Agriculture," de la Garza demonstrated a commitment to American

agriculture that was recognized on the House Floor by his colleagues' remarks celebrating his retirement.[45] In his honor, the USDA created the Kika de la Garza fellowship and designated its Subtropical Agricultural Research Center the Kika de la Garza Subtropical Agricultural Research Center. De la Garza also received the Texas Agricultural Lifetime Achievement Award.[46]

FOR FURTHER READING

Biographical Directory of the United States Congress, "Eligio (Kika) de la Garza II," http://bioguide.congress.gov.

Ralph Nader Congress Project. *Citizens Look at Congress: Eligio de la Garza, Democratic Representative from Texas* (Washington, D.C.: Grossman Publishers, 1972).

MANUSCRIPT COLLECTIONS

Texas State Library and Archives Commission (Austin). *Papers*: Texas Governor Allan Shivers Records, 1946–1964, 92 cubic feet. Persons represented include Eligio de la Garza.

The University of Texas–Pan American Library (Edinburg). *Papers*: 1965–1997, 656 linear feet. The papers in the Eligio "Kika" de la Garza collection are arranged chronologically in subgroups. The items in each subgroup are generally arranged in the order they were received by the repository.

NOTES

1 Carmen Enciso and Tracy North, eds., *Hispanic Americans in Congress, 1822–1995* (Washington, D.C.: Government Printing Office, 1996): 30. Representative Antonio M. Fernández chaired the Committee on Memorials in the 79th Congress (1945–1947).

2 Ward Sinclair, "That Fresh Breeze Blowing through Congress Is Named Kika," 27 December 1983, *Washington Post*: A7.

3 Matt Meier, *Mexican American Biographies* (New York: Greenwood Press, 1988): 87; Enciso and North, *Hispanic Americans in Congress*: 29–30; interview with Eligio (Kika) de la Garza by Oscar J. Martinez, 1975, "Interview no. 208," Institute of Oral History, University of Texas—El Paso: 1, 14.

4 Ben Guttery, *Representing Texas: A Comprehensive History of U.S. and Confederate Senators and Representatives from Texas* (n.p., 2008): 54.

5 Ralph Nader Congress Project, *Citizens Look at Congress: Eligio de la Garza, Democratic Representative from Texas* (Washington, D.C.: Grossman Publishers, 1972); interview with Eligio (Kika) de la Garza by Oscar J. Martinez, 1975, "Interview no. 208," Institute of Oral History, University of Texas–El Paso.

6 For more information on de la Garza's activities in the Texas house, see Legislative Reference Library of Texas, "Eligio de la Garza," http://www.lrl.state.tx.us/legeLeaders/index.cfm (accessed 11 April 2011); Ralph Nader Congress Project, *Eligio de la Garza*.

7 Enciso and North, *Hispanic Americans in Congress, 1822–1995*: 30.

8 Ralph Nader Congress Project, *Eligio de la Garza*.

9 *Almanac of American Politics, 1972* (Washington, D.C.: National Journal, Inc., 1971): 806; *Almanac of American Politics, 1974* (Washington, D.C.: National Journal, Inc., 1973): 995–996. For more information on the composition of Representative de la Garza's district, see David Montejano, *Anglos and Mexicans: In the Making of Texas, 1836–1986* (Austin: University of Texas Press, 1987): 79–82.

10 Robert E. Ford, "Texas Holds Runoff Today on Nominees," 6 June 1964, *Washington Post*: A6; "Texas Voters Decide Runoff Choices Today," 6 June 1964, *Los Angeles Times*: 6; "Election Statistics, 1920 to Present," http://history.house.gov/institution/election-statistics/election-statistics.

11 "Election Statistics, 1920 to Present," http://history.house.gov/institution/election-statistics/election-statistics.

12 Garrison Nelson, *Committees in the U.S. Congress, 1993–2010* (Washington, D.C.: CQ Press, 2011): 669.

13 *Congressional Record*, House, 89th Cong., 2nd sess. (1 September 1966): 21658.

14 Hearing before the House Committee on Agriculture, *Agricultural Legislation in the 90th Congress*, 90th Cong., 2nd sess. (9 November 1968): iv; *Congressional Directory*, 92nd–96th Congresses (Washington, D.C.: Government Printing Office). The name of this subcommittee varied during this period, as follows: Departmental Operations (90th–91st Congresses), Department Operations (92nd–93rd Congresses), Department Operations, Investigations and Oversight (94th Congress), and Department Investigations, Oversight, and Research (95th–96th Congresses).

15 *Congressional Record*, House, 92nd Cong., 1st sess. (4 October 1971): 34807–34809; *Congressional Record*, House, 95th Cong., 2nd sess. (12 April 1978): 9909; *Congressional Record*, House, 92nd Cong., 1st sess. (4 May 1978): 12613.

16 *Congressional Record*, House, 95th Cong., 1st sess. (22 July 1977): 24560.

17 Ibid., 24559–24560.

18 Dan Carney, "Untitled," 21 September 1989, States News Service.

19 Interview with Eligio (Kika) de la Garza by Oscar J. Martinez, 1975, "Interview no. 208," Institute of Oral History, University of Texas—El Paso.

20 Thomas J. Foley, "'Brown Power' Parley Opens This Weekend," 22 October 1971, *Los Angeles Times*: A18.

21 *Congressional Record*, House, 89th Cong., 1st sess. (9 July 1965): 16285; *Congressional Record*, House, 91st Cong., 2nd sess. (17 June 1970): 20199; *Congressional Record*, House, 94th Cong., 1st sess. (4 June 1975): 16917; *Congressional Record,* House, 90th Cong., 1st sess. (15 December 1967): 37174; *Congressional Record*, House, 100th Cong., 2nd sess. (22 March 1988): 4791.

22 Sinclair, "That Fresh Breeze Blowing through Congress Is Named Kika."

23 Whitney L. Jackson, "Out of Office, Still a Public Servant," 31 May 2001, *Roll Call*: 22.

24 Sinclair, "That Fresh Breeze Blowing through Congress Is Named Kika."

25 Seth King, "No One Seems Satisfied with the New Farm Bill," 19 December 1981, *New York Times*: 16.

26 Ward Sinclair, "House, over White House Objections, Votes Expensive Four Year Farm Bill," 23 October 1981, *Washington Post*: A12.

27 *Congressional Record*, House, 97th Cong., 2nd sess. (16 December 1981): 31812.

28 Ward Sinclair, "Farm Bill Squeaks through House by 205 to 203," 17 December 1981, *Washington Post*: A5.

29 *Congressional Record,* House, 101st Cong., 2nd sess. (25 July 1990): 19216.

30 *Congressional Record,* House, 101st Cong., 2nd sess. (24 July 1990): 18848.

31 Terry Atlas, "Congress Vows Farm Drought Relief," 23 June 1988, *Chicago Tribune*: 11.

32 Wendy Zentz, "Democrats Praise Drought Relief Bill," 13 August 1988, United Press International.

33 *Congressional Record,* House, 99th Cong. 2nd sess. (9 October 1986): 30054–30055.

34 Ibid., 30055.

35 Ibid., 30059.

36 *Congressional Record*, House, 103rd Cong., 2nd sess. (28 September 1994): 26293; *CQ Almanac,* 103rd Congress, 2nd Session, vol. L (Washington, D.C.: Congressional Quarterly, Inc., 1995): 191.

37 Lisa Richwine, "De La Garza Announces Formation of 'Ag for NAFTA'," 26 July 1993, States News Service; Lisa Richwine, "De La Garza Helping Secure Last Votes for NAFTA," 16 November 1993, States News Service.

38 *Congressional Record*, House, 103rd Cong., 1st sess. (16 November 1993): 29209.

39 Representative Harold Cooley of North Carolina chaired the Agriculture Committee for 16 years, from 1949 to 1953 and from 1955 to 1967. *Biographical Directory of the United States Congress*, "Harold Dunbar Cooley," http://bioguide.congress.gov.

40 "Major Cuts in Farm Bill Survive Test; House Panel Approves GOP Removal of Subsidies," 21 September 1995, *Dallas Morning News*: 1D.

41 Anne Hazard, "House Begins Historic Farm Bill Debate," 28 February 1996, States News Service.

42 All the entries for these bills proposing constitutional amendments can be found in the *Congressional Record,* Index, 89th–104th Cong.

43 Lisa Richwine, "Ortiz, de la Garza Adjust to Life in the Minority Party," 4 January 1995, States News Service.

44 "Rep. de la Garza Won't Run Again," 18 December 1995, United Press International.

45 *Congressional Record*, House, 104th Cong., 2nd sess. (28 February 1996): 3102.

46 E. Kika de la Garza Fellowship Program, USDA, www.hsi.usda.gov, (accessed September 16, 2011); Rod Santa Ana III, "Former Congressman Honored for Lifetime Service to Agriculture," *The Monitor*, www.themonitor.com (accessed 22 September 2011); Kika de la Garza Subtropical Agricultural Research Center, Weslaco, Texas, USDA, www.ars.usda.gov (accessed 24 October 2011).

"THE BIGGEST WEAPON KIKA HAS ARE THE LETTERS HE SENDS OUT TO PEOPLE ... EVERY KID WHO'S GOING TO GRADUATE HIGH SCHOOL GETS A LETTER FROM KIKA.... THEY GO THROUGH ALL THE AREA NEWSPAPERS TO SEE WHO'S DIED, AND THEY SEND A LETTER OF CONDOLENCE. EVERY TIME SOMEBODY GETS A SPECIAL AWARD OR SERVICE MEDAL, KIKA SENDS THE PARENTS A LETTER ... [RECIPIENTS] ARE VERY, VERY PROUD OF THE LETTERS."

A constituent of Eligio (Kika) de la Garza II, Ralph Nader Congress Project, 1972

Santiago Polanco-Abreu
1920–1988

RESIDENT COMMISSIONER 1965–1969
POPULAR DEMOCRAT FROM PUERTO RICO

Santiago Polanco-Abreu was one of the most powerful politicians in Puerto Rico during the 1960s. As committee chairman, speaker of the Puerto Rican house of representatives, and Resident Commissioner, Polanco-Abreu represented the next generation of the Partido Popular Democrático (Popular Democratic Party, or PPD). Known as "Chaguín," Polanco-Abreu had a 20-year political career that paralleled the peak of the PPD's influence mid-century and its fall in 1968. Committed to an expansive social agenda because of the poverty he experienced in childhood, Polanco-Abreu helped nurture Puerto Rico's commonwealth status and worked to ensure that the island's economic development was not disrupted by mainland policies. "I am not going to Washington hunting for a sinecure or material things," he said after winning the election for Resident Commissioner. "I am going to Washington as a first-class Puerto Rican citizen to defend the rights of my people and to serve in the cause of democracy."[1]

Polanco-Abreu was born in Bayamón, Puerto Rico, on October 30, 1920, to Santiago Polanco González, a farmer and a veteran of the Spanish-American War and World War I, and Anita Abreu.[2] As a child, Polanco-Abreu moved with his family to Barrio Bejucos in the town of Isabela along Puerto Rico's north shore. The region was dominated by subsistence farms and checkered with fields of beans, cotton, and vegetables. Polanco-Abreu grew up without electricity, running water, or paved roads. He worked his family's 20-acre plot and attended the local public schools, where he participated in drama productions and debates and served as class president. His parents, he said later, "knew perhaps by instinct that I should study." What little money they earned was used for his education. "My father was getting [a] $30 a month pension and he would give me the check the same day he received it, to go to the university," said Polanco-Abreu.[3] He attended the University of Puerto Rico in San Juan, earning a bachelor's degree in 1941 and a law degree two years later. In 1944 he married his college sweetheart, Viola Orsini. They adopted two children, José and Marta.[4]

Polanco-Abreu entered public service as soon as he finished school. He practiced law in Isabela and in San Juan, and from 1943 to 1944 he served as general counsel to the Tax Court of Puerto Rico. His first foray into electoral politics took place three years later. In 1947 Polanco-Abreu, then 28 years old and a firm supporter of PPD governor Luis Muñoz Marín, was elected to the Puerto Rican house of representatives to fill the vacancy resulting from the resignation of Esteban Susoni Lens. In the insular house, he sat on the rules and calendar committee and eventually became vice chairman of the committees on interior government, appointments, and impeachment proceedings.[5] Before long, the ruling party took note of his "clean-cut, self-possessed, amiable" personality and appointed him to the island's commonwealth convention in 1951.[6] Polanco-Abreu's political identity was consonant with his personal experiences. He referred to himself as a *jíbaro*, a salt-of-the-earth commoner, and readily identified with Puerto Rico's poor, once proudly telling reporters that his upbringing helped him "understand life."[7] But he was also comfortable in other strata of society and earned a reputation as "the only [member] who … exhibits definite ability to handle people at all levels—and who keeps in contact with that vast body of voters referred to as the masses."[8]

Eager to influence fiscal policy, Polanco-Abreu was quickly appointed chairman of the financial services committee. One of the most powerful groups in the legislature, the committee was responsible for the commonwealth's entire budget. It was said that he did 75 percent of the committee's work himself, rarely relinquishing control and refusing to create permanent

Image courtesy of the Library of Congress

subcommittees to manage the legislative workload. Polanco-Abreu oversaw huge increases in government spending, causing many to observe that he might be overly loyal to the Muñoz Marín administration.[9] "Polanco has been so close to Muñoz since he was a fledgling in the Legislature that it is difficult to distinguish the branch from the tree," went one assessment.[10]

Five days before the Puerto Rican house reconvened in January 1963, speaker Ernesto Ramos Antonini died of a heart attack, creating a power vacuum at the helm of the PPD.[11] As chairman of the financial services committee, Polanco-Abreu was quickly tapped by party leadership for inclusion on the short list of replacements. At 42, he was nearly a generation younger than the other candidates, including house vice president Jorge Font Saldaña, whom many viewed as the logical successor, but Polanco-Abreu's "dynamic drive and quick intelligence" won him respect as a dark horse candidate.[12]

In a vote predetermined at party headquarters earlier that day, Polanco-Abreu was formally elected speaker of the Puerto Rican house of representatives on January 17, 1963. His youth, his humble beginnings, and his party loyalty made him the overwhelming choice to lead the next generation of PPD brass.[13] The *San Juan Star Sunday Magazine* wrote, "For a politician, Polanco casts an immaculate image which inspires trust. One would never think of Polanco Abreu as foxy, cunning, or cagey. He appears like an open book."[14] Amid speculation that Muñoz Marín had influenced the vote, administration officials denied any involvement. "Polanco made it on his own," they said.[15] From the start, the young speaker maintained the furious energy that had fueled his climb to the top. After a breakfast of black coffee—"the staple of his diet," observed one journalist—Polanco-Abreu arrived at the capitol just before eight o'clock in the morning, worked 12 to 14 hours a day five days a week, and met with constituents on Saturdays. He was well liked by his house colleagues and often settled policy disputes over dinner at his home on McLeary Street.[16] Polanco-Abreu himself presided over nearly every legislative day. His duties as speaker forced him to abandon his law practice in San Juan, but he kept his Isabela district office open. "I want to dedicate all my time to public service," he said in spring 1963.[17]

As speaker, Polanco-Abreu never strayed far from the PPD's agenda, keeping the Puerto Rican house on a short tether. Along with Puerto Rico's secretary of state and the senate's majority leader, Polanco-Abreu made up the island's political "triumvirate," the governor's unofficial brain trust.[18] He oversaw the commonwealth's budget, continued to advocate for rural and underserved communities, supported Puerto Rico's involvement in Caribbean affairs, and championed the island's commonwealth status and cultural identity. "When a people is associated permanently with another country like the United States which is an economic giant, there are grave and serious risks that assimilation can occur," he said shortly after taking office, "but I have fought and will continue to fight so that the people of Puerto Rico conserve all their spiritual wealth and all their personality as a people."[19] Despite his efforts, Polanco-Abreu faced severe difficulties and was forced to admit, "The work facing Puerto Rico is not the task of men but of generations."[20]

The next generation of PPD leaders was pushed to take action sooner than Polanco-Abreu anticipated. On August 16, 1964, the speaker learned at the party's nominating convention that Governor Muñoz Marín would not run for re-election. Even more important, Polanco-Abreu had been handpicked to succeed the retiring Resident Commissioner in the U.S. House, Antonio Fernós-Isern.[21] Shocked and somewhat dismayed, he accepted the nomination.[22] Ever loyal, Polanco-Abreu insisted it was his "moral obligation to accept the mandate of the central committee of the party."[23]

There was little doubt about the outcome of the 1964 race. As speaker, Polanco-Abreu had wide name recognition, and as a party lieutenant he was able to marshal important campaign resources. He stumped primarily in Spanish and was frequently criticized for being deficient in English.[24] The party platform pushed for permanent commonwealth status, judicial and electoral reform, the decentralization of municipal planning boards, more funding for vocational training, and the expansion of the island's police force.[25] After directing orientations for local party leaders and giving a radio address on the eve of the election, Polanco-Abreu achieved a "crushing" victory, capturing 59 percent of the ballot and beating statehood Republican candidate Manuel Iglesias by nearly 205,000 votes.[26]

Polanco-Abreu made friends quickly in the U.S. House and throughout Washington, D.C., but as Resident Commissioner he lacked legislative power and voting privileges. The island press described his position as "little more than that of a 'cost-plus' lobbyist with the right to hang his hat in the House Office Building."[27] Just two months into his first session, Polanco-Abreu said, "It would be worth-while … to review the concept of the Resident Commissioner."[28] His frustration at being unable to vote on the floor continued to plague him throughout his House tenure. He sat on committees with jurisdictions relevant to Puerto Rico's major legislative concerns—Agriculture, Armed Services, and Interior and Insular Affairs—and although he supported President Lyndon B. Johnson's Great Society programs, Polanco-Abreu was limited to a supporting role because of his inability to vote.

Over the course of his House career, Polanco-Abreu focused on constituent services, introducing dozens of private relief bills, advocating for the extension of federal services, and seeking to fit Puerto Rico's interests into the President's social programs. When Congress moved to curtail subsidies for American rice exports in 1965, Polanco-Abreu testified about the devastating effects this policy would have on the island. Higher food prices "would be a step in retreat in today's war on poverty being waged by the administration and the Congress," he said.[29] The commonwealth's relaxed labor laws were key to its economic development, and Polanco-Abreu opposed amendments to the Fair Labor Standards Act that would raise the national minimum wage by 50 cents. Many felt this increase would be detrimental to current business and discourage potential industry.[30] The problem, Polanco-Abreu said on the House Floor, was that the island was being judged by mainland standards. "The economic intrinsics of Puerto Rico are so different from those of the United States as to be almost unfathomable," he said in May 1966.[31]

Polanco-Abreu compensated for his lack of voting privileges by testifying frequently before House and Senate committees. Because Polanco-Abreu knew the value of education, one of his main goals was to improve the island's school system. He helped procure millions in funding for local schools, predicting that the Elementary and Secondary Education Act of 1965 would affect Puerto Rico more dramatically than any previous education bill.[32] During a hearing on a 1966 education bill, he observed that education could help lower crime. "Our war against crime must be waged not with clubs and guns, but with books and tools," he said.[33] Later, when Congress considered reforming the Social Security system during the 90th Congress (1967–1969), Polanco-Abreu implored his colleagues to remember that Puerto Rico's residents were U.S. citizens and required the same protections as those on the mainland.

Polanco-Abreu never had the opportunity to tackle Puerto Rico's status question. On July 23, 1967, the people of Puerto Rico voted to remain a U.S. commonwealth, delaying any congressional debate about the island's independence or statehood. When the Resident Commissioner announced the results of the plebiscite on the House Floor the next day, Majority Leader Carl Albert of Oklahoma and Majority Whip Hale Boggs of Louisiana offered their congratulations. "I must pay tribute to the distinguished Resident Commissioner and his diligence in representing the interests of Puerto Rico here upon the floor and before the congressional committees," Boggs said. The peaceful vote, he added, was "something that all of us as Americans can be very proud of."[34]

Despite the pro-commonwealth vote and seemingly strong support for the PPD, the island's Partido Nuevo Progresista (New Progressive Party, or PNP) had grown more powerful during Polanco-Abreu's four years in Washington. By 1968 infighting had undercut the PPD's effectiveness, forcing Polanco-Abreu onto the short list of gubernatorial candidates. Given the rank and file's distrust of party leadership, Polanco-Abreu touted "his candidacy as the only way of reconciling" the PPD. "I represent the unity of the party," he said, emphasizing the theme of his campaign.[35] While the

other candidates indulged in personal attacks, Polanco-Abreu prided himself on running a clean, issues-oriented campaign and advocated for many of his congressional interests, including education, rehabilitation for drug users, and economic growth.[36] In early July he likened his campaign to "a rising river that is opening paths and filling ditches."[37] But running for governor while serving as Resident Commissioner was taxing; Polanco-Abreu spent four days a week in Puerto Rico and the remainder of the week in Washington, often giving interviews in the airport.[38] During the closed primary in late July, Polanco-Abreu failed to win the nomination, placing second to the senate's majority leader.[39] Instead he was nominated for re-election as Resident Commissioner, a race that many, including Polanco-Abreu, assumed he would win.[40] But after a contentious campaign in which his opponent Jorge Luis Córdova-Díaz of the PNP criticized him for missing subcommittee meetings and ignoring the island's booming middle class, Polanco-Abreu lost by roughly 15,000 votes, or only 1.7 percent.[41]

After his loss, Polanco-Abreu retired from politics and returned to his law practice in Isabela. He died 20 years later, on the morning of January 18, 1988. The island was plunged into mourning, and Polanco-Abreu's dedicated service to Puerto Rico was commemorated by friends and political foes alike. "He was a magnificent speaker and his record as resident commissioner was brilliant," reflected his former running mate, Luis Negrón Lopez. "Puerto Rico has lost a good man," said former governor Roberto Sanchez Vilella.[42] But Polanco-Abreu himself said it best: "I have served the Popular Democratic Party," he had noted after leaving politics in 1968. "I served the cause to which I have devoted my life."[43]

FOR FURTHER READING

Acevedo, Héctor Luis, ed., *Santiago Polanco Abreu: Compromiso y verticalidad en su lucha por Puerto Rico* (San Juan: Universidad Interamericana de Puerto Rico, 2010).

Biographical Directory of the United States Congress, "Santiago Polanco-Abreu," http://bioguide.congress.gov.

NOTES

1 "Yo no voy a Washington a caza de prebendas ni de bienes materiales. Voy a Washington como ciudadano de primera clase, a defender los derechos de mi pueblo y a servir a la causa de la democracia." Luis E. Agrait Betancourt, "La educación política de un Comisionado Residente," in Hector Luis Acevedo, ed., *Santiago Polanco Abreu: Compromiso y verticalidad en su lucha por Puerto Rico* (San Juan: Universidad Interamericana de Puerto Rico, 2010): 383–384. Translated as "The Political Education of a Resident Commissioner," by Translations International, Inc. (October 2011).

2 "Y Anita, la mamá de Chaguín.... El padre de Santiago Polanco Abreu, don Santiago Polanco González." José Enrique Ayoroa Santaliz, "El entorno familiar y emocional del joven Chaguin Polanco," in Acevedo, ed., *Santiago Polanco Abreu: Compromiso y verticalidad en su lucha por Puerto Rico*: 91, 93. Translated as "The Family and Emotional Background of Young Chaguin Polanco," by Translations International, Inc. (October 2011). See also Juan Manuel Ocasio, "The Man Called Polanco," 2 February 1964, *San Juan Star Sunday Magazine*: 8.

3 Alan Lupo, "A Jibaro in the Halls of Congress," 25 February 1965, *Baltimore Sun*: 18.

4 Manny Suarez, "Polanco Abreu Apparently Kills Self," 19 January 1988, *San Juan Star*: 1. "Durante la Segunda Guerra Mundial, Polanco Abreu inició dos etapas de importancia personal, obtuvo el grado de Licenciado en Derecho en 1943 y casó el año siguiente con Viola Orsini." Ruben Arrieta, "Un doloroso aniversario,"19 January 1988, *El nuevo dia*: 7. Translated as "A Painful Anniversary," by Translations International, Inc. (October 2011).

5 *Congressional Record*, 89th Cong. 1st sess. (28 April 1965): 8744.

6 Ocasio, "The Man Called Polanco."

7 Lupo, "A Jibaro in the Halls of Congress."

8 Ocasio, "The Man Called Polanco."

9 A. W. Moldonado, "Record P.R. Budget Goes to Legislature," 15 January 1963, *San Juan Star*: 1; "Polanco—Prospects Bright," 18 January 1963, *San Juan Star*: 15.

10 Ocasio, "The Man Called Polanco."

11 Eddie Lopez, "Ramos Antonini, 64, Dies Suddenly," 10 January 1963, *San Juan Star*: 1.

12 Eddie Lopez, "Key Topic at Capitol: Who'll Succeed Ramos?" 11 January 1963, *San Juan Star*: 1; A. W. Maldonado, "The New Leader," 13 March 1963, *San Juan Star*: 13.

13 A. W. Maldonado, "Polanco Abreu Voted New House Speaker," 18 January 1963, *San Juan Star*: 1.

14 Ocasio, "The Man Called Polanco."

15 A. W. Maldonado, "Munoz Did Not Take Sides in Speaker Election," 19 January 1963, *San Juan Star*: 4.

16 Margot Preece, "Polanco Abreu Has Firm Grip on House," 2 February 1963, *San Juan Star*: 7; Nory Segarra, "Speaker's Wife Trained in Politics But Her Main Job Is Their Home," 28 January 1963, *San Juan Star*: 10.

17 "Polanco Clarifies Remarks about Practice of Law," 4 April 1963, *San Juan Star*: 3.

18 Ocasio, "The Man Called Polanco."

19 Preece, "Polanco Abreu Has Firm Grip on House."

20 Normal Gall, "'Social Redemption' Confronts Puerto Rico—Polanco Abreu," 6 February 1963, *San Juan Star*: 3; Margot Preece, "House Sends Record Budget to Senate," 22 May 1963, *San Juan Star*: 3; "A Bigger Budget," 22 May 1963, *San Juan Star*: 15; Margot Preece, "Legislature Convenes; Vote Law Change Due," 14 January 1964, *San Juan Star*: 1.

21 Margot Preece, "House Speaker Gives Details of Nominating Convention," 15 August 1964, *San Juan Star*: 1.

22 A. W. Maldonado, "What Really Happened: Inside the Popular Convention," 30 August 1964, *San Juan Star Magazine*: 3.

23 "Polanco Abreu: 'I'm Not Upset,'" 26 August 1964, *San Juan Star*: 3.

24 Walter S. Priest, "What Lies Ahead for Polanco?" 15 November 1964, *San Juan Star Sunday Magazine*: 3; "P.D.P. to Orientate District Chiefs," 25 August 1964, *San Juan Star*: 6.

25 "Popular Leaders Launch Attacks on Republicans," 30 January 1964, *San Juan Star*: 3; "The Political Platforms: Popular Democratic Party," 2 November 1964, *San Juan Star*: 25.

26 "The Campaign Trail Today," 2 November 1964, *San Juan Star*: 3; Eddie Lopez, Frank Ramos, and Tomas Stella, "P.D.P. Rolls to Another Landslide Win," 4 November 1964, *San Juan Star*: 1; "Election Statistics, 1920 to Present," http://history.house.gov/institution/election-statistics/election-statistics.

27 Priest, "What Lies Ahead for Polanco?"

28 Lupo, "A Jibaro in the Halls of Congress."

29 Hearing before the House Subcommittee on Oilseeds and Rice of the Committee on Agriculture, *Rice*, 89th Cong., 1st sess. (11–13 May 1965): 167–168.

30 *Congressional Record*, House, 89th Cong., 2nd sess. (16 May 1966): 10584–10585; *Congressional Record*, House, 89th Cong., 2nd sess. (17 May 1966): 10850.

31 *Congressional Record*, House, 89th Cong., 2nd sess. (24 May 1966): 11274–11275.

32 *Congressional Record*, House, 89th Cong., 1st sess. (24 March 1965): 5764.

33 Hearing before the House Select Subcommittee on Labor, Committee on Education and Labor, *Manpower Development and Training Amendments of 1966*, 89th Cong., 2nd sess. (2 June 1966): 32–33.

34 *Congressional Record*, House, 90th Cong., 1st sess. (24 July 1967): 19870.

35 Henry Giniger, "Three Rivals Divide Ruling Party in Puerto Rico," 22 April 1968, *New York Times*: 68.

36 James McDonough, "PDP Candidates Continue on Trail: Polanco," 8 July 1968, *San Juan Star*: 3.

37 James McDonough, "Polanco: I'll Gain at Convention," 7 July 1968, *San Juan Star*: 3.

38 James McDonough, "Polanco's Campaign," 10 July 1968, *San Juan Star*: 21; James McDonough, "Polanco Kisses Off Sanchez' Chances," 11 July 1968, *San Juan Star*: 3.

39 Henry Giniger, "Puerto Rico Party Denies Governor Renomination," 22 July 1968, *New York Times*: 32.

40 James McDonough, "Polanco Mentions 'Sacrifice' in Renomination for Post," 22 July 1968, *San Juan Star*: 3.

41 "Election Statistics, 1920 to Present," http://history.house.gov/institution/election-statistics/election-statistics.

42 Quotes from Jaime Pieras, "Political Leaders Shocked by Death of Polanco Abreu," 19 January 1988, *San Juan Star*: 14; Suarez, "Polanco Abreu Apparently Kills Self."

43 McDonough, "Polanco: I'll Gain at Convention." In the days following his death, the press reported that Polanco-Abreu was believed to have taken his own life.

Jorge Luis Córdova-Díaz
1907–1994

RESIDENT COMMISSIONER 1969–1973
NEW PROGRESSIVE FROM PUERTO RICO

In just one term, Jorge Luis Córdova-Díaz, a lifelong proponent of Puerto Rican statehood, did more to transform the office of Resident Commissioner than nearly all of his predecessors, including his father, Resident Commissioner Félix Córdova Dávila. In 1970 as the House overhauled its rules and procedures, Córdova-Díaz pushed for and won the right to vote in committee. Though still prohibited from voting on the floor, the Resident Commissioner was able for the first time to influence the national lawmaking process. Bolstered by his landmark legislation, Córdova-Díaz did everything he could to strengthen federal programs on the island, and his tireless work won him respect from the Caribbean to Washington. "Mr. Córdova is present on the floor of the House more than most other Members," said Republican Robert McClory of Illinois in 1970, "and he is a most articulate and knowledgeable representative" of Puerto Rico's diverse interests.[1]

Córdova-Díaz was born in Manatí, Puerto Rico, on April 20, 1907, to Félix Córdova Dávila and Mercedes Díaz. As a boy, he attended the island's public schools, where he learned English. When Jorge Luis was 10, his father was elected Resident Commissioner to the U.S. House of Representatives, and in 1917 the Córdova-Díaz family moved to Washington, D.C., where Jorge Luis enrolled in the city's schools. The Resident Commissioner allowed his family to speak only Spanish at home, and Córdova-Díaz's bilingualism was the start of his political education.[2] Early on, he wrote speeches in English for his father, accompanying him to House sessions during the Warren G. Harding, Calvin Coolidge, and Herbert Hoover administrations.[3] He remained in the nation's capital for college, graduating with an A.B. from The Catholic University of America in 1928 and earning a law degree from Harvard University in 1931. Like his father, Córdova-Díaz returned to Puerto Rico and practiced law, until 1940, when he was selected to the supreme court of San Juan. In 1945 he was appointed to the bench of the supreme court of Puerto Rico, a move Resident Commissioner Jesús T. Piñero of the Partido Popular Democrático (Popular Democratic Party or PPD) adamantly opposed for political reasons.[4] Córdova-Díaz sat on the island's bench until 1946. He and his wife, Dora Rodríguez, had four children: Jorge Luis, Jr.; Elvira; Irene; and Fernando.[5]

Córdova-Díaz was a loyal advocate for statehood, but during the buildup to the election of 1960, he helped found the Partido Acción Cristiana (Christian Action Party, or PAC), whose ranks included individuals frustrated by "a government-sponsored recession of morality and spirituality."[6] Church officials quickly adopted the party's mantra.[7] Though they reassured the public that its involvement would not violate the separation of church and state, many voters were soon unable "to distinguish between clerical objectives and the broader aspects of the PAC program," asserts one historian.[8] Like many third parties, the PAC was short-lived. But in 1960 Córdova-Díaz ran as its candidate for Resident Commissioner, placing a distant third with roughly 7 percent of the vote, well behind the victor, Antonio Fernós-Isern of the Partido Popular Democrático.[9] After the election, Córdova-Díaz turned his attention back to Puerto Rican statehood. As a founding member of the nonpartisan Citizens for State 51, he was eventually catapulted back into the island's political scene.

Not long afterward, Córdova-Díaz joined up with members of the Partido Nuevo Progresista (New Progressive Party, or PNP), a pro-statehood faction that was sensitive to the ambitions of the island's booming middle class.[10] In 1968 the PNP nominated him for Resident Commissioner. With the incumbent Resident Commissioner, Santiago Polanco-Abreu of the PPD,

Image courtesy of the Library of Congress

dividing his time between Puerto Rico and Washington, Córdova-Díaz had a slight advantage during the campaign. Also in his favor, the PPD was in the middle of an identity crisis, struggling to craft an agenda after longtime party leaders had begun stepping aside.[11]

The 1968 campaign was about form as much as function; the dominant issue was the role of the Resident Commissioner. For the last four years, the PPD had emphasized that the nonvoting position reflected the island's unique status as a commonwealth. But the PNP wanted the Resident Commissioner to have more responsibility, like the other Members.[12] While Polanco-Abreu prioritized committee hearings and legislation that dealt explicitly with Puerto Rico, Córdova-Díaz promised to "share in the concern not only for national and international problems but also for local matters affecting other congressmen."[13] By inserting Puerto Rico's interests into an array of mainland concerns, he planned to compensate for the Resident Commissioner's inability to vote on national legislation. Supporting certain bills would give him more clout when he asked for help concerning "the problems affecting Puerto Rico," he explained.[14]

Regarding Puerto Rico's problems, Córdova-Díaz echoed the PNP's general platform, taking a long-term approach to the status question. Anticipating congressional resistance, he promised the party would not "ask Congress for statehood until the people have had an opportunity to decide for themselves in a plebiscite or a referendum."[15] With a healthy respect for the island's economy, which was becoming increasingly industrial, Córdova-Díaz favored a staggered revenue program—with various rates assigned to different sectors of the financial system—forcing the businesses with the lowest rates to abide by federal minimum wage laws. Also hoping to diversify the island's agricultural production, he asked farmers to give goods for local markets priority over exports of sugar and tobacco.[16]

On Election Day the PNP clinched a signal victory, taking the governorship, the office of Resident Commissioner, the Puerto Rican house, and the San Juan mayor's office. Pundits struggled to make sense of the results: "The enormity of what happened here Tuesday night is still sinking in," wrote the editors of the *San Juan Star*. "The depth and desire for change in the Puerto Rican electorate was underestimated by all the politicians." Córdova-Díaz edged out Polanco-Abreu in the general election by 2 points, taking 43.8 percent of the vote. "We think Jorge Luis Cordova Diaz … will be an excellent representative for the island in Washington. He is an outstanding lawyer, completely bilingual, and he understand[s] Washington," the editorial continued.[17] Córdova-Díaz's victory was a long time in the making, coming after nearly 30 years of one-party control. "I feel great joy and satisfaction in seeing that at last my people have awakened and have started to practice democracy," Córdova-Díaz said.[18] He promised to consult PPD leaders before taking action on certain pieces of legislation.[19]

Like the election, the transition for the new Resident Commissioner was cordial. Polanco-Abreu congratulated Córdova-Díaz and briefed the new Resident Commissioner and his staff when they visited Washington after the election. Also, Polaco-Abreu promised to introduce Córdova-Díaz later in the year to his new responsibilities and House colleagues, a courtesy he had not been shown by his predecessor.[20]

In the House, Córdova-Díaz was aligned with the Democrats at the start of the 91st Congress (1969–1971), sitting on their side of the chamber and being formally included on the Democratic committee rosters.[21] With the exception of his pro-statehood stance, much of his agenda echoed his PPD predecessors'. Like them, he was sent to Congress to ensure that Puerto Rico received its share of aid from the federal government, an assignment that grew increasingly difficult amid the island's growing prosperity.[22] He was placed on the Agriculture, Armed Services, and Interior and Insular Affairs Committees. These assignments, which symbolized Puerto Rico's main legislative concerns, were traditionally given to the Resident Commissioner, but since Córdova-Díaz could neither vote nor accrue seniority in committee, he was an observer more than anything else.[23] Córdova-Díaz nevertheless maintained a furious work schedule, beginning his day by attending the congressional prayer

breakfast with Members from both parties before logging a reported 16 hours at his office.[24] "I'm in the chamber, in the dining room, in the different groups up here," he said.[25]

Córdova-Díaz's tenure in Washington coincided with a major effort to reform the structure of the House, and he took advantage of this internal push for greater accountability by leveraging an amendment to the Legislative Reorganization Act of 1970 (H.R. 17654) to win the right to vote in committee. The *Washington Post* highlighted Córdova-Díaz's daily frustrations, and he used the publicity to lobby for reforms.[26] In September he made good on a campaign promise, introducing a revision to House Rule XII during debate on the Legislative Reorganization Act. The revision allowed the Resident Commissioner to "be elected to serve on standing committees in the same manner as Members of the House and ... possess in such committees the same powers and privileges as the other Members."[27] To Córdova-Díaz's surprise, Members from both sides supported the measure. "Let us take away a paper title and afford him the opportunity to voice the aspirations and hopes of his people," said Democrat Shirley Chisholm of New York. "This is an important and necessary change in the rules of this body," responded Ohio Republican Clarence Miller.[28] Despite the measure's success in the House, Córdova-Díaz felt sure it would fail in the Senate. "I can't complain that I've been ignored," he said after the House vote, "but I feel if the bill is passed [by the Senate] the chances are better that I'll be listened to. These department heads are well aware that I haven't had the vote and now they'll realize that someday they might need me. So I feel they'll be more responsive when I ask them for something."[29] With the Senate's passage of the amendment in early October, the office of Resident Commissioner became more powerful than ever before.[30]

At the start of the 92nd Congress (1971–1973), Córdova-Díaz was appointed to the Committee on Interior and Insular Affairs. His assignments to three subcommittees—Mines and Mining, National Parks and Recreation, and Territories—illustrated his efforts to involve himself as Resident Commissioner in the daily business of the House.[31] Córdova-Díaz rarely missed a hearing or a markup session, and his new ability to vote in committee necessitated his identification with a party. Córdova-Díaz chose to align himself with Republicans, who rewarded him with a seat in the party caucus in 1971. The PNP had no national affiliation, but with the upcoming election against the resurgent PPD, any affiliation with House Democrats could become a political liability.[32] Democratic freshman Herman Badillo, a Puerto Rican-born Member from New York City, criticized Córdova-Díaz's decision, arguing in island newspapers that he had further relinquished power in a Democratic-controlled House, but Ron de Lugo, the new Democratic Delegate from the Virgin Islands, was more sympathetic. "I don't know what else he could have done," he said.[33]

As a member of the Interior and Insular Affairs Committee, Córdova-Díaz was in a good position to advocate for funding for Puerto Rico. The existing laws prevented Congress from appropriating money to U.S. territories as it did to states, and since Puerto Ricans paid no federal income tax, many Members of Congress felt the practice was justified. In perhaps his most persistent legislative effort, Córdova-Díaz helped convince his colleagues to change this arrangement. During debate on the Economic Opportunity Act (S. 2007), Republican William Steiger of Wisconsin introduced an amendment as part of H.R. 10351 that would prioritize federal programs on the mainland and provide funding for territories only if there was a surplus. Córdova-Díaz immediately substituted his amendment "to place Puerto Rico, Guam, and the Virgin Islands in the same position as States." Córdova-Díaz's amendment garnered bipartisan support and passed the House 202 to 161 in a teller vote. Córdova-Díaz reported feeling "wonderful." "It's the most amazing success I've had yet in Congress," he said, "even more than getting the right to vote in committee."[34] But President Richard M. Nixon vetoed the final version of the legislation because he opposed the appropriation of nearly $2 billion for child development programs.[35] Long a supporter of Puerto Rican statehood, Córdova-Díaz viewed the veto as a "severe blow" and a major disappointment.[36]

Córdova-Díaz's four years in office were marked by increasingly unstable conditions in Puerto Rico: a sliding economy, rising prices, government corruption, and violence in the labor force.[37] The political atmosphere in 1972 was so toxic that San Juan's leading English-language newspaper refused to endorse candidates from either party. "The political process in Puerto Rico has been demeaned to a dangerously low point, there has been a grave clogging of public business, and grievous injury has been inflicted on the Puerto Rican spirit," said an editorial on the front page of the *San Juan Star*. "Puerto Rico cannot afford four more years like the past four years, from either the standpoint of programs to meet demands or from the damage done to a people's conception of itself." [38]

While voters directed much of their animosity toward the gubernatorial candidates, Córdova-Díaz found the race to be closer than he expected. He was renominated for Resident Commissioner and faced PPD candidate Jaime Benítez in the general election. After the House adjourned in mid-October, Córdova-Díaz returned to Puerto Rico to campaign, only weeks before the election. He kept his focus small and tried "to run a more personal campaign," visiting towns and communities scattered throughout the island.[39] Córdova-Díaz supported Puerto Rico's full participation in federal housing and welfare programs and remained a steadfast proponent of statehood.[40] Supporters praised his "caliber and sincerity" and commended his reform efforts in Washington.[41] While both candidates supported federal initiatives in Puerto Rico, Benítez reignited a 1968 debate when he announced, "The greatest strength of the Resident Commissioner in the United States lies in his own exceptional and peculiar responsibility."[42] While Córdova-Díaz had won concessions from Congress during the last four years, Benítez, like many in the PPD, sought to redirect federal policy by emphasizing Puerto Rico's unique position as a free and associated commonwealth.

Nearly 1.3 million people voted in the 1972 general election, and when the ballots were tallied, Córdova-Díaz had lost by more than 7 percent.[43] His association with an island administration that many considered corrupt weighed heavily on his chances for re-election, adding to the general pro-commonwealth sentiment.[44]

After his defeat, Córdova-Díaz returned to Puerto Rico. On September 18, 1994, he died at his home in Guaynabo at age 87.[45] In the House of Representatives Córdova-Díaz was remembered as "Don Jorge," a "distinguished leader" who "epitomized the virtues of a dedicated public servant."[46]

FOR FURTHER READING

Biographical Directory of the United States Congress, "Jorge Luis Córdova-Díaz," http://bioguide.congress.gov.

NOTES

1 *Congressional Record*, House, 91st Cong., 2nd sess. (15 September 1970): 31849.

2 Robert L. Asher, "'Congressman' without a Vote," 26 July 1970, *Washington Post*: B6; Harry Turner, "Cordova Diaz Pays Visit to Capitol," 6 December 1968, *San Juan Star*: 32; Marty Gerard Delfin, "Cordova Diaz, Former Resident Commissioner, Dies in Guaynabo," 18 September 1994, *San Juan Star*: 8.

3 Turner, "Córdova Díaz Pays Visit to Capitol": 32; Harry Turner, "Cordova Diaz Takes Oath for Washington Post," 4 January 1969, *San Juan Star*: 3.

4 Charles McCabe, "Sólo Piñero ha pedido ser oído sobre Córdova," 1 November 1945, *El mundo*: 1. Hearing before the Senate Judiciary Committee, *Nomination of Jorge Luis Cordova Diaz*, 79th Cong., 1st sess. (7 November 1945): 2–12.

5 *Congressional Record*, Extension of Remarks, 103rd Cong., 2nd sess. (26 September 1994): 25807.

6 As quoted in Jerome Fischman, "The Church in Politics: The 1960 Election in Puerto Rico," *Western Political Quarterly* 18 (December 1965): 821; "Jorge Luis Cordova Diaz," 22 September 1994, *Washington Post*: C5.

7 A. W. Maldonado, "Governor Scores 4th Straight Win," 9 November 1960, *San Juan Star*: 1.

8 Fischman, "The Church in Politics": 825, 828.

9 This publication reflects his official name at the time of his first election in 1968: Jorge Luis Córdova-Díaz. During his one term in the House (1969–1973), he served under the name Jorge L. Córdova, which is how it appears in the *Congressional Directory* and the *Congressional Record*. "Election Statistics, 1920 to Present," http://history.house.gov/institution/election-statistics/election-statistics.

10 For information on the PNP, see César Ayala and Rafael Bernabe,

Puerto Rico in the American Century: A History since 1898 (Chapel Hill: University of North Carolina Press, 2007): 224–226; Dimas Planas, "Where Does the PDP Go from Here?," 8 November 1968, *San Juan Star*: 30.

11 Ayala and Bernabe, *Puerto Rico in the American Century*: 226.

12 Harry Turner, "Polanco in Congress," 23 October 1968, *San Juan Star*: 25.

13 Harry Turner, "Cordova Diaz Talks of 'New Approach,'" 5 December 1968, *San Juan Star*: 1.

14 "Polanco Won't Talk about Ferre Taxes," 1 November 1968, *San Juan Star*: 6.

15 Frank Ramos, "Cordova Diaz Predicts Stall in Status Vote," 15 November 1968, *San Juan Star*: 1.

16 Ramos, "Cordova Diaz Predicts Stall in Status Vote."

17 "Depth of Change," 7 November 1968, *San Juan Star*: 29.

18 Pedro Roman, "Cordova Sees NPP Win Signaling End to 'One Man Rule,'" 7 November 1968, *San Juan Star*: 6.

19 Turner, "Cordova Diaz Talks of 'New Approach.'"

20 Harry Turner, "Polanco Salutes Ferre, But Also Criticizes Him," 12 November 1968, *San Juan Star*: 3.

21 Turner, "Cordova Diaz Takes Oath for Washington Post."

22 An editorial in the *San Juan Star* pointed out, "As Puerto Rico's prosperity increases it is becoming more difficult in Washington to convince congressmen of the continuing need for help and special understanding of the island's problems." See "New Approach," 6 December 1968, *San Juan Star*: 39.

23 Garrison Nelson, *Committees in the U.S. Congress, 1947–1992* Vol. 2 (Washington, D.C.: Congressional Quarterly, Inc., 1994): 192.

24 *Congressional Record*, Extension of Remarks, 103rd Cong., 2nd sess. (26 September 1994): 25807; Ralph Nader Congress Project, *Citizens Look at Congress: Jorge L. Córdova, Resident Commissioner from Puerto Rico* (Washington, D.C.: Grossman Publishers, 1972): 1.

25 Asher, "'Congressman' without a Vote."

26 Robert F. Levey, "A Nonvoting Delegate Tells of His Frustrations on Hill," 5 April 1970, *Washington Post*: 53; Asher, "'Congressman' without a Vote."

27 *Congressional Record*, House, 91st Cong. 2nd sess. (15 September 1970): 31848.

28 Ibid., 31852.

29 Despite the prospect of obtaining Córdova-Díaz's support, some outspoken Members opposed the plan. Córdova-Díaz believed the problem was that his winning the right to vote in committee would set a precedent, making it easier for the Delegate from the District of Columbia "to attain a similar status" against the wishes of other Members in the House. George Gedda, "House Gives P.R. Commissioner Vote," 16 September 1970, *San Juan Star*: 1.

30 For an early treatment of what one historian calls the "Córdova Amendment," see William R. Tansill, "The Resident Commissioner to the United States from Puerto Rico: An Historical Perspective," *Revista juridica de la Universidad de Puerto Rico* 47 (No. 1–2, 1978): 83, 98–100.

31 Ralph Nader Congress Project, *Citizens Look at Congress: Jorge L. Córdova, Resident Commissioner from Puerto Rico*: 7.

32 Ibid., 6–7.

33 Ibid., 6.

34 Ed Konstant, "Cordova Nips Poverty Aid Cutback Bid," 1 October 1971, *San Juan Star*: 3; "To the Rescue," 1 October 1971, *San Juan Star*: 27. See also Ralph Nader Congress Project, *Citizens Look at Congress: Jorge L. Córdova, Resident Commissioner from Puerto Rico*: 8.

35 "President Vetoes Bill on Child Care," 10 October 1971, *San Juan Star*: 20.

36 "Cordova Calls OEO Bill Veto Severe Blow to Puerto Rico," 12 December 1971, *San Juan Star*: 3.

37 Fernando Bayron Toro, *Elecciones y los partidos políticos de Puerto Rico, 1809–2000* (Mayagüez: Editorial Isla, 2003): 253.

38 "An Editorial: Our Position," 3 November 1972, *San Juan Star*: 1, 38.

39 Ed Konstant, "Cordova Sees Sure Win for NPP in Nov.," 8 October 1972, *San Juan Star*: 6.

40 "Resident Commissioner, Questions and Answers," 5 November 1972, *San Juan Star Sunday Magazine*: S-7.

41 Dimas Planas, "An Easy Choice," 4 November 1972, *San Juan Star*: 46.

42 "Resident Commissioner, Questions and Answers."

43 Córdova-Díaz captured 560,119 votes (43.4 percent) versus Benitez's 656,885 (50.9 percent). See "Election Statistics, 1920 to Present," http://history.house.gov/institution/election-statistics/election-statistics.

44 Frank Ramos, "Downfall of the NPP," 10 November 1972, *San Juan Star*: 25.

45 "Deaths: Jorge Luis Cordova Diaz, Resident Commissioner," 22 September 1994, *Washington Post*: C5.

46 *Congressional Record*, Extension of Remarks, 103rd Cong., 2nd sess. (26 September 1994): 25807.

Manuel Luján, Jr.
1928–

UNITED STATES REPRESENTATIVE 1969–1989
REPUBLICAN FROM NEW MEXICO

Manuel Luján, Jr., served 10 terms in the U.S. House, making him the second-longest-serving Representative in New Mexico's history and the longest-serving Hispanic Representative in New Mexico to date. A Republican in an era when nearly all the Hispanic Members of Congress were Democrats, he rarely faced stiff competition for re-election, despite the fact that his district leaned Democratic. Luján made his greatest mark as a member of the House Interior and Insular Affairs Committee, on which he was the Ranking Member from 1981 through 1985. Criticized by environmental groups for being pro-business, Luján sought to balance environmental conservation with development and public use, paving the way for his appointment as Secretary of the Interior after he retired from the House. While in Congress, Luján focused on regional issues and on the needs of his constituents. "If I'm remembered for anything, I'd rather be remembered for constituent service than national legislation," he said.[1]

Manuel Luján, Jr., was born on a small farm near the Indian pueblo of San Ildefonso on May 12, 1928, to Manuel Luján, Sr., and Lorenzita Romero. Lujan's mother was a teacher and served as county clerk in Santa Fe County, New Mexico. Also a teacher, Luján, Sr., later used his visibility as the successful owner of an insurance company to launch a career in politics, serving as mayor of Santa Fe, New Mexico, from 1942 to 1948.[2] Additionally, he made unsuccessful bids for a seat in the U.S. Congress in 1944 and the governorship of New Mexico in 1948.[3] Luján, Jr., attended Our Lady of Guadalupe in elementary and junior high school before graduating from St. Michael's High School in Santa Fe in 1946. He then attended St. Mary's College in California, earning a B.A. from New Mexico's College of Santa Fe in 1950. While an undergraduate, Luján married Jean Kay Couchman on November 18, 1948. The couple had four children: Terra Kay, Jay, Barbara, and Jeff.[4] After graduating from college, Luján worked at his father's insurance company and served in the National Guard Reserve.

With his father's strong roots in New Mexico, Luján, Jr., was well positioned for a career in politics. He bolstered his credentials by serving as vice chairman of the New Mexico Republican Party, and built strong community ties by serving on the Bernalillo County Crime Commission and holding leadership roles with the Coronado Kiwanis and the Knights of Columbus.[5] After an unsuccessful run for the New Mexico state senate in 1964, Luján sought the Republican nomination for the U.S. House four years later. The elections for the 91st Congress (1969–1971) marked the first time New Mexico had two distinct districts. (Previously New Mexico had two At-Large seats.) Luján campaigned for the seat in the district in northern New Mexico. Primarily rural, except for Albuquerque and Santa Fe, the area encompassed 14 counties. In a crowded primary, Luján bested five opponents—including Schuble Cook, the Republican nominee in 1966 for one of New Mexico's two At-Large seats—to secure the Republican nomination.[6]

In the 1968 general election, Luján challenged five-term Democratic Representative Thomas Morris. During the campaign, Luján represented himself as a newcomer who would bring change to New Mexico. He aligned himself with Republican presidential candidate Richard M. Nixon, who carried the state in the fall. Luján emphasized his strong attachment to the community, including his years in the family business, and accused Morris of ignoring northern New Mexico during his tenure in the House.[7] He also criticized his opponent's emphasis on the value of congressional experience, which he described as a "seniority symphony" with the "same old lyrics" but no

Collection of the U.S. House of Representatives, Photography Collection

real benefits for constituents.[8] Luján advocated a return to fiscally conservative principles, calling for more-efficient government expenditures. "We must fight to keep vital government installations in New Mexico and move forward to develop a diversified economy, government, tourism and agriculture," he observed. "We should emphasize private business to create jobs."[9]

Luján's campaign demonstrated the candidate's tireless effort. Luján had driven his father around the state during his political campaigns in the 1940s, and in his own 1968 campaign he adopted another personal approach: traversing the northern portion of the state, which rarely saw At-Large House candidates, and visiting the homes of thousands of constituents.[10] His strategy paid off. Luján won 53 percent of the vote to unseat the incumbent for a spot in the 91st Congress.[11] In the other New Mexico House race, businessman Ed Foreman (a former U.S. Representative from Texas) defeated incumbent Representative Johnny Walker. Luján and Foreman were the first Republicans from New Mexico who were elected to the U.S. House since Albert Simms in 1928.[12]

Luján's arrival in Washington, D.C., in 1969 began auspiciously; his freshman peers in the Republican Party selected him as a member of the executive committee of the Republican Committee on Committees, the body responsible for Republican committee assignments.[13] This influential assignment enabled Luján to secure a spot on the Interior and Insular Affairs Committee, a panel of major importance to his mostly rural district. Luján remained there his entire career and served as the Ranking Republican on the committee in the 97th and 98th Congresses (1981–1985).

Luján demonstrated his interest in environmental preservation during his second term in the House, urging the federal government to purchase the Vermejo Ranch, a 485,000-acre tract of private land that spread across New Mexico and Colorado.[14] After legislation that would have allowed the government to buy the land failed to reach the House Floor in the waning days of the 92nd Congress (1971–1973), Luján continued to voice his concern about the fate of what he called "some of the most scenic areas of the United States."[15] In the 93rd Congress (1973–1975), Luján introduced his own measure to authorize the acquisition of the Vermejo Ranch. Although the House never voted on his bill, Luján's resolve to reserve wilderness land for public use became a hallmark of his career. One of Luján's crowning achievements in the House was the passage of his New Mexico Wilderness Act in 1980. For two years, he worked to balance competing interests involved in incorporating more than 600,000 acres of land in New Mexico into the National Wilderness Preservation System. "Every effort has been made in it to satisfy the interests of everyone involved from the mining interests to the timber interests, from the cattlemen to the conservationists," Luján said. Later the New Mexico Representative called the new wilderness areas "one of the most complete packages in the United States."[16]

Despite these conservation efforts, Luján earned a reputation as an advocate for opening federal lands to recreation and commerce because he frequently supported increased mining, grazing, and logging on federal lands, including areas in New Mexico. Criticized by environmental groups that believed he valued business interests over conservation, Luján insisted he wanted "a balance between preservation and development."[17]

In 1981 Luján's interest in developing natural resources shifted temporarily when he learned that the Department of the Interior planned to lease 700 acres of New Mexico wilderness for oil and gas development. Furious that Secretary of the Interior James G. Watt and President Ronald W. Reagan had not informed him of their intention, Luján introduced legislation to prohibit further leases of wilderness area for development.[18] Not wanting to lose an important Republican ally on the Interior and Insular Affairs Committee, Watt attempted to make amends by proposing to ban federal mineral leasing until 2000, but exceptions that would open certain wilderness areas to development without congressional approval made the proposal objectionable to Luján, who responded by introducing the Wilderness Protection Act of 1982. "Everyone, even the hardliners, oppose[s] drilling in the wilderness," Luján observed. "This is just recognizing the fact that nobody wants it and putting it into writing."[19] Luján's bill, H.R. 6542, passed the House on August 12, 1982, but failed to reach a vote in the Senate.

Aside from his disagreement with Watt, Luján advocated additional exploration and development of nuclear energy during his time as Ranking Member of the Interior and Insular Affairs Committee. Concerned that "frivolous actions" by states would "impede the progress of a major Federal program," Luján proposed an amendment to the Nuclear Waste Policy Act of 1982 that would allow either the House or the Senate—rather than both chambers—to override a state's objection to an interim facility to store nuclear waste. The New Mexico Representative contended that his amendment would "achieve a proper balance" between states' rights and the need to develop a national solution for the disposal of nuclear waste.[20] Ultimately, the House narrowly defeated his amendment.[21] Luján worked closely for more than a decade with Interior and Insular Affairs Chairman Morris Udall of Arizona on the issue of nuclear waste disposal. Udall, a Democrat, praised his Republican colleague for avoiding partisanship.[22]

Early in his House career, Luján promised to focus on constituent service and the needs of his congressional district. "I think of myself more as a nuts and bolts type of individual rather than trying to push some federal program with far-reaching effects," Luján noted.[23] As the Representative of a district with high levels of structural unemployment, especially in the rural northern counties, he supported legislation to extend tax credits to businesses that would come to economically deprived states like New Mexico. Luján's district included several Indian reservations. Throughout his tenure, Luján supported tribal sovereignty and sponsored numerous laws to improve the lives of Native Americans in his state.[24] Like most Western Congressmen (of both parties), Luján sought to protect local water rights and opposed what he viewed as excessive federal control over New Mexico's water resources.[25]

During his time in office, Luján embraced fiscal conservatism and supported a balanced budget. The Congressman saw his fiscal agenda as vital to the country's economic well-being, believing that excessive federal spending would lead to dangerous levels of inflation. Since Luján generally favored military appropriations, he advocated cuts in discretionary domestic spending. He also argued that economic growth would result only from reduced taxes and the elimination of excessive federal regulations.[26] Luján also had a philosophical reason to reduce federal spending."This dependence on Government," he contended, "is a result of years of conditioning during which that very Government was too fast to try to solve every problem any individual, city, county or State might have."[27] In the end, the Congressman believed he failed to implement the fiscal aspect of his agenda. "I went there to balance the budget," Luján said after announcing his retirement in 1988. "In 20 years we haven't done that."[28]

Luján's regional focus and attention to his district were evident at the polls during the 1970s; although he was opposed by several prominent New Mexican Democratic candidates, he managed to win re-election by comfortable margins.[29] But in 1980, Luján's bid for a seventh term in the House was unexpectedly challenged by the former executive director of the state Democratic Party, Bill Richardson. Despite his lack of elective experience, Richardson ran an aggressive, well-financed campaign, attacking Luján's voting and attendance record and targeting Hispanic voters (he spoke Spanish and was Mexican American).[30] Luján touted his seniority, committee work, and focus on the district. "I believe my record of service to my constituents is unmatched in the Congress," he said.[31] Luján defeated Richardson by a razor-thin margin, with 51 percent of the vote, though Republican presidential nominee Ronald Reagan easily bested incumbent President James Earl (Jimmy) Carter in the state.[32] Luján blamed his close call on complacency, saying, "It had been too easy before. It won't happen again."[33]

Viewed by Democrats as vulnerable because of the tight race in 1980, Luján also had to contend with redistricting before the next election. A population increase necessitated the creation of a third congressional district for New Mexico. The legislature created a new, heavily Democratic district in northern New Mexico that included the state capital, Santa Fe.[34] Luján's new constituency was centered in Albuquerque and its immediate suburbs, an area that had seen considerable development of the aerospace, technology, and military industries after World War II. Despite the district's more favorable makeup, Luján encountered another tough Democratic challenge: Jan Hartke, the treasurer of New Mexico and the son of former Indiana Senator Vance Hartke.[35] But Luján had learned from the mistakes of his re-election bid in 1980, in which the incumbent had not even hired a campaign manager. He directed a well-financed, energetic campaign and defeated Hartke, winning 52 percent of the vote. In his remaining re-election bids, Luján earned 65 percent of the vote in 1984 and 71 percent in 1986.[36]

In 1985 Luján gave up his position as Ranking Republican on the Interior and Insular Affairs Committee to become the Ranking Republican on the Science and Technology Committee. He retained this position during the 99th and 100th Congresses (1985–1989).[37] A member of the Science and Technology panel since the 95th Congress (1977–1979), Luján recognized that the committee's work was increasingly meaningful in his newly drawn district. With his constituency shifting from a rural to an urban base and Albuquerque's growing emphasis on technology, Luján's position as Ranking Member on the Science and Technology Committee became an even more effective tool he could use to serve his district. Issues associated with nuclear development and energy were particularly important to central New Mexico. The Los Alamos National Laboratory was founded in 1942 to coordinate the development of an atomic bomb during World War II. After the war, the lab, which played a key role in the creation of the hydrogen bomb and other Cold War weapons, employed thousands of people and became vital to New Mexico's economy.

Luján's new prominence on the Science and Technology Committee also helped deflect criticism of what some perceived as a parochial focus at the expense of national issues.[38] Previously a steadfast supporter of the American space program, Luján had begun in the mid-1980s to question the direction and management of the National Aeronautics and Space Administration (NASA), and he pushed for more congressional oversight.[39] On January 28, 1986, the New Mexico Congressman watched the televised launch of the space shuttle *Challenger* in his House office with NASA's acting administrator, William Graham. Devastated by the shuttle's explosion and the loss of the seven astronauts on board, Luján became a leading critic of NASA during investigations of the tragic accident. "I think we have been too cozy over the years with NASA," he remarked. "We never really questioned what it is that they were doing."[40] Because he was knowledgeable about and interested in the space program, Luján was one of four Members of Congress (two Representatives and two Senators) who served as advisers to the National Commission on Space, a panel created before the *Challenger* disaster to develop long-term U.S. policy on space.[41]

During his first term in House, Luján served on the Mexico-United States Interparliamentary Group, an organization meant to promote dialogue between legislators in the two countries. He was also one of the five founding members of the Congressional Hispanic Caucus, which was created in 1976. The only Republican member of the caucus, Luján often found himself in a difficult position: having to choose between the policies of the Reagan administration and those of his Hispanic colleagues in the House. The New Mexico Republican defended the President, saying Reagan's "personal philosophy of working hard to succeed" appealed to Hispanic Americans.[42] Luján also criticized the Democratic Party's attitude toward Latinos. "Democrats tend to divide us and say, 'You poor unfortunate things,'" Luján commented. "'You were born Hispanic and you can't help it, but we have a government program that will help you.' I think it's demeaning."[43] But on occasion, Luján joined his Democratic colleagues on the caucus. He repeatedly spoke out against immigration reform proposals which could lead to discrimination against Spanish-speaking Americans. "Building a 'tortilla curtain' certainly is not the answer," he argued. Luján believed that identification cards, proposed to curb illegal immigration, were "offensive" and detrimental to the core American value of freedom.[44] In 1984 and 1986, Luján broke ranks with many Western Republicans, who wanted to revise federal immigration laws. Concerned that attempts to target illegal immigration would lead employers to discriminate against Hispanics, Luján worked with other Hispanic Members to defeat the legislation.[45]

In January 1988, Luján surprised political observers by announcing his decision to retire from the House at the end of the 100th Congress (1987–1989). The New Mexico Representative, who underwent coronary surgery in 1986, said health concerns played no part in his decision. "Twenty years is long enough," he mused. "It is time to come home."[46]

But Luján did not rule out resuming his political career. Frequently considered for a Cabinet position under President Reagan, Luján also made headlines as a candidate for President George H. W. Bush's Cabinet.[47] On December 22, 1988, President-elect Bush nominated Luján as Secretary of the Interior; the House veteran sailed through the Senate confirmation with minimal dissent. Luján retained his Cabinet position throughout President Bush's term in office, continuing to seek a balance between developing natural resources and preserving the environment. "We can do both," he said. "We do not have to choose between them."[48]

FOR FURTHER READING

Biographical Directory of the United States Congress, "Manuel Luján, Jr.," http://bioguide.congress.gov.

Ralph Nader Congress Project, *Citizens Look at Congress: Manuel Luján, Jr., Republican Representative from New Mexico* (Washington, D.C.: Grossman Publishers, 1972).

MANUSCRIPT COLLECTIONS

University of New Mexico Libraries, Center for Southwest Research (Albuquerque). *Papers*: 1971–1982, 24 cubic feet. The congressional papers of Manuel Luján include legislative files from the 92nd Congress (1971–1973) to the 97th Congress (1981–1983). These files normally contain printed copies of bills, revised and amended bills, resolutions, and occasionally other documents relative to a specific bill or piece of legislation. There are also some special files of legislative research that were established by Manuel Luján and his staff to provide background information on pending bills and social issues and topics including the Vermejo Park Ranch. The files contain a great deal of information on wilderness legislation and review, specifically on the Roadside Area Review and Evaluation (RARE II). Also included are constituent letters and other documents pertaining to the Equal Rights Amendment and background information on the Vietnam Veterans Memorial Chapel near Eagle's Nest, Colfax County, NM, also known as the Vietnam Veterans Peace and Brotherhood Chapel. Finally, Manuel Luján maintained a few files that reveal his stands and opinions on various legislative items. A finding aid is available in the repository and online.

Videocassette: 1983, one videocassette. An interview with Manuel Luján by Harold Rhodes.

Papers: Governor David Cargo Papers, 1967–1970, 86 linear feet. Other authors include Manuel Luján.

Papers: Governor Bruce King Papers, 1971–1974, 114 linear feet. Correspondents include Manuel Luján.

NOTES

1 John Robertson, "Lujan's Incumbency Looms over Hartke Campaign," 10 October 1982, *Albuquerque Journal*: A1.

2 Luján describes his early education, childhood, and parents in an interview conducted by the University of Texas at El Paso. Manuel Luján Oral History Interview, Oscar J. Martínez, University of Texas—El Paso, Institute of Oral History: 1–2.

3 In the 1944 election for one of the two At-Large New Mexico House seats, Luján, Sr., placed third out of four contenders, more than 14,000 votes behind second-place finisher and longtime New Mexico Congressman Antonio Fernández. "Election Statistics, 1920 to Present," http://history.house.gov/institution/election-statistics/election-statistics.

4 Mary Wiegers, "Home from the Hill," 8 June 1969, *Washington Post*: 149; *Congressional Directory*, 97th Cong., (Washington, D.C.: Government Printing Office, 1981): 112; Martin Tolchin, "Manuel Lujan Jr.," 23 December 1988, *New York Times*: A25.

5 David C. Williams, "Lujan Qualifications," 16 August 1968, *Albuquerque Journal*: A-5. Luján provides background on his precongressional political experience in an interview conducted in 1975; Luján, Oral History Interview, University of Texas—El Paso: 9–11.

6 "4 Democrats, 6 Republicans Seek Morris' Post," 26 August 1968, *Albuquerque Journal*: A-8; "Morris Wins; Walker Nips Sen. Runnels," 28 August 1968, *Albuquerque Journal*: A-15.

7 "Lujan Scores Morris' Use of Helicopter," 9 October 1968, *Albuquerque Journal*: A-11; Bob Beier, "Morris Cites His Seniority; Lujan Questions Its Value," 13 October 1968, *Albuquerque Journal*: C-1.

8 "'Same Old Song' Laid to Morris," 20 August 1968, *Albuquerque Journal*: A-2.

9 Beier, "Morris Cites His Seniority; Lujan Questions Its Value"; Wilson Cliff, "Stable Government Urged by Chavez," 19 September 1968, *Albuquerque Journal*: C-6.

10 Beier, "Morris Cites His Seniority."

11 "Election Statistics, 1920 to Present," http://history.house.gov/institution/election-statistics/election-statistics.

12 Ed Foreman represented a Texas congressional district in the 88th Congress (1963–1965).

13 "State's Frosh Congressmen Sworn In," 4 January 1969, *Albuquerque Journal*: B-8; "Lujan Gets House Boost," 7 January 1969, *Albuquerque Journal*: A-2.

14 *Congressional Record*, House, 93rd Cong., 2nd sess. (12 October 1972): 35636–35637.

15 "Scenic Area about Lost to Public," 14 December 1972, *Washington Post*: H1.

16 *Congressional Record*, House, 96th Cong., 2nd sess. (21 November 1980): 30567; "Lujan's Wilderness Plan Wins Approval of the House," 22 November 1980, *Albuquerque Journal*: A-14. The New Mexico Wilderness Act of 1980 became Public Law 96-550 on December 19, 1980.

17 William Kronholm, "Washington Dateline," 11 October 1983, Associated Press.

18 William Chapman, "West's Docile Conservatives Rebel against Big Oil in Wilderness," 7 February 1982, *Washington Post*: A21; *Politics in America, 1988* (Washington, D.C.: Congressional Quarterly, Inc., 1987): 988–989.

19 Dale Russakoff, "House Group Proposes Wilderness Leasing Ban," 9 June 1982, *Washington Post*: A4.

20 *Congressional Record*, House, 97th Cong., 2nd sess. (29 November 1982): 27779.

21 Judith Miller, "House Opens Debate on Settling National Policy on Nuclear Waste," 30 November 1982, *New York Times*: B9; "House Adopts N-Waste Site Location Plan," 1 December 1982, *Albuquerque Journal*: A-1.

22 Paul R. Wieck, "Space Program Draws Scrutiny of Congressman," 5 January 1988, *Albuquerque Journal*: A-6.

23 Luján, Oral History Interview, University of Texas—El Paso: 22.

24 Ralph Nader Congress Project, *Citizens Look at Congress: Manuel Luján, Jr., Republican Representative from New Mexico* (Washington, D.C.: Grossman Publishers, 1972): 8; *Congressional Record*, House, 92nd Cong., 2nd sess. (26 July 1972): 25482.

25 *Politics in America, 1982* (Washington, D.C.: Congressional Quarterly, Inc., 1981): 791.

26 Richard Beer, "Lujan Launches Re-Election Drive," 27 September 1980, *Albuquerque Journal*: B7.

27 "What You Should Expect of Congress: 28 Members Speak Out," 10 November 1975, *U.S. News & World Report*: 35.

28 John Robertson, "Manuel Lujan Won't Seek 11th Term," 5 January 1988, *Albuquerque Journal*: 1.

29 *Politics in America, 1982*: 791.

30 Richard Beer, "Senior Citizens, Toddlers Wooed in Lujan Campaign," 30 October 1980, *Albuquerque Journal*: E10; Bruce Campbell, "Richardson Says Lujan Doesn't Produce 'Clout,'" 23 October 1980, *Albuquerque Journal*: A8.

31 Beer, "Lujan Launches Re-Election Drive."

32 "Election Statistics, 1920 to Present," http://history.house.gov/institution/election-statistics/election-statistics.

33 Denise Tessier, "Congress Expected to Pass N.M. Wilderness Bill," 11 November 1980, *Albuquerque Journal*: A-9.

34 Bill Richardson, Luján's opponent in the 1980 general election, won a seat in the newly created New Mexico district in 1982.

35 "New Mexico," 3 November 1982, *Washington Post*: A31.

36 "Election Statistics, 1920 to Present," http://history.house.gov/institution/election-statistics/election-statistics; "Lujan's Incumbency Looms over Hartke Campaign."

37 In the 100th Congress, the Science and Technology Committee became the Science, Space, and Technology Committee.

38 Catherine C. Robbins, "In Retiring, Rep. Lujan Puts New Mexico in Tumult," 19 January 1988, *New York Times*: A18.

39 Gaylord Shaw and Rudy Abramson, "Serious Discord at Top Levels," 2 March 1986, *Los Angeles Times*: 1; Wieck, "Space Program Draws Scrutiny of Congressman."

40 "As Shuttle Inquiry Closes, Congress Is Set for Its Turn," 9 June 1986, *New York Times*: A20.

41 *Politics in America, 1988*: 987; Lujan joined Representative Don Fuqua of Florida and Senators Slade Gorton of Washington and John Glenn of Ohio on the National Commission on Space, "The National Commission on Space," http://history.nasa.gov/painerep/appendix.html (accessed 2 April 2012).

42 Ronald Smothers, "Two Parties Woo Votes of Hispanic Americans," 17 September 1983, *New York Times*: 1.

43 Carla Hall, "Courting Hispanic Power," 16 September 1983, *Washington Post*: D3.

44 "How the 1st District Candidates View the Key Issues," 12 October 1980, *Albuquerque Journal*: B-5.

45 Nancy J. Schwerzler, "Immigration Bill Unites, Mobilizes House Hispanics," 14 June 1984, *Baltimore Sun*: A1; *Politics in America, 1988*: 988–989.

46 "Rep. Manuel Lujan Served NM Proudly," 5 January 1988, *New Mexican* (Santa Fe): A-9; Robertson, "Manuel Lujan Won't Seek 11th Term."

47 Kronholm, "Washington Dateline."

48 Barbara Rosewicz, "Interior Secretary Nominee, Lujan, Sticks to Bush Vows," 27 January 1989, *Wall Street Journal*: A4.

Herman Badillo

1929–

UNITED STATES REPRESENTATIVE 1971–1977
DEMOCRAT FROM NEW YORK

Herman Badillo compiled a series of historic firsts, becoming the first Hispanic borough president in New York City and the first voting Member elected to the U.S. House of Representatives who had been born in Puerto Rico. During his seven years in Congress, Badillo used his position to draw attention to the plight of the inner cities and to urge federal assistance for numerous impoverished minorities residing in New York City. A four-time New York City mayoral candidate—twice while a Member of the House—Badillo was a major figure in local politics and policy for more than 40 years. "I represent the original immigrant," Badillo asserted. "Everybody says that their parents and grandparents came here and couldn't speak English and they were poor. And in my case it wasn't my parents and grandparents. It was me."[1]

Herman Badillo was born on August 21, 1929, in Caguas, Puerto Rico. His father, Francisco Badillo, taught in a public school, and his mother, Carmen Rivera, spent her time on charitable activities. In 1934 a tuberculosis epidemic swept through the island, claiming the lives of Badillo's parents and one of his grandmothers. Badillo's grandfather and aunt, Aurelia Rivera, who had two children of her own, raised him for the next several years. In 1941 Aurelia Rivera moved to New York City, along with Badillo and one of her sons. His aunt's financial problems forced young Badillo to move several times over the next few years, first to Chicago to live with an uncle and then to California to stay with another family member. Back in New York City in 1944, he attended Haaren High School. Placed in vocational classes because of his ethnicity, Badillo eventually switched to a more traditional academic track, and in 1947 he graduated with stellar grades.[2]

In the years after World War II, City College of New York offered free tuition to students with high grades, and the school became known as the Harvard of the Poor.[3] Badillo enrolled in City College in the fall of 1947, majored in business, and graduated with a bachelor's degree in business administration in 1951. He then worked as an accountant while attending night classes at Brooklyn Law School, where he won election to the law review. In 1954 he graduated as class valedictorian with an LL.B. He was admitted to the New York bar in 1955 and certified as a public accountant the following year; he worked as an accountant and a lawyer on Wall Street through the 1950s.[4] In 1949 Badillo married Norma Lit. The couple had a son, David Alan, before divorcing in 1960. A year later Badillo married Irma Liebling, who had two children from a previous marriage. After Irma's death in 1996, Badillo married Gail Roberts, a New York City schoolteacher.[5]

Badillo arrived in the United States on the cusp of the Great Migration, the postwar movement of Puerto Rican immigrants eager for better job opportunities who relocated to New York City. The beginning of Badillo's political career coincided with the growing importance and influence of Puerto Ricans in the city. He obtained his first political position in 1958, when he joined the Caribe Democratic Club. In 1960 he chaired John F. Kennedy's campaign committee for East Harlem. Badillo supported the 1961 re-election campaign of New York City Mayor Robert Wagner, Jr., and Wagner reciprocated by appointing him to a number of posts. In 1962 when Badillo took over as commissioner of the Department of Housing and Relocation, he became the highest-ranking Hispanic official in the city. Badillo stepped down from that position in 1965 to run for Bronx borough president.[6] After narrowly defeating a state senator backed by the county Democratic machine, he became, at age 36, the first Hispanic president of a New York City borough. "The margin of victory is small, but almost miraculous, considering that I did not have the support of the regular organization," Badillo remarked after his historic win.[7]

Collection of the U.S. House of Representatives, Photography Collection

In 1969, he entered the Democratic primary for New York City mayor. Proclaiming himself the "only liberal candidate" in the crowded race, Badillo captured 28 percent of the vote, narrowly trailing former mayor Wagner and primary winner Mario Procaccino, the New York City comptroller.[8]

Badillo's showing in the primary indicated that he was a strong mayoral candidate for 1973, although his political career appeared to have stalled. But in 1970 the New York legislature redrew the state's congressional districts, creating a new district that comprised portions of Queens, Manhattan, and the Bronx, connected by the Triborough Bridge. Described as "one of the more diverse urban Congressional districts in the country," it was inhabited by African Americans, whites, and Hispanics.[9] Badillo entered the race as the frontrunner, based on his background as borough president, his strong showing in the 1969 mayoral primary, and the district's many Puerto Rican constituents. He earned endorsements from the *Amsterdam News*, the city's leading African-American newspaper, and the *New York Times,* which described Badillo as "head and shoulders" above his competitors, a man who "believes in seeking change through the political process … an innovator, conciliator, and forceful leader."[10]

But the primary in the heavily Democratic district was far more competitive than expected. Former state senator Dennis Coleman, an African American, received the backing of Representative Shirley Chisholm of New York, the first black woman elected to Congress. Ramon Velez, an antipoverty administrator who had the support of the Bronx machine, heavily courted Puerto Rican voters in the district, as did Father Louis Gigante, a Roman Catholic priest from a parish in the Bronx. With multiple candidates competing for votes from Manhattan and the Bronx, Queens lawyer Peter Vallone—a future city council president and Democratic gubernatorial nominee—sought to consolidate Astoria's predominantly white, working-class voters. Badillo finished first, edging out Vallone by 587 votes and taking 30 percent of the primary tally. With no Republican contender, his victory in the fall seemed assured. Vallone challenged the result, however, and a lower-court judge in Queens ruled that 798 of the ballots had been cast by unregistered, Republican, or Liberal Party voters. As this total exceeded Badillo's margin of victory, the court invalidated the result and ordered a new primary. Badillo appealed, and on September 30, 1970, an appellate court sided with him, reinstating him as the nominee.[11] Coasting to victory in November, Badillo won 84 percent of the vote against Conservative Party candidate George Smaragdas, a Vietnam veteran who attacked Badillo for his antiwar stance.[12]

Badillo made history with his election to the 92nd Congress (1971–1973). The first person born in Puerto Rico to represent a district in the continental United States, Badillo was also the first person of Puerto Rican descent to serve as a voting Member of Congress. Badillo made headlines early in his first term when the Ways and Means Committee, which made committee assignments, rejected his request to serve on the Education and Labor Committee. Badillo was named to the Agriculture Committee instead, a move he deemed "an insult to those I represent."[13] The Democratic Study Group formally protested on Badillo's behalf, while a delegation of New York City Democrats met privately with Speaker Carl Albert of Oklahoma and Ways and Means chairman Wilbur Mills of Arkansas to recommend reversing Badillo's assignment. In a highly unusual move, the full Democratic Caucus, with Albert's backing, named Badillo to the Education and Labor Committee.[14] In the 94th Congress (1975–1977), Badillo switched from the Education and Labor Committee to the Judiciary and Small Business Committees. In the 95th Congress (1977–1979), Badillo retained his seat on Small Business but left the Judiciary Committee and joined the Banking, Finance and Urban Affairs Committee, a post of local importance given New York City's major financial crisis during the 1970s.

The Education and Labor Committee, which had jurisdiction over many antipoverty initiatives, served as the foundation for Badillo's highest-profile legislative work. On March 4, 1971, in his first major speech on the House Floor, Badillo urged a $20 billion federal government loan to the states and cities. "If we are going to save our cities from destruction," he said to his colleagues, "we must do it with a massive infusion of money if this Nation's cities are not to sink irretrievably into filth, decay, and crime."[15] According to the Congressman's proposal, New York City would receive $760 million from the federal government. "We lend money all the time to foreign governments," Badillo mused. "Why shouldn't we make loans to our cities and states which are on the verge of collapsing?"[16] As a member of the General Education Subcommittee, Badillo also championed more-aggressive federal action to aid minority students. In a 1971 hearing, he expressed support for mandatory school busing programs to achieve integration.[17]

Badillo also advocated equal rights for residents of Puerto Rico. On May 4, 1971, the New York Representative took to the House Floor to furnish detailed information on the economic woes of Puerto Rico and a multipart proposal to improve conditions there. Badillo called attention to the incongruity of Puerto Rican citizens' being subject to the draft but ineligible for federal benefits programs such as food stamps, the school milk program, and portions of Social Security. "I am fully prepared to offer amendments, where necessary and appropriate, to all pending and future measures to place Puerto Rico on a basis equal with the States," Badillo told his colleagues.[18] Keenly aware of the surging debate about whether Puerto Rico should pursue statehood or independence, Badillo remarked, "Only the people of Puerto Rico should decide, free of any outside influence or pressure." Regardless of the island's uncertain future status, however, Badillo urged Congress to provide Puerto Rico with the same federal aid as the United States.[19]

During his time in Congress, Badillo urged the Puerto Ricans in his community to seek change by working within the system. He reached out to the high school students in his district, scheduling a series of lectures by Puerto Rican professionals. "The Puerto Rican who grows up in the city of New York does not see the totality of Puerto Rican society," Badillo said. "He sees only people who are the poorest, who have the worst education, the worst employment and live in the worst housing conditions."[20] He criticized the naming of a Harlem public school after Pedro Albizu Campos, a Puerto Rican independence activist who endorsed terrorist activities in the 1930s.[21] Badillo also worried that federally funded antipoverty programs in New York City were encouraging ethnic enclaves rather than cooperation between differing groups.[22] He did what he could to promote conciliation—creating community councils in each part of his district to facilitate cooperation between local activists and the federal government—and to achieve consensus in his ethnically diverse electorate. He established joint district offices with state and local legislators to handle constituent complaints and to show his willingness to reach out to elected officials from various ethnic backgrounds.[23]

Badillo's more conciliatory approach to Puerto Rican identity politics met with resistance in the 1972 primary. Redistricting dramatically altered the boundaries of his congressional district, which lost its sections in Manhattan and Queens and consisted solely of the South Bronx, running from the downtrodden Mott Haven and Port Morris neighborhoods eastward to working-class Hunts Point and part of Soundview. The district was divided almost evenly between Puerto Rican and African-American constituents, with a small white minority.[24] "The working coalitions I have helped to form in my first term hold out real hope for the future of the city," Badillo stated when he announced his decision to run for re-election despite the redistricting.[25] Manuel Ramos, a New York assemblyman of Puerto Rican descent, launched a primary challenge against Badillo. During the campaign, Ramos dismissed Badillo as insufficiently militant, arguing, "Trying to work with others is no good." The challenger also attacked Badillo for living outside the district in the upscale Bronx neighborhood of Riverdale, ridiculed his polished speaking style, and claimed the Congressman "doesn't think like a Puerto Rican."[26] To hold off Ramos, Badillo rallied support from the district's small Jewish population, reached out to new African-American voters in the redrawn district, and bolstered Puerto Rican support by citing his standing as a pioneering politician. Badillo's strategy proved sufficient, and he easily rebuffed Ramos in the primary capturing 78 percent of the vote.[27] Ramos appeared on the November ballot as the Republican nominee, but Badillo earned an impressive 87 percent of the vote in the overwhelmingly Democratic district.[28]

In the 93rd Congress (1973–1975), Badillo championed the interests of Hispanic workers by ensuring that the Comprehensive Manpower Act of 1973 included funding for job training for unemployed U.S. citizens who spoke no English. In 1974 Badillo had a significant role in expanding federal support for bilingual education. During the debate on the bill to extend and amend the Elementary and Secondary Education Act of 1965, Badillo, concerned that the majority of the House might not back legislation seeking more money for bilingual education, offered an amendment on the House Floor to bolster bilingual education in American schools, but then quickly withdrew it. After the Senate approved funding for bilingual education, Badillo's amendment, with the help of the sympathetic chairman of the House Committee on Education and Labor, Carl Perkins of Kentucky, was added to the conference committee's report and remained part of the legislation that became law on August 21, 1974.[29]

Throughout his tenure in the House, Badillo demonstrated a community-centered approach. The New York Representative justified his decision to spend significant amounts of time in his district. Congress "will approve a program, but they will not fund it in significant enough amounts to make a difference," he explained.[30] In any case, he added, "Congress is at a standstill because of Watergate."[31] Badillo consistently supported initiatives to help his many disadvantaged constituents, including legislation regarding increased employment, comprehensive child care, and community development programs.[32] Badillo's high profile and frequent appearances in New York—including his public defense of prisoners' rights after the 1971 riots at the Attica State Correctional Facility—put him in a favorable position for the 1973 Democratic New York City mayoral primary.[33] Badillo carried both Manhattan and the Bronx, finishing 5 points behind New York City comptroller Abraham Beame. Neither candidate received 40 percent of the vote, necessitating a runoff, and Beame compiled huge margins among white voters in Brooklyn, Queens, and Staten Island, prevailing by 61 to 39 percent.[34]

Despite his loss in the mayoral primary, Badillo easily won re-election to his House seat in 1974, running unopposed in the Democratic primary and garnering 97 percent of the vote in the general election.[35] During the 94th Congress, Badillo introduced legislation to ease bankruptcy requirements for U.S. cities. An outspoken supporter of federal aid for New York City, Badillo believed cities seeking a way to escape major debt should not be held to the same rules as individuals in the same situation. "It is utterly irresponsible to put anything above the health and safety of New Yorkers—particularly the well-being of banks and other large creditors," Badillo pronounced.[36] His municipal bankruptcy legislation included language to prevent federal courts from obstructing local authorities in cities experiencing a financial crisis. "If we understand the limited jurisdiction that we have in this bill, we will be able to provide meaningful assistance to localities that need it," Badillo reminded his House colleagues.[37] After Badillo's bill easily passed the House and Senate, President Gerald Ford signed a version of the measure on April 8, 1976. "Now we can get something done in New York City," Badillo said.[38]

In the 1976 Democratic primary, Badillo's rivalry with Beame—which stemmed largely from his consistent criticism of the mayor's administration—persisted when Ramon Velez, a Beame ally and one of Badillo's 1970 challengers, battled him for the Democratic nomination. Badillo dismissed his opponent as Beame's "puppet" and "chosen hatchet man," and comfortably prevailed in his bid for a fourth term in the House.[39] He faced no Republican opposition in the general election and garnered 99 percent of the vote.[40] In the 95th Congress, Badillo focused mainly on city politics and geared up for another mayoral run. The 1977 Democratic mayoral primary attracted high-quality candidates, including Representative Ed Koch, former New York Representative Bella Abzug, New York secretary of state and future governor Mario Cuomo, and Manhattan borough president Percy Sutton. Badillo's campaign never gained traction, and he finished in sixth place.[41]

After his loss, Badillo endorsed Koch, who defeated Cuomo in a runoff and went on to win the general election. On November 29, 1977, Badillo stunned local political observers by announcing that he intended to resign from the House to serve as deputy mayor under Koch. Badillo said his new job, which involved a pay cut, would allow him to implement his agenda and to confront the "unpleasant tasks" that too many politicians avoided.[42] "I ran for Mayor because I felt that I had the talents, energies and programs to turn the city around and bring it out of its present crisis," Badillo said after making known his decision to leave the House. "I lost that race but now the winner has asked me to apply those very talents and energies in a way that will best serve the city. I did not see how I could refuse."[43] The New York Representative officially left the House on December 31, 1977. After his relationship with Koch soured, he resumed practicing law in 1979.

In 1986 Badillo attempted to revive his political career, but his run for a statewide comptroller position was unsuccessful. In 1993 he joined Rudy Giuliani's Republican-Liberal fusion ticket as a candidate for city comptroller. Though Giuliani narrowly won the mayoral election, Badillo lost to New York assemblyman Alan Hevesi. In 1998 Badillo officially switched his party affiliation to Republican. "As a lifelong Democrat, I did not make this decision lightly," Badillo said later.[44] In his last campaign, Badillo lost the Republican mayoral primary to Mike Bloomberg in 2001.

After his congressional career, Badillo held a variety of administrative positions and worked as an attorney. Consistent with his long-standing interest in education, he served as a trustee for the City University of New York (CUNY); Badillo served as vice chairman of the board from 1997 to 1999 and as chairman from 1999 to 2001.[45]

FOR FURTHER READING

Badillo, Herman. *Plain Talk: The Politics of Administration* (Greenvale, NY: Department of Health and Public Administration, C. W. Post Center, Long Island University, 1981).

_____. *One Nation, One Standard: An Ex-Liberal on How Hispanics Can Succeed Just Like Other Immigrant Groups* (New York: Sentinel, 2006).

_____, and Milton Haynes. *A Bill of No Rights: Attica and the American Prison System* (New York: Outerbridge and Lazard, Inc., 1972).

Biographical Directory of the United States Congress, "Herman Badillo," http://bioguide.congress.gov.

MANUSCRIPT COLLECTIONS

Columbia University, **Oral History Research Office** (New York, NY). *Oral History:* 1976, 34 pages. The interview includes Herman Badillo's memories of his childhood; his education, including college and law school; and his roles as a New York City Commissioner at the Department of Housing and Relocation, Bronx Borough President, and United States Congressman. The interview also includes Herman Badillo's observations on New York City politics in the 1960s and 1970s. Access to the interview is currently closed. A name index to the interview is available.

New York City Department of Records and Information Services, Municipal Archives (New York, NY). *Papers*: Deputy Mayor for Policy Records, 1979, 10 cubic feet. Includes correspondence and reports from Herman Badillo's tenure as deputy mayor of New York City.

NOTES

1 "Running for Mayor, in Perpetuity; Herman Badillo Is Hoping That the Timing Is Right," 9 May 2001, *New York Times*: B1. Herman Badillo was an official candidate for New York City mayor in 1969, 1973, 1977, and 2001. He also ran for the office in 1985 and 1993, but withdrew from these races after a short time.

2 Matt S. Meier, "Herman Badillo," *Notable Latino Americans: A Biographical Dictionary* (Westport, CT: Greenwood Press, 1997): 18–19; Herman Badillo, *One Nation, One Standard: An Ex-Liberal on How Hispanics Can Succeed Just Like Other Immigrant Groups* (New York: Sentinel, 2006): 9–14, 49–50; "Disputed Bronx Victor," 4 November 1965, *New York Times*: 51.

3 Herman Badillo, "Graduating to Higher Standards at City University," *Gotham Gazette,* http://www.gothamgazette.com/commentary/68.badillo.shtml.

4 Badillo, *One Nation, One Standard*: 15, 22; Meier, *Notable Latino Americans*: 19; "Puerto Rico Profile: Herman Badillo," 17 August 2001, *Puerto Rico Herald*.

5 'Youngest Commissioner," 17 November 1962, *New York Times*: 12; Vivian S. Toy, "Irma Badillo, 72, an Organizer for the Equal Rights Amendment," 18 May 1996, *New York Times*: 12; "Herman Badillo and Gail Roberts," 18 August 1996, *New York Times*: 56.

6 Meier, *Notable Latino Americans*: 20–21; Badillo, *One Nation, One Standard*: 22–23.

7 Peter Kihss, "Badillo Is Victor in Bronx by 2,086," 9 November 1965, *New York Times*: 38; Lyn Shepard, "Reform Tide Surges in Bronx," 25 September 1965, *Christian Science Monitor*: 2.

8 Clayton Knowles, "Badillo Joins Race as 'Only Liberal,'" 4 April 1969, *New York Times*: 1.

9 Richard L. Madden, "Badillo Innovates in His Diverse District," 26 August 1971, *New York Times*: 39. According to the *Almanac of American Politics*, the district was 34 percent African American and 30 percent Hispanic. *Almanac of American Politics, 1972* (Washington, D.C.: National Journal Inc., 1971): 548–549.

10 "Congressional Primaries," 17 June 1970, *New York Times*: 46; Alfonso A. Narvaez, "Badillo Expected to Be in Close House Race," 20 June 1970, *New York Times*: 16.

11 Peter Kihss, "Queens Court Voids Victory by Badillo," 24 September 1970, *New York Times*: 1; Will Lissner, "Appellate Division Upholds Badillo's Nomination in 21st District," 1 October 1970, *New York Times*: 37; "Top State Court Upholds Badillo," 8 October 1970, *New York Times*: 1; *Almanac of American Politics, 1972*: 549.

12 There was no Republican candidate in the 1970 general election; George Smaragdas ran as a Conservative. "Election Statistics, 1920 to Present," http://history.house.gov/institution/election-statistics/election-statistics; Murray Schumach, "Ex-Borough Leader Is Facing a Strong Conservative Bloc," 29 October 1970, *New York Times*: 50; Richard L. Madden, "Lowenstein Loses Seat in Congress," 4 November 1970, *New York Times*: 1.

13 Richard L. Madden, "2 in House Upset by Assignments," 29 January 1971, *New York Times*: 12.

14 David E. Rosenbaum, "Badillo Wins His Battle on House Committee Assignment, but Mrs. Abzug Loses," 4 February, 1971, *New York Times*: 21; "Badillo Gains Aid in Transfer Bid," 3 February 1971, *New York Times*: 38.

15 *Congressional Record*, House, 92nd Cong., 1st sess. (4 March 1971): 5141.

16 "Badillo Urges a $20-Billion U.S. Loan to States," 5 March 1971, *New York Times*: 31.

17 Gene I. Maeroff, "Delays Reported in Mixed Schools," 22 May 1971, *New York Times*: 29.

18 *Congressional Record*, House, 92nd Cong., 1st sess. (4 May 1971): 13344; Richard L. Madden, "Badillo Says U.S. Programs Are Excluding Puerto Ricans," 5 May 1971, *New York Times*: 16; "Badillo in Plea for Puerto Rico," 1 November 1971, *New York Times*: 30.

19 *Congressional Record*, House, 92nd Cong., 1st sess. (4 May 1971): 13344.

20 William E. Farrell, "Puerto Ricans Here Told to Aim High," 21 December 1970, *New York Times*: 37.

21 Peter Kihss, "Badillo Decries Name for School," 20 April 1976, *New York Times*: 9.

22 Murray Schumach, "New Congressional Panel Will Investigate City's Antipoverty Agencies," 4 April 1971, *New York Times*: 38.

23 "Badillo Innovates in His Diverse District," 26 August 1971, *New York Times*: 39.

24 *Almanac of American Politics, 1976* (Washington, D.C.: National Journal Inc., 1975): 699.

25 "2 N.Y. Liberals Battle for Redistricted Seat," 15 March 1972, *New York Times*: A12.

26 Tom Buckley, "Badillo-Ramos Contest Centers on Who Is More Puerto Rican," 13 June 1972, *New York Times*: 45.

27 Max H. Seigel, "Badillo-Ramos," 21 June 1972, *New York Times*: 29; "Results of Primary Contests in City and Suburbs," 22 June 1972, *New York Times*: 46.

28 "Election Statistics, 1920 to Present," http://history.house.gov/institution/election-statistics/election-statistics.

29 The bilingual education amendment proposed by Badillo enjoyed majority support in the Senate. For background and a personal reflection of the events surrounding the legislation, see Badillo, *One Nation, One Standard*: 59–63. For a comprehensive summary of the Elementary and Secondary Education Amendments, see *Congressional Quarterly Almanac, 1974* (Washington, D.C.: Congressional Quarterly, Inc., 1975): 441–474.

30 Stephen Isaacs, "Rep. Herman Badillo and His Strange Bedfellows," 14 November 1971, *Washington Post*: 2.

31 Martin Tolchin, "Badillo and Biaggi Staffs Toil On," 31 May 1973, *New York Times*: 36.

32 See, for example, Badillo's stance on unemployment, *Congressional Record*, House, 92nd Cong., 2nd sess. (2 March 1972): 6689–6690.

33 For background on Badillo and the prison riots, see Les Ledbetter, "Badillo Asks Prison School Aid and Union Rights for Convicts," 23 May 1972, *New York Times*: 20; Fred Ferretti, "Badillo Decries Attica 'Inaction,'" 2 December 1971, *New York Times*: 61. Based on his membership in a citizens' observation group brought to Attica at the inmates' request, Badillo coauthored *A Bill of No Rights: Attica and the American Prison System* (New York: Outerbridge and Lazard, Inc., 1972).

34 Stephen Isaacs, "Beame Wins N.Y. Mayor Runoff," 27 June 1973, *Washington Post*: A23; Frank Lynn, "Winning Edge 3–2," 27 June 1973, *New York Times*: 113.

35 There was no Republican candidate in the 1974 general election; Mary Lynch ran as a Conservative. "Election Statistics, 1920 to Present," http://history.house.gov/institution/election-statistics/election-statistics; Allan M. Siegal, "Republicans Offer Little Opposition for Congressional Races in the Bronx," 22 October 1974, *New York Times*: 32.

36 Nancy L. Ross, "Badillo Bill Would Ease City Bankruptcy Filings," 1 October 1975, *Washington Post*: D1.

37 *Congressional Record*, House, 94th Cong., 1st sess. (9 December 1975): 39413.

38 Badillo cosponsored the bankruptcy legislation, Public Law 94-260. According to the *New York Times*, Badillo was a principal author of the measure, which was sponsored by Representative Peter Rodino of New Jersey. Martin Tolchin, "Ford Signs Law to Ease Municipal Bankruptcies," 10 April 1976, *New York Times*: 30.

39 David Vidal, "Badillo Will Run Again, in 'Most Important Race,'" 16 June 1976, *New York Times*: 20.

40 "Election Statistics, 1920 to Present," http://history.house.gov/institution/election-statistics/election-statistics.

41 "Other Winners, Other Losers," 10 September 1977, *New York Times*: 20; Frank Lynn, "Beame Finishes Third," 9 September 1977, *New York Times*: 1.

42 Lee Dembart, "Why Did Badillo Give Up Seat?" 30 November 1977, *New York Times*: 31.

43 Maurice Carroll, "4 Appointed by Koch to Be Deputy Mayors; Equality Is Stressed," 30 November 1977, *New York Times*: 50.

44 Badillo, *One Nation, One Standard*: 174. In his book *One Nation, One Standard*, Badillo devotes an entire chapter to his gradual shift from the Democratic to the Republican Party: "From Kennedy Democrat to Giuliani Republican": 139–175. Alison Mitchell, "Green Wins Nomination for Advocate Post–Dinkins Has 68%," 15 September 1993, *New York Times*: A1; Bumiller, "Running for Mayor, in Perpetuity; Herman Badillo Is Hoping That the Timing Is Right"; Adam Nagourney, "Badillo Is Said to Be Switching to the Republicans," 25 June 1998, *New York Times*: B1.

45 Karen W. Arenson, "With Badillo Gone, CUNY Is Likely to Stay on Course He Set," 6 June 2001, *New York Times*: B4; Tracy Tully, "Badillo to Run CUNY Board, Eyes Shakeup," 30 May 1999, *Daily News* (New York): 2.

Jaime Benítez
1908–2001

RESIDENT COMMISSIONER 1973–1977
POPULAR DEMOCRAT FROM PUERTO RICO

Jaime Benítez was Puerto Rico's leading scholar for nearly 70 years. From his first teaching assignment in 1931, he rose to become a major influence on Puerto Rican and American education, serving nearly 30 years as chancellor and then president of the Universidad de Puerto Rico. Elected Resident Commissioner in 1972, Benítez focused on solidifying Puerto Rico's status as a commonwealth during his tenure in Congress. In many respects he was a consummate insider and a loyal member of the Partido Popular Democrático (Popular Democratic Party, or PPD), but Benítez never shied away from confrontations with party leadership. In the U.S. House, his animated personality and considerable intelligence won him friends on both sides of the aisle. Democrat Phillip Burton of California spoke of the "enormous commitment and concern and unique intellect [of] the Resident Commissioner … and [of] what a joy it is to listen to and associate with such a decent human being."[1]

Benítez was born on Vieques, an island east of Puerto Rico, on October 29, 1908, to Luis Benítez and Candida Rexach. He counted among his ancestors some of Puerto Rico's most respected 19th-century poets, Maria Bibiana Benítez, Alejandra Benítez, and Jose Gautier Benítez. When Jaime Benítez was seven, his mother, and then his father, died within a year of each other. Jaime went to live with an older sister in San Juan, where he enrolled in the public schools. In 1926 he moved to Washington, D.C., to begin studies at Georgetown University. He graduated in 1930, completing a master's degree in law the next year. After passing the District's bar exam, he returned to Puerto Rico in 1931 and accepted a teaching position at the Universidad de Puerto Rico. Benítez and his wife, LuLu Martinez, had two daughters, Clotilde and Margarita, and a son, Jaime.[2]

Founded in 1903, the Universidad de Puerto Rico was a middling institution when Benítez began teaching in its political and social science department during the Great Depression. After taking leave to earn a second master's degree from the University of Chicago in 1938, Benítez returned to Puerto Rico. He accepted another teaching position at the university, and three years later he became chancellor until 1966, when he became president of the university.[3]

Described by a contemporary as "vivid, voluble, ardent for his country's good and obviously talented," Benítez rebuilt the school's curriculum from the bottom up, implementing far-reaching reforms regarding the teaching of Puerto Rico's cultural heritage.[4] Enrollment surged from 5,000 to roughly 40,000 students, and by 1964, under Benítez's direction, the Universidad de Puerto Rico was known as "one of the great Spanish-language universities of the world."[5] The university opened campuses across the island and added professional schools for health care and architecture.[6] Benítez became a standard-bearer for academic freedom and sought to implement policies safeguarding students and faculty from political pressures in and out of the classroom. "Politicians out!" was one of Benítez's signature phrases; later, historians described his policies as "paternalistic."[7]

Early during his tenure at the university, Benítez began an association with the PPD that lasted throughout his career. He was known around the San Juan area as a party stalwart, and at least one historian suggests that Benítez was appointed chancellor so that he could help implement the PPD's broad agenda.[8] By mid-century, Benítez had assumed a larger role in the island's civic society and in international efforts to promote peace. From 1951 to 1952, Benítez was a member of Puerto Rico's constitutional convention; his familiarity with democratic political institutions and his theories on government earned him the chairmanship of the committee on the bill of rights—

Collection of the U.S. House of Representatives, Photography Collection

which worked to guarantee Puerto Ricans human, social, and economic liberties.[9] Benítez's role in shaping the curriculum at the Universidad de Puerto Rico paved the way for his membership on the United States' National Commission for the United Nations Educational, Scientific and Cultural Organization (UNESCO) from 1948 to 1954. Benítez also served as president of the national association of state universities from 1957 to 1958.[10]

By the late 1950s, Benítez's relationship with PPD leadership had begun to fray. Puerto Rico's charismatic and immensely popular governor, Luis Muñoz Marín, suspected Benítez was molding a competing political group at the university, and in 1957 Muñoz reported a complete "loss of confidence" in his college administrator.[11] By 1960 the two had reportedly reconciled, but in the next decade they engaged in what the *Washington Post* called a "distressing and undeclared feud." The two formidable personalities were likely more similar than they imagined. Benítez, said a later governor, "was to higher education what [Luis] Muñoz Marín was to politics."[12] In 1966 the insular legislature appointed Benítez university president—a post which some observers described as less influential. Benítez relinquished the seat five years later.[13]

After Muñoz Marín stepped down from the PPD in the late 1960s, the new leadership nominated Benítez for Resident Commissioner in the U.S. House of Representatives in 1972. The PPD had lost elections across the island four years earlier to the upstart pro-statehood Partido Nuevo Progresista (New Progressive Party, or PNP), but by 1972 the PPD had regrouped, and many islanders again favored commonwealth status. Benítez's opponent in the general election was PNP incumbent Jorge Córdova-Díaz, a popular and ambitious candidate who had transformed the office of Resident Commissioner. But the PNP had come under heavy criticism for mismanaging insular affairs, breathing new life into the all-important status question. The general assumption was that any vote for the PPD "meant a vote for commonwealth status and permanent union with the United States."[14] The election cycle that year was at all levels particularly and "untenably partisan," the *San Juan Star* lamented.[15]

"Benítez's vision of this island," wrote a political commentator during the election, "is deeply rooted in the era of the 40's when he made his greatest political and educational contributions to this island."[16] In the 1970s, as in the 1940s, Benítez favored a position of "limited autonomy"—a stance that was distinctly at odds with Córdova-Díaz's and with the PNP's platform supporting statehood.[17] Benítez reassured voters that all "Puerto Ricans are entitled … to full participation and equality of treatment in all federal welfare programs" and then emphasized the Resident Commissioner's unique position in the House.[18] Córdova-Díaz was known for his personable legislative style, and Benítez was equally popular for his "imagination, liberalism and intellectual creativity" which, the writer of an editorial hoped, would "help Puerto Rico to attain worldwide respect not merely for its social and economic attainments but for its cultural and human achievements as well."[19]

With a huge voter turnout, Benítez won almost 51 percent of the ballots in the general election.[20] Ever the educator, Benítez promised to inform his new House colleagues about the intricacies of Puerto Rico's political status. He also pledged to secure federal funding to help alleviate the island's "social problems."[21]

Benítez was the first Resident Commissioner to serve a full term under the new House Rules that were implemented as a result of the Legislative Reorganization Act of 1970, giving Resident Commissioners the right to be elected to committees and to vote therein. During the 93rd Congress (1973–1975), Benítez was assigned to the Committee on Education and Labor given his background at the Universidad de Puerto Rico. Benítez was an animated speaker, reported the *San Juan Star*, with a "distinctive oratorical style in that he often twisted his body and arms into unusual shapes as he punctuated his talks with quotes from Cervantes … Shakespeare, Ortega y Gasset," and other literary figures. "He was known for his histrionic style," the newspaper commented, "even when reading from the dry Congressional Record in 1973 as resident commissioner."[22] In his opening remarks to the House on January 30, 1973, Benítez began a rather lengthy talk on the U.S. military's continued use of the sparsely populated island of Culebra as a bombing range—an issue that defined his first session in office—by addressing the chamber in Spanish "to symbolize my deep feelings on this occasion," he explained.[23] Puerto Rican Democrat Herman Badillo of New York, who addressed the Resident Commissioner as "Don Jaime" and who later became one of his close advisors, said he was "delighted to have him with us in the Congress."[24]

Benítez immediately pushed for a solution to what he called "the Culebran question."[25] With support from a number of House Democrats, Benítez introduced H.R. 3224, seeking to hold the military accountable for promises to end training missions on Culebra. Two years earlier the navy had agreed to withdraw from the island, only to reverse course a short time later.[26] Benítez's predecessor had attempted to address this issue in 1972 but had run out of time. Many Members supporting Benítez's new legislation openly sympathized with Culebra's residents; Bella Abzug of New York declared that the events in the Caribbean demonstrated a "heartless attitude toward small and powerless groups."[27] Benítez's bill never made it out of committee, but earlier in the month, Republican Senator Howard Baker had introduced accompanying legislation (S. 156) charging the U.S. Navy with "a breach of faith with the people of Puerto Rico."[28] With pressure from Benítez and Baker, the outgoing Secretary of Defense stepped forward in May 1973 and promised the navy would withdraw within two years.[29] The final decision to relocate the testing range, Benítez said, "reinforces our faith in the basic integrity of the American system with its profound commitment to the fulfillment of understandings reached in good faith and in the pursuit of human values."[30]

Benítez kept a low profile for the rest of the 93rd Congress, but in a rare floor address in late July 1973, he spoke about the meaning and future of Puerto Rico's commonwealth. This became the foundation for his singular legislative effort in the 94th Congress (1975–1977). Attempting to explain the intricacies of the island's status, Benítez asserted that the frequent confusion and frustration experienced by both the United States and Puerto Rico was an important part of their association—an experiment in democratic self-governance, Benítez said, that "continues to develop ... from the needs, experiences, vicissitudes, conflicts, achievements, adjustments, contradictions, and aspirations inherent in 75 years of close relationship." Benítez asserted that the confederation between the United States and Puerto Rico had been allowed to develop without clear goals or boundaries, and to rectify what he called a policy of "benign neglect," Benítez began working with the White House to improve the federal-insular alliance.[31]

In the 94th Congress, Benítez continued to sit on the Education and Labor Committee, but in light of his recent effort to address Puerto Rico's status, he was also placed on the Interior and Insular Affairs Committee. After introducing a handful of unsuccessful education and revenue bills, Benítez submitted H.R. 11200, "a bill to approve the Compact of Permanent Union Between Puerto Rico and the United States," on December 17, 1975.[32] It was the most direct attempt to influence the state of Puerto Rican-U.S. relations since the constitutional convention (in which Benítez also played a role) in 1951. Puerto Rico would gain a greater measure of self-governance, including the prerogative to enter into binding agreements with other countries on a case-by-case basis pending presidential approval. The bill would also allow Puerto Rico one voting Member for both the U.S. House of Representatives and the U.S. Senate and would impose mainland standards for minimum wage at some point in the future. Finally, the bill would create a six-member commission to study and improve the federal-insular relationship.[33]

Benítez's bill, though actively pursued in the House, received a cold reception from executive branch officials. It was referred to the Subcommittee on Territorial and Insular Affairs, which held four days of hearings in both Washington and San Juan, with testimony from more than 60 witnesses. The subcommittee approved H.R. 11200 on August 23, 1976, but as the 94th Congress began to wind down, the bill never made it out of the full committee. Looking ahead, Benítez hoped his measure authorizing the compact of a permanent union between the United

States and Puerto Rico would "be one of the first pieces of legislation to be approved by the 95th Congress."[34]

After his disappointment in the House, Benítez returned to Puerto Rico to campaign for re-election against a surging Baltasar Corrada-del Río, the PNP candidate for Resident Commissioner. Benítez had taken a calculated gamble by introducing H.R. 11200, believing it had the support of a majority of the islanders. But in his four years in Washington, the PNP had again surged in popularity, largely in reaction to the island's poor economy. In a huge Election Day turnout—more than 1.44 million people voted for Resident Commissioner—Benítez lost to Corrada-del Río by about 3 percent (42,002 votes).[35] After the election, Benítez remained convinced that federal-insular relations played a negligible part in the outcome. "The fact is that the Commonwealth status has become so much part and parcel of life that Puerto Ricans don't take it into account in their political decisions. As a result," Benítez concluded, "the election turned on the bad condition of the Puerto Rican economy."[36]

After his electoral loss, Benítez returned to the classroom, teaching at the Inter-American University in Puerto Rico from 1980 to 1986 and consulting with PPD leaders when he was asked to. He retired to Condado Lagoon, outside Old San Juan, and spent a large part of his time in the city's bookstores or in his personal study. He suffered a stroke in 1994. On May 10, 2001, he died at Auxilio Mutuo Hospital of respiratory complications. "He was an extraordinary Puerto Rican," the island's governor said, "a great educator and outstanding among our people, for his personal and professional attributes.... The debt the Puerto Rican people owe to Benítez has no limits, because there are so many things we have to thank him for."[37]

FOR FURTHER READING

Benítez, Jaime. *Discursos* (San Juan: Universidad Interamericana de Puerto Rico, 2002).

_____. *La torre: Revista general de la Universidad de Puerto Rico* (Rio Piedras, 1956–1971).

Biographical Directory of the United States Congress, "Jaime Benítez," http://bioguide.congress.gov.

Sanjurjo, Carmen Hilda. "The Educational Thought of Jaime Benitez, Chancellor of the University of Puerto Rico from 1942 to 1966," (Ed.D. thesis, Columbia University Teachers College, 1986).

NOTES

1 *Congressional Record*, House, 93rd Cong., 1st sess. (30 January 1973): 2565.

2 Carmen E. Enciso and Tracy North, eds., "Jaime Benítez," *Hispanic Americans in Congress, 1822–1995* (Washington, D.C.: Government Printing Office, 1995); Paul Lewis, "Jaime Benítez, 92, Educator and Puerto Rican Politician," 1 June 2001, *New York Times*: C15.

3 *Biographical Directory of the U.S. Congress*, "Jaime Benítez," http://bioguide.congress.gov; Carmen Hilda Sanjurjo, "The Educational Thought of Jaime Benítez, Chancellor of the Universidad de Puerto Rico from 1942 to 1966," (Ed.D. thesis, Columbia Teachers College, 1986): 187.

4 Quotation from Rexford G. Tugwell, *The Stricken Land: The Story of Puerto Rico* (New York: Greenwood Press, 1968): 93; César J. Ayala and Rafael Bernabe, *Puerto Rico in the American Century: A History since 1898* (Chapel Hill: University of North Carolina Press, 2007): 134–135, 203–204.

5 "Storm Signal," 13 April 1964, *Washington Post*: A16.

6 Lewis, "Jaime Benítez, 92, Educator and Puerto Rican Politician"; "University Director Mourned," 3 June 2001, *Orlando Sentinel*: K8.

7 See Sanjurjo, "The Educational Thought of Jaime Benítez": 68–69, 77–78. For a detailed discussion of Benítez's educational thought, see Jaime Benítez, "Cultural Values in a Frontier: University Services in Puerto Rico," in A. Curtis Wilgus, ed., *The Caribbean: Its Culture*, Vol. 1 (Gainesville: University of Florida Press, 1955): 196–207.

8 For information about the relationship between Benítez and the PPD, see A. W. Maldonado, "Education Lives through Crisis," 2 November 1960, *San Juan Star*: S-17; and Manny Suarez, "Benítez, Top P.R. Educator and Reformer, Dies at Age 92," 31 May 2001, *San Juan Star*: 4. Carmen Hilda Sanjurjo notes that Benítez may have become an administrator at the university so that he "could 'guide' the institution towards helping this party [the PPD] carry out its social and economic reforms." See Sanjurjo, "The Educational Thought of Jaime Benítez," 59–60. See also Ayala and Bernabe, *Puerto Rico in the American Century*: 203–205.

9 Lewis, "Jaime Benítez, 92, Educator and Puerto Rican Politician."

10 *Biographical Directory of the U.S. Congress*, "Jaime Benítez," http://bioguide.congress.gov.

11 Lewis, "Jaime Benítez, 92, Educator and Puerto Rican Politician."

12 Fifty years later, after the two had died, the roots of their problems still had not been "made clear," according to another island newspaper. Manny Suarez, "Leaders Laud Benítez; Mourning Decreed," 31 May 2001, *San Juan Star*: 5.

13 Some mainland critics called the move to strip Benítez of his power "petty." See Maldonado, "Education Lives through Crisis"; "Storm Signal"; Lewis, "Jaime Benítez, 92, Educator and Puerto Rican Politician."

14 Margarita Babb, "Campaign Heads into Home Stretch: PDP," 23 October 1972, *San Juan Star*: 1; "An Editorial: Our Position," 3 November 1972, *San Juan Star*: 1.

15 "An Editorial: Our Position." See also "On Political Status," 3 November 1972, *San Juan Star*: 39.

16 Dimas Planas, "An Easy Choice," 4 November 1972, *San Juan Star*: 46.

17 Planas, "An Easy Choice."

18 "'72 Campaign: Resident Commissioner," 5 November 1972, *San Juan Star*: S-7.

19 Ursula Von Eckardt, "How I Shall Vote and Why," 6 November 1972, *San Juan Star*: 43.

20 "Election Statistics, 1920 to Present," http://history.house.gov/institution/election-statistics/election-statistics.

21 Manny Suarez, "Benítez Will Press for More Funding," 9 November 1972, *San Juan Star*: 3.

22 Suarez, "Benítez, Top P.R. Educator and Reformer, Dies at Age 92."

23 *Congressional Record*, House, 93rd Cong., 1st sess. (30 January 1973): 2563.

24 Ibid., 2566. Badillo, who had spent the last two years wrangling with Resident Commissioner Córdova-Díaz, was relieved to have Benítez in the House. Córdova-Díaz had caucused with the Republicans during the second half of his tenure.

25 Ibid., 2565.

26 Many believed the navy did not feel obligated to honor its agreement with Puerto Rico's former governor. See Manuel Suarez, "Navy Reported Set to Yield in Fight with Culebra," 11 January 1971, *New York Times*: 19; "Navy's 'War' with Culebra Ends in a Truce," 12 January 1971, *New York Times*: 14; "Culebra 'Treaty' Signed following Misunderstanding," 12 January 1971, *Washington Post*: A7; "A Cheer for Culebra," 15 January 1971, *Washington Post*: A24.

27 For the Culebra debate, see *Congressional Record*, House, 93rd Cong., 1st sess. (30 January 1973): 2563–2571. For Bella Abzug's quotation, see p. 2570.

28 *Congressional Record*, Senate, 93rd Cong., 1st sess. (4 January 1973): 96; *Congressional Record*, Senate, 93rd Cong., 1st sess. (15 March 1973): 8125–8129; Michael Getler, "Richardson Acts to Yield on Culebra," 25 May 1973, *Washington Post*: A1.

29 Getler, "Richardson Acts to Yield on Culebra"; "Navy to Quit Shelling Isle in 2 Years," 26 May 1973, *Chicago Tribune*: 5; "Culebra over Goliath," 28 May 1973, *New York Times*: 14; "On Culebra, a Promise Redeemed," 29 May 1973, *Washington Post*: A20.

30 As quoted in "On Culebra, a Promise Redeemed." Later, when people realized that no money had been set aside for the land transfer, Benítez introduced H.R. 8675 on June 14, 1973, which would have set aside "such funds as may be necessary" to complete the removal of the naval fortifications on Culebra.

31 *Congressional Record*, House, 93rd Cong., 1st sess. (31 July 1973): 27036; *Congressional Record*, House, 94th Cong., 2nd sess. (24 May 1976): 15133; *Congressional Record*, House, 93rd Cong., 2nd sess. (13 June 1974): 19300–19306.

32 For Benítez's lengthy introduction to the legislation and a history of U.S.-Puerto Rican relations, see *Congressional Record*, House, 94th Cong., 1st sess. (17 December 1975): 41451–41454. As during his election, Benítez viewed the 1970s through the lens of the 1940s. "We owe it to the new generations which did not participate in the struggles of the 1940s and 1950s to have for their own clarification a basic document reflecting the dignity and quality of our relationship," he said during his address on December 17th.

33 Congressional Research Service summary, THOMAS.gov (accessed 19 October 2011).

34 *Congressional Record*, House, 94th Cong., 2nd sess. (24 May 1976): 15133–15314; *Congressional Record*, Extension of Remarks, 94th Cong., 2nd sess. (1 October 1976): 35572–35573.

35 Henry L. Trewhitt, "Steamy Reception Looms for Ford at Puerto Rican Summit," 23 July 1976, *Baltimore Sun*: A2; "Election Statistics, 1920 to Present," http://history.house.gov/institution/election-statistics/election-statistics.

36 Interview with Jaime Benítez, Former Resident Commissioner of Puerto Rico, "Should Puerto Rico Be a State?: No," 11 April 1977, *U.S. News & World Report*: 47.

37 Suarez, "Benítez, Top P.R. Educator and Reformer, Dies at 92"; Suarez, "Leaders Laud Benítez; Mourning Decreed."

Ron de Lugo
1930–

TERRITORIAL DELEGATE 1973–1979; 1981–1995
DEMOCRAT FROM THE VIRGIN ISLANDS

Descended from an early Hispanic settler, Ron de Lugo became a fixture in territorial politics as the U.S. Virgin Islands gained greater autonomy in the late 20th century. A well-known radio personality and an early territorial senator, de Lugo successfully lobbied to create the position of Delegate to the U.S. House, which he held for a total of two decades. He proved to be a key figure in U.S. territorial policy. In the words of a contemporary, de Lugo "left an indelible mark on the history of the United States territories and the freely associated states."[1] Barred by the House Rules from voting on the floor for all but one Congress, he managed nevertheless to maneuver money and services to the Virgin Islands and to defend its economic and political interests. Describing his home territory as "a community of people of different origins and diverse cultural backgrounds," de Lugo sought for his constituents "the full benefits of our citizenship … just as we have met our responsibility as citizens."[2]

Ron de Lugo was born in Englewood, New Jersey, on August 2, 1930, to a family with deep roots in the Caribbean. The de Lugos had emigrated from Puerto Rico to the Virgin Islands in 1879. Ron de Lugo's grandfather, Antonio Lugo y Suarez, was a merchant on St. Thomas, and his father, Angelo, carried on the family business. Ron de Lugo attended Saints Peter and Paul School in St. Thomas, Virgin Islands, before transferring to the Colegio San José in Puerto Rico. He enlisted in the army for a two-year tour in 1948, working as a program director for the U.S. Armed Forces Radio network. After leaving the military, de Lugo worked in broadcasting as a civilian, helping to found WSTA, the first radio station in St. Thomas. De Lugo gained island-wide fame for his radio persona, the wisecracking comedian Mango Jones, as well as for appearances in local plays and benefit concerts.[3] In 1952 de Lugo used his radio show to revive the St. Thomas Carnival, a days-long celebration of the island's cultural heritage.[4] De Lugo and his first wife, Maria Morales Viera, had three children—James, Angela Maria, and Maria Cristina—before divorcing.[5] James (Jay) de Lugo died in a car accident in Virginia in 1972 at age 20.[6] Ron de Lugo later married Sheila Paiewonsky.

In 1955 de Lugo moved to St. Croix, where he won election to the Second Virgin Islands Legislature as an At-Large Democrat in 1956.[7] The youngest member of the legislature, he embarked on a career of nearly four decades in Virgin Islands politics. In 1960 de Lugo won election as the territory's representative to the Democratic National Committee. The following year, he took a break from the legislature when he was appointed by the territorial governor to act as a liaison for local concerns in St. Croix. De Lugo returned to the legislature from 1962 to 1966. In 1968 Virgin Islanders elected de Lugo the territorial representative to the U.S. government. Essentially working as a lobbyist for issues affecting the Virgin Islands, de Lugo set his sights on winning a congressional seat for the territory. In 1972 the House considered legislation that provided for popularly elected Delegates for the Virgin Islands and Guam, who would not be permitted a vote on the House Floor. Having testified in support of the bill before several congressional committees, and having lobbied intensely on its behalf, de Lugo called its signature into law on April 10, 1972, "a sweet victory" and considered this one of his greatest accomplishments as a territorial advocate.[8]

De Lugo subsequently set out to win the Territorial Delegate position he had lobbied to create, officially announcing his candidacy on May 23, 1972. De Lugo was unopposed in the Democratic primary almost until the June 1 filing deadline. But at the last minute, Leroy Mercer

Collection of the U.S. House of Representatives, Photography Collection

mounted a challenge, claiming that "scores of Democrats indicated a desire for a meaningful choice, not only in the general elections but in the primaries too."[9] Mercer campaigned aggressively against de Lugo, charging that the territorial representative had brought little economic change to the Virgin Islands during his tenure. De Lugo reminded his constituents of the federal programs and the money he had drawn to the islands.[10] With the support of the local Democratic organization, he handily defeated Mercer in the July 11 primary by a three to one margin.[11] The general election was even less competitive; the island's leading third party—Independent Citizens Movement, which was popular among the mostly poor, black population—did not field a candidate.[12] De Lugo faced black Republican George Schneider, a U.S. Army veteran, lawyer, and social worker.[13] Both candidates took stands that were popular with Virgin Islanders, campaigning on extending federal benefits to territorial residents and exempting them from the draft during the unpopular Vietnam War. De Lugo again prevailed with a nearly three to one victory, earning 73 percent of the vote. This "popular mandate," as he designated it, was representative of his re-election campaigns; throughout his career, de Lugo typically won by more than 70 percent of the vote.[14]

De Lugo's arrival in Washington for the start of the 93rd Congress (1973–1975) marked the fulfillment of one of his campaign promises. Minutes after he and Delegate Antonio Won Pat of Guam were sworn in as the first Delegates to represent their respective territories, the House narrowly voted to give the four Territorial Delegates a vote in their committees. De Lugo credited the "slick political maneuvering" of Representative Philip Burton of California—chairman of the Subcommittee on Territorial and Insular Affairs, an advocate for Delegate rights in Congress, and a leader in enacting congressional reform in the early 1970s—for the addition of this privilege to the package of changes in the House Rules.[15] The Democratic Caucus, which determined the direction of party policy and strategy, also supported giving Delegates a vote.[16]

Along with other representatives for U.S. territories, de Lugo sought and won a position on the Committee on Interior and Insular Affairs, where he could monitor and introduce legislation affecting the Virgin Islands. In his second term, he added a seat on the Merchant Marine and Fisheries Committee.[17] He was also a founding member of the House Territorial Caucus.

His first piece of legislation, introduced on February 5, 1973, and co-authored with Territorial Delegate Won Pat, proposed an amendment to the Constitution that granted citizens in the Virgin Islands and Guam the right to vote in U.S. presidential elections.[18] De Lugo pointed out that Virgin Islanders had earned this right, noting that election turnouts were routinely near 80 percent, "notably higher than in all but a few communities in the 50 states." He emphasized the islands' patriotism, particularly during the Vietnam War. "We in the Virgin Islands have recognized that the rights, obligations, and privileges of citizenship demand commitment and sacrifice," he told his colleagues. "We have unquestioningly risen to the defense of our country whenever and wherever it has been necessary to preserve America's Freedom and to secure liberty and the right to self-determination elsewhere."[19] The legislation ultimately died in the Judiciary Committee, but de Lugo obtained significant support from the Congressional Black Caucus as a show of solidarity with the black residents of the territory who made up nearly 80 percent of its population.[20]

De Lugo sought greater self-determination for the islands' territorial government, and he won for the Virgin Islands' legislature the right to determine procedure for filling vacancies. (Previously, vacancies were filled by the governor's appointees.) "Direct election by the people is the only method by which an individual may attain membership in the House of Representatives.... It is this fact which makes this body the most important democratic institution in the nation," he observed. "If the Legislature of the Virgin Islands is to truly be the people's forum at the territorial level, it must also maintain this qualification."[21] De Lugo also lobbied for a constitutional convention in the Virgin Islands, which would allow residents a chance to write their own governing document. He emphasized a greater need for autonomy in light of the islands' increasing prosperity, which paralleled a well-publicized increase in crime.[22] His request ultimately passed both houses with bipartisan support in October 1976.[23] De Lugo met with frustration at home, however, because Virgin Islands voters rejected the constitution to avoid higher local taxes and the costs associated with self-government.[24]

The islands' economic health depended on de Lugo's ability to obtain federal dollars, increase government spending, and gain greater control over private investment. Taxation was a significant issue for Virgin Islanders because they were subject to a unique system; since 1954 the islands' workforce had paid income taxes under a mirror structure wherein federal taxes were paid into the territory's general treasury.[25] The mirror tax system was a double-edged sword for the islands' coffers because while the Virgin Islands received federal money directly, its use of funds was regulated. Moreover, the territorial government lost money whenever the federal government reduced tax rates.[26] After major federal tax cuts in 1975, de Lugo helped shepherd a bill through the House that not only loaned the Virgin Islands money as a stopgap for its fiscal bleeding, but also granted the government the authority to levy a surtax of up to 10 percent of taxpayers' annual federal obligation.[27]

De Lugo also sought benefits from social services, including Social Security, Medicaid, and Medicare, for Virgin Islands residents when Congress left unchanged sections of the Social Security Act that capped spending limits. Stateside lawmakers noted that since Virgin Islanders did not pay federal taxes, they should receive fewer social services. Senator Bob Dole of Kansas expressed a viewpoint of the mirror tax system shared by many mainland politicians during a hearing before the Senate Finance Committee's Subcommittee on Public Assistance. "I think the record should be clear," Dole noted, "that taxes are not paid to the Federal Treasury; when we talk about discrimination against any citizen we have to make the record complete. That is a factor." De Lugo responded, "As you know, it has been the policy of the Congress of the United States that the territories should retain these tax moneys to help build their economies."[28] He noted that Virgin Islanders generally paid more taxes than the average American citizen and cited a 1976 report from the Department of Health, Education, and Welfare that said, "The current fiscal treatment of Puerto Rico and the territories under the Social Security Act is unduly discriminatory."[29] De Lugo's testimony convinced both houses to incorporate provisions to increase public assistance for the Virgin Islands, Puerto Rico, and Guam.[30]

De Lugo's attention to the Virgin Islands' economy also focused on securing greater command of its land and tourist trade. De Lugo sought to transfer the title to Water Island—the territory's fourth-largest island, which was then under the jurisdiction of the Department of the Interior—to the Virgin Islands' government to preserve its beaches for Virgin Islanders.[31] He also sought the ownership of submerged lands, requesting the use of the rules that applied to coastal states, which grant state sovereignty out to sea, three miles from the mean high-tide mark. Transferring ownership to the territorial governments, he argued, would "eliminate the present cumbersome and duplicative administrative processes which must be undertaken before these lands may be beneficially utilized."[32] He also offered an amendment to the Airport and Airway Development Act of 1970, calling for more federal funding for airport construction and expansion projects in the Virgin Islands, Guam, and American Samoa. "The Virgin Islands, because of their isolated position, are uniquely dependent upon air traffic for their economic survival," de Lugo told his colleagues. "The lack of fuel resources and raw material makes the islands particularly dependent upon the money generated by the tourist trade, much of which arrives by air."[33]

In 1978, de Lugo announced he would not seek re-election, in order to run against incumbent Juan Luis for territorial governor of the Virgin Islands, noting that he had "accomplished about everything I came for, and then some."[34] He officially announced his candidacy on March 28 and was confident enough to delay heavy campaigning until Congress recessed in August.[35] Luis ran as an Independent, although he had been appointed as an Independent Citizens Movement Party candidate when popular governor Cecil King died earlier that year.

De Lugo touted the federal money he had brought to the island, emphasizing his responsible fiscal management and his relationship with Washington. He challenged his opponent's spending habits and pointed to the higher rate of crime in the islands.[36] De Lugo hit Luis hard for delaying and eventually withholding his endorsement of de Lugo's pending immigration adjustment bill, and later criticized him for failing to offer an alternative plan.[37] The campaign soon turned vitriolic, with both candidates depending on the local courts and on mediators to arbitrate everything from the debate schedule to the structure of the ballots.[38] Voter weariness due to the candidates' quibbling, coupled with de Lugo's "overconfidence" and Luis's connections in St. Croix, ultimately led to the challenger's defeat; de Lugo garnered just 40 percent of the vote.[39] Most damaging was de Lugo's weak support from the Democratic machine—primarily his lack of key endorsements from the islands' senators, many of whom opposed his decision to run.[40]

After the election, de Lugo returned home to St. Croix and remained outside the public spotlight, claiming he was relieved to be "a private citizen" for the first time in two decades.[41] However, in 1980, citing "broad, grass-roots, bipartisan support," de Lugo announced he would run against Republican Territorial Delegate Mel Evans, the former Virgin Islands governor who had won de Lugo's vacant congressional seat in 1978. De Lugo criticized Evans's lack of bipartisanship, which he noted had alienated the Virgin Islands supporters de Lugo had lined up during his House service. Evans's party affiliation put the Virgin Islands "solidly in the Republican corner," in opposition to the Democratic majority, de Lugo observed, "When the crunch comes, the Democratic leadership can't count on him."[42] Particularly damaging was Evans's vote in the Interior Committee against an environmental protection bill; its failure essentially opened the Alaskan wilderness to oil exploration in 1979. Virgin Islands voters, most of whom supported environmental protection, were angered. De Lugo described the vote as "a major blunder." "All the Virgin Islands' friends wanted that bill," de Lugo said. "He voted against every ally he needs to get money for the territory." [43] De Lugo compared his congressional record to Evans's, noting that federal funds for the Virgin Islands had diminished during Evans's term. "When I was there, whenever we got money authorized, we got every penny appropriated," de Lugo noted. "It was taken for granted."[44] De Lugo defeated Evans in his closest election ever, with a narrow 53 percent of the vote. (He won his subsequent bids for Congress by comfortable margins.) De Lugo returned to the Interior and Insular Affairs Committee and also picked up assignments on the Post Office and Civil Service and the Public Works and Transportation Committees. He later served on the Education and Labor Committee and on the Select Committee on Narcotics Abuse and Control.[45]

Among de Lugo's first initiatives after returning to Washington was a bill on immigration that attempted to ease the resentment of many native Virgin Islanders toward a wave of Greater Caribbean immigrants. During the 1960s and 1970s, "down island" immigration from other Caribbean nations and territories increased dramatically as laborers moved to the Virgin Islands during the high tourist season to work in the hospitality industry; the islands' population grew 188 percent from 1960 to 1975.[46] These workers arrived under the H-2 provision of the 1954 Immigration and Naturalization Act, which permitted temporary residence.[47] Over the next two decades, as the islands became more dependent on foreign labor, Congress and the Department of Labor allowed family members to accompany alien workers. Schools, housing and welfare and health care services were overburdened by the surge in population, and the racial makeup of the labor force which was primarily black, increased tensions.[48] In 1976 de Lugo proposed an immigration adjustment act that would provide H-2 provision aliens a fast track to citizenship, but the Gerald R. Ford administration blocked the legislation.[49] In 1981 de Lugo pushed through the Virgin Islands Nonimmigrants Alien Adjustment Act, which became law on September 30, 1982. The bill addressed the issue of illegal immigration by ending the temporary worker program, except for temporary workers who performed at the annual carnival; by putting legal aliens who had resided in the Virgin Islands since June 30,

1975, on the path to citizenship; and by creating a task force composed of the governor of the Virgin Islands and six federal Cabinet officers to address the burdens caused by the addition of so many new citizens.[50] "The people of the Virgin Islands should be proud today," de Lugo noted just before the bill passed the House. Referring to Virgin Islanders' decade-long struggle with immigration issues, he continued, "For this bill is an honorable and equitable solution to a very difficult and long-standing problem. It tugged at their conscience. They wrestled with it publicly and privately. And, in the end reached this compromise solution which is uniquely ours—a product of our community for our community."[51]

De Lugo also initially supported President Ronald W. Reagan's Caribbean Basin Initiative, which called for eliminating taxes on goods from foreign countries in the Caribbean Sea.[52] However, he expressed concern about the advantage this agreement would give foreign competitors in the rum industry. "I simply cannot overemphasize the critical significance of the rum industry to the economic well-being of the U.S. citizens in the Virgin Islands," de Lugo told the House Committee on Ways and Means during a hearing. He noted that an excise tax on rum shipped to the mainland United States was the largest single source (18 percent) of the territorial government's revenue and that the rum industry employed numerous farmers and manufacturers. Eliminating duties on other Caribbean nations' rum exports would undercut the price of the taxed Virgin Islands product.[53] Though he preferred to abolish rum's favorable status, de Lugo admitted "a compromise is more realistic" and attempted to add to the initiative an amendment that set a quota for duty-free rum.[54] "I think it is great that the president has said the U.S. Virgin Islands and Puerto Rico must be enhanced by the policy towards the Caribbean Basin," he told the committee. "However, let's be realistic. No one looking at this legislation can say that the position of the flag territories is enhanced."[55] The amendment failed, 226 to 171. Most of its opponents felt the rum industry in the Caribbean territories was overly subsidized.[56] De Lugo continued to pursue the issue as debate on the legislation dragged into the 98th Congress (1983–1985). The final legislation, passed on July 28, 1983, included specific provisions inserted by the Senate to protect Virgin Islands rum.[57]

On September 18, 1989, Hurricane Hugo slammed into the Virgin Islands, crossing directly over St. Croix and inflicting catastrophic destruction. Most Virgin Islanders had no utilities, businesses were closed, and the airport on St. Croix was destroyed. Ninety percent of the buildings on St. Croix sustained major damage. Five people in Puerto Rico and the Virgin Islands were killed, and infrastructure repair costs for both territories exceeded $1 billion.[58] "[It is] beyond belief," de Lugo told the *Washington Post* after touring St. Croix, having arrived with Federal Emergency Management Agency (FEMA) crews on September 19. "The only thing you can liken it to is a war zone."[59] De Lugo's congressional office employed five staff members and five volunteers to answer the phone calls flooding his office.[60] Responding to reports of looting and threats to stranded tourists, 1,100 National Guardsmen arrived on the island a few days later.[61] De Lugo coordinated the Virgin Islands Hurricane Relief Fund, initially praising the "Herculean efforts by FEMA" to aid St. Croix's recovery.[62] However, he eventually criticized the relief agency's slow progress, noting in an open letter to his colleagues that 2,700 homes still lacked temporary cover more than a month after the storm.[63] The following November, de Lugo introduced the Hurricane Hugo Emergency Relief Act, which increased federal spending ceilings on road repair and flood control projects and permitted the Army Corps of Engineers to oversee reconstruction on the Virgin Islands and in Puerto Rico. The legislation passed by voice vote on November 17.[64]

De Lugo's seven terms in Congress during his second period of service, coupled with his three previous terms, made him the dean of the Territorial Delegates when Delegate Won Pat retired in 1985. Moreover, his long service on the Territorial and Insular Affairs Subcommittee on the Interior and Insular Affairs Committee allowed him to take the helm of that subcommittee in 1987, and he held that position until he left the House.[65] As chairman, de Lugo oversaw the political status and the budget for the Virgin Islands as well as those for all the other U.S. territories, thus enjoying a greater role shaping policy.

As subcommittee chairman, he was deeply involved in Palau's rocky path toward independence. An archipelago in the South Pacific that was captured from the Japanese during World War II, Palau had been a United Nations trust territory administered by the United States. In 1986, at the behest of President Reagan's administration, Congress passed the Compact of Free Association, which sought limited autonomy for Palau, the Federated States of Micronesia, and the Marshall Islands and provided for them, should they ratify the legislation.[66] However, de Lugo, then chairman of the Subcommittee on Territorial and Insular Affairs, sought to temporarily block Palau's ratification of the compact, citing corruption and bureaucratic problems that needed to be resolved before the island's independence could be considered. He asked the General Accounting Office to investigate Palau's finances and rumors of scandal. In an attempt to address these problems, on June 23, 1988, de Lugo introduced H.J. Res. 597, which provided aid and loans to Palau while requiring it to retain a special prosecutor and a public auditor to investigate corruption.[67]

De Lugo's legislation met with resistance among his congressional colleagues. Senator Bennett Johnston of Louisiana, chairman of the Senate Energy and Natural Resources Committee, and Representative Jim Leach of Iowa, the Ranking Republican Member on the House Foreign Affairs Committee, both proposed alternative legislation allowing Palauans greater independence in solving their economic and political difficulties. With both houses at an impasse, there was last-minute wrangling before the 100th Congress (1987–1989) adjourned on October 21, 1988. House supporters of the compromise provision exerted considerable pressure on de Lugo to accept Johnston's bill in exchange for the reconsideration of some of his provisions in 1989. Leach counted aloud as the minutes ticked off on his watch while he and others crowded around de Lugo on the House Floor during the final vote scheduled for the Congress, on an omnibus drug bill. By the time de Lugo accepted the compromise, the time had already expired. A compromise measure hammered out by de Lugo and Johnston passed the House in the final moments of the first session of the 101st Congress (1989–1991) at 2:40 a.m. on November 22, 1989. The measure granted Palau its independence and $478 million over 15 years while allowing the United States to maintain some military rights should Palauans accept the measure in a referendum. However, in February 1990 the vote fell short of the 75 percent minimum required by the Palauan constitution.[68]

In 1994 de Lugo retired from politics, returning to the Virgin Islands. Upon his departure from the House, other Delegates expressed their appreciation on the floor. Calling de Lugo "my greatest ally in Congress on political status issues," Territorial Delegate Robert Underwood of Guam said, "Few political leaders in the U.S. territories can claim the record of accomplishment of Ron de Lugo. Fewer still can boast of friends stretching from the far flung reaches of the Caribbean to the Pacific."[69] In 2001 the House passed legislation sponsored by Territorial Delegate Donna Christensen of the Virgin Islands to name a federal building in Charlotte Amalie, St. Thomas, after de Lugo.[70] "All of politics is not sweet," de Lugo noted at the Ron de Lugo Federal Building's dedication in 2003. "It is a mixture of sweetness and, to do it well, pain." Asked if he would return to politics, he responded, "I ain't running for a thing."[71]

FOR FURTHER READING

Biographical Directory of the United States Congress, "Ron de Lugo," http://bioguide.congress.gov.

MANUSCRIPT COLLECTION

The Virgin Islands Public Libraries, Territorial Archives (St. Thomas and St. Croix). *Papers*: Dates and amounts unknown.

NOTES

1 *Congressional Record*, House, 107th Cong., 1st sess. (21 May 2001): H2342.

2 "De Lugo Sees Election as Popular Mandate," 14 November 1972,

Virgin Island Daily News.

3 See, for example, "Mammoth Variety Show to Be Staged at Center," 16 January 1952, *Virgin Island Daily News*: 1; "Two Honored at Testimonial Dinners," 13 February 1952, *Virgin Island Daily News*: 1.

4 Leon Mawson, "Island Carnival," 24 August 1952, *New York Times*: X19; "Carnival Spotlight," 21 March 1953, *Virgin Island Daily News*; "The Carnival," 28 March 1953, *Virgin Island Daily News*.

5 *Congressional Directory*, 93rd Congress (Washington, D.C.: Government Printing Office, 1973): 203. The de Lugo family name appears in the photo captions for the following articles: "Supervisor of Elections Says Budget Unrealistic," 22 May 1972, *Virgin Island Daily News*: 1; No Title, 22 June 1973, *Virgin Island Daily News*: 6.

6 "Virginia Crash Kills Son of Washington Rep.," 21 March 1972, *Virgin Island Daily News*: 9.

7 In 1954 Congress passed the Revised Organic Act, allowing the Virgin Islands to elect its own legislature, an 11-member body of senators. With a near monopoly in the legislature, Virgin Islands Democrats split on factional lines into the Unity Democrats (Unicrats), previously a separate Unity Party, and the Donkey Democrats (Donkeycrats), sometimes called the Mortar and Pestle faction. Throughout the 1950s and 1960s, both sides fought for control over the legislature. De Lugo initially allied with the Donkeycrats, becoming the group's de facto leader, but later sided with the Unicrats. The two factions merged in the mid-1960s. A political history of the Virgin Islands is available in William W. Boyer, *America's Virgin Islands: A History of Human Rights and Wrongs* (Durham: Carolina Academic Press, 1983). For the development of political parties in the U.S. Virgin Islands, see Richard E. Sharpless, "Virgin Islands of the United States" in Robert J. Alexander, ed., *Political Parties of the Americas*, vol. 2 (Westport, CT: Greenwood Press, 1982): 743–749.

8 "De Lugo to Run for Delegate to Congress," 23 May 1972, *Virgin Island Daily News*: 1.

9 "Mercer, de Lugo Vie on Democratic Slate," 3 June 1972, *Virgin Island Daily News*.

10 See, for example, "Charges Washington Rep Neglects His Job," 20 June 1972, *Virgin Island Daily News*; "Campaign Roundup," 3 July 1972, *Virgin Island Daily News*; "Campaign Roundup," 10 July 1972, *Virgin Island Daily News*.

11 "De Lugo Overwhelms Demo Opponent; King, Roebuck Top," 13 July 1972, *Virgin Island Daily News*.

12 Appealing principally to the poorer, black voters, the Independent Citizens Movement emerged from the Democratic Party in the late 1960s. The party's creation was a reaction to growing racial and class tensions on the islands during a period of industrialization in the 1960s and 1970s; see Sharpless, "Virgin Islands of the United States": 746–747, 748.

13 The Republican Party had a small presence in the Virgin Islands from 1954 until the 1970s, when physician Melvin Evans became its first popularly elected governor. See Boyer, *America's Virgin Islands*: 266; Sharpless, "Virgin Islands of the United States": 746, 749.

14 "De Lugo Sees Election as Popular Mandate."

15 The 208 to 206 vote was close because the package of rules contained controversial clauses intended to fast track legislation. Minority Leader Gerald Ford of Michigan noted that the Republicans did not object to the Territorial Delegates' having the right to vote in committee. See *Congressional Record*, House, 93rd Cong., 1st sess. (3 January 1973): 17, 18, 26. For more information on Burton's role in advocating congressional reform, see Julian Zelizer, *On Capitol Hill: The Struggle to Reform Congress and Its Consequences, 1948–2000* (New York: Cambridge University Press, 2004).

16 De Lugo, Won Pat, District of Columbia Delegate Walter Fauntroy, and Puerto Rican Resident Commissioner Jaime Benítez all caucused with the Democrats in the 93rd Congress.

17 Garrison Nelson, *Committees in the U.S. Congress, 1947–1992*, vol. 2 (Washington, D.C.: CQ Press, 1994): 226.

18 The *Virgin Island Daily News* reported that de Lugo also sought to abolish the Electoral College, calling the organization "archaic, cumbersome, and undemocratic," and claimed there was "strong sentiment" for its elimination. No other sources mention de Lugo's desire to abolish the Electoral College. See "Delegates Broaden Efforts for V.I. Vote," 10 January 1973, *Virgin Island Daily News*: 6, 21.

19 *Congressional Record*, House, 93rd Cong., 1st sess. (5 February 1973): 3232.

20 *Congressional Record*, Index, 93rd Cong., 1st sess.: 2227; "Black House Members Back V.I. for Vote," 9 March 1973, *Virgin Island Daily News*: 3; see Table 17, U.S. Department of Commerce, Bureau of the Census, "General Population Characteristics, Virgin Islands of the United States: 1980 Census of Population," http://www.pacificweb.org/DOCS/usvi/1980%20VI%20_Census/1980%20General%20Population%20Characteristics.pdf (accessed 10 September 2009): 55–57. De Lugo renewed his request for a presidential vote for the insular territories in the 99th and 100th Congresses (1985–1989). Both bills were unsuccessful (99th Cong., 1st sess., H.J. Res. 23; 100th Cong., 1st sess., H.J. Res. 217).

21 *Congressional Record*, House, 93rd Cong., 1st sess. (10 May 1973): 15270.

22 *Congressional Record*, House, 93rd Cong., 2nd sess. (7 May 1974): 13438.

23 *Congressional Record*, House, 94th Cong., 1st sess. (9 September 1975): 28038–28039; *Congressional Record*, House, 94th Cong., 1st sess. (6 October 1975): 31858; Hearing before the House Subcommittee on

Territorial and Insular Affairs, Committee on Interior and Insular Affairs, *Constitution for the Virgin Islands and Constitution for Guam*, 94th Cong., 1st sess. (17 September 1975): 6–12.

24 Sharpless, "Virgin Islands of the United States": 746. The U.S. Virgin Islands has held five constitutional conventions. The most recent, in 2007, completed a draft in June 2009. Governor John DeJongh, Jr., forwarded the proposed constitution to President Barack Obama on December 31, 2009, for approval. See Aldeth Lewin, "Governor Ordered to Send Constitution Draft to the President," 29 December 2009, *Virgin Island Daily News*.

25 Steven Maguire, "Federal Taxes and the U.S. Possessions: An Overview," 19 May 2008, Rep. RL32708, Congressional Research Service, Library of Congress, Washington, D.C.: 5–7; Arnold H. Leibowitz, *Defining Status: A Comprehensive Analysis of United States Territorial Relations* (Dordrecht, Netherlands: Martinus Nijhoff, 1989): 288.

26 Leibowitz, *Defining Status*: 288–295.

27 Ibid., 288–295; *Congressional Record*, House, 94th Cong., 2nd sess. (10 August 1976): 26759.

28 Hearing before the Senate Subcommittee on Public Assistance, Committee on Finance, *Public Assistance Amendments of 1977*, 95th Cong., 1st sess. (12, 18, 19, 20 July 1977): 180.

29 Quoted in Hearing before the Senate Subcommittee on Public Assistance, Committee on Finance, *Public Assistance Amendments of 1977*, 95th Cong., 1st sess. (12, 18, 19, 20 July 1977): 180; Hearing before the House Subcommittee on Health and the Environment, Committee on Interstate and Foreign Commerce, *Increase Medicaid Assistance to Puerto Rico, the Virgin Islands, and Guam*, 95th Cong., 1st sess. (8 September 1977): 53–54. The two hearings contain different dates for the Health, Education, and Welfare report referenced by de Lugo. The correct date is listed in the September 8 hearing.

30 "Finance Committee Shapes a Welfare Bill." CQ Press Electronic Library, CQ Almanac Online Edition, cqal77-1203395. Originally published in *CQ Almanac 1977* (Washington, D.C.: Congressional Quarterly, Inc., 1978), http://library.cqpress.com/cqalmanac/cqal77-1203395 (accessed 14 January 2010).

31 *Congressional Record*, Extension of Remarks, 93rd Cong., 1st sess. (12 March 1973): 7381–7382.

32 *Congressional Record*, House, 93rd Cong., 2nd sess. (18 March 1974): 6956; Hearing before the Senate Subcommittee on Territories and Insular Affairs, Committee on Interior and Insular Affairs, *Submerged Lands Legislation Affecting Guam, the Virgin Islands, and American Samoa*, 93rd Cong., 2nd sess. (19 June 1974): 22.

33 *Congressional Record*, House, 93rd Cong., 1st sess. (1 May 1973): 3232.

34 Munroe, "Report from Washington," 28 January 1978, *Virgin Island Daily News*: 6.

35 "Exuding Confidence," 5 August 1978, *Virgin Island Daily News*: 6.

36 Penny Feuerzeig, "Delegate Sees Money in Islands by Next Summer," 8 August 1978, *Virgin Island Daily News*: 1; "De Lugo Assails Luis on Crime," 24 August 1978, *Virgin Island Daily News*: 5.

37 Penny Feuerzeig, "De Lugo Pushing Luis on Alien Bill," 2 May 1978, *Virgin Island Daily News*; "De Lugo Criticizes Luis over Silence on Alien Bill," 5 May 1978, *Virgin Island Daily News*. "Delegate Asks Luis for Details on Bill," 10 May 1978, *Virgin Island Daily News*.

38 See, for example, "Luis Sets Conditions for Debate with de Lugo," 11 October 1978, *Virgin Island Daily News*: 3; "Claims Luis Directed Probe," 27 October 1978, *Virgin Island Daily News*: 8; Penny Feuerzeig, "Investigator Silent on Leaflet Probe Results," 3 November 1978, *Virgin Island Daily News*: 3; Penny Feuerzeig, "De Lugo Going to Court on Spoiled Ballot Issue," 4 November 1978, *Virgin Island Daily News*: 1.

39 Jere Maupin, "Theories on Election Rampant," 9 November 1978, *Virgin Island Daily News*: 1.

40 Fred Clarke, "Virgin Island Democrats Will Never Be 'Family,'" 16 June 1980, *Virgin Island Daily News*: 10.

41 "There's No Place Like Home," 27 January 1979, *Virgin Island Daily News*: 6; Penny Feuerzeig, "De Lugo Considering Delegate Bid," 21 March 1980, *Virgin Island Daily News*: 3.

42 Feuerzeig, "De Lugo Considering Delegate Bid"; Penny Feuerzeig, "De Lugo Plans to Campaign for Delegate Evans' Seat," 13 June 1980, *Virgin Island Daily News*: 3.

43 Penny Feuerzeig, "Evans' Vote Rouses Colleagues' Ire," 3 March 1979, *Virgin Island Daily News*: 3.

44 Feuerzeig, "De Lugo Plans to Campaign for Delegate Evans' Seat."

45 Nelson, *Committees in the U.S. Congress, 1947–1992*, vol. 2: 226.

46 Leibowitz, *Defining Status*: 278.

47 Section 101 (a) (15) (H) (ii) of the act was known as the H-2 provision; see Boyer, *America's Virgin Islands*: 289.

48 See Leibowitz, *Defining Status*: 278–282; and Boyer, *America's Virgin Islands*: 287–292. The situation resulted in increased crime. The most infamous crime was the Fountain Valley Massacre, in which five black Crucians from prominent families who were angry about changes resulting from increased tourism and immigration robbed and murdered eight tourists and hotel workers, most of them white, at the Fountain Valley Golf Course, in broad daylight on September 6, 1972. The attackers' calm demeanor in these racially motivated killings made international headlines. See Leibowitz, *Defining Status*: 282n; and Boyer, *America's Virgin Islands*: 311–321.

49 Leibowitz, *Defining Status*: 283n.

50 Ibid., 283–284.

51 *Congressional Record*, House, 97th Cong., 2nd sess. (8 September 1982): 22858.

52 For more information, see "Caribbean Trade Plan." CQ Press Library, CQ Almanac Online Edition, cqal82-1163576. Originally published in *CQ Almanac 1983* (Washington, D.C.: Congressional Quarterly, Inc., 1983), http://library.cqpress.com/cqalmanac/cqal82-1163576 (accessed 27 April 2009).

53 Hearing before the House Subcommittee on Trade, Committee on Ways and Means, *Caribbean Basin Initiative*, 97th Cong., 2nd sess. (23 March 1982): 67.

54 Ibid.

55 Ibid., 66; Jane Seaberry, "Caribbean Policy Hit at Hearings," 24 March 1982, *Washington Post*: D9.

56 *Congressional Record*, House, 97th Cong., 2nd sess. (17 December 1982): 31930–31931.

57 Hearing before the Senate Committee on Natural Resources, *Caribbean Basin Initiative*, 98th Cong., 1st sess. (10 June 1983): 15; "Caribbean Trade Plan," *CQ Almanac 1983*.

58 National Oceanic and Atmospheric Administration, "Hurricane History: Hurricane Hugo 1989," http://www.nhc.noaa.gov/HAW2/english/history.shtml#hugo (accessed 11 September 2009).

59 Adela Gooch, "U.S. Troops Arrive on Ravaged Island," 22 September 1989, *Washington Post*: A1.

60 Molly Sinclair, "Area Residents Still Await Word on Friends and Relatives in Virgin Islands," 23 September 1989, *Washington Post*: A13.

61 Gooch, "U.S. Troops Arrive on Ravaged Island"; Jeffrey Schmalz, "3 Weeks after Storm, St. Croix Still Needs Troops," 9 October 1989, *New York Times*: A1. Though he admitted that some looting took place, de Lugo staunchly defended the island's reputation, claiming that media reports of violence were overblown and stressing the severity of the situation following the storm. "If you have a hurricane on the mainland … help comes from across the State line," de Lugo noted. "The little island of St. Croix … was completely cut off for at least 48 hours." *Congressional Record*, House, 101st Cong., 1st sess. (4 October 1989): 23295.

62 Remar Sutton, "In Hugo's Wake: A Move Is Afoot for the V.I. Events," 25 September 1989, *Washington Post*: B5; *Congressional Record*, House, 101st Cong., 1st sess. (17 October 1989): 24768.

63 Michael Wines, "U.S. Relief Agency Seeks Relief from Criticism," 25 October 1989, *New York Times*: A29.

64 *Congressional Record*, Extension of Remarks, 101st Cong., 1st sess. (7 November 1989): 27823. The bill was originally entitled "The Hurricane Hugo Disaster Reconstruction Bill" but was later re-titled by amendment. See *Congressional Record*, House, 101st Cong., 1st sess. (17 November 1989): 29993–29996.

65 The name of the Committee on Interior and Insular Affairs was changed to the Committee on Natural Resources in the 103rd Congress (1993–1995).

66 The legislation was originally introduced in 1983. Both the Federated States of Micronesia and the Marshall Islands ratified the Compact of Free Association and were granted independence in 1986. See "Micronesia Compact," CQ Press Electronic Library, CQ Almanac Online Edition, cqal85-1147328. Originally published in *CQ Almanac 1985* (Washington, D.C.: Congressional Quarterly, Inc., 1986), http://library.cqpress.com/cqalmanac/cqal85-1147328 (accessed 3 September 2009); "Palau Independence Dispute," CQ Press Electronic Library, CQ Almanac Online Edition, cqal88-1142501. Originally published in *CQ Almanac 1988* (Washington: Congressional Quarterly, Inc., 1989), http://library.cqpress.com/cqalmanac/cqal88-1142501 (accessed 27 April 2009).

67 "Palau Independence Dispute." *CQ Almanac 1988.* The aid included $30 million and an additional $25 million in loans for payment to creditors of a bankrupt power company with a plant in Palau.

68 "Palauans Reject Charter on Autonomy." CQ Press Electronic Library, CQ Almanac Online Edition, cqal90-1118789. Originally published in *CQ Almanac 1990* (Washington, D.C.: Congressional Quarterly, Inc., 1991). http://library.cqpress.com/cqalmanac/cqal90-1118789 (accessed 30 April 2009).

69 *Congressional Record*, Extension of Remarks, 103rd Congress, 2nd sess. (6 October 1994).

70 P.L. 107-175, 116 Stat. 576.

71 Jeremy W. Peters, "Federal Building Christened in Honor of de Lugo," 31 May 2003, *Virgin Island Daily News*.

Strength in Numbers, Challenges in Diversity

LEGISLATIVE TRENDS AND POWER SHARING AMONG HISPANIC AMERICANS IN CONGRESS, 1977–2012

When Congress debated new immigration legislation in 2006, Senator Mel Martinez of Florida was much in demand. If he was not speaking before an audience, Martinez was cornering his colleagues in the Capitol or talking to congressional staffers who were concerned about how the bill would affect them. "Hearing it from the guy behind the counter, they know the names of the bills, it's what everyone is talking about in the Hispanic community," he told a Miami reporter.[1]

The first Cuban American to serve in the U.S. Senate, Martinez immigrated to the United States in the 1960s. Part of a generation of Hispanic Americans that changed U.S. society and Congress's legislative focus, Martinez and many of his Hispanic colleagues during this period were immigrants or the children of immigrants, and their congressional ambitions were shaped by their stories and their families' stories. Martinez's policy preferences were informed by his childhood and by the experiences and observations of other Hispanic Members.[2]

Since their constituents frequently struggled with English and with discrimination, these issues became central to Hispanic Members' agendas. Other issues included the United States' relationship with Cuba and the federal government's relationship with its territories. But perhaps the most important topic of debate during the latter part of the 20th century was immigration. "There are those in the country who feel the country is 'full,'" Martinez observed in 2006. "Had that been the prevailing view in the 1960s, I would not be here."[3]

The Hispanic Americans who entered Congress between 1977 and 2012 represent the greatest increase in their ethnic group in congressional history.

At the 1981 Solidarity March in Washington, D.C., a migrant farm worker holds a sign in Spanish that reads, in part, "Do not snuff out the dreams of Hispanics!" Immigration reform remained a central, often controversial, national issue.

Image courtesy of the Library of Congress

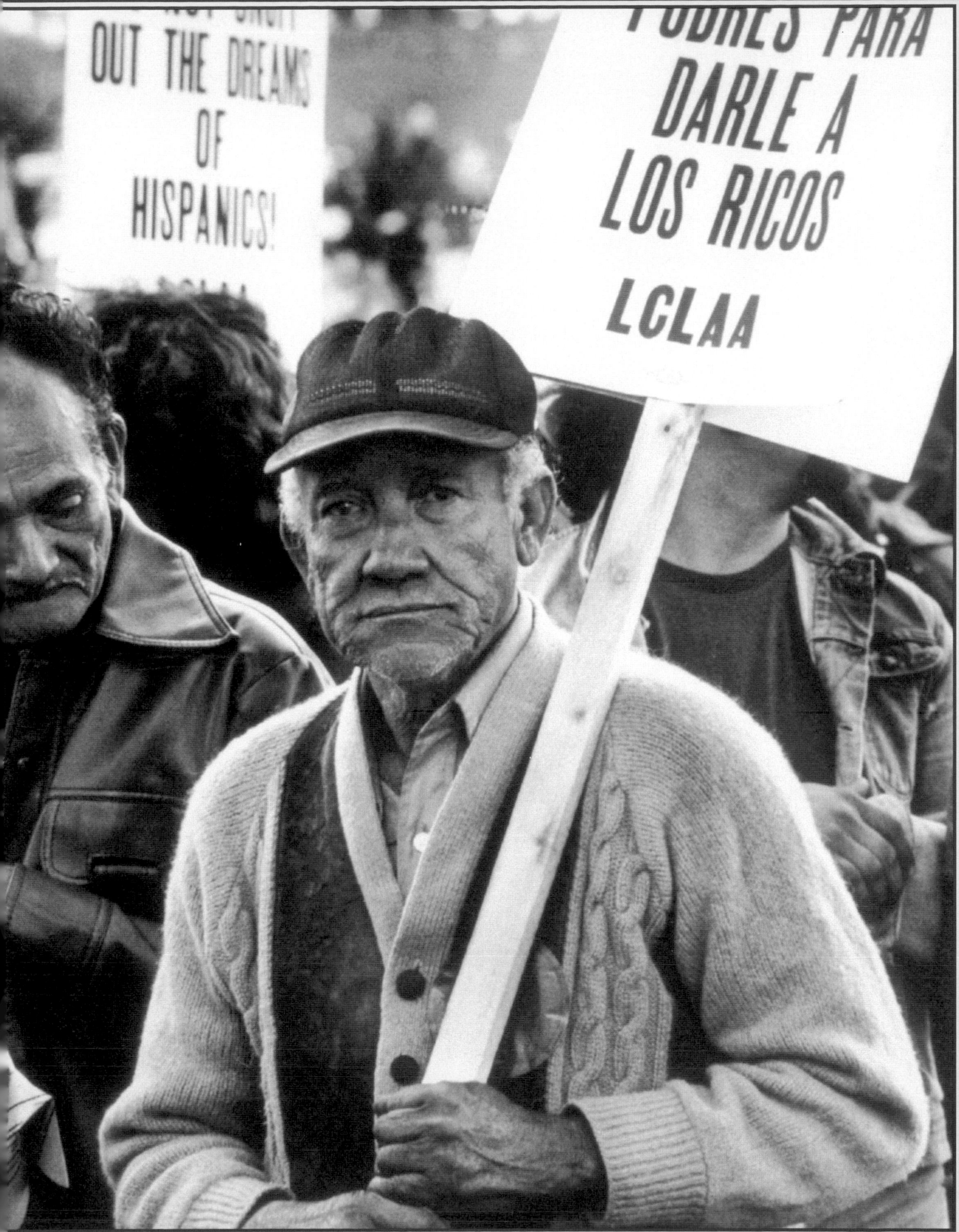

OUT THE DREAMS
OF
HISPANICS!
DARLE A
LOS RICOS
LCLAA

Of the 91 Hispanic Americans who served in Congress through August 2012, 37 were elected or appointed between 1822 and 1976, meaning that nearly 60 percent of the Hispanic Americans in congressional history (54 individuals) were elected in 1976 or later.

This increase was prompted by demographic changes and political reforms. Between the 1980 Census and 2010 Census, the number of Latinos in the United States nearly tripled, to 16 percent of the total population, making Hispanics the second largest ethnic group in the country.[4] Hispanic representation in Congress has also increased because of two major reforms to America's electoral system: the Voting Rights Act of 1965 and its extensions, and a series of Supreme Court decisions on redistricting that began in 1962.[5]

Hispanics' substantial presence in U.S. society did not translate immediately into a degree of comparative congressional representation.[6] Hispanic-American representation in Congress did not change proportionally from 1977 to 2012, despite the burgeoning ratio of Latinos in the U.S. population. In 1981 there were nine Hispanic Americans in Congress while Latinos constituted slightly more than 6 percent of the U.S. population. Thus, there was one Hispanic American in Congress for every 1.62 million Hispanics. Thirty years later that ratio remained unchanged—there were 31 Hispanic Americans in Congress, while Hispanic Americans made up 16 percent of the U.S. population.[7]

Nevertheless, Hispanics' rapid population growth has transformed their profile in a number of states. For most of the 19th century and early 20th century, Latinos were from the Southwest. But recent census data indicate that Hispanic Americans are settling in all the major urban areas in the country.[8] After reapportionment based on the 2010 Census, eight states gained House seats. The proportion of Hispanics in these growing states ranged from 37.6 percent (Texas) to 5.1 percent (South Carolina), with Hispanic growth rates

Members of the Congressional Hispanic Caucus meet, circa 1980s. From left to right: Solomon Ortiz of Texas; Robert Garcia of New York; Bill Richardson of New Mexico (standing); Albert Bustamante of Texas; Esteban Torres of California; and Matthew Martínez of California.

Image courtesy of the National Archives and Records Administration

ranging from 147.9 percent (South Carolina) to 41.8 percent (Texas). The 2010 Census also identified 10 states that lost House seats.[9] In these states, the Hispanic population ranges from 17.7 percent (New Jersey) to 3.1 percent (Ohio) with growth rates ranging from 83.7 percent (Iowa) to 19.2 percent (New York). In each one of these states, whether its population is growing or declining, the growth rate for Hispanics outstrips the growth rate for the general population, increasing the proportion of Hispanics in the total U.S. population.[10] This demographic trend has attracted the attention of both major political parties, which seek to win the loyalty of Hispanic voters.

As their numbers grew, particularly in the U.S. House of Representatives, Hispanic Americans in Congress were better positioned to influence the legislative process, both as individuals and as a bloc.[11] After the 1976 elections, for instance, five Members established the Congressional Hispanic Caucus, a legislative service organization that followed and influenced policy affecting America's Hispanic community. Unlike in other congressional caucuses, however, the diversity of the Hispanic Caucus limited its effectiveness. The caucus was open to both Republicans and Democrats, and its roster included Members from across the country. Competing regional interests often made the caucus an information clearinghouse and a communications network more than a vehicle for moving legislation through Congress.[12]

Hispanic Members during this period benefited from the privileges that were won by their predecessors. In congressional committees, these Members gained enough seniority to chair 11 committees and 16 subcommittees. A handful of Hispanic Members won spots in the leadership, where they helped make committee assignments, and track votes. Experience and exposure at many levels of American politics has made recent Hispanic-American Members attractive candidates for Cabinet-level posts and leadership positions at federal agencies. Senator Martinez's work as Secretary of Housing and Urban Development in the George W. Bush administration prior to his Senate service and his role as head of the Republican National Committee during his Senate tenure, exemplified Latinos' increasing participation in American politics by the early 21st century.

Secretary of Housing and Urban Development Mel Martinez addresses the League of United Latin American Citizens convention in Orlando, Florida. In 2004, Martinez won election to the U.S. Senate as the first Cuban American to serve in that body.

Image courtesy of the U.S. Department of Housing and Urban Development

BACKGROUND AND PRE-CONGRESSIONAL EXPERIENCE

From Congress's origins, its Members have tended to be better educated and wealthier than other Americans.[13] This pattern is evident in the Hispanic Americans elected to Congress after 1976.[14]

The occupations of this generation of Hispanic Members are heavily skewed toward the legal profession. Nearly 40 percent of this group, including all seven Puerto Rican Resident Commissioners who served during this era, practiced law or had studied law. This is consistent with the general characteristics of recent Congresses, in which law has been among the most frequently reported occupations. The 15 percent of Hispanic Members who worked in education, however, is twice as high as the percentage in Congress generally, and while the number of those engaged in business or banking pursuits hovered around 20 percent of the membership in recent Congresses, only 6 percent of Hispanics reported having such an occupation.[15]

Ken Salazar of Colorado served in the U.S. Senate from 2005 to 2009. Salazar resigned his Senate seat in 2009 to become Secretary of the Interior in President Barack Obama's Cabinet.

Image courtesy of the U.S. Department of the Interior

Consistent with earlier congressional trends, Hispanic Members arrived in Washington with more political experience than did previous generations. Half this group cited service in state or territorial legislatures before their arrival on Capitol Hill—the same percentage for all Members of Congress found in surveys conducted since 1987.[16] Seventy-one percent of Hispanic Members had prior political or public service, and many of these Members held prestigious positions before they arrived in Congress or after they left. Resident Commissioner Carlos Romero-Barceló served as governor of Puerto Rico before coming to Capitol Hill, and Aníbal Acevedo-Vilá and Luis G. Fortuño served as governors of Puerto Rico after their tenure in Washington. Two Hispanic Members of Congress were appointed to serve in President Barack Obama's Cabinet starting in 2009: Senator Ken Salazar of Colorado, as Secretary of the Interior, and Representative Hilda Solis of California, as Secretary of Labor.

Hispanic Members' experience meant they were slightly older than their colleagues. Notably, this development occurred at a time when Congress was aging. Contemporary Hispanic Members (1977–2012) were, on average, 56.41 years old when they arrived in Washington. The Congressional Research Service reports that the average age of all Members increased from 48.9 in 1981 to 56.65 in 2011.[17]

Family Connections, Gender, and Ethnic Roots

As in previous generations of Hispanic Members, politics in this generation was a family business. Three sets of siblings—the most common familial connection—served together during this period.[18] Representative Loretta Sanchez won election to a Southern California district in 1996. Her younger sister, Linda Sánchez, won a seat from a nearby district in 2002, making them the first pair of sisters to serve in Congress.[19] Brothers Mario and Lincoln Diaz-Balart served neighboring districts in South Florida between Mario's election in 2002 and Lincoln's departure from Congress in 2011. Colorado Senator Ken Salazar and Representative John Salazar were simultaneously elected to their respective chambers in 2004 and the brothers eventually shared a two-bedroom Washington apartment upon their election. Entering his congressional race four months after Ken announced his campaign for the Senate, older brother John joked, "He wore my hand-me-downs. I guess I can wear his."[20] Representative Edward Roybal of California and his daughter, Lucille Roybal-Allard, also of California, became the first Hispanic father-daughter pair to serve in Congress after she won election to represent part of his old district in 1992.

Increasing Diversity of Hispanic Members

The contemporary period also illustrates the geographical and gender diversity that began to characterize Hispanic Members of Congress. The expansion of territorial representation added Hispanics from the Virgin Islands with Territorial Delegate Ron de Lugo's election in 1972, followed by Ben Blaz and Robert Underwood from Guam and Gregorio Kilili Camacho Sablan from the Northern Mariana Islands. Another example of this growing heterogeneity was Tony Coelho of California. Not long after his election in 1978, Coelho, who was of Portuguese descent, had been denied membership by the Hispanic

Caucus reportedly because he was not considered Hispanic. But in 1985, he campaigned again and won admission to the caucus with the help of members such as Representative Bill Richardson of New Mexico.

The social changes of the 1970s opened the door for women Members. Up to this point all Hispanic Americans in Congress had been male and tended to be of Mexican or Puerto Rican ancestry. The election of Ileana Ros-Lehtinen, who succeeded Claude Pepper of Florida in 1989, marked two milestones: Ros-Lehtinen, who had been born in Cuba and had served in the Florida legislature for much of the 1980s, became the first Hispanic woman to serve in Congress, and the first Cuban American in Congress. Another seven women and seven Cuban Americans would follow her through 2012. Robert Menendez of New Jersey became the first Cuban American who was elected to Congresss from outside the state of Florida when he entered the House in 1993. In 2006 hewas appointed to the Senate, where he joined Cuban-American Senator Mel Martinez.

In 1985, Tony Coelho of California became the first person of Portuguese descent to join the Congressional Hispanic Caucus. He went on to become the Democratic Majority Whip, the highest elected House leadership position ever attained by a Hispanic American.

Image courtesy of the National Archives and Records Administration

CRAFTING AN IDENTITY

The educational, occupational, and political backgrounds of Hispanic Members resembled those of their congressional colleagues. Modern Hispanic Members benefited from the efforts of their female and African-American predecessors, who had arrived in Congress in greater numbers, pioneered strategies to influence legislation, and developed means to juggle their political interests with those of their geographic and ethnic constituencies.[21]

Representatives and Senators

Modern Hispanic-American Members have profited from the rights their predecessors won in Congress; long-serving Members such as Texans Henry González and Kika de la Garza, for example, rose to chair the powerful Banking, Housing, and Urban Affairs and Agriculture Committees, respectively.

Like other groups of congressional minorities, this generation of Latino Members faced a choice: to concentrate on their own legislative agendas without overtly embracing Hispanic issues, or to adopt Hispanic causes as their own and serve as surrogate representatives for Hispanics living in other districts or states.[22] Members like Bill Richardson of New Mexico, Robert Garcia of New York, and Albert Bustamante of Texas embraced these multiple roles. But surrogate representatives did not always represent national interests; often they championed issues that were unique to their districts. Other Members, such as Matthew Martínez of California, Henry Bonilla of Texas, and Ken Salazar, insisted they were not just "Hispanic politicians."

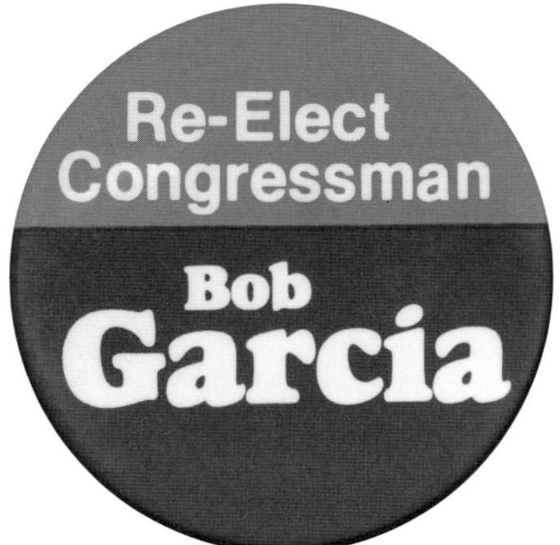

Robert Garcia of New York served seven terms in the U.S. House, representing a Bronx-centered district. Like his predecessor, Herman Badillo, Garcia was of Puerto Rican heritage.

Collection of the U.S. House of Representatives

Drawn by cultural ties, and responding to the wishes of New York City's large Puerto Rican constituency, Representative Robert Garcia, who was of Puerto Rican descent—as was his predecessor Herman Badillo—helped nonvoting Resident Commissioners such as Jaime Fuster with Puerto Rico's legislative agenda. Like their predecessors, the Resident Commissioners in this generation considered themselves to be ambassadors for Puerto Rico as well as active legislators. In addition to submitting legislation, they wrote editorials and spoke about Puerto Rico to a broad range of audiences.

Jaime Fuster served as Puerto Rico's Resident Commissioner from 1985 to 1992 before resigning to become an associate justice on the insular supreme court.

Collection of the U.S. House of Representatives, Photography Collection

Statutory Representatives

A major development after 1977 was the addition to the House of new Territorial Delegates. Many were of Hispanic descent. In addition to the Resident Commissioner, who represented Puerto Rico, Territorial Delegates of Hispanic descent represented the Virgin Islands, Guam, and the Northern Mariana Islands. The increased numbers of Territorial Delegates allowed them to work together and pursue greater political and economic autonomy for their respective territories. In the fall of 1981, they formed the Congressional Territorial Caucus in response to threats to cut territorial budgets.[23] Since they lacked a vote on the floor, Delegates and Resident Commissioners frequently testified before both House and Senate committees and subcommittees, hoping to influence legislation that was relevant to the territories. Delegates and Resident Commissioners concentrated on local issues much more often than their Hispanic colleagues who had a full vote.[24] Their distance from many national issues meant their experiences on Capitol Hill differed greatly from those of their voting colleagues. The job was humbling and often isolating, and almost all of them expressed the same frustrations. "When lobbyists learn that you don't have a vote, they don't talk to you. Maybe it's a blessing. I don't get harassed," Ben Blaz quipped in a 1986 *New York Times* feature on statutory representatives. Ron de Lugo said, "I can't afford to have a big ego." Resident Commissioner Jaime Fuster admitted, "There is a loneliness to this job," echoing the sentiments voiced by his predecessor Luis Muñoz Rivera decades earlier.[25] In 1993, when new House Rules gave statutory representatives the right to vote in the Committee of the Whole provided their vote did not determine the outcome of any particular measure, Puerto Rican Resident Commissioner Carlos Romero-Barceló noted that the new right was "not really a vote, just an opportunity to participate."[26] But their participation was short-lived. The new Republican majority repealed the privilege at the start of the 104th Congress (1995–1997), though Democrats restored it when they controlled the chamber during the 110th and 111th Congresses (2007–2011).[27]

Winning congressional attention for their local agendas, and simply expressing their patriotism, sometimes proved difficult for Territorial Delegates. Representing an island that was removed from the U.S. mainland presented Guamanian Delegate Robert Underwood with numerous challenges. "I always point this out, that in the course of trying to do legislative work here in Congress, frequently when legislation is passed, unless it specifically mentions Guam or it specifically mentions territories, it is normally ignored," he said.[28] Underwood often made a point of including his island in legislative discussions whenever possible, such as when he successfully lobbied for Guam's inclusion in the national World War II Memorial in Washington, D.C.[29]

Leadership Opportunities

House Party Leadership

House leadership opportunities for Hispanic Americans expanded as their numbers and length of service increased, allowing them to accrue the requisite seniority to participate in party leadership. For example, only three Hispanic Members won their first House election in 1982, but all of them went on to serve more than 10 years. In 1992, 10 Hispanic Members were first elected, and eight served more than 10 years. At the start of the 112th Congress (2011–2013), 31 total Hispanic Members of Congress served in the House and Senate, and 14 had served in Congress for 10 years or more.[30]

Leadership opportunities for Hispanic Members also increased as a result of the legislative reforms of the 1970s. These changes decentralized power in Congress, made individual House Members more influential, and provided greater coordinating authority within House leadership. To operate in this new environment, Speakers quickly learned that effective leadership required building a bigger, more diverse inner circle. In addition to the Speaker, the Majority Leader, and the Majority Whip, leadership in the House began to expand, including the chair and vice-chair of the party caucus and the four deputy whips.[31]

Speaker Thomas Foley of Washington (center) meets with members of the Congressional Hispanic Caucus. As post-Watergate reforms decentralized power in the House, Speakers began to broaden their leadership circles to appeal to a greater number of rank-and-file Members.

Image courtesy of the National Archives and Records Administration

Contemporary Hispanic Members of Congress were elected to a number of leadership positions in the House Democratic Caucus. In 1987, California's Tony Coelho became the first elected Democratic Whip. This is the highest congressional party leadership post that any Hispanic American has achieved to date. Coelho first came to the attention of party leaders through his fundraising talents, quickly leading to his appointment as chairman of the Democratic Congressional Campaign Committee (DCCC) as a sophomore Member.[32] This positioned him to recruit strong candidates for House races and build a broad base of support among Members during his rise to power.[33] In late 2002 Robert Menendez was elected chairman of the House Democratic Caucus after serving as its vice chairman since 1998. Menendez held the chairmanship until December 2005, shortly before he was appointed to the U.S. Senate in January 2006.

Beyond the elected leadership positions in the House and within the Democratic Caucus, the Speaker has the discretion to create new appointed positions with leadership responsibilities. In 1977, for instance, Speaker Thomas P. (Tip) O'Neill of Massachusetts authorized the Democratic Whip, John

Bill Richardson of New Mexico (left) confers with fellow House Members William Gray III of Pennsylvania (center) and Esteban Torres of California (right).

Image courtesy of the National Archives and Records Administration

Brademas of Indiana, to expand the whip organization to include a broader coalition. By the beginning of the 1990s, almost one in five Democratic Members served in the whip system.[34] Among the Hispanic Members appointed Chief Deputy Whip were Bill Richardson of New Mexico (1993), Robert Menendez of New Jersey (1997), and Ed Pastor of Arizona (1999); Esteban Torres of California became a Deputy Whip in 1991.[35] More recently, then-Minority Leader and future Speaker Nancy Pelosi of California appointed fellow Californian Xavier Becerra to the post of Assistant to the Speaker in 2006.[36]

Because of the smaller number of Hispanic Republican Members, only two Members served in a Republican leadership position. In 2001, Lincoln Diaz-Balart was appointed to the committee that develops policies for the Republican Conference. When the Republicans gained control of the House in 1995, Diaz-Balart was appointed to the Rules Committee, which determines the conditions under which major bills are debated. He remained there until his retirement from the House in 2011. Representative Devin Nunes of California was appointed assistant majority whip in his first term in the 108th Congress (2003–2005). He was later appointed vice chairman of the National Republican Congressional Committee.

Lincoln Diaz-Balart of Florida served in two Republican leadership positions during his service in the House from 1993 to 2011. In 1995, Diaz-Balart won a spot on the Rules Committee; in 2001, Speaker J. Dennis Hastert of Illinois appointed him to the Republican Policy Committee, which develops the party's legislative agenda.

Collection of the U.S. House of Representatives, Photography Collection

Senate Party Leadership

Four Hispanics served in the Senate during this period, making it improbable that any of them would hold a leadership position, but Robert Menendez became chairman of the Democratic Senatorial Campaign Committee in late 2008.[37] On the Republican side, Senator Mel Martinez was elected in early 2007 as chairman of the Republican National Committee, to raise funds and act as the party's principal spokesman. But after 10 months he left the position "to get back to my main job, my real obligation and passion"—serving Florida in the Senate.[38]

Hispanic Committee Leaders and Assignments

Members such as Robert Garcia and California's Edward Roybal used their positions as subcommittee chairmen to draw attention to legislative interests that benefited their districts and Hispanic Americans generally. Overall, many

Members of this generation gained institutional seniority during their long careers and held prominent committee assignments. Moreover, Hispanic Members' continuous service provided them a pathway to committee and subcommittee leadership by enabling them to gain expertise in certain policy areas.

House Committee Assignments

The Interior and Insular Affairs Committee (also called the Natural Resources or Resources Committee) was the most popular assignment for House Hispanic Members during this period. Twenty-six Hispanic Members served on this panel, which regulates the U.S. territories, public lands, and water and environmental issues.[39] These issues were popular among Southwestern and Western Members, as well as among Territorial Delegates and the Puerto Rican Resident Commissioners. A total of 10 Resident Commissioners and Hispanic Territorial Delegates served on this panel.[40]

Eighteen Hispanic Members served on the Education and Labor Committee (also called the Education and the Workforce Committee and the Economic and Educational Opportunities Committee) and the same number served on the Foreign Affairs Committee (also called the International Relations Committee). Clearly, those committees with jurisdiction over bilingual education, immigration, labor, loans for small businesses, and relations with Latin American countries provide numerous opportunities for Hispanic Members to shape policy.

Hispanic Members were also assigned to the House's most prestigious committees more often than in previous generations. The Appropriations, Rules, and Ways and Means Committees are exclusive assignments, meaning that Republican Conference and Democratic Caucus rules require Members serving on these committees to relinquish their other committee assignments. Additionally, the scope of these panels spans the entire federal government.[41] Thus, belonging to these committees immediately vaults a Member to the center of the House leadership circle.

In previous generations, only four Hispanic Members served on one of these choice panels; Joachim Octave Fernández of Louisiana, Antonio M. Fernández of New Mexico, Joseph Montoya of New Mexico, and Edward Roybal of California served on the Appropriations Committee. Of the Hispanic Members first elected since 1976, 20 have served on prestigious committees. (The Appropriations Committee has had 12 Hispanic members, Budget has had seven, Ways and Means has had three, and Rules has had two.)[42] Three Hispanic Members first elected since 1976 have risen to subcommittee chairmanships on one of these committees. Henry Bonilla of Texas became chairman of the Appropriations Subcommittee on Agriculture, Rural Development, Food and Drug Administration and Related Agencies. His 2001 appointment as one of the "cardinals" of the House—a reference to the 12 Appropriations subcommittee chairmen—passed over two more-senior colleagues.[43] Representative José Serrano of New York was another cardinal, chairing the Subcommittee on Financial Services and Government Reform in the 110th and 111th Congresses. Representative Lincoln Diaz-Balart of Florida also chaired the Legislative and Budget Process Subcommittee under the Rules Committee in the 109th Congress (2005–2007).

As the head of the Congressional Hispanic Caucus from 1981 to 1984, New York's Robert Garcia (right) represented Hispanic interests in meetings with President Ronald Reagan.

Image courtesy of the Ronald Reagan Library/National Archives and Records Administration

Edward Roybal of California (second from left), chairs a congressional hearing in 1992. Congressional Hispanic Caucus colleague Kika de la Garza of Texas (far left) sits next to Roybal.

Image courtesy of the National Archives and Records Administration

In previous generations, only a handful of Hispanic Members chaired subcommittees. Forty-one percent of Hispanic Members first elected since 1976 (22 of 54) chaired at least one subcommittee; eight have chaired multiple subcommittees. Representative Ileana Ros-Lehtinen of Florida chaired the most subcommittees, four under the International Relations Committee (she went on to chair the full committee): Africa; International Economic Policy and Trade; International Operations and Human Rights; and the Middle East and Central Asia.[44]

Senate Committee Assignments

The Senate has a less hierarchical structure and a much smaller membership than the House, so the role of committees and subcommittees in that chamber is very different. With far fewer Senators, each serves on many more committees, diluting the importance of a single prestigious panel.[45] The four Hispanic Senators serving in this era held committees assignments covering issues that were relatively similar to those covered by their House colleagues; three (Mel Martinez, Ken Salazar, and Robert Menendez) served on the Energy and Natural Resources Committee. Martinez, Menendez, and Marco Rubio of Florida have served on the Foreign Relations Committee.[46]

Two Hispanic Senators elected since 1976 have attained subcommittee leadership. Martinez chaired the Subcommittee on African Affairs (under the Foreign Relations Committee) in the 109th Congress. Menendez has chaired three subcommittees during his Senate career including two in the 112th Congress: Housing, Transportation and Community Development Subcommittee (under the Banking Committee); and of the Western Hemisphere, Peace Corps, and Global Narcotics Affairs Subcommittee (under the Foreign Relations Committee).[47]

Henry Bonilla of Texas served in the House from 1993 to 2007. During Bonilla's tenure, he chaired the Appropriations Committee's Subcommittee on Agriculture, Rural Development, Food and Drug Administration and Related Agencies.

Collection of the U.S. House of Representatives

Congressional Hispanic Caucus

The Congressional Hispanic Caucus followed patterns established by constituency caucuses using an informal group to serve as a clearinghouse for information and as a networking hub. Before the emergence of these caucuses, such groups served social or relatively narrow policy ends. The success of the Congressional Black Caucus in effecting policy change and increasing Black Americans' legislative input served as a model for other minority groups in Congress.[48]

The contemporary Congress retains a number of devices to bring Members together in ways that attempt to transcend parties and committees. The Hispanic Caucus provides an alternative to the party organizations and committee networks in that it is based on issues of common concern to the Hispanic community. Junior Members can develop leadership skills and policy strengths, but for most Hispanic Members, the caucus provides the opportunity to sort out their priorities.[49] Though they belonged to the same caucus, Hispanic Members often had a wide variety of agendas given their diverse constituencies.

The caucus worked by unanimous consent: If unanimity could not be achieved, its members were free to vote individually. On one level, this recognized the group's regional diversity enabling Members with different ideological and ethnic outlooks to reach a consensus in the caucus. The frequent inability to reach unanimous consent was attributed to the Hispanic Caucus's early bipartisan composition and the diverse legislative interests of its members. The lack of cohesiveness often circumscribed its ability to exercise power as a distinct bloc. On issues such as immigration reform, border control, and the North American Free Trade Agreement (NAFTA), Hispanic Members split because of their constituencies, their regional differences, and their ethnicities. When asked about the caucus's effectiveness as a coalition in 1992, Edward Roybal commented, "The word coalition to me would mean … a group of individuals that finally take a united action in support or against any particular subject matter. The Hispanic Caucus can not take a united action because the Hispanic Caucus … [includes] Republicans.… On the other hand, there are individuals within the caucus that have taken the opportunity to be supportive of one another on various issues … [which] have nothing to do with the caucus. We do it as individuals and we have been able to form a coalition of a sort."[50]

After its formation in December 1976, the Hispanic Caucus aggressively pursued its legislative interests. It criticized President James Earl (Jimmy) Carter after he nominated or appointed few of more than 600 Hispanic candidates to federal positions in his administration after the 1976 elections. Consequently, President Carter agreed to name more Latinos to administration positions. The caucus also worked to preserve programs for bilingual education and improve voter registration. Additionally, the caucus helped Members obtain desirable committee assignments, provided information to non-Hispanic Members with Hispanic constituencies, and brought public focus to issues that affected the Hispanic community as a whole.[51]

In the 1980s, caucus chairmen such as Robert Garcia and Bill Richardson seized on the group's increasing size to expand its institutional influence. During Garcia's tenure (1980–1984), the caucus delivered a concerted response to immigration reform. According to one scholar, Garcia used his position as chairman of the House Census and Population Subcommittee to bring the issue of immigration reform and its effects on Hispanics to prominent attention during Hispanic Heritage Week in 1981. Chairman Richardson (1984–1985) sought maximum media exposure for the caucus's opposition to an immigration

Members of the Congressional Hispanic Caucus meet with President Jimmy Carter in 1978. One of the caucus's first actions after its 1976 creation was to press the Carter administration to include more Hispanics in leadership positions in the federal government.

Image courtesy of the Jimmy Carter Library/National Archives and Records Administration reform bill and its first delegation trip to Latin America in December 1984. Richardson released a number of statements outlining the caucus's position on democratization in Latin America.[52]

The caucus had a conflicted relationship with the Ronald W. Reagan administration (1981–1989). At times it fought the White House over funding for domestic programs, immigration reform legislation, and its policies toward Nicaragua and El Salvador. At other times it worked alongside Hispanic officials within the Reagan administration. A caucus staffer recalled working with Republicans in "the White House, the campaign, the transition office, Senate staff, House staff, national organizations, everyone.... Probably every Hispanic that was appointed within the administration, we probably had some contact with."[53] Other divisions within the caucus emerged during this period as one of its founders, Henry González, had left the group by 1987.[54] Republicans Manuel Luján, Jr., of New Mexico and Delegate Ben Blaz of Guam also disagreed with their Democratic colleagues on a range of public policy matters.[55]

But during this period, the caucus gained additional institutional clout as its members held more-senior positions within the House committee and leadership structures.[56] Republican Ileana Ros-Lehtinen's membership in the caucus illustrated its growing diversity. Representative Luján, who retired at the end of the 100th Congress (1987–1989), served as Secretary of the Interior in the George H. W. Bush administration (1989–1993).[57]

The caucus began to publicize its legislative agenda in the 100th and 101st Congresses (1987–1991).[58] Before the 102nd Congress (1991–1993), caucus members submitted legislation individually when the caucus could not come to a unanimous decision. Chairman Solomon Ortiz of Texas pursued a more active agenda. "It seemed to me that we just talked about issues, and then everyone would go about their business," Ortiz recalled. "We weren't getting any legislation passed. So I said, 'Let's go out and get some legislation passed.'"[59] The caucus introduced bills such as the Hispanic Access to Higher Education Bill of 1991 (H.R. 3098) and the Voting Rights Improvement Act of 1992

In this undated photo, President Ronald Reagan speaks to members of the Congressional Hispanic Caucus (CHC). The CHC held different stances on issues such as domestic spending, immigration, and Latin America than those of the Reagan administration.

Image courtesy of the National Archives and Records Administration

(H.R. 4312; P.L. 102-344). Ortiz attributed the caucus's activity and institutional savvy to its maturity: "It used to be that we were very new to Congress and really didn't know our way around.... Now that a lot of us have been here for several years, we're more knowledgeable and self-confident."[60]

Hispanic Caucus growth reflected the rising number of Hispanics in the national legislature. At its inception, the caucus started with five Members, but grew to 14 at the start of the 100th Congress (11 voting Members, one Resident Commissioner, and two Delegates) and would remain constant until the start of the 103rd Congress (1993–1995).[61] In 1993, its ranks swelled to 19 (17 voting Members and two nonvoting Members), a result of the 1992 reapportionment that created six new districts favorable to Hispanic-American candidates.

The 103rd Congress marked other notable changes. The caucus garnered two voting members of Puerto Rican descent (Nydia Velázquez of New York and Luis Gutierrez of Illinois), two Republicans (Lincoln Diaz-Balart of Florida and Henry Bonilla of Texas), and a Cuban-American Democrat, Robert Menendez of New Jersey. Both Gutierrez and Menendez were the first Hispanic Representatives from their respective states. Velázquez was the first Puerto Rican woman elected to Congress. The caucus's institutional power increased when Esteban Torres, Ed Pastor, and José Serrano won seats on the House Appropriations Committee. Bill Richardson also became one of four chief deputy whips in the House.[62]

During the 103rd Congress, the caucus took advantage of its numbers and formed three task forces to better pursue its legislative agenda. Three members also sat on the Democratic Steering and Policy Committee, which assigns Members to House committees. However, a number of issues divided the caucus along regional lines. For example, although the caucus worked to block a $1 billion unemployment bill in October 1993, Hispanic Caucus members split on their support of the North American Free Trade Agreement (NAFTA).[63] With the shift to Republican control in the 104th Congress, many of the Democratic Members with senior posts as committee and subcommittee chairs lost their positions and began working against many Republican initiatives.[64]

The caucus's relationship with President William J. (Bill) Clinton was cordial. It sought to protect the interests of Hispanic Americans and often disagreed with the President's positions on social issues, but Clinton consulted the group about legislation, including a July 1993 meeting to discuss his budget proposal. The caucus also leveraged Hispanic electoral support for Democrats into policy concessions and pressured the President to use his influence to counter Republican legislative initiatives, particularly on welfare reform.[65] The caucus grew stronger after welcoming three new members during the 105th Congress (1997–1999) and after the rise of Robert Menendez and Ed Pastor to House party leadership positions (Democratic Party Caucus vice chairman and chief deputy whip, respectively).[66]

The caucus had more of a mixed record with the George W. Bush administration. The decision to deregulate parts of the economy split the caucus between Members of Rust Belt states and Sunbelt Members, who benefited more from recent Bush policies. President Bush met with the caucus in April 2001 to discuss immigration, education, and small business issues, but the President and the legislators disagreed

During Solomon Ortiz's tenure as chairman of the Congressional Hispanic Caucus, the group introduced the Voting Rights Improvement Act that became law in 1992. The Texas Representative attributed the caucus' active agenda to the fact that its members had accrued years of service and become "more knowledgeable and self-confident."

Image courtesy of the National Archives and Records Administration

Nydia Velázquez of New York, first elected in 1992, became the first woman of Puerto Rican descent to serve in Congress. Later, as chairwoman of the Small Business Committee (from 2007 to 2011), Velázquez became the first Hispanic woman to chair a full congressional committee.

Collection of the U.S. House of Representatives, Photography Collection

over their approaches to welfare reform, affirmative action, and education. By 2007 President Bush and Hispanic Members of Congress came together on changes to the immigration system, but that initiative was blocked by deadlock in the 109th and 110th Congresses (2005–2009).[67]

Congressional Hispanic Conference

For much of its history, the Congressional Hispanic Caucus has had a greater number of Democrats than Republicans. Manuel Luján, Jr., of New Mexico, who was the caucus's longest-serving Republican Member, found common ground with Democrats blocking immigration reform measures such as the Simpson–Mazzoli bill. As the numbers of Republican caucus members grew (Henry Bonilla, Ileana Ros-Lehtinen, and Lincoln Diaz-Balart), the decision to let Members vote individually kept partisan tensions to a minimum.

Bipartisanship dissolved in the Hispanic Caucus in the late 1990s, eventually precipitating a formal split between Democrats and Republicans. In 1997, two Democratic members of the caucus visited Cuba and met with Fidel Castro. In protest of the visit and of the absence of criticism of repressive aspects of the Castro regime, two Republican caucus members—both Cuban Americans from South Florida—announced their departure from the group.[68] From 1997 to 2003, Hispanic-American Republicans did not participate in the caucus, and a second episode led to the creation of a separate group entirely. In 2003, the Hispanic Caucus opposed President George W. Bush's nomination of Miguel Estrada to the U.S. Court of Appeals for the District of Columbia because of Estrada's record and perceived lack of sensitivity toward minority communities. The caucus also objected to Estrada's nomination partly because the appeals judgeship was regarded as a stepping stone to the U.S. Supreme Court.[69] Hispanic Republicans, who believed that the caucus's animus toward Estrada resulted from political partisanship, formed the Congressional Hispanic Conference.[70]

HISPANIC AMERICANS' LEGISLATIVE INTERESTS

Civil Rights

In the late 20th century, Hispanic Members built on the efforts of African-American Members and of the Congressional Black Caucus (CBC) in championing institutions within the federal government that protected the civil rights of racial and ethnic minorities. The Hispanic Caucus partnered with black Members on several legislative initiatives of mutual benefit. For example, caucus chairman José Serrano actively worked with CBC chairman Kweisi Mfume of Maryland in the 103rd Congress on legislation including the Clinton administration's health care overhaul and unemployment compensation.[71]

Framed within the experiences of Hispanic Members, civil rights took on new and different components. Using the language and imagery of the previous generation's civil rights movement, Hispanic Members debated issues like bilingual education, voting rights, Puerto Rican statehood, and immigration. The Congressional Hispanic Caucus helped drive policy in the House as it related to Hispanic Americans, but was often beset by internal debates over form and function.

In the latter 20th century, the Congressional Hispanic Caucus (CHC) partnered with the Congressional Black Caucus (CBC) on civil rights, health care, and unemployment issues. From left to right: the CHC's Lucille Roybal-Allard of California and José Serrano of New York meet with Maryland Representative Kweisi Mfume of the CBC.

Image copyright *Washington Post*; reprinted by permission of the National Archives and Records Administration

Voting Rights

The 1975 extension of the Voting Rights Act of 1965 (P.L. 94-73) reaffirmed the U.S. Attorney General's ability to veto election laws and regulations in areas of the U.S. where voting participation, especially among minority citizens, fell below a set standard. This extension also covered the North and West, and it brought "language minorities"—people who spoke English as a second language—within its protection. It required bilingual ballots and voting materials in areas where English literacy was below the national average.[72] This change made subsequent updates to the Voting Rights Act (VRA)—especially the 1982 version, which extended the VRA for 25 years and its bilingual requirement for 10 years—a major priority for Hispanic Members and for Hispanic civic groups that tracked legislative activity.[73]

Hispanic Members again played a major role in the debates over the Voting Rights Act extensions in 1992 and 2006. In 1992, the Hispanic Caucus sponsored and helped pass the Voting Rights Language Assistance Act (P.L. 102-344), which lengthened the bilingual requirements by 15 years. This major accomplishment dovetailed with a period of noted Hispanic political growth.[74] "The Congressional Hispanic Caucus," said Chairman Solomon Ortiz, "is committed to giving Americans, all Americans, including citizens whose first language is not English, the opportunity to fully participate in the electoral process."[75] In 2006, Hispanic Members fought attempts to shorten the shelf life of the VRA's bilingual requirements, arguing again that all citizens, whether native-born or naturalized, deserved a fair chance to vote.[76]

Bilingual Education

Contemporary Hispanic Members paid particular attention to the status of federal bilingual education programs, since many of these programs affected Spanish-speaking students. Legislation for bilingual education was often packaged in updates to the Elementary and Secondary Education Act (ESEA).

Puerto Rican Resident Commissioner Baltasar Corrada-del Río supported the creation of the U.S. Department of Education as well as bilingual education programs administered by the agency.

Collection of the U.S. House of Representatives, Photography Collection

Both Title VII of the ESEA of 1968 (P.L. 90-247) and the 1974 Supreme Court decision *Lau v. Nichols* (414 U.S. 563) required that special assistance be given to students whose ability to understand English was limited or nonexistent, but until the late 1970s, the United States lacked oversight of the public school system. President Carter's proposal for a separate Education Department included provisions for bilingual education programs. The initial Education Department bill was referred to the House Education and Labor Committee, where Puerto Rico's Resident Commissioner Baltasar Corrada-del Río spoke passionately in favor of creating the agency. "Bilingual education should be monitored, refined, and improved," Corrada-del Río said during the debate, "so that the high hopes which it has engendered in the hearts and the minds of those who need it are not thwarted."[77] Title VII had rarely come up in subsequent reauthorizations of ESEA, but when the new Education Department proposed guidelines for enforcing bilingual instruction in 1980, some Members of the House called it a federal power grab, setting the tone for much of the next decade.[78]

Throughout the 1980s and 1990s, the Congressional Hispanic Caucus and those who supported bilingual education came under increased pressure. Politicians began advocating English immersion programs and English as a Second Language programs as alternatives to bilingual instruction.[79] Conservatives in Congress also proposed replacing government-funded programs for speakers of other languages with block grants, which give states more control over how money is spent. Block grants became popular in Republican appropriations packages in the late 1990s, and supporters of bilingual instruction worried that these grants would fatally undercut bilingual education.

Congress did not renew the ESEA in 2000, but provided a stopgap measure until the 107th Congress (2001–2003) as they worked to create a long-term solution. Democrats focused on improving the accountability of education programs while Republicans favored converting programs into block grants.[80] On May 14, 2001, the House Education and the Workforce Committee

Representatives Frank Tejada of Texas (left) and Solomon Ortiz of Texas (right) meet with Treasury Secretary Lloyd Bentsen.

Image courtesy of the National Archives and Records Administration

reported the No Child Left Behind Act (H.R. 1), a complex bipartisan measure that combined several programs, including bilingual education, into block grants.[81] By December 2001, when the conference report for H.R. 1 arrived in the House, Hispanic Members emphasized the positive aspects of No Child Left Behind.[82]

Border Control and Immigration

Both voting rights and bilingual education were part of a larger debate over immigration and America's changing demographics in the late 20th century. In particular, the growth of illegal immigration from Latin America became one of the most explosive issues in Congress beginning in the 1970s.

Widespread political instability in Central and South America combined with an economic "push-pull" relationship with the United States fueled both legal and illegal migration from the region.[83] The nature of unauthorized entry into the United States makes it difficult to compile accurate statistics on how many people have crossed the border in the last few decades; however, citing a collection of published sources, the Congressional Research Service estimates the number of undocumented aliens in the United States as just short of 11 million, doubling estimates from 1996 and tripling those from 1986. According to 2010 figures, those in the United States illegally make up 28 percent of the foreign-born population.[84]

Hispanic Members of Congress serving in the late 20th century and early 21st century were universally wary that policies meant to curb illegal immigration had the potential to discriminate against Hispanic Americans or legal immigrants from Mexico, Central America, or South America. "Building a 'tortilla curtain' certainly is not the answer," argued Manuel Luján, Jr., of New Mexico in 1980, then the sole Republican in the Hispanic Caucus. Multiple attempts at immigration reform failed in the late 1970s and early 1980s, but divisions in the caucus over the terms of the debate and its legislative tactics often limited Hispanic Members' collective influence.

Unsuccessful Attempts at Immigration Reform

Alien Adjustment and Employment Act of 1977

On August 4, 1977, President Carter brought attention to the illegal immigration issue when he asked Congress to pass a comprehensive immigration reform package. Known as the "Carter Plan," the President's proposal adjusted the immigration status of undocumented aliens who registered with the federal government for permanent or temporary residency in the United States. Carter's proposal also included possible deterrents to illegal immigration: new penalties for U.S. businesses engaged in the "pattern or practice" of hiring undocumented workers; additional resources to patrol the U.S.-Mexican border; and binding agreements with Latin American governments to crack down on human smuggling.[85] The following October, H.R. 9531 and S. 2522, representing the President's proposal, were introduced in the House and Senate.

Members disagreed over various aspects of the bills, but both the House and the Senate versions of the bill met with firm resistance from Hispanic Members and Latino civil rights organizations.[86] Edward Roybal, then chairman of the

Manuel Luján, Jr., of New Mexico served in the U.S. House for nearly two decades. Luján left in 1989 to serve as Secretary of the Interior in President George H.W. Bush's Cabinet.

Collection of the U.S. House of Representatives, Photography Collection

Immigration reform remained a central and sometimes contentious issue even within the Congressional Hispanic Caucus. Caucus Chairman Edward Roybal of California, pictured at the center, was critical of immigration legislation that he thought might hurt employment opportunities for Hispanic Americans and legal immigrants.

Image courtesy of the U.S. House of Representatives Photography Office

South Texas Representative Kika de la Garza, who chaired the Agriculture Committee, disagreed with Hispanic colleagues representing urban constituencies over immigration reform efforts that would have negatively affected migrant farm workers.

Image courtesy of the National Archives and Records Administration

newly formed Congressional Hispanic Caucus, predicted that the policies would create "a segregated, card-carrying portion of our population," as the *New York Times* quoted him.[87] Moreover, he predicted that legal Hispanic immigrants and Hispanic Americans would suffer unfairly under employer penalties.[88] The legislation gained little traction in Congress, but in 1978 the Carter administration created the Select Commission on Immigration and Refugee Policy to study options for the future.[89]

Simpson–Mazzoli Legislation, 1982–1984

In March 1982, Senator Alan Simpson of Wyoming and Representative Romano Mazzoli of Kentucky, the chairmen of Senate and House subcommittees on immigration, introduced comprehensive immigration reform bills in their respective chambers (S. 2222 and H.R. 7357). This legislation included sanctions against employers who knowingly hired undocumented workers; sought to legalize the immigration status of millions of undocumented workers; created a temporary program for agricultural workers; and instituted new procedures restricting asylum and deportation cases.[90]

A majority of the members of the Hispanic Caucus opposed the bill, particularly employer sanctions, which they believed would discriminate against Hispanic Americans.[91] "It is easy to identify those people, and it is easy to assume immediately that those people are illegal and everybody else is legal," Representative Coelho said in an impassioned speech on the House Floor.[92]

Although the bill passed the Senate in August 1982, the House version stalled. Members had introduced nearly 300 amendments to the bill; according to one account, nearly 100 came from the Hispanic Caucus alone, and Edward Roybal threatened to stall consideration by requesting votes on every one of his measures.[93] Ultimately, the first version of the Simpson–Mazzoli legislation died at the end of the 97th Congress (1981–1983).

Simpson and Mazzoli resubmitted versions of their legislation in the 98th Congress (H.R. 1510 and S. 529), but the House version never made it out of the Rules Committee. Having nearly doubled their numbers in the 1982 election, Hispanic Members changed tactics. Instead of working against the legislation by flooding the bill with amendments, they attempted to work within the system by appealing directly to House leadership for a chance to weigh in on immigration reform.[94] After Speaker O'Neill pulled the bill from the House Floor, in part because of opposition from the Hispanic Caucus, he challenged Hispanic legislators to develop their own proposal to counter the Simpson–Mazzoli legislation in the next Congress. Freshman New Mexico Democrat and caucus member Bill Richardson said, "It's important that we not be viewed as obstructionist. We have to come up with a serious alternative."[95]

But Representative Roybal's alternative bill (H.R. 4909), introduced in the next session, did not have the caucus's full support.[96] The legislation attempted to modify the Simpson–Mazzoli bill by eliminating employer sanctions and easing restrictions to legalization.[97] Hispanic activists supported the bill, and Caucus Chairman Garcia promoted it at press conferences, but other members of the Hispanic Caucus were hesitant. Representative Luján, the caucus's sole Republican, opposed the legalization program. South Texas Representative

The Congressional Hispanic Caucus gathers on the East Front House steps of the U.S. Capitol, circa mid-1980s. From left to right: Henry B. González of Texas; Manuel Luján, Jr., of New Mexico; Jaime Fuster of Puerto Rico; Robert Garcia of New York; Bill Richardson of New Mexico; Tony Coelho of California; Ron de Lugo of the Virgin Islands; Matthew Martínez of California; Edward Roybal of California; and Esteban Torres of California.

Image courtesy of the National Archives and Records Administration

Eligio (Kika) de la Garza, who represented a large farming district, was frustrated that Roybal had removed provisions for temporary agricultural workers that were included in the Simpson–Mazzoli bill. Also, unlike Roybal, whose long-standing commitment to immigration reform had been vocal, other Hispanic legislators feared the political fallout from endorsing such a position and considered immigration reform a "no-win" issue at the polls.[98]

Roybal's bill never received a hearing, but the newest Simpson–Mazzoli bill, which was universally opposed by the Hispanic Caucus, narrowly passed the House 216 to 211, before dying in conference with the Senate.[99] Though it never became law, the Simpson–Mazzoli legislation revealed ideological and generational fissures within the caucus that caused some of its members to be more willing to compromise on future bills.[100]

The Immigration Reform and Control Act of 1986

The Simpson–Mazzoli proposal was infused with new life in the 99th Congress (1985–1987); bolstered by the sponsorship of House Judiciary Chairman Peter Rodino of New Jersey, the bill was also trimmed of some of its more controversial provisions. The bill (H.R. 3810) still fined employers for knowingly hiring undocumented workers, but offered legal status to those who had entered the United States before 1982 and had since lived in the country continuously.[101] The measure received support from a group of junior caucus members who wanted to call attention to issues affecting Hispanic communities and were willing to negotiate on portions of the proposal. Representative Richardson believed employer sanctions were a particularly grievous but inevitable part of any immigration reform, and he sought safeguards against discrimination.[102] Albert Bustamante regularly described the bill as "imperfect."[103] "We must start formulating an immigration policy. We have been vacillating from year to year," he told the *New York Times*. "That foments anger and misperceptions of which Hispanics are often the target."[104]

Esteban Torres, Solomon Ortiz, and Tony Coelho joined Richardson and Bustamante in voting for the legislation—breaking from the other six voting caucus members.[105] Opponents of the bill, such as Representative Garcia,

Members of the Congressional Hispanic Caucus were nearly evenly divided over the Immigration Reform and Control Act of 1986, which passed Congress and was signed into law by President Ronald Reagan. Albert Bustamante of Texas, pictured above, described it as "imperfect" but was one of five Hispanic Members to vote for it; six others opposed the bill.

Image courtesy of the U.S. House of Representatives Photography Office

likened the employer sanctions to "Jim Crow laws," setting up 20 million Hispanic Americans for "separate and unequal treatment."[106] Roybal, who had spent six years blocking immigration reform measures in the House, said the bill was "the worst piece of legislation we have passed in 25 years in Congress."[107] President Reagan signed the Immigration Reform and Control Act of 1986 (P.L. 99-603) into law on November 6, 1986.[108]

Immigration Reform in the 1990s

Increased migration across the U.S.-Mexico border, especially via human smuggling, renewed efforts at immigration control in the mid-1990s and led to calls to strengthen the Immigration Reform and Control Act.[109]

In 1990, Hispanic lawmakers played a key role in one of the largest immigration reforms in more than 60 years. With support from the Hispanic Caucus, Congress gradually increased quotas and issued a greater variety of visas aimed at admitting a larger pool of educated immigrants. The bill also streamlined the process for admitting family members of immigrants, stayed the deportations of Salvadoran refugees, and made discrimination based on immigrants' political beliefs or sexual orientation more difficult.[110] Working with the Congressional Black Caucus and a few California Members, Hispanic Members successfully lobbied for the removal of a national identification requirement that they felt would unfairly target minorities.[111]

The next major push for immigration reform occured in 1996. President Bill Clinton signed the Illegal Immigration Reform and Immigrant Responsibility Act of 1996 (P.L. 104–208) into law on September 30. The law strengthened federal control over the U.S.-Mexican border, streamlined deportation processes, and increased restrictions against undocumented workers.[112] Additionally, the Personal Responsibility and Work Opportunity Act of 1996 (P.L. 104-193)—popularly known as the Welfare Reform Act—restricted federal aid to legal immigrants, including Social Security, health care, public housing, education, and unemployment benefits.[113]

Caucus members opposed cuts to federal benefits. Representing a working-class Florida district, Lincoln Diaz-Balart was one of three Republicans who did not sign the Contract with America in 1994, because of its proposed welfare cuts to legal immigrants.[114] "When people follow the law and they pay taxes, they shouldn't be singled out for discrimination," he said, referring to the Welfare Reform Act.[115] Democrat Solomon Ortiz of Texas, too, implored his colleagues not to penalize legal immigrants. "The greatest danger to an immigration debate in this country is the merging and confusing of issues concerning legal and illegal immigration," he noted in 1996. "As [a] Representative of a border district, I am uniquely aware of the burden that illegal immigration poses on local communities."[116]

Border Control and Immigration after September 11, 2001

The terrorist attacks on September 11, 2001, largely reset the immigration debate. The U.S.-Mexico border, once the major focus of that debate, became part of a much larger national story as Congress turned its attention toward airport and homeland security.

Hispanic Members were concerned that the new focus would encroach on Hispanic-Americans' civil rights. Two Hispanic Senators became key figures in attempts at reshaping immigration laws. Drawing on his childhood experiences as a Cuban immigrant, Florida Senator Mel Martinez championed the Development, Relief and Education for Alien Minors (DREAM) Act (S. 1291), which provided a path to an education and permanent citizenship for the minor children of undocumented immigrants.[117] He also opposed efforts to build a 1,500-mile wall along the U.S. border with Mexico, noting, "What the wall symbolizes is not what we want—the face of America we want to show."[118] In 2005 and 2006, he teamed with then-Senator Barack Obama of Illinois to advance legislation that coupled border enforcement provisions and a guest-worker program to address the issue of illegal immigration "in a realistic fashion without providing amnesty."[119]

When conservatives attempted to re-draft immigration laws in 2006—making illegal immigration a felony and punishable by imprisonment—Democratic Senator Ken Salazar supported the Comprehensive Immigration Reform Act of 2006 (S. 2611) as a compromise. The crux of the reform included provisions for border security and a guest-worker program that would affect an estimated 12 million individuals who had immigrated illegally.[120] After a brief period of deadlock, the bill passed in the Senate but died in the House.[121]

Above is an image of the American flag which flew over the U.S. Capitol on the morning of September 11, 2001. Debates over border control and immigration were recast as national security issues after the terrorist attacks.

Image courtesy of the Architect of the Capitol

North American Free Trade Agreement (NAFTA)

In the late 1980s Mexico opened its markets to international investment, and Mexican President Carlos Salinas de Gortari, looking to reinforce his country's economic growth, proposed a free trade agreement with the United States. President George H.W. Bush, with Congress's initial backing, agreed to Salinas de Gortari's offer in September 1990.[122]

In a public letter, Bill Richardson advised the Bush administration to jump at the chance while it could and to "develop a long-term strategy for free trade throughout the hemisphere." Although the initiative began in the Bush administration, President Clinton subsequently supported such an agreement.[123] Representative Dan Rostenkowski of Illinois, then chairman of the Ways and Means Committee, introduced the North American Free Trade Agreement (NAFTA) as H.R. 3450 on November 4, 1993.

Organized labor unions tended to object to NAFTA because they feared losing jobs to Mexico where labor was cheap. Labor unions often supported congressional Democrats, who balked at the proposal. The Clinton administration coordinated with business groups, lobbyists, and allies inside and outside of Congress to convince undecided Members to support the legislation. On the floor and in the Capitol hallways, a handful of Senators and House Members, including Richardson, rounded up votes for the NAFTA bill. Interestingly, *Congressional Quarterly* has noted that Clinton "[owed] his House victory more to Republicans than to his own party."[124] Although the final vote was decisive (234 to 200), votes among Hispanic Caucus members split along regional lines, nine to eight. Most of the caucus members from the Southwest voted for NAFTA, while those from other regions of the country voted against it.[125]

President Bill Clinton, far right, meets Congressional Hispanic Caucus members in 1998. The Clinton administration heavily courted caucus members to support the North American Free Trade Agreement in 1993. Caucus members split on the issue along regional lines.

Image courtesy of the William J. Clinton Library/ National Archives and Records Administration

Ben Blaz of Guam was a highly decorated officer in the U.S. Marine Corps, retiring as a brigadier general in 1980. From 1985 to 1993, Blaz represented Guam as a Delegate in the U.S. House.

Collection of the U.S. House of Representatives, Photography Collection

Legislative Interests in the Territories

Hispanic Members representing overseas territories often balanced their desire for greater autonomy with their desire to maintain a political and economic connection with the mainland United States. While the nonvoting Members carefully reviewed legislation to ensure that their territories received the same benefits that were accorded to the states, they also sought greater self-government regarding local matters. After voters on the tiny South Pacific island of Guam overwhelmingly chose a commonwealth relationship with the United States in a 1982 plebiscite, Guam Delegate Ben Blaz said, "We in Guam have embarked on a voyage of political self-determination—a desire on our part for greater local autonomy and an equal place in the American political family."[126] The fact that their constituents had common experiences meant Territorial Delegates also looked after one another's interests. Speaking for the other Delegates, Puerto Rican Resident Commissioner Baltasar Corrada-del Río said, "We have to be constantly on alert to make sure we are included in bills."[127]

The geopolitical value of the offshore territories has traditionally been tied to America's defense policy, and virtually every Territorial Delegate and Resident Commissioner has negotiated with U.S. military officials. Few instances were as contentious as the one involving the death of a Puerto Rican citizen during a naval live-ammunition exercise on the island of Vieques in 1999.[128] The incident—which sparked protests against continued bomb training—happened just days after Resident Commissioner Carlos Romero-Barceló spoke on the House Floor about the island, its veterans, and its participation in federal programs.[129] The outgoing Clinton administration arranged with Puerto Rico to end the target practice on Vieques in 2003.[130] From his seat on the Armed Services Committee, Delegate Ben Blaz paid particular attention to issues that affected the numerous naval and air bases in Guam. In 1991, his unusual request to close an air base there made headlines. Blaz, a former Marine Corps General, asked the U.S. government to relocate the Agana Naval Air Station to the northern region of the island to make way for a major expansion of Guam's largest commercial airport.[131]

Puerto Rico, Section 936, and Statehood

The late 20th century was an era of political deadlock in Puerto Rico in which the future of the island's relationship with the federal government was a major issue in virtually every election. Puerto Rico's two major parties—the Partido Popular Democrático (Popular Democratic Party, or PPD), which supported commonwealth status, and the Partido Nuevo Progresista (New Progressive Party, or PNP), which supported statehood—alternately controlled the insular government. After PNP Resident Commissioner Jorge Luis Córdova-Díaz defeated PPD incumbent Santiago Polanco-Abreu in 1968, Resident Commissioners' political affliations alternated between the PPD and the PNP until 2008.[132]

Intertwined in the status debate was the future of section 936 of the United States Internal Revenue Code. Since 1952, Puerto Rico had been under the auspices of section 931, which stipulated that after liquidating operations on the island American corporations could move their profits from Puerto Rican banks without paying federal taxes. Amended under the Tax Reform Act of

1976, section 931 was replaced by section 936, which allowed corporations to move their profits tax-free at any time. So-called 936 corporations became the backbone of the Puerto Rican economy for the next 20 years.[133]

The tax breaks drew high-tech industries to the island, especially companies that manufactured precision instruments, alongside many pharmaceutical companies.[134] Because section 936 applied only while Puerto Rico remained a U.S. territory, the corporations that benefited from the policy tended to ally with the PPD.[135] Few seemed to support section 936 more than Antonio Colorado, who was handpicked by the PPD to protect the island's status as a tax-shelter in Washington from officials who wanted to rewrite the revenue code. Appointed after Resident Commissioner Jaime Fuster accepted a position on the insular supreme court, Colorado had served as Puerto Rico's chief economist and had spent years lobbying Congress in support of section 936. The *San Juan Star* noted that he knew "the ins and outs of Washington" and "more members of Congress than probably any other island resident."[136]

Governor-turned-Resident Commissioner Carlos Antonio Romero-Barceló, who defeated Colorado in the 1992 election, became the key figure for Puerto Rican statehood and an opponent of section 936 in Washington. Like his predecessors, he equated admission to the Union with recognition of the island's political maturity. "By and large we have emerged as a people justifiably possessed of optimism and self-confidence—a people no longer willing to continue tolerating political inferiority," he argued.[137] Statehood, he concluded in 1980, "could show the world that here is a Latin people who have been accepted in the United States as brothers."[138] Scholars César Ayala and Rafael Bernabe have also pointed out that Romero-Barceló framed statehood within America's civil rights movement and the war on poverty.[139] Romero-Barceló predicted that statehood would ensure the island received a larger share of federal money while "[giving] investors a feeling of greater security."[140]

Puerto Rican Resident Commissioner Carlos Antonio Romero-Barceló supported the effort for statehood, believing admission to the Union would signal an end to the island's "political inferiority."

Collection of the U.S. House of Representatives, Photography Collection

When Congress considered ways to offset new tax breaks for small businesses on the mainland, Puerto Rico's history as a longstanding tax shelter came under heavy scrutiny. In May 1996 Romero-Barceló had called the island's revenue policy little more than "corporate welfare." But, recognizing the need to protect the benefits that attended fostering industry there, he argued that it was "preposterous … that tax revenues collected on income earned in the Nation's poorest jurisdiction, Puerto Rico, be used to subsidize" industry in the states. He worked to replace the current arrangement with a system of wage-based credits for Puerto Rico, but the Small Business Job Protection Act, which became law in August 1996, rescinded what a business reporter for the *New York Times* called "the linchpin of this island's manufacturing-based economy."[141]

Despite Romero-Barceló's eight years in the House and the support of prominent mainland politicians, voters in two plebiscites in Puerto Rico in the 1990s favored maintaining the Estado Libre Asociado, the 1952 commmonwealth agreement.[142] "Commonwealth is only a name," a frustrated Romero-Barceló said in September 1997. "We're a territory. The biggest hoax in history was that Puerto Rico had a full measure of self-government."[143]

Yet, greater self-determination was a goal the PPD and the PNP could agree on, one that had been sought since the first Puerto Rican Resident Commissioner was elected in 1900. Faced with House and Senate bills calling for a congressionally mandated plebiscite in the late 1980s, exasperated PPD Resident Commissioner Jaime Fuster criticized the mainland politicians who, he said, had an "extraordinary propensity to get drawn into Puerto Rico's political status debate whenever it is to their advantage," especially "during presidential campaigns where island votes in national conventions are at stake."[144]

The Territorial Delegates and Resident Commissioners often faced an uphill battle representing their constituents. "I don't think you can be a Delegate in the House of Representatives," Guam's Robert Underwood mused, "and a day doesn't go by in which you're not reminded in some way, sometimes trivial, sometimes major, about not being able to vote on final passage of a bill."[145]

In the 103rd Congress (1993–1995), nonvoting Members won a symbolic victory when the House approved a change in the House Rules that allowed all Members a vote in the Committee of the Whole House. The Republican minority opposed the change since the four Delegates and one Resident Commissioner caucused with Democrats. To address these objections, the Democratic majority added a proviso that mandated an automatic re-vote if the Delegates and Resident Commissioner provided the winning margin. In the re-vote, statutory representatives would not be allowed to participate.[146] House Republicans unsuccessfully challenged the rule change in court. Initially during the 103rd Congress, Republicans demanded re-votes whenever a Delegate or Resident Commissioner voted in the Committee of the Whole. The votes from either Delegates or the Resident Commissioner, however, mattered in only three of 404 votes. Perhaps because of their limited power, Delegates and the Resident Commissioner voted in Committee of the Whole much more rarely than did the average House Member.[147]

When the Republican Party gained control of the House in 1995, for the first time in 40 years, the new majority rescinded the rule.[148] Stung by this quick reversal of fortune, Underwood called the ability of Delegates to vote on the House Floor "a recognition that you are not interlopers in the nation's affairs."[149]

CONCLUSION

Hispanic-American gains in the United States Congress over the last three decades have been remarkable, especially in the U.S. House of Representatives. Though their numbers on Capitol Hill are still disproportionately less than their percentage of the U.S. population, Hispanic Americans have steadily left their mark on Washington in both style and substance.[150] Since 1977, Hispanic Members have chaired powerful committees and subcommittees and have authored important legislation. They have been party leaders and directed national party organizations. They have held cabinet positions.

The development of congressional caucuses and interest groups that monitor and develop policies important to the Hispanic community has fostered its leaders' increasing political sway. Indeed, as the Hispanic population in the U.S. continues to grow and as their advocates win powerful seats at the federal level, Hispanic Americans have become one of the most influential voting blocs in the country. It is likely that Hispanic Americans will become more numerous and more powerful in Congress, especially if demographic trends continue as they have since the 1970s.

But gaining political representation has never been, and likely never will be, simple or straightforward. The experiences of Hispanic Members illustrate that no one person, party, or caucus can determine the needs, desires, or aspirations of America's Hispanic voters.[151] The emergence of both the Congressional Hispanic Caucus (composed of Democrats) and the Congressional Hispanic Conference (composed of Republicans) is perhaps the clearest sign that political debate within the Hispanic community is alive and well. Still, regardless of party, Hispanic Members of Congress share an interest in many issues, including immigration, health care, and education, and whatever the future holds, they can draw inspiration from their rich history and hard-won victories.[152]

A 2011 photograph of the Congressional Hispanic Caucus members on the steps of the U.S. Capitol shows their growing numbers. When the caucus was founded in late 1976 seven Hispanics served in Congress. By the start of the 112th Congress in January 2011, 29 served in the House and two in the Senate.

Image courtesy of the U.S. House of Representatives Photography Office

NOTES

1 Lesley Clark, "Senator Martinez Seeking Immigration Solution," 30 March 2006, *Miami Herald*: 5; see also, Libby Copeland, "Risky Political Waters," 8 April 2006, *Washington Post*: C1. William E. Gibson, "Immigrants Rally behind Senate Bill," 2 April 2006, *South Florida Sun-Sentinel*: n.p.

2 Martinez spoke often on the Senate Floor about immigration reform. See, for example, *Congressional Record*, Senate, 109th Cong., 2nd sess. (29 March 2006): S2519–S2520; *Congressional Record*, Senate, 109th Cong., 2nd sess. (7 April 2006): S3371–S3372.

3 Clark, "Senator Martinez Seeking Immigration Solution."

4 Sharon R. Ennis, Merarys Ríos-Vargas, and Nora G. Albert, "The Hispanic Population: 2010," http://www.census.gov/prod/cen2010/briefs/c2010br-04.pdf (accessed 22 August 2012): 2.

5 J. W. Peltason, "Reapportionment Cases," in Kermit L. Hall, ed., *The Oxford Companion to the Supreme Court of the United States*, 2nd ed. (New York: Oxford University Press, 2005): 826–827.

6 The foregoing figures are best understood within a three-tiered framework. First, there is the overall Hispanic population in the U.S., which these numbers reflect. But these numbers can be misleading. For instance, the population of Hispanic citizens is smaller when undocumented individuals and permanent residents are discounted. Moreover, electorally active individuals comprise an even smaller segment of the overall Hispanic population in the U.S. Also, Hispanics historically have had low voting rates and this varies by both region and group; Puerto Ricans, for example, have relatively low electoral participation rates. For more on this topic see two reports by the Pew Research Center, Mark H. Lopez, ed., "The Latino Electorate in 2010: More Voters, More Non-Voters," (Washington, D.C.: Pew Research Center, 2011): 4–6 ; and Roberto Suro, Richard Fry, and Jeffrey Passel, "Hispanics and the 2004 Election: Population, Electorate, and Voters," (Washington, D.C.: Pew Research Center, 2005): 1–5.

7 Jennifer E. Manning, "Membership of the 112th Congress: A Profile," 15 August 2012, Rep. R41647, Congressional Research Service (hereinafter referred to as CRS), Library of Congress, Washington, D.C.; Ennis et al., "The Hispanic Population: 2010": 2. As indicated in the previous footnote, these averages include *all* Hispanic individuals in the U.S., including the undocumented, permanent residents, and electorally inactive.

8 Ennis et al., "The Hispanic Population: 2010": 2.

9 States that gained seats were Arizona (1), Florida (2), Georgia (1), Nevada (1), South Carolina (1), Texas (4), Utah (1), and Washington (1). States that lost seats were Illinois (1), Iowa (1), Louisiana (1), Massachusetts (1), Michigan (1), Missouri (1), New York (2), Ohio (2), and Pennsylvania (1). Kristin D. Burnett, "Congressional Apportionment," http://www.census.gov/prod/cen2010/briefs/c2010br-08.pdf (accessed 23 August 2012): 3.

10 Ennis et al., "The Hispanic Population: 2010": 6. The Southwest Voter Registration Education Project (SVREP) has recently reported that registration growth rates have fallen in states with large Hispanic populations such as Arizona, California, Florida, and Texas. See "Hispanic Voter Registration Could Hit 20-Year Low," *HispanicBusiness.com*, http://www.hispanicbusiness.com/2012/7/13/hispanic_voter_registration_could_hit_20year.htm (accessed 23 July 2012).

11 Similar trends have been observed with regard to women and African Americans in Congress. See, for example, Office of History and Preservation, U.S. House of Representatives, "Assembling, Amplifying, and Ascending," in *Women in Congress, 1917–2006* (Washington, D.C.: Government Printing Office, 2007): 542–563; Office of History and Preservation, U.S. House of Representatives, "Permanent Interests," in *Black Americans in Congress, 1870–2007* (Washington, D.C.: Government Printing Office, 2008): 368–415.

12 For more information about the Congressional Hispanic Caucus, see Paul R. Wieck, "Different Interests, Personalities Hurt Unity of Hispanic Caucus," in F. Chris Garcia, ed., *Latinos and the Political System* (Notre Dame, IN: University of Notre Dame Press, 1988): 300–305; Maurilio E. Vigil, "The Congressional Hispanic Caucus: Illusions and Realities of Power," *Journal of Hispanic Policy* 4 (1989–1990): 19–30; Maurilio Vigil, *Hispanics in Congress: A Historical and Political Survey* (Lanham, MD: University Press of America, 1996): 88–97; John A. Garcia, "Congressional Hispanic Caucus," in Suzanne Oboler and Deena J. González, eds., *The Oxford Encyclopedia of Latinos and Latinas in the United States*, vol. 1 (New York: Oxford University Press, 2005): 396–398.

13 See, for example, Allan Bogue et al., "Members of the House of Representatives and the Processes of Modernization, 1789–1960," *Journal of American History* 63 (September 1976): 275–302.

14 For instance, 87 percent of the Latino Members of Congress in this period hold bachelor's degrees; another 8 percent attended college. More than a quarter also hold advanced degrees (doctorate, 28 percent; and masters, 26 percent).

15 R. Eric Peterson, "Representatives and Senators: Trends in Member Characteristics since 1945," 17 February 2012, Rept. R42365, CRS: 8–11.

16 Congressional statistics are from CRS Membership Profiles of the 100th–112th Congresses (1987–2012).

17 Petersen, "Representatives and Senators: Trends in Member Characteristics since 1945": 4.

18 More than 300 pairs of siblings have served in Congress. Since 1990, eight pairs have served in the House or in the House and the Senate, six of them simultaneously. See *Biographical Directory of the United States Congress*, http://bioguide.congress.gov.

19 See, for example, Roxanne Roberts, "House Mates: Loretta and Linda Sanchez Are Congress's First Sister Act," 12 December 2002, *Washington Post*: C1.

20 Valerie Richardson, "Colorado Brothers Set Sights on Hill," 30 August 2004, *Washington Times*: A2; Judith Kohler, "Brothers Elected to Congress Head to D.C.," 26 December 2004, Associated Press; Mark Leibovich, "Cramming Two Houses into One Apartment: Rep. John and Sen. Ken Salazar Hold Joint Session in Kitchen," 5 January 2005, *Washington Post*: C1; Eddie Pells, "'Colorado Kennedys' Going to Washington Together," 3 November 2004, Associated Press.

21 Office of History and Preservation, *Women in Congress, 1917–2006*; Office of History and Preservation, *Black Americans in Congress, 1870–2007*.

22 For a useful essay on surrogate representation within a larger discussion about "descriptive" versus "substantive" representation, see Michele L. Swers and Stella M. Rouse, "Descriptive Representation: Understanding the Impact of Identity on Substantive Representation of Group Interests," in *The Oxford Handbook of the American Congress*, Eric Schickler and Frances E. Lee, eds., (New York: Oxford University Press, 2011): 241–271.

23 It is unclear how long the Territorial Caucus operated. There is only one reference to the Territorial Caucus in the Spring 1985 *House Telephone Directory*. Newspaper references indicate that the Territorial Caucus may have lost funding in 1995. See Karla Vallance, "All Is Not Quiet with Far-Flung US Territories Either …," 12 May 1982, *Christian Science Monitor*: 4; *United States House of Representatives Telephone Directory*, Spring 1985 (Washington, D.C.: Government Printing Office, 1985): 288; Michael Ross, "GOP Plans to Cut Funds for Black Caucus, Others," 7 December 1994, *Los Angeles Times*: A1; Ann L. Brownson, ed., *1994 Congressional*

Staff Directory (Mt. Vernon, VA: Staff Directories Ltd., 1994): 968; Jeffrey L. Farrow, "'Benefits' in Puerto Rico," 8 November 2006, *New York Times*: A22.

24 Abraham Holtzman, "Empire and Representation: The U.S. Congress," *Legislative Quarterly Studies* 11 (1986): 249–273, especially p. 269.

25 Philip Shenon, "In the House, But without Votes," 12 April 1985, *New York Times*: A14.

26 Robert Friedman, "P.R. Commissioner Speaks His Piece on the House Floor," 6 January 1993, *San Juan Star*: 3; Friedman, "CBR Gets Diluted Right to Vote," 6 January 1993, *San Juan Star*: 3; Friedman, "Romero Co-Sponsors Bill to Permit Family Leave," 7 January 1993, *San Juan Star*: 4; Betsy Palmer, "Delegates to the U.S. Congress: History and Current Status," 29 April 2009, Rep. R40555, CRS: 10.

27 Palmer, "Delegates to the U.S. Congress: History and Current Status": 10; Peterson, "Resident Commissioner from Puerto Rico": 5–6.

28 *Congressional Record*, House, 105th Cong., 1st sess. (10 February 1997): H401.

29 *Congressional Record*, House, 107th Cong., 1st sess. (15 May 2001): 8074; Scott Radway, "Delegate Wants 'People to Come Back Home,'" 10 August 2001, *Pacific Daily News*: 3A.

30 For more information on the number of Hispanic Members by Congress, see Appendix A: Hispanic-American Representatives, Senators, Delegates, and Resident Commissioners by Congress, 1822–2012.

31 Barbara Sinclair, *Legislators, Leaders, and Lawmaking: The U.S. House of Representatives in the Postreform Era* (Baltimore: Johns Hopkins University Press, 1995): 82.

32 See Robin Kolodny, *Pursuing Majorities: Congressional Committees in American Politics* (Norman: University of Oklahoma Press, 1998).

33 *Politics in America, 1982* (Washington, D.C.: Congressional Quarterly Inc., 1983): 119; *Almanac of American Politics, 1990* (Washington, D.C.: National Journal, Inc., 1991): 118.

34 David W. Rohde, *Parties and Leaders in the Postreform House* (Chicago: University of Chicago Press, 1991): 86.

35 Bill Richardson with Michael Ruby, *Between Worlds: The Making of an American Life* (New York: G. P. Putnam's Sons, 2007): 106, 110–118.

36 *Almanac of American Politics, 2010* (Washington, D.C.: National Journal, Inc., 2011): 221; Jennifer Yachnin, "Becerra Takes Rare Tack in Caucus Race," 25 September 2006, *Roll Call*: 1; Carl Hulse, "Pelosi Names Maryland Congressman to Lead Democratic Campaign Efforts," 20 December 2006, *New York Times*: A27; "Official Biography of Xavier Becerra," http://becerra.house.gov/index.php?option=com_content&view=article&id=13&Itemid=16 (accessed 29 May 2012).

37 Emily Pierce, "A Super Day; Menendez Rises, Shines," 28 August 2008, *Roll Call*: 36; David M. Herszenhorn, "Schumer Out, Menendez In," 25 November 2008, *New York Times*: 20.

38 Anita Kumar, "Martinez Steps Up to Top GOP Role," 20 January 2007, *St. Petersburg Times*: 5A; Lesley Clark, "Some in GOP Oppose Martinez," 17 January 2007, *Miami Herald*: A3.

39 Garrison Nelson, ed., *Committees in the U.S. Congress, 1947–1992*, vol. 2 (Washington, D.C.: CQ Press, 1994): 1007–1008.

40 See Appendix C: Hispanic-American Members' Committee Assignments (Standing, Joint, Select) in the U.S. House and Senate, 1822–2012.

41 Christopher J. Deering and Steven S. Smith, *Committees in Congress*, 3d ed. (Washington, D.C.: CQ Press, 1997): 63–72.

42 See Appendix C. Several individuals served on more than one prestige committee.

43 Bree Hocking, "Bonilla: A 'Quiet Giant,'" 29 November 2004, *Roll Call*: n.p.; Lizette Alvarez, "Honoring '95 Vow, House Republicans Replace 13 Chiefs," 5 January 2001, *New York Times*: A1; Ben Pershing and John Bresnahan, "GOP Fills Panel Seats," 8 January 2001, *Roll Call*: n.p.; Gary Martin, "Texan Tops Agriculture Panel; Bonilla to Head Subcommittee," 6 January 2001, *San Antonio Express-News*: 15A. Edward Roybal of California was also a "cardinal," chairing the Treasury, Postal Service, and General Government Committee from 1981 to 1993. As he was first elected in 1963, he is not included in this discussion.

44 See Appendix E: Hispanic-American Chairs of Subcommittees of Standing and Select Committees in the U.S. House and Senate, 1949–2012.

45 Deering and Smith, *Committees in Congress*: 80.

46 See Appendix C.

47 See Appendix C.

48 See, for example, Susan Webb Hammond, *Congressional Caucuses in National Policy Making* (Baltimore: Johns Hopkins University Press, 1998): 96–98.

49 Hammond, *Congressional Caucuses in National Policy Making*: 74–79, 190; *Politics in America, 2010* (Washington, D.C.: Congressional Quarterly Inc., 2011): 190. Participation in congressional service organizations offered another opportunity for Hispanic Members to gain leadership experience. Guam's Robert Underwood was chairman of the Congressional Asian Pacific American Caucus (1999–2001), and Dennis Cardoza of California was co-chairman of the Blue Dog Coalition (2005–2007).

50 Quoted in David Rodriguez, *Latino National Political Coalitions: Struggles and Challenges* (New York: Routledge, 2002): 76–77; Vigil, *Hispanics in Congress*: 94–95; Arturo Vega, "Extrinsic Representation and Informal Groups in Congress—The Case of the Congressional Hispanic Caucus," Records of the Congressional Hispanic Caucus, Members of the Caucus, Biographical Files Relating to Former Caucus Members, 1983–1994, Becerra, X. to Richardson, Bill, Box 1, Record Group 233, National Archives and Records Administration, Washington, D.C. (hereinafter referred to as RG 233, NARA).

51 Ellen Hume, "Carter Agrees to Put Latins in More Top Posts," 2 March 1977, *Los Angeles Times*: B3; "Hispanic Group Asks Carter for More Jobs," 2 March 1977, *New York Times*: 14; Hume, "Carter to Name 13 More Latin Aides—Roybal," 8 March 1977, *Los Angeles Times*: B3; Steven V. Roberts, "Hispanic Caucus Is Flexing Its Muscle," 10 October 1983, *New York Times*: A14. Denice Darrow, "Congressional Hispanic Caucus Leads the Fight for Rights of Spanish-Speaking Citizens," *Reporter* (February–March 1977): 43–44; "History of the Caucus," History Files of the CHC, 1982–1994, Box 1, RG 233, NARA; Vega, "Extrinsic Representation and Informal Groups in Congress—The Case of the Congressional Hispanic Caucus," RG 233, NARA. The articles do not clearly indicate if the caucus operated as a unified group or if individual members spoke on its behalf.

52 Christine Marie Sierra, "In Search of National Power: Chicanos Working the System on Immigration Reform, 1976–1986," in David Montejano, ed., *Chicano Politics and Society in the Late Twentieth Century* (Austin: University of Texas Press, 1999): 140. See also "Statement of Bill Richardson, Re: Latin America-2/6/85," Press Releases, 1982–1994, Box 1, RG 233, NARA; "Congressman Richardson Urges Measures to Strengthen Democracy in Latin America," Legislative Update 1985–Folder 3 of 3, Caucus Monthly Publications 1985–1994, Box 1, RG 233, NARA.

53 For examples of the caucus's tepid relationship with the Reagan administration, see Karen Tumulty, "Reagan Record of Aiding Latinos Belittled," 16 September 1983, *Los Angeles Times*: B4; "Hispanic Caucus Chief Asks Congress to Kill Civil Rights Agency," 4 April 1984, Associated Press; Howard Kurtz, "HUD's Abrams Apologizes to Hill Hispanic Caucus," 16 May 1984, *Washington Post*: A10; Congressional Hispanic Caucus staffer quoted in Hammond, *Congressional Caucus in National Policy Making*: 143.

54 It remains unclear why González left the Congressional Hispanic Caucus, but multiple sources have speculated. See John Burgess, "Nakasone Apologizes to U.S. for Remarks on Minorities," 27 September 1986, *Washington Post*: A1; *Congressional Record*, House, 99th Cong., 2nd sess. (1 October 1986): 27460; Vigil, *Hispanics in Congress*: 123, endnote 11; Paul R. Wieck, "Different Interests, Personalities Hurt Unity of Hispanic Caucus," in F. Chris Garcia, ed., *Latinos and the Political System* (Notre Dame, IN: University of Notre Dame Press, 1988): 304; Christopher Hitchens, "No Fool on the Hill," *Harper's Magazine* (October 1992): 84–92; and Paul Houston, "Rep. Gonzalez: He Packs a Punch When It Gets Tense," 15 July 1990, *Los Angeles Times*: A1.

55 Wieck, "Different Interests, Personalities Hurt Unity of Hispanic Caucus": 303; Vigil, *Hispanics in Congress*: 92–93. Vigil does not list any specific pieces of legislation about which Blaz disagreed with the caucus.

56 David Rampe, "Power Panel in Making: The Hispanic Caucus," 30 September 1988, *New York Times*: B5; Vigil, *Hispanics in Congress*: 87.

57 William Garland, "Caucus Works at Collective Voice," 7 January 1990, *Corpus Christi Caller-Times*: A1.

58 "Congressional Hispanic Caucus: Legislative Agenda for the 100th Congress," Folder 7–1987, Press Releases, 1982–1994, Box 1, RG 233, NARA; Vigil, *Hispanics in Congress*: 93.

59 Ricardo Chavira, "Hispanic Caucus Comes of Age," *Hispanic Business*, May 1992.

60 Chavira, "Hispanic Caucus Comes of Age."

61 Roberts, "Hispanic Caucus Is Flexing Its Muscle"; Spencer Rich, "Hispanics Claim 11 House Seats," 11 November 1986, *Washington Post*: A5; Rampe, "Power Panel in Making: The Hispanic Caucus."

62 Kenneth J. Cooper, "Congress's Hispanic Membership Likely to Grow 50% for Next Term," 3 October 1992, *Washington Post*: A11; Kenneth J. Cooper, "An Experienced Freshman Class," 5 November 1992, *Washington Post*: A1; *Congressional Quarterly Almanac, 1992* (Washington, D.C.: Congressional Quarterly Inc., 1993): 21.

63 Kenneth J. Cooper, "Hispanic Caucus Shows Its New-Found Clout," 2 October 1993, *Washington Post*: A4.

64 Kenneth J. Cooper and Kevin Merida, "House Republicans Scrambling to Jettison Stereotypes of Party," 11 December 1994, *Washington Post*: A29; Michael Remez, "Some See Little Room for Hispanics in GOP 'Contract,'" 23 January 1995, *Hartford Courant*: A1; Christopher Lee, "Many Hispanics Unhappy with Welfare Law," 29 August 1996, *Dallas Morning News*: 25A; Lizette Alvarez, "For Hispanic Lawmakers, Time to Take the Offensive," 25 August 1997, *New York Times*: A14.

65 Susan Milligan, "A Caucus with Clout," 27 June 1993, *New York Daily News*: n.p.; Tim Lopes, "Hispanic Caucus Raps Welfare Bill," 31 March 1995, *Palm Beach Post* (FL): 7A; Gary Martin, "Hispanics Balk at Clinton's Cabinet Choices," 21 March 1997, *San Antonio Express-News*: 6B; Rich Hein, "Clout Translates in Spanish, Too," 8 October 1997, *Chicago Sun-Times*: 6; Alvarez, "For Hispanic Lawmakers, Time to Take the Offensive."

66 Susan Crabtree, "Hispanic Members Watch Their Political Clout Grow," 11 September 2000, *Roll Call*: A26.

67 For an overview of the George W. Bush administration's policies toward Hispanic Americans, see Gary Gerstle, "Minorities, Multiculturalism, and the Presidency of George W. Bush," in Julian E. Zelizer, ed., *The Presidency of George W. Bush: A First Historical Assessment* (Princeton University Press, 2010): 252–281. President Bush's meeting with the caucus is described in "Latinos Give Bush Meeting Mixed Reviews," 3 April 2001, Associated Press. The 2006 and 2007 immigration bill legislation debates are summarized in *Congressional Quarterly Almanac 2006* (Washington, D.C.: Congressional Quarterly Inc., 2007): 14–3; and *Congressional Quarterly Almanac, 2007* (Washington, D.C.: Congressional Quarterly Inc., 2008): 15-9–15-11.

68 Ed Henry, "Cuba Connection Jolts Hispanic Caucus as Two Republicans Quit," 9 January 1997, *Roll Call*: 40.

69 Darryl Fears, "For Hispanic Groups, A Divide on Estrada; Political, Geographical Fault Lines Exposed," 20 February 2003, *Washington Post*: A4; Gary Martin, "Estrada Opposition Fueled New Caucus; Partisanship Irked Hispanic GOPers," 20 March 2003, *San Antonio Express-News*: 4A; Sandra Hernandez, "Hispanics Show Political Diversity; Conservative Group Forms to Offer Another View of Latinos in Congress," 27 April 2003, *Fort Lauderdale Sun-Sentinel*: 1F.

70 Neil A. Lewis, "Battle Brews over a Hispanic Nominee to Appeals Court," 24 September 2002, *New York Times*: A23; Fears, "For Hispanic Groups, a Divide on Estrada; Political, Geographic Fault Lines Exposed"; Sheryl Gay Stolberg, "Battle over Judgeship Tests Congressman's Loyalties to People and Party," 15 March 2003, *New York Times*: A14; Martin, "Estrada Opposition Fueled New Caucus; Partisanship Irked Hispanic GOPers"; Frank Davies, "Three GOP House Members from Miami Help Organize New Hispanic Caucus," 19 March 2003, *Miami Herald*: n.p.

71 Michelle J. Meyers, "The Hispanic Caucus: United or Divided?" September 1994, *Hispanic*: 20–24; "Hillary Clinton Visits Minority Caucuses," 3 March 1993, *Washington Post*: A5; Cooper, "Hispanic Caucus Shows Its New-Found Clout"; Kenneth Cooper, "A Broken Barrier: Black, Hispanic Caucuses Meet on Capitol Hill," 14 October 1993, *Washington Post*: C2.

72 *Congressional Quarterly Almanac, 1975* (Washington, D.C.: Congressional Quarterly Inc., 1976): 521–532.

73 *Congressional Quarterly Almanac, 1982* (Washington, D.C.: Congressional Quarterly Inc., 1983): 373–377; Hearings before the House Subcommittee on Civil and Constitutional Rights of

the Committee on the Judiciary, *Extension of the Voting Rights Act, Part* 2, 97th Cong., 1st sess. (1981): 1486.

74 *Congressional Quarterly Almanac, 1992*: 330–331.

75 *Congressional Record*, House, 102nd Cong., 2nd sess. (24 July 1992): 19327.

76 *Congress and the Nation, 2005–2008*, vol. 7 (Washington, D.C.: CQ Press, 2010): 697–698.

77 *Congressional Record*, House, 96th Cong., 1st sess. (12 June 1979): 14474.

78 *Congress and the Nation 1977–1980*, vol. 5 (Washington, D.C.: CQ Press, 1981): 664–665, 677; *Congressional Record*, House, 96th Cong., 2nd sess. (27 August 1980): 23494.

79 *Congress and the Nation 1985–1989*, vol. 7 (Washington, D.C.: CQ Press, 1990): 655–656; Rampe, "Power Panel in Making: The Hispanic Caucus."

80 For the background of No Child Left Behind, see Andrew Rudalevige, "No Child Left Behind: Forging a Congressional Compromise," in Paul E. Peterson and Martin R. West, eds., *No Child Left Behind? The Politics and Practice of School Accountability* (Washington, D.C.: Brookings Institution Press, 2003): 23–54.

81 *Congressional Record*, House, 107th Cong., 1st sess. (22 May 2001): H2405.

82 *Congressional Record*, House, 107th Cong., 1st sess. (13 December 2001): H10090.

83 For an overview of scholarly theories on the causes of Latin American migration to the United States, see Héctor Cordero-Guzmán and Ted Henken, "Immigration" in Oboler and González, eds., *The Oxford Encyclopedia of Latinos and Latinas in the United States*, vol. 2.

84 William A. Kandel, "The U.S. Foreign-Born Population: Trends and Selected Characteristics," 15 February 2012, Rep. R41592, CRS: 9–10.

85 *Congressional Quarterly Almanac, 1977* (Washington, D.C.: Congressional Quarterly Inc., 1978): 43-E–45-E. Immigrants who had arrived before 1970 and lived continuously in the United States since then would be granted permanent resident alien status. Those who arrived between 1970 and January 1, 1977, would be given a new classification: "temporary resident alien." They would have permission to remain in the United States for five years but would not be eligible for federal social services. The proposal did not change the status of immigrants who arrived in 1977.

86 Sierra, "In Search of National Power: Chicanos Working the System on Immigration Reform, 1976–1986," in Montejano, ed., *Chicano Politics and Society in the Late Twentieth Century*: 132–133.

87 James T. Wooten, "President Seeks Legalized Status for Many Aliens," 5 August 1977, *New York Times*: 1.

88 Don Irwin, "Seeks More Guards for Border, Hiring Penalties," 5 August 1977, *Los Angeles Times*: 1.

89 *Congressional Quarterly Almanac, 1977*: 573–575; Sierra, "In Search of National Power: Chicanos Working the System on Immigration Reform, 1976–1986": 132–137.

90 *Congressional Quarterly Almanac, 1982*: 405–410.

91 Sierra notes that after the House referred the legislation to the Judiciary Committee, a letter to that panel's chairman, Peter Rodino of New Jersey, carried four individual signatories instead of the caucus's full endorsement. See Sierra, "In Search of National Power: Chicanos Working the System on Immigration Reform, 1976–1986," 140–141.

92 *Congressional Quarterly Almanac, 1982*: 405–410.

93 Ibid.

94 Sierra, "In Search of National Power: Chicanos Working the System on Immigration Reform, 1976–1986": 141.

95 Karen Tumulty, "Latinos Scramble to Come Up with Proposals," 1 December 1982, *Los Angeles Times*: B13.

96 Julia Malone, "Hispanic Americans Muster Political Clout in Washington," 22 April 1983, *Christian Science Monitor*: 1.

97 Sierra, "In Search of National Power: Chicanos Working the System on Immigration Reform, 1976–1986": 142.

98 Karen Tumulty, "Latino Caucus Seeks Weakened Immigration Bill," 17 January 1984, *Los*

Angeles Times: B5; Margaret Shapiro, "Hispanic Caucus Counters Bill on Aliens," 2 February 1984, *Washington Post*: A4; Shapiro, "Immigration Measure Produces Sharp Divisions in House Hispanic Caucus," 18 March 1984, *Washington Post*: A2; Sierra, "In Search of National Power: Chicanos Working the System on Immigration Reform, 1976–1986": 142–143.

99 *Congressional Quarterly Almanac, 1984* (Washington, D.C.: Congressional Quarterly Inc., 1985): 229–239.

100 During the 99th Congress, Roybal introduced a bill that was strikingly similar to the Simpson–Mazzoli legislation, which included the employer sanctions he had previously opposed. The California Congressman justified this surprising move by describing his bill as "bait"—an attempt to reveal the extremist intentions of immigration reformers, who, Roybal was certain, would counter with a more draconian measure. See Sierra, "In Search of National Power: Chicanos Working the System on Immigration Reform, 1976–1986": 144.

101 *Congressional Quarterly Almanac, 1985* (Washington, D.C.: Congressional Quarterly Inc., 1986): 223–228.

102 Sierra, "In Search of National Power: Chicanos Working the System on Immigration Reform, 1976–1986": 146.

103 See, for example, *Congressional Record*, House, 99th Cong., 2nd sess. (9 October 1986): 26403, 31644.

104 Robert Pear, "Immigration Bill: How 'Corpse' Came Back to Life," 13 October 1986, *New York Times*: A16.

105 The Hispanic Caucus comprised 11 voting members and three non-voting members: Territorial Delegates Ben Blaz of Guam and Ron de Lugo of the Virgin Islands, and Resident Commissioner Jaime Fuster of Puerto Rico.

106 "Hispanics Vow to Block Debate," 8 June 1984, United Press International.

107 Mary McGrory, "Still Gripped by Fear," 26 November 1987, *Washington Post*: 2; Marcia Chambers, "Many Questions Aimed at New Alien Law," 5 December 1986, *New York Times*: A21. For more on the law, see *CQ Almanac, 1986* (Washington, D.C.: Congressional Quarterly Inc., 1987): 61–67.

108 Sierra, "In Search of National Power: Chicanos Working the System on Immigration Reform, 1976–1986": 137–148; *Congressional Record*, House, 99th Cong., 2nd sess. (9 October 1986): 30075–30076.

109 *Congressional Quarterly Almanac, 1995* (Washington, D.C.: Congressional Quarterly Inc., 1996): 6-9–6-18.

110 *Congressional Quarterly Almanac, 1990* (Washington, D.C.: Congressional Quarterly Inc., 1991): 474–485.

111 Barbara Vobejda, "Immigration Bill Blocked in the House," 27 October 1990, *Washington Post*: A12; Robert Pear, "Major Immigration Bill Is Sent to Bush," 29 October 1990, *New York Times*: B10.

112 *Congressional Quarterly Almanac, 1996* (Washington, D.C.: Congressional Quarterly Inc., 1997): 5-3–5-17.

113 Nicholas De Genova, "Immigration Policy, Twentieth Century," in Oboler and González, eds., *Oxford Encyclopedia of Latinos and Latinas in the United States*, vol. 2; *Congressional Quarterly Almanac, 1996*: 6-3–6-24.

114 "No Fine Print; Republicans Put It in Writing: A New Way of Governing," 13 November 1994, Associated Press; Robert Pear, "House Backs Bill Undoing Decades of Welfare Policy," 25 March 1995, *New York Times*: 1.

115 Jill Miller, "Reforms May Halt Legal-Alien Welfare; GOP 'Contract' Hangs on Touchy Issue," 20 January 1995, *Fort Lauderdale Sun-Sentinel*: A1.

116 *Congressional Record*, House, 104th Cong., 2nd sess. (21 March 1996): H2602; see also, *Congressional Record*, House, 106th Cong., 2nd sess. (17 May 2000): H3275–H3276.

117 Milagros (Mimi) Aledo and Rafael J. López, interview with Senator Mel Martinez (R-Florida), *Harvard Journal of Hispanic Policy* 17 (2004–2005): 12–13.

118 Libby Copeland, "Risky Political Waters," 8 April 2006, *Washington Post*: C1.

119 "GOP Ends Rift, Moves Ahead on Immigration," 16 December 2005, *Miami Herald*: 6.

120 Elizabeth Aguilera, "Salazar Hopeful on Immigration, Saying 'Failure … Is not an Option,'" 10 June 2007, *Denver Post*: C6. See also Milagros (Mimi) Aledo, Rafael J. López, Liz Montoya, interview with Senator Ken Salazar (D-Colorado), *Harvard Journal of Hispanic Policy* 17 (2004–2005): 5–10.

121 Aguilera, "Salazar Hopeful on Immigration, Saying 'Failure … Is not an Option'"; *Congressional Record*, Senate, 109th Cong., 2nd sess. (29 September 2006): S10606. Salazar spoke frequently on the Senate Floor about immigration reform. See, for example: *Congressional Record*, Senate, 109th Cong., 2nd sess. (16 May 2006): S4577–S4579; *Congressional Record*, Senate, 109th Cong., 2nd sess. (20 September 2006): S9757–S9759.

122 *Congressional Quarterly Almanac, 1993* (Washington, D.C.: Congressional Quarterly Inc., 1994): 171–179.

123 Bill Richardson, "Free Trade with Mexico, Sí!," 22 March 1991, *Washington Post*: A25. See also Richardson, "Mexico—the Answer to Bush's Domestic Troubles," 12 December 1991, *Wall Street Journal*: A14; *Congressional Record*, House, 103rd Cong., 1st sess. (18 October 1993): 24868; *Congressional Record*, House, 103rd Cong., 1st sess. (1 November 1993): 26922–26923.

124 For a detailed explanation of efforts to influence undecided Members, see Frederick W. Mayer, *Interpreting NAFTA: The Science and Art of Political Analysis* (New York: Columbia University Press, 1998): 273–319; *Congressional Quarterly Almanac, 1993*: 171–179.

125 *Congressional Record*, House, 103rd Cong., 1st sess. (17 November 1993): 29949.

126 *Congressional Record*, House, 101st Cong., 1st sess. (9 March 1989): 4007.

127 Lynne Olson, "Territories Still Have Quiet Voices in Congress," 14 May 1978, *Baltimore Sun*: A3.

128 For background on Vieques and the protests surrounding its use by the U.S. Navy, see Katherine McCaffery, *Military Power and Popular Protest: The U.S. Navy in Vieques, Puerto Rico* (New Brunswick, NJ: Rutgers University Press, 2002); and César Ayala and José Bolívar, *Battleship Vieques: Puerto Rico from World War II to the Korean War* (Princeton, NJ: Markus Wiener Publishers, 2011).

129 *Congress and the Nation 1997–2001*, vol. 10 (Washington, D.C.: CQ Press, 2002): 290; *Congressional Record*, House, 106th Cong., 1st sess. (13 April 1999): 6270.

130 The House Armed Services Committee attempted to change the Clinton agreement with a provision in the 2001 defense authorization act, H.R. 4205 (H. Rep. 106-616), that would allow the navy to resume training "without interference" until 2003. Many Members, especially those of Puerto Rican descent, opposed the resumption of military training on Vieques. See *Congress and the Nation 1997–2001*: 291; *Congressional Record*, House, 106th Cong., 2nd sess. (18 May 2000): 8523; *Congressional Record*, House, 106th Cong., 2nd sess. (18 May 2000): 8520.

131 Gwen Ifill, "Guam, against the Tide, Wants Air Base Closed," 20 April 1991, *New York Times*: 6; Bernard E. Trainor, "Lack of Vote Doesn't Deter Delegate from Guam," 23 February 1988, *New York Times*: B6; Ron Scherer, "'Aviation Ghost Town': Guam Lobbies for US Base to Close," 20 August 1991, *Christian Science Monitor*: 6.

132 Resident Commissioners serving during this period alternated between PNP and PPD candidates, except for Jaime Fuster and Antonio Colorado. After Fuster, a PPD member, resigned his seat in 1992, Colorado (a member of the same party) was appointed as his replacement. Carlos Romero-Barceló of the PNP defeated Colorado in the 1992 election. In 2008 PNP Resident Commissioner Pedro Pierluisi broke the cycle by winning election after his fellow party member Luis G. Fortuño declined to run for re-election to make a (successful) bid for governor.

133 César J. Ayala and Rafael Bernabe, *Puerto Rico in the American Century: A History since 1898* (Chapel Hill: University of North Carolina Press, 2007): 268–269. For an in-depth look at section 936 and Puerto Rican politics, see Sara Lynn Grusky, "Political Power in Puerto Rico: Bankers, Pharmaceuticals, and the State," (Ph.D. diss., Howard University, 1994).

134 James L. Dietz, *Economic History of Puerto Rico: Institutional Change and Capitalist Development* (Princeton: Princeton University Press, 1986): 300–301.

135 For a discussion of 936 corporations and their connection to the PPD, see Maria Bird Pico, "Romero Leads Colorado in Campaign Fundraising," 22 October 1992, *San Juan Star*: 17.

136 Harry Turner, "Antonio Colorado Sworn In as Resident Commissioner," 5 March 1992, *San Juan Star*: 2. See also Harry Turner, "Section 936 Critics Fail to Awaken Opposition," 7 March 1992, *San Juan Star*: 3.

137 Carlos Romero-Barceló, "Puerto Rico, U.S.A.: The Case for Statehood," *Foreign Affairs* 59 (Fall 1980): 62–63.

138 Joanne Omang, "Puerto Rico in Political Turmoil," 20 August 1978, *Washington Post*: C1.

139 Ayala and Bernabe, *Puerto Rico in the American Century*: 277.

140 Interview with Carlos Romero-Barceló, Governor of Puerto Rico, "Should Puerto Rico Be a State?," 11 April 1977, *U.S. News & World Report*: 47.

141 First quotation from the *Congressional Record*, House, 104th Cong., 2nd sess. (21 May 1996): 11989. See also Dan Burton and Peter Deutsch, "It's Time to Reform the Puerto Rico Tax Credit," 16 January 1996, *Christian Science Monitor*: 18. Second quotation from, Doreen A. Hemlock, "Puerto Rico Loses Its Edge," 21 September 1996, *New York Times*: 31; see also, Larry Luxner, "Puerto Rico's Star Losing Its Luster," 8 December 1997, *Journal of Commerce*: C7.

142 In November 1993, an island-wide plebiscite revealed a razor-thin margin: 48 percent for commonwealth, 46 percent for statehood, and 4 percent for independence. The 1998 plebiscite ended with a similar result. Fernando Bayron Toro, *Elecciones y partidos políticos de Puerto Rico, 1809–2000* (Mayagüez: Editorial Isla, 2003): 354–355.

143 Guy Gugliotta, "Puerto Rico's State of Uncertainty," 16 September 1997, *Washington Post*: A15.

144 *Congressional Record*, Extension of Remarks, 100th Cong., 1st sess. (14 May 1987): 12552. See, for example, H. J. Res. 218 (100th Congress) introduced by Representative Ron Dellums of California calling for independence; S. 1182 (100th Congress) introduced by Senator Bob Dole of Kansas calling for statehood; and H.R. 3536 (101st Congress), introduced by Representative Robert Lagomarsino of California, calling for a referendum on status.

145 Jennifer Yachnin, "Guam Delegate Hopes to Exchange Long Flights for Governorship," 26 September 2002, *Roll Call*: n.p.

146 *Congress and the Nation 1993–1996*, vol. 9 (Washington, D.C.: Congressional Quarterly Inc., 1998): 881.

147 *Congress and the Nation 1993–1996*: 881–882.

148 When Democrats regained control of the chamber for the 110th and 111th Congresses (2007–2011), the rule was again changed to allow the vote in the Committee of the Whole House. When Republicans regained control of the chamber in the 112th Congress (2011–2013), it was again repealed.

149 *Congress and the Nation 1993–1996*: 888; Eamon Javers, "Samoan Delegate: I Fought in Vietnam But I Can't Vote in the U.S. Congress," 18 January 1995, *The Hill*: n.p.

150 Ennis et al., "The Hispanic Population: 2010": 2.

151 Kathryn Jean Lopez, "Power Struggle: Hispanic Republicans in Congress Have Banded Together to Challenge the Powerful Congressional Hispanic Caucus," 31 August 2003, *Hispanic*: 21.

152 Alan K. Ota, "Diversidad," 27 November 2010, *Congressional Quarterly Weekly*: n.p. See also Alan K. Ota, "Amid Gains, Hill Hispanics Look to Get Along," 29 November 2010, *Congressional Quarterly Weekly*, http://cq.com.doc/weeklyreport-3768531 (accessed 23 August 2012).

Party Divisions in the House of Representatives

95th–112th Congresses (1977–2012)*

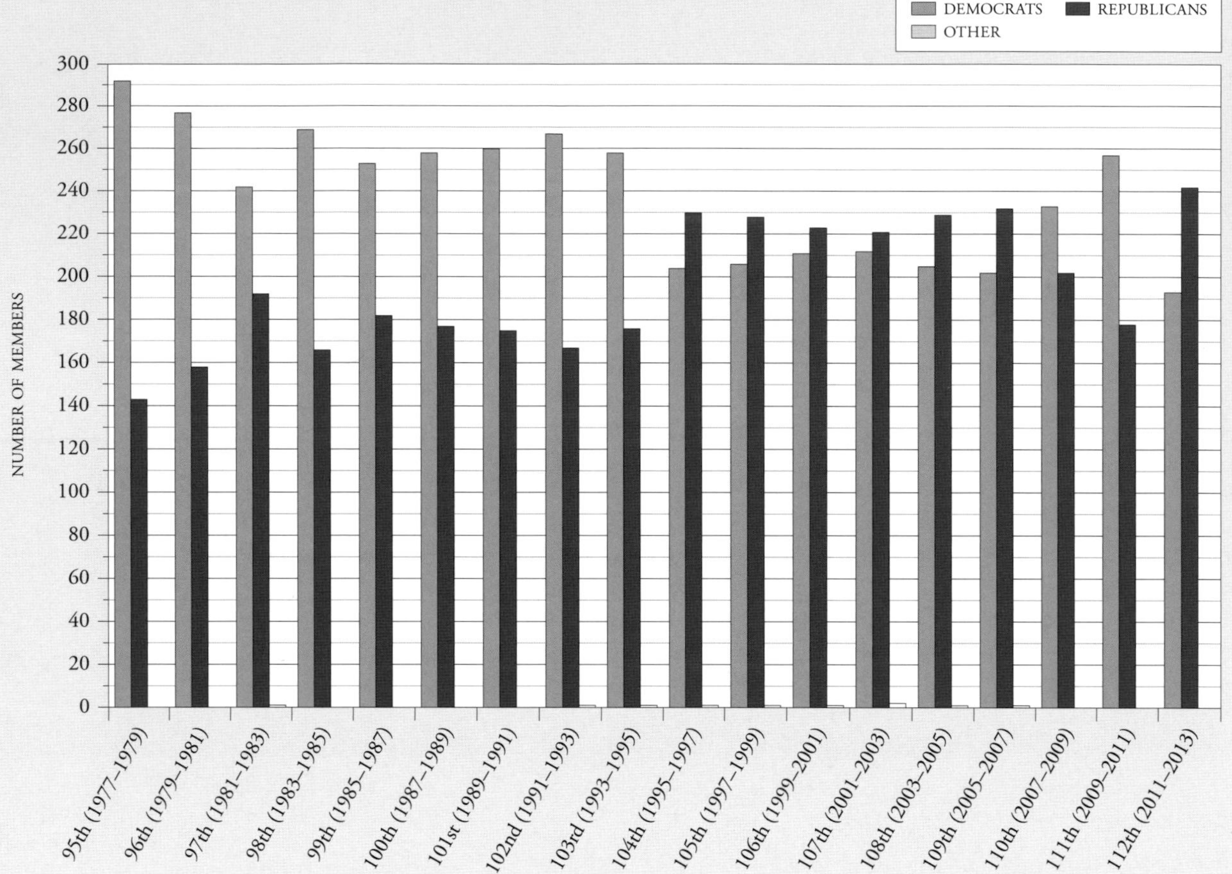

Source: Biographical Directory of the United States Congress, 1774–2005 (Washington, D.C.: Government Printing Office, 2005); also available at http://bioguide.congress.gov; Office of the Historian, U.S. House of Representatives

*Party division totals are based on election day results.

Party Divisions in the Senate

95th–112th Congresses (1977–2012)*

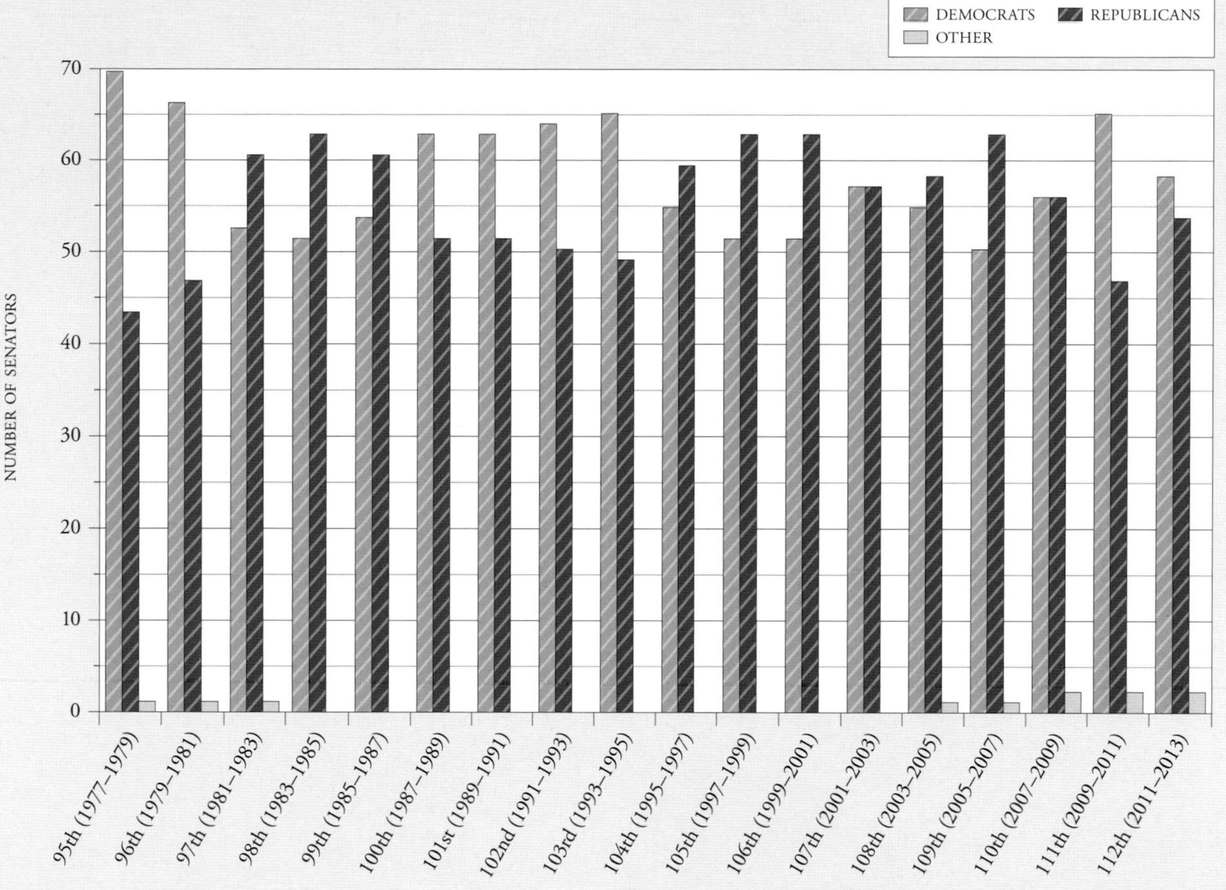

Source: Biographical Directory of the United States Congress, 1774–2005 (Washington, D.C.: Government Printing Office, 2005); also available at http://bioguide.congress.gov; U.S. Senate Historical Office.

*Party division totals are based on election day results.

Hispanic-American Members by Office

1977–2012*

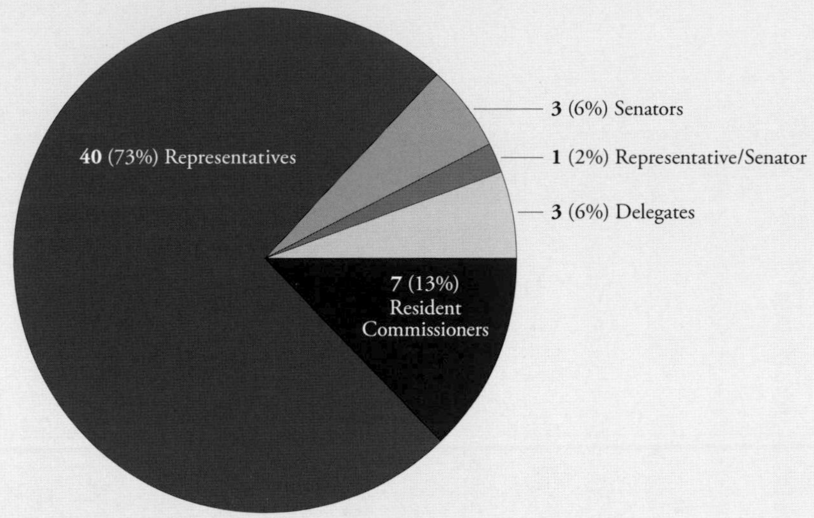

Hispanic-American Members by State and Territory

First Elected 1976–2012*

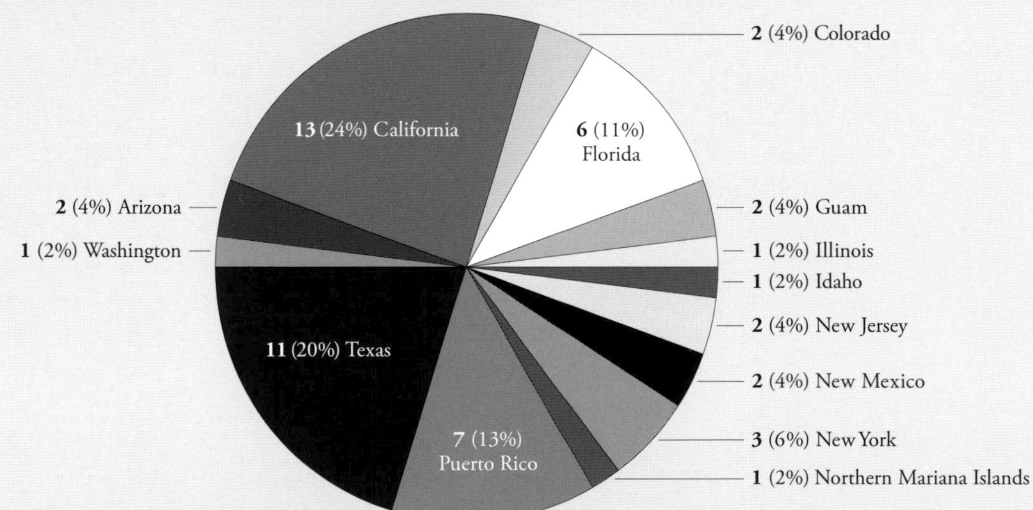

Source: Appendix A: Hispanic-American Representatives, Senators, Delegates, and Resident Commissioners by Congress, 1822–2012; Office of the Historian, U.S. House of Representatives; U.S. Senate Historical Office.

*112th Congress (2011–2013) as of September 1, 2012.

Congressional Service

For Hispanic Americans in Congress First Elected 1976–September 1, 2012*

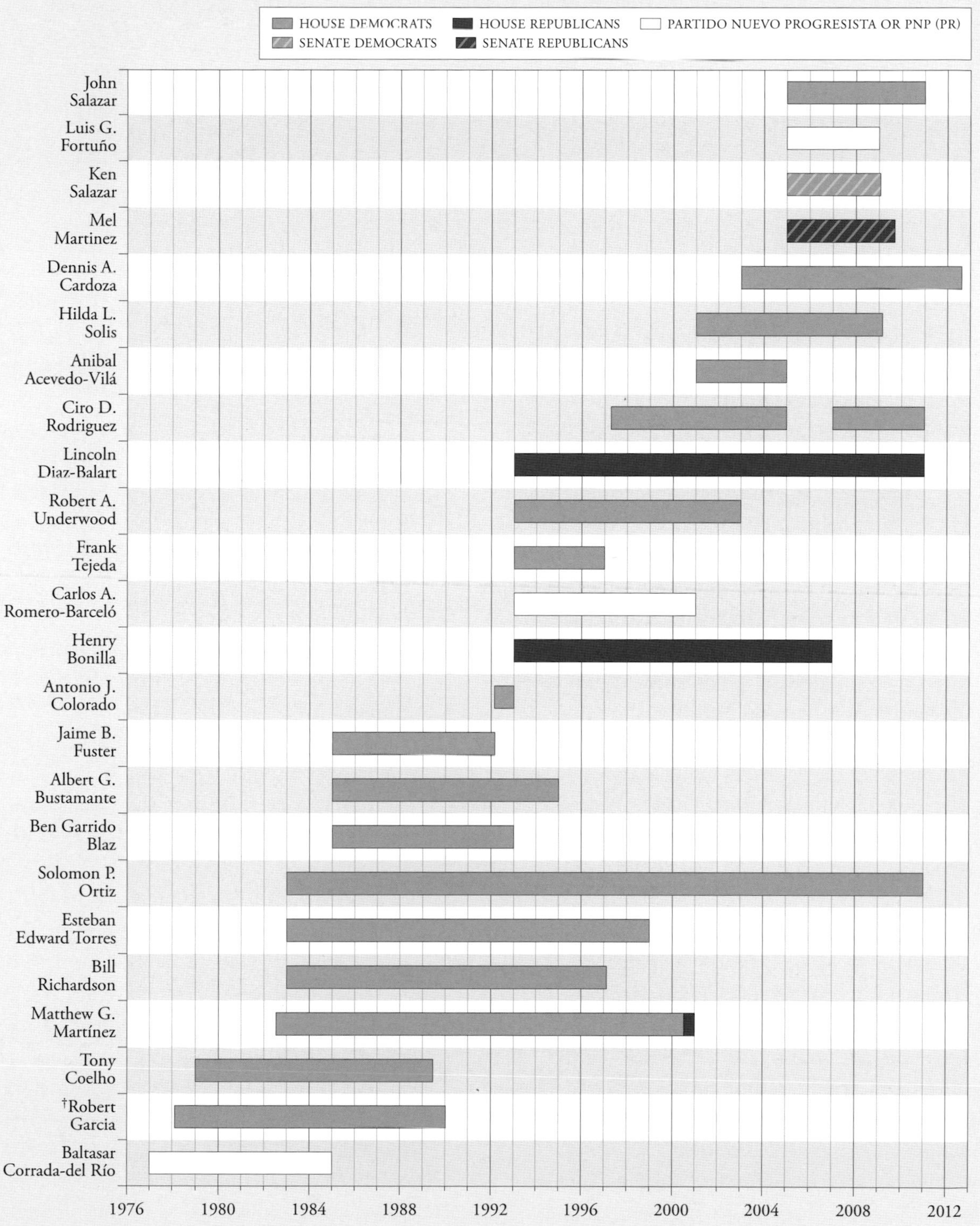

† Robert Garcia was a Republican-Liberal when elected to Congress in a special election on February 14, 1978. Seven days later, on February 21, he switched party affiliations to become a Democrat.

*Does not include Members whose service extends past September 1, 2012.

Baltasar Corrada-del Río

1935–

RESIDENT COMMISSIONER 1977–1985
NEW PROGRESSIVE FROM PUERTO RICO

Baltasar Corrada-del Río began his career as a leading human rights advocate in Puerto Rico and quickly became one of the island's most influential Resident Commissioners. A leading figure in the Partido Nuevo Progresista (New Progressive Party, or PNP) and a champion of Puerto Rican statehood, Corrada-del Río took an active interest in the concerns of minority citizens nationwide. Having helped found the Congressional Hispanic Caucus (CHC), he worked to ensure that Puerto Ricans and Hispanic Americans everywhere had access to important federal programs. "To me," he said toward the end of his career in the House, "it is quite an honor to be able to represent the interests of the Hispanic community."[1]

Corrada-del Río was born on April 10, 1935, in Morovis, Puerto Rico, to Rómulo Corrada and Ana María del Río. He attended the Morovis public grammar school until he was 13 and graduated from Colegio Ponceño de Varones high school in 1952. He immediately enrolled at the University of Puerto Rico in Rio Piedras, where he earned a bachelor's degree in social sciences four years later. He remained at the university and completed a law degree in 1959. That year he married Beatriz A. Betances. They had four children: Ana Isabel, Francisco Javier, Juan Carlos, and José B.[2]

Corrada-del Río was admitted to the bar in 1959, quickly made partner at a leading firm, and began a long and distinguished legal career. Unlike many Resident Commissioners, Corrada-del Río shied away from electoral office early on and often accepted leadership positions behind the scenes. In 1969, for instance, as the island's administration faced accusations of political suppression, Corrada-del Río was appointed to Puerto Rico's civil rights commission, which he chaired from 1970 to 1972.[3] In 1970 alone he was a member of the Advisory Committee to the Archbishop of Puerto Rico on Drug Abuse; the Puerto Rican Medical Association's Council of Public Health; and the Puerto Rican Bar Examination Board, having been appointed by the island's supreme court.[4]

By the mid-1970s, Corrada-del Río was one of the island's most respected human rights lawyers, known as "one of the bright young men of the New Progressive Party."[5] He wrote a regular column for *El mundo*, a leading island newspaper, and served as a member of the PNP's executive committee and as chairman of its committee on political status.[6]

Just 41 years old in 1976, Corrada-del Río had undergone a meteoric rise to become the PNP's front-runner for Puerto Rico's House seat in Washington. After he was formally nominated, Corrada-del Río faced incumbent Popular Democrat Jaime Benítez in the general election that year. Benítez was a well-known educator who had won by a landslide in 1972, but the island's economy had gone into a tailspin since his victory. "We think our chances are quite good," Corrada-del Río told the *Baltimore Sun* as Election Day neared.[7] In one of the closer elections in recent memory, he defeated Benítez by only 2.9 percent.[8]

When Corrada-del Río arrived in Washington, he broke with precedent to caucus with House Democrats. Since 1971, when Resident Commissioners won the right to vote in committee, they had essentially been required to join a mainland party caucus. New Progressives had loose ties to the GOP, and Jorge L. Córdova-Díaz, the last PNP official to serve in Washington, had elected to sit with Republicans. In the next Congress, Benítez, who was a member of the Partido Popular Democrático (Popular Democratic Party, or PPD), had caucused with Democrats to maintain parity. But Corrada-del Río broke that pattern, telling the *Washington Post* in 1977 that he was a "longtime Democrat." Paired with his membership

Collection of the U.S. House of Representatives, Photography Collection

in "the militantly pro-statehood wing of the [PNP]," Corrada-del Río's affiliation led him to support a strong federal state and its attendant public programs. "I like the Democratic Party['s] stand on social and economic issues," he said around the time of his swearing-in, "and feel I can accomplish a lot more for Puerto Rico by siding with the Democrats."[9] Corrada-del Río was appointed to the Committee on Education and Labor and the Committee on Interior and Insular Affairs, both traditional posts for Resident Commissioners. In mid-October 1977, the House appointed him to the Select Committee on Population, citing a need to study "the causes of changing population conditions and their consequences for the United States and the world."[10]

Corrada-del Río's tenure in the House marked a new chapter in the island's relationship with the federal government, reinvigorating the New Progressives' push for statehood. Corrada-del Río favored the outgoing Gerald Ford administration's decision to delay action on statehood, noting that he preferred "to be in power when these matters were decided." He refused to support any statehood measure originating in Congress that was not supported by an island plebiscite, and he criticized commonwealth supporters who fought to keep the government at a distance, only to structure insular policy around federal appropriations.[11] "Federal funds … must be understood and used as a complement and not as a substitute for Puerto Rican efforts," he said in a statement that dovetailed with his pro-statehood position.[12] Corrada-del Río promised that statehood would do little to impinge on Puerto Rico's unique culture. "We would continue doing the same things we do now," he said in 1977, "thinking, speaking, and praying in Spanish, without underestimating the importance of being bilingual.… In other words, we would continue practicing and enriching our customs, our traditions and our culture."[13]

For much of his first term in the 95th and 96th Congresses (1977–1981), Corrada-del Río defended Puerto Rico's participation in federal social programs, standing firmly in the vanguard of what became the PNP's standard policy in Washington: to convince Congress to treat Puerto Rico as if it were a state, especially regarding appropriations for education, Social Security, and labor. He opposed any cuts in food stamps, arguing such a decision "flies in the face of equal justice under law," particularly on "an island suffering the pains of a deep recession," he said a month later.[14] He championed bilingual education; sought to protect the benefits of disabled veterans living in U.S. territories; pushed to establish a minimum wage scale for Puerto Rico that was comparable to the mainland's; and actively backed raising the budget for executive agencies that helped Puerto Rico's rural communities, including the Farmers Home Administration, the Rural Electrification Administration, and the Agricultural Stabilization and Conservation Service.[15]

While only a handful of Corrada-del Río's bills ever made it out of committee, his activism resonated well beyond the Beltway, and his participation in the national fabric of Hispanic political activism surpassed his predecessors'. "Hispanics," he pointed out in 1979, "are becoming a force in almost every State and in almost every congressional district."[16] A founding member of the CHC, Corrada-del Río sought to reach an even broader audience by organizing the group Hispanic American Democrats (HAD).[17] As with the CHC, Corrada-del Río used HAD to push for greater political leverage. "If we Hispanics are to make it in the United States we must obtain an entrance to the front door of the economic temple," he said. "And that can hardly be arranged if we lack the political means, which is voter registration and the age-old practice of getting to the polls on voting day."[18]

A large part of Corrada-del Río's agenda concerned Puerto Rico's education system. In 1979 he supported a bill to create the U.S. Department of Education, a cabinet-level agency, to oversee the quality of the nation's schools and expand access to bilingual instruction "so that the high hopes … engendered in the hearts and the minds of those who need it are not thwarted."[19] Corrada-del Río's more notable successes included increasing federal funding for Puerto Rico's schools by more than $50 million and helping to augment the amount of money set aside by the government for college scholarships.[20]

In the buildup to the 1980 election, party infighting threatened to undercut the PNP's control over the insular government and nearly cost Corrada-del Río a second term. He found himself an unwitting pariah after Puerto Rico's secretary of state refused to attend an honorary dinner with President James Earl (Jimmy) Carter because he objected to a proposed immigration measure that was somewhat controversial. News of the secretary's snub traveled quickly, and while most PNP officials supported the president's rebuke, Corrada-del Río feared it might undermine communication between San Juan and Pennsylvania Avenue.[21] The Resident Commissioner publicly admonished the PNP administration for condoning the gesture, and while the party faithful responded in kind, Corrada-del Río tried to work past the criticism before Election Day.[22] He stumped on his record in the House, taking credit for sustaining the island's public works programs and school system with federal money.[23] Corrada-del Río complained about his opponents' "negative and confusing" campaigns attacking him for creating a "dependence" on federal funding, or "a welfare mentality." "One of the biggest errors we hear is that federal aid breeds dependence," Corrada-del Río responded. "We maintain these funds have been a blessing, not a substitute for our own development."[24]

Corrada-del Río won re-election by less than 1 percent in 1980, and ended up fighting many of the same battles he fought in his first term.[25] He was more vocal on the House Floor in his second term, fighting for access to food stamps and encouraging his colleagues to invest in the Caribbean Basin, even as the Ronald Reagan administration considered cutting billions from the national budget.[26] "Linked firmly to the U.S. economy, there is an axiom in our island that when Uncle Sam sneezes, Puerto Rico gets pneumonia," Corrada-del Río said in 1981.[27] In the scramble for federal aid, he warned that if the House targeted the island for block grants and across-the-board cuts—and it eventually did—Puerto Ricans would be singled out as "second class citizens … not deserving of equal treatment."[28]

With island unemployment still hovering above 20 percent, Corrada-del Río tried to help bolster the federal aid received by Puerto Rican sugar farmers, tuna canners, and rum sellers.[29] Hoping to protect both employers and employees, he took a firm stance on unauthorized labor, sponsoring an amendment to an unsuccessful immigration bill that required businesses to verify their employees' citizenship or face stiff penalties.[30] He also worked to extend unemployment benefits while backing the Job Training Partnership Act (H.R. 5320), which he described as a "comprehensive, coordinated approach to employment training," especially for underserved communities.[31] He continued to push for broader access to bilingual education and sought to bolster Puerto Rico's food stamp program, as he had for the past seven years.[32]

Corrada-del Río retired from the House at the end of the 98th Congress (1983–1985), opting not to run for re-election. Elected to serve Puerto Ricans, he took pride in promoting the concerns of Hispanic Americans throughout the United States.[33] The next year, Corrada-del Río was elected mayor of San Juan, Puerto Rico's capital and largest city, and served as the president of the PNP. In 1988 he waged an unsuccessful campaign for governor of Puerto Rico. Corrada-del Río was later appointed the island's secretary of state and eventually served as an associate justice on Puerto Rico's supreme court.[34] He has since retired from public service.

FOR FURTHER READING

Biographical Directory of the United States Congress, "Baltasar Corrada-del Río," http://bioguide.congress.gov.

NOTES

1 *Congressional Record*, House, 98th Cong., 2nd sess. (13 September 1983): 23913.

2 Baltasar Corrada to Denver Dickerson, Joint Committee on Printing, Congressional Directory Office, 23 November 1976, textual files of the *Biographical Directory of the United States Congress*, Office of the Historian, U.S. House of Representatives (hereinafter referred to as textual files of the *Biographical Directory of the United States Congress*).

3 "Puerto Rican Action on Equal Rights Urged by Law Panel," 22

August 1971, *Washington Post*: A18.

4 Baltasar Corrada to Denver Dickerson, Joint Committee on Printing, Congressional Directory Office, 23 November 1976, textual files of the *Biographical Directory of the United States Congress*.

5 Henry L. Trewhitt, "Steamy Reception Looms for Ford at Puerto Rican Summit," 23 June 1976, *Baltimore Sun*: A2.

6 Baltasar Corrada to Denver Dickerson, Joint Committee on Printing, Congressional Directory Office, 23 November 1976, textual files of the *Biographical Directory of the United States Congress*; William Claiborne, "Puerto Rican Officials Fear New Upswing of Terrorism," 25 March 1975, *Washington Post*: A4.

7 Trewhitt, "Steamy Reception Looms for Ford at Puerto Rican Summit"; Interview with Jaime Benítez, Former Resident Commissioner of Puerto Rico, "Should Puerto Rico Be a State?: No," 11 April 1977, *U.S. News & World Report*: 47.

8 "Election Statistics, 1920 to Present," http://history.house.gov/institution/election-statistics/election-statistics.

9 John Van Hyning, "Confronting an Island's Ills: Statehood Issue, Economic Depression Face New P.R. Governor," 2 January 1977, *Washington Post*: 3.

10 *Congressional Record*, House, 96th Cong., 1st sess. (21 March 1979): 5800; Garrison Nelson, *Committees in the U.S. Congress, 1947 to 1992*, vol. 2 (Washington, D.C.: CQ Press, 1994): 193.

11 Warren Brown, "Time May Run Out on Ford: Puerto Rico Bill Lagging," 4 January 1977, *Washington Post*: A1; James Nelson Goodsell, "Puerto Rico Struggling over Future," 27 July 1977, *Christian Science Monitor*: 9; Dave Smith, "Vote Dispute Leaves Puerto Rico in Limbo," 29 November 1980, *Los Angeles Times*: B1.

12 Beatriz Ruiz de la Mata, "Tripping over Puerto Rico's Bootstraps," 12 August 1979, *Boston Globe*: 45.

13 *Congressional Record,* Extension of Remarks, 95th Cong., 1st sess. (25 July 1977): 24837.

14 *Congressional Record*, House, 95th Cong., 1st sess. (21 June 1977): 20150; *Congressional Record*, House, 95th Cong., 1st sess. (20 July 1977): 24090.

15 *Congressional Record*, Extension of Remarks, 95th Cong., 1st sess. (6 December 1977): 38632; *Congressional Record*, Extension of Remarks, 95th Cong., 1st sess. (4 April 1977): 10330. See also *Congressional Record*, House, 96th Cong., 1st sess. (16 July 1979): 18765; Harry Turner, "Corrada 'Proud' of Helping P.R. Land U.S. Funds," 5 October 1980, *San Juan Star*: 6; "Corrada Asks P.R. Labor Force to Repudiate Torres' Wage Plan," 6 October 1980, *San Juan Star*: 8; *Congressional Record*, House, 95th Cong., 1st sess. (20 June 1977): 19802.

16 *Congressional Record*, Extension of Remarks, 96th Cong., 1st sess. (15 December 1979): 36371.

17 David Vidal, "Puerto Rico Aide Sees Statehood Hurt by Ford," 5 January 1977, *New York Times*: 12; "Hispanic Group Asks Carter for More Jobs," 2 March 1977, *New York Times*: 14.

18 *Congressional Record*, Extension of Remarks, 96th Cong., 1st sess. (15 December 1979): 36373.

19 *Congressional Record*, House, 96th Cong., 1st sess. (7 June 1979): 13971; *Congressional Record*, House, 96th Cong., 1st sess. (12 June 1970): 14474.

20 Harry Turner, "Corrada 'Proud' of Helping P.R. Land U.S. Funds," 5 October 1980, *San Juan Star*: 6.

21 Quotation from Harry Turner, "Corrada Gnashes at 'Immaturity' of Vazquez No-Show," 2 October 1980, *San Juan Star*: 1. On response by party, see Harold J. Lidin, "NPP Faithful Rake Corrada for Blast at Vazquez," 3 October 1980, *San Juan Star*: 3.

22 Harry Turner, "Corrada Won't Back Down in Flap over Vazquez Snub," 4 October 1980, *San Juan Star*: 3.

23 Turner, "Corrada 'Proud' of Helping P.R. Land U.S. Funds."

24 Harry Turner, "Corrada Claims PIP Desertions, No-Shows hurt NPP," 7 November 1980, *San Juan Star*: 6; Manny Suarez, "3 Resident-Commissioner Hopefuls Square Off in Debate," 24 October 1980, *San Juan Star*: 6.

25 "Election Statistics, 1920 to Present," http://history.house.gov/institution/election-statistics/election-statistics.

26 *Congressional Record*, Extension of Remarks, 97th Cong., 1st sess. (16 December 1981): 32367–32368.

27 *Congressional Record*, House, 97th Cong., 1st sess. (13 March 1981): 4397.

28 *Congressional Record*, House, 97th Cong., 1st sess. (25 June 1981): 14090; *Congressional Record*, House, 97th Cong., 1st sess. (26 June 1981): 14570. On food stamps and Puerto Rico, see *Congressional Record*, House, 97th Cong., 1st sess. (25 June 1981): 14089–14091; *Congressional Record*, House, 97th Cong., 1st sess. (26 June 1981): 14569–14570; *Congressional Record*, House, 97th Cong., 1st sess. (22 October 1981): 24868–24871; *Congressional Record*, House, 97th Cong., 2nd sess. (2 June 1982): 12767–12772.

29 *Congressional Record*, House, 97th Cong., 1st sess. (2 October 1981): 22950–22951; *Congressional Record*, House, 97th Cong., 2nd sess. (17 December 1982): 31890–31891, 31899, 31906, 31923, 31926, 31929; *Congressional Record*, House, 97th Cong., 1st sess. (15 October 1981): 24207–24208.

30 *Congressional Record*, House, 97th Cong., 2nd sess. (18 December 1982): 32168–32169.

31 *Congressional Record*, House, 98th Cong., 1st sess. (29 September 1983): 26426; quotation in *Congressional Record*, House, 97th Cong., 2nd sess. (4 August 1982): 19340.

32 *Congressional Record*, House, 98th Cong., 2nd sess. (2 March 1983): 3589–3590; *Congressional Record*, Extension of Remarks,

98th Cong., 2nd sess. (30 June 1983): 18392; *Congressional Record*, House, 98th Cong., 2nd sess. (15 November 1983): 32716.

33 *Congressional Record*, House, 98th Cong., 2nd sess. (13 September 1983): 23913.

34 Manny Suarez, "Ex-Governor's Bid Complicates Puerto Rico Race," 8 November 1987, *New York Times*: 41; Hearing before the House Subcommittee on Insular and International Affairs of the Committee on Natural Resources, *Articles of Relations for U.S. Territories,* 103rd Cong., 2nd sess. (24 May 1994): 41; Lance Oliver, "Political Battles Start New Year in Puerto Rico," 13 January 1997, *Orlando Sentinel*: A6.

Robert Garcia

1933–

UNITED STATES REPRESENTATIVE
REPUBLICAN-LIBERAL FROM NEW YORK 1978
DEMOCRAT FROM NEW YORK 1978–1990

A veteran of New York state politics for over a decade, Robert Garcia succeeded Herman Badillo in 1978 to represent a South Bronx district in the U.S. House. Eventually the chairman of two subcommittees, Garcia focused on federal programs to attract businesses to blighted urban areas. Garcia's signal piece of legislation—designating federal "enterprise zones" to promote job growth in depressed inner cities—highlighted a promising House career that ended abruptly when Garcia became enmeshed in the Wedtech scandal through his association with a defense contractor in his district.

Robert Garcia was born January 9, 1933, in Bronx, New York, to immigrants. His Puerto Rican father, Rafael Garcia, worked in a sugar mill before moving to New York City, where he founded an Assembly of God church in an aging storefront.[1] Garcia attended the local public schools, graduating from Haaren High School in 1950, and served overseas in the U.S. Army's Third Infantry from 1950 to 1953 during the Korean War, earning two Bronze Stars.[2] He attended City College of New York, the Community College of New York, and the RCA Institute in 1957, before becoming an engineer at two large computer corporations, where he worked from 1957 to 1965. Garcia married the former Anita Theresa Medina, and the couple raised sons Robert and Kenneth before separating in 1974 and divorcing several years later. In 1980 Garcia married the former Jane Lee, a longtime resident of Puerto Rico who had served as a staffer in the U.S. House in the late 1970s.[3]

Garcia first ran for political office in 1965 for the New York state assembly in the 83rd District, which encompassed Puerto Rican neighborhoods in and around Port Morris and Mott Haven in the South Bronx. In the September 14, 1965, Democratic primary he defeated Domingo Ramos, Jr., with 65 percent of the vote.[4] In the general election, Garcia faced Republican candidate Paul Spitaleri as well as two lesser-known challengers from the Liberal and Conservative Parties. Garcia prevailed handily with 74 percent of the vote in the four-way contest.[5] Since Garcia never had the full support of the regular Democratic organization, he faced a stiff primary challenge in 1966 from A. C. Acevedo, whom he defeated by roughly 70 votes out of the nearly 3,000 cast.[6] Garcia's base of support drew on local labor unions as well as on the Adlai E. Stevenson Independent Reform Democratic Club. In the state assembly, Garcia earned a reputation as an advocate for housing issues, sponsoring a bill, later signed into law, that gave the New York City buildings department the power to subpoena recalcitrant slumlords.[7]

In early 1967, Garcia entered a special election to represent portions of the South Bronx and Harlem in the New York state senate. Like his assembly district, the area was overwhelmingly Democratic. Its large Puerto Rican population (one-third of the district) was matched by equal numbers of African Americans and contingents of Irish and Jewish voters. The seat was left vacant when senator-elect Eugene Rodriguez was convicted and imprisoned for grand larceny, perjury, and conspiracy to murder a drug dealer. Rodriguez never claimed his seat because he was on trial when the legislative session opened. In the March 28, 1967, special election, Garcia—running as a Reform Democrat with the support of the regular Bronx Democratic organization—faced two weak candidates: Republican lawyer Dominick A. Fusco and Conservative Paul M. Patricola, a textile company employee. With little active campaigning, Garcia's name recognition and the endorsement of the Citizen's Union—which called him "a progressive and constructive legislator"—propelled him to an easy victory, with 73 percent of the vote. Garcia became the first Puerto Rican to serve in the state senate.[8]

Collection of the U.S. House of Representatives, Photography Collection

Serving over a decade in the New York state senate, Garcia built a reputation as a legislative "workhorse," according to a number of his colleagues. From 1975 to 1978, he served as deputy minority leader in Albany (an elected position). His legislative interests included prison reform, public housing, and narcotics control—all of which appealed to his inner-city constituents.[9] He also struck up a close relationship with U.S. Representative Herman Badillo, who represented a swath of the South Bronx that overlapped his senate and former assembly districts. Like Garcia, Badillo styled himself as a reformer, and he had been Bronx borough president before becoming the first person of Puerto Rican heritage elected to a full voting seat in the U.S. House in 1970.[10]

In 1977 Badillo resigned his House seat to become deputy mayor of New York City. The district, which was one of the most poverty-stricken and depressed in the nation, stretched northward from the East River and Mott Haven to Melrose, Morrisania, and West Farms in its northeastern quadrant. It had a reputation for being politically disorganized and had only 75,000 registered voters, a sign of its waning community cohesion. Initially, Garcia was among a field of seven candidates set to compete in the February 14, 1978, special election to fill the remainder of Badillo's term in the 95th Congress (1977–1979). Having failed to secure the Democratic nomination, Garcia ran as a Republican, making clear his intention to vote with the Democrats in Congress. His principal opponent was Democratic and Conservative nominee Louis Nine, a state assemblyman whose fortune from his liquor and real estate businesses provided him with ample personal resources to wage a campaign. Former city councilman Ramon S. Velez (a longtime rival of Badillo's who still had great influence in South Bronx antipoverty programs) ran as an Independent. Such party labels, the *New York Times* explained, were "little more than conveniences enabling rejected Democrats to obtain lines on the voting machines."[11] Badillo campaigned vigorously for Garcia, who also had the support of many leading city politicians, including the New York city council president, the city comptroller, and prominent African-American politicians such as Harlem Congressman Charles Rangel.[12] On a snowy Election Day with voter turnout higher than expected, Garcia prevailed handily over Nine and Velez, securing 55 percent of the vote versus his opponents' 25 and 16 percent of the vote, respectively. The *New York Times* called Garcia's majority "a victory for Badillo" that "reaffirmed" his status as leader of the city's Puerto Rican community.[13]

Garcia was sworn into the House and resumed his prior affiliation as a Democrat effective February 21, 1978. In a district that experienced intense economic and demographic instability, Garcia never faced serious electoral challenges. In the fall 1978 elections for the full term in the 96th Congress (1979–1981), he was unopposed in the Democratic primary and in the general election. Redistricting after the 1980 Census intended to preserve the Puerto Rican-majority district, adding areas in the Grand Concourse and blocks east of the South Bronx. It did not substantively change the constituency's strong Democratic tilt. Garcia won his five bids for re-election after 1978 with majorities of 89 percent of the vote or more.[14]

Garcia was assigned seats on the Banking, Finance, and Urban Affairs Committee and on the Post Office and Civil Service Committee and remained on both panels for the rest of his House career. He also temporarily served on the Foreign Affairs Committee during the 98th and 99th Congresses (1983–1987). He was quickly awarded the chairmanship of the Post Office and Civil Service Committee's Census and Population Subcommittee—an important assignment for a Member from one of the nation's poorest districts—and led that panel from 1979 to 1987. By the 100th Congress (1987–1989), he left to become chairman of the Banking panel's influential Subcommittee on International Finance, Trade, and Monetary Policy.

In 1979 Garcia gained national attention by sponsoring a bill to establish a national holiday in honor of slain civil rights leader Martin Luther King, Jr. The bill had been pushed by African-American Members for a decade before Garcia took it up, serving as floor manager during debate on December 5, 1979. Opponents decried the millions in wages that would be paid federal workers for a day of leave. "Some have argued that it would be too expensive to create another Federal holiday," Garcia told his colleagues. "This is, indeed, a concern. But when weighed against the need to honor all that Dr. King struggled for, prayed for, dreamed about, symbolized, and sought throughout his life, find that the scales of justice tilt decidedly in favor of a new Federal holiday to honor Dr. King." When opponents in the House passed an amendment requiring that the holiday be observed on a Sunday to avoid a federal holiday during the workweek, Garcia withdrew the bill from consideration, claiming such a designation would put King's holiday on a par with Leif Erickson Day and National Peanut Day. "We're not going to go with a commemorative day," Garcia said. "We're not going to place Martin Luther King into that situation."[15] The bill eventually passed the House and Senate and was signed into law by President Ronald W. Reagan in November 1983.[16]

Garcia was attuned to the interests of the larger Hispanic community. From his seat on the Foreign Affairs Committee, he weighed in on U.S.-Latin American policy. Garcia consistently opposed U.S. military aid to the Contras, insurgents who sought to overthrow Nicaragua's leftist government. Garcia was one of eight members of the Congressional Hispanic Caucus (CHC) who voted in February 1988 to stop arming the Contras; the measure narrowly passed the House, 218 to 211. Caucus opposition to the Reagan administration's foreign policy in Latin America, notes one scholar, represented a maturation of Latino political power.[17] From 1981 to 1984, during the 97th and 98th Congresses, Garcia served as chairman of the CHC. He was the CHC's second chairman as well as its longest-serving chairman; he served for two terms, partly because of his fundraising innovations.[18]

Garcia's principal focus was steering federal dollars, projects, and jobs into his economically distressed South Bronx district. Shortly after he took office, a major political publication described the district as "a sort of national slum." "Its many acres of abandoned and vandalized buildings in the South Bronx have become the symbol of contemporary urban decay," noted a companion publication.[19] Unemployment was rampant, and crime was exceedingly high. Additionally, a transition from older Jewish and Italian immigrants to younger Puerto Ricans and African Americans fueled a decline in the district's population, which according to one estimate decreased by half between 1972 and 1980.[20] As a junior House Member, Garcia described his district for political columnist David Broder. "There are parts … that are absolutely devastated, as bad as anything in Berlin in 1945." But "you talk to the people of the South Bronx and you're going to find many people who—in spite of the adversity, in spite of the tremendous odds, in spite of everything—have been able to raise families and bring forth young people who are making a contribution."

Garcia's legislative strategy was to leverage the influence of his seat on the Banking Committee to attract capital and industry to his district. He told Broder, "All I need are one or two successful projects. I think from that point on we can take off on our own. I think we'd get enough private money in so we wouldn't have to worry about the government's help."[21] This philosophy of limited government intervention to spark entrepreneurship had bipartisan appeal because it did not require another round of massive federal expenditures to solve the problem of poverty in the South Bronx.

In 1980 Garcia teamed with Republican Jack Kemp of Buffalo, New York, to co-author the Urban Jobs and Enterprise Zone Act. Introducing the bill on the House Floor on June 12, 1980, Garcia explained that it aimed to ameliorate "the plight of the cities … largely due to economic abandonment by businesses." The bill, Garcia said, sought "to begin the economic redevelopment of the slums by creating new reasons for entrepreneurs to want to set up businesses in them."[22] The Garcia–Kemp measure called for the creation of urban "free enterprise zones" where businesses would receive tax breaks for locating in economically depressed inner cities, such as the Bronx, and for hiring local residents. Payroll and capital gains taxes would be reduced to stimulate hiring. Additionally, the bill would establish duty-free foreign-trade zones for imports and exports fabricated in enterprise zones. Though Kemp and Garcia differed on many issues, both men, according to Garcia, agreed on the need for the "reestablishment of opportunity producing incentives in areas where they no longer exist but once did—and that it is proper for government to provide incentives to attract businesses to areas which face severe depression, unemployment, and poverty."[23] Garcia argued that such a program would benefit federal and local tax bases. "Our slums now produce little revenue either for their residents—that is, wages—or for their governments—that is, taxes," he explained. "I believe that it makes a great deal of sense to supplement existing programs with tax cuts to the poor and to those in impoverished neighborhoods who wish to become small business persons … to become active producers of revenue."[24]

For several Congresses the House refused to pass the tax breaks that were necessary to implement the enterprise zone project. Part of the problem in the Democratically controlled House was that conservative Republicans, including President Reagan, embraced the plan. Liberals believed this was cover for efforts to redline funding for longstanding urban renewal programs. Moreover, Ways and Means Chairman Dan Rostenkowski of Illinois, the gatekeeper for tax-related bills, opposed the plan. But many states adopted legislation that mirrored the proposed federal enterprise zone bill. Garcia persevered on the project until 1988, when a portion of his plan for inner-city economic development was enacted as part of a larger housing bill. While that bill authorized the creation of 100 enterprise zones—to be designated by the Secretary of Housing and Urban Development—it failed to provide tax incentives for businesses. In the 101st Congress (1989–1991), with Kemp ensconced as President George H. W. Bush's Secretary of Housing and Urban Development, Garcia, aided by Ways and Means Committee member and fellow New York Representative Rangel, launched a new effort to provide tax breaks to attract businesses.[25]

Garcia's promising House career unraveled in 1988 and 1989 when he was implicated in the Wedtech scandal. A small, Hispanic-owned defense contracting firm in Garcia's district that had received multimillion-dollar contracts, Wedtech was investigated by the U.S. Justice Department after it missed deadlines to produce military engines. Federal officials uncovered a massive bribery and extortion scheme that ensnared executive and legislative branch officials.[26] That year Garcia faced his first substantive primary challenge as an incumbent; two relatively obscure competitors won a combined 40 percent of the vote.[27] In November 1988, Garcia and his wife, Jane, were charged by investigators with accepting more than $80,000 from Wedtech as well as numerous loans and gifts. On October 20, 1989, the Garcias were convicted on extortion and conspiracy charges; they were acquitted of four counts of bribery and illegal gratuities. On January 7, 1990, before his sentencing and after the House Ethics Committee had launched an inquiry into the case, Representative Garcia resigned his seat. The Garcias were sentenced two weeks later to three years in prison, but the conviction was overturned on appeal. Garcia was tried a second time and convicted again in 1991, but that conviction too was overturned, and he spent no time in jail.[28]

FOR FURTHER READING

Biographical Directory of the United States Congress, "Robert Garcia," http://bioguide.congress.gov.

MANUSCRIPT COLLECTION

Special Collections and University Libraries, Rutgers University Libraries (New Brunswick, NJ). *Papers*: New Democratic Coalition of New York Records, 1960–1978, 49 cubic feet. Persons represented include Robert Garcia.

NOTES

1 For more on Garcia's youth and family background, see David Broder, *Changing of the Guard: Power and Leadership in America* (New York: Penguin Books, 1981): 291–292; Marilyn W. Thompson, *Feeding the Beast: How Wedtech Became the Most Corrupt Little Company in America* (New York: Charles Scribner's Sons, 1990): 178–188; Glenn Fowler, "New Representative from Bronx: Robert Garcia," 22 February 1978, *New York Times*: NJ24. No published source lists the name of Garcia's mother.

2 *Politics in America, 1990* (Washington, D.C.: Congressional Quarterly, Inc., 1989): 1047; Carmen E. Enciso and Tracy North, *Hispanic Americans in Congress, 1822–1995* (Washington, D.C.: Government Printing Office, 1995): 51.

3 Josh Barbanel, "A Streetwise Son of the Bronx Undergoes a Transformation on Capitol Hill," 22 November 1988, *New York Times*: A1; Nadine Brozan, "Verdict Dashes a Classic Success Story," 21 October 1989, *New York Times*: 28. The Garcias' marriage date is from James Traub, *Too Good to Be True: The Outlandish Story of Wedtech* (New York: Doubleday, 1990): 183.

4 "Prospective Primary Contests in City," 11 August 1965, *New York Times*: 23; Primary Voting Results, 16 September 1965, *New York Times*: 50.

5 List of Candidates, 1 November 1965, *New York Times*: 44; "Tally of Voting in Suburban and New Jersey Contests; State Assembly Results in City," 3 November 1965, *New York Times*: 33.

6 "Garcia Wins Unofficial Tally," 1 July 1966, *New York Times*: 14.

7 James F. Clarity, "Democrat Garcia Favored in Bronx: Special Election Today Will Fill Rodriguez's Seat," 28 March 1967, *New York Times*: 25; James F. Clarity, "Garcia Wins Seat Held by Rodriguez," 29 March 1967, *New York Times*: 33.

8 Clarity, "Garcia Wins Seat Held by Rodriguez"; Clarity, "Democrat Garcia Favored in Bronx: Special Election Today Will Fill Rodriguez's Seat." Rodriguez, too, was of Puerto Rican heritage, but never served in the New York state senate.

9 "Robert Garcia, The Winner in Bronx Race," 15 February 1978, *New York Times*: A22; Glenn Fowler, "Two Front-Runners Are Emerging in Race for Badillo's House Seat," 30 November 1977, *New York Times*: 32.

10 Puerto Rico had been represented by nonvoting Resident Commissioners in the U.S. House since the early 20th century.

11 "Black Vote Pivotal in South Bronx Race: Four Puerto Rican Candidates for Badillo's Congressional Seat Woo Other Minority Group," 5 February 1978, *New York Times*: 21.

12 Glen Fowler, "Garcia and Velez Rated in the Lead of Large Field Seeking Badillo Seat," 10 January 1978, *New York Times*: 37; "Black Vote Pivotal in South Bronx Race: Four Puerto Rican Candidates for Badillo's Congressional Seat Woo Other Minority Group."

13 Frank Lynn, "Mrs. Abzug Defeated Narrowly by Green; Garcia Wins in Bronx," 15 February 1978, *New York Times*: A1. See also Glenn Fowler, "Garcia's Victory Gives Added Leverage to Badillo," 16 February 1978, *New York Times*: B10.

14 "Election Statistics, 1920 to Present," http://history.house.gov/institution/election-statistics/election-statistics; *Almanac of American Politics, 1984*: 828.

15 *Congressional Record*, House, 96th Cong., 1st sess. (5 December 1979): quotation on p. 34749; for the full debate, see pp. 34747–34765. Mary Russell, "King Holiday Frustrated," 6 December 1979, *Washington Post*: A6; see also "Ducking a King Holiday Vote," 7 December 1979, *Washington Post*: A16.

16 Office of History and Preservation, U.S. House of Representatives, *Black Americans in Congress, 1870–2007* (Washington, D.C.: Government Printing Office, 2008): 385.

17 Antonio González, "Chicano Politics and U.S. Policy in Central America, 1979–1990," in *Chicano Politics and Society in the Late Twentieth Century*, David Montejano, ed. (Austin: University of Texas Press, 1999): 154–172.

18 Barbanel, "A Streetwise Son of the Bronx Undergoes a Transformation on Capitol Hill."

19 *Almanac of American Politics, 1980*: 614; *Politics in America, 1982*: 847.

20 Cited in *Politics in America, 1982*: 847.

21 Broder, *Changing of the Guard*: 292.

22 *Congressional Record*, House, 96th Cong., 2nd sess. (12 June 1980): 14468–14469.

23 *Congressional Record*, House, 96th Cong., 2nd sess. (2 October 1980): 29031–29033; quotation on p. 29033. See also Hon. Robert Garcia, "Toward a New Federal Role in Urban Redevelopment—A Policy of Opportunity Development," *Congressional Record*, Extension of Remarks, House, 96th Cong., 2nd sess. (19 August 1980): 22059–22061.

24 Hon. Robert Garcia, "Setting the Record Straight on the Kemp–Garcia Enterprise Zones Bill," *Congressional Record*, Extension of Remarks, House, 96th Cong., 2nd sess. (2 July 1980): 18682–18683.

25 See *Politics in America, 1990*: 1048.

26 Representative Mario Biaggi, who represented a Bronx district next to Garcia's, was convicted of bribery in August 1988. For contemporary news coverage, see Arnold H. Lubasch, "U.S. Indicts Rep. Garcia, His Wife, and a Lawyer in Wedtech Inquiry," 22 November 1988, *New York Times*: A1. Two major book-length accounts describe the rise and fall of Wedtech and its associates: Traub, *Too Good to Be True: The Outlandish Story of Wedtech*, especially pp. 183–185 and 270–273; and Thompson, *Feeding the Beast: How Wedtech Became the Most Corrupt Little Company in America*: 178–188.

27 *Politics in America, 1990*: 1049.

28 For more information, see "Historical Summary of Conduct Cases in the House of Representatives," Committee on Standards of Official Conduct, 9 November 2004, http://ethics.house.gov/Pubs/Default.aspx?Section=15 (accessed 6 May 2010); Mark Grossman, *Political Corruption in America: An Encyclopedia of Scandals, Power, and Greed*, vol. 1, (New York: Grey House Publishing, 2008): 185–186; William Glaberson, "Garcias' Extortion Convictions Are Reversed by Appeals Panel," 30 June 1990, *New York Times*: 1; Ronald Sullivan, "Convictions of Garcias in Wedtech Scandal Overturned Again," 23 April 1993, *New York Times*: B3; and "U.S. Will Not Retry Garcia in Extortion," 16 September 1993, *New York Times*: B3.

Tony Coelho

1942–

UNITED STATES REPRESENTATIVE 1979–1989
DEMOCRAT FROM CALIFORNIA

Departing from his original plan to become a Catholic priest, Tony Coelho instead dedicated himself to a political career, first as a staffer and then as a Member of the U.S. House of Representatives. During his six terms in office, Coelho led a push to revive the Democratic Party's fundraising abilities and became the first Hispanic American to attain a top-tier leadership position as Majority Whip. Coelho was unabashedly partisan, even by the standards of an already partisan age. "You know, politics reminds me of driving a car," he once remarked. "You put it in D and you go forward. You put it in R and you go backward."[1]

Anthony Lee (Tony) Coelho was born June 15, 1942, in Los Banos, California. His parents, Otto and Alice Branco Coelho, were the children of Portuguese immigrants.[2] As a teenager, Tony Coelho had an accident on his parents' dairy farm that caused him to black out sporadically for the rest of his life. Coelho attended the public schools in Dos Palos, California, before graduating from Loyola University in Los Angeles in 1964. Intent on attending law school, he changed his plans after President John F. Kennedy was assassinated, believing that the priesthood encapsulated Kennedy's vision of public service. But his plans were derailed when he learned on his 22nd birthday that his blackouts were caused by epilepsy. At the time, epileptics were barred from the priesthood.[3]

After suffering a bout of depression, Coelho worked briefly for comedian Bob Hope, who encouraged him to pursue a career in politics. A Jesuit acquaintance introduced Coelho to Hope, for whom Coelho did odd jobs. Coelho also lived for a while with the Hope family. Hope enjoyed nighttime drives on Los Angeles-area freeways and often took Coelho along for company. Hope once suggested that Coelho should work for a Congressman. "It's obvious that you have this burn to help people," Hope said. "If that's your bag, why don't you go work for a member of Congress?" Coelho sent his résumé and a letter of introduction to Congressman Bernie Sisk, whose district encompassed Coelho's hometown and much of the San Joachin Valley.[4] Shortly thereafter, Coelho began working as an intern in Representative Sisk's office. In June 1967, Coelho married Phyllis Butler, a legislative aide to Indiana Representative Andrew Jacobs. The couple raised two daughters, Nicole and Kristen.[5]

Sisk was an influential Democratic member of the California delegation with a decade of experience in the House when Coelho joined his staff in 1965. He held a post on the powerful Rules Committee and was a serious contender for Majority Leader in 1971.[6] An expert on Western water politics, Sisk directed millions of federal dollars to irrigation projects that helped establish central California as an ideal location for agricultural business. Moreover, as a native Texan who moved with his young family to California during the Great Depression, Sisk was popular with the Southern Members, who ruled the House at the time. He was particularly close to the Texas delegation—allowing Coelho, as a senior staffer, to establish important relationships with the group, notably with Representative Jim Wright from the Dallas-Ft. Worth area. In an era when the California and Texas delegations vied for influence in the House, Coelho was often on the outs with an alliance of California Democrats headed by one of the most skilled and powerful Members in the House, Phil Burton of San Francisco.[7]

For 14 years, Coelho worked his way up the ladder in Sisk's office. By 1970 he was Sisk's administrative assistant, the equivalent of a present-day chief of staff. He was also staff director of the Subcommittee on Cotton of the House Agriculture Committee, a consultant for the House Parking Committee, and a staff coordinator for the

Image courtesy of the National Archives and Records Administration

House Rules Committee's Subcommittee on Broadcasting. Coelho enjoyed a filial relationship with Sisk, who shared with him many of the eccentricities of the House and its Members. At one time Sisk chaired a three-man panel that assigned Members parking spaces while Coelho handled administrative duties. Coelho was astonished when he found out that a senior Texas member who was a close friend to his boss had routinely complained to the Speaker because Sisk had a more desirable spot than he did. Coelho considered the problem petty but informed Sisk, who immediately yielded the spot, saying, "You don't understand. Parking spaces are important." Coelho learned that such gestures, deference, and small favors cemented loyalty and turned the wheels of legislation.[8]

Sisk's district encompassed one of the most fertile stretches of farmland in the country, extending northward from the outskirts of Fresno to include Merced, Turlock, and at its far northern extreme, Modesto. More than 200 different crops were cultivated there, including cotton, grapes, walnuts, and peaches. The district's population was mixed; about one-fifth were Mexican Americans, and an equal number had roots in the South. Like Sisk, many of the residents were from families that had journeyed to the region during the Dust Bowl years. A growing population of Hmong refugees from Laos was centered in Merced. Over time, as the Central Valley leaned Republican, Coelho's district remained Democratic, though it was more conservative than coastal California on many social issues.

In 1978, by the time Sisk announced his decision to retire at the end of the 101st Congress (1989–1991), he had already chosen Coelho as his successor. Coelho had left his Washington post shortly beforehand to manage Sisk's district office and had forged strong political ties in the area.[9] Vincent Lavery, his only opponent in the Democratic primary, was a teacher from Fresno who had been defeated twice while seeking the party's nomination in the district. Coelho handily dispatched him, with 79 percent of the vote. In the general election, Coelho faced Chris Patterakis, a local celebrity and a former stunt pilot for the Air Force Thunderbirds. Coelho's epilepsy became a campaign issue. Describing Coelho as "a very sick man," Patterakis asked a crowd, "What would you think if Coelho went to the White House to argue a critical issue for you and he had a seizure?" Asked by the press for a response, Coelho quipped, "A lot of people have gone to the White House and had fits. At least I'd have an excuse." A Modesto native, Patterakis carried the district's largest city, but Coelho benefited from a two to one Democratic registration advantage and from his ties to the popular incumbent. Ultimately, Coelho prevailed in the bulk of the district and won the election, 60 to 40 percent.[10] According to the *Los Angeles Times*, Coelho's victory made him the first Portuguese American to serve in Congress.[11] In his subsequent five re-election campaigns, Coelho faced no serious challenges, winning between 64 and 72 percent of the vote.[12]

Coelho earned assignments on the Agriculture Committee and the Veterans' Affairs Committee.[13] The first panel was vital for his constituency, and he took over Sisk's role as the caretaker of the district's farming interests. He held several important subcommittee seats, including the Livestock, Dairy, and Poultry Subcommittee, which he chaired in the 99th Congress (1985–1987), and the Cotton, Rice, and Sugar Subcommittee. Also in the 99th Congress, Coelho earned a seat on the House Administration Committee, allowing him to influence election and campaign legislation. In his second term, he traded his Veterans' Affairs assignment for a seat on the Interior and Insular Affairs Committee and gained a critical spot on the panel's Subcommittee on Water and Power Resources, allowing him to monitor water and irrigation issues that were vital to the agriculture industry in the Central Valley. The industry was supported largely by government-sponsored public works projects that pumped water into the otherwise barren region.[14]

With the retirement of most of the other senior Representatives in California's Central Valley in the late 1970s and early 1980s, Coelho emerged as the defender of the region's large agribusiness sector. Early on, the battle lines were drawn around access to water, pitting Coelho against Democrat George Miller, who represented California's 7th Congressional District, to the northwest. Nearly a million acre-feet of water flowed through Miller's district into the valley's Westlands region. In the 1970s, small farmers backed by Representative Miller and supported by the James Earl (Jimmy) Carter administration sought to enforce a 1902 law that had been largely ignored, limiting the use of federally subsidized water to farmers who worked land in parcels of 160 acres or less. The large-scale agribusinesses in the San Joaquin Valley deemed this requirement unworkable, and Coelho sought to relax the requirements. Supported by a majority of the committee, he orchestrated a compromise with Representative Miller: Owners would pay higher fees but would qualify for federal water regardless of the size of their landholdings.[15]

Coelho's primary focus was to strengthen congressional Democrats' campaign fundraising capabilities. As a freshman Representative, he sold more tickets to the party's annual fundraising dinner than any other House Member. He then built up a considerable war chest for his 1980 re-election effort, and when his Republican challenger conceded the contest, Coelho used the money to fund other Democrats' campaigns. In 1981, at the start of his second term, party leaders selected Coelho to be chairman of the moribund Democratic Congressional Campaign Committee (DCCC), whose purpose was to raise funds and provide strategy for House Democratic candidates. Coelho was only the second junior Member ever tapped to lead the DCCC (the first was Lyndon B. Johnson of Texas).[16] Coelho proved to be an excellent fundraiser; he had the ability to work a crowd and speak to the issues. Under his chairmanship, the DCCC was revived from an organization that was nearly bankrupt—out funded 10 to 1 by Republicans—to a robust financing machine that helped propel Democrats to victory in 1982 and enabled them to retain their House majority throughout the Reagan presidency.[17] "We won the battle of the '80s," Coelho boasted. "They [Republicans] were determined they were going to take the House on Reagan's coattails. We have, in effect, destroyed the Reagan impact."[18]

In 1985 Coelho joined the Congressional Hispanic Caucus (CHC) after having been denied admission for unspecified reasons.[19] When reapplying for admission, Coelho emphasized his Portuguese roots and insisted that since Portugal is situated on the Iberian Peninsula (named Hispania by the Romans) many Europeans consider it a Hispanic country. "The dictionary definition of Hispanics includes those from the Iberian Peninsula," Coelho maintained.[20] Coelho's admission to the caucus, the first for a Portuguese American, provided the group with several benefits: his prodigious fundraising; his influential spot on the Agriculture Committee, which could be helpful for immigration measures to protect migrant farm workers; and his district's constituency, which was roughly one-fifth Hispanic.[21]

Many new Democratic Representatives looked to Coelho for support in their campaigns, and those who were elected to the House were indebted to him. In 1987 Coelho tapped into this growing network in an effort to ascend the leadership ladder. He succeeded Thomas Foley of Washington as Democratic Whip, handily winning a vote in the caucus to defeat Charles Rangel of New York and W. G. (Bill) Hefner of North Carolina. This was the first time the No. 3 Democratic leader was elected, rather than appointed.[22] With his election, Coelho became the first Hispanic American in House history to serve in a top party leadership post. Coelho's easy embrace of big-time donations left some observers ill at ease.[23] But Coelho maintained that his work was on the level. "I solve people's problems because I like to solve people's problems," he told the *Los Angeles Times*. "What people are used to in politics are people who deal under the table. I do things out in the open. I am an open book."[24]

The most significant piece of legislation Coelho sponsored was the Americans with Disabilities Act of 1990, which he introduced in the House on May 9, 1989. "The Americans with Disabilities Act provides a clear, comprehensive national mandate for the elimination of discrimination against individuals with disabilities. This mandate is urgently needed by our Nation's 43 million disabled citizens," he stressed.[25] His passion for this legislation stemmed from his experiences as an epileptic and from witnessing discriminatory behavior toward other epileptics. "My epilepsy is what makes me tick," he said.[26] "Discriminatory attitudes hold that you can't employ someone with epilepsy because they may have a seizure on the job, when today the overwhelming majority of people with epilepsy have their physical conditions under control through medication."[27] The act passed the House in May 1990 and was signed into law on July 26 of that year.

Though Coelho excelled at fundraising as chairman of the DCCC, some were uneasy about his financial dealings. *Newsweek* published a story alleging that Coelho had violated House Rules and federal law through his interactions with a savings and loan bank in Texas. The allegations focused on Coelho's use of a yacht he had borrowed from the bank, far exceeding the monetary limit set by House Rules and the contribution limit for federal political action committees. He was also criticized for failing to report a $100,000 junk bond on his financial disclosure forms. After the U.S. Department of Justice initiated an investigation, Coelho determined in May 1989 to resign from the House.[28] "I don't intend to put my party through more turmoil," he said. "And, more importantly, I don't intend to put my family through more turmoil."[29] On June 15, his 47th birthday, Coelho delivered his farewell address to the House. "The generosity of my constituents, and the good will of my colleagues, have enabled me to serve for 25 years: as a staffer, as a Member, as campaign chair, and as majority whip … I thank my colleagues for their friendship, hard work, and dedication to this great country."[30]

After leaving the House, Coelho worked as the head of the American mission to the 1998 Exposition in Lisbon, Portugal. He then managed Vice President Al Gore's 2000 presidential bid, resigning on June 15, 2000. Coelho later served as chairman of the Board of Directors of the Epilepsy Foundation.[31]

FOR FURTHER READING

Biographical Directory of the United States Congress, "Tony Coelho," http://bioguide.congress.gov.

Jackson, Brooks. *Honest Graft: Big Money and the American Political Process* (New York: Knopf, 1988).

MANUSCRIPT COLLECTION

Manuscript Division, Library of Congress (Washington, D.C.). *Oral History*: United States Capitol Historical Society Oral History Collection, 1976–1991, 13 items. Interviewees include Tony Coelho.

NOTES

1 Bob Secter, "Tony Coelho's Dramatic Rise Means a New Style in Democratic Leadership and New Clout for the California Delegation," 11 January 1987, *Los Angeles Times*: 10.

2 Linda Greenhouse, "Anthony L. Coelho," 9 December 1986, *New York Times*: B17.

3 Carmen E. Enciso and Tracy North, *Hispanic Americans in Congress, 1822–1995* (Washington, D.C.: Government Printing Office, 1995): 19; Mark Grossman, *Political Corruption in America: An Encyclopedia of Scandals, Power, and Greed,* vol. 1 (New York: Grey House Publishing, 2008): 84; Secter, "Tony Coelho's Dramatic Rise Means a New Style."

4 Betty Cuniberti, "Epileptic Congressman Finds a New Ministry," 21 November 1982, *Los Angeles Times*: G1; Ruth Shalit, "The Undertaker: Tony Coelho and the Death of the Democrats," *The New Republic* (2 January 1995): 17.

5 Cuniberti, "Epileptic Congressman Finds a New Ministry"; Shalit, "The Undertaker: Tony Coelho and the Death of the Democrats."

6 For more on Sisk's career, see B. F. Sisk, *A Congressional Record: The Memoir of Bernie Sisk* (Fresno, CA: Panorama West, 1980); and Robert L. Peabody, *Leadership in Congress: Stability, Succession, and Change* (Boston: Little, Brown and Company, 1976): 190–204.

7 Brooks Jackson, *Honest Graft: Big Money and the American Political Process* (New York: Alfred A. Knopf, 1988): 31–40; Peabody, *Leadership in Congress: Stability, Succession, and Change*: 190–204.

8 Jackson, *Honest Graft: Big Money and the American Political Process*: 46–47.

9 *Politics in America, 1990* (Washington, D.C.: Congressional Quarterly, Inc., 1989): 141.

10 David Hoffman, "Rep. Coelho: Democrats' Fund-Raiser Extraordinaire," 26 August 1982, *Washington Post*: A2; Ellen Hume, "Central Valley Farmers Face a New Game," 1 June 1978, *Los Angeles Times*: SD3; *Politics in America, 1982* (Washington, D.C.: Congressional Quarterly, Inc., 1981): 120.

11 Ellen Hume, "11 New Congressmen in State: 3 Incumbents Lose, 25% of Delegation Replaced," 9 November 1978, *Los Angeles Times*: B21.

12 "Election Statistics, 1920 to Present," http://history.house.gov/institution/election-statistics/election-statistics.

13 For a full listing of Coelho's committee assignments, see Garrison

Nelson, *Committees in the U.S. Congress, 1947–1992*, vol. 2 (Washington, D.C.: CQ Press, 1994): 175–176.

14 *Congressional Directory, 97th Congress* (Washington, D.C.: Government Printing Office, 1981): 295.

15 Hoffman, "Rep. Coelho: Democrats' Fund-Raiser Extraordinaire"; *Almanac of American Politics, 1982* (Washington, D.C.: Barone & Company, 1981): 119.

16 *Politics in America, 1982*: 119.

17 *Almanac of American Politics, 1990* (Washington, D.C.: National Journal Group, 1989): 118; Helen Dewar and Edward Walsh, "Arkansas Rep. Anthony Succeeds Coelho as Chief Democratic Fund-Raiser," *Washington Post,* 30 January 1987: A4.

18 Secter, "Tony Coelho's Dramatic Rise Means a New Style in Democratic Leadership and New Clout for the California Delegation."

19 Marjorie Hunter and Warren Weaver, Jr., "Washington Talk—Briefing: Señor Coelho," 25 March 1985, *New York Times*: A12.

20 Kenneth Weiss, No Title, 15 April 1985, States News Service.

21 Hunter and Weaver, "Washington Talk—Briefing: Señor Coelho."

22 *Politics in America, 1990*: 139.

23 Ellen Hume, "Freewheeling Rep. Coelho Rising Fast," 29 September 1982, *Los Angeles Times*: B3. "He's such a power broker, and he kind of shows off with it," noted a lobbyist. "He's got one foot in the fast lane and one on a banana peel. If he's not careful, he'll take a big fall."

24 Hume, "Freewheeling Rep. Coelho Rising Fast."

25 *Congressional Record*, House, 100th Cong., 1st sess. (9 May 1989): 8714.

26 Secter, "Tony Coelho's Dramatic Rise Means a New Style in Democratic Leadership."

27 *Congressional Record*, House, 100th Cong., 1st sess. (9 May 1989): 8712.

28 Grossman, *Political Corruption in America*: 85; David LaGesse, "Politicians Flew on Planes of Texas Thrift That Collapsed," 18 June 1987, *The American Banker*.

29 Michael Oreskes, "Coelho to Resign His Seat in House in Face of Inquiry—The No. 3 Democrat: In Surprising Decision He Speaks of Sparing His Party Turmoil," 27 May 1989, *New York Times*: 1.

30 *Congressional Record*, House, 101st Cong., 1st sess. (15 June 1989): 11952. See also Robert Shepard, "Coelho Says Goodbye to the House," 15 June 1989, United Press International; Steven Komarow, "Saying Goodbye to Congress with a Speech and a Bash,"15 June 1989, Associated Press.

31 Grossman, *Political Corruption in America*: 85–86.

Matthew G. Martínez
1929–2011

UNITED STATES REPRESENTATIVE
DEMOCRAT FROM CALIFORNIA 1982–2000
REPUBLICAN FROM CALIFORNIA 2000–2001

Matthew Martínez, whose career took him from East Los Angeles to Washington, won a special election to the U.S. House and later unseated a longtime incumbent, serving a total of 10 terms in Congress. Along the way, Martínez worked to address the education and labor concerns of his working-class district. "You know, a poor little ghetto kid from East Los Angeles standing in the hallowed halls of Congress—that's got to be the American Dream," Martínez said shortly after he was elected to the U.S. House.[1]

One of nine children born to Matthew and Helen Martínez, Matthew Gilbert (Marty) Martínez was born February 14, 1929, in Walsenburg, Colorado. His father was a Texas-born coal miner of Mexican heritage. The family moved to East Los Angeles when Martínez was a year old.[2] He attended local public schools and later told the *New York Times* he left home at age 12 because his mother beat him. "I ran away from home, hid out, bummed off friends, stole milk and bread, and learned how to survive," he said.[3] An older brother took him in and convinced him to return to school, and Martínez eventually graduated from Los Angeles' Roosevelt High School. From 1947 to 1950, he served in the U.S. Marine Corps, attaining the rank of private first class. In 1956, using the GI Bill to study business, he earned a certificate of competence from the Los Angeles Trade Technical School. Martínez married Elvira Yorba, and they raised five children: Matthew, Diane, Susan, Michael, and Carol Ann.[4] He opened a furniture upholstery shop in the 1950s, moving the business from Hollywood to Monterey Park in the Eastern Los Angeles suburbs. He also worked as a building contractor. Later, Martínez and his wife separated for many years, divorcing in the early 2000s. Martínez subsequently married Maxine Grant.[5]

Martínez's political career began at a Los Angeles hamburger stand, where he gathered with neighbors to discuss issues affecting Monterey Park. He was a member of the local Rotary Club, and during his years as a business owner he switched his political affiliation from Democratic to Republican. From 1971 to 1974, he served on the Monterey Park planning committee and embarked on a career in elective politics. Martínez changed his affiliation back to the Democratic Party shortly after winning a seat on the Monterey Park city council. He served on the council for six consecutive years, two of them (1974–1975) as mayor of Monterey Park. In 1977 he was appointed to the California Solid Waste Management Board.

In 1980 Martínez launched an uphill campaign against well-regarded California assemblyman Jack Fenton, an incumbent Democrat who represented a swath of suburbs east of Los Angeles for nearly two decades. Martínez, who maintained that Fenton had failed to keep in touch with the changing district, received an unexpected boost weeks before the Democratic primary; California Assemblyman Howard L. Berman of Los Angeles threw his support behind Martínez in a campaign blitz that propelled him to victory.[6] In the general election, Martínez prevailed with 72 percent of the vote in the heavily Democratic district.[7]

If Los Angeles' political machine propelled him into office, Martínez's decision to work with local Hispanic-American activists kept him there. He regained his proficiency in Spanish, which he had spoken as a child but abandoned because the Los Angeles public schools discouraged bilingualism.[8] At times Martínez was impatient with activists who worked outside the established political system. As a freshman state assemblyman, for instance, he assailed Californios for Fair Representation—a group of younger Latino activists pushing to create majority-Hispanic districts—for "a

Image courtesy of the National Archives and Records Administration

1st SESSION
1972
1st SESSION
1951
1st SESSION
1973
2d SESSION
1972
LIBRARY
H. of R.
13061-3
13017-3
13051-5
12971-1
A
HOUSE
REPORTS
Vol. 1-7
MISCELLANEOUS
PUBLIC
VII
92d CONGRESS
2d SESSION
1972
SENATE
REPORTS
UNITED STATES
REPORTS
VOL. 347
OCT. TERM 1953
11543
HOUSE
DOCUMENTS
9938
PT. 3
6
1954

total lack of sophistication" after they walked out of a reapportionment hearing in Sacramento.[9]

During his brief stint in the California assembly, Martínez compiled a notable record, serving on the agriculture and local government committees. He authored bills to promote safeguards for oil recycling and pharmacy prescriptions; both were signed into law. He also helped push through a measure reinvigorating a plan for the long-stalled completion of the Long Beach Freeway and promoted measures to curb gang violence.[10]

In 1982, when six-term Democratic incumbent U.S. Representative George E. Danielson resigned after being appointed to a state appellate court, Martínez declared his candidacy for the seat. Danielson, who had served five years as Deputy Majority Whip in the U.S. House, represented a district that overlapped a large section of Martínez's assembly district. Meanwhile, a redistricting plan backed by the leader of California's delegation in the U.S. House, Phil Burton of San Francisco, had created two new districts east of Los Angeles—California's 30th and 34th Districts—with the intention of getting more Hispanics elected to Congress. The new 30th District ran from the foothills of the San Gabriel Mountains in its far northeastern corner, swept southwestward along the valley east of Los Angeles, and enveloped towns including Alhambra, Montebello, Monterey Park, Bell Gardens, and El Monte. Some 54 percent of the population was of Hispanic descent, and the district had a healthy ratio of registered Democrats (nearly two to one). With his wide name recognition, Martínez enjoyed the support of many of the state's leading Hispanic politicians and civic organizations.[11]

Martínez faced an onslaught of opponents in the June 8 Democratic primary to decide the candidate for both the special election to fill the rest of Danielson's term as well as for the 1982 general election. Although former Danielson aide Dennis S. Kazarian came within roughly 400 votes of defeating him in the primary, Martínez prevailed before facing Republican lawyer Ralph R. Ramirez in the special election, which would be based on the old district boundaries. With the low voter turnout typical of special elections, Martínez repelled Ramirez's challenge by a margin of less than 1,000 votes—winning 51 to 49 percent in the July 13 contest. He was sworn in as a Member of the 97th Congress (1981–1983) on July 15, 1982, and was assigned to the Veterans' Affairs and the Education and Labor Committees.[12]

The redistricting plan that gave Martínez a seat in the 97th Congress ensured that he would have a difficult time returning in the 98th Congress (1983–1985). Part of Burton's plan to boost the number of Latino candidates for Congress involved disassembling the district of his longtime political foe Republican Representative John H. Rousselot, a one-time John Birch Society member and an eight-term House veteran. With his old district redrawn, Rousselot was faced with taking on a friend and fellow Republican in a neighboring district or challenging the up-and-coming Martínez.[13] Minutes after Martínez was sworn into the House on July 15, 1982, Rousselot challenged him to a series of 16 debates in the major towns in the new district. Martínez demurred, saying, "Rousselot's whole tactic is to bulldoze somebody and buffalo them, and he started in right away. I've got a surprise for him. He's going to know what it's like to be bowled over."[14]

Martínez was a formidable opponent, strolling through the precincts handing out campaign literature while portraying Rousselot as a carpetbagger who was unfamiliar with most of the district. Martínez was "rough around the edges" in the words of a Democratic activist, occasionally offering blunt assessments that his campaign staff scrambled to qualify.[15] But while Rousselot emphasized his experience and his service to the district's many Hispanic voters—being photographed with Los Angeles Dodgers ace pitcher Fernando Valenzuela and spending campaign funds for Spanish lessons—Martínez played down ethnic politics. "I'm not a Hispanic candidate," he said. "I'm an American candidate."[16]

To match Rousselot's spending during the campaign, Martínez again secured the backing of California's Democratic machine alongside party superstars like Senator Edward Kennedy of Massachusetts.[17] The race centered on Social Security reform, and Martínez attacked Rousselot for advocating cost-cutting measures during a weak economy. The high unemployment rate early in the Ronald W. Reagan administration made Rousselot's task even more difficult. Martínez prevailed 54 to 46 percent on Election Day as California Democrats picked up six new seats; overall, Democrats added 27 seats to their already solid House majority. In the 1984 primary, Martínez beat back a challenge by Gladys C. Danielson—the wife of the previous Representative of the 30th District—and defeated Republican Richard Gomez, 52 to 43 percent, with a third-party candidate taking the remaining 5 percent of the vote. In subsequent general elections he won by approximately 60 percentage points.[18]

Martínez left the Veterans' Affairs Committee after one term but retained his post on the Education and Labor Committee for his entire House career. He served as chairman of its Subcommittee on Employment Opportunities from the 99th through the 101st Congresses (1985–1991). He served as chairman of the Human Resources Subcommittee for the 102nd and 103rd Congresses (1991–1995) until Republicans gained the majority after the 1994 elections. He also served at various times on the Committees on Small Business, Government Operations, Foreign Affairs, and Transportation and Infrastructure as well as on the Select Committee on Children, Youth and Families. Additionally, he joined the Congressional Hispanic Caucus and served as its chairman for a portion of the 99th Congress (1985–1987).[19]

Throughout his career, Martínez was a strong advocate of the nation's public schools. In 1987 he strenuously opposed a proposal to divert funds for bilingual education to other programs for non–native English speakers, such as immersion. "You shouldn't dilute the bilingual education budget for what should be another federal program," he insisted.[20] "I am an immersion product. Fifty percent of students who started with me failed by the time they were in ninth or tenth grade."[21] Martínez was among the minority opposition to a 1997 effort by Republicans to authorize tuition vouchers to help low-income parents send their children to private schools. "Just like we abandoned the poor parts of our cities … this bill will leave our public schools in ruin in search of a panacea for just a few," he declared.[22]

Martínez also advocated for America's working class. In the 99th and 100th Congresses, he drafted legislation that prohibited private employers from making lie detector tests a condition for employment. Calling this practice "voodoo craft," Martínez claimed lie detectors had become "judge and jury and God in determining workers' fate."[23] The measure became law in 1988. Martínez also opposed a proposal to permit a subminimum training wage for minority groups and youth, characterizing this as "a way to get around paying the minimum wage to minorities and those who are at the very bottom of the employment ladder."[24] After the Republicans gained the House majority in 1995, he argued for a 90 cent increase in the minimum wage and opposed legislation that would have allowed businesses to save money by offering compensatory time instead of overtime pay.[25]

He also opposed the Teamwork for Employees and Managers (TEAM) Act because of a provision that would have undercut the power of labor unions, and his concern for the American worker led him to vote against the passage of the North American Free Trade Agreement (NAFTA) in 1993.[26] Martínez asserted, "Free trade is the best course for America as we try to maintain our economic leadership," but he refused to support NAFTA because he believed it lacked provisions to retain American jobs and protect American workers.[27] Martínez was one of 21 Representatives from the California congressional delegation to vote against the measure.

Martínez championed several significant pieces of legislation in the early 1990s. He sponsored the reauthorization of the Older Americans Act (first passed in 1965) in the 102nd Congress, including sustained funding for Meals on Wheels and the Administration on Aging, which implemented the act's programs.[28] In the 103rd Congress, he served as floor manager for the passage of H.R. 5194, to reauthorize the Juvenile Justice and Delinquency Prevention Act (first passed in 1974). The bill also created new programs for gang intervention and established the Runaway and Homeless Youth Act, which provided temporary shelter, support services, and counseling for "those young people, who have been cast off in a sea of distrust and exploitation."[29] He was the prime sponsor of the National Community Service Act (P.L. 103-82)—a priority of the William J. (Bill) Clinton administration—which offered educational incentives for community service and created AmeriCorps, a network of service-oriented programs modeled on the Civilian Conservation Corps of Martínez's youth.[30] "This [program provides] the opportunity for young people to earn and learn—to develop a sense of community and have confidence in themselves and others," he said.[31] Though pared down from the original version, the bill was signed into law by President Clinton on September 21, 1993.[32]

Usually a reliable liberal vote on economic and social issues, Martínez diverged from his party in several key areas. A supporter of abortion rights, he advocated allowing privately funded abortions at overseas military hospitals and allowing federal employee health plans to pay for abortions. He also supported requiring states to fund abortions through Medicaid for victims of rape or incest or to save a woman's life. [33] However, he supported a ban on "partial-birth" abortion and was one of 70 Democrats to vote to override Clinton's veto of the legislation. As a member of the National Rifle Association, he opposed passage of the Brady Bill—which required a five-day waiting period before the purchase of a handgun—but supported the 1994 assault weapons ban.[34] He also adopted a conservative position on the environment, opposing U.S. involvement in the U.N. conservation program while criticizing the Environmental Protection Agency for overregulation.[35]

In 2000 Martínez was challenged by state senator Hilda Solis, whose district overlapped with roughly 97 percent of his. Solis called Martínez's votes on abortion, gun control, and environmental regulations "dramatically out of touch."[36] She received endorsements from EMILY's list—a group dedicated to electing pro-choice women to Congress—and from significant labor organizations.[37] "They don't mean a damn thing," Martínez said of Solis' endoresements. "When I first ran for state Assembly in 1980, every single union endorsed the incumbent and I still won."[38] Still, Solis outraised Martínez four to one, and chipped away at his political backing, winning the support of many in California's congressional delegation.[39] Others remained neutral.[40] Martínez garnered just 28.5 percent of the primary vote to Solis's 62.2 percent.[41]

In his remaining months in the House, Martínez aligned himself with Republicans, opposing the Democrats on many votes. On July 27, 2000, Martínez formally switched political parties. "I didn't leave the Democrat Party, the Democratic Party left me," he said.[42] "I no l onger want to be part of a party where loyalty is not rewarded with support."[43] Noting that he agreed with many Republican positions, including tax cut proposals, he said "Republicans were more understanding of American values."[44] Despite vowing to run as a Republican in 2002, Martínez returned to private life.[45] He died in Fredericksburg, Virginia, on October 15, 2011.

FOR FURTHER READING

Biographical Directory of the United States Congress, "Matthew G. Martínez," http://bioguide.congress.gov.

NOTES

1 Kristina Lindgren, "Martinez Wins 30th District Race: Becomes 3rd California Latino Elected to Sit in U.S. House," 15 July 1982, *Los Angeles Times*: A28.

2 Dennis Hevesi, "Matthew G. Martinez, 82, Ex-Democratic Lawmaker," 27 October 2011, *New York Times*: A29; William McPhillips, "'Used to Achieving': Martinez Learning Fast in Assembly," 23 August 1981, *Los Angeles Times*: SG1.

3 Nadine Brozen, "Teens at the Covenant House Are Ready to Talk about Their Earlier Travails," 11 July 1992, *New York Times*: 20.

4 "Matthew Gilbert Martinez," *Marquis Who's Who, 2003*. On the GI Bill, see McPhillips, "'Used to Achieving': Martinez Learning Fast in Assembly."

5 T. Rees Shapiro, "California Congressman Left Democrats for GOP," 21 October 2011, *Washington Post*: B6.

6 McPhillips, "'Used to Achieving': Martinez Learning Fast in Assembly."

7 See, for example, Alan Maltun, "Democrat Martinez's Political Rise Is Fast," 24 October 1982, *Los Angeles Times*: SE1. Berman's support was part of a larger effort to unseat Assembly Speaker Leo T. McCarthy of San Francisco. Fenton had long been a McCarthy supporter in the state assembly. A portion of Martinez's constituency resented the fact that he had unseated the well-regarded Fenton,

and nurtured his political machine in the process.

8 McPhillips, "'Used to Achieving': Martinez Learning Fast in Assembly."

9 Kenneth Reich and Henry Mendoza, "Latinos Push for Political Power: But Even with 19% of State Population, Task Remains Difficult," 17 August 1981, *Los Angeles Times*: B3.

10 See, for example, Maltum, "Democrat Martinez's Political Rise Is Fast"; McPhillips, "'Used to Achieving': Martinez Learning Fast in Assembly."

11 *Almanac of American Politics, 1984* (Washington, D.C.: National Journal, Inc., 1983) 146–147; Kristina Lindgren, "Assemblyman Martinez Will Run for Congress," 11 February 1982, *Los Angeles Times*: LB1.

12 *Congressional Record,* House, 97th Cong., 2nd sess. (19 August 1982): 22248. During Martínez's tenure, the name of the Education and Labor Committee was changed to Economic and Educational Opportunities (1995–1997) and Education and the Workforce (1997–2007).

13 For more on the effects of redistricting in Southern California, see Ellen Hume, "Plan to Ensure Congress Seat for Latino May Be Backfiring," 18 April 1982, *Los Angeles Times*: B1.

14 Kristina Lindgren, "Martinez Sworn In, Gets First Challenge," 18 July 1982, *Los Angeles Times*: SG9.

15 Maltun, "Democrat Martinez's Political Rise Is Fast"; Alan Maltun, "Martinez–Rousselot Match Lives Up to Its Billing," 3 October 1982, *Los Angeles* Times: SE1.

16 Jay Mathews, "A Gringo's Gringo Moves His Border South," 15 October 1982, *Washington Post*: A5. According to this news report, Rousselot also joined the Hispanic Caucus, apparently as a dues-paying (but nonvoting) associate member.

17 For revised spending totals see, *Almanac of American Politics, 1986* (Washington, D.C.: National Journal Inc., 1985): 172. For campaign coverage and issues, see for example, Robert J. Gore, "Bitter Campaign by Congressmen Dominates Races," 31 October 1982, *Los Angeles Times*: SE1; Maltun, "Martinez–Rousselot Match Lives Up to Its Billing"; Alan Maltun, "Candidates Debate Jobless Issue: Martinez, Rousselot Also Clash over Social Security," 17 October 1982, *Los Angeles Times*: SG1; Ellen Hume, "Scramble for Congress Grows Madder," 24 May 1982, *Los Angeles Times*: B3.

18 *Politics in America, 1998* (Washington, D.C.: Congressional Quarterly Inc., 1997): 176; Tim Curran, "Rep. Martinez Will Run for L.A. Supervisor; Rep. Hopkins to Join Race for Ky. Governor," 19 November 1990, *Roll Call*: n.p.; Tim Curran, "Martinez Pulls Out of Contest for L.A. Board of Supervisors," 29 November 1990, *Roll Call*: n.p. Election results in several *Democratic primaries* indicated Martínez might be vulnerable to a strong primary challenger. He went from winning the 1986 primary with 81 percent to securing the 1994 nomination with only 55 percent. Nonetheless, he was unopposed in 1996 and won the 1998 primary with 67 percent of the vote.

19 *Almanac of American Politics, 1988–1996* (Washington, D.C.: National Journal Group, Inc., 1987–1995). During his career, the name of the Government Operations Committee was changed to Government Reform and Oversight (1995–1999) and Government Reform (1999–2001); Foreign Affairs was changed to International Relations (1995–2007).

20 Jill Lawrence, "Specialists Oppose Administration Plan to Ease Requirements," 24 March 1987, Associated Press.

21 *Politics in America, 2000* (Washington, D.C.: Congressional Quarterly, Inc., 1999): 169; *Politics in America, 1998*: 174.

22 Rene Sanchez, "House Votes against Bill to Provide School Vouchers," 5 November 1997, *Washington Post*: A8. Martínez was later appointed by Democratic Leader Richard Gephardt to an 18-member National Educational Goals Panel to monitor progress on education goals initially set by President George H. W. Bush and the nation's governors. See *Politics in America, 2000*: 169.

23 *Congressional Record*, House, 99th Cong., 2nd sess. (12 March 1986): 4515–4516; Larry Margasak, "House Votes to Restrict Lie-Detector Use," 12 March 1986, Associated Press.

24 *Politics in America, 1990* (Washington, D.C.: Congressional Quarterly, Inc., 1989): 185; Gene Grabowski, "Rite of Summer: Talk in Congress about Subminimum Wage for Teens," 27 May 1985, Associated Press.

25 *Politics in America, 1998*: 175.

26 Ibid; David R. Sands, "Worker-Participation Bill Tests Unions' Clout," 9 February 1995, *Washington Times*: B7.

27 *Congressional Record,* House, 103rd Cong., 1st sess. (16 November 1993): 29319.

28 *Congressional Record*, House, 102nd Cong., 1st sess. (26 June 1991): 16511; *Congressional Record*, House, 102nd Cong., 1st sess. (12 September 1991): H6468–6469; *Congressional Record*, House, 102nd Cong., 2nd sess. (9 April 1992): H2629–H2630; *Congressional Record*, House, 102nd Cong., 2nd sess. (22 September 1992): H9000.

29 *Congressional Record*, House, 102nd Cong., 2nd sess. (3 August 1992): H7246; *Almanac of American Politics, 1994* (Washington, D.C.: National Journal Group, Inc., 1993): 165; *Almanac of American Politics, 1998* (Washington, D.C.: National Journal Group, Inc., 1997): 165.

30 *Almanac of American Politics, 1996* (Washington, D.C.: National Journal Group, Inc., 1995): 174.

31 *Congressional Record,* House, 103rd Cong., 1st sess. (13 July 1993): 15434. See also *Congressional Record,* House, 103rd Cong., 1st sess. (13 July 1993): H4532–4533; *Congressional Record,* House, 103rd Cong., 1st sess. (20 May 1993): E1325.

32 "National Service Paired with Student Aid," *CQ Almanac, 1993* (Washington, D.C.: Congressional Quarterly, Inc., 1994): 400–404.

33 *Politics in America, 1998*: 174.

34 Ibid.

35 *Politics in America, 2000*: 170.

36 John Mercurio, "Martinez's Last Stand? Primary Threat Divides Hispanics, Could End 20-Year House Career," 20 January 2000, *Roll Call*: n.p.

37 Mary Lynn Jones, "Rep. Martinez Facing Tough Primary in Los Angeles CD," 1 March 2000, *The Hill*: 13.

38 Richard Simon and Antonio Olivo, "Two Incumbent Congressmen Facing Tough Challenges; 31st District: For Martinez, the Fight Is in the Primary—and in the Family," 23 February 2000, *Los Angeles Times*: B1.

39 Jones, "Rep. Martinez Facing Tough Primary in Los Angeles CD"; *Almanac of American Politics, 2002* (Washington, D.C.: National Journal Group, Inc., 2001): 242; John Mercurio, "California Feinstein Won't Back Martinez in Primary," 24 January 2000, *Roll Call*; Simon and Olivo, "Two Incumbent Congressmen Facing Tough Challenges."

40 Simon and Olivo, "Two Incumbent Congressmen Facing Tough Challenges"; Mercurio, "California Feinstein Won't Back Martinez in Primary."

41 *Politics in America, 2002* (Washington, D.C.: Congressional Quarterly, Inc., 2001): 125.

42 "Nicholson Applauds Rep. Martinez's Move, 478th Elected Official to Flee Clinton/Gore Party," 27 July 2000, PR Newswire.

43 "Martinez Joins GOP," 27 July 2000, *Bulletin's Frontrunner*.

44 "Martinez Joins GOP."

45 Ben Pershing, "Martinez Gets Star Treatment," 7 August 2000, *Roll Call*.

"NO POLITICIAN, NO MATTER WHAT HE TELLS YOU, KNOWS EVERYTHING. THE ONLY THING HE CAN DO IS KEEP AN OPEN MIND AND LEARN."

Matthew G. Martínez
Los Angeles Times, October 24, 1982

Solomon P. Ortiz
1937–

UNITED STATES REPRESENTATIVE 1983–2011
DEMOCRAT FROM TEXAS

After arriving in Washington in 1982, Solomon P. Ortiz joked that his "sense of direction" had become his biggest "weakness." "I went in one building, went out a different way and had to walk around the block three times before I figured out where I was," he said. Despite at first feeling "overwhelmed by the big buildings, the marble, the pillars and the responsibility," Ortiz earned a reputation as a moderate Democrat who was comfortable working behind the scenes and as a tireless champion of his district in southeast Texas. His ability to voice local concerns in national and international conversations was a staple of his legislative style in the House. "Here," he said shortly before taking the oath of office, "your vote may have an impact worldwide."[1]

Solomon Ortiz's path to the House began in Robstown, Texas, known as the "Biggest Little Town" in the state.[2] The eldest son of migrant workers, he was born on June 3, 1937.[3] His family struggled to make ends meet, and after his father died he left Robstown Public High School to work as a printer's aide at the *Robstown Record*.[4] In 1960 he enlisted in the U.S. Army and earned his general equivalency degree. The military sent Ortiz to France, where he learned the language and worked with the military police. After leaving the Army, Ortiz ran for the office of county constable back in Nueces, Texas, and won in an upset.[5] It was the year before Congress passed the Voting Rights Act, and America's electoral system was still segregated. "My mother took out a $1,000 loan—a fortune for a migrant family in 1964—to bankroll my first campaign," Ortiz remembered. "The money was mostly to help offset the poll tax for Hispanic voters whose priority was putting food on the table for their families."[6] After three years in the constable's office, Ortiz won election as Nueces County commissioner, becoming the first Hispanic American to sit on the county board. He remained in the commissioner's office until 1976, when he was elected the first Hispanic sheriff in county history.[7] During his early political career, Ortiz attended Del Mar College from 1965 to 1967.[8] Ortiz and his wife, Irme Roldan, were married in 1970 and had two children together, Yvette and Solomon, Jr., but the marriage ended in divorce.[9]

After the 1980 Census, Texas picked up three seats in the U.S. House.[10] One of the new districts, the 27th, had been drawn to include the region stretching from Corpus Christi south along the Gulf Coast to the city of Brownsville at the U.S.-Mexico border. Many of the district's residents were Hispanic middle-of-the-road Democrats, and after federal officials approved Texas' new federal congressional map in 1982, Ortiz emerged early in the race as a front-runner for the new House seat.[11]

He resigned from the sheriff's office to campaign full-time, and with 17 years' experience in local and county politics, he squeaked out a victory in the five-candidate Democratic primary. In the buildup to the general election, Ortiz, who was "very popular in South Texas," rode a wave of local support.[12] "If he's not elected, it may be a long time before another Mexican-American has a chance to be elected to Congress," worried one supporter.[13] The health of the U.S. economy weighed heavily on the race. Ortiz breezed through the general election; the district's Democratic majority gave him a 30,000-vote victory, and he took 64 percent of the total vote.[14] "People want to work and they can't find jobs so they turned to the Democrats for help," Ortiz said after the election.[15] Over the next 13 election cycles, Ortiz faced little opposition, and he ran unopposed in the general elections of 1986, 1988, and 1990. It was not until 1996 that he again faced opposition in the Democratic primary.[16]

From his first day in office, Ortiz seemed to have kept one foot planted firmly in his district. The Democratic

Collection of the U.S. House of Representatives, Photography Collection

leadership assigned him to the Armed Services and the Merchant Marine and Fisheries Committees to support Ortiz as he worked on behalf of the numerous military bases and vital fishing communities in the 27th District. In the winter of 1983 he joined the Select Committee on Narcotics Abuse and Control and remained on the panel until the House disbanded it a decade later. When the House abolished the Merchant Marine and Fisheries Committee in the early 1990s, Ortiz transferred to the Resources Committee. In the 111th Congress (2009–2011), he joined the Transportation and Infrastructure Committee.[17]

Never having served as a legislator, Ortiz felt out of place initially; Cold War arms policy usually "didn't matter to a sheriff," he said in 1982. "A sheriff puts in jail a person violating the law."[18] As a U.S. Representative, however, Ortiz was responsible for creating laws instead of enforcing them.

The junior Member from Texas quickly earned areputation as a centrist, a "Democratic fence-sitter," according to the *Wall Street Journal*. He often went out on a limb for his district, appealing to foreign governments and businesses to protect the interests of his constituents, especially those in the shrimp industry.[19] Because his district shared a border with Mexico, Ortiz had a unique perspective on immigration and on America's economic relationship with Latin America. In 1986, for instance, while the House and Senate considered reforms to the country's immigration policy, Ortiz, whose district had become a major entry point into the United States, voted for a measure that other Hispanic Representatives deemed too strict arguing that later attempts to reform immigration policy might result in an even harsher bill.[20] When those attempts occurred, in the mid-1990s, Ortiz implored his colleagues not to lose sight of the broader national picture: "The greatest danger to an immigration debate in this country is the merging and confusing of issues concerning legal and illegal immigration.... As [a] Representative of a border district, I am uniquely aware of the burden that illegal immigration poses on local communities."[21] He continued to champion immigration reform over the years, with the caveat that enforcing and strengthening America's borders needed to be done "in a responsible way."[22]

Ortiz made it a point to learn his colleagues' names and positions, and his personality endeared him to Democrats and Republicans alike, according to one of his closest aides.[23] He served as co-chairman of the House Border Caucus, and at the start the 102nd Congress (1991–1993) he was elected chairman of the Congressional Hispanic Caucus (CHC), a major assignment since Hispanic voters were becoming increasingly powerful nationwide.[24] The 1992 election, which Ortiz won by 13 percent, was a watershed year for minority representation. "I think we'll have a stronger voice, a louder voice," he said. Ortiz was a bridge builder; he worked to shape partnerships with non-Hispanic Members and other caucuses, especially those with similar legislative concerns. Calling the CHC's platform "an American agenda," he noted, "The problems we face as Hispanics will be the same—housing, jobs and health care."[25]

Despite his growing national profile, Ortiz's primary concern was the interests of his district. By 1993, Ortiz had accrued enough seniority to be named chairman of the Merchant Marine and Fisheries Committee's Subcommittee on Oceanography, Gulf of Mexico, and the Outer Continental Shelf. That year he also secured funding for military bases along the Gulf in exchange for supporting President William J. (Bill) Clinton's national budget—another testament to his growing influence.[26] He pushed back against later attempts by officials in the Clinton administration to privatize defense projects in his district and opposed a plan that would have required a hefty deposit for travel to and from Mexico.[27] By his 1996 campaign, Ortiz assessed his congressional tenure as "productive and effective," emphasizing his ability to steer new jobs to the 27th District while protecting existing industry.[28] After 14 years in the House, Ortiz remained committed to the aspirations he had expressed as a Member-elect. "We have great responsibilities here," he said in 1997. "I just hope ... we can focus on the issues that are good 0for America and my constituents."[29]

In 1992, Ortiz began a legislative battle that lasted nearly six years. The discovery that babies in South Texas

were being born with a high incidence of anencephaly, the failure of part or all of the brain to develop, prompted repeated investigations and underscored the need for more medical research. Though Ortiz had support in the CHC and in the Senate, the Birth Defects Prevention Act of 1992 (H.R. 5531), which he introduced on July 1, never made it out of committee.[30] In mid-March 1997, bolstered by more than 160 co-sponsors, Ortiz introduced his bill again (H.R. 1114), seven days after the Republicans introduced companion legislation in the Senate (S. 419). The measure provided for the creation of medical centers to study regional birth defects; the findings would be centralized in a national clearinghouse managed by the Center for Disease Control. Because the Senate passed its version of the bill in only four months, House leadership tabled Ortiz's measure and moved forward with the Senate's language. The Texas lawmaker's response was typical. "I don't care about credit," he reportedly said. "The important thing is to get the bill passed."[31] In a testament to Ortiz's leadership, the House voted 405 to 2 in favor of the Birth Defects Prevention Act, which was signed into law April 21, 1998.[32]

Ortiz had always looked out for the military personnel in his district, but veterans' issues and the state of America's armed forces became major priorities toward the end of his House career. He fought for better health care, support, training, equipment, and services for the military.[33] "The soldiers we send forth in today's war on terrorism are tomorrow's veterans," Ortiz said in 2003. "As liberty must be defended, the population of veterans in the United States and south Texas will continue to grow," making it incumbent upon the U.S. Congress to create and maintain an infrastructure to support future generations of military personnel.[34] When the Democrats regained control of the House in 2009, Ortiz became chairman of the Armed Services Committee's Readiness Subcommittee.

In 2010, Ortiz lost his re-election bid to Corpus Christi Republican Blake Farenthold. Ortiz ran on the strength of his productivity in the House, but the struggling economy and anti-incumbent sentiment sweeping the country that year made for a grueling campaign. Although Election Day results indicated that Ortiz had lost by only 800 votes, a recount, which took nearly three weeks, failed to give him the lead.[35]

During his 28 years in the House, Ortiz tended to keep a low profile, shying away from the limelight. But as one colleague noted, he "fought tirelessly to bring jobs and enhance the quality of life for residents of the Bay of Corpus Christi to the international border with Mexico."[36] Late in 2007 on the House Floor, Ortiz reflected on his upbringing and its effect on his political career. "It was in Robstown where my mother taught me my most important lesson: to always serve the community that gave you so many opportunities growing up," he said. "To whom much is given, much is expected."[37] After leaving the House, Ortiz returned to South Texas.

FOR FURTHER READING

Biographical Directory of the United States Congress, "Solomon P. Ortiz," http://bioguide.congress.gov.

Ortiz, Solomon P. "America's Third World: Colonias," *State Government News* 32 (January 1989): 20–22.

NOTES

1 Betty Cuniberti, "Orientation for Congress' New Members," 10 December 1982, *Los Angeles Times*: J1.

2 *Congressional Record*, House, 110th Cong., 1st sess. (11 December 2007): H15244.

3 Based on scattered state and federal records, it appears that Ortiz's parents were named Jose Ortiz and Feliciana Ocha. See "Salomon Porfirio Ortiz," *Texas Birth Index, 1903–1997*, Texas Department of State Health Services, Roll number 1937–0006, Library of Congress, Washington, D.C., http://search.ancestrylibrary.com (accessed 2 February 2012). See also *Fifteenth Census of the United States, 1930*, Robstown, Nueces, Texas, Roll 2381, page 37B, Library of Congress, Washington, D.C., http://search.ancestrylibrary.com (accessed 2 February 2012).

4 *Congressional Record*, House, 110th Cong., 1st sess. (11 December 2007): H15244.

5 "Arena Profile: Rep. Solomon Ortiz," *politico.com*, http://www.politico.com/arena/bio/rep_solomon_ortiz.html (accessed 23 February 2012); *Politics in America, 1994* (Washington, D.C.: Congressional Quarterly, Inc., 1993): 1528.

6 *Congressional Record*, House, 109th Cong., 2nd sess. (13 July 2006): H5174.

7 *Biographical Directory of the United States Congress*, "Solomon P. Ortiz," http://bioguide.congress.gov; *Politics in America, 1990* (Washington, D.C.: Congressional Quarterly, Inc., 1989): 1504.

8 *Biographical Directory of the United States Congress*, "Solomon P. Ortiz," http://bioguide.congress.gov.

9 According to state records, Ortiz and his wife were married on April 11, 1970. He filed for divorce on August 3, 1979. See *Texas Divorce Index, 1968–2002*, Texas Department of State Health Services, http://search.ancestrylibrary.com (accessed 2 February 2012).

10 John Herbers, "Minority Group Choices Pivotal in Some Contests," 1 November 1982, *New York Times*: D14.

11 *Politics in America, 1990*: 1504.

12 As quoted in Bob Ramsdell, "Police Union Picks Luby over Ortiz," 25 September 1982, *Corpus Christi Caller*: A1. See also Darla Morgan, "Demos Gather Here for Last-Minute Rally," 1 November 1982, *Corpus Christi Caller*: B1; Darla Morgan, "Large Turnout Sends Ortiz to Congress," 3 November 1982, *Corpus Christi Caller*: A1.

13 Morgan, "Demos Gather Here for Last-Minute Rally."

14 "Election Statistics, 1920 to Present," http://history.house.gov/institution/election-statistics/election-statistics.

15 Morgan, "Large Turnout Sends Ortiz to Congress."

16 "Election Statistics, 1920 to Present," http://history.house.gov/institution/election-statistics/election-statistics; Stefani Scott, "Veteran U.S. Rep. Solomon Ortiz Is Facing," 3 March 1996, *San Antonio Express-News*: B2.

17 See Garrison Nelson, *Committees in the U.S. Congress, 1947 to 1992*, vol. 2 (Washington, D.C.: CQ Press, 1994): 679; Garrison Nelson and Charles Stewart III, *Committees in the U.S. Congress, 1993–2010* (Washington, D.C.: CQ Press, 2011): 877. In 1995 the Armed Services Committee was renamed the Committee on National Security, and in 1999 it was renamed the Committee on Armed Services. The Resources Committee was renamed the Committee on Natural Resources in the 110th Congress (2007–2009).

18 Cuniberti, "Orientation for Congress' New Members."

19 Jackie Calmes, "The Clinton Tax Package: Hard Sell Is Finished, Now the Political Battle Is Due," 28 May 1993, *Wall Street Journal*: A4; Bryan Burrough, "Struggling South Texas Shrimpers Invade Mexican Waters in Search of Better Catch," 5 October 1984, *New York Times*: 35; "Arena Profile: Rep. Solomon Ortiz," *politico.com*, http://www.politico.com/arena/bio/rep_solomon_ortiz.html (accessed 23 February 2012); Lena Sun, "Congressional Democrats Tell China to Act on Rights of Face Stricture," 1 December 1992, *Washington Post*: A31.

20 Robert Pears, "Conferees on Bill on Immigration Pressing to Reconcile Differences," 11 October 1986, *New York Times*: 9; Peter Applebome, "Judge Halts Rule Stranding Aliens in Rio Grande Valley," 10 January 1989, *New York Times*: A14.

21 *Congressional Record*, House, 104th Cong., 2nd sess. (21 March 1996): H2602.

22 *Congressional Record*, House, 106th Cong., 2nd sess. (17 May 2000): H3275–H3276.

23 Liam Callanan, "Face Value," 9 February 1992, *Washington Post*: M7; *Politics in America, 2002* (Washington, D.C.: Congressional Quarterly, Inc., 2003): 1008.

24 On the Border Caucus, see *Congressional Record*, House, 107th Cong., 2nd sess. (7 May 2002): H2142.

25 Quotations are from Kenneth J. Cooper, "Congress's Hispanic Membership Likely to Grow 50% for Next Term," 3 October 1992, *Washington Post*: A11. See also Jonathan Moore, "Hispanics in Congress Begin to Find Their Voice," 15 March 1992, *Houston Chronicle*: A28; Richard Wolf, "House Remapping Benefits Minorities, Women and GOP," 8 June 1992, *USA Today*: A8; Alan K. Ota, "Hispanics on Verge of Making Political Presence Known," 16 August 1992, *Sunday Oregonian*: A16; Ben Johnson, "Congressional Results Mean Added Clout for Blacks, Hispanics," 6 November 1992, *St. Petersburg Times* (FL): A3; and Cara Tanamachi, "Face of Texas Politics Has Changed in 30 Years," 10 December 1995, *Dallas Morning News*: A31.

26 David Rogers and John Harwood, "No Reasonable Offers Refused as Administration Bargained to Nail Down Deficit Package in House," 6 August 1993, *Wall Street Journal*: A12.

27 Robert Bryce, "Uncle Sam Wants to Recruit a Few Good Contractors," 11 April 1996, *Christian Science Monitor*: 4; Sam Dillon, "Driving to Mexico?: $800 Deposit, Por Favor," 14 November 1999, *New York Times*: TR3.

28 Scott, "Veteran U.S. Rep. Solomon Ortiz Is Facing."

29 Gary Martin, "S. Texas Lawmakers Vote with Majority," 22 January 1997, *San Antonio Express-News*: A6.

30 *Congressional Record*, House, 102nd Cong., 2nd sess. (1 July 1992): 17309; *Congressional Record*, Extension of Remarks, 102nd Cong., 2nd sess. (1 July 1992): 17536.

31 *Congressional Record*, House, 105th Cong., 2nd sess. (10 March 1998): 3044–3045.

32 For the House debate and vote on S. 419, see *Congressional Record*, House, 105th Cong., 2nd sess. (10 March 1998): 3044–3051. For the law, see Birth Defects Prevention Act of 1998, P.L. 105-168, 112 Stat. 43–45.

33 *Congressional Record*, House, Extension of Remarks, 104th Cong. 1st sess. (5 January 1995): E45.

34 *Congressional Record*, House, 108th Cong., 1st sess. (29 October 2003): H10004.

35 Lynn Brezosky, "Ortiz Fighting Hard to Keep Seat," 28 October 2010, *San Antonio Express-News*: B1; Gary Martin, "S. Texas

Democrats Taking Fight to the Wire," 29 October 2010, *San Antonio Express-News*: B7; Lynn Brezosky, "Ortiz Refuses to Abandon Fight for District 27," 4 November 2010, *San Antonio Express-News*: B1; Lynn Brezosky, "Found Ballots Don't Help Ortiz," 5 November 2010, *San Antonio Express-News*: B3; Lynn Brezosky, "Ortiz Accepts His Loss," 23 November 2010, *San Antonio Express-News*: A9.

36 *Congressional Record*, Extension of Remarks, 106th Cong., 2nd sess. (28 September 2000): E1630.

37 *Congressional Record*, House, 110th Cong., 1st sess. (11 December 2007): H15244.

Bill Richardson
1947–

UNITED STATES REPRESENTATIVE 1983–1997
DEMOCRAT FROM NEW MEXICO

Bill Richardson's dual U.S.-Mexican heritage and his ability to interact in Washington's policy circles facilitated his success as a policy aide and as a Member of the U.S. House. During his 14 years in Congress, Richardson responded to constituent requests, burnished his foreign policy credentials, and raised the stature of the Congressional Hispanic Caucus. He also crafted a unique role as a diplomatic troubleshooter for the William J. (Bill) Clinton administration. Of the power that comes with public service, Richardson wrote, "Politics in a democracy is a competition over ideas, and it is inevitable there will be winners and losers. Any freely elected politician who says he doesn't crave power to get the laws and programs he thinks best for his city, state, or nation is either dissembling or belongs in a different business."[1]

The son of William Blaine Richardson, Jr., and Maria Louisa Lopez-Collada, William Blaine Richardson III was born in Pasadena, California, on November 15, 1947. As a manager for the National City Bank of New York (a predecessor to Citibank), Richardson's father worked in a number of foreign countries before settling in Mexico City, where he met his future wife Maria, who was a secretary at the bank. Richardson recalled his father "was proud of his American son, and my mother was very proud of her Mexican son. Their pride was passed down to me, and I grew up honoring both the United States and Mexico and the language and culture of each country." Richardson and his sister, Vesta, were raised in a bilingual household; his father spoke to the children in English, and his mother addressed them in Spanish.[2] Richardson attended school in Mexico City for seven years and then boarded at a private school in Concord, Massachusetts. He subsequently attended his father's alma mater, Tufts University, in Medford, Massachusetts. Majoring in political science and French, Richardson became active in politics when he ran for the presidency of his fraternity and won. Richardson recalled that experience as "my first taste of politics.... I liked all the organizing ... and I found that I was good at it. I started to appreciate that there was power that came with the office."[3] After receiving his B.A. in 1970, Richardson applied to the Fletcher School of Law and Diplomacy in Bedford, Massachusetts, where he participated in student government. He graduated with an M.A. in international affairs in 1971 and married his high school and college sweetheart, Barbara Flavin, in 1972. The Richardsons have no children.[4]

After college, Richardson moved to Washington, D.C., where he worked as a staff member for Representative F. Bradford Morse of Massachusetts, a moderate Republican, from 1971 to 1973. In 1974 Richardson left to work as a congressional relations aide for the State Department. "Human-rights issues at the State Department," he recalled, "were what made me a Democrat."[5] In 1976 Richardson returned to Capitol Hill to work as a staffer for the Senate Committee on Foreign Relations until 1978.[6]

Eight years of working as a staffer convinced Richardson that aides could affect the way legislation was implemented, but he decided that type of influence "was no substitute for the power to do good things for people that comes with elected office." Richardson's itinerant early life had prevented him from building an electoral base from which to launch a political career. After speaking with the staff of Senator Joseph Montoya, Richardson decided to move to New Mexico to "work hard in Democratic politics, make a contribution, and eventually run for office.... I told one and all that my ambition was to run for the United States Congress."[7]

Richardson introduced himself to the New Mexico political establishment and immersed himself in state

Image courtesy of the U.S. House of Representatives Photography Office

politics for two years. While establishing his political bona fides, Richardson opened a consulting firm, taught politics and government in Santa Fe, and prepared himself to run against six-term incumbent Manuel Luján, Jr., in New Mexico's First Congressional District.[8] A mixture of liberal and conservative areas encompassing Albuquerque and Santa Fe—two of the state's largest cities—the district spanned the northeastern and north-central portions of New Mexico.[9]

Richardson announced his candidacy in September 1979 and promised to bring industry and jobs to northern New Mexico using public and private resources.[10] He believed casting Lujan as a puppet of the energy industry—"an almost invisible presence in Washington" who "voted against the interests of his district"—would give him a decent chance of winning. Compensating for limited financial support from Democratic political organizers, and minimal name recognition, Richardson financed his campaign using donations from organized labor PACs and a $100,000 inheritance.[11] House Speaker Thomas P. (Tip) O'Neill of Massachusetts and prominent officials from the James Earl (Jimmy) Carter administration eventually backed him. "I was campaigning twelve or fourteen hours a day, seven days a week, and Lujan was doing nothing," Richardson recalled. Richardson lagged in the polls one week before the election but managed to gain ground. Luján clung to his seat, with 51 percent of the vote to Richardson's 49 percent.[12] Although the Democratic National Campaign Committee offered to pay for a recount, Richardson declined. "I was ecstatic," he said. "I had prepared myself to lose: All I wanted was to lose respectably so that my political prospects were not foreclosed." [13]

In 1982, Richardson ran in the newly created Third District, which covered much of northwestern New Mexico and included the major cities of Farmington and Santa Fe. Its majority-Hispanic population had sent many *nuevomexicano* Delegates, Representatives, and Senators to Washington. The district contained numerous American Indian reservations along the Rio Grande and its tributaries, a surplus of natural resources such as oil, gas, and coal, and the Los Alamos National Laboratory, a top-tier research lab and the birthplace of the atomic bomb. It also drew upon a mixture of political ideologies, with conservative San Juan County and Farmington offset by liberal voters in the state capital of Santa Fe.[14] Richardson described the district as "tailor-made for a Democrat and a Hispanic." He filed early to run for the seat, but met resistance from long-standing political bosses who encouraged their acolytes to run for the seat. The result was a fight for the June 1982 Democratic primary between Richardson, lieutenant governor Roberto Mondragon, district judge George Perez, and future Congressman and Senator Tom Udall.[15]

Behind in the early polls, Richardson reached beyond his *nuevomexicano* base by appealing to conservative Anglo Democrats in the district's larger cities and to Navajo voters who had backed his 1980 run.[16] Richardson recalled a frenetic primary finish: "We logged hundreds of miles of travel around the new Third, shoring up the Hispanic base, reinforcing my interest in Anglo voters, telling the Navajos that I meant it when I said I'd work their interests in Washington." Richardson won by a decisive plurality of 36 percent, ahead of Mondragon (30 percent), Perez (19 percent), and Udall (13.5 percent).[17]

Richardson's opponent in the general election was Republican Marjorie Bell Chambers, a two-time member of the Los Alamos county council, a former president of Colorado College, and a nationally recognized expert on civil rights and education issues. Both candidates promised to bring industry and economic opportunities to the district, pressing the state for tax incentives and the federal government for job training and environmental protection. Richardson criticized the Ronald W. Reagan administration's economic policies and garnered endorsements from Speaker O'Neill and Senator Edward (Ted) Kennedy of Massachusetts.[18] Chambers, a lifelong New Mexican, brought up Richardson's recent move to the state and compared him to a "Ping-Pong ball, first coming up on one side of an issue and then popping up on the other side." Richardson recalled, Chambers "came at me from the start with an odd and out-of-character bias: Let's send this guy back to Mexico."[19] Richardson canvassed the district—in which Democrats outnumbered Republicans nearly three to one—and won 64 percent of the vote on Election Day. In his victory speech, Richardson said he would begin working "tomorrow morning.... I promised to be a fighter, so I've got my work cut out for me," he added. In each of his six subsequent re-election campaigns, Richardson earned at least 60 percent of the vote.[20]

Richardson embraced a straightforward approach to his congressional career: "Err on the side of trying to do too much rather than the side of doing too little." Upon entering Congress, Richardson won seats on the Energy and Commerce and Veterans' Affairs Committees, but he quickly grew frustrated with the Veterans' Affairs assignment. He moved to the House Committee on the Interior (later Natural Resources), whose jurisdiction included Indian affairs, natural resources, and public lands. Between the Energy and Commerce and Interior Committees, Richardson could oversee some of New Mexico's most important interests. Richardson also served on the Education and Labor Committee and on two select committees, and he was the first Hispanic-American Member to serve on the Permanent Select Committee on Intelligence. He served as chairman of the Interior Committee's Subcommittee on Native American Affairs in the 103rd Congress (1993–1995).[21]

According to a popular political study, Richardson maintained a liberal voting record, with few exceptions. He tended to vote pro-business, especially on issues that affected his oil and gas constituencies in New Mexico. He also advocated for pro-business enterprise zones, especially between the United States and Latin American countries.[22] Between his duties in Washington and his constituent casework, Richardson maintained a punishing schedule. "During my fourteen years in Congress," Richardson recalled, "I averaged at least a couple of weekends a month in my home district." Consistent with his reputation, he described his approach as "moving a thousand miles an hour, hustling on all my committees and working my staff to death."[23]

Early in his congressional career, Richardson scored a victory for his American Indian constituents with the passage of two bills that entrusted a portion of federal lands to the Pueblos.[24] As chairman of the Subcommittee on Native American Affairs, Richardson proposed a number of bills involving health, education, and employment initiatives that became law. Richardson also shepherded to passage H.R. 4487, a bill that amended the Public Health Service Act by extending the National Health Service Corps and providing grants to states that supported rural health offices.[25]

Richardson took seriously his role as a Representative of Hispanic descent. He recalled that he "was not interested in becoming a professional Hispanic, but my heritage was central to my identity, and I was proud of it." Early in his first term, Richardson was elected chairman of the Congressional Hispanic Caucus (CHC). Later, he learned that Edward Roybal of California and Robert Garcia of New York, both previous chairs of the caucus, "settled on me as chairman, despite my rookie status, to avoid a divisive fight" for the seat. Richardson used his platform as chairman to feature legislation that affected Hispanic Americans and U.S. relations with Latin America. He also enhanced the CHC's influence and effectiveness by providing it with more public exposure.[26]

Richardson's strong interest in foreign affairs was manifest in his efforts to promote democratization and business interactions with Latin America in the 1980s. Richardson called for the United States to engage Latin American nations by providing economic aid and actively encouraging political democratization.[27] He noted that "military dictatorships were being cast aside ... one-party rule was getting competition at last ... and new leaders were committed to free elections that were emerging everywhere." Richardson viewed these changes as "developments to be encouraged by the United States, which wasn't always subtle or skillful in its application of carrots and sticks." Taking to the House Floor, Richardson criticized parts of the Reagan administration's approach, especially as it related to El Salvador and Nicaragua.[28] However, Richardson openly criticized Nicaraguan President Daniel Ortega, the leader of the communist Sandinista Party, both in the press and to Ortega's face. Ortega "promised land reform and an inclusive government," Richardson recalled. "Instead, he ruled as head of a junta that consolidated power and ran roughshod over all opposition." When a congressional delegation led by the CHC visited Nicaragua in December 1984, Richardson and Ortega "had a verbal fight: He defended his policies and I attacked his deteriorating record on human rights."[29] Richardson's position on supporting the Nicaraguan Contras changed over time. When he entered Congress, Richardson opposed the Reagan administration's efforts to undermine the Sandinista government by providing military support for the anti-communist Contras. But in his second term, Richardson criticized the Sandinista regime's human rights abuses. He eventually supported sending the Contras humanitarian aid with stipulations that the resources could not be used to buy weapons.[30]

Richardson served as a chief deputy whip for the House Democrats and an unofficial diplomatic envoy. As chief deputy whip in the 103rd Congress (1991–1993), Richardson helped maintain party discipline and count and round up votes to promote the agenda of House leadership. Two issues—the North American Free Trade Agreement (NAFTA) and the passage of the president's first budget plan—dominated that Congress, as President Clinton began his first term on an active note.[31] Richardson described his role as an envoy as a "fact-finding member of the (House) Intelligence Committee or a requested negotiator or an unofficial representative of the Clinton administration. Sometimes I was all three." Increasingly, the President asked him to serve abroad, and Richardson dubbed himself the "informal undersecretary for thugs" since he worked in countries with repressive regimes, such as Burma, Haiti, Iraq, Cuba, and North Korea.[32]

Richardson was a strong supporter of NAFTA and had long advocated enterprise free trade zones and emphasized improving business relations between the United States and New Mexico. With the economic liberalization of Mexico in the late 1980s, President Carlos Salinas de Gortari advocated for negotiating a free trade agreement with the United States to maintain Mexico's economic growth. In September 1990, President George H. W. Bush agreed to support the measure and fast-tracked the legislation per congressional approval in 1991.[33] In a public letter, Richardson advised the Bush administration to "develop a long-term strategy for free trade throughout the hemisphere."[34] Although this initiative began in the Bush administration, President Clinton also supported the bill's passage. "If we nix this NAFTA, there will be little or no hope of renegotiating another deal later next year or … in our lifetime," Richardson warned his colleagues.[35] Richardson was one of the chief deputy whips who rounded up votes for the bill to implement NAFTA (H.R. 3450). The "complex politics of NAFTA were best demonstrated by Clinton's owing his House victory more to Republicans than to his own party," *Congressional Quarterly* noted. Although Majority Leader Richard Gephardt of Missouri and Majority Whip David Bonior of Michigan opposed NAFTA, Richardson and other pro-NAFTA Democrats garnered Democratic support to ensure the bill's passage.[36]

In late 1992, Richardson had sought the nomination for Secretary of the Interior in the incoming Clinton administration, but he was passed over in favor of former Arizona governor Bruce Babbitt.[37] In 1997 President Clinton nominated Richardson to serve as the United States Ambassador to the United Nations. After a successful confirmation hearing in the U.S. Senate, Richardson resigned from the House on February 13, 1997.[38] In June 1998, President Clinton nominated Richardson to serve as Secretary of Energy. Confirmed in August 1998, Richardson served in that capacity for the remainder of President Clinton's second term.[39] Richardson later worked in the private sector while preparing for a gubernatorial run in New Mexico. Elected governor in 2002, he served for two terms (2003–2011).[40] In 2007 Richardson announced his candidacy for the Democratic nomination for U.S. President in the 2008 election, but he dropped out of the race in January 2008.[41] Richardson currently serves as chairman of Global Political Strategies, an international business consulting firm.[42]

FOR FURTHER READING

Biographical Directory of the United States Congress, "Bill Richardson," http://bioguide.congress.gov/.

Richardson, William B. "Hispanic American Concerns," *Foreign Policy* 60 (Autumn 1985): 30–39.

_____, with Michael Ruby. *Between Worlds: An American Life* (New York: G. P. Putnam's Sons, 2007).

_____. *Leading by Example: How We Can Inspire an Energy and Security Revolution* (Hoboken, NJ: Wiley, 2008).

NOTES

1 Bill Richardson with Michael Ruby, *Between Worlds: The Making of an American Life* (New York: G. P. Putnam's Sons, 2007): 120. Hereinafter referred to as Richardson, *Between Worlds: The Making of an American Life.*

2 Richardson, *Between Worlds: The Making of an American Life*: 12–24.

3 Ibid., 41–42. Richardson describes his experiences at Tufts on pp. 35–45.

4 Ibid., 43–45, 50–51.

5 Ibid., 48–59, quotation on p. 57; *Report of the Clerk of the House from January 1, 1972, to June 30, 1972*, 92nd Cong., 2nd sess., 1972, H. Doc 92-346: 88; U.S. Department of State Telephone Directory, various editions (Washington, D.C.: Government Printing Office, 1974, 1975); U.S. Department of State, *The Biographic Register* (Washington, D.C.: Government Printing Office, 1974): 286.

6 Richardson, *Between Worlds: The Making of an American Life:* 59–62; *Report of the Secretary of the Senate from January 1, 1976, to September 30, 1976, Part 1*, 94th Cong., 2nd sess., 1976, S. Doc. 94-279-Pt. 1: 801; Charles B. Brownson, ed., *Congressional Staff Directory*, 1977 (Washington, D.C.: Staff Directories, Ltd., 1977): 170; Brownson, ed. *Congressional Staff Directory*, 1978: 181.

7 Richardson, *Between Worlds: The Making of an American Life*: 63–65.

8 Ibid., 65–70.

9 *Congressional Directory*, 97th Congress (Washington, D.C.: Government Printing Office, 1981): 956; *Almanac of American Politics, 1980* (New York: E. P. Dutton, 1979): 566; Richardson, *Between Worlds: The Making of an American Life*: 65.

10 Bruce Campbell, "Richardson Says Lujan Doesn't Produce 'Clout,'" 23 October 1980, *Albuquerque Journal*: A8; Robert Storey, "Richardson Criticizes Lujan Campaign," 4 September 1980, *The New Mexican* (Santa Fe): B1; Bruce Campbell, "Determined Richardson Stays in There Pitching against Lujan," 26 October 1980, *Albuquerque Journal*: A1; Bruce Campbell, "Richardson, Lujan Ease Up on Barbs," 1 November 1980, *Albuquerque Journal*: C2.

11 Richardson, *Between Worlds: The Making of an American Life*: 75; Robert V. Beier, "Campaign Short of Funds But Richardson Optimistic," 5 September 1980, *Albuquerque Journal*: C7; Paul R. Wieck, "Lujan, Richardson Even in Spending on Campaigns," 23 October 1980, *Albuquerque Journal*: E1; "Lujan-Richardson Race Most Aggressive in Decade," 2 November 1980, *The New Mexican* (Santa Fe): B2.

12 "Election Statistics, 1920 to Present," http://history.house.gov/institution/election-statistics/election-statistics. Richardson recalled that "Lujan had won by less than one percent"; see Richardson, *Between Worlds: The Making of an American Life*: 77.

13 Richardson, *Between Worlds: The Making of an American Life*: 71–76; Steve Terrell, "Richardson Arrived in N.M. with Eye toward Congress and Beyond," 23 November 2007, *The New Mexican* (Santa Fe). For an analysis of the race, see Robert Storey, "Richardson Comes Oh, So Close," 5 November 1980, *The New Mexican* (Santa Fe): A1.

14 Albuquerque Convention & Visitors' Bureau, "Indian Pueblos and Reservations," http://www.itsatrip.org/travel-tools/maps/pueblos/default.aspx (accessed 30 May 2012); *Congressional Directory*, 98th Congress (Washington, D.C.: Government Printing Office, 1983): 1020; *Politics in America, 1982* (Washington, D.C.: Congressional Quarterly, Inc., 1981): 1000; Robert Storey, "New Congressional District as Diverse as the Issues," 17 May 1982, *The New Mexican* (Santa Fe): A1.

15 Bill Feather, "Bingaman, Anaya, Richardson Grab Top Demo Spots," 22 March 1982, *The New Mexican* (Santa Fe): A1. For two examples of debates during the primary, see Robert Storey, "Congressional Hopefuls Agree on Arms Sales," 13 May 1982, (Santa Fe) *The New Mexican*: A1; Robert Storey, "Candidates Propose Solutions to High Interest Rates," 15 May 1982, *The New Mexican* (Santa Fe): A5. In March 1982 the Democratic nominating convention had selected Richardson, Mondragon, Perez, and Udall as candidates for the primary.

16 Richardson's campaign nearly derailed on two occasions. He backtracked from a statement in his official campaign biography that he was the "top" foreign policy aide to Senator Hubert Humphrey of Minnesota, insisting that he was Humphrey's principal aide on a Senate Foreign Affairs subcommittee. "Richardson Backs Off on Job History," 13 April 1982, *The New Mexican* (Santa Fe): A1. For an editorial that chastised Richardson for this statement, see "Richardson's Gaffe," 15 April 1982, *The New Mexican* (Santa Fe): A6. In another incident, the Federal Election Commission (FEC) confronted Richardson with questions about a series of personal loans he had made to his campaign totaling more than $170,000. Richardson denied any wrongdoing and was eventually cleared, though the charges cast a long shadow over

the election. See Robert Storey, "Richardson's Campaign Loan Questioned," 25 May 1982, *The New Mexican* (Santa Fe): A1; Denise Kessler, "New Facts Muddle Richardson Finances," 28 May 1982, *The New Mexican* (Santa Fe): A1; Denise Kessler, "Former Candidate Seeks Explanations from Richardson," 29 May 1982, *The New Mexican* (Santa Fe): A1; Denise Kessler, "Election Board Dismisses Complaint on Richardson," 9 June 1982, *The New Mexican* (Santa Fe): A1; Denise Kessler, "FEC Clears Richardson in Probe of Campaign Finances," 4 August 1982, *The New Mexican* (Santa Fe): A1; Paul R. Wieck, "Richardson Explains Mother Was behind Loan Guarantee," 13 August 1982, *Albuquerque Journal*: A1.

17 Office of the Secretary of State, New Mexico. *State of New Mexico Official Returns, 1982 General, Special, and Primary Returns* (Santa Fe: n.p., 1982). Out of a total of 63,845 votes, Richardson earned 23,123, Mondragon earned 19,691, Perez earned 12,412, and Udall earned 8,619. "Richardson Formally Enters Race for Congress," 28 January 1982, *The New Mexican* (Santa Fe): A3; "This Weekend Is No Holiday for NM's Primary Candidates," 29 May 1982, *The New Mexican* (Santa Fe): A1; Richardson, *Between Worlds: The Making of an American Life*: 77–81. As one observer noted, a key difference was that Richardson's 1982 campaign was better organized. See Robert Storey, "Richardson's New Campaign Strategy Paying Off," 16 May 1982, *The New Mexican* (Santa Fe): A1.

18 Robert Storey, "Candidates Appear to See Eye-to-Eye on Most Big Issues," 18 September 1982, *The New Mexican* (Santa Fe): A1. For Chambers's background, see Robert Storey, "Chambers: Artist of Compromise," 10 October 1982, *The New Mexican* (Santa Fe): A1; Polly Summar, "Marjorie Bell Chambers: Los Alamos Politician Was a 'Powerhouse,'" 26 August 2006, *Albuquerque Journal*: D8; Robert Storey, "Kennedy Thrills Democrats," 27 September 1982, *The New Mexican* (Santa Fe): A1.

19 Robert Storey, "Chambers Lambasts Richardson," 11 September 1982, *The New Mexican* (Santa Fe): A1; Richardson, *Between Worlds: The Making of an American Life*: 81.

20 "Lack of Party Support Disappoints Chambers," 2 November 1982, *The New Mexican* (Santa Fe): A4; Jon Bowman, "Richardson Coasts Past Chambers," 3 November 1982, *The New Mexican* (Santa Fe): A1; "Election Statistics, 1920 to Present," http://history.house.gov/institution/election-statistics/election-statistics.

21 Garrison Nelson, *Committees in the U.S. Congress, 1947–1992*, vol. 2 (Washington, D.C.: Congressional Quarterly, Inc., 1994): 743–744; Garrison Nelson and Charles Stewart III, eds., *Committees in the U.S. Congress, 1993–2010* (Washington, D.C.: CQ Press, 2011): 906–907; Richardson, *Between Worlds: The Making of an American Life*: 82–86.

22 *Politics in America, 1994*: 1011. For a detailed outline of the enterprise zone, see Bill Richardson, "Hispanic American Concerns," *Foreign Policy* 60 (Autumn 1985): 30–39, especially p. 35.

23 Richardson, *Between Worlds: The Making of an American Life*: 83–84, 87, 92–93. See also *Politics in America, 1992*: 979.

24 *Congressional Record*, Index, 99th Cong., 2nd sess.: 2863, 2875. Richardson successfully sponsored H.R. 4090, a bill that established the Glorieta National Battlefield to commemorate a pivotal battle of the Civil War in New Mexico. See *Congressional Record*, Index, 101st Cong., 2nd sess.: 2644. Richardson also sponsored H.R. 40 (P.L. 100-225), a bill that established the El Malpais National Monument Park in northwestern New Mexico.

25 *Congressional Record*, Index, 102nd Cong., 2nd sess.: 2662; *Politics in America, 1994*: 1012. For a detailed example of Richardson's successful sponsorship of public lands legislation, see "Congressman Bill Richardson and the 1984 Creation of the Bisti and De-Na-Zin Wilderness Areas in Northwest New Mexico," in Ferenc M. Szasz, *Larger Than Life: New Mexico in the Twentieth Century* (Albuquerque: University of New Mexico Press, 2006): 50–66.

26 Richardson, *Between Worlds: The Making of an American Life*: 96–97; Jacqueline Trescott, "Rallying around Richardson," 21 September 1984, *Washington Post*: A1; John Dillin, "US Hispanics Want to Stop Flood of Aliens," 9 October 1985, *Christian Science Monitor*: 3. Richardson voiced his opposition to a constitutional amendment requiring the use of English. See *Congressional Record*, House, 99th Cong., 1st sess. (30 April 1985): 9970.

27 Richardson, *Between Worlds: The Making of an American Life*: 97; "A New Role for the Hispanic Caucus," *Hispanic Review of Business*, March 1985: 20–21. For an overview of Richardson's approach toward U.S. foreign policy in Latin America, see Richardson, "Hispanic American Concerns": 30–39. For a unique recommendation of providing aid and promoting democratization short of military force, see Bill Richardson, "Here's How to Get Noriega," 11 May 1989, *New York Times*: A29.

28 See *Congressional Record*, House, 98th Cong., 1st sess. (27 April 1983): 9864–9865; *Congressional Record*, House, 99th Cong., 1st sess. (6 February 1985): 1860–1861. Richardson criticized (and voted against) the CIA's funding of the Nicaraguan Contras during the House Floor debate over H.J. Res. 239. See *Congressional Record*, House, 99th Cong., 1st sess. (23 April 1985): 8989–8997, 9085–9086; but supported the implementation of a peace process and humanitarian aid in H.J. Res. 247. See *Congressional Record*, House, 99th Cong., 1st sess. (24 April 1985): 9256–9257. Two months later, Richardson voted in favor of sending humanitarian aid (in an amendment to H.R. 2577) to the Contras because of his opposition to the Daniel Ortega regime in Nicaragua, bipartisan coordination with Republican Members on the details of the amendment, and support for President Reagan's negotiation attempts with the Sandinista government, but the amendment did not pass. He also voted for the final passage of H.R. 2577, which passed in a 271 to 156 vote. See *Congressional Record*, House, 99th Cong., 1st sess. (12 June 1985): 15399–15400, 15419–15420.

29 Richardson, *Between Worlds: The Making of an American Life*:

98. The debate became so heated that "Arcy Torres, wife of Representative Esteban Torres ... pinched my arm and asked me to cool it," Richardson recalled.

30 *Politics in America, 1987*: 994. Richardson criticized the Ortega government on the House Floor. See *Congressional Record*, House, 99th Cong., 1st sess. (3 April 1985): 7442.

31 Roger H. Davidson and Walter J. Oleszek, *Congress and Its Members*, 10th ed. (Washington, D.C.: CQ Press, 2006): 166–167; Richardson, *Between Worlds: The Making of an American Life*: 106, 110–118.

32 Richardson, *Between Worlds: The Making of an American Life*: 121, 199. For an extensive chronicle of Richardson's diplomatic missions, see pp. 121–197. For a contemporary account, see Bill Richardson, "Diary of a Reluctant Diplomat," 15 January 1995, *Washington Post*: C1.

33 "Congress OKs North American Trade Pact," in *CQ Almanac 1993*, 49th ed. (Washington, D.C.: Congressional Quarterly, Inc., 1994): 171–179.

34 Bill Richardson, "Free Trade with Mexico, Sí!", 22 March 1991, *Washington Post*: A25. See also Bill Richardson, "Mexico—the Answer to Bush's Domestic Troubles," 12 December 1991, *Wall Street Journal*: A14.

35 *Congressional Record*, House, 103rd Cong., 1st sess. (18 October 1993): 24868; *Congressional Record*, House, 103rd Cong., 1st sess. (1 November 1993): 26922–26923.

36 *CQ Almanac*, "Congress OKs North American Trade Pact."

37 Adam Clymer, "Push for Diversity May Cause Reversal on Interior Secretary," 23 December 1992, *New York Times*: A1; Dan Balz, "Picking the Clinton Cabinet: The Winners, the Losers and Those Who Got Lost in the Shuffle," 9 May 1993, *Washington Post*: M6. Richardson writes that environmental groups' criticisms of his voting record and Vice President Al Gore's endorsement of Babbitt were deciding factors in Clinton's choice for Secretary of the Interior. See Richardson, *Between Worlds: The Making of an American Life*: 106–109.

38 For Richardson's experiences at the U.N., see *Between Worlds: The Making of an American Life*: 198–232; James Brooke, "Traveling Troubleshooter Is Ready to Settle Down, at the UN," 14 December 1996, *New York Times*: 11; Eric Pianin, "Richardson: A Daring Diplomat," 14 December 1996, *Washington Post*: A10; Faye Bowers, "America's Nimble New Ambassador to the UN," 13 February 1997, *Christian Science Monitor*: 1; Barbara Crossette, "Richardson Reflects on His U.N. Days: As U.S. Delegate, His Informality Often Startled His Colleagues," 8 September 1998, *New York Times*: A6.

39 For Richardson's recollections as Secretary of Energy, see *Between Worlds: The Making of an American Life*: 242–280; Philip Shenon, "Chief U.N. Delegate May Get Energy Post," 9 May 1998, *New York Times*: A1; Neil A. Lewis, "Derring-Do at Energy: William Blaine Richardson," 19 June 1998, *New York Times*: A26.

40 For Richardson's experiences as a gubernatorial candidate and as governor, see Richardson, *Between Worlds: The Making of an American Life*: 281–282, 286–350; Michael Janofsky, "A Candidate Tries to Keep His Troubles behind Him," 10 April 2002, *New York Times*: A20; Michael Janofsky, "Resume and Message Help Ex-Clinton Official to Victory," 8 November 2002, *New York Times*: A26.

41 Matthew Wald, "Democratic Governor of New Mexico Joins Race," 22 January 2007, *New York Times*: A14; Leslie Wayne, "Richardson Officially Enters '08 Democratic Presidential Race," 22 May 2007, *New York Times*: A18; Jodi Kantor, "Personal Touch for Richardson in Envoy Role," 21 December 2007, *New York Times*: A1; Leslie Wayne, "Richardson Is Expected to Drop Out of Primaries," 10 January 2008, *New York Times*: A25; Leslie Wayne and Dennis J. Carroll, "Seeing the Good in Everyone," 11 January 2008, *New York Times*: A16.

42 Bill Richardson, "Biography," http://www.billrichardson.com/about-bill/biography (accessed 2 April 2012).

Esteban Edward Torres

1930–

UNITED STATES REPRESENTATIVE 1983–1999
DEMOCRAT FROM CALIFORNIA

A Korean War veteran and a longtime antipoverty activist in East Los Angeles with strong ties to unions, Esteban Torres served eight terms in the U.S. House. His career on Capitol Hill put him in the vanguard of Latino influence in U.S. politics. "When he took this seat in Congress, it was a period when we didn't have much representation in the Hispanic community," noted Vic Fazio of California, a longtime House colleague. "Now the gates are down, their political power is on the rise. It's a career like Esteban Torres' that has really made it possible for these younger people to have the opportunities for public service."[1]

Esteban Edward Torres was born in Miami, Arizona, on January 27, 1930, at a mining camp owned by the Phelps–Dodge Company. When Torres was five years old, his father was deported to Mexico and he never saw him again. Esteban, along with his mother, Rena Gómez, and his younger brother, Hugo, moved to East Los Angeles in 1936, where he attended the public schools and graduated from James A. Garfield High School in 1949.[2] He was brought up by his mother and grandmother, Teresa Baron-Gómez, who instilled in him a sense of cultural pride. "My mother and my grandmother were very strong women, very educated and very proud to be Mexicans," Torres remembered years later. "They were the ones that taught me to defend my rights, to shame me for not being Mexican." Torres grew up in tough neighborhoods, crediting his survival to a structured family life anchored by his mother and his ability to find a middle ground among competing factions. "I was a barrio kid," Torres recalled. "I grew up in the toughest environment anybody could grow up in. A lot of gangs. It was a depression. It was tough to get decent housing.... I was able to move between gangs and not alienate one group or the other. I had rapport with everybody. People always felt I was a peacemaker."[3] From 1949 to 1953, Torres served in the U.S. Army, fought in the Korean War, and was honorably discharged with the rank of sergeant first class. Torres used his benefits from the GI Bill to study at the Los Angeles Art Center in 1953. Over the next decade, he took courses at East Los Angeles College and California State University at Los Angeles. He took graduate-level courses, at the University of Maryland in economics and at American University in Washington, D.C., in international relations. Torres married Arcy Sanchez of Los Angeles on January 22, 1955. The couple raised five children: Carmen, Rena, Camille, Selina, and Esteban.[4] "I thought about teaching in fine arts, but we had started raising a family and I had to go to work as a welder on the [assembly line at an auto plant]," Torres recalled. "I would take home pieces of metal, especially junk parts that were going to get scrapped, and develop larger pieces, labeled by the kind of car it was; Dodge, DeSoto, all those." His interest in metal sculpting remained part of his life. "I saw so much conflict in the fight for social justice, in this country and abroad," Torres recalled, "I couldn't help being affected.... There's a lot of frustration and revolt in me that comes out in my work."[5]

Torres was introduced to politics by way of his activism in the local branch of the United Auto Workers (UAW) Union. In 1958 his coworkers elected him chief steward of the Local 230. He was later appointed the UAW organizer for the western region of the United States. In 1963 he was tapped by Walter Reuther as a UAW international representative in Washington, D.C., and from 1964 to 1968 he served as the union's director of the Inter-American Bureau for Caribbean and Latin American Affairs. In 1968 Torres returned to Los Angeles, founding The East Los Angeles Community Union (TELACU), a community action organization that grew under his

Collection of the U.S. House of Representatives, Photography Collection

E PLURIBUS

stewardship into one of the nation's largest antipoverty agencies. While serving as TELACU's chief executive officer, Torres also was active in other local organizations, such as the Los Angeles County Commission on Economic Development, the Mexican-American Commission on Education, and the Plaza la Raza Cultural Center.

In 1974 Torres made his first bid for elective office, running in the Democratic primary for a U.S. House seat representing California's 30th Congressional District. He faced George E. Danielson, a two-term incumbent who had been an FBI agent, an attorney, and a member of the California state assembly and senate. The district was 42 percent Hispanic and covered a large swath of suburbs east of Los Angeles. Danielson benefited from being an incumbent and from the visibility he had gained as a member of the House Judiciary Committee during the Watergate investigation.[6] Danielson prevailed in the June 1974 primary election, with roughly 54 percent of the vote to Torres's 37 percent.[7]

Torres returned to the UAW and for several years was assistant director for International Affairs. In 1976 he was appointed as a delegate to the International Metalworkers Federation Central Committee meetings in Geneva, Switzerland. When President James Earl (Jimmy) Carter took office in 1977, Torres was considered for Assistant Secretary of State for Latin America, but instead he served from 1977 through 1979 as Carter's Permanent Representative to the United Nations Educational, Scientific and Cultural Organization (UNESCO). The person who filled the position, whose rank was comparable to that of an ambassador, was required to be confirmed by the U.S. Senate. Torres served as a White House aide from 1979 through 1981.

In 1982 Torres considered running in the 30th District after Representative Danielson was appointed to a seat on the California court of appeals, but Matthew Martínez, the former mayor of Monterey Park, decided to run in the special election to fill that vacancy. House Democrats, led by California Representatives Phillip Burton and Edward Roybal, convinced Torres to run in the newly created 34th Congressional District. As the state's Democratic powerhouse, Burton had orchestrated the decadal statewide redistricting plan, which supporters hailed as masterful and detractors deemed maniacal. One political observer described Burton's effort—which netted the Democrats six more congressional seats in the 1982 elections—as a "jigsaw puzzle designed by the inmate of a mental institution."[8] The editors of the *Almanac of American Politics* noted that the new 34th District "was Burton's *pièce de résistance*" along with two other majority-Hispanic Los Angeles-area districts.[9]

The new crescent-shaped district included a large swath of suburban East Los Angeles that was bounded roughly by the Interstate 10 corridor to the north and the Interstate 5 corridor running south and east; West Covina, Valinda, and La Puente lay on its northern side, and Norwalk and South Whittier lay on its southern borders. The district was 48 percent Hispanic. Torres secured the support of the local political machine, led by U.S. Representative Henry Waxman and California assemblyman Howard Berman (who won a Los Angeles-area seat in the U.S. House in the fall of 1982). His platform was pro-labor, but he took a more conservative approach on social issues, such as abortion, which he opposed. In the Democratic primary, he faced former Representative Jim Lloyd, a three-term veteran and a former mayor of West Covina, who had lost a bid for re-election to the House in 1980. Torres stressed his experience in Washington and won the endorsement of most House Democrats in the California delegation.[10] But Lloyd, who had the backing of some prominent Democrats, such as Ways and Means Committee Chairman Dan Rostenkowski of Illinois, argued that Torres was a "carpetbagger," who had not registered in the district until early 1982 after declaring his candidacy. Torres, who was a longtime resident of East Los Angeles (just west of the new district), responded that Lloyd had "never picked walnuts or cabbage or lived in the barrios here."[11] Torres was better funded than Lloyd, and in a sometimes-bitter race that political observers predicted would be neck-and-neck, he prevailed over Lloyd by 51 to 36 percent. A third candidate received 13 percent of the vote.

In a district where roughly two-thirds of the residents were registered Democrats, Torres was heavily favored in the November general election against Republican candidate Paul Jackson. Jackson had lived in the district for decades, served on a number of civic associations, and enjoyed a long career on the Los Angeles police force. The two candidates clashed on major issues. Torres derided President Ronald W. Reagan's supply-side economics, supported a bilateral nuclear freeze between the superpowers, and advocated pumping more federal dollars into urban infrastructure improvements. "Our cities are really in a state of decay—our road systems, our bridges, our waterways, our court facilities," Torres said.[12] Jackson, whose platform embraced the policies of the Reagan administration, including a massive defense buildup, hoped to tap into the large number of blue-collar Democrats who helped give Reagan a 13 percent margin of victory in the district in 1980. But with a plethora of built-in advantages, including the poor economic conditions, which he pinned on the President's policies, Torres prevailed, 57 to 43 percent.

Reapportionment after the 1990 Census made the district "an almost ideal place for someone like Torres to run," observed a political almanac.[13] The new district was 62 percent Hispanic and added Montebello, an upper middle-class Hispanic town, to Torres's existing base. In his subsequent seven re-election campaigns, Torres won by healthy margins, garnering at least 60 percent of the vote. In his final election in 1996, he won 68 percent of the vote against Republican candidate David Nunez and two minor party candidates.[14]

When Torres took his seat in the House in January 1983, he won assignments on the Banking, Finance and Urban Affairs Committee (later renamed Banking and Financial Services) and the Small Business Committee. He chaired two subcommittees during his tenure: In the 102nd Congress (1991–1993), he chaired the Banking panel's Subcommittee on Consumer Affairs and Coinage, and in the 101st Congress (1989–1991), he chaired the Small Business Subcommittee on Environment and Labor. At the start of the 103rd Congress (1993–1995), Torres lobbied for and won a seat on the exclusive Appropriations Committee, leaving his other assignments. He served on the Foreign Operations, Export Financing and Related Programs Subcommittee and eventually gained a seat on the Transportation Subcommittee.

Torres chaired the Congressional Hispanic Caucus in late 1988, before the start of the 101st Congress (1989–1991). Torres's Democratic colleagues from the California delegation elected him whip for the Southern California area, giving him an entry-level position on the party leadership ladder. In the 102nd Congress (1991–1993) Torres was tapped by the Democratic leadership as a deputy whip.

Torres's position as an early advocate of environmental justice for minorities developed from his efforts to close a neglected landfill in his district. He helped craft the Hazardous Waste Control Act of 1983, which required landfill owners to conduct studies on the health risks their properties posed to nearby communities. He served as chairman of the Small Business Subcommittee on Environment and Labor in the 101st Congress.

As chairman of the Banking panel's Subcommittee on Consumer Affairs and Coinage, Torres pushed measures to empower customers of financial institutions. In the 102nd Congress, Torres authored the Truth in Savings Act, which required banks to clearly disclose information about fees, terms, and conditions for savings deposits.[15] The measure was signed into law. He also advocated for legislation that would give consumers better access to their credit histories and allow them to more easily challenge errors in their credit reports—a reform prompted by changes in financial recordkeeping practices made possible by new computer technology. That bill languished in the 102nd Congress but was enacted into law as part of a fiscal omnibus bill in the 103rd Congress.[16] "Today, consumers' lives are an open book. Sensitive personal and financial data is bought and sold with little or no regard for the privacy of the consumer," Torres noted. "Workers are denied employment or even blackballed because of erroneous information in their files.… Clearly, it is time to regain the balance to protect American consumers against the abuses of the

credit reporting industry."[17] Torres also had a hand in major housing legislation in the 102nd Congress, inserting language that provided assistance to low-income victims of disasters. After Torres gave up his Banking post for a seat on the Appropriations Committee, Democratic leaders temporarily reassigned him to the Banking panel in the 105th Congress (1997–1999) as the Republican majority sought to overhaul national housing programs.[18]

A key vote in Torres's career took place in 1993, when he supported the bill to implement the North American Free Trade Agreement (NAFTA) between the U.S., Mexico, and Canada, that created a regional trade bloc and eliminated tariffs on finished imports and agricultural products. It also dispensed with barriers and deterrents to investments within and among the three countries.[19] NAFTA's proponents believed it would spur U.S. job growth by increasing exports while improving the standard of living in Mexico; its opponents believed NAFTA would endanger American wages and jobs. The treaty was signed in late 1992 in San Antonio, Texas, and by mid-1993 a bill to fund and implement the treaty began making its way through Congress.

Many Americans in unions and the manufacturing sector opposed NAFTA because they believed it would send working-class jobs overseas. The William J. (Bill) Clinton administration sought to rally support for NAFTA by targeting key lawmakers, identifying Torres as an important ally because of his background as an autoworker, his membership in the UAW, and his ties to the Hispanic community. A Clinton advocate in Congress commented, "The symbolism of Torres supporting NAFTA is powerful."[20] To woo Torres, the Clinton administration agreed to include a provision to create and fund a North American Development Bank (NADBank) in the legislation to implement NAFTA. NADBank, which the Clinton administration promised to finance up to $225 million, would help initiate badly needed infrastructure and environmental cleanup projects—particularly in the Southwest along the border with Mexico—and through a Community Adjustment and Investment Program assist communities whose economies were negatively affected by NAFTA. The Mexican government would match U.S. contributions, and the bank would secure international loans of approximately $3 billion. With the NADBank commitment, Torres swung his support behind NAFTA. "What has surprised me is that my friends on the North American labor movement, so far, have failed to grasp the enormous opportunity and potential in the NAFTA for spreading the vision and reality of industrial democracy throughout this hemisphere," Torres remarked, announcing his decision.[21] While he understood union members' opposition, he told the *Los Angeles Times*, "They have to live in the real world. I believe this [NAFTA] is the future."[22] Torres's influence on fellow Hispanic lawmakers was unclear; roughly half voted for the measure, and half voted against it when the bill passed the House by a vote of 234 to 200 on November 17, 1993.

Torres and a group of other Hispanic Representatives later expressed disappointment with NAFTA and its implementation by the Clinton administration. "I've taken a lot of heat," Torres said. "Certain promises were made about helping the adjustment to free trade, and they were not kept."[23] Impatient and disillusioned because the administration had been slow to fund NADBank projects, Torres conceded, "One could argue that the Administration used 'bait and switch' tactics to secure our support for NAFTA."[24]

In 1990 Torres had given serious consideration to running for a seat on the Los Angeles County board of supervisors, but he was unable to register as a candidate because the incumbent held onto the seat until just before the filing deadline, by which time Torres had already filed papers to seek another term in the U.S. House.[25] In 1996, during President Clinton's transition to a second term, Torres's name appeared on a short list of candidates for Secretary of Labor and Secretary of Housing and Urban Development, but he was not chosen for either position and remained in the House.[26]

In early March 1998, days before the filing deadline for the fall elections, Torres announced that he would retire from the House at the end of the 105th Congress, in January 1999. "I have reached the pinnacle of success

in my own eyes," he told reporters. "I'm leaving while in good health. My wife and I want to enjoy life, my family, my grandchildren and pursue personal goals."[27] Torres endorsed his chief of staff and son-in-law, Jamie Casso, to succeed him in the Democratic primary, but Casso lost to longtime community leader Grace Napolitano, who garnered the support of the AFL-CIO. She went on to win the general election.[28] In retirement, Torres has pursued his passion for sculpting and painting.

FOR FURTHER READING

Biographical Directory of the United States Congress, "Esteban Edward Torres," http://bioguide.congress.gov.

NOTES

1 Daniel Yi and Jodi Wilgoren, "Rep. Torres Says He Will Not Seek Reelection to 9th term," 4 March 1998, *Los Angeles Times*: B1.

2 For information on Torres's parents, see Jose Luis Sierra, "Chopped Lives: Part Three of a Three-Part Series on Deportation," 12 November 2004, http://news.ncmonline.com/news/view_article.html?article_id+e2c898c82671fc971ec46d6fef3845bf (accessed 17 July 2009).

3 Mike Ward, "Contrasting Political Philosophies Clash in 34th District Race," 17 October 1982, *Los Angeles Times*: SE1.

4 Family information published in the 1983 *Congressional Directory*.

5 Eric Brace and Jacqueline Trescott, "Art of the Congressman," 19 April 1983, *Washington Post*: C7.

6 See, for example, *Almanac of American Politics, 1976* (Washington, D.C.: National Journal, 1975): 103.

7 Steven C. Smith, "Incumbents Win Renomination in Light Turnout," 6 June 1974, *Los Angeles Times*: SE1.

8 John Jacobs, *A Rage for Justice: The Passion and Politics of Phillip Burton* (Berkeley: University of California Press, 1995): 432–440, quotation on p. 434.

9 *Almanac of American Politics, 1984* (Washington, D.C.: National Journal Inc., 1983): 154–155.

10 Ellen Hume, "House Democrats Back Two Latino Candidates," 11 February 1982, *Los Angeles Times*: B23; Kristina Lindgren, "Torres Kicks Off Race for Congress," 4 March 1982, *Los Angeles Times*: LB1.

11 Ellen Hume, "Plan to Ensure Congress Seat for Latino May Be Backfiring," 18 April 1982, *Los Angeles Times*: B1; Mike Ward, "After 2 Losses, Jim Lloyd Gets 'the Idea They Don't Want You,'" 13 June 1982, *Los Angeles Times*: LB1.

12 Ward, "Contrasting Political Philosophies Clash in 34th District Race."

13 *Politics in America, 1998* (Washington, D.C.: Congressional Quarterly, Inc., 1997): 184.

14 "Election Statistics, 1920 to Present," http://history.house.gov/institution/election-statistics/election-statistics.

15 *Congressional Record*, House, 102nd Cong., 1st sess. (13 June 1991): E2218.

16 *Politics in America, 1998*: 184; Rick Bragg, "Anxiously Looking South; NAFTA," 16 November 1993, *Los Angeles Times*: n.p.

17 *Congressional Record*, House, 103rd Cong., 2nd sess. (27 September 1994): H9811.

18 See Carmen E. Enciso and Tracy North, eds., *Hispanic Americans in Congress, 1822–1995* (Washington, D.C.: Government Printing Office, 1995): 130; *Politics in America, 1998*: 183.

19 For more on the history of NAFTA, see Maxwell A. Cameron and Brian W. Tomlin, *The Making of NAFTA: How the Deal Was Done* (Ithaca, NY: Cornell University Press, 2000); John R. MacArthur, *The Selling of "Free Trade": NAFTA, Washington, and the Subversion of American Democracy* (Berkeley: University of California Press, 2000).

20 MacArthur, *The Selling of "Free Trade"*: 158–159.

21 *Politics in America, 1998*: 183.

22 Bragg, "Anxiously Looking South; NAFTA"; James Gerstenzang, "Clinton Offers NAFTA Enticement for Wary Lawmakers," 28 October 1993, *Los Angeles Times*: A20.

23 John Maggs, "Before and NAFTA: Hispanic Discontent and Free Trade," 1 September 1997, *The New Republic*: 11.

24 MacArthur, *The Selling of "Free Trade"*: 305–306.

25 Timothy Curran, "Torres Is Bluffed out of Race for L.A. Post; Misses Filing Deadline for Board of Supervisors," 19 March 1990, *Roll Call*.

26 *Politics in America, 1998*: 183.

27 Yi and Wilgoren, "Rep. Torres Says He Will Not Seek Reelection to 9th Term."

28 See Norah M. O'Donnell, "Torres Backs Aide, Son-in-Law, for Seat," 5 March 1998, *Roll Call*; Norah M. O'Donnell, "California Split Labor Reversal Spells Trouble for Torres's Son-in-Law," 16 April 1998, *Roll Call*: n.p.

Ben Garrido Blaz
1928–

TERRITORIAL DELEGATE 1985–1993
REPUBLICAN FROM GUAM

In 1985, Ben Garrido Blaz became the first Hispanic American to represent the Western Pacific island of Guam in Congress. A decorated military veteran who became a politician later in life, Blaz focused on issues of local importance to the island territory. Acutely influenced by the Japanese invasion of Guam during World War II, Blaz used his national position to bring attention to the sacrifices and hardships of the era, including his own imprisonment. During his four terms in the House, Blaz led the charge for commonwealth status for his native land. "We in Guam have embarked on a voyage of political self-determination—a desire on our part for greater local autonomy and an equal place in the American political family."[1]

Vicente Tomas (Ben) Garrido Blaz was born February 14, 1928, in Agana, the capital of Guam.[2] Thirteen years old when the Japanese invaded Guam during World War II, Blaz worked in labor camps building aviation fields, planting rice, and digging trenches until American forces retook the island in 1944.[3] After the war ended in 1945, Blaz returned to school. In 1947 he left Guam after earning an academic scholarship to the University of Notre Dame. Blaz majored in physics and chemistry.[4] While in school, he joined the U.S. Marine Corps Reserve at the onset of the Korean War. After graduating from Notre Dame in 1951 with a B.S. degree, he was commissioned a second lieutenant. Blaz served two overseas tours in Japan and one in Vietnam. In 1963 he earned an M.A. in management from The George Washington University, and in 1971 he graduated from the Naval War College in Newport, Rhode Island. Blaz rose to the rank of brigadier general in 1977, becoming Guam's highest-ranking military officer.[5] That same year he headed the Marine information division that was tasked with improving public relations in the post–Vietnam War era.[6] Blaz's military honors include the Legion of Merit, the Bronze Medal with Combat "V," the Navy Commendation Medal, and the Vietnamese Cross of Gallantry.[7] Blaz married Ann Evers, a teacher, and the couple had two sons, Mike and Tom. After retiring from the military in 1981, Blaz returned to his native island, where he taught at the University of Guam. Blaz received an honorary LL.D. degree from the University of Guam in 1974.

On August 1, 1950, President Harry S. Truman signed the Organic Act of Guam, granting U.S. citizenship and limited self-government to the inhabitants of Guam. In 1972 the House of Representatives granted congressional representation to Guam and the Virgin Islands. Territorial Delegates were permitted to serve on and vote in committee, but they could not vote on the House Floor. In the 93rd Congress (1973–1975) Antonio Won Pat became the first Delegate to represent Guam in the U.S. House of Representatives. Despite Won Pat's popularity and his impressive political résumé, which included service as speaker of the Guam assembly, Blaz challenged the longtime Delegate in 1982. "One reason I decided to run," Blaz revealed, "is that I did not get the sense that bureaucrats understand and appreciate Guam's uniqueness.... We're 100,000 American citizens who deserve a rightful spot in the American family."[8] Blaz attempted to offset his opponent's experience by emphasizing the need for a new, more aggressive strategy to represent Guam—especially with regard to the island's political status.[9] Although his first run for Congress was not successful, Blaz earned an impressive 48 percent of the vote against incumbent Won Pat.[10]

Encouraged by his strong showing at the polls, Blaz challenged Won Pat again in 1984. Both candidates ran unopposed in the primary, but voters had the option of crossing party lines. Tellingly, Blaz polled nearly 2,000 more votes than the incumbent.[11] During the general

Collection of the U.S. House of Representatives, Photography Collection

election campaign, 75-year-old Won Pat stressed his seniority in Congress. The challenger countered by reminding voters that his Republican Party affiliation would be an asset for Guam under the Ronald W. Reagan administration.[12] "Although I'll be a junior I'm not exactly without friends," Blaz added. "There are many ways to explain clout—seniority is just one of them."[13]

During the tightly contested campaign, Blaz criticized his opponent's attendance record in Congress and accused Won Pat of missing opportunities to improve Guam's economy while serving as its Delegate.[14] He also promised to ensure that Guamanians enjoyed the same privileges as U.S. citizens on the mainland. After the ballots were tallied on Election Day, Blaz had a razor-thin lead of about 300 votes, leading the Guam Election Commission to authorize a recount. On November 11, 1984, the commission certified the election, declaring Blaz the winner by 354 votes.[15] "I'm ready," Blaz remarked. "I've been ready for 40 years. I'm on a mission."[16]

Though eager to start his new career, Blaz still had to contend with the remnants of a competitive and heated campaign. Initially conciliatory, Won Pat ultimately contested the election. Citing "substantial irregularities," Won Pat asked the House to overturn the election results, claiming Blaz had not received a majority of the votes. (Unlike in most congressional races in the United States, in which Representatives need only capture a plurality, Delegates in Guam must win a majority of votes to avoid a runoff election.) The House denied Won Pat's challenge on July 24, 1985, by a voice vote, citing insufficient evidence.[17] "Deep down inside I didn't have doubts, but the House of Representatives is hard to predict," Blaz commented afterward.

At the beginning of the 99th Congress (1985–1987), the freshman class elected Blaz as its president, marking the first time a Territorial Delegate held this informal leadership position.[18] Blaz received two committee assignments, Armed Services and Interior and Insular Affairs. Both fit his legislative interests and allowed him to oversee and influence legislation affecting Guam. Blaz retained these two assignments during his eight years in the House. In the 100th Congress (1987–1989), he also had a spot on the Foreign Affairs Committee, which he kept until he left Congress in 1993. From 1985 until 1993, he served on the Select Committee on Aging.

Guam's strategic location in the Western Pacific Ocean significantly affected Blaz's legislative focus in Congress. After the Americans regained control of Guam during World War II, the island became a military bastion for the United States and a vital Cold War defense point. Guam's economy prospered with the influx of federal spending for the island's conversion to a military outpost. It continued to flourish after the Vietnam War, with a construction boom sparked by a budding tourism industry—fueled mainly by Japan. Blaz, however, questioned the need for the U.S. military's vast land holdings on Guam throughout the latter half of the 20th century. In 1992 he introduced the Guam Excess Lands Act, which called for the United States to return to Guam specified areas that had been appropriated by the military during World War II. According to the Guam Delegate, the U.S. forces increased their presence after they regained control of Guam, instead of downsizing at the war's end. "These lands have remained unjustly inaccessible to my constituents ever since, even though much of it has not been used since the war for any military purpose," Blaz stated. He went on to say that returning the land to the people of Guam would help the nation's economy and "close the books on the issue of excess lands since the military has repeatedly indicated that it has no further use for them."[19]

Throughout his tenure in the House, Blaz sought to publicize Guam's role during World War II. Blaz offered a firsthand account of the hardships the people endured during Japan's nearly three-year occupation. "There are many horrible and appalling stories I could tell about the atrocities inflicted upon our people," he said, "about mysterious disappearances of friends, about discoveries of decapitated corpses tied to trees, about clearing jungles under the barrel of a gun and about the hunger and deprivation of concentration camps."[20] Blaz also recalled serving as commanding officer of the same Marine regiment that rescued him and eventually liberated Guam in 1944. "Taking command of the Ninth Marines was and remains the proudest moment of my life," he observed.[21] Building upon legislation drafted by Won Pat in 1983, Blaz introduced a bill to establish a Commission on War Claims to examine assertions of damages that were suffered by the people of Guam at the hands of Japanese occupation forces. Although he did not attain this goal while he was serving in Congress, Blaz continued to fight for federal reparations for Guam. In 2005 he testified before the House Committee on Resources in favor of the Guam World War II Loyalty Recognition Act. "Loyalty and appreciation for their liberation made many of them hesitant to seek compensation for death, injuries, and damages in the years immediately following liberation," Blaz explained.[22]

While in the House, Blaz worked on a range of issues to fortify Guam's economy. The island relied heavily on the fishing industry. During the 99th Congress, Blaz introduced a bill to amend the Immigration and Nationality Act to allow alien crewmen working on U.S. fishing boats to go ashore while working in Guam. As Guam was the home port for America's Western Pacific tuna fleet, which supplied much of the tuna for the United States, the fleet's presence had a major impact on Guam's economy. Blaz's measure called for the continued presence of U.S. fishing fleets and the same shore leave privileges for all crew members, regardless of their national origin. "Since Guam is America's bridge to the Pacific and its finest symbol it is essential that the free enterprise system flourish there," Blaz observed.[23] Blaz's bill became law on October 21, 1986. The Guam Delegate also sought to extend supplemental security income (SSI)—federal benefits for low-income, disabled, or elderly American citizens—to his constituents. Blaz introduced legislation to "reverse the meaningless discrimination" of SSI funding, which included residents of the District of Columbia and the Commonwealth of the Northern Mariana Islands but not the residents of other U.S. territories like Guam. "Affording these benefits to residents of one island and not to another is tantamount to extending benefits to residents of Chicago's North Side but not to fellow Americans in the South side," Blaz concluded.[24] Blaz also supported federal assistance for educational programs in Guam, including funding for vocational education and improvements to elementary and secondary education. To help the many veterans residing in Guam, Blaz introduced the Veterans' Educational Assistance Act during his first term in the House. The measure called for expanded eligibility for basic assistance under the GI Bill.

Throughout his tenure, Blaz's most consistent and fervent cause remained improving Guam's political status. He routinely introduced legislation to establish Guam as an American commonwealth rather than an unincorporated U.S. territory. "Commonwealth is the principal issue for Guam," Blaz asserted. "It's not a Democratic issue and it's not a Republican issue. It's a distinctly Guam issue with political, civil and human rights issues in it."[25] On March 7, 1988, the same week as Discovery Day—a holiday commemorating the founding of Guam by Portuguese explorer Ferdinand Magellan—Blaz introduced the Guam Commonwealth Act. Resulting from the work of the bipartisan Commission on Self-Determination, and ratified by Guam's voters, the measure called for complete self-government for the people of Guam, the preservation of the indigenous Chamorro culture, and consultation with the United States about matters that would affect the island. Advocating a partnership with the United States, Blaz reminded his House colleagues of Guam's sacrifices throughout the 20th century. "We on Guam paid our dues—as heavily in war as in peace—to prove our loyalty and pride as members of the American family. Still, we have never enjoyed equal status with other Americans—either politically or economically."[26] Although the Guam Commonwealth Act never made it out of committee, Blaz reintroduced it twice.[27]

Blaz did not limit his quest for equal rights to Guam. In 1991 he came out in support of statehood for the District of Columbia and compared the plight of his constituents with that of the residents of D.C. "Yet the people of Guam—Americans all—remain second-class citizens. Like the people of the District of Columbia, they are denied the fundamental rights afforded their counterparts elsewhere," he said.[28] He also backed

legislation sponsored by Virgin Islands Delegate Ron de Lugo that called for increased sovereignty of the U.S. territories of the Virgin Islands, Guam, American Samoa, and the Northern Mariana Islands. "The measure before us is the result of careful consideration and comes to the floor with bipartisan support," Blaz observed. "It contains several items of importance to each of the territorial representatives and the American citizens from the territories and I urge approval of its passage."[29] The final version of the bill, which became law on August 27, 1986, provided additional funding for and greater autonomy over Guam's education system. During the 99th Congress, Blaz demonstrated further solidarity for his nonvoting colleagues and their constituents by introducing legislation to authorize inclusion in the Capitol's National Statuary Hall Collection of statues from Washington, D.C.; Puerto Rico; Guam; the Virgin Islands; and American Samoa.[30]

Until his last election in 1992, Blaz encountered only modest competition in his campaigns to serve as Guam's Delegate. In 1986 he trounced Frank Torres, a former adjutant general of the National Guard, with 65 percent of the vote; in his subsequent two elections he easily defeated Vicente Pangelinan, a political veteran who worked for Delegate Won Pat, and Guam governor Ricardo Bordallo, capturing 55 percent of the ballots cast in both contests.[31] In his bid for a fifth term in the House, Blaz faced a strong challenge from Robert Underwood, a longtime educator with strong community ties in Guam. Underwood ran an effective grass-roots campaign, criticizing Blaz for not spending enough time in Guam. Blaz countered by emphasizing his military and congressional record.[32] Constituting an unexpected obstacle to Blaz's re-election, a typhoon postponed voting in Guam for nearly a week. By the time voters cast their ballots for Delegate, they knew that William J. (Bill) Clinton had been elected President; this was significant because Blaz had underscored the value of Guam's Delegate being from the same party as the U.S. President.[33] On Election Day, Blaz garnered only 45 percent of the vote. He later offered to help his successor during the transition, remarking that his political career "started and ended on the high road."[34]

After leaving the House, Blaz taught at the University of Guam. He currently resides in Fairfax, Virginia.[35]

FOR FURTHER READING

Biographical Directory of the United States Congress, "Ben Garrido Blaz," http://bioguide.congress.gov.

NOTES

1 *Congressional Record*, House, 101st Cong., 1st sess. (9 March 1989): 4007.

2 Formerly called Agana, Guam's capital was renamed Hagatna, which is Chamorro. The names of Blaz's parents did not appear in any secondary sources, campaign materials, or newspaper articles. The 1930 Census listed a Vicente G. Blar (Blas) born in Guam in 1928, to Vicente and Rita Blar (Blas). *Fifteenth Census of the United States, 1930:* Piti, Piti, Guam, Roll 2629, page 1A, Library of Congress, Washington, D.C., http://search.ancestrylibrary.com (accessed 25 May 2012).

3 "Vicente Tomas (Ben) Blaz," http://bisitaguam.com/bio/index.html (accessed 9 January 2012).

4 Neither the name of the high school Blaz attended nor the date of his high school graduation is available on his website, "Vicente Tomas (Ben) Blaz," http://bisitaguam.com/bio/index.html (accessed 11 April 2011). Newspaper accounts provide contradictory information about the high school Blaz attended. See, for example, "Election 1992, a Special Project of the *Pacific Daily News*," 2 November 1992, *Pacific Daily News*: 2; Jeremiah O'Leary, "Guam Delegate's Rise Parallels Struggle for Civil Rights," 17 July 1989, *Washington Times*: B1.

5 Elaine Santos, "The Delegate," 4 November 1984, *Pacific Daily News*: 3.

6 Harold J. Logan, "Information Head Says Marines Must Be Open to Scrutiny," 2 July 1977, *Washington Post*: A6.

7 "Vicente Tomas (Ben) Blaz," http://bisitaguam.com/bio/index.html (accessed 11 April 2011); O'Leary, "Guam Delegate's Rise Parallels Struggle for Civil Rights."

8 Susan Kreifels, "'We Deserve a Rightful Spot,'" 29 October 1982, *Pacific Daily News*: 3.

9 Paul J. Borja, "'No Substitute for Experience,'" 29 October 1982, *Pacific Daily News*: 3; Kreifels, "'We Deserve a Rightful Spot.'"

10 "Election Statistics, 1920 to Present," http://history.house.gov/institution/election-statistics/election-statistics.

11 "Rival's Tally in Guam Overshadows Incumbent," 3 September 1984, *New York Times*: 9.

12 Elaine Santos, "Won Pat, Blaz Face Off," 1 November 1984, *Pacific Daily News*: 1.

13 Santos, "The Delegate."

14 Campaign Material for Ben Blaz; "Issues Facing Guam Now," 3 November 1984, *Pacific Daily News*: 41.

15 Kate Pound, "Recount Set for Delegate Race," 8 November 1984, *Pacific Daily News*: 1; Yvonne Martinez, "It's Blaz by 354 Votes," 11 November 1984, *Pacific Daily News*: 1; "Election Statistics, 1920 to Present," http://history.house.gov/institution/election-statistics/election-statistics.

16 Paul J. Borja, "Blaz: On a New Mission," 12 November 1984, *Pacific Daily News*: 1.

17 *Congressional Record*, House, 99th Cong., 1st sess. (24 July 1985): 20180–20181; "House Rejects Bid to Overturn Election of Guam Delegate," 25 July 1985, *Los Angeles Times*: 23; "House Denies Won Pat Challenge," 26 July 1985, *Pacific Daily News*: 1; Stephen Labaton, "Guam Delegate Resists Demand for Runoff Vote," 6 June 1985, *Washington Post*: A7; Stephen Labaton, "Guam's Seat in Congress Still Disputed," 4 June 1985, *Washington Post*: A12.

18 "Minority Reports," 16 December 1984, *New York Times*: E20.

19 *Congressional Record*, House, 102nd Cong., 2nd sess. (5 February 1992): 1691.

20 *Congressional Record*, House, 99th Cong., 2nd sess. (26 November 1991): 35435.

21 Blaz took command of the Ninth Regiment of the Marines 27 years after the liberation of Guam. Blaz recalled escaping with several companions from a Japanese concentration camp shortly after U.S. troops invaded Guam in 1944. The Marines mistook Blaz for a Japanese soldier and briefly held him as a prisoner of war. According to Blaz, the Japanese captured and killed two Guamanians in his group who ran in a different direction. Bernard E. Trainor, "Lack of Vote Doesn't Deter Delegate from Guam," 3 February 1988, *New York Times*: B6.

22 The Honorable Ben Garrido Blaz, "Testimony before the Committee on Resources, United States House of Representatives," April 20, 1985, Hearing on H.R. 1595; James Brooke, "Decades after Abuses by the Japanese, Guam Hopes the Military Will Make Amends," 14 August 2005, *New York Times*: 16.

23 *Congressional Record*, House, 99th Cong., 2nd sess. (12 May 1986): 10276.

24 *Congressional Record*, House, 102nd Cong., 2nd sess. (18 February 1992): 2452.

25 Tambra A. Bryant, "Guam Dems: Clinton Win Would Help Underwood," 4 November 1992, *Pacific Daily News*: 3.

26 *Congressional Record*, House, 100th Cong., 2nd sess. (7 March 1988): 3500.

27 For detailed information on the commonwealth movement in Guam, see Robert F. Rogers, "Guam's Quest for Political Identity," Pacific Studies 12 (November 1988): 49–70; Robert F. Rogers, *Destiny's Landfall: A History of Guam* (Honolulu: University of Hawai'i Press, 1995): 271–290.

28 Ben Blaz, "Guam: Equal in War, But Not in Peace," 19 October 1991, *New York Times*: 22.

29 *Congressional Record*, House, 99th Cong., 2nd sess. (1 August 1986): 18622.

30 *Congressional Record*, House, 99th Cong., 1st sess. (19 November 1985): 32463.

31 "Election Statistics, 1920 to Present," http://history.house.gov/institution/election-statistics/election-statistics; "Senator Vicente (Ben) Cabrera Pangelinan," official biography of Guam Senator Pangelinan, http://senbenp.com/?page_id=6 (accessed 4 January 2012); "Guamanians Cast Ballots in U.S. Territory's Primary Election," 6 September 1986, Associated Press.

32 Donovan Brooks, "New Turn on the 'High Road,'"10 November 1992, *Pacific Daily News*: 1; Donovan Brooks, "Grassroots, Media Use Called Key to Success," 11 November 1992, *Pacific Daily News*: 7. For an example of Blaz's campaign advertisements, see "Ben Blaz for U.S. Congress," 1 November 1992, *Pacific Daily News*: 14.

33 Bryant, "Guam Dems: Clinton Win Would Help Underwood"; Frale Oyen, "Election Postponed," 3 November 1992, *Pacific Daily News*: 1.

34 Brooks, "New Turn on the 'High Road.'"

35 "Vicente Tomas (Ben) Blaz," http://bisitaguam.com/bio/index.html (accessed 9 January 2012).

Albert G. Bustamante
1935–

UNITED STATES REPRESENTATIVE 1985–1993
DEMOCRAT FROM TEXAS

Born to migrant workers and unable to speak English until he was nine years old, Albert Bustamante was eventually elected to Congress from the poor Hispanic suburbs in South Texas where he grew up. A self-described political "moderate who hugs the middle and can go either way," and an active member of the Congressional Hispanic Caucus (CHC), Bustamante was the swing vote on important Latin American issues such as aid to Nicaraguan rebels and immigration control during his four terms in Congress.[1]

The oldest of 11 children in a family of migrant workers, Albert Garza Bustamante was born April 8, 1935, in Asherton, Texas. As a child, he picked crops with his family in Oregon from May to September. "I know the vicious cycle of migrant life," he later recalled. "What we earned in the five months before returning to Texas in September had to support us the rest of the year."[2] Bustamante began school at age nine, speaking an "in-between Spanish dialect" and unable to read or speak English.[3] Hampered by this late start, Bustamante struggled academically, but managed to graduate from Asherton High School in 1954. He joined the U.S. Army that same year, serving as a paratrooper until 1956. Bustamante attended San Antonio College from 1956 to 1958 before transferring to Sul Ross State College in Alpine, Texas. Financing his final semester of education with a $250 loan from a school janitor, he graduated with a degree in secondary education in 1961. Bustamante taught at Cooper Junior High School in San Antonio and coached football and basketball for seven years. He married Rebecca Pounders, and the couple raised three children: Albert, John, and Celina.

In 1968 Bustamante got his start in politics as a constituent aide in the San Antonio-based district office of U.S. Representative Henry González. He worked there for three years. But in 1971, believing the liberal Democratic incumbent on the county commission "had polarized the community, pitting Anglo against Mexican-American," Bustamante won his first elective office to a five-year term in the Bexar County Commission.[4] In 1978 Bustamante became the first Hispanic American elected to a major Bexar County office when he won a judgeship. He was soon recognized as one of the leading conservative Democrats in the county, which included San Antonio and its suburbs.[5]

In 1984 Bustamante took on Abraham Kazen, an 18-year incumbent, for a House seat representing the northwest San Antonio suburbs in Bexar County. The diverse district included many middle-class, primarily white communities outside the city as well as the rural, mostly Hispanic towns near Laredo, on the Mexican border. Though its voters leaned Democratic, socially conservative Hispanics as well as a large military presence from several nearby air force bases generally made the district more competitive.[6] Bustamante's greatest obstacle proved to be the Democratic primary race against the entrenched incumbent. Bustamante criticized what he said were Kazen's scarce accomplishments during his long career, playing up his ethnicity and the possible increase of Hispanics in Congress. This strategy was particularly effective since the primary fell on Cinco de Mayo (May 5), the widely celebrated date of Mexico's victory over French invaders in 1862. "Help me on Cinco De Mayo to declare our independence from an old political family who has controlled the destiny of this area," he told a crowd of Hispanic voters.[7] Bustamante upset Kazen in the Democratic primary, winning every county in the district and taking 59 percent of the vote to his opponent's 37 percent. He was unopposed in the general election.

When Bustamante arrived in Washington in 1985, he was elected president of his Democratic freshman class.

Image courtesy of the U.S. House of Representatives Photography Office

He was the first Hispanic to be so honored.[8] During his first term he also received a position on the Democratic Steering and Policy Committee, which assigned committees and set party policy. Bustamante was assigned to the Government Operations and Armed Services Committees, on which he served his entire congressional career. The latter proved beneficial for serving the large military population in his district. In his final two terms Bustamante also served on the Select Committee on Hunger.

Bustamante's position as a moderate Democrat often defined his congressional career, and he sought to balance the needs of his Anglo and Hispanic constituents. He was an active member of the CHC, eventually serving as chairman in the 100th Congress (1987–1989). Bustamante firmly believed in the caucus's power to improve the lives of Hispanic Americans, especially those in the impoverished border communities. He brought attention to the *colonias*, or rural Hispanic neighborhoods, along the U.S.-Mexico border, arguing in favor of more funding for food for the poor and increased economic opportunities. "We … want to upgrade the economic status of our group because as you enhance that economic status you bring about jobs to that community," Bustamante said. "And hopefully they can identify with our roots and invest within the community."[9] Yet he took an unpopular stance within the Hispanic community by opposing bilingual education in border schools. "I'm for bringing about a system of education that will help a child to live in the business climate we have in this area of the country," he argued. "And that is [in] English."[10]

Bustamante's middle-of-the-road approach to combating communism in Central America ultimately placed him in the middle of difficult votes during legislative showdowns between President Ronald W. Reagan and the Democratic majority in the 99th Congress (1985–1987) over the provision of humanitarian and military aid to Contra rebels attempting to overthrow Nicaragua's leftist Sandinista regime.[11] Caught between the negative effect of Central American unrest on trade and immigration along the Texas border and his uneasiness with an increased U.S. military presence in the region, Bustamante wavered between supporting legislation to provide the Contras solely with humanitarian assistance and supporting legislation to provide them both financial and military aid.[12] On April 23, 1985, he joined the Democratic majority, who rejected the Reagan administration's proposed $14 million package, fearing that funding for humanitarian aid would be redirected for military purposes.[13] The following June, however, Bustamante, along with a handful of moderate Democrats, bucked Party leaders to support a $27 million White House-backed aid package including both humanitarian and nonlethal military support.[14] Bustamante cited the desperate need for humanitarian assistance in the war-torn region—even when tied to military support—as his primary motive for switching his vote.[15]

When the issue of aid for the Nicaraguan Contras came up again in early 1986, however, Bustamante was undecided about a Reagan-backed proposal for $100 million, 30 percent of which would be humanitarian aid, with the remainder earmarked for military assistance. He was among the 31 moderate Democrats who wrote to the President asking him to delay seeking military assistance and focus instead on peace talks. Both the White House and liberal Democrats pressured the signatories. Of Reagan's televised address to the nation on March 16, Bustamante noted, "If you were on the right, you applauded. If you were on the left, you tried to shoot holes in it. Those of us in the middle are looking at both sides and saying 'My God, what is going on?'"[16] Bustamante was among more than a dozen Democrats who were summoned to the White House and courted by the President's top aides.[17] In the face of sharp partisan bickering Bustamante helped narrowly defeat the bill, 222 to 210, on March 20, 1986.[18] But when the $100 million package came up again in June, Bustamante was among six Democrats and five Republicans who changed their positions, providing a substantial victory for the Reagan administration when the legislation passed, 221 to 209.[19] Bustamante credited his change of mind to observations he made on a trip to Central America. "There will be no peace in Central America until internal reform is forced [on the Nicaraguan government]," he admitted, after meeting with Contra leaders and Nicaraguan President Daniel Ortega. "I came away convinced that we need to continue to pressure the Sandinistas."[20]

The public revelation of the Iran-Contra scandal in November 1986 changed Bustamante's mind once again. When reports surfaced that arms and funding sent to Iran to aid in its ongoing war with Iraq had been diverted to the Nicaraguan Contras without Congress's knowledge, the administration came under withering scrutiny from Capitol Hill and the Justice Department. Citing these revelations, Bustamante expressed distrust about the allocation of any future aid, demanding to "know where the money is going." "We've got too many free agents setting policy in Central America," he observed.[21] Bustamante also became the target of attack ads during the 1986 election cycle that painted moderates who voted against Reagan's original Contra aid package as unpatriotic. These "underhanded tactics" further convinced Bustamante to vote on March 11, 1987, to withhold the $40 million remaining in the original $100 million aid package.[22] Thereafter, Bustamante regularly opposed military aid for the Nicaraguan Contras.[23]

Bustamante sided with the Reagan administration on the issue of immigration. He and four other Hispanic Members—Esteban Torres and Tony Coelho of California, Solomon Ortiz of Texas, and Bill Richardson of New Mexico—out of the 11 voting members of the CHC approved the administration's Immigration Reform and Control Act on October 9, 1986.[24] Proposed in response to rising illegal immigration, the legislation fined employers for knowingly hiring undocumented workers, but offered legal status to those who had entered the United States before 1982 and had lived there continuously. The legislation was aimed at Hispanic immigration, which had increased dramatically after an economic recession in Mexico in the early 1980s. Bustamante favored regulating immigration to benefit the economy of the border towns in his district, which were flooded with workers.[25] He also feared that Hispanic-American workers would be discriminated against because of the fines levied on the employers of undocumented workers. "The demonstrated tendency of businesses to play it safe while hiring could jeopardize the employment of as many as 150,000 Hispanic job seekers every week," Bustamante told his colleagues. "The consequence … is the violation of a fundamental right of all Americans, including Hispanic Americans—the right to work."[26] Bustamante protested the higher-than-expected fee proposed by the Reagan administration for those applying for legal status; the fee was $150 to $200 versus the original figure of $100. In 1990 Bustamante called for the repeal of all employer sanctions when the General Accounting Office reported that those seeking employment who had a "foreign appearance or accent" were often discriminated against under the 1986 law.[27]

Bustamante warily supported increased military spending. Though he favored projects that positively affected the military bases in his district, he often voiced concern about their impact on the environment and about the safety of nuclear production plants.[28] Because Bustamante served on two subcommittees that oversaw the manufacture of nuclear power and weapons—Procurement and Military Nuclear Systems (Armed Services Committee) and Environment, Energy, and Natural Resources (Government Operations)—he had a platform from which to critique the management and proliferation of such facilities. In 1988 he noted the ailing Savannah River weapons plant in South Carolina "has been living on the edge of a major disaster for 30 years" when fires, equipment failure, and plutonium leaks inspired an investigation by the Department of Energy.[29] Bustamante eventually supported closing the Savannah plant and other plants, castigating the oversight committees for their lack of action regarding faulty facilities. "The Armed Services Committee has done very little," he scolded. "Anytime we get into a problem … nobody on the committee knows what is what. We just delegate things to the Department of Energy," which he noted was already stretched thin having to regulate 17 plants across a dozen states.[30] In 1987 and 1988, Bustamante supported the Nuclear Test-Ban Treaty amendments put forth by liberal Democrats.

In 1992 Bustamante faced Republican Henry Bonilla, a local television producer, in an attempt to win a fifth term.

Though he raised significantly more money than Bonilla did in the first half of the year, Bustamante's electoral chances were later dimmed by scandal.[31] In December 1990, he admitted that the Federal Bureau of Investigation (FBI) had been questioning his friends and family as part of a three-year probe into his receipt of monetary bribes in exchange for federal contracts. Bustamante denied the charges, but Bonilla highlighted the ongoing investigation throughout the campaign.[32] He also underscored Bustamante's 30 overdrafts from the House "Bank," an informal institution run by the Sergeant at Arms in which some Members deposited their congressional pay. Though Bustamante's overdrafts were modest compared to those of the worst offenders in the House "Bank" scandal, he was one of a handful of Members with overdrafts who did not receive a letter from the U.S. Attorney special counsel clearing him of criminal wrongdoing before the election.[33] Redistricting further hampered Bustamante's re-election bid; Hispanic neighborhoods in the southwest sections of San Antonio were sliced out of his district, increasing the leverage of heavily Republican and Anglo neighborhoods northwest of the city.[34] Additionally, Bonilla's media work, linked with a popular television news program, gave him greater name and face recognition than Bustamante. Campaigning on reducing government regulations and taxes, Bonilla defeated Bustamante by a margin of 59 to 39 percent. In a year of incumbent losses nationwide, Bustamante was the only Latino incumbent who was not re-elected. He blamed his loss on the negative press generated by the scandals. "I could not sustain the tremendous amount of publicity that went against me," he said.[35]

Shortly after Bustamante left Congress, the FBI investigation resulted in an indictment on 10 counts of accepting bribes amounting to more than $300,000 in exchange for his official activities. On July 21, 1993, Bustamante was convicted on two of these 10 charges. A federal judge in San Antonio sentenced him to three and a half years in prison and ordered him to pay $55,100 in fines and legal fees.[36] After a series of unsuccessful appeals, Bustamante began serving out his prison term in El Paso, Texas, in May 1995. Upon his release from prison in 1998, Bustamante returned to San Antonio, where he manages a shopping center and works on projects related to affordable housing and education.[37]

FOR FURTHER READING

Biographical Directory of the United States Congress, "Albert G. Bustamante," http://bioguide.congress.gov.

Broder, David S. *Changing of the Guard: Power and Leadership in America* (New York: Penguin Books, 1980).

Rodriguez, David. *Latino National Political Coalitions: Struggles and Challenges* (New York: Garland Publishing, 2000).

MANUSCRIPT COLLECTION

The University of Texas at San Antonio Library, UTSA Archives (San Antonio). *Papers*: 1980–1992, 13 boxes, 5 linear feet. The collection documents Albert Bustamante's career from 1980 to 1992 as a Bexar County judge and as a U.S. Congressman. The bulk of the collection consists of incoming and outgoing correspondence from constituents and colleagues. The remainder of the records compile Congressman Bustamante's legislative record through vote books, a legislative profile, and his weekly newspaper column. The collection is divided into two series: papers from his tenure as a Bexar County judge and papers from his tenure as a U.S. Congressman.

NOTES

1 David S. Broder, *Changing of the Guard: Power and Leadership in America* (New York: Penguin Books: 1980): 286.

2 Spencer Rich, "The Cutting Edge: Migrant Workers Suffer Nutritional Deficiencies," 11 April 1989, *Washington Post*: 5.

3 Broder, *Changing of the Guard*: 286.

4 Ibid.

5 See, for example, Broder, "Texas, Vital to a Carter Victory, Presents Many Obstacles," 14 September 1980, *Washington Post*: A2; Rowland Evans and Robert Novak, "Keeping Glenn Moderate," 13 July 1983, *Washington Post*, A19.

6 *Almanac of American Politics, 1986* (Washington, D.C.: National Journal Inc., 1985): 1339.

7 *Politics in America, 1990* (Washington, D.C.: Congressional Quarterly, Inc., 1989): 1493.

8 "Minority Reports," 16 December 1984, *New York Times*: E20.

9 Antoinette Sedillo Lopez, ed., *Latino Communities: Emerging Voices* (New York: Routledge, 2002): 102.

10 Broder, *Changing of the Guard*: 286.

11 For more information on the Hispanic Caucus's perspective on Central American policy, see Antonio González, "Chicano Politics and U.S. Policy in Central America, 1979–1990," in David Montejano, ed., *Chicano Politics and Society in the Late Twentieth Century* (Austin: University of Texas Press, 1999): 154–172.

12 *Politics in America, 1990*: 1493.

13 *Congressional Quarterly Almanac, 1985* (Washington, D.C.: Congressional Quarterly, Inc., 1986): 22-H–25-H; *Congressional Record*, House, 99th Cong., 1st sess. (23 April 1985): 9085–9086; *Congressional Record*, House, 99th Cong., 1st sess. (24 April 1985): 9255–9257; Jacquelyn Swearingen, [No title], 23 April 1985, State News Service.

14 Bustamante voted with President Reagan in all five crucial votes on the bill that took place June 12. *Congressional Record*, House, 99th Cong., 1st sess. (12 June 1985): 15419–15420, 15431, 15436–15437, 15466, 15468–15469; *Congressional Quarterly Almanac, 1985*: 46-H–49-H.

15 Jacquelyn Swearingen, [No title], 12 June 1985, State News Service.

16 Jacquelyn Swearingen, [No title], 19 March 1986, State News Service.

17 Robert Parry, "Centrist Democrats Seek Delay on Contra Aid," 3 February 1986, Associated Press; Edward Walsh and Milton Coleman, "Reagan Twists Arms as Aides Seek Pact on Aid to Contras," 19 March 1986, *Washington Post*: A27; Lea Donsky, "Contra Deal Rides on a Few Votes," 18 March 1986, *Chicago Tribune*; Swearingen, [No title], 5 June 1986, State News Service.

18 *Congressional Record*, House, 99th Cong., 2nd sess. (20 March 1986): 5770–5771; *Congress and the Nation, 1985–1988* (Washington, D.C.: CQ Press, 1990): 178.

19 *Congressional Record*, House, 99th Cong., 2nd sess. (25 June 1986): 15562–15563; Linda Greenhouse, "Lobbying Succeeds," 26 June 1986, *New York Times*: A1.

20 Edward Walsh, "House Reverses Vote, Approves Reagan Plan for Aid to the Contras," 26 June 1986, *Washington Post*: A1.

21 Karen Tumulty, "House Votes to Bar Funds for Contras," 12 March 1987, *Los Angeles Times*: 1.

22 R. W. Apple, Jr., "North Role Cited in Bid to Unseat Contra Aid Foes," 15 December 1986, *New York Times*: A1; *Congress and the Nation, 1985–1988*: 211; *Congressional Record*, House, 100th Cong., 1st sess. (11 March 1987): 5467.

23 See, for example, the final vote on H. J. Res. 484, *Congressional Record*, 100th Cong., 2nd sess. (3 March 1988): 3257, and the amendment proposed by Henry Hyde of Illinois to H.R. 4387. See *Congressional Record*, 100th Congress, 2nd sess. (26 May 1988): 12526.

24 *Congressional Record*, House, 99th Cong., 2nd sess. (9 October 1986): 30075–30076.

25 See, for example, *Congressional Record*, House, 99th Cong., 2nd sess. (9 October 1986): 26403, 31644; Robert Pear, "Immigration Bill: How 'Corpse' Came Back to Life," 13 October 1986, *New York Times*: A16.

26 *Congressional Record*, House, 99th Cong., 2nd sess. (9 October 1986): 30051.

27 Robert Pear, "Study Finds Bias, Forcing Review of 1986 Alien Law," 30 March 1990, *New York Times*: A1.

28 Richard Haller, "Budget Cuts? 'Not in My District!'," 11 February 1988, *New York Times*: A20.

29 Keith Schneider, "Inquiry Ordered at Nuclear Arms Site," 7 October 1988, *New York Times*: A18.

30 Fox Butterfield, "Trouble at Atomic Bomb Plants: How Lawmakers Missed the Signs," 28 November 1988, *New York Times*: A1.

31 Jonathan Moore, "Bustamante Warchest Larger Than Bonilla's," 3 June 1992, State News Service.

32 See, for example, Jennifer Dixon, "Bustamante Says FBI Questioning People about His Links to Bingo," 6 December 1990, Associated Press; Hugh Aynesworth, "Bustamante Calls Probe GOP Political Vendetta," 1 October 1992, *Washington Times*: A5.

33 See, for example, Karen J. Cohen, "Rep. Bustamante Has No Problems with Releasing Names in the Check-Cashing Scandal," 11 March 1992, State News Service; William E. Clayton, Jr., and Damon Gardenhire, "House Unmasks Check-Kiters; Names of 21 Texas Members Listed in 'Rubbergate' Report," 17 April 1992, *Houston Chronicle*: A1; Dante Chinni, "3 Texans Unable to Shake House Banking Scandal," 10 October 1992, *Houston Chronicle*: A4; Dante Chinni, "3 in Check Case Hope the All-Clear Really in the Mail," 31 October 1992, *Houston Chronicle*: A16.

34 Hugh Aynesworth, "Bustamante Calls Probe GOP Political Vendetta," 1 October 1992, *Washington Times*: A5; *Almanac of American Politics, 1994* (Washington, D.C.: National Journal Inc., 1993): 1263.

35 James Rubin, "Scandal the Deciding Factor for Many of Congress' Losing Incumbents," 4 November 1992, The Associated Press.

36 Bustamante's wife, Rebecca, was also charged with seven counts of bribery. She was acquitted on all charges. See, for example, "Ex-Congressman Indicted on Charges of Accepting Bribes," 19 February 1993, *New York Times*: A11; Federal Jury Convicts Ex-Texas Congressman, 22 July 1993, *New York Times*: A21; "Ex-Congressman Is Sentenced," 2 October 1993, *New York Times*: 9.

37 University of Texas at San Antonio, Archives and Special Collections, "A Guide to the Albert Bustamante Papers, 1980–1992," http://www.lib.utexas.edu/taro/utsa/00006/utsa-00006.html (accessed 14 July 2009).

Jaime B. Fuster

1941–2007

RESIDENT COMMISSIONER 1985–1992
POPULAR DEMOCRAT FROM PUERTO RICO

Described as "a serious tennis player and a voracious reader," Jaime Fuster brought a scholarly demeanor to Capitol Hill during his House tenure of a little less than two terms.[1] With his academic background, Fuster focused his legislative energies on educational opportunities in Puerto Rico and the mainland. But he spent most of his time in the House vigorously defending the Estado Libre Asociado (Free Associated State, or ELA)—the commonwealth relationship between the United States and Puerto Rico—against advocates for statehood, whom he accused of indulging in "rhetorical flourishes and pie-in-the-sky prophecies."[2] As the first Puerto Rican chairman of the Congressional Hispanic Caucus (CHC), Fuster appreciated the growing caucus's diversity. "We Hispanics are peoples of all colors and all hues," he boasted.[3] "We Mexican-Americans, Cuban-Americans, Puerto Ricans and others—we are all, first and foremost, Hispanic brothers and sisters with a common heritage, with common problems and with common challenges. Far more binds us together than separates us."[4]

Jaime B. Fuster was born on January 12, 1941, in Guayama, on the southeast coast of Puerto Rico. Fuster attended Saint Anthony High School in Guayama, graduating as valedictorian in 1958.[5] He earned a B.A., magna cum laude, from Notre Dame University in South Bend, Indiana, in 1962. He earned a J.D. from the Universidad de Puerto Rico in 1965 and a specialized post-law degree from Columbia University a year later. Fuster began working as a law professor at the Universidad de Puerto Rico in 1966. He received a fellowship in law and the humanities from Harvard from 1973 to 1974. When he returned to Puerto Rico, he served as dean of his law school through 1978. Throughout his tenure, Fuster took a particular interest in interamerican policy throughout Latin America, traveling extensively throughout the region.[6] In 1980 he left the university to serve as a U.S. deputy assistant attorney general. The next year he started a four-year tenure as president of Pontificia Universidad Católica de Puerto Rico. Fuster married Mary Jo Zalduondo, and the couple raised two children, María Luisa and Jaime José.[7]

In the wake of the 1980 election—in which the U.S. Supreme Court decided the makeup of the Puerto Rican house of representatives after two years of electoral dispute—the 1984 election appeared to be another close referendum on the island's status in relation to the United States.[8] Three parties—the Partido Popular Democrático (Popular Democratic Party, or PPD), the Partido Nuevo Progresista (New Progressive Party, or PNP), and the Partido Independentista Puertorriqueño (Independence Party, or PIP)—represented three respective options for Puerto Rican status: commonwealth status, statehood, and independence. Fuster accepted the PPD nomination for Resident Commissioner after PNP Resident Commissioner Baltasar Corrada del-Río declared his candidacy for mayor of San Juan. Running unopposed in the PPD primary in June, Fuster sought the post of Resident Commissioner as a political ally of gubernatorial candidate Rafael Hernández Colón's. He vowed to "improve the over-all tenor of Puerto Rican relations in Washington," which he believed had been "bruised" by incumbent PNP Governor Carlos Romero-Barceló's accusations that Puerto Rico remained a "colony." Fuster's primary objectives were to defend the ELA and to maintain the flow of federal dollars to the island.[9]

Fuster and the PPD had an advantage when the PNP split over a crisis of leadership. After insurgents attempted to remove PNP leader Carlos Romero-Barceló from power, they were humiliated by Romero-Barceló and his fellow *penepeistas* (PNP members) at the Party assembly in November 1982. The insurgents subsequently formed the

Collection of the U.S. House of Representatives, Photography Collection

Partido Renovación Puertorriqueña (Puerto Rican Renewal Party), presenting their own candidates for governor, the Puerto Rican legislature, and Resident Commissioner. With a turnout of nearly 90 percent of registered voters, Fuster won the Resident Commissioner position, garnering 48.5 percent of the vote—a slim victory over Nelson Famadas of the PNP, who won 45.4 percent. The race would have been even closer had Partido Renovación Puertorriqueña candidate Angel Viera-Martinez not siphoned off 2.3 percent of the vote. PIP candidate Francisco Catala took 3.8 percent.[10] The PPD swept the election, winning the gubernatorial contest and a majority in both the Puerto Rican house and senate in addition to Fuster's victory.[11]

Upon his arrival in Washington, Fuster won seats on the Committee on the Interior and Insular Affairs and the Committee on Banking, Finance and Urban Affairs. In the following Congress, he traded his seat on the Banking panel for a seat on the Foreign Affairs Committee. In the 101st Congress (1989–1991), he also picked up a seat on the Education and Labor Committee.[12] Unable to vote in the House, Fuster depended on friends and fellow Congressional Hispanic Caucus (CHC) members, frequently reminding his colleagues that he represented three million Americans. Representative Robert Garcia, who served a South Bronx district in New York City with a large Puerto Rican population, proved to be Fuster's closest congressional ally. "In some kind of crazy way, I consider myself something of a representative of Puerto Rico," Garcia once remarked.[13] Fuster regularly submitted editorials and letters to the editor in response to coverage of Puerto Rican politics in major U.S. newspapers.[14]

On September 8, 1988, the CHC unanimously elected Fuster chairman, a post in which he served from 1988 to 1989. He became the first Puerto Rican to chair the caucus, which consisted at that time of 13 Hispanic members and 67 dues-paying non-Hispanic members. "It is … a tribute to Puerto Rico, and I look forward to this new assignment," Fuster noted in a caucus press release.[15] As chairman, Fuster focused on education, employment, and affordable housing for many of the caucus's urban constituents. CHC members also focused on increasing American exports across the southern border of the United States.[16] "Every year we're more successful than the year before," Fuster said of the caucus's work. "When we work together we can have a fairly strong influence despite our size."[17]

Fuster's legislative agenda was focused southward toward his home in the Caribbean. He supported the Caribbean Basin Initiative, which called for the duty-free entry of goods from countries in the Caribbean Sea.[18] He also backed aspects of the 1986 Omnibus Drug Act that provided additional radar coverage for Puerto Rico to fight drug trafficking.[19] He was barred from serving as an election monitor in Haiti in November 1987 because he was a congressional signatory to an October 14 letter accusing the government in Port-au-Prince of human rights abuses.[20] The Haitian Foreign Affairs Ministry returned the letter, unopened, on November 29, 1987.[21]

Education was also key for Fuster, especially given his academic background. "Not until we have a better understanding of ourselves can we move forward," he said regarding his education initiatives.[22] Fuster spearheaded a plan to make Puerto Rico the educational and training hub for Central America and the Caribbean by introducing the Caribbean Basin Scholarship Act (H.R. 3806) in 1988; the bill would authorize the creation of 1,000 scholarships for students earning higher degrees at Puerto Rican institutions. After the House scheduled hearings on the bill in the Subcommittee on Human Rights and International Organizations under the House Foreign Affairs Committee, Fuster observed that the attention was "a sign of American recognition of the maturity of Puerto Rico's leadership and … of the enduring nature of Puerto Rico's accomplishments economically and politically." In addition, Fuster pointed out, the program would enhance American leadership in the region.[23]

Fuster and his CHC colleagues advocated bilingual education in the United States. "We want to make sure that Hispanics who don't speak English will have the opportunity in some stages at least to learn in Spanish, while they pick up enough English language skills to be able to do well," he noted. "The goal eventually is to fully integrate in social life in English."[24] When the Puerto Rican legislature submitted a bill making Spanish the island's official language, thereby endangering U.S. support for the commonwealth, Fuster was unapologetic. "We should not delude someone in Congress over who we are and what we are. We are a Spanish-speaking country. If this happens to give people … more concern, so be it," he said.[25]

The need to educate other Members about Puerto Rico's unique relationship with the United States dominated Fuster's career. The Resident Commissioner grew frustrated with the general lack of knowledge about the island in Congress, a situation he vowed to change. "The main problem I have," he lamented, "is not only the lack of information [others have about the island], but [that] Puerto Rico is not in the mainstream of mainland concerns, but we are part of the United States."[26]

Like the tenures of previous Resident Commissioners, Fuster's was dominated by Puerto Rico's status. Despite his frustration at not having a vote in Congress, Fuster firmly supported the ELA over statehood.[27] "At first glance, you might think that the people of Puerto Rico are somehow being held back from exercising their right to have the island become the 51st State," he noted in the *Congressional Record*. "That is simply not true.… It is appalling that some Members of Congress would want to open up this thorny and explosive issue when the people of Puerto Rico themselves do not." [28] Fuster warned against "toying with Puerto Rico" and in the late 1980s bemoaned a spate of bills seeking adjustments in Puerto Rico's relationship with the United States.[29] "Pandering to political currents with one upmanship in submitting bills about Puerto Rico's status is not the way to assist the people of Puerto Rico to exercise their right to self-determination," he said, accusing his colleagues of using Puerto Rican issues as a political tool.[30]

Despite Fuster's warning, political maneuverings both on the island and on the mainland pushed Puerto Rico toward a plebiscite on status. In 1988, PPD Governor Hernández Colón won re-election with a slim plurality, but for the fourth consecutive time, no candidate won more than 50 percent of the vote in the gubernatorial race, indicating a divided electorate.[31] Fuster, too, won re-election with another narrow plurality, taking 49 percent over PNP candidate Pedro J. Rosselló, who won 47 percent, and PIP candidate Luis Pio Sanchez Longo.[32] Both the PNP and the PIP showed their strength on the island. The PNP won a larger swath of the municipal election, and the PIP, for the first time, triumphed in a mayoral election when Santos (El Negro) Ortiz won in the municipality of Cabo Rojo.[33] The two minority parties took advantage of the close elections to create an alliance with the pro-statehood PNP.[34]

At the same time, President George H. W. Bush shined a spotlight on Puerto Rican statehood in Washington. The President surprised observers by announcing his support for a self-determination plebiscite in Puerto Rico during his February 9, 1989, State of the Union address. Bush's Senate ally, J. Bennett Johnston of Louisiana, drafted S. 712 in response. Johnston chaired the Senate Energy and Natural Resources Committee, which had direct oversight over Puerto Rico. His self-executing bill put the three "well-formed" options—continuation under commonwealth status, statehood, and independence—to a vote in Puerto Rico whose results would take effect immediately.[35] The Committee on Energy and Natural Resources favorably reported the bill to the Senate on August 2, 1989.

Fuster complained that advocates presented statehood as a magical solution to Puerto Rican economic problems. "Statehood is portrayed as the panacea for the many complex and intractable social and economic problems that Puerto Rico has suffered for centuries," he explained. "Puerto Ricans are being told that with statehood, unemployment will nearly disappear, education and healthcare will be of the highest quality possible, our local roads will be like the best interstate highways, there will be no homeless, even crime will diminish. We in Puerto Rico have a right to know whether or not the United States Congress shares these alluring expectations about the bonanza that allegedly will accompany statehood."[36]

Delegate Ron de Lugo of the Virgin Islands—Chairman of the Committee on Territories—countered the Senate bill by introducing his own version (H.R. 4765) collaborating closely with Fuster, on May 9, 1990. The bill authorized a "non-binding referendum" and required Congress—specifically, the House Interior and Senate Energy Committees—to follow up on the results and enact the status chosen by voters.[37] The House legislation cobbled together the disparate interests of the island's multiple political parties as well as the various desires of mainland lawmakers, leading Fuster to label the bill "imperfect." The compromises "do not all share the sense of purpose and high-mindedness that should have prevailed," he noted.[38] Yet he supported the House version of the bill—with increased congressional oversight—over the Senate version. "It is crucial to the plebiscite process that the Congress spell out to the voters of Puerto Rico precisely what it is prepared to offer under each of the three formulas for political status," he wrote in an opinion piece for the *Washington Post*. "Otherwise, the whole thing could be an empty gesture."[39] The House passed de Lugo's bill by voice vote on October 10. It was the first time since the creation of the ELA in 1952 that a referendum on Puerto Rican status had cleared either chamber.[40]

Reaching a compromise between the House and Senate versions of the bill proved "an uphill battle," Fuster noted in June 1990, and he feared the legislation would not pass in time. "It's going to be dicey. If we have one more delay, that's it," he warned.[41] Lobbying over the bill became increasingly intense, with a deadlock between the two chambers. More than 70 U.S. companies doing business on the island—and enjoying tax breaks—formed the Puerto Rico U.S.A. Foundation, which fought the Bush administration's pro-statehood stance.[42] Advocates for ELA and advocates for statehood hired more than a dozen lobbying firms that hit Capitol Hill "with the force of Hurricane Hugo," according to the *Wall Street Journal*.[43] But Johnston was dissatisfied with the House version of the bill and refused to take action on it, effectively killing the measure at the end of the 101st Congress. "The Senate's position is that we have waited 30 years. Another year is not going to matter," Johnston said.[44]

Though de Lugo re-introduced his plebiscite bill on the first day of the new Congress, the momentum from the previous Congress had been lost. Puerto Rican officials were wary of holding a vote on status during 1992, an island-wide election year, because they feared the plebiscite would likely promote a charged and disruptive atmosphere. Cost was also an issue. After a 10 to 10 vote in the Senate Energy Committee on legislation equivalent to that promoted in the 101st Congress, Johnston again admitted defeat, despite pressure from President Bush to continue pursuing the plebiscite. Acknowledging inadequate GOP support, de Lugo did not push his legislation further.[45] "I'm more convinced than ever that there is going to be no plebiscite," Fuster noted.[46] "There is a stalemate in Congress, and we don't see any signs that it's going to change," he added. "The people of Puerto Rico have been left dangling with great expectations. We're saying 'Take us seriously or let us be.'"[47]

Fuster's final term in the House was truncated. In early 1992, Governor Hernández Colón nominated him as an associate justice on the Puerto Rican supreme court. Confirmed by a 14 to 5 decision in the island's senate, Fuster resigned from the House on March 3, 1992.[48] He served as an associate justice until his death on December 3, 2007, in his home in Guaynabo, Puerto Rico.[49]

FOR FURTHER READING

Biographical Directory of the United States Congress, "Jaime B. Fuster," http://bioguide.congress.gov.

Fuster, Jaime B. *Los derechos civiles reconocidos en el sistema de vida puertorriqueño* (San Juan, PR: Comisión de Derechos Civiles, 1972).

NOTES

1 Robin Toner, "Explain, Explain, Explain," 8 May 1986, *New York Times*: B22.

2 *Congressional Record*, Extension of Remarks, 101st Cong., 1st sess. (25 April 1989): 7472.

3 David Rampe, "Power Panel in Making: The Hispanic Caucus," 30 September 1988, *New York Times*: B5.

4 Congressional Hispanic Caucus, "Remarks of Jaime B. Fuster at Congressional Banquet," Press Release 13 September 1988; Fuster, Jaime, Former Caucus Members, Folder 2; Records of the Congressional Hispanic Caucus, 97th–103rd Congress; Record Group 233; National Archives Building, Washington, D.C.

(hereinafter referred to as RG 233; NARA).

5 "Curriculum Vitae," Fuster, Jaime, Former Caucus Members, Folder 1; Biographical Files Relating to Former Caucus Members, 1983–1984, Becerra, X. to Richardson, Bill, Box 1; Records of the Congressional Hispanic Caucus, 97th–103rd Congress; RG 233; NARA.

6 Ibid.

7 "Supreme Court Justice Jaime Fuster Dies at 66," *Caribbean Business* 35, no. 48 (6 December 2007); Camile Roldán Soto, "Destacan la trayectoria del jurist," 4 December 2007, *El nueva dia*, http://www.adendi.com/ (accessed 29 March 2012).

8 Fernando Bayron Toro, *Elecciones y partidos políticos de Puerto Rico, 1809–2000* (Mayagüez, PR: Editorial Isla, 2003): 302.

9 Harold Lidin, "50,000 Turnout Seen for PDP Primaries Sunday," 6 June 1984, *San Juan Star*: 10; Lidin, "Fuster Sees a Role in Island-U.S. Relations," 25 June 1984, *San Juan Star*: 16.

10 "Election Statistics, 1920 to Present," http://history.house.gov/institution/election statistics/election-statistics.

11 Bayron Toro, *Elecciones y partidos políticos de Puerto Rico, 1809–2000*: 310.

12 Garrison Nelson, *Committees in the U.S. Congress, 1947 to 1992*, vol. 2 (Washington, D.C.: CQ Press, 1994): 318.

13 Toner, "Explain, Explain, Explain."

14 Jaime B. Fuster, Letter to the Editor, "The Politics of Governing Puerto Rico," 16 July 1986, *Washington Post*; Fuster, Letter to the Editor, "Promise in Puerto Rico," 20 March 1987, *Christian Science Monitor*: 15; Fuster, Letter to the Editor, "Puerto Rico Enjoys Commonwealth Status," 2 May 1988, *Wall Street Journal*: 25.

15 "Congressional Hispanic Caucus Elects Fuster Chairman," Press Release 8 September 1988, Folder 1, Former Caucus Members, Fuster, Jaime, RG 233; NA.

16 For a rundown of Fuster's goals as CHC chairman, see "Congressional Hispanic Caucus Legislative Agenda for the 100th Congress," Official Memorandums, 1989, Folder 1 of 2; Official Memorandums 1985–1992, Box 2; RG 233, NA.

17 Rampe, "Power Panel in Making: The Hispanic Caucus."

18 For more information, see "Caribbean Trade Plan." CQ Press Library, CQ Almanac Online Edition, cqal82-1163576. Originally published in *CQ Almanac 1982* (Washington, D.C.: Congressional Quarterly, Inc., 1983). http://library.cqpress.com/cqalmanac/cqal82-1163576 (accessed 27 April 2009).

19 *Congressional Record*, House, 99th Cong., 2nd sess. (10 September 1986): 22730.

20 "3 U.S. Legislators Barred," 29 November 1987, *New York Times*: 16.

21 Julia Preston, "Haitians Set to Vote Despite Violence," 29 November 1987, *Washington Post*: A31.

22 Congressional Hispanic Caucus, "Legislative Review," Fall 1988, p. 1; Official Memorandums, 1988, Folder 2 of 2; RG 233, NA.

23 Congressional Hispanic Caucus, "House Foreign Affairs Subcommittee to Hold Hearings on Puerto Rico Scholarships Bill," Press Release 9 August 1988, Fuster, Jaime, Former Caucus Members, Folder 2, CHC Records, RG 233. See also Hearing before the House Subcommittee on Human Rights and International Organizations, *Development Policy in the Caribbean*, 100th Cong., 2nd sess. (28 July 1988).

24 Rampe, "Power Panel in Making: The Hispanic Caucus."

25 Bill McAllister, "Puerto Rican Bill on Spanish Called Statehood Setback," 6 March 1991, *Washington Post*: A6.

26 Toner, "Explain, Explain, Explain."

27 Ibid.

28 *Congressional Record*, Extension of Remarks, 100th Cong., 1st sess. (15 July 1987): 20115–20116.

29 See, for example, H.J. Res. 218 (100th Congress, 1987–1989), introduced by Representative Ron Dellums of California, calling for independence; S. 1182 (100th Congress), introduced by Senator Bob Dole of Kansas, calling for statehood; and H.R. 3536 (101st Congress, 1989–1991), introduced by Representative Robert Lagomarsino of California, calling for a referendum on status.

30 *Congressional Record*, Extension of Remarks, 100th Cong., 1st sess. (7 August 1987): 23488.

31 Bayron Toro, *Elecciones y partidos políticos de Puerto Rico, 1809–2000*: 261–265, 271–291, 310, 333–334.

32 "Election Statistics, 1920 to Present," http://history.house.gov/institution/election-statistics/election-statistics.

33 Bayron Toro, *Elecciones y partidos políticos de Puerto Rico, 1809–2000*: 335, 337.

34 "Puerto Rico's Status Remains Unresolved." CQ Press Electronic Library, CQ Almanac Online Edition, cqal90-1113003. Originally published in *CQ Almanac 1990* (Washington, D.C.: Congressional Quarterly, Inc., 1991). http://library.cqpress.com/cqal90-1113003 (accessed 8 October 2009).

35 "Puerto Rico's Status Remains Unresolved."

36 *Congressional Record*, Extension of Remarks, 101st Cong., 1st sess. (16 November 1989): 3872. Earlier that year Fuster accused statehood supporters of upholding an "Alice-in-Wonderland mileu [*sic*]." Fuster asked his colleagues, "Would Congress and President Bush really be prepared to accept ... that Puerto Rico be admitted to the Union with Spanish as our official language, with our own limited international personality preserved, paying no Federal income taxes? Would they accept statehood to be portrayed as the panacea for many complex and intractable social and economic problems that Puerto Rico has suffered for centuries?" See

Congressional Record, Extension of Remarks, 101st Cong., 1st sess. (25 April 1989): 7472.

37 "Puerto Rico's Status Remains Unresolved."

38 Ibid.

39 Jaime B. Fuster, "Statehood Could Ruin Puerto Rico's Economy," 31 July 1989, *Washington Post*: A15.

40 Robert Pear, "House Votes Bill for Puerto Rico to Decide Status," 11 October 1990, *New York Times*: A1.

41 Bill McAllister, "Puerto Rico Bill Wording Is Criticized," 29 June 1990, *Washington Post*: A11.

42 "Puerto Rico's Status Remains Unresolved."

43 Jill Abramson, "Plan for 1991 Referendum on Puerto Rico Status Spurs Rival Factions to Blitz Lawmakers in U.S.," 10 October 1989, *Wall Street Journal*: A20. Jaime B. Fuster, Letter to the Editor, "Throwing Weight for Puerto Rico Statehood," 4 November 1990, *Washington Post*: C6.

44 Bill McAllister, "Puerto Rico Referendum in Jeopardy," 11 October 1990, *Washington Post*: A10.

45 "No Progress Made on Puerto Rico Plebiscite." CQ Press Electronic Library, CQ Almanac Online Edition, cqal91-1110291. Originally published in *CQ Almanac 1991* (Washington, D.C.: Congressional Quarterly, Inc., 1992). http://library.cqpress.com/cqal91-1112109 (accessed 27 April 2009).

46 Bill McAllister, "Administration Backs Puerto Rico Bill, But Seeks Changes," 8 February 1991, *Washington Post*: A3. See also Martin Tolchin, "Constitutionality of a Choice for Puerto Rico's Future Is Challenged," 8 February 1991, *New York Times*: A18.

47 Martin Tolchin, "Shift in San Juan on Vote on Status," 23 November 1990, *New York Times*: A27.

48 Robert Friedman, "Senate Gives Fuster OK for Top Court," 14 February 1992, *San Juan Star*: 5; Associated Press, "Fuster Takes Oath as Justice of High Court," 4 March 1992, *San Juan Star*: 8. Though Fuster's resignation letter submitted to the Speaker of the House indicates he resigned on March 4, 1992, he took the oath of office for the Puerto Rican supreme court on March 3, 1992. Thus, he would have submitted his official resignation as Resident Commissioner to the governor before his swearing-in. Other official sources indicate he resigned March 3, 1992. See, for example, Clerk of the House of Representatives, "Official List of Members of the House of Representatives of the United States and Their Places of Residence," 102nd Cong., 2nd sess. (5 January 1993), http://clerk.house.gov/102/olm102.pdf (accessed 28 March 2012).

49 "Former Resident Commissioner Dies at Age 66 in Puerto Rico," 4 December 2007, *National Journal's CongressDaily*.

"Hispanics must communicate to all segments of society the fact that our growing numbers are a positive trend in American development. To convey that idea persuasively, we must be fully convinced of it ourselves.... Only when we ourselves feel the strength that comes from the achievements of others in our community will we be able to set new precedents and create the sorely needed role models for our young."

Jaime B. Fuster
Hispanic Business, September 1988

Antonio J. Colorado

1939–

RESIDENT COMMISSIONER 1992–1993
POPULAR DEMOCRAT FROM PUERTO RICO

Antonio J. Colorado had the shortest tenure of any Puerto Rican Resident Commissioner in nearly 56 years. Nevertheless, he used his expertise in tax policy to influence national legislation and protect Puerto Rico's unique revenue-sharing arrangement with the federal government.

Colorado was born in New York on September 8, 1939, but grew up in Puerto Rico after his family moved back to the island for his early education. Colorado's father was a major influence in the genesis of the island's modern political system and an early backer of the Partido Popular Democrático (Popular Democratic Party, or PPD). Colorado's father designed the PPD's logo and was a close friend of Luis Muñoz Marín, Puerto Rico's most powerful governor and the party's founder. The younger Colorado was groomed for political stardom alongside Muñoz Marín's daughter, Victoria Muñoz Mendoza, who later served in the insular senate and ran for governor.[1] Colorado attended the primary and high school affiliates of the Universidad de Puerto Rico and returned to the mainland for college. He graduated from Boston University in Massachusetts with a bachelor of science degree in 1962. Two years later, having gone back to the island, he earned a law degree from the Universidad de Puerto Rico. In 1966, he earned a master's degree from Harvard University.[2]

Colorado passed the bar in 1966 and began working in tax law, a specialty that fueled his rise to the heights of Puerto Rican politics. From 1966 to 1969, he worked as a legal tax aide for and an executive assistant to the Economic Development Administration of Puerto Rico. He left in 1969 to join a private law firm, where he practiced for the next 15 years. A respected policy advisor, Colorado served on Puerto Rico's Tax Reform Commission in 1973 and later lectured at the law schools of the Universidad de Puerto Rico and Inter-American University.[3]

In 1985 Colorado was appointed Puerto Rico's administrator of economic development, solidifying his status as the island's foremost financial mind. Over the next five years, Colorado worked to protect Puerto Rico's unique revenue-sharing relationship with the federal government, which used tax breaks to lure major industry to Puerto Rican shores. The corporations that set down roots in Puerto Rico were known as "936 companies," after the Internal Revenue Code governing the insular tax shelter.[4]

Colorado's defense of the tax break was part of the PPD's broader agenda to keep the federal government at arm's length, giving the island more control over its domestic economy. Puerto Rico's main English-language newspaper called Colorado "smart, hard-driving, and approachable," qualities that made him a key player in the PPD's ongoing feud with members of the Partido Nuevo Progresista (New Progressive Party, or PNP), which wanted to reform Puerto Rico's unique tax incentives and pave the way for statehood. Equally important, according to the *San Juan Star*, Colorado's demeanor made him "a highly effective one-on-one salesman," and he had "immense confidence in" the island's financial capacities. As Puerto Rico's chief economist, he was well versed in international finance and had traveled widely in the Caribbean, and often to Washington, to lobby members of the House and Senate.[5] In 1990, Colorado was named Puerto Rico's secretary of state, enabling him to directly engage nations in the Caribbean Basin that struggled with similar problems.

When Puerto Rico's Resident Commissioner, Jaime B. Fuster, accepted a position on the island's supreme court in late February 1992, Colorado was recommended for the post. Replacing a Resident Commissioner did not require a special election; the candidate needed only to be nominated and confirmed by the insular senate.[6] Given his long career in tax policy, Colorado seemed a logical choice

Collection of the U.S. House of Representatives, Photography Collection

to the island's sitting PPD administration. With Congress set to consider whether to delete section 936 from the tax code and quit providing incentives to big pharmaceutical companies (one of the largest employers in Puerto Rico), Colorado was in a better position than nearly anyone else to lobby on the island's behalf. His confirmation hearings were so straightforward, that one newspaper described the process as "smooth sailing."[7] Even before taking office late in the winter of 1992, Colorado began speaking with members of the Senate's Finance Committee to prepare for the upcoming debate.[8] "If a man and a place were meant to meet," wrote one of San Juan's leading newspapers that March, "it's Antonio [J.] 'Tito' Colorado and the United States Congress."[9]

Colorado was sworn in on March 4, 1992, and like many of his predecessors, he caucused with the Democrats. Around two-thirty in the afternoon, dressed in "a dark gray suit and red tie," Colorado began the briefest tenure of any Puerto Rican Resident Commissioner since 1932.[10] His first priority, he said, was to protect his island's "very special relationship" with the mainland. "I look to the next months as the most important days of my life," he told the chamber, "and I will work with you intensively to better the quality of life in Puerto Rico, in the mainland United States, in the Caribbean and Central America, and everywhere else in the world where we may be needed."[11] Colorado was assigned to the Committee on Foreign Affairs. "With my experience in the Caribbean and as a tax lawyer, I think I've got something to offer Foreign Affairs," Colorado said.[12]

Colorado quickly eased himself into the ongoing debates over tax policy and the profits generated by Puerto Rico's major pharmaceutical companies. In Washington, the push to delete section 936 from the Internal Revenue Code was popular among Senators intent on lowering the cost of medicine, even if they had to strong-arm certain drug makers along the way.[13] But Colorado thought the proposal would have done little more than punish Puerto Rican companies and their employees.[14] As it had elsewhere, the cost of health care had skyrocketed in Puerto Rico, and since Colorado's main concern was to protect the island's economic development, he lobbied the Senate Finance Committee to reform the tax code so that drug manufacturers across the country would be affected equally.[15] Colorado's decision to single out the industry troubled many corporate executives but seemed to have an impact.[16] The general sense in Congress was that reforming section 936 would do more harm than good, making it harder for those who opposed the incentives to take the lead.[17] In July, during consideration of the Foreign Income Tax Rationalization and Simplification Act of 1992 (H.R. 5270), Colorado testified before the House Ways and Means Committee that any reduction in section 936 "would be an economic calamity for Puerto Rico" since over the last 40 years, one-third of the jobs on the island were created because of the shelter policy.[18] The bill died in committee after the hearings.

That summer, Colorado introduced the second of the two bills he sponsored during his House career. His first measure, H.R. 5030, sought to facilitate trade between the mainland and Puerto Rico; introduced in April, it died in committee.[19] His second bill, the Puerto Rico Medicaid Improvement Act of 1992, would have boosted the island's health funding by nearly $30 million. Though it had the support of the George H. W. Bush administration, and though Puerto Rico needed more services to combat one of the country's highest rates of new AIDS cases, Colorado's bill never received a hearing in committee.[20]

Adding to the hectic pace of his first few months in office, Colorado decided to run for re-election after receiving the blessing of the PPD leadership.[21] Colorado spent his weekends stumping across Puerto Rico when the House was in session, returning to the island to "be out on the streets"after the House recessed on October 9th.[22]

As it had in Washington, the fate of section 936 influenced the 1992 election, crystallizing Puerto Rico's anxiety about its status. Though Colorado had managed to protect the island's tax shelter and the jobs he claimed it created, those debates appeared likely to begin anew in the next Congress. For those who favored commonwealth status, Colorado was again the logical choice for Resident Commissioner. "One of my objectives is to try to get people

to understand what 936 is all about," he said, citing the general confusion that was often associated with insular tax policy. "We need to create a constituency of people who understand that [936] is positive for them."[23] But the insurgent statehood movement had rallied behind Colorado's PNP challenger, former San Juan mayor and Puerto Rican governor Carlos Romero-Barceló, who advocated reforming the tax policy to offset federal appropriations.[24]

The 1992 election was one of the closest in recent memory. Despite his ties to the island's business community, Colorado raised less money than Romero-Barceló, and despite early polls showing a sizable lead for Colorado, the incumbent couldn't match his opponent's populist message.[25] Colorado countered criticism that in supporting commonwealth status, he was sacrificing access to federal aid. "We have great problems, crime, the economy and health.... These programs will depend greatly on Washington and there we can get the help and benefits needed," he said.[26] "We are going to seek equality," Colorado stated later, "but without undermining our economic program and our tax incentives." On Election Day he lost by less than 1 percent.[27] Almost immediately, there was talk that statehood and the foreign policy requirements that come with it would force the island to "slash ties" with friendly nations in the Caribbean, damaging relationships Colorado had helped build. With his experience as Puerto Rico's secretary of state, Colorado seemed poised to accept an appointment to a diplomatic position. "I'd like to work with something that has to do with Puerto Rico, the United States, the Caribbean and Latin America, either on the level of the federal government or an international organization," he admitted.[28]

After finishing his term in Washington, Colorado moved back to Puerto Rico, but the hoped-for diplomatic position never materialized.[29] In 1994 he ran for president of the PPD, promising to "lead the transformation of Puerto Rico to a new future."[30] He remained involved in the economic health of the Caribbean Basin, and in 1996 he accepted the executive directorship of a private lobbying firm working in Caribbean and Latin American affairs.[31] Around the same time, federal officials began gradually phasing out section 936, effectively ending the island's long-standing tax incentives. "It's the end and Puerto Rico will suffer," Colorado said in the summer of 1996.[32] "What companies are going to come to Puerto Rico without 936?"[33] He remained a strong supporter of the PPD's status platform, and in 1998 celebrated a victory in the pro-commonwealth plebiscite vote.[34]

FOR FURTHER READING

Biographical Directory of the United States Congress, "Antonio J. Colorado," http://bioguide.congress.gov.

Colorado, Antonio J. *Democracia y socialismo: Dos ensayos politicos* (San Juan, PR: Editorial Raíces, 1990).

_____. *The First Book of Puerto Rico* (New York: F. Watts, 1965).

_____. *Puerto Rico: La Tierra y otros ensayos* (San Juan, PR: Editorial Cordillera, 1972).

_____. *Puerto Rico y tú; libro de estudios sociales para la escuela elemental* (San Juan, PR: Departamento de Instrucción, 1952).

_____. *Semblanzas de ayer y de hoy* (San Juan, PR: Editorial Raíces, 1990).

NOTES

1 Doreen Hemlock and Jorge Luis Medina, "Colorado Tapped for D.C. Post in '92," 11 March 1992, *San Juan Star*: 2.

2 *Biographical Directory of the United States Congress*, "Antonio J. Colorado," http://bioguide.congress.gov; Harry Turner, "Antonio Colorado Sworn in as Resident Commissioner," 5 March 1992, *San Juan Star*: 2.

3 *Biographical Directory of the United States Congress*, "Antonio J. Colorado," http://bioguide.congress.gov.

4 In 1987 a lobby group for the Caribbean Basin purchased a three-page advertisement in the *New York Times*. Included in the spread was an article published under Colorado's name (and including his headshot) arguing how the 936 policy encouraged investment throughout the region. See the advertisement "Central America, Caribbean Development Program: Peace Prosperity and Business," 1 December 1987, *New York Times*: D11.

5 "Colorado in Congress," 5 March 1992, *San Juan Star*: 51; Turner, "Antonio Colorado Sworn in as Resident Commissioner"; Doreen Hemlock, "Colorado Is Possible Clinton Appointee," 5 November 1992, *San Juan Star*: 4.

6 Several other Resident Commissioners were appointed to the House. Appointments from Puerto Rico to fill vacancies are

permitted under the Jones Act of 1917 (39 Stat. 964). The following Resident Commissioners were also appointed to their first terms: José Pesquera of Puerto Rico (1932), Quintin Paredes of the Philippines (1935), Joaquin Elizalde of the Philippines (1938), Bolívar Pagán of Puerto Rico (1939), Carlos Romulo of the Philippines (1944), and Antonio Fernós-Isern of Puerto Rico (1946). See also, *Biographical Directory of the United States Congress*, http://bioguide.congress.gov.

7 "Smooth Sailing for Colorado," 20 February 1992, *San Juan Star*: 4.

8 Harry Turner, "Pryor Set to File New Anti-936 Legislation," 3 March 1992, *San Juan Star*: 5.

9 "Colorado in Congress."

10 Turner, "Antonio Colorado Sworn in as Resident Commissioner."

11 *Congressional Record*, House, 102nd Cong., 2nd sess. (4 March 1992): 4386–4387.

12 Harry Turner, "Colorado: Section 936 Safe in Congress," 14 March 1992, *San Juan Star*: 6. It was rumored that Colorado was being considered for a more prestigious spot on the Committee on Ways and Means given his familiarity with federal tax policy. See *Congressional Record*, House, 102nd Cong., 2nd sess. (4 March 1992): 4386.

13 Some Puerto Rican activists also opposed section 936. See Miriam J. Ramirez de Ferrer, "Section 936 vs. the People of Puerto Rico," 20 March 1992, *San Juan Star*: 16. See also Harry Turner, "Indiana Congressman Joins Battle against 936 Benefits," 23 March 1992, *San Juan Star*: 4. Some Members of Congress wanted to punish the "runaway" company that, according to the *San Juan Star*, "changes locations for tax or other economic advantages and costs people jobs at the original site," usually on the mainland. See Harry Turner, "Section 936 Critics Fail to Awaken Opposition," 7 March 1992, *San Juan Star*: 3.

14 Harry Turner, "Pryor to File Anti-936 Bill," 5 March 1992, *San Juan Star*: 2; Harry Turner, "P.R. Not out of the Woods with Defeat of 936 Attack," 13 March 1992, *San Juan Star*: 6.

15 Turner, "Pryor to File Anti-936 Bill."

16 Harry Turner, "Colorado's Letter Angers Pharmaceutical Industry," 11 March 1992, *San Juan Star*: 4; Turner, "Colorado: Section 936 Safe in Congress."

17 Turner, "P.R. Not out of the Woods with Defeat of 936 Attack"; Turner, "Colorado: Section 936 Safe in Congress."

18 Hearing before the House Committee on Ways and Means, *Foreign Income Tax Rationalization and Simplification Act of 1992*, 102nd Cong., 2nd sess. (21 and 22 July 1992): 191; Harry Turner, "Battle Lines Being Drawn in 936 Review," 22 July 1992, *San Juan Star*: 6; Harry Turner, "Colorado 'Behaves' in Seat of Power," 22 July 1992, *San Juan Star*: 6. For background on the congressional opposition to section 936, see Turner, "Section 936 Critics Fail to Awaken Opposition" and A. W. Maldonado, "The U.S. Senate Debate on 936," 29 March 1992, *San Juan Star*: 26. See also Turner, "Colorado: Section 936 Safe in Congress."

19 For Colorado's remarks on H.R. 5030, see *Congressional Record*, House, 102nd Cong., 2nd sess. (29 April 1992): 9823.

20 *Congressional Record*, Extension of Remarks, 102nd Cong., 2nd sess. (18 June 1992): 15585; Harry Turner, "Colorado Hopeful Congress Will Increase Medicaid Funds," 20 June 1992, *San Juan Star*: 6.

21 Hemlock and Medina, "Colorado Tapped for D.C. Post in '92."

22 Robert Friedman, "Colorado Considers Effects of a Victory without Muñoz," 14 September 1992, *San Juan Star*: 2.

23 John Marino, "936 Catches Heat from TV Lights," 4 October 1994, *San Juan Star*: B1.

24 Robert Friedman, "CRB Says He Will Back Cutting 936," 6 August 1992, *San Juan Star*: 3. See also Robert Friedman, "Romero Links 936 Changes to Funding for P.R. Programs," 6 December 1992, *San Juan Star*: 4.

25 Maria Bird Pico, "Romero Leads Colorado in Campaign Fund-Raising," 22 October 1992, *San Juan Star*: 17.

26 Miglisa Capo, "Muñoz Files Her Candidacy for '92 Gubernatorial Race," 16 March 1992, *San Juan Star*: 2.

27 Jorge Luis Medina, "Poll Shows Romero Trailing Colorado," 20 May 1992, *San Juan Star*: 10. Quotations from Robert Friedman, "Colorado, Romero Face Off, But Throw No Body Punches," 14 August 1992, *San Juan Star*: 2; "Election Statistics, 1920 to Present," http://history.house.gov/institution/election-statistics/election-statistics. See also Friedman, "CRB Says He Will Back Cutting 936."

28 Hemlock, "Colorado Is Possible Clinton Appointee."

29 Robert Friendman, "Colorado Says Battle Looms for Party Control," 26 November 1992, *San Juan Star*: 2; Doreen Hemlock, "Caribbean Needs Strategy to Keep Role in Global Trade," 26 November 1992, *San Juan Star*: 30.

30 Larry Luxner, "Campaigning Starts for Puerto Rican Governor," 3 January 1994, *Miami Herald*: A8.

31 Larry Luxner, "Puerto Rico's Commonwealth Status under Fire," 31 March 1996, *Washington Times*: A8.

32 Larry Luxner, "Puerto Rico Loses Tax Incentive; Wage Bill Axes Corporate Breaks," 22 August 1996, *Washington Times*: A3.

33 David Beard, "Wage Bill Damages Tax Break; Caribbean Will Feel the Pinch," 11 July 1996, *Sun-Sentinel* (Fort Lauderdale, FL): D1.

34 Juan O. Tamayo, "For Third Time, Puerto Rico Rejects Becoming 51st State," 14 December 1998, *Miami Herald*: A1.

"If a man and a place were meant to meet, it's Antonio R. 'Tito' Colorado and the United States Congress … he can walk out of his office, stride down one of the most important corridors of power in the universe and lobby the 435 members of the House of Representatives for benefits for Puerto Rico."

Editors of the *San Juan Star*, March 5, 1992

Henry Bonilla

1954–

UNITED STATES REPRESENTATIVE 1993–2007
REPUBLICAN FROM TEXAS

Born and raised in southwest Texas, Henry Bonilla left his career in television and ran for public office in 1992 after being inspired by then-Minority Whip Newt Gingrich. From his perch on the Appropriations Committee, where he eventually served as one of 13 powerful subcommittee chairmen, Bonilla championed deregulation and espoused fiscal conservatism. Portrayed as the GOP's inroad into a primarily Democratic Hispanic electorate, Bonilla played down his ethnicity. "[When I] look in the mirror in the morning, I'm American first," he noted.[1]

The son of a civil service worker at Kelly Air Force Base, Henry Bonilla was born in San Antonio, Texas, on January 2, 1954. Bonilla was the oldest of three boys and two girls. He lived two blocks away from South San Antonio High School, from which he graduated in 1972. Bonilla admitted to being a lackluster student in a school rocked by teacher walkouts and a high dropout rate. "My school didn't motivate me, but I watched a lot of TV and realized that there was a lot more to the world than what I experienced within the one-mile radius of where I lived," he said. Coverage of President Richard M. Nixon's trip to China in 1972 solidified Bonilla's conservative beliefs. "I realized that all of the overarching ideals I had about politics—a belief in the free enterprise system, a strong defense, less government—did not have a thing in common with the Democratic Party," he noted. "So I became a Republican." An essay Bonilla wrote about Nixon's China diplomacy won him a college scholarship.[2] He earned his B.A. from the University of Texas at Austin in 1976 and then began a career in television news. Bonilla started as a reporter for two stations in Austin from 1976 to 1980 before moving to Philadelphia to serve as press secretary for Pennsylvania governor Dick Thornburgh for a year in 1981; this post would be his only experience in politics before he was elected to Congress. He stayed in the Northeast, working as a news producer for a flagship ABC station in New York City. In 1985 he returned to Philadelphia for a year to serve as an assistant news director for a local station, before becoming an executive producer for KENS-TV and settling in San Antonio in 1986. There he met his future wife, Deborah Knapp, a television anchor in a highly rated San Antonio news program. The couple had two children, Alicia and Austin.

In 1992, Bonilla cited Minority Whip Newt Gingrich of Georgia as his inspiration to run for a seat in the U.S. House.[3] Supporting the conservative platforms espoused by the Georgia leader proved difficult in the overwhelmingly Democratic district, the birthplace of the La Raza Unida activist movement. Drawn after the 1990 Census as an "incumbency protection plan" for Democratic Congressman Albert Bustamante, the district covered 58,000 square miles across a wide swath of southwest Texas. A mix of Hispanic *barrios* (low-income neighborhoods) near Laredo—including eight of the 20 poorest counties in the state—and wealthy areas such as the San Antonio suburbs in Bexar County, El Paso desert, and Midland Oil Fields (home to affluent ranchers and oil industry executives) made up the district.[4] With more than 60 percent of its population being of Mexican-American origin, the district was the largest in the Texas delegation—measuring roughly the size of Illinois—and shared a longer stretch of the Mexican border (800 miles) than any other congressional district.[5] Bonilla immediately contrasted himself with Bustamante, who had more than 30 overdrafts in the House "Bank," an informal institution run by the Sergeant at Arms in to which some Members deposited their congressional pay. Though Bustamante had few overdrafts compared with some of the worst offenders, Bonilla hit his opponent hard in an attempt to

Collection of the U.S. House of Representatives, Photography Collection

appeal to frugal working-class immigrants, using the term "*cheques calientes*" (hot checks) throughout his campaign and evoking gangster Al Capone.[6] An untarnished political newcomer, Bonilla was attractive because of his personality and his skill as a news producer. "Blitzing" the district with well-crafted TV advertisements, Bonilla appealed to small business owners and conservative Democrats.[7] He took a leave of absence from the TV station to drive across Southern Texas, meeting with voters and conversing in Spanish with locals in coffee shops and cafes.

Bonilla also faced scrutiny in the hard-fought campaign. On September 28, Bustamante a filed a complaint with the Federal Election Commission (FEC) claiming that the San Antonio news station employing Bonilla provided biased campaign coverage in the challenger's favor.[8] The FEC eventually determined that the Bonillas had no intention of violating campaign law, and the couple later turned the scandal into an asset. Working full-time for the campaign, Deborah Bonilla added local celebrity star power to her husband's appearances.[9]

Bonilla's cross-party appeal ultimately secured his victory. Democratic presidential candidate William J. (Bill) Clinton narrowly won the district with 42 percent of the vote, versus 41 percent for President George H. W. Bush and 17 percent for Independent Ross Perot. Voters crossed party lines and were frequently seen sporting Bonilla's campaign buttons alongside Clinton's.[10] Bonilla defeated the incumbent with 59 percent of the vote by sweeping the more conservative San Antonio suburbs, coming closer than expected in Laredo, and taking other border counties.[11] Part of a wave of anti-incumbency that swept in the largest freshman class in 60 years, Bonilla was confident that his conservative platform had reached national prominence. "The gravity is clear with this [Republican] side because the philosophy of our party is more in sync with the working man," he noted.[12] In subsequent elections, Democrats had difficulty getting candidates to run against Bonilla.[13] The district supported Clinton and Bonilla again in 1996, the latter winning with 63 percent of the vote. For the next three election cycles, Bonilla won easily, with close to 60 percent of the vote. The district was so safe in 1998, the *San Antonio Express-News* described Bonilla's political clout as "strong as [an] acre of garlic."[14]

Bonilla was active in the House Republican Conference throughout his congressional career, and his leadership earned him the title the "Quiet Giant."[15] House Republicans came to appreciate his media savvy; in 1993 they selected Bonilla to deliver the GOP response to President Clinton's radio address advocating his proposals for health care reform.[16]

Despite his national appeal, Bonilla kept his Texas district at the forefront of his legislative interests. He was a strong supporter of the North American Free Trade Agreement (NAFTA), which passed in 1993 with the firm backing of President Clinton and many congressional Republicans. Bonilla believed that the agreement—which would eliminate tariffs on goods moving across the Mexican border over the next 15 years—would increase business traffic and make goods cheaper in Texas' beleaguered border towns. "We must take a stand for economic growth and opportunity. When we enter new markets—such as the ones NAFTA will give us—we win," he told his colleagues on the House Floor. "This is a nation of competitors—and winners. When Americans compete, they win."[17] Bonilla traveled with Senate Minority Leader Bob Dole of Kansas throughout South Texas to rally support for the agreement. Bonilla's backing the bill, however, rested on assurances of improvements to the safety of Mexican trucks.[18] He later obtained $10 million in aid for garment and farm workers who lost jobs because of the flood of cheap Mexican goods into the U.S. market.[19]

On national issues, Bonilla's fiscal conservatism defined his career, particularly his belief that government overregulation inhibited the growth of private business. "The greatest burden that … entrepreneurs and those who wish to pursue the American dream have today," Bonilla declared, "is the regulatory burden they face every time they walk out the door, trying to create more jobs, trying to be more productive in this country."[20] His positions often put him at odds with the Occupational Safety and Hazards Administration (OSHA)—the federal agency charged with enforcing safety standards in the workplace—

over its regulatory power.[21] After the GOP gained a majority in the House in the 1994 elections, Bonilla first addressed the federal regulation of safety standards, advocating amending the 1938 Fair Labor Standards Act to allow children under 18 to operate cardboard balers and box compactors.[22] He also took on the United Parcel Service (UPS) after it received a number of OSHA complaints from workers who frequently lifted heavy packages.[23] Bonilla continued to fight OSHA's regulatory power, opposing an attempt by the House in 1998 to require tougher flame retardant standards for infant pajamas.[24] He also attempted to block Democratic efforts to require the inclusion of country of origin on beef labels during the height of the nationwide scare over Mad Cow disease, an illness that affected British beef cows. Despite arguments that such labels would help the American beef industry, Bonilla sided with packers, because he thought the new regulations would be too expensive and burdensome for them.[25]

Bonilla also expressed his disapproval of government regulation by introducing a bill placing a moratorium on the addition of animals to the Endangered Species Act (ESA), claiming the 1973 act unduly burdened landowners. "In its current form the Endangered Species Act—though well intentioned—works contrary to, and often against one particular species—the human being," he told his colleagues. Referencing ESA-protected species in his district, he said, "Many hardworking ranchers, farmers, and homeowners in Texas have a greater fear of the gold cheeked warbler than they do of tax hikes and tornadoes."[26] After the Committee on Resources held up his bill, Bonilla eventually attached the legislation to a defense spending bill. Regarding critics who questioned the amendment's relevance to the Pentagon's budget, Bonilla said, "I reminded them that in addition to being used against private property owners, ESA regulations have been used to curtail training exercises at some of our military installations."[27] After the amendment was pulled from the defense appropriations, Senator Kay Bailey Hutchison of Texas added it to Department of the Interior appropriations, but as part of a compromise with the Clinton administration, the final legislation gave the President authority to lift the moratorium if he saw fit. Bonilla was among a small minority that opposed the bill based on this provision. Clinton exercised his prerogative the same day he approved the law, April 26, 1996.[28]

Bonilla won appointment to the powerful Appropriations Committee in his freshman term, a position he held throughout his Capitol Hill career.[29] In 2001, benefiting from term limits imposed on committee chairs by the Republican Conference, Bonilla leapfrogged two senior Republicans on the committee to chair the Subcommittee Agriculture, Rural Development, Food and Drug Administration, and Related Agencies for the 107th Congress (2001–2003), serving in that position for the rest of his congressional career.[30] From his new perch as a "cardinal"—the designation given the powerful Appropriations subcommittee chairmen—Bonilla exercised even greater influence on fiscal matters.

Fights over government spending, however, pitted Bonilla and other GOP appropriators against party leadership in a battle over appropriations legislation that highlighted fissures within the GOP and between the legislative and executive branches in the early 2000s. The George W. Bush administration advocated restraint in congressional budget proposals, and the House Republican leadership felt pressure to comply. But Bonilla proved to be a staunch defender of lawmakers' ability to add earmarks in appropriations bills. Bonilla's subcommittee's first appropriation bill in 2001 included $1.6 billion more than the President requested, including $20 million earmarked by Bonilla for the sheep and goat ranchers in his district.[31] Bonilla and several other cardinals found themselves in a showdown over the spending limitations established by House leadership and the White House. The battle came to a head in May 2002 over a typically straightforward procedural move: approving the rules of debate for a $29.4 billion fiscal year 2002 emergency spending bill, which provided money for domestic defense against bioterrorism as well as for the military campaign in Afghanistan. The popular bill had the strong support of Bush administration officials, who warned of an imminent terrorist attack like those of September 11, 2001. Bonilla and three other Republicans on the Appropriations Committee supported the legislation but protested last-minute changes limiting discretionary spending in fiscal year 2003, sweetening the legislation for fiscal conservatives. Despite heavy courting from Speaker J. Dennis Hastert of Illinois and Majority Leader Tom DeLay of Texas, Bonilla, along with colleagues George Nethercutt of Washington and Zach Wamp of Tennessee, held firm, voting "present" in the final tally. Other appropriators voted against the rule, which passed, 216 to 209.[32] The GOP retaliated against its intransigent cardinals by mandating that henceforth their selection would be by Party leadership instead of by seniority.[33]

Bonilla's support among Hispanics in his district dropped precipitously throughout his career, and in his victory against Democrat Henry Cuellar by a slim 52 percent in 2002, only 8 percent of Latinos supported him.[34] Texas GOP lawmakers attempted to make Bonilla's district safer for him by slicing out more than 100,000 Hispanic voters in Webb County.[35] The new map also added Republican strongholds in Bandera, Kerr, and Kendall counties, northwest of San Antonio. Moreover, it isolated Hispanics who were formerly Bonilla's constituents in one of several long, narrow districts 10 miles wide and more than 300 miles north to south.[36] Bonilla's new district also kept most of the West Texas ranchers and oil and gas executives who had solidly supported him in the past.[37] Within the new borders, Bonilla won with a comfortable 69 percent of the vote over Democrat Joe Sullivan.[38]

Yet the Supreme Court ruled against the Texas redistricting plan, arguing that Bonilla's district had violated the 1965 Voting Rights Act in June 2006.[39] Bonilla initially lobbied for the change to take place after the 2006 elections, months away. "Logistically, it is so difficult now to make a huge change before the November election," he told the *Fort Worth Star-Telegram*. "It would probably be wise to wait for the Legislature to do it when they convene next year."[40] The court's decision changed the November 7 general election to a "blanket primary" in which candidates from both parties appeared on the same ballot, inspiring six Democratic challengers and one Independent challenger. Bonilla drew high-ranking Republicans to South Texas to campaign for him. He had the ardent support of Majority Leader DeLay.[41] Vice President Richard (Dick) Cheney also held a fundraiser for him in October, and political strategist Karl Rove campaigned on his behalf.[42] Bonilla's substantial war chest of more than $2 million dwarfed those of his opponents.[43] In the November election, he took 48.6 percent of the vote, narrowly missing the 50 percent required by state law to seal a victory. Former Democratic Representative Ciro Rodriguez, who had narrowly lost a primary election in 2004 against Henry Cuellar, was the closest challenger, with 19.9 percent of the vote. The two faced each other in a runoff election scheduled for December 12, 2006.

The cash-strapped Rodriguez, who had considered dropping out of the race, received an infusion of support and money from the national Democratic Party, fresh from winning a new House majority in the 110th Congress (2007–2009).[44] Dubbed a "coconut"—a Hispanic who forgets his ethnic roots—by some of his opponents, Bonilla touted his pro-business legislative record, noting, "Job growth is not along ethnic lines."[45] Large financial contributions quickly spawned a series of negative television ads featuring both candidates. Rodriguez attempted unsuccessfully to change the date of the runoff since it fell on the Feast of the Virgin of Guadalupe, a Mexican Catholic holiday that would occupy his Hispanic base with church services, parades, and celebrations. But despite the holiday, Hispanic voters catapulted Rodriguez to a surprising victory; he took 53.3 percent of the vote to Bonilla's 46.7 percent.[46] Bonilla lost four counties in his West Texas stronghold because of low voter turnout.[47]

Shortly after Bonilla left Congress, President Bush nominated him to be ambassador to the Organization of American States, a body of delegates from nations in the Western Hemisphere that discuss policy affecting the region. Bonilla withdrew his nomination three months later, citing the U.S. Senate's failure to confirm him for the position. He subsequently joined a lobbying firm.[48]

FOR FURTHER READING

Biographical Directory of the United States Congress, "Henry Bonilla," http://bioguide.congress.gov.

NOTES

1 Bree Hocking, "Bonilla: A 'Quiet Giant,'" 29 November 2004, *Roll Call.*

2 "The Other Henry," *Texas Monthly* 21, no. 12 (December 1993): 110.

3 *Almanac of American Politics, 1996* (Washington, D.C.: National Journal Inc., 1995): 1320.

4 Scott Pendleton, "Inspired by 'Superstar' Congressman, Hispanic Republicans Run for Office," 16 March 1994, *Christian Science Monitor*: 12; *Politics in America, 1994* (Washington, D.C.: Congressional Quarterly, Inc., 1993): 1517.

5 *Politics in America, 2000* (Washington, D.C.: Congressional Quarterly, Inc., 1999): 1346; "Remember the Alamo: San Antonio Foes in Shootout," 22 October 1992, *National Journal's Congress Daily*; *Politics in America, 2004* (Washington, D.C.: Congressional Quarterly, Inc., 2003): 1577.

6 *Politics in America, 1994*: 1516.

7 "The Other Henry": 110.

8 Bustamante also noted that Bonilla's wife had used the station's computers, phones, and faxes to raise funds for her husband in violation of campaign finance laws. Deborah Bonilla subsequently apologized for her actions and took a leave of absence, and the campaign repaid the station for the use of the equipment. The station also issued an on-air apology and explanation. "Deborah made some mistakes by not following the guidelines I laid down when Henry first announced," acknowledged news director Bob Rogers. "I told them they had to be pure as the driven snow." See, for example, James Cox, "Congressman: TV station biased," 1 October 1992, *USA Today*: 2B; David McLemore, "No Liberal Media Bias in San Antonio Cases," 4 October 1992, *Dallas Morning News*: 46A; Howard Kurtz, "Big Apple Gets Plum Spot," 9 October 1992, *Washington Post*: B4.

9 *Politics in America, 1994*: 1516. The entire complaint filed by the Bustamante campaign is available at Federal Election Commission, *Matter under Review Archive–1975 through 1998*, MUR no. 3631, http://mur.nictusa.com/mur/3631.pdf (accessed 23 February 2010).

10 *Politics in America, 1994*: 1516, 1517.

11 *Almanac of American Politics, 1994* (Washington, D.C.: National Journal Inc., 1993): 1263; "Election Statistics, 1920 to Present," http://history.house.gov/institution/election-statistics/election-statistics.

12 Kelley Shannon, "Texas House Race Casts Doubt on Belief Hispanics Loyal Democrats," 20 October 1992, Associated Press. Data on the freshman class were gleaned from the *Congressional Directory*, various years.

13 "The Other Henry": 110.

14 "Election Statistics, 1920 to Present," http://history.house.gov/institution/election-statistics/election-statistics; *Almanac of American Politics, 1998* (Washington, D.C.: National Journal Inc., 1997): 1393.

15 Hocking, "Bonilla: A 'Quiet Giant.'"

16 Al Kamen, "In the Loop," 15 October 1993, *Washington Post*: A23.

17 *Congressional Record*, House, 103rd Cong., 1st sess. (17 November 1993): H10036.

18 *Politics in America, 2000*: 1347.

19 *Almanac of American Politics, 2002*: 1502.

20 *Congressional Record*, House, 104th Cong., 1st sess. (23 February 1995): H2094.

21 Ibid; Steve Lohr, "A Compromise Plan to Address Workplace Ergonomics Stays on the Shelf," 8 April 1996, *New York Times*: D5.

22 *Congressional Record*, House, 104th Cong., 1st sess. (24 October 1995): H10665.

23 Maria Recio, "Legislator Seeks to Block Rules on Repetitive Stress Disorders," 25 April 1996, *Fort Worth Star-Telegram*: 1; Curt Suplee, "House to Consider 'Ergo Rider' Restraints on OSHA," 11 July 1996, *Washington Post*: A4.

24 *Politics in America, 2000*: 1346.

25 Sheryl Gay Stolberg, "Mad Cow Case Heightens Debate on Food Labeling," 8 January 2004, *New York Times*: A16.

26 *Congressional Record*, Extension of Remarks, 103rd Cong. 1st sess. (30 September 1994): E2014.

27 *Politics in America, 1998* (Washington, D.C.: Congressional Quarterly, Inc., 1997): 1425.

28 "Omnibus FY96 Bill Ties Loose Ends." CQ Press Electronic Library, CQ Almanac Online Edition, cqal96-841-24596-1091488. Originally published in *CQ Almanac 1996* (Washington, D.C.: Congressional Quarterly, Inc., 1997), http://library.cqpress.com/cqalmanac/cqal96-841-24596-1091488 (accessed 8 April 2010); Robert Dodge, "Clinton Signs Budget Measure," 27 April 1996, *Dallas Morning News*: 3A.

29 The Appropriations Committee was Bonilla's only assignment to a standing committee. He also served on the Select Bipartisan Committee to Investigate the Preparation for and Response to Hurricane Katrina in the 109th Congress (2005–2007). See Garrison Nelson and Charles Stewart III, *Committees in the U.S. Congress, 1993–2010* (Washington, D.C.: CQ Press, 2011): 595.

30 Hocking, "Bonilla: A 'Quiet Giant'"; Lizette Alvarez, "Honoring '95 Vow, House Republicans Replace 13 Chiefs," 5 January 2001, *New York Times*: A1; Ben Pershing and John Bresnahan, "GOP Fills

Panel Seats," 8 January 2001, *Roll Call*; Gary Martin, "Texan Tops Agriculture Panel; Bonilla to Head Subcommittee," 6 January 2001, *San Antonio Express-News*: 15A.

31 *Politics in America, 2004*: 996; Robert Pear, "Fiscal Conservatives Heighten Fight over Pet Projects," 25 May 2006, *New York Times*: A18.

32 "Key Votes of 2002: Strategic Muscle, Political Will." CQ Press Electronic Library, CQ Almanac Online Edition, cqal02-236-30557-1462194. Originally published in *CQ Almanac 2002* (Washington, D.C.: Congressional Quarterly, Inc., 2003), http://library.cqpress.com/cqalmanac/cqal02-236-30557-1462194 (accessed 9 April 2010); Alison Mitchell, "House Leaders Quell Revolt to Advance Spending Bill," 23 May 2002, *New York Times*: A22.

33 "Key Votes of 2002: Strategic Muscle, Political Will"; David Firestone, "G.O.P.'s 'Cardinals of Spending' Are Reined in by House Leaders," 2 December 2002, *New York Times*: A1.

34 "Election Statistics, 1920 to Present," http://history.house.gov/institution/election-statistics/election-statistics; David M. Drucker, "Ruling Could Hurt Bonilla," 26 June 2006, *Roll Call*: 1.

35 "Election Statistics, 1920 to Present," http://history.house.gov/institution/election-statistics/election-statistics.

36 Hocking, "Bonilla: A 'Quiet Giant.'" For maps, see Bickerstaff, *Lines in the Sand*: 392–393. For a multi-layered interactive map that outlines all the changes that took place in Texas congressional districts from 2001 to 2010, see Texas Legislative Council, "DistrictViewer," http://gis1.tlc.state.tx.us/ (accessed 17 February 2010).

37 Texas Legislative Council, "DistrictViewer." The exception was half of Sutton County and several other counties southwest of Midland, all Bonilla strongholds with natural gas and ranching as their main industries. The new plan moved those counties to a district that was eventually represented by Representative Michael Conaway. "A West Texas Hamlet Adjusts to Being Split by Redistricting," 30 November 2003, *New York Times*: N34.

38 "Election Statistics, 1920 to Present," http://history.house.gov/institution/election-statistics/election-statistics.

39 "Redistricting Has Mixed Results for GOP." CQ Press Electronic Library, CQ Almanac Online Edition, cqal05-766-20107-1042509. Originally published in *CQ Almanac 2005* (Washington, D.C.: Congressional Quarterly, Inc., 2006), http://library.cqpress.com/cqalmanac/cqal05-766-20107-1042509 (accessed 13 April 2010).

40 John Moritz, "Panel to Oversee Redrawing District," 30 June 2006, *Fort Worth Star-Telegram*: B4.

41 Bonilla was also one of DeLay's strongest backers following the Majority Leader's indictment for felony campaign finance violations. Bonilla proposed a rule change in the GOP Conference that would allow DeLay to keep his leadership post even after his indictment. He also was the second-largest contributor to the embattled Majority Leader's legal defense fund in March of 2005, having donated $15,000. Bonilla's American Dream Political Action Committee, created to raise funds to support minority GOP candidates, eventually faced scrutiny because much of the money went toward DeLay's legal fees. Hocking, "Bonilla: A 'Quiet Giant'"; Carlos Guerra, "Bonilla Has Benefited Greatly from His Loyalty to Tom DeLay," 30 November 2006, *San Antonio Express-News*: 1B.

42 Guillermo X. Garcia, "Cheney Is Stopping in San Antonio to Raise Funds for Bonilla," 3 October 2006, *San Antonio Express-News*: 3B; Greg Jefferson, "Election 2006: Bonilla Plays It Safe in a Crowded Field," 5 November 2006, *San Antonio Express-News*: 1A.

43 Jefferson, "Election 2006: Bonilla Plays It Safe in a Crowded Field."

44 David M. Drucker, "DCCC Senses Another Pickup in Texas Runoff," 7 December 2006, *Roll Call*: 11.

45 Greg Jefferson, "Bonilla's Hispanic Standing at Issue," 9 December 2006, *San Antonio Express-News*: 1A.

46 *Politics in America, 2006* (Washington, D.C.: Congressional Quarterly, Inc., 2005): 995.

47 Greg Jefferson et al., "Bonilla Falls Short in Runoff," 13 December 2006, *Houston Chronicle*: B1; Greg Jefferson, "Ciro in Landslide," 13 December 2006, *San Antonio Express-News*: 1A.

48 Todd J. Gillman, "Bush Nominates Bonilla for OAS Ambassadorship," 16 March 2007, *Dallas Morning News*: 9A; "Former Congressman Bonilla Withdraws Ambassador Nomination," 5 June 2007, Associated Press.

"All too often Hispanics are portrayed as victims, cowering in the neighborhoods waiting for the federal government to rescue them. This is simply not the case. There is a booming Hispanic middle class, with good prospects for future growth.... I don't know about the people who represent these 'professional minority' groups, but when I look in the mirror every morning I first see an American. I'm proud of my culture, but more proud and grateful to say that I live in this country."

Henry Bonilla
Almanac of American Politics, 2004

Lincoln Diaz-Balart

1954–

UNITED STATES REPRESENTATIVE 1993–2011
REPUBLICAN FROM FLORIDA

A refugee of the 1959 Cuban Revolution with deep family ties to the island's politics in the era before Fidel Castro, Lincoln Diaz-Balart was a leading congressional voice for reform in the Cuban government and for immigrants' rights. Beginning with his election to the U.S. House of Representatives in 1992, he advocated for the fair treatment of legal immigrants and refugees and for the maintenance of vigorous economic sanctions against Cuba. "I'm friends with anyone who's fighting Castro because that's the supreme cause," Diaz-Balart once said.[1]

Lincoln Diaz-Balart was born in Havana, Cuba, on August 13, 1954, to Rafael Lincoln and Hilda Caballero Diaz-Balart. He and his brothers, Rafael, Jose, and Mario, were born into a family that had long been involved in Cuba's government. Diaz-Balart's grandfather, father, and uncle served in Cuba's house of representatives, and his father was president of the senate under President Fulgencio Batista.[2] Diaz-Balart's aunt was briefly married to Fidel Castro and was the mother of Castro's only recognized child. In 1959 Diaz-Balart and his family fled Cuba after their home was looted and burned by pro-Castro forces during the Cuban Revolution. They lived in New York, Fort Lauderdale, Venezuela, and Spain before settling in Miami.[3] Lincoln attended the American School in Madrid, Spain, and graduated from the University of South Florida in Sarasota with a degree in international relations in 1976. He went on to study British politics in Cambridge, England, and earned his law degree from Case Western University in Cleveland, Ohio, in 1979. Diaz-Balart worked in private practice in Miami before serving as an assistant state's attorney. He and his wife Cristina raised two sons, Lincoln and Daniel.

Diaz-Balart got his start in politics leading the Florida Young Democrats and running an unsuccessful campaign for the Florida legislature as a Democrat in 1982. But he began to identify with the Republican Party during the Ronald W. Reagan administration, co-chairing the Democrats for Reagan Campaign in 1984. He formally switched his party allegiance in 1985, citing what he described as Democrats' lenient policy toward communism in Nicaragua and El Salvador. He was elected to the state house of representatives in 1986, and three years later he won a special election for a seat in the state senate.[4] While in the Florida legislature, Diaz-Balart sponsored laws strengthening sentences for crimes against law enforcement officers, increasing penalties for drug-related money laundering, providing low-interest loans for home construction, creating a statewide program to combat substance abuse, and establishing disclosure rules for Florida companies doing business with Cuba.[5]

After the 1990 Census, Florida created a new congressional district encompassing portions of Kendall, Westchester, Sweetwater, and Hialeah and stretching to the west and south of downtown Miami. Hispanic Americans constituted 71 percent of the voting-age population. In the Republican primary, Diaz-Balart faced fellow state senator Javier Souto, who was also Cuban-born. Each candidate attempted to portray himself as the greater champion of Cuba's freedom.[6] Diaz-Balart proved a more efficient fundraiser and secured the party's nomination with 69 percent of the vote. He had no opposition in the general election.[7] In four of his next five re-election bids, Diaz-Balart was unopposed. In 1998 Democrat Patrick Cusack ran against him but lost, 74 to 26 percent. In his final three general election campaigns, Diaz-Balart faced opposition but won by wide margins.[8]

Diaz-Balart was sworn in as a Member of the 103rd Congress (1993–1995) on January 5, 1993, and was placed on the Foreign Affairs and Merchant Marine and Fisheries Committees. Leaders quickly tapped him for

Collection of the U.S. House of Representatives, Photography Collection

prominent assignments after the Republicans regained the House majority during the 1994 election, and Diaz-Balart relinquished his initial assignments for seats on the House Oversight Committee and the powerful Rules Committee.[9] He left the former at the end of the 104th Congress (1995–1997) but retained the Rules Committee assignment—where he worked closely with leadership to shape and pulse bills for consideration on the floor—for the rest of his House career. Diaz-Balart eventually chaired two subcommittees: the Rules Committee's Legislative and Budget Process Subcommittee in the 109th Congress (2005–2007) and the Select Committee on Homeland Security's Rules Subcommittee in the 108th Congress (2003–2005). In 2001 Speaker J. Dennis Hastert of Illinois appointed him to the Republican Policy Committee, which was in charge of developing the GOP's legislative agenda. In the 108th Congress, Diaz-Balart also served on the Select Committee on Homeland Security, but left the panel when it became a standing committee in the next Congress.[10]

Representing a solidly conservative working-class district, Diaz-Balart occasionally demonstrated his willingness to break with his party to support immigrant rights and worker protections. He was one of only three Republicans who did not sign the Contract with America in 1994, and he opposed the 1996 welfare reform legislation—a pillar of the Contract with America—because of scheduled cuts to Supplemental Security Income (SSI) for legal immigrants.[11] "When people follow the law and they pay taxes, they shouldn't be singled out for discrimination," he said.[12] He successfully championed legislation postponing the SSI cuts, which passed the House by a vote of 345 to 74 on May 15, 1997.[13] He also strenuously opposed efforts to prevent the children of undocumented immigrants from enrolling in public schools and fought successfully to get the provision dropped from the 1996 Immigration Act. The House voted to pass the provision as a stand-alone measure, but it never cleared the Senate.[14]

On this and other immigration issues, Diaz-Balart often allied with two Floridians, fellow Cuban-American Representative Ileana Ros-Lehtinen and Democrat Carrie Meek, whose congressional district included a large Haitian population. In the 105th and 106th Congresses (1997–2001), Diaz-Balart helped shape legislation that prevented the deportation of thousands of refugees from countries in Latin America, the Caribbean, and the former Eastern Bloc under retroactively applied provisions of the Illegal Immigration Reform and Immigrant Responsibility Act (IIRIRA) of 1996.[15] "I think it is our moral obligation and a requirement of elemental fairness that at the very least these refugees be considered under the rules in existence when they filed their applications," he said of Nicaraguan immigrants on the House Floor while arguing for a measure that eventually passed as the Nicaraguan Adjustment and Central American Relief Act. "I have witnessed in South Florida how they have made significant social, economic and cultural contributions to my community.... My bill ensures that these refugees will be able to obtain basic procedural justice in recognition of their historically unique and important circumstances."[16] In 2007 Diaz-Balart sponsored legislation to allow two Colombian college students whose parents brought them to the United States illegally when they were two and three years of age to remain in the country. He used their example to support legislation that would allow in-state tuition for the children of undocumented immigrants and provide them a path to citizenship.[17]

Diaz-Balart's central objective in the House was to promote freedom and democracy in Cuba, and he organized the Cuba Democracy Group to rally support.[18] He strongly advocated preserving and strengthening economic sanctions against the Castro regime. In the 104th Congress, Diaz-Balart sponsored the Cuban Liberty and Democratic Solidarity Act of 1996 (H.R. 927), which codified the existing trade embargo against Cuba.[19] On the House Floor, Diaz-Balart declared, "Mr. Speaker, the Cuban people are facing an avalanche of collaborationism by governments and investors in the international community who are seriously considering, and in a few instances, accepting, the Cuban dictator's invitation to come in and partake of his oppression of Cuban workers, his guaranteed denial of all labor rights, and his fire sale of the island at dirt cheap prices to foreign capitalists."

He lashed out at the Cuban military for shooting down two unarmed civilian U.S. planes in international waters in early 1996, arguing that this action justified continued economic sanctions.[20] He said that opponents of a hard-line policy toward the Castro regime—many of whom supported sanctions in the 1980s against South Africa's apartheid regime—displayed a "double standard" that was "insidious, hypocritical, and objectionable."[21]

Diaz-Balart was an early and a strong critic of the William J. (Bill) Clinton administration's movement toward engagement with Cuba's communist regime, and in 1995 he was arrested outside the White House in a peaceful protest.[22] He decried the Clinton administration's 1998 decision to ease some of the provisions of the embargo, while refusing to automatically grant Cuban refugees safe haven in the United States. "All this does is send a political victory to Castro," Diaz-Balart argued. "While Castro is throwing people in dungeons, President Clinton looks for wiggle room under current law to send a signal of good relations to Castro."[23] In 2000 Diaz-Balart and Representative Ros-Lehtinen of Florida opposed efforts by farm-state Members to ease the Cuban embargo. While failing to completely preserve the embargo, Diaz-Balart and his pro-embargo colleagues succeeded in imposing limitations on sales to Cuba and in preserving the prohibition on travel to Cuba. They also forced restrictions to prevent federal or U.S. commercial financing for food exports.[24] Additionally, Diaz-Balart opposed legislation benefiting governments that replicated or supported Cuba's oppressive policies. "International capitalism is pouring billions of dollars into the coffers of the communist oppressors, billions that they use to maintain their oppressive apparatus," he said.[25] Diaz-Balart opposed the North American Free Trade Agreement (NAFTA) in 1993, principally because the governments of Mexico and Canada had closer ties to the Cuban regime.[26]

In late 1999, the story of a young Cuban boy named Elián González riveted the nation. The U.S. Coast Guard rescued the child at sea after the boat carrying Elián, his mother, and a dozen other refugees sank. Elián's mother perished, and his father, who had remained in Cuba, sought his son's return. When the Immigration and Naturalization Service removed González from the home of relatives in Miami in April 2000 so that the boy could be returned to his family—an event that was widely covered by the media—Diaz-Balart called the government's action "a monstrosity."[27] Castro disdained Lincoln and his brother, Mario—elected to the U.S. House in 2002—as "miserable Judases."[28]

Diaz-Balart's years in public service earned him a reputation as a skilled legislator and politician who was unwilling to shy away from controversy when his priorities were at stake. In his freshman year, he successfully defunded a $23 million project from the district of an appropriator who had defunded anti-communist radio broadcasts into Cuba.[29] In January 1997, when the chairman of the Hispanic Caucus traveled to Cuba to meet with Castro, Diaz-Balart and Representative Ros-Lehtinen quickly announced that they would withdraw from the caucus and would rejoin only if the chairman called for free and fair elections in Cuba.[30] "There has to be a limit to insensitivity, and going to meet the Cuban tyrant … is beyond the pale. It's unacceptable. It's too much," Diaz-Balart said.[31] In March 2003, Diaz-Balart, Ros-Lehtinen, and three other Republican Members formed the Congressional Hispanic Conference as an alternative to the Hispanic Caucus.[32]

While the Democrats made significant gains in the House in 2006, Diaz-Balart nonetheless won election, with nearly 60 percent of the vote.[33] In 2008 he faced his most serious challenger, Raul Martinez, formerly a mayor of Hialeah. Martinez criticized Diaz-Balart for focusing too much on Cuba and for supporting restrictions on family travel and remittance to the island. Highlighting his record of supporting immigrants and bringing federal money to the district for highway construction, Diaz-Balart prevailed with a comfortable 58 percent of the vote.[34] However, midway through the 111th Congress (2009–2011), Diaz-Balart announced his retirement from the House, citing his desire to continue advocating for Cuban democracy as a private citizen. "I am convinced that in the upcoming chapter of the struggle, I can be

more useful to the inevitable change that will soon come to Cuba, to Cuba's freedom, as a private citizen dedicated to helping the heroes within Cuba," he said.[35] Mario Diaz-Balart, who had served a neighboring congressional district to the southwest for nearly a decade, won election in 2010 to succeed his brother in the 21st Congressional District.

FOR FURTHER READING

Biographical Directory of the United States Congress, "Lincoln Diaz-Balart," http://bioguide.congress.gov.

NOTES

1 Andres Viglucci, "Former Friends Now Foes in Hot Congressional Race," 16 August 1992, *Miami Herald*: B1.

2 Matt Meier, *Notable Latino Americans: A Biographical Directory* (Westport: Greenwood Press, 1997): 118; Mirta Ojito, "Mr. Diaz-Balart Goes to Washington, Miamian Brings Unique Heritage to House," 4 January 1993, *Miami Herald*: A1.

3 Ojito, "Mr. Diaz-Balart Goes to Washington; Miamian Brings Unique Heritage to House"; *Almanac of American Politics, 2000* (Washington, D.C.: National Journal Group, 1999): 443.

4 *Notable Latino Americans*: 118; William Gibson, "Miami Maverick; Lincoln Diaz-Balart, A Freshman in Washington," 21 August 1994, *Sun-Sentinel*: 1E.

5 *Almanac of American Politics, 2000*: 443.

6 Viglucci, "Former Friends Now Foes in Hot Congressional Race."

7 Karen Branch, "Diaz-Balart Beats Colleague Souto," 9 September 1992, *Miami Herald*: A15; "Election Statistics, 1920 to Present," http://history.house.gov/institution/election-statistics/election-statistics.

8 "Election Statistics, 1920 to Present," http://history.house.gov/institution/election-statistics/election-statistics.

9 *Congressional Directory,* 103rd Congress (Washington, D.C.: Government Printing Office, 1993): 442, 451; *Congressional Directory,* 104th Congress (Washington, D.C.: Government Printing Office, 1995): 403, 413. See also Paul Anderson, "Miami Congressman Named to Rules Panel," 7 December 1994, *Miami Herald*: A7.

10 Garrison Nelson et al., *Committees in the U.S. Congress, 1993–2010* (Washington, D.C.: Congressional Quarterly, Inc., 2011): 674–675.

11 "No Fine Print; Republicans Put It in Writing: A New Way of Governing," 13 November 1994, *Dallas Morning News*: 1J; Robert Pear, "House Backs Bill Undoing Decades of Welfare Policy," 25 March 1995, *New York Times*: 1.

12 Jill Miller, "Reforms May Halt Legal-Alien Welfare; GOP 'Contract' Hangs on Touchy Issue," 20 January 1995, *Sun Sentinel*: A1.

13 *Congressional Record*, House, 105th Cong., 1st sess. (15 May 1997): H2691–H2692, H2742.

14 *Politics in America, 1998* (Washington, D.C.: Congressional Quarterly, Inc., 1997): 363.

15 *Politics in America, 2002* (Washington, D.C.: Congressional Quarterly, Inc., 2001): 248–249.

16 *Congressional Record*, House, 105th Cong., 1st sess. (16 September 1997): H7352; "Hope for Nicaraguans," 12 October 1997, *Miami Herald*: 2L; *Almanac of American Politics, 2000*: 444.

17 Sergio R. Bustos, "Lawmakers Push Pro-Immigrant Bill," 12 March 2007, *Miami Herald; Almanac of American Politics, 2010* (Washington, D.C.: National Journal Group, Inc., 2009): 398.

18 *Notable Latino Americans*: 120; *Politics in America, 2010* (Washington, D.C.: Congressional Quarterly, Inc., 2009): 259.

19 *Congressional Record*, House, 104th Cong., 2nd sess. (6 March 1996): H1724–H1725; *Almanac of American Politics, 2002* (Washington, D.C.: National Journal Group, Inc., 2001): 419.

20 *Congressional Record*, House, 104th Cong., 2nd sess. (6 March 1996): H1735.

21 *Congressional Record*, House, 104th Cong., 1st sess. (20 September 1995): H9328–H9329.

22 See, for example, *Congressional Record*, House 104th Cong., 1st sess. (7 March 1995): H2789; *Congressional Record*, House, 104th Cong., 1st sess. (3 April 1995): H4076.

23 Jorge Banales, "UPI Focus: Mixed Reaction to Clinton's Cuba Shift," 20 March 1998, United Press International.

24 Jim Landers, "Farm-State Republicans Cheer Cuba Trade Deal; Party Leaders Concede Defeat on Easing of Embargo," 28 June 2000, *Dallas Morning News*: 1A; "Deal Set to Ease Cuba Embargo," 6 October 2000, *Sun-Sentinel*: 3A.

25 Carol Rosenberg, "Wheeling and Dealing in D.C.; Diaz-Balart's Immigration Bill Is a Victory of Behind-the-Scenes Politicking," 15 November 1997, *Miami Herald*: 8A.

26 Tim Goldens, "Cuban Refugees Tangle Mexican Diplomacy," 21 September 1993, *New York Times*: A10; *Politics in America, 1994* (Washington, D.C.: Congressional Quarterly, Inc., 1993): 379.

27 David Adams, "Amid Protests, Miami Debates Elian's Fate," 7 January 2000, *St. Petersburg Times*: A1.

28 Maya Bell, "Brothers' Ascent to Power: Part Destiny, Part Dynasty," 6 January 2003, *Orlando Sentinel*: A1.

29 Timothy J. Burger, "Freshman Rep. Diaz-Balart Gets Revenge on Rep. Skaggs, to the Tune of $23 Million," 5 July 1993, *Roll Call.*

30 Peter Janhunen, "House Hispanics Split over Cuba Trade Policy," 25 June 1997, *The Hill*; Phil Willon, "Cuban Issues Create Rift with Hispanic Lawmakers," 13 January 1997, *Tampa Tribune*: 1.

31 Tom Carter, "Cuban-Americans from Florida Quit Hispanic Caucus," 9 January 1997, *Washington Times*: A4; "Hispanic Caucus Loses 2 Floridians," 12 January 1997, *St. Petersburg Times*: 4A.

32 Suzanne Gamboa, "GOP Hispanics Form Congressional Group," 18 March 2003, Associated Press.

33 "Election Statistics, 1920 to Present," http://history.house.gov/institution/election-statistics/election-statistics.

34 Alfonso Chardy and Laura Figueroa, "Candidates Commence Fight," 23 January 2008, *Miami Herald*: B1; Alfonso Chardy, "Ex-Mayor to Run for Congress," 22 January 2008, *Miami Herald*: B1; "Election Statistics, 1920 to Present," http://history.house.gov/institution/election-statistics/election-statistics.

35 Josh Krauschaar, "Lincoln Diaz-Balart Opts Out of 2010," 11 February 2010, *Politico*, http://www.politico.com/news/stories/0210/32829.html (accessed 31 January 2011).

Carlos A. Romero-Barceló
1932–

RESIDENT COMMISSIONER 1993–2001
NEW PROGRESSIVE FROM PUERTO RICO

With only a few breaks, Carlos Antonio Romero-Barceló served in public office for nearly 40 years. A leading figure in the Partido Nuevo Progresista (New Progressive Party, or PNP), Romero-Barceló served two terms as Resident Commissioner in the U.S. House of Representatives, promoting Puerto Rico's statehood and working to strengthen the island's relationship with the federal government.

Romero-Barceló, who became the most distinguished member of a prominent political family, was born September 4, 1932, in San Juan, Puerto Rico. His maternal grandfather, Antonio R. Barceló, was president of the insular senate, and his mother, Josefina Barceló, was the last president of the island's Partido Liberal (Liberal Party) before it dissolved. As a young man, Romero-Barceló moved to New Hampshire to attend Phillips Exeter Academy, from which he graduated in 1949. He earned a B.A. from Yale University in 1953, with a double major in political science and economics. Returning to Puerto Rico, he earned a law degree from the Universidad de Puerto Rico in 1956, passed the bar, and began working for a private law firm. He married and had two sons, Carlitos and Andres. Romero-Barceló and his second wife, Kate Donelly, also had a son, Juan Carlos.[1]

Romero-Barceló started his political career as the director of the pro-statehood group Citizens for State 51. From 1965 to 1967, he worked his way up to the PNP leadership. Only 36 years old, but increasingly popular, he ran for mayor of San Juan in 1968 against elder statesman Jorge Font Saldaña of the Partido Popular Democrático (Popular Democratic Party, or PPD). According to a city newspaper, the election quickly became "a battle between the generations at a time in which age probably has a bigger role to play in an island election than at any time in its history."[2] An enthralling speaker, Romero-Barceló visited San Juan's housing projects and schools as he talked about his ambitious economic program, "Operation Rescue."[3] In "the most interesting, stimulating, and, at times, gaudiest campaign the city has had in recent history," Romero-Barceló, who stumped with armed security personnel, crushed Font Saldaña in the general election.[4]

As mayor, Romero-Barceló modernized the city's waste disposal services, and he worked to combat drug addiction and poor housing in San Juan.[5] He advocated for a stronger tourism bureau and remade the mayor's office, transforming it from what one newspaper called "a political outpost." Romero-Barceló's combined initiatives made him widely popular, and he was re-elected in 1972 by a comfortable margin.[6]

Romero-Barceló's tenure as mayor made him a household name, and in 1976 the PNP picked him as its gubernatorial candidate. His opponent was incumbent Rafael Hernández Colón of the PPD, who earlier had instituted a handful of controversial financial reforms. Romero-Barceló emphasized his plan to create jobs and downplayed the PNP's position on Puerto Rico's status. That fall he rode a wave of anti-incumbent frustration to a convincing victory in the general election.[7]

By the late 1970s, Romero-Barceló had become the consummate politician. "His personality fills the room. He's 100 percent political," admitted one member of the press. And he acted the part, too. "The brawny governor, who looks like a silver-haired movie idol," said the *Washington Post*, seemed to captivate an audience the way few others in Puerto Rico could.[8]

The new governor inherited an economy in utter ruin. Even with an annual allowance from the federal government of more than one billion dollars, Puerto Rico was still twice as impoverished as the poorest U.S.

Collection of the U.S. House of Representatives, Photography Collection

state.[9] There were no immediate solutions to the island's unemployment problem, but Romero-Barceló began putting together a long-term agenda so that Puerto Rico could "become more self-sufficient." The plan included education and vocational training for the rapidly growing population.[10] Romero-Barceló emphasized growing more and different foodstuffs for domestic markets, and as part of his push to win greater borrowing privileges from Washington, he worked to curtail generous tax exemptions for many of the island's businesses.[11]

Romero-Barceló also made statehood a pillar of his administration. The governor had long viewed the island's commonwealth status as a deliberately nebulous concept that was little more than an outdated "interim compromise."[12] Statehood, he believed, would finally generate some stability. It would end Puerto Rico's "political inferiority," he said, and open doors to all sorts of federal programs.[13] However, no amount of lobbying could withstand the pressure of another recession and a new oppositional majority in the island's legislature.[14] Though Romero-Barceló won re-election in 1980 by a razor-thin 0.2 percent, he was never able to muster the popular support that was needed for a referendum on statehood.[15] Four years later he was ousted from the governor's mansion by his longtime rival, Hernández Colón of the PPD.[16]

After the election Romero-Barceló returned to private law practice, but he was not away from politics for long.[17] He was elected to the Puerto Rican senate and served from 1986 to 1989, having lost the gubernatorial primary election in 1987 to San Juan mayor and future Resident Commissioner Baltasar Corrada-del Río. After his senate term, a brief hiatus from public office helped him regain control of the party, and he was re-elected PNP president from 1989 to 1992 (he had served earlier from 1974 to 1985).[18]

In 1992 Romero-Barceló became the New Progressives' candidate to challenge Antonio J. Colorado, the incumbent Resident Commissioner in the U.S. House of Representatives. After fighting a smear campaign by the insular legislature, Romero-Barceló began positioning himself more as a populist than as a party stalwart: "As resident commissioner," he said, "I would not be representing the government of Puerto Rico. I would be representing the people of Puerto Rico."[19] Opponents criticized his rather gruff political style, but the former governor was a seasoned fundraiser.[20] He sought to reform the island's tax code and promised to bolster Medicare and Medicaid, establish a minimum wage, and secure Pell grants for the island's schools. On Election Day, Romero-Barceló captured 48.5 percent of the vote, besting Colorado by less than 1 percent.[21] In 1993, when Romero-Barceló took his seat in the U.S. House, he became the first former Puerto Rican governor to serve as Resident Commissioner.

Though the federal-insular relationship was downplayed during the election, securing statehood for Puerto Rico moved to the top of Romero-Barceló's agenda after he arrived in Washington. He framed the island's political status, and his own unique position in the House, as part of a larger civil rights narrative, caucusing with the Democratic Party because he had "no doubt that it is easier to work with Democrats than Republicans on civil rights."[22] In addition to the constitutional limits placed on the Resident Commissioner's ability to vote, another part of the problem, especially as Romero-Barceló saw it, had to do with taxes. Since the territories and the commonwealth of Puerto Rico paid no federal income taxes, their representatives in the House—the Territorial Delegates and the Resident Commissioner—had been denied the right to vote on pending legislation, preventing them from raising taxes, which their constituents did not pay. Romero-Barceló found the pay-to-play mentality unfair, noting that he had "never heard of such a thing as no representation without taxation." The final version of the House Rules adopted in 1993 gave Romero-Barceló and the other Delegates a vote in the Committee of the Whole as long as they did not determine the outcome of any particular measure. While Romero-Barceló appreciated the modest amount of leverage he had acquired, he said it was "not really a vote, just an opportunity to participate."[23]

In his first four-year term, Romero-Barceló was placed on the Committee on Natural Resources and the Committee on Education and Labor, where he focused most of his legislative energy on improving Puerto Rico's school system.[24] He sat on multiple conference committees but struggled to increase funding for the island. In early March 1994, as the House debated the specifics of the Improving America's Schools Act (H.R. 6), Romero-Barceló introduced an amendment to lift the cap on the island's funding. Federal policy, he said, had created a "second-class, underfunded educational system" in Puerto Rico, but though Romero-Barceló won support from more-progressive House Members, his amendment was voted down, 358 to 70.[25] The next day a similar amendment failed to pass by a similar margin.[26] For years, Romero-Barceló had also wanted to replace the island's corporate tax breaks with wage-based credits, but he opposed the Small Business Job Protection Act of 1996 because it promised to upend Puerto Rico's revenue program.[27]

Though Romero-Barceló's legislative record was modest during his first few years in the House, he often pursued policy that was outside Puerto Rico's immediate interests. An active member of the Congressional Hispanic Caucus (CHC), Romero-Barceló was elected vice chairman at the start the 104th Congress (1995–1997). At a time when Hispanic voters were growing increasingly powerful—every Hispanic Member who ran for re-election in 1994 had won—Romero-Barceló and the CHC worked to shape national policy.[28] He readily backed William J. (Bill) Clinton's presidency, hoping his plans to stimulate the economy and reform health care would improve living conditions in the poorest areas of the United States.[29] He pushed to limit occupational hazards, spoke passionately about protecting Medicare benefits, and argued to raise the minimum wage.[30] In spring 1996, Romero-Barceló attacked the English Language Empowerment Act of 1996 (H.R. 123), which would have required all federal documents to be printed only in English. He called the measure "absurd" and questioned its constitutionality. House Rules prevented him from voting against it, however, and the bill passed but died in the Senate Judiciary Committee.[31]

Romero-Barceló won re-election in 1996 with 50 percent of the vote and returned to Washington on the eve of the 100th anniversary of America's sovereignty over Puerto Rico.[32] The timing intensified the federal government's effort to permanently define America's insular policy, and in late February 1997, the 105th Congress began considering the United States-Puerto Rico Political Status Act (H.R. 856).[33] Co-sponsored by Romero-Barceló, the bill would "provide the first Congressionally-sponsored process leading to full self-government for Puerto Rico," a later committee report argued.[34] Months of horse trading in Congress and heated discussions in Puerto Rico preceded a contentious debate on the House Floor that lasted nearly 12 hours. Romero-Barceló helped manage the bill, which passed the House 209 to 208, but died in the Senate. "What is regrettable in the saga of Puerto Rico's century-old colonial relationship with the United States is not the recent one-vote majority in the House to permit Puerto Rico to begin a process of self-determination," Romero-Barceló said, "but rather Congress's long history of indifference to and inaction on the political status of Puerto Rico."[35]

Romero-Barceló continued to sit on the Education and Resources Committees in the 105th and 106th Congresses (1997–2001) and became the Ranking Minority Member of Resources' Subcommittee on National Parks and National Lands. In addition to statehood, Romero-Barceló devoted his attention to health policy, resource conservation, and education. His bill to remove the caps on funding for veterans' Medicaid programs in Puerto Rico faltered from the start, and he found "it unconscionable that the Federal Government would uphold a policy where the health and lives of the people of Puerto Rico are considered to be of less value than the lives of other citizens."[36] Neither of his bills to conserve and protect Puerto Rico's sensitive ecosystems passed committee review. Romero-Barceló adamantly opposed the English Language Fluency Act, which required non-native speakers of English to master the language in just two years. The bill, he said, amounted to outright discrimination and threatened to overturn nearly 30 years of more progressive policy.[37]

At the end of his House career, Romero-Barceló was still fighting the same battles he had fought at the start. "Puerto Ricans are first-class citizens in times of war," he said, observing that the island's residents had fought and died in U.S. conflicts, but "second-class citizens in times of peace."[38] He called the island's unequal privileges with regard to federal health programs an "abomination," questioning how America could "stand as a model for the world when it maintains a policy of discrimination, a policy of economic and political apartheid."[39] When the U.S. Navy accidently killed a Puerto Rican civilian during a training mission on the island of Vieques, debates about the island's self-governance began anew. Romero-Barceló supported moving naval operations elsewhere, calling the Vieques question "a defining moment in Puerto Rico's relationship" with the federal government.[40] Despite a tenuous agreement with the Clinton administration that would allow the U.S. Navy to continue using the island, Puerto Rico's new pro-commonwealth administration began calling for the navy to leave.[41]

Romero-Barceló was one of the many New Progressives who were swept out of office in 2000; he lost the election to Aníbal Acevedo-Vilá of the PPD by about 4 percent.[42] Though Romero-Barceló received endorsements from President Clinton and a handful of sitting Members and raised significantly more money than his opponent, accusations of corruption against the PNP's entire roster cost him the race. "Theirs was a campaign of insults and defamation," he said of the PPD before vowing to support the New Progressive agenda in the coming years. "We are going to fight to bring statehood to the island because we want equality."[43] After the election, he returned home to Puerto Rico, becoming president of the Puerto Rican delegation to the League of United Latin American Citizens.[44] In 2003 he was passed over for the New Progressive nomination to his former post as Resident Commissioner, but he remained active in the party's leadership.[45]

FOR FURTHER READING

Biographical Directory of the United States Congress, "Carlos A. Romero-Barceló," http://bioguide.congress.gov.

Romero-Barceló, Carlos. *Camino a la igualdad: Puerto Rico: Ante una nueva jornada* (Ponce, PR: Partido Nuevo Progresista, Junta Central Estatal, 1995).

_____. *El hombre, el amigo, el politico* (Puerto Rico: Oficina de Información de la Campaña Carlos '76, 1976).

_____. *La estadidad es para los pobres* (San Juan, PR: n.p., 1976).

_____. "Puerto Rico, U.S.A.: The Case for Statehood," *Foreign Affairs* 59 (Fall 1980): 58–81.

NOTES

1 Martha Dreyer, "Romero—New Generation Man," 7 November 1968, *San Juan Star*: 21; "'Fraud' Smelled by Romero as He Slams Election Board," 6 November 1968, *San Juan Star*: 6.

2 Manny Suarez, "Font v. Romero," 17 August 1968, *San Juan Star*: 21.

3 Manny Suarez, "Candidates for Mayor Debate on TV," 11 October 1968, *San Juan Star*: 1; Martha Dreyer, "Romero: Plan Board OK'd Bridge," 18 October 1968, *San Juan Star*: 24; James McDonough, "Romero Shows Appeal to Youth," 21 October 1968, *San Juan Star*: 3.

4 "'Fraud' Smelled by Romero as He Slams Election Board"; "The Choice for Mayor," 4 November 1968, *San Juan Star*: 43. See also "San Juan," 6 November 1968, *San Juan Star*: 23; Frank Ramos, "Win Margin Surprises Romero," 7 November 1968, *San Juan Star*: 3.

5 Dimas Planas, "Mayor-Elect Unveils Part of City Cabinet," 31 December 1968, *San Juan Star*: 3; Pedro Roman, "Romero to Wage War against Drugs," 20 December 1968, *San Juan Star*: 10; Frank Ramos,"Romero Urges P.R. Culture Center," 11 December 1971, *San Juan Star*: 6; Margarita Babb, "Romero Slates New Poverty Program," 15 October 1972, *San Juan Star*: 3; "'72 Campaign: Mayors of San Juan," 5 November 1972, *San Juan Star*: S-4.

6 "Romero Barcelo for Mayor," 3 November 1972, *San Juan Star*: 38; Tomas Stella, "Romero Apparently Wins Re-Election," 9 November 1972, *San Juan Star*: 1.

7 "Romero has become a political figure at an island-wide level," observed a newspaper even before he won election in 1968. See Dimas Planas, "Romero's Future," 31 October 1968, *San Juan Star*: 41. See also David Vidal, "Change in Puerto Rico Vowed," 4 November 1976, *New York Times*: 22; "Statehood Advocates Sweep Puerto Rico," 4 November 1976, *Washington Post*: A11; John Van Hyning, "Confronting an Island's Ills," 2 January 1977, *Washington Post*: 3; Charles A. Krause, "New Governor of P.R. Ignores Statehood Issue," 3 January 1977, *Washington Post*: A1.

8 Joanne Omang, "Puerto Rico in Political Turmoil," 20 August 1978, *Washington Post*: C1.

9 Andrew Jaffe, "Puerto Rico: Vote for Change," 22 November 1976, *Newsweek*: 46; "Puerto Rico: Getting Things Taped," 4 December

1976, *Economist*: 52.

10 Interview with Carlos Romero-Barceló, Governor of Puerto Rico, "Should Puerto Rico Be a State?" 11 April 1977, *U.S. News & World Report*: 47.

11 Charles A. Krause, "Romero Says P.R. Should Control Offshore Minerals," 22 January 1977, *Washington Post*: A10; Interview with Carlos Romero-Barceló, Governor of Puerto Rico, "Should Puerto Rico Be a State?"; William C. Bryant, "Puerto Rico Loses Some of Its Business Allure," 10 July 1978, *U.S. News & World Report*: 55; "New Look for Puerto Rico," 10 March 1979, *Economist*: 116.

12 Carlos Romero-Barceló, "Puerto Rico, U.S.A.: The Case for Statehood," *Foreign Affairs* 59 (Fall 1980): 61.

13 Omang, "Puerto Rico in Political Turmoil." For background on Romero-Barceló's position on Puerto Rican statehood, see César J. Ayala and Rafael Bernabe, *Puerto Rico in the American Century: A History since 1898* (Chapel Hill: University of North Carolina Press, 2007): 277. See also Romero-Barceló, "Puerto Rico, U.S.A.: The Case for Statehood": 60–81 (quotation on p. 62); and Interview with Carlos Romero-Barceló, Governor of Puerto Rico, "Should Puerto Rico Be a State?"

14 Warren Brown, "Puerto Rico Bill Lagging," 4 January 1977, *Washington Post*: A1; "Ford Asks for Referendum on Puerto Rico Statehood Plan," 15 January 1977, *Washington Post*: B3; Charles Krause, "Showdown Viewed as Certain in Puerto Rico's Ties to U.S.," 11 January 1977, *Washington Post*: A15; "Puerto Rico: Stalled," 17 January 1981, *Economist*: 31; "Puerto Rican Leader Re-Elected," 11 November 1980, *Chicago Tribune*: 10; Alfonso Chardy, "Puerto Rico: The Soul Is Latin," 11 September 1982, *Miami Herald*: A10.

15 Romero-Barceló won by only 3,503 of the roughly 1.6 million votes cast in 1980. See "Governor Is Sworn In," 3 January 1981, *Washington Post*: A4. See also Joanne Omang, "Puerto Rico Unable to Find Way to Escape Commonwealth Status," 3 August 1982, *Washington Post*: A2.

16 Sonia L. Nazario, "Candidate on Horseback," 14 September 1984, *Wall Street Journal*: 62; Harold Lidin, "Ex-Puerto Rican Governor Regains Post," 8 November 1984, *Miami Herald*: A25. See also Joan O'Neill, "Puerto Rico's Governor's Race Reflects Pro-State, Commonwealth Tensions," 11 November 1984, *Washington Post*: A1.

17 Mireya Navarro, "Puerto Rico Gripped by Its Watergate," 30 January 1992, *New York Times*: A18.

18 The 1987 race had the island's first-ever gubernatorial primary election. See Manuel Suarez, "Ex-Governor's Bid Complicates Puerto Rico Race," 8 November 1987, *New York Times*: 41. See also *Biographical Directory of the United States Congress*, "Carlos Antonio Romero-Barceló," http://bioguide.congress.gov.

19 The tax legislation had been introduced by Rep. Dan Rostenkowski of Illinois and sought to recoup the estimated $2.5 billion the island lost every five years because of the loopholes in section 936. Regarding the office of Resident Commissioner, Romero-Barceló argued, "During the years of Popular Democratic Party power, the resident commissioner has been a tool of the party, a puppet. The governor pulled the strings and the resident commissioner spoke." See Robert Friedman, "CRB Says He Will Back Cutting 936," 6 August 1992, *San Juan Star*: 3.

20 Robert Friedman, "Colorado, Romero Face Off, But Throw No Body Punches," 14 August 1992, *San Juan Star*: 2; Maria Bird Pico, "Romero Leads Colorado in Campaign Fund-Raising," 22 October 1992, *San Juan Star*: 17.

21 Robert Friedman, "Romero Appears to Have Won Race," 5 November 1992, *San Juan Star*: 3; "Election Statistics, 1920 to Present," http://history.house.gov/institution/election-statistics/election-statistics; Robert Friedman, "Romero Links 936 Changes to Funding for P.R. Programs," 6 December 1992, *San Juan Star*: 4; Jenifer McKim, "New Commissioner Vows to Fight Law Barring Pell Grants," 18 December 1992, *San Juan Star*: 2.

22 Friedman, "Romero Appears to Have Won Race"; Friedman, "Romero Links 936 Changes to Funding for P.R. Programs."

23 Robert Friedman, "P.R. Commissioner Speaks His Piece on the House Floor," 6 January 1993, *San Juan Star*: 3; Robert Friedman, "CBR Gets Diluted Right to Vote," 6 January 1993, *San Juan Star*: 3; Robert Friedman, "Romero Co-Sponsors Bill to Permit Family Leave," 7 January 1993, *San Juan Star*: 4.

24 During the 104th Congress (1995–1997), the Committee on Education and Labor was renamed the Committee on Economic and Educational Opportunities. It was renamed the Committee on Education and the Workforce in 1997, and remained so until 2007 when Democrats regained the majority and the panel was renamed Education and Labor. The Committee on Natural Resources was renamed the Committee on Resources from the 104th Congress through the 111th Congress.

25 *Congressional Record*, House, 103rd Cong., 2nd sess. (2 March 1994): 3669–3670.

26 *Congressional Record*, House, 103rd Cong., 2nd sess. (3 March 1994): 3800–3801.

27 The legislation, he said, also offered "no increase in the Federal benefits provided to the U.S. citizens of Puerto Rico." See, *Congressional Record*, House, 104th Cong., 2nd sess. (21 May 1996): 11989. Dan Burton and Peter Deutsch, "It's Time to Reform the Puerto Rico Tax Credit," 16 January 1996, *Christian Science Monitor*: 18; Doreen A. Hemlock, "Puerto Rico Loses Its Edge," 21 September 1996, *New York Times*: Business Day, 31.

28 Ana Gershanik, "Caucus Takes Stock of Its Successes," 15 December 1994, *Times-Picayune* (New Orleans): G6.

29 *Congressional Record*, House, 103rd Cong., 1st sess. (18 February 1993): 2973; *Congressional Record*, House, 103rd Cong., 1st sess. (29 July 1993): 17702; *Congressional Record*, House, 103rd Cong., 2nd sess. (2 February 1994): 745–746; *Congressional Record*,

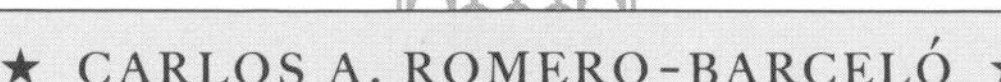

House, 103rd Cong., 2nd sess. (29 June 1994): 15092.

30 *Congressional Record*, House, 104th Cong., 1st sess. (1 August 1995): 21332; *Congressional Record*, House, 104th Cong., 1st sess. (11 May 1995): 12645; *Congressional Record*, House, 104th Cong., 1st sess. (26 July 1995): 20518; *Congressional Record*, House, 104th Cong., 2nd sess. (23 April 1996): 8560–8561.

31 *Congressional Record*, House, 104th Cong., 2nd sess. (1 August 1996): 21175, quotation on p. 21198.

32 "Election Statistics, 1920 to Present," http://history.house.gov/institution/election-statistics/election-statistics.

33 Stephen S. Rosenfeld, "Forgotten Isles of Empire," 24 January 1997, *Washington Post*: A23.

34 House Committee on Resources, *United States-Puerto Rico Political Status Act*, 105th Cong., 1st sess., 1997, H. Rep. 131, 30.

35 Carlos Romero-Barceló, "Puerto Rico: Still Only a Colony," 3 April 1998, *Washington Post*: A30. For the debate, which lasted nearly 12 hours, see *Congressional Record*, House, 105th Cong., 2nd sess. (4 March 1998): 2484–2551. Many islanders complained that the bill's language would have precluded the appearance of the island's commonwealth status on the ballot. For a brief explanation, see Ayala and Bernabe, *Puerto Rico in the American Century*: 293–294.

36 *Congressional Record*, House, 105th Cong., 1st sess. (25 June 1997): 12255; *Congressional Record*, House, 106th Cong., 1st sess. (23 June 1999): 14062.

37 Romero-Barceló's conservation bills were H.R. 4668, introduced on June 14, 2000, and H.R. 5651, introduced on December 8, 2000. For the English Language Fluency Act, see *Congressional Record*, House, 105th Cong., 2nd sess. (10 September 1998): 19952.

38 *Congressional Record*, House, 106th Cong., 1st sess. (13 April 1999): 6270.

39 *Congressional Record*, House, 106th Cong., 1st sess. (23 February 1999): 2688.

40 Juan O. Tamayo, "Island's Naval Battle Escalates, Puerto Rico Resists U.S. Firing Range," 30 August 1999, *Miami Herald*: A1.

41 Mimi Whitefield, "Vieques Clash Back on Front Burner," 4 December 2000, *Miami Herald*: A1.

42 "Election Statistics, 1920 to Present," http://history.house.gov/institution/election-statistics/election-statistics.

43 Carlos Antonio Otero, "Romero Says Clinton, 5 Members of Congress Endorse His Candidacy," 31 October 2000, *San Juan Star*: 6; Maria Soledad Calero and Carlos Antonio Otero, "Acevedo Vilá Defeats Incumbent CRB for Resident Commissioner," 8 November 2000, *San Juan Star*: 7. Quotation from Laura Albertelli, "Pesquera to Go Back to Private Life," 8 November 2000, *San Juan Star*: 6.

44 Maria T. Padilla, "League Seems to Be Naïve on Statehood Issue," 18 June 2003, *Orlando Sentinel*: B1.

45 "Puerto Rico Hopefuls Start Bids for Office," 2 August 2003, *Orlando Sentinel*: A14.

"I am convinced, both as a Latin American and as a U.S. citizen, that statehood for Puerto Rico would constitute a boon for the nation, as well as for the island."

Carlos A. Romero-Barceló
Foreign Affairs, 1980

Frank Tejeda
1945–1997

UNITED STATES REPRESENTATIVE 1993–1997
DEMOCRAT FROM TEXAS

Frank Tejeda served slightly more than two terms as a Texas Representative in the U.S. House before his life was cut short by a severe illness. Tejeda was a decorated U.S. Marine with a long and influential career in the Texas state legislature when he arrived in Washington. Tejeda's military service, in which he specialized in national security, greatly influenced his career in politics. His humble beginnings led to his desire to improve conditions in his majority-Hispanic district. "His story is very much the American story, about the ingenuity and creativity of one man's rise from obscurity to power," said Representative Solomon Ortiz of Texas after his colleague died in 1997.[1]

Frank Mariano Tejeda was born in San Antonio, Texas, on October 2, 1945, to Frank Tejeda, Sr., a disabled veteran of World War II, and Lillie Tejeda, a housekeeper and an employee of a local beauty shop.[2] Tejeda attended St. Leo's Catholic School and then Harlandale High School, a public school in San Antonio's South Side. In 1963, at age 17, he dropped out of school and joined the Marine Corps.[3] This "was probably the turning point in my life," Tejeda reflected later.[4] His valiant tour of duty in Vietnam earned him a Bronze Star and a Purple Heart. "I was a grunt, and proud of it," Tejeda recalled. "I wouldn't have it any other way."[5] He credited his Marine service and guidance from his parents as the primary factors that helped him overcome a difficult childhood in an impoverished neighborhood. "They always instilled in me that many people can deprive you of many things ... but you can never be deprived of an education," Tejeda said of his parents.[6] Heeding their advice, Tejeda attained his high school equivalency degree while serving in the Marines; upon his return to San Antonio in 1967, he enrolled at St. Mary's University, graduating with a B.A. in 1970. Tejeda went on to law school at the University of California at Berkeley, receiving his J.D. in 1974. He returned to San Antonio after law school to work as an attorney, remaining in the Marine Reserves and eventually earning the rank of major. Tejeda married Cecelia Gaitan; the couple had three children, Marissa, Sonya, and Frank III, before divorcing.[7]

In 1976, at age 31, Tejeda won a seat in the Texas state house of representatives in a district that included the South Side of San Antonio. "I'd see the streets that never got repaired, the poor drainage," Tejeda said, explaining why he ran for political office. "I'd see other people get things done because they had influence. I got involved because it was the only way, I felt, to get things done."[8] Auguring the bipartisan support he enjoyed throughout his career, his first campaign contribution from outside his family came from Lamar Smith, who chaired the Bexar County Republican Party before joining Tejeda in the U.S. House.[9] Tejeda spent a decade in the Texas house before advancing to the state senate. While serving in the legislature, Tejeda continued working as a lawyer and pursued two advanced degrees. In 1980 he obtained a Master's of Public Administration degree from Harvard, and in 1989 he earned an LL.M. degree from Yale.

In the state legislature, Tejeda developed a reputation as a dedicated and tenacious public servant. Tejeda pledged to "serve all the people and all groups and to serve the South Side to the best of my ability," and his concern for his constituents contributed to his solid voting base and popularity.[10] He also cultivated alliances with politicians from San Antonio's South Side and emerged as a leader of a formidable political coalition with a strong grass-roots base aimed at reform and community activism.[11] Tejeda rejected criticism that the association he helped create resembled a political machine. "It's just a group of people concerned about how people live," he said. "There's no formal meetings, no divvying up of political spoils. We talk with

Image courtesy of the U.S. House of Representatives Photography Office

each other about problems and keep each other honest to a commitment to the South Side."[12] During his 16 years in the Texas house and senate, Tejeda attempted to boost state aid for women- and minority-owned businesses, sought to provide housing for veterans, and backed increased government protection of voting rights for minority groups. Tejeda also championed worker's compensation reform, leading to a direct confrontation with the state's trial lawyers, who were unhappy about new arbitration guidelines that prevented civil law suits.[13] In 1990 Texas attorneys groups helped finance a primary challenger against Tejeda, but he ultimately prevailed with more than three-quarters of the vote.[14]

Texas gained three U.S. congressional seats as a result of reapportionment after the 1990 Census; a high rate of population growth ensured that at least one new seat would come from heavily Hispanic South Texas. The newly created district, anchored in Bexar County, included Tejeda's political base in the Harlandale neighborhood as well as Republican-leaning northeastern San Antonio, which was mostly white and middle class. The district stretched south from San Antonio to a predominantly Hispanic region of Texas on the Mexican border with a high unemployment rate and many residents below the poverty line.[15] The seasoned Texas politician faced no opposition from his own party or from the Republicans when he declared his intent to run for the House in the 1992 elections, demonstrating his political strength. With no major-party contenders, Tejeda's campaign focused less on specific policy topics than on his style of governing. "My message is that I'm a hard worker, I'm a caring and compassionate individual," Tejeda noted. "And I will listen. I'm here to serve the people, not to dictate."[16] In the November election, Tejeda squared off against Libertarian Party candidate David Slatter, a field service engineer.[17] Tejeda easily defeated Slatter, earning 87 percent of the vote. Although the national and state political environments diverged from the Democratic Party in the 1994 midterm elections, Tejeda sailed to victory. The Republicans nominated Slatter. The incumbent prevailed by more than 45,000 votes, capturing 71 percent of the final tally.[18]

Reflecting his personal background and his interest in national security policy, Tejeda received assignments to the Armed Services and Veterans' Affairs Committees. During his short tenure in the House, Tejeda focused much of his attention on the military and veterans. In 1993 he enthusiastically backed increased disability compensation for veterans, their dependents, and surviving family members. "We owe a tremendous debt to those disabled veterans who stood the long watches and sacrificed for our Nation's defense," Tejeda reminded his House colleagues.[19] During the 103rd Congress (1993–1995) and again in the 104th Congress (1995–1997), the Texas Representative introduced legislation to increase educational assistance and opportunities for veterans.

A lifelong Democrat, Tejeda earned a reputation as an independent thinker. Though a strong supporter of increased federal funding for education and initiatives to combat poverty, he also opposed gun control and military budget cuts.[20] Asked if he thought his positions aligned better with those of the Republican Party, Tejeda responded, "I didn't go to Washington to march in lockstep with the president or the party."[21] While in the House, Tejeda did break from the Democratic majority and Democratic President William J. (Bill) Clinton on certain issues. He voted against President Clinton's highly publicized crime bill and against the Brady Bill, which restricted the purchase of handguns. In 1993 he came out against "Don't ask, don't tell," the President's proposal to allow gays and lesbians to serve in the military provided they did not reveal their sexual orientation. "I don't know if anything would be changed," Tejeda commented. "My bottom line is looking at military effectiveness."[22]

Preferring to work behind the scenes and out of the limelight, Tejeda had a reserved personality and a strong work ethic that complemented his focus on constituent service, the hallmark of his tenure in Congress. As a Representative, he often worked on routine affairs for his constituents, such as sorting out their problems with Social Security or Veterans Administration benefits. "You know that you've helped someone," he explained. "And you know that in the long run it will be politically helpful, too."[23]

Tejeda rarely made speeches on the House Floor, adopting a more vocal role in the House only when he believed it would benefit his district. During his first term, for example, he made an impassioned plea to his colleagues to vote in favor of the North American Free Trade Agreement (NAFTA). "If we do not take advantage of this tremendous opportunity, Japan and the European Economic Community certainly will," Tejeda said. "Let us not slam the window shut on our children's economic futures."[24] Tejeda's vote in favor of NAFTA reflected his belief that the agreement would open up economic opportunities for his district, which hugged the Mexican border.[25]

During his second term in the House, Tejeda focused on a matter that was of great importance to his district and to the state of Texas. By the 1990s, San Antonio's Kelly Air Force Base, which dated from World War I, was the Air Force's oldest continuously active air field.[26] It also had developed into a crucial component of San Antonio's economy. The largest single-site employer in Tejeda's job-starved district, it helped build San Antonio's Hispanic middle class.[27] When Tejeda first entered the House, Kelly employed half the Hispanics in the air force.[28] As the Cold War wound down, hopes for a "peace dividend" led Congress to create the Base Realignment and Closure Commission (BRAC). The purpose of the commission was to provide an "objective, non-partisan, and independent review and analysis" of Department of Defense recommendations of military bases that could be consolidated or closed without compromising national security. Congress could reject the BRAC list by passing a resolution of disapproval but could not modify the recommendations.[29] Kelly Air Force Base had survived three BRAC cuts, but the 1995 list recommended its closure, since San Antonio had five military bases. Joined by colleagues from California, which also had several bases on the 1995 BRAC list, Tejeda launched a long-shot effort to persuade Congress to reject the BRAC recommendations. He received little support, however, and on July 26, 1995, by a 43 to 10 tally, the National Security Committee (later named the Armed Services Committee) rejected Tejeda's motion to disapprove of the BRAC recommendations.[30] Despite the defeat, Tejeda carried his fight to the House Floor, where he contended that the commission had overlooked significant security and economic concerns. "I have no illusions about the final outcome of this matter," Tejeda admitted. "It is the bottom of the ninth and we are behind by a lot of runs. But this does not mean we give up and walk off the field."[31] On September 8, 1995, the House rebuffed Tejeda's resolution to set aside the BRAC recommendations by a vote of 343 to 75. "It's over," Tejeda conceded after the vote. "We'll take the lemons that have been handed to us and make some outstanding lemonade."[32] The Congressman moved on to explore ways of privatizing the base's operations, hoping to preserve as many local jobs as possible.[33]

Tejeda's attempt to save Kelly Air Force Base was his last significant political venture. After experiencing severe headaches in the fall of 1995, Tejeda went for a medical checkup; doctors discovered a malignant brain tumor. In October 1995, surgeons removed 90 percent of the tumor but could not reach the remainder, which was lodged in Tejeda's left temporal lobe. Doctors told the 50-year-old Tejeda that he would need at least six weeks to recuperate, but he returned to the House Floor only two weeks after surgery, just before a roll call vote on a Republican proposal to reduce Medicare funding. House Majority Whip Tom DeLay of Texas interrupted the proceedings to acknowledge Tejeda's presence, and his colleagues cheered.[34]

Though Tejeda resumed a normal schedule for most of 1996, during the fall campaign for his third term in the House his health deteriorated. Speaking and completing his thoughts became increasingly difficult. "If you've heard me speak recently, you may have noticed a few changes," he said. "I know exactly what I want to say, but the words just don't come out like I want."[35] Despite the setback, Tejeda easily defeated his opponents, Republican Mark Cude, a local businessman, and third-party candidate Clifford Finley—with 75 percent of the vote—for a seat in the 105th Congress (1997–1999).[36]

In December 1996, Tejeda's doctors discovered that his brain tumor had metastasized; surgery was impossible. Since Tejeda's poor health prevented him from traveling to Washington for the beginning of the 105th Congress, the House allowed a judge in San Antonio to swear him in for a third term.[37] "I'll do my best to recuperate quickly and join my colleagues in the House chamber," Tejeda promised in a statement. "The Marine in me intends to attack this thing with full vigor."[38] But the cancer had spread, and 17 months after his initial diagnosis, Tejeda passed away in San Antonio on January 30, 1997, at age 51. The next day, Navy Secretary John Dalton announced that Tejeda would be posthumously awarded the Silver Star for his efforts to save a wounded Marine in Vietnam. "What made Frank special was his quiet and unpretentious manner despite his distinguished accomplishments," New Mexico Congressman Bill Richardson said upon hearing of his colleague's death.[39] President Clinton also reflected on the Texas Representative's passing: "He endeared himself to all who knew him, always looking out for the best interests of his constituents, members of the military, and the Hispanic and veterans' communities in particular."[40] Tejeda was buried with full military honors at the Fort Sam Houston National Cemetery in San Antonio, Texas.[41]

FOR FURTHER READING

Biographical Directory of the United States Congress, "Frank Tejeda," http://bioguide.congress.gov.

MANUSCRIPT COLLECTIONS

University of Oklahoma, The Julian P. Kanter Political Commercial Archive, Department of Communication (Norman). *Videocassette:* 1990, two commercials on one videocassette. The Democratic Party commercials were used during Frank Tejeda's campaign for a 1990 state senatorial election in Texas.

University of Texas at Austin, Briscoe Center for American History. *Papers*: Lawrence C. Pope Collection, 1961–1989, 90 feet. Persons represented include Frank Tejeda.

University of Texas at San Antonio, Archives and Special Collections. *Papers*: Cyndi Taylor Krier Papers, 1956–2002, 176.4 linear feet, and the San Antonio Hispanic Chamber of Commerce Records, 1931–2008, 66.7 linear feet. Persons represented include Frank Tejeda.

NOTES

1 *Congressional Record,* 105th Cong., 1st sess. (4 February 1997): 1384.

2 Carol J. Castaneda, "Texan Is a Sure Shot for Congress," 17 March 1992, *USA Today*: 2A; David McLemore, "U.S. Rep. Frank Tejeda of San Antonio Dies at 51," 31 January 1997, *Dallas Morning News*: 24A.

3 Several sources indicate that Tejeda was expelled from high school. See McLemore, "U.S. Rep. Frank Tejeda of San Antonio Dies at 51."

4 McLemore, "U.S. Rep. Frank Tejeda of San Antonio Dies at 51."

5 Benjamin Sheffner, "Rep. Frank Tejeda Dies at Age 51"; Special Election Expected in March," 3 February 1997, *Roll Call.*

6 Castaneda, "Texan Is a Sure Shot for Congress."

7 *Congressional Directory*, 104th Congress (Washington, D.C.: Government Printing Office, 1996): 273; Ben R. Guttery, *Representing Texas: A Comprehensive History of U.S. and Confederate Senators and Representatives from Texas* (Austin, TX: Eakin Press, 2008): 146.

8 Ron Hutcheson, "San Antonio Representative Battling against Brain Tumor," 12 January 1997, *Fort Worth Star-Telegram*: 2.

9 *Congressional Record,* 105th Cong., 1st sess. (4 February 1997): 1384.

10 "Congressman Frank Tejeda Dead at 51," 31 January 1997, *Houston Chronicle*: 27.

11 Robert McG. Thomas, Jr., "Frank Tejeda, 51, Congressman from Texas and Former Marine," 2 February 1997, *New York Times*: 39; Bruce Davidson, "Tejeda Death Imperils South Side Coalition," 2 February 1997, *San Antonio Express-News*: 1A.

12 McLemore, "U.S. Rep. Frank Tejeda of San Antonio Dies at 51."

13 *Politics in America, 1994* (Washington, D.C.: Congressional Quarterly, Inc., 1993): 1531.

14 Scott Pendelton, "Frank Tejeda: A Candidate Who Sidesteps Stereotypes,"4 February 1992, *Christian Science Monitor*: 7.

15 "Presenting the First Freshman of Class of 1993: Texas Democrat Frank Tejeda," 26 January 1992, *Roll Call.* According to several sources, while serving in the Texas state senate, Frank Tejeda helped to draw the lines for the district he would later represent in the U.S. House. See "Congressman Frank Tejeda Dead at 51."

16 Pendelton, "Frank Tejeda: A Candidate Who Sidesteps Stereotypes."

17 *Politics in America, 1996* (Washington, D.C.: Congressional Quarterly, Inc., 1995): 1322.

18 "Election Statistics, 1920 to Present," http://history.house.gov/institution/election-statistics/election-statistics.

19 *Congressional Record*, House, 103rd Cong, 1st sess. (27 April 1993): 8277.

20 McLemore, "U.S. Rep. Frank Tejeda of San Antonio Dies at 51."

21 Ibid.

22 William Clayton, Jr., "Far from Consensus on Military Gay Ban; Both Sides Inflexible as Ever on Issue," 13 May 1993, *Houston Chronicle*: 9A; *Politics in America, 1996*: 1322.

23 George Rodrigue, "Taking Constituent Service Seriously; Helping the Folks Back Home Can Transcend Party Politics, Texans Find," 14 December 1995, *Dallas Morning News*: 33A.

24 *Congressional Record*, House, 103rd Cong., 1st sess. (9 November 1993): 27967.

25 Jonathan Moore, "Hispanics in Congress Begin to Find Their Voice," 15 March 1992, *Houston Chronicle*: 28A; *Almanac of American Politics, 1996* (Washington, D.C.: National Journal Inc., 1995): 1334.

26 "Kelly AFB, Texas," http://www.globalsecurity.org/military/facility/kelly.htm (accessed 25 July 2012).

27 "Base Privatization Review Urged," 11 February 1996, *San Antonio Express-News*: B1.

28 *Politics in America, 1994* (Washington, D.C.: Congressional Quarterly, Inc., 1993): 1532.

29 "Defense Base Closure and Realignment Commission," http://www.brac.gov/index.html (accessed 13 February 2012).

30 "Panel OK's Military Base Closing List," 27 July 1995, *Morning Call* (Allentown, PA): A3.

31 *Congressional Record*, House, 104th Cong., 1st sess. (8 September 1995): 24130.

32 "House OK's Shutting Down 79 Bases, Including Kelly," 9 September 1995, *Dallas Morning News*: 7A.

33 "Base Privatization Review Urged."

34 "Surgery Can't Stop Tejeda from Voting," 20 October 1995, *Dallas Morning News*: 6A.

35 "Lawmaker's Speech Worsens as Tumor Grows," 4 January 1997, *Fort Worth Star-Telegram*: 8; Ken Dilanian, "Tejeda to Miss Swearing-In after Fall at S. Side Home," 6 January 1997, *San Antonio Express-News*: A1.

36 "Election Statistics, 1920 to Present," http://history.house.gov/institution/election-statistics/election-statistics; Thaddeus Herrick, "Even in Death, Tejeda's Influence Dominates," 9 March 1997, *Houston Chronicle*: 1.

37 On January 8, 1997, U.S. District Judge Orlando Garcia swore Tejeda in as a Member of the 105th Congress. The private ceremony took place in a San Antonio hospital. Bruce Davidson, "Ailing Tejeda Takes Oath," 9 January 1997, *Houston Chronicle*: 24; Bruce Davidson, "Tejeda Returns Home from Stay in Hospital," 10 January 1997, *San Antonio Express-News*: 8B.

38 McLemore, "U.S. Rep. Frank Tejeda of San Antonio Dies at 51."

39 *Congressional Record,* House, 105th Cong., 1st sess. (4 February 1997): 1378.

40 "Peers Mourn San Antonio Congressman," 1 February 1997, *Fort Worth-Telegram*: 10.

41 David McLemore, "Tejeda Mourned; San Antonio Lawmaker's Services Draw Thousands," 4 February 1997, *Dallas Morning News*: 17A.

Robert A. Underwood
1948–

TERRITORIAL DELEGATE 1993–2003
DEMOCRAT FROM GUAM

Robert Underwood served five terms as Guam's Delegate in the U.S. House of Representatives before running unsuccessfully for governor. As Guam's third Delegate, Underwood continued his two predecessors' push for commonwealth status for the tiny island in the Western Pacific. His experience as an educator, along with his respect for Guam's Chamorro culture, shaped much of his legislative agenda during his time in the House. Using his position to draw attention to the pressing needs of the territory, Underwood fought for increased recognition for Guam and for its inclusion in federally funded programs. "When you're a small territory, the nexus of your relationship to the federal government is the basis for your representation in Washington," Underwood noted. "It's always trying to understand that and take advantage of it and try to fix the problems with that. That's the nature of the representation that comes from a small territory."[1]

Robert Underwood was born July 13, 1948, in Tamuning, a town on the west coast of Guam. Both his father, John, and his mother, Esther Flores Taitano, were teachers.[2] After graduating from Tamuning's John F. Kennedy High School in 1965, Underwood attended California State University in Los Angeles, earning a B.A. in history in 1969 and an M.A. in history in 1971. Influenced by his mother's vocation as a teacher, Underwood embarked on a 20-year career in education.[3] From 1972 to 1976, he was employed as a high school teacher, a school administrator, and a curriculum writer for Guam's public schools. He then worked at the University of Guam from 1977 to 1992 as an instructor for and a director of the Bilingual Bicultural Training Program, a director of Project BEAM (Bilingual Education Assistance from Micronesia), a professor of education, the dean of the College of Education, and the academic vice president of the university. During this period, Underwood also earned an Ed. D. from the University of Southern California in 1987 and graduated from Harvard's Management Development Program in 1988.[4] Underwood married Lorraine Aguilar, a teacher, and the couple had five children: Sophia, Roberto, Ricardo, Ramon, and Raphael.[5]

In 1992, Underwood left the University of Guam to challenge four-term incumbent Ben Blaz in the election for Guam's congressional Delegate. Long active in the debate on Guam's political status, Underwood was familiar with the issues affecting the island and pledged to use his experience in public policy to help Guam at the national level.[6] He used his strong ties to the community, built during his career as an educator, and his familial connections, which included his grandfather James H. Underwood, a former U.S. Marine and the postmaster of Guam.[7] He directed a successful grass-roots campaign, walking to small villages and meeting with voters.[8] Underwood's electoral prospects received an unanticipated boost when an impending typhoon postponed voting in Guam for nearly a week. Thus, Guamanians knew before going to the polls that William J. (Bill) Clinton had succeeded in his bid to unseat President George H. W. Bush. This was an important development since both Underwood and Blaz had emphasized the significance of Guam's having a Delegate from the same party as the President.[9] Ultimately, Underwood benefited from a desire for political change and bested Blaz with 55 percent of the vote.[10] "I feel gratified, but that has to end real quick," Underwood remarked. "There's a lot of work ahead."[11] In subsequent elections, Underwood cruised to victory. In 1994 and 1996 he ran unopposed. He faced minimal opposition in his final two elections, defeating Manuel Cruz, a labor union president, with 76 and 78 percent of the vote, respectively.[12]

Collection of the U.S. House of Representatives, Photography Collection

GUA

During his first term in the House, Underwood was assigned to the Armed Services, Natural Resources, and Education and Labor Committees. He remained on Armed Services and Natural Resources throughout his five terms in the House but left Education and Labor after the 103rd Congress (1993–1995).[13] Lacking the ability to vote on the final passage of legislation, Underwood used his committee work as a vital tool to represent his constituents. His spot on Natural Resources—an essential seat for Territorial Delegates—allowed him to weigh in on and influence legislation affecting Guam and the other U.S. territories. Located west of the International Date Line, Guam was a strategic U.S. military stronghold because of its proximity to East Asia. As the U.S. military presence on the island grew after World War II and the Cold War, Guam's economy became closely linked to the armed forces. Underwood's seat on the Armed Services Committee allowed him to cultivate military connections and monitor any changes that might affect the island. In addition to his committee workload, Underwood also chaired the Congressional Asian Pacific American Caucus during the 106th Congress (1999–2001).

Underwood wasted no time taking up the issue of Guam's political status. Since the passage of the Organic Act in 1950, which granted Guamanians U.S. citizenship and limited self-government, the island's political future remained a significant topic of debate. Underwood, a longtime advocate of Chamorro rights and increased independence for Guam, backed the commonwealth movement. On March 30, 1993, he introduced his first piece of legislation, the Guam Commonwealth Act. The measure called for the creation of a commonwealth with full self-government, the preservation of Chamorro culture, and the "mutual consent" of Guam and the United States for federal policies affecting the territory. Although the measure did not make it to the floor for a vote, Underwood introduced the legislation multiple times during his House tenure. In 1997 he took to the House Floor asking his colleagues to consider commonwealth status for Guam. "The 100th anniversary of the Spanish-American War marks an important time period for the United States to, in a sense, come face to face with its imperial past and come face to face with what hopefully will be in the next century a more perfect union not only for the 50 States and the District of Columbia, but all the people who live under the American flag," Underwood declared.[14]

As a nonvoting Delegate, Underwood faced unique challenges. "So essentially we are Members, but not entirely," Underwood said, explaining the role of Territorial Delegates. "The island or jurisdiction each respective delegate represents is not often afforded the attention that their jurisdictions deserve, and by our unique status we must introduce very unique legislation tailor-made for our respective jurisdictions."[15] Underwood drafted legislation that focused primarily on issues that pertained solely to Guam, and particularly on protecting the interests of its native inhabitants. One such matter concerned lands that had been taken from the Chamorros by the U.S. military after World War II. "Returning Federal excess lands to the people of Guam is not just a good thing to do," Underwood told his House colleagues. "It is the right thing to do, the just thing to do."[16] The freshman Delegate achieved a major legislative victory when his bill, the Guam Excess Lands Act, became law in 1994. The new law transferred more than 3,000 acres of federal land to Guam for parks, new schools, and affordable housing.

Bolstered by this success, Underwood sought to tackle a related long-standing dispute between Guam and the United States. The federal government owned a substantial portion of the island, whose land mass was little more than 200 square miles. In the wake of security demands after World War II, the U.S. military took control of large tracts of land in Guam. With the end of the Cold War, the local government called for the return of the unused land. Criticism of the American government intensified after the U.S. military relinquished a substantial stretch of land in 1994 to the U.S. Fish and Wildlife Service for use as a refuge.[17] In response to frustration over U.S. land practices, Underwood introduced the first Guam omnibus legislation in congressional history. He considered the Guam Land Returns Act, a provision giving Guam the right of "first refusal of declared excess lands" by the federal government, the most important segment of the bill. The Guam Delegate hoped to develop a process for acquiring excess land that would differ from the standard practice, which gave federal agencies interested in obtaining the unused property priority over the local government.[18] Labeling the topic "one of the most contentious issues in Guam history since the end of World War II," Underwood guided his bill through the House. It became law in 2000.[19]

Following the lead of his predecessors, Antonio Won Pat and Ben Blaz, Underwood drew attention to the hardships Guamanians endured during World War II. During Japan's three-year occupation, the people of Guam suffered forced labor and internment. Although he was born a few years after the war ended, Underwood had a personal connection to the period; he had lost his two older siblings (as infants) during the occupation. Reflecting on his parents' reaction to their loss, Underwood said, "They taught me that in the midst of difficult circumstances, we should learn lessons about dignity and courage and not bitterness or resentment."[20] Inspired by the Chamorros' strength, Underwood focused his legislative energy on reparations for the victims of the occupation. During the 107th Congress (2001–2003), he oversaw the passage of the Guam War Claims Review Commission Act. The bill, which became law in 2002, established a commission to oversee and settle claims made by Guamanians after World War II. Although the law did not authorize any payments, it was viewed as an important step in the eventual monetary compensation of the victims of the war.[21] In the interest of his constituents' safety, Underwood also asked American military personnel to search for unexploded mustard gas bombs left in Guam during World War II.[22]

Underwood's goal of ensuring fair treatment for all Americans often extended to other U.S. territories. In 1996 he inserted language into a telecommunications bill that would extend domestic rates and access to new technology to Guam and other Pacific territories.[23] He also introduced legislation to extend federal benefits for low-income, disabled, and elderly U.S. citizens to qualifying residents of Guam and the Virgin Islands. As a lifelong educator, Underwood wanted U.S. territories included in national education policy, and he expressed frustration when Guam, the Virgin Islands, Puerto Rico, and the Commonwealth of the Northern Mariana Islands were omitted from President George W. Bush's No Child Left Behind proposal.[24] "We will not be ignored and we will be included so that every child, whether they are from California, Texas or more familiar locations like Guam will not be left behind," Underwood said.[25] Although he was able to secure more federal funding to build schools and train teachers, Underwood wanted additional federal money for public education in Guam.[26]

Underwood also fought to preserve Guam's unique cultural identity. Underwood had chaired the Chamorro Language Commission before coming to Congress, and had led a movement to incorporate the Chamorro language and culture into the curriculum at the University of Guam.[27] His commitment to protect Guam's indigenous customs and traditions continued during his House tenure. In 2001 Underwood achieved an important victory when he convinced the Food and Drug Administration to allow the importation of betel nuts into the U.S. mainland. Chewed by many Pacific Islanders, the betel nut, a product of the areca palm tree, was a significant part of the Chamorro culture.[28] In the 106th Congress (1999–2001), Underwood introduced a bill to establish a standard time zone for Guam and the Northern Mariana Islands. Signed into law in 2000, the new legislation "will prove to be a source of pride when people refer to our time zone as Chamorro Standard Time," Underwood remarked.[29] Rather than criticizing legislation that would declare English the official language of the U.S. government, Underwood sent House Members a "Dear Colleague" letter poking fun at the bill by offering a mock "Ketchup-Only" measure. "I was surprised to learn salsa has replaced ketchup in sales as our nation's leading condiment," Underwood wrote. "I hope you share my concern that a country built on ketchup should take steps to ensure the predominance of this vegetable as our national condiment."[30] Speaking at the Democratic National Convention in 2000, Underwood highlighted the unique nature of Guam and the other Pacific Islands, concluding his speech in Chamorro as a tribute to his native land.[31]

In 2002 Underwood announced his decision to not seek a sixth term in the House. "Ten years in Washington is a long time, and I had hoped to have a good career in Congress, and I felt that I've done well, but it's also time to come back home," Underwood observed.[32] Still interested in public service, he entered the race for governor of Guam in 2002. In the campaign against Guam senator Felix Camacho, Underwood, heavily outspent by his Republican opponent, employed a grass-roots strategy like the one he used when he ran for Delegate.[33] Underwood ultimately lost the election, garnering 45 percent of the vote to Camacho's 55 percent.[34] "This is not the end. It is just another chapter," he told his supporters after the loss.[35] But four years later he again lost to Camacho. Named professor emeritus by the University of Guam in 2000, Underwood was selected as the university's president in 2008.

FOR FURTHER READING

Biographical Directory of the United States Congress, "Robert A. Underwood," http://bioguide.congress.gov.

NOTES

1 Jennifer Yachnin, "Guam Delegate Hopes to Exchange Long Flights for Governorship," 26 September 2002, *Roll Call*: 14.

2 Biographical information about Delegate Underwood appeared on his 2002 campaign website for governor of Guam, "Underwood & Ada for Governor and Lt. Governor," http://www.underwoodada.com/?ua=profiles (accessed 7 November 2002).

3 Yachnin, "Guam Delegate Hopes to Exchange Long Flights for Governorship."

4 Underwood's curriculum vitae was posted on the University of Guam's website, http://www.uog.edu/dynamicdata/PresidentsOffice.aspx (accessed 11 January 2012).

5 Biographical information was obtained from press coverage of Underwood's initial run for Congress in 1992. "Robert Underwood," 2 November 1992, *Pacific Daily News*: 3.

6 Underwood's campaign materials underscored his familiarity with important issues in Guam and his desire to bring change to the island. See "The Time Is Right for a Change," 4 November 1992, *Pacific Daily News*: 27.

7 Robert F. Rogers, *Destiny's Landfall: A History of Guam* (Honolulu: University of Hawai'i Press, 2011): 267.

8 Marshall Santos, "Democrats Win 2–1 Advantage," 9 November 1992, *Pacific Daily News*: 3.

9 Tambra A. Bryant, "Guam Dems: Clinton Win Would Help Underwood," 4 November 1992, *Pacific Daily News*: 3; Frale Oyen, "Election Postponed," 3 November 1992, *Pacific Daily News*: 1. According to the Constitution, only states can participate in the electoral process.

10 "Election Statistics, 1920 to Present," http://history.house.gov/institution/election-statistics/election-statistics.

11 Donovan Brooks, "Grassroots, Media Use Called Key to Success," 11 November 1992, *Pacific Daily News*: 7.

12 "Election Statistics, 1920 to Present," http://history.house.gov/institution/election-statistics/election-statistics; Jacob Leon Guerrero, "Underwood to House: Halt A–76," 12 April 2000, *Pacific Daily News*: 5A.

13 When the Republican Party took control of the House in 1995, many committee names were changed, including Armed Services, which was renamed National Security during the 104th and 105th Congresses, and Natural Resources, which was renamed Resources for the rest of Underwood's tenure. Before the 104th Congress, Natural Resources was known as the Interior and Insular Affairs Committee—a name dating back to 1951. For information on committee histories and name changes, see Garrison Nelson, *Committees in the U.S. Congress, 1947 to 1992*, vol. 2 (Washington, D.C.: CQ Press, 1994).

14 *Congressional Record*, House, 105th Cong., 1st sess. (10 February 1997): H401.

15 *Congressional Record*, House, 106th Cong., 1st sess. (29 June 1999): 4999.

16 *Congressional Record*, House, 103rd Cong., 1st sess. (18 May 1993): 2500.

17 During World War II, the U.S. military seized a large tract of land in northern Guam that made up nearly one-third of the island. In 1994 the military relinquished the land it no longer needed to the U.S. Fish and Wildlife Service, which added the area to an existing national wildlife refuge. Many Guamanians thought the land should have been returned to them. There was also concern that the new wildlife reserve would lead to more destruction by the brown tree snake, which was introduced to the island during World War II and which devastated many indigenous bird species. William Branigin, "Guam Sees Predator in Wildlife Effort: Expansion of Refuge Acreage Smacks of Colonialism," 15 April 1994, *Washington Post*: A21.

18 *Congressional Record*, House, 106th Cong., 2nd sess. (30 October 2000): 11574.

19 Yachnin, "Guam Delegate Hopes to Exchange Long Flights for Governorship"; *Congressional Record*, House, 106th Cong., 2nd sess. (30 October 2000): 11574.

20 Robert Underwood, "Recognize Chamorro Character," 13 July 2011, *Pacific Daily News*.

21 *Congressional Record*, House, 107th Cong., 1st sess. (30 January 2001): E49–E50; *Almanac of American Politics, 1998* (Washington, D.C.: National Journal Inc., 1997): 1565; Dionesis Tamondong, "Delegate Returns to Hall," 6 July 2000, *Pacific Daily News*: 2A.

22 Steve Limtiaco, "Delegate Urges Federal Action on Buried Weapons," 4 October 2000, *Pacific Daily News*: 5A; *Almanac of American Politics, 2002* (Washington, D.C.: National Journal Inc., 2001): 1698.

23 *Congressional Record*, House, 104th Cong., 2nd sess. (1 February 1996): 2237.

24 Tanya M. C. Mendiola, "Underwood Wants Guam Included in Education Plan," 2 February 2001, *Pacific Daily News*: 7A.

25 Scott Radway, "Delegate Wants Unity," 9 August 2001, *Pacific Daily News*: 1A; Mendiola, "Underwood Wants Guam Included in Education Plan."

26 Radway, "Delegate Wants Unity."

27 "Robert Underwood," http://guampedia.com/robert-underwood/ (accessed 7 January 2011).

28 Theresa Merto, "Delegate's Address Encourages Listeners," 9 August 2001, *Pacific Daily News*: 3A; *Congressional Record*, House, 106th Cong., 2nd sess. (30 October 2000): H11574.

29 Theresa Merto, "Chamorro Time Measure Awaits Clinton's OK," 17 December 2000, *Pacific Daily News*: 5A.

30 Emily Hancock, "Guam Delegate Pours It on English-Only Measure," 20 October 1995, *Houston Chronicle*: 14.

31 Steve Limtiaco and Dionesis Tamondong, "Underwood Steps Up," 19 August 2000, *Pacific Daily News*: 1A.

32 Limtiaco and Tamondung, "Underwood Steps Up."

33 Theresa Merto, "The Count Continues," 6 November 2002, *Pacific Daily News*: 1.

34 "Results," 6 November 2002, *Pacific Daily News*: 3.

35 Scott Radway, "Underwood Keeps Spirits High upon Defeat," 6 November 2002, *Pacific Daily News*: 2.

Ciro D. Rodriguez
1946–

UNITED STATES REPRESENTATIVE 1997–2005; 2007–2011
DEMOCRAT FROM TEXAS

Known for his resilience in the political arena, Ciro Rodriguez represented two Texas districts in the U.S. House. In the Texas legislature and in Congress, Rodriguez championed a variety of veterans' issues and advocated for increased federal funding for education. "The greatest equalizer is education," he observed. "We must ensure that our children have access to the best education."[1] Convinced of the importance of public service, Rodriguez continued to seek elective office even after redistricting transformed his constituency.

Ciro D. Rodriguez was born in Piedras Negras, Mexico, on December 9, 1946, to Luvin and Aurora (Davis) Rodriguez. Before settling in Texas, the Rodriguez family moved between Mexico and the United States, during which time Rodriguez's father worked on industrial refrigeration units. After living in Eagle Pass, Texas, the Rodriguezes settled in San Antonio in 1951. One of six children, Ciro Rodriguez held a series of jobs, including selling vegetables in his neighborhood, to help support his family. When his mother passed away, Rodriguez dropped out of high school at age 13 and worked at a gas station. He returned to Harlandale High School, where he graduated with his class in 1966. Rodriguez enrolled in San Antonio College before attending St. Mary's University in San Antonio, where he earned a B.A. in political science in 1973. Two years later he won a seat on the Harlandale Independent School District Board and served until 1987. In 1978 Rodriguez earned a master's degree in social work from Our Lady of the Lake University. He later worked as an educational consultant and a county caseworker. From 1987 to 1996, he returned to Our Lady of the Lake University, where he taught at the Worden School of Social Work. Rodriguez married Carolina Peña, an elementary school teacher and a librarian; the couple had one daughter, Xochil.[2]

In 1987 Rodriguez won election to the Texas house of representatives. During his decade in the state house, he sought to equalize funding between Texas school districts and to promote employment through the private redevelopment of San Antonio's Kelly Air Force Base, which was closed in 1995.[3] When Representative Frank Tejeda succumbed to brain cancer shortly after being sworn into the 105th Congress (1997–1999), Rodriguez entered the March 1997 special election to fill the vacant seat. "It's comforting to see such a groundswell of support and to know that our campaign will clearly be the most aggressive grass-roots effort out there," Rodriguez remarked.[4] Nine Democrats, five Republicans, and an Independent entered the contest to represent the predominantly Hispanic district, which stretched from the southern half of San Antonio to the Mexican border. Rodriguez and Democratic San Antonio councilman Juan Solis quickly distanced themselves from the rest of the pack.[5] Rodriguez earned the backing of many influential Democratic groups and politicians, but the heated campaign was overshadowed by Tejeda's untimely death.[6] Forced into a runoff election since he failed to garner a majority of the vote, Rodriguez easily defeated Solis, 67 to 33 percent.[7] "It was a humbling experience, in all honesty," Rodriguez admitted.[8]

Sworn into Congress on April 17, 1997, Rodriguez, like his predecessor, served on the Committee on National Security (later named Armed Services) and Veterans' Affairs. Both panels were a good fit for his district, which included several military bases and thousands of active and retired military personnel. During the 108th Congress (2003–2005), Rodriguez also was assigned to the Resources Committee and was elected chairman of the Congressional Hispanic Caucus (CHC), at which time he vowed to make education and health care his top priorities.[9]

Collection of the U.S. House of Representatives, Photography Collection

In Congress, Rodriguez focused on a range of issues that affected his constituents. A vocal supporter of veterans, the Texas Representative advocated increased educational opportunities and improved health care for current and retired military personnel. Rodriguez also fought to minimize job losses at Kelly Air Force Base by converting its operation to the private sector, an initiative he had backed as a state representative.[10] Concerned about the well-being of his constituents, he proposed tighter security along the U.S.-Mexico border, with expanded law enforcement authority. "Along the border we face a flood of drugs, weapons and human smuggling in addition to coping with illegal immigration," Rodriguez said.[11] The Texas Representative also advocated a series of education and health care initiatives for Hispanic Americans. In his maiden speech on the House Floor, he expressed his desire to improve the education system for all Americans. "What is going to be the strength of this country is going to be its people, and we need to invest in ourselves and in our people," Rodriguez observed.[12] Recognizing his commitment to education and his experience in the field, the Democratic leadership in the 106th Congress (1999–2001) appointed him to a task force charged with drafting Party strategy for education programs.[13]

After winning a seat in the 105th Congress, Rodriguez faced minimal opposition in his first three bids for re-election, earning more than 70 percent of the vote in each contest.[14] But redistricting in 2003 drastically changed Rodriguez's constituency; half the voters were new to the district. In the Democratic primary, Rodriguez squared off against a longtime ally, attorney and former Texas secretary of state Henry Cuellar. While the newly drawn district still encompassed southern San Antonio and snaked south to the Mexican border, the addition of several white suburbs east of San Antonio and the inclusion of a substantial portion of Laredo, Cuellar's hometown, altered the composition of the district, making for a competitive race.[15] On election night, Rodriguez emerged as the front-runner with a margin of 145 votes, but a recount determined that Cuellar had narrowly bested the incumbent.[16] After a four-month battle that included a lawsuit and a second recount, Rodriguez lost the nomination to Cuellar by 58 votes.[17] In 2006 Rodriguez tried to recapture his seat but lost to Cuellar, 40 to 53 percent.[18]

Rodriguez's political fortunes received an unexpected boost in the summer of 2006 after a Supreme Court decision invalidated the boundaries of a district in southwestern Texas on the grounds that the redistricting violated the Voting Rights Act by decreasing the number of Hispanic voters.[19] Federal judges subsequently redrew the district held by seven-term Republican incumbent Henry Bonilla. Running along the Mexican border by the Rio Grande River, the new district stretched from El Paso to San Antonio. With the addition of more voters who were Democratic and Hispanic, especially in his Bexar County power base, Rodriguez entered the November 2006 election. He placed a distant second, capturing only 20 percent of the vote in the field of eight contenders, but since Bonilla narrowly failed to secure a majority—with 49 percent of the vote—a runoff ensued. Rodriguez secured the backing of local and national Democrats and pulled off an upset, winning 54 percent of the vote.[20] "It's a totally different ball game," Rodriguez mused after his victory. "Although my basic values haven't changed, what changes is that I am responding to views of different constituents."[21]

In the 110th Congress (2007–2009), Rodriguez received a spot on the Veterans' Affairs Committee. He also secured a seat on the influential Appropriations Committee and served on both panels through the 111th Congress (2009–2011). Rodriguez won his re-election bid in 2008—by 56 to 42 percent—against Republican Lyle Larson, a San Antonio county commissioner.[22] Two years later, he lost—44 to 49 percent—to Republican lawyer and banker Francisco (Quico) Canseco in the general election for the 112th Congress (2011–2013).[23]

FOR FURTHER READING

Biographical Directory of the United States Congress, "Ciro D. Rodriguez," http://bioguide.congress.gov.

NOTES

1 Rebecca Rodriguez, "Rodriguez to Lead Caucus; Fellow Hispanics Elect Him to Post," 14 November 2002, *San Antonio Express-News*: 16A.

2 "About Ciro," http://www.cirodrodriguez.com/index.php/about (accessed 14 February 2012); Edmund S. Tijerina, "Rodriguez Proves There Is Hope; U.S. Representative Who Left School Works to Ensure That Others Don't," 29 May 2001, *San Antonio Express-News*: 7A; *Politics in America, 2004* (Washington, D.C.: Congressional Quarterly, Inc., 2003): 1005.

3 *Politics in America, 1998* (Washington, D.C.: Congressional Quarterly, Inc., 1997): 1440.

4 Bruce Davidson, "Wing Decides Not to Seek Tejeda's Seat–Rodriguez Formally Enters Race; Aide Says Morales Plans to Run," 11 February 1997, *San Antonio Express-News*: 1A.

5 Bruce Davidson, "15 Seeking Tejeda Slot," 13 February 1997, *San Antonio Express-News*: 1A.

6 Brenda Rodriguez, "Coalition of Democratic Politicians Backs Rodriguez," 15 February 1997, *San Antonio Express-News*: 12B; Thaddeus Herrick, "Even in Death, Tejeda's Influence Dominates; Top Two in Crowded Race Staking Claim to Late Congressman's Mantle," 9 March 1997, *Houston Chronicle*: 1.

7 Rodriguez won 46 percent of the vote in the initial special election. *Almanac of American Politics, 2000* (Washington, D.C.: National Journal Inc., 1999): 1589.

8 Bruce Davidson, "Rodriguez Captures Runoff to Claim Spot in U.S. House," 13 April 1997, *San Antonio Express-News*: 1A.

9 Rodriguez, "Rodriguez to Lead Caucus; Fellow Hispanics Elect Him to Post."

10 Scott Huddleston, "The Crisis at Kelly: Rep. Rodriguez Says Aid Falls Short of the Mark," 26 November 1997, *San Antonio Express-News*: 1A; *Politics in America, 2002* (Washington, D.C.: Congressional Quarterly, Inc., 2001): 1010.

11 Gary Martin, "Rep. Rodriguez Backs Border Bill," 7 November 2007, *San Antonio Express-News*: 7A.

12 *Congressional Record*, House, 105th Cong., 1st sess. (17 April 1997): H1627.

13 *Politics in America, 2002*: 1010.

14 "Election Statistics, 1920 to Present," http://history.house.gov/institution/election-statistics/election-statistics.

15 Gary Martin, "S.A., Laredo Dist. 28 Keys; Cuellar, Rodriguez Campaigns Banking on Local Support," 14 February 2004, *San Antonio Express-News*: 1A; *Almanac of American Politics, 2006* (Washington, D.C.: National Journal Inc., 2005): 1659–1660.

16 Rebecca Rodriguez, "District 28 Recount Will Get Under Way Today; New Tally Requested by Cuellar to Start in Atascosa and Wilson," 26 March 2004, *San Antonio Express-News*: 5B.

17 "Court Won't Decide Vote–Fraud Appeal," 4 August 2004, *Houston Chronicle*: B3; Rebecca Rodriguez, "Rep. Rodriguez Throws in the Towel; Cuellar to Be on Ballot; S.A. Lawmaker Looks to '06," 12 August 2004, *San Antonio Express-News*: 1A.

18 *Almanac of American Politics, 2008* (Washington, D.C.: National Journal Inc., 2007): 1611.

19 Greg Jefferson, "Rodriguez Back in the Running," 2 September 2006, *San Antonio Express-News*: 1B; Gary Martin, "Democrats Hail Old Pal's Return to Capitol Hill," 14 December 2006, *San Antonio Express-News*: 1A.

20 *Politics in America, 2008* (Washington, D.C.: Congressional Quarterly, Inc., 2007): 995–996; "Election Statistics, 1920 to Present," http://history.house.gov/institution/election-statistics/election-statistics; Greg Jefferson, "Democrats Unite behind Rodriguez," 10 November 2006, *San Antonio Express-News*: 1B; Greg Jefferson, "Clinton Duc in S.A. to Boost Rodriguez," 9 December 2006, *San Antonio Express-News*: 4A.

21 "People in the News: Ciro D. Rodriguez," *Washington Post*, http://www.washingtonpost.com/politics/ciro-d-rodriguez/gIQAMKoVBP_topic.html (accessed 14 February 2012).

22 Libertarian Lani Connolly captured the remaining 2 percent of the vote. "Election Statistics, 1920 to Present," http://history.house.gov/institution/election-statistics/election-statistics; Gary Martin and Guillermo X. Garcia, "Rodriguez Wins 2nd Term in High-Profile Campaign," 5 November 2008, *San Antonio Express-News*: 5AA.

23 Five candidates, three of whom represented third parties, ran in the general election. "Election Statistics, 1920 to Present," http://history.house.gov/institution/election-statistics/election-statistics; Gilbert Garcia, "A Tale of Two Democrats," 4 November 2010, *San Antonio Express-News*: 1B.

Aníbal Acevedo-Vilá
1962–

RESIDENT COMMISSIONER 2001–2005
POPULAR DEMOCRAT FROM PUERTO RICO

Aníbal Acevedo-Vilá served a single four-year term as Puerto Rico's Resident Commissioner, advocating for the island's commonwealth status and its cultural and political autonomy. "I'm going to Washington to reaffirm that we are Puerto Ricans first. I'm going to Washington to defend the sovereignty of the Puerto Rican people," Acevedo-Vilá declared shortly after his election to the U.S. House of Representatives in 2000.[1]

Aníbal Acevedo-Vilá was born on February 13, 1962, in Hato Rey, Puerto Rico, to state senator Salvador Acevedo and Elba Vilá. He earned a degree in political science from the Universidad de Puerto Rico in 1982 and graduated from its law school three years later. After clerking for the supreme court of Puerto Rico, he moved to the mainland United States, where he earned a masters degree from Harvard Law School in 1987. For the next two years, he clerked for the chief judge of the U.S. Court of Appeals for the First Circuit, returning to Puerto Rico in 1989. He married Luisa Gándara, and the couple had two children, Gabriela and Juan Carlos.

Acevedo-Vilá began his career as an aide for Puerto Rican Governor Hernández Colón of the Partido Popular Democrático (Popular Democratic Party, or PPD), which he called "the longstanding defender of the commonwealth of Puerto Rico."[2] In 1992 at the age of 30, he won election as a Popular Democrat to the Puerto Rican house of representatives, and after only five years in the insular legislature, he was elevated to minority leader and elected president of the PPD—a major vote of confidence.[3] As party head, Acevedo-Vilá became a leading critic of the island's 1998 status referendum—which had support in the U.S. House of Representatives—complaining that it gave those who favored statehood an unfair advantage. On multiple occasions, Acevedo-Vilá asked Congress to scrap referendum bills H.R. 856 and S. 472, and in 1997 he argued heatedly with Puerto Rican Resident Commissioner Carlos Romero-Barceló during a House subcommittee hearing on the island's political status.[4] Testifying before the U.S. Senate's Committee on Energy and Natural Resources roughly a year later, Acevedo-Vilá blamed mainland administrators for the island's nebulous federal relationship. "It is not our fault. It was the United States that invaded Puerto Rico. It was Congress that granted U.S. citizenship back in 1917. It was Congress that granted Commonwealth back in 1952," he said. "By harmonizing the fact that we are a people, a Nation, with our own identity, history, and culture, with the preservation of the permanent bond of the U.S. citizenship, Commonwealth represents an alternative to the extremes of complete integration and total separation."[5] In December 1998, much to Acevedo-Vilá's satisfaction, a majority on the island voted in favor of commonwealth status. "This vote," he declared, "means that we have here people who are proud of their history, proud of their relationship with the United States, proud of their American citizenship, but, above all, proud of their Puerto Ricanness."[6]

Not long after the contentious plebiscite debates, Acevedo-Vilá received some unexpected support in the PPD primaries and ran for Resident Commissioner against Romero-Barceló.[7] The earlier status vote had set the stage for the 2000 election, crystallizing the major differences between the island's two main parties. According to the San Juan press, the race was notably "confrontational," with attacks on character, accusations of dirty money, complaints filed with the Federal Election Commission (FEC), and threats of disbarment.[8] Acevedo-Vilá put everything he had and then some into the campaign; by late October, he was nearly half a million dollars in debt and struggling to match the fundraising pace set by Romero-Barceló.[9] In a televised debate days before

Image courtesy of the U.S. House of Representatives Photography Office

the election, Acevedo-Vilá chided the incumbent for his aggressive position on statehood, faulted him for the federal government's military training on the island of Vieques, and accused him of wasting time in Congress.[10] Acevedo-Vilá won the support of powerful labor unions and campaigned on promises to strengthen Puerto Rico's economy, revamp certain environmental regulations, open access to affordable housing, curtail crime, and improve the island's education system.[11] The PPD's frequent charges of corruption against the sitting Nuevo Progresista (New Progressive) administration weighed heavily on the race. Despite early polls that showed him trailing Romero-Barceló, Acevedo-Vilá eventually pulled ahead with a 49.3 percent plurality, besting the incumbent by about 4 percent.[12]

Acevedo-Vilá was sworn in as the 18th Resident Commissioner from Puerto Rico on January 3, 2001. He caucused with the Democrats and was selected by his first-term peers to serve as their vice president. Like those of his predecessors, Acevedo-Vilá's committee assignments gave him a voice in economic and territorial issues before Congress. He served on the Agriculture, Resources, and Small Business Committees and also joined the Congressional Hispanic Caucus, where he chaired the Livable Communities Task Force.[13]

Underlying Acevedo-Vilá's time in the House was an aggressive campaign to change how Congress understood its relationship with Puerto Rico. Romero-Barceló had cast the federal-insular connection as a struggle for equality, but Acevedo-Vilá sought "a fresh start" in which Puerto Rico would lobby for more control over its affairs, almost as if it were a separate nation. The island's press called Acevedo-Vilá's plan "a concept that could run into trouble with federal bureaucrats." "No longer will Puerto Rico be portrayed on Capitol Hill as a politically put-upon colony whose citizens are deprived of full civil rights within the American system," wrote the Washington correspondent of the *San Juan Star*.[14]

The first test was Acevedo-Vilá's attempt to convince the navy to cease bombing exercises on the nearby island of Vieques before May 2003, the deadline set by the previous Resident Commissioner and the outgoing William J. (Bill) Clinton administration.[15] Acevedo-Vilá had been working on the issue for the better part of two years as PPD president, and in 1999, a year before he ran for the U.S. House, Acevedo-Vilá called on the U.S. Senate to withdraw the navy for good. An accident in which a resident of Vieques was killed by a stray bomb sparked new calls for the Defense Department to cede its portion of the island to Puerto Rico. Moreover, the continual bombings were reportedly sickening Vieques' residents and destroying the environment.[16] "It's not a national security issue, it's a health and human-rights issue," Acevedo-Vilá said.[17] Despite the Resident Commissioner's efforts, the U.S. military upheld the original settlement, ceasing all operations on Vieques in spring 2003 before transferring much of the land to the National Wildlife Refuge System.[18]

The situation in Vieques cast a long shadow over Acevedo-Vilá's legislative agenda in the House, which included securing new tax-based incentives for industry seeking to establish roots in Puerto Rico. Many in Washington suspected that Congress would delay any new tax package as long as Puerto Rico pressured the navy to leave Vieques—especially a tax proposal that could easily be construed as "corporate welfare," according to the island's press.[19] But Acevedo-Vilá framed the incentives as a way to create jobs on an island suffering from high unemployment.[20] In a *Washington Times* editorial, he proposed new tax breaks with safeguards to prevent big companies from exploiting possible loopholes, "thereby maximizing the economic benefits of the legislation." Since Puerto Rico was a major consumer of U.S. goods, any policy that benefited the island would also benefit the mainland's economy, Acevedo-Vilá explained, calling his plan "a win-win proposition."[21]

Acevedo-Vilá often emphasized Puerto Rico's unique relationship with the federal government in the hopes of winning more autonomy while seeking equal treatment in relation to the national budget. As the *Washington Post* pointed out in September 2002, he sought leeway to enact independent trade pacts with nearby Caribbean countries, which the PPD hoped would raise much-needed revenue, even as the PPD "also [was] working to achieve parity with states in federally funded programs, such as nutritional assistance and health care."[22] In the 108th Congress (2003–2005), Acevedo-Vilá worked to improve the services available to veterans on the island, especially at the San Juan VA Medical Center, which had lost many of its resources. He supported amendments to H.R. 1261, the Workforce Reinvestment and Adult Education Act of 2003, and advocated bolstering Medicare on the island, declaring, "U.S. citizens in Puerto Rico pay the same Federal payroll taxes as any other jurisdiction. They deserve equity."[23]

Acevedo-Vilá also highlighted Puerto Rico's environment, introducing a bill in mid-March 2002 to protect a swath of land known as El Yunque, "the only tropical rain forest within the U.S. National Forest System." Known as the Caribbean National Forest Wild and Scenic Rivers Act of 2002 (H.R. 3954)—and based on the Wild and Scenic Rivers Act of 1968—the bill provided "maximum protection" for three river systems containing "critical habitat for endangered species and sensitive tropical plant species." As Acevedo-Vilá noted during its consideration that May, his measure insulated the designated rivers from future commercial development. The bill was reported favorably out of the Resources Committee and passed the House by voice vote on May 7th. The measure was approved by the Senate in the fall and was signed into law by President George W. Bush on December 19, 2002.[24]

Midway through his four-year term, Acevedo-Vilá announced he would not seek re-election to the House.[25] Opting instead to run for governor of Puerto Rico, he won the PPD's nomination and prevailed in the general election in fall 2004 by a razor-thin margin. After a lengthy legal battle, with multiple appeals and overturned rulings, the federal courts declared Acevedo-Vilá the victor by about 0.2 percent, or approximately 3,500 of the nearly two million votes cast.[26] As governor, he continued to oppose calls for statehood and supported efforts in the U.S. Congress proposing a new Puerto Rican constitutional convention. Facing mounting budget deficits, Acevedo-Vilá fought with the Nuevo Progresista-controlled house over a loan to keep the government operational, only to see part of the insular government shut down in May 2006.[27]

In 2008 Resident Commissioner Luis Fortuño of the Partido Nuevo Progresista challenged Acevedo-Vilá in the gubernatorial election. From the start, Acevedo-Vilá's re-election prospects were weakened by the controversial race four years earlier, the government shutdown, and the resulting financial difficulties. Worse, federal authorities indicted him on multiple counts of fraud, along with a handful of other charges, in what the *New York Times* described as "an elaborate scheme to pay off more than $500,000 in campaign debts" dating to his time as Resident Commissioner.[28] The prosecution denied any underlying motivation, but Acevedo-Vilá remained convinced that the case was politically motivated—a "spectacle designed to harm me." Acevedo-Vilá lost the gubernatorial election that fall. He was eventually acquitted of all the charges.[29]

FOR FURTHER READING

Biographical Directory of the United States Congress, "Aníbal Acevedo-Vilá," http://bioguide.congress.gov.

NOTES

1 Roberto Santiago, "Statehood's Out under P.R. Leader," 9 November 2000, *Daily News*: 29.

2 Hearing before the Senate Committee on Energy and Natural Resources, To Consider the Results of the December 1998 Plebiscite on Puerto Rico, 106th Cong., 1st sess. (6 May 1999): 22. For more on Acevedo-Vilá's political philosophy and his support for commonwealth status, see *Congressional Record*, Extension of Remarks, 107th Cong., 2nd sess. (24 July 2002): E1338–E1339.

3 Aníbal Acevedo Vilá, "Biography," http://webarchive.loc.gov/lcwa0005/20040125060636/http://www.house.gov/acevedo-vila/xp/eng/biography.htm (accessed 14 February 2011).

4 For Acevedo-Vilá's testimony, see Hearing before the House Committee on Natural Resources, H.R. 856: A Bill to Provide a Process Leading to Full Self-Government for Puerto Rico, 105th Cong., 1st sess. (19 March 1997); Workshop before the Senate Committee on Energy and Natural Resources, To Provide the Committee with an Overview of the Political Status Discussion in Puerto Rico, 105th Cong., 2nd sess. (2 April 1998); Hearing before the Senate Committee on Energy and Natural Resources, H.R. 856: A Bill to Provide a Process Leading to Full Self-Government for Puerto Rico, S. 472: To Provide for Referenda in Which the

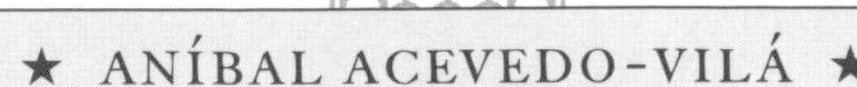

Residents of Puerto Rico May Express Democratically Their Preferences Regarding the Political Status of the Territory, and for Other Purposes, 105th Cong., 2nd sess. (14, 15 July 1998). For Acevedo-Vilá's testimony after the plebiscite, see Hearing before the Senate Committee on Energy and Natural Resources, To Consider the Results of the December 1998 Plebiscite on Puerto Rico, 106th Cong., 1st sess. (6 May 1999).

5 Workshop before the Senate Committee on Energy and Natural Resources, To Provide the Committee with an Overview of the Political Status Discussion in Puerto Rico, 105th Cong., 2nd sess. (2 April 1998): 20, 22.

6 Mireya Navarro, "Puerto Ricans Vote for the Status Quo," 14 December 1998, *New York Times*: A1.

7 Frank Ramos, "Election Campaign Is a Roller Coaster Ride," 29 October 2000, *San Juan Star*: 28.

8 Romero-Barceló even expressed doubts about the patriotism of Acevedo-Vilá and other PPD officials during hearings on H.R. 856 in 1997. Regarding the nature of the election, see Eva Llorens Velez, "Jabs on Vieques, Status Dominate Debate," 30 October 2000, *San Juan Star*: 8. For more on the election, see "Campaign Briefs: CRB Asked to Cut Personal Attacks," 2 October 2000, *San Juan Star*: 10; Marty Gerard Delfin, "Complaints on Morey, CRB Dismissed," 5 October 2000, *San Juan Star*: 8; Maria Soledad Calero, "Acevedo Vilá: I Preferred to Let Complaint Run Its Course," 6 October 2000, *San Juan Star*: 5; "Campaign Briefs: Rodríguez: CRB Aided by Proposed Disbarment," 9 October 2000, *San Juan Star*: 8; Marty Gerard Delfin, "CRB, Acevedo Vilá File Memorandums Defending Positions," 11 October 2000, *San Juan Star*: 12; Leslie Donaldson, "Attack Ads Flourish in Last Weeks of Campaigns," 15 October 2000, *San Juan Star*: 5.

9 Robert Friedman, "FEC: CRB Tops Acevedo in Stump Funds," 22 October 2000, *San Juan Star*: 5.

10 Eva Llorens Velez, "Jabs on Vieques, Status Dominate Debate," 30 October 2000, *San Juan Star*: 8.

11 "Campaign Briefs: Acevedo-Vilá Gets Union Backing," 25 October 2000, *San Juan Star*: 15; "Campaign Briefs: Acevedo-Vilá: Less U.S. Control," 3 October 2000, *San Juan Star*: 6; "Campaign Briefs: Acevedo Unveils Environment Plan," 16 October 2000, *San Juan Star*: 6; "Hopefuls for D.C. Post Debate Vieques, Status," 20 October 2000, *San Juan Star*: 12; "Campaign Briefs: Acevedo-Vilá Plan Is Also on Internet," 13 October 2000, *San Juan Star*: 6; "Campaign Briefs: Acevedo Unveils Environment Plan," 16 October 2000, *San Juan Star*: 6.

12 Eva Llorens Velez, "D.C. Post Hopefuls Prepare to Vote," 7 November 2000, *San Juan Star*: 6; Maria Soledad Calero and Carlos Antonio Otero, "Acevedo-Vilá Defeats Incumbent CRB for Resident Commissioner," 8 November 2000, *San Juan Star*: 7; Rachel Van Dongen, "Puerto Rico's Man on the Hill Ousted," 13 November 2000, *Roll Call*. "Election Statistics, 1920 to Present," http://history.house.gov/institution/election-statistics/election-statistics.

13 "Local Briefs: Acevedo Chosen for Dem Caucus," 17 November 2000, *San Juan Star*: 13; Aníbal Acevedo-Vilá, "Biography," http://webarchive.loc.gov/lcwa0005/20040125060636/http://www.house.gov/acevedo-vila/xp/eng/biography.htm (accessed 14 February 2011). For information on his larger agenda, see Jose A. Delgado, "Acevedo-Vilá Will Be Sworn In Today as Resident Commissioner," 3 January 2001, *San Juan Star*: 8; "Securing Section 30A Would Be True Test for PDP's Acevedo-Vilá," 29 November 2000, *San Juan Star*: 25.

14 Robert Friedman, "Acevedo's Portrayal of P.R. as a Nation May Confuse Many in D.C.," 8 January 2001, *San Juan Star*: 4. See also Robert Friedman, "Acevedo-Vilá Agrees to Cosponsor Medicaid Bill," 4 January 2001, *San Juan Star*: 8. For criticism of Acevedo-Vilá's decision, see Guillermo Moscoso, "Like It or Not, P.R. Not Free from U.S. Congress," 17 January 2001, *San Juan Star*: 22; Guillermo Moscoso, "The Time Is Now For P.R. to Make Decision," 7 February 2000, *San Juan Star*: 38.

15 Robert Friedman, "Acevedo: Vote Shows P.R. Status Stance," 13 November 2000, *San Juan Star*: 5; Robert Becker, "PDP Needs Friends in Washington, D.C.," 13 November 2000, *San Juan Star*: 25; Karen Carrillo, "Viequens Reach Milestone in Bombing Struggle, Still Remain Vigilant," 15 March 2001, *New York Amsterdam News*: 5; Ivan Roman, "Vieques Parties, Calls for Cleanup; On Thursday, the Navy Will Leave Its Bombing Range, But Remnants of Weapons Will Remain," 30 April 2003, *Orlando Sentinel*: A1; John McPhaul, "Acevedo-Vilá Blasts Navy," 16 January 2001, *San Juan Star*: 6.

16 Robert Friedman, "Bush: I 'Fully Support' Vieques Vote," 27 January 2001, *San Juan Star*: 5; "Editorial: President Starts on Good Terms With P.R.," 28 January 2001, *San Juan Star*: 21; Roman, "Vieques Parties, Calls for Cleanup."

17 Hearing before the Senate Committee on Energy and Natural Resources, To Consider the Results of the December 1998 Plebiscite on Puerto Rico, 106th Cong., 1st sess. (6 May 1999): 22; Larry Luxner, "Calderón Invites Fox to Island; Acevedo Hopes Ties Improve," 22 February 2001, *San Juan Star*: 10.

18 *Congressional Record,* House, 108th Cong., 1st sess. (1 May 2003): H3621; *Congressional Record*, House, Extension of Remarks, 108th Cong., 2nd sess. (24 April 2004): E709–E710; Roman, "Vieques Parties, Calls for Cleanup."

19 Robert Friedman, "Push for Tax Relief May Face Hurdles," 4 February 2001, *San Juan Star*: 5; Robert Friedman, "Bush Plan Unlikely to Include P.R. Tax Proposal," 7 February 2001, *San Juan Star*: 9.

20 Robert Friedman, "Acevedo-Vilá: 936 Phase Out Has Had Disastrous Effects," 8 February 2001, *San Juan Star*: 8; John McPhaul, "Acevedo-Vilá Will Prod Congress to Give P.R. a

Piece of the Tax-Cut Pie," 10 February 2001, *San Juan Star*: 4; *Congressional Record*, House, 107th Cong., 1st sess. (13 March 2001): H834–H835.

21 Aníbal Acevedo-Vilá, "Sunny Economic Returns; Tax Revision Would Revitalize Puerto Rico and America," 10 October 2002, *Washington Times*: A21.

22 John Marino, "Puerto Rico's New War on Poverty; Critics Fault $1 Billion Proposal as Paternalistic and No Substitute for Statehood," 4 September 2002, *Washington Post*: A3.

23 For veterans' benefits, see *Congressional Record*, House, 108th Cong., 1st sess. (21 November 2003): H12156. For the workforce bill, see *Congressional Record*, House, 108th Cong., 1st sess. (8 May 2003): H3787. For Medicare, see *Congressional Record*, House, 108th Cong., 1st sess. (5 June 2003): H5039.

24 Quotations from *Congressional Record*, House, 107th Cong., 2nd sess. (7 May 2002): H2125–2127. For the committee report, see House Committee on Resources, Caribbean National Forest Wild and Scenic Rivers Act of 2002, 107th Cong., 2nd sess. H. Rep. 107-441. For the final law, see Caribbean National Forest Wild and Scenic Rivers Act of 2002, P.L. 107-365, 116 Stat. 3027–3029.

25 Chris Wright, "Puerto Rico's Delegate Won't Run Again," 4 June 2003, *Roll Call*; "Puerto Rican Delegate in D.C. Will Run for Seat in Territory," 10 June 2003, *Orlando Sentinel*: A11; "Puerto Rico; Resident Commissioner Will Run for Governor," 21 July 2003, *Roll Call*.

26 On the gubernatorial election, see Abby Goodnough, "Puerto Rico's Election Has Extra Dose of Drama," 25 July 2004, *New York Times*: 12; Nancy San Martin, "Close Governor's Race Requires a Recount," 4 November 2004, *Miami Herald*: A9; Abby Goodnough, "Governor's Race Keeps Puerto Rico in Suspense," 17 November 2004, *New York Times*: 16; "Commonwealth Backer Wins in Puerto Rico," 24 December 2004, *Pittsburgh Post-Gazette*: A6; Abby Goodnough, "Officials Call Disputed Race for Governor of Puerto Rico," 29 December 2004, *New York Times*: A16; *Almanac of American Politics, 2008* (Washington, D.C.: National Journal Group Inc., 2007): 1806.

27 Matthew Hay Brown, "New Puerto Rico Governor Faces Challenges," 2 January 2005, *Orlando Sentinel*: A13; Ray Quintanilla, "Governor, Lawmakers Must End Stalemate," 17 April 2005, *Orlando Sentinel*: A11; Pablo Bachelet, "Party Sets in Motion a Push for Statehood," 7 February 2006, *Miami Herald*: A10; Anibal Acevedo-Vilá, "When Puerto Ricans Vote, They Choose Commonwealth," 19 March 2006, *Miami Herald*: L1; Frances Robles, "Lawyer Hopes to Beat Odds to Win Statehood," 3 April 2006, *Miami Herald*: A10; Frances Robles, "Lawmakers Try to Avert Government Shutdown," 28 April 2006, *Miami Herald*: A10; Frances Robles, "Thousands Are Idled; No Solution Seen," 2 May 2006, *Miami Herald*: A1; Rick Lyman, "Compromise Resolves the Fiscal Crisis in Puerto Rico," 9 May 2006, *New York Times*: A18.

28 As quoted in Damien Cave and Omaya Sosa-Pascual, "Puerto Rico Ex-Governor Acquitted of Graft," 21 March 2009, *New York Times*: A13. See also Kirk Semple, "Puerto Rico's Political Melodrama Plays On, with Its Governor in the Lead Role," 24 February 2008, *New York Times*: A24; Carrie Johnson and Matthew Mosk, "Puerto Rico's Governor Is Charged with Corruption," 28 March 2008, *Washington Post*: A1; Frances Robles, "Puerto Rico's Governor Is Indicted on New Charges," 20 August 2008, *Miami Herald*: A13; Jeannette Rivera-Lyles, "Puerto Rico's Governor: Latest Charges Are Bogus, Too," 21 August 2008, *Orlando Sentinel*: D3; Susan Anasagasti Akus and Frances Robles, "Indicted Governor Faces Tough Challenge," 3 November 2008, *Miami Herald*: A16.

29 As quoted in William Bender, "Gladwyne Fundraiser Charged in Campaign-Contribution Scam," 28 March 2008, *Philadelphia Daily News*: 13. See also Jeannette Rivera-Lyles, "Puerto Rican Governor Vows He'll Stay Despite 19 Fundraising Charges," 28 March 2008, *Orlando Sentinel*: A2; Devlin Barrett, "Justice Dept. under Scrutiny after Stevens' Trial," 5 April 2009, *Virginian-Pilot* (Norfolk): A4; Cave and Sosa-Pascual, "Puerto Rico Ex-Governor Is Acquitted of Graft."

Hilda L. Solis

1957–

UNITED STATES REPRESENTATIVE 2001–2009
DEMOCRAT FROM CALIFORNIA

An accomplished legislator in the California assembly, Hilda Solis was elected to the U.S. House from a district in Southern California after she defeated an 18-year incumbent in the primary. In Congress, Representative Solis championed the interests of working families and women and focused on legislation about health care and environmental protection. "People need to better understand that environmental justice issues are issues of better health care, better education, and an opportunity to begin to clean up their communities and enhance economic development in a positive way so that everybody can grow and prosper, and children, whether they are rich or poor, can live in a clean environment," Solis once remarked.[1]

The third of seven children, Hilda Lucia Solis was born to Raul and Juana Sequiera Solis in Los Angeles, California, on October 20, 1957. Solis's father and mother were immigrants from Mexico and Nicaragua, respectively, who met in a class on U.S. citizenship. Her parents worked blue-collar jobs—her father at a battery plant and mother on a toy assembly line—and Solis assumed many domestic duties early in life. "It wasn't what you would call the all-American life for a young girl growing up," she said. "We had to mature very quickly."[2] She later remarked, "They came here with that hope—esperanza—of coming to a country that would allow their children to prosper. I was born here. But I still have the notion that my parents have instilled in me, that they want a better life and they know that there's opportunities for us here."[3] After earning a B.A. in political science in 1979 from California State Polytechnic University, Pomona, Solis worked in the White House Office of Hispanic Affairs during the James Earl (Jimmy) Carter administration. In 1981 she earned an M.A. in public administration from the University of Southern California. Later that year, she worked as a management analyst in the civil rights division of the Equal Opportunity Program at the Office of Management and Budget. In June 1982, Solis married Sam Sayyad, a small business owner, and returned to Southern California, where she became a field representative in the office of Assemblyman Art Torres. She also worked as the director of the California Student Opportunity and Access Program in Whittier from 1982 until 1992.

Solis's first venture into politics was at the local level. In 1985 she ran an intensive grass-roots campaign against better-known candidates for a position as a trustee of Rio Hondo Community College. She walked the local precincts tirelessly and gained an upset victory as the top vote-getter.[4] Solis served as a trustee for seven years, winning re-election in 1989. In 1992 she won election to the California assembly, serving there until 1994, when she was elected to the state senate. She was the youngest member in that body at the time of her election and its first-ever Latina. Solis chaired the industrial relations committee, where in 1996 she led the fight to raise California's minimum wage standards. As a state senator, Solis also authored environmental protection legislation, including a bill that created the San Gabriel and Los Angeles Rivers and Mountains Conservancy to preserve open spaces and habitat, restore the watershed, and promote recreational activities that did not harm the environment.[5] Her environmental justice legislation earned her a John F. Kennedy Profile in Courage Award in 2000. She was the first woman to receive this award.[6]

Facing term limits in the California senate, Solis decided in 2000 to challenge Matthew Martínez, a nine-term Democratic incumbent whose U.S. congressional district encompassed much of her state senate district in the San Gabriel Valley. Just east of Los Angeles, the district swept across the lower two-thirds of the valley, taking in El

Collection of the U.S. House of Representatives, Photography Collection

Monte and West Covina and part of Monterey Park. Labor unions, with which Solis had closely allied herself, and the state party switched their support to the challenger. The campaign split local Latino leaders as well as members of the California congressional delegation.[7] Portraying herself as an active progressive, in contrast to Martínez, with his low-key style, Solis prevailed in the March 7 primary, 62 to 29 percent.[8] She had no Republican challenger in the general election and captured 80 percent of the vote while three third-party candidates split the remainder. She easily won re-election four times, earning a fourth term in the House with 83 percent of the vote in 2006 and running unopposed for a fifth term in 2008.[9]

When Solis took her seat in the House in January 2001, she won assignments on the Education and Workforce Committee and the Resources Committee. Solis also was tapped as the Democratic freshman class whip in the 107th Congress (2001–2003). In the 108th Congress (2003–2005), she left those committees to become the first Latina member of the powerful Energy and Commerce Committee and the Ranking Member on the Environment and Hazardous Materials Subcommittee.[10] She also was elected chairwoman of the Congressional Hispanic Caucus Task Force on Health, and Democratic vice chair of the Congressional Caucus on Women's Issues. In the 109th Congress (2005–2007), she was elected Democratic chair of the Congressional Caucus on Women's Issues and chair of the Democratic Women's Working Group. She was the first Latina to hold these positions.

When the Democrats gained control of the House in the 110th Congress (2007–2009), Solis was assigned to the Natural Resources Committee and the Select Committee on Energy Independence and Global Warming. Solis retained her assignment on Energy and Commerce, serving as vice chair of the Environment and Hazardous Materials Subcommittee. She was also appointed vice chairman of the Democratic Steering and Policy Committee, which made committee assignments.[11]

In the U.S. House, Solis advanced the environmental justice agenda she had championed at the state level. In 2003 her San Gabriel River Watershed Study Act was signed into law with bipartisan support. The bill authorized the Secretary of the Interior to study the San Gabriel River to find out how the federal government could improve the area's recreational and environmental opportunities. Solis believed this was particularly important in an area that had been overbuilt, in which 25 percent of the water was contaminated and a disproportionately high number of children suffered from asthma.[12] "This will hopefully provide some type of relief for over 2 million people that reside along the San Gabriel River," Solis noted on the House Floor. "I grew up there as a child and spent many Saturday afternoons and vacations in this area. Something we like to talk about is the fact that so many people in that area come from largely low-income, underrepresented areas, and do not have the ability or the economic means to go to Sequoia, to go to Yosemite, to even go to the beach.... Their recreation occurs in this particular geographic area."[13] In 2005 Solis authored an amendment to prevent the testing of pesticides on humans; the amendment was later enacted into law. She carefully monitored Environmental Protection Agency policies that affected her district, where several Superfund sites (areas deemed by the federal government to be especially polluted) were located and where numerous water wells had been shut down because rocket fuel had seeped into the water table.[14]

Solis was also a longtime advocate for women's rights, particularly for victims of violence and domestic abuse. During her tenure in the House, she raised awareness about the murders, dating to 1993, of nearly 400 girls and women in Ciudad Juárez, Mexico. She led a congressional delegation to the city, located just five minutes from the U.S. border, to help publicize the brutality and the families' heart-wrenching losses. In 2006 Solis, with support from House colleagues Ileana Ros-Lehtinen of Florida and Tom Lantos of California, authored a resolution to condemn the murders, to express sympathy for the families of the victims, and to urge the United States to increase its efforts to end such human rights violations. "I have always believed that attacks on women are attacks on women everywhere," Solis told colleagues on the House Floor. "I felt compelled as a woman, as a Latina, as someone who felt very strongly that, if we are going to stand up for women's rights in other continents of the world and the Middle East and to defend Afghani women who are being tortured by the Taliban, why not then also come forward and support the women of Ciudad Juárez?"[15] The House passed the measure. In the 110th Congress, Solis sponsored a similar measure expressing sympathy and concern about the violence that had claimed the lives of more than 2,000 women and girls in Guatemala since 2001.[16] This measure also passed the House.

As chair of the Congressional Hispanic Caucus Task Force on Health, Solis traveled across the country to educate policymakers, advocates, and community leaders about health needs in the Latino community. In the 109th Congress, Solis was a lead coauthor of a bicameral bill addressing minority health, The Healthcare Equality and Accountability Act.[17] During her eight years in the House, she introduced more than 75 measures, many of which pertained not only to environmental and women's issues but also to the concerns of recent immigrants, labor, and access to health care. "I've always been a big believer that government, if done right, can do a lot to improve the quality of people's lives," Solis observed.[18]

In December 2008, President-elect Barack Obama chose Representative Solis to serve as Secretary of Labor.[19] Solis resigned her seat in the House on February 24, 2009, shortly after the U.S. Senate confirmed her appointment.

FOR FURTHER READING

Biographical Directory of the United States Congress, "Hilda L. Solis," http://bioguide.congress.gov.

NOTES

1 *Congressional Record*, House, 108th Cong., 1st sess. (8 April 2003): H2924.

2 *Politics in America, 2008* (Washington, D.C.: Congressional Quarterly, Inc., 2007): 134.

3 Dan Morian and Evelyn Larrubia, "Roots of Solis' Belief in Unions Run Deep," 9 January 2009, *Los Angeles Times*: A1. See also *Congressional Record*, Extensions of Remarks, House, 111th Cong., 1st sess. (24 February 2009): E337.

4 Jean Merl, "Solis Prepares to Take Another Step Up," 28 December 2000, *Los Angeles Times*: B1.

5 *Congressional Record*, Extensions of Remarks, House, 109th Cong., 1st sess. (4 January 2005): E16.

6 *Almanac of American Politics, 2002* (Washington, D.C.: National Journal Inc., 2001): 241–242; "Official Biography of Hilda Solis," http://www.house.gov/solis/bio.htm (accessed 21 November 2001).

7 John Mercurio, "Martinez Fights for Survival; Calif. Member Battles Solis, Former Allies," 2 March 2000, *Roll Call*; Mary Lynn Jones, "Rep. Martinez Facing Tough Primary in Los Angeles CD," 1 March 2000, *The Hill*: 13.

8 Jean Merl and Antonio Olivo, "Solis Trounces Martinez in Bitter Race; Challenger Ousts 18-Year Veteran in a Fight That Split the Latino Leadership," 8 March 2000, *Los Angeles Times*: A3; Richard Simon and Antonio Olivo, "Two Incumbent Congressmen Facing Tough Challenges; 31st District: For Martinez, the Fight Is in the Primary—and in the Family," 23 February 2000, *Los Angeles Times*: B1.

9 See "Election Statistics, 1920 to Present," http://history.house.gov/institution/election-statistics/election-statistics.

10 For all Solis's committee assignments, see Garrison Nelson and Charles Stewart III, *Committees in the U.S. Congress, 1993–2010* (Washington, D.C.: CQ Press, 2011): 958.

11 *Politics in America, 2008*: 133.

12 *Congressional Record*, Extensions of Remarks, House, 108th Cong., 1st sess. (31 January 2003): E117.

13 *Congressional Record*, House, 108th Cong., 1st sess. (19 March 2003): H1964. Solis first introduced the measure during her freshman term; see *Congressional Record*, House, 107th Cong., 1st sess. (17 July 2001): H4022–H4023.

14 *Politics in America, 2008*: 133.

15 *Congressional Record*, House, 109th Cong., 2nd sess. (2 May 2006): H1945–H1946.

16 H. Res. 100, 110th Cong., 1st sess.: "Expressing the Sympathy of the House of Representatives to the Families of Women and Girls Murdered in Guatemala and Encouraging the Government of Guatemala to Bring an End to These Crimes."

17 *Congressional Record*, House, 109th Cong., 1st sess. (21 July 2005): H6208–H6209.

18 Merl, "Solis Prepares to Take Another Step Up."

19 Anne E. Kornblut, "Obama to Announce Final Cabinet Picks," 19 December 2008, *Washington Post*: A2.

Dennis A. Cardoza

1959–

UNITED STATES REPRESENTATIVE 2003–2012
DEMOCRAT FROM CALIFORNIA

Dennis Cardoza was elected as a Democrat to the U.S. House of Representatives in 2002 after defeating his former boss in the Democratic primary, and became a staple on the powerful Agriculture Committee. A self-styled "raging moderate," Cardoza often enlisted bipartisan support for his projects while pursuing the interests of his largely agricultural-based constituency in central California. "You're paid to make the tough choices," he commented shortly after his election, "and you're paid to do the right thing."[1]

The son of dairy farmers turned business owners, Cardoza was born in Merced, California, on March 31, 1959. Like many in California's Central Valley, Cardoza was of Portuguese descent; his grandparents emigrated from the Azores during the 1920s.[2] After interning on Capitol Hill and graduating from the University of Maryland, College Park, with a bachelor's degree in government and politics, Cardoza returned to California, where he won a spot on the Atwater city council in 1984. He worked for then-state assemblyman Gary Condit, transferring to Washington when Condit won election to the U.S. House of Representatives. After his stint as an aide, Cardoza returned to California, where he took over his family's bowling alley company. He moved back to Merced and served on its city council from 1994 to 1996, when he was elected to California's general assembly. Cardoza served in the state assembly for six years, eventually chairing its rules committee.[3] But when Condit's congressional career unraveled amid a highly publicized scandal, Cardoza, who was facing a term limit in the state assembly, challenged the incumbent in the district's Democratic primary in 2002.[4] One of the year's few competitive races, the election for California's recently redrawn 18th District attracted widespread attention.[5] Cardoza won the primary election handily and then defeated his Republican challenger in the general election, taking 51 percent of the vote. After that, he faced virtually no opposition in the party primary and dominated each of his subsequent general elections.[6] Cardoza married Dr. Kathleen McLoughlin, and they have three children: Joey, Brittany Mari, and Elaina.

Known as an energetic lawmaker willing to pursue bipartisan compromise, Cardoza initially used appointments to the Agriculture, Resources, and Science Committees in the 108th Congress (2003–2005) to legislate on pollution and water-access issues that were of great importance to his agricultural district. During the 109th Congress (2005–2007), Cardoza continued his tenure on the Agriculture Committee and the Resources Committee (later renamed Natural Resources) but left the Committee on Science for a seat on International Relations (later renamed Foreign Affairs). He worked to improve the conditions for the nation's farmers, introducing efforts to facilitate communication between local, state, and federal authorities during environmental disasters and crop failures. Early on, Cardoza championed renewable sources of energy such as solar power. He also took a notable interest in reforming the country's foster care system after he and his wife repeatedly experienced frustrations as adoptive parents.[7] Cardoza also was committed to helping homeowners and mortgage holders and successfully spearheaded efforts to erect a University of California campus in Merced, which opened in 2005.[8] His skill as a legislator earned him a coveted spot on the Rules Committee for the 110th Congress (2007–2009). Although he gave up seats on Foreign Affairs and Natural Resources, he kept his spot on the Committee on Agriculture, having become chairman of its Subcommittee on Horticulture and Organic Agriculture in time to help draft the 2008 Farm Bill. In the 112th Congress (2011–2013), Cardoza sat on the Foreign Affairs and Agriculture Committees.

Collection of the U.S. House of Representatives, Photography Collection

In addition to his committee work, Cardoza took an active role in caucus and party leadership. A member of the Blue Dog Coalition, which he co-chaired during the 109th Congress, Cardoza opposed continued federal borrowing and advocated offsetting costs in real time, writing "quite simply it's high time our country starts paying for what it buys."[9] A member of the Congressional Hispanic Caucus (CHC) for his entire congressional career, Cardoza also was elected to the powerful Democratic Steering and Policy Committee, a leadership group responsible for Members for committee assignments. In 2008 Cardoza co-chaired a program initiated by the Democratic Congressional Campaign Committee, which helps fund and support Democratic campaigns in the House.[10]

In October 2011, Representative Cardoza announced that he would retire from the House at the conclusion of the 112th Congress in January 2013. He resigned his seat on August 15, 2012.[11]

FOR FURTHER READING

Biographical Directory of the United States Congress, "Dennis A. Cardoza," http://bioguide.congress.gov.

NOTES

1 *Politics in America, 2002* (Washington, D.C.: Congressional Quarterly, Inc., 2001): 102; as quoted in Jim Miller, "Cardoza Ready to Tackle New Job in Congress," 9 November 2002, *Fresno Bee*: B2.

2 *Politics in America, 2008* (Washington, D.C.: Congressional Quarterly, Inc., 2007): 106–107.

3 "Official Biography of Dennis Cardoza," http://cardoza.house.gov/biography/ (accessed 29 May 2012); *Almanac of American Politics, 2006* (Washington, D.C.: National Journal, 2005): 214–215; *Politics in America, 2012* (Washington, D.C.: CQ-Roll Call, Inc., 2011): 99–100.

4 Jim Miller, "Cardoza to Reveal Bid for Condit Seat," 23 October 2001, *Fresno Bee*: B4.

5 B. Drummond Ayres, Jr., "Political Briefing," 27 January 2002, *New York Times*: A24; Evelyn Nieves, "Condit Loses House Race to Former Aide," 6 March 2002, *New York Times*: A15; Michael Doyle, "Cardoza Enjoying Political Capital: Condit's Challenger Gets Endorsements Usually Reserved for Incumbents," 5 February 2002, *Fresno Bee*: A1.

6 *Politics in America, 2002*: 102; "Election Statistics, 1920 to Present," http://history.house.gov/institution/election-statistics/election-statistics; Mark Grossi, Matt Leedy and Marc Benjamin, "Condit Loses House Re-Election Run: Dennis Cardoza to Face Republican Dick Monteith in November," 6 March 2002, *Fresno Bee*: A1.

7 Michael Doyle, "Close to His Heart: Adoptive Parent Rep. Cardoza Writes Bill Targeting Foster Care," 16 May 2003, *Fresno Bee*: B1; Nicole Gaouette and Jerry Hirsch, "Proposed Farm Bill May Benefit California," 1 February 2007, *Los Angeles Times*: C1; "A Warming World," 17 September 2007, *Los Angeles Times*: A14; *Politics in America, 2006* (Washington, D.C.: Congressional Quarterly, Inc., 2005): 106–107.

8 "Official Biography of Dennis A. Cardoza," http://cardoza.house.gov/biography/ (accessed 29 May 2012).

9 As quoted in "Official Biography of Dennis A. Cardoza," http://cardoza.house.gov/biography/ (accessed 29 May 2012); *Politics in America, 2008*: 106.

10 *Politics in America, 2010* (Washington, D.C.: Congressional Quarterly, Inc., 2009): 190.

11 *Biographical Directory of the United States Congress, 1774 to Present*, http://bioguide.congress.gov; Kyle Trygstad, "Dennis Cardoza Makes Retirement Official," 20 October 2011, *Roll Call*: n.p.; Seung Min Kim, "Dennis Cardoza's Surprise Resignation," 14 August 2012, *Politico*: n.p.

"You're paid to make the tough choices ... and you're paid to do the right thing."

Dennis A. Cardoza,
on being a Member of Congress
Fresno Bee, November 9, 2002

Luis G. Fortuño
1960–

RESIDENT COMMISSIONER 2005–2009
NEW PROGRESSIVE FROM PUERTO RICO

The first Resident Commissioner to caucus with the Republican Party since the 92nd Congress (1971–1973), Luis G. Fortuño served one term in the U.S. House of Representatives before becoming governor of Puerto Rico in 2009. As a principal figure in Puerto Rico's Partido Nuevo Progresista (New Progressive Party, or PNP), he was the primary advocate for Puerto Rican statehood during his tenure in Washington and an outspoken critic of the island's limited influence in Congress. "After 106 years of territorial status, and 88 years of being U.S. citizens, we are tired of waiting," Fortuño said in March 2005. "The people of Puerto Rico deserve better. We have earned the right to be heard."[1]

Luis G. Fortuño was born October 31, 1960, in San Juan, Puerto Rico. The son of a dentist, Fortuño was educated at a private high school and graduated from Georgetown University with a bachelor's of science in foreign service in 1982.[2] He attended law school at the University of Virginia in Charlottesville, earning a J.D. in 1985, after which he returned to Puerto Rico and began practicing at one of the island's premier law firms.[3] He made a name for himself in the legal world of corporate finance, and in 1993 he was appointed executive director of the Puerto Rico Tourism Company, where he worked to attract new business to the island.[4] In 1994 PNP governor Pedro Rosselló selected Fortuño to lead Puerto Rico's Department of Economic Development and Commerce, an umbrella agency that was responsible for the oversight of several government bureaus.[5] Fortuño and his wife, Lucé, have triplets (two sons and a daughter).[6]

Fortuño left the Rosselló administration a short while later and "became something of a white knight for his party, symbolizing youth and fresh ideas," according to the *Miami Herald*.[7] In what appeared to be a changing of the guard, Rosselló declined to run for re-election, and Fortuño joined a crowded field seeking the PNP nomination. He withdrew in June 1999, however, and resumed practicing law for clients as far away as Florida.[8] A member of the Republican National Committee from Puerto Rico, Fortuño kept a low profile until 2003, when he entered the race for Resident Commissioner.[9]

The island's incumbent Resident Commissioner, Aníbal Acevedo-Vilá of the Partido Popular Democrático (Popular Democratic Party, or PPD), opted to run for governor in 2004, clearing the way for the PNP's bold campaign to re-take the seat. Roughly a year before the general election, Fortuño beat out three other candidates for the PNP nomination, including former Resident Commissioner Carlos Romero-Barceló. His opponent in the general election was Roberto Prats of the PPD.[10]

As in every election on the island since the 1950s, the future of Puerto Rico's relationship with the federal government emerged as a dominant issue early on.[11] In the early 2000s, the George W. Bush administration began laying out options for Puerto Rico's future status; commonwealth status, the island's longstanding arrangement with the federal government, was not initially included. An advocate for Puerto Rican statehood, Fortuño supported the Bush administration's proposal. "The federal government can have a relationship with a state, or with a sovereign nation," the PNP candidate said that December. "At the end of the day, you really have two options, I believe: either statehood or independence."[12]

Unlike most Puerto Rican elections, the 2004 race attracted national attention. For the first time in more than 30 years, there was a chance that Puerto Rico's next Resident Commissioner would caucus with the GOP.[13] Although Fortuño had identified with the Republican Party since college, his House campaign signaled a larger political trend. "It's been a priority of the Republican Party

Collection of the U.S. House of Representatives, Photography Collection

and the House leadership to recruit more Hispanics into the party and Luis Fortuño was pretty much a dream candidate for this Resident Commissioner spot in Puerto Rico," said a national GOP official.[14] Fortuño campaigned from San Juan to Madison Square Garden and spoke at the Republican National Convention three months before the election.[15]

At home, Fortuño campaigned on his belief that Puerto Rico was more conservative than most people realized. He focused his platform on lowering taxes, limiting government influence, and achieving statehood.[16] The race was extremely close, and early results put Fortuño ahead with a slight lead. His margin shrank throughout the evening, but by the end of the week he had squeaked by Prats with 48.8 percent of the vote—a victory of one-half of 1 percent.[17]

At the start of the 109th Congress (2005–2007), the Republicans appointed Fortuño to the Committees on Education and the Workforce, Resources, and Transportation and Infrastructure, all of which had jurisdiction over issues that were important to Puerto Rico. Early in the first session, he supported the Job Training Improvement Act of 2005 as well as the Transportation Equity Act.[18] The first bill Fortuño introduced—the Caribbean National Forest Act of 2005 (H.R. 539), placing Puerto Rico's El Toro Wilderness under the National Wilderness Preservation System—became law in December 2005, capping an ambitious first session in which Fortuño also worked to reform the island's tax code and its Medicare system. "There are 100 different issues people have been trying to get on the table since the 1980s," he told the *Miami Herald* in 2006. "The big difference is that as a member of the Republican conference, I sit at the table."[19]

With a four-year term as Resident Commissioner, Fortuño did not have to think about re-election right away, and in summer 2005 he created a political action committee called L.U.I.S.— "Leading Us in Success"—to defray his travel costs while he campaigned for other members of the GOP. "Being a Hispanic, a Puerto Rican and a Republican, certainly I believe I can be helpful in a number of places," he told a Capitol Hill newspaper that July.[20]

In the second session Fortuño offered his defining piece of legislation: the Puerto Rico Democracy Act of 2006 (H.R. 4867). Together with 110 co-sponsors, Fortuño introduced the bill on the 89th anniversary of Puerto Ricans' American citizenship in hopes of renegotiating the island's relationship with the federal government. The measure recommended two plebiscites and "[guaranteed] that the terms and conditions of Puerto Rico's future be developed jointly and democratically by the people of Puerto Rico and the Congress and not by the whims of an elite few," Fortuño said. The first plebiscite would determine whether Puerto Rican voters wanted "to remain a U.S. territory." If voters chose what Fortuño called a "constitutionally viable permanent non-territorial status," the second plebiscite would be held to determine whether they favored independence or statehood.[21] Fortuño believed that statehood would galvanize the people of Puerto Rico, and he pointed to Hawaii as a model for what could happen in the Caribbean.[22] The House referred his bill to the Resources Committee, but it was not acted on.

In the 110th Congress (2007–2009), Fortuño lost his spot in the majority after the Democrats regained control of the House for the first time since 1995. He kept his seats on the Education and Resources Committees but moved from Transportation to the Committee on Foreign Affairs.[23] GOP House leaders also named Fortuño Ranking Member of Natural Resources' Subcommittee on Insular Affairs, which oversaw the federal government's relationship with its territories. This assignment carried additional weight after Fortuño was named chairman of the Congressional Hispanic Conference in 2007.[24]

The 110th Congress opened with a debate after Democrats proposed allowing statutory representatives to vote on amendments in the Committee of the Whole.[25] Fortuño was the only Republican who would be affected by the bill, and he supported it alongside the Delegates from the District of Columbia, American Samoa, Guam, and the U.S. Virgin Islands. The measure passed and was celebrated for its "symbolic importance," but its limited scope meant the measure had little influence on the legislative process. Nevertheless, Fortuño hoped the vote would be the first step toward resolving America's often-nebulous insular-federal relationship. "What the House really needs to do for the almost 4 million U.S. citizens that I represent before the Senate, the executive branch, as well as this House is to authorize a self-determination process for Puerto Rico.... What my constituents really deserve is the opportunity to seek equal representation and equal responsibilities in the Federal system or, alternatively, the freedom of a sovereign nation," he said.[26]

Fortuño spent much of the rest of the 110th Congress pushing to reform Puerto Rico's status, along with its tax code and its Medicare and Medicaid systems.[27] With legislation like the Puerto Rico Economic Stimulus Act of 2007 (H.R. 1339), Fortuño fought to improve health care and general services for the island's military personnel and veterans.[28]

In 2008, Fortuño ran for governor of Puerto Rico against incumbent Aníbal Acevedo-Vilá. Federal prosecutors had indicted Acevedo-Vilá earlier in the year on multiple counts of violating campaign finance law, and though he was cleared of all wrongdoing a few months later, the incident cast a long shadow over the campaign. The island needed new leadership in order to "re-establish the people's confidence in their government," Fortuño said.[29] That November Fortuño won the governor's mansion by a wide margin.[30]

FOR FURTHER READING

Biographical Directory of the United States Congress, "Luis G. Fortuño," http://bioguide.congress.gov.

NOTES

1 *Congressional Record*, House, 109th Cong., 1st sess. (2 March 2005): H918.

2 Damien Cave, "Puerto Rico Governor Promises Change," 28 November 2008, *New York Times*: A28.

3 "Puerto Rico's Governor Appoints Secretary for New Umbrella Department," 11 July 1994, Business Wire.

4 "Puerto Rico's Governor Appoints Secretary for New Umbrella Department"; "Puerto Rico Hotel Plans Announced," 17 February 1994, *Miami Herald*: A24; "Tourism," 11 October 1994, *Orlando Sentinel*: B1; Don Long, "Travel Notes," 4 June 1995, *Denver Post*: T2.

5 "Puerto Rico's Governor Appoints Secretary for New Umbrella Department."

6 Alicia Colon, "Untapped Conservatives," 9 August 2004, *New York Sun*: 10.

7 Susan Anasagasti and Frances Robles, "Indicted Governor Faces Tough Challenge; Puerto Rico Gov. Aníbal Acevedo Vilá Is in a Tight Race to Keep His Job," 3 November 2008, *Miami Herald*: A16. For more on the Rosselló administration, see César J. Ayala and Rafael Bernabe, *Puerto Rico in the American Century: A History since 1898* (Chapel Hill: University of North Carolina Press, 2007): 291–315, especially 302–303.

8 Ivan Roman, "Party Pushes Pesquera for Governor's Job," 14 June 1999, *Orlando Sentinel*: A10; quotation from Kathy Bushouse and Doreen Hemlock, "Puerto Ricans Expand Donations to GOP, Bush; Some Islanders See Governor as Friendly to Their Issues," 14 October 2002, *Sun-Sentinel* (Ft. Lauderdale, FL): A1.

9 Ed Silverman, "Despite Troubling Questions, the Drug Industry Is Booming in Puerto Rico," 21 July 2002, *The Star-Ledger* (Newark, NJ): Business, 1.

10 "Puerto Rico Hopefuls Start Bids for Office," 2 August 2003, *Orlando Sentinel*: A14.

11 Matthew Hay Brown, "Puerto Rico's Commonwealth Could Slip Away; Some See Signs That Washington Will Seek a Vote on Statehood or Independence," 25 July 2004, *Orlando Sentinel*: A22.

12 Matthew Hay Brown, "Puerto Ricans May Have to Choose; President Bush Named a Panel to Look into Settling the Political Status of the Island," 12 December 2003, *Orlando Sentinel*: A17.

13 The last Resident Commissioner to sit with Republicans was New Progressive Jorge Luis Córdova-Díaz, who won the right to vote in committee during the early 1970s and then had to choose sides in Washington. Since 1973, every Puerto Rican representative in Washington has chosen to sit with the Democrats, regardless of whether he belonged to the PPD or the PNP. Neither of the island's two main political parties had formal ties to Democrats or Republicans on Capitol Hill, but during the 1990s PNP officials in the Rosselló administration, including Fortuño, implemented economic principles favored by the GOP to align their push for statehood with policy on the mainland, according to historians César J. Ayala and Rafael Bernabe. See Ayala and Bernabe, *Puerto Rico in the American Century*: 291–315.

14 Quotation from Jennifer Yachnin, "GOP Makes History with Puerto Rican's Election," 4 November 2004, *Roll Call*: 10. It was also a presidential election year, and officials from both mainland parties expected the campaign in Puerto Rico to gauge the political leanings of what *Roll Call* termed "the all-important Latino voting bloc." See also Nicole Duran, "Both Parties Now Interested in Puerto Rico," 15 December 2003, *Roll Call*: 11. See also Teddy

Davis, "Fortuño Latest Member to Start His Own PAC," 5 July 2005, *Roll Call*: 9; *Politics in America, 2008* (Washington, D.C.: Congressional Quarterly, Inc., 2007): 1130.

15 Colon, "Untapped Conservatives"; Luiza Ch. Savage, "Praise of Bush Opens Convention," 31 August 2004, *New York Sun*: 3; Lindsey Kerr, "Profile: Del. Luis Fortuño, R-Puerto Rico," 12 March 2005, United Press International.

16 Colon, "Untapped Conservatives"; Kerr, "Profile: Del. Luis Fortuño"; Yachnin, "GOP Makes History with Puerto Rican's Election."

17 Ray Quintanilla, "Puerto Rico Governor's Race in Virtual Deadlock," 3 November 2004, *Orlando Sentinel*: A13; "Election Statistics, 1920 to the Present," http://history.house.gov/institution/election-statistics/election-statistics.

18 *Congressional Record*, House, 109th Cong., 1st sess. (2 March 2005): H877; *Congressional Record*, House, 109th Cong., 1st sess. (9 March 2005): H1047.

19 Frances Robles, "Lawyer Hopes to Beat Odds to Win Statehood; Resident Commissioner Luis Fortuño Is Latest Hope to Win Statehood for U.S. Territory," 3 April 2006, *Miami Herald*: A10.

20 Davis, "Fortuño Latest Member to Start His Own PAC."

21 *Congressional Record*, Extension of Remarks, 109th Cong., 2nd sess. (2 March 2006): E265–E266. See also Vanessa Bauzá, "Island Debates Its State; Will They Join U.S.? Bills May Help Decide," 16 July 2007, *Sun-Sentinel* (Fort Lauderdale, FL): A1.

22 Frances Robles, "Bills Address Thorny Issue of Puerto Rico's Status," 3 April 2006, *Miami Herald*: A10.

23 In the 110th Congress, the Education and the Workforce Committee became the Education and Labor Committee, and the Resources Committee was renamed the Natural Resources Committee.

24 Gary Martin, "Hispanic Groups Hail the Growing Clout of Latinos," 4 January 2007, *San Antonio Express-News*: A4; *Politics in America, 2008*: 1130; Garrison Nelson and Charles Stewart III, *Committees in the U.S. Congress, 1993–2010* (Washington, D.C.: CQ Press, 2011): 710.

25 *Congressional Record*, House, 110th Cong., 1st sess. (24 January 2007): 2135–2136. Delegates and Resident Commissioners were last given voting privileges on the floor about a decade before, when Democrats controlled the House. For more information, see Jim Abrams, "Non-State House Delegates Gain Limited Votes; Republicans Say Democrats' Move Unconstitutional," 25 January 2007, *Sun-Sentinel* (Ft. Lauderdale, FL): A3.

26 *Congressional Record*, House, 110th Cong., 1st sess. (24 January 2007): H899.

27 As Fortuño wrote to the editors of *New York Times* in May 2008, "Puerto Ricans … have never had the chance to vote on whether they are satisfied with the existing arrangement in the context of a fair and orderly self-determination process sponsored by Congress." See Luis G. Fortuño, "Puerto Rico's Status," 29 May 2008, *New York Times*: A24. On status issues, see David Lightman, "Wider Puerto Rican Vote Proposed; Would Include Those Living on Mainland," 28 February 2007, *Hartford Courant*: A2; Vanessa Bauzá, "Island Debates Its State; Will They Join the U.S.? Bills May Help Decide," 16 July 2007, *Sun-Sentinel* (Ft. Lauderdale, FL): A1; Mike Williams, "Puerto Rico Mulls Statehood, Commonwealth: A Bill for a Referendum on Becoming the 51st State Triggers the Debate," 23 December 2007, *Atlanta Journal-Constitution*: A12. Other prominent bills of Fortuño's included the Puerto Rico Medicare Reimbursement Equity Act of 2007 (H.R. 615); the Puerto Rico Hospitals Medicare DSH Equity Act of 2007 (H.R. 616); the Caribbean Basin Trade Enhancement Act of 2007 (H.R. 762); and the National Enterprise Zone Act of 2007 (H.R. 1340).

28 *Congressional Record*, House, 109th Cong., 1st sess. (3 May 2005): H2787. For Fortuño's support of the VA hospital in San Juan, see *Congressional Record*, House, 109th Cong., 1st sess. (13 September 2006): H6457–H6458.

29 Anasagasti and Robles, "Indicted Governor Faces Tough Challenge; Puerto Rico Gov. Aníbal Acevedo Vilá Is in a Tight Race to Keep His Job."

30 Frances Robles, "Embattled Puerto Rico Governor Soundly Defeated; Aníbal Acevedo Vilá, the Governor of Puerto Rico Who's Facing Charges of Campaign Finance Fraud, Lost by a Sizable Margin to Resident Commissioner Luis Fortuño," 5 November 2008, *Miami Herald*: A12.

"I am a firm believer in statehood for Puerto Rico, but I respect the right of my constituents to choose freely the status of choice of their preference, be it as a state of the Union, an independent republic or a republic associated with the United States.... Until this process of self-determination is completed, Congress will not have fully discharged its responsibility."

Luis G. Fortuño
The Hill, July 14, 2005

Mel Martinez
1946–

UNITED STATES SENATOR 2005–2009
REPUBLICAN FROM FLORIDA

After fleeing Cuba in 1962 to escape an outbreak of violence in his hometown, Mel Martinez settled in Florida. He served in local government and in President George W. Bush's Cabinet before being elected the first Cuban American to serve in the U.S. Senate. While staunchly conservative on many issues, he was a moderate voice in support of comprehensive immigration reform. "Bringing people together is my nature," noted Martinez, the only immigrant among his Senate colleagues. "There is nothing I'd rather do in the United States Senate than work to reach a consensus, build a bridge, seek and maintain common ground."[1]

Melquiades R. (Mel) Martinez was born October 23, 1946, in Sagua la Grande, Cuba, to Melquiades and Gladys Ruiz Martinez, who raised their three children in a devout Roman Catholic family. Melquiades, Sr., was a veterinarian.[2] In the face of the Castro regime's increased hostility toward Catholics, Martinez's parents sent him to the United States in 1962 through Operation Pedro Pan, a program organized by the U.S. government and the Catholic Church.[3] Martinez was placed with a foster family in Orange County, Florida, until his parents arrived in the United States in 1966. He earned a bachelor's degree in international affairs from Florida State University in 1969 and a law degree from that institution in 1973. He worked in private practice for nearly two decades and was president of the Florida Academy of Trial Lawyers from 1988 to 1989. He also chaired the Orlando Housing Authority and served on the board of directors of the Orlando Utilities Commission. Martinez met his future wife, Kitty, while they were students at Florida State. The couple raised three children: Lauren, John, and Andrew.[4]

Initially affiliated with the Democratic Party, Martinez switched his allegiance to the Republican Party when President Ronald W. Reagan took office. In 1998 he won election as Orange County chairman. Martinez also took an active role in the 2000 presidential campaign as co-chairman of the Florida operation of Republican nominee George W. Bush. After the election, President Bush nominated Martinez as Secretary of the Department of Housing and Urban Development (HUD), and he was unanimously confirmed by the U.S. Senate on January 23, 2001. As Secretary, Martinez was a forceful advocate for homeownership and for the advancement of public-private initiatives with faith-based and community services. At HUD he established a $1.7 billion tax credit program for investors building affordable housing and a $1 billion program to help 650,000 low-income families make down payments.[5]

In 2003 three-term incumbent Democratic Senator Bob Graham of Florida announced his intention to not seek re-election in 2004, setting off a scramble in both parties to recruit candidates. At the urging of President Bush and Senate Republicans, Martinez resigned his position at HUD on December 12, 2003, to run for the open seat.[6] In the Republican primary, he faced 10-term U.S. Representative Bill McCollum.[7] After prevailing in the primary with 44.9 percent of the vote, Martinez faced Betty Castor, a former state legislator, state education commissioner, and president of the University of Florida, in the general election. The candidates differed on virtually every issue, from abortion to the Iraq War.[8] Martinez won, with 49.4 of the vote versus Castor's 48.3 percent.[9] "Only in America can a 15-year-old boy arrive on our shores alone, not speaking the language—with a suitcase and the hope of a brighter future—and rise to serve in the Cabinet of the President of the United States. And only in America can that same boy today stand one step away from making history as the first Cuban-American to serve in the United States Senate," Martinez said.[10]

Mel Martinez was sworn in as a Member of the 109th Congress (2005–2007) on January 4, 2005, and

Image courtesy of the U.S. Senate Historical Office

acquired seats on the committees on Banking, Housing, and Urban Affairs; Energy and Natural Resources; and Foreign Relations. He also served on the Select Committee on Aging, and later secured seats on the Armed Services Committee and the Commerce, Science, and Transportation Committee.[11]

On national issues, he attempted to forge agreement with Senators of both parties. "You get things done by reaching for the middle," Martinez said.[12] On energy policy, for instance, he took a middle position on opening up more offshore areas for deep drilling, though he noted that such expansion was only a "component … of a comprehensive energy policy."[13] Martinez supported drilling in Alaska's Arctic National Wildlife Refuge (ANWR) on the condition that Florida's Gulf Coast would be sheltered from oil and gas exploration. He introduced a measure to permanently ban drilling in the outer continental shelf off the Florida coastline, adding, "I can clearly state that [Floridians] do not want drilling now, and I do not see a scenario anywhere on the horizon where we would change that position."[14]

An issue on which Senator Martinez cast himself as a centrist was immigration reform. His childhood experiences shaped his approach, which differed from his party's opposition to the establishment of a path to citizenship for undocumented immigrants.[15] He opposed efforts to build a 1,500-mile-long wall along the U.S. border with Mexico. "What the wall symbolizes is not what we want—the face of America we want to show," Martinez said.[16] In 2005 and 2006, he teamed up with Senator Barack Obama of Illinois to advance legislation using provisions for border enforcement and a guest worker program to address the issue of illegal immigration "in a realistic fashion without providing amnesty."[17] Among the proposals Martinez supported was an initiative that was introduced in the Senate as early as 2001. The purpose of the Development, Relief and Education for Alien Minors (DREAM) Act was to provide a path to education and permanent citizenship for the minor children of undocumented immigrants. "I'm very empathetic towards giving opportunity to children who have lived in this country all their lives … to reach their dreams and not be held back in any way," Martinez said.[18] While a comprehensive version of the immigration reform bill eventually passed the Senate, competing proposals in the House prevented its enactment into law.

At the opening of the 110th Congress (2007–2009), after Republicans had suffered heavy losses in the 2006 elections, President Bush nominated Martinez for chairman of the Republican National Committee, with responsibility for fundraising and communicating the party's message to the public. Political observers viewed the appointment partly as an effort to court Hispanic voters. Martinez was elected to the post in early 2007, but some Republicans opposed him because of his position on immigration. His goal was to "deliver a message that conveys to the American people that we are a party that has renewed itself and that has answers to their everyday problems." To allow Martinez to continue performing Senate duties, his post as chairman of the Republican National Committee was structured so that he could serve as general chairman while a directing chairman ran daily operations.[19] Ultimately, however, Martinez served only 10 months. Announcing his decision to leave the post on October 19, 2007, Martinez insisted he had rebuilt the party and its fundraising capacity, noting, "It was probably a good moment to get back to my main job, my real obligation and passion."[20]

In December 2008, Martinez announced his intention to not seek re-election to the U.S. Senate in 2010. Then, in August 2009, he announced he would resign as soon as a replacement could be appointed, citing a desire to return to Florida and his family.[21] "This is of my own free will," Martinez said, "only my desire to move on and get on with the rest of my life."[22] Martinez retired September 9, 2010, after Florida governor Charlie Crist selected his chief of staff, George S. Lemieux, to complete the term. Delivering his farewell address, Martinez stated, "Having lived through the onset of tyranny in one country and played a part in the proud democratic traditions of another, I leave here today with a tremendous sense of gratitude for the opportunity to give back to the Nation that I love—the Nation not of my birth, but the Nation of my choice."[23]

FOR FURTHER READING

Biographical Directory of the United States Congress, "Mel Martinez," http://bioguide.congress.gov.

Martinez, Mel, with Ed Breslin. *A Sense of Belonging: From Castro's Cuba to the U.S. Senate, One Man's Pursuit of the American Dream* (New York: Crown Forum, 2008).

MANUSCRIPT COLLECTION

University of Miami, Special Collections (Miami). *Papers*: 1998–2009 (bulk 2005–2009), 89 boxes. Senatorial papers including legislative and committee files, campaign files, administrative records, photographs, audiovisual materials, and electronic records. Topics include Florida projects; immigration; U.S.-Cuba relations; services to the elderly; and Florida environment, including issues relating to offshore oil drilling.

NOTES

1 Allison North Jones and Ellen Gedalius, "Martinez 'Humbled to Be' U.S. Senator," 4 November 2004, *Tampa Tribune*: 5.

2 Mel Martinez, *A Sense of Belonging: From Castro's Cuba to the U.S. Senate, One Man's Pursuit of the American Dream* (New York: Crown Forum, 2008): 3–12.

3 Official Biography of Senator Mel Martinez, http://martinez.senate.gov/public/index.cfm?FuseAction=AboutMartinezBiography&CFID=7934585&CFTOKEN=17985484 (accessed 3 July 2007, inactive website).

4 Mark Schlueb, "Immigrant's Rise to Success Appeals to GOP; Sent from Castro's Cuba as a Teen, Mel Martinez Pulled Himself Way Up," 6 December 2003, *Orlando Sentinel*: A6; Keith Epstein, "Humble Origins Are Key to Martinez's Persona," 10 August 2004, *Tampa Tribune*: 1; Libby Copeland, "Risky Political Waters," 8 April 2006, *Washington Post*: C1.

5 Matthew Vadum, "Bush Cabinet: Senate Unanimously Confirms Mel Martinez as New HUD Secretary," 24 January 2001, *Bond Buyer*: 4; *Almanac of American Politics, 2006* (Washington, D.C.: National Journal Group, Inc., 2005): 403–404.

6 Bill Adair and Steve Bousquet, "Martinez Quits Cabinet; Is Poised for Senate Run," 10 December 2003, *St. Petersburg Times*: 1B; Tamarz Lytle, "Martinez to Make Senate Bid; Cabinet Member Will Resign, Head Back to Orlando," 6 December 2003, *Orlando Sentinel*: A1; John Kennedy and Mike Silva, "Martinez Mulls Bid for U.S. Senate," 13 November 2003, *Orlando Sentinel*: A1.

7 Steve Bousquet, "Rival Pans Martinez's History as Trial Lawyer," 11 August 2004, *St. Petersburg Times*: 6B; Steve Bousquet, "GOP Senate Candidate Attacks as Election Nears," 20 August 2004, *St. Petersburg Times*: 5B.

8 Anita Kumar and Steve Bousquet, "Castor, Martinez Now Set Sights on Middle," 2 September 2004, *St. Petersburg Times*: 1B; Beth Reinhard, "Storms Don't Derail Castor, Martinez," 12 September 2004, *Miami Herald*: 2B.

9 "Election Statistics, 1920 to Present," http://history.house.gov/institution/election-statistics/election-statistics.

10 Lesley Clark and Frank Davies, "Mel Martinez Says He's Proof of American Dream," 3 September 2004, *Miami Herald*: 3A.

11 Garrison Nelson and Charles Stewart III, *Committees in the U.S. Congress: 1993–2010* (Washington, D.C.: CQ Press, 2011): 830; *Almanac of American Politics, 2006*: 404–406.

12 Wes Allison, "Sen. Martinez Makes a Move toward the Middle," 5 January 2005, *St. Petersburg Times*: 1A.

13 *Congressional Record*, Senate, 110th Cong., 2nd sess. (31 July 2008): S7812.

14 *Congressional Record*, Senate, 109th Cong., 1st sess. (20 June 2005): S6802. See also *Congressional Record*, Senate, 109th Cong., 1st sess. (14 June 2005): S6451–S6453.

15 Martinez spoke often on the Senate Floor about immigration reform. See for example, *Congressional Record*, Senate, 109th Cong., 2nd sess. (29 March 2006): S2519–S2520; *Congressional Record*, Senate, 109th Cong., 2nd sess. (7 April 2006): S3371–S3372; *Congressional Record*, Senate, 109th Cong., 2nd sess. (17 May 2006): S4672; *Congressional Record*, Senate, 109th Cong., 2nd sess. (24 May 2006): S5087; *Congressional Record*, Senate, 110th Cong., 1st sess. (28 June 2007): S8647–S8648.

16 Copeland, "Risky Political Waters."

17 "GOP Ends Rift, Moves Ahead on Immigration," 16 December 2005, *Miami Herald*: 6.

18 "Latino Leadership in the U.S. Senate—A Life of Public Service," an Interview with Senator Mel Martinez, 18 February 2005, *Harvard Journal of Hispanic Policy* 17 (2004–2005): 12–13.

19 Anita Kumar, "Martinez Steps Up to Top GOP Role," 20 January 2007, *St. Petersburg Times*: 5A; Lesley Clark, "Some in GOP Oppose Martinez," 17 January 2007, *Miami Herald*: A3.

20 Lesley Clark, "Martinez Resigns as Republican Party Chief," 20 October 2007, *Miami Herald*: 5; Larry Lipman, "Martinez Resigns as Republican Chairman," 20 October 2007, *Palm Beach Post*: 10A.

21 Josh Hafenbrack, Aaron Deslatte, and Mark Matthews, "Sen. Mel Martinez Resigns; Gov. Charlie Crist Will Pick His Replacement," 7 August 2009, *South Florida Sun-Sentinel*: n.p.; Joe Follick, "Martinez Giving Up Senate Seat Early," 8 August 2009, *Sarasota Herald-Tribune*: A1.

22 David M. Herszenhorn, "Martinez of Florida Says He Is Leaving Senate," 8 August 2009, *New York Times*: n.p.

23 *Congressional Record*, Senate, 111th Cong., 1st sess. (9 September 2009): S9147.

John Salazar

1953–

UNITED STATES REPRESENTATIVE 2005–2011
DEMOCRAT FROM COLORADO

With his election to the U.S. House of Representatives in 2004, John Salazar became one of a handful of farmers serving in Congress. From his seat on the Agriculture Committee, Salazar used his experience as a seed-potato farmer and a state legislator to defend his district's interests in agriculture and conservation. "There are only four, maybe six of us [farmers] here in Congress," he said. "If we can't stand up for farmers, we shouldn't be here."[1]

John Salazar was born July 21, 1953, in Alamosa, Colorado, to Emma and Henry Salazar. A fifth-generation resident of the San Luis Valley, he was raised with his seven siblings on the 52-acre family ranch on the western slope of the Rocky Mountains. Salazar grew up poor—his family's home did not have electricity until the 1980s—and he learned to love farming by working on his father's alfalfa and potato farm. After three years at St. Francis Seminary in Cincinnati, Colorado, Salazar served four years in the U.S. Army. He went on to earn his business degree from Adams State College in Alamosa, Colorado, in 1981.[2] He married after leaving the military. Salazar and his wife, Mary Lou, had three children: Jesus, Esteban, and Miguel.[3]

Salazar returned to the family ranch and began a career as a seed-potato farmer. His success landed him on the cover of the potato growers' journal *Spudman* in 1990, and he was named Colorado seed-potato grower of the year from 1995 to 1996.[4] While a farmer, Salazar became active in local agricultural organizations. He served on the Rio Grande water conservation district, where he successfully opposed a private company's effort to buy local water rights to divert water to Denver's suburbs. He was appointed to the Colorado agricultural commission in 1999. In 2002 he was elected to the Colorado state house of representatives, where he continued to oppose measures to divert water out of the region.[5] "We shouldn't develop a garden spot on the Front Range while drying up the West Slope and the [San Luis] Valley," he argued.[6]

In November 2003, Republican U.S. Representative Scott McInnis announced his retirement from the U.S House of Representatives, and Salazar announced his intent to run for the open seat in the general election the following year.[7] "Being a potato farmer, I've learned that if you want to increase your harvest, you have to rotate your crops from time to time," he said. "Well, now it's time for Colorado to rotate its congressional crop, so we can get more of a harvest out of our representatives."[8] Colorado's 3rd Congressional District was at its largest during that time, spanning an area that was roughly the size of Arkansas. The district extended east of the Front Range, including the city of Pueblo and most of the Western Slope.[9] Salazar had no opposition in the Democratic primary. In the general election, Salazar faced the Republican candidate, Colorado department of natural resources director Greg Walcher.

During the campaign, Salazar highlighted his experience as a farmer and businessman, voicing his support for agriculture, renewable energy, health care reform, balanced budgets, tax incentives for small businesses, and the repeal of the federal inheritance tax. But he focused on local issues, particularly water access.[10] He highlighted his opposition to a highly unpopular referendum—supported by Walcher the previous year—that guaranteed up to $2 billion in revenue bonds to fund water projects, characterizing it as a "billion-dollar grab of the Western Slope and rural water by the Front Range."[11] He also advocated for the creation of a federally funded water conservation program to keep water in the region.[12] Walcher attempted to tie Salazar to presidential candidate John Kerry and criticized him for supporting the elimination of tax cuts for high-income earners.[13] The race was highly competitive, and

Image courtesy of the U.S. House of Representatives Photography Office

both parties spent millions.[14] Salazar narrowly defeated his opponent, with 51 percent of the vote, becoming one of only five Democrats nationally to win a seat that had been Republican in the previous Congress. He was re-elected with more than 60 percent of the vote in 2006 and 2008. His younger brother, Ken Salazar, was elected in 2004 as the junior Senator from Colorado.[15]

John Salazar was sworn in as a Member of the 109th Congress (2005–2007) on January 4, 2005, and was assigned to the Committee on Agriculture and the Committee on Transportation and Infrastructure.[16] There he sought to protect agricultural interests, push for renewable energy development, and improve the infrastructure in his district. "As a lifelong farmer and rancher, it's my responsibility to make sure that rural Coloradans are properly represented as Congress develops national agriculture policy," he said.[17] In 2007 he defended his constituents' interests against an effort by the U.S. Army to expand one of its Colorado training bases by displacing numerous ranchers and farmers. Salazar and other members of the Colorado delegation successfully sponsored an amendment to block the military's efforts. "No one can support the taking by force of their constituents' land, homes, ranches, and towns," he declared.[18] As a member of the Transportation and Infrastructure Committee, he worked to improve local infrastructure; as a freshman, he secured $32 million for his district in the 2005 highway bill.[19]

The only veteran in the Colorado delegation during his first two terms, Salazar was seated on the Veterans' Affairs Committee in the 110th Congress. As a member of the committee, he sponsored the Stolen Valor Act, legislation to criminalize the fraudulent receipt of a military honor, especially the highest awards, such as the Medal of Honor and the Distinguished Service Medals. "This piece of legislation will make it easier for Federal law enforcement officials to prosecute phonies and imposters and restore the true meaning of these illustrious awards," Salazar said on the House Floor.[20] The measure passed the House in December 2006 and was signed into law by President George W. Bush. "This day has been a long time coming," Salazar said. "The brave men and women who have earned awards for service to our country should not have these honors tarnished by frauds."[21] In June 2012, the U.S. Supreme Court struck down the law as overreaching; a revised act was quickly passed by the House.[22]

In the 111th Congress (2009–2011), Salazar relinquished the committee seats he held previously for a seat on the powerful Appropriations Committee, where he served on the Subcommittees on Energy and Water Development, and Related Agencies and Military Construction, Veterans Affairs, and Related Agencies. He was also selected to sit on the Select Committee on Energy Independence and Global Warming, a position he used to safeguard coal-fired electricity providers seeking to reduce greenhouse gas emissions.[23] In the midst of the economic crisis in 2008, Salazar opposed legislation to stabilize the financial markets but approved loans to the automobile industry. He also was a reliable vote for the Democratic leadership in the House, supporting the American Recovery and Reinvestment Act, the American Clean Energy and Security Act, the Wall Street Reform and Consumer Protection Act, and the Patient Protection and Affordable Care Act.[24]

In the 2010 midterm elections, Salazar faced state legislator Scott Tipton, who had challenged him in the 2006 general election. In a contest that propelled Republicans back into the House majority, Tipton defeated Salazar, with 50.1 percent of the vote.[25] Salazar was appointed by Colorado Governor John Hickenlooper to lead the state department of agriculture on January 5, 2011.[26]

FOR FURTHER READING

Biographical Directory of the United States Congress, "John Salazar," http://bioguide.congress.gov.

NOTES

1 Anne Mulkern, "'He's a Real Farmer,'" 4 December 2008, *Denver Post*: A6.

2 Berny Morson, "Salazar Roots Run Deep; 3rd District Hopeful Is Longtime Advocate for Area's Agriculture," 18 October 2004, *Rocky*

Mountain News: 16A; *Politics in America, 2010* (Washington, D.C.: Congressional Quarterly, Inc., 2009): 185.

3 John Salazar for Congress, "About John," http://webarchive.loc.gov/lcwa0016/20040917003900/ http://www.salazar2004.com/about_john.asp (accessed 24 January 2011).

4 Morson, "Salazar Roots Run Deep; 3rd District Hopeful Is Longtime Advocate for Area's Agriculture."

5 *Politics in America, 2008* (Washington, D.C.: Congressional Quarterly, Inc., 2007): 187.

6 Electa Draper, "Profiles: 3rd Congressional District," 14 October 2004, *Denver Post*: B4.

7 Sarah Huntley, "Second Democrat Enters Race to Replace McInnis," 17 November 2003, *Rocky Mountain News*: 21A.

8 T. R. Reid, "Democrats Eye Colorado and See Chance to Tweak Republican Noses," 9 October 2004, *Washington Post*: A14.

9 *The Almanac of American Politics, 2010* (Washington, D.C.: National Journal Group, Inc., 2009): 286.

10 Draper, "Profiles: 3rd Congressional District."

11 Electa Draper, "U.S. House of Representatives 3rd District, Salazar and Walcher Survived Wide Field of Candidates, Now Face Off on Water, War, Taxes," 17 October 2004, *Denver Post*: V7.

12 Draper, "Profiles: 3rd Congressional District."

13 Electa Draper, "Salazar, Walcher Tout Ties, Each Claims to Be Best Fit for Sprawling Region," 5 October 2004, *Denver Post*: B4.

14 M. E. Sprengelmeyer, "Money Revs Up 3rd District Race," 25 October 2004, *Rocky Mountain News*: 20A.

15 "Election Statistics, 1920 to Present," http://history.house.gov/institution/election-statistics/election-statistics.

16 Garrison Nelson, *Committees in the U.S. Congress, 1993–2010* (Washington, D.C.: CQ Press, 2011): 923.

17 "Congressman John Salazar Named to Agriculture, Transportation and Veterans Committees," 29 January 2007, States News Service, http://w3.nexis.com/new/auth/signoff.do (accessed 1 February 2011).

18 Anne C. Mulkern, "House Blocks Piñon Expansion," 17 June 2007, *Denver Post*: C4.

19 *The Almanac of American Politics, 2010*: 287.

20 *Congressional Record*, House, 109th Cong., 1st sess. (12 July 2005): H5643; *Congressional Record*, House, 109th Cong., 2nd sess. (6 December 2006): H8819–H8823.

21 Anne C. Mulkern, "Rep. Salazar's Bill on Falsely Claiming Medals Now a Law," 21 December 2006, *Denver Post*: B3.

22 The court found that lying about military service was protected by the First Amendment. The new legislation was written to specifically address instances in which individuals benefitted from fraudulent claims of military service.

23 *Congressional Directory, 111th Congress* (Washington, D.C.: Government Printing Office, 2008): 398–399, 453.

24 Office of the Clerk, "U.S. House of Representatives Roll Call Votes, 111th Congress, 1st Session (2009)," http://clerk.house.gov/evs/2009/index.asp (accessed 4 May 2011); Office of the Clerk, "U.S. House of Representatives Roll Call Votes, 111th Congress, 2nd Session (2010)," http://clerk.house.gov/evs/2010/index.asp (accessed 4 May 2011).

25 *New York Times*, "Election 2010," http://elections.nytimes.com/2010/results/house (accessed 19 January 2011).

26 Joe Hanel, "John Salazar New Colorado Ag Leader," 5 January 2011, *Durango Herald*, http://durangoherald.com/article/20110106/NEWS01/701069954/-1/s (accessed 19 January 2011).

Ken Salazar
1955–

UNITED STATES SENATOR 2005–2009
DEMOCRAT FROM COLORADO

With his election in 2004, Ken Salazar became the first Hispanic American from Colorado to serve in the U.S. Senate. A fifth-generation Coloradan, Salazar crafted a reputation as an independent voice supporting agricultural and conservation interests and an advocate for comprehensive immigration reform. "My view is that U.S. Senators are elected for a six-year period because we are supposed to exercise our own independent judgment," Salazar noted en route to becoming one of the Senate's key centrists.[1]

Kenneth Salazar was born March 2, 1955, in Alamosa, Colorado, to Henry Salazar and Emma M. Montoya Salazar.[2] He and his seven siblings were raised on the family ranch in the San Luis Valley, where his ancestors settled in the 1850s. Salazar grew up poor—his family's house was not equipped with electricity until the 1980s—and the foundation for his future was his experience on the family farm. He graduated from Centauri High School in Conejos County, Colorado. Raised in a devout Catholic family, Salazar spent two years in the seminary before attending Colorado College, graduating in 1977 with a degree in political science. He went on to earn his law degree from the University of Michigan in 1981. Salazar met Hope Hernandez in Denver in 1980. The couple married in 1985 and raised two children, Melinda and Andrea.[3]

After practicing law in Denver for several years, Salazar served as chief legal counsel for Colorado Governor Roy Romer from 1987 to 1990. He then accepted an appointment to head the state department of natural resources, where he gained bipartisan acclaim for authoring the state constitutional amendment creating the Great Outdoors Colorado program. It was, Salazar said, "the only tool ever created at state level to help in the preservation of farmlands, open spaces and river corridors."[4] Funded through lottery proceeds, the program became one of the most successful land conservation efforts in the United States.[5] Salazar's knowledge about and passion for land issues prompted Senator Ben Campbell of Colorado to recommend him as head of the federal government's Bureau of Land Management, but Salazar declined this opportunity and returned to private practice in Denver.

On November 3, 1998, Salazar won election as Colorado's 36th attorney general, making him the first Hispanic to win statewide office.[6] He established a Fugitive Prosecutions and Gang Prosecution Unit and an Environmental Crimes Unit within the attorney general's office.[7] In the wake of the shooting at Columbine High School, Salazar joined the governor in organizing a summit on youth violence and supporting a ballot measure to limit the sale of firearms at gun shows.[8] As in his initial victory, Salazar was re-elected in 2002 as a centrist candidate who drew unaffiliated and crossover voters.[9]

In early 2004, Senator Campbell announced his intention to retire from the Senate, triggering a scramble in both parties to produce a nominee. Salazar announced in March that he planned to run for the open seat.[10] After soundly defeating Colorado Springs educator Mike Miles in the Democratic primary, with 73 percent of the vote, Salazar faced Pete Coors, chairman of the Coors Brewing Company, in the general election.[11] The candidates agreed on the need for investment in renewable energy and domestic exploration for oil and gas. Both candidates also supported the PATRIOT Act and gun rights, but Salazar backed additional privacy protections and a ban on assault weapons. The candidates differed principally on tax policy. Salazar proposed allowing federal tax rates to return to their pre-2001 levels for those earning more than $250,000 a year and supported the inheritance tax for estates worth more than $10 million. Coors, on the other hand, proposed making all President George W. Bush's tax cuts permanent

Image courtesy of the Senate Historical Office

and further reducing dividend and capital gains taxes.[12] Salazar defeated Coors on November 2, 2004, with 51.3 versus 46.5 percent of the vote.[13]

Salazar and newly elected Senator Mel Martinez of Florida became the first Hispanics to serve in the U.S. Senate since 1977. Salazar's older brother, John, was elected to the U.S. House of Representatives the same day to represent a Colorado district, making the Salazar brothers the second pair of Hispanic brothers to serve simultaneously in Congress. Ken Salazar consistently resisted attempts to label him as an advocate for Hispanic issues. "It wasn't the Hispanic community that voted me in," he said. "I have to work on all the issues that affect the state of Colorado. I don't see myself working on a specific Hispanic agenda."[14]

Salazar was sworn in as a Member of the 109th Congress (2005–2007) on January 4, 2005, and received assignments on the Agriculture, Nutrition and Forestry; Veterans' Affairs; and Energy and Natural Resources Committees. Two years later, he relinquished his seat on the Veterans' Affairs Committee for a spot on the influential Finance Committee. He also served on the Select Committee on Ethics and on the Special Committee on Aging.[15]

Salazar's self-description as "a moderate Democrat with an independent streak" was evidenced throughout his Senate service.[16] He was a member of the "Gang of 14," a group of seven Republicans and seven Democrats who forged a compromise on judicial nominees. Salazar also joined several other Senators to filibuster the reauthorization of the PATRIOT Act on the basis of civil rights. He voted with Republicans to protect gun manufacturers from lawsuits, enhance bankruptcy rules, and confirm Judge John G. Roberts as Chief Justice of the Supreme Court.[17] Salazar's independent streak gave him more clout in a Senate that was evenly and sharply divided along party lines. A seasoned political observer noted, "The relatively small number of people who are near the center become significant players. And he's done that. He's now one of the go-to guys."[18]

Salazar used his position to weigh in on two of the day's most contentious issues: energy development policy and immigration reform. Based on his earlier work at the state level and on his experience as a longtime sportsman, he emerged as one of the Senate's leading advocates for balancing energy development with environmental sustainability. In 2005 he worked with colleagues from both parties to pull from a defense bill language that would have authorized drilling for oil and gas in Alaska's Arctic National Wildlife Refuge (ANWR). As the debate about exploration in the ANWR intensified, Salazar pushed his colleagues to seek long-term solutions to meet energy needs. "Ultimately, this fight is not about barrels of oil, it's about the deeper moral decisions we make as a nation about how best to address our energy needs," Salazar said.[19] He was a primary cosponsor of the Renewable Fuels, Consumer Protection, and Energy Efficiency Act of 2007, which sought to increase America's use of renewable fuels.

Salazar was also intimately involved in grueling negotiations in 2006 and 2007 within the Senate and with President George W. Bush to craft comprehensive immigration legislation. "Failure on immigration reform is not an option," he said.[20] The resultant proposal—the Comprehensive Immigration Reform Act of 2006—passed the Senate in May 2006. The bill featured provisions for border security and a guest worker program for the estimated 12 million undocumented immigrants in the United States.[21] Salazar described the effort, which he helped advance with leading Democrats like Edward (Ted) Kennedy of Massachusetts and Republicans like John McCain of Arizona, as one "that dealt with creating a system of law and order, that would have taken us out of the lawlessness we currently have in our country with respect to immigration and have created a comprehensive system to deal with these major issues of national security, economic security, and moral values."[22] Ultimately, the immigration measure did not clear the House, and efforts to revive it in the following Congress failed.

Salazar was nominated December 17, 2008, to serve in President Barack Obama's Cabinet as the nation's 50th Secretary of the Interior. He was unanimously confirmed by the Senate on January 20, 2009.[23] "I look forward to helping build our clean energy economy, modernize our interstate electrical grid and ensure that we are making wise use of our conventional natural resources," he said after his nomination.[24] Salazar worked to reform regulatory agencies, particularly the Minerals Management Service, after he took office. He also continued to support the forms of renewable energy that he had championed as a legislator.[25]

FOR FURTHER READING

Biographical Directory of the United States Congress, "Ken Salazar," http://bioguide.congress.gov.

MANUSCRIPT COLLECTION

University of Colorado (Boulder). *Papers*: Senatorial papers. Collection size is unspecified and access may be restricted.

NOTES

1 Judith Kohler, "Colorado's Salazar Confounding Colleagues on Both Sides of the Aisle," 15 July 2005, Associated Press.

2 *Congressional Record*, Senate, 111th Cong., 1st sess. (16 January 2009): S637. In his farewell address, Salazar traced his North American ancestry back to the 1520s.

3 Colleen O'Conner, "Salazar's Hope: A Devoted Mom and Budding Businesswoman," 26 September 2004, *Denver Post*: L1.

4 Lynn Bartels, "Ken Salazar's Story Is Made for Political Campaign," 12 July 2004, *Rocky Mountain News*: 14A; John Sanko, "Salazar's Appeal May Aid Dems; Front-Runners for the Senate," 16 March 2004, *Rocky Mountain News*: 18A; Berny Morson, "Salazar Roots Run Deep," 18 October 2004, *Rocky Mountain News*: 16A.

5 U.S. Department of the Interior, "About Secretary Salazar," http://www.doi.gov/whoweare/secretarysalazar.cfm (accessed 19 January 2011).

6 Bartels, "Ken Salazar's Story Is Made for Political Campaign."

7 "About Secretary Salazar," http://www.doi.gov/whoweare/secretarysalazar.cfm.

8 Bartels, "Ken Salazar's Story Is Made for Political Campaign."

9 Ibid.

10 Karen E. Crummy, "Salazar Gets Dems' Blessing Udall, Bridges Drop Out of U.S. Senate Race to Endorse State Attorney General," 11 March 2004, *Denver Post*: A1.

11 Mark P. Couch, "It's Coors vs. Salazar, Nation's Eyes Turn to Colorado as a Key to Balance of Senate Power," 11 August 2004, *Denver Post*: A1; *Politics in America, 2006* (Washington D.C.: Congressional Quarterly, Inc., 2005): 181; Kirk Johnson, "Politics Are Both Local and National in Colorado Race," 16 October 2004, *New York Times*: A10.

12 Tom Kenworthy, "In Colorado Race, Two Very Different Choices," 5 October 2004, *USA Today*: 13A; Karen Crummy, "Coors, Salazar Debate Drinking Age, Abortion Issues; Senate Candidates Also Touch on Assault Weapons," 19 September 2004, *Denver Post*: C5.

13 "Election Statistics, 1920 to Present," http://history.house.gov/institution/election-statistics/election-statistics; See also Stephen Kiehl, "Democrat Salazar Wins Open Seat over Coors; Ex-Rancher Will Succeed Republican Campbell, Who Is Retiring," 3 November 2004, *Baltimore Sun*: 16B.

14 Mike Soraghan, "Salazar Reluctant to Wave Hispanic Banner," 5 December 2004, *Denver Post*: A1.

15 Garrison Nelson, *Committees in the U.S. Congress, 1993–2010* (Washington, D.C.: CQ Press, 2011): 923.

16 Mike Soraghan, "Salazar's Aisle-Crossings Have Some Democrats Fuming," 20 March 2005, *Denver Post*: A34. See also M. E. Sprengelmeyer, "Salazar Remains a Maverick," 23 December 2005, *Rocky Mountain News*: 5A.

17 Anne C. Mulkern, "Salazar Cuts His Own Trail in the Senate," 26 December 2005, *Denver Post*: A1; Judith Kohler, "Salazar Discusses Spying Flap, Patriot Act, First Year in Office," 22 December 2005, Associated Press.

18 The quotation is political scientist Norman Ornstein's. See Mulkern, "Salazar Cuts His Own Trail in the Senate."

19 *Congressional Record*, Senate, 109th Cong., 1st sess. (3 November 2005): S12338–S12339.

20 Elizabeth Aguilera, "Salazar Hopeful on Immigration, Saying 'Failure … Is Not an Option,'" 10 June 2007, *Denver Post*: C6.

21 Aguilera, "Salazar Hopeful on Immigration, Saying 'Failure … Is Not an Option.'" See also Salazar's interview of 17 February 2005, "Across the Spectrum: Latino Leadership in the U.S. Senate," *Harvard Journal of Hispanic Policy* 17 (2004–2005): 5–10.

22 *Congressional Record*, Senate, 109th Cong., 2nd sess. (29 September 2006): S10606.

23 "About Secretary Salazar," http://www.doi.gov/whoweare/secretarysalazar.cfm (accessed 2 April 2012); Karen Crummy and Anne C. Mulkern, "New Direction at Interior, Salazar Given Charge," 18 December 2008, *Denver Post*: A6.

24 Peter Roper, "Salazar Receives Nod for Interior Post," *The Pueblo Chieftain,* 18 December 2008, http://www.chieftain.com/news/local/article_d7c63bc2-fbda-56a0-8e91-d7a9f735e1ea.html (accessed 24 January 2011). See also Crummy and Mulkern, "New Direction at Interior: Salazar Given Charge."

25 "About Secretary Salazar," http://www.doi.gov/whoweare/secretarysalazar.cfm (accessed 2 April 2012).

★ PART TWO ★

Current Hispanic-American Members

★ INTRODUCTION ★

Current Hispanic-American Members

Nearly two centuries ago, Territorial Delegate Joseph Marion Hernández of Florida became the first Hispanic American to serve in the national legislature. Since then, 90 Hispanic Americans have followed in his footsteps.[1] The history of Hispanic representation in Congress contains many of the same themes that resonate in the larger chronicle of American democracy: a pioneering spirit, times of struggle and times of perseverance, the gradual attainment of power, and outstanding legislative achievements.

The 30 Hispanic Americans who currently serve in the 112th Congress (2011–2013) have inherited that long historical legacy which extends to Hernández. These 26 Representatives, one Delegate, one Resident Commissioner, and two Senators make up one of the largest groups of Hispanic legislators to serve in the history of the institution. Remarkably, they also account for nearly one-third of all the Hispanics who have ever served in Congress.

The 30 profiles in this section contain information on precongressional careers, elections, committee and leadership assignments, and legislative achievements. Because these Members are incumbent, comprehensive accounts of their congressional careers must await a later date. Their profiles are arranged into two distinct groups. First, the 24 Hispanic Americans who have served two or more terms in Congress are arranged in alphabetical order and profiled in 750-word entries. Second, the six freshman Hispanic Members of the 112th Congress appear at the end of this section and are profiled in résumé format entries. All current Members were given the opportunity to review their profiles before the book was published.

Among the current Members profiled in this section is Representative Ileana Ros-Lehtinen of Florida who, with 23 years of service as of the closing date of this volume, is the longest-serving current Hispanic Member of Congress. First elected to the House in a special election in August 1989, Ros-Lehtinen was also the first Cuban American to serve in Congress and eventually became one of the first Hispanic women to chair a standing committee (Foreign Affairs in the 112th Congress). Also included in this section is Robert Menendez of New Jersey, who became one of the highest ranking Hispanics ever to serve in the House, chairing the Democratic Caucus from 2002 until his appointment to the U.S. Senate in 2006.

As incumbent Members retire, we will expand their profiles in the hopes of detailing and analyzing their congressional careers. For the foreseeable future, their profiles will be updated in an online version of *Hispanic Americans in Congress*—located at http://history.house.gov—and will reflect their individual contributions to the rich history of Hispanic Americans in Congress.

1 The closing date for this volume was September 1, 2012.

KEY TO MEMBER TITLES

SENATOR

REPRESENTATIVE

TERRITORIAL DELEGATE/ RESIDENT COMMISSIONER

Image courtesy of the Member

Joe Baca
1947–

UNITED STATES REPRESENTATIVE 1999–
DEMOCRAT FROM CALIFORNIA

Joe Baca won election to the U.S. House of Representatives in 1999 in a special election to replace one of California's longest-serving Members. Since then, the former semi-pro baseball player has become a primary advocate to diversify America's business leadership and has helped procure funding for institutions working for the country's minority students.

Born the youngest of 15 children in Belen, New Mexico, Baca moved to Barstow, California, at age four. The son of a Santa Fe Railroad worker, Baca shined shoes and worked as a janitor before serving as a paratrooper during the Vietnam era. He graduated with a bachelor's degree in sociology from California State University, Los Angeles, in 1971 and worked for a telephone company until 1989, when he and his wife Barbara became co-owners of a travel agency.[1] The couple raised four children: Joe, Jr.; Jeremy; Natalie; and Jennifer. Baca's son Joe Baca, Jr., was elected to the Rialto city council after two years in the California state assembly.[2]

Joe Baca's political career began in 1979 when he was elected to the San Bernardino community college board. He spent the next 14 years on the board, waging two unsuccessful campaigns for a seat in the California state assembly in 1988 and 1990. When he won an assembly seat in 1992, Democrats in Sacramento quickly placed Baca in the leadership, electing him speaker pro tempore in 1995.[3] "Some people tell me I'm too small to do some things," Baca once remarked. "But I'm not too small. I just have to work harder than the bigger guys."[4] Two years later he nearly challenged 18-term Democratic U.S. Congressman George E. Brown, Jr., for California's 42nd District before winning a spot in the state senate in 1998. Brown died only a few months later, and Baca won the Democratic primary and then the special election in a November runoff to fill the remainder of Brown's unexpired term in the U.S. House during the 106th Congress (1999–2001).[5] He won again in 2000 for the full term to the 107th Congress (2001–2003). Baca now represents California's 43rd District—located in southwestern California at the foot of the San Bernardino Mountains—and since his first victory more than a decade ago he has cruised to victories in the general elections.[6]

Since his swearing-in, Baca has served on four House committees: Agriculture (106th–112th Congresses, 1999–2013), Science (106th–107th Congresses, 1999–2003), Financial Services (108th–112th Congresses, 2003–2013), and Resources (108th Congress, 2003–2005, and in the 110th–111th Congresses,

2007–2011, after it was renamed Natural Resources). In 2007 when the Democrats gained control of the House, Baca became chairman of the Agriculture Committee's Subcommittee on Department Operations, Oversight, Nutrition and Forestry.[7]

Baca's working-class roots have made him a champion both of organized labor and of the farmers throughout his district. His legislative interests have spanned everything from health care, to education, to transportation. Baca has used his position on the Agriculture Committee, to support the interests of low-income farmers and has worked to make Agriculture Department programs more accessible to minority growers.[8] He has used his seat on Natural Resources to help decontaminate groundwater throughout the Santa Anna River Watershed.[9] As a member of the Financial Services Committee, Baca has advocated for homeowners threatened by foreclosure.[10]

Baca is a member of numerous caucuses, including the Blue Dog Coalition and the Congressional Hispanic Caucus (CHC). Regarded as one of the more influential Hispanic legislators, Baca moved to the top of the CHC, serving as vice chairman in 2005 and as chairman in 2007 and 2008. Immigration has become a signal issue for Baca in the House, and he has pushed for thorough reform of the country's immigration and naturalization policies.[11] Also, throughout his tenure in Washington and in the CHC, Baca has supported access to bilingual education, helped ensure the continuation of food stamps and dietary programs for legal immigrants, and assisted in procuring millions in funding for educational institutions that serve large populations of Hispanic students.[12] "I'm a fighter," Baca has noted, "because I know what it's like to struggle."[13]

FOR FURTHER READING

Biographical Directory of the United States Congress, "Joe Baca," http://bioguide.congress.gov.

NOTES

1 *Politics in America, 2002* (Washington, D.C.: Congressional Quarterly, Inc., 2001): 144–145; Lauren V. Burke and Mary Shaffrey, "Rep. Baca Joins the 106th," 1 December 1999, *The Hill*: 12.

2 "Official Biography of Joe Baca," http://www.house.gov/baca/meetjoe/bio.htm (accessed 16 March 2010); "Mayor Pro Tem: Joe Baca, Jr.," http://www.ci.rialto.ca.us/citycouncil_285.php (accessed 25 May 2010).

3 Patrick J. McDonnell, "State Assembly/San Bernardino and Riverside; Diversity of Districts Helps Make Contests Competitive," 24 May 1992, *Los Angeles Times*: B2.

4 Jerry Gillam, "Eaves' Foe Looks to Willie Brown for Help," 7 May 1988, *Los Angeles Times*: 32.

5 David Wert, "Battle to Succeed Brown Taking Shape," 30 July 1999, *Press Enterprise*: B4; *Politics in America, 2002*: 145.

6 *Politics in America, 2012* (Washington, D.C.: CQ-Roll Call, Inc., 2011): 146.

7 Garrison Nelson and Charles Stewart III, *Committees in the U.S. Congress, 1993–2010* (Washington, D.C.: CQ Press, 2011): 568; Claire Vitucci, "Inland Members Get House Assignments," 10 January 2001, *Press Enterprise*: B6.

8 Onell R. Soto, "Adjournment Vote Note on Baca's Agenda," 19 November 1999, *Press Enterprise*: B6; *Almanac of American Politics, 2010* (Washington, D.C.: National Journal Group, 2009): 248.

9 *Politics in America, 2006* (Washington, D.C.: CQ Press, 2005): 155; *Politics in America, 2008* (Washington, D.C.: Congressional Quarterly, Inc., 2007): 155.

10 *Almanac of American Politics, 2010*: 248; *Almanac of American Politics, 2006* (Washington, D.C.: National Journal Inc., 2005): 283, 285.

11 *Politics in America, 2012*: 146.

12 "Official Biography of Joe Baca," http://www.house.gov/baca/meetjoe/bio.htm (accessed 16 March 2010); *Almanac of American Politics, 2004* (Washington, D.C.: National Journal Inc., 2003): 275.

13 Official Biography of Joe Baca," http://www.house.gov/baca/meetjoe/bio.htm (accessed 16 March 2010); as quoted in *Politics in America, 2002*: 144.

Image courtesy of the Member

Xavier Becerra
1958–

UNITED STATES REPRESENTATIVE 1993–
DEMOCRAT FROM CALIFORNIA

Xavier Becerra had barely completed one term in the California state assembly when he was elected to the U.S. House of Representatives in 1992. During his career in Washington, Becerra has emerged as a Democratic leader, becoming the first Latino in the history of the House to sit on the powerful Ways and Means Committee and being elected twice by his colleagues to serve as the Vice Chairman of the House Democratic Caucus.

Xavier Becerra was born in Sacramento, California, on January 26, 1958, the third of four children to working-class parents Maria Teresa and Manuel Becerra. He majored in economics and graduated in 1980 from Stanford University, near Palo Alto, California, becoming the first member of his family to earn a bachelor's degree.[1] He stayed on at Stanford, earning a law degree in 1984, before working as an aide to a California state senator and then becoming a California deputy attorney general. After Becerra moved to Los Angeles, community leaders encouraged him to run for the state assembly in 1990.[2] Becerra was young and relatively unknown, and his victory that year galvanized a new generation of Latino politicians.[3] Before the expiration of Becerra's first term in the state assembly, venerable Los Angeles Democrat Edward R. Roybal retired from the U.S. House. California had just redrawn its congressional districts, shifting the border of Roybal's 30th District westward from East Los Angeles to Hollywood. When one of Roybal's top aides declined to run, Becerra entered the race, receiving the outgoing Congressman's support. In a crowded primary, the 34-year-old Becerra—self-described as "pro-active" and "independent"—won the party nod with 58 percent of the vote and easily captured the general election that fall.[4] Currently representing California's 31st District, he has won every congressional election since 1992 by overwhelming majorities.[5] In 2001 Becerra ran for mayor of Los Angeles but lost in a heated election. Becerra and his wife, Dr. Carolina Reyes, have three daughters: Clarisa, Olivia, and Natalia.[6]

In the House, Becerra continues to champion the causes of underprivileged communities, aided in large measure by powerful committee assignments. Early in his congressional career, he served on the Committee on Science, Space, and Technology (103rd Congress, 1993–1995), the Committee on Education and Labor (103rd–104th Congresses, 1993–1997), and the Committee on the Judiciary (103rd–104th Congresses).[7] He has supported educational programs in areas with disadvantaged children, including Los Angeles, and from his seat on the Judiciary Committee, Becerra has become a leader in debates about America's immigration and welfare systems. Recognizing his determined early efforts, Democratic leaders placed Becerra on the influential Committee on Ways and Means, where he has served since the 105th Congress (1997–1999).[8] He joined the Committee on the Budget in the 110th and 111th Congresses (2007–2011), and in the 112th Congress (2011–2013), Becerra was appointed to the Joint Select Committee on Deficit Reduction.

An advocate of tighter gun regulations, Becerra also has opposed English-only education and supported tax measures to keep jobs in the entertainment industry in the United States.[9] As a more senior member of the Ways and Means Committee, Becerra continues to work to broaden the scope of Social Security, bolster Medicare, and make more opportunities available to the needy.[10] In 2008 Becerra was considered by then-President-elect Barack Obama for the Cabinet office of U.S. Trade Representative, to advise him on international trade issues.[11]

Representative Becerra is active in numerous House organizations, including the Congressional Progressive Caucus (CPC), the Congressional Hispanic Caucus (CHC), and the Congressional Asian Pacific American Caucus (CAPAC). His early success led one Latino California politician to call Becerra "our shining star."[12] The CHC elected him chairman in 1997 (105th Congress), and in the spring of 2008, he worked across the aisle with Representative Ileana Ros-Lehtinen (R-FL) to push through a measure to add a national museum for the American Latino to the Smithsonian Institution.[13] Becerra was elected one of three freshman whips in 1993, and he remains active in the House Democratic Caucus. His colleagues approved his appointment as Assistant to the Speaker in 2006, a position that involved working closely with party leadership to craft policy. Becerra was elected Vice Chair of the House Democratic Caucus in November 2008 and was re-elected for a second term in November 2010. Additionally, Becerra sits on the Smithsonian Board of Regents, which manages the institution's collection of art and artifacts.[14]

FOR FURTHER READING

Biographical Directory of the United States Congress, "Xavier Becerra," http://bioguide.congress.gov.

NOTES

1 James Bornemeier, "Rising Star Builds a More Visible Platform," 24 November 1996, *Los Angeles Times*: A3; *Politics in America, 2004* (Washington, D.C.: Congressional Quarterly, Inc., 2003): 127; Matea Gold, "Profile: Xavier Becerra; Congressman Tests His Winning Streak," 12 March 2001, *Los Angeles Times*: A1.

2 Tina Griego, "California Elections," 7 June 1990, *Los Angeles Times*: J1.

3 Rodolfo Acuña, "The Candidate Who Upset Latino Politics," 8 June 1990, *Los Angeles Times*: B7; Griego, "California Elections."

4 *Politics in America, 1996* (Washington, D.C.: Congressional Quarterly, Inc., 1995): 157; Guy Gugliotta, "Stakes Are Enormous in Contest for California's 52 House Seats," 1 June 1992, *Washington Post*: A6; George Ramos, "Assemblyman Becerra to Seek Rep. Roybal's Seat," 29 February 1992, *Los Angeles Times*: B3; Michael S. Arnold, "Latinos Make Political Gains," 18 June 1992, *Los Angeles Times* (nuestro tiempo edition): 1. As quoted in Andres Chavez, "Hot Contest Shaping up for Congress Seat," 21 May 1992, *Los Angeles Times* (nuestro tiempo edition): 1.

5 "Election Statistics, 1920 to Present," http://history.house.gov/institution/election-statistics/election-statistics.

6 "Official Biography of Xavier Becerra," http://becerra.house.gov/index.php?option=com_content&view=article&id=13&Itemid=16 (accessed 29 May 2012).

7 Garrison Nelson and Charles Stewart III, *Committees in the U.S. Congress, 1993–2010* (Washington, D.C.: CQ Press, 2011): 579.

8 "Welcome Teamwork on Immigration," 16 March 1994, *Los Angeles Times*: B6; Ruben Navarrette, Jr., "Immigration Ghosts Haunt the Hispanic Caucus," 20 March 1994, *Los Angeles Times*: M2; Alan C. Miller, "The Washington Connection: Two Faces of Immigration Debate," 2 July 1993, *Los Angeles Times*: A3; *Politics in America, 1996*: 156; Karen Tumulty, "Jobless Bill Snared in Immigration Issue," 15 October 1993, *Los Angeles Times*: A14; *Politics in America, 1998* (Washington, D.C.: Congressional Quarterly, Inc., 1997): 171; James Bornemeier, "Rising Star Builds a More Visible Platform," 24 November 1996, *Los Angeles Times*: A3.

9 *Almanac of American Politics, 2002* (Washington, D.C.: National Journal Group, 2001): 239; *Almanac of American Politics, 2004* (Washington, D.C.: National Journal Group, 2003): 246–247.

10 "Official Biography of Xavier Becerra," http://becerra.house.gov/HoR/CA31/About+Xavier/ (accessed 3 March 2010).

11 *Almanac of American Politics, 2010* (Washington, D.C.: National Journal Group, 2009): 221.

12 As quoted in Arnold, "Latinos Make Political Gains."

13 *Almanac of American Politics, 2010*: 221.

14 Ibid; Jennifer Yachnin, "Becerra Takes Rare Tack in Caucus Race," 25 September 2006, *Roll Call*: 1; Carl Hulse, "Pelosi Names Maryland Congressman to Lead Democratic Campaign Efforts," 20 December 2006, *New York Times*: A27; S. A. Miller and Tom LoBianco, "Waxman Bid to Head Energy Boosted," 20 November 2008, *Washington Times*: A1; "Official Biography of Xavier Becerra," http://becerra.house.gov/index.php?option=com_content&view=article&id=13&Itemid=16 (accessed 29 May 2012).

Image courtesy of the Member

Jim Costa

1952–

UNITED STATES REPRESENTATIVE 2005–
DEMOCRAT FROM CALIFORNIA

Jim Costa has dedicated his career to improving the quality of life and opportunities for the people of California's San Joaquin Valley so they can realize the promise of the American Dream. Costa is the grandson of Portuguese immigrants. Three of his four grandparents could neither read nor write, and his parents did not speak English until they were in first grade. Costa's grandparents scratched out a living working in dairies until they were able to save enough money to establish their own. Growing up, Costa worked on the family dairy and he now farms almonds. "Agriculture continues to be one of the major economic engines in California, providing the country with California's finest products," Costa said on the House floor in 2008. "As agriculture evolves, it is essential that our policies be based on current needs of this vital industry."

James Manuel Costa was born in Fresno, California, on April 13, 1952, to Manuel and Lena Cardoso Costa. He graduated from San Joaquin Memorial High School in 1970 and earned his bachelor's degree in political science from California State University, Fresno, in 1974. While in college, Costa worked as an intern in the office of U.S. Representative B. F. Sisk (D-CA). After college, Costa spent two years working as an aide to U.S. Representative John Krebs (D-CA), before becoming chief of staff to California state assemblyman and future U.S. Representative Richard Lehman (D-CA).

In 1978, Costa won a seat in the state assembly alongside his former boss Lehman. Over the next 16 years, he championed his district's agricultural and water interests and pushed for better rail access and health care services. In 1994, he was elected to the state senate, where he served for eight years until term limits forced him to retire in 2002. He was named the Kenneth L. Maddy Institute of Public Affairs Professor at California State University, Fresno, in 2003. He also started a successful consulting firm during that period.

When U.S. Representative Calvin M. Dooley (D-CA) announced his retirement from the House at the end of the 108th Congress (2003–2005), Costa entered the race to fill the open seat. As a lifelong native of the San Joaquin Valley, Costa launched his campaign with strong credentials, including wide name recognition. He defeated Dooley's former chief of staff in the hotly-contested primary, before defeating Republican state senator Roy Ashburn by 4.47 percent in the general election. Costa ran unopposed in 2006, and in 2008, he won with an overwhelming 74.3 percent of the vote. His closest re-election to date came in 2010, when he defeated his Republican opponent by 3.4 percent of the vote.

Costa represents the Democratic-leaning 20th District of California, comprising all of Kings and parts of Fresno and Kern counties in the Central Valley. Costa's district is one of the richest agricultural regions in the world with all three counties ranking among the top-10 agricultural producing counties in the United States.

During his tenure in the House, Costa has served on three committees: Agriculture (109th–112th, 2005–2013), Natural Resources (109th–112th, 2005–2013), and Foreign Affairs (109th–111th, 2005–2011).[1] He was Chairman of the Natural Resources' Subcommittee on Energy and Mineral Resources from the 110th–111th Congress (2007–2011), and in the 112th Congress (2011–2013) he serves as the Ranking Member of the Agriculture Committee's Subcommittee on Rural Development, Research, Biotechnology and Foreign Agriculture.

Costa's committee assignments reflect his chief legislative priorities and the needs of his district. He is dedicated to protecting and enhancing agricultural production in the U.S. Costa has also been a strong advocate for bringing additional water to the Valley and expediting the construction of water infrastructure projects. His focus on water reliability and water quality issues led him to co-found the Congressional Water Caucus. On the Foreign Affairs panel, he has worked each Congress to pass a resolution to officially recognize the Armenian genocide. In 2006, Costa co-founded the bipartisan Congressional Victims' Rights Caucus, and has consistently introduced legislation to draw awareness to National Crime Victims' Rights Week. The Victims' Rights Caucus has also been vocal on improving the Violence Against Women Act and the Victims of Crime Act.

Costa is a member of the Blue Dog Coalition, a caucus of fiscally-conservative Democrats, and believes it is important to work with his colleagues across the aisle. "I'm not pollyannish about it, but I would like to be part of the force encouraging bipartisanship in Congress."

FOR FURTHER READING

Biographical Directory of the United States Congress, "Jim Costa," http://bioguide.congress.gov.

NOTES

1 At the conclusion of the 109th Congress, the Resources Committee was renamed Natural Resources.

Image courtesy of the Member

Henry Cuellar

1955–

UNITED STATES REPRESENTATIVE 2005–
DEMOCRAT FROM TEXAS

Henry Cuellar hails from one of America's busiest border crossings, a Texas town where different people and ideas move back and forth between Mexico and the U.S. every day. In a sense, this constant exchange has given Cuellar a unique perspective on the American experience, one that appreciates solutions which benefit people of all stripes and political persuasions. "I'm just a big believer in bipartisanship," he said in 2011.[1]

Henry Cuellar, the oldest of eight children, was born in Laredo, Texas, on September 19, 1955, to Martin and Odilia Cuellar, migrant workers from Tamaulipas, Mexico. Though his parents had little more than an elementary-level education, Cuellar became a voracious reader while driving cattle in central Texas. He earned an associate's degree in political science from Laredo Community College in 1976 before graduating two years later from Georgetown University in Washington, D.C., with a bachelor of science degree in Foreign Service. In 1981 he earned a law degree from the University of Texas, Austin. He then opened a practice specializing in customs and worked as an adjunct professor of international commercial law at Texas A&M International from 1984 to 1986.[2] He earned a master's degree in international trade from Texas A&M International and a Ph.D. in government from the University of Texas, Austin, in 1998. Cuellar and his wife Imelda are the parents of two daughters, Christy and Catie.

Cuellar's political career began in 1987 when voters from his native Laredo elected him to the Texas state house of representatives, where he served for the next 14 years. In the state legislature, Cuellar found his way into the Democratic leadership and earned spots on powerful committees. In 2001 he was appointed Texas secretary of state, but he quickly resigned to challenge incumbent Republican Henry Bonilla for a seat in the U.S. House of Representatives. Cuellar lost in the general election that year, but after redistricting in 2003, he ran again, this time in Texas' new 28th U.S. Congressional District, where he faced incumbent Democrat Ciro D. Rodriguez in the primary. At the time, only the eastern half of Laredo was located in the 28th District, which ran north from the border with Mexico up and around the city of San Antonio. The close Democratic primary necessitated two recounts before a state court ruled Cuellar the victor. In his predominantly Hispanic and Democratic district, Cuellar won the general election by 20 points. In 2006 federal courts redrew the 28th District to include all of Laredo and Webb County.[3] Since his first victory,

Cuellar has faced increasingly less opposition in the party primary (running unopposed in 2008 and 2010) and has won by comfortable margins in the general elections.

Upon taking his seat in the House during the 109th Congress (2005–2007), Cuellar was assigned to the influential Budget and Agriculture Committees. During the 110th Congress (2007–2009), Cuellar's committee workload grew as he moved from the Budget to the Homeland Security and the Oversight and Government Reform Committees. His push for compromise—in 2006 Cuellar noted that "we've got to legislate from the middle"—won him the chairmanship of Homeland Security's Subcommittee on Emergency Communications, Preparedness, and Response, where he worked to combat gang violence and to strengthen laws governing sex offenders who violate parole.[4] As subcommittee chair, Cuellar also helped build relationships and facilitate communication between federal and local law enforcement agencies along the country's southern border. In 2010 Cuellar became chairman of the Subcommittee on Border, Maritime and Global Counterterrorism.[5] During Cuellar's tenure on the Agriculture Committee he has used his seat to provide drought relief and to combat the damaging effects of cattle fever ticks.[6]

With his background in customs law and having come from a district contiguous with Mexico, Cuellar has emerged as a prominent voice on international issues, especially trade. A member of the Blue Dog Coalition, Cuellar supports a self-styled "fiscally conservative" approach to government spending, supporting Pay-As-You-Go legislation to offset costs.[7] In 2005 Cuellar backed the Central American Free Trade Agreement, a corollary to the long-standing North American Free Trade Agreement, to open trade and capital investments in Central American markets. He founded and has co-chaired the House Pro-Trade Caucus, and his independent streak prioritizes the interests of his district. As he told one Texas newspaper in 2005, "I have always put my community first before any political party."[8]

FOR FURTHER READING

Biographical Directory of the United States Congress, "Henry Cuellar," http://bioguide.congress.gov.

NOTES

1 Gary Martin, "Cuellar Shies away from Endorsement," 30 October 2011, *San Antonio Express-News*: B3.

2 Gary Martin, "Mr. Cuellar Goes to Washington," 5 January 2005, *San Antonio Express-News*: 1A; Chuck Lindell, "Cuellar's First Days in Office Will Be Test," 19 January 2005, *Austin American-Statesman*: A1; *Almanac of American Politics, 2010* (Washington, D.C.: National Journal Group, 2009): 1476; "Official Biography of Henry Cuellar," http://cuellar.house.gov/Biography/ (accessed 28 May 2010).

3 *Almanac of American Politics, 2010*: 1478; *Politics in America, 2008* (Washington, D.C.: Congressional Quarterly, Inc., 2007): 1006; "Election Statistics, 1920 to Present," http://history.house.gov/institution/election-statistics/election-statistics.

4 Todd J. Gillman, "Balance of Power Is Shifting to the Center," 19 November 2006, *Dallas Morning News*: 11A; Jesse Bogan, "Cuellar Plan Gets a Tepid Response," 3 September 2005, *San Antonio Express-News*: B1; Hernán Rozemberg, "Millions for Containing Violence Closer," 5 October 2005, *San Antonio Express-News*: B8.

5 *Almanac of American Politics, 2010*: 1478; "Official Biography of Henry Cuellar," http://cuellar.house.gov/Biography/ (accessed 28 May 2010).

6 "Official Biography of Henry Cuellar," http://cuellar.house.gov/Biography/ (accessed 28 May 2010).

7 Ibid; Henry Cuellar, "We Are PAYGOing Our Way out of Federal Debt," 25 February 2010, *San Antonio Express-News*: 4.

8 As quoted in Lindell, "Cuellar's First Days in Office Will Be a Test."

Image courtesy of the Member

Mario Diaz-Balart

1961–

UNITED STATES REPRESENTATIVE 2003–
REPUBLICAN FROM FLORIDA

Growing up, Mario Diaz-Balart and his family "didn't go to sporting events," he remembered shortly after his 2002 election to the U.S. House of Representatives. "We talked politics." Like his father and older brother, Diaz-Balart has prioritized public service. In fact, "service," he said, "is what drives the family."[1]

Mario Diaz-Balart was born on September 25, 1961, in Ft. Lauderdale, Florida, to Rafael Diaz-Balart and Hilda Caballero. The Diaz-Balarts had been one of Cuba's most powerful political families in the mid-20th century: Rafael had been majority leader in the island's national legislature, and his sister—Mario Diaz-Balart's aunt—had married a young politician named Fidel Castro. But when Fulgencio Batista came to power in Cuba, the elder Diaz-Balart joined the new administration, and Castro rebelled against it. With Castro's rise, the Diaz-Balarts left the island and moved repeatedly before settling in the Miami area shortly before Mario was born.[2]

After completing his early education, Diaz-Balart enrolled at the University of South Florida but withdrew in 1982 to campaign and work for Miami Mayor Xavier Suarez. After his stint in the mayor's office, Diaz-Balart won election to the Florida state house of representatives in 1988. He served in the house until 1992, when at age 31 he became the youngest successful candidate for the state senate. Diaz-Balart moved quickly through the leadership, becoming chairman of the ways and means committee and earning a reputation for fighting government waste and protecting the rights of the state's minority residents. Florida's term limits forced him out of the senate in 2000, but that year he again won election to the state house, where he chaired the redistricting committee. While in the state legislature, Diaz-Balart was also a public relations executive for a private firm. He is married to Tia Diaz-Balart. They live in Miami with their son.[3]

In 2002 Diaz-Balart ran for Florida's 25th District seat in the U.S. House. One of two districts Florida gained after the 2000 Census, the 25th District encompassed a large swath of produce farmland and the Everglades in southern Florida between the cities of Naples to the west and Miami to the east.[4] He campaigned unopposed in the Republican primary and overwhelmed his Democratic opponent in the general election, winning by 29 percent. Diaz-Balart supported the country's hard line against Castro's Cuba, and he received support from many incumbent House Republicans, including his brother,

Representative Lincoln Diaz-Balart.[5] In the eight years he represented the 25th District, Diaz-Balart faced little opposition on the campaign trail. His closest race was in 2008, when he won the general election by about 6 percent. In the fall of 2010, he ran unopposed for Florida's 21st District seat in the House, a predominantly suburban district just to the west of Miami which had been represented by Mario's brother Lincoln for 18 years.[6]

Diaz-Balart's committee assignments in the House have been few but powerful: the Budget Committee (108th–111th Congresses, 2003–2011), the Transportation and Infrastructure Committee (108th–111th Congresses), the Science Committee (later renamed Science and Technology: 109th–111th Congresses, 2005–2011), and the exclusive Appropriations Committee (112th Congress, 2011–2013).[7] The jurisdiction of his initial committee seats dovetailed with Diaz-Balart's legislative interests and South Florida has benefitted accordingly. Diaz-Balart has won billions in funding for highway and metro rail development in and around the Miami area, and in 2003 he successfully protected additional billions in federal funds for the rehabilitation of the Everglades' fragile ecosystem. He has supported efforts to reform the internal revenue code by making permanent certain deductions, including commuting costs, and has sought similar ways to help struggling U.S. homeowners.[8]

Also, Diaz-Balart has emerged as a prominent voice on immigration and trade issues, fighting to protect access to bilingual government services, opposing efforts to criminalize illegal immigration, and supporting the Central American Free Trade Agreement.[9] He has remained ardently opposed to Castro's regime in Cuba, and, in 2003, that stance became the underlying reason for his decision to create the Congressional Hispanic Conference, a predominantly Republican caucus he continues to chair. Diaz-Balart's legislative interests have taken root in other caucuses outside the House chamber: He founded and is co-chair of the Everglades Caucus, and he helped establish the Washington Waste Watchers to combat government fraud.[10]

FOR FURTHER READING

Biographical Directory of the United States Congress, "Mario Diaz-Balart," http://bioguide.congress.gov.

NOTES

1 Oscar Corral, "New Diaz-Balart in Congress Adds to Family's Growing Political Dynasty," 6 January 2003, *Miami Herald*: A1.

2 Maya Bell, "Brothers' Ascent to Power: Part Destiny, Part Dynasty," 6 January 2003, *Orlando Sentinel*: A1; Abby Goodnough, "All in the Family, Brothers Wage War on Uncle Fidel," 8 March 2006, *New York Times*: A18; *Politics in America, 2006* (Washington, D.C.: CQ Press, 2005): 274.

3 *Politics in America, 2006*: 273–274; "Official Biography of Mario Diaz-Balart," http://mariodiazbalart.house.gov/index.cfm?sectionid=37§iontree=7,37 (accessed 17 May 2012); *Politics in America, 2012* (Washington, D.C.: CQ-Roll Call, Inc., 2011): 251.

4 *Almanac of American Politics, 2010* (Washington, D.C.: National Journal Group, 2009): 407–408.

5 Oscar Corral, "Policy Toward Cuba Is Ripped," 4 October 2002, *Miami Herald*: B1; Elaine DeValle, "2 Familiar Faces Hope to Capture Seat in Congress," 8 September 2002, *The Miami Herald*: B6; Oscar Corral, "U.S. House Speaker Hastert Backs Diaz-Balart in Hialeah," 6 October 2002, *Miami Herald*: B4.

6 *Politics in America, 2004*: 264; *Politics in America, 2010* (Washington, D.C.: Congressional Quarterly, Inc., 2009): 266; "Official Biography of Mario Diaz-Balart," http://mariodiazbalart.house.gov/index.cfm?sectionid=37§iontree=7,37 (accessed 17 May 2012).

7 Garrison Nelson and Charles Stewart III, *Committees in the U.S. Congress, 1993–2010* (Washington, D.C.: CQ Press, 2011): 675.

8 *Politics in America, 2006*: 274; *Politics in America, 2008* (Washington, D.C.: Congressional Quarterly, Inc., 2007): 266; *Politics in America, 2010*: 266.

9 *Politics in America, 2010*: 266.

10 "Official Biography of Mario Diaz-Balart," http://mariodiazbalart.house.gov/index.cfm?sectionid=37§iontree=7,37 (accessed 3 August 2010).

Image courtesy of the Member

Charles A. Gonzalez

1945–

UNITED STATES REPRESENTATIVE 1999–
DEMOCRAT FROM TEXAS

As a former judge, Charles Gonzalez has a unique, straight-forward way of finding common ground in the U.S. House of Representatives. "I'm not for pomp and circumstance," he said in 2001. "Let's get into the nitty-gritty and discuss our differences."[1]

Charles A. Gonzalez was born the third of eight children on May 5, 1945, in San Antonio, Texas, to Henry B. and Bertha González. As a child, he attended Catholic parochial schools while his father served in the San Antonio City Council and then in the state senate. When Charlie Gonzalez was in high school, his father became the first Mexican American from Texas elected to the U.S. House of Representatives. (He is the longest-serving Hispanic American in congressional history, 1961–1999.) With his father in Washington, the younger Gonzalez remained in San Antonio, and after graduating from Thomas A. Edison High School, he attended the University of Texas, Austin, receiving a bachelor of arts degree in government in 1969. Three years later he earned a law degree from St. Mary's School of Law in San Antonio. From 1969 to 1975, Gonzalez was also a reservist in the Texas Air National Guard.[2] He is divorced, with a son, Leo, from his previous marriage.

Gonzalez spent one year teaching school before practicing law in the private sector for roughly a decade. In 1983 he became a municipal court judge before being elected to the Bexar County Court at Law. After five years as a county judge, Gonzalez was elected to the bench of Texas' 57th District Court and served from 1988 until 1997.[3] When Henry B. González announced his retirement from national politics in 1997, Charlie Gonzalez resigned his judgeship to campaign for his father's seat. Texas' traditionally Democratic and predominantly Hispanic 20th District cuts a diagonal through the city of San Antonio, encompassing much of the downtown area, including the Alamo, before stretching south and westward into the suburbs.[4] The 1998 election featured a crowded Democratic primary, and after Gonzalez captured the party nod in the runoff election, he defeated his Republican challenger in the general election by nearly 30 percent.[5] Since his first victory more than a decade ago, Gonzalez has faced little competition in either primary or general elections.[6]

Gonzalez has sat on multiple committees during his career in the House: Banking and Financial Services (later renamed Financial Services, 106th–108th Congresses, 1999–2005); Small Business (106th–110th Congresses, 1999–2009), where from 2007 to 2009 he chaired the Subcommittee on Regulation,

Healthcare and Trade; Energy and Commerce (108th–112th Congresses, 2003–2013); House Administration (110th–112th Congresses, 2007–2013); Judiciary (111th Congress, 2009–2011); and the Select Committee on Homeland Security (108th Congress, 2003–2005).[7]

Gonzalez earned a reputation as a respected mediator in the national legislature, underscoring his efforts to protect the civil rights of individuals across the country.[8] He has worked to protect homebuyers and family businesses in his district, especially small and independent health care providers. His work on behalf of the nation's Hispanic community has placed him in leadership positions across Capitol Hill, and his advocacy for Spanish-language telecommunications and support for the nation's education system have contributed to his popularity in Texas.[9] "You don't make the public schools stronger by taking the funds away," Gonzalez told the *San Antonio Express-News* in 2001.[10]

With his no-frills approach to the national lawmaking process, Gonzalez was elected vice president of his class of first term lawmakers in 1999. Shortly thereafter, the Democratic Party appointed him chairman of a task force investigating the results of the 2000 presidential election. He has also been an active member of the Congressional Hispanic Caucus (CHC), chairing its civil rights task force during the 107th Congress (2001–2003) and helping to organize opposition against several administration nominees. In addition, the CHC made him responsible for investigating claims that the 2000 Census inaccurately calculated the size of the country's minority population, a problem Gonzalez called "the civil rights issue of the decade."[11] In the 112th Congress (2011–2013), the CHC elected him chairman. He is also a member of the New Democrat Coalition, the 21st Century Health Care Caucus, the High Speed Rail Caucus, the Air Force Caucus, the Infrastructure and Transportation Caucus, and the Missing and Exploited Children's Caucus.[12]

FOR FURTHER READING

Biographical Directory of the United States Congress, "Charles A. Gonzalez," http://bioguide.congress.gov.

NOTES

1 Gary Martin, "Bush Reaching to Other Side," 4 February 2001, *San Antonio Express-News*: A1.

2 Christopher Marquis, "Henry Gonzalez, 84; Served 37 Years in House," 29 November 2000, *New York Times*: A33; *Politics in America, 2000* (Washington, D.C.: Congressional Quarterly, Inc., 1999): 1339; *Politics in America, 2010* (Washington, D.C.: Congressional Quarterly, Inc., 2009): 994; "Official Biography of Congressman Charlie A. Gonzalez," http://gonzalez.house.gov/index.php?option=com_content&view=article&id=19&Itemid=9 (accessed 4 August 2010).

3 "New District Judge," 9 January 1998, *San Antonio Express-News*: B3; *Politics in America, 2000*: 1339.

4 *Politics in America, 2012* (Washington, D.C.: CQ-Roll Call, Inc., 2011): 957; *Almanac of American Politics, 2006* (Washington, D.C.: National Journal Group, 2005): 1634; *Almanac of American Politics, 2010* (Washington, D.C.: National Journal Group, 2009): 1459–1460; *Politics in America, 2000*: 1339.

5 *Politics in America, 2000*: 1339.

6 *Politics in America, 2002* (Washington, D.C.: Congressional Quarterly, Inc., 2001): 994; *Politics in America, 2004* (Washington, D.C.: Congressional Quarterly, Inc., 2003): 990; *Politics in America, 2006* (Washington, D.C.: Congressional Quarterly, Inc., 2005): 1004; *Politics in America, 2008* (Washington, D.C.: Congressional Quarterly, Inc., 2007): 989; *Politics in America, 2010*: 993.

7 Garrison Nelson and Charles Stewart III, *Committees in the U.S. Congress, 1993–2010* (Washington, D.C.: CQ Press, 2011): 725–726; *Politics in America, 2008*: 989.

8 Sherry Sylvester, "Son Steps Out of Dad's Shadow in Washington," 25 November 2001, *San Antonio Express-News*: A12; *Politics in America, 2000*: 1339; *Politics in America, 2002*: 994; *Politics in America, 2008*: 990; *Politics in America, 2010*: 993–994.

9 *Politics in America, 2004*: 990–991; *Politics in America, 2008*: 989–990.

10 Gary Martin, "Hispanic Caucus Will Meet Bush," 2 April 2001, *San Antonio Express-News*: A1.

11 Sherry Sylvester, "Census Tally Will Not Be Adjusted," 7 March 2001, *San Antonio Express-News*: A1.

12 *Politics in America, 2004*: 991; *Politics in America, 2008*: 989; "Official Biography of Congressman Charlie A. Gonzalez," http://gonzalez.house.gov/index.php?option=com_content&view=article&id=19&Itemid=9 (accessed 6 August 2010).

Image courtesy of the Member

Raúl M. Grijalva
1948–

UNITED STATES REPRESENTATIVE 2003–
DEMOCRAT FROM ARIZONA

For Raúl Grijalva, serving in the U.S. House of Representatives is about more than pursuing the interests of a particular constituency. "We are not only required to produce," he said shortly after winning his third term in the House, "but we are required to lead."[1] Grijalva has led by advocating for better educational opportunities and by becoming one of the most prominent environmentalists in Congress.

During World War II, Grijalva's father immigrated to the United States from Mexico as part of the Bracero labor program, an agreement between the two countries permitting U.S. farmers to hire Mexican workers to remedy the wartime labor shortage.[2] Sponsored by an employer, his father became an American citizen, married, and settled in Tucson, Arizona. Raúl M. Grijalva was born in Tucson on February 19, 1948, and grew up in the southwest side of the city. He graduated from Sunnyside High School in 1967 and attended the University of Arizona before withdrawing to marry Ramona F. Grijalva, a librarian.[3] Early in his career, Grijalva was an active community organizer and social worker, and was later an assistant dean for Hispanic Student Affairs at the University of Arizona.[4] In 1974 he won election to the governing board of the Tucson unified school district and served until 1986. In 1987 he returned to the University of Arizona and completed his bachelor of arts degree in sociology. The following year, he won election to the Pima County board of supervisors and served as its chairman in 1997 and from 2001 to 2002.[5] He and his wife have three daughters: Adelita, Raquel, and Marisa.

After Arizona gained two seats in the U.S. House of Representatives following the 2000 Census, Grijalva resigned from the Pima County board to run from the new 7th District. Located south of Phoenix and west of Tucson, the majority-Hispanic, Democratic-leaning district covered nearly 23,000 square miles and shared a 300-mile border with Mexico.[6] Though part of the region's economy is supported by seasonal farm labor, many residents live in Tucson and work for the University of Arizona. The district also contains seven American Indian reservations. "We're a place where frontier crashed into frontier," Grijalva said of his district in early 2002. "We have a history of being fairly diverse."[7] He ran on a platform advocating environmental protection, immigration reform, better access to education and health care, and economic stimulus.[8] In the race for the House seat, Grijalva captured the party primary before taking the general election by more than 20 percent later that fall.[9] "I am not one to avoid traveling the path least traveled," he said a few months before the election. "The personal risk is well worth the community reward."[10] Since his first victory in 2002, he has run unopposed in every Democratic primary and has won each subsequent general election.[11]

In the House, Grijalva continues to champion the issues he supported during his time in local government, including education, labor, and the environment, and his committee assignments have bolstered his legislative activities. For his entire congressional career, starting in the 108th Congress (2003–2005), Grijalva has sat on the Committee on Education and Labor and the Committee on Natural Resources.[12] He has worked to overhaul the nation's immigration policy, advocating for the Safe, Orderly, Legal Visas and Enforcement Act (SOLVE), and has sought to fully fund education programs for the families of seasonal workers and non-native English speakers. Grijalva has also successfully introduced bills returning nearly 16,000 acres to four American Indian tribes in his district and spurring economic development on tribal lands.[13] He joined the Committee on Small Business during the 109th and 110th Congresses (2005–2009), and in 2007 he became the chairman of Natural Resources' Subcommittee on National Parks, Forests and Public Lands. While chairman, he sought to maintain funding for the country's national parks and worked to protect public lands and their resources.[14]

Grijalva has co-chaired the Congressional National Landscape Conservation Caucus and previously chaired the Democratic Environmental Task Force Caucus from 2003 to 2006.[15] A member of the Congressional Hispanic Caucus (CHC), Grijalva served as its first vice chairman at the start of the 110th Congress (2007–2009).[16] Grijalva has served as co-chair of the Congressional Progressive Caucus since the start of the 111th Congress (2009–2011).

FOR FURTHER READING

Biographical Directory of the United States Congress, "Raúl M. Grijalva," http://bioguide.congress.gov.

NOTES

1 Josh Brodesky, "Grijalva Stands to Gain More Influence," 24 November 2006, *Arizona Daily Star*.

2 Nicole Santa Cruz, "He's Standing His Ground: An Arizona Lawmaker Feels the Backlash after Calling for a Boycott of His State," 25 May 2010, *Los Angeles Times*: A8; Gilbert Paul Carrasco, "Bracero Program," in Suzanne Oboler and Deena J. González, eds., *The Oxford Encyclopedia of Latinos and Latinas in the United States Vol. 1* (New York: Oxford University Press, 2005): 220–221.

3 *Politics in America, 2010* (Washington, D.C.: Congressional Quarterly, Inc., 2009): 46; Garry Duffy, "Grijalva Resigns County Job," 6 February 2002, *Tucson Citizen*: C1.

4 "Official Biography of Congressman Raúl M. Grijalva," http://grijalva.house.gov/index.cfm?sectionid=87§iontree=2,87 (accessed 16 March 2010); *Almanac of American Politics, 2004* (Washington, D.C.: National Journal Group, 2003): 121; *Politics in America, 2004* (Washington, D.C.: Congressional Quarterly, Inc., 2003): 42.

5 *Politics in America, 2010* (Washington, D.C.: Congressional Quarterly, Inc., 2009): 45.

6 *Almanac of American Politics, 2010* (Washington, D.C.: National Journal Group, 2009): 105.

7 Michael Lafleur, "Tucson Living King's Dream," 21 January 2002, *Tucson Citizen*: A1.

8 Duffy, "Grijalva Resigns County Job"; "Ask the Candidates; Topics: Immigrants, Economy," 11 August 2002, *Arizona Daily Star*: A7.

9 *Politics in America, 2004*: 42.

10 Duffy, "Grijalva Resigns County Job."

11 *Politics in America, 2010*: 45.

12 In the 108th Congress, the names of these panels were the Education and the Workforce Committee and the Resources Committee, respectively. When Democrats won the House majority at the start of the 110th Congress in 2007, they were renamed Education and Labor and Natural Resources. When Republicans regained the House majority for the 112th Congress in 2011, Education and Labor was again renamed Education and the Workforce; the Natural Resources name remained unchanged.

13 Sheryl Gay Stolberg, "Two Sides of Political Reality for New Lawmakers," 30 June 2003, *New York Times*: A14; Luke Turf, "Grijalva Unveils Immigration Reform," 5 May 2004, *Tucson Citizen*: A7; C. T. Revere, "Grijalva Gets 1st Bill through House," 29 September 2004, *Tucson Citizen*: A4; *Politics in America, 2006* (Washington, D.C.: Congressional Quarterly, Inc., 2005): 47–48; *Politics in America, 2010*: 45.

14 C. T. Revere, "Bush Plan for Forest Land Irks Grijalva, Activists," 3 December 2002, *Tucson Citizen*: A7; "Official Biography of Congressman Raúl M. Grijalva," http://grijalva.house.gov/index.cfm?sectionid=87§iontree=2,87 (accessed 16 March 2010); *Almanac of American Politics, 2010*: 106.

15 "Official Biography of Congressman Raúl M. Grijalva," http://grijalva.house.gov/index.cfm?sectionid=87§iontree=2,87 (accessed 16 March 2010).

16 *Politics in America, 2010*: 45.

Image courtesy of the Member

Luis V. Gutierrez

1953–

UNITED STATES REPRESENTATIVE 1993–
DEMOCRAT FROM ILLINOIS

Luis Gutierrez has a straightforward approach to the national lawmaking process, especially when it comes to the country's immigration policy. "The value of getting something done that is not worthy of our immigrants is not anything," he told the *Chicago Tribune* in 2007. "It's more important to get it done right."[1]

Luis Vicente Gutierrez was born on December 10, 1953, in Chicago, Illinois, the first of two children. His father drove taxicabs, and his mother worked in a factory. The Gutierrezes, who hailed from Puerto Rico, moved the family back to the island after Luis's freshman year of high school in 1968. After completing his early education, he enrolled at the University of Puerto Rico.[2]

While visiting friends in Chicago in the early 1970s, Gutierrez decided to transfer to Northeastern Illinois University. He graduated with a bachelor of arts degree in English in 1974 and returned to Puerto Rico, where he married Soraida Arocho and began teaching elementary school. He moved back to Chicago in 1978, taking a job as a social worker with the Illinois state department of children and family services. He left in 1983 to run for a position on the city council, losing that election before being hired by the Chicago mayor's office to work on infrastructure issues.[3] Gutierrez and his wife have two daughters: Omaira and Jessica.

In 1985 Gutierrez lived in a new ward, cofounded a grass-roots political organization, and embarked on another run for city council. The race involved a recount and a runoff, but Gutierrez prevailed and quickly became a force on the council for the next six years, championing "affordable housing, tougher ethics rules, and a law to ban discrimination based on sexual orientation."[4] He was named chairman of the council's housing committee and was appointed the board's president pro tempore.[5]

Gutierrez ran for a seat in the U.S. House of Representatives after Illinois redrew its district boundaries following the 1990 Census. Chicago's 4th District was famously "C-shaped"—some observers said it resembled "a snake or a pair of earmuffs"—and linked the city's two major Hispanic neighborhoods.[6] Inhabited by a mixture of white-collar and blue-collar residents working in transportation and manufacturing, the district as a whole was, and remains, overwhelmingly Democratic. Gutierrez announced his candidacy in late 1991 and won the Democratic primary in March of 1992. He promised to "commit … to being a commuter congressman," keeping his focus on Chicago rather than on "the back rooms of Washington, D.C." His platform included causes he had dealt with on the city council, including affordable housing, drug awareness, crime prevention, and tax policy.[7] With no incumbent in the race, Gutierrez dominated the general election, taking 76 percent of the vote.[8] Since 1992, Gutierrez has often run unopposed in the Democratic primary and has faced little competition in the general election.

Gutierrez has served on multiple committees in the House: the Committee on Financial Services (103rd–112th Congresses, 1993–2013); the Committee on Veterans' Affairs (103rd–109th Congresses, 1993–2007); the Committee on Foreign Affairs (103rd Congress, 1993–1995); the Judiciary Committee (110th–111th Congresses, 2007–2011); and the Permanent Select Committee on Intelligence (112th Congress, 2011–2013). His tenure on Financial Services has been marked by steady advancement. In the 110th Congress (2007–2009), Representative Gutierrez was chairman of the Committee on Financial Services' Subcommittee on Domestic and International Monetary Policy, Trade, and Technology. In the 111th Congress (2009–2011) he served as chairman of Financial Services' Subcommittee on Financial Institutions and Consumer Credit.[9]

Such assignments have allowed Gutierrez to pursue an ambitious legislative agenda, working to improve the nation's immigration policy, protecting the victims of sexual assault, and maintaining funding for health care research. He has also sought to combat congestion on Chicago's roadways by bolstering the city's mass transit services. Gutierrez has had perhaps his biggest influence on the Financial Services Committee, contributing to the overhaul of the nation's banking industry by shaping the Dodd–Frank Wall Street Reform Act and the Consumer Financial Protection Bureau. Gutierrez has been an active member of the Congressional Hispanic Caucus (CHC) during his time in Washington, spearheading its Immigration Task Force and encouraging minority employment throughout the banking sector.[10] Immigration reform has become a primary cause; Gutierrez once referred to it as his "unfinished business."[11]

FOR FURTHER READING

Biographical Directory of the United States Congress, "Luis V. Gutierrez," http://bioguide.congress.gov.

NOTES

1 Jim Tankersly, "Gutierrez's Last Immigration Stand," 21 May 2007, *Chicago Tribune*: C1.

2 Jorge Casuso and Ben Joravsky, "'El Gallito': Luis Gutierrez Carves a Major Role for Himself in Chicago Politics," 4 June 1989, *Chicago Tribune Sunday Magazine*: C10.

3 Casuso and Joravsky, "'El Gallito': Luis Gutierrez Carves a Major Role for Himself in Chicago Politics."

4 For more on the election, see Teresa Córdova, "Harold Washington and the Rise of Latino Electoral Politics in Chicago, 1982–1987," in David Montejano, ed., *Chicano Politics and Society in the Late Twentieth Century* (Austin: University of Texas Press, 1999): 31–57. "Official Biography of Congressman Luis V. Gutierrez," http://www.gutierrez.house.gov/index.php?option=com_content&view=article&id=450&Itemid=24 (accessed 23 April 2012).

5 For more on Gutierrez's council district and his term in office, see David K. Fremon, *Chicago Politics Ward by Ward* (Bloomington: University of Indiana Press, 1988): 171–178; Casuso and Joravsky, "'El Gallito': Luis Gutierrez Carves a Major Role for Himself in Chicago Politics."

6 Thomas Hardy, "Former Ald. Soliz Joins Crowded Congress Race," 6 December 1991, *Chicago Tribune*: C4; John Kass, "Gutierrez Picks Up Daley's Backing for Congress," 10 December 1991, *Chicago Tribune*: C3; Melita Marie Garza, "Winner Sure to Make History in Hispanic District," 28 September 1992, *Chicago Tribune*: C3.

7 Susan Kuczka, "Gutierrez Vows to Be 'Commuter' Congressman in Hispanic District," 9 December 1991, *Chicago Tribune*: C3.

8 Melita Marie Garza, "'Hispanic' District Really Isn't: 4th's Voter Rolls Primarily White," 5 February 1992, *Chicago Tribune*: C2; Steve Johnson, "Gutierrez Builds Big Lead Thanks to Non-Hispanics," 5 March 1992, *Chicago Tribune*: C1; Steve Johnson, "Reynolds, Lipinski Win," 18 March 1992, *Chicago Tribune*: C1; Steve Johnson, "Gutierrez Breezes to Victory," 4 November 1992, *Chicago Tribune*: N1; "Election Statistics, 1920 to Present," http://history.house.gov/institution/election-statistics/election-statistics.

9 See also Garrison Nelson and Charles Stewart III, *Committees in the U.S. Congress, 1993–2010* (Washington, D.C.: CQ Press, 2011): 739.

10 "Official Biography of Congressman Luis V. Gutierrez," http://www.gutierrez.house.gov/index.php?option=com_content&view=article&id=450&Itemid=24 (accessed 23 April 2012).

11 As quoted in *Politics in America, 2012* (Washington, D.C.: CQ-Roll Call, Inc., 2011): 320–321.

Image courtesy of the Member

Rubén Hinojosa

1940–

UNITED STATES REPRESENTATIVE 1997–
DEMOCRAT FROM TEXAS

Since 1997, when he took over the House seat previously held by a powerful Democratic committee chairman, Rubén Hinojosa has been a tireless champion in the U.S. Congress for progressive education policy. "We must refocus our energies on the unfinished business of providing for the education of our youth," he said in 2003, noting that Hispanic-American children were particularly at risk for being overlooked during national lawmaking. "If we do not invest in education and training for this emerging population, we put our nation's economic foundation at risk."[1]

Rubén Hinojosa was born on August 20, 1940, the eighth of 11 children, raised by Mexican immigrants who settled in Edcouch, Hidalgo County, Texas. Hinojosa's parents established a major food-distributing company in the Lower Rio Grande Valley. Their leadership in the business sector soon made them a powerful force in the Mercedes community of south Texas.[2] English was a second language for the entire Hinojosa family, and Rubén attended a segregated elementary school in South Texas before graduating from Mercedes High School. Education became his lifelong obsession. Hinojosa enrolled at the University of Texas, Austin, graduating with a bachelor's degree in business administration in 1962, and went on to earn a master's degree in business administration from the University of Texas–Pan American in Edinburg in 1980. His first marriage ended in divorce. He is married to Martha Lopez Hinojosa and has five children: Rubén, Jr.; Laura; Iliana; Kaitlin; and Karén.[3]

After college, Hinojosa went to work for his family's company, a prominent employer in the region, eventually serving as its chief executive. After a brief stint on the Mercedes school board from 1972 to 1974, Hinojosa was elected to the Texas state board of education, where he served until 1984. He returned to the University of Texas–Pan American as an adjunct professor in its business school and was elected chairman of the board for South Texas Community College in 1993.[4]

In early 1996, long-serving Texas Democrat Eligio (Kika) de la Garza announced his retirement from the U.S. House of Representatives. His predominantly rural and Hispanic 15th District stretched northward from the U.S. border with Mexico, curving up and to the east between San Antonio and Corpus Christi.[5] Given Hinojosa's prominent position in South Texas' business community and his respected work on the board of education, he emerged as an early front-runner to replace the longtime chairman of the House Agriculture

Committee. He made education initiatives in South Texas his top campaign priority and promised to "support legislation that benefits the small and large businesses" throughout the Rio Grande Valley.[6] In the race to fill the 15th District seat, Hinojosa failed to capture a majority in the Democratic primary but took the runoff election in early April 1996.[7] Hinojosa cruised to an easy victory in the general election later that fall.[8] Since 1996, he has either run unopposed or faced nominal opposition in the primary and general elections.

In the House, Hinojosa has spent the majority of his career on the Committee on Education and the Workforce (renamed the Committee on Education and Labor from 2007 to 2011) and the Committee on Financial Services. He has also served for briefer periods on the Small Business Committee (105th–107th Congresses, 1997–2003), the Resources Committee (108th Congress, 2003–2005), and the Foreign Affairs Committee (110th Congress, 2007–2009).[9]

When Democrats gained control of the House at the start of the 110th Congress, Hinojosa was appointed chairman of the Education and Labor Committee's Subcommittee on Higher Education, Lifelong Learning, and Competitiveness. His leadership on national education policy has helped many of the country's underprivileged communities gain access to better schools and resources, which he has long believed would generate broader economic stability. "We must have an educated work force if we are to build upon initiatives such as the Rio Grande Valley Empowerment Zone to enhance our economy and create jobs," he said not long after winning his first election.[10] In recognition of his efforts, the Congressional Hispanic Caucus (CHC) named him chairman of its educational task force.[11] Hinojosa also has worked tirelessly to reform the country's immigration policy to open paths to citizenship, and he has attempted to illuminate the inner workings of the country's financial system.[12] In 2006 Hinojosa admitted that he probably works too much, "but I take my job very seriously," he quickly followed up, "and approach it with passion."[13]

FOR FURTHER READING

Biographical Directory of the United States Congress, "Rubén Hinojosa," http://bioguide.congress.gov.

NOTES

1 Rubén Hinojosa, "Hispanics' Prosperity Depends on Education: Key Programs Need More Money," 3 September 2003, *The Hill*: 30.

2 "Footnotes," 31 October 1999, *Houston Chronicle*: State, 2.

3 *Biographical Directory of the United States Congress*, "Rubén Hinojosa," http://bioguide.congress.gov; "Official Biography of Congressman Rubén Hinojosa," http://hinojosa.house.gov/biography (accessed 10 May 2012); *Politics in America, 2012* (Washington, D.C.: CQ-Roll Call, Inc., 2011): 947; *Almanac of American Politics, 2012* (Washington, D.C.: University of Chicago Press, 2011): 1570–1571. See also Emily Cahn, "Hinojosa Puts Education First," 6 April 2011, *The Hill*.

4 *Biographical Directory of the United States Congress*, "Rubén Hinojosa," http://bioguide.congress.gov; "Official Educational Biography of Congressman Rubén Hinojosa," http://hinojosa.house.gov/about-me/educational-biography (accessed 10 May 2012); *Politics in America, 2012*: 947.

5 *Politics in America, 1998* (Washington, D.C.: Congressional Quarterly, Inc., 1997): 1404; *Politics in America, 2012*: 947.

6 Gary Martin, "Hinojosa to Seek Input on Education Proposal," 18 February 1997, *San Antonio Express-News*: B1; Gary Martin, "Hinojosa Named to Education Committee," 26 November 1996, *San Antonio Express-News*: A8.

7 Catalina Camia, "Primaries Set Stage for Fight to Control Congressional Delegation," 11 March 1996, *Dallas Morning News*: A10; "Primary '96," 14 March 1996, *Houston Chronicle*: A36; Stefanie Scott, "Ex-Demo Laughlin Loses GOP Runoff Bid," 10 April 1996, *San Antonio Express-News*: A1.

8 "Election Statistics, 1920 to Present," http://history.house.gov/institution/election-statistics/election-statistics.

9 Garrison Nelson and Charles Stewart III, *Committees in the U.S. Congress, 1993–2010* (Washington, D.C.: CQ Press, 2011): 757.

10 Martin, "Hinojosa Named to Education Committee."

11 *Politics in America, 2006* (Washington, D.C.: CQ Press, 2005): 994.

12 "Official Financial Literacy Biography of Rubén Hinojosa," http://hinojosa.house.gov/about-me/financial-literacy-biography (accessed 10 May 2012); *Politics in America, 2012*: 947–948.

13 Cameron Joseph, "What Is Your Greatest Vice?," 21 September 2006, *The Hill*: 24.

Image courtesy of the Member

Ben Ray Luján

1972–

UNITED STATES REPRESENTATIVE 2009–

DEMOCRAT FROM NEW MEXICO

Ben Ray Luján won election to the U.S. House of Representatives from his hometown district in northern New Mexico in 2008, continuing a family tradition of public service highlighted by his father, a speaker of the New Mexico state house. The younger Luján has become a vocal advocate for American Indian and Hispanic communities as well as for alternative energy and technology industries. "We need to out-educate and out-innovate the rest of the world in order to grow our economy and put people back to work," Luján has said.[1]

Ben Ray Luján was born June 7, 1972, in Santa Fe, New Mexico, to Carmen and Ben Luján. The family—the future Representative, his brother, and their two sisters—lived in the small community of Nambé, about 20 miles north of Santa Fe. His mother worked in the local schools, and his father was an ironworker before entering politics.[2] Following his graduation from Pojoaque High School in 1990, Luján attended the University of New Mexico in Albuquerque. After working in human resources at an Albuquerque racetrack and casino, Luján entered public service as deputy state treasurer in 2002. A year later, he became director of administrative services and chief financial officer for the New Mexico department of cultural affairs. In 2004 he was elected to the state public regulation commission, a watchdog for utilities and insurance companies, and served as its chairman. Three years later, Luján completed his bachelor's degree in business administration at New Mexico Highlands University.[3]

Luján began his campaign for the U.S. House in December 2007 after incumbent Democratic Representative Tom Udall announced his bid for the U.S. Senate. The seat, which includes Santa Fe and most of northern New Mexico, had been held by a Democrat for all but one year since its creation in 1982.[4] In a six-way primary campaign, Luján defeated his closest Democratic competitor by nearly 16 percent before capturing the November 2008 general election with 57 percent of the vote.[5] Luján was unopposed in the 2010 Democratic primary and won re-election that fall with 57 percent of the vote.[6]

In the 111th Congress (2009–2011), Luján served on the Homeland Security and Science and Technology Committees. He was also a member of the Congressional Hispanic Caucus (CHC), the Native American Caucus, and the Sustainable Energy and Environment Coalition.[7] He introduced legislation to train workers for jobs in sustainable energy industries, and he has sought to help consumers lower their utility costs by improving access to solar panels and other energy saving devices. Similarly, Luján has worked to strengthen "net-metering," a practice energy companies use to reimburse consumers for the wattage they produce at home. He has also sponsored legislation that would create an environmental research park at Los Alamos National Laboratories, which is located in his district.[8] "With investments in renewable energy," Lujan said during his first term, "we can create jobs in a variety of industries across New Mexico."[9] In October 2009, *Hispanic Business Magazine* named him one of the 100 most influential Hispanics in the country.[10]

Luján served on the Natural Resources and Science, Space, and Technology Committees during the 112th Congress (2011–2013). He continued his advocacy for the Los Alamos National Laboratory and alternative energy development. Luján was also elected second vice chair of the CHC, was co-chair of the Technology Transfer Caucus, and continued his membership with the Native American Caucus and Sustainable Energy and Environment Coalition.[11] "I am humbled my colleagues have entrusted me with this position," Luján said after being elected to the CHC's leadership. "I look forward to working on issues of importance to the Hispanic community including empowering students through educational opportunities, strengthening small businesses and our middle class, and looking out for our seniors and veterans."[12]

FOR FURTHER READING

Biographical Directory of the United States Congress, "Ben Ray Luján," http://bioguide.congress.gov.

NOTES

1 "Official Biography of Congressman Ben Ray Luján," http://lujan.house.gov/index.php?option=com_content&view=article&id=47&Itemid=54 (accessed 30 April 2012); *Congressional Record*, House, 112th Cong., 1st sess. (16 February 2011): H988.

2 Jessica Dyer, "Immigration among Differences; Nominees Agree on Little in Dist. 3," 10 October 2010, *Albuquerque Journal*: 1.

3 Kate Nash, "Luján: Happy to Follow N.M. House Speaker Dad, Points to Work on Public Regulatory Commission," 18 May 2008, *Santa Fe New Mexican*: A8.

4 "Election Statistics, 1920 to Present," http://history.house.gov/institution/election-statistics/election-statistics.

5 "Canvass of Returns of Primary Election Held on June 3, 2008," State of New Mexico, http://www.sos.state.nm.us/sos-2008PrimResults.html; "Election Statistics, 1920 to Present," http://history.house.gov/institution/election-statistics/election-statistics.

6 "Election Statistics, 1920 to Present," http://history.house.gov/institution/election-statistics/election-statistics.

7 *Congressional Directory*, 111th Congress (Washington, D.C.: Government Printing Office, 2009): 176.

8 Michael Coleman, "House OKs Landmark Energy Bill," 27 June 2009, *Albuquerque Journal*: A1; Steve Terrell, "U.S. House: Luján Poised to Make Mark," 8 September 2009, *Santa Fe New Mexican*: A1; *Politics in America, 2012* (Washington, D.C.: CQ-Roll Call, Inc., 2011): 654; Michael Coleman, "Rep. Lujan Chalks up Victory for Labs," 3 August 2009, *Albuquerque Journal*: A6.

9 "Around Northern New Mexico," 30 June 2009, *Albuquerque Journal*: 5.

10 Carol A. Clark, "Luján Named amongst Influentials," 9 October 2009, *Los Alamos Monitor*, http://www.lamonitor.com/content/lujan-named-amongst-influentials (accessed 30 April 2012).

11 *Congressional Directory*, 112th Congress (Washington, D.C.: Government Printing Office, 2011): 177; Congressional Hispanic Caucus, "Caucus Membership," http://chc-gonzalez.house.gov/membership (accessed 2 May 2012).

12 Congressional Hispanic Caucus, "Congressional Hispanic Caucus Elects Leadership for the 112th Congress," 18 November 2010, http://chc-gonzalez.house.gov/press-release/congressional-hispanic-caucus-elects-leadership-112th-congress (accessed 2 May 2012).

Image courtesy of the Member

Robert Menendez

1954–

UNITED STATES REPRESENTATIVE 1993–2006
UNITED STATES SENATOR 2006–
DEMOCRAT FROM NEW JERSEY

The son of Cuban immigrants with a keen mind for foreign policy, Robert Menendez rose steadily through the world of New Jersey politics to fulfill his childhood dream of becoming a United States Senator. "I have walked in the shoes of the average New Jerseyan all of my life," Menendez said in 2005, "and I know the challenges they face."[1]

Robert Menendez was born on January 1, 1954, in New York City, one of three children born to Mario, a carpenter, and Evangelina Menendez, a seamstress. The couple emigrated from Havana, Cuba, to New York, eventually settling across the Hudson River in Union City, New Jersey. Menendez graduated from Union Hill High School in 1972 and went on to earn his bachelor's degree in political science from St. Peter's College in Jersey City in 1976. Three years later, he was awarded a J.D. from Rutgers University's School of Law in Newark. Menendez is divorced, with two children, Alicia and Robert, Jr.

Menendez became involved in community issues early on, and in college he won a spot on the Union City Board of Education. He served on the school board from 1974 to 1978, and once he completed his law degree, he took a job with Union City's mayor. After racketeering charges were leveled against his boss, Menendez ran for mayor in 1982 but lost to his embattled mentor. Four years later, he ran again and won; he served as mayor until 1992. Beginning in 1987, Menendez also served in the state assembly, stepping down in 1991 when he was appointed to a vacant state senate seat; he was elected to a full term later that year.[2]

Congressional redistricting in 1992 created a majority-Hispanic district in northern New Jersey, running along the Hudson River from North Bergen to Perth Amboy. That year incumbent Representative Frank J. Guarini, Jr., declined to seek re-election, clearing a path for Menendez.[3] Menendez defeated the mayor of Jersey City in the Democratic primary and won the general election with 64.3 percent of the vote, becoming the first Hispanic elected to represent New Jersey in the U.S. Congress. Menendez easily topped Republican opponents in each subsequent re-election campaign for the House, securing between 70 and 80 percent of the vote.[4]

Menendez served on two standing committees in the House: Public Works and Transportation (later renamed Transportation and Infrastructure) and Foreign Affairs (later renamed International Relations). From the 107th until he left the House in the 109th Congress (2001–2006), he was Ranking

Member of the International Relations Committee's Western Hemisphere Subcommittee. He sought to bolster state building initiatives in Latin America and supported the United States' travel and trade restrictions against Cuba's communist government.[5] On Public Works and Transportation, Menendez emerged as a leading proponent of public mass transit and of a new commuter tunnel connecting New Jersey to Manhattan under the Hudson River. In 2001 party leadership appointed him to chair the Democratic Homeland Security Taskforce; a year later he joined the new Select Committee on Homeland Security for the 107th Congress (2001–2003).[6] In addition to his committee duties, Menendez served as one of the Democrats' chief deputy whips (105th Congress, 1997–1999) and as vice chair of the House Democratic Caucus (106th–107th Congresses, 1998–2002). In late 2002, he became the first Hispanic Member to chair the House Democratic Caucus.

In 2005 Senator Jon S. Corzine won his bid for Governor of New Jersey and announced that he would appoint Menendez to his vacant Senate seat. Menendez was sworn in as the junior Senator from New Jersey on January 18, 2006. That fall in the general election he defeated his Republican challenger by 9 points in the contest for the full six-year term.[7]

In the Senate, Menendez has served on five committees: Banking, Housing, and Urban Affairs (109th–112th Congresses, 2006–2013); Budget (109th–111th Congresses, 2006–2011); Energy and Natural Resources (109th–111th Congresses); Foreign Relations (110th–112th Congresses, 2007–2013); and Finance (111th–112th Congresses, 2009–2013). He currently chairs the Banking Committee's Subcommittee on Housing, Transportation and Community Development and the Foreign Relations' Subcommittee on Western Hemisphere, Peace Corps, and Global Narcotics Affairs. He has remained a hawk on Cuba, challenged America's military operations in Iraq, and opposes efforts to privatize Social Security and Medicare.[8] Respected as a prodigious organizer and fundraiser, Menendez was named as Chairman of the Democratic Senatorial Campaign Committee in November 2008 and held this position for the 111th Congress (2009–2011).[9] He currently serves as Chairman of the Democratic Hispanic Task Force.

FOR FURTHER READING

Biographical Directory of the United States Congress, "Robert Menendez," http://bioguide.congress.gov.

NOTES

1 David W. Chen, "Menendez Basks in Appointment to the Senate, if Only Briefly," 10 December 2005, *New York Times*: B6

2 Jeffrey Gettleman, "William Musto, 88, a Mayor Re-Elected on His Way to Jail," 1 March 2006, *New York Times*: 16.

3 "Menendez to Seek Congressional Seat," 8 April 1992, *New York Times*: B4.

4 "Election Statistics, 1920 to Present," http://history.house.gov/institution/election-statistics/election-statistics.

5 Alain L. Sanders, "Crafting an American Agenda for Hispanics and for the Nation: Interview with Congressman Robert Menendez (D-NJ)," *Harvard Journal of Hispanic Policy* 16 (2003–2004): 19–29.

6 Miguel Perez, "Menendez Says Nation Must Guard Its People and Their Rights," 10 October 2001, *The Record*: A11.

7 CQ Press, *Guide to U.S. Elections,* sixth edition, vol. 2 (Washington, D.C.: CQ Press, 2009): 1456.

8 "Official Biography of Senator Robert Menendez," http://www.menendez.senate.gov/biography/ (accessed 2 May 2012).

9 Emily Pierce, "A Super Day; Menendez Rises, Shines," 28 August 2008, *Roll Call*, 36; David M. Herszenhorn, "Schumer Out, Menendez In," 25 November 2008, *New York Times*: 20.

Image courtesy of the Member

Grace Flores Napolitano
1936–

UNITED STATES REPRESENTATIVE 1999–
DEMOCRAT FROM CALIFORNIA

Grace Napolitano entered community politics in the 1980s, built wide name recognition as a city mayor and California assemblywoman, and won election to the U.S. House in 1998. In Washington, Napolitano has focused on water, mental health, transportation, and securing federal dollars for her district.

Graciela (Grace) Flores was born in Brownsville, Texas, on December 4, 1936, to Miguel Flores and Maria Alicia (Ledezma) Flores. After graduating from Brownsville High School in 1954, she married Federico Musquiz and had five children: Yolanda, Federico, Edward, Miguel, and Cynthia. The family moved to Southern California, where she continued her education at Cerritos College. In 1982, several years after her first husband passed away, she married California restaurateur Frank Napolitano. The two live in the Los Angeles suburb of Norwalk in the home Grace has maintained for more than 50 years.

Napolitano worked for four years for the California Department of Employment before moving to Ford Motor Co., where she spent 22 years. In 1974 Napolitano was appointed a commissioner on the International Friendship Commission, a sister city program in which Norwalk was paired with the Mexican town of Hermosillo. The program focused on cultural exchanges, and the experience pulled Napolitano into public service.[1]

In 1986 Napolitano was first elected to the Norwalk City Council by a 28-vote margin. Four years later, she won her second term by the largest margin in city history. In 1989 Napolitano's council colleagues elevated her to mayor. In 1992 she was elected to the California Assembly, where she served until 1998. There she emerged as a leader on international trade, environmental protection, transportation, and immigration issues. Napolitano earned a reputation as a champion for small business, women, economic expansion, and job creation. She chaired the Women's Caucus and the International Trade Committee and served as vice chair of the Latino Caucus.

In 1998, upon the retirement of Representative Esteban Torres, Napolitano entered the primary race to succeed him. She used $200,000 of her retirement funds and drew from the political base of her assembly district, which encompassed much of the largely Hispanic middle-class Democratic congressional district. She won the primary by 619 votes and captured the general election with 67 percent of the vote. Napolitano has been re-elected six times, running unopposed in 2004 and winning her other elections by margins of 70 percent or higher in a district stretching from East Los Angeles to Pomona.[2]

Napolitano has served on the Natural Resources Committee since entering the House in January 1999. In the 106th Congress (1999–2001), she also served on the Small Business Committee. In the 107th Congress (2001–2003), she won an additional post on the International Relations Committee. In the 110th Congress (2007–2009), she took a seat on the Transportation and Infrastructure Committee, where she still sits. Napolitano was unanimously selected chair of the Congressional Hispanic Caucus for a two-year term during the 109th Congress (2005–2007).[3] She also serves as co-chair of the Congressional Mental Health Caucus, having been prompted to take action on the issue by a report showing that Latina teenagers have the highest suicide rate of any ethnic or racial group in the country. Napolitano is focused on the effect of post-traumatic stress disorder on our troops and on seniors suffering from depression.

Constituent service tops Napolitano's congressional agenda. "As far as passing legislation, that is not the main reason I went to Washington," Napolitano said. "I want to be able to open the doors like I have at the county and state level."[4] Napolitano also has worked with the Small Business Administration assisting minorities to gain financial assistance to grow their businesses.

On the Natural Resources Committee, Napolitano worked with the U.S. Energy Department to clean up a 10-million-ton uranium tailings pile in Utah that leaches into the Colorado River, which is the source of one-third of Southern California's drinking supply. She also has teamed with regional members of Congress to help secure $55 million in federal funds to continue the cleanup of key Superfund sites in Los Angeles-area aquifers. In the 110th and 111th Congresses (2007–2011), she chaired the Natural Resources Subcommittee on Water and Power, and she is currently its Ranking Member. Napolitano's major accomplishments on the Transportation Committee have been securing funding for the Alameda Corridor East project, the I-5 freeway expansion, separating railroads from roadways to reduce accidents and congestion, purchasing clean-energy buses for local cities, and extending the Metro Gold Line into East Los Angeles.

FOR FURTHER READING

Biographical Directory of the United States Congress, "Grace Flores Napolitano," http://bioguide.congress.gov.

Polanco, Richard G. and Grace Napolitano. *Making Immigration Policy Work in the United States* (Sacramento: California Latino Legislative Caucus, 1993).

NOTES

1 *Politics in America, 2002* (Washington, D.C.: Congressional Quarterly, Inc., 2001): 129.

2 "Election Statistics, 1920 to Present," http://history.house.gov/institution/election-statistics/election-statistics.

3 "Napolitano Selected to Lead Congressional Hispanic Caucus," 18 November 2004, http://www.napolitano.house.gov/press_releases/pr111804.htm (accessed 29 December 2004).

4 Norah M. O'Donnell, "The Votes Are In After Battling Torres, Napolitano Claims His Seat," 15 June 1998, *Roll Call.*

Image courtesy of the Member

Devin Nunes

1973–

UNITED STATES REPRESENTATIVE 2003–
REPUBLICAN FROM CALIFORNIA

In 2002 Devin Nunes told a group of high school students, "All I wanted to be was a dairy farmer."[1] Later that fall, however, he won election to the U.S. House of Representatives from California's 21st District, starting a career that has made him a powerful figure in the national legislature.

The first of two sons, Devin Nunes was born in Tulare, California, on October 1, 1973, to Anthony and Diane Nunes, second-generation Portuguese-American dairy farmers in California's Central Valley.[2] He grew up working the family farm and graduated from Tulare Union High School. He then earned an associate's degree from the College of the Sequoias in Visalia, California. In 1995 he graduated from California Polytechnic with a bachelor's of science degree in agricultural business. The next year he completed a master's of science degree in agriculture.[3] After school Nunes returned to farming. He is married to Elizabeth Tamariz; together they have three daughters: Evelyn, Julia, and Margaret.[4]

Nunes's first political victory occurred almost by accident. In 1996 after a candidate vying for a seat on the board of the College of the Sequoias backed out, Nunes, then only 22 years old, decided to run at the last minute and won. In 1998 he set his sights on Washington and ran as a Republican for California's 20th District seat in the U.S. House of Representatives. He lost that year in the primary election, but in 2001 Nunes was appointed the California Director of Rural Development for the U.S. Department of Agriculture.[5]

Redistricting by the California assembly following the 2000 Census created an open district encompassing Nunes's hometown in the San Joaquin Valley.[6] The new 21st District is one of the most productive agricultural regions in the country and is solidly Republican. Because of his previous tenure in public office, Nunes entered the GOP primary with an early advantage over his opponents. On the campaign trail, he made water use and access his foremost priority, with trade, job creation, and health care running close behind. He won the primary before crushing his Democratic opponent in the general election.[7] "I'm most proud of growing up in a country where a son of recent immigrants can actually be elected to the United States Congress," he said shortly after being sworn in as the second-youngest Member of the House at the time.[8] Since 2002, Nunes has won by lopsided margins in general elections.

Nunes has sat on varied and powerful committees: Agriculture (108th–109th Congresses, 2003–2007); Resources (108th–109th Congresses, 2003–2007);

Veterans' Affairs (briefly in the 109th Congress, 2005–2007); Budget (111th Congress, 2009–2011); Ways and Means (109th–112th Congresses, 2005–2013); and the Permanent Select Committee on Intelligence (112th Congress, 2011–2013).[9] With large swaths of federal parkland surrounding his district, Nunes was appointed chairman of the Resources Committee's Subcommittee on National Parks, Recreation, and Public Lands in his sophomore term.[10]

Managing California's water supply, which Nunes once called "the most important issue facing the Valley and the state," has been at the forefront of his agenda.[11] He has sought funding for studies and dam projects along the San Joaquin River and has worked to bolster state and federal programs that manage California's water resources. He has fought to assist the dairy industry in his home district, supported timber harvesting in nearby national parks to prevent wildfires, and spearheaded efforts to fund programs working to curb drug trafficking in central California.[12] Trade and transportation have also been key considerations during Nunes's career, and he has worked to improve the condition of Highway 99, his district's major thoroughfare.[13]

Nunes has quietly emerged as one of the more influential members of his party. Republican leadership appointed him assistant Majority Whip during his first term, and he has positions on influential committees and caucuses, including his current appointment as vice chairman of the National Republican Congressional Committee. He is also a member of the Congressional Hispanic Conference.[14]

FOR FURTHER READING

Biographical Directory of the United States Congress, "Devin Nunes," http://bioguide.congress.gov.

NOTES

1 Justin Stoner, "Nunes Holds Advantages in Race for 21st Congressional District," 4 November 2002, *Fresno Bee*: A1.

2 Rick Elkins, "Mr. Nunes Goes to Washington," 1 January 2003, *Tulare Advance-Register*: A1.

3 *Biographical Directory of the United States Congress*, "Devin Nunes," http://bioguide.congress.gov; Elkins, "Mr. Nunes Goes to Washington"; Tim Sheehan, "Nunes Learns to Navigate Congress," 18 October 2004, *Fresno Bee*: B1; Charles Case, "House Call," 6 September 2005, *The Hill*: 23.

4 Lewis Griswold, "Nunes Pops Question; She Says Yes," 2 July 2003, *Fresno Bee*: B1; *Politics in America, 2006* (Washington, D.C.: CQ Press, 2005): 112; Marty Burleson, "Rep. Devin Nunes and Wife Get an Election Day Delivery — a Baby Girl!," 4 November 2009, *Tulare Advance-Register*: A1.

5 *Politics in America, 2000* (Washington, D.C.: Congressional Quarterly, Inc., 1999): 139; *Biographical Directory of the United States Congress*, "Devin Nunes," http://bioguide.congress.gov; Jim Steinberg, "Unruh Gets News at 2 A.M.—He'll Face Dooley in November," 4 June 1998, *Fresno Bee*: A14.

6 Elkins, "Mr. Nunes Goes to Washington."

7 Stoner, "Nunes Holds Advantages in Race for 21st Congressional District"; Cindy Carcamo, "Nunes Dishes up Issues at Gathering," 26 April 2003, *Fresno Bee*: B1; "Election Statistics, 1920 to Present," http://history.house.gov/institution/election-statistics/election-statistics.

8 Michael Doyle, "Nunes Hits the Office Running," 8 January 2003, *Fresno Bee*: B1.

9 Nunes had been reserved a seat on the Ways and Means Committee to begin the 109th Congress, but could not formally join the panel until a spot opened. He officially took his seat on Ways and Means on May 5, 2005. See Lewis Griswold, "Golden West Kicks Out Soccer League; Power Perch: It's Official," 6 May 2005, *Fresno Bee*: B1; Michael Doyle, "Valley Loses Key Parks Position on Capitol Hill," 10 May 2005, *Fresno Bee*: B5.

10 Garrison Nelson and Charles Stewart III, *Committees in the U.S. Congress, 1993–2010* (Washington, D.C.: CQ Press, 2011): 873.

11 Bethany Clough, "Valley Water Projects Advance," 19 July 2003, *Fresno Bee*: A1.

12 Kerri Ginis, "Hearing to Study Valley Water Needs," 26 June 2003, *Fresno Bee*: B1; Laura Florez, "Farmers: Build Another Dam," 30 June 2003, *Tulare Advance-Register*: A1; *Politics in America, 2008* (Washington, D.C.: Congressional Quarterly, Inc., 2007): 112; Michael Doyle, "Congress to Look at Sierra Drug Role," 8 October 2003, *Fresno Bee:* B1; Michael Doyle, "White House Helps Valley's Drug Battle," 25 August 2006, *Fresno Bee:* B4.

13 "Official Biography of Congressman Devin Nunes," http://nunes.house.gov/Biography/ (accessed 5 May 2012); Amee Thompson, "Nunes Pushes to Widen Hwy. 99," 15 March 2003, *Visalia Times-Delta*: C1; Bethany Clough, "$158m Sought to Widen Hwy. 99; Plan Would Add a Third Lane from Tulare to Kingsburg," 15 March 2003, *Fresno Bee*: A1.

14 *Congressional Staff Directory, Spring 2010* (Washington, D.C.: CQ Press, 2010): 589; "Congressman Devin Nunes," Congressional Hispanic Conference, http://canseco.house.gov/CHC/Members/RepNunes.htm (accessed 4 June 2012).

Image courtesy of the Member

Ed Pastor

1943–

UNITED STATES REPRESENTATIVE 1991–
DEMOCRAT FROM ARIZONA

As the dean of Arizona's House delegation—and the state's first Hispanic American elected to Congress—Ed Pastor has set many milestones during his career. But while he acknowledges the gains Hispanics have made in the House, Pastor keeps his focus on the task at hand. "The fact is I am Hispanic, the fact is there is a lot of pride in the Hispanic community. And I join the enthusiasm," he said after first winning election in 1991, "but as an elected official you represent the entire community."[1]

The oldest of three children, Ed López Pastor was born on June 28, 1943, to Enrique and Margarita Pastor. He grew up in the copper mine town of Claypool, Arizona, and attended the public schools in nearby Miami, Arizona.[2] Pastor received a scholarship to Arizona State University in Tempe and became the first in his family to go to college, earning a bachelor's degree in chemistry in 1966. He took a teaching job at North High School in Phoenix after graduation, but left in 1969 to become deputy director of the community nonprofit Guadalupe Organization, Inc. He served as vice president of the Maricopa Legal Aid Society in 1971 and returned to school, earning his J.D. in 1974 from Arizona State College of Law in Tempe. He then joined the staff of Arizona's first Hispanic governor, Raul Héctor Castro, and worked on civil rights and equal opportunity issues. Pastor is married to Verma Mendez Pastor. They have two daughters, Laura and Yvonne, and four grandchildren.[3]

In 1976 Pastor, seeking to build on his time with the governor's office, won election as a Democrat to the Maricopa County Board of Supervisors. When 15-term Representative Morris Udall resigned from the U.S. House of Representatives in May 1991, Pastor stepped down from the county board to enter the race for the open seat. Facing four other challengers, including Tucson Mayor Tom Volgy, Pastor won the special Democratic primary that August with 37 percent of the vote. He then defeated Republican Pat Conner in the special general election on September 24, 1991, with 56 percent.[4] Despite redistricting after the 2000 Census, Pastor has won each of his 10 succeeding elections with more than 62 percent of the vote.[5]

Pastor's committee assignments in the House have been notably powerful: the Education and Labor Committee (102nd Congress, 1991–1993); the Small Business Committee (102nd Congress); the Appropriations Committee (103rd Congress, 1993–1995; 105th–112th Congresses, 1997–2013); the Agriculture Committee (104th Congress, 1995–1997); the House Oversight Committee

(104th Congress, 1995–1997); and the Standards of Official Conduct Committee (105th Congress–107th Congresses, 1997–2003). He was also a member of the House Select Committee on Aging during the 102nd Congress. In addition to his committee duties, Pastor served as chairman of the Congressional Hispanic Caucus (CHC) in the 104th Congress, and in 1999 Democratic leaders tapped Pastor to be one of the party's chief deputy whips—a position he continues to hold.

In his two decades in the House, Pastor has supported a variety of issues concerning his district, but immigration and education reform have been the two causes he is most passionate about. Since 2001 Pastor has advocated for the Development, Relief, and Education for Alien Minors (DREAM) Act. The bill, he said on the House Floor, "would create a pathway to citizenship for undocumented young people, who were brought to the U.S. as children, raised in this country, have excelled in our education systems, and have expressed a clear commitment to pursue higher education or military service."[6] From his post on Appropriations, Pastor has also championed numerous infrastructure projects in his home state, especially those concerned with energy development, water access, and mass transit.[7] "Whatever my constituents ask for, I try to meet their needs," he told an Arizona newspaper in 2009. "When you're an appropriator, obviously, you are able to do things, so I try to help as much as I can."[8] He has supported many of the Southwest's environmental programs, and he has been a frequent advocate for Arizona's American Indian communities.[9] On the national level, Pastor has backed the North American Free Trade Agreement in 1993 (Public Law 103-182), the Children's Health Insurance Program Reauthorization Act of 2009 (Public Law 111-3), and the Patient Protection and Affordable Care Act of 2010 (Public Law 111-148).

FOR FURTHER READING

Biographical Directory of the United States Congress, "Ed Pastor," http://bioguide.congress.gov.

MANUSCRIPT COLLECTION

Arizona State University Libraries, Chicano Research Collection, Hayden Library (Tempe, AZ). *Papers*: 1977–1992, amount unknown. The collection consists of correspondence, reports, budget records and appointment books from Edward Pastor's political career dating back to 1977. These papers contain a record of Pastor's efforts to provide a voice for the Mexican-American community in Arizona. The papers also document his years as a member of the Maricopa County Board of Supervisors and include examples of his efforts to represent his constituency. Additionally, there are a number of congressional research papers on domestic and foreign issues. A guide to the papers is available in the repository.

NOTES

1 "Hispanic Candidate Elected to Congress from Arizona," 26 September 1991, *New York Times*: B12.

2 *Congressional Directory*, 106th Congress (Washington D.C.: Government Printing Office, 1999): 11.

3 "Official Biography of Congressman Ed Pastor," http://www.pastor.house.gov/index.php?option=com_content&view=article&id=77&Itemid=84, (accessed 2 May 2012).

4 Maralee Schwartz, "Hispanic Victor in Primary Likely to Succeed Udall," 15 August 1991, *Washington Post*: A9; Karen Foerstel, "Pastor Victory in Arizona Narrower than Expected," 26 September 1991, *Roll Call*; Maralee Schwartz and Lou Cannon, "More Hispanics in Office," 29 September 1991, *Washington Post*: A14; Mary Benanti and Desda Moss, "Hispanic to Fill Udall's Seat in the U.S. House," 3 October 1991, *USA Today*: A9.

5 "Election Statistics, 1920 to Present," http://history.house.gov/institution/election-statistics/election-statistics.

6 *Congressional Record*, House, 111th Cong., 2nd sess. (8 December 2010): H8227.

7 *Politics in America, 2012* (Washington, D.C.: CQ-Roll Call, Inc., 2011): 36.

8 Dan Nowicki, "Rep. Pastor Doesn't Shy away from Earmarks," 11 March 2009, *The Arizona Republic*: 1.

9 Garry Duffy, "Locals Back O'odham Push for Citizenship," 8 August 2001, *Tucson Citizen*: C4; Judith Graham, "Border Crackdown Vexes Tribe," 30 December 2001, *Chicago Tribune*: C14; Shaun McKinnon and Billy House, "Historic AZ Water Deal: Congress OKs Settlement Empowering Tribes," 18 November 2004, *The Arizona Republic*: A1; Billy House, "Tribes Getting Back Land After 90 Years," 3 August 2005, *The Arizona Republic*: B1; *Politics in America, 2000* (Washington, D.C.: Congressional Quarterly, Inc.: 1999): 49–50.

Image courtesy of the Member

Pedro Pierluisi

1959–

RESIDENT COMMISSIONER 2009–
NEW PROGRESSIVE FROM PUERTO RICO

According to Pedro Pierluisi, Puerto Rico's Resident Commissioner in the U.S. House of Representatives, "Puerto Rico's relationship with the United States is as close as it is complex." "But like so many American stories, this is a chronicle of progress and a determined march towards a more perfect union," he said early in the 111th Congress (2009–2011). "For me, as for millions of my constituents, the pride we feel in being Puerto Rican is matched by the pride we feel in being American citizens."[1]

Pedro R. Pierluisi was born in San Juan, Puerto Rico, on April 26, 1959, to Jorge Pierluisi, a former Puerto Rican housing secretary, and Doris Urrutia.[2] After completing his early studies, Pierluisi attended Tulane University in New Orleans, Louisiana, graduating with a bachelor's degree in U.S. history in 1981. He moved to the nation's capital to attend law school at George Washington University, earning a J.D. in 1984. He remained in Washington, D.C., and worked as an aide to former Puerto Rican Resident Commissioner Baltasar Corrada-del Río before joining a law firm in the city. He is married to Maria Elena Carrión and has four children.[3]

After six years as a litigator in an internationally recognized law firm, Pierluisi moved back to Puerto Rico, and in 1993 he was appointed the island's Secretary of Justice (otherwise known as the Attorney General).[4] In his three years as Puerto Rico's top lawyer, Pierluisi worked to uncover and end corruption in the insular government and earned a reputation for his tireless efforts to fight crime. (His younger brother was murdered during a carjacking near their parents' San Juan home in 1994.) Later, he worked with officials in Congress to strengthen national crime prevention policies, and returned to private law practice in 1996.[5]

In 2008, Pierluisi was nominated for the Office of Resident Commissioner after incumbent Republican Luis G. Fortuño decided to run for governor of Puerto Rico. The Resident Commissioner is the sole representative for the Commonwealth of Puerto Rico and the interests of its nearly four million residents. Unemployment and poverty have long plagued the Caribbean island, and since the mid-20th century, its relationship with the federal government has been the driving force behind political debates there. As a member of the Partido Nuevo Progresista (New Progressive Party, or PNP), Pierluisi campaigned behind calls for statehood and full participation in federal aid programs and defeated his opponent from the Partido Popular Democrático (Popular Democratic Party, or PPD) in the general election.[6] Neither of Puerto

Rico's two major political parties has an official affiliation on the mainland, and Pierluisi has caucused with the Democratic Party in the House.

Resident Commissioners serve four-year terms (two Congresses). During his time on Capitol Hill, Pierluisi has sat on powerful committees indicative of his earlier legal career: Education and Labor (111th Congress, 2009–2011); Ethics (112th Congress, 2011–2013); and the Judiciary and Natural Resources Committees (both from the 111th through the 112th Congresses).[7] He has also made inroads into the Democratic Party's national leadership, serving as the community mobilization chairman for the Democratic Congressional Campaign Committee.

In the House, Pierluisi has made Puerto Rican statehood a priority. In the spring of 2009, he submitted the Puerto Rico Democracy Act—which passed the House in late April 2010 with bipartisan support—calling for an island-wide plebiscite in the hopes of settling the status question, and he has worked to increase federal funding for health care and economic stimulus programs in Puerto Rico. From his post on the Natural Resources Committee, Pierluisi has championed the protection of America's marine environments and introduced legislation to protect El Yunque National Forest near the northeastern coast of Puerto Rico.[8] In both the 111th and the 112th Congresses, he has worked to create teacher exchange programs to serve high-need areas of the country.

In addition to his official legislative assignments, Pierluisi has been actively involved in several caucuses, including the Congressional Hispanic Caucus, the Congressional Caribbean Caucus, the Congressional Friends of Spain Caucus, the House Nursing Caucus, the Art Caucus, and the Friends of Job Corps Congressional Caucus.[9]

FOR FURTHER READING

Biographical Directory of the United States Congress, "Pedro Pierluisi," http://bioguide.congress.gov.

NOTES

1 *Congressional Record*, House, 111th Cong., 1st sess. (3 March 2009): H2891.

2 "Official Biography of Resident Commissioner Pedro R. Pierluisi," http://pierluisi.house.gov/english/biography.html (accessed 5 May 2012).

3 *Politics in America, 2012* (Washington, D.C.: CQ-Roll Call, Inc., 2011): 1091.

4 *Biographical Directory of the United States Congress*, "Pedro Pierluisi," http://bioguide.congress.gov; "Official Biography of Resident Commissioner Pedro R. Pierluisi," http://pierluisi.house.gov/english/biography.html (accessed 5 May 2012).

5 "Deaths Last Week," 12 June 1994, *Chicago Tribune*: C6; "Killings Break Puerto Rico's Record for Violent Deaths," 26 December 1994, *Sun-Sentinel* (Fort Lauderdale, FL): A19.

6 Sarah Weaton, "Democrats' Campaign in Puerto Rico Becomes Entangled in Statehood Issue," 3 April 2008, *New York Times*: A22; *Politics in America, 2012*: 1091; "Election Statistics, 1920 to Present," http://history.house.gov/institution/election-statistics/election-statistics.

7 Garrison Nelson and Charles Stewart III, *Committees in the U.S. Congress, 1993–2010* (Washington, D.C.: CQ Press, 2011): 891.

8 *Politics in America, 2012*: 1091; Jeannette Rivera-Lyles, "Obama Vows to Solve Puerto Rico's Status," 13 January 2009, *Orlando Sentinel*: A5; Frances Robles, "Congress Considers Referendum on Puerto Rico's Political Status," 23 June 2009, *Miami Herald*.

9 "Official Biography of Resident Commissioner Pedro R. Pierluisi," http://pierluisi.house.gov/english/biography.html (accessed 5 May 2012).

Image courtesy of the Member

Silvestre Reyes

1944–

UNITED STATES REPRESENTATIVE 1997–

DEMOCRAT FROM TEXAS

Representative Silvestre Reyes went from the cotton fields of West Texas to popular Border Patrol chief before heading to Congress and becoming the first Hispanic chairman of the House Permanent Select Committee on Intelligence. Throughout his U.S. House career, Reyes has advocated for border security and a strong national defense. "Imagining that I would one day be in politics and Congress never occurred to me," Reyes once said. "All my life, I've focused on the tasks in front of me."[1]

The oldest of 10 children, Silvestre Reyes was born on November 10, 1944, to Rafael and Estela Reyes in Canutillo, Texas. He was raised in a farming community and did not learn English until age six. Reyes graduated from Canutillo High School in 1964 and attended the University of Texas at Austin on a debate scholarship.[2] He interrupted his studies in 1965 to help take care of the family farm, but soon enrolled at Texas Western College (now the University of Texas at El Paso). Reyes again returned to help run the family farm but was drafted by the U.S. Army in 1966. For more than a year, he served as a helicopter crew chief in Vietnam, returning to Canutillo after his father died.[3] He married Carolina Gaytan in 1968, and they raised three children.[4]

In 1969 Reyes became a United States Border Patrol agent in Del Rio, Texas. He earned an associate's degree in criminal justice from El Paso Community College in 1976, and eight years later he became the country's first Hispanic sector chief in the Border Patrol. Reyes achieved national recognition for clamping down on illegal immigration and related crime near El Paso. In 1993 he implemented "Operation Hold the Line," which increased the Border Patrol's presence in West Texas and lowered the crime rate there.[5] In 1995 he ended his 26½-year career in the Border Patrol to run for Congress.[6]

Campaigning in 1996 on his tough immigration record, Reyes ran in a five-way Democratic primary for the El Paso House seat that opened when Representative Ron Coleman retired. On March 12, 1996, Reyes placed first in the close party contest and defeated his strongest Democratic opponent, former Coleman aide Jose Luis Sanchez, with 51 percent of the vote in the runoff election.[7] In the largely Hispanic and heavily Democratic district, Reyes defeated Republican Rick Ledesma and a third-party candidate in the general election with more than 70 percent of the vote, becoming the first Hispanic to represent the district in the U.S. House.[8] Reyes won by large margins in his seven subsequent general election campaigns.[9]

During his first term, in the 105th Congress (1997–1999), Reyes served on the National Security and Veterans' Affairs Committees.[10] He worked to keep Fort Bliss, located outside El Paso, from planned military cuts and advocated for increased immigration security, sponsoring a bill to make the Border Patrol a stand-alone agency in the Department of Justice.[11] In the 107th Congress (2001–2003), Reyes was appointed to the Permanent Select Committee on Intelligence in addition to his assignments on Armed Services and Veterans' Affairs. He also assumed the chairmanship of the Congressional Hispanic Caucus (CHC). Reyes was an outspoken critic of the Iraq War and helped organize the CHC's unanimous opposition to the use of force there.[12]

After Democrats won the House majority in the 110th Congress (2007–2009), Reyes became chairman of the Intelligence Committee; he was the first Hispanic to serve in that role and the seventh to chair a full House committee.[13] Reyes had been an outspoken critic of the intelligence failures in the run up to the Iraq War, and he put oversight of intelligence agencies at the top of his agenda. "One of the first things we're going to have to do is reclaim our turf," Reyes said at the time. "We have ceded and abdicated our role as a co-equal branch of government."[14] In 2010 Reyes shepherded into law the first intelligence reauthorization bill in six years, expanding what spy agencies are required to disclose to Congress.[15] When Democrats returned to the minority in the 112th Congress (2011–2013), Reyes gave up his seat on the Intelligence Committee but continued to serve on Armed Services and rejoined Veterans' Affairs.[16]

FOR FURTHER READING

Biographical Directory of the United States Congress, "Silvestre Reyes," http://bioguide.congress.gov.

NOTES

1 Ramón Rentería, "Reyes Poised for Real Power in New Position," 9 December 2006, *El Paso Times*.

2 Suzanne Gamboa, "Rep. Reyes: 1st Hispanic Intel. Chairman," 2 December 2006, Associated Press; Nicholas W. Malinowski, "Reyes, Silvestre," *Current Biography* (New York: H. W. Wilson Company: 2007): 417.

3 "Official Biography of Congressman Silvestre Reyes," http://reyes.house.gov/Biography (accessed 8 May 2012); Malinowski, *Current Biography*: 417.

4 *Congressional Directory*, 112th Congress (Washington, D.C.: Government Printing Office, 2011): 259; "Official Biography of Congressman Silvestre Reyes," http://reyes.house.gov/Biography (accessed 8 May 2012).

5 Malinowski, *Current Biography*: 417; Tim Golden, "U.S. Blockade of Workers Enrages Mexican Town," 1 October 1993, *New York Times*: A3; Joel Brinkley, "A Rare Success at the Border Brought Scant Official Praise," 14 September 1994, *New York Times*: A1.

6 "Official Biography of Congressman Silvestre Reyes," http://reyes.house.gov/Biography (accessed 8 May 2012); Malinowski, *Current Biography*: 417.

7 Eduardo Montes, "Popular Ex-Border Chief Makes Congressional Run," 6 April 1996, Associated Press; Office of the Secretary of State (Texas), "1996 Democratic Party Primary Runoff Election Race Summary Report," 9 April 1996, http://elections.sos.state.tx.us/elchist.exe (accessed 9 May 2012).

8 "Election Statistics, 1920 to Present," http://history.house.gov/institution/election-statistics/election-statistics; *Politics in America, 1998* (Washington, D.C.: Congressional Quarterly, Inc., 1997): 1405.

9 "Election Statistics, 1920 to Present," http://history.house.gov/institution/election-statistics/election-statistics. Reyes lost the Democratic primary in May 2012.

10 The Committee on Armed Services was renamed the Committee on National Security during the 104th and 105th Congresses.

11 "Official Biography of Congressman Silvestre Reyes," http://reyes.house.gov/Biography (accessed 8 May 2012); *Politics in America, 2000* (Washington, D.C.: Congressional Quarterly, Inc., 1999): 1328.

12 Malinowski, *Current Biography*: 419.

13 Mark Mazzetti and Jeff Zeleny, "Next Chairman for Intelligence Opposed War," 2 December 2006, *New York Times*: A11.

14 David Montgomery, "The Chairman's Turf," 4 January 2007, *Washington Post*: C01.

15 *Politics in America, 2012* (Washington, D.C.: CQ-Roll Call, Inc., 2011): 949.

16 *Politics in America, 2012*: 949. Reyes left the House Committee on Veterans' Affairs during the 110th and 111th Congresses (2007–2011) while he was chairman of the intelligence panel.

Image courtesy of the Member

Ileana Ros-Lehtinen

1952–

UNITED STATES REPRESENTATIVE 1989–
REPUBLICAN FROM FLORIDA

A childhood refugee from Fidel Castro's communist regime, Ileana Ros-Lehtinen emerged as a powerful voice in her South Florida community and a major critic of the tyrannical regime. Her historic 1989 election to the U.S. House of Representatives made her the first Hispanic woman and the first Cuban American elected to the U.S. Congress.

Ileana Ros was born in Havana, Cuba, on July 15, 1952, and moved with her family to the United States shortly after Castro came to power in 1959. After graduating from Southwest Miami High School in 1970, she earned an Associate of Arts degree from Miami-Dade Community College in 1972, a B.A. in Higher Education from Florida International University (FIU) in 1975, and an M.A. in Educational Leadership from FIU in 1985. In 2004 she received her Doctorate in Higher Education from the University of Miami. She also founded a private elementary school, serving as a teacher and as its chief administrator. From 1982 to 1986, she served in the Florida House of Representatives as a Republican (she was its first Hispanic woman), and from 1986 to 1989, she served in the Florida Senate. During her time in the State Senate, she helped create the Florida Pre-Paid Program and met and married State Representative Dexter Lehtinen, who later went on to serve as the U.S. Attorney for the Southern District of Florida. Ros-Lehtinen is mother and stepmother to four adult children.

After the death of Representative Claude Pepper on May 30, 1989, Ileana Ros-Lehtinen sought the Republican nomination for the vacant seat and won the special election on August 29, 1989. Ros-Lehtinen defeated her Democratic rival by a 53 to 47 percent margin. Her victory put the seat in Republican hands for the first time since its creation in 1962. In 1990 and 1992, Ros-Lehtinen comfortably won re-election by 60 and 64 percent, respectively.[1] From 1994 to 2000, she was re-elected without opposition. In her last five re-election campaigns, she won against Democratic candidates with between 58 and 69 percent of the vote.

After Ros-Lehtinen took the oath of office on September 6, 1989, she was assigned to the Foreign Affairs and Government Reform Committees. She served on the Government Reform Committee until 2007, and in the 112th Congress (2011–2013) Ros-Lehtinen was selected to chair the House Foreign Affairs Committee, making her just the second Hispanic-American woman to chair a standing congressional committee.

During her career, Ros-Lehtinen also has chaired several Foreign Affairs subcommittees, including Africa, International Economic Policy and Trade, International Operations and Human Rights, and Middle East and Central Asia. In this respect, Representative Ros-Lehtinen has been a leading advocate for the promotion of human rights in countries like Syria, Iran, Saudi Arabia, and China. She is a steadfast supporter of Israel's right to exist in peace and security as a democratic Jewish state. She has also served as Vice Chair of the Subcommittee on the Western Hemisphere and has served on the Budget Committee.

Ros-Lehtinen's well-known leadership and service to the South Florida community have included a number of initiatives that have safeguarded the environment, promoted job creation, and shaped local infrastructure and transportation. She has worked tirelessly to reinvigorate the Miami River in downtown Miami and to expand PortMiami so that it can serve larger Post-Panamax ships. Ros-Lehtinen also has been a strong supporter of expanding Miami International Airport so it can serve the growing South Florida community and continue to be the gateway to the Americas.

Representative Ros-Lehtinen has also worked to restore the housing market while protecting affordable housing. As the wife of a Vietnam veteran and the stepmother of Marine aviators, Ros-Lehtinen is passionate about supporting our nation's military, bolstering veterans' health care, and ensuring that returning veterans have access to a college education.

Valuing the trust between government and its citizens, Ros-Lehtinen has been a strong advocate for strengthening Medicare. She aims to guarantee the promise of Medicare that is efficient, solvent, and sustainable.

As a mother and a grandmother, Representative Ros-Lehtinen has championed anti-bullying legislation and the prevention of child trafficking. Furthermore, her support for modernizing the Coast Guard fleet ensures that the hardworking men and women of the Coast Guard have the tools they need to effectively patrol the Florida coast from trafficking of narcotics.

On the civil rights front, Ros-Lehtinen is a founding member of the LGBT Equality Caucus and continues to strive for equality for all people regardless of race, religion, gender, or sexual orientation.

FOR FURTHER READING

Biographical Directory of the United States Congress, "Ileana Ros-Lehtinen," http://bioguide.congress.gov.

Fernández, Mayra. *Ileana Ros-Lehtinen, Legisladora* (Cleveland, OH: Modern Curriculum Press, 1994).

NOTES

1 "Election Statistics, 1920 to Present," http://history.house.gov/institution/election-statistics/election-statistics.

Image courtesy of the Member

Lucille Roybal-Allard

1941–

UNITED STATES REPRESENTATIVE 1993–
DEMOCRAT FROM CALIFORNIA

Following her family's tradition of public service, Lucille Roybal-Allard pioneered new political ground in 1992, becoming the first Mexican-American woman to be elected to the U.S. Congress. Running in a new congressional district, Roybal-Allard also was one of a handful of daughters who followed her father to Congress. Like her father, Edward Roybal, she serves on the Appropriations Committee and has chaired the Congressional Hispanic Caucus. She is the first Latina to hold both positions.

Lucille Roybal was one of three children born to Lucille Beserra and Edward Roybal in Los Angeles, California, on June 12, 1941. Edward Roybal served in the U.S. House of Representatives for 30 years, chairing the Congressional Hispanic Caucus (CHC) and rising to chair the Appropriations' Subcommittee on Treasury, Postal Service, and General Government. Roybal-Allard graduated from California State University in Los Angeles in 1965 with a B.A. in speech therapy. She worked in alcohol and drug treatment programs in Los Angeles, as a public relations and fundraising executive for the United Way, and as the executive director of a national trade association for Hispanic certified public accountants in Washington, D.C. Lucille Roybal married Edward T. Allard III in 1981. Together they have four children: Ricardo, Lisa, Angela, and Guy Mark.

In 1987 Roybal-Allard followed her father into public office, winning a special election to fill a vacancy in the California Assembly, where she served until 1992. In the state legislature, Roybal-Allard advocated for women's rights and passed key legislation to protect victims of rape and domestic violence. She also was a proponent of environmental justice, successfully leading a campaign against the building of a commercial hazardous waste incinerator in her urban district. The battle led her to author several environmental bills that became law, including a measure requiring environmental impact reports. Roybal-Allard also worked to advance Hispanic entrepreneurship and has strived to provide economic and political control to local communities.[1]

Following the 1990 Census, a new congressional district encompassing most of her assembly district was created. In 1992 Lucille Roybal-Allard ran for Congress in the new district, capitalizing on family name recognition and on her legislative record in the state assembly. She easily won the primary with 73 percent of the vote. In the general election, she defeated Republican Robert Guzman with 63 percent of the vote. Since her first campaign, Representative

Roybal-Allard has been re-elected nine times with margins higher than 70 percent.[2]

When Roybal-Allard was sworn into the House in January 1993, she was assigned to the Banking, Finance, and Urban Affairs Committee (later renamed Financial Services) and the Small Business Committee. Starting in the 104th Congress (1995–1997), she took a post on the Budget Committee in exchange for her seat on the Small Business panel. In the 105th and 106th Congresses (1997–2001), Roybal-Allard served on the House Select Committee on U.S. National Security and Military/Commercial Concerns with the People's Republic of China. She also has served on the Committee on Standards of Official Conduct. Roybal-Allard's reputation as a respected consensus builder won her the chairmanship of the California Democratic Congressional Delegation in 1997 and 1998. In assuming this position, she became the first woman to serve at the delegation's helm and the first Member to achieve this role through election rather than seniority.

Representing a district with one of the largest Hispanic populations in the nation (77.2 percent), Roybal-Allard followed in her father's footsteps in 1999 and 2000 when she became chair of the CHC. Under her leadership, the CHC played a major role in passing immigration reforms; increasing funding for Hispanic-Serving Institutions; and the partial restoration of food stamps, Social Security benefits, and Medicaid for legal immigrants.

Roybal-Allard gave up all her prior committee assignments in 1999 for a seat on the prestigious Appropriations Committee, where she remains. Roybal-Allard serves on two influential Appropriations subcommittees: Homeland Security; and Labor, Health and Human Services, and Education. From these panels, she oversees funding for the Department of Homeland Security, including Citizenship and Immigration Services and Customs Service; and the Departments of Labor, Health and Human Services, and Education.

In Congress, Roybal-Allard concentrates on social and domestic legislation. Her legislative priorities include public health, immigration reform, reducing underage drinking, promoting maternal and child health, and making college affordable and accessible to all, including immigrant youth. She has also focused on promoting infrastructure and urban redevelopment. She works to meet the needs of her constituents by bringing millions in federal dollars to her district for key priorities such as transportation, economic development, infrastructure, housing, public safety, health care, and education.

FOR FURTHER READING

Biographical Directory of the United States Congress, "Lucille Roybal-Allard," http://bioguide.congress.gov.

MANUSCRIPT COLLECTION

California State Archives (Sacramento). *Papers*: Office files of Lucille Roybal-Allard, 1989–1990, one cubic foot. Includes chronological correspondence and schedules for appearances. *Papers*: Author's bill and correspondence files of Lucille Roybal-Allard, 1987–1988, four cubic feet. Includes chronological correspondence, invitations, and schedules.

NOTES

1 *Politics in America, 2004* (Washington, D.C.: Congressional Quarterly, Inc., 2003); Associated Press Candidate Biography, 2004.

2 "Election Statistics, 1920 to Present," http://history.house.gov/institution/election-statistics/election-statistics.

Image courtesy of the Member

Gregorio Kilili Camacho Sablan

1955–

TERRITORIAL DELEGATE 2009–
DEMOCRAT FROM THE NORTHERN MARIANA ISLANDS

Representing a territory including more than a dozen volcanic islands that is 15 time zones away from Washington, D.C., Gregorio Kilili Camacho Sablan is the first Delegate for the Northern Mariana Islands in the U.S. House of Representatives. Early in his first term, Sablan, who prefers to be called Congressman Kilili, noted, "We've been a commonwealth for 33 years, and we became citizens in 1986. We've got a lot of catching up to do."[1]

Gregorio Kilili Camacho Sablan, born on the island of Saipan on January 19, 1955, is the oldest of seven children of Jesus Diaz Sablan and Victorina Camacho Sablan.[2] Sablan graduated from Marianas High School before attending the University of Guam, Armstrong University at Berkeley, and the University of Hawaii at Manoa. He served in the United States Army from 1981 to 1986. Sablan and his wife, Andrea, have six children and four grandchildren.

In 1976, when Sablan was 21 years old, President Gerald Ford approved P.L. 94-241, formalizing a covenant between the Northern Mariana Islands and the United States. The new Commonwealth government was established on January 9, 1978, and three years later, Sablan began working for the first governor, Carlos S. Camacho. Sablan hailed from a political family—his uncle, Vicente D. Sablan, and his grandfather, SN. Sablan, were both mayors of Saipan—and like them, he gravitated to public service. In 1982 Sablan was elected to the Commonwealth legislature, where he served until 1986. After his stint in the legislature, Sablan worked as an aide to Senator Daniel Inouye of Hawaii and later as an aide to the governor of the Commonwealth. Sablan was appointed Executive Director of the Commonwealth Election Commission in 1999.[3]

In May 2008, more than 30 years after the original covenant, President George W. Bush signed P.L. 110-229, granting the Islands a Delegate in the U.S. House of Representatives. Later that fall, Sablan left his position with the election commission and entered a nine-way race for the new seat.[4] In the early 1980s, he was chairman of the Northern Marianas' Democratic Party, but by the time of the 2008 general election, Sablan had grown frustrated with what he considered a highly unorganized Democratic Party and opted to run as an Independent instead. His biggest competition came from Republican Pete A. Tenorio, the incumbent Washington representative.[5] Sablan edged out Tenorio by 357 votes, winning 24 percent of the total vote. In 2010 he won re-election in a four-way contest with 43 percent of the vote.[6]

Sablan was assigned to the Committee on Natural Resources and the Committee on Education and Labor for the 111th Congress (2009–2011). He caucused with the Democratic Party. In the 112th Congress (2011–2013), Sablan serves on the Natural Resources and Agriculture Committees. Focusing on the basic needs of his territory, he has introduced more than 40 bills during his career to bolster educational, environmental, and labor programs on or affecting the islands. Moreover, he has made it a point to educate Congress on the conditions in the Northern Marianas, especially the lack of fresh, potable drinking water. "[W]e just don't have 24-hour water," he said on the House Floor, noting that many residents of the Northern Marianas lack simple access to sewer systems. "And not just that, but if you're lucky enough to get two to three hours of water a day, you can't drink that water anyway," he added.[7]

In both the 111th and 112th Congresses, Sablan has introduced legislation to convey submerged land rights to the Northern Mariana Islands.[8] The bill passed the House in the 111th Congress but died in the Senate. "The Northern Mariana Islands is the only U.S. jurisdiction that does not have ownership of the submerged lands three miles off its shores," he noted upon reintroducing the bill in the 112th Congress.[9] Delegate Sablan also seeks equal treatment for the Northern Mariana Islands regarding other federal legislation and entitlements.

FOR FURTHER READING

Biographical Directory of the United States Congress, "Gregorio Kilili Camacho Sablan," http://bioguide.congress.gov.

NOTES

1 Kris Kitto, "This Man Is No Island," April 20, 2009, *The Hill*; quotation from *Congressional Record*, House, 111th Cong., 1st sess. (14 May 2009): H5657.

2 "Official Biography of Congressman Gregorio Kilili Camacho Sablan," http://sablan.house.gov/about-me/full-biography, (accessed 21 May 2012); "About," Kilili for Congress Facebook Page, http://www.facebook.com/pages/Kilili-for-Congress/112096108825189?sk=info (accessed 9 May 2012).

3 "Progress in the Pacific," 15 November 1986, *Christian Science Monitor*: 19; "Official Biography of Congressman Gregorio Kilili Camacho Sablan," http://sablan.house.gov/about-me/full-biography (accessed 24 May 2012); *Politics in America, 2012* (Washington, D.C: CQ-Roll Call, Inc., 2011): 1090.

4 *Congressional Record*, House, 111th Cong., 1st sess. (24 March 2009): H3785; "Official Biography of Congressman Gregorio Kilili Camacho Sablan," http://sablan.house.gov/about-me/full-biography (accessed 24 May 2012).

5 From 1978 to 2008, the Northern Mariana Islands elected a Resident Representative to the United States. This representative was not a Member of the House of Representatives, but served as an advocate for the Northern Mariana Islands. Frank S. Rosario, "Sablan Leads CNMI's U.S. Congress Delegate Race," *Pacific Magazine*, www.pacificmagazine.net (accessed 5 November 2008).

6 *Politics in America, 2010* (Washington, D.C.: Congressional Quarterly, Inc., 2009): 1130; *Politics in America, 2012*: 1090.

7 *Congressional Record*, House, 111th Cong., 1st sess. (14 May 2009): H5656–H5657.

8 H.R. 934, 111th Congress; H.R. 670, 112th Congress.

9 *Congressional Record*, House, 112th Cong., 1st sess. (10 February 2011): E203.

Image courtesy of the Member

Linda T. Sánchez

1969–

UNITED STATES REPRESENTATIVE 2003–
DEMOCRAT FROM CALIFORNIA

Recognized by her colleagues and the national media as a leading voice for working families, judiciary, and trade matters, Linda Sánchez has served in the U.S. House of Representatives since 2003. When she won her bid to become a United States Representative from Los Angeles County, she not only earned a seat in Congress, she also made history; Linda and her older sibling Loretta Sanchez, who was first elected to the U.S. House in 1996, became the first sisters to serve simultaneously in Congress.[1] Re-elected to the U.S. House four times, Sánchez is a strong advocate for California's working families. She is committed to reducing crime, making schools safe, providing quality education, and decreasing unemployment. She holds the distinction of being the first Latina to serve on the House Judiciary Committee and the Committee on Ways and Means.

The sixth of seven children, Sánchez was born on January 26, 1969, in Orange, California, to immigrant parents from Mexico. Her father, Ignacio Sandoval Sánchez, worked as a mechanic at a plastics and rubber plant, and her mother, Maria Socorro Macias, taught elementary school. Sánchez and her parents challenged the gender typecasts of their culture that encouraged boys to attend college and girls to marry and have children. Maria Sánchez, who decided to attend night school to further her education, cultivated Linda's refusal to accept the status quo by suggesting that she work to change societal inequalities.[2] When reflecting upon the importance that her family and parents had in her life, Sánchez commented, "In every Latino family, there's a sense of 'We need to stick together.' It's us against the world." She went on to add, "But I think in our particular family, that's even stronger because our folks expected great things from us. They wanted us to take advantage of all the opportunities they never had."[3] Heeding her parents' advice and her mother's example, Sánchez enrolled in the University of California, Berkeley, where she earned a Bachelor of Arts in Spanish literature with an emphasis in bilingual education. After working her way through school as a bilingual aide and an ESL instructor, she earned her law degree from the University of California, Los Angeles.

After law school, she practiced law in the areas of appellate law, civil rights, and employment law. Committed to political activism, she worked extensively on her sister Loretta's 1996 and 1998 campaigns.

After the 1998 election, Sánchez worked for the International Brotherhood of Electrical Workers (IBEW) Local 441 and the National Electrical Contractors

Association (NECA) as a compliance officer on public works and prevailing wage issues. Representative Sánchez has been a proud, active member of IBEW Local 441 since 1998. Prior to coming to Congress, Sánchez served as the first Latina to head a countywide central labor council when she was named Executive Director of the Orange County Central Labor Council, AFL-CIO.[4]

Motivated by a desire to serve her community, Sánchez decided in 2002 to run for Congress in a newly created district encompassing southeast Los Angeles County. Sánchez joined a tight race as one of three Latino contenders in a field of five.[5] She won the Democratic primary on March 5, 2002, and went on to defeat Republican Tim Escobar in the general election with 55 percent of the vote.[6]

During her first term, Sánchez served on the Judiciary, Government Reform, and Small Business Committees and became a member of the Congressional Hispanic Caucus. She has held seats on the Education and Labor and Foreign Affairs Committees. In the 111th Congress (2009–2011), she served on the powerful Ways and Means Committee. She currently serves on the Veterans' Affairs and Judiciary Committees, and is the Ranking Member of the House Ethics Committee.

As the only freshman Democrat to earn a seat on the Judiciary Committee during the 108th Congress (2003–2005), Sánchez remarked, "Having worked with laws in the courtroom, I've really seen how legislation impacts people."[7] Sánchez sponsored measures to improve school safety and to assist women, minorities, and veterans establish small businesses. In 2008, as chairwoman of the Commercial and Administrative Law Subcommittee, Sánchez led an investigation into the politicization of the Justice Department and another investigation into the firing of nine U.S. attorneys during the George W. Bush administration.[8]

Sánchez and her husband, James Sullivan, are the proud parents of Joaquín Sánchez Sullivan, who joins his Sullivan brothers: Brendan, Jack, and Seamus.

FOR FURTHER READING

Biographical Directory of the United States Congress, "Linda T. Sánchez," http://bioguide.congress.gov.

NOTES

1 Chelsea J. Carter, "L.A. Representative's Sibling Wins Primary; Sisters May Become First to Serve in House Together," 7 March 2002, *San Mateo County Times*.

2 "First Person Singular: Rep. Linda Sanchez (D-Calif.)," 25 April 2004, *Washington Post*: W09.

3 Roxanne Roberts, "House Mates," 12 December 2002, *Washington Post*.

4 "Linda Sanchez for Congress," http://www.lindasanchez2002.com/about.shtml (accessed 6 November 2002); "New Members Guide: Linda Sanchez," 18 November 2002, *The Hill*.

5 Richard Marosoi, "Battle Shapes up in Latino District," 19 February 2002, *Washington Post*: 1.

6 "Election Statistics, 1920 to Present," Office of the Clerk, http://history.house.gov/institution/election-statistics/election-statistics.

7 "CQ Member Profile, 108th Congress: Linda Sanchez," http://www.cq.com (accessed 5 March 2004).

8 "Official Biography of Congresswoman Linda Sánchez, http://lindasanchez.house.gov/index.php/about-linda (accessed 6 December 2011).

Image courtesy of the Member

Loretta Sanchez

1960–

UNITED STATES REPRESENTATIVE 1997–
DEMOCRAT FROM CALIFORNIA

Loretta Sanchez won election to the U.S. House, her first political office, by defeating a longtime incumbent. During her tenure in the House, Representative Sanchez has established herself as an advocate for economic development, a strong military, homeland security, and education issues. In 2003, when Loretta's sister, Linda, won election to the House, the two became the first sisters to serve concurrently in Congress.

Loretta Sanchez was born in Lynwood, California, on January 7, 1960. She is the oldest daughter of Ignacio Sandoval Sánchez and Maria Socorro Macias.[1] She graduated in 1982 with a B.S. in economics from Chapman University, and in 1984 she earned an MBA from American University. Sanchez settled in Orange County, California. From 1984 to 1987, she worked as a special projects manager at the Orange County Transportation Authority. Sanchez then entered the private sector in the investment banking industry and later worked as a strategist at a leading consulting company. A registered Republican and a fiscal conservative, she broke with the GOP in 1992, believing the party had marginalized immigrants and women.

In 1996 Sanchez declared her candidacy in the race for a California district encompassing central Orange County. During the campaign, she touted her business credentials, particularly her effort to secure funding from national companies to establish programs between local grade schools and state colleges in Orange County.[2] Despite her lack of political experience, she defeated three male contenders in the Democratic primary with 35 percent of the vote. In the general election she faced longtime incumbent Republican Bob Dornan, a controversial and outspoken conservative. Her platform included support for small- and medium-sized businesses, investment in high tech research, and federal funding for school improvements. Sanchez also appealed to the district's traditionally conservative voters with a tough-on-crime agenda, advocating a ban on assault weapons and the elimination of gun show loopholes. Sanchez prevailed with a 984-vote margin out of more than 100,000 cast—eking out a 47 to 46 percent win.[3] For more than a year, Sanchez contended with Dornan's challenge to her election. In February 1998, the House voted overwhelmingly to dismiss Dornan's complaint.[4] Later that year, she faced Dornan again in the general election in one of the most expensive races in the country. Her clash with Dornan provided Sanchez with national exposure, making her one of the Democratic Party's primary congressional conduits for appealing to Latinos, women, and young voters. Sanchez prevailed with a 56 to 39 percent margin of victory. She won her six subsequent re-election bids comfortably, garnering as much as 69 percent of the vote.[5]

When Sanchez took her seat in the House on January 7, 1997, she received assignments on the Education and Workforce Committee and the National Security Committee (later renamed Armed Services). She is currently the highest-ranking woman on the Armed Services Committee and the second-ranking Democrat on the Homeland Security Committee, which she joined in the 109th Congress (2005–2007) after she left her seat on the Education and Workforce Committee.

A former member of the United Food and Commercial Workers with family roots in the union movement, Representative Sanchez is a congressional friend of organized labor despite her strong ties to business. She voted against "fast track" trade authority that authorized the President to negotiate trade agreements without congressional approval, oversight, or amendment. Sanchez also broke with the William J. (Bill) Clinton administration when she voted against granting China permanent normal trade relations. Sanchez has a mixed position on trade agreements, basing her approval on whether such treaties constitute "fair trade." Sanchez also is a congressional leader on global human rights issues.[6]

In line with her fiscally conservative principles, Sanchez joined the Democratic Blue Dog Caucus, advocated a major overhaul of the IRS, and supported reductions in the federal budget deficit. Nevertheless, she believed the federal government should play a role in improving local life, particularly in the area of education. A graduate of the Head Start program, Sanchez vowed to make federally funded education programs available to low-income children. She also authored legislation to encourage tax-free bonds to spur funding for school construction. As a Representative, Sanchez has enjoyed success steering federal money and projects into her California district that have benefitted both the local and the state economy.

FOR FURTHER READING

Biographical Directory of the United States Congress, "Loretta Sanchez," http://bioguide.congress.gov.

NOTES

1 *Politics in America, 2002* (Washington, D.C.: Congressional Quarterly, Inc., 2001): 152–153.

2 *New Members of Congress Almanac for the 105th Congress*: 32.

3 "Election Statistics, 1920 to Present," http://history.house.gov/institution/election-statistics/election-statistics.

4 "House Formally Dismisses Dornan Challenge to Sanchez," 13 February 1998, *Washington Post*: A6; Jodi Wilogren, "House Gives Sanchez Reason for Celebration: Task Force Drops Inquiry, Leaving Her with Incumbency, National Celebrity and Fund-Raising Prowess," 5 February 1998, *Los Angeles Times*: A1.

5 "Election Statistics, 1920 to Present," http://history.house.gov/institution/election-statistics/election-statistics.

6 *Politics in America, 2002*: 152–153.

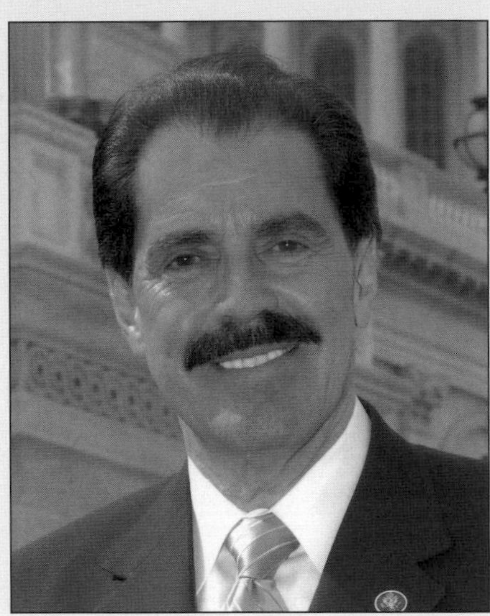

Image courtesy of the Member

José E. Serrano

1943–

UNITED STATES REPRESENTATIVE 1990–
DEMOCRAT FROM NEW YORK

When José E. Serrano won election to the U.S. House of Representatives on March 20, 1990, he requested that his swearing-in be postponed until the 28th, since that was exactly 38 years to the day, since José, his mother, and his brother, Eli, arrived in New York City from Puerto Rico to join his father, who was working there. "Let the message go from here today to those children who live in the projects and to those children who are still on the street corners, that there is indeed a better tomorrow," Serrano said after taking the oath of office.[1]

José Enrique Serrano was born in Mayaguez, Puerto Rico, on October 24, 1943, to José and Hipólita Serrano, but grew up in the Millbrook public housing project in the South Bronx. He graduated from Dodge Vocational High School in 1961 and served in the U.S. Army Medical Corps from 1964 to 1966.

Serrano spent his early career pushing to improve New York's school system. He worked for the New York City Board of Education as a paraprofessional from 1969 to 1974, before running for and winning a seat in the New York State Assembly. Serrano served in Albany for 15 years (1975–1990), chairing the Education Committee from 1983 to 1990. In 1985 he waged an unsuccessful campaign for Bronx borough president, and he was denied an appointment to the position two years later.[2] When Democratic Representative Robert Garcia resigned from Congress in January 1990, Serrano immediately entered the race to fill the vacancy. Predominantly Hispanic, New York's 16th Congressional District is located in the South Bronx between the Harlem and Bronx Rivers.[3] Serrano handily defeated his Republican opponent in the special election that year, winning 92 percent of the vote. Since then, he has consistently polled more than 90 percent of the vote in his 11 re-election bids. Today Serrano is the longest-serving Member of Congress of Puerto Rican descent, the longest-serving elected official in the history of the Bronx, and the most senior member of the Congressional Hispanic Caucus.[4]

Serrano has served on four House committees: Small Business (100th–102nd Congresses, 1987–1993), Education and Labor (100th–102nd Congresses), Judiciary (104th Congress, 1995–1997), and Appropriations (103rd Congress, 1993–1995; 104th–112th Congresses, 1996–2013).[5] On Education and Labor, Serrano, building on his earlier work on education policy in New York, sponsored the School Dropout Prevention and Basic Skills Improvement Act of 1990, and the Voting Rights Language Assistance Act of 1992. The 1992 law broadened the scope of the Voting Rights Act of 1965, guaranteeing access to bilingual ballots and voter assistance for minority communities that were not included in the earlier legislation.[6]

Serrano lost his seat on Appropriations with the majority change in the 104th Congress, but returned to the panel in March 1996. Between 1996 and 2006, Serrano served as the Ranking Member of two subcommittees: Legislative (105th Congress, 1997–1999) and the Departments of Commerce, Justice, and State, the Judiciary, and Related Agencies (106th–108th Congresses, 1999–2005). Serrano used his position to secure funding for many projects in the Bronx, including help for local nonprofits and a major clean-up effort of the Bronx River.

In the 110th Congress (2007–2009), Serrano became Chairman of the Appropriations Committee's Financial Services and General Government Subcommittee, serving until the 112th Congress (2011–2013). When Republicans regained control of the chamber, he became Ranking Member. While Chairman, Serrano worked to increase funding for federal agencies that help protect consumers, such as the Securities and Exchange Commission, and supported efforts to improve economic development and access to financial services for economically distressed communities.

In the 103rd Congress (1993–1995), Serrano was elected chairman of the Congressional Hispanic Caucus (CHC). With a record number of Hispanics serving that Congress, he worked to expand the CHC's profile—holding its first national conference, establishing issue-specific subcommittees, and working to identify policy goals it shared with other caucuses.[7] Serrano has consistently criticized the United States' embargo on Cuba. He also supports an improved relationship between the United States and his native Puerto Rico; he supported the island's 1998 plebiscite and was arrested outside the White House in 2000 while protesting U.S. Navy bombing exercises on the neighboring island of Vieques.[8]

Despite his national profile, Serrano's diverse district has been his top priority in the House. "It's traditionally the place where new groups come," he said to a New York newspaper in 2004. "So this part of the Bronx is where you make your first stop, be it 20 or 30 years."[9]

FOR FURTHER READING

Biographical Directory of the United States Congress, "José E. Serrano," http://bioguide.congress.gov.

NOTES

1 *Congressional Record*, House, 101st Cong., 2nd sess. (28 March 1990): 5696–5697.

2 Frank Lynn, "Candidates for Borough Chief Split over State of the Bronx," 7 August 1985, *New York Times*: B1; Frank Lynn, "2 Rivals for Bronx Post Questioned on Integrity," 24 March 1987, *New York Times*: B4.

3 *Politics in America, 2012* (Washington, D.C.: CQ-Roll Call, Inc., 2011): 692–693.

4 "Election Statistics, 1920 to Present," http://history.house.gov/institution/election-statistics/election-statistics; "Official Biography of Congressman José E. Serrano," http://serrano.house.gov/about-me/full-biography (accessed 1 May 2012).

5 Garrison Nelson and Charles Stewart III, *Committees in the U.S. Congress, 1993–2010* (Washington, D.C.: CQ Press, 2011): 939.

6 *Congressional Record*, House, 102nd Cong., 2nd sess. (24 July 1992): 19321.

7 Kenneth J. Cooper, "A Broken Barrier; Black, Hispanic Caucuses Meet on Capitol Hill," 14 October 1993, *Washington Post*: C2.

8 Kenneth R. Bazinet, "Bronx Dem Arrested in 1-Man D.C. Protest," 5 May 2000, *New York Daily News*: 32.

9 Bob Kappstatter, "Serrano S. Bx. Guardian Angel," 17 December 2004, *New York Daily News*: 3.

Image courtesy of the Member

Albio Sires

1951–

UNITED STATES REPRESENTATIVE 2006–
DEMOCRAT FROM NEW JERSEY

"I am in a good position for New Jersey and my district," Albio Sires told a Newark reporter in 2009. With seats on powerful committees overseeing the interests of his busy upstate district, Sires has been able to champion transportation and immigration issues that hit close to home. As he said, "You're always trying to help your constituents."[1]

Albio Sires was born on January 26, 1951, in Bejucal, Cuba. His family fled Fidel Castro's government in 1962 and settled in West New York, New Jersey, where his parents, who had a grade school education, worked in the factories. He graduated from West New York's Memorial High School in 1970 and earned a bachelor's degree from St. Peter's College in Jersey City in 1974. Sires returned to his old high school to teach Spanish and English as a Second Language, coaching the basketball team after classes. In 1985 Sires received a master's degree in Spanish from Middlebury College in Vermont. He is married to Adrienne Sires and has a stepdaughter, Tara Kole.[2]

In his first bid for public office, Sires ran as a Democrat for mayor of West New York in 1983, losing to longtime incumbent Anthony DeFino. Three years later he ran as a Republican for New Jersey's 14th U.S. Congressional District seat held by Democrat Frank J. Guarini, Jr. Sires lost that year, but New Jersey Governor Thomas Kean soon hired him to improve the communication between his administration and the Hispanic community. Sires eventually opened an insurance company, before running unsuccessfully for the West New York Town Commission in 1991 and 1993.[3]

In 1995 DeFino retired, and Sires again ran for mayor of West New York—this time as an Independent—and won. He served three terms in city hall (1995–2006), where he worked to spur residential and commercial investment while opening access to affordable housing.[4] In 1999 Sires re-registered as a Democrat and, while serving as mayor, ran as a Democrat for a seat in the New Jersey assembly, defeating the incumbent candidate in the primary before easily winning the general election that fall. He served as speaker of the assembly from 2002 until 2006—the first Hispanic official to hold the position—where he worked to increase access to higher education for New Jersey students and to bolster homeland security in the wake of the terrorist attacks on September 11, 2001.[5]

When U.S. Representative Robert Menendez was appointed to the Senate after Jon S. Corzine resigned in 2006, Sires announced his candidacy to fill the

Velázquez has served on the Financial Services (formerly Banking, Finance, and Urban Affairs) and Small Business Committees during her House career. She currently serves on the Financial Services Subcommittees on Insurance, Housing and Community Opportunity and Financial Institutions and Consumer Credit. In 1998 she became the Ranking Member on the Small Business Committee and in 2007, when Democrats regained control of the House, she became chairwoman until the Republicans regained majority status in the House after the 2010 elections.

The Small Business Committee oversees federal programs and contracts that total more than $200 billion annually, and Velázquez has used her position as Ranking Member to cultivate more federal support for small business and entrepreneurship in her district and nationally. She has sought to steer federal agencies toward contracting with small businesses, to help the owners of small firms provide medical and retirement benefits to their employees, and to make federal loans and grants more accessible to small firms. She has criticized federal agencies for what she views as their unsatisfactory efforts to do business with private companies, issuing an annual report card on such practices. In the 107th Congress (2001–2003), Velázquez called attention to the effects of sweatshop industries on the working-class poor in her district. After the September 11, 2001, terrorist attacks, she introduced legislation that required the hiring of small businesses to clean up and reconstruct lower Manhattan.

Velázquez is keenly interested in immigration matters and in U.S. foreign policy in the Caribbean. Much of her district casework centers on immigration issues, as many of her constituents have family in Caribbean countries. She has worked for increased funding to reduce the immigration backlog at the Bureau of Citizenship and Immigration Services. Velazquez consistently advocated for ending practice bombing on the U.S. Navy's test range on the island of Vieques, just off the Puerto Rican coast, and for liberating Puerto Rican political prisoners. In 1994, she protested the Clinton administration's policy of refusing Haitian refugees entrance into the United States.[5]

FOR FURTHER READING

Biographical Directory of the United States Congress, "Nydia M. Velázquez," http://bioguide.congress.gov.

NOTES

1 Deborah Sontag, "Puerto Rican-Born Favorite Treated Like Outsider," 2 November 1992, *New York Times*: B1.

2 Biographical Resource Center, www.Galenet.com; *Politics in America, 2004* (Washington, D.C.: Congressional Quarterly, Inc., 2003): 705.

3 Maria Newman, "From Puerto Rico to Congress, a Determined Path," 27 September 1992, *New York Times*: 33.

4 Newman, "From Puerto Rico to Congress, a Determined Path"; "Election Statistics, 1920 to Present," http://history.house.gov/institution/election-statistics/election-statistics.

5 Associated Press Candidate Biography, 2000; Douglas Jehl, "Clinton's Options on Haiti: Ever Harsher Choices Ahead," 6 May 1994, *New York Times*: A10.

First Term Hispanic-American Members of the 112th Congress

Francisco (Quico) Canseco

UNITED STATES REPRESENTATIVE
REPUBLICAN FROM TEXAS

HOUSE COMMITTEE: Financial Services

BORN: July 30, 1949, Laredo, Texas

FAMILY: Spouse: Gloria Canseco; children: Anna, Francisco, Jr., Carlos

EDUCATION: B.A., St. Louis University, St. Louis, Missouri, 1972; J.D., St. Louis University, St. Louis, Missouri, 1975

MILITARY: N/A

POLITICAL CAREER: N/A

PROFESSIONAL CAREER: Lawyer, banking executive, real estate development

PUBLICATIONS: N/A

Bill Flores

UNITED STATES REPRESENTATIVE
REPUBLICAN FROM TEXAS

HOUSE COMMITTEES: Budget; Natural Resources; Veterans' Affairs

BORN: February 25, 1954, Cheyenne, Wyoming

FAMILY: Spouse: Gina Flores; children: Will, John

EDUCATION: B.B.A., Texas A&M University, College Station, Texas, 1976; M.B.A., Houston Baptist University, Houston, Texas, 1985

MILITARY: N/A

POLITICAL CAREER: N/A

PROFESSIONAL CAREER: Accountant, energy company executive

PUBLICATIONS: N/A

Jaime Herrera Beutler

UNITED STATES REPRESENTATIVE
REPUBLICAN FROM WASHINGTON

HOUSE COMMITTEES: Transportation and Infrastructure; Small Business

BORN: November 3, 1978, Glendale, California

FAMILY: Spouse: Daniel Beutler

EDUCATION: A.A., Bellevue Community College, Bellevue, Washington, 2003; B.A., University of Washington, Seattle, Washington, 2004

MILITARY: N/A

POLITICAL CAREER: Washington state house of representatives, 2007–2010

PROFESSIONAL CAREER: Legislative aide

PUBLICATIONS: N/A

Raúl R. Labrador

UNITED STATES REPRESENTATIVE
REPUBLICAN FROM IDAHO

HOUSE COMMITTEES: Oversight and Government Reform; Natural Resources

BORN: December 8, 1967, Carolina, Puerto Rico

FAMILY: Spouse: Rebecca Labrador; children: Michael, Katerina, Joshua, Diego, Rafael

EDUCATION: B.A., Brigham Young University, Provo, Utah, 1992; J.D., University of Washington, Seattle, Washington, 1995

MILITARY: N/A

POLITICAL CAREER: Idaho state house of representatives, 2006–2010

PROFESSIONAL CAREER: Lawyer

PUBLICATIONS: N/A

David Rivera

UNITED STATES REPRESENTATIVE
REPUBLICAN FROM FLORIDA

HOUSE COMMITTEES: Foreign Affairs; Natural Resources

BORN: September 16, 1965, Brooklyn, New York

FAMILY: Single

EDUCATION: B.A., Florida International University, Miami, Florida, 1986; M.P.A., Florida International University, Miami, Florida, 1994

MILITARY: N/A

POLITICAL CAREER: Florida state house of representatives, 2002–2010

PROFESSIONAL CAREER: Legislative and campaign aide

PUBLICATIONS: N/A

Marco Rubio

UNITED STATES SENATOR
REPUBLICAN FROM FLORIDA

SENATE COMMITTEES: Commerce, Science, and Transportation; Foreign Relations; Intelligence (Select); Small Business and Entrepreneurship

BORN: May 28, 1971, Miami, Florida

FAMILY: Spouse: Jeanette Dousdebes Rubio; children: Amanda, Daniella, Anthony, Dominick

EDUCATION: B.S., University of Florida, Gainesville, Florida, 1993; J.D., University of Miami, Coral Gables, Florida, 1996

MILITARY: N/A

POLITICAL CAREER: West Miami city commission, 1998–2000; Florida state house of representatives, 2000–2008, serving as majority leader (2003–2004) and speaker (2007–2008)

PROFESSIONAL CAREER: Lawyer

PUBLICATIONS:

Rubio, Marco. *An American Son: A Memoir* (New York: Sentinel, 2012).

____. *100 Innovative Ideas for Florida's Future* (Washington, D.C.: Regnery Publishing, 2006).

SOURCES

Online *Biographical Directory of the United States Congress, 1774–Present*: http://bioguide.congress.gov; individual Member offices.

The closing date for this volume was September 1, 2012.

★ PART THREE ★
Appendices

★ APPENDIX A ★

Hispanic-American Representatives, Senators, Delegates, and Resident Commissioners by Congress, 1822–2012

The total membership listed in this appendix applies to the number of Members, House and Senate, in a particular Congress. It does not take into consideration deaths, departures, or special elections over the course of a Congress. For details about each Congress, please consult the footnotes.

CONGRESS	TOTAL MEMBERSHIP	HOUSE	SENATE
17th (1821–1823)	1	Joseph Marion Hernández (FL)[1]	N/A
18th–32nd (1823–1853)	N/A	N/A	N/A
33rd (1853–1855)	1	José Manuel Gallegos (NM)	N/A
34th (1855–1857)	2	José Manuel Gallegos (NM)[2] Miguel Antonio Otero (NM)[3]	N/A
35th (1857–1859)	1	Miguel Antonio Otero (NM)	N/A
36th (1859–1861)	1	Miguel Antonio Otero (NM)	N/A
37th (1861–1863)	N/A	N/A	N/A
38th (1863–1865)	1	Francisco Perea (NM)	N/A
39th (1865–1867)	1	José Francisco Chaves (NM)	N/A
40th (1867–1869)	1	José Francisco Chaves (NM)	N/A
41st (1869–1871)	1	José Francisco Chaves (NM)	N/A
42nd (1871–1873)	1	José Manuel Gallegos (NM)	N/A
43rd–44th (1873–1877)	N/A	N/A	N/A
45th (1877–1879)	2	Romualdo Pacheco (CA)[4] Trinidad Romero (NM)	N/A
46th (1879–1881)	2	Mariano Sabino Otero (NM) Romualdo Pacheco (CA)	N/A

1 Elected as a Delegate upon the formation of the Florida Territory and served from September 30, 1822, to March 3, 1823.
2 Presented credentials to the 34th Congress and served from March 4, 1855, to July 23, 1856, when he was succeeded by Miguel Antonio Otero, who contested his election.
3 Successfully contested as a Democrat the election of José Manuel Gallegos to the 34th Congress and served from July 23, 1856, to March 3, 1857.
4 Presented credentials to the 45th Congress and served from March 4, 1877, to February 7, 1878, when he was succeeded by Peter D. Wigginton, who contested his election.

CONGRESS	TOTAL MEMBERSHIP	HOUSE	SENATE
47th (1881–1883)	2	Tranquilino Luna (NM) Romualdo Pacheco (CA)	N/A
48th (1883–1885)	2	Tranquilino Luna (NM)[5] Francisco Antonio Manzanares (NM)[6]	N/A
49th–55th (1885–1899)	N/A	N/A	N/A
56th (1899–1901)	1	Pedro Perea (NM)	N/A
57th (1901–1903)	1	Federico Degetau (PR)	N/A
58th (1903–1905)	1	Federico Degetau (PR)	N/A
59th (1905–1907)	1	Tulio Larrínaga (PR)	N/A
60th (1907–1909)	1	Tulio Larrínaga (PR)	N/A
61st (1909–1911)	1	Tulio Larrínaga (PR)	N/A
62nd (1911–1913)	1	Luis Muñoz Rivera (PR)	N/A
63rd (1913–1915)	2	Ladislas Lazaro (LA) Luis Muñoz Rivera (PR)	N/A
64th (1915–1917)	3	Benigno Cárdenas Hernández (NM) Ladislas Lazaro (LA) Luis Muñoz Rivera (PR)[7]	N/A
65th (1917–1919)	2	Félix Córdova Dávila (PR) Ladislas Lazaro (LA)	N/A
66th (1919–1921)	3	Félix Córdova Dávila (PR) Benigno Cárdenas Hernández (NM) Ladislas Lazaro (LA)	N/A
67th (1921–1923)	3	Félix Córdova Dávila (PR) Ladislas Lazaro (LA) Néstor Montoya (NM)[8]	N/A
68th (1923–1925)	2	Félix Córdova Dávila (PR) Ladislas Lazaro (LA)	N/A

5 Presented credentials to the 48th Congress and served from March 4, 1883, until March 5, 1884, when he was succeeded by Francisco Antonio Manzanares, who contested his election.
6 Successfully contested the election of Tranquilino Luna to the 48th Congress and served from March 5, 1884, to March 3, 1885.
7 Died in office on November 15, 1916.
8 Died in office on January 13, 1923.

CONGRESS	TOTAL MEMBERSHIP	HOUSE	SENATE
69th (1925–1927)	2	Félix Córdova Dávila (PR) Ladislas Lazaro (LA)	N/A
70th (1927–1929)	3	Félix Córdova Dávila (PR) Ladislas Lazaro (LA)[10]	Octaviano A. Larrazolo (NM)[9]
71st (1929–1931)	1	Félix Córdova Dávila (PR)	N/A
72nd (1931–1933)	4	Dennis Chavez (NM) Félix Córdova Dávila (PR)[11] Joachim Octave Fernández (LA) José Lorenzo Pesquera (PR)[12]	N/A
73rd (1933–1935)	3	Dennis Chavez (NM) Joachim Octave Fernández (LA) Santiago Iglesias (PR)	N/A
74th (1935–1937)	3	Joachim Octave Fernández (LA) Santiago Iglesias (PR)	Dennis Chavez (NM)[13]
75th (1937–1939)	3	Joachim Octave Fernández (LA) Santiago Iglesias (PR)	Dennis Chavez (NM)
76th (1939–1941)	4	Joachim Octave Fernández (LA) Santiago Iglesias (PR)[14] Bolívar Pagán (PR)[15]	Dennis Chavez (NM)
77th (1941–1943)	2	Bolívar Pagán (PR)	Dennis Chavez (NM)
78th (1943–1945)	3	Antonio M. Fernández (NM) Bolívar Pagán (PR)	Dennis Chavez (NM)
79th (1945–1947)	4	Antonio M. Fernández (NM) Antonio Fernós-Isern (PR)[16] Jesús T. Piñero (PR)[17]	Dennis Chavez (NM)
80th (1947–1949)	3	Antonio M. Fernández (NM) Antonio Fernós-Isern (PR)	Dennis Chavez (NM)

9 Elected on November 6, 1928, to fill the vacancy caused by the death of Andrieus A. Jones.
10 Died in office on March 30, 1927.
11 Resigned on April 11, 1932, having been appointed an associate justice of the supreme court of Puerto Rico.
12 Appointed on April 15, 1932, to fill the vacancy caused by the resignation of Félix Córdova Dávila.
13 Appointed on May 11, 1935, to fill the vacancy caused by the death of Bronson M. Cutting.
14 Died in office on December 5, 1939.
15 Appointed on December 26, 1939, to fill the vacancy caused by the death of Santiago Iglesias for the term ending January 3, 1941.
16 Appointed on September 11, 1946, to fill the vacancy caused by the resignation of Jesús T. Piñero.
17 Resigned on September 2, 1946, having been appointed Governor of Puerto Rico.

CONGRESS	TOTAL MEMBERSHIP	HOUSE	SENATE
81st (1949–1951)	3	Antonio M. Fernández (NM) Antonio Fernós-Isern (PR)	Dennis Chavez (NM)
82nd (1951–1953)	3	Antonio M. Fernández (NM) Antonio Fernós-Isern (PR)	Dennis Chavez (NM)
83rd (1953–1955)	3	Antonio M. Fernández (NM) Antonio Fernós-Isern (PR)	Dennis Chavez (NM)
84th (1955–1957)	3	Antonio M. Fernández (NM)[18] Antonio Fernós-Isern (PR)	Dennis Chavez (NM)
85th (1957–1959)	3	Antonio Fernós-Isern (PR) Joseph M. Montoya (NM)[19]	Dennis Chavez (NM)
86th (1959–1961)	3	Antonio Fernós-Isern (PR) Joseph M. Montoya (NM)	Dennis Chavez (NM)
87th (1961–1963)	4	Antonio Fernós-Isern (PR) Henry B. González (TX)[21] Joseph M. Montoya (NM)	Dennis Chavez (NM)[20]
88th (1963–1965)	4	Antonio Fernós-Isern (PR) Henry B. González (TX) Joseph M. Montoya (NM)[22] Edward R. Roybal (CA)	Joseph M. Montoya (NM)
89th (1965–1967)	5	Eligio (Kika) de la Garza II (TX) Henry B. González (TX) Santiago Polanco-Abreu (PR) Edward R. Roybal (CA)	Joseph M. Montoya (NM)
90th (1967–1969)	5	Eligio (Kika) de la Garza II (TX) Henry B. González (TX) Santiago Polanco-Abreu (PR) Edward R. Roybal (CA)	Joseph M. Montoya (NM)

18 Re-elected on November 6, 1956, to the 85th Congress but died in office on November 7, 1956.
19 Elected on April 9, 1957, by special election, to fill the vacancy caused by the death of Antonio M. Fernández.
20 Died in office on November 18, 1962.
21 Elected on November 4, 1961, by special election, to fill the vacancy caused by the resignation of Paul J. Kilday.
22 Resigned on November 3, 1964, having been elected to the Senate to complete the unexpired term of Dennis Chavez for the term ending January 3, 1965.

CONGRESS	TOTAL MEMBERSHIP	HOUSE	SENATE
91st (1969–1971)	6	Jorge Luis Córdova-Díaz (PR) Eligio (Kika) de la Garza II (TX) Henry B. González (TX) Manuel Luján, Jr. (NM) Edward R. Roybal (CA)	Joseph M. Montoya (NM)
92nd (1971–1973)	7	Herman Badillo (NY) Jorge Luis Córdova-Díaz (PR) Eligio (Kika) de la Garza II (TX) Henry B. González (TX) Manuel Luján, Jr. (NM) Edward R. Roybal (CA)	Joseph M. Montoya (NM)
93rd (1973–1975)	8	Herman Badillo (NY) Jaime Benítez (PR) Eligio (Kika) de la Garza II (TX) Ron de Lugo (VI) Henry B. González (TX) Manuel Luján, Jr. (NM) Edward R. Roybal (CA)	Joseph M. Montoya (NM)
94th (1975–1977)	8	Herman Badillo (NY) Jaime Benítez (PR) Eligio (Kika) de la Garza II (TX) Ron de Lugo (VI) Henry B. González (TX) Manuel Luján, Jr. (NM) Edward R. Roybal (CA)	Joseph M. Montoya (NM)
95th (1977–1979)	8	Herman Badillo (NY)[23] Baltasar Corrada-del Río (PR) Eligio (Kika) de la Garza II (TX) Ron de Lugo (VI) Robert Garcia (NY)[24] Henry B. González (TX) Manuel Luján, Jr. (NM) Edward R. Roybal (CA)	N/A

23 Resigned on December 31, 1977, to become a deputy mayor of New York City.
24 Elected on February 14, 1978, by special election, to fill the vacancy caused by the resignation of Herman Badillo.

CONGRESS	TOTAL MEMBERSHIP	HOUSE	SENATE
96th (1979–1981)	7	Tony Coelho (CA) Baltasar Corrada-del Río (PR) Eligio (Kika) de la Garza II (TX) Robert Garcia (NY) Henry B. González (TX) Manuel Luján, Jr. (NM) Edward R. Roybal (CA)	N/A
97th (1981–1983)	9	Tony Coelho (CA) Baltasar Corrada-del Río (PR) Eligio (Kika) de la Garza II (TX) Ron de Lugo (VI) Robert Garcia (NY) Henry B. González (TX) Manuel Luján, Jr. (NM) Matthew G. Martínez (CA)[25] Edward R. Roybal (CA)	N/A
98th (1983–1985)	12	Tony Coelho (CA) Baltasar Corrada-del Río (PR) Eligio (Kika) de la Garza II (TX) Ron de Lugo (VI) Robert Garcia (NY) Henry B. González (TX) Manuel Luján, Jr. (NM) Matthew G. Martínez (CA) Solomon P. Ortiz (TX) Bill Richardson (NM) Edward R. Roybal (CA) Esteban Edward Torres (CA)	N/A
99th (1985–1987)	14	Ben Garrido Blaz (GU) Albert G. Bustamante (TX) Tony Coelho (CA) Eligio (Kika) de la Garza II (TX) Ron de Lugo (VI) Jaime B. Fuster (PR) Robert Garcia (NY) Henry B. González (TX) Manuel Luján, Jr. (NM) Matthew G. Martínez (CA)	N/A

25 Elected on July 13, 1982, by special election, to fill the vacancy caused by the resignation of George E. Danielson.

CONGRESS	TOTAL MEMBERSHIP	HOUSE	SENATE
99th (1985–1987) *continued*		Solomon P. Ortiz (TX) Bill Richardson (NM) Edward R. Roybal (CA) Esteban Edward Torres (CA)	
100th (1987–1989)	14	Ben Garrido Blaz (GU) Albert G. Bustamante (TX) Tony Coelho (CA) Eligio (Kika) de la Garza II (TX) Ron de Lugo (VI) Jaime B. Fuster (PR) Robert Garcia (NY) Henry B. González (TX) Manuel Luján, Jr. (NM) Matthew G. Martínez (CA) Solomon P. Ortiz (TX) Bill Richardson (NM) Edward R. Roybal (CA) Esteban Edward Torres (CA)	N/A
101st (1989–1991)	15	Ben Garrido Blaz (GU) Albert G. Bustamante (TX) Tony Coelho (CA)[26] Eligio (Kika) de la Garza II (TX) Ron de Lugo (VI) Jaime B. Fuster (PR) Robert Garcia (NY)[27] Henry B. González (TX) Matthew G. Martínez (CA) Solomon P. Ortiz (TX) Bill Richardson (NM) Ileana Ros-Lehtinen (FL)[28] José E. Serrano (NY)[29] Edward R. Roybal (CA) Esteban Edward Torres (CA)	N/A

26 Resigned on June 15, 1989.
27 Resigned on January 7, 1990.
28 Elected on August 29, 1989, by special election, to fill the vacancy caused by the death of Claude D. Pepper.
29 Elected on March 20, 1990, by special election, to fill the vacancy caused by the resignation of Robert Garcia.

CONGRESS	TOTAL MEMBERSHIP	HOUSE	SENATE
102nd (1991–1993)	15	Ben Garrido Blaz (GU) Albert G. Bustamante (TX) Antonio J. Colorado (PR)[30] Eligio (Kika) de la Garza II (TX) Ron de Lugo (VI) Jaime B. Fuster (PR)[31] Henry B. González (TX) Matthew G. Martínez (CA) Solomon P. Ortiz (TX) Ed Pastor (AZ)[32] Bill Richardson (NM) Ileana Ros-Lehtinen (FL) Edward R. Roybal (CA) José E. Serrano (NY) Esteban Edward Torres (CA)	N/A
103rd (1993–1995)	20	Xavier Becerra (CA) Henry Bonilla (TX) Eligio (Kika) de la Garza II (TX) Ron de Lugo (VI) Lincoln Diaz-Balart (FL) Henry B. González (TX) Luis V. Gutierrez (IL) Matthew G. Martínez (CA) Robert Menendez (NJ) Solomon P. Ortiz (TX) Ed Pastor (AZ) Bill Richardson (NM) Carlos A. Romero-Barceló (PR) Ileana Ros-Lehtinen (FL) Lucille Roybal-Allard (CA) José E. Serrano (NY) Frank Tejeda (TX) Esteban Edward Torres (CA) Robert A. Underwood (GU) Nydia M. Velázquez (NY)	N/A

30 Appointed on February 21, 1992, to fill the vacancy that would ensue on March 4, 1992, with the resignation of Jaime B. Fuster.
31 Resigned on March 4, 1992.
32 Elected on September 24, 1991, by special election, to fill the vacancy caused by the resignation of Morris K. Udall.

CONGRESS	TOTAL MEMBERSHIP	HOUSE	SENATE
104th (1995–1997)	19	Xavier Becerra (CA) Henry Bonilla (TX) Eligio (Kika) de la Garza II (TX) Lincoln Diaz-Balart (FL) Henry B. González (TX) Luis V. Gutierrez (IL) Matthew G. Martínez (CA) Robert Menendez (NJ) Solomon P. Ortiz (TX) Ed Pastor (AZ) Bill Richardson (NM) Carlos A. Romero-Barceló (PR) Ileana Ros-Lehtinen (FL) Lucille Roybal-Allard (CA) José E. Serrano (NY) Frank Tejeda (TX) Esteban Edward Torres (CA) Robert A. Underwood (GU) Nydia M. Velázquez (NY)	N/A
105th (1997–1999)	22	Xavier Becerra (CA) Henry Bonilla (TX) Lincoln Diaz-Balart (FL) Henry B. González (TX) Luis V. Gutierrez (IL) Rubén Hinojosa (TX) Matthew G. Martínez (CA) Robert Menendez (NJ) Solomon P. Ortiz (TX) Ed Pastor (AZ) Silvestre Reyes (TX) Ciro D. Rodriguez (TX)[33] Bill Richardson (NM)[34] Carlos A. Romero-Barceló (PR) Ileana Ros-Lehtinen (FL) Lucille Roybal-Allard (CA) Loretta Sanchez (CA) José E. Serrano (NY) Frank Tejeda (TX)[35]	N/A

33 Elected on April 12, 1997, by special election, to fill the vacancy caused by the death of Frank Tejeda.
34 Resigned on February 13, 1997.
35 Died in office on January 30, 1997.

CONGRESS	TOTAL MEMBERSHIP	HOUSE	SENATE
105th (1997–1999) *continued*		Esteban Edward Torres (CA) Robert A. Underwood (GU) Nydia M. Velázquez (NY)	
106th (1999–2001)	21	Joe Baca (CA)[36] Xavier Becerra (CA) Henry Bonilla (TX) Lincoln Diaz-Balart (FL) Charles A. Gonzalez (TX) Luis V. Gutierrez (IL) Rubén Hinojosa (TX) Matthew G. Martínez (CA) Robert Menendez (NJ) Grace Flores Napolitano (CA) Solomon P. Ortiz (TX) Ed Pastor (AZ) Silvestre Reyes (TX) Ciro D. Rodriguez (TX) Carlos A. Romero-Barceló (PR) Ileana Ros-Lehtinen (FL) Lucille Roybal-Allard (CA) Loretta Sanchez (CA) José E. Serrano (NY) Robert A. Underwood (GU) Nydia M. Velázquez (NY)	N/A
107th (2001–2003)	21	Aníbal Acevedo-Vilá (PR) Joe Baca (CA) Xavier Becerra (CA) Henry Bonilla (TX) Lincoln Diaz-Balart (FL) Charles A. Gonzalez (TX) Luis V. Gutierrez (IL) Rubén Hinojosa (TX) Robert Menendez (NJ) Grace Flores Napolitano (CA) Solomon P. Ortiz (TX) Ed Pastor (AZ) Silvestre Reyes (TX) Ciro D. Rodriguez (TX)	N/A

36 Elected on November 16, 1999, by special election, to fill the vacancy caused by the death of George E. Brown.

CONGRESS	TOTAL MEMBERSHIP	HOUSE	SENATE
107th (2001–2003) *continued*		Ileana Ros-Lehtinen (FL) Lucille Roybal-Allard (CA) Loretta Sanchez (CA) José E. Serrano (NY) Hilda L. Solis (CA) Robert A. Underwood (GU) Nydia M. Velázquez (NY)	
108th (2003–2005)	25	Aníbal Acevedo-Vilá (PR) Joe Baca (CA) Xavier Becerra (CA) Henry Bonilla (TX) Dennis A. Cardoza (CA) Lincoln Diaz-Balart (FL) Mario Diaz-Balart (FL) Charles A. Gonzalez (TX) Raúl M. Grijalva (AZ) Luis V. Gutierrez (IL) Rubén Hinojosa (TX) Robert Menendez (NJ) Grace Flores Napolitano (CA) Devin Nunes (CA) Solomon P. Ortiz (TX) Ed Pastor (AZ) Silvestre Reyes (TX) Ciro D. Rodriguez (TX) Ileana Ros-Lehtinen (FL) Lucille Roybal-Allard (CA) Linda T. Sánchez (CA) Loretta Sanchez (CA) José E. Serrano (NY) Hilda L. Solis (CA) Nydia M. Velázquez (NY)	N/A
109th (2005–2007)	30	Joe Baca (CA) Xavier Becerra (CA) Henry Bonilla (TX) Dennis A. Cardoza (CA) Jim Costa (CA) Henry Cuellar (TX) Lincoln Diaz-Balart (FL)	Mel Martinez (FL) Robert Menendez (NJ) Ken Salazar (CO)

CONGRESS	TOTAL MEMBERSHIP	HOUSE	SENATE
109th (2005–2007) *continued*		Mario Diaz-Balart (FL)	
		Luis G. Fortuño (PR)	
		Charles A. Gonzalez (TX)	
		Raúl M. Grijalva (AZ)	
		Luis V. Gutierrez (IL)	
		Rubén Hinojosa (TX)	
		Robert Menendez (NJ)[37]	
		Grace Flores Napolitano (CA)	
		Devin Nunes (CA)	
		Solomon P. Ortiz (TX)	
		Ed Pastor (AZ)	
		Silvestre Reyes (TX)	
		Ileana Ros-Lehtinen (FL)	
		Lucille Roybal-Allard (CA)	
		John Salazar (CO)	
		Linda T. Sánchez (CA)	
		Loretta Sanchez (CA)	
		José E. Serrano (NY)	
		Albio Sires (NJ)[38]	
		Hilda L. Solis (CA)	
		Nydia M. Velázquez (NY)	
110th (2007–2009)	30	Joe Baca (CA)	Mel Martinez (FL)
		Xavier Becerra (CA)	Robert Menendez (NJ)
		Dennis A. Cardoza (CA)	Ken Salazar (CO)
		Jim Costa (CA)	
		Henry Cuellar (TX)	
		Lincoln Diaz-Balart (FL)	
		Mario Diaz-Balart (FL)	
		Luis G. Fortuño (PR)	
		Charles A. Gonzalez (TX)	
		Raúl M. Grijalva (AZ)	
		Luis V. Gutierrez (IL)	
		Rubén Hinojosa (TX)	
		Grace Flores Napolitano (CA)	
		Devin Nunes (CA)	
		Solomon P. Ortiz (TX)	
		Ed Pastor (AZ)	

37 Resigned on January 16, 2006, to fill the Senate vacancy caused by the resignation of Jon S. Corzine.
38 Elected on November 7, 2006, by special election, to fill the vacancy caused by the resignation of Robert Menendez.

CONGRESS	TOTAL MEMBERSHIP	HOUSE	SENATE
110th (2007–2009) *continued*		Silvestre Reyes (TX)	
		Ciro D. Rodriguez (TX)	
		Ileana Ros-Lehtinen (FL)	
		Lucille Roybal-Allard (CA)	
		John Salazar (CO)	
		Linda T. Sánchez (CA)	
		Loretta Sanchez (CA)	
		José E. Serrano (NY)	
		Albio Sires (NJ)	
		Hilda L. Solis (CA)	
		Nydia M. Velázquez (NY)	
111th (2009–2011)	32	Joe Baca (CA)	Mel Martinez (FL)[39]
		Xavier Becerra (CA)	Robert Menendez (NJ)
		Dennis A. Cardoza (CA)	Ken Salazar (CO)[40]
		Jim Costa (CA)	
		Henry Cuellar (TX)	
		Lincoln Diaz-Balart (FL)	
		Mario Diaz-Balart (FL)	
		Charles A. Gonzalez (TX)	
		Raúl M. Grijalva (AZ)	
		Luis V. Gutierrez (IL)	
		Rubén Hinojosa (TX)	
		Ben Ray Luján (NM)	
		Grace Flores Napolitano (CA)	
		Devin Nunes (CA)	
		Solomon P. Ortiz (TX)	
		Ed Pastor (AZ)	
		Pedro Pierluisi (PR)	
		Silvestre Reyes (TX)	
		Ciro D. Rodriguez (TX)	
		Ileana Ros-Lehtinen (FL)	
		Lucille Roybal-Allard (CA)	
		Gregorio Kilili Camacho Sablan (MP)	
		John Salazar (CO)	
		Linda T. Sánchez (CA)	
		Loretta Sanchez (CA)	
		José E. Serrano (NY)	

39 Resigned on September 9, 2009.
40 Resigned on January 20, 2009, to serve as Secretary of the Interior in the Cabinet of President Barack Obama.

CONGRESS	TOTAL MEMBERSHIP	HOUSE	SENATE
111th (2009–2011) *continued*		Albio Sires (NJ) Hilda L. Solis (CA)[41] Nydia M. Velázquez (NY)	
112th (2011–2013)	31	Joe Baca (CA) Xavier Becerra (CA) Francisco (Quico) Canseco (TX) Dennis A. Cardoza (CA)[42] Jim Costa (CA) Henry Cuellar (TX) Mario Diaz-Balart (FL) Bill Flores (TX) Charles A. Gonzalez (TX) Raúl M. Grijalva (AZ) Luis V. Gutierrez (IL) Jaime Herrera Beutler (WA) Rubén Hinojosa (TX) Raúl R. Labrador (ID) Ben Ray Luján (NM) Grace Flores Napolitano (CA) Devin Nunes (CA) Ed Pastor (AZ) Pedro Pierluisi (PR) Silvestre Reyes (TX) David Rivera (FL) Ileana Ros-Lehtinen (FL) Lucille Roybal-Allard (CA) Gregorio Kilili Camacho Sablan (MP) Linda T. Sánchez (CA) Loretta Sanchez (CA) José E. Serrano (NY) Albio Sires (NJ) Nydia M. Velázquez (NY)	Robert Menendez (NJ) Marco Rubio (FL)

41 Resigned on February 24, 2009, to serve as Secretary of Labor in the Cabinet of President Barack Obama.
42 Resigned on August 15, 2012.

★ APPENDIX B ★

Hispanic-American Representatives, Senators, Delegates, and Resident Commissioners by State and Territory, 1822–2012

States and territories are listed in descending order according to the number of Hispanic Americans that each has sent to Congress.

STATE/TERRITORY	MEMBER	YEAR MEMBER TOOK OFFICE
Puerto Rico (19)	Federico Degetau[a]	1901
	Tulio Larrínaga[a]	1905
	Luis Muñoz Rivera[a]	1911
	Félix Córdova Dávila[a]	1917
	José Lorenzo Pesquera[a]	1932
	Santiago Iglesias[a]	1933
	Bolívar Pagán[a]	1939
	Jesús T. Piñero[a]	1945
	Antonio Fernós-Isern[a]	1946
	Santiago Polanco-Abreu[a]	1965
	Jorge Luis Córdova-Díaz[a]	1969
	Jamie Benítez[a]	1973
	Baltasar Corrada-del Río[a]	1977
	Jaime B. Fuster[a]	1985
	Antonio J. Colorado[a]	1992
	Carlos A. Romero-Barceló[a]	1993
	Aníbal Acevedo-Vilá[a]	2001
	Luis G. Fortuño[a]	2005
	Pedro Pierluisi[a]	2009
California (15)	Romualdo Pacheco	1877
	Edward R. Roybal	1963
	Tony Coelho	1979
	Matthew G. Martínez	1982
	Esteban Edward Torres	1983
	Xavier Becerra	1993
	Lucille Roybal-Allard	1993
	Loretta Sanchez	1997
	Joe Baca	1999
	Grace Flores Napolitano	1999
	Hilda L. Solis	2001
	Dennis A. Cardoza	2003
	Devin Nunes	2003

STATE/TERRITORY	MEMBER	YEAR MEMBER TOOK OFFICE
California (15) *continued*	Linda T. Sánchez	2003
	Jim Costa	2005
Texas (13)	Henry B. González	1961
	Eligio (Kika) de la Garza II	1965
	Solomon P. Ortiz	1983
	Albert G. Bustamante	1985
	Henry Bonilla	1993
	Frank Tejeda	1993
	Rubén Hinojosa	1997
	Silvestre Reyes	1997
	Ciro D. Rodriguez	1997
	Charles A. Gonzalez	1999
	Henry Cuellar	2005
	Francisco (Quico) Canseco	2011
	Bill Flores	2011
New Mexico Territory (9)	José Manuel Gallegos[b]	1853
	Miguel Antonio Otero[b]	1856
	Francisco Perea[b]	1863
	José Francisco Chaves[b]	1865
	Trinidad Romero[b]	1877
	Mariano Sabino Otero[b]	1879
	Tranquilino Luna[b]	1881
	Francisco Antonio Manzanares[b]	1884
	Pedro Perea[b]	1899
New Mexico (9)	Benigno Cárdenas Hernández	1915
	Néstor Montoya	1921
	Octaviano A. Larrazolo[d]	1928
	Dennis Chavez[c]	1931
	Antonio M. Fernández	1943
	Joseph M. Montoya[c]	1957
	Manuel Luján, Jr.	1969
	Bill Richardson	1983
	Ben Ray Luján	2009

a Resident Commissioner

b Delegate

c Senator and Representative

d Senator

Note: The following states and territories have never elected a Hispanic American to Congress: Alabama, Alaska, American Samoa, Arkansas, Connecticut, Delaware, District of Columbia, Georgia, Hawaii, Indiana, Iowa, Kansas, Kentucky, Maine, Maryland, Massachusetts, Michigan, Minnesota, Mississippi, Missouri, Montana, Nebraska, Nevada, New Hampshire, North Carolina, North Dakota, Ohio, Oklahoma, Oregon, Pennsylvania, Rhode Island, South Carolina, South Dakota, Tennessee, Utah, Vermont, Virginia, West Virginia, Wisconsin, Wyoming.

STATE/TERRITORY	MEMBER	YEAR MEMBER TOOK OFFICE
Florida (6)	Ileana Ros-Lehtinen	1989
	Lincoln Diaz-Balart	1993
	Mario Diaz-Balart	2003
	Mel Martinez[d]	2005
	David Rivera	2011
	Marco Rubio[d]	2011
New York (4)	Herman Badillo	1971
	Robert Garcia	1978
	José E. Serrano	1990
	Nydia M. Velázquez	1993
Arizona (2)	Ed Pastor	1991
	Raúl M. Grijalva	2003
Colorado (2)	John Salazar	2005
	Ken Salazar[d]	2005
Guam (2)	Ben Garrido Blaz[b]	1985
	Robert A. Underwood[b]	1993
Louisiana (2)	Ladislas Lazaro	1913
	Joachim Octave Fernández	1931
New Jersey (2)	Robert Menendez[c]	1993
	Albio Sires	2006
Florida Territory (1)	Joseph Marion Hernández[b]	1822
Idaho (1)	Raúl R. Labrador	2011
Illinois (1)	Luis V. Gutierrez	1993
Northern Mariana Islands (1)	Gregorio Kilili Camacho Sablan[b]	2009
Virgin Islands (1)	Ron de Lugo[b]	1973
Washington (1)	Jaime Herrera Beutler	2011

a Resident Commissioner

b Delegate

c Senator and Representative

d Senator

Note: The following states and territories have never elected a Hispanic American to Congress: Alabama, Alaska, American Samoa, Arkansas, Connecticut, Delaware, District of Columbia, Georgia, Hawaii, Indiana, Iowa, Kansas, Kentucky, Maine, Maryland, Massachusetts, Michigan, Minnesota, Mississippi, Missouri, Montana, Nebraska, Nevada, New Hampshire, North Carolina, North Dakota, Ohio, Oklahoma, Oregon, Pennsylvania, Rhode Island, South Carolina, South Dakota, Tennessee, Utah, Vermont, Virginia, West Virginia, Wisconsin, Wyoming.

★ APPENDIX C ★

Hispanic-American Members' Committee Assignments (Standing, Joint, Select) in the U.S. House and Senate, 1822–2012

This appendix lists alphabetically all the congressional committees on which Hispanic-American Members served. Several features will help readers track Hispanic membership on committees over time:

- In instances where a committee's name (rather than its primary jurisdictional duties) has changed, a "See also" note refers researchers to prior or latter committee name iterations. These name iterations are listed in chronological order.
- In instances where a committee on which a Hispanic Member served was disbanded and its jurisdiction subsumed by another committee, a "Jurisdiction reassigned" note is provided. Not all reassigned jurisdictions are listed. Researchers are referred only to the committees with expanded jurisdictions on which Hispanic Members later served.
- In instances where a committee was disbanded and no jurisdictional transfer occurred, only the Congress and date ranges of the committee are provided.
- Members' terms of service on committees reflect the years they served on the committees; the Congress range is provided in a separate column. Because this appendix accounts for Members joining or leaving committees because of deaths, resignations, and special elections, in some instances service dates are not coterminous with Congress dates.
- Delegates from the New Mexico and Florida Territories did not receive committee assignments until the 1880s.
- The closing date for this volume was September 1, 2012.

HOUSE STANDING COMMITTEE	TERM	CONGRESS
AGRICULTURE [1820–Present]		
16th Congress–Present		
Santiago Iglesias	1933–1939	73rd–76th
Bolívar Pagán	1939–1945	76th–78th
Jesús T. Piñero	1945–1946	79th
Antonio Fernós-Isern	1947–1965	80th–88th
Santiago Polanco-Abreu	1965–1969	89th–90th
Eligio (Kika) de la Garza II	1965–1997	89th–104th
Jorge Luis Córdova-Díaz	1969–1971	91st
Tony Coelho	1979–1989	96th–101st
Ed Pastor	1995–1997	104th
Joe Baca	1999–	106th–112th
Aníbal Acevedo-Vilá	2001–2005	107th–108th
Devin Nunes	2003–2007	108th–109th
Dennis A. Cardoza	2003–	108th–112th
John Salazar	2005–2009	109th–110th
Jim Costa	2005–	109th–112th
Henry Cuellar	2005–	109th–112th
Gregorio Kilili Camacho Sablan	2011–	112th
APPROPRIATIONS [1865–Present]		
39th Congress–Present		
Joachim Octave Fernández	1937–1941	75th–76th
Antonio M. Fernández	1949–1956	81st–84th
Joseph M. Montoya	1959–1964	86th–88th
Edward R. Roybal	1971–1993	92nd–102nd
Esteban Edward Torres	1993–1999	103rd–105th
Henry Bonilla	1993–2007	103rd–109th
Ed Pastor	1993–	103rd–112th
APPROPRIATIONS *continued*		
José E. Serrano	1993–	103rd–112th
Lucille Roybal-Allard	1999–	106th–112th
Ciro D. Rodriguez	2007–2011	110th–111th
John Salazar	2009–2011	111th
Mario Diaz-Balart	2011–	112th
ARMED SERVICES [1947–1995; 1999–Present]		
80th through 103rd Congresses; 106th Congress–Present		
(See also the following standing committee: National Security)		
Antonio Fernós-Isern	1947–1965	80th–88th
Santiago Polanco-Abreu	1965–1969	89th–90th
Jorge Luis Córdova-Díaz	1969–1971	91st
Solomon P. Ortiz	1983–1995	98th–103rd
	1999–2011	106th–111th
Ben Garrido Blaz	1985–1993	99th–102nd
Albert G. Bustamante	1985–1993	99th–102nd
Frank Tejeda	1993–1995	103rd
Robert A. Underwood	1993–1995	103rd
	1999–2003	106th–107th
Ciro D. Rodriguez	1999–2005	106th–108th
Silvestre Reyes	1999–	106th–112th
Loretta Sanchez	1999–	106th–112th
BANKING AND CURRENCY [1865–1975]		
39th through 93rd Congresses		
(See also the following standing committees: Banking, Currency, and Housing; Banking, Finance, and Urban Affairs; Banking and Financial Services; Financial Services)		
Henry B. González	1961–1975	87th–93rd

HOUSE STANDING COMMITTEE	TERM	CONGRESS

BANKING, CURRENCY, AND HOUSING [1975–1977]
94th Congress
(See also the following standing committees: Banking and Currency; Banking, Finance, and Urban Affairs; Banking and Financial Services; Financial Services)

Henry B. González	1975–1977	94th

BANKING AND FINANCIAL SERVICES [1995–2001]
104th through 106th Congresses
(See also the following standing committees: Banking and Currency; Banking, Currency, and Housing; Banking, Finance, and Urban Affairs; Financial Services)

Henry B. González	1995–1999	104th–105th
Lucille Roybal-Allard	1995–1999	104th–105th
Luis V. Gutierrez	1995–2001	104th–106th
Nydia M. Velázquez	1995–2001	104th–106th
Esteban Edward Torres	1997–1999	105th
Charles A. Gonzalez	1999–2001	106th

BANKING, FINANCE, AND URBAN AFFAIRS [1977–1995]
95th through 103rd Congresses
(See also the following standing committees: Banking and Currency; Banking, Currency and Housing; Banking and Financial Services; Financial Services)

Herman Badillo	1977	95th
Henry B. González	1977–1995	95th–103rd
Robert Garcia	1978–1990	95th–101st
Esteban Edward Torres	1983–1993	98th–102nd
Jaime B. Fuster	1985–1987	99th
Luis V. Gutierrez	1993–1995	103rd
Lucille Roybal-Allard	1993–1995	103rd
Nydia M. Velázquez	1993–1995	103rd

BUDGET [1974–Present]
93rd Congress–Present

Lucille Roybal-Allard	1995–1999	104th–105th
Mario Diaz-Balart	2003–2011	108th–111th
Henry Cuellar	2005–2007	109th
Ileana Ros-Lehtinen	2005–2007	109th
Xavier Becerra	2007–2011	110th–111th
Devin Nunes	2009–2011	111th
Bill Flores	2011–	112th

CLAIMS [1794–1947]
3rd through 79th Congresses

Antonio M. Fernández	1943–1947	78th–79th

COINAGE, WEIGHTS, AND MEASURES [1864–1947]
38th through 79th Congresses
(Jurisdiction reassigned to the following standing committees: Banking and Currency; Interstate and Foreign Commerce)

Mariano Sabino Otero	1880–1881	46th
Tranquilino Luna	1881–1884	47th–48th
Francisco Antonio Manzanares	1883–1885	48th
Ladislas Lazaro	1913–1919	63rd–65th
	1921–1923	67th

COMMERCE [1995–2001]
104th through 106th Congresses
(See also the following standing committees: Energy and Commerce)

Bill Richardson	1995–1997	104th–105th

ECONOMIC AND EDUCATIONAL OPPORTUNITIES [1995–1997]
104th Congress
(See also the following standing committees: Education and Labor; Education and the Workforce)

Xavier Becerra	1995–1997	104th
Matthew G. Martínez	1995–1997	104th
Carlos A. Romero-Barceló	1995–1997	104th

HOUSE STANDING COMMITTEE	TERM	CONGRESS

EDUCATION AND LABOR [1867–1883; 1947–1995; 2007–2011]
40th through 47th Congresses; 80th through 103rd Congresses; 110th and 111th Congresses
(See also the following standing committees: Economic and Educational Opportunities; Education and the Workforce)

Herman Badillo	1971–1975	92nd–93rd
Jaime Benítez	1973–1977	93rd–94th
Baltasar Corrada-del Río	1977–1985	95th–98th
Matthew G. Martínez	1982–1995	97th–103rd
Bill Richardson	1987–1989	100th
Jaime B. Fuster	1989–1992	101st–102nd
José E. Serrano	1990–1993	101st–102nd
Ed Pastor	1991–1993	102nd
Ron de Lugo	1991–1995	102nd–103rd
Xavier Becerra	1993–1995	103rd
Carlos A. Romero-Barceló	1993–1995	103rd
Robert A. Underwood	1993–1995	103rd
Luis G. Fortuño	2007–2009	110th
Linda T. Sánchez	2007–2009	110th
Raúl M. Grijalva	2007–2011	110th–111th
Rubén Hinojosa	2007–2011	110th–111th
Pedro Pierluisi	2009–2011	111th
Gregorio Kilili Camacho Sablan	2009–2011	111th

EDUCATION AND THE WORKFORCE [1997–2007; 2011–Present]
105th through 109th Congresses; 112th Congress
(See also the following standing committees: Economic and Educational Opportunities; Education and Labor)

Matthew G. Martínez	1997–2001	105th–106th
Carlos A. Romero-Barceló	1997–2001	105th–106th
Loretta Sanchez	1997–2005	105th–108th
Rubén Hinojosa	1997–2007	105th–109th
	2011–	112th
Hilda L. Solis	2001–2003	107th
Raúl M. Grijalva	2003–2007	108th–109th
	2011–	112th
Luis G. Fortuño	2005–2007	109th

ELECTIONS NO. 1 [1895–1947]
54th through 79th Congresses
(Jurisdiction reassigned to the following standing committee: House Administration)

Antonio M. Fernández	1943–1947	78th–79th

ENERGY AND COMMERCE [1981–1995; 2001–Present]
97th through 103rd Congresses; 107th Congress–Present
(See also the following standing committee: Commerce)

Bill Richardson	1983–1995	98th–103rd
Charles A. Gonzalez	2003–	108th–112th
Hilda L. Solis	2003–2009	108th–110th

ENROLLED BILLS [1876–1947]
44th through 79th Congresses
(Jurisdiction reassigned to the following standing committee: House Administration)

Ladislas Lazaro	1913–1923	63rd–67th

ETHICS [2011–Present]
112th Congress
(See also the following standing committee: Standards of Official Conduct)

Pedro Pierluisi	2011–	112th
Linda T. Sánchez	2011–	112th

HOUSE STANDING COMMITTEE	TERM	CONGRESS
FINANCIAL SERVICES [2001–Present] *107th Congress–Present* *(See also the following standing committees: Banking and Currency; Banking, Currency, and Housing; Banking, Finance, and Urban Affairs; Banking and Financial Services)*		
Charles A. Gonzalez	2001–2005	107th–108th
Luis V. Gutierrez	2001–	107th–112th
Rubén Hinojosa	2001–	107th–112th
Nydia M. Velázquez	2001–	107th–112th
Joe Baca	2003–	108th–112th
Albio Sires	2007–2009	110th
Francisco (Quico) Canseco	2011–	112th
FOREIGN AFFAIRS [1822–1977; 1981–1995; 2007–Present] *17th through 94th Congresses; 97th through 103rd Congresses; 110th Congress–Present* *(See also the following standing committee: International Relations)*		
Edward R. Roybal	1965–1971	89th–91st
Robert Garcia	1983–1987	98th–99th
Jaime B. Fuster	1987–1992	100th–102nd
Ben Garrido Blaz	1987–1993	100th–102nd
Ileana Ros-Lehtinen	1989–1991	101st–103rd
	2007–	110th–112th
Antonio J. Colorado	1992–1993	102nd
Lincoln Diaz-Balart	1993–1995	103rd
Luis V. Gutierrez	1993–1995	103rd
Matthew G. Martínez	1993–1995	103rd
Robert Menendez	1993–1995	103rd
Luis G. Fortuño	2007–2009	110th
Rubén Hinojosa	2007–2009	110th
Linda T. Sánchez	2007–2009	110th
Jim Costa	2007–2011	110th–111th
Albio Sires	2007–	110th–112th
Dennis A. Cardoza	2011–	112th
David Rivera	2011–	112th
GOVERNMENT OPERATIONS [1953–1995] *83rd through 103rd Congresses* *(See also the following standing committees: Government Reform; Oversight and Government Reform; Government Reform and Oversight)*		
Albert G. Bustamante	1985–1993	99th–102nd
Matthew G. Martínez	1985–1993	99th–102nd
Ileana Ros-Lehtinen	1989–1995	101st–103rd
GOVERNMENT REFORM [1999–2007] *106th through 109th Congresses* *(See also the following standing committees: Government Operations; Government Reform and Oversight; Oversight and Government Reform)*		
Ileana Ros-Lehtinen	1999–2007	106th–109th
Linda T. Sánchez	2003–2007	108th–109th
GOVERNMENT REFORM AND OVERSIGHT [1995–1999] *104th and 105th Congresses* *(See also the following standing committees: Government Operations; Government Reform; Oversight and Government Reform)*		
Ileana Ros-Lehtinen	1995–1999	104th–105th
HOMELAND SECURITY [2005–Present] *109th Congress–Present* *(See also the following select committee: Homeland Security)*		
Loretta Sanchez	2005–	109th–112th
Henry Cuellar	2007–	110th–112th
Ben Ray Luján	2009–2011	111th
HOUSE ADMINISTRATION [1947–1995; 1999–Present] *80th through 103rd Congresses; 106th Congress–Present* *(See also the following standing committee: House Oversight)*		
Tony Coelho	1983–1989	98th–101st
Charles A. Gonzalez	2007–	110th–112th
HOUSE OVERSIGHT [1995–1999] *104th and 105th Congresses* *(See also the following standing committee: House Administration)*		
Lincoln Diaz-Balart	1995–1997	104th
Ed Pastor	1995–1997	104th
INDIAN AFFAIRS [1821–1947] *17th through 79th Congresses* *(Jurisdiction reassigned to the following standing committee: Public Lands, which later became Interior and Insular Affairs)*		
Benigno Cárdenas Hernández	1915–1917	64th
	1919–1921	66th
Néstor Montoya	1921–1923	67th
Dennis Chavez	1931–1935	72nd–73rd
Antonio M. Fernández	1943–1947	78th–79th
INSULAR AFFAIRS [1899–1947] *56th through 79th Congresses* *(Jurisdiction reassigned to the following standing committee: Public Lands, which later became Interior and Insular Affairs)*		
Federico Degetau	1904–1905	58th
Tulio Larrínaga	1905–1911	59th–61st
Luis Muñoz Rivera	1911–1913	62nd
	1915–1916	64th
Félix Córdova Dávila	1917–1932	65th–72nd
José Lorenzo Pesquera	1932–1933	72nd
Santiago Iglesias	1933–1939	73rd–76th
Bolívar Pagán	1939–1945	76th–78th
Antonio M. Fernández	1943–1947	78th–79th
Jesús T. Piñero	1945–1946	79th
INTERIOR AND INSULAR AFFAIRS [1951–1993] *82nd through 102nd Congresses* *(See also the following standing committees: Public Lands; Natural Resources; Resources)*		
Edward R. Roybal	1963–1965	88th
Santiago Polanco-Abreu	1965–1969	89th–90th
Jorge Luis Córdova-Díaz	1969–1973	91st–92nd
Manuel Lújan, Jr.	1969–1989	91st–100th
Ron de Lugo	1973–1979	93rd–95th
	1981–1993	97th–102nd
Jaime Benítez	1975–1977	94th
Baltasar Corrada-del Río	1977–1985	95th–98th
Tony Coelho	1981–1989	97th–101st
Bill Richardson	1984–1993	98th–102nd
Jaime B. Fuster	1985–1992	99th–102nd
Ben Garrido Blaz	1985–1993	99th–102nd
INTERNATIONAL RELATIONS [1977–1981; 1995–2007] *95th and 96th Congresses; 104th through 109th Congresses* *(See also the following standing committee: Foreign Affairs)*		
Eligio (Kika) de la Garza II	1977–1979	95th
Matthew G. Martínez	1995–2001	104th–106th
Robert Menendez	1995–2006	104th–109th
Ileana Ros-Lehtinen	1995–2007	104th–109th
Grace Flores Napolitano	2001–2007	107th–109th
Dennis A. Cardoza	2005–2007	109th

HOUSE STANDING COMMITTEE	TERM	CONGRESS

IRRIGATION AND RECLAMATION [1925–1947]
69th through 79th Congresses
(See also the following standing committee: Irrigation and Reclamation. Jurisdiction reassigned to the following standing committee: Public Lands, which later became Interior and Insular Affairs)

Dennis Chavez	1931–1935	72nd–73rd
Antonio M. Fernández	1943–1947	78th–79th

IRRIGATION OF ARID LAND [1893–1925]
53rd through 68th Congresses
(See also the following standing committee: Irrigation and Reclamation)

Benigno Cárdenas Hernández	1915–1917	64th
	1919–1921	66th

JUDICIARY [1813–Present]
13th Congress–Present

Joseph M. Montoya	1957–1959	85th
Herman Badillo	1975–1977	94th
Xavier Becerra	1993–1997	103rd–104th
José E. Serrano	1995–1997	104th
Linda T. Sánchez	2003–	108th–112th
Luis V. Gutierrez	2007–2011	110th–111th
Charles A. Gonzalez	2009–2011	111th
Pedro Pierluisi	2009–	111th–112th

LABOR [1883–1947]
48th through 79th Congresses
(See also the following standing committees: Education and Labor; Education and the Workforce)

Santiago Iglesias	1935–1939	74th–76th
Bolívar Pagán	1941–1945	77th–78th
Jesús T. Piñero	1945–1946	79th

MEMORIALS [1929–1947]
70th through 79th Congresses
(Jurisdiction reassigned to the following standing committee: House Administration)

Antonio M. Fernández	1945–1947	79th

MERCHANT MARINE AND FISHERIES [1947–1995]
80th through 103rd Congresses
(Jurisdiction reassigned to the following standing committees: National Security; Resources; Science; Transportation and Infrastructure)

Ladislas Lazaro	1913–1927	63rd–69th
Eligio (Kika) de la Garza II	1971–1981	92nd–96th
Ron de Lugo	1975–1979	94th–95th
Solomon P. Ortiz	1983–1995	98th–103rd
Lincoln Diaz-Balart	1993–1995	103rd

MILITARY AFFAIRS [1822–1947]
17th through 79th Congresses
(Jurisdiction reassigned to the following standing committee: Armed Services)

Pedro Perea	1899–1901	56th
Bolívar Pagán	1943–1945	78th
Jesús T. Piñero	1945–1946	79th

MINES AND MINING [1865–1947]
39th through 79th Congresses
(Jurisdiction reassigned to the following standing committee: Public Lands, which later became Interior and Insular Affairs)

Antonio M. Fernández	1943–1945	78th
Jesús T. Piñero	1945–1946	79th

HOUSE STANDING COMMITTEE	TERM	CONGRESS

NATIONAL SECURITY [1995–1999]
104th through 105th Congresses
(See also the following standing committee: Armed Services)

Solomon P. Ortiz	1995–1999	104th–105th
Frank Tejeda	1995–1999	104th–105th
Robert A. Underwood	1995–1999	104th–105th
Silvestre Reyes	1997–1999	105th
Ciro D. Rodriguez	1997–1999	105th
Loretta Sanchez	1997–1999	105th

NATURAL RESOURCES [1993–1995; 2007–Present]
103rd Congress; 110th Congress–Present
(See also the following standing committees: Insular Affairs; Interior and Insular Affairs; Resources)

Ron de Lugo	1993–1995	103rd
Bill Richardson	1993–1995	103rd
Carlos A. Romero-Barceló	1993–1995	103rd
Robert A. Underwood	1993–1995	103rd
Luis G. Fortuño	2007–2009	110th
Solomon P. Ortiz	2007–2009	110th
Hilda L. Solis	2007–2009	110th
Joe Baca	2007–2011	110th–111th
Jim Costa	2007–	110th–112th
Raúl M. Grijalva	2007–	110th–112th
Grace Flores Napolitano	2007–	110th–112th
Pedro Pierluisi	2009–	111th–112th
Gregorio Kilili Camacho Sablan	2009–	111th–112th
Bill Flores	2011–	112th
Raúl R. Labrador	2011–	112th
Ben Ray Luján	2011–	112th
David Rivera	2011–	112th

NAVAL AFFAIRS [1822–1947]
17th through 79th Congresses
(Jurisdiction reassigned to the following standing committee: Armed Services)

Joachim Octave Fernández	1931–1937	72nd–74th
Bolívar Pagán	1943–1945	78th
Jesús T. Piñero	1945–1946	79th

OVERSIGHT AND GOVERNMENT REFORM [2007–Present]
110th Congress–Present
(See also the following standing committees: Government Operations; Government Reform; Government Reform and Oversight)

Henry Cuellar	2009–2011	111th
Raúl R. Labrador	2011–	112th

POST OFFICE AND CIVIL SERVICE [1947–1995]
80th through 103rd Congresses
(See also the following standing committee: Post Office and Post Roads. Jurisdiction reassigned to the following standing committees: Government Reform and Oversight; House Oversight)

Edward R. Roybal	1963–1965	88th
Robert Garcia	1978–1990	95th–101st
Ron de Lugo	1981–1991	97th–101st

POST OFFICE AND POST ROADS [1808–1947]
10th through 79th Congresses
(See also the following standing committee: Post Office and Civil Service)

Pedro Perea	1899–1901	56th

HOUSE STANDING COMMITTEE	TERM	CONGRESS
PRIVATE LAND CLAIMS [1816–1911] *14th through 61st Congresses*		
Romualdo Pacheco	1879–1883	46th–47th
Pedro Perea	1899–1901	56th
PUBLIC BUILDINGS AND GROUNDS [1837–1947] *25th through 79th Congresses* *(Jurisdiction reassigned to the following standing committee: Public Works)*		
Dennis Chavez	1931–1933	72nd
PUBLIC EXPENDITURES [1814–1880; 1881–1883] *13th through 46th Congresses; 47th Congress*		
Romualdo Pacheco	1879–1881	46th
PUBLIC LANDS [1805–1951] *9th through 81st Congresses* *(See also the following standing committees: Interior and Insular Affairs; Natural Resources; Resources)*		
Romualdo Pacheco	1877–1879	45th
Benigno Cárdenas Hernández	1919–1921	66th
Néstor Montoya	1921–1923	67th
Dennis Chavez	1931–1935	72nd–73rd
Antonio M. Fernández	1943–1949	78th–80th
Antonio Fernós-Isern	1947–1965	80th–88th
PUBLIC WORKS AND TRANSPORTATION [1975–1995] *94th through 103rd Congresses* *(See also the following standing committees: Public Works; Transportation)*		
Ron de Lugo	1981–1995	97th–103rd
Robert Menendez	1993–1995	103rd
RESOURCES [1995–2007] *104th through 109th Congresses* *(See also the following standing committees: Insular Affairs; Interior and Insular Affairs; Natural Resources)*		
Bill Richardson	1995–1997	104th–105th
Carlos A. Romero-Barceló	1995–2001	104th–106th
Robert A. Underwood	1995–2003	104th–107th
Solomon P. Ortiz	1995–2007	104th–109th
Grace Flores Napolitano	1999–2007	106th–109th
Hilda L. Solis	2001–2003	107th
Aníbal Acevedo-Vilá	2001–2005	107th–108th
Joe Baca	2003–2005	108th
Rubén Hinojosa	2003–2005	108th
Ciro D. Rodriguez	2003–2005	108th
Dennis A. Cardoza	2003–2007	108th–109th
Raúl M. Grijalva	2003–2007	108th–109th
Devin Nunes	2003–2007	108th–109th
Jim Costa	2005–2007	109th
Luis G. Fortuño	2005–2007	109th
RULES [1849–Present] *31st Congress–Present*		
Lincoln Diaz-Balart	1995–2011	104th–111th
Dennis A. Cardoza	2007–2011	110th–111th
SCIENCE [1995–2007] *104th through 109th Congresses* *(See also the following standing committees: Science, Space, and Technology; Science and Technology)*		
Joe Baca	1999–2003	106th–107th
Dennis A. Cardoza	2003–2005	108th
Jim Costa	2005–2007	109th
Mario Diaz-Balart	2005–2007	109th

HOUSE STANDING COMMITTEE	TERM	CONGRESS
SCIENCE AND TECHNOLOGY [1975–1987; 2007–2011] *94th through 99th Congresses; 110th and 111th Congresses* *(See also the following standing committees: Science, Space, and Technology; Science)*		
Manuel Lújan, Jr.	1977–1987	95th–99th
Mario Diaz-Balart	2007–2011	110th–111th
Ben Ray Luján	2009–2011	111th
SCIENCE, SPACE, AND TECHNOLOGY [1987–1995; 2011–Present] *100th through 103rd Congresses; 112th Congress* *(See also the following standing committees: Science; Science and Technology)*		
Manuel Lújan, Jr.	1987–1989	100th
Xavier Becerra	1993–1995	103rd
Ben Ray Luján	2011–	112th
SMALL BUSINESS [1975–Present] *94th Congress–Present* *(See also the following select committee: Small Business)*		
Herman Badillo	1975–1977	94th–95th
Henry B. González	1975–1989	94th–100th
Esteban Edward Torres	1983–1993	98th–102nd
Matthew G. Martínez	1985–1989	99th–100th
José E. Serrano	1990–1993	101st–102nd
Ed Pastor	1991–1993	102nd
Lucille Roybal-Allard	1993–1995	103rd
Nydia M. Velázquez	1993–	103rd–112th
Xavier Becerra	1995–1997	104th
Rubén Hinojosa	1997–2003	105th–107th
Grace Flores Napolitano	1999–2005	106th–108th
Charles A. Gonzalez	1999–2009	106th–110th
Aníbal Acevedo-Vilá	2001–2005	107th–108th
Linda T. Sánchez	2003–2007	108th–109th
Raúl M. Grijalva	2005–2009	109th–110th
Henry Cuellar	2007–2009	110th
Jaime Herrera Beutler	2011–	112th
STANDARDS OF OFFICIAL CONDUCT [1967–2011] *90th through 111th Congresses* *(See also the following standing committee: Ethics)*		
Ed Pastor	1997–2003	105th–107th
Lucille Roybal-Allard	2003–2009	108th–110th
TERRITORIES [1825–1847] *19th through 79th Congresses* *(Jurisdiction reassigned to the following standing committee: Public Lands)*		
Pedro Perea	1899–1901	56th
Santiago Iglesias	1937–1939	75th–76th
Bolívar Pagán	1939–1945	76th–78th
Jesús T. Piñero	1945–1946	79th
TRANSPORTATION AND INFRASTRUCTURE [1995–Present] *104th Congress–Present* *(See also the following standing committees: Public Works; Public Works and Transportation)*		
Robert Menendez	1995–2006	104th–109th
Matthew G. Martínez	1999–2001	106th
Mario Diaz-Balart	2003–2011	108th–111th
Luis G. Fortuño	2005–2007	109th
John Salazar	2005–2009	109th–110th
Grace Flores Napolitano	2007–	110th–112th
Albio Sires	2007–	110th–112th
Solomon P. Ortiz	2009–2011	111th
Jaime Herrera Beutler	2011–	112th

HOUSE STANDING COMMITTEE	TERM	CONGRESS
VETERANS' AFFAIRS [1947–Present]		
80th Congress–Present		
(See also the following standing committee: World War Veterans' Legislation)		
Edward R. Roybal	1969–1971	91st
Tony Coelho	1979–1981	96th
Matthew G. Martínez	1982–1985	97th–98th
Bill Richardson	1983–1984	98th
Frank Tejeda	1993–1997	103rd–104th
Luis V. Gutierrez	1993–2007	103rd–109th
Ciro D. Rodriguez	1997–2005	105th–108th
	2007–2011	110th–111th
Silvestre Reyes	1997–2007	105th–109th
	2011–	112th
Devin Nunes	2005	109th
John Salazar	2005–2009	109th–110th
Bill Flores	2011–	112th
Linda T. Sánchez	2011–	112th
WAR CLAIMS [1873–1947]		
43rd through 79th Congresses		
(Jurisdiction reassigned to the following standing committee: Judiciary)		
Dennis Chavez	1931–1933	72nd
WAYS AND MEANS [1795–Present]		
4th Congress–Present		
Xavier Becerra	1997–	105th–112th
Devin Nunes	2005–	109th–112th
Linda T. Sánchez	2009–2011	111th
WORLD WAR VETERANS' LEGISLATION [1924–1947]		
68th through 79th Congresses		
(Jurisdiction reassigned to the following standing committee: Veterans' Affairs)		
Dennis Chavez	1931–1933	72nd
DELEGATES AND REPRESENTATIVES WHO SERVED FULL OR PARTIAL TERMS WITHOUT COMMITTEE ASSIGNMENTS		
Joseph Marion Hernández	1822–1823	17th
José Manuel Gallegos	1853–1856	33rd–34th
	1871–1873	42nd
Miguel Antonio Otero	1856–1861	34th–36th
Francisco Perea	1863–1865	38th
José Francisco Chaves	1865–1871	39th–41st
Trinidad Romero	1877–1879	45th
Federico Degetau	1901–1903	57th
Luis Muñoz Rivera	1913–1915	63rd
Antonio Fernós-Isern	1945–1947	79th
Ed Pastor	1991–1992	101st
Albio Sires	2006–2007	109th

HOUSE SELECT COMMITTEE	TERM	CONGRESS
SELECT COMMITTEE ON AGING [1975–1993]		
94th through 102nd Congresses		
Edward R. Roybal	1975–1993	94th–102nd
Bill Richardson	1983–1993	98th–102nd
Ben Garrido Blaz	1985–1993	99th–102nd
Ed Pastor	1991–1993	102nd
SELECT COMMITTEE ON ASSASSINATIONS [1976–1979]		
94th and 95th Congresses		
Henry B. González	1976–1977	94th
SELECT COMMITTEE ON CHILDREN, YOUTH, AND FAMILIES [1983–1993]		
98th through 102nd Congresses		
Bill Richardson	1983	98th
Matthew G. Martínez	1984–1993	98th–102nd
SELECT COMMITTEE ON ENERGY INDEPENDENCE AND GLOBAL WARMING [2007–2011]		
110th and 111th Congresses		
Hilda L. Solis	2007–2009	110th
John Salazar	2009–2011	111th
SELECT COMMITTEE ON HOMELAND SECURITY [2002–2005]		
107th and 108th Congresses		
(Jurisdiction reassigned to the following standing committee: Homeland Security)		
Robert Menendez	2001–2003	107th
Lincoln Diaz-Balart	2003–2005	108th
Charles A. Gonzalez	2003–2005	108th
Loretta Sanchez	2003–2005	108th
SELECT COMMITTEE ON HUNGER [1984–1993]		
98th through 102nd Congresses		
Albert G. Bustamante	1989–1993	101st–102nd
PERMANENT SELECT COMMITTEE ON INTELLIGENCE [1977–Present]		
95th Congress–Present		
Bill Richardson	1987–1997	100th–104th
Silvestre Reyes	2001–2011	107th–111th
Luis V. Gutierrez	2011–	112th
Devin Nunes	2011–	112th
SELECT BIPARTISAN COMMITTEE TO INVESTIGATE THE PREPARATION FOR AND RESPONSE TO HURRICANE KATRINA [2005–2006]		
109th Congress		
Henry Bonilla	2005–2006	109th
SELECT COMMITTEE ON NARCOTICS ABUSE AND CONTROL [1976–1993]		
94th through 102nd Congresses		
Herman Badillo	1976–1977	94th–95th
Eligio (Kika) de la Garza II	1976–1981	94th–96th
Solomon P. Ortiz	1983–1993	98th–102nd
Ron de Lugo	1991–1993	102nd
SELECT COMMITTEE ON U.S. NATIONAL SECURITY AND MILITARY/COMMERCIAL CONCERNS WITH THE PEOPLE'S REPUBLIC OF CHINA [1998–1999]		
105th and 106th Congresses		
Lucille Roybal-Allard	1998–1999	105th–106th
SELECT COMMITTEE ON THE OUTER CONTINENTAL SHELF (AD HOC) [1975–1980]		
94th through 96th Congresses		
Eligio (Kika) de la Garza II	1975–1977	94th
SELECT COMMITTEE ON POPULATION [1977–1979]		
95th Congress		
Baltasar Corrada-del Río	1977–1979	95th

HOUSE SELECT COMMITTEE	TERM	CONGRESS
SELECT COMMITTEE ON MISSING PERSONS IN SOUTHEAST ASIA [1975–1977] *94th Congress*		
Henry B. González	1975–1977	94th
SELECT COMMITTEE ON SMALL BUSINESS [1947–1975] *80th through 93rd Congresses* *(Jurisdiction reassigned to the following standing committee: Small Business)*		
Manuel Luján, Jr.	1971–1973	92nd

JOINT COMMITTEE	TERM	CONGRESS
JOINT COMMITTEE ON ATOMIC ENERGY [1947–1977] *80th through 95th Congresses*		
Manuel Luján, Jr.	1973–1977	93rd–94th
Joseph M. Montoya	1973–1977	93rd–94th
JOINT COMMITTEE ON BICENTENNIAL ARRANGEMENTS [1975–1976] *94th Congress*		
Joseph M. Montoya	1975–1976	94th
JOINT SELECT COMMITTEE ON DEFICIT REDUCTION [2011] *112th Congress*		
Xavier Becerra	2011	112th
JOINT COMMITTEE ON DISPOSITION OF EXECUTIVE PAPERS [1947–1970] *80th through 91st Congresses*		
Dennis Chavez	1947–1948	80th
JOINT ECONOMIC COMMITTEE [1947–Present] *80th Congress–Present*		
Loretta Sanchez	2005–	109th–112th
JOINT COMMITTEE ON THE LIBRARY OF CONGRESS [1806–Present] *9th Congress–Present*		
Ed Pastor	1995–1997	104th
JOINT COMMITTEE ON PRINTING [1947–Present] *80th Congress–Present*		
Charles A. Gonzalez	2011–	112th
JOINT COMMITTEE ON TRUST TERRITORIES OF THE PACIFIC [1948–1949] *80th Congress*		
Antonio M. Fernández	1948–1949	80th

SENATE STANDING COMMITTEE	TERM	CONGRESS
AGRICULTURE AND FORESTRY [1884–1977] *48th through 94th Congresses* *(See also the following standing committee: Agriculture, Nutrition, and Forestry)*		
Octaviano A. Larrazolo	1928–1929	70th
Joseph M. Montoya	1965–1969	89th–90th
AGRICULTURE, NUTRITION, AND FORESTRY [1977–Present] *95th Congress–Present* *(See also the following standing committee: Agriculture and Forestry)*		
Ken Salazar	2005–2009	109th–110th
APPROPRIATIONS [1867–Present] *40th Congress–Present*		
Dennis Chavez	1939–1947	76th–79th
	1948–1962	80th–87th
Joseph M. Montoya	1969–1977	91st–94th
ARMED SERVICES [1947–Present] *80th Congress–Present*		
Mel Martinez	2007–2009	110th–111th
BANKING, HOUSING, AND URBAN AFFAIRS [1971–Present] *92nd Congress–Present*		
Mel Martinez	2005–2009	109th–111th
Robert Menendez	2006–	109th–112th
BUDGET [1974–Present] *93rd Congress–Present*		
Robert Menendez	2006–2011	109th–111th
COMMERCE, SCIENCE, AND TRANSPORTATION [1977–Present] *95th Congress–Present*		
Mel Martinez	2009	111th
Marco Rubio	2011–	112th
EDUCATION AND LABOR [1869–1946] *41st through 79th Congresses*		
Dennis Chavez	1941–1947	77th–79th
ENERGY AND NATURAL RESOURCES [1977–Present] *95th Congress–Present*		
Mel Martinez	2005–2009	109th–110th
Ken Salazar	2005–2009	109th–110th
Robert Menendez	2006–2011	109th–111th
FINANCE [1947–Present] *80th Congress–Present*		
Ken Salazar	2007–2009	110th
Robert Menendez	2009–	111th–112th
FOREIGN RELATIONS [1947–Present] *80th Congress–Present*		
Dennis Chavez	1935–1939	74th–75th
Mel Martinez	2005–2007	109th
Robert Menendez	2007–	110th–112th
Marco Rubio	2011–	112th
GOVERNMENT OPERATIONS [1953–1977] *83rd through 95th Congresses*		
Joseph M. Montoya	1965–1969	89th–90th
INDIAN AFFAIRS [1820–1947] *16th through 79th Congresses*		
Dennis Chavez	1935–1947	74th–79th
IRRIGATION AND RECLAMATION [1891–1905; 1921–1947] *52nd through 58th Congresses; 67th through 79th Congresses*		
Dennis Chavez	1935–1947	74th–79th

SENATE STANDING COMMITTEE	TERM	CONGRESS
POST OFFICE AND CIVIL SERVICE [1947–1977] *80th through 95th Congresses*		
Dennis Chavez	1947–1948	80th
POST OFFICE AND POST ROADS [1816–1947] *14th through 79th Congresses* *(Jurisdiction reassigned to the following standing committee: Post Office and Civil Service)*		
Dennis Chavez	1935–1947	74th–79th
PUBLIC BUILDINGS AND GROUNDS [1857–1947] *35th through 79th Congresses*		
Dennis Chavez	1935–1941	74th–76th
PUBLIC LANDS AND SURVEYS [1921–1947] *67th through 79th Congresses*		
Octaviano A. Larrazolo	1928–1929	70th
PUBLIC WORKS [1947–1977] *80th through 95th Congresses*		
Dennis Chavez	1947–1962	80th–87th
Joseph M. Montoya	1965–1977	89th–94th
SMALL BUSINESS AND ENTREPRENEURSHIP [2001–Present] *107th Congress–Present*		
Marco Rubio	2011–	112th
TERRITORIES AND INSULAR AFFAIRS [1929–1947] *71st through 79th Congresses* *(See also the following standing committee: Territories and Insular Possessions)*		
Dennis Chavez	1941–1947	77th–79th
TERRITORIES AND INSULAR POSSESSIONS [1921–1929] *67th through 70th Congresses* *(See also the following standing committee: Territories and Insular Affairs)*		
Octaviano A. Larrazolo	1928–1929	70th
VETERANS' AFFAIRS [1971–Present] *92nd Congress–Present*		
Ken Salazar	2005–2007	109th

SENATE SELECT COMMITTEE	TERM	CONGRESS
SPECIAL COMMITTEE ON AGING [1961–Present] *87th Congress–Present*		
Mel Martinez	2005–2009	109th–111th
Ken Salazar	2005–2009	109th–110th
PERMANENT SELECT COMMITTEE ON ETHICS [1977–Present] *95th Congress–Present*		
Ken Salazar	2005–2009	109th–110th
PERMANENT SELECT COMMITTEE ON INTELLIGENCE [1976–Present] *94th Congress–Present*		
Marco Rubio	2011–	112th
SELECT COMMITTEE ON NATIONAL WATER RESOURCES [1959–1961] *86th Congress*		
Dennis Chavez	1959–1961	86th
SELECT COMMITTEE ON PRESIDENTIAL CAMPAIGN ACTIVITIES [1973–1974] *93rd Congress*		
Joseph M. Montoya	1973–1974	93rd
SELECT COMMITTEE ON SENATE ROOF AND SKYLIGHTS AND REMODELING OF SENATE CHAMBER [1947–1951] *80th through 82nd Congresses*		
Dennis Chavez	1949–1951	81st–82nd
SELECT COMMITTEE ON SMALL BUSINESS [1950–1981] *81st through 97th Congresses* *(Jurisdiction reassigned to the following standing committee: Small Business)*		
Joseph M. Montoya	1965–1973	89th–92nd

Sources: David T. Canon, Garrison Nelson, and Charles Stewart III, *Committees in the U.S. Congress, 1789 to 1946*, 4 volumes (Washington, D.C.: CQ Press, 2002); various editions of the *Congressional Directory* (Washington, D.C.: Government Printing Office); various editions of the *Congressional Quarterly Almanac* (Washington, D.C.: Congressional Quarterly, Inc.); various editions of the *Congressional Record*; Garrison Nelson, *Committees in the U.S. Congress, 1947 to 1992*, 2 volumes (Washington, D.C.: Congressional Quarterly Press, 1994); Garrison Nelson and Charles Stewart III, *Committees in the U.S. Congress, 1993 to 2010* (Washington, D.C.: CQ Press, 2011); various editions of Congressional Committee Prints (Washington, D.C.: Government Printing Office).

Hispanic Americans Who Have Chaired Congressional Committees, 1881–2012

CONGRESS	MEMBER (PARTY-STATE)	HOUSE COMMITTEE
47th (1881–1883)	Romualdo Pacheco (R-CA)	Private Land Claims
48th–63rd (1883–1915)	N/A	N/A
64th (1915–1917)	Ladislas Lazaro (D-LA)	Enrolled Bills
65th (1917–1919)	Ladislas Lazaro (D-LA)	Enrolled Bills
66th–72nd (1919–1933)	N/A	N/A
73rd (1933–1935)	Dennis Chavez (D-NM)	Irrigation and Reclamation
74th–78th (1935–1945)	N/A	N/A
79th (1945–1947)	Antonio M. Fernández (D-NM)	Memorials
80th–94th (1947–1977)	N/A	N/A
95th (1977–1979)	Henry B. González (D-TX)*	Select Assassinations
96th (1979–1981)	N/A	N/A
97th (1981–1983)	Eligio (Kika) de la Garza II (D-TX)	Agriculture
98th (1983–1985)	Eligio (Kika) de la Garza II (D-TX) Edward R. Roybal (D-CA)	Agriculture Select Aging
99th (1985–1987)	Eligio (Kika) de la Garza II (D-TX) Edward R. Roybal (D-CA)	Agriculture Select Aging
100th (1987–1989)	Eligio (Kika) de la Garza II (D-TX) Edward R. Roybal (D-CA)	Agriculture Select Aging
101st (1989–1991)	Eligio (Kika) de la Garza II (D-TX) Henry B. González (D-TX) Edward R. Roybal (D-CA)	Agriculture Banking, Finance, and Urban Affairs Select Aging
102nd (1991–1993)	Eligio (Kika) de la Garza II (D-TX) Henry B. González (D-TX) Edward R. Roybal (D-CA)	Agriculture Banking, Finance, and Urban Affairs Select Aging
103rd (1993–1995)	Eligio (Kika) de la Garza II (D-TX) Henry B. González (D-TX)	Agriculture Banking, Finance, and Urban Affairs

* Henry B. González resigned from the Select Committee on Assassinations on March 8, 1977.

CONGRESS	MEMBER (PARTY-STATE)	HOUSE COMMITTEE
104th–109th (1995–2007)	N/A	N/A
110th (2007–2009)	Silvestre Reyes (D-TX) Nydia M. Velázquez (D-NY)	Permanent Select Intelligence Small Business
111th (2009–2011)	Silvestre Reyes (D-TX) Nydia M. Velázquez (D-NY)	Permanent Select Intelligence Small Business
112th (2011–Present)	Ileana Ros-Lehtinen (R-FL)	Foreign Affairs

CONGRESS	MEMBER (PARTY-STATE)	SENATE COMMITTEE
79th (1945–1947)	Dennis Chavez (D-NM)	Post Office and Post Roads
80th (1947–1949)	N/A	N/A
81st (1949–1951)	Dennis Chavez (D-NM)	Public Works
82nd (1951–1953)	Dennis Chavez (D-NM)	Public Works
83rd (1953–1955)	N/A	N/A
84th (1955–1957)	Dennis Chavez (D-NM)	Public Works
85th (1957–1959)	Dennis Chavez (D-NM)	Public Works
86th (1959–1961)	Dennis Chavez (D-NM)	Public Works
87th (1961–1963)	Dennis Chavez (D-NM)†	Public Works

† Dennis Chavez died on November 18, 1962.

Hispanic-American Chairs of Subcommittees of Standing and Select Committees in the U.S. House and Senate, 1949–2012

CONGRESS	MEMBER (PARTY-STATE)	COMMITTEE	SUBCOMMITTEE
81st (1949–1951)	Dennis Chavez (D-NM)[a]	Appropriations	Labor-Federal Security
82nd (1951–1953)	Dennis Chavez (D-NM)[a]	Appropriations	Labor-Federal Security
83rd (1953–1955)	N/A	N/A	N/A
84th (1955–1957)	Dennis Chavez (D-NM)[a]	Appropriations	Department of Defense
85th (1957–1959)	Dennis Chavez (D-NM)[a]	Appropriations	Department of Defense
86th (1959–1961)	Dennis Chavez (D-NM)[a]	Appropriations	Department of Defense
87th (1961–1963)	Dennis Chavez (D-NM)[a]	Appropriations	Department of Defense
88th–89th (1963–1967)	N/A	N/A	N/A
90th (1967–1969)	Eligio (Kika) de la Garza II (D-TX)	Agriculture	Departmental Oversight
	Joseph M. Montoya (D-NM)[a]	Select Small Business	Government Procurement
91st (1969–1971)	Eligio (Kika) de la Garza II (D-TX)	Agriculture	Departmental Operations
	Joseph M. Montoya (D-NM)[a]	Appropriations	Legislative Branch
	Joseph M. Montoya (D-NM)[a]	Public Works	Special Subcommittee on Economic Development
	Joseph M. Montoya (D-NM)[a]	Select Small Business	Government Procurement
92nd (1971–1973)	Eligio (Kika) de la Garza II (D-TX)	Agriculture	Department Operations
	Henry B. González (D-TX)	Banking and Currency	International Finance
	Joseph M. Montoya (D-NM)[a]	Appropriations	Treasury and Post Office and General Government
	Joseph M. Montoya (D-NM)[a]	Public Works	Economic Development
	Joseph M. Montoya (D-NM)[a]	Select Small Business	Government Procurement

a Denotes U.S. Senator

CONGRESS	MEMBER (PARTY-STATE)	COMMITTEE	SUBCOMMITTEE
93rd (1973–1975)	Eligio (Kika) de la Garza II (D-TX)	Agriculture	Department Operations
	Henry B. González (D-TX)	Banking and Currency	International Finance
	Joseph M. Montoya (D-NM)[a]	Joint Atomic Energy	Agreements for Cooperation
	Joseph M. Montoya (D-NM)[a]	Appropriations	Treasury, Post Office, and General Government
	Joseph M. Montoya (D-NM)[a]	Public Works	Economic Development
	Joseph M. Montoya (D-NM)[a]	Select Small Business	Government Procurement
94th (1975–1977)	Eligio (Kika) de la Garza II (D-TX)	Agriculture	Department Operations, Investigations, and Oversight
	Henry B. González (D-TX)	Banking, Currency, and Housing	International Development, Institutions, and Finance
	Henry B. González (D-TX)	Small Business	Ad Hoc Subcommittee on Antitrust, the Robinson-Patman Act, and Related Matters
	Edward R. Roybal (D-CA)	Select Aging	Housing and Consumer Interests
95th (1977–1979)	Eligio (Kika) de la Garza II (D-TX)	Agriculture	Department Investigations, Oversight, and Research
	Henry B. González (D-TX)	Banking, Finance, and Urban Affairs	International Development, Institutions, and Finance
	Edward R. Roybal (D-CA)	Select Aging	Housing and Consumer Interests
96th (1979–1981)	Eligio (Kika) de la Garza II (D-TX)	Agriculture	Department Investigations, Oversight, and Research
	Robert Garcia (D-NY)	Post Office and Civil Service	Census and Population
	Henry B. González (D-TX)	Banking, Finance, and Urban Affairs	International Development, Institutions, and Finance
	Edward R. Roybal (D-CA)	Select Aging	Housing and Consumer Interests
97th (1981–1983)	Robert Garcia (D-NY)	Post Office and Civil Service	Census and Population
	Henry B. González (D-TX)	Banking, Finance, and Urban Affairs	Housing and Community Development
	Edward R. Roybal (D-CA)	Select Aging	Housing and Consumer Interests
	Edward R. Roybal (D-CA)	Appropriations	Treasury, Postal Service, and General Government
98th (1983–1985)	Robert Garcia (D-NY)	Post Office and Civil Service	Census and Population
	Henry B. González (D-TX)	Banking, Finance, and Urban Affairs	Housing and Community Development
	Edward R. Roybal (D-CA)	Select Aging	Retirement Income and Employment
	Edward R. Roybal (D-CA)	Appropriations	Treasury, Postal Service, and General Government

CONGRESS	MEMBER (PARTY-STATE)	COMMITTEE	SUBCOMMITTEE
99th (1985–1987)	Tony Coelho (D-CA)	Agriculture	Livestock, Dairy, and Poultry
	Robert Garcia (D-NY)	Post Office and Civil Service	Census and Population
	Henry B. González (D-TX)	Banking, Finance, and Urban Affairs	Housing and Community Development
	Matthew G. Martínez (D-CA)	Education and Labor	Employment Opportunities
	Edward R. Roybal (D-CA)	Select Aging	Retirement Income and Employment
	Edward R. Roybal (D-CA)	Appropriations	Treasury, Postal Service, and General Government
100th (1987–1989)	Ron de Lugo (D-VI)[b]	Interior and Insular Affairs	Insular and International Affairs
	Robert Garcia (D-NY)	Banking, Finance, and Urban Affairs	International Finance, Trade and Monetary Policy
	Henry B. González (D-TX)	Banking, Finance, and Urban Affairs	Housing and Community Development
	Matthew G. Martínez (D-CA)	Education and Labor	Employment Opportunities
	Edward R. Roybal (D-CA)	Appropriations	Treasury, Postal Service, and General Government
101st (1989–1991)	Ron de Lugo (D-VI)[b]	Interior and Insular Affairs	Insular and International Affairs
	Henry B. González (D-TX)	Banking, Finance, and Urban Affairs	Housing and Community Development
	Matthew G. Martínez (D-CA)	Education and Labor	Employment Opportunities
	Edward R. Roybal (D-CA)	Select Aging	Retirement Income and Employment
	Edward R. Roybal (D-CA)	Appropriations	Treasury, Postal Service, and General Government
	Esteban Edward Torres (D-CA)	Small Business	Environment and Labor
102nd (1991–1993)	Ron de Lugo (D-VI)[b]	Interior and Insular Affairs	Insular and International Affairs
	Henry B. González (D-TX)	Banking, Finance, and Urban Affairs	Housing and Community Development
	Matthew G. Martínez (D-CA)	Education and Labor	Human Resources
	Edward R. Roybal (D-CA)	Select Aging	Health and Long-Term Care
	Edward R. Roybal (D-CA)	Appropriations	Treasury, Postal Service, and General Government
	Esteban Edward Torres (D-CA)	Banking, Finance, and Urban Affairs	Consumer Affairs and Coinage

a Denotes U.S. Senator

b Denotes Delegate

CONGRESS	MEMBER (PARTY-STATE)	COMMITTEE	SUBCOMMITTEE
103rd (1993–1995)	Ron de Lugo (D-VI)[b]	Natural Resources	Insular and International Affairs
	Henry B. González (D-TX)	Banking, Finance, and Urban Affairs	Housing and Community Development
	Matthew G. Martínez (D-CA)	Education and Labor	Human Resources
	Solomon P. Ortiz (D-TX)	Merchant Marine and Fisheries	Oceanography, Gulf of Mexico, and the Outer Continental Shelf
	Bill Richardson (D-NM)	Natural Resources	Native American Affairs
104th (1995–1997)	Ileana Ros-Lehtinen (R-FL)	International Relations	Africa
105th (1997–1999)	Ileana Ros-Lehtinen (R-FL)	International Relations	International Economic Policy and Trade
106th (1999–2001)	Ileana Ros-Lehtinen (R-FL)	International Relations	International Economic Policy and Trade
107th (2001–2003)	Henry Bonilla (R-TX)	Appropriations	Agriculture, Rural Development, Food and Drug Administration, and Related Agencies
	Ileana Ros-Lehtinen (R-FL)	International Relations	International Operations and Human Rights
108th (2003–2005)	Henry Bonilla (R-TX)	Appropriations	Agriculture, Rural Development, Food and Drug Administration, and Related Agencies
	Lincoln Diaz-Balart (R-FL)	Select Homeland Security	Rules
	Ileana Ros-Lehtinen (R-FL)	International Relations	The Middle East and Central Asia
109th (2005–2007)	Henry Bonilla (R-TX)	Appropriations	Agriculture, Rural Development, Food and Drug Administration, and Related Agencies
	Lincoln Diaz-Balart (R-FL)	Rules	Legislative and Budget Process
	Mel Martinez (R-FL)[a]	Foreign Relations	African Affairs
	Devin Nunes (R-CA)	Resources	National Parks, Recreation, and Public Lands
	Ileana Ros-Lehtinen (R-FL)	International Relations	The Middle East and Central Asia
110th (2007–2009)	Joe Baca (D-CA)	Agriculture	Department Operations, Oversight, Nutrition, and Forestry
	Dennis A. Cardoza (D-CA)	Agriculture	Horticulture and Organic Agriculture
	Jim Costa (D-CA)	Natural Resources	Energy and Mineral Resources
	Henry Cuellar (D-TX)	Homeland Security	Emergency Communications, Preparedness, and Response
	Charles A. Gonzalez (D-TX)	Small Business	Regulations, Healthcare and Trade
	Raúl M. Grijalva (D-AZ)	Natural Resources	National Parks, Forests, and Public Lands
	Luis V. Gutierrez (D-IL)	Financial Services	Domestic and International Monetary Policy, Trade and Technology

CONGRESS	MEMBER (PARTY-STATE)	COMMITTEE	SUBCOMMITTEE
110th (2007–2009) *continued*	Ruben Hinojosa (D-TX)	Education and Labor	Higher Education, Lifelong Learning, and Competitiveness
	Robert Menendez (D-NJ)[a]	Foreign Relations	International Development and Foreign Assistance, Economic Affairs and International Environmental Protection
	Grace Flores Napolitano (D-CA)	Natural Resources	Water and Power
	Solomon P. Ortiz (D-TX)	Armed Services	Readiness
	Linda T. Sánchez (D-CA)	Judiciary	Commercial and Administrative Law
	Loretta Sanchez (D-CA)	Homeland Security	Border, Maritime, and Global Counterterrorism
	José E. Serrano (D-NY)	Appropriations	Financial Services and General Government
111th (2009–2011)	Joe Baca (D-CA)	Agriculture	Department Operations, Oversight, Nutrition, and Forestry
	Dennis A. Cardoza (D-CA)	Agriculture	Horticulture and Organic Agriculture
	Jim Costa (D-CA)	Natural Resources	Energy and Mineral Resources
	Henry Cuellar (D-TX)*	Homeland Security	Emergency Communications, Preparedness, and Response
	Henry Cuellar (D-TX)	Homeland Security	Border, Maritime, and Global Counterterrorism
	Raúl M. Grijalva (D-AZ)	Natural Resources	National Parks, Forests, and Public Lands
	Luis V. Gutierrez (D-IL)	Financial Services	Financial Institutions and Consumer Credit
	Rubén Hinojosa (D-TX)	Education and Labor	Higher Education, Lifelong Learning, and Competitiveness
	Robert Menendez (D-NJ)[a]	Banking, Housing, and Urban Affairs	Housing, Transportation, and Community Development
	Robert Menendez (D-NJ)[a]	Foreign Relations	International Development and Foreign Assistance, Economic Affairs and International Environmental Protection
	Grace Flores Napolitano (D-CA)	Natural Resources	Water and Power
	Solomon P. Ortiz (D-TX)	Armed Services	Readiness
	Loretta Sanchez (D-CA)*	Homeland Security	Border, Maritime, and Global Counterterrorism
	José E. Serrano (D-NY)	Appropriations	Financial Services and General Government
112th (2011–Present)	Robert Menendez (D-NJ)[a]	Banking, Housing, and Urban Affairs	Housing, Transportation, and Community Development
	Robert Menendez (D-NJ)[a]	Foreign Relations	Western Hemisphere, Peace Corps, and Global Narcotics Affairs

a Denotes U.S. Senator

b Denotes Delegate

* In January 2010, Henry Cuellar replaced Loretta Sanchez as the chair of the Homeland Security Subcommittee on Border, Maritime, and Global Counterterrorism. Cuellar retained membership on the Subcommittee on Emergency Communications, Preparedness, and Response but no longer served as chair.

*Hispanic Americans in U.S. House Party Leadership Positions, 1987–2012**

CONGRESS	MEMBER (PARTY-STATE)	CAUCUS/CONFERENCE	POSITION
100th (1987–1989)	Tony Coelho (D-CA)	Democratic Caucus	Majority Whip
101st (1989–1991)	Tony Coelho (D-CA)	Democratic Caucus	Majority Whip
102nd (1991–1993)	N/A	N/A	N/A
103rd (1993–1995)	Bill Richardson (D-NM)	Democratic Caucus	Chief Deputy Whip
104th (1995–1997)	Bill Richardson (D-NM)	Democratic Caucus	Chief Deputy Whip
105th (1997–1999)	Robert Menendez (D-NJ)	Democratic Caucus	Chief Deputy Whip
106th (1999–2001)	Robert Menendez (D-NJ)†	Democratic Caucus	Vice Chair
	Ed Pastor (D-AZ)	Democratic Caucus	Chief Deputy Whip
107th (2001–2003)	Robert Menendez (D-NJ)†	Democratic Caucus	Vice Chair
	Ed Pastor (D-AZ)	Democratic Caucus	Chief Deputy Whip
108th (2003–2005)	Robert Menendez (D-NJ)†	Democratic Caucus	Chair
	Ed Pastor (D-AZ)	Democratic Caucus	Chief Deputy Whip
109th (2005–2007)	Robert Menendez (D-NJ)†**	Democratic Caucus	Chair
	Ed Pastor (D-AZ)	Democratic Caucus	Chief Deputy Whip
110th (2007–2009)	Ed Pastor (D-AZ)	Democratic Caucus	Chief Deputy Whip
111th (2009–2011)	Xavier Becerra (D-CA)†	Democratic Caucus	Vice Chair
	Ed Pastor (D-AZ)	Democratic Caucus	Chief Deputy Whip
112th (2011–Present)	Xavier Becerra (D-CA)†	Democratic Caucus	Vice Chair
	Ed Pastor (D-AZ)	Democratic Caucus	Chief Deputy Whip

* No Hispanic American has served in a party leadership position in the Senate.

† While elections for Democratic Caucus leadership positions take place in the final months of a preceding Congress, this chart does not include service that predates the beginning of a new Congress. For example, Robert Menendez was elected Vice Chair for the 106th Congress (1999–2001) in the fall of 1998.

** After being appointed to the U.S. Senate, Menendez left his leadership position in the House in December 2005.

★ APPENDIX G ★

Hispanic-American Familial Connections in Congress

CHILDREN WHO HAVE SUCCEEDED THEIR PARENTS

Resident Commissioner Jorge Luis Córdova-Díaz of Puerto Rico (1968–1973), son of Resident Commissioner Félix Córdova Dávila of Puerto Rico (1917–1932)

Representative Charles A. Gonzalez of Texas (1999–Present), son of Representative Henry B. González of Texas (1961–1999)

Representative Lucille Roybal-Allard of California (1993–Present), daughter of Representative Edward R. Roybal of California (1963–1993)

SIBLINGS WHO HAVE SERVED IN CONGRESS

Representative Linda T. Sánchez of California (2003–Present) and Representative Loretta Sanchez of California (1997–Present)

Representative Lincoln Diaz-Balart of Florida (1993–2011) and Representative Mario Diaz-Balart of Florida (2003–Present)

Representative John Salazar of Colorado (2005–2011) and Senator Ken Salazar of Colorado (2005–2009)

COUSINS WHO HAVE SERVED IN CONGRESS

Delegate José Francisco Chaves of New Mexico (1865–1867; 1869–1871), cousin of Delegate Francisco Perea of New Mexico (1863–1865), and Delegate Pedro Perea of New Mexico (1899–1901)

MISCELLANEOUS FAMILIAL CONNECTIONS IN CONGRESS*

Delegate Miguel Antonio Otero of New Mexico (1856–1861), uncle of Delegate Mariano Sabino Otero of New Mexico (1879–1881)

Resident Commissioner Santiago Iglesias of Puerto Rico (1933–1939), father-in-law of Resident Commissioner Bolívar Pagán of Puerto Rico (1939–1945)

* A number of Delegates from the New Mexico Territory had family ties through marriage. For instance, Miguel Antonio Otero, was related by marriage to José Francisco Chaves and Tranquilino Luna. Otero's nephew Mariano Sabino Otero was related by marriage to Francisco Perea and Pedro Perea. For a detailed description, see Miguel Otero, Jr., to Ansel Wold, 9 November 1928, textual files of the *Biographical Directory of the United States Congress*, Office of the Historian, U.S. House of Representatives. For background and detailed explanations about the family ties between the New Mexico Delegates, see Carlos Brazil Ramirez, "The Hispanic Political Elite in Territorial New Mexico: A Study of Classical Colonialism," (Ph.D. Diss., University of California, Santa Barbara, 1979): 22–26, 284–288, 298, 300–301, 306–307.

★ APPENDIX H ★

Congressional Hispanic Caucus and Congressional Hispanic Conference Chairmen and Chairwomen, 1976–2012

Below are the Chairmen and Chairwomen for both the Congressional Hispanic Caucus and the Congressional Hispanic Conference. The Congressional Hispanic Caucus was formed in December 1976. The Congressional Hispanic Conference was formed in March 2003. From 1984 through 1990, the Chair of the Hispanic Caucus was elected in September, to correspond with Hispanic Heritage Month rather than the beginning of the new Congress. These Chairmen served for a one-year term, September to September. Beginning with Solomon P. Ortiz, the Chair served for a term that corresponded with a Congress. Although the elections almost always took place in the months before the end of the preceding Congress, the chart below does not include service that predates the beginning of a new Congress. For example, Ed Pastor was elected Caucus Chairman in November of 1994 for 104th Congress (1995–1997).

CONGRESS	MEMBER'S NAME
CONGRESSIONAL HISPANIC CAUCUS CHAIRMEN AND CHAIRWOMEN, 1976–2012	
94th (1975–1977)	Edward R. Roybal (D-CA)
95th (1977–1979)	Edward R. Roybal (D-CA)
96th (1979–1981)	Edward R. Roybal (D-CA)
97th (1981–1983)[1]	Edward R. Roybal (D-CA) Robert Garcia (D-NY)
98th (1983–1985)[2]	Robert Garcia (D-NY) Bill Richardson (D-NM)
99th (1985–1987)[3]	Bill Richardson (D-NM) Matthew G. Martínez (D-CA) Esteban Edward Torres (D-CA)
100th (1987–1989)[4]	Esteban Edward Torres (D-CA) Albert G. Bustamante (D-TX) Jaime B. Fuster (Resident Commissioner-PR)
101st (1989–1991)[5]	Jaime B. Fuster (Resident Commissioner-PR) Eligio (Kika) de la Garza II (D-TX) Solomon P. Ortiz (D-TX)
102nd (1991–1993)	Solomon P. Ortiz (D-TX)
103rd (1993–1995)	José E. Serrano (D-NY)
104th (1995–1997)	Ed Pastor (D-AZ)
105th (1997–1999)	Xavier Becerra (D-CA)
106th (1999–2001)	Lucille Roybal-Allard (D-CA)
107th (2001–2003)	Silvestre Reyes (D-TX)
108th (2003–2005)	Ciro D. Rodriguez (D-TX)
109th (2005–2007)	Grace Flores Napolitano (D-CA)
110th (2007–2009)	Joe Baca (D-CA)
111th (2009–2011)	Nydia M. Velázquez (D-NY)
112th (2011–2013)	Charles A. Gonzalez (D-TX)
CONGRESSIONAL HISPANIC CONFERENCE CHAIRMEN AND CHAIRWOMEN, 2003–2012	
108th (2003–2005)	Mario Diaz-Balart (R-FL)
109th (2005–2007)	Ileana Ros-Lehtinen (R-FL)
110th (2007–2009)	Luis G. Fortuño (NP-PR)
111th (2009–2011)	Mario Diaz-Balart (R-FL)
112th (2011–2013)	Mario Diaz-Balart (R-FL)

1 In the 97th Congress, Edward R. Roybal served as chair from January to February 1981. Robert Garcia served as chair from February 1981 to January 1983.

2 In the 98th Congress, Robert Garcia served as chair from January 1983 to September 1984. Bill Richardson served as chair from September 1984 to January 1985.

3 In the 99th Congress, Bill Richardson served as chair from January 1985 to September 1985. Matthew G. Martínez served as chair from September 1985 to September 1986. Esteban Edward Torres served as chair from September 1986 to January 1987.

4 In the 100th Congress, Esteban Edward Torres served as chair from January to September 1987. Albert G. Bustamante served as chair from September 1987 to September 1988. Jaime B. Fuster served as chair from September 1988 to January 1989.

5 In the 101st Congress, Jaime B. Fuster served as chair from January 1989 to September 1989. Eligio (Kika) de la Garza II served as chair from September 1989 to September 1990. Solomon P. Ortiz served from September 1990 to January 1991.

Constitutional Amendments, Treaties, and Major Acts of Congress Referenced in the Text

AMENDMENT/ACT	PUBLIC LAW/U.S. CODE	MAIN PROVISIONS
NORTHWEST ORDINANCE OF 1787	1 Stat. 50-53	Provided for a territorial government in the Northwest Territory. Created the framework for territories to apply for statehood. Approved by the Second Continental Congress on July 13, 1787. Re-enacted by the 1st Federal Congress (1789–1791) on July 21, 1789.
LOUISIANA PURCHASE TREATY (1803)	8 Stat. 200-206	For approximately $15 million, France ceded Louisiana to the United States, roughly encompassing the territory between the Mississippi River in the east and the Rocky Mountains in the west. Approved by the Senate during the 8th Congress (1803–1805) on October 20, 1803.
ADAMS–ONÍS (TRANSCONTINENTAL) TREATY OF 1819	8 Stat. 252-273	Provided for Spain's cession of Florida to the United States, and set the western boundary of the Louisiana Purchase. The United States renounced claims to Texas and took responsibility for $5 million in American citizens' claims against Spain. Approved by the Senate during the 16th Congress (1819–1821) on February 19, 1821.
THE TREATY OF GUADALUPE HIDALGO OF 1848	9 Stat. 922-943	Ended the war between Mexico and the United States. Mexico ceded to the United States control of Texas north of the Rio Grande River, and the territory that eventually made up the states of California, Nevada, Utah, the bulk of New Mexico and Arizona (the Gadsden Purchase of 1853 secured the rest of the territory that comprises these states), and portions of Colorado and Wyoming. The United States paid the Mexican government $15 million and assumed $3.25 million in war claims by American citizens. Guaranteed Mexican citizens in those territories U.S. citizenship and property rights. Approved by the Senate during the 30th Congress (1847–1849) on March 10, 1848.
TEXAS AND NEW MEXICO ACT (1850)	9 Stat. 446-452	Provided Texas with $10 million, and in return Texas ceded all claims on New Mexico, formally setting the border between the two states. Stipulated that New Mexico could enter the Union either as a free or slave state based on its constitution. Passed by the 31st Congress (1849–1851) on September 9, 1850.
FOURTEENTH AMENDMENT (1868)	14 Stat. 358-359	Declared that all persons born or naturalized in the United States were citizens and that any state that denied or abridged the voting rights of males over the age of 21 would be subject to proportional reductions in its representation in the U.S. House of Representatives. Approved by the 39th Congress (1865–1867) as H.J. Res. 127; ratified by the states on July 9, 1868.

AMENDMENT/ACT	PUBLIC LAW/U.S. CODE	MAIN PROVISIONS
THE TREATY OF PARIS (1899)	30 Stat. 1754-1762	Ended the Spanish-American War and Spain ceded Cuba, Guam, Puerto Rico, and portions of the West Indies to the United States. Additionally, Spain surrendered the Philippines to the U.S. for $20 million. Approved by the Senate during the 55th Congress (1897–1899) on February 6, 1899.
FORAKER ACT OF 1900 (THE ORGANIC ACT)	31 Stat. 77-86	Established a Puerto Rican government administered by the U.S. President and Congress, with an 11-member executive council, a house of delegates, and a governor; the governor and executive council were all appointed by the U.S. President. Designated the island an "unorganized territory," granting inhabitants "U.S. national" status but not full U.S. citizenship. Provided for biennial elections for a Resident Commissioner, with a non-voting seat in the U.S. House. Passed by the 56th Congress (1899–1901) as H.R. 8245.
SECOND JONES ACT OF 1917 (THE JONES–SHAFROTH ACT)	39 Stat. 951-968	Designated Puerto Rico as a U.S. territory and granted U.S. citizenship to Puerto Ricans. Created a bicameral legislature with U.S. congressional oversight to annul or amend legislation. Term for Resident Commissioner lengthened to four years. Passed by the 64th Congress (1915–1917) as H.R. 9533.
ELECTIVE GOVERNOR ACT OF 1947 (THE CRAWFORD–BUTLER ACT)	P.L. 80-362	Amended the Foraker Act to permit Puerto Ricans to elect their governor. Passed by the 80th Congress (1947–1949) as H.R. 3309.
PUERTO RICAN FEDERAL RELATIONS ACT (1950)	P.L. 81-600	Mandated a Puerto Rican plebiscite on the territory's future relationship with the United States. Presented three options: independence, statehood, or commonwealth. With approval of a status option, the Puerto Rican legislature would convene a constitutional convention to draft a constitution for the island, including a bill of rights, to be submitted to the U.S. President and Congress for approval. Passed by the 81st Congress (1949–1951) as S. 3336.
ORGANIC ACT OF 1950	P.L. 81-630	Granted U.S. citizenship to inhabitants of Guam, and allowed for limited self-government, with a unicameral legislature and a governor appointed by the U.S. President. Oversight transferred from the U.S. Navy to the Department of the Interior. Passed by the 81st Congress (1949–1951) as H.R. 7273.
CIVIL RIGHTS ACT OF 1957	P.L. 85-315	Created the six-member Commission on Civil Rights and established the Civil Rights Division in the U.S. Department of Justice. Authorized the U.S. Attorney General to seek court injunctions against deprivation and obstruction of voting rights by state officials. Passed by the 85th Congress (1957–1959) as H.R. 6127.

AMENDMENT/ACT	PUBLIC LAW/U.S. CODE	MAIN PROVISIONS
CIVIL RIGHTS ACT OF 1960	P.L. 86-449	Expanded the enforcement powers of the Civil Rights Act of 1957 and introduced criminal penalties for obstructing the implementation of federal court orders. Extended the Civil Rights Commission for two years. Required that voting and registration records for federal elections be preserved. Passed by the 86th Congress (1959–1961) as H.R. 8601.
CIVIL RIGHTS ACT OF 1964	P.L. 88-352	Prohibited discrimination in public accommodations, facilities, and schools. Outlawed discrimination in federally funded projects. Created the Equal Employment Opportunity Commission to monitor employment discrimination in the public and private sectors. Provided additional capacities to enforce voting rights. Extended the Civil Rights Commission for four years. Passed by the 88th Congress (1963–1965) as H.R. 7152.
VOTING RIGHTS ACT OF 1965	P.L. 89-110	Suspended the use of literacy tests and voter disqualification devices for five years. Authorized the use of federal examiners to supervise voter registration in states that used tests or in which less than half the voting-eligible residents registered or voted. Directed the U.S. Attorney General to institute proceedings against use of poll taxes. Provided criminal penalties for individuals who violated the act. Passed by the 89th Congress (1965–1967) as S. 1564.
BILINGUAL EDUCATION ACT (TITLE VII OF THE ELEMENTARY AND SECONDARY EDUCATION ACT AMENDMENTS OF 1967)	P.L. 90-247	Granted federal money to local school districts to develop and provide bilingual education programs and teacher training. Passed by the 90th Congress (1967–1969) as H.R. 7819.
CIVIL RIGHTS ACT OF 1968 (FAIR HOUSING ACT)	P.L. 90-284	Prohibited discrimination in the sale or rental of approximately 80 percent of the housing in the United States. Prohibited state governments and Native-American tribal governments from violating the constitutional rights of Native Americans. Passed by the 90th Congress (1967–1969) as H.R. 2516.
VOTING RIGHTS ACT AMENDMENTS OF 1970	P.L. 91-285	Extended the provisions of the Voting Rights Act of 1965 for five years. Made the act applicable to areas where less than 50 percent of the eligible voting age population was registered as of November 1968. Passed by the 91st Congress (1969–1971) as H.R. 4249.
DELEGATE TO THE HOUSE OF REPRESENTATIVES FROM GUAM AND VIRGIN ISLANDS (1972)	P.L. 92-271	Created Delegate positions in the U.S. House of Representatives for Guam and the U.S. Virgin Islands beginning in the 93rd Congress (1973–1975). Passed by the 92nd Congress (1971–1973) as H.R. 8787.
VOTING RIGHTS ACT AMENDMENTS OF 1975	P.L. 94-73	Extended the provisions of the Voting Rights Act of 1965 for seven years. Established coverage for other minority groups including Native Americans, Hispanic Americans, and Asian Americans. Permanently banned literacy tests. Passed by the 94th Congress (1975–1977) as H.R. 6219.

AMENDMENT/ACT	PUBLIC LAW/U.S. CODE	MAIN PROVISIONS
VOTING RIGHTS ACT AMENDMENTS OF 1982	P.L. 97-205	Extended for 25 years the provisions of the Voting Rights Act of 1965. Allowed jurisdictions that could provide evidence of maintaining a clean voting rights record for at least 10 years, to avoid preclearance coverage (the requirement of federal approval of any change to local or state voting laws). Provided for aid and instruction to disabled or illiterate voters. Provided for bilingual election materials in jurisdictions with large minority populations. Passed by the 97th Congress (1981–1983) as H.R. 3112.
IMMIGRATION REFORM AND CONTROL ACT OF 1986	P.L. 99-603	Offered legal status to those immigrants who entered the United States illegally prior to 1982 and had lived continuously in the country. Fined employers for knowingly hiring undocumented workers. Passed by the 99th Congress (1985–1987) as S. 1200.
CIVIL RIGHTS RESTORATION ACT OF 1987	P.L. 100-259	Established that antidiscrimination laws are applicable to an entire organization if any part of the organization receives federal funds. Passed by the 100th Congress (1987–1989) as S. 557.
FAIR HOUSING ACT AMENDMENTS OF 1988	P.L. 100-430	Strengthened the powers of enforcement granted to the Department of Housing and Urban Development in the 1968 Fair Housing Act. Passed by the 100th Congress (1987–1989) as H.R. 1158.
CIVIL RIGHTS ACT OF 1991	P.L. 102-166	Reversed nine U.S. Supreme Court decisions (rendered between 1986 and 1991) that had raised the bar for workers who alleged job discrimination. Provided for plaintiffs to receive monetary damages in cases of harassment or discrimination based on sex, religion, or disability. Passed by the 102nd Congress (1991–1993) as S. 1745.
VOTING RIGHTS LANGUAGE ASSISTANCE ACT OF 1992	P.L. 102-344	Broadened the scope of the Voting Rights Act of 1965, guaranteeing access to bilingual ballots and voter-assistance for minority communities not covered by the earlier legislation. Passed by the 102nd Congress (1991–1993) as H.R. 4312.
VOTING RIGHTS ACT OF 2006	P.L. 109-478	Extended the provisions of the Voting Rights Act of 1965 for 25 years. Extended the bilingual election requirements through August 5, 2032. Directed the U.S. Comptroller General to study and report to Congress on the implementation, effectiveness, and efficiency of bilingual voting materials requirements. Passed by the 109th Congress (2005–2007) as H.R. 9.

★ APPENDIX J ★

Original Text of Political Poems and Songs Referenced in Contextual Essays

Referenced in *From Democracy's Borderlands: Hispanic-American Representation, 1822–1898,* on page 37.

Homilia En Verso

El dia 30 de Julio
Se reunió la convención
Para escojer Delegado
Al Congreso de la Unión.

Convención republicana
Al que bien has acordado
Que Don Mariano S. Otero
Sea nuestro Delegado.

Pues bien, Nuevo Mejicanos
Tenéis amor por la Patria
Votad por Mariano Otero
Dejad a Benito Baca.

Dando una Mirada cierta
Reflejando la cuestión
El Nuevo Méjico grita
Electo nuestro campeón!

Partido republicano
Que tienes la garantía
Que todos vuestros amigos
Trabajan de noche y día.

Atención buenos amigos
Inteligencia y valor
Y que nuestro candidato
Reciba su posición.

"Un Viajero" (A Traveler)."Homilia En Verso" (excerpt). Santa Fe *Weekly New Mexican* (Santa Fe, NM), 21 November 1878: 2. Translated as "Homily in Verse" by Translations International, Inc. (December 2009).

Homily in Verse

On July 30th
The convention met
To elect a delegate
To the Congress of the Union.

Republican Convention
You have come to good accord,
That Don Mariano S. Otero
Be our delegate.

So then New Mexicans,
Love your country,
Vote for Mariano Otero,
Drop Benito Baca.

Taking a closer look
And reflecting on the issue
New Mexico declares,
Elect our champion!

Republican Party,
You are assured
That all your friends
Work night and day.

Pay attention our friends,
Be intelligent and valiant,
Make sure the job goes
To our candidate.

Excerpt of campaign poem about Territorial Delegate Mariano S. Otero of New Mexico. From the Santa Fe *Weekly New Mexican*, November 21, 1878.

Referenced in *From Democracy's Borderlands: Hispanic-American Representation, 1822–1898,* on page 42.

Miguel Antonio Otero

El Sol con sus rayos baña
Desde lo alto del imperio
A nuestra fiel democracia
A nuestro ilustre partido
A Miguel Antonio Otero
A este joven tan querido
A quien se ha dignado el cielo
Colmarle de beneficios
Proclamamos sin recelo
Y sin cobardía a mi juicio
Viva MIGUEL, viva ANTONIO
Y viva también OTERO.

Terrible administración
Que gobierna este Condado
Que nos ha subordinando
De la libertad y acción
Ahora hay tiempo, hay ocasión
Para librarnos del mal
Democracia Nacional
Alerta, alerta, estaremos
La sangre derramaremos
Nacionales con esmero
Viva MIGUEL, viva ANTONIO
Y viva también OTERO.

En el próximo Septiembre
Tendremos nuestra elección
Para nuestro Delegado
Al Congreso de la Unión
Y también la remoción
De todo official perverso
Que todo el interés nuestro
Sea bien representado
Por medio del Delegado
Que nos ha donado el cielo
Viva MIGUEL, viva ANTONIO
Y viva también OTERO

J. L. "Miguel Antonio Otero" Santa Fe *Weekly Gazette* (Santa Fe, NM), 22 August 1857: 4. Translated as "Miguel Antonio Otero" by Translations International, Inc. (December 2009).

Miguel Antonio Otero

From high up in the empire,
the sun casts its rays
on our true democracy,
on our illustrious party,
on Miguel Antonio Otero;
on this beloved young man
showered with gifts
by the heavens;
we proclaim without apprehension
and, in my own judgment, without cowardice,
long live MIGUEL, long live ANTONIO
and long live OTERO as well.

This terrible administration
that governs this County
has subordinated
our liberty and action.
Now it is time and it is our chance
to be free from evil.
National Democracy
alert, alert we will be,
we nationals with greatest care,
will shed the blood
long live MIGUEL, long live ANTONIO
and long live OTERO as well.

Next September
we will have the elections
for our Delegate
to the Congress of the Union
and, also to remove
every corrupt official.
That all of our interests
be well represented
by our Delegate
a gift from the heavens,
long live MIGUEL, long live ANTONIO
and long live OTERO as well.

Translation of an excerpt of a campaign poem about Delegate Miguel Antonio Otero of New Mexico. From the Santa Fe *Weekly Gazette*, August 22, 1857.

Referenced in *"Foreign in a Domestic Sense," 1898–1945,* on page 162.

Sisifo (Sisyphus) excerpt

V.

Resignado
pero indomable; con la altiva y ruda
dignidad de quien cumple su destino
y en su valor descansa, poco a poco
llega el titán a la planicie y busca
el peñón que sus fuerzas desafía.
Lo contempla hito en hito; gira en torno;
estudia sus cavernas seculares
y aplica el hombre a su gigante masa.
Todo inútil. Los monstruos le acometen
con infernal estruendo y los reptiles
clavan en él su envenenada lengua.
La multitud, del éxito dudosa,
le aplaude sin cesar; pero a distancia,
cual si temiese al rápido desplome.
Resiste el bloque al temerario impulso;
redoblan su tremenda algarabía
las bestias que en sus cóncavos se ocultan
y Sísifo jadeante se detiene,
medita y vuelve a comenzar.

Luis Muñoz Rivera, "Sisifo" in *Tropicales* (New York: H.M. Call Printing, Co., 1902). Translated as "Sisyphus" by Translations International, Inc. (December 2009).

V.

Resigned
but indomitable, with the proud and rough
dignity of someone who is fulfilling his destiny
and that relies on his valor, little by little
the titan arrives at the plain and looks
for the crag that defies his strength.
He stares at it, walks around it,
studies its centuries-old caves
and puts his shoulder to the giant mass.
It's all useless. He is attacked by monsters
with infernal thunder and stung by reptiles
with their venomous tongues.
The crowd, doubtful of success,
applauds the whole time but from a distance
as if they were fearful of a fast collapse.
The block resists the bold push,
the beasts that hide in its cavities
redouble their enormous joy
and Sisyphus, breathless, stops,
reflects, and starts all over again.

By Luis Muñoz Rivera (1902), referencing Greek mythology in speaking of Puerto Rico's political position after the United States won control of the island from Spain.

Glossary

A

Antebellum The era that preceded the American Civil War, 1861–1865.

At-Large Representative A Representative elected to the U.S. House in statewide voting when a majority of the state delegation is elected by single-member, geographically-defined districts. This method for electing differs from the general ticket, in which an entire delegation is elected statewide. Until the mid-20th century, At-Large Representatives were often elected immediately following decennial apportionment. At-Large elections were abolished by federal law in 1968.

B

Barrio A neighborhood defined by geographical location, particular feature, or history.

C

Caucus A meeting of party members used primarily to select candidates for office and to consider other important business for furthering party interests. House and Senate Democrats refer to their meetings as caucuses. House and Senate Republicans describe their gatherings as "Conferences." The term also describes an organization of House and Senate Members that is devoted to a special interest or legislative area.

Census An official count of a population that includes various related statistics. The U.S. Constitution mandates that a census be taken every 10 years.

Chicano Used by Americans of Hispanic and/or *mestizo* descent in the 1960s and 1970s as a term of self-identification that emphasized working-class origins as well as indigenous influences. The term is also used to describe the historical study of citizens of Mexican descent and a civil rights initiative that pushed the government to acknowledge civil rights issues that relate to Chicanos.

Cold War The state of ideological, economic, political, military, and cultural warfare between the United States and the Soviet Union (USSR) from 1947 until 1991. Developing from divergent United States and Soviet foreign policies concerning the restoration of Europe after World War II, the conflict spread from Europe to the rest of the world. Although there were no direct military conflicts, the Soviet and U.S. superpowers tried to alter the international balance of power in their favor by competing globally for allies, strategic locations, natural resources, and influence in Asia, Africa, and Latin America. The Cold War ended with the collapse and disintegration of the USSR in 1991.

Committee (Standing, Joint, Select or Special) A Standing Committee is permanently established by House and Senate Rules and has the ability to receive and report bills and resolutions to the full chamber. A Joint Committee is also established by House and Senate Rules, with membership comprised of an equal number of Representatives and Senators and a chairperson that traditionally rotates between a House and a Senate member each Congress. A Select or Special Committee is established by resolution for a defined period of time, is usually created to investigate a specific legislative issue, and may or may not have legislative authority.

Commonwealth (in Puerto Rico, Estado Libre Asociado) A nation, state, or political unit founded on law and united by compact or tacit agreement of the people for the common good. Used to refer to self-governing political units voluntarily associated with the United States, namely Puerto Rico and the Northern Mariana Islands. The commonwealth agreement between the United States and Puerto Rico is the Estado Libre Asociado (Free Associated State or ELA), first enacted in 1952.

Compromise of 1850 The Compromise of 1850 was a series of bills organizing land ceded by Mexico to the United States in the Treaty of Guadalupe Hidalgo in 1848. After President Zachary Taylor proposed carving two free states out of the land, Southern opponents threatened secession. Senator Henry Clay of Kentucky responded with a package of compromises that was later made into a single omnibus bill. Clay's resolutions proposed admission of California as a free state; establishment of the territories of Utah and New Mexico without restrictions on slavery; adjustment of the Texas-New Mexico boundary; assumption of the debt of the Republic of Texas; enactment of a stronger fugitive slave law; abolition of the slave trade in the District of Columbia; and approval of a resolution stating that Congress had no power over the interstate slave trade. Although his proposals failed to pass as one bill, each gained a majority on its own. By September 17, 1850, all of these proposals were signed into law by President Millard Fillmore.

Constituents People living within the geographic area that a Member of Congress represents.

Cortes Spain's parliament that consists of two houses: the lower house (*Congreso de los Diputados*), and the upper house (*El Senado*).

D

Delegate A non-voting official in the U.S. House representing the following territories: the District of Columbia, Guam, American Samoa, the U.S. Virgin Islands, and the Northern Mariana Islands. Delegates serve two-year terms. Delegates cannot vote in the full House but are permitted to vote in committees and can introduce and cosponsor legislation. Under a House rule in place in 1993 and 1994, and restored in 2007, delegates are permitted to vote in the Committee of the Whole, in which the House considers appropriations, authorization and tax bills for amendment. If the votes of the delegates are decisive on any vote in the Committee of the Whole, the amendment is automatically voted on again in the full House, where the delegates cannot vote.

Disfranchisement The act of depriving an eligible citizen or a portion of the population of voting rights.

District A geographical area represented by a U.S. Representative.

G

Great Depression The economic crisis and period of minimal business activity in the United States and other industrialized nations that began in 1929 and continued through the 1930s. During the 1920s in the United States, speculation on the stock market led to changes in the federal monetary policy. The subsequent decline in personal consumption and investments triggered the stock market crash of 1929, which, along with World War I debts and reparations, precipitated the Great Depression.

Great Society A wave of social reform legislation championed by President Lyndon Johnson in the mid-1960s and passed in the wake of a Democratic sweep in the 1964 presidential and congressional elections. The crowning legislation of Johnson's reforms included increased aid for education; the establishment of Medicare and Medicaid which provided healthcare for the elderly and the poor; immigration reform; and the 1965 Voting Rights Act, which outlawed literacy tests and provided federal monitoring of elections in southern states.

H

Hispano A 19th-century term describing a person of Hispanic and/or *mestizo* descent native to the American West and Southwest.

House Rules The rules and precedents that govern the conduct of business in the House. These rules address duties of officers, the order of business, admission to the floor, parliamentary procedures on handling amendment and voting, and jurisdictions of committees. Whereas the House re-adopts its rules, usually with some changes, at the beginning of each Congress, Senate rules carry over from one Congress to the next.

I

Incumbency The holding of an office or the term of an office (usually political).

J

Jim Crow A system of segregation enforced by law and custom that aimed at the social control and the political and economic subjugation of African Americans in the South from the late 1800s to the 1960s. Hispanic Americans experienced varying degrees of Jim Crow segregation in the Southwest during this period.

M

Manifest Destiny A term used in the 1840s to justify U.S. expansion into Texas, Oregon, and Mexico, on the theory that Providence had designated North America as a stage for demonstrating history's larger trajectory. Jacksonian journalist John O'Sullivan is reputed to have coined the term and wrote that Manifest Destiny was "to overspread the continent allotted by Providence for the free development of our yearly multiplying millions."

Mestizo A person of American Indian and Caucasian ancestry.

N

New Deal A period of political, economic, and social activity spanning President Franklin D. Roosevelt's first two terms in office (1933–1941). In response to the Great Depression, the Roosevelt administration worked with Congress to provide an unprecedented level of emergency intervention to revive the economy and provide basic welfare to citizens.

Nominating Convention A meeting of local party officials to select the delegates who eventually designate party nominees for elective office or represent the locality at state or national conventions. Developed in the 1820s and 1830s, the system ensured that only one party member would run for an elective position while it provided structure and publicity for the party. In the early 20th century the modern primary election replaced the nominating convention as the principal method for selecting congressional candidates.

Nuevomexicano A 19th-century term used to describe Hispanics and Caucasians living in New Mexico. This publication uses the term to describe New Mexicans of Hispanic and/or *mestizo* descent.

O

Omnibus Bill A term used to refer to a package of numerous, often unrelated, bills that are bundled together and considered in Congress as a single measure.

P

Patrón The master or owner of an estate; also used to describe a political boss.

Plebiscite A vote by which the people of an entire country or district express an opinion for or against a proposal especially on a choice of government or ruler.

Primary A preliminary election, usually between aspirants from the same political party held to determine who will serve as the party's candidate in the general election.

R

Redistricting The redrawing of U.S. House districts within states, following the constitutionally mandated decennial census and the apportionment of seats. State legislatures draw new districts based on population declines or increases that result in the addition or subtraction of House seats apportioned to the state.

Resident Commissioner of Puerto Rico Puerto Rico's non-voting delegate, elected by the people of Puerto Rico for a four-year term. Puerto Rico has had a Resident Commissioner in the House since 1901.

Rico Literally "the rich"; a term used to describe affluent *Hispanos* and Anglos in 19th-century New Mexico.

S

Seniority Priority or precedence in office or service; superiority in standing to another of equal rank by reason of earlier entrance into the service or an earlier date of appointment.

Special Election An election held by a state to fill a vacancy created when a Member of Congress dies, resigns, or is expelled. All House vacancies must be filled by election; Senate vacancies usually are filled by temporary appointments until a special election can be organized.

Statutory Representation A position defined by congressional mandate rather than by the United States Constitution. Territorial Delegates and Resident Commissioners are statutory representatives. Senators and Representatives are Constitutional Representatives.

W

Whip An assistant House or Senate Floor leader who helps round up party members for quorum calls and important votes. Coined in the British Parliament, this term is derived from "whipper-in," a person who keeps the dogs from straying during a fox hunt.

Index

Member names appear in **bold** (surnames in **ALL CAPS**)
Bold page numbers denote Member profiles
Italicized page numbers denote references to figure legends

A

Abzug, Bella, 452, 459, 461n
Acevedo, A.C., 516
ACEVEDO-VILÁ, Anibal, 476, 509, 600, **620–625**, 634, 637
Adams, John Quincy, 25–26, *26*, 29, 33, 72–74
Adams-Onís (Transcontinental) Treaty of 1819, *26*, 25–27. *See*, Appendix I: Constitutional Amendments, Treaties, and Major Acts of Congress Referenced in the Text.
Agricultural Adjustment Act of 1933, 170, 186n, 273, 302
Albert, Carl, 354, *354*, 358n, 385, 431, 450
Alianza (Alliance), 160, 193, 246, 288, 301, 305n
  Hispanic representation, 246–53
Alianza Agricultural (Agricultural Alliance), 290
Alien Adjustment and Employment Act of 1977, 489–90
Alinsky, Saul, 410
Allen, Charles H., *164*
Allen, O. K., 286n
Allison, W. H. H., 105
American Federation of Labor (AFL), 150, 160, 300–301, 303, 331, 337, 342, 555, 695
American Indians, 27, 30–31, *34*, 47–49, 73, 93, 138n. *See also*, Apache Indians; Hopi Indians; Navajo Indians; Pueblo Indians; Seminole Indians.
  conflicts and, 34, 38, 48, 70, 74, 93, 100, 102, 115n
  legislation and, 112, 130, 142, 257, 319–20, 329, 392–93, 396n, 545, 669, 683
  peonage. *See*, Peonage.
  removal and, 47–49, *48*, 75, 102, 104, 110–11
  reservation system, 30, *34*, 47–49, 74, 85–86, 100, 102–105, 110–11, 115n, 257, 329. *See also*, Bosque Redondo Reservation.
  slavery. *See*, Slavery.
  treaties and. *See*, Treaty of Guadalupe Hidalgo; Treaty of Moultrie Creek.
  tribal sovereignty and, 329, 443
  voting rights, 61n, 82–83, 319
American Party. *See*, New Mexico Territory.
American Revolution, 72
Americans with Disabilities Act of 1990, 525
Anderson, Clinton, *7*, 316, 392–93, 395n
Andrews, William H., Jr., 267n
Apache Indians, 37, 48, *48*, 50, 102, 108, 110–11
Apportionment and redistricting, 7, 316, 403, 410, 415, 443–44, 451, 474, 485, 518, 528, 530, 552–53, 566, 586, 606, 616, 618, 662, 664, 676, 680, 682
Arcelay, Maria Luisa, 303
Arctic National Wildlife Refuge (ANWR), 642, 650
Arizona, Hispanic representation, 668–69, 682–83. *See also*, Appendix B: Hispanic-American Representatives, Senators, Delegates, and Resident Commissioners by State and Territory, 1822–2012.
Armijo, Manuel, 80, 108
Arny, William F. M., 85, 103, 106–107n, 115–16n
Arredondo, Felipe Cuebas, 202, 207n
Articles of Confederation, 32
Ashburn, Roy, 606
Ashley, James, 104, 107n, 115n
Aspinall, Wayne, 327, 385
At-Large Representative, 256, 258, 272, 316, 320, 327, 390, 392, 440, 442, 445n. *See also*, Appendix K: Glossary.
Atchison, Topeka, Santa Fe Railroad, 44, 95, 99n, 112, 140, 254
Austin, Stephen, 28
Ayers, James, 121

B

Babbitt, Bruce, 546, 549n
Baca, Benito, *37*, 130, 131n, 140, 143n, 751
BACA, Joe, 656–57
Baca, Juan, 134
BADILLO, Herman, 8, *8*, 325–26, *328*, 328–30, *330*, 344, *344*, 355–57, 358–59n, 368n, 371, 422, 437, **448–55**, 459, 461n, 477, *477*, 516, 518
Baird, Spruce McCoy, 93, 97n
Baker, Howard, 459
Baldorioty de Castro, Román, 218, 220
Balzac v. Porto Rico. *See*, Supreme Court, United States.
Bankhead, William B., 284, 303
Barbee, Alfred, 229
Barbosa, José Celso, 300
Barceló, Antonio R., 250, 305n, 596
Barkley, Alben, 334–35
Bartlett, Robert, 352
Batista, Fulgencio, 590, 664
Bay of Pigs, 406
Beame, Abraham, 452
Beauchamp, Elías, 173
BECERRA, Xavier, 8, 480, **658–59**
Bell, C. Jasper, 178–79, 375
Benedict, Kirby, 85, 117n
BENÍTEZ, Jaime, 325–26, 350, *350*, 356–57, 365n, 371, 438, 439n, **456–61**, 469n, 510
Bennet, Hiram, 106n
Benton, Thomas Hart, 29, 83, 88n
Bentsen, Lloyd, 348, *488*
Berman, Howard L., 528, 532n, 552
Bethune, Farquar, 74
Beveridge, Albert J., 54, *54*, 66n
Beverley, James, 288, 290, 293, 296n, 305n
Biaggi, Mario, 521
Bilingual Education Act (Title VII of the Elementary and Secondary Education Act Amendments of 1967), *340*, 340–41, 393, 413, 423, 452, 487–89. *See also*, Appendix I: Constitutional Amendments, Treaties, and Major Acts of Congress Referenced in the Text.
Blackwood, Mary Josephine, 43
BLAZ, Ben Garrido, 422, 476, 478, 484, 494, *494*, 500n, 503n, 509, **556–61**, 610, 613
Bliss, Cornelius Newton, 197n
Bloomberg, Michael, 453
Blue Dog Coalition, 500, 632, 657, 661, 663
Boggs, Hale, 285, 431
Bolack, Thomas, 390, 392, 395–96n
Bone, Homer, 179
BONILLA, Henry, 477, 481, *482*, 485–86, 509, 565–66, **582–89**, 618, 662
Bonior, David, 546
Booth, John Wilkes, 103
Booth, Newton, 120
Bordallo, Ricardo, 560
Border Patrol, United States, 331, 337–38, 686–87
Bosone, Reva, 348n
Bosque Redondo Reservation, 47–49, 62n, 104–105, 106n, 110–11, 115n
Boxer, Barbara, 414
Bracero Program, 335–38, 361n, 403, 408n, 413, 668
Brademas, John, 479–80
Bratton, Sam Gilbert, 262, 273, 277n
Breeden, William A., 142
Broder, David, 519
Brooke, John, 153, 300
Brown Power movement, 403, 422
Brown, E. L., 117n
Brown, George E., Jr., 656, 719n
Brown, Henry, 151
Brownell, Herbert, Jr., 337
Buchanan, James, 51
Bursum, Holm O., 240, 257, 260n
Burton, Phillip, 456, 464, 469n, 522, 530, 552
Bush, George H. W., 404–406, 423, 445, 484, *489*, 493, 520, 533n, 546, 571–72, 573n, 578, 584, 610
Bush, George W., 475, 485–86, 501n, 585–86, 613, 623, 634, 640, 642, 646, 648, 650, 692, 695
BUSTAMANTE, Albert G., *474*, 477, 491, *492*, 509, **562–67**, 582, 584, 587n
Butler, Hugh, 345, 365n, 383
Byrns, Joseph W., 286n

C

Cadwalader, John, 84
CAFTA. *See*, Central American Free Trade Agreement (CAFTA).
Calhoun, John C., 28, 33, *53*, 74
California, Hispanic representation, 118–23, 328, 410–19, 522–27, 528–35, 550–55, 626–29, 630–33, 656–57, 658–59, 660–61, 678–79, 680–81, 690–91, 694–95, 696–97. *See also*, Appendix B: Hispanic-American Representatives, Senators, Delegates, and Resident Commissioners by State and Territory, 1822–2012.
Californios for Fair Representation, 528, 530
Call, Richard Keith, 74
Camacho, Felix, 614
Campbell, Ben, 648
Campbell, Philip, 176
Campos, Pedro Albizu, 173, 334, 451
Canby, Edwin, 95
Cannon, Joseph Gurney, *163*, 163–64, 184n, 214
CANSECO, Francisco (Quico), 618, **704**
Cantinflas, 402
Capone, Al, 584
CARDOZA, Dennis A., 500n, 509, **630–33**
Caribbean Basin Initiative, 467, 570
Caribe Democratic Club, 448
Carleton, James H., 48, 105, 107n, 110–11, 115n
Carranza, Venustiano, 239, 243n
Carroll, Charles, 43, 90
Carson, Kit, 48, 110
Carter, James Earl (Jimmy), 413, 443, 483, *483*, 487–90, 513, 525, 544, 552, 626
Cass, Lewis, 115n
Casso, Jamie, 555
Castor, Betty, 640
Castro, Fidel, 424, 486, 590, 592–93, 640, 664–65, 688, 700
Catala, Francisco, 570
Catron, Thomas Benton, 38, *38*, 60n, 117n, 130, 194, 196, 238–39, 242–43n, 256
Celler, Emanuel, 336
Census Bureau, 414. *See also*, Apportionment and redistricting.

Central America, foreign policy, 122, 564–65, 570, 578, 592. *See also*, Central American Free Trade Agreement (CAFTA); Nicaragua; Contras; Immigration.
Central American Free Trade Agreement (CAFTA), 663, 665
Chambers, Marjorie Bell, 544, 548n
Chappius, Phillip J., 228
Chardón, Carlos, 172
Chase, Salmon, 107n, 115n
Chaves, Francisco Xavier, 35, 100, 108
CHAVES, José Francisco, *34*, 34–44, *35*, *39*, 47–50, 52–54, 58–59n, 64–65n, 69, 86, 100, 105, 107n, **108–17**, 130, 134, 137, 139n, 144n
Chaves, Mariano, 108
Chávez, César, *340*, 340
CHAVEZ, Dennis, 167–68, *168*, *178*, 193, 233n, **270–79**, 313, 319, *327*, 327–28, 392–93, 395n, 409n
"Chavez Committee," 177–79
civil rights and, 179–80, 270, 275–76, 324, 334
Cold War and, 275–76, 354–55, *355*
committee assignments, 7, 169, 272–75, 354
early background, 270, 272
Fair Employment Practices Committee, 274, *334*, 334–35
legislative interests, 272–76, 327–28, 337
legislative style, 273
New Deal and, 272–75
Puerto Rico and, 177–79, 274, 322, 348, 358n, 375
surrogate representation and, 6, *6*, 148, 322
Cheney, Richard (Dick), 586
Chisholm, Shirley, 437, 450
Christensen, Donna, 468
Christensen, Parley P., 410
Citizens for State 51, 434, 596
Civil Rights, 3, *6*, 6–8, 180, 200, 256, 262, 264–65, 270, 322, *322*, 324, *327*, 329, *330*, 330–32, 335, *340–41*, 360n, 363n, 393–94, 410, 413–14, 486, *487*, 489, 493, 598, 622, 650, 667, 689
See also, Civil Rights legislation; Civil Rights Movement; Cold War; Democratic Party; Discrimination; Disfranchisement; Elections; Republican Party; Segregation; Senate, United States; Supreme Court, United States.
Civil Rights legislation, 328–29, 403, 413, 422–23
See also, Appendix I: Constitutional Amendments, Treaties, and Major Acts of Congress Referenced in the Text.
Civil Rights Act of 1964, 329, 357, 397n, 403
Civil Rights Restoration Act of 1987, 423
Civil Rights Movement, 7–8, 63n, 325, 338–41, 344, 354, 357, 397n, 495, 598
Civil War, *24*, *34*, 35–38, *38*, 43, 47–49, *52*, 54, 59n, 64–65n, 85, 89n, 90, 95, 98n, 106n, 108, 122, 143, 151, *156*, 265, 335, 548. *See also*, Military service, Hispanic-American Members of Congress.
Civilian Conservation Corps (CCC), 273, 410, 532
Clancy, Frank W., 114
Clark, Clarence, 198n
Clark, James Beauchamp (Champ), 39, 163, 204, 214
Clay, Henry, 36, *36*, *53*, 752
Cleveland, Grover, 122, 151
Clever, Charles P., 39, 85, 111–12, 116n
Clinton, William J. (Bill), 424, 485–86, 492–94, *493*, 504n, 532, 538, 542, 546, 549n, 554, 560, 584–85, 593, 599–600, 606, 608, 610, 622, 697, 703
Club político independiente de Nuevo Mexico, 272
Coalición (Coalition), 160, 193, 248, 291, 293, 301, 303, 308, 310, 313, 315n, 374, 380
Hispanic representation, 298–315
COELHO, Tony, 8, *8*, 476, *477*, 479, 490–91, *491*, 509, **522–27**, 565
Coffee, Harry, 177
Cold War, 275, 322, 344, 348, 354–56, 390, 394, 412, 444, 538, 558, 564, 590, 607, 612
Coleman, Dennis, 450
Coleman, Ron, 686
Coll y Toste, Cayetano, 210
Collier, John, 319
Collins, James L., 85, 94
COLORADO, Antonio J., 294n, 314n, 386n, 495, 504n, 509, **576–81**, 598
Colorado, Hispanic representation, 644–51. *See also*, Appendix B: Hispanic-American Representatives, Senators, Delegates, and Resident Commissioners by State and Territory, 1822–2012.
Committee assignments. *See*, Appendix C: Hispanic-American Members' Committee Assignments (Standing, Joint, Select) in the U.S. House and Senate, 1822–2012; Hispanic-American Members of Congress, characteristics.
Commonwealth of Puerto Rico. *See*, Estado Libre Asociado (Free Associated State).
Communism. *See*, Cold War.
Community Service Organization (CSO), 6, 338–39, 410, 412–13, 416n
Compromise of 1850, *31*, 36, *36*, 40, 50, 52, *53*, 137, 752
Conaway, Michael, 588n
Condit, Gary, 630
Congress of Mexican-American Unity, 414
Congressional Asian Pacific American Caucus (CAPAC), 500n, 612, 659
Congressional Black Caucus (CBC), 414, 418n, 464, 483, 486, *487*, 492
Congressional Caucus on Women's Issues, 628
Congressional districts. *See*, Apportionment and redistricting.
Congressional Drought Relief Task Force, 423
Congressional Hispanic Caucus (CHC), *9*, *10*, *322*, 413, *477*, *479*, *481–84*, *487*, *491*, 497, *497*, 562, 599, 632, 657, 659, 674, 685, 695, 698, 701. *See also*, Appendix H: Congressional Hispanic Caucus and Congressional Hispanic Conference Chairmen and Chairwomen, 1976–2012.
committee assignments and, 484–85
diversity of, 475, 483–85, 525, 568
formation of, 8, 180, 324–25, 357, 403, 413, 422, 444, 475, 483, 485, 510
immigration and, 483–86, 490, *490*, *492*
leadership of, 410, 422, 483, *485*, 489–90, 531, 538, 542, 545, 553, 570, 599, 616, 669, 679, 683, 687, 690, 699
legislative interests of, 482–88, *492*, *493*, 519, 687
legislative strategy of, 324, 357, 403, 413, 475, 482–86, 538, 570
partisanship and, 444–45, 484, 486
relationship with Presidents, *483*, 483–86, *493*
task forces and, 485, 622, 628–29, 667, 671, 673
Congressional Hispanic Conference, 8–9, 486, 497, 593, 636, 665, 681. *See also*, Appendix H: Congressional Hispanic Caucus and Congressional Hispanic Conference Chairmen and Chairwomen, 1976–2012.
Connecticut, 343, 726n
Connelly, Henry, 58–59n, 100, 103, 107n, 115n
Conner, Pat, 682
Connolly, Lani, 619
Conservative Party (Puerto Rico), 218
Constitution, United States, 2, *25*, 29, 31–32, *32*, 38, 47, 78n, 93–94, 102, 148, 155, 157, 161
Constitutional Historical Party, 248
Contested elections, 38–42, 46, 78n, 80, 84, 92, 103, 112, 117n, 120, 130, 137, 140, 142, 273, 275, 286n, 558
Continental Congress, 32, 745
Contract with America, 492, 592. *See also*, Republican Party.
Contras, 519, 546, 548–49n, 564–65
Cook, Schuble, 440
Cooley, Harold Dunbar, *7*, 426n
Coolidge, Calvin, *5*, 230, 250, 434
Cooper, Henry, 162, 203, 207n, 213–14
Coors, Pete, 648, 650
CÓRDOVA DÁVILA, Felix, *5*, 149–50, 157, 159–60, 164–66, 169, *175*, 175–76, 183n, 193, 233n, **246–53**, 288, 291, 325, 409n, 434
CÓRDOVA-DÍAZ, Jorge Luis, 149, 325–26, 350, 353–54, 356, 358n, 367–68n, 371, 409n, 432, **434–39**, 458, 461n, 494, 510, 637n
Cornell, Dudley, 320
CORRADA-DEL RÍO, Baltasar, 8, 357, 460, 488, *488*, 494, 509, **510–15**, 598, 684
Cortes (Spain), 153–54, 200, 220, 753
Corzine, Jon S., 677, 700, 721n
COSTA, Jim, **660–61**
Coulter, Joe, 422
Cranston, Alan, 412
Crawford, Fred L., 177, 345–46, *347*, 376, 382–83
Crawford–Butler Act. *See*, Elective Governor Act.
Crespo, Domingo S., 303
Crist, Charlie, 642
Crittenden, John, 29, 57n
Cruz, Manuel, 610
Cuba, 8–9, 56n, 70, 72, 76n, *146*, 152–53, 170, *174*, 220, 486, 590, 593, 644
United States trade with, 170–71, 186n, 214, 302, 311, 382, 424, 592–93, 664, 677, 699, 701
Cuba Democracy Group, 592
Cude, Mark, 607
CUELLAR, Henry, 586, 618, **662–63**
Cuevas Zequeira, Rafael, 288, 294n
Culebra, 459, 461n
Cummings, Amos, 146
Cuomo, Mario, 452
Cusack, Patrick, 590
Cutting, Bronson, 168, 266, 268n, 273, 277n, 712n
Cwiklik, Robert, 406

D

Dallinger, Frederick, 251
Dalton, John, 608
Dalzell, John, 162, 203
Danielson, George E., 530, 552, 715n
Danielson, Gladys C., 531
Davis, Garrett, 29, 57n
Davis, George W., 153
Davis, Jefferson, 43, 94
Dayton, Jonathan, 32, *32*
de Baca, Ezquiel C., 265, 270
de Diego, José, 221
DE LA GARZA, Eligio II (Kika), 325–26, *326*, 371, **420–27**, *490*, 672
agriculture policy, 422–24
committee assignments and, *7*, 327, 420, 422–23, 477, 482
Congressional Hispanic Caucus and, 8, 357, 422, 482
legislative interests, 329–30, 422–24, 490–91
legislative style, 422, 424
Vietnam War and, 356
DE LUGO, Ron, 325–26, 328, 352–54, *353*, 357, 358n, 371, 437, **462–71**, 476, 478, *491*, 503n, 560, 571–72
de Onís, Luis, 25, 72
De Rouen, René Louis, 226, 232n

de Santa Anna, Antonio López, 28, *28*
Debs, Ernest, 417n
Declaration of Independence, 202, 335
Decolonization, 345, 349, 354, 383. *See also*, Cold War.
DeFino, Anthony, 700
DEGETAU, Federico, 5, 146, 149, 152–53, 159–60, 162–63, *163*, 168, 193, **200–209**, 210, 212, 214, 221
DeJongh, John, Jr., 470n
DeLay, Tom, 586, 588n, 607
Delegate. *See*, Territorial Delegate.
Dellums, Ronald V., *328*, 418n, 505n, 573n
Democratic Congressional Campaign Committee (DCCC), 8, 479, 525–26, 632, 685, 701
Democratic National Committee, 273, 462
Democratic National Convention, 94, 106n, 228, 339, 613
Democratic Party, 28–29, 39, 56n, 67–69, 93, 120–21, 177, 190–91, 193, 369, 371, 506–507, 509
  American South and, 280
  Civil Rights movement and, 344
  Congressional Hispanic Caucus and, 485
  Hispanic Americans and, 264, 267n, 270, 324, 339–40, 344, 444
  Hispanic representation and, 80–99, 140–45, 226–35, 270–87, 316–21, 390–427, 448–55, 462–71, 516–55, 562–67, 604–19, 626–33, 644–51, 656–63, 666–79, 682–83, 686–87, 690–703
  See also, Hispanic American Democrats (HAD); New Deal; New Mexico Territory, party politics and.
Democratic Senatorial Campaign Committee (DSCC), 480, 677
Democratic Steering and Policy Committee, 485, 564, 628, 632
Democratic Study Group, 358n, 450
Democratic Women's Working Group, 628
Dempsey, John J., 274, 278n, 316, 320, 392
Department of Agriculture, United States, 170, 177, 424
Department of Labor, United States, 233n, 302, 333, 337, 466
Department of State, United States, 159, 161, 170, 276, 333, 335, 542
Department of the Interior, United States, 47, 172, 257, 329, 375, 392, 442, 465, 585
Department of War, United States, 164, 172, 215, 274, 292–93
Deutsch, Hermann B., 282
Development, Relief, and Education for Alien Minors (DREAM) Act, 493, 642, 683
DIAZ-BALART, Lincoln, 424, 476, *480*, 480–81, 485–86, 492, 509, **590–95**, 665
DIAZ-BALART, Mario, 476, **664–65**
Diaz-Balart, Rafael, 664
Dillon, W. B., 241
Discrimination, 36, 40, 51–54, 87n, 167, 180n, 197n, 264, 267n, 274, 318, 324, 330–34, 336, 341, 357, 393, 396n, 402, 410, 415, 472, 525, 536, 592, 599, 670
  hiring practices and, 274, 330, 334, 525–26
  immigration legislation, fears of, 332–33, 415, 444–45, 489–92, 565
  Territories, federal programs and, 291, 382, 465, 559, 600
  See also, Hispanic-American Members of Congress, discrimination against.
Disfranchisement, 2, 39, 148, 264, 324. *See also*, Appendix K: Glossary.
  poll tax, 56n, 324, 536. *See also*, Appendix I: Constitutional Amendments, Treaties, and Major Acts of Congress Referenced in the Text.
District of Columbia, 319, 439n, 559, 612, 726n
  Delegate, 44, 367n, 439n, 469n, 636
Dole, Robert, 465, 505n, 573n, 584
Dominican Republic, 153
Donelson, Andrew Jackson, 29
Dooley, Calvin M., 660
Dornan, Bob, 696
Dorr v. United States. *See*, Supreme Court, United States.
Douglas, Stephen A., *24*
Downes v. Bidwell. *See*, Supreme Court, United States.
Dred Scott v. Sanford. *See*, Supreme Court, United States.
Dust Bowl, 168–69, 332, 524
DuVal, William Pope, 72–73

E

East Harlem, New York, 312, 326, 342, 344, 363n, 448. *See also*, New York, Hispanic representation.
Economic policy. *See*, Central American Free Trade Agreement (CAFTA); Civilian Conservation Corps (CCC); Congressional Hispanic Caucus; Congressional Hispanic Conference; Cuba, United States trade with; Fair Employment Practices Committee (FEPC); Immigration; New Deal; North American Free Trade Agreement (NAFTA).
Education policy
  bilingual education, 330, *340*, 393, 413, 452, 454, 481, 483, 486–89, 512–13, 528, 531, 564, 570, 657, 665, 669. *See also*, Bilingual Education Act.
  GI Bill of Rights and, 318, 528, 550, 559
  legislation. *See*, Bilingual Education Act; Development, Relief, and Education for Alien Minors (DREAM) Act; Elementary and Secondary Education Act (ESEA); Vocational Education Act of 1963.
  veterans and, 606, 618, 689
Edwards, T. Arthur, 229
Eighteenth Amendment, 231, 234n, 256, 290. *See also*, Prohibition.
Eisenhower, Dwight D., 275, 337, 351, 354, 368, 390, 402
El Salvador, foreign policy, 484, 545, 590
El Toro Wilderness, 636
El Yunque, 623, 685
Elections
  1932 election, 172, 272–73, 288, 290–93, 300–301
  1940 election, 274, 284–85, 310, 374, 380
  1960 election, *339*, 339–40, 434
  1968 election, 353, 434, 436, 440, 442, 494
  1976 election, 394–95, 459–60, 475, 483, 510
  1982 election, 478, 490, 530
  1992 election, 7–8, 422, 476, 479, 485, 495, 504n, 538, 565, 579, 582, 590, 598, 606, 610, 658, 670, 676, 688, 690, 702
  conventions and, 167, 185n, 339, 496
  Foraker Act and, 153–54, 161
  See also, individual states; individual Hispanic-American Members of Congress; Apportionment and redistricting; Contested elections; Democratic Party; Disfranchisement; Machine politics; Republican Party; Voting Rights.
Elective Governor Act (Crawford–Butler Act), 7, *172*, 325, 328, 345–47, 376, 383. *See*, Appendix I: Constitutional Amendments, Treaties, and Major Acts of Congress Referenced in the Text.
Elementary and Secondary Education Act (ESEA) of 1965, 393, 431, 452
Elizalde, Joaquin, 294n, 314n, 386n, 580n
Elkins, Stephen B., 38, 52, *52*, 54, 60n, 65n, 86, 89n, 116n, 124, 130, 197n
Ellis Island, New York, 204
Ellison, Samuel, 87–88n
Ely, Charles, 238
Emigration. *See*, Puerto Rico, migration to mainland U.S.
Endangered Species Act of 1973, 585
England, 29, 298
Equal Employment Opportunity Commission (EEOC), 340, 747
Escobar, Tim, 695
Estado Libre Asociado (Free Associated State)
  antecedents, 158–59, 310, 344–45, 375–76
  creation of, 7, 180, 322, 324–25, 328, *343*, 345–49, 380, 383–85, 428, 456, 458. *See also*, Appendix I: Constitutional Amendments, Treaties, and Major Acts of Congress Referenced in the Text.
  effect on Office of Resident Commissioner, 351–54
  initial reactions to, 349–51
  opposition to. *See*, Statehood, Puerto Rico; Puerto Rico, independence and.
  support for, 160, 428, 430–31, 456, 458–60, 495, 505n, 568, 571, 578–79, 620
Estrada, Miguel, 486
Evans, Melvin, 466, 469n
Executive Order 8802. *See*, Fair Employment Practices Committee.

F

Fair Employment Practices Commission (FEPC), 274, 334, *334*
Fair Employment Practices Committee, 334
Fajardo Cardona, Mateo, 212
Famadas, Nelson, 570
Familial connections. *See*, Appendix G: Hispanic-American Familial Connections in Congress; Hispanic-American Members of Congress, characteristics.
Farenthold, Blake, 539
Farm Subsidy Administration (FSA), 177
Farrington, Joseph, 352
Fauntleroy, Thomas T., 115n
Fauntroy, Walter Edward, 469n
Fazio, Vic, 550
Federación Libre (Free Federation), 160, 300
Federación Libre de Trabajadores (Free Federation of Laborers), 160, 300, 342
Federación Regional de los Trabajadores (Puerto Rican Federation of Laborers), 300
Federal Deposit Insurance Corporation (FDIC), 170, 302, 405
Federal Election Commission (FEC), 547n, 584, 587, 620
Federal Emergency Management Agency (FEMA), 467
Federal Savings and Loan Insurance Corporation, 404
Fenton, Jack, 528, 532n
Fergusson, Harvey Butler, 194, 196, 197n, 236, 238, 242n
Fernández García, Benigno, 301
FERNÁNDEZ, Antonio M., 169, 193, **316–21**, 327–28, 336, 338, 375, 390, 395n, 425n, 445n, 481
FERNÁNDEZ, Joachim Octave, 6, 149, 168, 193, **280–87**, 481
FERNÓS-ISERN, Antonio, 294n, 310, 314n, 327, 345, 371, 376, **380–89**, 430, 434, 580n
  Estado Libre Asociado (Free Associated State) and, 7, 324, 328, 345–47, *346*, 349–52, *352*, 364n, 380, 383–85
  legislative style, 3
  Puerto Rican migration and, 343, *343*
Fillmore, Millard, 36, 92, 97n, 753
Financial Institutions Reform, Recovery, and Enforcement Act of 1989, 404
Finley, Clifford, 607

First Federal Congress, 32
First Jones Act, 157
Fitzgerald, William F., 412
FLORES, Bill, 705
Florida Territory, Hispanic representation, 70–79. *See also*, Appendix B: Hispanic-American Representatives, Senators, Delegates, and Resident Commissioners by State and Territory, 1822–2012.
Florida, Hispanic representation, 590–95, 640–43, 664–65, 688–89, 706–707. *See also*, Appendix B: Hispanic-American Representatives, Senators, Delegates, and Resident Commissioners by State and Territory, 1822–2012.
Flynn, Dennis, 198n
Foley, Thomas, 408n, 423, *479*, 525
Font Saldaña, Jorge, 430, 596
Font, Manuel, 313, 374
Foraker Act of 1900 (The Organic Act), 5, 146, 153–58, 160–61, *164*, 184n, 202–203, 205, 210, 212–214, 216n, 221, 246, 291, 300, 305n, 385. *See also*, Appendix I: Constitutional Amendments, Treaties, and Major Acts of Congress Referenced in the Text.
Foraker, Joseph, *153*, 154. *See also*, Foraker Act of 1900.
Ford Foundation, 341
Ford, Gerald R., 452, 466, 469n, 512, 692
Foreman, Ed, 409n, 442, 446n
Fort Craig, 108
Fort Union, 108
Fort Wingate, 110, 115n
FORTUÑO, Luis G., 476, 504n, 509, 623, **634–39**, 684
Fountain Valley Massacre, 470n
Fourteenth Amendment, 208n, 397. *See also*, Appendix I: Constitutional Amendments, Treaties, and Major Acts of Congress Referenced in the Text.
France, 25, 120, 152, 200, 214, 239, 376, 536, 745
Franqui, Victor Gutierrez, *346*
Froebel, 200
Fulmer, Hampton, 310, 314n
Fuqua, Don, 446n
Fusco, Dominick A., 516
FUSTER, Jaime B., 477–78, *478*, *491*, 495–96, 503n, 504n, 509, **568–75**, 576

G

Gadsden Purchase, 30, 745
Gadsden, James, 74–75
GALLEGOS, José Manuel, 4, 22, 24, 34–44, *39*, 46, 49–50, 54, 55n, 58n, 60n, 62n, 64, 69, **80–89**, 90, 92–93, 96–98n, 102–103, 106n, 113, 117n, 140
García Méndez, Miguel Angel, 176, 303, 310
García, Felix, 265
Garcia, Orlando, 609n
GARCIA, Robert, *474*, 477, *477*, 480, *481*, 483, 490–92, *491*, 509, **516–21**, 545, 570, 698
Garfield, James A., 120, 123n
Garfield, James R., 215
Garner, John Nance, 272
Gatell, Manuel, 202, 207n
Geether, Greenbury, 77n
Georgia, 25, 70, 76n
Gephardt, Richard, 533n, 546
GI Bill of Rights, 318, 528, 550, 559
GI Forum, 338–40
Giddings, Joshua, 29–30
Gigante, Father Louis, 450
Gilbert, Ralph, 251
Gingrich, Newt, 582
Giuliani, Rudy, 453
Glenn, John, 446n
Glenn, Otis F., 266
Goldwater, Barry, 393
Gómez Quiñones, Juan, 328, 338–40, 396n
Gómez, Laura, 42, 51, 61n, 65n, 98n
Gomez, Richard, 531
Gompers, Samuel, 300
Gonzalez v. Williams. *See*, Supreme Court, United States.
GONZALEZ, Charles A., 400, 407, **666–67**
González, Elián, 593
GONZÁLEZ, Henry B., 270, *322*, 327, 371, **400–409**, 562, 666
Chicano movement and, 340–41, *341*
committee assignments, 7, 327, 403–404, 477
Congressional Hispanic Caucus, 8, 357, 403, 408n, 422, 484, *491*, 500n
discrimination against, 402
early background, 6, 325–26, 339–40, 400
González amendment, 404
legislative interests, 394, 397n, 403–406
legislative style, 3, 329–30, 341, *341*, 400, 402–403, 406
Savings and Loan crisis, 404
Viva Kennedy clubs, 339–40, *339*
González, Isabel, 204
Good Neighbor Policy, 172, 422
Goode, John, Jr., 402
Gore, Al, 526, 549n
Gorton, Slade, 446n
Gossett, Ed, 312
Graham, Bob, 640
Graham, William, 444
Grant, Ulysses S., 86, 117n
Gray, William III, *480*
Great Depression, 168–73, 272, 280, 288, 291–92, 301, *331*, 332–33, *333*, *337*, 342, 372, 400, 404, 456, 522, 550. *See also*, New Deal.
Great Society, 403, 431
Greeley, Horace, 51, *51*
Greenspan, Alan, 408n
GRIJALVA, Raúl M., 668–69
Gruening, Ernest, 171–72, 186n
Guam, 5, *146*, 152, *154*, 203, 352, 368, 437, 462, 464–65, 478
commonwealth, 494, 559
education policy, 560, 613
Hispanic representation, 556–61, 610–15. *See also*, Appendix B: Hispanic-American Representatives, Senators, Delegates, and Resident Commissioners by State and Territory, 1822–2012.
Organic Act of 1950, 556, 612
Guarini, Frank J., Jr., 676, 700
Guerra, Miguel, 250
Guillory, Isom, 151
Gulf Coast, 25–26, 536, 642
Gulf War, 406
GUTIERREZ, Luis V., 485, **670–71**
Guzman, Robert, 690

H

H.J. Res. 149, 165–66, 253n
Hall, Luther, 228
Hamilton, Alexander, 74
Hanna, Richard, 256
Harding, Warren G., *174*, 174–76, 241, 248–49, 257, 265, 434
Harrison, Benjamin, 122
Harrison, William Henry, 33
Hartke, Jan, 444
Hartke, Vance, 444
Hastert, J. Dennis, *480*, 586, 592
Hatch, Carl A., 274, 277n, 334
Haugen, Gilbert N., 230, 233n
Hawaii, 162, 171, 204, 302, 352, 378n. *See also*, Statehood.
Hawaii v. Mankichi. *See*, Supreme Court, United States.
Hébert, F. Edward, 284–85, 286n
Hefner, W. G. (Bill), 525
Henry, Guy V., 153, 200, 221
Herbert, Hilary, 163
Hernández Colón, Rafael, 568, 571–72, 596, 598, 620
HERNÁNDEZ, Benigno Cárdenas, *2*, 167, 193, **236–45**, 258
HERNÁNDEZ, Joseph Marion, 1, 4, 22, 26, 33–34, 46–47, 49, 55n, 69, **70–79**, 655
HERRERA BEUTLER, Jaime, 705
Hevesi, Alan, 453
Hickenlooper, John, 646
HINOJOSA, Rubén, 672–73
Hispanic American Democrats (HAD), 512
Hispanic Heritage Month, 744
Hispanic-American Members of Congress, characteristics
committee assignments, 44–46, 168–69, 327, 480–82. *See also*, Appendix C: Hispanic-American Members' Committee Assignments (Standing, Joint, Select) in the U.S. House and Senate, 1822–2012; Appendix D: Hispanic Americans Who Have Chaired Congressional Committees, 1881–2012; Appendix E: Hispanic-American Chairs of Subcommittees of Standing and Select Committees in the U.S. House and Senate, 1949–2012.
discrimination and, 2, 40, 53, 163–65, 393, 396n, 410, 413, 472
District of Columbia, experience in, 42–44, 148, 150–51, 327–28
early backgrounds of, 3, 34–36, 49–50, 58n, 149–50, 475–76
education, 35, 149–50, 326
family and ethnic roots, 34–35, 149, 325, 476. *See also*, Appendix G: Hispanic-American Familial Connections in Congress.
interpreter and, 4, 22, 24, 41, 55n, 83
language barrier, 164–65
leadership positions, 8–9, 478–81. *See also*, Appendix F: Hispanic Americans in U.S. House Party Leadership Positions, 1987–2012.
legislative interests, 44–54, 148, 168–74, 328–29, 482–96
legislative style, 3–8, 44–46, 148, 161–62, 328–29, 477–78. *See also*, individual Hispanic-American Members of Congress.
military service. *See,* Military Service, Hispanic-American Members of Congress.
pre-congressional careers and political experience, 34–36, 149–50, 180n, 326, 475–76
See also, Congressional Hispanic Caucus; Congressional Hispanic Conference; Democratic Party; Elections; Incumbency and seniority, influence of; Republican Party; Senate, United States; Surrogate representation.
Hispanic-majority congressional districts. *See*, Apportionment and redistricting.
Hitler, Adolph, 283, 312
Hooper, Joseph, 251
Hoover, Herbert, 164, 169, 274, 288, 291–93, 296n, 333, 434
Hope, Bob, 522
Hopi Indians, 319
Houghton, Joab, 60n, 87–88n, 97n, 102
House "Bank" scandal, 566, 582–83
House Border Caucus, 538
House Democratic Caucus, 8, 162–63, 221, 229, 408n, 418n, 423, 450, 464, 479, 481, 496, 505n, 578, 622, 636–37, 655, 658–59, 677, 701
House Office Building (Cannon), 150, *151*
House Republican Conference, 162–63, 221, 358n, 437, 461n, 478, 480–81, 484, 496, 505n, 584, 585, 634, 636, 637n
House Rules. *See*, Resident Commissioner, right to vote in committee; Territorial Delegate, status and rights of.
House Territorial Caucus, 464, 478, 498n
House Un-American Activities Committee (HUAC), 335, 368n, 392, 409n

Houston, Sam, 28, *28*
Hubbell, Frank A., 240, 256–57, 259–60n
Hughes, Charles Evans, 240
Hull, Cordell, 310–11
Hull, John, 214
Humphrey, Hubert, 547n
Humphreys, Benjamin G., 175
Hurley, Patrick J., 274–75, 278n
Hurricanes
Hugo (1989), 467, 471n
Katrina (2005), 587n
San Cipriano (1932), 164, 169, 292, 301, 372
San Felipe (1928), 169, 372
Hussein, Saddam, 406
Hutchison, Kay Bailey, 585

I

Ickes, Harold, 176, 310, 312
Idaho, Hispanic representation, 706. *See also*, Appendix B: Hispanic-American Representatives, Senators, Delegates, and Resident Commissioners by State and Territory, 1822–2012.
Iglesias, Manuel, 431
IGLESIAS, Santiago, 3, *13*, 149–50, 152, 160, 164, 168, 170–74, *176*, 186n, 193, 212, 290, 292–93, **298–307**, 308, 313n, 342
Illegal Immigration Reform and Immigrant Responsibility Act of 1996, 492, 592
Illinois, Hispanic representation, 670–71. *See also*, Appendix B: Hispanic-American Representatives, Senators, Delegates, and Resident Commissioners by State and Territory, 1822–2012.
Immigration
"Operation Wetback," 338, 362n
Depression and World War II era, 331–38
illegal immigration, 331, 336–38, 415, 444–45, 489–93, 513, 538, 565, 618, 642, 650, 665, 686
labor and, 331, 336–38, 415, 444–45, 466, 489–91, 513, 565, 642, 650
legislation. *See*, Alien Adjustment and Employment Act of 1977; Bracero Program; Congressional Hispanic Caucus; Congressional Hispanic Conference; Hispanic-Americans in Congress, legislative interests; Illegal Immigration Reform and Immigrant Responsibility Act of 1996; Immigration Reform and Control Act of 1986; Simpson–Mazzoli legislation.
See also, Insular cases.
Immigration and Naturalization Service (INS), 337, 593
Immigration and Naturalization Act of 1954, 466
Immigration Reform and Control Act of 1986, 414–15, 491–92, *492*, 565. *See also*, Simpson–Mazzoli legislation.
Imperialism. *See*, Decolonization; Manifest Destiny; Mexican-American War; Spanish-American War; Treaty of Guadalupe Hidalgo; Treaty of Paris.
Incumbency and Seniority, influence, 7–8, 33, 168–69, 221, 301, 327, 353–54, 357, 382, 475, 478, 481. *See also*, Appendix D: Hispanic Americans Who Have Chaired Congressional Committees, 1881–2012; Appendix E: Hispanic-American Chairs of Subcommittees of Standing and Select Committees in the U.S. House and Senate, 1949–2012.
Inouye, Daniel, 692
Insular Cases, 5, 155–56, 158, 182n, 250. *See also*, Supreme Court, United States.
Inter-Agency Cabinet Committee on Mexican-American Affairs, 340
Iran-Contra affair, 406, 565

J

Jackson, Alexander, 94, 127n
Jackson, Andrew, 25, 28–29, *29*, 47, *48*, 72–75
Jackson, Paul, 553
Jacobs, Andrew, 522
Javits, Jacob, 346, 365n
Jefferson, Thomas, 25, *25*, 50, 72
Jeffersonian Republican Party, Hispanic representation, 70–79
Jesup, Thomas Sidney, 75–76, 78n
Jim Crow, 59n, 264, 331, 338, 492. *See also*, Discrimination.
Johnson, Andrew, 52, 85, 105
Johnson, Hiram, 273
Johnson, Lyndon B., *7*, 276, 340, 357, 393–94, 397n, 402–403, 413, 420, 431, 525, 753
Johnston, J. Bennett, 468, 571–72
Johnston, Olin, 348, 358n, 366n
Jones, Andrieus A., 266, 270, 272
Jones, Ed, 423
Jones, Sam H., 284–85
Jones, Wesley L., 234n
Jones, William A., *156*, 156–57, 222–23
Jones-Shafroth Act. *See*, Second Jones Act of 1917.
Joseph, Antonio, 65n, 117n, 130, 144n, 254
Juárez, Benito, 118, 262

K

Kahn, Julius, 241
Kapp, Harry, 229
Kazarian, Dennis S., 530
Kazen, Abraham, 562
Kean, Thomas, 700
Kearny, Stephen W., 87–88n, 124
Keating, Charles, 409n
Kemp, Jack, 519–20
Kennedy, Edward (Ted), 530, 544, 650
Kennedy, Jacqueline B., *339*
Kennedy, John F., 276, *339*, 339–40, *348*, *356*, 357, 385, 392, 402, 406, 408–409n, 412–13, 448, 522
"Viva Kennedy" clubs, *339*, 339–40, 409n
Kerry, John, 644
Kiess, Edgar, 251
Kilday, Paul, 402
Kilgore, Joe, 420
King, Cecil, 465
King, Martin Luther, Jr., 406, 518–19
King, William, 250
Koch, Ed, 452–53
Koreagate scandal, 395, 414
Korean War, 354, 420, 516, 550, 556
Krebs, John, 660
Krueger, J.W., 292–93, 296n
Krug, Julius, 376

L

La Follette, Robert Marion, 273
La Guardia, Fiorello Henry, 291
La Raza Unida, 324, 341, 582
LABRADOR, Raúl R., 706
Lagomarsino, Robert, 505n, 573n
Lamy, John Baptiste, 80, 82–85, 87n, 92
Lane, William Carr, 60n, 82–83, 85, 88n, 90
Lantos, Tom, 628
Larrazolo, Marie, *150*
LARRAZOLO, Octaviano A., 6, 114, 149, *150*, 164, *166*, 167, 180n, 193, 242n, 254, **262–69**, 270
LARRÍNAGA, Tulio, 5, *5*, 154, 160, *163*, 164, 193, **210–17**, 221, 300
Las Gorras Blancas (the White Caps), 254, 259n
Latin America, foreign policy, 171–72, 175, 225n, 250, 274, 278n, 311–12, *339*, 348, 354–55, 390, 413, 481, 484, *484*, 489, 502n, 519, 538, 545, 550, 562, 568, 579, 592, 677
Lau v. Nichols. *See,* Supreme Court, United States.
Lavery, Vincent, 524
Lazaro, Elaine, 150, 226
Lazaro, Eloise, 150, 226
LAZARO, Ladislas, 3, *3*, 148, *148*, 150–51, 164, 169, 193, **226–35**
Leach, Jim, 407, 468
Leach, Wallace, 121
League of United Latin American Citizens (LULAC), 333, 338–40, 362n, *475*, 600
Leahy, William B., *13*, *176*, 308, 310
Ledesma, Rick, 686
Legislative Reorganization Act of 1946, 275, 318, 327, 387n
Legislative Reorganization Act of 1970, 325, 354, 437, 458
Legislative style. *See*, Hispanic-American Members of Congress, characteristics; Surrogate representation.
Lehman, Richard, 660
Lemieux, George S., 642
Levy, David, 76
Lewis, John W., 228
Lewis, Meriwether, 25
Lincoln, Abraham, 37, 95, 98n, 100, 102–105, 107n, 115n, 424
Livable Communities Task Force, 622, 701
Lloyd, Jim, 552
Long, Huey P., 149, 168, 280, 282–84, 285n, 286n
Long, Leonard, 366n
López Antongiorgi, J. A., 303
Los Alamos National Laboratory, 444, 544, 675
Louisiana Purchase, 25–26, 72. *See also*, Appendix I: Constitutional Amendments, Treaties, and Major Acts of Congress Referenced in the Text.
Louisiana Territory, 22, 25, 72
Louisiana, Hispanic representation, 226–35, 280–87. *See also*, Appendix B: Hispanic-American Representatives, Senators, Delegates, and Resident Commissioners by State and Territory, 1822–2012.
Lucero, Antonio J., 167, 256–57, 260n
Luis, Juan, 465–66
LUJÁN, Ben Ray, 674–75
LUJÁN, Manuel, Jr., *10*, 325, 327, 329, 338, 357, 371, 390, **440–47**, 484, 486, *489*, 489–90, *491*, 544
Luna, Melchior, 138, 139n
LUNA, Tranquilino, 34, 39–40, *40*, 42, 45, 50, 61n, 64n, 69, 95–96, 99n, 117n, **134–39**, 140, 142, 144n, 197n, 243–44n
Lusk, Georgia Lee, 316, 320n
Lynch, Mary, 455n

M

Machebeuf, J. Projectus, 80, 82, 87n
Machine politics, 167, 236, 242n, 256, 262, 264, 280, 282–84, 286n, 448, 466, 530, 532–33n. *See also*, Santa Fe Ring.
Madison, James, 25, *25*, 72
Maestri, Robert, 284–85, 286n
Magellan, Ferdinand, 559
Mahan, Alfred, 222
Maloney, Paul, 282, 285
Manifest Destiny, 26–27, 31, 56n, 151. *See also*, Appendix K: Glossary.
MANZANARES, Francisco Antonio, *38*, 38–39, 45, 69, 117n, 137–38, 139n, **140–45**, 197n, 259n
Marcantonio, Vito, 312, 315n, 344, 346, *347*, 365n, 378n, 386n
Marín y Solá, Ramón, 218
Martínez Nadal, Rafael, 290, 292, 296n
Martínez, Antonio José, 80, 82, 87n, 140
MARTÍNEZ, Matthew G., *474*, 477, *491*, 509, **528–35**, 552, 626, 628
MARTINEZ, Mel, 8, 472, 475, *475*, 477, 480, 482, 493, 497n, 509, **640–43**, 650
Martinez, Raul, 593
Mathews, George, 72
McAdoo, William, 53–54, *54*
McCain, John, 650
McCarthy, Eugene, 337, 361n
McCarthy, Joseph R., 276, 355, *355*
McCarthy, Leo T., 532n
McClellan, George B., 107n, 115n

McClory, Robert, 434
McCollum, Bill, 640
McCormack, John, 320, 403
McDonald, A. J., 257
McDonald, William, 242n, 270
McDonough, Gordon L., 412
McFadden, Louis, 291
McFall, John, 414
McGovern, George, 337
McInnis, Scott, 644
McKinley, William, *40*, 90, 152, *152*, 154, *164*, 194, 197n, 221, 300
McLemore, Jeff, 239
McNary, Charles, 230, 233n, 257, 260n
Mechem, Edwin L., 393, 396–97n
Medicaid, 465, 532, 578, 598–99, 637, 691, 753
Medicare, 465, 598–99, 607, 623, 636–37, 638n, 659, 677, 689, 753
Medina González, Julio, 301, 305n
Meek, Carrie, 592
Méndez, Miguel Angel García, 176, 303, 310
MENENDEZ, Robert, 8–9, 424, 477, 479–80, 482, 485, 655, **676–77**, 700
Mercer, Leroy, 462, 464
Meriwether, David, 24, 83, 96n
Mexican American Political Association (MAPA), 339–40
Mexican American Youth Organization (MAYO), 341
Mexican Revolution, 239, 400
Mexican-American War, *24*, 26, 28–30, 34, 49–50, 80, 84, 90, 100, 103, 108, 118
Mexico, foreign policy, 3, 22, 24, 27–31, 34, 41–42, 47, 49–50, 56–57n, 340
immigration and, 330–33, *332*, 335–38, 362n, 489, 492–93
See also, Bracero program; Immigration; Mexican-American War; North American Free Trade Agreement (NAFTA); Treaty of Guadalupe Hidalgo.
Mexico-United States Interparliamentary Group, 444
Mfume, Kweisi, 486, *487*
Miles, John E., 316
Miles, Mike, 648
Military service, Hispanic-American Members of Congress, 440, 462, 536, 692
Civil War, 100, 102, 108, 110
First Seminole War, 26
Korean War and era, 420, 516, 550, 556, 562
Patriot War, 26, 72, 77n
Seminole Wars, 26, 47, 75–76
Vietnam War and era, 556, 604, 608, 656, 666, 686, 698
World War I, 372
World War II, 285, 410
Miller, Clarence, 163, 437
Miller, George, 524–25
Miller, Henry R., 122
Mills, Wilbur, 450
Missouri, 35, 51, 59n, 83, 89, 93–94, 100, 108, 124, 134, 140, 273, 497n
Mobile Act, 25, 77n
Mondell, Frank, 163, 204, 239, 241, 243n
Mondragon, Roberto, 544, 547–48n
Monroe Doctrine, 26, 103, 151
Monroe, James, 26, 34, 73–74, 77n
Montoya, Frances, 256
MONTOYA, Joseph M., *7*, 7–8, 320, 325–30, *330*, 338, *340*, 340–41, 355, 358n, 371, **390–99**, 481, 542
MONTOYA, Néstor, 149–50, 167, 193, **254–61**
Morris, Thomas, 440
Morrison, DeLesseps (Chep), 285
Morrow, John, 258
Morse, F. Bradford, 542
Morton, Jackson, 76
Moseley, George Van Horn, 164, 293
Muñocistas (Puerto Rico), 221
Muñoz Marín, Luis, 7, 149, *149*, 160, 172, *172*, 177, 218, 301, 303, 310–11, 313, 326, *339*, 345, *345*, *346*, 347, *348*, 349–52, *352*, 364n, 366n, 372, 374–77, 377n, 380, 383–85, 386n, 388n, 428, 430, 458, 576
Muñoz Mendoza, Victoria, 576
MUÑOZ RIVERA, Luis, 3, 7, 148–50, 152–53, 155, 157–58, 160, *162*, 163–64, 172, 180, 181–82n, 193, 202, 210, **218–25**, 246, 248, 298, 300, 372, 374, 478
Murdock, John, 347–48
Murphy, John B., 282
Murray, James, 352
Mussolini, Benito, 312

N

NAFTA. *See*, North American Free Trade Agreement (NAFTA).
NAPOLITANO, Grace Flores, 555, **678–79**
National Aeronautics and Space Administration (NASA), 444
National Association for the Advancement of Colored People (NAACP), 397n
National Association of Latino Democratic Officials (NALADO), 414
National Association of Latino Elected and Appointed Officials (NALEO), 414
National Commission on Space, 444, 446n
National Council of La Raza, 414
National Democrats, 37, 84, 92, 94, 134
National Geographic, 165
National Housing Trust, 405
National Republican Congressional Committee (NRCC), 480, 681
National Spanish-Speaking Coalition Conference, 330
National Youth Administration, 284
Navajo Indians, 38, 48, 63n, 102–105, 107n, 108, 110, 114n, 115n, 319, 392, 396n, 544
Negrón Lopez, Luis, 432
Nethercutt, George, 586
Nevada, 22, 30, 120, 275, 302, 497n
New Deal, 160, 168–71, *169*, *176*, 177, 270, 273–75, 278n, 284, 302, 308, *327*, *332*, 405. *See also*, Civilian Conservation Corps (CCC); Fair Employment Practices Commission (FEPC); Appendix K: Glossary.
New Frontier, 402–403
New House Office Building (Longworth), 351, 382, 386n
New Jersey, Hispanic representation, 676–77, 700–701. *See also*, Appendix B: Hispanic-American Representatives, Senators, Delegates, and Resident Commissioners by State and Territory, 1822–2012.
New Mexico
American Indians and. *See*, American Indians.
civil rights and. *See*, Civil Rights.
Hispanic representation, 236–45, 254–79, 316–21, 390–99, 440–47, 542–49, 674–75. *See also*, Appendix B: Hispanic-American Representatives, Senators, Delegates, and Resident Commissioners by State and Territory, 1822–2012.
"Little Texas" and, 261n
nominating conventions, 167, 185n
Organic Act, 137
party politics and, 167, 236, 256, 262, 272, 390, 392
statehood. *See*, Statehood, New Mexico.
New Mexico Territory
"Little Texas" and, 196
American Indians and, 47–49
Civil War and, 37–38
Hispanic representation, 80–117, 124–45, 194–99. *See also*, Appendix B: Hispanic-American Representatives, Senators, Delegates, and Resident Commissioners by State and Territory, 1822–2012.
land grants and, 46–47
party politics and, 2, 30–31, 36–38, 40–43, 52, 54, 65–66n, 86, 88n, 93-94, 100, 104, 107n, 124, 128. *See also*, Santa Fe Ring.
slavery and. *See*, Slavery.
statehood and. *See*, Statehood, New Mexico.
statutory representation, 33–34, 43–44
New York, Hispanic representation, 328, 448–55, 516–21, 698–99, 702–703. *See also*, Appendix B: Hispanic-American Representatives, Senators, Delegates, and Resident Commissioners by State and Territory, 1822–2012.
Nicaragua, 484, 519, 545–46, 548–49n, 562, 564–65, 590, 592, 626
Nine, Louis, 518
Nineteenth Amendment, 231, 248, 258, 265
Nixon, Richard M., 355–56, 394, 398n, 437, 440, 582
No Child Left Behind Act, 489, 502n, 613
Noe, James, 284
Norris, George, 273
North American Free Trade Agreement (NAFTA), 424, 483, 485, 493, *493*, 531, 546, 554, 584, 593, 607, 683
Northern Mariana Islands, 476, 478, 508, 559–60, 613, 692–93, 726, 752–53
Hispanic representation, 692–93. *See also*, Appendix B: Hispanic-American Representatives, Senators, Delegates, and Resident Commissioners by State and Territory, 1822–2012.
Northwest Ordinance of 1787, *32*, 32–33, 58n, 155. *See*, Appendix I: Constitutional Amendments, Treaties, and Major Acts of Congress Referenced in the Text.
Northwest Territory, 33, 50, 745
NUNES, Devin, 480, **680–81**
Nunez, David, 553
Nye, Gerald P., 273

O

O'Connor, James, 282, 286n
O'Dwyer, William, 376
O'Mahoney, Joseph, 365n
O'Neill, Thomas P., Jr. (Tip), 479, 490, 544
O'Sullivan, John L., 56n, 753
Obama, Barack, 470n, 476, *476*, 493, 629, 642, 650, 659
Office of Price Administration, 176
Olmsted, Marlin, 213
Operation Bootstrap, 345
Oregon, 26, 29, 48, 94
Organic Act of 1900 (Puerto Rico). *See*, Foraker Act of 1900.
Organic Act of 1950 (Guam), 556, 612. *See also*, Appendix I: Constitutional Amendments, Treaties, and Major Acts of Congress Referenced in the Text.
Organization of American States (OAS), 349, 586
Ortega, Daniel, 545–46, 549n, 565
Ortiz, Santos, 571
ORTIZ, Solomon P., *474*, 484–85, *485*, 487, *488*, 491–92, 509, **536–41**, 565, 604
Osceola, 75, 78n
Osias, Camilo, 166, 251
OTERO, Mariano Sabino, 35, *35*, *37*, 43–46, 50, 58n, 64n, 69, **128–33**, 137, 138n, 140, 149, 194, 197n
Otero, Miguel A., Jr., 40, *40*, 44, 59n, 137, 139n, 194, 196, 197n, 273
OTERO, Miguel Antonio, 35–44, *39*, *41–42*, 51–52, 54, 61n, 64n, 69, 83–85, 89n, **90–99**, 100, 102, 106n, 114n, 127n, 134, 136–37, 139, 194
Otero-Warren, Adelina, 167, 258

P

PACHECO, Romualdo, 3, 22, *22*, 34–36, *36*, 39, 43, 45–47, 69, **118–23**,

137, 139n, 232–33n
PAGÁN, Bolívar, *13*, 149–50, 160, 161n, 165, 168, 170, *176*, 176–77, 186n, 193, 292, 294n, 304, 306n, **308–15**, 374, 380, 386n, 580n
Palacio de González, Romualdo, 200, 205n, 220
Pan American Federation of Labor (PAFL), 300, 303
Pan American Progressive Association (PAPA), 6, 400
Panama Canal, 156, *157*, 176, 213, 233n
Pangelinan, Vicente, 560
Paredes, Quintin, 294n, 314n, 386n, 580n
Paria Capo, Ledo Francisco, 212
Park, Tongsun, 414
Parker, John, 229
Partido Acción Cristiana (Christian Action Party), 358n, 434
Partido Agrícola Pura (Pure Agriculture Party), 310
Partido Autonomista (Autonomist Party), 152–53, 218, 220
Partido de Unión (Union Party), 160, 173, 193, 210, 212, 218–22, 246–50, 300
Hispanic representation, 210–25, 246–53
Partido Federal (Federal Party), 154, 160, 202, 206–207n, 210, 221, 300
Partido Independentista Puertorriqueño (Independence Party), 367n, 568
Partido Liberal (Liberal Party), 153, 160, 172–73, 210, 218, 220, 224n, 290–92, 296n, 301–303, 305n, 310, 313, 315n, 372, 374, 596
Partido Nacionalista (Nationalist Party), 160, 173–74, 301, 305n, 344, 350–51, 384
Partido Nuevo Progresista (New Progressive Party, or PNP), 353, 371, 431–32, 434, 436–37, 458, 460, 494–96, 504n, 509–10, 512–13, 568, 571, 576, 579, 596, 598, 600, 622–23, 634, 637n, 684. *See also*, Statehood, Puerto Rico.
Hispanic representation, 358n, 434–39, 510–15, 596–603, 634–39, 684–85
Partido Popular (Popular Party), 254, 256
Partido Popular Democrático (Popular Democratic Party, or PPD), 160, 177, 180, 310–11, 313, 326, 343, 345–46, 350, 352–53, 371–72, 374–75, 379n, 380, 382–83, 385, 388n, 428, 430–32, 434, 436–38, 456, 458, 460n, 494–96, 504n, 510, 568, 570, 576, 578–79, 596, 600, 601n, 620, 622, 634, 637n, 684. *See also*, Estado Libre Asociado (Free Associated State).
Hispanic representation, 372–89, 428–33, 456–61, 568–81, 620–25
Partido Renovación Puertorriqueña (Puerto Rican Renewal Party), 568, 570
Partido Republicano (Republican Party, Puerto Rico), 160, 205, 206n, 221, 248, 288, 300
Hispanic representation, 200–209, 288–97
Partido Socialista (Socialist Party), 160, 161n, 246, 248, 252n, 290–93, 300–301, 305–306n, 308, 310, 313, 315n, 374
Partido Unificación Tripartita (Tripartite Unification Party), 310, 374
Partido Unión Republicana (Republican Union Party), 160, 288, 290–93, 295n, 300–301, 305n, 308, 310, 313, 315n
Hispanic Representation, 288–97
PASTOR, Ed, 9, 480, 485, **682–83**
Patman, Wright, 403
Patricola, Paul M., 516
Patriot War, 26, 72, 77n
Patterakis, Chris, 524
Payne, Sereno, 153–54
Pearl Harbor, 274, 284, 311
Pearson, Drew, 366n
Peonage, 49–52, 63–65n, 98n. *See also*, Slavery.
Pepper, Claude, 7, 477, 688
PEREA, Francisco, *34*, 34–35, 39, 48, 50, 54, 58n, 64n, 69, 85–86, **100–107**, 108, 110–111, 115–16n, 126, 149
Perea, José Leandro, 100, 194, 197n
PEREA, Pedro, 35, 108, 114, 128, 149, 167–68, 193, **194–99**
Perez, George, 544, 547–48n
Perkins, Carl, 452
Perot, Ross, 584
Pershing, John J., 239
PESQUERA, José Lorenzo, 149, 160, 164–65, 169, 193, **288–97**, 305n, 313n, 386n, 580n
Pettis, Solomon N., 112, 116n
Phelps, John Smith, 22, *24*
Philippines, 5, 58n, 146, *146*, 152, *154*, 155, 159, 166, 171, *174*, 183n, 203, 212, 251, 294n, 302, 314n, 318, 386n, 580n
Pierce, Franklin, 36, 51, 96n, 138n
PIERLUISI, Pedro, 504n, **684–85**
PIÑERO, Jesús T., 6, *6*, 160, *171*, *172*, 187n, 313, 345, *345*, 352, 371, **372–79**, 380, 382, 434
Plan Chardón, 172, 187n
Pleasant, Rufus, 229
Poage, William, 312, 314n
POLANCO-ABREU, Santiago, 326, 352, 356, 367n, 371, **428–33**
Political Association of Spanish-Speaking Organizations (PASSO), 339, 420
Political machines. *See*, Machine politics.
Polk, James K., 28–31, *29*, *30*
Poll tax. *See*, Disfranchisement.
Poore, Benjamin Perley, 42, *43*
Pope Pius IX, 80, 87n
Post, Regis H., 156, 215, 216n
Potter, Clarkson, 123n
Prats, Roberto, 634, 636
Prince, L. Bradford, 117n, 144n
Procaccino, Mario, 450
Prohibition, 231, 256, 272, 290
Public Law 600 (Puerto Rican Federal Relations Act), 347–50, 352, 384–85, 386n. *See also*, Appendix I: Constitutional Amendments, Treaties, and Major Acts of Congress Referenced in the Text.
Pueblo Indians, 30, *30*, 49, 60n, 83, 86, 108, 130, 257, 273, 329, 545
Pueblo Revolt of 1837, 108
Puerto Rican Federal Relations Act. *See*, Public Law 600.
Puerto Rican Women's Club, 382
Puerto Rican Women's Suffrage Association, 248
Puerto Rico, 151–59
Commonwealth status. *See*, Estado Libre Asociado (Free Associated State).
continental governors of, 174–77
education policy, 172, 202, 248–49, 431–32, 512, 570, 598–99
Great Depression and, 169–73
Hispanic representation, 200–25, 246–53, 288–15, 372–89, 428–39, 456–61, 510–15, 568–81, 596–603, 620–25, 634–39, 684–85. *See also*, Appendix B: Hispanic-American Representatives, Senators, Delegates, and Resident Commissioners by State and Territory, 1822–2012.
independence and, 158–60, 173–74, 179, 202, 220–22, 224n, 246, 249, 301–303, 310, 312–13, 344–46, *347*, *349*, 350–51, 374–75, 378n, 380, 431, 451, 568, 571, 634, 636. *See also*, Estado Libre Asociado (Free Associated State); Statehood, Puerto Rico.
migration to mainland U.S., 342–44, 363n
plebiscites in, 173, 303, 306n, 313, 346–47, 350, 353, 375–76, 378n, 383–85, 431, 436, 495–96, 505n, 512, 571–72, 579, 620, 624n, 636, 685, 699
section 936 and, 494–95, 504n, 576, 578–79, 580n, 599, 601n
Spanish rule in, 152–53, 203–204, 208n, 212, 220, 298, 349
statehood. *See*, Statehood, Puerto Rico.
United States citizenship, 5, 154–59, *158*, 163–64, 200, 202–205, 208n, 213–14, 222–23, 224–25n, 251, 253n, 290, 298, 342–43, 353, 375–76, 378n, 620, 636
Puerto Rico Reconstruction Administration, 172, 372
Puerto Rico U.S.A. Foundation, 572
Pujo, Arsène, 228, 232n
Putnam, Otis, 228

R

Race, 331, 334, 397n, 689
continental expansion and, 31, 52, 54
elections and, 39–42, 111, 136, 196, 238, 264
Puerto Rico and, 163, 175
See also, Discrimination; Segregation; Civil Rights.
Racism. *See*, Discrimination.
Ramirez, Ralph R., 530
Ramos Antonini, Ernesto, 430
Ramos, Domingo, Jr., 516
Ramos, Manuel, 451
Rangel, Charles, 518, 520, 525
Rasmussen v. United States. *See*, Supreme Court, United States.
Rayburn, Samuel, 284
Reagan, Ronald W., 404, 406, 423, 442–45, 467–68, *481*, 484, *484*, 492, 500n, 513, 519–20, 525, 531, 544–46, 549n, 553, 558, 564–65, 567n, 590, 640
Reconstruction Finance Corporation (RFC), 170, 272, 291, 296n
Redistricting. *See*, Apportionment and redistricting.
Reily, E. Montgomery, *174*, 174–76, 249
Rencher, Abraham, 115n
Republican National Committee, 475, 480, 634, 642. *See also*, Republican Party.
Republican National Convention, 103, 106n, 138, 194, 236, 636
Republican Party, 67–69, 190–91, 344, 354, 369, 371, 488, 496, 506–507, 509
1994 election, 403, 422, 480, 531, 585, 592
Congressional Hispanic Caucus and, 475, 483, 486, 490
Congressional Hispanic Conference and, 8, 486, 497, 593, 636, 665, 681. *See also*, Appendix H: Congressional Hispanic Caucus and Congressional Hispanic Conference Chairmen and Chairwomen, 1976–2012.
contested elections and, 38–40
Hispanic representation and, 100–39, 194–99, 236–45, 254–69, 440–47, 480, 528–35, 556–61, 582–95, 637n, 640–43, 664–65, 680–81, 688–89, 704–707
See also, Santa Fe Ring; New Mexico Territory, party politics.
Republican Policy Committee, *480*, 592
Resident Commissioner, 200–25, 246–53, 288–15, 372–89, 428–39, 456–61, 510–15, 568–81, 596–603, 620–25, 634–39, 684–85
appointment of, 294n, 313n, 576, 578
changing role of, 2–3, 5, 7, 148, 223, 325, 352–54
committee assignments and, 162, 168–69, 221, 301, 354
Commonwealth status and, 345–49, *346*, 351–52
creation of. *See*, Foraker Act.
discrimination against, 163–64
incumbency and, 168–69, 327, 353–54
language barrier and, 164–65
legislative interests, 158–59, 164, 169–74, 1346
legislative style, 5, 148, 159, 161–63

right to vote in committee, 353–54, 437
right to vote in the Committee of the Whole, 478, 496, 598, 636–37
See also, Elective Governor Act; Jones-Costigan Act of 1934; Legislative Reorganization Act of 1970; Second Jones Act.
Resolution Funding Corporation (RFC), 404
Reuther, Walter, 550
REYES, Silvestre, **686–87**
Richards, John K., 204
RICHARDSON, Bill, 8–9, 443, 446n, *474*, 477, 480, *480*, 483–85, 490–91, *491*, 493, 509, **542–49**, 565, 608
Richardson, G. A., 241
Richardson, William A., 24, *24*
Riggs, E. Francis, 173, 302
Rios, Cancel, 386
Rios, José, 352, 367n
Ritchie, Thomas, 31
RIVERA, David, **706**
Roberts, John G., 650
Robertson, Alice, 258, 261n
Rodey, Bernard S., 267n
RODRIGUEZ, Ciro D., 509, 586, **616–19**, 662
Rodriguez, Eugene, 516, 521n
Rodríguez, Juan, 204
Rodriguez, Lindsey, 420
Romer, Roy, 648
Romero, Miguel, 124
ROMERO, Trinidad, *43*, 43, 69, **124–27**
Romero, Vicente, 112, 116n
ROMERO-BARCELÓ, Carlos A., 476, 478, 494–95, *495*, 504n, 509, 568, 579, **596–603**, 620, 622, 634
Romulo, Carlos, 294n, 314n, 386n, 580n
Roosevelt, Franklin D., *169*, 170–72, 177, 272–74, 284, 286n, 292–93, 301–302, 310–12, 333–334, 336
Roosevelt, Theodore (Teddy), 134, 212–15, 216n, 234n, 300
Roosevelt, Theodore, Jr., 174
Root, Elihu, 163, 214
ROS-LEHTINEN, Ileana, 7, 422, 424, 477, 482, 484, 486, 592–93, 628, 655, 659, **688–89**
Rosado, Hiram, 173
Rosselló, Pedro, 571, 634, 637n
Rostenkowski, Daniel, 493, 520, 552, 601n
Rough Riders, 134
Rousselot, John H., 530–31
Rove, Karl, 586
ROYBAL, Edward R., 371, 409n, **410–19**, 476, 552, 658, 690
committee assignments, 7, 413–15, 480–82, *482*, 499n
Congressional Hispanic Caucus and, 8, 357, 413–14, 422, 483, 489–90, *490–91*, 545
early background, 6, *326*, 326–27, *338–39*, 338–40
immigration and, 414–15, 489–92, 503n
legislative interests, 329, 394, 412–15, 489–92
legislative style, 3, 6, 412–14
surrogate representation and, 328, 412, 414
Unidos Meeting of 1971, 329–30, *330*
Vietnam War and, 355, 413
Viva Kennedy Clubs and, *339*, 339–40
ROYBAL-ALLARD, Lucille, 409n, 415, 476, *487*, **690–91**
RUBIO, Marco, 482, **707**
Rynerson, William L., 117n, 144n

S

SABLAN, Gregorio Kilili Camacho, 476, **692–93**
Sagasta, Praxedes M., 220
Salazar, E. H., 254
SALAZAR, John, 476, 509, **644–47**, 650
SALAZAR, Ken, 8, 415, *476*, 476–77, 482, 493, 504n, 509, 646, **648–51**
Salinas de Gortari, Carlos, 493, 546
Salpointe, John B., 262
Sánchez Vilella, Roberto, 432
Sanchez, Jose Luis, 686
SÁNCHEZ, Linda T., 476, **694–95**
SANCHEZ, Loretta, 476, **696–97**
Sanchez, Manuel, 138
Sanders, Jared Y., Jr., 283
Sandinista, 545–46, 549n, 564–65
Santa Fe Ring, *35*, 38, *38*, 44, 47, 52–54, 60n, 86, 113, 124, 130, 139n, 140, 143, 144n, 194, 238
Santa Fe Trail, 35, 59n, 100, 124, 254
Schmitt, Harrison (Jack), 395
Schneider, George, 464
Second Jones Act of 1917 (Jones–Shafroth Act), 156–58, 162–63, 170, 174–75, 218, 222–23, 246, 248–49, 251, 252n, 290–291, 294n, 302, 308, 312, 313n, 325, 342, 345, 348–49, 383, 385, 386n, 580n. *See also*, Appendix I: Constitutional Amendments, Treaties, and Major Acts of Congress Referenced in the Text.
Second Spanish Period (1783–1821), 70
Segregation, 2, 148, 324, 331–33, 338, 339–40, 362n, 400, 402–403.
Seminole Indians, 34, 47, 72–76
First Seminole War, 25–26, 72–73
Second Seminole War, 26, 48, 75–76
Sena, José D., 86, 113
Senate, United States, 16n, 29, *29*, 32–33, 36, *53*, 54, 73–74, *164*, 231, 241, 274, 318–19, 329, 334–35, 354, 452, 454n, 479-80, 490, 493, 650. *See also*, Senators, Hispanic-American.
appointment of Hispanic Americans to, 8, 233n, 273, 477, 479, 655, 677, 700
committees, 6–7, 47, 54, 64–65n, 98n, 163, *168*, 169, 177–78, *178*, 188n, 210–13, 248, 250, 274–75, 303, 327, 348, 353–54, 465, 468, 480–82, 542, 547n, 571–72, 578
confirmations and, 37, 95, 376, 445, 546, 629, 640, 650
elections, 26, 76, 78n, *166*, 266, 273–74, 328, 393, 640, 648, 650, 677
Puerto Rico and, 153–55, 161, 173–74, 222, 250–51, 291, 322, 375–76, 459
treaties and, 27–28, *29*, 30, *31*, 50, *51*, 72
Senators, Hispanic-American, 262–79, 390–99, 640–43, 648–51, 676–77, 707
Seniority. *See*, Incumbency and seniority.
SERRANO, José E., 481, 485–86, *487*, **698–99**
Servicemen's Readjustment Act. *See*, GI Bill of Rights.
Seven Years' War, 70
Seventeenth Amendment, 78n
Seward, William Henry, 95, 103, 106n
Sheldon, Lionel, 46, 144n
Shipstead, Henrik, 273
Sibley, Henry L., 60n, 85, 95, 108
Simms, Albert G., 272, 442
Simpson–Mazzoli legislation, 486, 490–91. *See also*, Immigration.
SIRES, Albio, **700–701**
Sisk, Bernie, 522, 524, 660
Slatter, David, 606
Slavery, 26–30, 36, 49–52, 64–65n, 72, 84, 90, 94, 98n, 106 107n, 118, 134, 264
Small Business Job Protection Act of 1996, 495, 599
Smaragdas, George, 450, 454n
Smith, Lamar, 604
Smith, William L., 32
Social Security legislation, 170, 273, 277n, 302, 382, 392, 415, 431, 451, 465, 492, 512, 530, 606, 659, 677, 691
Solarz, Stephen, 702
SOLIS, Hilda L., 476, 509, 532, **626–29**
Solis, Juan, 616
South America, foreign policy, 250, 311, 348, *348*, 489
Southern Pacific Railroad, 47, 94–95, 99n, 121
Souto, Javier, 590
Spain, foreign policy. *See*, Adams–Onís (Transcontinental) Treaty; Spanish-American War; Treaty of Paris.
Spanish-American War, 5, 22, 25, 55, 56n, 134, *146*, 152–53, 164–65, 168, 200, 241, 298, 349, 380, 428, 612. *See also*, Appendix I: Constitutional Amendments, Treaties, and Major Acts of Congress Referenced in the Text; Treaty of Paris.
Spearing, James Z., 232
Spitaleri, Paul, 516
Spooner, John C., 154, *154*, 161
Sprague, Richard A., 406, 409n
St. Germain, Fernand J., 404
Stalin, Joseph, 283
Stanford, Leland, 118
Stanton, Frederick P., 24
State constitutional conventions. *See*, Statehood.
Statehood
Florida, 47, 70, 74, 76, 77n
Hawaii, 154, 385, 636
New Mexico, *39*, 50–54, 60n, 65n, 85, 87n, 90, 93–94, 97–98n, 102, 108, 111–13, 134, 142, 194, 196, 198n, 264, 267n
Puerto Rico, post-Estado Libre Asociado (Free Associated State), 353, 385, 431, 434, 436, 451, 458, 486, 494–95, 505n, 510, 512, 568, 571–72, 573n, 576, 579, 596–600, 620, 622, 623, 634–36, 637n, 684
Puerto Rico, pre-Estado Libre Asociado (Free Associated State), 161, 164, 202–203, 206n, 221–23, 246, 248–50, 298, 301, 301–303, 308, 345–46, 349–50
United States Virgin Islands, 352–53
Statutory Representation. *See*, Resident Commissioner; Territorial Delegate.
Steiger, William, 437
Stevenson, Adlai E., 516
Stokes, Louis, 409n
Stolen Valor Act of 2006, 646
String, Jack, 282
Sugar Act of 1934 (Jones–Costigan Act), 170–71, 186n, 302, 372, 382, 422
Sullivan, Joe, 586
Supreme Court, United States
Balzac v. Porto Rico, 155, 251
Dorr v. United States, 155
Downes v. Bidwell, 151, 155–56
Dred Scott v. Sanford, 94
Gonzalez v. Williams, 204–205
Hawaii v. Mankichi, 204
Lau v. Nichols, 488
Rasmussen v. United States, 155
Surrogate representation, 2, 4, 6, 16n, 148, 178–80, 254, 412, 477. *See also*, Hispanic-American Members of Congress, characteristics; Congressional Hispanic Caucus; Congressional Hispanic Conference.
Susoni Lens, Esteban, 428
Sutherland, William A., 316
Sutton, Percy, 452
Swift, Zephaniah, 32
Swing, Joseph, 338
Swope, Guy, 177, 311

T

Taft, Robert, 334
Taft, William Howard, *4*, 156
Tappan, Benjamin, 28
TEJEDA, Frank, 509, **604–609**, 616
Tenorio, Pete A., 692
Territorial Delegate, *26*, *34*, *38*, *39*, 70–117, 124–45, 194–99, 462–71, 556–61, 610–15, 692–93
committee assignments, 33, 44–46, 137, 142, 168–69, 327–28, 481–82
creation of, 32–34, 352–53, 367n
legislative interests, 44–54, 168, 481, 494
legislative style, 33–34, 162–63, 478,

496
status and rights of, 2–5, 22, 24, 33–34, 44–45, 61n, 168–69, 184n, 352–54, 478, 496, 598, 636, 638n
Texas
annexation, 26–29, *29*
Hispanic representation, 400–409, 420–27, 536–41, 562–67, 582–89, 604–609, 616–19, 662–63, 666–67, 672–73, 686–87, 704–705. *See also*, Appendix B: Hispanic-American Representatives, Senators, Delegates, and Resident Commissioners by State and Territory, 1822–2012.
Texas and New Mexico Act. *See*, Appendix I: Constitutional Amendments, Treaties, and Major Acts of Congress Referenced in the Text.
Thirteenth Amendment, 52, *52*
Thornburgh, Dick, 582
Tingley, Clyde, 273, 278n
Tipton, Scott, 646
Todd, Roberto, 212
Tompkins, Daniel D., 73
Torres, Arcy, 549n
Torres, Art, 626
TORRES, Esteban Edward, *474*, 480, *480*, 485, 491, *491*, 509, **550–55**, 565, 678
Torres, Frank, 560
Towner, Horace M., *175*, 176, 223, 224n, 248–250, 253n
Towns, Edolphus, 702
Travis, William, 28
Treaty of Guadalupe Hidalgo of 1848, 30–31, *31*, 41, 48, 57–58n, 61n, 80, 82, 84, 92, 118, 136. *See also*, Mexican-American War; Appendix I: Constitutional Amendments, Treaties, and Major Acts of Congress Referenced in the Text.
Treaty of Moultrie Creek, 34, 74
Treaty of Paris, 152, 165, 200, 204. *See also*, Appendix I: Constitutional Amendments, Treaties, and Major Acts of Congress Referenced in the Text; Spanish-American War.
Trimble, South, 150
Trosclair, J. P., 151
Truman, Harry S., 6, 187n, 276, 319, 335, 337, 345, *345*, 347, 349–51, 354, 372, 375–76, 378n, 383–84, 556
Tugwell, Rexford Guy, *169*, 171, *171*, *176*, 176–79, 311–13, 374, 376, 383
Tydings, Millard, 160, *173*, 173–74, 248, 302–303, 375
Tyler, John, 28, *29*

U

U.S.-Mexican War. *See*, Mexican-American War.
U.S.S. Maine, 152, *152*, 181n, 220
Ubarri, Pablo, 210
Udall, Morris, 443, 682
Udall, Tom, 544, 547–48n, 674
Un-American Activities Commitee. *See*, House Un-American Activities Committee (HUAC).
Unconditional Party, 210
Underhill, Charles Lee, 251
Underwood, Oscar, 229
UNDERWOOD, Robert A., 468, 476, 478, 496, 500n, 509, 560, **610–15**
Unidos Meeting of 1971, 329–30
Union Party, 105, 110, 118
United Farm Workers, 340, *340*
United Nations, 345, 347, 349, 355, 384, 392, 468, 546
United Nations' Educational, Scientific, and Cultural Organization (UNESCO), 458, 552
United States Virgin Islands
Hispanic representation, 462–471. *See also*, Appendix B: Hispanic-American Representatives, Senators, Delegates, and Resident Commissioners by State and Territory, 1822–2012.
Organic Act, 375, 469n
United States-Puerto Rico Commission on the Status of Puerto Rico, 385
Upham, William, 57n
Upshur, Abel, 28

V

Valdez, Pedro, 126, 127n
Valdez, Robert, 316
Valenzuela, Fernando, 530
Valles, Domingo, 114
Vallone, Peter, 450
Valverde, battle of, 37, 85, 108
Van Buren, Martin, 28
Vandenberg, Arthur, 177
VELÁZQUEZ, Nydia M., 485, *485*, **702–703**
Velez, Ramon, 450, 452, 518
Victoria, Manuel, 118
Vieques, 456, 494, 504n, 600, 622, 699, 703
Viera-Martinez, Angel, 570
Vietnam War, 335–36, 355–56, 394, 413, 464, 556, 558, 604, 608, 656, 686, 689. *See also*, Military service, Hispanic-American Members of Congress.
Villa, Francisco (Pancho), 239, 265
Vinson, Carl, 283, 286n
Virgin Islands Nonimmigrants Alien Adjustment Act of 1982, 466–67
Vocational Education Act of 1963, 392
Volcker, Paul, 405
Volgy, Tom, 682
Voter registration drives, 324, 338, 340, *342*, 410, 414, 483, 498n, 512
Voting rights, 231, 248, 264, 402, 486–87, 489, 606
Voting Rights Act of 1965, 329, 357, 423, 474, 487, 536, 586, 618. Appendix I: Constitutional Amendments, Treaties, and Major Acts of Congress Referenced in the Text.
Voting Rights Language Assistance Act of 1992, 484–85, *485*, 487, 698–99. Appendix I: Constitutional Amendments, Treaties, and Major Acts of Congress Referenced in the Text.

W

Wagner, Robert F., 292
Wagner, Robert, Jr., 448, 450
Walcher, Greg, 644
Walker, Johnny, 442
Walton, William, 240, 243n
Wamp, Zack, 586
War of 1812, 25, *48*, 283
War with Mexico. *See*, Mexican-American War.
Warren Commission, 406
Washington, D.C. *See*, District of Columbia.
Washington, Hispanic representation, 705. *See also*, Appendix B: Hispanic-American Representatives, Senators, Delegates, and Resident Commissioners by State and Territory, 1822–2012.
Watergate scandal, 398n, 406, 418n, 452, *479*, 552
Watt, James G., 442–43
Watts, John S., 103, 107n, 115n
Waxman, Henry, 552
Weaver, Jim, 423
Webster, Daniel, *30*, *53*
Webster, William, 406
Wedtech scandal, 516, 520
Weightman, Richard H., 60n, 82, 87–88n, 97–98n
Welfare policy, 170, 332, 424, 438, 458, 466, 485–86, 492, 513, 592, 658
Westcott, James D., 76
Whig Party, 28–30, 37, 49, 57n, 59n, 67, 76, 92, 97n, 138n
White, James, 32–33
White, Joseph M., 74–75
Wickard, Claude, 310
Williams, Guinn, 250
Willoughby, William F., 216n
Wilmot Proviso, 50, *51*
Wilmot, David, 50, *51*
Wilson, Charles H., 414
Wilson, Francis C., 238
Wilson, Henry, 52
Wilson, John F., 198
Wilson, Woodrow, *148*, 156, 158, 217n, 222, 226, 228, 239–40, 242n, 246, 265
Windom, William, 103
Winthrop, Robert, 26
Won Pat, Antonio, 464, 467, 469n, 556, 558–60, 613
Wood, John, 348
Wood, John W., 406
Works Progress Administration (WPA), 273, 284
World War I, 156, *157*, 170, 221–22, 230, 239–41, 250, 256–57, 265, 282. *See also*, Military service, Hispanic-American Members of Congress.
World War II, 2–3, 55, 148, 168, 180, 233n, 274–75, 283, 308, 311, 318, 324, 333–35, *335*, 357, 375, 380, 382–83, 403, 415, 444, 468, 614n, 668. *See also*, Military service, Hispanic-American Members of Congress.
Wright, Hendrick, 24
Wright, Herbert, *178*
Wright, Jim, 522

Y

Yarborough, Ralph, 393–94, 397n

Z

Zioncheck, Marion, 187n
Zubiría y Escalante, Antonio, 80